Warman's
ANTIQUES
AND THEIR PRICES
25th Edition

---

*The Standard Price Reference for antiques
and collectibles, for collectors, dealers
and professionals in the trade.*

Edited by
Harry L. Rinker

**Completely illustrated
and authenticated**

**Wallace-Homestead Book Company
Radnor, Pennsylvania**

ISBN 0-87069-592-4
ISSN 0196-2272
Library of Congress Catalog Card No. 82-643542
Manufactured in the United States of America

1 2 3 4 5 6 7 8 9 0   9 8 7 6 5 4 3 2 1 0

Additional copies of this book may be obtained from your book-
store or directly from Wallace-Homestead Book Company, 201
King of Prussia Rd., Radnor, PA 19089. Enclose $13.95 plus
$2.50 for postage and handling for the first book and $.50 for each
additional book. Add applicable state sales tax.

EDITORIAL STAFF

Harvey Duke
115 Montague St.
Brooklyn, NY 11201
(718) 625-3536
Hall China

Arthur M. Feldman
1815 St. Johns Avenue
Highland Park, IL 60035
(312) 432-2075
Judaica

Regis and Mary Ferson
122 Arden Rd.
Pittsburgh, PA 15216
(412) 563-1964
Milk Glass

Doug Flynn and Al
Bolton
Holloway House
P. O. Box 547
Mesilla, NM 88046-0547
(505) 527-4555
*British Royalty
Commemoratives*

Ron Fox
Fox-Terry Steins, Inc.
416 Throop St.
N. Babylon, NY 11704
(516) 669-7232
Mettlach, Steins

Roselyn Gerson
12 Alnwick Rd.
Malverne, NY 11565
Compacts

Walter Glenn
Geode Ltd.
3393 Peachtree Rd.
Atlanta, GA 30326
(404) 261-9346
Frankart

Dan Golden
5375-C Avendia Encinas
Carlsbad, CA 92008-
4362
(619) 438-8383
Telephones

Ted Hake
Hake's Americana &
Collectibles
P. O. Box 1444
York, PA 17405
(717) 848-1333
*Disneyana, Political
Items*

John High
415 E. 52nd St.
New York, NY 10022
(212) 758-1692
Stevengraphs

Joan Hull
1376 Nevada
Huron, SD 57350
(605) 352-1685
Hull Pottery

David and Sue Irons
Irons Antiques
R. D. #4, Box 101
Northampton, PA 18067
(215) 262-9335
Irons

William J. Jenks
Golden Webb Antiques,
Inc.
P. O. Box 1274
Wilkes-Barre, PA 18703
(717) 288-3039
Pattern Glass

Judy Knauer
1224 Spring Valley Lane
West Chester, PA 19380
(215) 431-3477
Toothpick Holders

Edward W. Leach
381 Trenton Ave.
Paterson, NJ 07503
(201) 684-5398
Shaving Mugs

Ron Lieberman
The Family Album
R. D. #1, Box 42
Glen Rock, PA 17327
(717) 235-2134
Books, Americana

Elyce Litts
P. O. Box 394
Morris Plains, NJ 07950
(201) 361-4087
Geisha Girl Porcelain

H. Thomas Laun
215 Paul Ave.
Syracuse, NY 13206
Firehouse Collectibles

Elaine J. Luartes
Athena Antiques
100 Beta Drive
Franklin, TN 37064
(615) 377-3442
Jewelry

Clarence and Betty
Maier
The Burmese Cruet
P. O. Box 432
Montgomeryville, PA
18936
(215) 855-5388
*Burmese Glass, Crown
Milano, Royal Flemish*

James S. Maxwell, Jr.
P. O. Box 367
Lampeter, PA 17537
(717) 464-5573
Banks, Mechanical

Joan Collett Oates
5912 Kingsfield Dr.
W. Bloomfield, MI
48322
(313) 661-2335
Phoenix Bird Pattern

Evalene Pulati
National Valentine
Collectors Association
P. O. Box 1404
Santa Ana, CA 92702
Valentines

John D. Querry
R. D. 2, Box 137B
Martinsburg, PA 16662
(814) 793-3185
Gaudy Dutch

Darryl K. Reilly
Dendara's Antiques
P. O. Box 1203
Pepperel, MA 01463
(508) 433-8718
Pattern Glass

Ferill J. Rice
302 Pheasant Run
Kaukauna, WI 54130
(414) 766-9176
Fenton

Julie Rich
Tea Leaf Readings
9720 Whiskey Run
Laurel, MD 20707
(301) 490-7604
*Tea Leaf Ironstone
China*

Mark Saville
26 Brookmawr Rd.
Newtown Square, PA
19073-2001
(215) 353-5506
Canton

Mark Supnick
8524 NW 2nd St.
Coral Springs, FL 33071
(305) 755-3449
Shawnee Pottery

George Theofiles
Miscellaneous Man
Box 1776
New Freedom, PA 17349
(717) 235-4766
Posters

Kathy Wojciechowski
P. O. Box 230
Peotone, IL 60468
(708) 258-6105
Nippon

INTRODUCTION
"Warman's Is The Key"

Warman's provides the keys needed by auctioneers, collectors, and dealers to open the doors to understanding and dealing with the complexities of the antiques market. A price list is only one of the many keys needed today. **Warman's 25th Edition** contains many additional keys, including histories, reference books, periodicals, collectors' clubs, and museums. Useful buying and collecting hints also are provided.

Warman's is designed to be your first key to the exciting world of antiques. As you use the keys provided to advance beyond this book in specialized collecting areas, **Warman's** hopes you will remember with fondness where you received your start. When you encounter items outside your area of specialty, remember **Warman's** remains your key to unlocking the information you need, just as it has for over forty-two years.

ORGANIZATION

Listings: Objects are listed alphabetically by category, beginning with ABC Plates and ending with Zsolnay Pottery. If you have trouble identifying the category in which your object belongs, use the extensive index in the back of the book. It is designed to guide you to the proper category.

We have attempted to make the listings descriptive enough so that specific objects can be identified. We also have placed emphasis on those items which are actively being sold in the marketplace. Nevertheless, some harder-to-find objects are included in order to demonstrate the market spread.

Each year as the market changes, we carefully consider which categories to include, which to drop, and which to add. **Warman's** is a direct response to the developing trends in the marketplace. To further help collectors and dealers, Wallace-Homestead Book Company also publishes *Warman's Americana & Collectibles*, an excellent source for information and prices on 20th century collectibles.

History: Every collector should know something about the history of his object. We have presented a capsule background for each category. In many cases the background contains collecting hints or tips to spot reproductions.

References: Special references are listed for each category to help collectors learn more about their objects. Included are author, title, publisher [if published by a small firm or individual, we have indicated "published by author"], and date of publication or most recent edition.

Finding these books may present a problem. The antiques and collectibles field is blessed with a dedicated core of book dealers who stock these specialized publications. You will find them at flea markets, antiques shows, and advertised in leading publications in the field. Many dealers publish annual or semi-annual catalogs. Ask to be put on their mailing lists. Books go out-of-print quickly, yet many books printed over twenty-five years ago remain the standard work in a category. Used book dealers often can turn up many of these valuable reference sources.

Periodicals: Generally, the newsletter or bulletin of a collectors' club focuses on the specific publication needs within a category. However, there are other publications, not associated with collectors' clubs, of which the collector and dealer should be aware. These are covered under specific categories.

In addition, there are general interest newspapers and magazines which deserve to be brought to our users' attention. These are:

Antique Review, P. O. Box 538, Worthington, OH 43085
Antique Trader Weekly, P. O. Box 1050, Dubuque, IA 52001
Antique Week, P. O. Box 90, Knightstown, IN 46148
Antiques (The Magazine Antiques), 551 Fifth Avenue, New York, NY 10017
Antique & The Arts Weekly, Bee Publishing Company, 5 Church Hill Road, Newton, CT 06470
Antiques & Collecting Hobbies, 1006 South Michigan Avenue, Chicago, IL 60605
Collector News & Antique Reporter, Box 156, Grundy Center, IA 50638
Collectors Journal, P. O. Box 601, Vinton, IA 52349
Collectors' Showcase, P. O. Box 837, Tulsa, OK 74101
Maine Antique Digest, P. O. Box 358, Waldoboro, ME 04572
MidAtlantic Monthly Antiques Magazine, P. O. Box 908, Henderson, NC 27536
New England Antiques Journal, 4 Church Street, Ware, MA 01082
New York-Pennsylvania Collector, Drawer C, Fishers, NY 14453
Southern Antiques, P. O. Box 1107, Decatur, GA 30031
West Coast Peddler, P. O. Box 5134, Whittier, CA 90607
Yesteryear, P. O. Box 2, Princeton, WI 54968

It is impossible to list all the national and regional publications in the antiques and collectibles field. A check with your local library will bring many other publications to your attention.

Collectors' Clubs: The large number of collectors' clubs adds vitality to the antiques and collectibles fields. Their publications and conventions produce knowledge which often cannot be found anywhere else. Many of these clubs are short-lived; others are so strong that they have regional and local chapters.

Museums: The best way to study a specific field is to see as many documented examples as possible. For this reason, we have listed museums where significant collections in that category are on display. Special attention must be directed to the complex of museums which make up the Smithsonian Institution in Washington, D.C.

Reproductions: Reproductions are a major concern to all collectors and dealers. Most reproductions are unmarked; the newness of their appearance is often the best clue to uncovering them. Specific objects known to be reproduced are marked within the listings with an asterisk (*).

Index: A great deal of effort has been expended to make our index useful. Always try to find the most specific reference. For example, if you have a piece of china, look first for the maker's name and second for the type. The key is to ask the right questions of yourself.

Photographs: You may encounter a piece you cannot identify well enough to use the index. Consult the photographs and marks. If you own the last several editions of **Warman's**, you have assembled a valuable photographic reference to the antiques and collectibles field.

PRICE NOTES

In assigning prices we assume the object is in very good condition. If otherwise, we note this in our description. It would be ideal to suggest that mint, or unused, examples of all objects do exist. The reality is that objects from the past were used, whether they be glass, china, dolls, or toys. Because of this, some normal wear must be expected. In fact, if an object such as furniture does not show wear, its origins may be suspect.

Whenever possible, we have tried to provide a broad listing of prices within a category so you have a "feel" for the market. We emphasize the middle range of prices within a category, while also listing some objects of high and low value to show the market spread.

We do not use ranges because they tend to confuse rather than help the collector and dealer. How do you determine if your object is at the high or low end of the range? There is a high degree of flexibility in pricing in the antiques field. If you want to set ranges, add or subtract 10% from our prices.

One of the hardest variants with which to deal are the regional fluctuations of prices. Victorian furniture brings widely differing prices in New York, Chicago, New Orleans, or San Francisco. We have tried to strike a balance. Know your region and subject before investing heavily. If the best prices for cameo glass are in Montreal or Toronto, then be prepared to go there if you want to save money or add choice pieces to your collection. Research and patience are key factors to building a collection of merit.

Another factor that affects prices is a sale by a leading dealer or private collector. We have tempered both dealer and auction house figures.

PRICE RESEARCH

Everyone asks—where do we get our prices? They come from many sources.

First, we rely on auctions. Auction houses and auctioneers do not always command the highest prices. If they did, why would so many dealers buy from them? The key to understanding auction prices is to know when a price is high or low in the range. We do this and think we do it well.

Second, we work closely with dealers. We screen our contacts to make certain they have a full knowledge of the market. Dealers make their living from selling antiques; they cannot afford to have a price guide which is not in touch with the market.

Over forty antiques and collectibles magazines, newspapers, and journals come into our office regularly. They are excellent barometers of what is moving and what is not. We don't hesitate to call an advertiser and ask if listed merchandise sold.

When the editorial staff is doing field work, we identify ourselves. Our conversations with dealers and collectors around the country have enhanced this book. Teams from Warman's are in the field at antiques shows, flea markets, and auctions, recording prices and taking photographs.

Collectors work closely with us. They are specialists whose devotion to research and accurate information is inspiring. Generally, they are not dealers. Whenever we have asked them for help, they have responded willingly and admirably.

BOARD OF ADVISORS

Our Board of Advisors are specialists, both dealers and collectors, who feel a commitment to accurate information. You'll find their names listed in the front of the book. Several have authored a major reference work on their subject.

Members of the Board of Advisors file lists of prices in their categories for which they are responsible. They help select and often supply the photographs used. If you wish to buy or sell an object in their field of expertise, drop them a note along with an SASE. If time or interest permits, they will respond.

BUYER'S GUIDE, NOT SELLER'S GUIDE

Warman's is designed to be a buyer's guide to what you would have to pay to purchase an object on the open market from a dealer or collector. **It is not a seller's guide to prices.** People frequently make this mistake. In doing so, they deceive themselves. If you have an object listed in this book and wish to sell it to a dealer, you should expect to receive approximately fifty percent of the listed value. If the object is not anticipated to be resold quickly, expect to receive even less.

A private collector may pay more, perhaps seventy to eighty percent of our list price. Your object will have to be something needed for his or her collection. If you have an extremely rare object or an object of exceptionally high value, these guidelines do not apply.

Examine your piece as objectively as possible. As an antiques and collectibles appraiser, I spend a great deal of time telling people their treasures are not "gold" at all, but items readily available in the marketplace.

In respect to buying and selling, a simple philosophy is that a good purchase occurs when the buyer and seller are happy with the price. Don't look back. Hindsight has little value in the antiques field. Given time, things tend to balance out.

COMMENTS INVITED

Warman's Antiques and Their Prices continues to be the leader in the antiques and collectibles price guide field because we listen to our readers. Readers are encouraged to send their comments and suggestions to Harry L. Rinker, Consulting Editor, Wallace-Homestead, c/o Rinker Enterprises, Inc., P. O. Box 248, Zionsville, PA 18092.

ACKNOWLEDGMENTS

The 25th edition of *Warman's Antiques and Their Prices* is the first general price guide to mark its silver anniversary. It would not have been possible without the loyal support of five decades of *Warman's* users. On behalf of the Warman's staff, I thank you for your continuing support and pledge not only to preserve the high Warman's standards of the past but to continue to pioneer those changes that make *Warman's* the industry's standard.

I call your attention to the traditional author photograph in the back of the book. Of course, I am pictured, but with a group known affectionately throughout the trade as the "Rinkettes." These individuals are the heart and soul of Rinker Enterprises, Inc., the researchers, sorters, and compilers of the information in Warman's guides. Each brings a unique touch to this enterprise.

The 25th edition marks the completion of Warman's first year under the leadership of Wallace-Homestead Book Company, a division of Chilton Book Company. Edna Jones, Troy Vozzella, and Tim Scott brought an increased level of professionalism to the production area. Neil Levin and his staff have produced record sales. Hallelujah! The book deserves both. Thanks gang.

Warman's future has been brightened by strong support from Ronald A. Hoxter, Senior Vice President, and Christopher Kuppig, General Manager, of Chilton. Recognizing the value of the Warman's format, Chilton has approved publication of a multivolume series of Warman's encyclopedias, the first of which will appear in late 1991.

For the past ten years, *Warman's* has literally been prepared at a cabin in the woods. Early in 1991 the Warman's editorial staff will move to the former Vera Cruz (Pennsylvania) Elementary School as part of Rinker Enterprises' Institute for the Study of Antiques and Collectibles, the largest independent antiques and collectibles research center in the United States. We are all excited.

Annually, I thank all those who sent price lists and letters, allowed their material to be photographed, and took time to discuss the business with me when I talked with them on the phone or saw them in the field. Rest assured you are not taken for granted. We recognize that you are an essential element in the preparation of *Warman's*.

Finally, a tribute on our silver anniversary to Edwin G. Warman, who had the foresight and courage to publish the first edition of *Warman's* in 1948. Long after my tenure as editor, the Warman name will continue, a honor justly deserved.

Rinker Enterprises, Inc.   Harry L. Rinker
P. O. Box 248   Editor
Zionsville, PA 18092
January 1991

STATE OF THE MARKET

The "State of the Market" report in the 24th edition of *Warman's Antiques and Their Prices* began: "The 1980s were a boom time for the antiques and collectibles business. No one, even those whose involvement in the field extends back into the 1940s and 1950s, remembers a period of such sustained growth over such a wide portion of the market. Many, and I am one, feel a technical correction in pricing is long overdue. Signs of such a correction do not appear on the horizon. Let the good times roll." *Things have certainly changed in one year.*

Unlimited prosperity throughout the antiques and collectibles market is a thing of the past. While gloom and doom proponents are not yet a majority, their mental thought process is in ascendancy. Recession and war in the Persian Gulf fuels their mind-set. Rumors of the collapse of dealers, malls, and shows abound. A number of individuals, particularly dealers and show promoters, are attempting to stem the tide by being good news cheerleaders. The antiques and collectibles market is tottering. "Uncertainty" best describes the state of the market as 1991 begins.

Many claim the first signs of trouble appeared at the Atlantique City show in March 1990. Sales did not meet dealers' expectations. The real slowdown occurred in the summer when many dealers did not replace low and middle range material that they sold. Dealer to dealer sales are a critical element in the strength of the antiques and collectibles market.

Confusion arose from the absolute unpredictability of the market. A dealer who took the same merchandise to two shows did terrible business at one and spectacular business at the other. There were no logical explanations "why." Dealers were not able to make corrections that kept their sales volume consistent. By early fall 1990 the general rule of thumb was that, on average, show gates and sales were off by one-quarter to one-third from a year earlier.

The thing that saved the market during the last half of 1990 was the continuing strength of the "high-end" material. The best examples, whether antique or collectible, continued to sell well. In fact, the sale of this material permitted many dealers to make their "nut." In order to maintain cash flow, dealers offered many premier pieces from their personal collections. However, they found it next to impossible to replace these items with fresh merchandise.

A major downturn struck twentieth century and contemporary American paintings, folk art, oriental rugs, and aspects of the Continental market in late fall 1990. The New York auction houses came under heavy attack. Their bastions crumbled. All of a sudden, high-end material was no longer recession proof.

The auction houses became victims of their own hype. Their public relations departments heavily stressed the concept of record prices throughout the 1980s. Auctions became media events. The media reported regularly on all levels of the antiques and collectibles market. As long as the prices skyrocketed and news from the field was good, media coverage was an advantage. As the market receded and news from the field soured, media coverage fueled the increasing negativism. The media also became more sophisticated. Instead of simply running auction house, dealer, and show promoter press releases verbatim, they did their own analysis. All too often they found their conclusions did not match those in the press releases.

The increasing attitude shrouding the market is that antiques and collectibles are no longer affordable. Many feel that prices have reached the point of ridiculousness. In many categories, especially in the antiques sector, this is true. I am a price reporter and observer. The prices in this book reflect what sellers are asking and buyers are paying. Never make the assumption that they represent what I personally feel the items are worth.

The antiques and collectibles market is soft in almost every category, with low and middle priced objects being harder hit than high-end items. In the last quarter of 1990, several sellers began reducing prices. At the moment, they are in a minority. The bulk of the dealers are rallying around 1990s market prices, content with a stable market. But, the pressure on this pricing dam is increasing at an alarming rate. The only question in most observers' minds is, "When will it burst?"

Within the present soft market, there are a number of categories that are gaining and declining at a pace greater than the majority. You will find them listed below. You may not agree with my conclusions, but you would be well advised to think about them.

Gaining	*Declining*
Grueby (Art Pottery)	Folk Art
Lalique	Jewelry, Costume
Little Golden Books	Miniatures, especially Doll
Radios, 1930s and 1940s	House Furnishings
Russian Items	Ohr Pottery (Art Pottery)
Silver, Danish	Oriental Rugs
Space Adventure Collectibles	Paintings, Contemporary
Sports Collectibles other than	Paintings, Twentieth Century
Baseball	Silver, English
Toys, 19th and Early 20th	Toy Trains, Williams
Century Tin	
TV Collectibles	

There are positive signs in this negative market. The antiques and collectibles market has survived previous recessionary cycles to emerge strong and viable. There is absolutely no reason to believe this will not happen again. Give the technical corrections time to work.

First, collectors are once again major players in the antiques and collectibles marketplace equation. In the 1980s sellers controlled the market and set prices. One bought or else. While interior decorators, investors, and speculators willingly paid the ever increasing prices, many collectors were forced to the sidelines when their pocketbooks became exhausted. In 1991 the interior decorators, investors, and speculators have vanished. All of a sudden, sellers need the collector in order to survive. Collectors realize that the only valid price is what they are willing to pay. More and more, they are holding firm and refusing to pay more. Collectors with cash in their pocket in June 1991 will be in the driver's seat.

Second, the 1980s market was auction, dealer, mall, and show top heavy. A decline already has begun in all four major categories. The key is dealer decline, since this decline seriously affects the other three categories. The three dealer groups most likely to show attrition are shop-show dealers, collector-dealers (collectors who deal to support their habit), and mall dealers. Weak malls and shows will fail as the number of dealers declines. Recently, a brochure for a New Jersey antiques center had six of the fifteen original dealers crossed out and only one new one added. Expect more of this in the year ahead.

Third, in 1991 the principal sales vehicles will become the telephone and mail as opposed to the mall, shop, and show. The sellers best able to utilize these vehicles are dealers with a strong collector base. The 1991 antiques and collectibles seller's life jacket is customer service—something that was badly neglected in the 1980s. Do not be surprised if some collectors have long memories.

Fourth, there are plenty of affordable categories. The catch is that they are primarily in the collectibles field. Like it or not, traditionalists are going to have to deal in twentieth century material, especially post-1945 items, if they hope to survive. Justice is served. Since pricing for this material falls within a much narrower range than the antiques sector, dealers will need to sell a greater volume of material to maintain their annual income levels. They are going to earn their money the old-fashioned way.

One segment of the market that seems to be resisting much of the current market decline is paper ephemera. There is plenty of action for the heavy spender, e.g., posters. Some categories, such as letter and bill heads, are reaching a point where collectors are questioning the values being asked. But, overall, the bulk of the material sells from a few cents to a few dollars. Twenty-five dollars still buys plenty of great paper ephemera.

Fifth, although the soft market appears to have discouraged many speculators and investors, it certainly has not rid itself of market manipulators, individuals who attempt to corner and drive up a specific collecting category in a relatively short period of time. Four areas where this is happening at the moment are: Baseball Gloves, Cereal Boxes, Late 19th and Early 20th Century Tin Toys, and 1930s and 1940s Radios.

The 1991 antiques and collectibles market is not a place for the individual with a weak heart. The first six months should prove to be a real roller coaster ride. Join me for the ride; just hang on tight.

AUCTION HOUSES

The following auction houses cooperated with Warman's by providing catalogues of their auctions and price lists. This effort is most appreciated.

Sanford Alderfer Auction
Company
501 Fairgrounds Rd.
Hatfield, PA 19440
(215) 368-5477

W. Graham Arader III
1000 Boxwood Court
King of Prussia, PA
19406
(215) 825-6570

Ark Antiques
Box 3133
New Haven, CT 06515
(203) 387-3754

Arman Absentee
Auctions
P.O. Box 174
Woodstock, CT 06281
(203) 928-0873

Arthur Auctioneering
R. D. 2
Hughesville, PA 17737
(717) 584-3697

Noel Barrett Antiques
and Auctions Ltd.
P.O. Box 1001
Carversville, PA 18913
(215) 297-5109

Robert F. Batchelder
1 West Butler Avenue
Ambler, PA 19002
(215) 643-1430

Richard A. Bourne Co.,
Inc.
Corporation St.
P.O. Box 141
Hyannis Port, MA 02647
(508) 775-0797

Butterfield's
220 San Bruno Ave.
San Francisco, CA
94103
(415) 861-7500

Christie's
502 Park Avenue
New York, NY 10022
(212) 546-1000

Christie's East
219 E. 67th St.
New York, NY 10021
(212) 606-0400

Marvin Cohen Auctions
Box 425, Routes 20 &
22
New Lebanon, NY
12125
(518) 794-9333

Marlin G. Denlinger
RR 3, Box 3775
Morrisville, VT 05661
(802) 888-2774

William Doyle Galleries,
Inc.
175 E. 87th St.
New York, NY 10128
(212) 427-2730

Early Auction Co.
123 Main St.
Milford, OH 45150
(513) 831-4833

Fine Arts Co. of
Philadelphia, Inc.
1808 Chestnut St.
Philadelphia, PA 19103
(215) 563-9275

William A. Fox
Auctions, Inc.
676 Morris Ave.
Springfield, NJ 07081
(201) 467-2366

Ron Fox
F. T. S. Inc.
416 Throop St.
N. Babylon, NY 11704
(516) 669-7232

Garth's Auction, Inc.
2690 Stratford Rd.
P.O. Box 369
Delaware, OH 43015
(614) 362-4771 or 369-
5085

Guerney's
136 East 73rd St.
New York, NY 10021
(212) 794-2280

Hake's Americana and
Collectibles
P.O. Box 1444
York, PA 17405
(717) 848-1333

Harmer Rooke
Numismatists, Inc.
3 East 57th St.
New York, NY 10022
(212) 751-4122

Hart Galleries
2311 Westheimer
Houston, TX 77098
(713) 524-2979 or 523-7389

Norman C. Heckler &
Company
Bradford Corner Rd.
Woodstock Valley, CT
06282
(203) 974-1634

Leslie Hindman, Inc.
215 West Ohio St.
Chicago, IL 60610
(312) 670-0010

Michael Ivankovich
Antiques
P.O. Box 2458
Doylestown, PA 18901
(215) 345-6094

James D. Julia, Inc.
P.O. Box 830
Fairfield, ME 04937
(207) 453-7904

Les Paul's
2615 Magnolia St., Suite
A
Oakland, CA 94607
(415) 832-2615

Milwaukee Auction
Galleries
318 N. Water
Milwaukee, WI 53202
(414) 271-1105

Neal Alford Company
4139 Magazine St.
New Orleans, LA 70115
(504) 899-5329

New England Auction
Gallery
Box 2273
W. Peabody, MA 01960
(508) 535-3140

New Hampshire Book
Auctions
Woodbury Rd.
Weare, NH 03281
(603) 529-1700

Nostalgia Publications,
Inc.
21 South Lake Dr.
Hackensack, NJ 07601
(201) 488-4536

Pettigrew Auction
Company
1645 South Tejon St.
Colorado Springs, CO
80906
(719) 633-7963

David Rago Arts &
Crafts
P.O. Box 3592 Station E
Trenton, NJ 08629
(609) 585-2546

Lloyd Ralston Toys
173 Post Road
Fairfield, CT 06432
(203) 255-1233 or 366-3399

R. Niel & Elaine
Reynolds
Box 133
Waterford, VA 22190
(703) 882-3574

Roan Bros. Auction
Gallery
R.D. 3, Box 118
Cogan Station, PA 17728
(717) 494-0170

Robert W. Skinner Inc.
Bolton Gallery
357 Main St.
Bolton, MA 01740
(508) 779-6241

Smith House Toy Sales
26 Adlington Rd.
Eliot, ME 03903
(207) 439-4614

Sotheby's
1334 York Avenue
New York, NY 10021
(212) 606-7000

Swann Galleries, Inc.
104 E. 25th St.
New York, NY 10010
(212) 254-4710

Winter Associates
21 Cooke St. Box 823
Plainville, CT 06062
(203) 793-0288

Wolf's Auction Gallery
13015 Larchmere Blvd.
Shaker Heights, OH
44120
(216) 231-3888

Woody Auction
Douglass, KS 67039
(316) 746-2694

ABBREVIATIONS

The following are standard abbreviations which we have used throughout this edition of **Warman's**.

ah =	applied handle	litho =	lithograph
C =	century	ls =	low standard
c =	circa	MIB =	mint in box
circ =	circular	mkd =	marked
cov =	cover	MOP =	mother of pearl
d =	diameter or depth	NE =	New England
dec =	decorated	No. =	number
DQ =	Diamond Quilted	opal =	opalescent
emb =	embossed	orig =	original
ext. =	exterior	os =	orig stopper
FE =	first edition	pat =	patent
ftd =	footed	pcs =	pieces
ground =	background	pr =	pair
h =	height	rect =	rectangular
hp =	hand painted	sgd =	signed
hs =	high standard	sngl =	single
imp =	impressed	SP =	silver plated
int. =	interior	SS =	Sterling silver
irid =	iridescent	sq =	square
IVT =	inverted thumbprint	w =	width
j =	jewels	yg =	yellow gold
K =	karat	# =	numbered
l =	length		

ABC PLATES

History: The majority of early ABC plates were manufactured in England, imported into the United States, and achieved their greatest popularity from 1780 to 1860. Since a formal education was limited in the early 19th century, the ABC plate was a method of educating the poor for a few pennies.

ABC plates are found in glass, pewter, porcelain, pottery, and tin. Porcelain plates range in diameter from 4⅜ to slightly over 9½ inches. The rim usually contains the alphabet and/or numbers; the center features animals, great men, maxims, or nursery rhymes.

Reference: Susan and Al Bagdade, *Warman's English & Continental Pottery & Porcelain, 1st Edition,* Warman Publishing Co., Inc., 1987; Mildred L. and Joseph P. Chalala, *A Collector's Guide to ABC Plates, Mugs and Things,* Pridemark Press, 1980.

GLASS

6" d
Barley pattern	45.00
Garfield, President, frosted center	60.00
Westward Ho, pattern glass	50.00
6¼" d, Christmas Morning, frosted center scene, stippled alphabet border	175.00
8" d, Stork, pattern glass	65.00

Porcelain, brown alphabet, green transfer of man standing in front of canal, titled "Nations of the World," white ground, marked "Tunstall, England," 7¼" d, $55.00.

PORCELAIN OR POTTERY

5½" d, children, dog, parrot, and verse, multicolored transfer center, emb alphabet border	35.00
5¾" d, girls in flower garden, black	

transfer center, emb alphabet border, marked "J & G Meakin," 1851	50.00

6" d
Fox and Grapes, black and white, red trim, marked "J Meir & Son, Tunstall, England"	40.00
Dr Franklin Maxim Proverb, "If You Would Know The Value Of Money Try To Borrow Some—Creditors Have Better Memories Than Debtors," two men in office	115.00
The Drive, center scene, couple in open horse drawn carriage, raised alphabet border, Staffordshire	115.00
6⅛" d, zebra, black transfer, polychrome enamel, Staffordshire	85.00
6¼" d, Buster Brown	85.00
6½" d, Noah and the Ark, religious transfer center, emb alphabet border	45.00

7" d
Seal Hunters, Elsmore	135.00
Step Child's, boy with dog	60.00
Teddy Bears, playing tennis, multicolored transfer center, printed alphabet border	100.00
7¼" d, Boy Scouts, woodland scene, c1918	125.00
7½" d, cricket game, multicolored transfer center, Staffordshire	125.00
7¾" d, Who Killed Cock Robin	45.00

TIN

2⅞" d, emb, two children playing hoops scene	100.00

3" d
Girl and boy rolling hoop	140.00
Tom Thumb	35.00
5½" d, Liberty	55.00
5⅝" d, Washington	145.00
6" d, two kittens playing with yarn	35.00
6⅛" d, Jumbo	125.00
7⅞" d, Who Killed Cock Robin	100.00

8" d
Mary Had A Little Lamb	160.00
Monkey on Barrel, litho	60.00
Who Killed Cock Robin	110.00
9" d, Hey Diddle Diddle	50.00

ADAMS ROSE

History: Adams Rose, made c1820–40 by Adams and Son in the Staffordshire district of England, is decorated with brilliant red roses and green leaves on a white ground.

G. Jones and Son, England, made a variant known as "Late Adams Rose." The colors are not as brilliant and the ground is a "dirty" white. It commands less than the price of the early pattern.

Reference: Susan and Al Bagdade, *Warman's English & Continental Pottery & Porcelain, 1st Edition,* Warman Publishing Co., Inc., 1987.

Plate, late, marked "England," 7½" d, $25.00.

Bowl, 9" d, early, mint, rare size	450.00
Creamer, 5¾" h, early	300.00
Cup and Saucer, handleless	
Early	200.00
Late, rose dec on saucer, blue spatter	80.00
Plate	
8" d, early, vine border, imp mark	225.00
8½" d, early	200.00
9" d, early	200.00
9¼" d, late, emb scalloped rim	75.00
Platter	
12" l, late	90.00
17⅝" l, early, emb scalloped rim	425.00
Soup Plate	
10¼" d, early	200.00
10½" d, late	65.00
Sugar Bowl, cov, early	300.00
Tea Bowl and Saucer, early	185.00
Teapot, cov	
Early	600.00
Late	250.00
Vegetable Dish, cov, 12⅝" l, early	500.00

ADVERTISING

History: Before the days of mass media, advertisers relied on colorful product labels and advertising giveaways to promote their products. Containers were made to appeal to the buyer by the use of stylish lithographs and bright colors. Many of the illustrations showed the product in the advertisement so that even an illiterate buyer could identify a product.

Advertisements were put on almost every household object imaginable and were constant reminders to use the product or visit a certain establishment.

References: Al Bergevin, *Drugstore Tins And Their Prices,* Wallace-Homestead, 1990; Al Bergevin, *Food And Drink Containers And Their Prices,* Wallace-Homestead, 1988; Ray Klug, *Antique Advertising Encyclopedia,* Vol. 1 (1978) and Vol. 2 (1985), L-W Promotions; Ralph and Terry Kovel, *Kovels' Advertising Collectibles Price List,* Crown Publishers Inc., 1986; L-W Promotions (ed.), *Antique Advertising Handbook and Price Guide,* L-W Book Sales, 1988; Robert W. and Harriet Swedberg, *Tins 'N Bins,* Wallace-Homestead, 1985.

Collectors' Clubs: The Ephemera Society of America, P.O. Box 37, Schoharie, NY 12157; Tin Container Collectors Association, P.O. Box 440101, Aurora, CA 80014.

Periodical: *National Association of Paper and Advertising Collectibles,* P.O. Box 500, Mount Joy, PA 17552.

Additional Listings: See *Warman's Americana & Collectibles* for more examples.

Box, Aberdeen Creamery Co, "Bossie's Best Brand Butter," 1 pound box, $5.00.

Ashtray	
General Tire, rubber tire, glass insert, inscribed "Goes A Long Way To Make Friends"	35.00
Taittinger Champagne, France	75.00
Banner	
Kellogg's Corn Flakes, 48 x 23", 1919–23	260.00
Sickle Plug Tobacco, 36 x 18"	210.00
Blotter, Peter's Weatherbird Shoes	10.00
Bookends, pr, Hartford Fire Insurance Company, bronze, dated 1935	90.00
Booklet, Honest Scrap Tobacco, 1910, dog and cat illus	30.00
Bottle Opener	
Old Falstaff, wall type, orig box	12.00
Whelans Ginger Ale, figural	12.00
Bowl	
Boone Dairy Products, stoneware, blue and gray, 7", 1928	60.00
Geneva, Iowa General Store, spongeware, blue, rust, and cream	125.00

Button, pinback, cello, Infalliable Smokeless Shotgun, blue lettering, white flag, 1¼" d, $20.00.

L Mankowitz Cloaks, Chicago, glass	38.00
Bread and Crumb Tray, Freihofers Bread	45.00

Calendar
Aetna Insurance Co, 1894, Brownies illus, full pad, 6¾ x 9½"	275.00
Cliquot Club, 1942, 12 x 24"	23.00
M. Soffan, T. Dabian and A. Abda Dry Goods Store, 1918, full pad, 15 x 19½"	90.00
Mass & Steffen Fur Co, 1944, 26½ x 13¾"	110.00
Metropolitan Insurance Co, 1903, celluloid	35.00
New York Life Insurance Co, 1890–91	10.00
Springfield Fire and Marine Insurance Co, perpetual, tin, sailing ship scene, green	20.00
Standard Oil Co, 1929, gas globe, 13½ x 27"	250.00
Wester World's Champion Ammunition, 1928, flying snow geese, 14¾ x 28"	300.00

Change Tray
De Laval Cream Separators, 4¼", farm wife using product	75.00
Prudential Insurance Co, oval, 3½"	75.00
Cigar Rest, Spohn & Walters Edelweiss Cigar	45.00

Doll
G. E. Bandy, wood	300.00
Poll Parrot, 3½"	55.00
Western Union Dolly-Gram	20.00
Door Push, Sweetheart Products, metal, heart shape	60.00
Fan, Moxie, celluloid	130.00
Humidor, Hayner Cigars, Dayton, OH	95.00
Jar, Horlick Milk, emb, zinc lid	35.00
Jug, Tome Kellar Rye, Utica, NY, stoneware, qt	100.00

Letter Opener
DeLaval	26.00

Fuller Brush, figural, man, plastic, pink	8.00
Protective Fire Insurance Co, Seward, Nebr	10.00

Match Holder
Dockash Stove Factory, 3⅜ x 5"	10.00
Moxie, 7 x 2½"	100.00
Match Safe, Wetherill & Brother, Philadelphia, lead	70.00

Menu Board
Alka-Seltzer, tin, wood frame	175.00
Butter Nut Bread, fiberboard, diecut, loaf of bread at top	140.00
Kayo, boy in one corner	95.00

Mirror, Beautyskin, Chichester Chemical Co, Phila, girl wearing pink dress, yellow flowers, green ground, 2½ x 1½", $35.00.

Mirror
Baileys Music Room, man, woman, girl, and piano	30.00
Continental Cube Pipe Tobacco, pretty lady with red hair	55.00
Dr.'s Bureson and Burleson Rectal Specialist, Grand Rapids, Mich	140.00
Duffy's Malt Whiskey, pocket	65.00
Gates Hotel, hotel illus and rates	25.00
Golden Wedding Liquor, gold	125.00
Mascot Tobacco, dog in center	35.00
Munsingwear, pocket, silver	55.00
Princess Stoves	35.00
Utz & Dunn's Footwear, adv on re-	

verse painted glass on other side, oak frame with cast iron legs, 44 x 32" **1,600.00**

Y & N Corsets, 21 x 30" **110.00**

Napkin Holder, Rolling Rock Beer, mountain stream scene **20.00**

Noisemaker, Buster Brown Shoes, wood and metal **15.00**

Paper Doll

Kis-Me Gum, orig sheet **35.00**

Pepsodent **35.00**

Paperweight, The Duff Manuf. Co., Allegheny, PA, glass, black and white, 4 x 2⅝", $20.00.

Paperweight

Oil Well Supply Co, lead, oil well figure **45.00**

Puritan Coke, brass, figural, pilgrim **185.00**

Sandell Beer Pumps & Coolers, brass **35.00**

Pin, Lawrence's 5¢ Cigar **35.00**

Pitcher, Moxie, 5", pretty girl **250.00**

Plate

Clarke's Pyramid Night Lights, 2¼", black and white, light illus **40.00**

Lincolnshire Boot Stores, 7½", white, red border, adv stores in various cities, c1880 .... **110.00**

Walter Baker Co, tin, 10" d **150.00**

Plaque

Hartford Fire Insurance Company, bronze and oak, dated 1909 .... **110.00**

Watlings Pic-Nic Pies, porcelain, black transfer, celebrating appointment to Crystal Palace Co 1851, hanging wire, 9½ x 12" **900.00**

Pocket Knife

Home Insurance Co, North Wind design, Victorian SS switchblade ... **90.00**

West End Brewing Co, Utica, NY, lady's leg **95.00**

Poker Chip, Lorillard Plug Tobacco, pr **10.00**

Postcard, Ruder Brewing Co **30.00**

Poster

B Stuebners Son's Shaving Mug, 12¾ x 19" **50.00**

Cetacolor, "Prevents Wash Goods from Fading 10¢ package," pretty woman, 35 x 23" **145.00**

Cognac Cocktails, cardboard, sexy woman, 9¾ x 17½" **250.00**

Cow Brand Baking Soda, hunting dog and landscape scene, product box in lower right corner, 17 x 25½" .. **85.00**

Dupont Shotgun Powder, "End of a Good Day," hunting scene, 27 x 18", Robert Robinson copyright 1910 .... **1,600.00**

Egyptienne Cigarette, paper, bright colors, framed, 19 x 25" **175.00**

Gold Dust Washing Powder, paper, two black boys in tub of water, framed, 13½ x 26" **5,000.00**

Druso Pastry and Biscuit Flour, old man on beach with parrot, 25½ x 18" **325.00**

Marlin Repeating Rifles and Shotguns, paper, man in boat shooting ducks scene, 16¼ x 24¾" **200.00**

O B Joyful Tobacco, paper, hunting scene, 15 x 19½" **320.00**

OFC Rye, two hunters having drink, titled "A Stag Party," 27 x 18" ... **25.00**

Old English Curve Cut Tobacco, linen, metal bands, man smoking pipe, 25 x 21" **125.00**

Overland Car, family riding in car, 24 x 17" **90.00**

Putnam Nail Co, blond lady, 14 x 21", 1890 .... **70.00**

Ragged Edge Cigars, cardboard, cigar box illus, 11 x 14¾" **525.00**

Sapolo Soap, cardboard, lovely lady, orig hanging string, 11¾ x 15" ... **55.00**

Shamrock Tobacco, canvas frame back, 23 x 17" **190.00**

Pouch, Climax Plug Tobacco **22.00**

Ruler, Lowney's Peanut Chew, metal **35.00**

Sack

Fairy Flour **20.00**

Snow White Flour, Snow White rolling dough, unused **20.00**

Salt and Pepper Shakers, Nipper dog, inscribed "RCA Victor Master's Voice," pr **55.00**

Shoe Horn

Claridge Hotel, Atlantic City **18.00**

Sears & Roebuck, "World's Largest Store" **15.00**

Sign

American Rubbers, pretty girl on swing, 25" h **800.00**

Barbee Whiskey, tin, distillery scene, framed, 31 x 19" **3,200.00**

Barne's Cafe, tin, diecut, pointed arm shape **125.00**

Beshores Dandruff Cure, celluloid, beautiful woman, 9 x 12" **350.00**

Shoehorn, Shinola Shoe Polish, Chas. W. Shonk Co., Chicago, lithographed tin, multicolored, $40.00.

Bickmore Shave Cream, stand-up, cardboard, 31 x 24"	35.00
Blatz Old Heidelberg Beer, tin, emb, framed, 35 x 22"	65.00
Bradley and Company Farm Machinery, paper, various farm machines, framed, 27 x 13"	300.00
Buffalo Brewing Co, Sacramento, CA, tin, bottles on table illus, framed, 22 x 28"	650.00
Cheer Up, diecut, bottle shape, cardboard, 9" h	10.00
Clysmic Water, oval, topless girl sitting by stream holding bottle, 14½ x 12"	1,200.00
Columbian Propellers, tin, 18½ x 26½"	80.00
Columbian Rope, stand-up, diecut, cardboard, man seated with parrot on shoulder, 52" h	135.00
El Principal Cigars, standup, cardboard	70.00
Elgin Watches, "My Elgin's All Right," wood, boy standing, strap with attached watch around neck, 22 x 15"	225.00
Fontella Perfectos Cigars, Spanish lady holding cigar box, framed, 23⅛ x 28½"	85.00
Green River Whiskey, 36 x 19½", black man with horse, framed . . .	65.00
Harvard Beer, tin, beautiful woman sitting by table pouring product in glass, gold leaf frame, 27 x 35" . .	4,000.00
Heinz Soup, "15 cents per bowl, ready in 2 min," tin, diecut	155.00
High Admiral Cigarette, diecut, cardboard, 14½" h	85.00

Honesty Tobacco, canvas, dog	550.00
Honey Bee Snuff, "Sweet as Honey," tin, emb, beehive, 11¾ x 18"	90.00
Hood's Royal Oak Rubber Boots, tin, emb, orig hanging string, 13 x 9"	250.00
Hotel Lincoln, "Rooms $1.00, $1.50 with bath-elevator service," tin . . .	130.00
J F Burnham Shoe Store, paper, black and white, 18 x 24"	45.00
Japp's Hair Rejuvenator, celluloid, includes hair samples, 13 x 9¼" . . .	475.00
Johnson Straw Hat, paper, matted and framed, 44 x 25"	1,950.00
Kayo Chocolate, tin, boy in plaid pants	100.00
Klondike Gold & Aluminum Paint, oval, two men panning gold and two women using product, 22½ x 17"	2,450.00
Kohlsaat Bread, tin, wood frame . . .	150.00
Kool Cigarette, tin, 30 x 12"	60.00
L & M Cigarette, 17¾ x 22½"	50.00
Norseman Coal, tin, Viking	150.00
Orange Crush, tin, chalkboard, 1937	125.00
Otto Friedrick Watch, Clocks, and Jewelry, Cape Girardeau, MI, tin, 28 x 18"	150.00

Sign, Buster Brown Shoes, reverse painting on glass, framed, 9½ x 9¾", $200.00.

Painters and Decorators, Expert Grainers and Paper Hangers, J. P. Shaw Co, polychrome, wood, 30" w, 71" h	1,800.00
Richmond Cigarettes, oval, tin, man wearing black coat and hat, framed, 28 x 22½"	450.00
Russell's Ice Cream, tin, flange	125.00
Sakrete Concrete Mortar Mixes, emb, yellow and black, 28¾ x 17¾" . . .	45.00

Satin Cigarettes, tin, pretty lady wearing hat, 19" d **1,400.00**
Schepps Cocoanut, two monkeys, one holding product, 16½ x 11½" **150.00**
Soldier Boy French Briar Pipe Smoking, cardboard, color, 11 x 6" **25.00**
Spanish Segaros, open cigar box illus, litho, 18 x 23", c1897 ..... **275.00**
The Doctor, Compliments of Liquid Peptonoid, 17¾ x 13", framed ... **60.00**
Turf Club Gin, jockey riding horse, reverse painted glass, framed, 15½ x 19½" **3,000.00**
Turkish Trophies Cigarettes, 36½ x 26¼", Turkish girl, wood frame, c1900 .... **700.00**
Uncle Walbash Cupcake, cardboard, black **50.00**
White House Shoes, reverse painted glass, 18" d **1,650.00**
White Loaf Baking Powder, tin **850.00**
Wm J Moxley's High Grade Butterine, woman in kitchen, litho on canvas, 36 x 58" **225.00**
Zeigler's Beer, tin over cardboard .. **120.00**
Spoon, Towles Log Cabin Syrup **15.00**
Stickpin
Case Plow Works, sunburst, hand holding plow blade **55.00**
Emerson Foot Lift Farm Implements, plated foot **40.00**
Grand Detour Plow, copper oval ... **40.00**
Lion Buggy, bronze lion **30.00**
RCA Victor, Nipper dog **55.00**
United Munitions Co, copper arrow . **25.00**
Store Bin
Fairy Soap, wood, paper ad on lid .. **175.00**
Rice's Flower Seeds, wood, paper ad of girl on lid **125.00**
Tape Measure, Hoover Vacuum Cleaner, 1950s **30.00**
Thermometer
Butter Nut Bread, tin **25.00**
Duquesne Beer, figural, Duke with beer in hand **40.00**
E. C. Atkins and Co, "Finest Saws on Earth," wood **100.00**
Hardy's Salt, round **125.00**
Kentucky Club Tobacco **55.00**
Old Colony Beverage, tin **35.00**
Pepsi **40.00**
Ramon's Brownie Pills, wood, 21" .. **100.00**
Tin
Cardinal Cut Plug **35.00**
Good Luck Baking Powder, 1901 .. **20.00**
Jacob's Biscuit, children caroling ... **30.00**
Jays Potato Chips **45.00**
McLaughlin Moca Java, 1 lb **22.00**
Old Chum Tobacco, 1919 .... **85.00**
Pickwick Coffee, 1 lb **35.00**
Queen Cigarettes, woman selling cigarettes **45.00**

Radium Nutex Condom **85.00**
Sioux Bee Honey **55.00**
Sir Walter Raleigh Pipe Tobacco, 11" **65.00**
Southern Rose Shortening, pail shape **20.00**
States Mixture Tobacco **65.00**
Sultana Ground Red Pepper **60.00**
Taj Mahal Phonograph Needles, black with red letters **20.00**
Tuxedo Tobacco, pocket, curved shape, man smoking **30.00**
Wills Bullwark Tobacco, domino illus **40.00**
Yankee Boy Plug, pocket **50.00**
Tray
Aurora Brewing Company, Dutch boy, 1915 .... **45.00**
Calumet Brewing, Chilton, Wisconsin, "Hearts Are Trump," 17 x 12" ... **65.00**
Cordia Club Whiskey, "A Helping Hand," Dutch girl, 1914 .... **45.00**
De Laval Cream Separators, 4¼", farm wife using product, tip **75.00**
Garland Stoves, multicolored, logo **20.00**
Green River Whiskey, black man and horse, 12" d **375.00**
Heils Extra, tin, sq, pretty blond girl, 13 x 13," copyright 1909 .... **375.00**
Indianapolis Brewing Company, Gold Medal **65.00**
Jersey Creme, hanging holes, 1910 **80.00**
Moxie, woman surrounded by purple flowers, 6" d **210.00**
Prudential Insurance Co, tip, oval, 3½" **75.00**
Red Fox Beer, Waterbury, Conn ... **250.00**
Reliable Coffee, man smoking pipe . **30.00**
Rock Island Brewing Company **120.00**
Texatone, oval, girl wearing red shirt riding horse **750.00**
Tumbler, Hygeia Spring Water, etched **10.00**
Washboard, child's, "2 In 1 Junior Carolina Washboard," glass, clear **35.00**
Watch Fob
Northwestern Hide & Fur Co **150.00**
S. Silberman & Son Fur Co **150.00**
Savage Pistol **80.00**

ADVERTISING TRADE CARDS

History: Advertising trade cards are small, thin cardboard cards made to advertise the merits of a product and usually bear the name and address of a merchant.

With the invention of lithography, colorful trade cards became a popular advertising media in the late 19th and early 20th centuries. They were made especially to appeal to children. Young and old alike collected and treasured them in albums and scrapbooks. Very few were dated; 1880 to 1893 were the prime years for trade cards; 1810 to 1850 cards can be found, but rarely. By 1900 trade cards were rapidly losing their popularity. By 1910 they had all but vanished.

References: Kit Barry, *The Advertising Trade Card*, Book 1, Iris Publishing Co., 1981; Robert Jay, *The Trade Card In Nineteenth-Century America*, University of Missouri Press, 1987; Jim and Cathy McQuary, *Collectors Guide To Advertising Cards*, L-W Promotions, 1975; Murray Card (International) Ltd., *Cigarette Card Values: Murray's 1990 Guide To Cigarette & Other Trade Cards*, published by author, 1990.

Additional Listings: See *Warman's Americana & Collectibles* for more examples.

CLOTHING

Beals, Torrey & Co., "Boots and Shoes," Palmer Cox brownies	6.50
Buster Brown Shoe, children and dog, 1909	10.00
Edwin Burt Fine Shoes, children's tea party scene	5.00
Prevost, M.V. Fine Millinery, fan shape, diecut, comical animals	2.00
Wheeler & Wilson, two ladies making dress	5.00

COFFEE

Great Atlantic & Pacific Tea Co., Dinah praises A & P teas and coffees, black landlord and renter's conversation on bottom, adv on back, 1884, 8 x 9" . .	20.00
Victor Coffee, four horses pulling chariot	6.00

FARM MACHINERY

McCormick, hand shape, diecut	10.00
Princess Plow Co, Canton, OH, The Princess of Wales Plow, full color, four pgs, Princess on cov, farm plow illus on three pages	12.00
Sharples Bros, Philadelphia, cream separator, chromolitho of girl and bunny	12.00

FOOD

Dixon's Ice Cream, Kearny Statue in Military Park	6.00
Eagle Brand Condensed Milk, three children seated at table	
Greenfield's Chocolate Sponge, child carrying box with policeman directs traffic, 1915	10.00
Hecker's Buckwheat, hold to light type	18.00
Homogenized Bond Bread, set of 52, movie star series	25.00
Quaker Oats, mechanical	35.00

Ridge's food, child shakes rattle over baby's head	4.00
Thurber's Canned Vegetables	5.00

Medicine, Bush's Liquid Beef, A. P. Bush & Co, Boston, MA, black shoe shine boy, sepia, J. Ottmann Litho Co., NY, $7.50.

MEDICINE

Ayer's Hair Vigor	13.00
Carter's Little Nerve Pills, boy and girl hugging large dog	5.00
Evarosa, portrait of woman	3.00
Jayne's Expectorant, children begging, 1890	6.00
Krauter Bitters, elaborate center panel, three folds	4.00
Schenk's Pulmonic Syrup, hold to light type, sleeping children and kitten . .	10.00

MISCELLANEOUS

Buckingham's Dye For The Whiskers, metamorphic, gentleman with chest length white beard changes to black beard, adv on back, 3 x 3½" closed	10.00
Columbus Watch Company, little girl, white dancing dog with blue collar, "Time flies, to keep pace with it, buy a New Columbus watch"	8.00
Dutch Boy Paints, mechanical, feet move, diecut, blue, white, yellow, and red, 6" h	12.00
Glenwood Ranges & Heaters, pretty girl in hat	6.00
McAuslan & Wahelin Co. Toyland, Holyoke, MA, mechanical, Santa writes on blackboard, black, white, and red, adv on back	35.00

Metropolitan Life, diecut chromolitho of three little girls having tea party, boy wearing baker's hat, c1900 . . . . 25.00
Nevius & Haviland Shades, hunting dog 8.50
New Home, hold to light, rags to riches 8.00
Royal Glue, Capitol building, Washington DC 6.00
Thomas's Electric Oil 6.00

PIANOS AND ORGANS

Jesse French & Sons Piano Co., bookmark, lady, rose in hair, full color, black and white vignette of factory 5.00
Patterson Organs, parlor scene 4.00
Waterloo Organs, Malcolm Love & Co., lady seated in front of ornate parlor organ, full color 5.00

SOAP AND CLEANERS

Bon-Ton Polish, two girls playing with dolls and dog 4.00
Geneva Hand Fluter, young lady fluting her petticoat, two kittens playing under table, 3¾" 5.00
Niagara Starch, well dressed, long haired lady holding box, full color, 3 x 4½" 4.00
Packer's Tar Soap, mother washing baby, full color 2.00
Star Soap, The Best For Family Use, elegantly dressed lady, full color . . . 2.00

STOVES AND RANGES

Dixon's Stove Polish, child listening to watch 6.00
Happy Thought Range, diecut jelly roll 4.00
Noble Cook Stoves, early wood stove, happy chef 10.00

THREAD AND SEWING

Clark's O.N.T. Thread, children around spool of thread, 19th C 5.00
J & P Coats, Nancy Hanks, famous trotting mare 9.50
Merrick's Thread, titled "In Search of the North Pole," hot air balloon 5.00
Wheeler & Wilson, delivery of sewing machine by buggy to prosperous rural family, full color, black and white illus on back with adv, horizontal, 3 x 5" 6.00

TOBACCO

Horsehead Tobacco, horse's head, plug in mouth 8.50
King Bull 3¢ Cigar, risque metamorphic, diecut opening, adv on back, 3 x 5½" closed 25.00
Lang's Plug, barometer card, before and after chewing 8.00
Newsboy Plug, "Where is Mother," five puppies 5.00
Veteran Tobacco, soldier, windmill . . . 8.00

AGATA GLASS

History: Agata glass was invented in 1887 by Joseph Locke of the New England Glass Company, Cambridge, Massachusetts.

Agata glass was produced by using a piece of peachblow glass, coating it with metallic stain, spattering the surface with alcohol, and firing. The result was a high gloss, mottled appearance of oil droplets floating on a watery surface. Shading usually ranged from opaque pink to dark rose. Pieces are known in a pastel opaque green. A few pieces have been found in a satin finish.

Thread, Kerr, Santa at chimney, 4¹¹⁄₁₆ x 3⅛", $8.50.

Juice tumbler, 3¾" h, $800.00.

Bowl, 4" d, green opaque body, mottled
border with scalloped gold tracery .. **600.00**
Cruet, 6" h, acid finished pale green
opaque bulbous body, random oil
spot dec, applied handle, orig faceted
darker green stopper **550.00**
Finger Bowl, 4½" d, ruffled rim, pronounced mottling, deep pink int. ... **800.00**
Lemonade Tumbler, 1⅝" d base, 2½"
top, 5⅛" h, New England peachblow
shading, pronounced mottling, gold
tracery **1,250.00**
Plate, 6⅝" d, ribbon candy fluted rim **875.00**
Punch Cup, 3" d, 2¾" h, deep color, oily
spots with blue highlights, applied
handle with mottling **600.00**
Salt Shaker, delicate shading **525.00**
Spooner, 3¾" h, green opaque body,
mottled upper band and narrow gold
band **950.00**
Tumbler, pronounced mottling **550.00**
Vase, 7¼" h, baluster, random oil spot
dec, satin finish **1,450.00**

AMBERINA GLASS

History: Joseph Locke developed Amberina
glass in 1883 for the New England Glass Works.
"Amberina," a trade name, describes a transparent glass which shades from deep ruby to amber
color. It was made by adding powdered gold to the
ingredients for an amber glass batch. A portion of
the glass was reheated later to produce the shading effect. Usually it was the bottom which was
reheated to form the deep red; however, reverse
examples have been found.

Most early Amberina is of flint quality glass,
blown or pattern molded. Patterns include Diamond Quilted, Daisy and Button, Venetian Diamond, Diamond and Star, and Thumbprint.

In addition to the New England Glass Works,
the Mt. Washington Glass Company of New Bedford, Massachusetts, copied the glass in the 1880s
and sold it at first under the Amberina trade name
and later as "Rose Amber." It is difficult to distinguish pieces from these two New England factories. Boston and Sandwich Glass Works never
produced the glass.

Amberina glass also was made in the 1890s by
several Midwest factories, among which was
Hobbs, Brockunier & Co. Trade names included
"Ruby Amber Ware" and "Watermelon." The Midwest glass shaded from cranberry to amber and
resulted from a thin flashing of cranberry applied
to the reheated portion. This created a sharp de-
markation between the two colors. This less expensive version caused the death knell for the New
England variety.

In 1884 Edward D. Libbey was assigned the

trade name "Amberina" by the New England Glass
Works. Production occurred in 1900, but ceased
shortly thereafter. In the 1920s Edward Libbey renewed production at his Toledo, Ohio, plant for a
short period. The glass was of high quality. Amberina from this era is marked "Libbey" in script
on the pontil.

Reproduction Alert: Reproductions abound.

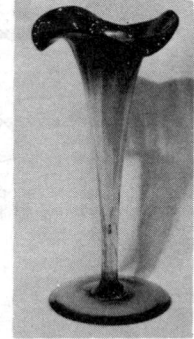

**Vase, New England, lily, tricorn top, 8¼"
h, $375.00.**

NEW ENGLAND

Bowl
5" l, 4½" w, 1½" h, oblong, slight ribs,
Mt Washington **425.00**
5½" d, 3" h, bulbous base, slight ribs,
wide flaring ruffled rim, ground pon-
til **375.00**
Carafe, 8½" h, DQ, Sandwich **225.00**
Celery Vase, 6½" h, 3" w, sq top, Vene-
tian Diamond pattern **475.00**
Champagne, 4" h, hollow stem **200.00**
Creamer, 4" h, tricorn, applied reeded
loop handle, designed by Joseph
Locke **475.00**
Finger Bowl, 4¼" d, deep color **275.00**
Hair Receiver, 2⅛" h, 4" d, fuchsia, sgd
pontil, paper label, Libbey **200.00**
Lamp Shade, 5" d, 4¼" h, 2" fitting ring,
DQ, fuchsia shading to deep blue, Mt
Washington **575.00**
Lemonade, DQ, applied ring handle .. **285.00**
Marmalade, cov, 5½" h, IVT, white metal
cov, Mt Washington **185.00**
Pickle Castor, 11½" h, deep colored am-
berina hobnail insert, fancy silver-
plated frame and cov, Mt Washington **1,100.00**
Pitcher, 5" h, Melon Herringbone, sq,
applied amber handle **245.00**

Punch Cup, DQ, deep color, applied
  amber reeded handle **120.00**
Spooner, 4½" h, DQ, sq scalloped top **235.00**
Sugar Shaker, 4" h, globular, IVT, emb
  floral and butterfly lid **400.00**
Toothpick, tricorn, Mt Washington **365.00**
Tumbler, 4" h, Swirl pattern, ground
  pontil **125.00**
Vase
  7" h
    Lily, ribbed body **375.00**
    Trumpet, 3" ruby red top fades to
      honey amber stem, applied
      wafer foot **475.00**
    10" h, lily, ribbed body **450.00**
    12" h, trumpet, ribbed body **350.00**
    23" h, trumpet, ribbed body, knobbed
      stem, raised circular base **1,250.00**
Water Set, 9" h pitcher, three matching
  tumblers, 4 pcs **1,150.00**
Whiskey Taster, 2½" h, barrel shape,
  Venetian Diamond pattern, deep
  fuchsia color **225.00**
Wine, barrel shaped bowl **385.00**

MIDWESTERN

Bowl
  4" d, 5¼" h, cov, swirled ribbing,
    thumbprints **350.00**
  4⅜" d, Hobnail pattern, ruffled edge **100.00**
Butter Dish, cov, 7" d, 5" h, IVT, amber
  knob, amber Daisy and Button tray **300.00**
Butter Pat, Daisy and Button, Hobbs,
  Brockunier, set of six **650.00**
Creamer
  4½" h, Hobnail, applied clear reeded
    handle **180.00**
Cruet
  5" h, Coin Spot, faceted cut amber
    stopper, amber handle **250.00**
  5½" h, DQ, tricorn rim, faceted cut
    amber stopper, amber handle . . . **350.00**
Finger Bowl, 4½" d, DQ, trefoil rim . . . **125.00**
Ice Cream Set, Daisy and Button, 14½"
  l x 9¼" w tray, eight 6" d plates,
  Hobbs, Brockunier **1,275.00**
Pitcher
  7½" h, inverted swirl, cylindrical neck,
    amber handle **175.00**
  8" h, IVT, quad spouts, amber handle **185.00**
Punch Cup, Expanded Diamond, ap-
  plied amber handle **90.00**
Sauce, 5¾" sq, Daisy and Button, fuch-
  sia, scalloped edge **110.00**
Toothpick, 4½" h, DQ, fuchsia, triple
  plated holder with pond lilies and
  leafy stems **325.00**
Vase
  7" h, cylindrical, Thumbprint, ruffled
    rim **125.00**

9" h, 5" d, gourd, IVT, applied clear
  glass cherries and leaves, thorn
  handle, Hobbs **575.00**
10½" h, inverted swirled bulbous
  body, flared rim, applied pinched
  amber rigaree, ftd **175.00**

AMBERINA GLASS—PLATED

History: The New England Glass Company,
Cambridge, Massachusetts, first made Plated Amberina in 1886; Edward Libbey patented the process for the company in 1889.

Plated Amberina was made by taking a gather
of chartreuse or cream opalescent glass, dipping
it in Amberina and working the two, often utilizing
a mold. The finished product had a deep amber to
deep ruby red shading, a fiery opalescent lining,
and often vertical ribbing for enhancement. Designs ranged from simple forms to complex pieces
with collars, feet, gilding, and etching.

A cased Wheeling glass of similar appearance
had an opaque white lining, but is not opalescent
and the body is not ribbed.

Tumbler, 3¾" h, $2,000.00.

Bowl, 8" d, 3¼" h, ruffled **1,600.00**
Cream Pitcher, 2¾" h, 3½" w, bulbous,
  raspberry shades two–thirds down,
  elaborate strap handle, deep oil spots
  dec **1,800.00**
Cruet, 6¼" h, deeply ribbed, trefoil top,
  amber handle and faceted stopper **3,600.00**
Pitcher, 6½" h, paneled, applied clear
  amber handle **4,500.00**
Punch Cup, 2¾" h, barrel shape, ribbed,
  nine alternating panels of light and
  darker mahogany, deep polished pon-
  til, applied clear amber pigtail handle **2,250.00**
Spooner, 4" h, paneled, ground pontil **1,900.00**
Tumbler, ribbed **1,600.00**
Vase, 3¼" h, bulbous **2,400.00**

AMPHORA

History: The Amphora Porcelain Works was one of several pottery companies located in the Teplitz-Turn region of Bohemia in the late 19th and early 20th centuries. It is best known for art pottery, especially Art Nouveau and Art Deco pieces.

Several markings were used, including the name and location of the pottery and the Imperial mark which included a crown. Prior to WWI Bohemia was part of the Austro-Hungarian Empire, so the word "Austria" may appear as part of the mark. After WWI the word "Czechoslovakia" may be part of the mark.

Reference: Susan and Al Bagdade, *Warman's English & Continental Pottery & Porcelain, 1st Edition*, Warman Publishing Co., Inc., 1987.

Additional Listings: Teplitz.

Basket, 17" h, ovoid, three applied putti climbing floral vines, imp and faint printed marks, c1900 . . . . **500.00**
Bowl, 8" d, beige, raised apples, vines, and leaves, ftd **160.00**
Compote, 11" d, 9½" h, speckled rose, blue, and cream body, accented with blue, green, and rose jewels, incised black linear motifs, stamped mark "Amphora Made in Czecho–Slovakia," incised "W" **100.00**
Figure, 15½" h, Arab holding lion cub, seated on camel, fending attack by lion, marked "Reissner, Stellmacher, and Kessel" **750.00**

Pitcher, Art Deco, blue, red, yellow, and orange, green mottled ground, marked "Stellmacher," c1900, $225.00.

Mug, 5¾" h, fox and bear, imp crown mark, c1891 . . . . **100.00**
Vase
  3¼" h, compressed spherical form, four looping handles, applied grapes and leafy vines, purple and mauve, irid green ground, imp "Amphora 8558," inscribed monogram of Reissner, Stellmacher, and Kessel **275.00**
  6⅛" h, gourd, multicolored jewels, gilt spiderweb ground on upper body, pastel butterflies on lower body, "Turn–Teplitz" and "Amphora" marks **825.00**
  8" h, tapered cylinder, three scrolled handles at rim, metallic gray ground, bright orange painted lobster, gilt printed mark "Reissner, Stellmacher, and Kessel" **250.00**
  9", Art Nouveau style, irid gold and yellow floral encrusted vines, blue–green irid ground **245.00**
  14¾" h, lobed bulbous base, cylindrical neck, inverted rim, white poppies, pink, silver, and gold ground, imp "Amphora" **385.00**

ANIMAL COLLECTIBLES

History: The representation of animals as a theme in fine arts, decorative arts, and utilitarian products dates back to antiquity. Some religions endowed certain animals with mystical properties. Authors throughout written history embodied them with human characteristics.

Collecting by animal theme has been practiced for centuries. Until the early 1970s most collectors were of the closet variety. However, the formation of collector's clubs and marketing crazes, e.g., flamingo, pig, and penguin, brought most collectors out into the open.

The animal collector differs from other collectors in that they care little about the date when an object was made or even its aesthetic quality. The key is that the object is in the image of their favorite animal.

References: Peter Johnson, *Cats & Dogs: Phillips Collectors Guides*, Dunestyle Publishing Ltd., 1988; Alice Muncaster and Ellen Yanow, *The Cat Made Me Buy It*, Crown, 1984; Alice Muncaster and Ellen Yanow Sawyer, *The Cat Sold It!*, Crown, 1986.

Periodicals: *The Canine Collector's Companion*, P.O. Box 2948, Portland, OR 97208; *The Owl's Nest*, Howards Alphanumeric, P.O. Box 5491, Fresno, CA 93755.

Collector's Clubs: Cat Collectors, 31311 Blair Drive, Warren, MI 48092; Equine Collectors Club, Box 4764 New River Stage II, Phoenix, AZ 85027; The Frog Pond, P.O. Box 193, Beech Grove, IN

46107; The National Elephant Collector's Society, 89 Massachusetts Avenue, Box 7, Boston, MA 02115; Russell's Owl Collector Club, P.O. Box 1292, Bandon, OR 97411.

Additional Listings: See specific animal collectible categories in *Warman's Americana & Collectibles*.

BEARS

Advertising, pinback button, 7/8" d, cello, Remington UMC, red rim, white letters, black and white center of bears with ammunition case, bottom rim inscribed "Lesmoke Cartridges," c1910 .... **75.00**

Bank, still

Cast Iron, 4" l, emb "Teddy," worn black paint **90.00**

White Metal, 2¾" h, bronzed, trap missing **10.00**

Candy Mold, 6½" h, bear against tree trunk, clamp type two pc chocolate mold **25.00**

Cookie Jar

American Bisque Co, blue coveralls, marked "USA" **40.00**

Morton Pottery, 10½" h, panda, black ground, white spray glaze **25.00**

Figure, 11" h, Teddy, pink, blue, and brown spray glaze, white ground, Morton Pottery **20.00**

Planter, 3", tan and brown, Niloak Pottery **15.00**

BIRDS, EXOTIC

Egret, lamp, table, 14¾" h, figural, wrought iron and glass, egret poised on one leg, pyramidal base, black–gray marble plinth, reticulated body, blue and white translucent glass with metallic inclusions, iron sgd "Chapelle Nancy," glass inscribed "Muller Freres Luneville" **8,800.00**

Macaws, vase, 9" h, ovoid, amber frosted glass, molded macaws among berried branches, molded "R Lalique," inscribed "France" **8,360.00**

Parakeets, vase, 10" h, spherical, frosted amber glass, molded parakeets on branches, tiny blossoms, wheel cut "R Lalique" **8,800.00**

Pheasants, sculpture, 12½" h, 21½" l, damascened bronze, cast from model by Alexander Kelety, Belgian marble base, French, early 20th C **4,000.00**

BULLS

Advertising, pinback button, 1¾" d, cello, "Aberdeen Angus," black and

white center photo, rim inscribed for breeder, Denison, IA, c1900 ...... **20.00**

Carving, 11" l, wood, orig paint, fake ruby eyes, clothes line tail, mid 20th C folk art, Ohio **200.00**

Windmill Weight, cast iron

14" l, Dempster, full bodied, emb "Boss," welded base **450.00**

24½" l, marked "Fairbury Nebr," wood base **650.00**

Cat, pottery, hand molded, blue glazes, oval base, marked "R. R. Stahl, 1/6/1950," 3¾" h, $175.00.

CATS

Advertising Mirror, White Cat Union Suits, oval **30.00**

Bank, still, 4¾" h, cast iron, worn polychrome **85.00**

Candy Container, papier mache **60.00**

Candy Mold, 6½", metal, clamp type two pc chocolate mold **30.00**

Door Stop, 10½" l, Angora cat, reclining, orig cream paint, Hubley **115.00**

Netsuke, 1¼" h, Japanese, Good Luck cat, painted black spots, red ribbon **150.00**

Pin Cushion, 4", Bakelite, black cat, pin cushion head, tape measure tail, marked "Bavaria" **25.00**

Sculpture, 11¾" h, bronze, brown patina, standing feline, holding tray, titled "Le Chat Maitre–D'Hotel: Version Au Plateau Creux," artist Diego Giacometti, stamped "Diego," c1970 .. **24,750.00**

Tape Measure, brass, circular, emb cat's head, glass eyes, c1910 ..... **75.00**

Teapot, 7" h, figural, orange and brown, blue ribbon, marked "Hand Painted Japan" **35.00**

Toy, litho tin wind up, cat with sweeper, Line Mar **45.00**

CHICKENS

Bank, still
    4⅝" h, tin, marked "Baldwin" 30.00
    6⅛" h, cast iron, worn polychrome   45.00
Candy Container
    2", papier mache, gray hen, chick on
      each side, bottom closure 85.00
    3½", composition, white hen sitting on
      box, two colored eggs, wood base,
      German 100.00
Candy Mold, tin, clamp type two pc
    chocolate mold 20.00
Hen on Nest, Staffordshire, seated hen
    with chicks, polychrome enamel
    9" l, basketweave base, stains and
      chips on inner lid flange, small chip
      on beak 375.00
    9½" l, unglazed area on tail, stains   175.00
    10¾" l, basketweave base 400.00
Tape Measure, celluloid, hen with
    chicks 40.00

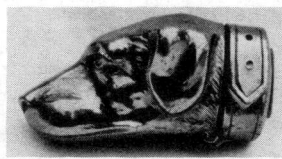

Dog, match safe, plated metal, English, 2⅛" l, $200.00.

DOGS

Bank, still
    Aluminum, 3¼" h, dog cart, modern   40.00
    Cast Iron
      3⅜" h, Retriever with pack, traces
        of black paint 50.00
      4¾" l, Scottie, black paint 130.00
      5¼" h, Fido, seated on pillow base,
        polychrome 200.00
      5½" h, Retriever with pack, brown
        japanning and gold paint 40.00
    Tin and Cast Metal, 1¾" h, dog and
      drum, worn polychrome, trap miss-
      ing 45.00
    White Metal, 4⅝" h, forlorn, seated,
      polychrome, minor wear 20.00
Candy Container, 11", Dalmatian puppy   30.00
Figure
    6½" h, Ohio white clay, clear glaze,
      brown and blue trim, wear and
      chips on base 200.00
    8" h
      Ceramic, Foo, polychrome glaze,
        chips on base, Oriental, pr 250.00

    10" h, Ohio White Clay, seated, brown
      spots, emb stag and dog on base,
      minor chips on base 750.00
    10¼" h, Borzoi, chrome plated metal,
      cast from model by Hagenauer, un-
      derside stamped "Hagenauer
      Wien," Hagenauer/Wiener Werk-
      state seal, Austria, early 20th C ..   3,300.00
Print, 24⅞ x 14⅞", Louis Icart, titled
    "Speed (Vitesse)," three leaping sight
    hounds with woman in flowing dress,
    etching and drypoint, printed in
    colors, cream wove paper, sgd in pen-
    cil, artist's blindstamp, laid down,
    framed, c1927 ....   7,700.00

DONKEYS

Bank, mechanical, 10⅛" l, cast iron, "Al-
    ways did 'spise a mule," polychrome
    paint, whip and one back leg missing   325.00
Bank, still
    4½" h, cast iron, worn blue paint ...   50.00
    7" h, cast iron, worn polychrome, sad-
      dle and harness 150.00
Candy Container, 5", papier mache,
    glass eyes, blanket, German 225.00
Candy Mold, 7", wire clamps, two pc
    chocolate mold 30.00
Cookie jar, donkey and milk wagon,
    American Bisque Co 65.00

DUCKS

Advertising, pinback button, 1¼" d, mul-
    ticolored, "Ducks Unlimited 1948" ..   20.00
Bank, 4" h, cast iron, round, poly-
    chrome, small flakes, trap replaced   175.00
Candy Container
    7", composition, wearing pink bonnet,
      purple int., German 85.00
    10", papier mache, spring neck, black
      top hat, glittered red coat, green
      floral lapels, green bow tie, carrying
      stick, German 65.00
Napkin Ring, figural, yellow, Bakelite ..   5.00
Planter, 5", blue and pink, Niloak Pottery   15.00
Toy, 7½" l, tin, wind up, duck pulling
    cart, marked "Lehmann, Quack,
    Quack," minor wear 300.00
Wall Pocket, 7 x 7", mallard in flight,
    naturalistic colors, Morton Pottery ..   10.00

EAGLES

Figure, 8½" h, Bald Eagle, naturalistic
    colors, spray glaze, Cliffwood Art Pot-
    tery 75.00
Nutcracker, 4½ x 10", head, c1860 ...   125.00
Weather Vane, 36" l, 85" h, hollow cop-
    per body, cast iron head and talons,
    sheet copper wings, emb feathers,

old worn polychrome repaint, mismatched stand, attributed to Boston, c1870 .... **2,500.00**

ELEPHANTS

Bank, still
  Cast Iron
    2½" h, howdah, traces of gold paint **45.00**
    3" h, standing, worn gray paint .. **35.00**
    4" h, gold and red paint, replaced tin wheels **180.00**
  Nickel Plated, 3⅝" l, standing, worn plating **90.00**
  White Metal, 3½" h, hinged top, dark patina, repaired hasp **90.00**
Bottle Opener, cast iron, worn white paint, 3" h **15.00**
Candy Mold, 4" clamp type two pc chocolate mold **15.00**
Carving
  20½" l, ivory tusk, six graduated elephants **75.00**
  32" l, wood, fully dimensional, crouching, trunk raised, worn old brown and gold repaint, age cracks, tusks missing **400.00**
Cookie Jar, pink, Shawnee Pottery ... **40.00**
Figure, 11¼" h, Sung porcelain, clear dark rouge flambe glaze on raised head and trunk, ears, body and legs red and black, mottled blue running down sides, white glazed tusks, black painted mark "Doulton, Burslem/ Sung/Noke/F Allen," imp "7855," c1920 .... **1,100.00**

Elephant, ice cream mold, pewter, three piece mold, marked "S. & Co," $600.00.

Inkwell, 5⅜" h, cast metal, worn bronze finish, glass insert, marked "Germany" **45.00**
Paperweight, advertising, cast iron, emb "Independent Stove Co" **45.00**
Planter, 6" h, circus drum, pink and gray, Niloak Pottery **20.00**

HORSES

Advertising
  Pinback Button
    1¼" d, Oak Park Horse Show, red and yellow, c1900 .... **15.00**
    1½" d, Thoroughbred Work Clothing, multicolored, horse head center, light blue ground **20.00**
  Trade Card, National Wax Thread Sewing Machine, diecut, black and yellow **5.00**
  Tray, 10 x 13", Bevo–Anheuser Busch, team and wagon **75.00**
Bank, still, cast iron
  4⅛" h, standing, emb "Beauty," black and silver **45.00**
  4¼" h, standing, emb "My Pet," worn black paint **60.00**
  7½" h, prancing, pebbled base, two layers of gold paint **85.00**
Calendar, 15 x 20", 1889, E. L. McClain Mfg Co, Greenfield, OH, horse seated at desk **145.00**
Figure, 4 x 3", colt, apricot and white glaze, short tail, Midwest Pottery, c1940 .... **5.00**
Inkwell, cast iron, double, figural head lids, glass wells **50.00**
Painting, oil on canvas, facing pr, horse portraits, sgd "W Fincher 1854," brass frame plates "Young England, by W Fincher 1854," minor wear and crazing, 24¼" h, 28¼" w, framed ... **1,300.00**
Sculpture, 23⅜" h, gilt bronze, equestrian group, rearing horse with armor clad maiden riding bareback, right arm extended, grasping sword, cast from model by Louis Chalon, green marble base, French, late 19th C .. **6,000.00**
Sign, trade, 19" h, figural head, flowing mane, zinc, gold repaint **450.00**
Tile, man on horse, holding falcon, Persian **40.00**
Wax Seal, 2⅜", brass, horsehead **140.00**
Weather Vane, 41½" l, running horse, hollow copper body, cast iron head, green patina, minor dents, repairs, replaced tubular iron rod, modern stand **1,700.00**
Windmill Weight, cast iron, modern wood base
  16½" h, Dempster, good detail, long tail **450.00**
  16¾" h, Dempster, emb mane and short tail, traces of white paint ... **400.00**

INSECTS

Butterflies
  Jewelry, pin, 18 karat yellow gold, pave wings set with fifty round dia-

monds, small round rubies, sapphires, and emeralds 950.00
Lamp, table, 27½" h, 12½" d conical shade, double overlaid glass, peach and white ground, brown and green overlay, etched butterflies and stylized swirling motif, baluster base with wooded landscape, cameo sgd shade, base engraved "Galle" 82,500.00
Vase, 6" h, cov, cameo glass, egg shape, yellow and white frosted ground, purple and blue overlay, etched butterflies and clematis, cameo sgd "Galle" 4,200.00
Fly, toy, tin wind up, worn polychrome, 6" l 45.00
Lady Bug, clicker, round, black and red bug, green ground, c1946 .... 8.00
Wasp, paperweight, 5¼" h, pate–de–verre glass, open wings, brown and green, sucking pollen from yellow centered flower, sgd "A Walter Nancy" 6,380.00

Owl, pottery, wall pocket, shades of green and brown, marked "Weller Pottery," 11" h, 5¾" w, $145.00.

OWLS

Andirons, 14" h, cast iron, copper wash, owls perched on branch, yellow glass eyes, c1920, pr 125.00
Bank, still, cast iron
  3¾" h, polychrome, minor wear, modern 50.00
  5" h, "Be Wise Save Money," worn gold paint 95.00
Bookends, pr, brass, Frankart 40.00

Calendar Plate, owl on open book, 1912, Berlin, NE 25.00
Figure, 5" h, pottery, rouge ground, gray–blue luster glaze, opalescent jeweled eyes, perched on mound base, c1905 .... 100.00
Lamp, table, 34¼" h, 16¼" d shade, cameo glass, conical carved and etched shade, baluster base, opaque martele ground overlaid in green–beige and deep red, moonlight sky, owl grasping pine tree branch, patinated bronze standard with owl faces, base with pine cones and needles, foot below martele knop with fallen pine needles, cameo sgd "Daum Nancy," c1903 .... 880,000.00
Lamp Base, table, 17¼" h, etched and enameled glass, baluster, opaque ground, enameled turquoise, pea green, navy, and oxblood, etched forest scene with owl resting on tree branch, enameled "Muller Croismare" 7,700.00
Match Holder, 8" h, metal, hanging type 18.00
Mustard Jar, 5" h, milk glass, screw top, glass insert, Atterbury 150.00
Napkin Ring, owl sitting on stump, Nippon 225.00
Paperweight, cast iron, owl family, three babies 35.00
Pitcher, 8" h, pressed glass, figural ... 115.00
Ring Tree, 3¼" d, 4" h, shallow brown dish, blue lining, brown and tan owl perched on back, marked "Doulton Stoneware" 325.00
Stein, half liter, Bibite on shield held between claws, Mettlach #2036 ..... 950.00
Vase, 12" h, etched and enameled glass, flattened bulbous body, long attenuated neck, everted rim, enameled oxblood, navy, turquoise, mustard, amber, and fuchsia, etched owl on tree branch, nighttime sky, enameled "Muller Croismare" 6,600.00
Watch Fob, brass, figural, braided human hair chain 125.00

PIGS

Advertising, mirror, 2⅛" d, Newton Collins Short Order Restaurant, St Joe, MO, pastel yellow and orange 35.00
Ashtray, heart shape, two pigs with sheet music on each side, marked "Germany" 60.00
Bank, still
  Bronze, 7" l, sleek 45.00
  Cast Iron
    4" l, worn black paint 85.00
    4⅜" l, emb "Decker Iowana," repainted gold 30.00

5¼" l, laughing, worn polychrome 100.00
Nickel Plated, 5¼" l, wearing bow .. 135.00
Pottery, two tone marbleized glaze
  4¼" l, minor flakes, marked "Made in Checho–slov" 25.00
  6¼" l, marked "Austria" 25.00
Clicker, blue and white, marked "O.I.C." 15.00
Cutting Board, 14 x 9½", wood, figural, marked "Arnold, Kent Feeds" 12.00
Figure
  2½" h, pig pushing cart, marked "Porker Sausage Makers Are The Best Value" 65.00
  4" h, pink pig poking out of open green purse, orange medallion, German 60.00
  4½" h, schoolhouse, bell, orange roof, pig teacher, book in hands, piglet student 80.00
Inkwell, 3" h, pink pig sitting on top, green well 85.00
Nodder, dressed as man and woman, ceramic 55.00
Pitcher, 4", figural, dressed in tie and tails, brown 18.00
Salt, master, 3½", two pigs alongside bucket, stamped "Made in Germany" 50.00
Tape Measure, brass, figural 48.00
Toothpick Holder, 2" h, two pink pigs, inverted green top hat, stamped "Made in Germany" 50.00

RABBITS

Advertising, pinback button, ⅞" d, "Cuties Club," white rabbit, light blue center, red letters "Sox For Tots," light blue rim stripe, c1930 .... 7.50
Bank, cast iron
  5⅛" h, sitting, worn gold paint 135.00
  6½" h, standing, worn gold paint ... 250.00
Candy Container, 6" h, composition, wearing sailor shirt, holding yellow basket, German, marked "US Zone" 85.00
Candy Mold, 5 x 7½", landscape, rabbit pulling cart, flat chocolate tray mold 25.00
Cookie Jar, brown, California Originals 10.00
Planter, 3", green, Niloak Pottery 10.00

ROOSTERS

Box, cov, 4¼" d, black glass, circular, strutting rooster on cov, molded highly stylized wheat motif on sides, green patina, engraved "R Lalique" 9,900.00
Candy Mold, 9", clamp type two pc chocolate mold 30.00
Carving, 15½" h, wood, chip carving, silhouette, old orange and black repaint, minor edge damage 50.00
Game, shooting gallery, 10¼" l, cast iron and steel, bull's-eye and two

roosters, worn orig red and white paint 100.00
Nutcracker, brass 20.00
Wall Pocket, 9 x 7½", white ground, red, blue, green, and yellow spray glaze, Morton Pottery 15.00
Weather Vane, 16½" h, sheet iron, silhouette, old worn yellow and black paint 300.00
Windmill Weight, cast iron, wood base
  9¼" h, Elgin, marked "Hummer E 184," old red and white repaint, light rust 600.00
  10¼" h, Elgin, marked "Hummer E 184," red comb, varnished 325.00
  17½" h, Elgin, three dimensional, relief detail, pitted surface 1,600.00
  22¾" h, full bodied, relief detail, removable base 1,300.00

SQUIRRELS

Jewelry, pin, platinum, baroque fresh water pearl body, pave head, tail, and feet, 185 round cut diamonds, ruby eye, c1935 .... 4,250.00
Nutcracker, cast iron 40.00
Planter, 6", brown glaze, Niloak Pottery 15.00
Windmill Weight, 16½" h, cast iron, Elgin, tail damaged and ground 750.00

TURKEYS

Bank, 4¼" h, cast iron, brown japanning with red paint 285.00
Candy Container, 8", papier mache ... 25.00
Candy Mold, pewter, clamp type two pc chocolate mold 35.00
Planter, 7½" sq, white glaze, cold painted red head and wattle, Morton Pottery 20.00

WILD ANIMALS

Cougar, vase, 2½" h, cameo glass, spherical, waisted flared neck, burnt orange frosted ground, enameled black cougar, foliate neck dec, engraved "Daum Nancy" 2,000.00
Leopards, sculpture, 12" h, 35¾" l, parcel silvered and damascened bronze, group of five leopards, walking, cast from model by Alexandre Kelety, inscribed "A Kelety," French, early 20th C 37,400.00
Lions
  Bank, still, cast iron
    2½" h, worn gold paint 80.00
    5¼" l, gold and red paint, minor wear 45.00
  Candy Mold, clamp type two pc chocolate mold 25.00

Door Stop, cast iron, full body, old
gold repaint **175.00**
Figure
9½" l, Ohio white clay, rect base,
old chips **200.00**
12¼" h, Royal Doulton porcelain,
long bushy mane, naturalistic
glazed, tawny brown and black,
open mouth, teeth bared, stalking prey, shaped gray glazed earthenware rock base, printed lion
above crowned factory mark,
c1902–30 . . . . **525.00**
Nutcracker, brass **30.00**

ARCHITECTURAL ELEMENTS

History: Architectural elements are those items
which have been removed or salvaged from buildings, ships, or gardens. Many are hand crafted.
Frequently they are carved in stone or exotic
woods. Part of their desirability is due to the fact
that it would be extremely costly to duplicate the
items today.

The current trend of preservation and recycling
architectural elements has led to the establishment
and growth of organized salvage operations who
specialize in removal and resale of elements. Special auctions are now held to sell architectural elements from churches, mansions, office buildings,
etc. Today's decorators often design an entire
room around one architectural element, such as a
Victorian marble bar or mural, or use several as
key accent pieces.

References: J.L. Mott Iron Works, *Mott's Illus-
trated Catalog of Victorian Plumbing Fixtures for
Bathrooms and Kitchens*, Dover Publications,
1987; Alan Robertson, *Architectural Antiques*,
Chronicle Books, 1987; J.P. White's Pyghtle
Works, Bedford, England, *Garden Furniture and
Ornament*, Apollo Books, 1987.

Additional Listings: Stained Glass.

**Valance, Art Deco, bronzed cast iron,
24¼" l, 5½" h, 4 pcs, marked, $450.00.**

Arch, 96 x 206", Eastlake, cornice, dentils, anthemion leaf brackets, incised
panels, fluted columns, paneled base **475.00**
Architectural Ornament
Art Deco, 35¼ x 38¾", cast aluminum, scene of farmer sharpening
scythe, plate glass mirror backing **900.00**

Eagle, 68", cast iron, orig finish,
spread wings, perched on half
globe base, Gettysburg, PA ceme-
tery gate type, American, c1870 **4,000.00**
Barber Pole
34½" l, turned and rope carved, old
worn red and white repaint, back
slightly flattened with two mortises
for attachment, pr **400.00**
64" h, turned wood, half round, layers
of old polychrome paint, wear and
age cracks **250.00**
77" h, turned wood, traces of old
paint, weathered, age cracks, base
added **275.00**
101" h, striped red and white paint,
gilt painted wood ball **550.00**
Barn Door, 39½ x 71", pine, three
boards, two wide battens, orig
wrought iron strap hinges, midsection
with seven slots cut with curved scallop, traced of old red paint, PA **100.00**
Bathtub, cast iron, ball and claw feet **65.00**
Bird Cage
14½ x 23¼ x 21½", rect, wire and
wood, replaced pull out copper tray,
old black paint **160.00**
20" h, onion dome shape, wire and
wood, white paint, blue trim, minor
damage **75.00**
Ceiling Medallion, 31" d, plaster, acan-
thus leaf dec **100.00**
Doors, pr, 89" h, 21" w, stained and
painted glass, finches and flowers,
Renaissance style fretwork border,
French, 20th C **2,500.00**
Down Spout Collection Box, 17" h, tole,
old black repaint, red and gold trim,
gold numbers "1860," minor damage **425.00**
Fire Board, punched birds and grapes,
Victorian **1,650.00**
Floor Register, 8 x 12", cast iron, scroll-
ing vines **25.00**
Fountain, 64" d, 48" h, cast iron, fluted
bowl, everted rim, lappets, pedestal
base of four cranes **375.00**
Fountain Ornament, 18" l, Art Nouveau,
bronze, figural, winged nymph standing over spigot opening, back cast
with single tulip framed by morning
glories, cast from model by G Obiols,
sgd in bronze and with tag "E Blot,
Paris Vrai Bronze" **675.00**
Garden Figure
Crane, bronze, Italian, base marked
"Campaiola," late 19th C **900.00**
Stag, brown painted cast iron, Whit-
man Foundry, Whitman, MA, late
19th C, minor imperfections, pr . . **8,500.00**
Garden Furniture
Bench, 48" l, cast iron, rococo, Amer-
ican, mid 19th C **1,500.00**

Chair
Arm, cast iron, rustic branches and foliage, American, mid 19th C — 700.00
Side, cast iron, vintage dec, old worn blue repaint with rust, pr — 400.00
Settee, wire, Victorian, old white repaint, 55" l . . . . — 225.00
Table, 24" d, 16" h, cast iron, vintage dec, old worn blue repaint, board replacement top . . . . — 160.00
Garden Urn
17 x 34", cast iron, rect base, open grill work panels, florentine handles — 425.00
21" h, cast iron, marked "The Kreamer Bros, Dayton, OH," black repaint, pr . . . . — 550.00
24 x 59½", picket fence, paneled section in base, various sized spires, orig cast iron hardware and latch, Southern, weathered . . . . — 150.00
28 x 20", cast iron, ornamental, scrolling branches, central face, Baltimore area, 19th C . . . . — 700.00
Gate Post, 44" h, cast iron, ear of corn finials, scrolled bases at back, modern steel base, pitted posts, black, green, and yellow repaint, pr . . . . . . — 800.00
Hitching Post, cast iron, horse head
13" h, early 20th C, pr . . . . — 110.00
44" h, orig mounting post . . . . — 90.00
Ladder, 66" h, primitive, pine, old worn patina . . . . — 115.00
Mantel
44" w, 47½" h, 9¼" d, 44" l shelf, 24⅜ x 35" opening, poplar, applied folk art dec, worn brown graining, ebonized areas, yellow striping . . . . . . — 300.00
63" h, 6" d, 48½" w, Adam, 48½ x 43" opening, deal pine, relief urns, swags, birds, oak leaf foliage . . . . — 600.00
Panel
59" h, 71" w, lacquered and gilded, two native riders in pursuit of five wild horses, gold ground, lower right inscribed "Jean Dunand" . . . — 14,300.00
64¼" h, 53½" w, mosaic, multicolored harvest scene, three maidens carrying baskets on heads, designed by Kay Nebel, made by Ravenna Mosaics Company, c1929, orig paper inventory label wood frame . . — 12,100.00
Planter
12" h, 16" w, 7" d, paneled canoe form, continuous Chinoiserie dec of sage and attendants, molded base — 700.00
39¾" h, 52" w, 14½" d, Adirondack, orig green paint, orange and gold dec, minor paint wear . . . . — 550.00
Plaque
18½" d, cast iron, round, high relief horse's head, black repaint . . . . . — 100.00
24" d, brass, emb, relief portraits, Rubens and Holbein, battered, minor repairs, dark patina . . . . — 100.00
Sign, trade
19" h, figural, horse head, zinc, gold repaint . . . . — 450.00
21" h, 33½" w, rect, painted wood, shaded black, worn gilded letters "Philip A Wood, Dentist," scrolled dec in corners, painted on both sides . . . . — 100.00
29" h, boot shape, sheet metal, wrought iron hanger, old reddish brown paint . . . . — 275.00
34½" h, 29¾" w, shield shape, pressed board, wood frame, red, white, blue, silver, and gold paint — 150.00
72" l, scrolled banner, painted wood, black ground, blue and gold, "Drug Store Est'b 1842," mortar and pestle center, painted on both sides, minor restoration . . . . — 700.00
Staircase, Victorian, 21 steps, curved, newel post, 52 spindles . . . . — 1,000.00
Wall Sconce
13½" h, 5" d, gilt bronze, three sides with central panel of pierced rect devices, linear framework supporting rect green irid glass panels, cast cubes at each corner, stepped, rect wall bracket, Frank Lloyd Wright for Francis W Little House, Peoria, IL, c1902 . . . . — 7,700.00
20" h, Art Deco, gilt and green patinated bronze, stylized devil mask, face flanked by drapery rising to two curving brackets hung with two small prism molded light bulbs, from Wiltern Theatre, Los Angeles, designed by G. Albert Lansburgh, 1931, pr . . . . — 1,875.00

ART DECO

History: The Art Deco period was named for an exhibition, "l'Exposition Internationale des Arts Décorative et Industriels Modernes," held in Paris in 1927. It is a later period than Art Nouveau, but sometimes the two styles overlap since they were closely related in time.

Art Deco designs are angular and of simple lines. This was the period of skyscrapers, movie idols, and the cubists works of Picasso and Legras. Art Deco motifs were used for every conceivable object being produced in the 1920s and 1930s, including ceramics, furniture, glass, and metals, not only in Europe but in America as well.

References: Victor Arwas, *Glass: Art Nouveau To Art Deco*, Rizzoli, 1977; Lillian Baker, *Art Nouveau & Art Deco Jewelry: An Identification & Value Guide*, Collector Books, 1981; Bryan Catley, *Art Deco And Other Figures*, Antique Collectors' Club;

Tony Fusco, *The Official Identification And Price Guide To Art Deco*, House of Collectibles, 1988; Mary Gaston, *Collector's Guide To Art Deco*, Collector Books, 1989; Katherine Morrison McClinton, *Art Deco: A Guide For Collectors*, reprint, Clarkson N. Potter, 1986; Wolf Uecker, *Art Nouveau and Art Deco Lamps and Candlesticks*, Abbeville Press, 1986.

Collectors' Club: Art Deco Societies of America, 3447 Sheridan Avenue, Miami Beach, FL 33140.

Museums: Art Institute of Chicago, Chicago, IL; Corning Museum of Glass, Corning, NY; Jones Museum of Glass and Ceramics, Sebago, ME.

Additional Listings: Furniture and Jewelry. Also check glass, pottery, and metal categories.

Ashtray and Cigarette Box, pottery, 4½" h, $50.00.

Beverage Set, frosted glass, cameo overlay, red bamboo and stylized leaf dec, twelve tumblers, matching ice bucket 175.00
Bowl, 3" h, sterling silver, low ftd, pierced flat handles, monogram, Richard Dimes Co, retailed by A. Stowell, c1930, 20 troy oz 400.00
Chandelier
　26" l, 15" d, six radiating chrome ribs with gilded accents, base of six triangular peach frosted glass shield shaped wing forms, trumpet form ceiling cap with stepped cone and ball at base, shades sgd in cameo "Maynadier," French, c1930 . . . . . 3,000.00
　31½" l, rect center, four molded rect glass panels depicting child reading book, four radiating arms, shallow circular shades with scenic panels, molded sgd "Herriter–Vincent France," shades cameo sgd "Muller Fres Luneville" 1,650.00

Cigarette Case, 4¼" h, enamel and silver–gilt, rect, black ground, two red bands, white metal geometric inlay, gilt int., inscribed, French 225.00
Clock, mantel
　10½" h, French, rect case, gilt clock face, black painted Arabic chapters, polished onyx steps with triangular gilt edged reserves, enameled red and black geometric formation, c1925 . . . . 2,000.00
　11" h, French, chromed metal case, conforming black onyx handles, rect green marble base, two polished onyx cushion feet 600.00
　14½" h, French, rect base, white and veined marble, diamond shaped face, Arabic chapters, mounted bronze fox on haunches and crow perched in tree, light brown patina, sgd "P Sega," French title plaque 750.00
Cocktail Picks, silver and enamel, chevron enameled terminals, simulated blue lizard triangular case, marked "Silver," Chinese, set of six 90.00
Cup, 2¾" h, cylindrical, waisted body, slightly flaring everted lip, flat base, monogrammed, Danish silver, Georg Jensen, 1925–30 . . . . 350.00

Dresser Set, black and chrome stripes, mirror, brush, cov powder box, $75.00.

Figure
　12¼" h, dancer, nude, bronze, cast from model by D. Charol, sgd . . . 300.00
　16" h, nude young woman, holding garland above her head, bronze, stepped brown stone base, cast from model by Joe Descomps, sgd "Descomps" 900.00
　29½" l, muscular male moving marble block with pole, marble and black onyx base, sgd "Bezin" 1,300.00
Furniture
　Armoire, French, rosewood veneer, silvered bronze mounts, mirrored, 82½" h 1,500.00
　Bed, German, c1925, ebonized and inlaid walnut, arched founded

headboard and conforming footboard, pr 3,100.00
Chair, side, French, carved walnut, arched back, reeded fans, bowed seat rail, reeded tapering cylindrical legs, c1925, pr 700.00
Stand, bedside, rosewood veneer, silvered bronze mounts, mirrored, 18¼" h 700.00
Table
  Center, French, c1925, hexagonal walnut top, ebony edge, ebonized hexagonal pedestal with relief carved trees, vegetation and tribesmen, mounted ivory masks, three large relief carved African ivory tusks, tapering hexagonal walnut and ebony base, 31" d, 28" h 3,850.00
  Dining, American, c1930, burled walnut, double rect top, pedestal base, open geometric design, 54" l, 22" d, 31" h 1,320.00
Inkwell, 2¾" h, 14 karat gold, glass inkwell with gold hinged lid, sq gold platform, engine turned parallel striated lines, monogrammed, marked "William B Kerr, Newark, NJ," retailed by Brand Chatillon Co, c1925 350.00
Jug, 9" h, 4¾" d, pottery, green bands, green and gold leaves, mottled light gray ground, marked "Charlotte Rhead" 175.00

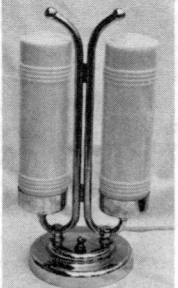

Lamp, chrome, white milk glass cylindrical shades, ring motif, 5" d, 12½" h, $125.00.

Mirror, 40½" d, oval, silvered wood, white silk tassels suspended from carved fruit and flowers, marked "M Roger" and "E Ferron" 1,650.00
Stationery Holder, 5" l, 2⅞" h, 14 karat gold, two upright vertical sides, horizontal base with four cushion feet, monogrammed, marked "William B Kerr, Newark, NJ," retailed by Brand Chatillon Co, c1925 .... 225.00
Tea Caddy, 3¾" h, ovoid, waisted tapering neck, Danish silver, Georg Jensen, 1925–30 .... 435.00
Tea Set
  Silver, 5¼" h teapot, hemispherical base, conical top, angular belly, lap–over edge chased base, engraved conjoining rect segments on top, C scroll handles, bud finial, ring collet base, Reed and Barton, Providence, RI, 1928, 25 ozs, 16 dwts, 3 pcs 700.00
  Silverplated, 6¾" h teapot, creamer, cov sugar, 17" l tray, upright disc form, ebony C scroll handles, half moon ebony finial, incurved rect plinth bases, D shaped cov sugar, rect tray with raised border, C scroll ebony handles, designed by Fjerdingstad for Christofle, 6 pcs 2,475.00
Vase
  5⅝" h, 6⅞" d, pottery, mottled gold ground, bright black and orange Indian type dec, marked "Charlotte Rhead" 200.00
  5⅞" h, opalescent glass, ovoid, everted rim, molded, spike artichoke leaves from shoulder, molded signature "Muller" 130.00
  8¼" h, 5¾" d, pottery, Manchu pattern, green handle and rim, green satin finish ground, large green dragon with gold trim, marked "Crown Ducal, Charlotte Rhead" 200.00
  8¾" h, 5½" d, pottery, green bands, pink, blue, and lavender spring flowers, green leaves, mottled light beige ground, marked "Charlotte Rhead" 185.00
  9" h, glass, orange, Poppy pattern, Paul D'Avesn 725.00
  10⅞" h, wide conical body, everted gilted rim, raised, banded circular gilted foot, forest green int. shading to deep lavender, random, free form gilt lozenges ext., emerald green and crystalline gilt ground, imp "Les Ateliers De Ceramique/ Sevres/Made in France," c1925 .. 900.00

ART NOUVEAU

History: Art Nouveau is the French term for the "new art" which had its beginning in the early 1890s and continued for the next 40 years. The flowing and sensuous female forms used in this period were popular in Europe and America.

Among the most recognized artists of this period were Galle, Lalique, and Tiffany.

Art Nouveau can be identified by its flowing, sensuous lines, floral forms, insects, and the feminine form. These designs were incorporated on almost everything produced at that time, from art glass to furniture, silver, and personal objects.

References: Victor Arwas, *Glass: Art Nouveau To Art Deco*, Rizzoli, 1977; Lillian Baker, *Art Nouveau & Art Deco Jewelry: An Identification & Value Guide*, Collector Books, 1981; Giovanni Fanelli and Ezio Godoli, *Art Nouveau Postcards*, Rizzoli International Publication, Inc., 1987; Albert Christian Revi, *American Art Nouveau Glass*, reprint, Schiffer Publishing, 1981; Wolf Uecker, *Art Nouveau and Art Deco Lamps and Candlesticks*, Abbeville Press, 1986.

Additional Listings: Furniture and Jewelry. Also check glass, pottery, and metal categories.

Bookends, pr, cast metal, green finish, bronze seated maidens, 7½" h, $200.00.

Clock, white metal case, bronze finish, floral motif, 1890 and 1894 patent dates, 8½" h, $85.00.

Bowl, 13" d, sterling silver, everted rim, applied grapevine dec, hammered, made by "Gorham Mfg Co, Providence, RI, retailed by F W Drosten, c1905, 49 ozs, 8 dwts 1,225.00
Bust, 12½" h, polychromed earthenware, golden haired maiden, lilies in her hair, arms folded across chest, Austrian, c1900 .... 1,400.00
Candlesticks, pr, 12", bronze, bobeche suspended on baluster tripod standard, leaf form legs 750.00
Chandelier, 21" d, pyramidal, sq edge, textured mottled amber, white, and green slag glass panels, openwork bronze frame, cast honeysuckle, chain cast as gnarled vines 2,530.00
Clock, mantel, 14⅞" h, gilt bronze, arched top, undulating sides, cast high relief, poppy blossoms and leaves, openwork ball feet, black painted arabic numerals, young woman in center, crowned by blossoms, matted ground, inscribed "Charles Honchery," c1900 .... 3,850.00
Clothes Brush
5½" l, silverplated, sultry maiden reclining, rosebud spray in right hand, marked "Derby Silver Co" 115.00
7" l, silver, deeply chased repousse, youth and maiden on swing, undulating foliage and branches, monogrammed, marked "Foster & Bailey" 125.00
Desk Set, copper, spherical inkwell on ball feet, round calendar frame, 11" l shaped rect pen tray, ink blotter, ivory handled sealing wax lamp, seal, and four desk blotter corners, cerise enamel, applied enamel cherries and silver branches, marked "La Pierre Mfg Co," c1920 .... 1,450.00
Dresser Set
Silver, 9" l hand mirror, clothes brush, and hat brush, woman in Greek clothes, crayfish outline, holding flowers, scalloped borders, monogrammed, c1900, 3 pcs 175.00
Silverplated, 10½" l hand mirror, hair brush, and comb, chased repousse, maiden in backless gown, long flowing tresses, wave scrolls and flowers border, Britannia Artistic Silver Co, Chicago, c1905, 3 pcs 165.00
Figure
8¾" h, ivory, young nude woman, poised on right foot, drapery, ebony

base, inscribed "R Middegaels," c1925 .... **2,750.00**

18¾" h, polychromed bronze, woman, long flowing skirt, close fitting patterned blouse, body arched, poised on right foot, carved ivory hands and face, stepped onyx base, titled "Dancer, Ayouta," inscribed "D Chiparus," c1925 .... **12,100.00**

22" h, parcel gilt, silvered, and patinated bronze, partly draped figure seated on crescent moon, star at forehead, arms raised above head holding flowing robes, plinth base, inscribed "H Levasseur," plaque inscribed "Etoile du Berger Par Levasseur," c1900 .... **5,000.00**

24½" l, bronze, equestrian group, turbanned man, exotic costume, racing on horseback with young maiden, mustard, black, and brown patina, multicolored onyx base, inscribed "Niomel," c1920 .... **4,650.00**

Frame, 11½" h, sterling silver, easel support back, arched crest, chased pendant husks, clusters of fruit, velvet cov back, marked "Walker & Hall, Birmingham," 1911 .... **1,125.00**

Furniture

Bedroom Suite, double bed, 74" w, 56" h headboard and footboard inlaid with trumpet creeper, floral carved crestrails, carved whiplash borders, marbletop dresser with carved mirror, pair of night tables, 5 pcs **7,700.00**

Cabinet, vitrine, French, walnut, rect top, out curved supports with carved flowering vines and ivy tendrils, ivy carved glazed door, three glass shelves, splayed feet with carved poppies and oak leaves, 29" w, 78" h **4,125.00**

Chair, arm, Karpen Bros, Chicago, c1900, mahogany, reed and tendril carved frame, undulating crestrail with high relief carving of female heads and poppy blossoms, poppy carved scrolled armrests, conforming seat rail, cabriole legs, upholstered **1,200.00**

Desk, Majorelle, fruitwood, lobed rect top, stylized Queen Anne's lace on scalloping apron, three desk drawers, hardware cast with matching foliate motif, four carved legs, replaced leather top, 51" l, 30" w, 32½" h **8,800.00**

Stand, Majorelle, three tiers, three twisted carved legs, marquetry pond lilies, sgd "L. Majorelle," 46¼" h **4,000.00**

Table, occasional, Galle, marquetry, rect top, molded serpentine edge, two inlaid sparrows pecking at seed, large falling leaves, inscrolled and rect legs, shaped rect platform stretcher with large leaf inlay, sgd in marquetry, 22" w, 29" h **1,100.00**

Glove Box, silverplated, 15½" l, 6" w, 6½" h, rect, hinged domed lid, chased sides, repeating band of dragonflies **425.00**

Goblet, 6⅝" h, Russian silver, gilt int., maker's marks "NC," Moscow hallmarks, c1890 .... **85.00**

Handbag, 10¼" l, rect, leather, diamond shaped studs on edges, monogrammed, gilt metal hammered emb and chased surface with beadwork, florets, faux tortoiseshell fittings, braided leather handle, suede int., Tiffany & Co, NY, c1880 .... **825.00**

Jardiniere, 18" h, terra cotta, figural, rect, nymph in flowing gown holding blossom, standing against vine cov wall, sgd "J Causse," orig liner **500.00**

Lamp

81" h, torchere, twelve light, wrought iron, cut and beaded glass, elaborately scrolling blossoming vines, hung with pods, pierced peacock on tree trunk, leafy foliage, electrified **19,800.00**

86" h, patinated cast metal, winged nymph emerging from marsh vegetation, three lights above, rockwork pedestal **1,870.00**

Tea Set, porcelain, four cups and saucers, 10½" teapot, sugar, and creamer, painted pink and green thistle leaves, acorns and dragonflies on white ground, printed J & C Kopenhagen mark **275.00**

Tray, 11¼" l, bronze, shaped oval, nude long haired woman and mermaid, two bodies form sides of rippled pool, medium green and green patination, c1900 .... **900.00**

Urn, 16½" h, bronze, figural, ovoid, waisted neck, C scroll handle, cast full relief, nude woman seated on river bank, drawing fishing net, cast gushing waves, gnarled tree handle, brown patination, inscribed "A Vibert," imp circular seal "Siot Decauville/Fondeur/Paris," c1900 .. **3,500.00**

Vase

9", pottery, young male hunter, gilt dec, c1890, marked "Forester & Sons Phoenix Pottery" **200.00**

9⅜" h, pottery, portrait, triangular, three leaf form handles, painted maiden with downcast eyes, painted poppies, sgd "Salvini, Italy" **900.00**

10½" h, pottery, ovoid, incised and painted, blue, white, and green high glazes, stylized pairs of birds, matte mocha ground, incised "Gres Keramis" **500.00**

14" h, molded lacy rims, stylized green, mottled blue and brown flowers and leaves, designed by Eliza Simmace, Jane Rumbol Jr Assistant, imp Doulton Lambeth marks, pr **800.00**

20¼" h, pottery, ovoid, incised and glazed grazing deer, blue, aqua, turquoise, stamped Boch Freres Keramis mark, marked "Ch. Catteau" ....·........ **2,100.00**

24" h, silver, trumpet, wavy mouth, pierced border, weighted pierced circular foot, applied chrysanthemum blossoms, applied blossoms and leaves, engraved sinuous stems, monogrammed, Shreve & Co, San Francisco, c1900, 72 ozs, 14 dwts **4,125.00**

Wall Sconce, 16" l, bronze, spade shaped wall mount, tulip blossom sprouting three curved stems, green patina, set of 3 .... **1,125.00**

ART PEWTER

History: Pewter objects produced during the Art Nouveau, Arts and Crafts, and Art Deco periods are gaining in popularity. These mostly utilitarian objects, e.g., tea sets, trays, and bowls, were elaborately decorated and produced in the Jugendstil manner by German firms, such as Kayserzinn, and Austrian companies, such as Orivit. In England, Liberty and Company marketed Tudric Pewter, which often had a hammered surface and was embellished with enameling or semi-precious stones. Most pieces of art pewter contain the maker's mark.

FIEN ZINN

Bowl, 9½" d, large open rim handles, marked "S Rothhan, Fien Zinn" ... **50.00**
Pitcher, 12" h, marked "Wien, Fien Zinn" **85.00**
Plate, three angels, marked **35.00**

JUGENDSTIL

Tray On Stand, 9" h, oval tray, relief lily pads and frog, figural maiden perched on end, raising blossoms to her hair, waisted branching pedestal, spreading oval base with low relief lily pads and buds, imp "WMF" box, c1900 .... **880.00**

Bowl, cov, 7½" d, sunflowers dec, ftd, handled, marked "Kayzerzinn," numbered, $150.00.

KAYSERZINN

Basket, 6⅛" l, everted ovoid, cast stylized blossoms and leaves, organic handle pierced with buds, stamped "Kayserzinn 4415" **200.00**
Bowl, 10" d, scalloped, water lily center, dragonflies **75.00**
Chamberstick, Art Nouveau floral dec **85.00**
Knife Rest, dachshund **60.00**
Plate, 8½" d, lattice design, relief scrolls and strawberries **75.00**
Vase, 7¾" h, wheat and butterflies ... **125.00**

TUDRIC

Clock, 6½" h, tapering rect body, sq peaked top, circular copper clock face, blue–green enameled center, curvilinear blue, green, and deep red enameled medallion, designed by Archibald Knox for Liberty & Co, stamped "Tudric, Made In England" **1,500.00**
Compote, 10½ x 10", three part pedestal, c1900 .... **375.00**
Tea and Coffee Service, 8" h cov coffee pot, cov teapot, creamer, and sugar, oviform, hammered finish, flattened ball feet, imp "Tudric/English Pewter/Liberty & Co" **250.00**
Vase, 9⅞" h, two leafy handles, floriform, designed by Archibald Knox for Liberty & Co, c1903, circular foot stamped "Tudric" **500.00**

ART POTTERY (GENERAL)

History: The period of art pottery reached its zenith in the late 19th and early 20th century. Over a hundred companies produced individually designed and often decorated wares which served a utilitarian as well as a aesthetic purpose. Artists moved about from company to company, some forming their own firms.

Quality of design, beauty in glazes, and condition are the keys in buying art pottery. This category covers companies not found elsewhere in the guide.

References: Paul Evans, *Art Pottery of the United States, Second Edition*, Feingold & Lewis Publishing Co., 1987; Lucile Henzke, *Art Pottery of America*, Schiffer Publishing, Ltd., 1982; Ralph and Terry Kovel, *The Kovels' Collector's Guide to American Art Pottery*, Crown Publishers, Inc., 1974.

Periodical: *Arts & Crafts Quarterly*, Station E, P.O. Box 3592, Trenton, NJ 08629.

Collectors' Club: American Art Pottery Association, 9825 Upton Circle, Bloomington, MN 55431.

Additional Listings: See Cambridge, Clewell, Clifton, Cowan, Dedham, Fulper, Grueby, Jugtown, Marblehead, Moorcroft, Newcomb, North Dakota School of Mines, Ohr, Owens, Paul Revere, Peters and Reed, Rookwood, Roseville, Van Briggle, Weller, and Zanesville.

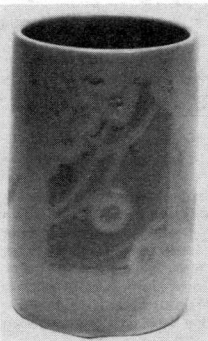

Overbeck, vase, 5¾″ h, cylindrical, beige ground, pale green, marked "Thrown by Elizabeth, decorated by Mary F.," $850.00.

American Art Clay Co, (1892–1903), Edgerton, WI, figure, stylized female nude, borzoi at feet, sq self base, turquoise blue glaze, stamped mark, c1930 .... 100.00
Arequipa Pottery, (1911 to 1918), Marin County, CA
  Bowl, 9″ d, 4¾″ h, light blue glossy glaze, molded flower and leaf dec, rolled over rim, marked 40.00
  Vase
    6¼″ h, tapering cylindrical, wide mouth, carved chestnut tree branches, shaded blue glaze, imp mark, artist's initials, base chips, c1915 .... 900.00

    8⅛″ h, sq tapered cylindrical, sq mouth, angled shouldered, vertical fluted dec on corners, gray–plum glaze, imp mark, base chip, c1915 .... 600.00
California Faience
  Bowl, 4½″ d, medium blue, glossy glaze 125.00
  Flower Frog, sailboat shape 25.00
  Vase, 5″ h, 7″ d, pumpkin shape, luminous turquoise glaze, marked 115.00
Merrimac Pottery, Newburyport, MA, mug, 4½″ h, cylindrical, loop handle, figural frog inside, dark green matte glaze, imp mark, c1905 .... 275.00
Overbeck Pottery, Cambridge City, IN, vase, 4½″ h, squat bulbous, rolled up and short neck, dark mauve glaze, three vertical bands of molded Oriental type geometric dec, imp "OBK," cipher and "EH," dec by Hannah Overbeck, c1915 .... 475.00
Pewabic Pottery (1903–61), Detroit, MI
  Ashtray, 3⅞″ d, lustered burgundy glaze, imp mark and paper label 135.00
  Box, cov, 5 x 4″, rect
    Stylized bird, mossy green and burgundy glazes, imp mark 350.00
    Stylized prancing deer on lid, green and beige glaze, imp mark, pr 675.00
  Candleholders, 3⅞″ h, flower shape, lustered moss green glaze, imp marks, paper labels, pr 125.00
  Cup, 4″ h, matte beige, lustrous green glaze dripping from rim, imp mark 450.00
  Furniture, tile top table, rect top inlaid with plain lustered blue tiles, some molded geometric tiles, 30¼″ l, 23″ d, 24¾″ h 1,100.00
  Lamp, 28½″ h, bulbous thrown pottery base, matte orange glaze, twisted finial, copper insert, scroll metal base, stamped mark, pr ... 1,600.00
  Vase
    2⅛″ h, flared cylinder, grooved rim, crazed gold and green glaze, imp mark, paper label 385.00
    2⅜″ h, cabinet, baluster, lustrous green, gray, and blue mottled glazes, imp marks 245.00
    4½″ h, cylindrical, flared rim, lustrous aqua and rose glaze, paper label 675.00
Pisgah Forest (1913–present), Mt. Pisgah, NC
  Creamer and Sugar, 2¼″ h, pink, 1942 .... 25.00
  Ginger Jar, 1942 .... 60.00
  Vase
    5¼″ h, squat baluster, green and blue brilliant crystalline glaze over beige, molded marks 900.00

13⅛" h, baluster, maize to ivory, blue crystalline glaze over body, pink int., molded marks 825.00

Shawsheen Pottery, Mason City, IA, vase, ovoid, wide mouth, molded stylized leaf dec, matte green glaze, incised marks "SP 1911" 650.00

Teco Pottery, (1886–1930), Terra Cotta, IL

Bookends, gargoyle, ivory, c1910 .. 300.00

Bowl, 6" h, four buttress leg supports, white int. glaze, matte green glaze, designed by Holmes Smith, stamped "Teco" five times and "400" 4,620.00

Jardiniere, 7⅝" h, flaring rim, molded frieze of sq and lines around collar, matte green glaze, designed by William J Dodd, stamped "Teco" twice, incised "75" 1,650.00

Vase

9⅞" h, molded amphora seated in four rect buttresses, matte green glaze, Model No. 431, designed by W D Gates, stamped "Teco" three times 4,400.00

10" h, molded basketweave neck, frieze of tulips and blossoms around body, Model No. 154, designed by William Le Baron Jenney, stamped "Teco" twice 1,650.00

13" h, triple gourd shape, four buttress supports, matte green glaze, Model No. 287, designed by William Bryce Mundie, stamped "Teco" twice 7,700.00

16¾" h, conical vase, molded vortex of lily leaves, cylindrical shaft, matte green glaze, Model No. 310, designed by Fritz

Albert, stamped "Teco" twice and "310" 28,600.00

Tiffany Pottery, (1898–1920), Corona, NY

Jardiniere, 13½" d, 8" h, squatty bulbous seven lobed tomato form body, raised cuff rim, white clay, molded raised leafy tomato laden vines, bisque finish, glazed green int., "LCT" monogram 2,000.00

Pitcher, 12½" h, elongated tankard, folded clay handle and spout, relief carved cat o'nine tails, white clay, bisque finish, glazed green int., Tiffany monogram 1,200.00

Vase, 8" h, oval, green glazed, high relief carved apple branches, leaves, and fruits, bark textured ground, sgd "L. C. Tiffany Inc., Favrile Pottery/P1131," Tiffany monogram 2,000.00

Walley Pottery, Sterling, MA, early 20th century

Vase

5¾" h, bud, elongated cylindrical neck flaring to bulbous base, matte green glaze, brown glaze at neck, imp mark "W. J. W." .. 200.00

12¼" h, tapering cylindrical, short neck, angled shoulder, two applied loop handles, molded design of two trout, imp mark "W. J. W.," paper label 2,300.00

ARTS AND CRAFTS MOVEMENT

History: The Arts and Crafts Movement in American decorative arts took place between 1895 and 1920. Leading proponents of the movement were Elbert Hubbard and his Roycrofters, the brothers Stickley, Frank Lloyd Wright, Charles and Henry Greene, George Niedecken, and Lucia and Arthur Mathews.

The movement was marked by individualistic design (although the movement was national in scope) and re-emphasis on handcraftsmanship and appearance. A reform of industrial society was part of the long range goal. Most pieces of furniture favored a rectilinear approach and were made of oak.

References: Steven Adams, *The Arts & Crafts Movement,* Chartwell Books, Inc., 1987; David M. Cathers, *Furniture Of The American Arts and Crafts Movement,* New American Library, 1981; Paul Evans, *Art Pottery Of The United States,* 2nd Edition, Feingold & Lewis Publishing, 1987; Malcolm Haslam, *Collector's Style Guides: Arts and Crafts,* Ballantine Books, 1988; Bruce Johnson, *The Official Identification And Price Guide To Arts And Crafts,* House of Collectibles, 1988; Wendy Kaplan, *The Art That Is Life: The Arts And Crafts*

Walrath Pottery, candleholder, seated cherub on pedestal warming hands over candle opening, light green, imp "Walrath Pottery/914," 7¼" h, $465.00.

Movement In America 1875–1920, Boston Museum of Fine Arts, 1987; Coy L. Ludwig. *The Arts and Crafts Movement In New York State, 1890s–1920s,* Gallery Association of New York State, 1983.

Periodical: *Arts and Crafts Quarterly,* Station E, P.O. Box 3592, Trenton, NJ 08629.

Museum: Museum of Modern Art, New York, NY.

Additional Listings: Roycroft Items, Stickleys, and art pottery categories.

Tankard, 14″ h, copper and brass, pewter lined, wheat dec, $350.00.

Andirons, pr
  16¼″ h, wrought iron, inverted "Y" form, ball finial, cast Bradley & Hubbard mark **225.00**
  21″ h, cast iron, faceted domed finial, tapering faceted standard, angular scrolled feet, applied gilt diamond shaped mounts, English **275.00**
Ashtray, 6″ d, hammered copper low bowl, repousse center dec, ext. wrapped by animal antlers, attached smoking accessories, sgd "Albert Berry, Seattle" on base, c1905 . . . . **400.00**
Box, 10¼″ l, 7″ w, 4¾″ h, hammered copper, oval mounting, hinged rect cov, handles, canted sides, stylized floral dec, ball feet, velvet lining . . . **175.00**
Bowl, 10″ d, cylindrical, tapered, copper, hammered, inverted flattened fold–over rim, brown patina, stamped "A Heineman" within a rect, c1910 . . . **440.00**
Candlesticks, pr
  8¼″ h, 5¼″ d, enameled copper, floriform socket, slender stem, green and red enameled disk base, Art Crafts Shop, Buffalo, NY, 1905 . . **800.00**

  11¼″ h, brass, disc bobeche, egg shaped socket, slender stem, disc base, sgd "Jarvie," Chicago, c1905 **1,200.00**
  14¼″ h, brass, conical bowls with removable ring bobeches, delicate stems, large disc foot, Jessie Preston **825.00**
Chandelier, 16¼″ d, leaded glass, flared rect form, stylized sunray motif, yellow, aqua, and lavender slag glass, rim imp several times "Pat'd Oct 20 08," Prairie School, attributed to Bradley & Hubbard **275.00**
Clock, mantel, floriform finial, four strapwork arms framing rect hammered copper form, flared base, English, c1905, 13½″ h, 9¼″ w, 7″ d **275.00**
Cocktail Shaker, 10″ h, International Co, sterling silver, knobbed cov, cylindrical form, corked spout, loop handle, strapwork decanter, sgd "Wilcox S. P. Co., International Co," bent rim **75.00**
Desk Set, copper, red patina, applied sterling silver leaf and cherry design, pen tray, inkwell, blotter, frame, stamp box, clip, letter opener, blotter corners, pen wiper, glue pot, and writing implement, imp logo of "La Pierre Mfg Co, NY, Newark, NJ," and "Silver and Copper," 15 pcs **950.00**
Furniture
  Cabinet, two glazed doors each with twenty panels, two top drawers, three int. shelves, 42″ w, 13″ d, 61½″ h **500.00**
  Daybed, oak, rect, angular raised end, William Morris green floral fabric upholstered cushions, 85″ l, 28¼″ w, 24″ h **1,100.00**
Table
  Tile Top, rect top inlaid with geometric and figural Pewabic tiles, lustered polychrome glazes, 25½″ l, 18¾″ d, 25½″ h **1,100.00**
  Writing, oak, rect, four post legs, two top drawers, undershelf stretcher, crown decal mark for Grand Rapids, MI, 56½″ l, 34″ w, 29¼″ h **750.00**
Lamp
  Floor, 57″ h, wrought iron, three part columnar shaft, double strap base, double, graduated sq collar, attributed to Frank Lloyd Wright for Arizona Biltmore Hotel, c1927 . . . . . **1,760.00**
  Table, 10″ h, wrought iron, three part columnar shaft, double strap base, double, graduated sq collar, attributed to Frank Lloyd Wright for Arizona Biltmore Hotel, c1927 . . . . . **770.00**
Lantern, 12″ h, 11″ w, four sided copper

framework, four amber glass panels, Prairie School, pr **350.00**

Loving Cup, 5⅜" h, bulbous cylindrical copper body, three handles, silver rim, three shell appliques, gilt int., imp "Tiffany & Co 15033 Makers 4573 Sterling Silver 925–1000 T And Other Metals 2 Pints" **350.00**

Mirror, frame of fifty–nine turtleback tiles, peacock blue irid, Tiffany Studios, 44 x 17 x 68" **5,720.00**

Tray, 13¼" d, copper, hammered and acid etched, two rocks among leaves and branches, early 20th C **150.00**

Vase, 7" h, Chicago Art Silver Shop, hammered sterling silver, everted quatrefoil, vertical body with straight sides, applied monogram, imp "Sterling Handmade C. A. S. S.," 8 troy oz **475.00**

Waste Paper Basket, 16" h, octagonal, oak, leather thongs joining sides . . . **350.00**

AUSTRIAN WARE

History: Over a hundred potteries were located in the Austro-Hungarian Empire in the late 19th and early 20th centuries. Although Carlsbad was the center of the industry, the factories spread as far as modern day Czechoslovakia.

Many of the factories were either owned or supported by Americans; hence, their wares were produced mainly for export to the United States. Responding to the 1891 law that imported products must be marked as to country of origin, many wares do not have a factory mark, but only the word "Austrian."

Reference: Susan and Al Bagdade, *Warman's English & Continental Pottery & Porcelain, 1st Edition,* Warman Publishing Co., Inc., 1987.

Additional Listings: Amphora, Carlsbad, Royal Dux, and Royal Vienna.

Cake Plate, 11½" d, multicolored daisies, white ground, Carlsbad, $85.00.

Bowl
8½" h, irid glass, pinched and folded in trefoilate mouth, waisted cylindrical stem, spreading cushioned circular foot, claret shading to striated and mottled light green, purple, green, and amber irid, lightly ribbed and swirled **275.00**

9¾" h, light green irid rim with all–over hexagon pattern, patinated metal fluted cylindrical standard, circular base with pierced rim, two applied arching lotus leaf cast handles, c1900 . . . . **250.00**

Chocolate Pot, cov, hp grapes dec, gold mark **60.00**

Creamer, 7⅛" h, blue glaze, floral dec panel **45.00**

Demitasse Cup and Saucer, Alhambra pattern **48.00**

Dresser Set, tray, two boxes, pin tray, multicolored floral dec **115.00**

Jar, cov, 5⅜" h, rect, pebbled pale green glass, gold oil spot dec, SP rim, domed SP cov **200.00**

Pitcher, 4⅛" h, striped gold irid dec, applied handle **120.00**

Tray, 15" l, pierced handles, beaded rim, ornate gold, green, and purple grape clusters, sgd "Koch" **90.00**

Vase
5" h, cylindrical form, mottled shaded amber irid dec, c1900 . . . . **110.00**

8⅛" h, pottery, cylindrical, wide mouth, band of raised circular flowers in gold, blue centers, gold stems, blue ground, imp maker's mark "Paul Dachsel," early 20th C **450.00**

9¾" h, conical form, deep red, purple irid shaded to amber and blue, relief thistle plant dec, tripod stand with patinated metal ring with three applied dragonflies, c1900 . . . . . . **360.00**

20" h, elongated baluster form, light moss green, shaded amber, blue and violet irid, attenuated neck, everted ruffled rim, c1900 . . . . **165.00**

21½" h, porcelain, polychrome floral swags and baskets, gilded trim, dragon handles, marked "Austria" **450.00**

AUTOGRAPHS

History: Autographs occur in a wide variety of formats—letters, documents, photographs, books, and cards, etc. Most collectors focus on a particular person, country, or category, e.g. signers of the Declaration of Independence.

The condition and content of letters and documents bears significantly on value. Collectors should know their source since forgeries abound, and copy machines compound the problem. Further, some signatures of recent presidents and movie stars are done by machine rather than by the persons themselves. A good dealer or advanced collector can help one spot the differences.

The leading auction sources for autographs are Swann Galleries, Sotheby's, and Christie's, all located in New York City.

References: Mary A. Benjamin, *Autographs: A Key To Collecting*, reprint, Dover, 1986; Charles Hamilton, *American Autographs*, University of Oklahoma Press, 1983; Robert W. Pelton, *Collecting Autographs For Fun And Profit*, Betterway Publications, 1987; George Sanders, Helen Sanders, Ralph Roberts, *Collector's Guide To Autographs*, Wallace-Homestead, 1990; George Sanders, Helen Sanders, Ralph Roberts, *The Price Guide To Autographs*, Wallace-Homestead, 1988.

Collectors' Clubs: Manuscript Society, 350 Niagara Street, Burbank, CA 95105; Universal Autograph Collectors Club, P.O. Box 6181, Washington, DC 20044.

Additional Listings: See *Warman's Americana & Collectibles* for more examples.

The following abbreviations denote type of autograph material and their sizes.

ADS	Autograph Document Signed
ALS	Autograph Letter Signed
AQS	Autograph Quotation Signed
CS	Card Signed
DS	Document Signed
LS	Letter Signed
PS	Photograph Signed
TLS	Typed Letter Signed

Sizes (approximate):

Folio	12 x 16 inches
4to	8 x 10 inches
8vo	5 x 7 inches
12mo	3 x 5 inches

COLONIAL AMERICA

Baldwin, Abraham, signer of Constitution, 4to, address panel, "Henry Baldwin Esq/Meadsville/Pennsylvania" and "Free Abr Baldwin," 1801 ..... **1,200.00**

Burnside, General Ambrose, ALS, 4to, to Col. E.B. Tompkins, sgd approvals by George McClellan and M.C. Meigs, January 25, 1862 .... **750.00**

Fitzsimons, Thomas, signer of Constitution, ALS 2 pgs 4to, to John Anderson, concerning land in Pennsylvania, Philadelphia, Aug 2, 1792 .... **200.00**

Harrison, Benjamin, signer of Declaration, ADS, 8vo, certifying John Mc-Dougal entitled to proportion of land, April 1, 1783 .... **275.00**

Heyward, Thomas, signer of Declaration of Independence, folio, ordering Jacob Bailey summoned to court, Jan 27, 1787 .... **250.00**

Martin, Luther, American revolutionary leader, ADS, 4to, concerning last will of George Leggett of Chester County, PA, June 29, 1814 .... **100.00**

Trumbull, Johnathan, Jr, Revolutionary War official and secretary, ADS, 4to, regarding famous Trumbull family of Connecticut, Sept 18, 1788 ...... **275.00**

White, John, Commanding Col. of 4th Georgia Brigade, Philadelphia, Oct 20, 1780, concerning a deserter he sgd as an apprentice **250.00**

EUROPEAN

Baring-Gould, Sabine, English author and hymn writer, manuscript, folio, 1 pg, eight stanzas from "On the Resurrection Morning" **300.00**

Ben Gurion, David, First Prime Minister of Israel, TLS, 8vo, 1 pg, to Abba Eban, Israeli Ambassador to US, Sept 16, 1955 .... **900.00**

Bonaparte, Josephine, wife of Napoleon I, note, 12mo, inlaid on 10 x 12" sheet, 1802 .... **2,750.00**

Churchill, Sir Winston, TLS, 4to, 1 pg, to Capt. Archilbald Cooper, Oct 12, 1952 .... **900.00**

Coward, Sir Noel, British Actor, PS, 4to, matte finish, inscribed and sgd with ball point ink **200.00**

Louis Philippe, last King of France, ALS, 1 pg 4to, to Comte de Berenger, advising next session of the Assembly open on July 26, Paris, July 16, 1842 **200.00**

North, Lord Frederick, Prime Minister of England, ADS, folio, receipt of 400 pounds due to him for past services as Chancellor of Exchequer, July 11, 1777 .... **200.00**

Piaf, Edith, French singer, PS, 4to, black and white, inscribed and sgd "For Joseph, very friendly, Edith Piaf" **475.00**

Stravinsky, Igor, Russian composer, musical quotation, 12mo, three bars, New York, Feb 22, 1945 .... **1,150.00**

Wagner, Richard, German composer, ALS, 2 pgs 8vo, to Mr. Anderson, concerning a score for performance at Royal Court London, Zurich, Dec 12, 1857 .... **1,300.00**

Verdi, Giuseppe, Italian composer, ALS, 8vo, emb initial letterhead, "Pardon, pardon. I thought I had returned your 'place reserve' but I find it on my desk. I want you to get it in time" **1,700.00**

GENERAL

Anthony, Susan B. and Elizabeth Cady Stanton, leader of women's rights, 4 x 5″ pg from book *History of Woman Suffrage*, written "Presented to Harriet Cady Eatin, May 1881," sgd by Stanton and Anthony **450.00**

Audubon, John James, American artist and ornithologist, ALS, 4to, 2½ pgs, mentions his work on the quadrupeds of North America and includes some writting from his son Victor to Benjamin Philips of London, Nov 25, 1845 **4,500.00**

Bell, Alexander Graham, TLS, 8vo, thank you note to James Lewis Howe of Smithsonian Institute, March 18, 1898 . . . . **375.00**

Buchman, Frank N.D., American evangelist, TLS, 8vo, to Mrs. Bird **300.00**

Greeley, Horace, journalist, presidential candidate, folio, manuscript, 3½ pgs, Civil War damage claim **375.00**

Edison, Thomas, TLS, 4to, 1 pg, laboratory letterhead, to Mr. Straus thanking him for his congratulations and good wishes on his birthday, Feb 16, 1915 . . . . **500.00**

Hawks, Frank, American aviator, book *Speed* sgd, inscribed and sgd on flyleaf above collector's bookplate . . . **200.00**

James, William, American philosopher, ALS, 4to, to Mrs. MacKaye, advising her to stay in Europe, mentions McKinleyism in America and Dreyfus affair in France, July 5, 1900 . . . . . **650.00**

Madison, Dolley, first lady, ALS, 8vo, note of apology, Jan 12, 1849 . . . . . **985.00**

Nast, Thomas, political cartoonist, pen and ink drawing, two men in overcoats attempting to open cavernous door, sgd "Th Nast/1889," 11 x 14″ gold and black wood frame **950.00**

Penney, James Cash, department store chain founder, TLS, 4to, to Woodrow Lane sending his autograph, December 6, 1933 . . . . **200.00**

Rockwell, Norman, TLS, to Mr. Rosenthal with pen and ink drawing of small dog, Aug 8, 1973 . . . . **900.00**

Seabury, Samuel, First Episcopal Church Bishop in America, manuscript, 8vo, sermon text, Nov 5, 1772 **400.00**

Smith, Jessie Wilcox, pen and ink drawing, inscribed and sgd "Marching on to a great future! Jessie Wilcox Smith" **350.00**

Vanderbilt, Cornelius, American financier, CS, sgd "C Vanderbilt" **250.00**

LITERATURE

Alcott, Louisa May, ALS, 8vo, note of apology to Mrs. Armstrong **500.00**

Bierce, Ambrose, American author, ALS, 8vo, 2 pgs, to Edwin Markham, June 4, 1897 . . . . **650.00**

Day, Clarence S., ALS 2 pgs 4to, to Mr. Nock, New York, Sept 22, 1935 . . . **200.00**

Dickens, Charles, ALS, 1 pg 8vo, to Mr. Knight, London, June 15, 1858 . . . **750.00**

Holmes, Oliver Wendell, AQS, 4to, poem to commemorate seventieth birthday of poet John Greenleaf Whittier, Nov 1, 1881 . . . . **500.00**

Longfellow, Henry Wadsworth, ALS, 1 pg 8vo, Cambridge, March 26, 1881 **225.00**

Mencken, Henry Louis, PS, 4to, black and white, seated at his desk, bold pencil signature "For James Cargill, H L Mencken, 1943," mounted **300.00**

Stowe, Harriett Beecher, AQS, 1 pg 12mo, May 18, 1893 . . . . **2,500.00**

White, E.B., PS, 4 x 6″, black and white, sgd "E b White," 8 x 10″ white mat mount, c1955 . . . . **250.00**

Wilder, Thornton, 4to, typescript, closing lines to *The Long Christmas Dinner* play, bold signature **200.00**

MUSIC

Caruso, Enrico, PS, 6½ x 8½″, sepia, seated in tuxedo, boldly inscribed, sgd, and dated 1914 . . . . **775.00**

Cole, Nat King, PS, 4to, black and white glossy, sgd "Best wishes/Nat King Cole" **200.00**

Crawford, Robert, sheet music, Off We Go, into the Wild Blue Yonder, "To my gracious hostess Elizabeth Weaver-with deep appreciation, Robert Crawford, Maxwell Field, 1939" **200.00**

Dorsey, Jimmy, postcard, black and white photograph of Dorsey as young man, inscribed and sgd **45.00**

Ellington, Duke, PS, 4to, black and white glossy, Ellington and orchestra, bold signature **200.00**

Farrar, Geraldine, postcard, shows her in Juliet costume, Metropolitan Opera debut, boldly sgd green ink **100.00**

Gershwin, George, TLS, 1 pg 4to, to Walter W. Clark, RCA Victor Co, New York, Sept 14, 1931 . . . . **2,000.00**

Herbert, Victor, operetta composer, CS, musical quote, three bars from "Kiss Me Again," July 1906 . . . . **300.00**

Lind, Jenny, opera singer, 8vo, poem, sgd in French, Aug 28, 1849 . . . . . . **200.00**

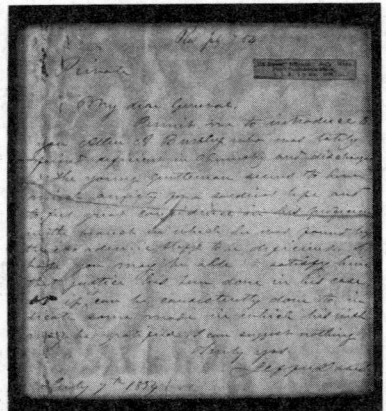

Jefferson Davis, ALS, letter of introduction, 8¼ x 9¼", $600.00.

PRESIDENTIAL, AMERICAN

Arthur, Chester, DS, folio, appointing Jay Knox as commissioner of Internal Revenue, Executive Mansion, May 11, 1883 .... 800.00
Coolidge, Calvin, ALS, 4to, 1 pg, to Charles Scott, March 31, 1930 .... 750.00
Garfield, James A., ALS, 4to, 1 pg, to Rev. E.P. Ingersoll, Sept 6, 1880 ... 500.00
Harrison, Benjamin, TLS, 1 pg 4to, to publisher S. S. McClure, Indianapolis, May 28, 1898 .... 300.00
Johnson, Andrew, note, 1 pg, 8vo, referred to Sec. of War for consideration when a vacancy occurs 800.00
Johnson, Lyndon B., TLS, 1 pg 4to, to Commander W. I. Causey of New Orleans, concerning application of Charles Zivley for commission as lieutenant in the Naval Reserves, US House of Representatives, Committee on Naval Affairs letterhead, July 8, 1940 .... 325.00
Lincoln, Abraham, ADS, folio, vellum, commissioning James A. Ekin with the rank of Captain, Feb 21, 1862 .. 3,000.00
McKinley, William, ADS, folio, appointing William Barnard a Notary Public, May 28, 1895, sgd as Governor ... 200.00
Monroe, James, ALS, 4to, discussing possible appointments for Marshall's post in Tennessee, Oct 20, 1817 .. 2,800.00
Roosevelt, Theodore, ADS, 1 pg folio, appointing Jacob F. Kreps Major of Infantry in the US Army, Sept 4, 1906, matted and framed 450.00
Taft, William Howard, 8vo, sgd "W H Taft/Washington March, 1909," red wax Presidential seal 275.00
Taylor, Zachary, ADS, 4to, certifying requisition for fuel from the office of commanding officer, sgd "Z Taylor, col 1st Infy comdg, February, 1833" 975.00
Washington, George, ADS, 4to, "Rec'd from Doctr Carter one year's interest on Mrs. McKenzies bond due the month, being ten pounds sixteen shillings, G Washington," May 2, 1766 4,000.00

SHOW BUSINESS

Barrymore, Ethel, PS, 4to, black and white, bold signature 200.00
Dietrich, Marlene, PS, 4to, boldly sgd "Dietrich," c1936 .... 85.00
Gable, Clark, PS, 10 x 12", black and white, matte finish, inscribed and sgd 650.00
Hart, William S, PS, 4to, black and white, standing in Western garb, inscribed and sgd in black ink "To Goldie Keller, from her friend, Bill Hart" 350.00
Hayworth, Rita, PS, 4to, black and white, bold signature "Rita Hayworth Martinez" 350.00
Leigh, Viven, postcard, black and white, dressed as Scarlett O'Hara 775.00
Russell, Lillian, postcard, photograph, sgd "very truly yours, Lillian Russell," 1897 .... 150.00
Sullavan, Margaret, PS, 4to, black and white glossy, wearing "Back Street" costume, inscribed and sgd 225.00
Taylor, Robert, PS, 8vo 75.00
Valentino, Rudolph, PS, 18th C French costume, framed, 10 x 12¼" 35.00
Wild Bill Elliott, PS, 4to 90.00

SPORTS

Clemente, Roberto, baseball player, PS, 4 x 6", black and white, wearing Pirates uniform, bold signature 200.00
Johnson, Jack, heavyweight boxing champion, postcard, sgd "Jack Johnson/Former Heavyweight/Champion of the World/Good Luck" in black ink, Oct 14, 1937 postmark 250.00

STATESMEN, AMERICAN

Blaine, James G., Speaker of the House and Sec of State, ALS, 8vo, to Mr. Brown concerning amelioration of Russian Jews, June 14, 1884 ..... 225.00
Clay, Henry, ALS, 4to, to William Mc-

Conkey, commenting on current campaign for President, Sept 28, 1844 .... **500.00**

Johnston, Samuel, Governor, ALS, 1 pg 4to, to his sister, family matters, Hermitage, June 4, 1800 .... **200.00**

Lincoln, Robert T, TLS, 2 pgs 8vo, to publisher S. S. McClure, June 25, 1900 .... **150.00**

Muhlenberg, Frederick A.C., first speaker of the US House of Representatives, ADS, order for Treasurer David Rittenhouse to pay George Woods 43 pounds for 43 days, Sept 26, 1783 .... **200.00**

Pierce, William, ADS, 1 pg 4to, certification to quantity and value of sugar and coffee from Philadelphia merchant, Savannah, Jan 6, 1786 .... **500.00**

Rittenhouse, David, ADS, 4to, noting receipt from William Henry, Treasurer of Lancaster county, Jan 29, 1783 .. **375.00**

Washington, Bushrod, Associate Justice of Supreme Court, ADS, 1 pg 8vo, promissory note for 1248 dollars to George C. Washington, Jan 26, 1815 .... **450.00**

Webster, Daniel, ALS, 1 pg 4to, to Alexander Ross, Washington, Feb 1, 1851 .... **150.00**

AUTOMOBILES

History: Automobiles can be classified into several categories. In 1947 the Antique Automobile Club of America devised a system whereby any motor vehicle (car, bus, motorcycle, etc.) made prior to 1930 is an "antique" car. The Classic Car Club of America expanded the list focusing on luxury models from 1925 to 1948. The Milestone Car Society developed a list for cars in the 1948 to 1964 period.

Some states, such as Pennsylvania, have devised a dual registration system for older cars—antique and classic. Models from the 1960s and 1970s, especially convertibles and limited production models, fall into the "classic" designation depending how they are used.

References: Quentin Craft, *Classic Old Car Value Guide, 23rd Edition,* published by author, 1989; Editors of Old Cars Weekly, *Old Cars Auction Results Worldwide Model Years 1905–1988, 1989 Edition,* Krause Publications, 1989; James M. Flammang, *Standard Catalog of American Cars, 1976–1986, 2nd Edition,* Krause Publications, 1989; Beverly Kimes and Henry Austin Clark, Jr., *Standard Catalog of American Cars, 1805–1942, Second Edition,* Krause Publications, 1989; *Standard Guide to Cars & Prices, 1989 Edition,* Krause Publications, 1989.

Periodicals: *Hemmings Motor News,* Box 100, Bennington, VT 05201; *Old Cars Price Guide,* 700 E. State Street, Iola, WI 54990; *Old Cars Weekly,* 700 E. State Street, Iola, WI 54990.

Collectors' Clubs: Antique Automobile Club of America, 501 W. Governor Road, Hershey, PA 17033; Classic Car Club of America, P.O. Box 443, Madison, NJ 07940; Milestone Car Society, P.O. Box 50850, Indianapolis, IN 46250.

Note: The prices below are based upon a car in running condition, with a high percentage of original parts, and somewhere between 60 and 80% restored. *Prices can vary by as much as 30% in either direction.*

Many older cars, especially if restored, now exceed $15,000.00. Their limited availability makes them difficult to price. Auctions, more than any other source, are the true determinant of value at this level. Especially helpful are the catalogs and sale bills of Kruse Auctioneers, Inc., Auburn, IN 46706.

AUTOMOBILES

AMC
1957, Rambler, Custom Sedan, 8 cyl **2,250.00**
1962, American, Station Wagon, 5 door **1,750.00**
Abingdon, 1902, Meredith, 2 cyl **6,000.00**
Alfa Romeo, GTV, 1973, Convertible .. **6,500.00**
Auburn
1921, Model 6-39, Sedan **10,000.00**
1934, Model 652X, Standard, Brougham, 6 cyl. **9,000.00**
Austin-Healey, 1958, Sprite MK I, Roadster, 4 cyl., 80" wheel base ... **6,000.00**
BMW, 1957, 502/2.6, Sedan, 4 door, V-8, 2580 cc **6,000.00**
Bentley
1951-52, Freestone & Webb, Coupe, 6 cyl **15,000.00**
1962-65, S3 type, Park Ward, Coupe, V-8, 6230 cc **24,000.00**
Bradley, 1981, GT, electric car **3,000.00**
Bricklin, 1975, SV-1 GW, Coupe **9,000.00**
Buick
1916, Model D-54, Touring, 6 cyl .. **12,000.00**
1956, Century Series 60, Convertible, V-8 .... **14,000.00**
1965, Wildcat, Hardtop, 4 door, V-8 . **1,800.00**
Cadillac
1917, Model 55, Victoria, V-8 ..... **8,000.00**
1937, Series 75, Touring Sedan, Fleetwood body, V-8 .... **19,000.00**
1957, Series 62, Convertible, V-8 .. **18,500.00**
1972, Calais, Hardtop, 4 door **2,400.00**
Checker, 1964, Marathon, Sedan **1,750.00**
Chevrolet
1920, Series 490, Roadster, 4 cyl .. **7,500.00**
1937, Master, Coupe, 6 cyl **5,000.00**
1957, Model 150, Sedan, V-8 ..... **3,000.00**
1957, Bel-Air, Convertible, V-8 .... **22,500.00**
1960, Corvette, Convertible, fuel injected **25,000.00**

1963, Corvair, Series 700, 6 cyl . . . **1,600.00**
1969, Chevy II, Nova, Sedan, V-8 . . **1,500.00**
Chrysler
  1926, Series G-70, Crown Sedan, 6
    cyl **5,000.00**
  1947, Windsor Series, Coupe, 6 cyl **4,500.00**
  1965, Newport Series, Hardtop, 4
    door, V-8 . . . . **1,350.00**
Citroen, 1973, SM, 2 door **3,500.00**
Cord
  1932, Series L-29, Sedan, 5 passen-
    ger, 8 cyl **35,000.00**
  1936, Westchester, Sedan, 4 door . . **17,500.00**
Crosley, 1950, Standard, Convertible, 4
  cyl **1,500.00**
Daimler, 1952, Royal, 4 door **8,500.00**
Dagmar, 1924, Model 6T, Sedan, 6 cyl **10,000.00**
Datsun, 1966, 1600 Roadster, SPL 311,
  4 cyl **2,000.00**
DeLorean, 1981, GW, Coupe **9,000.00**
DeSoto
  1931, Model SA, Coupe, 6 cyl **4,000.00**
  1938, S-5, Convertible, 6 cyl **14,500.00**
  1955, Firedome, Sedan, V-8 . . . . . . **2,500.00**
Dodge
  1923, Touring, 4 cyl **4,000.00**
  1941, Deluxe Series D19, Sedan, 6
    cyl **3,000.00**
  1956, Royal, Station Wagon, 8 pas-
    senger, V-8 . . . . **2,500.00**
Duesenburg, 1929, J BT, Speedster . **700,000.00**
Eagle, 1909, Roadster, air cooled, 2 cyl **9,500.00**
Edsel, 1959, Corsair Series, Converti-
  ble, V-8 . . . . **8,000.00**
Empire, 1912, Model 20, Touring, 6 cyl **12,000.00**
Essex, 1929, Challenger Series,
  Roadster, 6 cyl **12,500.00**
Ferrari, 1962, 250GT Belinetta Lusso,
  V-12 . . . . **70,000.00**

Ford, 1956, Thunderbird, $17,500.00.

Ford
  1926, Model T, Touring, 4 cyl **6,000.00**
  1935, Model 48, Roadster, V-8 . . . . **13,000.00**
  1950, Custom DeLuxe, Station Wa-
    gon, V-8 . . . . **9,000.00**
  1957, Fairlane 500, Sky Hardtop
    Convertible, V-8 . . . . **12,500.00**
  1961, Thunderbird, Hardtop, 2 door . **6,000.00**
  1967, Mustang, Convertible **6,500.00**

1968, Falcon Futura, Sedan, 6 cyl . . **1,400.00**
Franklin
  1909, Model H, Touring, 7 passenger,
    6 cyl **15,000.00**
  1931, Series 15, Coupe, 6 cyl, 125"
    wheel base **14,000.00**
Frazer, 1948, Manhattan, Sedan, 6 cyl **3,500.00**
Graham, 1939, Sedan, 4 door, 6 cyl . . **7,000.00**
Haynes, 1914, Model 26, Roadster, 6
  cyl **16,000.00**
Henry J, 1952, Vagabond, Sedan, 2
  door, 6 cyl **3,000.00**
Horch, 1938, Convertible Sedan **55,000.00**
Horstman, 1923, Model 11, Touring, 4
  passenger **10,000.00**
Hudson
  1921, Super Six, Cabriolet, 6 cyl . . . **7,000.00**
  1949, Commodore Series 492, Con-
    vertible, 6 cyl **13,500.00**
  1956, Super Hornet, Sedan, 6 cyl,
    121" wheel base **2,000.00**
Hupmobile, 1928, Century 6 . . . . **6,500.00**
Jaguar
  1953, XK-120S, Coupe, 6 cyl **14,000.00**
  1964, XKE, Roadster, 6 cyl **17,500.00**
Jeffery, 1917, Model 472, Sedan, 7 pas-
  senger, 4 cyl **6,000.00**
Kaiser, 1948, Vagabond, Sedan, 4 door,
  6 cyl **7,000.00**
Lamborghini, 1970, P400 Miura S,
  Coupe, V-12 . . . . **28,000.00**
LaSalle
  1928, Series 303, Sport Phaeton, V-
    8 . . . . **45,000.00**
  1936, Series 50, Sedan, 2 door, 8 cyl **10,000.00**
Lincoln
  1925, Model L, Sedan, 5 passenger,
    V-8 . . . . **14,000.00**
  1948, 8th Series, Convertible, V-12 . **18,000.00**
  1967, Continental, Sedan, 4 door, V-
    8 . . . . **3,500.00**
MG, 1958, MG-A, 1500 Roadster, 4 cyl **4,500.00**
Marmon, 1921, Model 34, Touring, 4
  passenger, 6 cyl **12,500.00**
Maserati, 1964, 3500GT **11,000.00**
Maxwell, 1914, Sedan, 2 door **5,500.00**
Mercedes-Benz
  1954, Model 300S, Roadster **90,000.00**
  1964, Model 220S, Sedan, 4 door . . **6,500.00**
Mercury
  1951, Monterey, leather Coupe, V-8 **6,000.00**
  1959, Parklane, Hardtop, 4 door, V-8 **3,000.00**
  1964, Comet 404, Convertible, 6 cyl **4,000.00**
Morgan, 1962, Roadster **10,000.00**
Morris Minor, 1966, 1000, Station Wa-
  gon, 2 door **2,000.00**
Nash
  1923, Series 690, Touring, 6 cyl . . . **7,000.00**
  1941, Ambassador 600, Deluxe Busi-
    ness Coupe, 6 cyl **2,000.00**
  1956, Metropolitan, Series 1500,
    Hardtop, 4 cyl **1,250.00**

Oakland, 1913, Greyhound 6-60, Touring, 7 passenger, 6 cyl 12,000.00
Oldsmobile
  1917, Model 37, Roadster, 6 cyl . . . **7,000.00**
  1936, Model L-36, Sports Coupe, 8 cyl **4,000.00**
  1961, Super 88, Convertible, V-8 . . **8,500.00**
Opel, 1973, GT, Coupe **3,250.00**
Packard
  1912, Model 1-38, Phaeton, 6 cyl . . **30,000.00**
  1933, 10th Series, Model 1002, Sedan, Eight 20,000.00
  1955, 55th Series, Clipper Custom 5560, Sedan **4,250.00**
Pierce-Arrow
  1911, Model 48T, Touring, 7 passenger, 6 cyl 38,000.00
  1933, Model 1236, Club Sedan, 5 passengers, 12 cyl 27,500.00
Plymouth
  1934, DeLuxe PE, Coupe, 6 cyl . . . **4,500.00**
  1955, Plaza, Sedan, 4 door. V-8 . . . **2,250.00**
  1966, Satellite, Convertible, V-8 . . . **6,000.00**
Pontiac
  1935, Master Series 701, Touring Sedan, 2 door, 6 cyl **3,000.00**
  1959, Catalina, Hardtop, 4 door, V-8 **2,500.00**
  1970, LeMans Sport, Convertible, 6 cyl **4,000.00**
Porsche
  1956, Model 356A, Cerrera, Coupe **15,000.00**
  1975, Model 914, Coupe/Targa, 4 cyl, 2 liter **5,000.00**
Renault
  1919, Type K2, Roadster **10,000.00**
  1961, Model 4CV, Sedan, 4 door . . . **1,250.00**
Reo, 1923, Model T-6, Sedan, 5 passenger, 6 cyl **6,500.00**
Rolls-Royce
  1950, Freestone & Webb, Saloon, 6 cyl 18,000.00
  1960, Silver Cloud II, Standard Steel Saloon, V-8 . . . . 15,000.00
Saab, 1958, GT 750, Sedan, 2 door, 3 cyl **1,400.00**
Star, 1924, Coupe, 4 cyl **7,500.00**
Studebaker
  1914, Series 14, Model 1 SC, Touring, 4 cyl **7,000.00**
  1932, Model 62 Dictator, Sports Coupe, 8 cyl 11,000.00
  1961, Lark Rega, Convertible, V-8 **4,500.00**
  1968, Cruiser, Sedan, 4 door, V-8 . . **1,500.00**
Sunbeam
  1925, Touring, 4 door 50,000.00
  1965, Tiger, Convertible **9,000.00**
Triumph, 1950, Renown, Sedan, 4 door **4,000.00**
Volkswagen
  1956, DeLuxe, Sedan, 2 door **4,000.00**
  1964, Beetle, DeLuxe Sedan, 2 door, 4 cyl **2,250.00**
  1973, Karmann Ghia, Convertible . . **3,500.00**

Volvo, 1962, 122S, Sedan, 4 door, 4 cyl **1,250.00**

MISCELLANEOUS

Fire Truck
  Aheren-Fox, 1921, Pumper **5,000.00**
  American-LaFrance
    1926, Hook and Ladder **3,000.00**
    1937, Pumper **2,500.00**
  GMC, Pumper **3,000.00**
  Hahn, 1923, Pumper **10,000.00**
  Mack, 1945, Pumper **1,750.00**
  Packard, 1921, Pumper **4,500.00**
  Pirsch, 1938, Pumper **3,750.00**
  Seagrave
    1932, Pumper Ladder Truck **1,500.00**
    1946, Hook and Ladder **3,000.00**
Motorcycles
  Ariel, 1954, Square Four **6,500.00**
  BMW, 1962 . . . . **6,000.00**
  Cleveland, 1921 . . . . **3,000.00**
  Harley Davidson, 1931, Model VL . . **4,000.00**
  Indian
    1916, Power Plus, side car, trailer **15,000.00**
    1947 . . . . **5,000.00**
    Monarch, 1919 . . . . **6,500.00**
  Triumph, 1965, Bonneville, 650cc **1,750.00**
  Vincent, 1951, Rapide CV Twin, 1000cc **9,500.00**
Truck
  Chevrolet
    1938, Series HD, Panel **4,000.00**
    1952, Series 3100, Pickup **4,250.00**
    1961, Corvair Series 95, Rampside **2,000.00**
    1966, El Camino, Custom Sports Pickup **4,250.00**
  Crosley, 1950, Pickup, 4 cyl **1,200.00**
  Diamond, 1932, Model T, Stake . . . **6,000.00**
  Dodge
    1930, Series UI-B-124, Pickup, 4 cyl **2,000.00**
    1942, Series WD, Stake, ¾ ton . . **2,500.00**
    1956, Series C-3-B, Highside Pickup, ½ ton **2,500.00**
    1967, A100 Compact, Van, ½ ton **1,800.00**
  Ford
    1936, Pickup **2,500.00**
    1947, Panel, ½ ton **2,750.00**
    1959, Ranchero, Pickup **3,500.00**
    1972, Bronco, Wagon **2,400.00**
  GMC
    1941, Pickup, ½ ton **3,250.00**
    1957, Series 350, Dump **2,500.00**
  Hudson, 1936, Terraplane Series 61, Custom Panel Delivery **4,500.00**
  Mack, 1926, Stake **9,000.00**
  Titan, 1918 . . . . **10,000.00**
  White, 1910 . . . . **10,000.00**
  Willys
    1925, Overland Torpedo **7,500.00**
    1942, Jeep, military, trailer **15,000.00**
    1943, Jeep, military **2,500.00**

1953, Jeepster **1,750.00**
1955, Bermuda, Hardtop **2,500.00**

AUTOMOBILIA

History: The amount of items related to the automobile is endless. Collectors seem to fit into three groups—those collecting parts to restore a car, those collecting information about a company or certain model for research purposes, and those trying to use automobile items for decorative purposes. Most material changes hands at the hundreds of swap meets and auto shows around the country.

Reference: Scott Anderson, *Check The Oil: Gas Station Collectibles With Prices,* Wallace-Homestead, 1986; Brian Jewell, *Motor Badges & Figureheads,* Midas Books, 1978.

Periodical: *Hemmings Motor News,* Box 100, Bennington, VT 05201.

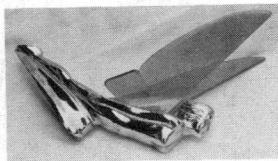

Hood Ornament, chrome, yellow plastic wings, marked #511 on base, 7½ x 4¼ x 9", $75.00.

Advertising
  Blotter, Goodyear Tires **5.00**
  Mirror, Studebaker Vehicle Works, South Bend, IN, 1910, 2¾" oval .. **125.00**
  Sign
    Dodge Brothers Service Station, porcelain, c1930, 15 x 45" **125.00**
    Ford Dealer's, neon **750.00**
    United Motor Dealer, neon outline of early auto **1,250.00**
  Thermometer, Kendall Oil, round ... **25.00**
Ashtray, Buick, dash type **20.00**
Bank, Phillips 66 Motor Oil, tin, 3½" .. **15.00**
Calendar, White Rose Gasoline, 1933 **10.00**
Carburetor, Buick, 1924–25 .... **25.00**
Catalog
  Auburn, 1935, part color, 9 x 16", 16 pgs **35.00**
  Kissel Kar, 10 x 13", 36 pgs **125.00**
Chauffeur's Badge, 1936, Missouri ... **15.00**
Clock, Motor, "Luna," 8 day, luminous dial, brass and bronze, 1914 ...... **120.00**
Display Case, Autolite, glass front, for sparkplugs **125.00**
Engine
  Maxwell, 1914, complete **200.00**

Packard, 1935 .... **800.00**
Gas Pump Globe
  Mobil, glass and metal **250.00**
  Standard Oil, crown, glass globe, one piece, good paint **200.00**
Gearshift Knob, glass swirl, blue and white **15.00**
Grill, Packard, 1941 .... **125.00**
Headlamp, bullseye, Marchal, 12", orig **700.00**
Horn, Pierce Arrow, 1915-20, cowl mounted, correct bracket **175.00**
Hubcaps, Plymouth, 1939–40, set of 4 **250.00**
License Plate, 1933, North Dakota, orig wrapper, pr **7.50**
Literature
  Owner's Manual, Ford, 1914, Model T **15.00**
  Sales Brochure, Buick, 1933, Series 90, orig photos, 8 x 10", black and white **8.00**
  Shop and Parts Manual
    Cadillac, 1941 .... **110.00**
    DeSoto, 1936, master **45.00**
Magazine Advertisement, Wayne Cut 278, 1912 .... **85.00**
Oil Can, Texaco, 1927, orig spout ... **35.00**
Ornament, radiator
  Buick, front grill emblem, 1934 .... **30.00**
  Plymouth, 1933 .... **45.00**
  Pontiac, feather headdress, 1958 .. **15.00**
Pinback Button, Buick, "Looking Fine For 39" **45.00**
Postcards, DeSoto, 1939, full color, one with four door Sedan, other with two door Sedan, pr **8.00**
Poster, Buick, "Kansas City," 1921–22, 25 x 38", black and white **85.00**
Radio, Cadillac, 1937 .... **250.00**

BACCARAT GLASS

History: The Sainte-Anne glassworks at Baccarat in the Voges, France, was founded in 1764 and produced utilitarian soda glass. In 1816 Aime-Gabriel d'Artiques purchased the glassworks, and a Royal Warrant was issued in 1817 for the opening of Verrerie de Vonĉhe á Baccarat. The firm concentrated on lead crystal glass products. In 1824 a limited company was created.

From 1823 to 1857 Baccarat and Saint-Louis glassworks had a commercial agreement and used the same outlets. No merger occurred. Baccarat began the production of paperweights in 1846. In the late 19th century the firm achieved an

international reputation for cut glass table services, chandeliers, display vases and centerpieces, and sculptures. Products eventually included all forms of glassware. The firm still is active today.
Additional Listing: Paperweights.

Water Bottle, Rose Tiente, rose shading to amber, 7″ h, $75.00.

Animal
Dolphin, crystal, sgd	75.00
Shark, crystal, sgd	110.00
Wild Boar, crystal, sgd	145.00

Atomizer, 5″ h, 3½″ l, oval, etched crystal body, chrome top, marked 85.00
Beverage Set, 9¾″ h pitcher, six 4¾″ h tumblers, 11½″ d tray, Rose Tiente, marked 600.00
Biscuit Jar, 6″ h, etched ground, cranberry flowers, leaves, and vines, lid marked 400.00
Bowl, 5½″ d, cameo, clear etched leaf ground, chartreuse floral dec 80.00
Calling Card Holder, 5½″ h, fan shape, pedestal base, relief butterflies, trees, and flowers, opal, sgd 150.00
Candelabra, pr, 22½″ h, amberina socket and bobeche, clear cut base, cut prisms 450.00
Candlesticks, pr, 14½″ h, clear, baluster form, spiral, dome base 200.00
Chandelier, 32″ w, 25″ h, electric, four branches, baluster column, 20th C 800.00
Cologne Bottle, 8″ h, Rose Tiente, pinwheel 90.00
Decanter, 14″ h, amphora shape, lightly ribbed, collared stem, slightly domed foot, conforming stopper, factory acid stamp mark 250.00
Dresser Set, Art Deco, amberina, swirl, brass rack with beveled mirror, marked, 5 pcs 650.00

Epergne, 14″ h, twig and floriform SP mounts, fluted glass bowl and vase, c1900 ..... 300.00
Fairy Lamp, 5½″ h, Rose Tiente, sunburst, matching base, clear candle insert 245.00
Goblet, 6½″ h, cranberry over green, cameo floral cutting, double teardrop stem, gold trim 325.00
Paperweight, Gridel Series
Deer	195.00
Pelican	195.00
Pheasant	195.00

Perfume
4¼″ h, Rose Tiente, swirl, marked .. 70.00
5½″ h, amberina, shell pattern, orig stopper 75.00
8″ h, Art Deco, geometric cut crystal, orig stopper 115.00
Rose Bowl, 3″ d, cranberry, lace enamel dec 150.00
Scent Bottle, 3½″ h, Art Deco, Toujours Fidele, c1930 ..... 500.00
Tumbler, 3½″ h, Rose Tiente, marked 60.00
Vase
8½″ h, cylindrical, molded bamboo branch, insect crawling to top, coiled serpent, circular base, molded rocks and leaves, rust, blue, and black enamel, gilding, molded "Baccarat," c1890 ..... 450.00
13″ h, molded, fish breaking the waves, Japanese taste, gilt bronze mount 2,700.00
Wine, D'Assas pattern, crystal 50.00

BANKS, MECHANICAL

History: Banks which display some form of action while utilizing a coin are considered mechanical banks. Although mechanical banks are known which date back to ancient Greece and Rome, the majority of collectors center their interests in those made between 1867 and 1928 in Germany, England, and the United States. Recently there has been an upsurge of interest in later types, some of which date into the 1970s.

Initial research suggested that approximately 250 to 300 different or variant designs of banks were made in the early period. Today that number has been revised to 2,000–3,000 types and varieties. The field remains ripe for discovery and research.

Over 80% of all cast iron mechanical banks produced between 1869 and 1928 were made by J.E. Stevens Co., Cromwell, Connecticut. Tin banks tend to be German in origin.

While rarity is a factor in value, appeal of design, action, quality of manufacture, country of origin, and history of collector interest also are important. Radical price fluctuations may occur with an imbalance of these factors. Rare banks may sell for a few hundred dollars while one of more common design with greater appeal will sell in the thousands.

The prices on our list represent fairly what a bank sells for in the specialized collectors market. Some banks are hard to find and establishing a price outside auction is difficult.

The prices listed are for original old mechanical banks with minor repairs, in sound operating condition, and with a majority of the original paint intact.

References: Al Davidson, *Penny Lane, A History Of Antique Mechanical Toy Banks,* Long's Americana, 1987; Bill Norman, *The Bank Book: The Encyclopedia of Mechanical Bank Collecting,* Collectors' Showcase, 1984.

Collectors' Club: Mechanical Bank Collectors of America, P.O. Box 128, Allegan, MI 49010.

Reproduction Alert: Reproductions, fakes, and forgeries exist for many banks. Forgeries of some mechanical banks were made as early as 1937, so age alone is not a guarantee of authenticity. In our listing two asterisks indicate banks for which serious forgeries exist and one asterisk indicates banks for which casual reproductions have been made.

Advisor: James S. Maxwell, Jr.

Boys stealing watermelons, cast iron, Kyser & Rex Co., Frankford, PA, c1894, $850.00.

African Native, tin	600.00
Alligator, pot metal, spring jawed	400.00
Artillery Bank, eight sided block house, cannon shoots	625.00
Aunt Dinah and the Good Fairy	20,000.00
Automatic Coin Savings, iron	1,500.00
Baby Elephant, unlocks at 10 o'clock, lead and wood	5,750.00
Bamboula, iron	750.00
Bank Teller, iron, tall man behind three sided lattice work grill	8,000.00

Bear, tin	900.00
**Bear and Tree Stump, iron	675.00
**Bill E. Grin, iron	650.00
**Bird on Roof, iron	875.00
Blacksmith, lead	2,875.00
Bowling Alley, wood and iron, ball knocks down wooden pins and rings bell	16,000.00
**Boy and Bull Dog, brass	850.00
**Boy Robbing Bird's Nest, iron	1,350.00
Boy Scout with Tray, tin	950.00
Breadwinners, iron	5,500.00
**Bucking Mule, iron	1,050.00
**Bull and Bear, brass	5,000.00
**Bulldog Standing, coin on tongue	450.00
**Bull with Movable Horns, iron	450.00
Bureau, iron, Ideal	750.00
Bureau, wood, Serrill patent	975.00
**Butting Goat, tree stump	650.00
*Cabin, iron	275.00
Called Out, brass pattern	3,600.00
**Called Out, iron, painted	6,000.00
Calumet with Calumet Kid, cardboard and tin can	150.00
Calumet with Sailor, cardboard and tin can	350.00
Calumet with Soldier, cardboard and tin can	650.00
**Camera, iron	2,200.00
Carnival, iron	1,275.00
**Cat & Mouse, iron, cat stands on hands	980.00
Cat, pot metal, spring jawed	325.00
**Chief Big Moon, iron	845.00
Chinaman with Queue, tin	975.00
Circus, iron	4,450.00
Clever Dick, tin	850.00
Clown, tin, white faced	875.00
Clown Bust with Acorn Shaped Hat, iron	1,650.00
Clown on Lattice Base, tin clown with tray on iron base, does flip	5,800.00
Coasting, iron	7,500.00
Columbian Magic Savings, iron	460.00
*Creedmoor, iron	450.00
Crossed Legged Minstrel, tin	450.00
Cupola, iron, man in circular building .	1,350.00
*Darktown Battery, iron	1,150.00
Darky Fisherman, lead	11,500.00
Dinah, iron	425.00
Ding Dong Bell, tin, windup	6,375.00
Dog on Turntable, iron	400.00
Dog Standing, tin, nods head	475.00
Droste's, tin	360.00
*Eagle and Eaglettes, iron	750.00
**Elephant, iron, Hannibal	540.00
Elephant, iron, made in Canada, trunk moves	625.00
**Elephant, iron, tusks on wheels	1,250.00
Elephant, tin, safe deposit	4,200.00
*Elephant and Three Clowns	850.00
**Elephant with Howdah, iron, pull tail . .	300.00
Feed the Goose, pot metal	280.00
Feed the Kitty, pot metal	1,400.00

**Ferris Wheel, iron and tin, no markings (smaller than Bowen's Pat. model)	1,500.00
Five Cent Adding, iron	750.00
**Football, iron, boy and shed	1,900.00
Fortune Wheel, tin	875.00
Freedman, wood, pewter, cloth, etc., man sitting at desk	20,000.00
Frogs on Rock, iron	270.00
**Gem, iron	350.00
Giant in Tower, iron	5,500.00
**Girl Skipping Rope, iron	6,000.00
**Glutton, iron, lifts turkey	725.00
**Goat, Frog, and Old Man, iron	2,800.00
Grenadier, iron	720.00
Guessing, lead and iron, woman's figure	7,800.00
Hall's Excelsior, iron and wood, monkey figure	200.00
Hall's Lilliput, Type I	450.00
Hall's Lilliput, Type III	350.00
Hall's Yankee Notion, iron	2,300.00
Hardwig and Vogel Candy Dispenser, tin	660.00
Hen and Chick, iron	1,125.00
**Hindu, iron	1,450.00
**Hold the Fort, iron, seven holes	1,500.00
Home, tin	240.00
Hoop-la, iron	950.00

Lighthouse, pot metal, $600.00.

**Horse Race, iron with tin horses, straight base	1,450.00
Horse Race Savings Bank, tin, Pat. Oct. 5, 1897	3,500.00
Huntley and Palmers Biscuit Tin, drawer pulls out	1,280.00
*I Always Did 'Spise A Mule, iron, jockey	650.00

*Indian and Bear, iron, brown bear	750.00
Indian Chief, aluminum, bust, black face with headdress	4,500.00
Japanese Ball Tosser, tin, windup	5,000.00
John Bull's Money Box, iron	8,000.00
**Jolly Nigger	
Aluminum	
Bar and screw side	165.00
Moves ears, high hat	250.00
With fez	400.00
Iron	
Butterfly tie	190.00
Fixed eyes	240.00
*Jonah and Whale, iron, rect base	950.00
**Jumbo, iron, elephant on wheels	975.00
Key, iron, Golden Gate Exposition	450.00
Kilte, iron	850.00
Lehmann London Tower, tin	1,700.00
Lighthouse, pot metal	600.00
Lion, tin	1,150.00
**Lion and Two Monkeys, iron	575.00
Little Jack Horner, tin, windup	5,000.00
Little Joe, iron	205.00
**Lost Dog, iron	725.00
**Magic Man, iron	750.00
Magic Safe, tin	675.00
**Mama Katzenjammer, iron, 1905–08, dark blue dress painted to neck	2,750.00
Mammy and Child, iron	1,000.00
Man in Chair with Dog near Feet, wood	3,600.00
Man standing wearing Top Hat, wood	1,050.00
Memorial Liberty Bell, iron	750.00
**Merry-Go-Round, iron, semi-mechanical version	400.00
Mickey Mouse with Accordion, tin	2,700.00
**Milking Cow, iron	1,400.00
Model Railroad Drink Dispenser, tin	2,200.00
Model Railroad Ticket Dispenser, tin	2,200.00
**Monkey, iron, drop coin in stomach	1,250.00
Monkey Face	1,125.00
Moody and Sanky, iron and paper	700.00
Moonface, tin	1,150.00
Motor, iron, trolley car	3,750.00
Musical, tin	875.00
Musical Savings, wood and tin, Regina music box	4,500.00
National, iron	1,000.00
New, iron, lever on side	400.00
North Pole, iron	5,500.00
Novelty, iron, Johnson's Pat	400.00
Old Woman in Shoe, iron	100,000.00
*Organ, iron, boy and girl	575.00
Owl, iron, slot in book	425.00
*Owl, iron, turns head	270.00
Panorama, iron	1,800.00
Patronize the Blind Man, iron	1,600.00
**Pelican with Arab, iron	900.00
**Pelican with Man Thumbing Nose, iron	1,125.00
**Perfection Registering, iron, girl at blackboard	2,900.00
**Piano, iron, modern conversion to musical	1,600.00

Picture Gallery Bank	1,875.00
Pistol, cast iron	650.00
Popeye Knockout, tin	375.00
Preacher in Pulpit, iron	15,000.00
Presto, iron, small building with drawer	380.00
Professor Pug Frog, iron	2,100.00
Punch and Judy, cast iron front, tin back	1,550.00
Puss and Boots, iron	20,000.00
Queen Victoria, brass, bust	5,000.00
Rabbit, iron, small	475.00
Registering Dime Savings	475.00
Robot, aluminum	1,800.00
**Rooster, iron	315.00
Sailor Face, tin	850.00
Sambo, iron	625.00
**Santa Claus, iron	780.00
Savo, tin, rect with lines	210.00
Savo, tin, rect with soldiers	275.00
Schley Bottling Up Cervera, iron	3,750.00
Seek Him Frisk, iron, dog chases cat up tree	18,000.00
Sentry, tin, raises bugle	1,200.00
Shoot That Hat, iron	12,000.00
Shoot the Chute, iron	6,500.00
**Smyth X-Ray, iron	3,750.00
**Snap It, iron	450.00
Springing Cat, lead	4,250.00
Squirrel, lead	550.00
Starkies Aeroplane	8,500.00
Stollwerk, tin, Vending	480.00
*Stump Speaker	875.00
**Tabby, iron	500.00
Tank and Cannon, iron	585.00
Target Building, iron	750.00
*Teddy and the Bear, iron	840.00
Thrifty Animal, tin	420.00
Tid-Bits Automatic Money Box, tin	1,850.00
Time Is Money, iron, embossing of man bent over	2,400.00
Toad on Stump, iron	440.00
Tommy, iron	2,300.00
*Trick Dog, iron, six part base	540.00
**Trick Donkey, iron	625.00
Trick Savings, wood, end drawer	285.00
**Tricky Pig, iron, risque	1,800.00
**Turtle, iron	4,000.00
Twentieth Century Savings Bank	950.00
U. S., iron	1,250.00
Uncle Sam, iron, standing figure	1,000.00
**Uncle Tom, iron, no star	540.00
Uncle Tom, iron, no lapels	510.00
Village School Master, tin, windup	3,750.00
Watch, tin, dime disappears, several varieties	675.00
Watch Dog Savings, wood	950.00
*William Tell, iron	650.00
Winner Savings, tin and glass, horse race	4,000.00
Wishbone, iron	12,500.00
Woodchopper, iron	810.00
Woodpecker, tin, 1940s	425.00
World's Fair, iron	775.00

BANKS, STILL

History: Banks with no mechanical action are known as still banks. The first still banks were made of wood, pottery, or from gourds. Redware and stoneware banks, made by America's early potters, are prized possessions of today's collectors.

Still banks reached a "golden age" with the arrival of the cast iron bank. Leading manufacturing companies include Arcade Mfg. Co., J. Chein & Co., Hubley, J.& E. Stevens and A.C. Williams. The banks often were ornately painted to enhance their appeal. During the cast iron era, banks and other businesses used the still bank as a form of advertising for attracting customers.

The tin lithograph bank, again frequently with advertising, did not reach its zenith until the 1930 to 1955 period. The tin bank was an important premium, whether it be a Pabst Blue Ribbon beer can bank or a Gerber's Orange Juice bank. Most tin advertising banks resembled the packaging shape of the product.

Almost every substance has been used to make a still bank–diecast white metal, aluminum, brass, plastic, glass, etc. Many of the early glass candy containers also converted to a bank when the candy was eaten. Thousands of varieties of still banks were made, and hundreds of new varieties appear on the market each year.

References: Earnest Ida and Jane Pitman, *Dictionary of Still Banks*, Long's Americana, 1980; Andy and Susan Moore, *Penny Bank Book, Collecting Still Banks*, Schiffer Publishing, Ltd., 1984; Hubert B. Whiting, *Old Iron Still Banks*, Forward's Color Productions, Inc. 1968, out of print.

Collectors' Club: Still Bank Collectors Club of America, 62 South Hazelwood, Newark, OH 43055.

Museum: Margaret Woodbury Strong Museum, Rochester, NY.

CHALK

Dove, 11" h, worn green, red, and yellow ochre paint	225.00
Pig, 7⅛" l, old white repaint, pink ears	85.00

GLASS

Bank of Independence Hall, 7¼" h, clear, tin base, chips	55.00
Clock, 3¾" h, mantle type, painted, tin closure	25.00
Log Cabin, 3⅞" h, milk glass, paper label, worn gold, lid glued	15.00
Pig, 4¼" l, painted gold	25.00
Radio, clear, emb details	25.00
Skookum, 3½" h, clear, marked "S Sears 1916"	20.00

Metal, cast iron, Battleship *Maine*, 4½″ l, $300.00.

METAL. Cast iron unless otherwise noted.

Barrel of Money, 5″ l, orig dolly, nickel plate	260.00
Battleship *Maine*, 10¼″ l, flaked polychrome, damaged masts	175.00
Billiken, 4⅛″ h, gold traces	30.00
Black Boy, 4″ h, two faces, polychrome repaint	55.00
Boy Scout, 5⅞″ h, gold and red	135.00
Building	
Administration Building, Columbian Exposition, 5″ h, nickel plate	85.00
Blackpool Tower, 7½″ h, no paint	45.00
Egyptian Tomb, 6¼″ h, worn nickel plate	700.00
House, 4⅛″ h, two story, green and silver	110.00
Independence Hall, 11¼″ l, worn gold, 1875 patent	700.00
The Villa Bank, 4″ h, worn japanning	125.00
Clock, 3¾″ h, "Time is Money, Save It," black and gold, marked "The Ohio Foundry Co, Cleveland, OH"	115.00
Coronation, 6⅝″ h, worn bronze japanning, "Our Empire Bank," monarchs in round medallion	110.00
Devil, 4¼″ h, worn red, screw replaced	110.00
Dog	
4⅛″ h, sitting on drum	75.00
4⅜″ h, Bulldog, seated	65.00
Donkey, 7″ h, polychrome	130.00
Duck, 4″ h, round, polychrome, trap replaced	175.00
Elephant, 4″ h, gold and red, replaced tin wheels, minor wear	180.00
Ferris Wheel, 4½″ h, nickel plate	1,025.00
Fez, 5⅜″ h, "Baby Smiles...," aluminum with polychrome	85.00
Gas Stove, 5½″ h, black paint, traces of gold	125.00
General Sheridan, 5¾″ h, gold repaint	200.00
Globe, 5½″ h, red and gold	90.00
Graf Zeppelin, 6¾″ l	145.00
Horse	
4¾″ l, prancing	45.00
5⅜″ h, front legs on tub, black and silver	75.00
7⅛″ h, rearing, gold	25.00
7½″ h, prancing, pebbled base, two layers of gold paint	55.00
Lion, 5½″ l, gold, cracked belly	30.00
Mammy, 6″ h, polychrome	155.00
Merry Go Round, 4⅝″ h, worn and faded polychrome	140.00
Mulligan, 5¾″ h, polychrome	135.00
Organ Grinder, 6¼″ h, worn polychrome over red paint	135.00
Owl, 5″ h, "Be Wise Save Money," worn gold	95.00
Rabbit	
5⅛″ h, sitting, worn gold	135.00
6½″ h, standing, worn gold	250.00
Safe	
Army–Navy, 6″ h, double safe, worn nickel plate, Kenton	250.00
Bank of Columbia, 5½″ h, worn nickel plate	85.00
Coin Deposit Bank, 5½″ h, nickel plate	55.00
Daisy Safe, 3½″ h, tin sides and back, nickel plate	25.00
Dome top, 5″ h, nickel plate	65.00
Star Safe, 3½″ h, tin sides and back, nickel plate	25.00
Sailor, 5¼″ h, worn polychrome	130.00
Santa, 5⅞″h, white metal, worn polychrome and flocking	50.00
Turkey, 4¼″ h, brown japanning with red	285.00

PAPIER MACHE

Charlie McCarthy, "Feed Me...," worn polychrome	35.00
James Bank, 7″ h, taffy ad on tin top	10.00
Kewpie, 5″ h, worn polychrome, trap missing	35.00
Scottie, 5¾″ h, pink and white	15.00

POTTERY

Acorn, 4″ h, redware, brown fleck glaze, chips	20.00
Cat, head, white clay, green glaze, 3″ h	95.00
Dog, Scottie, head, white clay, green glaze, 3⅜″ h	55.00
Dutch Girl, 4¾″ h, worn polychrome, chips	50.00
Elf, head, white clay, brown glaze, 3⅜″ h	55.00
Elephant, 5¼″ l, white clay, green glaze	40.00
Grass Hut, 4″ h, sewer pipe, chips	30.00
Pig	
3¾″ l, brown and blue sponging	125.00

Pottery, die, ochre coloring, 2¾″ sq, $35.00.

4¼″ l, two tone marbleized glaze, marked "Checho-slov"	25.00
5¾″ l, brown and yellow mottled glaze	30.00
6″ l, white clay, brown glaze, yellow dots	40.00
6¼″ l, two tone marbleized glaze, marked "Austria"	25.00
Safe, 3½″ h, Marvel, brown glaze, marked "Austria"	35.00
Uncle Sam, 4½″ h, white and blue	5.00

WOOD

Fidelity Trust, 8½″ h, black and gold, decoupage scenes sides and top, drawer	95.00
First National Bank, 5¾″ h, worn decoupage	80.00
Fort, 6⅛″ h, oak, pull out coin slot, chips on roof	15.00

BARBER BOTTLES

History: Barber bottles, colorful glass bottles found on shelves and counters in barber shops, held the liquids barbers used daily. A specific liquid was kept in a specific bottle which the barber knew by color, design, or lettering.

The bulk liquids were kept in utilitarian containers under the counter or in a storage room.

Barber bottles are found in many types of glass: art glass with varied decoration, pattern glass, and commercially prepared and labeled bottles.

References: Richard Holiner, *Collecting Barber Bottles*, Collector Books, 1986; Ralph & Terry Kovel, *The Kovels' Bottle Price List, Eighth Edition* Crown Publishers, Inc. 1987; Philip L. Krumholz, *Value Guide For Barberiana & Shaving Collectibles*, Ad Libs Publishing Co., 1988.

Note: Prices are for bottles without original stoppers unless otherwise noted.

Amber
7¼″ h, Coin Spot pattern, melon shape, rolled lip, smooth base	65.00
8″ h, IVT, enamel dec	160.00

Amethyst
7½″ h, Mary Gregory type, white enamel figure	250.00
7¾″ h, enameled flowers	160.00
8⅝″ h, enameled and gilt Art Nouveau style dec, formed lip and pontil	160.00

Canary, 7¼″ h, Hobnail, three pouring rings, round lip, smooth base	45.00

Cobalt Blue, 8″ h
Loetz, irid purple streaks, sheared mouth, smooth base, 1870	175.00
Mary Gregory type white enameled scene of young girl holding tennis racquet, gold trim	375.00

Cranberry
6¾″ h, 3½″ d, rings of hobnails on neck	175.00
7¼″ h, opalescent, coin spot	140.00

Milk Glass, gold initials, hexagonal base, 7⅝″ h, $45.00.

Opalescent
6⅞″ h, Coin Spot pattern, light blue, fluted, tooled mouth, smooth base	85.00
8⅜″ h, Spanish Lace, cranberry, rolled lip, polished pontil	110.00
9¼″ h, Waffle pattern, light blue, rolled lip	80.00

Spatter Glass, 8¼″ h, light blue and white, polished mouth and base	200.00
Violet Blue, 8¹⁄₁₆″ h, applied Art Nouveau enamel dec	275.00

BAROMETERS

History: A barometer is an instrument which measures atmospheric pressure which, in turn, aids weather forecasting. Low pressure indicates the coming of rain, snow, or storm; high pressure signifies fair weather.

Most barometers use an evacuated and graduated glass tube which contains a column of mercury and are classified by the shape of the case. An aneroid barometer has no liquid and works by a needle connected to the top of a metal box in which a partial vacuum is maintained. The movement of the top moves the needle.

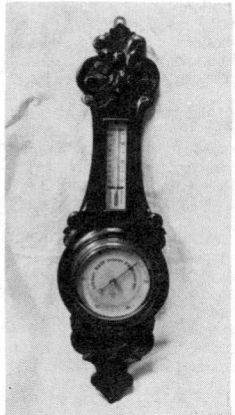

Short and Mason, London, #2404, 26½" l, $250.00.

Aneroid, 5½", Holosteric, brass, ring hanging mount, marked "France, USLH Establishment" from New London Lighthouse 275.00

Banjo
  34" h, 13" d, Louis XVI style, ormolu, rect molded cornice, foliate wreath crest above thermometer, flanked by disengaged colonettes, circular barometric dial sgd "Colin a Paris," conforming cove molded case flanked by putti, urn crest flanked by fruiting branches 900.00
  37" h, 10" w, George III, circular brass molded barometric dial, thermometer, inlaid foliage ovals, stamped "Dominico Gally" 500.00
  38½" h, Victorian, mahogany, inlaid case, thermometer, and silvered dial, sgd "Pastorelli, Bowling St, Westminster" 600.00
  45" h, Louis XVI, bouelle marquetry, ormolu dial, white enamel, surmounted by figure of Vanity, ve-

neered pedestal, brass mounts, blue tortoiseshell ground 2,000.00
Clock, 37½" h, Louis XVI style, ormolu and kingwood, circular enamel dial, conforming cove case flanked by fruiting cornucopia, suspended by foliate wrapped drapery, ribbon tied bow crest, base with drapery framing acorn vine, conforming mahogany backplate with beaded rim, 19th C 4,450.00
Stick
  28" h, rosewood case, orig label on back, Timby, Model #4, c1860 . . . 350.00
  37" h, William IV, rosewood, waisted case, ivory scale with brass border, sgd "S A Caile, Newcastle," c1835 1,600.00
  38¾" h, inlaid mahogany case, dial, and thermometer, sgd "Smith & Sons, Scarboro" 600.00
  39" h, mahogany, engraved ivory dials, thermometer, sgd "G Tagliabue, New York" 900.00
  58" h, Georgian, mahogany, split baluster, thermometer 750.00
Wheel
  39" d, George III, inlaid mahogany, broken arch pediment, baluster body, silvered dial thermometer, convex mirror and level, inscribed "J Hood Watchmaker Cupar Fife," restoration, early 19th C 425.00
  40½" d, Victorian, walnut, sgd "Abraham & Co, Liverpool" 300.00

BASKETS

History: Baskets were invented when man first required containers to gather, store, and transport goods. Today's collector, influenced by the country look, focuses on baskets made of splint, rye straw, or willow. Emphasis is placed on handmade examples. Nails or staples, wide splints which are thin and evenly cut, or a wire bail handle denote factory construction which can date back to the mid-19th century. Painted or woven decorated baskets rarely are handmade, unless American Indian.

Baskets are collected by (a) type—berry, egg, or field, (b) region—Nantucket or Shaker, and (c) composition—splint, rye, or willow. Stick to examples in very good condition; damaged baskets are a poor investment even at a low price.

References: Frances Johnson, *Wallace-Homestead Price Guide To Baskets, Second Edition,* Wallace-Homestead, 1989; Martha Wetherbee and Nathan Taylor, *Legend of the Bushwhacker Basket,* published by author, 1986; Christoph Will, *International Basketry For Weavers and Collectors,* Schiffer Publishing, Ltd., 1985.

Reproduction Alert: Modern reproductions

abound, made by diverse groups ranging from craft revivalists to foreign manufacturers.

Bushel, 18 x 11", stave construction, wrapped with wire bands, wooden rim, bentwood rim handles, old varnish finish **150.00**

Cheese
12½" d, woven splint **225.00**
14" d, woven splint, dark brown stain ext. **55.00**
16½ x 18¼", woven splint, repaired **150.00**
30" d, woven splint, scrubbed finish **400.00**

Creel, 11¾" h, woven splint, worn red paint, no lid **175.00**

Drying, 14½ x 15", round, open weave wire bottom, bentwood handle branded "Dr. Webb" **70.00**

Egg
13 x 14 x 6¾", woven splint, radiating ribs, bentwood handle **200.00**
16 x 17¾", woven splint **65.00**

Flower, 6" h, woven splint, bentwood handle **85.00**

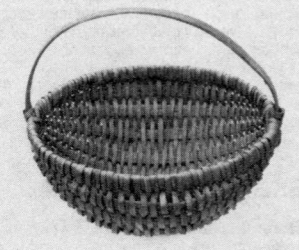

Splint, center rib, $130.00.

Gathering
8½" h, woven splint, bentwood handle, old white paint **175.00**
13" h, woven splint, bentwood handle **200.00**
15½ x 20½ x 10" h, woven splint, two bentwood rim handles, one perpendicular handle **145.00**
15½ x 27", rect, woven splint, bentwood handle **110.00**

Herb Drying, 20½ x 21", woven splint **355.00**

Knife, 9 x 12 x 3½" h, woven splint, divided int., polychrome water-color floral design, bentwood handle **225.00**

Laundry, 21" d, 10" h, round, woven splint, bentwood rim handles **65.00**

Loom
7½" l, woven splint **250.00**
11" h, woven splint, hanging, two sections, black painted design **300.00**

14¼ x 17", hanging, woven splint . . **350.00**

Market, 15 x 6", woven splint, oval rim tapers to rect base, bentwood handle, painted dark green, 19th C **285.00**

Miniature
4¼" h, buttocks form **120.00**
4¾ x 5¼ x 3", buttocks form, twelve rib construction, woven splint **155.00**

Nantucket
8 x 5", oval, swing handle **1,815.00**
8½", swing handle, incised rings in wood bottom **1,650.00**
9¾ x 10¾", woven splint, turned wood bottom, cane and bentwood swivel handle, brass ears **1,000.00**
10¼" d, circular, label "Mitchell Ray," 18th C **700.00**
11 x 7¾", lightship, label "Alfred D Williams," 18th C **1,100.00**
12" d, incised turned base, shaped swing handle, paper label "Lightship Basket made by William D Appleton, Nantucket, Mass," early 20th C **1,700.00**
14½" d, oval, turned wood base, bentwood handle, 19th C **990.00**

Picnic, 9¾ x 15 x 7", woven splint, swivel handle, red paint over earlier black paint **65.00**

Potato, ash splint **35.00**

Sewing, 12 x 5¾", Shaker, woven splint, rim handle, orig white cotton liner and needle **145.00**

Wash
20 x 11½", woven splint, rim handle holds **125.00**
22 x 27 x 12½", oval, woven splint, rim hand holds **100.00**

Work, 11½ x 18", woven splint, bentwood rim handle, attached small woven oval basket int. corner, light blue paint **110.00**

BATTERSEA ENAMELS

History: Battersea enamel is a generic term for English enamel-on-copper objects of the 18th century.

In 1753 Stephen Theodore Janssen established a factory to produce "Trinkets and Curiosities Enamelled on Copper" at York House, Battersea, London. Here the new invention of transfer printing developed a high degree of excellence, and the resulting trifles delighted fashionable Georgian society.

Recent research has shown that enamels actually were being produced in London and the Midlands several years before York House was established. However, most enamel trinkets still are referred to as "Battersea Enamels," even though they were probably made in other workshops in London, Birmingham, Bilston, Wednesbury, or Liverpool.

All manner of charming items were made, including snuff and patch boxes bearing mottos and memory gems. (By adding a mirror inside the lid, a snuff box became patch box). Many figural whimsies, called "toys," were created to amuse a gay and fashionable world. Many other elaborate articles, e.g., candlesticks, salts, tea caddies, and bonbonnieres, were made for the tables of the newly rich middle classes.

Reference: Susan Benjamin, *English Enamel Boxes*, Merrimack Publishers Circle, 1978.

Advisors: Barbara and Melvin Alpren.

Bird, blue speckled head, rose breast, green, purple, red, black, yellow, and green wings, dec on base with bird, dandelion, hallmarked, 2½ x 1½ x 2½", $3,750.00.

Bonbonnier, Spaniel, King Charles, oval, black and white, yellow ground, pastoral scene lid, c1770, Bilston	2,900.00
Candlestick, 10½" h, white ground, landscape vignettes within pink ground, gilt scroll borders, c1770, Bilston	3,900.00
Cloak Hooks, 2" l, oval, rose festooned anchors, white ground, c1775, South Staffordshire	500.00
Counter Box, 1½" d, ivory, fanned playing cards top, center inscribed "Lady Luck," tortoiseshell lined, c1770	950.00
Patch Box	
3/4", round, "Keep this for my Sake," slip lid, c1775, Bilston	350.00
1¼", "Always the same," oval, love birds on white lid, pink base, c1780, Bilston	500.00
1½", "A Trifle from Abroad," oval, white, blue ship, red wavy border, c1775, Bilston	550.00
1⅞" l, oval, "A Trifle from Buston," pale blue, waisted body, high river bands scene on hinged top	200.00
2" l, oval, "May we join hands In Hymens bands," elongated, pink base, hinged top with painted pastoral church and motto	220.00

2¼", oval, red checked gingham, green hinge holder, c1770, Bilston	650.00
Scent Bottle Holder, ½ x 1¼ x 2¼", pink all-over floral with trellis, leafy green, c1775, Bilston	350.00
Snuff Box, 2½" l, white, lovers in pastoral setting, ruin background, c1780, Bilston	800.00

BAVARIAN CHINA

History: Bavaria, Germany, was an important porcelain production center, similar to the Staffordshire district in England. The name Bavarian China refers to companies operating in Bavaria, among which were Hutschenreuther, Thomas, and Zeh, Scherzer & Co. (Z. S. & Co.). Very little of the production from this area was imported into the United States prior to 1870.

Reference: Susan and Al Bagdade, *Warman's English & Continental Pottery & Porcelain, 1st Edition*, Warman Publishing Co., Inc., 1987.

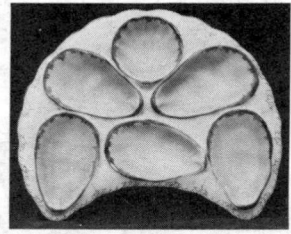

Oyster Plate, shaded blue, gold border, 9" w, $90.00.

Ashtray, 5¼" sq, full figure Peter Pan seated on corner, legs extended to opposite corner, marked "Hutschenreuther"	145.00
Berry Set, master bowl and six individual serving bowls, pink chrysanthemums dec, marked "JS Bavaria"	60.00
Bowl, 7¼" d, octagonal, two parrots decal dec, reticulated lavender rim	35.00
Celery Tray, hp, multicolored parrots, white ground	35.00
Chocolate Pot, cov, green flowers, gold handle	95.00
Compote, 8¼" d, openwork edge, fruit dec	30.00
Creamer and Sugar, green band, roses dec, gold rim	35.00
Cup and Saucer, soft pink roses, light blue ground, gold handle and rim, marked "J & C Bavaria"	95.00
Dish, 10" oval, hp, pink and white roses,	

shaded green ground, gilding, handle, artist sgd **75.00**
Dresser Set, 11 x 7½" dresser tray, powder dish, hair receiver, 3 x 4½" pin tray, hp, white roses, shaded green ground **135.00**
Fish Set, 9½" serving bowl, attached underplate, 9 x 14" platter, six 10½" d plates, cobalt blue ground, gold rim, 9 pcs **125.00**
Hair Receiver, pink roses, green leaves, gold trim, marked "Z S & Co" **30.00**
Luncheon Service, Vienna Rose pattern, 58 pcs **375.00**
Marmalade Jar, 6" h, cov, underplate, two handles, hp, pink roses, cream ground, black and gold trim **100.00**
Pitcher, 9" h, bulbous, burnished gold lizard handle, hp blackberry dec, shaded ground, artist sgd **120.00**
Plate, 9" d, portrait of young girl, maroon ground, lacy gold border, marked "Z S & Co" **65.00**
Toothpick, pink flowers, green leaves, shaded ground, gold rim, marked "Versailles/R C Bavaria" **30.00**
Wall Pocket, figural, woman **80.00**

BELLEEK

History: Belleek, a thin, ivory colored, almost iridescent-type porcelain, was first made in 1857 in county Fermanagh, Ireland. Production continued until World War I, was discontinued for a period of time, and then resumed. The Shamrock pattern is most familiar, but many patterns were made, including Limpet, Tridacna, and Grasses.

Irish Belleek has several identifying marks, e.g., the Harp and Hound (1865–80) and Harp, Hound, and Castle (1863–91). After 1891 the word "Ireland" or "Erie" was added. Some pieces are marked "Belleek Co., Fermanagh."

There is an Irish saying: If a newly married couple receives a gift of Belleek, their marriage will be blessed with lasting happiness.

Several American firms made a Belleek-type porcelain. The first was Ott and Brewer Co. of Trenton, New Jersey, in 1884, followed by Willets. Other firms included The Ceramic Art Co. (1889), American Art China Works (1892), Columbian Art Co. (1893), and Lenox, Inc. (1904).

Reference: Mary Frank Aston, *American Belleek,* Collector Books, 1984.

Additional Listings: Lenox.

Abbreviations: 1BM = 1st Black Mark; 2BM = 2nd Black Mark; 3BM = 3rd Black Mark; 4GM = 4th Green Mark; 5GM = 5th Green Mark.
Advisor: Mary Beth Appert.

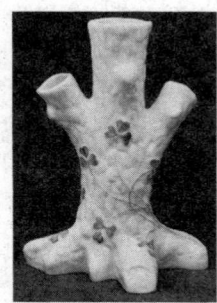

Irish, vase, tree trunk, green clover dec, 3rd black mark, 6¼" h, 4½" w, $175.00.

AMERICAN

Blotter Ends, paste dec, primroses, CAC lavender palette mark, 4 pcs . . **150.00**
Bowl, hp, acorns and oak leaves, Willets **150.00**
Buttermilk Service, pitcher, twelve cups, matching tray, grapes and leaves dec, Lenox green wreath marks **500.00**
Creamer
  3¾" h, gold florals, scalloped rim, CAC lavender palette mark **120.00**
  4" h, scalloped rim, woody thumbprint base, ivory matte, gold paste florals, sponged gold, branch handle, Ott & Brewer **200.00**
Cup and Saucer
  Band of florals, Willets **100.00**
  Morning glories, blue and pink flowers, Morgan **100.00**
  Roses, scalloped gold rim, gold handle, CAC **225.00**
Demitasse Cup and Saucer
  Gold border, sterling silver filigree holder, sterling silver saucer, Willets **35.00**
  Gold rim and handle, magenta body, Gordon **50.00**
Desk Set, rolling blotter, large ruffled pen tray, cov stamp box, sealing wax holder, violets dec, CAC lavender palette mark **375.00**
Figure, swan
  4" l, pink, gold trim, Lenox green wreath mark **45.00**
  9" l, cream, Lenox green wreath mark **90.00**

Hatpin Holder, 5¼" h, ribbed, creamy ivory ground, Willets **100.00**
Honey Jar, cov, 6" h, cream ground, gold bees, Lenox palette mark **135.00**
Lamp, 12" h, Armstrong vase base, swan handles, cream, Lenox green wreath mark **165.00**
Mug, pink, coral, and plum pomegranates dec, c1890, CAC **165.00**
Orb Vase, hp, roses, gold paste dec, ruffled top, Willets **225.00**
Pitcher, hp, grapes, gold dec, Willets **200.00**
Rose Bowl, 8" h, orange flowers, artist sgd, Willets **265.00**
Salt, master, 2" d, three feet, gold painted stem with leaves, gold rim, cream ground, Lenox palette mark, dated Oct 11, 1905 on bottom **20.00**
Tankard, 14" h, Indian corn dec, CAC **350.00**
Tea Set, 6" h cov teapot, 4" h cov creamer and sugar, sq pedestal base, angular handles, gold trim, cream ground, monogrammed "B," Lenox palette mark **215.00**
Vase, Venus and swan decal, Willets **175.00**

IRISH

Basket
4½" d, Heart, floral dec, four strands, pearl finish, two pads imp "Belleek" and "Co. Fermanagh" **450.00**
6" d, Erne, applied floral rim, four strands, pearl finish, one pad imp "Belleek, Co. Fermanagh" **475.00**
8½" d, Twig, three strands, pearl finish, applied twig handles, applied floral dec around rim, two pads imp "Belleek" and "Co. Fermanagh," minor chip on one rose **2,250.00**
12½" l, oval, cov, handles, applied floral dec to cov, four strands, painted finish, two pads imp "Belleek R," and "Co. Fermanagh" **2,500.00**
Bowl, 4½" d, Shamrock–Basket Weave pattern, 3BM **100.00**
Candleholder, cherub on dolphin, gold mark **115.00**
Creamer
Echinus pattern, tinted, 1BM **275.00**
Ivy pattern, painted, 1BM **100.00**
Lily pattern, 1BM **75.00**
Vintage pattern, 2GM **50.00**
Cup and Saucer
Artichoke pattern, gilt, 1BM **250.00**
Erne pattern, 1BM **85.00**
Lily pattern, imp "Belleek Co, Fermanagh," 1BM **300.00**
Limpet pattern, pink, ftd, 2BM **250.00**
Neptune pattern, green trim, 2BM .. **125.00**
Shamrock–Basket Weave pattern, 3BM **80.00**

Demitasse Cup and Saucer
Limpet pattern, 3BM **85.00**
Mask pattern, 3BM **115.00**
Egg Cup Set, 6" d, 5½" h, six egg cups, matching holder, center hand holding ring handle, Sydney pattern, Basket Weave **1,200.00**
Figure
3" h, Spaniel on cushion, bisque and pearl finish, 6GM **85.00**
6½" h, Greyhound, bisque and pearl finish, sitting on base, 3BM **375.00**
Frame, 12 x 11½", two photograph openings, elaborate applied floral dec, pearl finish, 1BM **4,500.00**
Honey Pot, cov, Grass pattern, 1BM .. **350.00**
Kettle, 6½" d, Grass Tea Ware, painted finish, repaired spout, 1BM **450.00**
Marmalade Jar, cov, Shamrock–Basket Weave pattern, twig handles, 2GM **135.00**
Mug, Shamrock pattern, 2BM **100.00**
Teapot
Limpet pattern, 6½" h, cob luster, 6GM **175.00**
Neptune pattern, 4½" h, cob luster, repaired, 2BM **165.00**
Shamrock pattern, 4¼" h, 3BM **165.00**
Tridacna pattern, 3¾" h, tinted, 1BM **600.00**
Tobacco Box, 6½ x 3¾", Mask Tea Ware, cob luster, 3BM **275.00**
Tumbler, black mark, 2nd Deg 283 ... **110.00**
Vase
7½" h, Aberdeen, applied floral dec, pearl finish, 2BM **550.00**
9" h, Tulip, triple, painted, 2BM **1,500.00**
12" h, Fish, double, painted and gilt finish, 1BM **1,000.00**
13½", Nile, pearl finish, 2BM **225.00**

BELLS

History: Bells have been used for centuries for many different purposes. They have been traced as far back as 2697 B.C., though at that time they did not have any true tone. One of the oldest bells is the "crotal," a tiny sphere with small holes and a ball or stone or metal inside. This type now appears as sleigh bells.

True bell making began when bronze, the mixing of tin and copper, was discovered. There are now many types of materials of which bells are made—almost as many materials as there are uses for them.

Bells of the late 19th century show a high degree of workmanship and artistic style. Glass bells from this period are examples of the glass blower's talent and the glass manufacturer's product.

Collectors' Club: American Bell Association, Rt. 1, Box 286, Natronia Heights, PA 15065.

Additional Listings: See *Warman's Americana & Collectibles* for more examples.

Cigar Counter Bell, brass, cast iron base, marked "Russel & Erwin Mfg. Co, New Britain, CT, USA, Pat'd Aug 1, 96, Rd. No. 269895," $275.00.

Altar, 2½" h, brass, emb, angels and Latin script	75.00
Church	
Steeple, 20" d, molded signature, "Made by Meneeley Bell Co. at Troy, NY, 1911," orig mounting bracket, wooden base	300.00
Triple, 27" h, graduated stand, domed cross finial	75.00
Desk	
Side Tap, bronze, white marble base, c1875	40.00
Turtle, cast iron, 6½" l	200.00
Twirler Type, double chime, c1850	75.00
Door, brass, metal netting hung with small spheres, larger center sphere, orig mounting bracket	85.00
Fire, 11½" l, hand, metal, iron spring loaded clapper, turned handle	210.00
Hand	
Brass, figural	
Napoleon, 6¼" h, raised scene of Battle of Waterloo	70.00
Queen Elizabeth, 5¼" h, crown on head, high ruffled collar	65.00
Victorian Lady, plumed hat	75.00
Bronze, figural	
Dutch Girl, 4½" h	125.00
Windmill, turning blades, emb brickwork	90.00
China	
Delftware, 4" h, Dutch boy, girl, and windmill, marked "Holland"	50.00
Limoges, hp, roses	50.00
Glass	
Bohemian, 5" h, overlay, pink ext., cream int., amber glass handle, rigaree, and clapper, applied pink and cream flower, green glass leaves	175.00
Cranberry, wedding	110.00
Fostoria, American pattern	65.00
Pottery, 5¼" h, Southern Belle, Ceramic Arts Studio	65.00

Silver, sterling, 4⅝" h, cupid blowing horn, figural handle, frosted finish, foliate strapwork border, Gorham Mfg Co, c1870	725.00
Mechanical, figural, Colonial boy, turn knob to ring	100.00
School	
Desk type	25.00
Hand held, brass	
No 7, wood handle	30.00
No 9, teak handle	40.00
Ship, bronze, 30" d, wooden stand	175.00
Sleigh, brass, leather strap, 33 graduated bells	85.00
Trolley Car, brass	125.00

J. NORTON
BENNINGTON
VT.

BENNINGTON AND BENNINGTON-TYPE POTTERY

History: In 1845 Christopher Webber Fenton joined Julius Norton, his brother-in-law, in the manufacturing of stoneware pottery in Bennington, Vermont. Fenton sought to expand the company's products and glazes; Norton wanted to concentrate solely on stoneware. In 1847 Fenton broke away and established his own factory.

Fenton introduced the famous Rockingham glaze, developed in England and named after the Marquis of Rockingham, to America. In 1849 he patented a flint enamel glaze, "Fenton's Enamel," which added flecks, spots, or streaks of color (usually blues, greens, yellows, and oranges) to the brown Rockingham glaze. Forms included candlesticks, coachman bottles, cow creamers, poodles, sugar bowls, and toby pitchers.

Fenton produced the little known scroddled ware, commonly called lava or agate ware. Scroddled ware is composed of different colored clays, mixed with cream colored clay, molded, turned on a potter's wheel, coated with feldspar and flint, and fired. It was not produced in quantity, as there was little demand for it.

Fenton also introduced Parian ware to America. Parian was developed in England in 1842 and known as "Statuary ware." Parian is a translucent porcelain which has no glaze and resembles marble. Bennington made the blue and white variety in the form of vases, cologne bottles, and trinkets.

Five different marks were used, with many variations. Only about twenty percent of the pieces carried any mark; some forms were almost always marked, others never. Marks: (a) 1849 mark (4 variations) for flint enamel and Rockingham; (b) E. Fenton's Works, 1845–47, on Parian and occasionally on scroddled ware; (c) U. S. Pottery Co., ribbon mark, 1852–58, on Parian and blue and white porcelain; (d) U. S. Pottery Co., lozenge mark, 1852–58, on Parian; and (e) U. S. Pottery, oval mark, 1853–58, mainly on scroddled ware.

The hound handled pitcher is probably the best known Bennington piece. Hound handled pitchers also were made by some 30 potteries in over 55 different variations. Rockingham glaze was used by over 150 potteries in 11 states, mainly the Mid-West, between 1830 and 1900.

References: Richard Carter Barret, *How To Identify Bennington Pottery*, Stephen Greene Press, 1964; Laura Woodside Watkins, *Early New England Potters And Their Wares*, Harvard University-Press, 1950.

Museums: Bennington Museum, Bennington, VT; East Liverpool Museum of Ceramics, East Liverpool, OH.

Additional Listings: Stoneware.

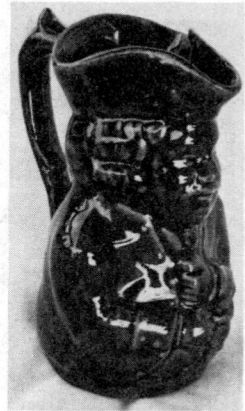

Bennington, Toby Jug, Fenton, 5⅞″ h, $525.00.

BENNINGTON POTTERY

Book Flask, flint enamel
"Bennington Ladies," 5¾″ h 850.00
"Hermit's Companion," 1849 mark .. 850.00
Untitled, marked "L. F. & Co/Patent" on spine, Lyman Fenton Co circular mark 500.00
Bottle, 9⅜″ h, figural, coachman, brown and tan, Rockingham glaze, c1850 190.00
Bowl, 11⅞″ d, flint enamel, impressed 1849 mark on bottom 100.00
Bust, 5″ h, parian, girl with bird on shoulder 50.00

Chamber Pot, 9⅛″ d, flint enamel, scalloped rib pattern 600.00
Coffeepot, 12″ h, flint enamel, scalloped rib pattern, crack in base 650.00
Curtain Tiebacks, 4½″ l, flint enamel, 1849–58, pr 250.00
Cuspidor
8¼″ d, scalloped rib pattern, 1849 mark, tiny hole in one panel 100.00
9½″ d, flint enamel, rare 1849 mark 450.00
Ewer, 7″ h, parian, raised grapevines 150.00
Figure, poodles, 9½″ l, 8¼″ h, flint enamel, one professionally repaired leg, one half of basket handle missing, pr 5,500.00
Jar, 4⅜″ h, 4¼″ d, parian, blue and white, acanthus leaf pattern, lid missing 70.00
Nameplate
7⅞″ l, white, numerals "702" 100.00
8″ l, Rockingham glaze 125.00
Paperweight, 5 x 3 x 2¾″, flint enamel, imp 1849 mark 350.00
Pie Plate, 8¼″ d, impressed 1849 mark on bottom 160.00
Pipkin, 9″ h, flint enamel, lid 2,600.00
Pitcher
6¼″ h, brown, scroddle, alternate rib pattern, U.S. Pottery oval mark, age cracks 400.00
8¾″ h, white, tulip and sunflower, U.S. Pottery ribbon mark 1,300.00
8⅞″ h, white, cascade pattern, highly glazed, U.S. Pottery raised lozenge mark 300.00
9″, hunting scene, c1850 .... 200.00
10″ h
Flint enamel, tulip and heart pattern, sgd, 1849 mark 600.00
Parian, Pond Lily pattern, U.S. Pottery ribbon mark 175.00
10½″ h, flint enamel, octagonal paneled, imp 1849 mark 300.00
Relish Dish, 10″ l, Rockingham glaze 350.00
Snuff Jar, dark greenish-brown glaze, flint enamel, lidded, minor repair ... 600.00
Sugar Bowl, 3¾″ h, parian, blue and white, repeated oak leaves pattern, raised grapevine dec lid 125.00
Syrup Jug, 8½″ h, spinning wheel pattern 70.00
Teapot, flint enamel, alternate rib pattern, pierced pouring spout, period lid 400.00
Toby
Coachman, 10⅜″ h, Rockingham glaze, honey colored, 1849 mark 475.00
General Stark, Rockingham glaze, 1,200.00
Toby Jar, Rockingham glaze, 1849 mark 175.00
Toothbrush Holder, flint enamel, alternate rib pattern, lid 500.00

Bennington Type, pitcher, tulip, New Jersey, medium brown, 5″ h, $125.00.

BENNINGTON-TYPE

Cake Mold, 9½ x 4″, Rockingham glaze	150.00
Curtain Tieback, 4¼″ d, 4½″ l, flint enamel	30.00
Frame, 8 x 7″, oval, Rockingham glaze	325.00
Mixing Bowl, 14¼ x 5¼″, Rockingham glaze	190.00
Plate, 9″, sq, emb design, Rockingham glaze	290.00
Trinket Box, 5″ l, natural colors, flowers and grapes dec	50.00

BISCUIT JARS

History: The biscuit or cracker jar was the forerunner of the cookie jar. They were made of various materials by leading glassworks and potteries of the late 19th and early 20th centuries.

Note: All items listed here have silver plated mountings unless otherwise noted.

Bristol Glass, 6¼″ h, 5¼″ d, satin finish, opaque beige ground, pink roses, gold leaves, gray foliage, SP top, rim, and handle	150.00
Carlton Ware, 9½″ h, pottery, multicolored floral dec, cobalt trim, SP handle, Staffordshire	110.00
Cased Glass, 6¼″ h, 5¼″ d, blue, enameled pink roses, green leaves, SP top, rim, and handle	150.00
Crown Milano	
6″ h, 5½″ d, barrel shaped, pale yellow ground shades to creamy white, cluster of deep pink apple blossoms, green leaves, gray–green branches, Pairpoint SP lid	
and collar, "P" in diamond logo emb in floral motif	685.00
9″ h, 5½″ d, cylindrical body of sixteen panels, two molded in scrolls at top, molded in scroll at base, painted Johnny Jump–Up dec, base sgd "3922/263," Pairpoint SP lid incised with "P" in diamond mark and "3932"	635.00
Limoges, roses, blue forget–me–nots, gold trim, handle	120.00
Mount Washington, satin glass, blown out pulled drapery, Burmese int., salmon pink, gold highlights, fancy SP cov and bail handle, sgd "MW"	875.00
Opalescent Glass, 7¾″ h, William and Mary pattern, English	300.00
Royal Bonn, 7″ h, sq, floral design, SP top and handle	95.00
Royal Worcester, 7″ h, Swirl pattern, daisies and fuchsias	275.00

Wavecrest, floral dec, emb swirls, 7½″ h, $450.00.

Smith Bros, melon ribbed, cream ground, pink spider mums, brown and gray leaves, gold flowers and bud highlights, fancy SP cov and bail	825.00
Wavecrest, pink and blue ground, robins and violets dec	300.00
Wedgwood, 7″ h, 5″ d, Jasperware, tricolor, dark blue, light blue, and white, resilvered SP mountings, c1910	385.00

BISQUE

History: Bisque or biscuit china is the name given to wares that have been fired once and are not glazed.

Bisque figurines and busts were popular during the Victorian era, being used on fireplace mantels, dining room buffets, and end tables. Manufacturing was centered in the United States and Europe. By the mid-20th century the Japanese were the principal source of bisque items, especially character related items.

Reference: Susan and Al Bagdade, *Warman's English & Continental Pottery & Porcelain, 1st Edition,* Warman Publishing Co., Inc., 1987.

Bank, 3″ h, fox head, wearing eye glasses **375.00**
Bust
   10″ h, pr, Spring and Autumn, circular bases, sgd "L Kley" on side, blue monogram on base, French **325.00**
   25″ h, Duchess de Lambelle, mid 18th C dress, draped bodice, tresses at shoulders, pencil identification on base, late 19th C, base chip **500.00**
Candleholder, 8″ h, double, figural, girl leaning against bridge in woods, Germany, late 19th C **55.00**
Cigar Holder, 4¼″ h, tree stump, bird chasing insect, German, 19th C . . . **40.00**

Match Holder, seated baby with chamber pot, gold lettering on pot reads "Scratch my back," 4¾″ h, $75.00.

Figure
   10″ h, children playing dress up, girl in lavender shawl, plumed hat, boy in pink dunce cap, sticking out tongue and making face in removable mirror, Heubach, pr **735.00**
   11½″ h, dancing girl, aqua dress, sanded ground, pink bow, white lace collar, multicolored base, Heubach **510.00**
   13½″ h, young woman wearing long full waisted gown, flowers in hair, group of six, different dancing poses, sgd "E Quinter," Continental, c1900 . . . . **3,575.00**
   14½″, girl, white blouse, blue lapels,

pink trim, blue dress, holding kitten in left arm, blue hat, pink bow, German, c1920 . . . . **250.00**
   21″ h, Edwardian Couple, girl in light blue flowing dress, pink sash, man in light blue striped trousers, long tan coat, pink jacket, pr **1,150.00**
Nodder
   Chinese man and woman, pr **650.00**
   Poodle and bulldog, oval base, 4¾″ h **150.00**
Piano Baby
   8″ l, 5½″ h, crawling infant, white gown, chubby legs, Heubach **420.00**
   9″ l, 5½″ h, little girl, sitting on side, hands extended, curly wig **275.00**
Snow Baby, 1″ h, sitting, arms outstretched, marked "Germany" **45.00**
Toothpick Holder, 4½″ h, figural, dwarf, blue pants, green hat **25.00**
Vase, 6⅜″ h, Dutch boy standing by sq container, blue shirt, tan pants and hat, Heubach **110.00**

BITTERS BOTTLES

History: Bitters, a "remedy" made from natural herbs and other mixtures with an alcohol base, often was viewed as the universal cure-all. The names given to various bitter mixtures were imaginative, though the bitters seldom cured what their makers claimed.

The manufacturers of bitters needed a way to sell and advertise their products. They designed bottles in many shapes, sizes, and colors to attract the buyer. Many forms of advertising, including trade cards, billboards, signs, almanacs, and novelties proclaimed the virtues of a specific bitter.

During the Civil War a tax was levied on alcoholic beverages. Since bitters were identified as medicines, they were exempt from this tax. The alcohol content was never mentioned. In 1907 when the Pure Foods Regulations went into effect, "an honest statement of content on every label" put most of the manufacturers out of business.

References: Carlyn Ring, *For Bitters Only,* 1980; J. H. Thompson, *Bitters Bottles,* Century House, 1947; Richard Watson, *Bitters Bottles,* Thomas Nelson and Sons, 1965.

Periodical: *Antique Bottle and Glass Collector,* P.O. Box 187, East Greenville, PA 18041.

A S Hopkins Union Stomach Bitters, yellow green, applied tapered lip, smooth base, emb, 9¾″ h, c1880 . . **275.00**
Atwoods' Jaundice Bitters, twelve sided, aqua, applied sq collar lip, open pontil base, 6⅜″ h, c1850 . . . . **40.00**
Brown's Celebrated Indian Herb Bitters, figural, Indian queen, golden amber, rolled lip, smooth base, 12¼″ h, c1870 . . . . **425.00**

Digestive Bitters P J Bowlin Liquor Co, rect, fancy corners, golden amber, tooled lip, smooth base, 8¼" h, 1880–90 . . . . **260.00**

Dr. C D Warner, honey amber, tooled lip, smooth base, emb "Dr. C D Warner, Reading, Mich/German Hop Bitters/ Warner 1880/Warner/1880," 9⅞" h, c1880 . . . . **325.00**

Dr. Caldwell's Herb Bitters, triangular, beveled and lattice work panels, golden amber, applied tapered lip, smooth base, 12¾" h, c1870 . . . . . **130.00**

Dr. J Hostetter's Stomach Bitters, olive green, applied tapered lips, smooth base, 8½" h, 1865–75 . . . . **150.00**

Dr. John Bull's Compound Cedron Bitters, Louisville, KY, sq olive green, applied taper lip, smooth base, 9¾" h, 1865–75 . . . . **1,000.00**

Abbotts Bitters, pewter top, raised letters, 9" h, $125.00.

Dr. Jones Linament, emb, beaver, label **15.00**

Dr. Stephen Jewetts' Celebrated Health Restoring Bitters, rect, beveled corners, honey yellow, sq collar lip, iron pontil base, orig label, 7⅛" h, c1840 **1,400.00**

E J Roses' Magador Bitters For Stomach Kidney & Liver, golden amber, tooled tapered lips smooth base, 9¾" h, 1880–90 . . . . **65.00**

East India Root Bitters, Geo P Clapp, sq, tapered, golden amber, applied tapered lip, smooth base, emb, 9½" h, 1865–70 . . . . **425.00**

G W Day's Stomach Bitters, sq, indented panels front and back, aqua,

applied tapered ring lip, smooth base, 9½" h, c1865 . . . . **750.00**

Hertrich's Gesundheits Bitter, yellow green, tooled double ring lip, smooth base, emb, 12" h, 1880–1900 . . . . . **1,900.00**

J C & Co, pineapple, golden amber, applied ring lip, open pontil base, 8¾" h, c1850 . . . . **325.00**

J P Brady's Family Bitters, sq, yellow amber, indented panels, applied tapered lip, smooth base, 9⅝" h, 1865–75 . . . . **650.00**

McKeevers' Army Bitters, stylized drum with cannon balls on top, golden amber, applied tapered lip, smooth base, 10¾" h, 1870–80 . . . . **1,700.00**

Old Dr. Warren's Quaker Bitters, Flint & Co, aqua, applied sq collar lip, smooth base, orig label, 9⅝" h, 1872–80 . . . . **300.00**

Old Homestead Wild Cherry Bitters, cabin shape, golden amber, applied tapered lip, smooth base, 9¾" h, c1870 . . . . **220.00**

Old Sachem Bitters and Wigwam Tonic, aqua, applied sq collar lip, pen pontil base, emb, 10³⁄₁₆" h, c1850 . . . . **650.00**

St Drake's 1860 Plantation Bitters, Drakes Cabin, greenish yellow, applied tapered lip, smooth base, 9⅞" h, 1865–75 . . . . **350.00**

Simons Centennial Bitters, figural, George Washington bust, golden amber, applied ring lip, smooth base, 10" h, c1876 . . . . **1,450.00**

Sol Frank's Panacea Bitters, figural, light house, golden amber, applied tapered lip, smooth base, 10¼" h, c1876 . . . . **1,400.00**

Steinfeld's French Cognac Bitters, golden amber, applied tapered lip, smooth base, 11¼" h, c1865 . . . . . **160.00**

Suffolk Bitters/Philbrook & Tucker, Boston, figural, pig, yellowish amber, ground lip, emb, 10" l, c1870 . . . . . **150.00**

Tippecanoe, 9" h, figural, canoe, honey amber, mushroom lip, smooth base, 1870–80 . . . . **60.00**

W F Severa Stomach Bitters, golden amber, tooled tapered lip, smooth base, 8⅞" h, 1880–90 . . . . **65.00**

W H Ware Patented 1866/The Fish Bitters, clear, tooled lip, smooth base, emb, 11½" h, c1870 . . . . **475.00**

BLACK MEMORABILIA

History: The term "Black memorabilia" refers to a broad range of collectibles that often overlap other collecting fields, e.g., toys, postcards, etc. It also encompasses African artifacts, items created by slaves or related to the slavery era, modern Black cultural contributions to literature, art, etc., and material associated with the Civil Rights Movement and the Black experience throughout history.

The earliest known examples of Black memorabilia include primitive African designs and tribal artifacts. Black Americana dates back to the arrival of African natives upon American shores.

The advent of the 1900s launched an incredible amount and variety of material depicting Blacks, most often in a derogatory and dehumanizing manner that clearly reflected the stereotypical attitude held toward the Black race during this period. The popularity of Black portrayals in this unflattering fashion flourished as the century wore on.

As the growth of the Civil Rights Movement escalated and aroused public awareness to the Black plight, attitudes changed. Public outrage and pressure eventually put a halt to the offensive practice during the early 1950s.

Black representations still are being produced in many forms, but no longer in the demoralizing designs of the past. These modern objects, while not as historically significant as earlier examples, will become the Black memorabilia of tomorrow.

References: Patiki Gibbs, *Black Collectibles Sold In America*, Collector Books, 1987; Patiki Gibbs and Tyson Gibbs, *The Collector's Encyclopedia of Black Dolls*, Collector Books, 1987; Dawn Reno, *Collecting Black Americana*, Crown Publishing Co., 1986; Darrell A. Smith, *Black Americana: A Personal Collection*, Black Relics, Inc., 1988.

Periodical: *Black Ethnic Collectibles*, 1401 Asbury Court, Hyattsville, MD 20782.

Reproduction Alert. Reproductions are becoming an increasing problem, from advertising signs (Bull Durham Tobacco) to mechanical banks (Jolly Nigger). If the object looks new to you, chances are that it is new.

Tobacco Humidor, chalkware, olive jacket, mustard hat and pants, 10½" h, $225.00.

Architectural Element, cast iron	
Hitching Post, jockey, ring on outstretched hand, polychrome	125.00
Lawn Ornament, black child with watermelon, 24" h, pr	300.00
Ashtray, pot metal, boy on potty	75.00
Autograph	
Diddley, Bo, card, 5 x 3" plain white card	10.00
Domino, Fats, color photograph, 5 x 3"	15.00
LaBelle, Patti, black and white glossy photograph, 8 x 10"	15.00
Washington, Booker T, Oct 6, 1908, letter, 11 x 12", matted and framed	150.00
Automata, 20 x 15", clockwork, black man's face, eyes roll, nods head, opens his mouth and smiles, Hoyt, late 19th C, framed	3,500.00
Baseball Pennant, NY Black Yankees, felt, 25" l	125.00
Children's Book	
A Story of Our Gang, Whitman, 1929, 20 pgs, hardcover	65.00
Beloved Belinda, Johnny Gruelle, 1926, 90 pgs, 2nd edition	48.00
New Story of Little Black Sambo, CB Thurston, 1926	45.00
Ten Little Niggers, McLoughlin, c1880	185.00
The Story of Little Black Sambo, McLoughlin Brothers, Inc., Springfield, MA, 1931, 16 pgs	15.00
Turkey Trott Kate G Dyer, 1942, hardcover	30.00
Cigarette Holder, ceramic, three black children on clothesline	20.00
Clock	
9½" h, cast iron and wood, top hatted black banjo player, eyes move from side to side	1,500.00
16" h, cast iron, standing black man holding banjo with inset clock	1,200.00
Cookbook	
Aunt Jemima's Magical Recipes, 1952, 26 pgs	35.00
Metachol, Mammy cover, 1921	15.00
New Orleans Recipes, Mammy cover, 6 x 8½"	20.00
Decanter, 8" h, ceramic, figural, butler, cork neck	185.00
Doll,	
10" h, Topsy Turvy, black composition head and body, three pigtails	65.00
12½" h, Topsy Turvy, cloth body, c1940	50.00
14" h, cloth body, hard head, hands, and boots, dress, kerchief, and orig apron	85.00
Flour Sack, Aunt Jemima, 25 lbs, c1940	65.00

Game

Chocolate Splash, Willis G Young
Mfg, Chicago, 1916 copyright ... 100.00
Ten Little Niggers, Parker Bros 125.00
Lunch Box, Dixie Kid Tobacco, tin ... 150.00
Map, 21 x 28", Cream of Wheat pre-
mium, Jolly Bill and Jane Moon Map,
black and white cartoon illus, center
Rastus illus, 1933 .... 80.00
Paperweight, 5½" l, cast iron, alligator
swallowing black boy 60.00
Pipe Rack, 12" l, brass, figural, man's
head, large hat 200.00

Puzzle

Amos and Andy, Pepsodent Co,
1932, 8 x 10" 85.00
Little Black Sambo, sgd "Fern Bisel
Peat," 7½ x 9½" 40.00

Sheet Music

Aunt Jemima's Picnic Day, 1914 ... 20.00
Little Alabama Coon, 1893 .... 25.00
*They'll Be Mighty Proud In Dixie Of
Their Old Black Joe*, music by
Harry Carrol, published by Shapiro,
Bernstein & Co, multicolored cover,
1917 .... 10.00
Three Little Words, 1930 .... 15.00
Smoking Stand, 25" h, figural, butler
holding green ashtray, painted wood 100.00

Textile

Laundry Bag, 24 x 16½", Mammy .. 45.00
Tablecloth, 52 x 48", cotton, Mammy
serving pie 85.00
Towel, 26 x 15", boy playing harmonica, dancing children 40.00

Toy

Alabama Corn Jigger, litho tin windup,
10" h, Strauss, minor paint touch
up 200.00
Amos 'N' Andy Fresh Air Taxi, Louis
B Marx C, MIB, 1930 .... 650.00
Be–Bob Jigger, tin and plastic, Marx,
c1940 .... 100.00
Dancin' Dan, 11" h, stick, painted
wood, orig instructions 50.00
Mule Cart, black driver, cast iron,
c1890 .... 175.00
Porter, pushing two wheeled cart, tinplate, keywind, Straus 250.00
Preacher At The Pulpit, litho tin keywind, cloth dressed black preacher,
waving hands, thumps Bible, on
platform, Ives, 10" h 2,450.00
Two Man Band, tinplate, two seated
black musicians, one playing accordion, other flute and cymbals,
keywind platform, Gunthermann,
c1895 .... 2,000.00
Walking Lady, litho tin windup, hp,
black woman, wide full skirt, carrying umbrella and wicker basket,
Gunthermann 750.00

Wall Pocket, 5½" l, man and woman,
exaggerated features, polka dot cap
and bandana, pr 50.00

BLOWN THREE MOLD

History: The Jamestown colony in Virginia introduced glass making into America. The artisans
used a "free blown" method.

Blowing molten glass into molds was not introduced into America until the early 1800s. Blown
three mold glass used a pre-designed mold that
consisted of two, three, or more hinged parts. The
glass maker placed a quantity of molten glass on
the tip of a rod or tube, inserted it into the mold,
blew air into the tube, waited until the glass cooled,
and removed the finished product. The three part
mold is the most common and lends its name to
this entire category.

The impressed decorations on blown mold glass
usually are reversed, i.e., what is raised or convex
on the outside will be concave on the inside. This
is useful in identifying the blown form.

By 1850 American made glassware was in relatively common usage. The increased demand led
to large factories and the creation of a technology
which eliminated the smaller companies.

Reference: George S. and Helen McKearin,
American Glass, reprint, Crown Publishers, 1941,
1948.

Collectors' Club: National Early American
Glass Club, 7417 Allison Street, Hyattsville, MD
20784.

Basket

3⅛" d, 3½" h, cobalt blue, traces of
gold dec, plain base, solid applied
handle, pontil scar 115.00
4" d, 4½" h, clear, rayed base, solid
applied handle, pontil scar 275.00
Bottle, 9" h, gold–amber 700.00

Bowl, clear

5" h, 1⅝" h, rounded sides, outward
folded rim, rayed base, pontil scar 165.00
6¼" d, folded rim, twelve diamond
base, pontil scar 185.00
Carafe, 9½" h, dark yellow–amber,
rayed base, deep pontil scar 2,300.00
Cordial, 3" h, clear, stemmed 750.00

Creamer

2⅞" h, clear, fifteen diamond base,
pontil scar, applied ribbed handle 200.00
3½" h, clear, ringed base, formed
mouth and spout, applied solid
handle with curled end 375.00
Cruet, sapphire blue, molded neck
rings, rayed base, pontil scar, orig
solid tam stopper 465.00
Cup Plate, 3⅞" d, folded rim, rayed
base, pontil scar, three McKearin labels, ex–collection George McKearin

and TMR Culbertson, McKearin GII–1 . . . . 600.00
Decanter, qt, clear
McKearin GII–18, flaring lip, three pairs of quilled neck rings, pontil scar, type two stopper, New England 150.00
McKearin GIII–5, clear, pontil scar, type two stopper, New England, 1825–40 . . . . 150.00

Decanter, three ring rigaree neck, ground sunburst stopper, McKearin GII–22, 8¼″ h, $175.00.

Dish
5⅜″ w, 1¾″ l, clear, lead glass, folded over lip, pontil scar, New England, 1825–40, McKearin GIII–25 . . . . . 125.00
6⅜″ d, folded rim, rayed base, iron pontil 100.00
Flip Glass
4½″ h, clear, gray tint, pontil scar, New England, 1825–40, McKearin GII–18 . . . . 135.00
5¾″ h, clear, pontil scar, New England, 1825–40, McKearin GII–18 150.00
Hat
2⅛″ h, clear, fifteen diamond base, folded rim, pontil scar 275.00
2⅝″ h, 2¼″ d, sapphire blue, folded rim, ringed and pontil base 850.00
Inkwell
1⅜″ h, 2¼″ d, olive amber, disc mouth, plain base, rough pontil . . 100.00
1⅞″ h, 2¾″ d, amber, drum shape, faint ringed base, pontil scar 115.00
Lamp, 6½″ h, fluid, clear, double paw pressed base, orig brass collar, marked "BTM font/Mt Vernon Works/GI–30," ex–collection George McKearin 900.00
Mustard Jar, cov
5¼″ h, clear, plain base, orig pressed finial, hollow blown cov, pontil scar, McKearin GI–24 . . . . 100.00
5½″ h, clear, pontil scar, chip on bottom cov edge, New England, McKearin GIII–23 . . . . 175.00
Pan, 1½″ h, 5″ d, McKearin GI–6 . . . . 165.00
Pitcher
3¾″ h, clear, bulbous, fifteen diamond base, pontil scar, solid applied handle 275.00
7″ h, clear, rayed base, manipulated mouth, pontil scar, hollow applied handle 250.00
Plate, 5⅜″ d, clear, plain base, folded rim, pontil scar 150.00
Salt, master
2¼″ h, purple blue, rayed and ringed base, pontil scar 750.00
2½″ h, sapphire blue, rayed base, galleried rim, pontil scar 1,500.00
Toilet Bottle
6⅝″ h, yellow green, tapering ovoid shape, plain base, pontil scar, orig matching stopper, McKearin GI–3, type II 2,750.00
6¾″ h, violet, smooth base, flanged lip, orig tam stopper 650.00
Tumbler
3⅛″ h, clear, lead glass, blue rim, pontil scars, New England, 1825–40, McKearin GI–24 . . . . 1,800.00
3¾″ h, clear, pontil scar, New England, 1825–40, McKearin GII–18 130.00
Whiskey Taster, 1⅝″ h, clear, ringed base, pontil 185.00

BOEHM PORCELAINS

History: Edward Marshall Boehm was born on August 21, 1913. Boehm's childhood was spent at the McConogh School, a rural Baltimore County, Maryland, school dedicated to caring for homeless boys. He studied animal husbandry at the University of Maryland, serving as manager of Longacre Farms on the Eastern Shore of Maryland upon graduation. During World War II, Boehm joined the Air Force and was assigned as a therapist to a convalescent center in Pawling, New York. After the war, he moved to Great Neck, Long Island, and worked as an assistant veterinarian.

In 1949 Boehm quit his job to open a potter studio in Trenton, New Jersey. His initial sculptures consisted of Herefords, Percherons, and dogs done in hard-paste porcelain. The first five to six years were a struggle, with several partnerships beginning and ending during the period. In the early 1950s Boehm's art porcelain sculptures began appearing in major department stores. When Eisenhower presented a Boehm sculpture to Queen Elizabeth and Prince Philip during their visit to the United States in 1957, Boehm's career accelerated.

Boehm was a character—opinionated, prejudiced, and unforgiving. Boehm's contributions were the image concepts and techniques used to produce the sculptures. Thousands of prototype sculptures were made, with over 400 put into actual production. The actual work was done by skilled artisans. Boehm died on January 29, 1969.

In the early 1970s a second production studio was opened in Malvern, England. As Boehm Studios, the tradition begun by Boehm continues today.

Reference: Reese Palley, *The Porcelain Art of Edward Marshall Boehm*, Harrison House, division of Crown Publishers, 1988.

BIRDS

American Eagle, #498	950.00
American Redstarts, #40138	750.00
Black Capped Chickadee, #438, holly leaves base, 9" h	500.00
Blue Heron, #200–19	275.00
Blue Jay, fledgling, 4½" h	175.00
Bluebird, baby, #442, 4½" h	155.00
Bobwhite Quail, #407	1,200.00
Brown Thrasher, #400–26R, black feather mark	825.00
Cardinal, female, #415, 15" h	600.00
Canada Warbler, fledgling, #491	1,500.00
Canadian Geese, #408, pr	575.00
Cedar Waxwing, #432	115.00
Crested Flycatcher, baby, #458C	170.00
Cygnet	165.00
Downy Woodpeckers, #427	1,000.00
Eastern Bluebird, #442	135.00
English Nuthatch, #1001	650.00
Goldfinch, thistle, #457	1,000.00
Horned Lark, grapes, #400–25	2,500.00
Hummingbird, #440, cactus base, 8½" h	900.00
Indigo Bunting, #429	725.00
Kingfisher, #449, 6" h	135.00
Lesser Prairie Chicken, #464	2,750.00
Magpie, fledgling, 6" h	225.00
Nuthatch, #469, ivy and moneywort base, 11" h	485.00
Oven Bird, 10" h	725.00
Prothonotary Warbler, #445	575.00
Ring Neck Pheasants, #409	800.00
Robin	
#472, daffodils base, 14" h	2,000.00
#4375, baby, 3½" h	135.00
Song Sparrow, #400–59	475.00
Western Bluebirds, #494, pr	350.00

FLOWERS

Alex Red Rose, #300–39	1,250.00
Daisies, #3002	750.00
Gold Rose, #G7	600.00
Pussy Willows, #200–28, pr	175.00
Queen Elizabeth Rose, #30091	1,200.00
Royal Blessings Rose, #300–99	1,200.00
Tiger Lilies, #30077	850.00

BOHEMIAN GLASS

History: The once independent country of Bohemia, now a part of Czechoslovakia, produced a variety of fine glassware: etched, cut, overlay, and colored. Their glassware was first imported into America in the early 1820s and continues today.

Bohemia is known for its "flashed" glass that was produced in the familiar ruby color, as well as amber, green, blue, and black. Common patterns include "Deer and Castle," "Deer and Pine Tree," and "Vintage."

Most of the Bohemian glass encountered in today's market is of the 1875–1900 period. Bohemian–type glass also was made in England, Switzerland, and Germany.

Reproduction Alert.

Decanter, Vintage pattern, hollow teardrop stopper, 15" h, $100.00.

Beaker
4⅛" h, amber flashed, three panels, engraved named scenes of Prague, flaring base, mid 19th C	300.00
4½" h	
Blue and white overlay, arched panels with gilt ivy and stylized foliage on oval white overlay, flaring base, mid 19th C	225.00

Blue and white overlay, multicolored spring floral bouquet on oval white overlay, gilt foliage, arched panels, mid to late 19th C 250.00

Clear, continuous hunters in landscape, band of flowering branches 350.00

4⅝" h, waisted cylindrical, multicolored enameled morning glories between cut roundels, pink overlay, white ground 600.00

4¾" h

Green Flashed, circular and oval cut windows, multicolored enameled flowers, gilt lines 200.00

White overlay, multicolored enameled peasant girl, oval cartouche edged with gilt ivy, loose bouquet of flowers on reverse 450.00

5" h, pink flashed opaline, cut stylized leaves and drapery, enamel and gilt flowering branches, flaring base, late 19th C 465.00

5⅛" h, blue and white overlay, rect panel engraved with stag landscape, oval roundels, named scenes, gilt highlights, late 19th C 300.00

5¼" h, white on amethyst overlay, quatrefoil and circular cut windows, painted trailing roses 225.00

5½" h, amber and ruby flashed, alternating panels engraved with cornucopia, flowers, beehive, and urn, cut panels, scalloped foot 200.00

Decanter, 8¼" h, octagonal, triple ringed neck, windows engraved with named scenes of Prague on alternating pink and blue flashed, yellow flashed ground, enameled black foliage 950.00

Goblet

5½" h, ruby, engraved stag, rocky landscape, enameled stylized foliage and flowers, flaring base 200.00

5¾" h, paneled, ruby flashed roundels, engraved named scenes, white enamel flowers, flaring foot 185.00

6¼" h, Annagelb, hexagonal bowl, raised enameled bosses, gilt named scenes, conforming knop and petal base 420.00

Tumbler, 4¼" h, clear, lead glass, pontil scar, enameled German inscription, florals, heart, two hands shaking, dated 1727 .... 550.00

Vase

5" h, molded Bacchanalian dancing female and foliage, deep green glass, faceted foot, c1930 ...... 150.00

6⅛" h, waisted cylindrical, cut oval panels engraved with symbols of Prosperity, amber flashed reserved on amethyst ground, allover flowering branches engraving 450.00

12" h, ruby overlay cut to crystal ... 235.00

BOOKS—ANTIQUES AND COLLECTIBLES

History: The first books about antiques appeared at the end of the nineteenth century. By the 1920s books about antiques were standard fare among publishers. Topics ranged from books on antique furniture and English Staffordshire to "how-to" books on collecting and going to auctions. Many of the books from this period, e.g., George and Helen McKearin's *Two Hundred Years of American Blown Glass,* have become classics.

In the 1960s the antiques and collectibles field witnessed the birth of a publishing explosion. The number of books issued yearly increased many fold. Today there are few topics not covered by a specialized book.

Because of the specialized nature of many books about antiques and collectibles, titles tend to go out-of-print very rapidly. Many are privately published by the authors or small firms.

Many books were published in several printings and editions. Since most collectors' primary reason for acquiring these books is for the information that they contain, it is best to acquire the last, not the first edition, since it most likely contains the most complete information.

Many books about antiques and collectibles prior to 1950 had dust jackets. The book should not be considered complete if the jacket has been lost. Also check to make certain that all illustrations are present.

Many popular editions were issued. These were printed on lesser quality paper and have poorer bindings. Avoid them whenever possible.

There are a number of dealers who specialize in out-of-print books about antiques and collectibles. You will find their advertisements in the trade magazines and newspapers. Do not hesitate to contact them with your needs. It may take from a few months to several years, but eventually they will find the book or books you are seeking.

References: *American Book Prices Current, Volume 95, 1989,* Bancroft-Parkman, Inc., 1990; Editors of Collector Books, *The Old Book Value Guide, Second Edition,* Collector Books, 1990; Marjorie M. and Donald L. Hinds, *How To Make Money Buying & Selling Old Books,* published by authors, 1974.

See *Warman's Americana and Collectibles* for additional listings in the Books: Antiques and Collectibles, Cookbooks, Paperback Books, and Pulp Magazine categories.

Advisor: Ron Lieberman.

CERAMICS AND POTTERY

Barrett, *Bennington Pottery And Porcelain*, Bonanza, NY, 1958, 8 x 10", 342 pgs, 462 black and white illus, worn dj **55.00**

Brankston, A. D., *Early Ming Wares Of Chingtechen, Fully Illustrated*, Henri Vetch, Peking, 1938, 5 x 7", silk, color frontis, 120 pgs, map, halftone plates, first edition, limited to 650 copies .. **40.00**

Bushell, Stephen W. and William M. Laffan, *Catalogue Of The Morgan Collection Of Chinese Porcelains*, Metropolitan Museum of Art, NY, 1910, 5 x 7", orig blue wrappers, 195 pgs, 76 halftone plate illus **25.00**

Haines, Flora E., *A Keramic Study. A Chapter In The History Of Half A Dozen Dinner Plates*, Bangor, ME, 1895, 3 x 5", cloth, 127 pgs **35.00**

James, *The Potters And Potteries Of Chester County, Pennsylvania*, West Chester, 1945, 5 x 7", 116 pgs, limited to 600 copies **135.00**

Langenbeck, Karl, *The Chemistry Of Pottery*, Chemical Publ. Co., Easton, PA, 1895, 3 x 5", cloth, 197 pgs, ads, first edition **75.00**

McLaughlin, M. Louise, *China Painting. A Practical Manual For The Use of Amateurs In The Decoration Of Hand Porcelain*, Clarke, Cincinnati, 1892, 3 x 5", cloth, 103 pgs, ads **35.00**

Ramsay, *American Potters And Pottery*, Clinton, 1939, 5 x 7", 304 pgs, 87 black and white plates, worn dj **85.00**

Schwartz & Wolfe, *A History Of American Art Porcelain*, NY, 1967, 8 x 10", 93 pgs, 7 color, 68 black and white illus, dj **35.00**

Sparkes, John C. L., *A Hand Book To The Practice Of Pottery Painting*, Harper, NY, 1877, printed wrappers, 79 pgs **35.00**

FASHION

Beck, S. William, *Gloves, Their Annuals And Associations: A Chapter Of Trade And Social History*, Hamilton, Adams, London, 1883, small 5 x 7", cloth, 263 pgs, owner blind stamp on title **100.00**

Lester & Oerke, *Accessories Of Dress*, Peoria, 1940, 7 x 10½", 587 pgs, 60 black and white plates, 644 black and white illus **100.00**

Liberty & Co, *Liberty's Dresses And Jumpers For Ladies And Frocks For Children*, London, 1932, 5 x 9", 32 pgs, softcover **30.00**

Parsons, Frank Alvah, *The Psychology Of Dress*, Garden City, 1920, 5 x 7", cloth dull, rubbed, 358 pgs **35.00**

Percival, *The Fan Book*, NY, 1971, 6 x 9", 344 pgs, 32 black and white plates **50.00**

FURNITURE

Bissell, *Antique Furniture In Suffield, Connecticut, 1670–1835*, Suffield, 1956, 7 x 11", 128 pgs, 60 black and white plates, limited to 750 copies .. **125.00**

Blackie & Son, *The Cabinetmakers Assistant—A Series Of Original Designs For Modern Furniture, With Descriptions And Details Of Construction*, London, 1853, 11 x 15", 123 pgs, 101 engraved plates, quarter leather ... **375.00**

Blanchard, *How To Restore And Decorate Chairs*, New York, 1952, 8 x 11", 128 pgs, black and white illus, dj ... **15.00**

Cescinsky, *English Furniture From Gothic To Sheraton*, Grand Rapids, 1929, 9 x 12", 438 pgs, 900 black and white illus **150.00**

Curtis Companies Service Bureau, *Permanent Furniture For Better Built Homes*, Clinton, IA, 1923, 3 x 5", color picture wrappers, 48 pgs, illus **15.00**

Eberlein, Harold Donaldson and Roger Wearne Ramsdell, *The Practical Book Of Italian, Spanish And Portuguese Furniture*, Philadelphia, 1927, thick 5 x 7", 254 pgs, first edition .. **20.00**

Kirk, *American Chairs, Queen Anne and Chippendale*, NY, 1972, 11 x 12", 208 pgs, color frontis, 204 black and white illus, dj **250.00**

Lamp, George N., *The Mahogany Book*, Chicago, 1936, 5 x 7", wrappers, 80 pgs, illus, second edition .. **15.00**

Lea, *The Ornamented Chair, Its Development In America 1700–1890*, Rutland, 1966, 8 x 11", 173 pgs, 7 color plates, 290 black and white illus, dj . **85.00**

Longnon, Henri and Frances Wilson Huard, *French Provincial Furniture*, Philadelphia, 1927, 5 x 7", 167 pgs, illus, first edition **20.00**

Luther, *The Hadley Chest*, Hartford, 1935, 8 x 11", 144 pgs, black and white illus, dj, supplemental list **350.00**

Macquoid & Edwards, *The Dictionary Of English Furniture*, London and New York, 1924–27, 3 volumes, 11 x 15", 962 pgs, 51 color plates, green cloth cover, gilt titles, first edition **650.00**

FOLK ART

Bird, *Ontario Fraktur–A Pennsylvania–German Folk Tradition In Early Can-*

ada, Toronto, 1977, 10 x 8", 144 pgs, color and black and white illus, dj . . **30.00**

Black and Lipman, *American Folk Painting,* NY, 1966, 9 x 12", 244 pgs, 86 color plates, 146 black and white illus, dj **50.00**

Christensen, *Early American Wood Carving,* NY, 1952, 6 x 9", 149 pgs, 5 color and 50 black and white illus, special first edition limited to 1,250 copies, slipcase **50.00**

Doty, *American Folk Art In Ohio Collections,* Akron, 1976, 9 x 8', 10 pgs of text, 11 color and 58 black and white plates, dj **20.00**

Earle, *Scrimshaw, Folk Art Of The Whalers,* Cold Spring Harbor, 1957, 6 x 9", 36 pgs, 8 black and white plates, softcover **15.00**

Fitzgerald, *Weathervanes and Whirligigs,* NY, 1967, 6 x 9", 186 pgs, line drawings **15.00**

Little, *The Abby Aldrich Rockefeller Folk Art Collection,* Boston/Williamsburg, 1957, 8 x 10", 402 pgs, 165 color plates, boxed **100.00**

Museum of Modern Art, *American Folk Art—The Art Of The Common Man In America, 1750–1900,* NY, 1932, 7 x 10", 52 pgs, 79 black and white plates, card cov **50.00**

Stoudt
Early Pennsylvania Arts and Crafts, South Brunswick, 1964, 9 x 12", 364 pgs, 21 color and 344 black and white illus, dj **50.00**

Sunbonnets and Shoofly Pies, A Pennsylvania Dutch Cultural History, Castle, NY, 1973, 10 x 12", 272 pgs **40.00**

Glass, Edwin G. Warman, *American Cut Glass,* **11th Printing, E. G. Warman Publishing Inc., 1978, $30.00.**

GLASS

Faber, William Frederic, *Stained Glass Windows. An Essay With A Report To The Vestry On Stained Glass Windows For Grace Church, Lockport, New York,* Lockport, NY, 1900, 3 x 5", slight edge chips, 41 pgs **35.00**

Heiges, *Henry William Stiegel,* Manheim, 1937, 5 x 7", 80 pgs, 15 black and white plates, dj **25.00**

Hunter, *Stiegel Glass,* Boston, 1914, 7 x 10", 272 pgs, 12 color plates, 159 black and white illus, pictorial covers, limited to 420 copies, inscribed **300.00**

McKearin, G., *Two Hundred Years Of American Blown Glass,* Bonanza, NY, nd, 8 x 11", 382 pgs, 10 color plates, 105 black and white illus, dj . **40.00**

Wilson, *New England Glass and Glassmaking,* Sturbridge, 1972, 8 x 10", 401 pgs, black and white illus, dj . . . **65.00**

MISCELLANEOUS

Conningham, Frederic A., *Currier & Ives Prints,* 1970, hardbound **100.00**

Dennis, Lee, *Warman's Antique American Games, 1840–1940,* 1986 . . . . **25.00**

Gottesman, *The Arts & Crafts In New York, 1726–1804,* 3 volumes, NY, 1938, 1948, 1965, 6 x 9", 1471 pgs, green and red cloth cov **250.00**

Hannas, *The English Jigsaw Puzzle 1760 to 1890,* London, 1972, 8 x 10", 164 pgs, color and black and white illus, dj **50.00**

Hayward, *Colonial Lighting,* Boston, 1923, 6 x 9", 159 pgs, 114 black and white illus, first edition **75.00**

Hughes, Elizabeth and Lester, Marion, *The Big Book of Buttons,* 1981, hardbound **275.00**

Luckey, Carl F., *Collector Prints, Old and New,* Books Americana, 1982 **25.00**

Punchard, Lorraine M., *Child's Play,* privately printed, 1982 . . . . **50.00**

TEXTILES

Bolton & Coe, *American Samplers,* Weathervane, NY, 1973, 6 x 9", 416 pgs, 76 black and white plates, dj . . **40.00**

Di Brazza, Cora A., *A Guide To Old And New Lace In Italy, Exhibited At Chicago In 1893,* Conkey, Chicago, 1893, 5 x 7", morocco spine labels, 186 pgs **75.00**

Hall, *A Book Of Handwoven Coverlets,* Boston, 1912, 6 x 9", 279 pgs, 16 color and 48 black and white plates, pictorial cloth covers, first edition . . . **150.00**

Kent, *The Hooked Rug*, NY, 1973, 8 x 10", 210 pgs, 172 black and white illus, dj 50.00

Little, *Early American Textiles*, NY, 1931, 6 x 8", 267 pgs, 62 black and white illus, dj 85.00

Orlofsky, *Quilts In America*, NY, 1974, 8 x 10", 3768 pgs, 109 color, 205 black and white illus, dj 300.00

Parnell, Edward Andrew, *Dyeing And Calico–Printing*, London, 1849, 5 x 7", cloth, 288 pgs, ads on end papers, 23 orig fabric samples, first edition 175.00

Peto, *Historic Quilts*, NY, 1939, 6 x 9", 210 pgs, 62 black and white plates 125.00

Pushman Bros, *Arts Panels From The Handlooms Of The Far Orient. As Seen By A Native Rug Weaver*, Chicago, 1911, 5 x 7", 88 pgs, halftone plate illus, color illus 25.00

Swygert, *Heirlooms From Old Looms, A Catalogue of Coverlets Owned By The Colonial Coverlet Guild Of America And Its Members*, Chicago, 1955, 6 x 10", 406 pgs, second edition ... 200.00

BOOTJACKS

History: Bootjacks are metal or wooden devices that facilitate the removal of boots. Bootjacks are used by placing the heel of the boot in the "U" shaped opening, putting a foot on the back of the bootjack, and pulling the front boot off the foot.

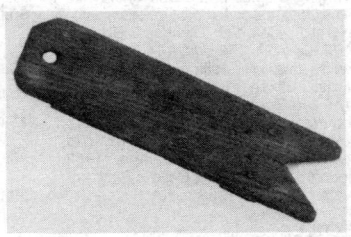

Wood, pine, 17″ l, $30.00.

Advertising, Mussleman's Plug Tobacco, cast iron 130.00

Cast Iron
Beetle, 9¼", black paint 35.00
Closed Loop, cast iron, large 70.00
Downs & Co, cast iron 85.00

Heart and Diamond, 22" l, walnut, openwork 40.00

Open heart and circle, scalloped sides, cast iron, 13" l 220.00

Pheasants, 19" l, two birds, cast iron, brushes 225.00

Scissor action, cast iron, marked "Pat 1877" 85.00

V shape, cast iron, ornate 45.00

Wood
Bentwood, arched 85.00
Birch, folding, hinged 30.00
Mahogany, folding type, c1860 .... 40.00
Pine, 25", oval ends, sq nails 30.00

BOTTLES, GENERAL

History: Cosmetic bottles held special creams, oils, and cosmetics designed to enhance the beauty of the user. Some also claimed, especially on their colorful labels, to cure or provide relief from common ailments.

A number of household items, e.g., cleaning fluids and polishes, required glass storage containers. Many are collected for their fine lithograph labels.

Mineral water bottles contained water from a natural spring. Spring water was favored by health conscious people between the 1850s and 1900s.

Nursing bottles, used to feed the young and sickly, were a great help to the housewife because of graduated measures, replaceable nipples, ease of cleaning, sterilizing, and reuse.

References: Ralph & Terry Kovel, *The Kovels' Bottle Price List, Eighth Edition*, Crown Publishers, Inc., 1987; Carlo & Dorothy Sellari, *The Illustrated Price Guide To Antique Bottles*, Collector Books, 1989.

Periodicals: *Antique Bottle And Glass Collector*, P.O. Box 187, East Greenville, PA 18041.

Collectors' Club: Federation of Historical Bottle Collectors, 14521 Atlantic, Riverdale, IL 60627.

Museum: National Bottle Museum, Ballston Spa, NY.

Additional Listings: Barber Bottles, Bitter Bottles, Figural Bottles, Food Bottles, Ink Bottles, Medicine Bottles, Poison Bottles, Sarsaparilla Bottles and Snuff Bottles. Also see the bottle categories in *Warman's Americana & Collectibles* for more examples.

COSMETICS

Boswell & Warner's Colorific, rect, indented panels, cobalt blue, tooled sq lip, 5½" h, c1880 .... 80.00

Hinds' Honey and Almond Cream, 5½" 5.00

The Mexican Hair Renewer, oval, cobalt blue, tooled double ring lip, side strap, 7¼" h, c1880 .... 120.00

Violet Dulce Vanishing Cream, 2½", eight panels 12.00

HOUSEHOLD

E Z Stove Polish, 6", aqua 10.00

Golden Key Ammonia, 8″, paper label 2.00
Jennings Blueing, 7″, aqua, blob top 5.00
Parsons Ammonia, aqua, 1882 . . . . . 18.00
Sanford's Library Paste, amber, emb, label, 1 pt 15.00

Mineral Water, Superior Mineral Water, graphite bottle, Twitchel, Philadelphia, 7⅛″ h, $42.50.

MINERAL OR SPRING WATER

Artesian Water, round, twelve paneled base, golden chocolate amber, iron pontil, pint, 1850–60 . . . . 450.00
Boyd & Beard Mineral Water, squat, iron pontil, green 65.00
Champlain Spring, Alkaline Chaaly-beate, Highgate, VT, round, deep green, applied collar lip, qt, c1870 . . 150.00
E M Keane Ale, round, golden amber, applied lip, 9⅛″ h, c1870 . . . . 600.00
F & L Schaum Baltimore Glass Works, round, olive green, rect slug plate reverse, iron pontil, 7⅛″ h, 1850–60 . . 375.00
Lancaster Glass Works, round, sapphire blue, applied blob lip, iron pontil, 7″ h, 1850–60 . . . . 100.00
Middletown Mineral Spring Co, round, emerald green, applied tapered lip, orig label, c1870 . . . . 425.00
Pavilion, United States Spring, emerald green 210.00
Saratoga Seltzer Water, cylinder shape, teal blue green, applied ring lip, 7½″ h, c1890 . . . . 75.00
Stirlings Magnetic Mineral Spring, Eaton Rapids, Mich, round, golden am-

ber, applied tapered collar lip, qt, 1870–80 . . . . 150.00
Wm W Lappeus, Premium Soda or Mineral Water, Albany, ten sided, blue, blob top, iron pontil base, 7″ h, 1850–60 . . . . 725.00

NURSING

Baby's Delight, glass straw 45.00
Happy Baby, baby outline, big letters, 8 oz 5.00
Manx Feeding Bottle, bulbous, clear, tooled sq collar, 3″ h, emb "Patent July 4, 1876" 200.00
Miller Sanitate 35.00
Sweet Babee Nurser, clear, emb "Easy Clean," Patd May 3, 1910 . . . . 12.00
True Temp, thermometer 30.00

BRASS

History: Brass is a durable, malleable, and ductile metal alloy consisting mainly of copper and zinc. It achieved its greatest popularity for utilitarian and decorative art items in the eighteenth and nineteenth centuries.

References: Mary Frank Gaston, *Antique Brass: Identification and Values*, Collector Books, 1985; Peter, Nancy, and Herbert Schiffer, *The Brass Book*, Schiffer Publishing, Ltd, 1978.

Additional Listings: Bells, Candlesticks, Fireplace Equipment, and Scientific Instruments.

Reproduction Alert: Many modern reproductions are being made of earlier brass forms, especially in the areas of buckets, fireplace equipment, and kettles.

Vase, triangular, flared, three handles, 8⅜″ h, $75.00.

Andirons, pr
  15½" h, steeple top, repaired **200.00**
  16½" h, urn finial, sq plinth, molded base, spurred arched legs, penny feet, Federal, American, early 19th C **700.00**
  16¾" h, double ball turned finials, cylindrical plinth, spurred arched legs, ball feet, Federal, American, early 19th C **800.00**
  18¾" h, acorn style, ball feet, American, late 18th C, early 19th C . . . **500.00**
Bed Warmer
  44" l, engraved and pierced lid, orig maple handle **175.00**
  44½" l, oversized lid with tooled designs and heart, turned wood handle **75.00**
  46" l, pierced and engraved lid, turned wood handle **110.00**
  48½" l, pierced lid, engraved floral design, turned wood handle **325.00**
Bell
  Kewpie **65.00**
  School **40.00**
Candlestick
  6⅜" h, side pushup, saucer base . . **100.00**
  7½" h, pushup, sgd "J T & Co" **30.00**
  9", diamond and beehive detail, pushup, pr **145.00**
  9½" h, engraved, Continental, 19th C **25.00**
  9¾" h, Jack of Diamond pattern, pushups, pr **125.00**
  10" h, trumpet shape, pushups, 19th C, pr **185.00**
  10¾" h, Queen of Diamond pattern, pushups, English, 19th C **200.00**
  10⅝" h, pr, Jack of Diamond pattern, pushups, pr, English, 19th C **100.00**
  19" h, trumpet shape, English, 19th C, pr **150.00**
Chamberstick
  4½" h, side pushup **135.00**
  5" h, plated, ejector, English **35.00**
  5½" h, pushup, holders for snuffer and wick trimmer **75.00**
  8" l, pushup, includes wick trimmer and snuffer **275.00**
Clock Jack, 12½" l, marked "G Salter & Co, Improved" **85.00**
Doorstop, 10¾" h, lion attacked by snake, lead weighted, English **80.00**
Figure, 15½" l, leaping cat, black lacquered wood base, attributed to Hagenauer **900.00**
Fireplace Fender
  48" w, D shape, brass rail surmounted by three brass finials over wire screen, meandering floral vine and intertwined circle band, vertical bar ground, brass paw feet, late Federal, American, early 19th C **1,550.00**

51" d, 14" d, English, c1820 . . . . . . **225.00**
Heater, 8¼" d, 7½" h, octagonal shape, pierced, four turned feet, bail handle, four inscribed "Dutch" script lines on lid **300.00**
Lamp
  Fluid
    6½", marked "Dyott/Philadelphia" **60.00**
    7¾", pear shape font, weighted base, electrified, pr **120.00**
    8½" h, iron weighted base, molded pear shape font, etched globe, orig luster **60.00**
    12" h, frosted and etched globe, weighted base, orig luster finish **110.00**
  Grease, 7¼" h, open font, tin wick support, engraved "FMO 1857" . . **90.00**
  Hand, 6½", cast brass dolphin handle, orig luster **50.00**
  Student, 20½" h, orig **275.00**
Noodle Maker Roller, 8½" w, marked "F H Crafts, Rochester NY" **45.00**
Pail
  9½" d, 6" h, spun, iron bale handle, marked "Haydens Patent" **65.00**
  11" d, 7½" h, iron bale handle, "Haydens Patent" label **75.00**
Pendant, 12", Art Nouveau, stylized insect, turquoise and brown glass accents **75.00**
Skimmer, star flower shape holes, wrought iron handle, 18¼" l **55.00**
Stand, 9¾" h, reticulated top, cast iron weighted base, English, 19th C **60.00**
Taper Jack, 6¼" h, clamp spring missing **195.00**
Tea Kettle, 8" h, gooseneck spout, turned handle **55.00**
Trivet
  5½ x 10", reticulated top, foliage design, paw feet, marked "England" **65.00**
  7¼ x 12¼", 5½" h, reticulated lion and unicorn, English **175.00**
  7½" d, 5¼" h, reticulated top, worn tooling **95.00**
  10⅝" l, punch engraved date "1826," replaced feet **65.00**
Warming Pan, orig turned handle **175.00**
Wick Trimmer
  6" l **30.00**
  9¼" l, includes tray **115.00**
  9½" l, includes tray **85.00**

BREAD PLATES

History: Beginning in the mid-1880s, special trays or platters were made for serving bread and rolls. Designated by collectors as "bread plates," these small trays or platters can be found in porcelain, glass (especially pattern glass), and metals.

Bread plates often were part of a china or glass set. However, many glass companies made special plates which honored national heroes, commemorated historical or special events, offered a moral maxim, or supported a religious attitude. The theme on the plate could be either in a horizontal or vertical format. The favorite shape for these plates is oval, with a common length being ten inches.

Reference: Anna Maude Stuart, *Bread Plates And Platters*, published by author, 1965.

Additional Listings: Pattern Glass.

Last Supper, clear glass, frosted grape leaf border, 10⅞ x 7″, $70.00.

Advertising, Pioneer Flour Mill, San Antonio, clear pressed glass	45.00
Historical Glass	
Garfield Memorial	40.00
Liberty and Freedom	65.00
McKinley, oval	40.00
Three Presidents	65.00
U.S. Grant	45.00
Majolica	
Etruscan, 11½″ d, emb fern leaves and wheat sheaves	250.00
Pond Lily pattern, 13″ l	165.00
Pattern Glass	
Actress, Miss Neilson	80.00
Basketweave, amber	35.00
Beaded Loop	30.00
Crying Baby	50.00
Deer and Pine Tree	45.00
Double Vine	20.00
Faith, Hope, and Charity, plain center, imp "Patd Nov 23, 1875"	30.00
Finecut and Panel, amber, 13″ l	45.00
Frosted Lion, 10½″ d, round, Cable border	75.00
Garden of Eden	30.00
Grapes, slogan	45.00
Minerva	60.00
Royal Lady, vaseline	135.00
Scroll with Flowers	25.00
Swan with Flowers	35.00

Three Graces	45.00
Wheat	25.00
Silver, plated, 11″ l, 7¾″ w, 2¼″ h, rounded rect, Asian head pattern border, center scenic panel of gypsy dancer, four small feet, Meriden Britannia Co, Meriden, CT, late 19th C	250.00

BRIDE'S BASKETS

History: A ruffled edge glass bowl in a metal holder was a popular wedding gift in the 1880–1910 era, hence, the name of "bride's basket." The glass bowls can be found in most glass types of the period. The metal holder was generally silver plated with a bail handle, thus enhancing the basket image.

Over the years bowls and bases became separated, and married pieces resulted. When the base has been lost, the bowl is sold separately.

Reference: John Mebane, *Collecting Bride's Baskets And Other Glass Fancies,* Wallace-Homestead, 1976.

Reproduction Alert: The glass bowls have been reproduced.

Note: Items listed have silver plated holder unless otherwise noted.

Cased glass, white ext., pink int., stand marked "Middletown Plate, Quad Plate," 11¼″ d, 11″ h, $250.00.

Amberina, 9″ d, 12″ h, rose–amber Coin Spot bowl, silver plated sgd Pairpoint stand, Mt Washington, c1880	875.00
Cased Glass, 11½″ d, 13½″ h, ruffled, white shading to pink to raspberry, cased in white, plum dec, gold branches, hanging ferns, gold dotted florals, double handled ornate silver	

frame, figural flowers on handle and base 375.00

Crown Milano
10" d, 2¾" h, painted Burmese ground, four pansy bouquets, gold scrolls, eighty flutes, crimped rim, Mt Washington 875.00
11" d, tricorn, 11½" h, six large pansies, pale purple and orange tracery medallions, pale yellow int., orig tricorn ftd sgd Pairpoint stand 3,000.00

Peachblow
9" d, amber applied rim, shiny finish, SP holder marked "Wilcox" 185.00
11" d, pink ext. with gold stylized flowers, peachblow int., ornate SP holder with aquatic marine life motif, marked "Pairpoint Mfg Co" ... 800.00

Satin Glass
8" d, pink, lemon yellow ribbon rim 150.00
9" d, MOP, herringbone, rainbow ... 220.00
9½" sq, MOP, DQ, deep blue shading to pale blue int., blue shading to white ext., applied frosted crimped edge, Mt Washington 585.00
10" d, 2½" h, deep rose shading to pink, ruffled, enameled floral dec 225.00
10¼" d, lemon yellow, applied cranberry rim 150.00
11" d, 12" h, 17½" w, baby blue, herringbone, MOP, melon ribbed, gold chrysanthemum blossoms and foliage, golden yellow enamel, gold scrolls, applied gold highlights, frilly crimped rim, attributed to Mt Washington Glass decorators, SP holder with applied metal leaves, emb details, sgd "The Acme Silverplate Co, Boston Quadruple Plate 854" 1,850.00

Spangled Glass, Vasa Murrhina
10½" d, blue and white, applied clear twist handle 275.00
11" d, pink and white, applied clear thorn handle 250.00

BRISTOL GLASS

History: Bristol glass is a designation given to a semi–opaque glass, usually decorated with enamel and cased with another color.

Initially the term referred only to glass made in Bristol, England, in the 17th and 18th centuries. By the Victorian era forms on the Continent and in America copied the glass and its forms.

Biscuit Jar, cov, 7" h, 4¼" d, gray–brown ground, enameled running ostrich and stork, florals, bail handle 275.00
Cologne Bottle, 8⅞" h, white ground, hp butterfly and flowers, Victorian 40.00
Compote, fluted, hp, cat scene, metal base 65.00

Vase, cream ground, green, yellow, and blue dec, bird and white scene, 12¼" h, $100.00

Cruet
5½" h, yellow over white, floral dec, pint int., applied handle 40.00
5¾" h, blue ground, hp swallow, orig stopper 45.00
Decanter, 11½" h, rose shading to deep rose, purple flowers, gilt butterfly on neck, applied handle, marbleized rose and white stopper 110.00
Flask, 8⅞" h, moon shape, cream ground, stepped handles, hp birds and flowers, English, late 19th C, pr 325.00
Goblet, 10¾" h, pedestal base, opaque blue, polychrome enamel floral dec, gilt trim 85.00
Ring Box, cov, 1¾" d, 1¾" h, turquoise, gold flowers and leaves 50.00
Salt, 2⅜" d, light gray ground, enameled herons and foliage, silverplated rim and handle 40.00
Sweetmeat Jar, 4" h, hp ducks and cranes, robin egg blue, cow finial .. 350.00
Vase
6½" h, baluster, ftd, wide flaring scalloped neck, light gray ground, blue, yellow, and green enameled flowers 30.00
10" h, apple green ground, cottage and water scene, gilt scrolling and flowers, deep rust shading on base, neck, and top 80.00
10½" h, squatty, long cylindrical neck, ruffled rim, cream shaded to forest green ground, hp mill scene, brown banding, fired gold trim 110.00
14½" h, cone shape, folds, blue, white enamel floral dec and beading, Webster Bros silverplate holder .. 275.00
17¼" h, baluster, ftd, cut scalloped top, creamy opaque ground, enameled mill scene, enameled pink floral border, gold trim, pr 400.00

BRITISH ROYALTY COMMEMORATIVES

History: British commemorative china, souvenirs to commemorate coronations and other royal events, dates from the 1600s, with the early pieces being rather crude in design and form. The development of transfer printing, c1780, led to a much closer likeness of the reigning monarch on the ware.

Few commemorative pieces predating Queen Victoria's reign are found today at popular prices. Items associated with Queen Elizabeth II and her children, e.g., the wedding of HRH Prince Andrew and Miss Sarah Ferguson and the subsequent birth of their daughter HRH Princess Beatrice are very common.

Some British Royalty commemoratives are easily recognized by their portraits of past or present monarchs. Some may be in silhouette profile. Other royal symbols include crowns, dragons, royal coats of arms, national flowers, swords, scepters, dates, messages, and initials.

References: Malcolm Davey and Doug Mannion, *50 Years of Royal Commemorative China 1887–1937,* Dayman Publications, 1988; Peter Johnson, *Royal Memorabilia: A Phillips Collectors Guide,* Dunestyle Publishing Ltd., 1988; John May, *Victoria Remembered, A Royal History 1817–1861,* London, 1983; John and Jennifer May, *Commemorative Pottery 1780–1900, A Guide for Collectors,* Charles Scribner's Sons, 1972; Josephine Jackson, *Fired For Royalty,* Heaton Moor, 1977; David Rogers, *Coronation Souvenirs and Commemoratives,* Latimer New Dimensions, Ltd., 1975; Sussex Commemorative Ware Centre, *200 Commemoratives,* Metra Print Enterprises, 1979; Geoffrey Warren, *Royal Souvenirs,* Orbis, 1977; Audrey B. Zeder, *British Royal Commemoratives,* Wallace-Homestead, 1986.

Additional Listings: See *Warman's Americana & Collectibles* for more examples.

Advisors: Douglas Flynn and Alan Bolton.

Mug, King George V, Silver Jubilee, white ground, 4⅛″ h, $55.00.

Beaker	
Elizabeth II, 1953 Coronation, 3½″ h, Poole	30.00
Elizabeth II, 60th Birthday, 4½″ h, limited edition 250, Caverswall	90.00
George V/Mary, 1911 Coronation, 3½″ h, Bishop and Stonier	75.00
George VI/Elizabeth, 1937 Coronation, 4⅛″ h, Grindley	40.00
Bowl	
Edward VIII, 1937 Coronation, 6¼″ d, Grindley	40.00
Elizabeth II, 1959 Canada Visit, 1½″ h, Royal Albert	50.00
George VI/Elizabeth, 1937 Coronation, coat of arms, 5½″ d, Paragon	45.00
Victoria, 1901, In Memoriam, 9½″ d, pressed glass	100.00
Box, Elizabeth II, 1977 Jubilee, raised flowers, 1⅞″ d, Crown Staffordshire	20.00
Cake Plate, Victoria, 1897 Jubilee, sepia portraits, residences, Man of War, 10¾″ d	130.00
Cup and Saucer	
Andrew/Sarah, 1986 Wedding, Colclough	25.00
Charles/Diana, 1981 Wedding, Duchess	30.00
Edward VII/Alexandra, 1888 Silver Wedding Anniversary, coat of arms, oversize	175.00
George VI/Elizabeth, 1937 Coronation, sepia portraits with Princess Elizabeth and Margaret, Welworth	50.00
Jug	
Elizabeth II, 1953 Coronation, emb crowning scene, 8¼″ h, Burleigh Ware	240.00
George VI/Elizabeth, 1937 Coronation, musical, sepia portraits, Princess Elizabeth/Margaret on reverse, Shelley	260.00
Lithophane	
Alexandra, 1902, cup, crown, and cypher, 2¾″ h	180.00
Edward VII, 1902, mug, crown, and cypher, 2¾″ h	90.00
George V, 1911, mug, crown, and cypher, 2¾″ h	150.00
Mary, 1911, cup, crown, and cypher, 2¾″ h	270.00
Loving Cup	
Andrew/Sarah, 1986 Wedding, color portraits in wedding attire, 2⅞″ h, Fenton	60.00
Elizabeth II, 1972 Silver Wedding Anniversary, 3″ h, Paragon	175.00
George VI/Elizabeth, 1937 Coronation, brown portrait, 3¼″ h, Marcus Adams, Sampson Smith	140.00

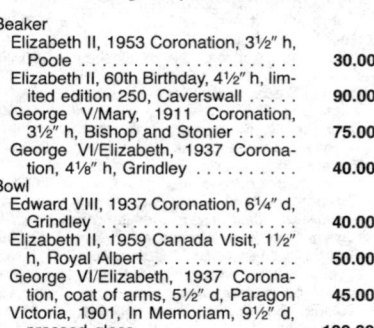

Henry, 1984 Birth, 3" h, Paragon . . .   **110.00**
Victoria, 1897 Jubilee, brown portrait,
  4" h, Victoria **175.00**

Mug

Charles, 1969 Investiture as Prince of
  Wales, gold dragon, feathers, black
  ground, 4" h, Portmeirion Pottery   **60.00**
Duke/Duchess of Windsor, In Memo-
  riam, black and white portraits, im-
  portant dates, 3⅜" h, Dorincourt   **55.00**
Edward VIII, 1937 Coronation, etched
  crystal, accession and coronation
  dates, T Goode & Co **140.00**
Elizabeth II, 40th "Ruby" Wedding
  Anniversary, color portraits, 3" h,
  Coalport **45.00**
George V/Mary, 1911 Coronation, se-
  pia portraits, 4" h, Ridgway **100.00**
Victoria, 1887 Jubilee, color beaded
  crown and ribbon, 3¼" h, William
  Whiteley **90.00**
Victoria, 150th Anniversary of Coro-
  nation, 3⅝" h, Caverswall **40.00**

Paperweight

Charles/Diana, 1981 Wedding, black
  and white portraits, 2¾" d **25.00**
Edward VIII, 1937 Coronation, black
  and white portrait, 4¼ x 1⅛" **20.00**
Victoria/Albert, black and white portraits, color and glitter, 2⅞" **30.00**

Pin Tray

Edward VIII, 1937 Coronation, color
  portrait, 4" d **25.00**
Edward VII/Alexandra, 1902 Corona-
  tion, sepia portraits, 4" d **40.00**
George VI, 1937 Coronation, sepia
  portrait, 3" sq, Royal Crown Derby   **40.00**
Victoria, 1897 Jubilee, sepia portrait,
  5" d **45.00**

Pitcher

Elizabeth, 1953 Coronation, brown
  portrait, 6¼" h, Royal Doulton . . .   **190.00**
Victoria, 1887 Jubilee, black and
  white portrait, 5" h **120.00**

Plate

Charles, 1969 Investiture as Prince of
  Wales, sepia portrait, 8" d, Coronet   **70.00**
Charles/Diana, 1981 Wedding, sepia
  portraits, 6¼" d, Weatherby **20.00**
Edward VII/Alexandra, 1902 Corona-
  tion, color portraits, 7" d **50.00**
Elizabeth II, 60th Birthday, large color
  portrait, limited edition 20,000,
  Coalport **80.00**
George VI/Elizabeth, 1937 Corona-
  tion, black and white portraits, 6" d,
  Royal Doulton **50.00**
Princess Margaret, Birth, parakeets,
  flowers, 6" d, Paragon **75.00**
Victoria, 150th Anniversary of Coro-
  nation, gold portrait, 10½" d, limited
  edition 150, Caverswall **135.00**

Plate, Queen Elizabeth, June, 1953, redware, stamped "Dartmouth Pottery, Devon, England," 5⅝" d, $25.00.

Victoria, 1897 Jubilee, brown and
  white young and mature portraits,
  7½" d **70.00**

Playing Cards

Andrew/Sarah, 1986 Wedding, color
  portraits, double deck, Wadding-
  tons **30.00**
Edward VIII, 1919 Canada Visit, color
  portrait, single deck, C Goodall &
  Co **75.00**
Elizabeth II, 1977 Jubilee, sepia por-
  trait, single deck, Waddingtons . . .   **25.00**
George V/Mary, 1911 Coronation,
  color portraits, double deck **75.00**

Shaving Mug

Edward VII/Alexandra, 1902 Corona-
  tion, color portraits, 3¾" h **100.00**
Edward VIII, 1937 Coronation, sepia
  portrait, 4" h **75.00**
Elizabeth II, 1953 Coronation, color
  portrait, 4" h **70.00**
George VI/Elizabeth, 1937 Corona-
  tion, sepia portraits, 4½" h, Shelley   **100.00**

Teapot

Charles/Diana, 1981 Wedding, sepia
  portraits, 5" h, Price **55.00**
Charlotte, In Memoriam, black and
  white dec, 6" h **260.00**
Edward VII/Alexandra, 1902 Corona-
  tion, color portraits, 4¾" **65.00**
Elizabeth II, 1953 Coronation, relief
  portraits, Jasperware, white on
  royal blue, 5" h, Wedgwood **225.00**
George V/Mary, 1911 Coronation,
  color portraits with Prince of Wales,
  6" h, bone china **255.00**
Victoria, 1897 Jubilee, color portraits,
  4" h **130.00**

Victoria, 1897 Jubilee, color coat of arms, 6" h, Aynsley **250.00**
Tea Set, Elizabeth II, 1953 Coronation, teapot, cream and sugar, relief portraits, Jasperware, white on royal blue, Wedgwood **325.00**
Tin
  Andrew/Sarah, 1986 Wedding, color portraits, 8" d **20.00**
  Edward VII/Alexandra, 1902 Coronation, color portraits, hinged lid, 4¼ x 5½" **65.00**
  Edward VII/Alexandra, 1902 Coronation, color portrait, 5 x 3½", Ridgway Ltd. Tea **100.00**
  Edward VIII, 1937 Coronation, color portrait, hinged lid, 5¾ x 3¾", Riley's Toffee **45.00**
  Elizabeth II, 1953 Coronation, color portrait, hinged lid, 5½ x 4¼", Rowntree **25.00**
  George V/Mary, 1935 Jubilee, color portraits, 6¾ x 4½" **45.00**

Tin, Queen Victoria, 1900, "I Wish You A Happy New Year," red ground, blue border, 6¼ x 3⅜ x 1⅛", $50.00.

George VI/Elizabeth, 1937 Coronation, gold portraits, 3" h, Oxo **18.00**
George VI/Elizabeth, 1937 Coronation, sepia Vandyk portrait, 5¾" h, 4½ x 3¼" **50.00**
Princess Mary, 1914 Christmas, brass, emb profile, hinged lid, 4¾ x 3 x 1" **50.00**
Princess Mary, 1922 Wedding, color portraits, 4¼ x 4" **45.00**
Victoria, 1897 Jubilee, color dec, accession picture on lid, 5½ x 3½ x 3½" **100.00**
Victoria, color portrait on hinged lid, 6¾ x 4½ x 3¼" **75.00**

BRONZE

History: Bronze is an alloy of copper, tin, and traces of other metals. It has been used since Biblical times not only for art objects, but also for utilitarian purposes. After a slump in the Middle

Ages, bronze was revived in the 17th century and continued in popularity until the early 20th century.
  Reference: Anita Jacobsen (ed.), *Jacobsen's Painting and Bronze Price Guide*, published by author.
  Notes: Do not confuse a "bronzed" object with a true bronze. A bronzed object usually is made of white metal and then coated with a reddish–brown material to give it a bronze appearance. A magnet will stick to it.
  A signed bronze commands a higher market price than an unsigned one. There also are "signed" reproductions in the market. It is very important to know the history of the mold and the background of the foundry.

Plaque, Marat, 8½" d, $300.00.

Andirons, pr, 13¾" h, Diego Giacometti style, stamped "Made In France" .. **1,800.00**
Animal
  Deer, pr, 48", standing, patina, Oriental **5,500.00**
  Horse, 11½" h, French, sgd "Mene," 19th C **2,400.00**
  Whippet, pr, 20½" h, 27" l, full bodied, good detail, dark patina **1,050.00**
Blotter, Zodiac pattern, rocker type, sgd "Tiffany Studios" **90.00**
Box, 8" l, Oriental, keg shape, mouse on lid, gold tassel, orig worn red finish, gilt trim **275.00**
Bust
  6¼" h, smiling old man, brown patina, cast from model by Vincenzo Gemito, Italian, late 19th C, inscribed "Gemito Proprieta Artistica" **450.00**
Candelabra, Louis XV style
  14½" h, pr, gilt and patinated, three light **550.00**

27½" h, cupid bearing leafy spray, six
light 500.00
Candlesticks, pr, 12½" h, onion shape
socket, slender stem, flat bobeche,
disc foot, Jarvie, Chicago, IL, c1910 1,200.00
Clock, mantel, 17" h, gilt, Louis XV style 350.00
Ewer, 21¾" h, cast Bacchanalian putti,
grape leaves, and cluster dec, golden
patina, conforming handle with
winged cherub, 19th C 500.00
Figure
4¼" h, 11" l, reclining tiger licking its
paw, black patina, cast from model
by Charles Valton, late 19th or early
20th C, inscribed "C Valton" and "F
Barbedienne, Fondeur" 715.00
7¾" h, crowing rooster, golden brown
patina, cast from model by Auguste
Nicholas Cain, late 19th C, inscribed "A Cain," and imp Susse
Freres foundry seal 800.00
12" h, 19" l, walking lion, dark green
patina, cast from model by Paul
Edouard Delabrierre, late 19th C,
inscribed "E Delabrierre" 1,325.00
14" h, two old women, green patina,
sgd "Plessner Perrugia 1902" . . . 700.00
15" h, parrot perched on branch, reddish brown patina, cast from model
by Ferdinand Pautrot, late 19th C,
inscribed "F Pautrot" 1,980.00
18½" l, tiger, brown patina, Japanese
marks, pr 850.00
22" h, nude young girl balanced on
one foot, circular base with four
frogs 1,900.00
25" h, equestrian group, battling Arab
and British general, dark brown patina, cast from model by Jean Francois Theodore Gechter, inscribed
"T Gechter, 1837" 3,300.00
29½" l, 8½" h, stalking panther, laid–
back ears, snarling jaws, granite
oblong base, inscribed "Andre Bas-
seire, Cire Perdu Leblanc Barbe-
dienne A Paris 18/25" 1,650.00
30½" h, Moroccan Falconer, dark
brown patina, cast from model by
Pierre–Jules Mene, 19th C, in-
scribed "P J Mene" 7,150.00
Inkwell, 7½", sparrow on branch,
painted, c1910 . . . . 350.00
Jardiniere, 8" h, cast Bacchanalian
scenes, Bacchus mask handles,
stamped "Copyright by E Soleau,
Paris, 1893," 19th C 880.00
Lamp
Astral, 29" h, frosted and engraved
globe, electrified 200.00
Floor, 59½" h, harp form, green patina 300.00
Table, 22½" h, braised dragons on
base, brass font, opaque white

shade with gold painted dragons,
electrified, 19th C 350.00
Medal, bust, George Washington, emb,
old patina 35.00
Paperweight, elf on horseshoe 100.00
Pitcher, 12½" h, oak leaves and acorns,
nude figure shape handle, legs form
tree roots, golden brown patina,
c1900 . . . . 1,050.00
Pot, 8" h, birds and flowering branches
in relief, dragon handles, old dark pa-
tina, Oriental 90.00
Sconces, pr, three light, gilt, frosted
glass petal shades 45.00
Spoon Mold, dessert size 325.00
Statue, 26" h, girl with bow, green patina, bow end glued, artist sgd 800.00
Tiebacks, set of 4, rococo, American,
c1860–65 . . . . 70.00
Tray, 9" d, Abalone pattern, sgd "Tiffany
Studios" 190.00
Urn, 25", animal scenes, brown patina 325.00
Vase
5½" h, waisted cylindrical, cast Art
Nouveau nymph in bower 125.00
9" h, bud, swelled cylindrical, handles
cast as stems, arrow root leaves on
sides 160.00
11¾" h, elephants, brown patina, sgd
"A Barye" 750.00

BUFFALO POTTERY
1907

DELDARE WARE
UNDERGLAZE

BUFFALO POTTERY

History: Buffalo Pottery Co., Buffalo, New York,
was chartered in 1901. The first kiln was fired in
October 1903. Larkin Soap Company established
Buffalo Pottery to produce premiums for its extensive mail order business. Wares also were sold to
the public by better department and jewelry stores.
Elbert Hubbard and Frank L. Wright, who designed
the Larkin Administration Building in Buffalo in
1904, were two prominent names associated with
the Larkin Company.

Early production consisted mainly of dinner sets
of semi–vitreous china. Buffalo was the first pottery
in the United States to produce successfully the

Blue Willow pattern, marked "First Old Willow Ware Mfg. in America." Buffalo also made a line of hand decorated, multicolored willow ware, called Gaudy Willow. Other early items include a series of game, fowl, and fish sets, pitchers, jugs, and a line of commemorative, historical, and advertising plates and mugs.

In 1908–09 and 1921–23, Buffalo Pottery produced the line for which it is most famous, Deldare Ware. The earliest of this olive green, semi–vitreous china depicts hand decorated scenes from the English artist Cecil Aldin's *Fallowfield Hunt*. Hunt scenes only were done in 1908–09. English village scenes also were characteristic and found throughout the series. Most are artist signed.

In 1911 Buffalo Pottery produced Emerald Deldare, which used scenes from Goldsmith's *The Three Tours of Dr. Syntax* and an Art Nouveau type border. Completely decorated Art Nouveau pieces also were made.

In 1912 Abino was born. Abino was done on Deldare bodies and showed sailing, windmill, and seascape scenes. The main color was rust. All pieces are artist signed and numbered.

In 1915 the pottery was modernized, giving it the ability to produce vitrified china. Consequently, hotel and institutional ware became their main production, with hand decorated ware de–emphasized. Buffalo china became a leader in producing and designing the most famous railroad, hotel, and restaurant patterns. These wares, especially railroad items, are eagerly sought by collectors.

In the early 1920s fine china was made for home use, e.g., the Bluebird pattern. In 1950 Buffalo made their first Christmas plate. They were given away to customers and employees from 1950–60. Hample Equipment Co. ordered some in 1962. The Christmas plates are very scarce.

The Buffalo China Company made "Buffalo Pottery" and "Buffalo China," the difference being one is semi–vitreous ware and the other vitrified. In 1956 the company was reorganized, and Buffalo China became the corporate name. Today Buffalo China is owned by Oneida Silver Company. The Larkin family no longer is involved.

Reference: Seymour and Violet Altman, *The Book Of Buffalo Pottery,* reprinted by Schiffer Publishing, 1987.

Note: Numbers in parenthesis refer to plates in the Altman's book.

Advisor: Seymour & Violet Altman.

ABINO WARE

Dresser Tray, 10½ x 13¾", rect, herd of sheep on village street, blue highlights, 1913 (238)	1,500.00
Hair Receiver, sailing ship, blue highlights, 1913, sgd "WE Simpson" (237)	600.00
Pitcher, 7", Portland Head Light (256)	950.00
Plaque, 12¼", sailing ship (241)	1,000.00

Jug, emerald green, Mason, 1907, 8¼" h, $675.00.

Tile, 6", nautical scene (259)	700.00
Vase, 6¾", windmill scene (258)	875.00

BLUE AND GAUDY WILLOW

Blue Willow	
Bowl, 14 oz	18.00
Cup and Saucer (26)	30.00
Plate, 9¼" (75)	25.00
Platter, 13 x 16" (24)	60.00
Teapot, round	100.00
Vegetable Bowl	45.00
Gaudy Willow	
Butter Pat	25.00
Pitcher, 8" (C8)	385.00
Plate, 10½" (28)	140.00

COMMERCIAL SERVICES

Bowl, 8½", Ahwahnee, Yosemite Park (299)	75.00
Cake Plate, 10", Roycroft Inn (288)	200.00
Cup and Saucer, George Washington (276)	275.00
Plate	
9", Fairview Golf Club (298)	80.00
10½", Skier (305)	100.00

DELDARE

Bowl, Fallowfield Hunt, 9" d, 1909 (125)	475.00
Calling Card Tray, 7¾", Ye Lion Inn (173)	300.00
Candlestick	
6¾", shield back, Art Nouveau dec (193)	1,000.00
9", bayberry motif, pr (192)	950.00

Creamer, Scenes of Village Life In Ye
Olden Days (138) **200.00**
Cup and Saucer, Ye Olden Days (150)   **235.00**
Dressing Tray, Dancing Ye Minuet, 12"
l, 9" w (144) **450.00**
Fruit Bowl, Ye Village Tavern, 9¼" d,
1908 (152) **400.00**
Mug, Ye Lion Inn, 4¼" d, 1909, G Eaton
(178) **250.00**
Pitcher
Fallowfield Hunt, Hunt Supper, 12½"
h, 1909 (118) **700.00**
Their Manner of Telling Stories, 6" h,
1908 (165) **400.00**
Plaque, Ye Lion Inn, 12" d, 1905 (171)   **500.00**
Plate
Fallowfield Hunt, 10" d (124) **165.00**
Ye Olden Times, 9" d (145) **145.00**
Ye Village Gossip, 10" d (142) **150.00**
Relish, 12 x 6½", The Fallowfield
Hunt—The Dash (135) **475.00**
Sugar, cov, Village Scenes, 1925 (138)   **225.00**
Tea Tray, 10½ x 12", Heirlooms, 1908
(141) **675.00**
Teapot, 3¼", Village Life, 1909 (138)   **300.00**

DELDARE SPECIALS

Humidor, 8", There Was An Old Sailor
(227) **875.00**
Salt and Pepper, Art Nouveau (194) . .   **600.00**

**Emerald Deldare, Dr. Syntax Robbed Of
His Property, plate, 7" d, $525.00.**

EMERALD DELDARE

Cup and Saucer, Dr. Syntax At Liverpool
(181) **400.00**
Fern Dish, 8", butterflies and flowers
(186) **750.00**
Mug, 4¼", Dr. Syntax Again Filled Up
His Glass (200) **450.00**

Plate, 8¼", Art Nouveau dec (214) . . .   **375.00**
Plaque
13½", Penn's Treaty With The Indi-
ans, 1911 (217) **2,000.00**
16½", The Garden Trio (211) **5,000.00**
Toothpick, 2¼", Art Nouveau dec (197)   **385.00**
Vase, 8", kingfisher, dragonflies, iris,
and waterlilies (188) **1,000.00**

HISTORICAL, COMMEMORATIVE, AND ADVERTISING WARE

Mug, 3½", Beechland Farms (112) . . .   **100.00**
Plate
7½"
Gates Circle, Buffalo, NY (97) . . .   **125.00**
George Washington (101) **250.00**
Old Fellows Hall, Cambridge, MA
(96) **85.00**
Trinity Church, New York City (94)   **85.00**
10"
Faneuil Hall, Boston (84) **60.00**
New Bedford, MA, made for Bliss
& Nye, 1908 (85) **160.00**
Niagara Falls (81) **60.00**

MISCELLANEOUS

Cake Plate, 6" (324) **35.00**
Chocolate Pot, 11½" (334) **150.00**
Creamer and Sugar, (332) **55.00**
Cup and Saucer (340) **50.00**
Dinner Sets, 100 pcs
Maple Leaf (314) **400.00**
Vienna (319) **500.00**
Feeding Dish, Mary Had A Little Lamb
(331) **50.00**
Pitcher, Tea Rose **90.00**
Plate, 9"
Erie County SPCA, 1967 . . . .   **25.00**
Rouge Lamelle, garden scene (349)   **115.00**
Rose Bowl, 3¾" (358) **125.00**
Tea Set, child's Baby Bunting (315) . .   **250.00**
Wash Bowl and Pitcher Set, 11 pcs
Chrysanthemum (326) **650.00**
Tea Rose **500.00**

BURMESE GLASS

History: Burmese glass is a translucent art
glass originated by Frederick Shirley and manufactured by the Mt. Washington Glass Co., New
Bedford, Massachusetts, from 1885 to c1891.

Burmese glass shades from a soft lemon to a
salmon pink. Uranium was used to attain the yellow color and gold was added to the batch so that
on reheating one end turned pink. Upon reheating
again, the edges would revert to the yellow coloring. The blending of the colors was so gradual that
it was difficult to determine where one color ended
and the other began.

Although some of the glass has a surface that is glossy, most of it is acid finished. The majority of the items were free blown, but some were blown molded in a ribbed, hobnail, or diamond quilted design.

American–made Burmese is quite thin, fragile, and brittle. The only factory licensed to make Burmese was Thos. Webb & Sons in England. Out of deference to Queen Victoria, they called their wares "Queen's Burmese."

Reproduction Alert: Reproductions abound in almost every form. Since uranium can no longer be used, some of the reproductions are easy to spot. In the 1950s Gunderson produced many pieces in imitation of Burmese.

MW = Mount Washington
Wb = Webb
a.f. = acid finish
s.f. = shiny finish
Advisors: Clarence and Betty Maier.

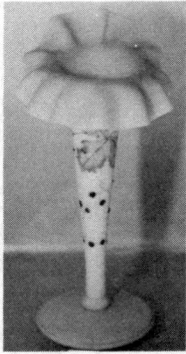

Vase, lily, autumn leaves dec, blue berries, 6¾" h, $500.00.

Bowl
6" d, s.f., fluted edge 250.00
6⅜" l, MW, s.f., Diamond Quilted pattern, folded edge, basket shape, paper label 300.00
Creamer
4" h, s.f., applied handle and pedestal base 200.00
4¼" h, MW, s.f., Diamond Quilted pattern 300.00
Cup and Saucer, s.f., applied handle 325.00
Fairy Lamp
Double skirted, ruffled Burmese base, bowl, candle cup, and shade, clear glass candle cup marked "S Clarke Trade Mark Fairy," orig candle stamped in wax "S Clarke Fairy Pyramid," orig paper wrapper

printed "Icco Night Light, Manufactured by Ibbestson, Stevenage, Herts" 2,450.00
Pyramid, 8½" h, 8" w, twin pyramid fairy lamps, prunus dec, sgd clear glass candle cups, twin Burmese dec bud vases, surmounted by larger dec bud vase, gilted metal stand stamped "Clarke's Patent Fairy Lamp" 2,750.00
Lemonade Glass, 5" h, s.f., applied handle 225.00
Perfume Bottle, 5¼" h, s.f., branches and pine cone dec, hallmarked monogrammed sterling silver cap 725.00
Rose Bowl, 3½" h, s.f., scalloped edge, three applied feet 225.00
Rose Jar, cov, 6⅞" h, a.f., flower and leaf dec, applied gold handles, gold painted cov 275.00
Scent Bottle, 4" h, six delicate glossy yellow vertical rigaree ribbons, tiny yellow stopper and button on base, blush body 750.00
Sugar Shaker, MW, deep salmon to yellow, all–over beaded white and blue flowers, orig top, Timothy Canty style 1,285.00
Syrup, 4⅝" h, s.f., enameled daisy and vine dec, applied handle with gold dec 520.00
Toothpick Holder, 2¼" h, s.f., tricorn shape, quilted design, 3½" d undertray 275.00
Tumbler, 3¾" h, ivy leaves dec, folded rim, satin finish 250.00
Vase
7¼" h, s.f., pinched top, three applied feet, berry pontil 600.00
8" h, MW
Lily, blush throat, narrow band of pastel yellow, refired yellow border 585.00
Trumpet, a.f., gauffered rim 275.00
8" h, 6¼" d, MW, Burns "Auld Lang Syne" verse, grape vine frames black enameled verse, purple grapes, autumn leaves 3,450.00
9" h, s.f., cylindrical, ftd 450.00
10" h, a.f., stick, autumn leaf and enameled blueberries dec, gold accent stripe edge 800.00
10" h, 5" w, MW, a.f., stick type, deep color, oak leaf and blue dot dec, traceries of natural fall color leaves 1,750.00
12½" h, MW, bowling pin shape, trefoil top 485.00

BUSTS

History: The portrait bust has its origins in pagan and Christian tradition. Greek and Roman heroes, and later images of Christian saints, dominate the early examples. Busts of the "ordinary man" first appeared in the Renaissance.

Busts of the nobility, poets, and other notable persons dominated the 18th and 19th centuries, especially those designed for use in a home library. Because of the large number of these library busts, excellent examples can be found at reasonable prices, depending on artist, subject, and material.

Reference: Anita Jacobsen (ed.), *Jacobsen's Painting and Bronze Price Guide,* published by author.

Additional Listings: Ivory, Parian Ware, Soapstone, and Wedgwood.

Jesus Christ, parian ware, 9″ h, $145.00.

Bronze
- Athena, wearing helmet, defined facial features, fishscale yoke with relief Medusa head, 9½″ h, 19th C 200.00
- Benjamin Franklin, green patina, after Jean–Antoine Houdon, French, 19th C, 23¼″ h 700.00
- King Vittorio Emanuele II, brown patina, inscribed and dated "Roman Bronze Works N–Y–1910," 37″ h 1,000.00
- Gentleman, well dressed, rich brown patina, stamped "Roman Bronze Works, NY," 17″ h 250.00
- Maiden, parcel gilt, gilt and dark brown patina, socle base, inscribed "G," 17¾″ h 1,980.00
- Negro, young, patina, mounted on gilt bronze socle, Belgian marble base, 12¼″ h 1,045.00
Bronze and Marble, young girl, classically dressed, mounted on amber veined base, sgd "A Gori," 8¾″ h .. 4,250.00
Creamware, Reverend John Wesley, gray hair, pink tinged flesh, black and white clerical robes, black self socle base, inscribed "The Revd John Wesley M, Died Mar 2 1791, Aged 88, Enoch Wood Sculp, Burslem," Staffordshire, chips to base, c1791, 12¼″ h 385.00
Majolica, gentleman wearing scale pattern armor, blue breastplate with yellow scrolling foliage, woman in white ruff flowered blouse, blue bodice, yellow scrolling foliage, waisted rect marbled socle, inscribed "Hercules I. Est DVX. Ferrarae" and "Eleonora.Ara Gonensis.D.F.," 19th C, Deruta style, 25″ h 1,650.00
Marble
- Apollo Belvedere, raised pedestal base, 19th C, 24½″ h 1,600.00
- Athena, raised pedestal base, 23½″ h, 19th C 1,300.00
- Benjamin Franklin, after Jean–Antoione Houdon, late 19th C, white bust, white marble socle, 18¼″ h 4,650.00
- Caesar Augustus, carved, Continental, c1900, 21¼″ h 1,980.00
- Goddess Tyche, carved, 8″ h 1,045.00
- Mademoiselle Adelaide, young girl wearing chemise, after Jean–Antoine Houdon, French, 19th C, white bust, gray marble socle and separate base, 20⅛″ h 5,000.00
- Maiden, medieval, carved and gilded, white, sgd "E Fiaschi," Italian, 19th C, 24¾″ h 3,000.00
- Old Man, holding wine jug, Jafet Torelli, Italian, late 19th C, sgd "Torelli," 19½″ h 5,000.00
- Young woman, carved, Roman style, wood base, 13″ h 1,430.00
- Venus, white, inscribed "V Vincitrice," 18″ h 350.00
Porcelain, Napoleon, green tunic, medals, black hat, gray cloak, marked "Schiebe–Alsbach," marked "N" on base, 10½″ h 225.00
Terra Cotta
- Antoine–Pierre Bernave, after Jean–Antoione Houdon, French, 19th C, terra cotta socle, 27½″ h 1,875.00
- Maiden, sgd "A Carrier–Belleuse," French, 1824–87, 24″ h 6,000.00
- Noble Woman, polychrome, red velvet cov socle, 7″ h 3,850.00

BUTTER PRINTS

History: Butter prints divide into two categories: butter molds and butter stamps. Butter molds are generally of three piece construction—the design, the screw-in handle, and the case. Molds both mold and stamp the butter at the same time. Butter stamps are of one piece construction, sometimes two pieces if the handle is from a separate piece of wood. Stamps decorate the top of butter after it is molded.

The earliest prints were one piece and hand carved, often thick and deeply carved. Later prints were factory made with the design forced into the wood by a metal die.

Some of the most common designs are sheaves of wheat, leaves, flowers, and pineapples. Animal designs and Germanic tulips are difficult to find. Rare prints include unusual shapes, such as half-rounded and lollipop, and those with designs on both sides.

Reference: Paul E. Kindig, *Butter Prints And Molds*, Schiffer Publishing, Ltd., 1986.

Reproduction Alert: Reproductions of butter prints date as early as the 1940s.

MOLD

Acorn, Double, 4 x 7", cased, turned handle	135.00
Acorn and Strawberries, 5½ x 6", hinged case, brass latch hooks	75.00
Cow, 3¼" d, cased	180.00
Eight Square Design, 5½ x 11", cased	225.00
Heart, 3¾" d, cased	180.00
Leaves and berries, 5¼ x 6", hinged case, brass latch hooks	75.00

Stamp, stylized thistle carving, rope edge, 3¼ x 7" d, $85.00.

STAMP

Cow, 2½ x 4¾", grain and chip carved edge, inserted turned handle	200.00
Eagle, 4½" d, deep carved, cross hatching and scratch carved initials, marked "E D C 1841"	695.00
Eagle	
3⅛" d, stylized, turned handle	200.00
4⅝" d, stylized, foliage and star, turned handle	450.00
Fish, 3" d, scrubbed finish	150.00
Floral Design	
3½ x 7", semicircular, stylized, inserted turned handle	185.00

9¾" l, recessed scalloped edge, lollipop handle, old finish	60.00
Foliage	
3½" d, rayed rim, turned handle	100.00
4 x 6½", stylized, varnished	150.00
Flower and Fruit, 3⅞" d, stylized, turned handle, gray finish, white wash	75.00
Four Birds, flower center, 4¾" d, flat turned handle	225.00
Four designs, 4 x 13", carved sheaf, berries, and ear of corn, cased	175.00
Geometric Design, 4¼" d, natural patina	75.00
Heart with foliage and cross, hatched carved, turned inserted handle	300.00
Leaf, 2½" sq, varnished	30.00
Paisley and floral design, 4¼" d, stylized	65.00
Pineapple, double, 2⅝ x 5"	25.00
Pinwheel, 3¾" d, deeply carved, dark finish	115.00
Pomegranate, 3⅝", stylized, dark varnished finish	30.00
Sheaf, 4½" d, turned handle, varnish	225.00
Star Flower, double, 5⅛ x 5⅜", turned	175.00
Star pattern, 2¾" d, pine, hand hewn and carved, 19th C	150.00
Strawberry, double, 2⅝ x 5"	25.00
Sunflower and leaves, 4¼" d, turned inserted handle, dark finish	430.00
Tree, 3½ x 4½", stylized	25.00
Tulip, 4½" d, stylized, knob handle, varnished	200.00
Tulip and Heart, 3⅞" d, stylized, dark patina	165.00

CALENDAR PLATES

History: Calendar plates were first made in England in the late 1880s. They became popular in the United States after 1900, the peak years being 1909 to 1915. The majority of the advertising plates were made of porcelain or pottery with a calendar, the name of a store or business, and either a scene, portrait, animal, or flowers. Some also were made of glass or tin.

Additional Listings: See *Warman's Americana & Collectibles* for more examples.

1907, Christmas holly edge	80.00
1908, 8" d, holly sprays, Russell Clothing House adv	18.00
1909, 7¼", peaches and blackberries design, months form border, Otto Stelse Merchant adv	30.00
1909, 8½", flower girl, souvenir, Abrams, WI	40.00
1909, 9½", Gibson girl type portrait, calendar months, fruit, and floral border, WI adv	25.00
1909, Iowa Falls, IA	35.00
1910, 7", emb edge, gold scalloped	

1910, compliments of Geo. H. Fargu-hasson, Cooperstown, NY, marked "Semi Porcelain," 6⅞" d, $35.00.

The cards themselves were small, embossed or engraved with the caller's name, and often carried a floral design. Many hand done examples, especially in Spencerian script, can be found. The cards themselves are considered collectible and range in price from a few cents to several dollars.

Note: Don't confuse a calling card case with a match safe.

American coin silver, scenic center cartouche with mountain and lake scene, scale and herringbone design, 2¼ x 3⅜", $125.00.

edge, violets with ribbon banner, J. L. McCue adv	25.00
1910, 9", portrait, ME adv	30.00
1910, 9½", bust of woman, large hat, calendar months, fruit, and floral border	50.00
1910, 10", woman in garden center, calendar months border	30.00
1911, 8", red open touring car, Buffalo Pottery	38.00
1911, 8½", gray fence with three rabbits, two birds on top, J. W. Mowry adv	30.00
1912, 8½", hot air balloons	75.00
1912, 9", glider plane	25.00
1913, 8", calendar months center, rose garland and holly border	20.00
1913, 8¼", sweet peas, pink and lavender ground	45.00
1914, 9¼", Washington's Tomb, Milford, DE, artist sgd "A Smith"	32.00
1916, 8¼", eagle with shield, American flag	32.00
1917, 9", American Old Glory, emb design, scalloped edge, J. J. Shutt, Benld, IL adv	25.00
1919, 8¼", American flag, John J. Rutgers Co, Holland, MI adv	38.50
1920, American flag center	38.00

CALLING CARD CASES AND RECEIVERS

History: Calling cards, usually carried in specially designed cases, played an important social role in the United States from the period of the Civil War until the end of World War I. When making a formal visit, a caller left their card in a receiver (card dish) in the front hall. Strict rules of etiquette developed. For example, the lady in a family was expected to make calls of congratulations, visits to the ill, and condolence.

CALLING CARD CASES

Abalone Shell	
3¾" h, inlaid diamond shaped pearl	75.00
4¼" h, pearl, engraved shield and flowers	85.00
Ivory, 4½" h, intricate floral carving	235.00
Mother of Pearl, 3¾" h, floral relief ivory like insert	125.00
Pearl, 4" h, engraved silver diamond medallion	65.00
Silver	
3½" h, machine dec and engraving, "Carrie," marked "Sterling"	75.00
3⅞ x 2⅜", rounded rect case, repousse and chased as imitation pressed leather, gilt pansies, Japanese lantern dec, loops and suspension chain, marked "Wood & Hughes," c1880	800.00
Tortoise Shell, 3⅝" h, nacre, wire floral inlay	115.00

CALLING CARD RECEIVERS

Glass, 9½″ h, 6″ d top plate, 8″ d base plate, deep rose DQ MOP satin glass plates, tightly ruffled, applied glass edge, flowers and butterflies dec, one side of each turned up to fit into metal frame with leaves and flowers	925.00
Silver, plated	
7⅛″ h, aesthetic taste, oak branch form stand, surmounted by two cast owls on fan shaped dish, chased foliage in Japanese taste, inscription "Should Owl'd Acquaintenance Be Forgot," rect base, bracket feet, marked "Derby Silver Co, Derby, CT," late 19th C	250.00
10½″ h, tray for calling cards, mirror, and fancy ornate stand with name of jeweler engraved on bottom, orig paper label adv on back of mirror, marked "James W Tufts"	600.00

CAMBRIDGE GLASS

History: Cambridge Glass Company, Cambridge, Ohio, was incorporated in 1901. Initially the company made clear tableware, later expanding into colored, etched, and engraved glass. Over 40 different hues were produced in blown and pressed glass.

Five different marks were employed during the production years, but not every piece was marked.

The plant closed in 1954. Some of the molds were later sold to the Imperial Glass Company, Bellaire, Ohio.

References: National Cambridge Collectors, Inc., *The Cambridge Glass Co., Cambridge, Ohio* (reprint of 1930 catalog and supplements through 1934), Collector Books, 1976; National Cambridge Collectors, Inc., *The Cambridge Glass Co., Cambridge, Ohio, 1949 Thru 1953* (catalog reprint), Collector Books, 1976; National Cambridge Collectors, Inc., *Colors In Cambridge Glass,* Collector Books, 1984; Mark Nye, *Cambridge Stemware,* published by author, 1985.

Collectors' Club: National Cambridge Collectors, Inc., P.O. Box 416, Cambridge, OH 43725.

Ashtray	
Caprice, Moonlight blue, ftd	10.00
Statuesque, clear nude lady stem	
Amber bowl	325.00
Clear bowl	200.00
Asparagus Plate, Deco, crystal	20.00

Basket, Inverted Strawberry, 6″ h, 7″ l	45.00
Brandy, Statuesque, clear nude lady stem	
Forest Green bowl	115.00
Gold Krystol bowl	120.00
Moonlight Blue bowl	150.00
Candlesticks, pr	
Dolphin, two light, Crown Tuscan . .	245.00
Ram's Head, crystal	80.00
Rose Point, keyhole, two light	40.00
Candy Dish, cov	
Caprice, Moonlight blue	70.00
Chantilly, etched, sterling silver base, three part	125.00
Crown Tuscan, gold trim, three part	48.00
Wild Flower, gold trim	68.00
Cocktail, amber bowl, Farberware chrome holder, 5⅜″ h	10.00
Cocktail Shaker	
Amber, gray cutting, #3400/158 . . .	85.00
Chantilly, metal top	95.00
Elaine, metal top	85.00
Compote	
Elaine Gadroon	58.00
Seashell	
6″, Crown Tuscan, gold trim	65.00
7″, Forest Green bowl and nude lady stem	600.00
Console Bowl, Deco, Heron flower frog, ebony flip bowl	135.00
Cordial, Stradivari/Regency, Moonlight Blue	45.00
Cordial Decanter Set	
Mt Vernon, six matching cordials . . .	75.00
#3400, upright, four matching cordials, assorted colors, Farberware holders	100.00
Creamer and Sugar, Rose pattern, amber	50.00
Cruet	
Deco, green, 7¾″ h	75.00
Rose Point, etched, sterling silver stopper	85.00
Cup and Saucer	
Chantilly, Martha blank, silver overlay	165.00
Jubilee, yellow	20.00
Flower Holder, figural	
Bashful Charlotte	
Cinnamon, frosted, 11″ h	300.00
Crystal, 6½″ h	75.00
Peach–Blo, frosted, 11″ h	200.00
Draped Lady	
Amber, 13″ h	225.00
Crystal, 8½″ h	70.00
Green, 13″ h	250.00
Mandolin Lady, 9″ h	
Crystal	200.00
Green	275.00
Rose Lady, 8½″ h	
Amber	250.00
Two Kid, 8¾″ h	
Crystal	150.00

Green	200.00
Peach–Blo	225.00

Goblet
Caprice, pale pink, 9 oz	35.00
Mt Vernon	9.00
Tally Ho, amber, 14 oz	15.00

Ice Tub, Candlelight	95.00
Muddler, rooster, crystal	18.00
Mug, Tally Ho, Carmen	38.00
Pitcher, King Edward cutting, sterling foot	100.00

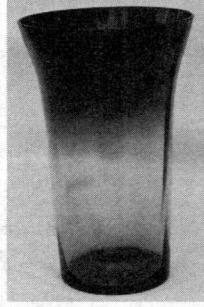

Tumbler, rubena, 5½″ h, $125.00.

Plate
Cleo, 9½″, amber	10.00

Jubilee, yellow
7″ d	10.00
8¾″ d	12.00
11″ d, handles	30.00
Tally Ho, Carmen, 9½″ d, dinner	28.00
Relish, Diane, etched	45.00

Salt and Pepper Shakers, pr, Rose Point, #3400	68.00

Sherbet
Candlelight, etched	20.00
Rose Point, low, ftd	20.00
Wildflower, low	15.00

Tray
Cleo, 11″, amber	13.00
Rose Point, 11″, handled	110.00

Tumbler
Caprice, crystal, ftd	24.00
Georgian	13.00
Gloria, forest green	30.00
Vase, Roxbury cutting, bud, 8″ h	27.00

Wine
Bacchus, nude frosted stem	75.00
Caprice, crystal	25.00
Diane, crystal	20.00
Ebony, nude stem	75.00
Valencia	30.00

CAMBRIDGE

CAMBRIDGE POTTERY

History: The Cambridge Art Pottery was incorporated in Ohio in 1900. Between 1901 and 1909 the firm produced the usual line of jardinieres, tankards, and vases with underglazed slip decorations and glazes similar to other Ohio potteries. Line names included Terrhea, Oakwood, Otoe, and others.

In 1904 the company introduced Guernsey kitchenware. It was so well received that it became the plant's primary product. In 1909 the company's name was changed to Guernsey Earthenware Company.

All wares were marked.

Bowl, matte green glaze, four sgd imp acorn marks, 8½″ d, 5¾″ h, $100.00.

Bank, 6″ l, pig shape, brown mottled glaze	75.00

Bowl
6½ x 3″, Acorn, green glossy glaze, marked	50.00
8½ x 5¾″, matte green glaze, four sgd imp acorn marks	100.00
Ewer, 7½″ h, Oakwood, cream, yellow, and green blended glaze, numbered	65.00
Pitcher, 6″ h, dark brown ground, honeysuckle dec, sgd "DL," marked "Cambridge" and "CAP"	200.00
Tile, 6″, floral, high relief, majolica type	25.00

Vase
7¼" h, bud, brown streaked ground, molded flowers, marked "Oakwood" **100.00**
8" h, two handles, brown ground, flower dec **90.00**
9" h, dog portrait, brown glaze, sgd "AV Lewis" **675.00**

CAMEO GLASS

History: Cameo glass is a form of cased glass. A shell of glass was prepared; then one or more layers of glass of a different color(s) was faced to the first. A design was then cut through the outer layer(s) leaving the inner layer(s) exposed.

This type of art glass originated in Alexandria, Egypt, 100–200 A.D. The oldest and most famous example of cameo glass is the Barberini or Portland vase which was found near Rome in 1582. It contained the ashes of Emperor Alexander Serverus who was assassinated in 235 A.D.

Emile Gallé is probably one of the best known artists of cameo glass. He established a factory at Nancy, France, in 1884. Although much of the glass bears his signature, he was primarily the designer. On many pieces assistants did the actual work, even to signing his name. Glass made after his death in 1904 has a star before the name Gallé. Other makers of French cameo glass include D'Argental, Daum Nancy, LeGras, and Delatte.

English cameo does not have as many layers of glass (colors) and cuttings as do French pieces. The outer layer is usually white, and cuttings are very fine and delicate. Most pieces are not signed. The best known makers are Thomas Webb & Sons and Stevens and Williams.

References: Victor Arwas, *Glass Art Nouveau to Art Deco*, Rizzoli International Publications, Inc., 1977; Ray and Lee Grover, *English Cameo Glass*, Crown Publishers, Inc., 1980; Albert C. Revi, *Nineteenth Century Glass*, reprint, Schiffer Publishing, 1981; John A. Shuman, III, *The Collector's Encyclopedia of American Art Glass*, Collector Books, 1988.

ENGLISH

Stevens and Williams
Perfume Bottle, 4" h, bulbous, red ground, carved white trailing fuchsias, hinged spherical silvered metal cap, c1900 .... **375.00**
Vase
4" h, barrel, bright blue ground, white overlay, cameo ferns, grasses, and wild thistle, sod border, circular trademark on base "Stevens & Williams Art Glass" **1,200.00**
7½" h, broad ovoid, lustrous red

cased to clear ground, white overlay, hand carved leafy wild flowers and grasses, elaborate borders, circular trademark on base "Stevens & Williams Art Glass Stourbridge" **3,300.00**
12" h, vasiform, cinnamon orange–red ground, white overlay, cameo blackberry blossoms, buds, fruits, and thorny branches above and below medial floral border, butterfly and insect in flight, marked "Stevens & Williams Stourbridge Art Glass" .. **4,300.00**
Unknown Maker
Biscuit Jar, 5¾ x 5⅜", frosted deep red ground, opaque white carved flowers, SP top **2,100.00**
Bowl, 8¼ x 4", frosted blue ground, opaque white carved flowers, leaves, and branches **2,250.00**
Sweetmeat Jar, 4¾" d, 3" h, frosted deep cranberry ground, opaque white carved apple blossoms and leaves, SP top, rim, and handle .. **1,000.00**
Vase
5" h, baluster shape, robin's egg blue cased in opal glass, white cameo enamel leaves and buds **200.00**
5¾" h, 2½" d, cylinder, frosted red ground, opaque white carved flowers and leaves, white band at top and base **900.00**
7½" h, 5¼" d, baluster shape, white neck band, carved foliated white clematis branch, stippled blue ground **3,750.00**
8¼" h, 5" l, 2¾" w, bud, orig gilt mount, crimson inverted teardrop shaped body, white leafed poppy, fully opened blossom and bud, wheat stalk, graceful oak stalk sweeps across back, two white rings just above holder, holder held between paws of rampant lion, burnished gold polish on lion, shield, and shaped platform base, base sgd "England," "56," "1704," "EP," and unidentified maker's stamp **1,835.00**
11⅞" h, 6" d, attributed to Woodall, baluster shape, everted lip, dark brown ground, very deeply carved, three white dancing girls with outstretched arms, foliage carved around neck and upper section **4,750.00**
Webb
Cologne Bottle, 7½" h, bulbous, pastel yellow body, white overlay hand carved florabunda roses, buds, leaves, thorny branches, and but-

terfly, leaf spike border, matching glass stopper with rose bud and leaf dec, Webb four sided medallion on base **4,600.00**

Creamer and Sugar, 3½" h creamer, 1¾" h x 4" d open sugar, Fish Scale pattern, white lining revealed through pink ext., gold enamel butterfly and ivy dec, attributed to Thomas Webb, each pc sgd "G. L. F.," pr **485.00**

Perfume Bottle, 3¼" h, ball shape, cornflower blue ground, white carved overlay apple blossoms and leafy branches, threaded rim, hallmarked silver monogrammed cap, circular base mark "Thomas Webb & Sons Cameo" **1,000.00**

Rose Bowl, lime green ground, heavy cameo carved raspberries and leaves, Webb butterfly on reverse **1,435.00**

Vase, 6¼" h, oval body, pastel yellow ground, white carved overlay lily blossoms, spiked leaves, and two butterflies, four sided Webb medallion **2,200.00**

Daum Nancy, tumbler, frosted ground, white floral dec, gold trim, 4¾" h, $475.00.

FRENCH

Daum Nancy
Bowl, 5½" h, canary yellow and orange mottled ground, lime and umber overlay, etched ships at sea, etched "Daum Nancy" **4,400.00**
Cruet, 7¼" h, green ground, stylized foliate branch with white enamel berries, gold enamel accents, applied brushed gold highlights, sterling silver edged matching flat

sided stopper, orig silver holder with cut out edge, gold enamel sgd "Daum Nancy," Cross of Lorraine mark **1,750.00**
Ewer, 12" h, peach and white frosted ground, etched and enameled green and yellow blossoms, applied frosted white handle with enameled swirled green dec, sgd in cameo **9,350.00**
Vase
4" h, mottled mustard, gray invested with brown base, yellow overlay and cut, green and ironred, fruiting branches and leafage, sgd "Daum/Nancy" and "croix de Lorraine" **1,210.00**
7⅜" h, cylindrical, everted rim, cushion foot, double overlay, mottled orange overlaid in orange and brown, carved riverside scene with mountains in distance, sgd in cameo **1,650.00**
D'Argental
Box, cov, 6⅞" d, compressed spherical form, central knop on lid, yellow ground, mauve overlay, carved roses, lid sgd in cameo **1,100.00**
Perfume Bottle, 5¼" h, lime green ground, light and dark burgundy overlay, carved flowers, buds, and leaves, carved signature, gold washed metal top sgd "LeParisien" **1,150.00**
D'Aurys, Haag, vase, 7" h, oviform, white ground, pink and brown overlay, carved scene, mother stork feeding young in nest, rooftops and steeples, sgd in cameo **600.00**
DeGue
Lamp
Boudoir, Bedouin priests, one riding camel with pyramids and palm trees, desert ground **7,200.00**
Table, 16½" h, 10⅜" d domed shade, pale yellow ground, red shading to dark purple overlay, carved flowering vines, cylindrical standard with knopped circular base, shade and base sgd in cameo, base also engraved "Made In France" **4,400.00**
Vase
7⅞" h, low, tapered cylinder, yellow ground, orange and brown overlay, base with triangular border, curling vines and blossoms descending from rim, engraved "Degue" **1,870.00**
11⅜" h, baluster, everted rim, ftd, clear ground, purple overlay, deeply carved zigzag motif, engraved "Degue" **550.00**

14½″ h, ovoid, matte black ground, brick red overlay, carved horizontal bands and triangular motif, sgd in cameo **2,200.00**

16¾″ h, baluster, cushion foot, bright yellow ground, brown shaded to bright orange overlay, carved stylized leaves and blossoms, engraved "Degue" **3,200.00**

18¾″ h, gourd form, cushion foot, pale blue ground, lapis blue and black overlay, carved trees, sgd in cameo, foot sgd "Made In France" **2,420.00**

Devez, pieces sgd "de Vez" in cameo, c1920

Tumbler, 5″ h, barrel shape, amber frosted ground, red star flowers, green leaves **775.00**

Vase

4¾″ h, baluster, opaline cased in pink and green, carved house on tree lined lake, sgd in cameo .. **500.00**

5″ h, ovoid, tapered neck, white translucent body, cased shaded lavender, two growing violet sprays, sgd "de Vez" in cameo **200.00**

Galle, vase, Pilgrim flask shape, peach shading to light olive green frosted ground, green overlay, cut acorns and leaves, 5¾″ h, $1,250.00.

Galle, pieces sgd "Galle" in cameo

Box, cov, 4⅜″ d, compressed spherical shape, flat lid, amber ground, purple overlay, carved stalk of starflowers, lid and base sgd, lid cracked **125.00**

Perfume Bottle, 4½″ h, dark autumn green ferns, mottled green ground, frosted ribbed stopper **2,200.00**

Vase

2½″ h, cabinet, frosted glass, orange overlay, carved nasturtiums **350.00**

2¾″ h, cabinet, squatty baluster, frosted glass, purple overlay, carved leafy vines and berries, pr **600.00**

3″ h, ovoid, cabinet, purple waisted foot, translucent amber and gray splashed glass, deep purple overlay, berry branches and leafage dec **470.00**

3¼″ h, cabinet, candlestick shape, frosted body, purple overlay, carved wisteria **385.00**

3½″ h, cabinet, baluster, ftd, dusty rose, purple overlay, carved violets **715.00**

3¾″ h, cabinet, tapered cylinder, pale gray, purple overlay, carved morning glories **350.00**

4½″ h, cabinet, baluster, pink ground cased in clear, lavender and green overlay, carved pendant wisteria branches **1,150.00**

5″ h, compressed baluster, pale gray ground, purple overlay, deeply carved Japanese iris, fire polished surface, engraved "Cristallerie de Galle, modele et decor deposes" **2,450.00**

5¼″ h, tapered cylinder, everted rim, amber ground, lavender overlay, carved buttercup **600.00**

5¾″ h, bulbous, trumpet neck, pale pink ground, green and brown overlay, carved oak branches and acorns **800.00**

6½″ h, bowl shape, pink tinted ground, purple and green overlay, carved hydrangea **1,150.00**

8¼″ h, 5½″ w, baluster, yellow ground, dark lotus flower, foliage, and band carved dec **5,800.00**

8½″ h, slender trumpet neck, spreading circular base, pale amber ground, cherry red overlay, carved carnations **1,320.00**

9⅛″ h, candlestick shape, pale blue ground, amber and green overlay, carved honeysuckle vines **1,450.00**

13″ h, swelled cylinder, tapering to circular foot, cantaloupe ground, brown overlay, carved snapdragon stalks **1,200.00**

13½″ h, candlestick shape, pink tinted ground, white and green overlay, carved pendant maple leaves and pods **1,650.00**

14″ h, 10⅜″ d, for 1889 Exposition Universelle Internationale in Paris, ftd cylinder, martele ground, dark brown overlay, carved entrelac design, rim carved "En Deuil Jusqua Ce Que," pontil sgd "Emile Galle

Nancy 1889, Exposition, Paris"
and "E. G." within vase, base
cracked **9,000.00**
16¼" h, ovoid, everted rim, pale
yellow, cherry red and burgundy
overlay, carved hydrangea **17,600.00**
Lamartine, vase, 9" h, 2" d, 4" w, birch
trees by roadside dec **1,500.00**
Legras
Vase
7⅛" h, cylinder, U form rim, spreading circular base, pale pink
ground, white, lime, and dark
green overlay, carved trees along
riverbank, sgd in cameo **700.00**
10¼" h, modified trumpet shape,
deep red leaves and cherries,
semi–martele frosted ground,
sgd in cameo **500.00**
Muller Freres
Bowl, 6" d, bulbous, sloped sides,
shaped oval mouth, mottled translucent white glass, cased shades of
brown, eight tiny finches perched on
branches, etched "Muller Fres/
Luneville" **330.00**
Lamp, table, 14¾" h, domed cameo
shade, mottled orange ground,
brown overlay, carved leaves and
berries on tendril vines, sgd in
cameo, openwork wrought iron four
arm base, curling vine motif **3,850.00**
Vase
8¼" h, ovoid, everted rim, salmon
ground, pink and burgundy overlay, carved roses and thorny
stems, sgd in cameo **2,200.00**
14¼" h, slender baluster, rim folded
back at sides to form handles,
orange ground, brown overlay,
carved trees and mountains
scene, sgd in cameo "Muller
Fres., Luneville" **1,980.00**
Richard
Atomizer, 7" h, baluster shape,
cameo, raspberry leaves, deep
pink ground, wafer foot, worn hard-
ware **750.00**
Lamp, table, 14" h, 8¼" d domed
shade, mottled orange ground,
dark purple overlay, carved detailed
mountain and river scene, conforming baluster body on circular foot,
shade and base sgd in cameo . . . **4,750.00**

CAMERAS

History: The collecting of cameras, except in
isolated instances, started about 1970. Although
photography generally is considered to have had

its beginning in 1839, it is very unusual to find a
camera made before 1880. These cameras and
others made before 1925 are considered to be
antique cameras. Most cameras made after 1925
that are no longer in production are considered to
be classic cameras. American, German, and Japanese cameras are found most often.

Value of cameras is affected by both exterior
and mechanical conditions. Particular attention
must be given to the condition of the bellows if
cameras have them.

References: Jim and Joan McKeown, *Price
Guide To Antique And Classic Still Cameras,
1989–90, Seventh Edition,* published by authors,
1990; *Jason Schneider On Camera Collecting,
Book Three,* Wallace-Homestead, 1985; Myron
Wolf, *Blue Book Illustrated Price Guide to Collec-
tible & Useable Cameras, Second Master Edition,*
Photographic Memorabilia, 1985.

Periodical: Camera Shopper, One Magnolia
Hill, West Hartford, CT 06117.

Collectors' Clubs: National Stereoscopic As-
sociation, P.O. Box 14801, Columbus, OH 43214;
Photographic Historical Society, P.O. Box 9563,
Rochester, NY 14604.

Museum: George Eastman Museum, Rochester, NY; Smithsonian Institution, Washington, DC.

Additional Listings: See *Warman's Americana
& Collectibles* for more examples.

**Eastman Kodak, Brownie #2A, orig
box, 3¼ x 5 x 6", $35.00.**

Adlake Plate, 3 x 4", sliding knob, side
door, c1898 . . . . **60.00**
Akeley, lightweight aluminum, hand
crank, designed for wildlife photog-
raphy, tripod, c1917 . . . . **600.00**
American Optical Co, Henry Clay Cam-
era, 5 x 7 cut film, 1896 . . . . **280.00**
Ansco No 4, Model D, wood case . . . **65.00**

Baby Hawkeye, roll film box, c1897 .. **160.00**

Bell's Straight Working Panorama camera, BG 100, horizontal format, folding bellows, 5 panoramic exposure **250.00**

Biflex, 35mm, 2cm f2.5 Tritar lens, 200 exposure, Mfg in Switzerland, Made for British intelligence, c1945 ..... **425.00**

Blair, No 3 Weno Hawkeye, box type, c1900 **25.00**

Ciro 35T, 35mm, Wollensak Anastigmat 50mm f2.8 coated lens, Rapax shutter, c1950 .... **30.00**

Conley Camera Co, Rochester, NY
   Junior, folding plate, 1900–10 .. **35.00**
   Kewpie, side load, early 1900 ..... **20.00**

Devin One-Shot Color Camera, 6.5 x 9 cm sheet film, Goerz Dogmar 5½" f4.5 lens, Compur dialset shutter, c1940 .... **300.00**

Eastman Kodak
   Autographic Folding Cartridge 2A, Model B, 1920s **75.00**
   Petite, Model B, vest pocket, Meniscus lens, rotary shutter, 127 roll film, blue, brown, gray, green, or red, c1929–33 .... **60.00**
   No 2, factory loaded, sixty exposures, 1890 .... **225.00**
   Six-20 Camera, Kodak Anastigmat 10mm f4.5 coated lens, No 1 Diodak shutter, 620 roll film, c1932–37 **15.00**
   3B Quick Focus, Meniscus Achromatic lens, rotary shutter, 125 roll film, c1906–11 .... **125.00**

Fallowfield Hand Camera, Moroccan crocodile skin valise, c1892 ...... **425.00**

Franke
   Rollei 16S, subminiature, Tessar 25mm f2.8 lens, first Rollei with one lens, black **75.00**
   Rolleidoscop Reflex Stereo Camera, Zeiss Tessar 75mm f4.5 lens, c1926 .... **650.00**
   Rolleiflex New Standard 1939, Zeiss Tessar 75mm lens, Synchro-Compur shutter, c1939–41 .... **50.00**

Goerz
   Minicord, 16mm, Helgro 25mm f2.0 lens, 16mm cassettes film, eye level viewing through roof prism, c1951 .... **150.00**
   Stereo Ango, Goerz Dagor 120mm f6.8 lens, film pack adapter, rising and sliding lens panel, c1906 ... **225.00**

Guthe & Thorsche, Germany, Pilot 6, box type, 120 film **45.00**

Jumbo Century Studio Camera, No 4A, wood, lens, hand held rubber squeeze bulb, brass hardware, orig label, made by Folmer Graphflex Corp, Rochester, NY, 12½ x 25", 16½" h **100.00**

Mycro, miniature, brown, leather case, stamped "Made in Occupied Japan" **65.00**

Polaroid Land Camera, Model 95B, unused **50.00**

J Robinson & Sons, England, Luzo Detective Camera, Aplanat 2½" f11 lens, variable speed sector shutter, used Eastman roll type film, first British made box camera, c1890 .... **1,500.00**

Ross Twin Lens Reflex, Ross Homocentric 7" f6.3 lens, Bausch & Lomb pneumatic shutter, rotating back, c1891 .... **575.00**

Samei Sangyo, Japan, Samoca 35III, 35mm, c1957 .... **15.00**

Schmitz & Thienemann, Dresden, Germany, Uniflex, Unar 75mm f4.5 lens, self cocking Pronto shutter coupled to mirror, c1933 .... **120.00**

Scovill 4 x 5" Vertical View Camera, R Morrison, NY, lens, rotating stops, holder and case, c1881 .... **225.00**

A G Taylor Tailboard Camera, brass Clement Gilmer lens, mahogany finish, brass fittings, leather bellows, c1890 .... **250.00**

Universal Camera Corp (New York)
   Iris, miniature, Ilex Vitar 50mm f7.9 lens, T B I shutter **10.00**
   Mercury I, 35 mm half frame, Tricor 35mm f3.5 lens, rotary sector, c1947 .... **30.00**

Voigtlander A G, Braunschweig, Germany, Bergheil, Heliar 12cm f4.5 lens, Compur shutter, folding plate, c1930 **50.00**

Watson View Camera, Bush Rapid Symmetrical lens, Thornton Pickard behind lens shutter, mahogany finish, brass fittings, reversible and tilting back, c1890 .... **375.00**

Wirgin, Germany, Edinex, 127 film, compact viewfinders **30.00**

Zeiss
   Adoro, folder, 6 x 9 cm plates, 1920s **25.00**
   Contraflex, Walz filter kit, wide angle and telephoto lens, instruction book and case **250.00**

CAMPHOR GLASS

History: Camphor glass derives its name from its color. Most pieces have a cloudy white appearance, similar to gum camphor; the remainder has a pale colored tint. Camphor glass is made by treating the glass with hydrofluoric acid vapors.

Biscuit Jar, cov, brass fittings **65.00**
Bookends, pr, horse heads **80.00**
Bowl, 7½" d, flared, scalloped rim, ftd **75.00**
Goblet, 7" h, butterscotch bowl, gold dec, blue ring, red jewels **90.00**

Creamer, 2½″ h, Button Arches pattern, "Souvenir of Youngstown, Ohio," gold lettering, $35.00.

Hair Receiver, gold scroll dec	50.00
Jar, cov, blue	35.00
Mustard, cov, Wild Rose and Bowknot	40.00
Plate, 6½″ d, hp, Easter greeting	30.00
Powder jar, cov, sq, blue, bird finial, c1920	60.00
Ring Tree, 4¾″ h, floral dec	20.00
Rose Bowl, hp, blue forget–me–not dec, gold trim	45.00
Salt and Pepper Shakers, pr, 3½″ h, hand holding torch, orig tops, c1876	45.00
Shoe, 5″ l, lady's, Libbey Glass, World's Fair, 1893	35.00
Vase, 8″ h, nude molded relief	25.00

CANDLESTICKS

History: The domestic use of candlesticks is traced to the 14th century. The earliest was a picket type, named for the sharp point used to hold the candle. The socket type was established by the mid-1660s.

From 1700 to the present, candlestick design mirrored furniture design. By the late 17th century, a baluster stem was introduced, replacing the earlier Doric or clustered column stem. After 1730 candlesticks reflected rococo ornateness. Neoclassic styles followed in the 1760s. Each new era produced a new grouping of candlesticks.

However, some styles became universal and remained in production for centuries. For this reason, it is important to examine the manufacturing techniques of the piece when attempting to date a candlestick.

Reference: Margaret and Douglas Archer, *The Collector's Encyclopedia Of Glass Candlesticks,* Collector Books, 1983; Tom Felt and Bob O'Grady, *Heisey Candlesticks, Candelabra, and Lamps,* Heisey Collectors of America, 1984; Wolf Uecker, *Art Nouveau and Art Deco Lamps and Candlesticks,* Abbeville Press, 1986.

Art Deco, nude lady, 9″ h, Krome Kraft Farber Brothers, pr	100.00
Brass	
4¾″ h, plain nozzle and stem, triangular base, Spanish, mid 17th C, pr	1,100.00
5″ h, plain nozzle and stem, raised trumpet base, English, late 17th C	700.00
5½″ h, plain nozzle with aperture, drip pan, bell shaped base, southern European, c1600	400.00
5⅝″ h, shaped nozzle, knopped stem, octagonal stepped base, seamed, traces of silvering, French, mid 18th C, pr	950.00
6¼″ h, spiral stem, saucer base, Continental, 18th C	150.00
6½″ h, plain nozzle with aperture, baluster stem, octagonal base, Spanish, late 17th C	350.00
7″ h, baluster turned stem, step molded shaped base, 18th C, pr	1,000.00
7½″ h	
Cylindrical nozzle with everted rim, trumpet turned rim, petal form base, English, imp "Geo. Grove," c1748, pr	1,980.00
Plain shaped nozzle with aperture, central circular drip pan, knopped stem, circular base, Heemserk, c1600	750.00
8¼″ h, baluster turned stem, petal base, 18th C	350.00
8½″ h, baluster turned stem, swirl base, stamped "Geo Grove," England, 18th C, pr	2,750.00
10½″ h, bold design, mid drip pan, Dutch	700.00
12½″ h, bulbous bobeche, narrow ring turning on stem flaring towards base, raised circular foot, Arts and Crafts, 20th C, pr	650.00
Brass and Copper, 8¾″ h, pr, flaring copper sockets, brass standards, copper disk bases, cut–out details, Roycroft logo, early 20th C	150.00
Brass and Silver, banded nozzle, plain stem, circular drip pan, bell shaped base, damascening with silver, overall arabesques, coat of arms, and lions dec, Venetian, late 15th C	7,500.00
Bronze	
10¼″ h, three bladed discs on stem, circular dished drip pan, bell shaped base, overall arabesque dec, Venetian, 15th C, pr	4,250.00
11″ h, Empire style, gilded, paw feet, c1880, pr	475.00
17¾″ h, urn shape candle socket, shallow circular drip pan, long spiral stem, domed circular base, three ball feet, Arts and Crafts, early 20th C, pr	125.00

Glass, Doric column, clambroth petal socket, medium blue sand finish base, attributed to Sandwich Glass, $350.00.

Glass
Flint, 9⅝" h, clear, pewter insert, Pittsburgh 160.00
Opalescent, 7" h, pressed 100.00
Heisey, 7½" h, paneled, polished, pr 110.00
Sandwich
  6¾" h, canary yellow, loop pattern,
    pr 200.00
  10⅞" h, opaque, blue and white,
    acanthus leaf pattern, pr 400.00
  Translucent, 9" h, powdery blue, hexagonal, opaque white mottling, pr 800.00
Iron
  7¼" h, hog scraper, pushup, tin plate 100.00
Pewter
  8" h, beaded detail, pushups, one
    stem resoldered, pr 100.00
  9" h, attributed to Henry Hooper, pr 175.00
  10¾" h, removable bobeche, pr . . . 250.00
Porcelain, Meissen, 8⅞" h, blue and
  white 70.00
Silver
  Plated, Sheffield, English, 19th C, pr
    8½" h 125.00
    9" h 100.00
  Sterling
    4¾" h, Persian taste, scalloped circular nozzle, urn shaped candle
      cup, spreading cylindrical support, dished circular base with
      pierced and scalloped border,
      niello inlaid mounts on handle,
      candle cup, and base, marked
      "Tiffany & Co.," 1889, 8 oz, 10
      dwt 6,400.00
    6¾" h, Japanese taste, serpentine
      removable nozzle, shaped cylindrical stem, sq dished base with
      shaped brim, four scroll feet, applied beetle on base, spot ham-

mered surface, engraved monogram, marked "Tiffany & Co,"
c1885, pr 6,600.00

CANDY CONTAINERS

History: In 1876 Croft, Wilbur and Co. filled a small glass Liberty Bell with candy and sold it at the Centennial Exposition in Philadelphia. From that date until the 1960s glass candy containers remained popular and served to outline American and American transportation history.

Jeannette, Pennsylvania, a center for the packaging of candy in containers, was home for J. C. Crosetti, J. H. Millstein, T. H. Stough, and Victory Glass. Other early manufacturers included: George Borgfeldt, New York, New York; Cambridge Glass, Cambridge, Ohio; Eagle Glass, Wheeling, West Virginia; L. E. Smith, Mt. Pleasant, Pennsylvania; and West Brothers, Grapeville, Pennsylvania.

Candy containers with original paint, candy, and closures command a high premium, but be aware of reproduced parts and repainting. The closure is a critical part of each container; its loss detracts significantly from the value.

Small figural perfumes and other miniatures often are sold as candy containers.

References: George Eikelberner and Serge Agadjanian, *The Compleat American Glass Candy Containers Handbook,* revised and published by Adele L. Bowden, 1986; Jennie Long, *An Album Of Candy Containers,* published by author, Volume I: 1978, Volume II: 1983.

Collectors' Club: Candy Container Collectors Of America, P.O. Box 1088, Washington, PA 15301.

Museums: Cambridge Glass Museum, Cambridge, OH; L. E. Smith Glass, Mt. Pleasant, PA.

Additional Listings: See *Warman's Americana & Collectibles* for more examples.

Airplane, glass
  P-38, cardboard closure, Play Toy Co 140.00
  Spirit of St Louis, tin wings and
    wheels, West Bros 375.00
Automobile
  Sedan, glass, emb, tin wheels, tin closure, V G Co 70.00
  Station Wagon, glass, Woodie style,
    cardboard closure, J H Millstein . . 30.00
Baby, glass, nude 50.00
Bank, tin, litho, glass insert 30.00
Basket, milk glass, hanging type, emb
  grapes and vines 40.00
Boat
  Glass, battleship, miniature, four
    guns, cardboard closure 20.00
  Tin, submarine, glass hull 275.00
Bug, 8½", composition, sitting up, smil-

ing, black top hat and glasses, red
umbrella, German 125.00
Bunny, 6", composition, sailor shirt,
holding yellow basket, German,
marked "US Zone" 90.00
Bus, glass, Victory Lines Special, gray
paint, cardboard closure 50.00
Cannon, 3¾" l, pressed glass, red tin
carriage, two pierced wheels, tin
screw on cap 400.00
Cash Register, 2⅝" h, glass 300.00
Cat, black, green glass eyes, arched
back 100.00
Chicken on egg, German 35.00
China Man, 4", papier mache, sitting on
log, German 250.00
Church, tin, litho, glass insert 25.00
Dog
  Bulldog, 3¾" h, clear pressed glass,
  sitting, open base, inside flanges 30.00
  Dalmatian, 11", papier mache, pup 30.00
  Scotty, clear pressed glass, head
  down, open base, inside flanges 20.00
Donkey, 5", papier mache, glass eyes,
blanket, German 220.00
Duck
  Composition, 7", lady, pink bonnet,
  purple int., German 90.00
  Papier Mache, 10", spring neck, black
  top hat, glittered red coat, green
  floral lapels, green bowtie, carrying
  stick, German 55.00
Egg, with emerging rabbit, pint 40.00
Fire Engine, 5" l, glass, Fire Dept in
circle on top, J C Crosetti 25.00
Football, tin 15.00
Foxy Grandpa, riding rabbit 125.00
Frog, 4¼" h, milk glass, sitting upright,
green and brown traces, protruding
glass eyes, tin screw on cap 300.00
Globe, clear glass, raised degree lines
and continents, metal screw-on cap,
spins in metal frame stand, marked
"Pat appl'd For" 375.00
Golf Club, 4⅝" l, clear glass, un-
threaded neck, marked "D R G M" 40.00
Gun, glass, JR 22 pistol, Whitling Jim,
T H Stough 20.00
Hat, Uncle Sam, milk glass, painted red,
white, and blue, slotted closure 50.00
Hen, 2", papier mache, gray, chick on
each side, bottom swivel closure . . . 90.00
Irish Boy, 4" h, composition, standing,
green shamrock on gray fez, green
jacket, red vest, yellow pants, purple
socks, small oval wood box, German 100.00
Iron, glass, electric type, closure and
paper cord, Play Toy Co 50.00
Jack O'Lantern, 2½" h, clear pressed
glass, ribbed, red intaglio nose and
mouth, raised white teeth, black
ringed protruding pop eyeballs, all-

over pumpkin yellow paint, wire bail,
slotted metal screw on cap 300.00
Kangaroo, 5¼" h, clear pressed glass,
sitting holding cricket bat, black paint
traces, metal screw on cap 2,000.00
Kettle, glass, paper handle, slotted
cardboard closure, T H Stough 25.00

**Lantern, glass, clear, J. C. Crosetti Co.,
$20.00.**

Lantern, glass, ribbed base, green tin
reflector, red cap, T H Stough 15.00
Liberty Bell, glass, amber, hanger 50.00
Mailbox, 3¼" h, clear pressed glass,
"Souvenir—Dubua IA" in gilt, alumi-
num painted, tin slide closure 125.00
Milk Bottle, glass, emb "Dolly's Milk," V
G Co 40.00
Mug, 3½" h, glass, large "M" on base,
T H Stough 40.00
Owl, paint traces, tin cap closure, un-
makred, 1920s 70.00
Pipe, 4¼" h, ornate bowl, swirl stem
base 50.00
Powder Horn, 4⅞", blown two part mold,
clear, rough lip, rubber like composi-
tion cork, metal screw on cap, marked
"Pat appd for" 40.00
Rabbit, figural, brown, painted eyes . . . 60.00
Radio, glass, emb, tune-in buttons, tin
closure, V G Co 90.00
Rocking Horse and Clown, glass, blue 225.00
Rolling Pin, 7" l, glass, metal cap ends,
turned wood handles, marked "VG
Co Jnet Pa ¾ oz" 175.00
Santa, glass, standing, cap closure, V
G Co 70.00
School House, tin, litho, glass insert . . 20.00
Soldier, 5⅛" h, clear pressed glass,
scarlet tunic, gray pants, silver sword
and scabbard, gilted belt and sword
sash, white painted helmet, un-

painted plinth type base, tin slide clo-
sure, marked "1¼ AV. OZ" **800.00**
Suitcase, 2½" h, glass, emb straps and
patent, tin closure, wire handle **35.00**
Table, 2⅛" h, clear pressed glass, gilt
table edge and drawer outline, knob
feet, tin snap closure **650.00**
Telephone, glass, French desk type,
Crosetti **15.00**
Turkey, marked "Germany" **30.00**
Wheelbarrow, glass, red tin wheels, tin
closure, V G Co **50.00**
Windmill, 4⅞" h, Dutch type, six sided
tower, tin arms, cardboard closure
marked "Play-Toy Co," 1940s **60.00**

CANES

History: Canes and walking sticks were important accessories in a gentleman's wardrobe in the
18th and 19th centuries. They often served both
a decorative and utilitarian function. Collectors frequently view carved canes in wood and ivory as
folk art and pay higher prices for them. Glass
canes and walking sticks were glass makers'
whimsies, ornamental rather than practical.
References: Joyce E. Blake, *Glasshouse
Whimsies,* published by author, 1984; Catherine
Dike, *Cane Curiosa,* published by author, 1983;
Catherine Dike, *La Canne: Objet d'Art,* published
by author, 1987.

CANES

Ebony, 35", chip carved shaft, elephant
head handle, ivory tusks and eyes,
horn tip, India **500.00**
Glass, 34", clear, red and blue swirls,
gilded int. **250.00**
Ivory
34¾" l, carved fist clenching coiled
snake with inset red glass eyes,
acanthus leaf and beaded ring
base, tapered whalebone shaft,
American, late 19th C **1,650.00**
Scrimshaw
33" l, rope and diamond point carved
whalebone shaft, "L" shape whale
ivory handle, wood separators,
19th C **550.00**
33¾" l, wood shaft, turned whale ivory
knob, 19th C **150.00**
34" l, coconut wood shaft, carved
whale ivory clenched hand, 19th C **400.00**
35⅝" l, whalebone shaft, "L" shape
handle with alternating hardwood
and whale ivory, 19th C **350.00**
36⅝" l, coconut wood shaft, whale
ivory tooth form handle, 19th C . . **250.00**
Wood
32½" l, carved speckled fish handle,

relief carved snake and incised owl
head shaft, American, late 19th C **1,430.00**
34¼" l, two blue birds with relief
carved and painted wing detail handle, red bead inset eyes, tapered
blue painted root shaft, American,
late 19th C **770.00**
35" l, horn handle, tapered shaft with
relief carved trotter Nancy Hanks
with famous race horses, sgd "T W
Moore," American, late 19th C . . . **1,540.00**
35¾" l, carved animal bone handle
with lion and two dogs, 19th C . . . **125.00**
39½" l, black and white painted pig
eating painted ear of corn handle,
standing on cage enclosing a puzzle ball, black and yellow snake
with bearded man on side, cloved
hoof end, sgd "Herbert Borders,"
American, late 19th C **6,600.00**
48" l, horned man's head, relief
carved features, glass button eyes,
twisted root shaft, American, late
19th C **2,090.00**

**Walking Stick, blue enameled handle,
chased silver overlay, rose quartz set
in bezel on top, hallmarked "900" and
hand, French, $575.00.**

WALKING STICKS

Baleen, 39½" h, woven baleen turk's
head knob, mother-of-pearl on top,
19th C **250.00**
Folk Art, 37½", tattoo type, pony, ga-
zelle, fish, crane, lizard, and snake,
knob handle **35.00**
Scrimshaw
31½" l, seven whale ivory sections
shaft, eight sided balloon shape
knob, 19th C **375.00**

34¼" l, paneled whalebone shaft,
gold knob with gold connector, 19th
C **125.00**
35¾" h, paneled whalebone shaft,
turned tapered ivory knob, 19th C **200.00**
Wood, 36", lady's, walnut, twisted shaft,
two grooved sides **30.00**

CANTON CHINA

History: Canton china is a type of oriental porcelain made in the Canton region of China from the late 18th century and early 19th century to the present and produced largely for export. Canton china is hand decorated in light to dark blue underglaze on white. Design motifs include houses, mountains, trees, boats, and a bridge. A design similar to "willow china" is the most common.

Borders on early Canton feature a rain and cloud motif (a thick band of diagonal lines with a scalloped bottom). Later pieces usually have a straight line border. The markings "Made in China" and "China" indicate wares which date after 1891.

Early, c1790–1840, plates are very heavy and often have an unfinished bottom, while serving pieces have an overall "orange peel" bottom. Early covered pieces, such as tureens, vegetable dishes, sugars, etc., have strawberry finials and twisted handles. Later ones have round finials and straight, single handles.

Reference: Sandra Andacht, *Oriental Antiques & Art: An Identification And Value Guide,* Wallace-Homestead, 1987.

Reproduction Alert: Several museum gift shops and private manufacturers are issuing reproductions of Canton china.

Advisor: Mark Saville.

Basket, 9¾" l, fruit, reticulated, matching undertray, c1840 . . . . **1,100.00**

Cup and Saucer, loop handle, $125.00.

Bowl, 10"
Round, scalloped, c1830 . . . . **775.00**
Square, cut corners, c1830 . . . . . . **1,200.00**
Butter Dish, 3 pcs, c1840 . . . . **700.00**
Butter Pat, early **80.00**
Candlesticks, pr, 7", trumpet shape . . . **2,850.00**
Charger, 14", early, c1835 . . . . **800.00**
Coffeepot, 10", domed lid, c1850 . . . . **900.00**
Creamer, 4", pear shape, c1840 . . . . . **235.00**
Egg Cup, 2½", early, c1840 . . . . **125.00**
Ginger Jar
4", c1840 . . . . **135.00**
6", cov, c1840 . . . . **275.00**
Hot Water Dish, 8½", c1845 . . . . **400.00**
Kettle Stand, 7", c1830 . . . . **225.00**
Pie Dish, early, c1840
7" **300.00**
9" **425.00**
Plate, early, c1820–30
6", butter **60.00**
7½", salad **75.00**
8"
Dessert **90.00**
Pierced **275.00**
9", lunch **110.00**
10", dinner **150.00**
Platter, early, c1830–40
13", rect **375.00**
16", rect **650.00**
17", Well-in-tree **750.00**
Salt, master, c1830 . . . . **500.00**
Saucer
Straight line border, late, c1875 . . . . **75.00**
Twig shape handle, c1850 . . . . **105.00**
Serving Dish, early, c1840
10", open **300.00**
12", rect, open **450.00**
Leaf shape **285.00**
Spoon, firemarks, early, c1835 . . . . . . **50.00**
Sugar, Cov, twisted handles **360.00**
Teapot
6", drum shape, c1830 . . . . **500.00**
7", lighthouse shape, c1825 . . . . . . **650.00**
Tile, sq, early, c1820 . . . . **325.00**
Tureen, 13", undertray, c1820 . . . . . . **2,400.00**
Vegetable Dish, cov, 8½ x 9½", sq,
c1840 . . . . **475.00**
Water Pitcher, 10", c1830 . . . . **1,300.00**

CAPO-DI-MONTE

History: In 1743 King Charles of Naples established a soft paste porcelain factory near Naples which made figures and dinnerware. In 1760 many of the workmen and most of the molds were taken to Buen Retiro, near Madrid, Spain. A new factory opened in Naples in 1771 and added hard paste porcelains. In 1834 the Doccia factory in Florence purchased the molds and continued their production in Italy.

Capo-di-Monte was copied heavily by factories in Hungary, Germany, France, and Italy.

Reference: Susan and Al Bagdade, *Warman's English & Continental Pottery & Porcelain, 1st Edition*, Warman Publishing Co., Inc., 1987.

Reproduction Alert: Many of the pieces in today's market are of recent vintage. Do not be fooled by the crown over the "N" mark; it also was copied.

Figurine, child with comb, sgd "G. Armanis," late $165.00.

Box, cov, 4¾" l, emb, polychromed frolicking cherubs, crowned "N" mark ... 145.00
Dresser Box, bonbonnier, oblong, scalloped corners, serpentine shaped sides, bas–relief Greek mythological dec, underglaze blue "N" surmounted by crown mark 1,500.00
Figure
  8 x 11", boy and girl on teeter–totter, girl in pink dress and hat, boy in tan coat, blue pants, sgd "B Martino," crossed feathers mark 125.00
  8½ x 9½", boy kneeling with camera, taking photo of young girl on brick wall, crowned N and initials mark ... 125.00
  10 x 12", old man in wheelbarrow, white jug, pushed by man in tattered clothes, platform base, sgd "G Armani" 350.00
  10½ x 10½", fisherman, seated man, red tassel cap, smoking pipe, holding net to be mended, sgd "G Armani" 175.00
Plate, 8¾" d, shaped edge, gilt rim, multicolored classical figures in relief, ionic scroll framing center bunch of flowers, gilt ground, underglaze blue crowned N mark, 18 pcs 2,200.00

Tea Set, 9" h cov teapot, creamer, cov sugar, four cups, saucers, and cake plates, relief molded, enameled, continuous landscape scenes of classical figures, crowned N mark, c1900, 15 pcs 275.00
Urn
  13½" h, 8½" w, semi–nude women and men with grapes and jugs, floral leaf rim border, two gold loop handles, blue and yellow pedestal base 325.00
  15" h, 7½" w, cov, molded body, cherubs and grapes, Bacchus head handles, floral leaf cov, pr 375.00
Vase, 13" h, cylindrical, pedestal base, ring and domed foot, relief molded, classical figures, polychrome dec, relief molded putti around foot, pr 250.00

CARLSBAD CHINA

History: Because of changing European boundaries, German–speaking Carlsbad found itself located in the last hundred years first in the Austro-Hungarian Empire, next in Germany, and currently in Czechoslovakia. Carlsbad was one of the leading pottery manufacturing centers in Bohemia.

Wares from the numerous Carlsbad potteries are lumped together under the term "Carlsbad China." Most pieces on the market are post-1891, although several potteries date to the early 19th century.

Reference: Susan and Al Bagdade, *Warman's English & Continental Pottery & Porcelain, 1st Edition*, Warman Publishing Co., Inc., 1987.

Bowl
  6¾ x 3¼", irid gold, pink int., four gold handles, marked "Karlsbad, Austria" 160.00
  12 x 2", sq, pale peach shading to pale blue, center transfer of five classical maidens, gold foliage, marked "Victoria–Carlsbad" 75.00
  16 x 9", oval, fluted top, hp, purple and blue flowers, gold trim 45.00
Box, cov, diamond shape, amethyst cut to clear, marked 400.00
Cake Plate, 12" d, violets, pierced gold handles, marked "Victoria, Carlsbad, Austria" 40.00
Chocolate Pot, 10" d, multicolored daisies, gold trim, white ground, marked ... 100.00
Dessert Set, 9½" d master bowl, twelve

Vase, handled, cobalt blue top and base with gold circles, white and pink chyrsanthemums, cream ground, small blue flowers, marked "Victoria, Carlsbad, Austria," 10¼" h, 4½" d base, $150.00.

CARNIVAL GLASS

History: Carnival glass, an American invention, is colored pressed glass with a fired on iridescent finish. It was first manufactured about 1905 and was immensely popular both in America and abroad. Over 1,000 different patterns have been identified. Production of old carnival glass patterns ended in 1930.

Most of the popular patterns of carnival glass were produced by five companies—Dugan, Fenton, Imperial, Millersburg, and Northwood. Northwood patterns frequently are found with the "N" trademark. Dugan used a diamond trademark on several patterns.

In carnival glass color is the most important factor in pricing. The color of a piece is determined by holding the piece to the light and looking through it.

References: Bill Edwards, *The Standard Encyclopedia of Carnival Glass, Revised Second Edition*, Collector Books, 1988; Bill Edwards, *The Standard Carnival Glass Price Guide, Revised Seventh Edition*, Collector Books, 1989; Marion T. Hartung, *First Book of Carnival Glass to Tenth Book of Carnival Glass* [series of 10 books], published by author, 1968 to 1982; Thomas E. Sprain, *Carnival Glass Tumblers, New and Reproduced*, published by author, 1984.

Collectors' Club: American Carnival Glass Association, 4579 Clover Hill Circle, Walnutport, PA 18088; Collectible Carnival Glass Association, 2360 N. Old S.R.9, Columbus, IN 47203; Heart of America Carnival Glass Association, 3048 Tamarak Drive, Manhattan, KS 66502; International Carnival Glass Association, Inc., R.D. #1, Box 14, Mentone, IN 46539; New England Carnival Glass Club, 12 Sherwood Road, West Hartford, CT 06117.

5½" d bowls, scalloped and fluted, four winter scenes, apple blossom boughs, cream ground, 13 pcs	165.00
Gravy Boat, 5⅝" h, 9¼" l, open handled underplate, yellow and pink roses, green leaves, gold rims, white ground, c1908	65.00
Miniature Lamp, 8½" h, porcelain base, Bristol glass shade, orange, blue, and lavender flowers, scrolling gold trim, nutmeg burner, marked "Victoria, Carlsbad, Austria"	425.00
Mug, 4" h, decal portrait of monk, violin, marked "Victoria–Carlsbad"	65.00
Pitcher, 11" h, cobalt blue bands, gold trim, pink ground	100.00
Plate, 7⅝" d, scalloped, spray of pink and yellow roses, green buds and leaves, gold trim, white ground, c1905	30.00
Portrait Plate, 9" d, portrait of blonde woman, heavy gold trim	50.00
Relish, pierced handles, multicolored flowers, pink border, cream ground	32.00
Sugar Shaker, Bluebird pattern, marked "Victoria–Carlsbad"	40.00
Teapot, cov, relief scrolls, hp, marked "Carlsbad 1892"	45.00
Vase	
8½" h, portrait of monk reading newspaper, pink and gold, two handles, sgd "Carlsbad Victoria"	50.00
9" h, baluster, shaded pink and red roses, blue violets, green leaves, gold trim, cream ground	75.00

Acorn Burrs, Northwood	
Berry Set, 7 pcs, blue	300.00
Bowl, 5" d, pastel	60.00
Butter Dish, cov, marigold	125.00
Creamer, purple	100.00
Punch Bowl, matching base, aqua opal	19,000.00
Punch Cup, aqua opal	1,800.00
Spooner, marigold	75.00
Tumbler, purple	50.00
Apple Blossom Twigs, Dugan	
Bowl, three in one edge, peach opal	95.00
Plate, marigold	75.00
Beads, Northwood, dish, 8", green . . .	40.00
Blackberry Spray, Fenton	
Bonbon, green	50.00
Compote, marigold	40.00
Hat, red irid	400.00
Bushel Basket, basket, aqua opal . . .	475.00
Butterfly and Berry, Fenton	
Sauce, 5" d, ftd, marigold	24.50

Tumbler, marigold	20.00
Vase, 6″ h, marigold	40.00
Water Set, 7 pcs, blue	500.00

Butterfly and Fern, Fenton, tumbler,
green	40.00

Butterfly and Tulip, Dugan, bowl, ftd,
marigold	475.00

Captive Rose, Fenton, plate, 9″ d, blue — 160.00

Carolina Dogwood, Dugan
Bowl
Collar base, 8″ d, 3″ h, blue opal	320.00
Pie crust edge, peach opal	115.00
Plate, white, irid	300.00

Cherry, sauce, 6″ d, ruffled, marigold
opal	24.50

Cherry Circles, Fenton, bonbon, mari-
gold	45.00

Coin Dot, Fenton, bowl, lavender — 50.00

Daisy Wreath, Westmoreland
Bowl
8″ d, blue opal	380.00
9″ d, moonstone	250.00
Plate, 9″ d, ruffled, aqua	350.00

Dandelion, Northwood
Mug, electric blue	550.00
Pitcher, water, tankard, green	750.00
Tumbler
Blue	50.00
Green	90.00
Marigold	45.00
White	150.00

Diamond Lace, Imperial
Bowl
5″ d, marigold	18.00
8″ d, purple	50.00
Pitcher, water, purple	190.00
Tumbler, purple	50.00

Water Set, 7 pcs, blue	525.00

Diamonds, Millersburg
Pitcher, water
Green	185.00
Marigold	275.00
Purple	175.00
Punch Bowl, matching base, marigold	1,600.00
Tumbler
Amber	45.00
Marigold	45.00
Purple	50.00

Embroidered Mums, Northwood
Bowl, ruffled, 8″ or 9″ d
Blue	400.00
Ice green	1,000.00
Marigold	225.00
Purple	245.00
Plate, ice green	2,400.00

Fentonia, Fenton
Berry Set, marigold, 5 pcs	175.00
Butter Dish, cov, ftd, blue	150.00
Creamer, marigold	60.00
Pitcher, water, marigold	225.00
Spooner, marigold	60.00
Sugar, cov, blue	125.00
Tumbler
Blue	45.00
Marigold	50.00

Fisherman's Mug, Dugan, mug, peach
opal	1,100.00

Fishscale and Beads, Dugan
Banana Boat, peach opal	35.00
Bonbon, marigold	35.00
Calling Card Tray, peach opal	70.00
Plate
7″ d, marigold	50.00
7½″ d, amethyst	600.00

Left: Dandelion, tumbler, purple, $50.00; center: Diamond Lace, pitcher and tumbler, purple, $200.00 pitcher, $50.00 tumbler; right: Fisherman's Mug, marigold, $235.00.

Flute, Northwood
Creamer, purple 40.00
Pitcher, water, clambroth 175.00
Salt, master, blue 45.00
Tumbler, marigold 50.00
Vase, funeral, green 175.00
Four Flowers, Dugan
Berry Bowl, peach opal
Individual 65.00
Master 125.00
Fruits and Flowers, Northwood
Berry Set, 7 pcs, blue 600.00
Bonbon, blue 100.00
Bowl, 7" d, purple 60.00
Calling Card Tray, green 125.00
Plate, 7" d, green 175.00
Sauce, marigold 30.00
Garden Path, Dugan
Bowl
6" d, ruffled, purple 45.00
10" d, ruffled, marigold 75.00
Chop Plate, purple, 11" d 1,700.00
Plate, 6" d
Peach opal 625.00
White 250.00
Gay Nineties, Millersburg
Pitcher, green 6,550.00
Tumbler, purple 750.00
Good Luck, Northwood
Bowl
Clambroth, pie crust rim, 8" d . . . 450.00
Electric blue, ruffled, 7" d 275.00
Green, ruffled, 7" d 275.00
Lavender, pie crust rim, 9" d 700.00
Marigold, basketweave ext., 7" d 145.00
Plate, 9" d
Blue 425.00
Green 500.00

Marigold 235.00
Purple 350.00
Grape and Cable, Northwood
Bowl
Aqua opal, pie crust rim 3,500.00
Blue, Persian Medallion int., three
ftd, 9¾" d, 5" h 230.00
Green, pie crust rim, 8" d 125.00
Purple, spatula foot, 7½" d 75.00
Butter Dish, cov, purple 175.00
Candle Lamp, marigold 475.00
Plate, 9", purple 100.00
Grape & Gothic Arches, Northwood,
berry set, 3 pcs, blue 195.00
Hearts and Flowers, Northwood
Bowl, ice blue 500.00
Plate, blue 950.00
Heavy Grape, Dugan
Bowl 48.00
Chop Plate, blue 315.00
Hobstar Band, Imperial, pitcher, mari-
gold 155.00
Honeycomb and Hobstar, Millersburg,
vase, amethyst 6,500.00
Kittens, Fenton
Bowl, cereal, blue 200.00
Cup and Saucer, marigold 285.00
Dish, marigold 85.00
Plate, 4½" d, marigold 150.00
Toothpick Holder, blue 285.00
Lily of the Valley, Fenton, water
pitcher, blue 4,000.00
Lions, Fenton, bowl, blue 315.00
Mitered Ovals, Millersburg, vase, green 4,500.00
Orange Tree, Fenton
Bowl, ftd
5½" d, blue, irid 26.00
10" d, blue 200.00

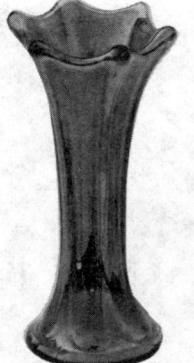

Left: Flute, vase, marigold, 6¾" h, $30.00; center: Kittens, plate, marigold, 4½" d, $85.00; right: Three Fruits, plate, basketweave ext., marigold, 9" d, $150.00.

Goblet, water, marigold	30.00
Plate, 9¼" d, cobalt blue	300.00

Panther, Fenton
Berry Set, marigold	550.00
Centerpiece Bowl, marigold	600.00

Peacock and Urn, Millersburg
Chop Plate, amethyst	5,000.00
Goblet, marigold	75.00
Plate, 9" d, marigold	175.00
Sauce, blue	125.00

Peacock and Urn, Northwood, ice
cream bowl, sapphire	9,500.00

Peacock at the Fountain, Northwood
Bowl, master berry, marigold	100.00
Compote, blue	500.00
Creamer, purple	95.00
Orange Bowl, ftd, lavender	350.00
Spooner, purple	90.00
Tumbler, purple	50.00

Peacock on Fence, Northwood
Bowl, 8¾" d, 2" h, pie crust rim, purple	380.00
Plate, 9" d, marigold	315.00

Peacocks, Northwood, plate, blue . . .	600.00
Plaid, Fenton, bowl, green	575.00
Pods and Posies, plate, 9" d, purple	500.00

Poinsettia, Imperial, pitcher, milk size,
marigold	55.00

Poppy Show, Northwood, plate, aqua
opal	20,000.00

Raindrops, Dugan, bowl, 9" d, fluted,
purple	50.00

Rose Show, Northwood
Bowl, marigold	275.00
Plate, 9" d, white irid	385.00

Stag and Holly, Fenton
Bowl, ftd, 9½" d, marigold	70.00
Rose Bowl, green	245.00
Plate, marigold	875.00

Strawberry, Northwood, plate, green	175.00
Ten Mums, Fenton, tumbler, marigold	55.00
Thistle, Fenton, plate, green	3,000.00

Three Fruits, Northwood
Bonbon, marigold	50.00
Bowl, 9" d, fluted, purple, marked . .	75.00
Plate, aqua opal	3,750.00

Two Flowers, Fenton, bowl, spatula
foot, 8" d, 3½" h, amberina	1,925.00

Vintage, Fenton
Calling Card Tray, marigold	45.00
Cup, green	35.00
Epergne, blue	50.00
Fernery, blue	50.00

Wild Strawberry, Northwood, plate,
handle, purple	175.00

Wine and Roses, Fenton, goblet, mar-
igold	95.00

Wishbone, Northwood
Bowl, 10" d, amethyst	85.00
Tumbler, amethyst	120.00

Wreathed Cherry, Dugan
Banana Bowl, amethyst–black	300.00
Berry Bowl, master, purple	125.00

Creamer, marigold	75.00
Toothpick Holder, amethyst	150.00
Tumbler, white	100.00

CAROUSEL FIGURES

History: By the late 17th century carousels were found in most capital cities of Europe. In 1867 Gustav Dentzel carved America's first carousel. Other leading American manufacturers include Charles I. D. Looff, Allan Herschell, Charles Parker, and William F. Mangels.

Original paint is not critical, since figures were repainted annually. Park paint indicates layers of accumulated paint; stripped means paint removed to show carving; restored involves stripping and repainting in the original colors.

References: Charlotte Dinger, *Art Of The Carousel,* Carousel Art, Inc., 1983; Tobin Fraley, *The Carousel Animal,* Tobin Fraley Studios, 1983; Frederick Fried, *The Pictorial History Of The Carousel,* Vestal Press, 1964; William Manns, Peggy Shank, and Marianne Stevens, *Painted Ponies: American Carousel Art,* Zon International Publishing, 1986.

Periodicals: *Carrousel Art,* P.O. Box 992, Garden Grove, CA 92642; *The Carousel News & Trader,* 87 Park Avenue West, Suite 206, Mansfield, OH 44902.

Collectors' Clubs: The American Carousel Society, 60 East 8th Street, #12K, New York, NY 10003; National Amusement Park Historical Association, P.O. Box 83, Mount Prospect, IL 60056; National Carousel Association, P.O. Box 8115, Zanesville, OH 43702.

Camel
49" l, Arabian, strolling pose, two sad- dles, fringed blanket and tassels, French, Matthieu, c1932	3,850.00
66" l, outside row, deep carved fur detail, layered jeweled trappings, draped blanket and fabric swags, elaborate carved scalloped straps, bird on saddle cantle, American, Looff, c1900	31,900.00
75" l, running, fur detail, layered trap- pings with tassels, European, c1910	6,600.00

Cat, finely carved fur detail, fish in
mouth, 54" l, American, Dentzel, c1903	27,500.00

Chicken, standing, feather detail, ex-
pressive face, orig brass handle, 39" l, French, c1910	11,550.00

Deer, outside row, standing, dec trap-
pings, dog head cantle, deep carved fur, real antlers, 58" l, American, Her- schell-Spillman, c1910	23,100.00

Dog, jumping, expressive face, 54" l,
American, Herschell-Spillman, c1905	6,875.00

Donkey
  52″ l, standing, nodding head, layered trappings, Bayol plaque, French, Bayol, c1902 . . . . **7,425.00**
  60″ l, standing on hind legs, whimsical expression, long perky ears, neck strap with bell, carved bells on trappings, orig handles, French, Bayol, c1895 . . . . **16,500.00**
Dragon, leaping, fierce expression, etched mirrored-jeweled eye, hinged neck, double saddle, 69″ l, English, Anderson, c1900 . . . . **11,000.00**
Elephant
  42″ l, walking, raised trunk, rippled blanket with tassels, French, Matthieu, c1930 . . . . **3,850.00**
  52″ l, walking, expressive face, scalloped blanket, tusks, American, c1880 . . . . **11,550.00**
Giraffe
  48″ l, criss-cross blanket, saddle with eagle heads at cantle, American, Looff, c1895 . . . . **13,200.00**
  50″ l, criss-cross blanket, two eagle heads on saddle cantle, American, Looff, c1895 . . . . **16,500.00**
  70″ h, outside row, whimsical expression, deep carved trappings, with leaves, draped blanket, American, Dentzel **42,900.00**

Pig, French, wood, iron corkscrew tail, glass eyes, orange body, red saddle, attributed to Alfred Chanvin, c1930, $3,000.00.

Goat
  Jumping
    36″ l, fur carved body, straps and blanket, expressive face, French, Henri Devos, c1920 . . . . **3,300.00**
    45″ l, animated pose, carved fur detail, layered trappings, American, PTC, c1906 . . . . **5,500.00**
  Standing, fur detail, whimsical expression, 32″ l, French, Bayol, c1920 . . . . **5,500.00**
Horse
  Galloping, double seat, elaborate carved leaves, scrolls, and ribbon dec, 73″ l, English, Anderson, c1895 . . . . **4,400.00**
Jumper
  40″ l, windblown mane, layered trappings, American, Illions, c1910 . . . . **4,950.00**
  48″ l, animated pose, layered trappings, raised forelock, flowing mane, American, PTC, c1916 . . **5,500.00**
  50″ l, alert expression, full mane, scalloped straps, American, Looff, c1895 . . . . **5,500.00**
  58″ l
    PTC, American, animated pose, tucked head, flowing mane, oversized saddle, tassels and flower bouquet dec blanket, c1919 . . . . **10,450.00**
    Spillman, American, jeweled trappings, fringed blanket, rose on breast strap, c1924 **5,500.00**
Prancer
  54″ l, inner row, flowing mane, scalloped straps, draped blanket, painted, American, Dentzel, c1900 . . . . **16,500.00**
  64″ l, alert expression, intricately carved mane, layered straps, rippled blanket, and Western saddle, American, Dentzel, c1900 **13,200.00**
  66″ l, gentle expression, full mane, checkered blanket, two eagle heads with glass eyes at saddle cantle, American, Looff, c1895 **7,700.00**
Stander
  43″ l, alert expression, windswept mane, jeweled scalloped trappings, American, Carmel, c1905 **8,800.00**
  60″ l, outside row, reverse flowing windswept mane, layered jeweled trappings, detailed rifle on saddle cantle, American, PTC, c1914 . . . . **22,000.00**
  64″ l, outside row, leader, flowing mane, jeweled trappings, sword and scabbard, fish scale armor, fringed fabric and layered straps, American, Charles Carmel, c1915 . . . . **29,700.00**
  65″ l, outside row, blowing mane, draped forelock, tucked head, multi-layered strap dec with star motif, bridle rosette with jewel, 65″ l, American, PTC, c1919 . . **22,000.00**
Lion, roaring expression, intricate carved mane, 33″ l, German, c1890 **3,190.00**
Mule, animated pose, pleasant expression, folded blanket, 52″ l, American, Herschell-Spillman, c1914 . . . . **6,600.00**
Organ Facade, carved roses, butterfly, and scroll work, 81″ h, European, early 1900s **5,500.00**

Ostrich, running, feathered detail, hinged neck, double saddle, 61″ l, English, Savage, c1880 . . . . **3,575.00**
Pig
Jumping, deep rippled blanket, ribbon and bow on neck, curly metal tail, 44″ l, American, Herschell-Spillman, c1914 . . . . **16,500.00**
Running, collar and blanket dec, protruding tongue, 42″, French, Chanvin, c1895 . . . . **3,520.00**
Rabbit
42″ l, tail with bow, breast strap, orig brass handles, French, Henri Devos, c1920 . . . . **2,750.00**
46″ l, animated racing pose, fur detail, layered trappings with tassel dec, German, Hubner, c1890 . . . . **4,950.00**
Rhinoceros, charging pose, carved detail, 47″ l, German, Heyn, c1880 . . . **7,425.00**
Rooster, running, feather detail, hinged neck, double saddle, factory name plate, 57″ l, English, Spooner, c1890 **4,400.00**
Sea Dragon, fierce expression, shell saddle, jeweled straps and blanket, fish scale tail, 66″ l, American, Looff, c1900 . . . . **20,900.00**
Seal, ball on nose, saddle, mounted on pedestal, 31″ l, 38″ h, European, unknown carver, c1925 . . . . **1,760.00**
Swan, arched neck, full feather detail, int seat, French, Henri Devos, c1920 **4,125.00**
Zebra, proud stance, layered blanket, fringed straps, 56″ l, American, PTC/E Joy Morris, c1903 . . . . **22,000.00**

CASTLEFORD

History: Castleford is a soft paste porcelain made in Yorkshire, England, in the 1800s for the American trade. The ware has warm, white ground, scalloped rims (resembling castle tops), and is trimmed in deep blue. Occasionally pieces are decorated further with a coat of arms, eagles, or Lady Liberty.

Bowl, 5″ d, scalloped, white ground, blue bands **185.00**
Creamer, 3½″ h, three brown oval medallions, one with white applied eagle and shield, second with Lady Liberty, and third with cherubs and eagle on cloud **300.00**
Sugar, cov, round, mythological scenes, vertical panels, twisted rope band near top, scalloped edge with oval medallions, blue enamel lines, dome lid, floral knob **200.00**
Teapot, cov, mythological scenes, flanked by floral panels, acanthus leaf

Teapot, saltglaze, cobalt blue borders, 7 x 10½″, $225.00.

borders top and bottom, blue enamel lines on body, lid, and handle, leaf shape spout, floret knob **265.00**

CASTOR SETS

History: A castor set consists of matched condiment bottles within a frame or holder. The bottles are for condiments such as salt, pepper, oil, vinegar, and mustard. The most commonly found castor set consist of three to five glass bottles in a silver plated frame.

Although castor sets were known as early as the 1700s, most of the sets encountered today date from the 1870 to 1915 period when they enjoyed great popularity.

3-bottle, IVT, amber, SP holder, brass ring handle **125.00**
3-bottle, milk glass, salt and pepper shakers, mustard container, orig matching undertray **225.00**
3-bottle, opaque, Mt Washington bottles, floral on salt and pepper, hummingbird on mustard, pastels, round hammered SP frame, marked "Pairpoint 724" **185.00**
3-bottle, ribbed acid finished Burmese glass, salt and pepper shakers, matching mustard pot with spoon, silverplated holder **400.00**
3-bottle, satin glass, white, ribbed, SP holder marked "Pairpoint" **225.00**
4-bottle, blown-three mold, cruet with solid ball stopper, mustard with ribbed cov, 2 shakers with orig metal caps, red painted sq tin frame, GI-7 . . . . . **400.00**
4-bottle, clear, octagon paneled pressed glass bottles, pewter stand, attributed to Israel Trask, 7½″ **200.00**

4-bottle, Daisy and Button, blue, glass holder 100.00
4-bottle, milk glass, turquoise, Fenton ... 75.00
4-bottle, Mt Washington, Burmese, acid finish, ribbed, salt, pepper, mustard, and vinegar, SP holder marked "F. B. Rogers" 625.00
5-bottle, Bellflower pattern, two bottles with ribbed period stoppers, pewter stand, 11¼" h 300.00
5-bottle, blue satin ribbon glass, revolving frame 270.00
5-bottle, 8" h, boat shaped silver stand, gadroon rim, central handle, bracket feet, pr of cut glass silver mounted bottles, pr of cut glass silver mounted casters, cut glass mustard pot with silver domed lid, Regency, Thos Holland, London, 1813–14, foot repair, minor chips 750.00
5-bottle, china, Blue Willow pattern, matching holder 125.00
5-bottle, cut glass, cut lunar and geometric cutting, SS mountings, SS stand, Warwick form, shell shaped foot, English, hallmarks, c1750, 8½" ... 600.00

6-bottle, cut and edged glass bottles, SP holder, 14" h, $150.00.

5-bottle, Gothic pattern, one bottle replaced, pewter frame 125.00
5-bottle, Heavy Paneled Finecut pattern, SP holder 90.00
5-bottle, ivory, mahogany case, SP tops 150.00
5-bottle, Sandwich Glass, Cable pattern, pewter frame, Rufus Dunham, Westbrook, ME, 19th C 350.00
5-bottle, vaseline, fern engraving, orig tops and stoppers, sgd Meriden handled frame 275.00
6-bottle, amberina, metal holder, marked "Aurora, 487," 18" d 2,000.00
6-bottle, cut glass, ribbed trim on ped-

estal base, deep skirt, bale handle holds bell and plunger, marked "Meriden B Co," 7" h 225.00
6-bottle, cut glass, Sheffield SP oval holder, baluster stem, loop handle, 9¾" 375.00
6-bottle, 10" h, oval silver plated stand, center handle, pierced reticulated sides and scroll feet, four glass bottles, castor, and mustard pot with spoon, George III, early 19th C 200.00
6-bottle, 11½" h, circular form cast and chased sterling silver stand, floral dec, paw feet, rotating bottle rack, matched set of cut glass bottles with silver mounts, marked "Gorham," 1880, 58 troy oz 2,000.00
7-bottle, cut glass bottles, SS collars and caps, George III silver galleried canoe shaped tray, scroll feet, marked "Peter, Ann & William Bateman, London," 1801, 8½" 1,250.00
7-bottle, oval, silver frame, clear bottles, silver tops, chased dec, Georgian style 1,000.00

CATALOGS

History: The first American mail order catalog was issued by Benjamin Franklin in 1744. This popular advertising tool helped to spread inventions, innovations, fashions, and other necessities of life to rural America. Catalogs were profusely illustrated and are studied today to date an object, identify its manufacturer, study its distribution, and determine its historical importance.

References: Don Fredgant, *American Trade Catalogs: Identification and Value Guide*, Collector Books, 1984; Lawrence B. Romaine, *A Guide To American Trade Catalogs 1744–1900*, R. R. Bowker, 1960.

Additional Listings: See *Warman's Americana & Collectibles* for more examples.

Adironack Lumber Co, Wells, NY, 34 pgs, 8½ x 11½", floor plans of forty summer homes and lodges, c1933 ... 18.00
American Tube Works, Boston, MA, 51 pgs, 4¼ x 7¼", 1900 .... 8.00
Bausch & Lomb Optical, Microscopes, and Accessories, 1919 .... 35.00
Carr, Ryder & Adams Co, Dubuque, IA, 351 pgs, 11 x 8", hard cover, 54 colored pages 48.00
Crane Bros, Water, Gas & Steam Accessories, 1883 .... 20.00
Excelsior Mantel Co, Grafton, WV, 288 pgs, 7 x 10¼", hard cover, 17 color illus, 27 black and white illus, five complete house plans, 1924 ...... 50.00
Fisher Scientific Co, 1934 .... 40.00

R. M. Kellogg Co., Three Rivers, MI, 1922, 67 pgs, $10.00.

Globe Iron Works, Stockton, CA, 28 pgs, 6 x 9½", 1905	24.00
Green's Nursery Co, Rochester, NY, 64 pgs, 7½ x 9½", illus, 1917	15.00
International Harvester Co of America, Chicago, Il, 112 pgs, 6¾ x 9½", 1934	25.00
International Projector Corporation, NY, 61 pgs, 6 x 9¼", 1929	32.00
Kelly, J, Fire Fighting Equipment, 38 pgs, 6½ x 10", color, 1925	65.00
Larkin Christmas Catalog, 1931	13.00
Louden Machinery, 1929	20.00
Lufkin Tools, 1940s	18.50
Lyman Gun Sights, 1914	30.00
McCutcheon Fashion, 1919	25.00
Montgomery Ward	
1903, 104 pgs, 7 x 10"	65.00
1920, #92	55.00
National Style Fashion, 1910	25.00
Noonan Co, barber supplies, 176 pgs, c1925	45.00
Purintan Malt, 1928	28.00
Radio Trading Co., Radio & Short Wave Treatise, 1933	15.00
Rochester Can Co, 50 pgs, 8 x 11", color, c1920	45.00
South Bend Bait Co, 116 pgs, 5¼ x 6", four colored sheets, 1925	44.00
Star Brass Manufacturing Co, Boston, MA, 91 pgs, 6 x 8¼", hard cover, blue ink, 1889	65.00
Starrett Tools, 1910s	28.00
Sterlinger, Chas, Wood Worker's Tools, c1880	40.00
Tucker Duck & Rubber Co, Fort Smith, Ar, 75 pgs, 5½ x 8¾", 1931	35.00
United Merchandise Co, Tyrone, PA, 64 pgs, 1926	40.00
Wheeler & Wilson Mfg Co, Bridgeport, CT, 12 pgs, 6 x 9", c1900	12.00
Winchester Tool, 1923	30.00

CELADON

History: The term celadon, meaning a pale grayish green color, derives from a theatrical character Celadon, who wore costumes of varying shades of grayish green, in Honore d'Urfe's 17th century pastoral romance, "L'Astree." French Jesuits living in China applied it to a specific type of Chinese porcelain.

Celadon divides into two types. Northern celadon, made during the Sung Dynasty up to the 1120s, has a gray to brownish body, relief decoration, and monochrome olive green glaze.

Southern (Lung-ch'uan) celadon, made during the Sung Dynasty and much later, is paint decorated with floral and other scenic designs and found in forms which would appeal to the European and American export market. Many of the Southern pieces date from 1825 to 1885. A blue square with Chinese or pseudo-Chinese characters appears on pieces after 1850. Later pieces also have a larger and sparser decorative patterning.

Reproduction Alert.

Vase, baluster, molded lingzhi, reticulated foliage, stick neck with acanthus band, bamboo molded handles, 14" h, $1,500.00.

Bowl
3⅞" d, petal rim, fifteen fluted molded side panels, raised slip int. dec, peaches and leaf scrolls, olive green glaze with bubbles, recessed unglazed base, Sung Dynasty, minute rim chip	6,600.00
7½" d, 3½" h, molded leaf design, Longquan, early Ming Dynasty, China	900.00
10½" d, white raised enamel emblems and scholar's implements, everted rim, cylindrical foot, 19th C	245.00

Charger, 14½" h, octagon shape, peacock and blossoms **200.00**
Dish, 10½" d, incised peony blossom, crackled deep green glaze, everted rim, Ming Dynasty **250.00**
Ewer, 3⅝", ovoid, ribbed, plain shoulder, loop handle, upright spout, bluegreen glaze, burnt orange foot rim, Southern Sung Dynasty **900.00**
Figure, elephant, 6" h, porcelain, Chinese **200.00**
Jar
  5" h, globular form, pale green glaze, Yongzheng mark, 1723–35 . . . . . **4,950.00**
  5½" h, relief molded, blue, pink, and red flowers, green leaves, gold trim, lid **95.00**
Lamp Base, 17½" h, vase, ovoid, long slender neck flaring to wide rim, flared foot, large blossoming peony sprigs, fluted base, overall pale green glaze, wide crackle pattern, Ming Dynasty **825.00**
Platter, oval, floral and bird design, gold trim, 19th C **350.00**
Rose Jar, 5¾ x 4¼", three part, bulbous, pink, relief red and blue flowers, green foliage, gold trim, cov **120.00**
Sake Pot, 5¼" h, ribbed, dome cov, green foliage, pink flowers **75.00**
Vase
  6" h, Moghul style, low relief carved Indian lotus motif, exotic bloom carved handles, surmounted lotus form knot cov **2,860.00**
  7¼" h, stick type, incised dragon, lingzhi and scrolling clouds, flared rim, rolled foot, 19th C **355.00**
  11½" h, hand thrown, prunus blossoms **75.00**
  13" h, baluster, stepped neck, flaring mouth, carved and incised flowers and leaf scroll, crackled sea green glaze, Chinese **200.00**
  28", double gourd, incised flowers panels, lotus scroll ground, soft pea green glaze, mounted as lamp, pr **2,800.00**

CELLULOID ITEMS

History: In 1869 brothers J. W. Hyatt and I. S. Hyatt developed celluloid, the world's first synthetic plastic, as an ivory substitute because elephant herds were being slaughtered for their ivory tusks.

Known as "Ivorine" or "French Ivory," celluloid was made of nitrocellulose and camphor. Early pieces have a creamy color with stripes and grooves to imitate the texture of ivory or bone. The 1897 Sears catalog featured celluloid items. Celluloid was used widely until synthetics replaced it in the early 1950s. Celluloid often is used as a generic term for all early plastics.

Advertising
  Compact, Kremola Skin Cream mirror, girl pictured, dated 1915 . . . . **15.00**
  Pinback Button, Heinz Pickle, round **15.00**
  Tape Measure, People's National Bank **12.00**
Animal
  Cat, black and white **40.00**
  Elephant, 3½" gray **25.00**
Bodkin **20.00**
Bottle Opener, pipe wrench shape, Coes Wrench Company, c1910 . . . . **22.50**
Collar Box, horses on cov **45.00**
Corkscrew, 4" l, nude mermaid, marked "Geschutz," Germany **320.00**
Dresser Set, 6 pcs, French ivory, includes tray, mirror, hair receiver, cov powder jar, buttonhook, and talcum shaker **75.00**
Dresser Tray, 11¼" l **20.00**
Frame, 7", oval, easel type **25.00**
Glove Box
  Beautiful lady dec on cov **45.00**
  Roses, 1900 . . . . **30.00**
Letter Opener, monkey, carved **38.00**
Manicure Set, 15 pc, elephant skin case **55.00**
Pencil Sharpener, airplane **35.00**
Pin Cushion, 4" d, lift off plush cov top **10.00**

Pocket Scorer, baseball, *Chicago Tribune,* American Art Works, Coshocton, Ohio, $30.00.

Rattle
  Doll, blue dress and pink hat, 1920–30 . . . . **15.00**
  Turtle **20.00**
Ring Box, 5" h, 3" d, cov, creamy ivory, ftd **15.00**
Shoe Horn, figural, lady's leg, wearing high-heeled shoe and rhinestone garter **15.00**
String Holder, 3", Lydia Pinkham, black on white **35.00**
Teething Ring, 5½" h, girl holding lamb and basket of flowers, pink and blue on white, emb "VCO USA" on back . **16.00**
Toy, 4½" l, 4" h, Prince on pig, jointed legs **30.00**
Vase, 6" h, pansy **30.00**

CHALKWARE

History: William Hutchinson, an Englishman, invented chalkware in 1848. It was a substance used by sculptors to imitate marble. It also was used to harden plaster of Paris, creating a confusion between the two products.

Chalkware often copied many of the popular Staffordshire items of the 1820 to 1870 period. It was cheap, gayly decorated, and sold by vendors. The Pennsylvania German "folk art" pieces are from this period.

Carnivals, circuses, fairs, and amusement parks used chalkware pieces as prizes during the late 19th and 20th centuries. They often were poorly made and gaudy. Don't confuse them with the earlier pieces. Prices for these chalkware items range from ten to fifty dollars.

References: Thomas G. Morris, *Carnival Chalk Prize,* Prize Publishers, 1985; Ted Soufe, *Midway Mania: A Collectors Guide To Carnival Plaster Figurines, Prizes, and Equipment 1900–1950,* L-W, Inc., 1985.

Additional Listings: See Carnival Chalkware in *Warman's Americana & Collectibles.*

Figure, Jiggs, flesh tones, black suit, ochre vest, red tie, brown cane, green base, stamped "Geo McManus/Manufactured by YETOWN E. GOSSIP, San Francisco," 8½" h, $150.00.

Bank, 9½" h, dove form, repaired	100.00
Bookends, pr, buccaneer busts, sgd "Herzel"	265.00
Bust, 11¼" h, woman, titled "Micaela," pedestal, painted	135.00
Figure	
Buddha	25.00
Cat	
4" h, laying on oval pillow base,	
mouse in mouth, orig polychrome paint	375.00
5⅜" h, seated, orig polychrome paint	425.00
9" h, holding ball, polychrome paint	110.00
10¼" h, pipe in mouth, polychrome paint	235.00
Frog, 13" l, green and white repaint, impressed "M McKinzie" on base	75.00
Lamb, 11" l, polychrome paint and varnish	150.00
Parrot, 8¼" h, standing on plinth	250.00
Snow White, 14"	25.00
Squirrel, 6¼" h, polychrome paint	300.00
Stag, 6 x 9½", painted and smoked dec, PA, c1850	400.00
Note Pad Holder, 10½" h, mammy	35.00
Plaque	
Amish couple, pr	12.00
Indian with feathers	15.00
Scottish man wearing tam	15.00
Statue, W C Fields	50.00
Vase, 9", squirrel holding nut, 1930s	25.00

CHARACTER ITEMS

History: In many cases, toys and other products, using the image of fictional comic, movie, and radio characters occur simultaneously with the origin of the character. The first Dick Tracy toy was manufactured less than a year after the strip first appeared.

The "golden age" of character material is the TV era of the mid-1950s through the late 1960s. Some radio premium collectors might argue this point. Today television and movie producers often have their product licensing arranged well in advance of the initial release.

Do not overlook the characters created by advertising agencies, e.g., Tony the Tiger. They represent a major collecting subcategory.

This category includes only objects related to fictional characters. Sometimes the line can become very blurred. Bill Boyd's portrayal of Hopalong Cassidy turned Clarence Mulford's fictional hero into a real life entity in the minds of many.

References: Fred Grandinetti, *Popeye: The Collectible,* Krause Publications, 1990; David Longest, *Character Toys and Collectibles,* Collector Books, 1984; David Longest, *Character Toys And Collectibles, Second Series,* Collector Books, 1987; Richard O'Brien, *Collecting Toys, A Collector's Identification & Value Guide, No. 5,* Books Americana, 1990.

Additional Listings: See *Warman's Americana & Collectibles* for expanded listings in Cartoon Characters, Cowboy Collectibles, Movie Personalities and Memorabilia, Shirley Temple, and Space Adventurers.

Amos and Andy
 Figure, bisque, stamped "Pieffer Porzellan," crown mark, marked "Germany," pr **300.00**
 Script, radio episode, Amos' Wedding, 9 x 11" booklet, orig envelope **45.00**
 Toy, litho tin windup, taxicab, Amos driving, dog shakes back and forth, Andy seated on back, 3½ x 5 x 8", Marx **600.00**

Barney Google and Sparkplug, Schoenhut, wood bodies, painted features, felt, leather, and rope trim, copyright 1922 by King Features, pr, $725.00.

Betty Boop
 Animation Art, 8½ x 11", Betty in top hat, ink on paper, Max Fleicher Studios, c1930, unframed **935.00**
 Carnival Chalkware, 14½" h, c1930 **185.00**
 Figure, 3" h, bisque, holding French horn, "Fleischer Studios copyright and Made In Japan C407" stamped on back, c1930 . . . . **175.00**
 Perfume, 3½", glass, clear, figural, painted facial features, dark red plastic cap, c1930 . . . . **50.00**
Buck Rogers
 Member Badge, brass **70.00**
 Watch, pocket, copper lightning bolt hands, one-eyed monster on reverse **300.00**
Bugs Bunny
 Animation Art, 10 x 12", gouache on multi–cel, watercolor production background, "Slick Hare," Bugs Bunny lies on platter at Lauren Bacall's table, Warner Bros Studios, 1947, unframed **14,300.00**
 Big Little Book, *Bugs Bunny In Risky Business,* Whitman Better Little Book, 1948, 288 pgs, hardcover **25.00**
 Carnival Chalkware, 9¼" h, flat back, c1940 . . . . **45.00**
 Cartoon Art, directorial layout drawing, "Bugs Bunny and Roadrunner Comedy Hour," graphite on paper, Bugs and Daffy Duck take bow on stage, Warner Bros Studios/Chuck Jones, c1960, 10½ x 14", unframed **1,650.00**
 Coloring Book, Whitman, 1957, unused **15.00**
 Doll, talking, Mattel Toys, c1960 . . . **30.00**
Buster Brown
 Blotter, unused **18.00**
 Bowl, 3½" d, Buster pouring hot milk into Tige's bowl **12.00**
 Children's Dishes, cookware set, tin, red handles **125.00**
 Clicker, 1¼" l, Buster Brown Shoes, multicolored, c1900 . . . . **40.00**
 Napkin Ring, celluloid, Buster Brown and Tige **30.00**
 Pinback Button, 1", Buster Brown Blue Ribbon Shoes, sepia, back paper with text, c1900 . . . . **28.00**
 Whistle, 1 x 2⅝", litho tin, brown ground, yellow and green accents, c1920–30 . . . . **45.00**
Campbell Kids
 Ashtray **25.00**
 Children's Feeding Dish, Buffalo Pottery **50.00**
 Cup, 2½" h, silverplated, engraved illus, William Rogers **35.00**
 Doll, cloth, straw stuffed, painted eyes, 1909 . . . . **250.00**
 Placemat Set, Campbell Kids Eat–O–Mats, six illus placemats, Milton Bradley, c1960, unused **25.00**
 Photograph, 7½ x 11", lighting display by Westinghouse, window display in Wanamakers, Philadelphia, dolls seated at table, 1912 . . . . **35.00**
 Spoon, 6" l, silverplated, boy on handle, c1950 . . . . **15.00**
Captain America, shield, brass, red and blue, 1941–42 . . . . **350.00**
Captain Marvel
 Bank, dime register **150.00**
 Membership Club Card, 1940 . . . . . **75.00**
Captain Midnight, figure, 6½", plaster, holster belt, aviator cap, and goggles detail, etched wing insignia, Captain Midnight and Wader Co copyright on base, 1940s **75.00**
Daffy Duck
 Animation Art, 8½ x 11", gouache on full celluloid, watercolor production background, "Daffy Duck Slept Here," Porky Pig gets angry at Hotel Plaza, Warner Bros Studios, 1948 . . . . **4,400.00**
 Pinback Button, Great American Theme Park, 1976 . . . . **8.00**
Dick Tracy
 Big Little Book, *The Super Detective,*

Whitman Better Little Book, 1939, Chester Gould artist and author, 432 pgs, hardcover 25.00
Candy Bar Wrapper, color picture, premium offer, c1950 . . . . 10.00
Children's Book, *Dick Tracy Meets the Night Crawler,* orig dust jacket 25.00
Crime Stoppers Kit, detective items, glossy photo, member card, 1961 15.00
Flashlight, 5" l, plastic, black, dimensional plastic head on front glows when operated, 1975 copyright . . 20.00
Handcuffs, orig card 40.00
Lunch Box, Aladdin, 1967 . . . . 15.00
Pinback Button, 1¼", back paper "Read Dick Tracy Every Day In The Chicago Tribune," Chester Gould signature, 1930s 30.00
Record, 78 rpm, Dick and Sparkle Plenty, illus cov, 1947 . . . . 75.00
Ring, brass, star and shield design, Tracy portrait on top, green enamel paint, red enamel band, mid 1930s 150.00
Tie Clip, 2½" l, silvered brass, blue lettering and center star 60.00

Felix the Cat
Carnival Chalkware, 12½" h 75.00
Doorstop, wood 50.00
Ruler, wood, 10", 1930 . . . . 15.00
Valentine, mechanical, German, framed 60.00

Flintstones, The, Hanna–Barbera Studios
Animation Art, unframed
9 x 24", gouache on multi–cel, watercolor pan production background, Fred, Barney, and Dino having breakfast 660.00
9½ x 12½", gouache on multi–cel, watercolor production background, Fred and Barney outside The Slate Rock and Gravel Co., top sgd by Hanna and Barbera 715.00
Cartoon Art, model sheet, 12 x 15½", graphite, ink, and colored crayon on paper, various poses of Fred and Wilma, c1960, unframed 1,980.00
Cookie Jar 25.00
Mug, Bam–Bam, marked "F & S Co" 7.50
Store Display, characters on fiberglass base, 17 x 24" 150.00

Green Hornet, pinback button, 1¼", red, blue, and black hornet center, yellow ground, yellow lettering with green ground rim 250.00
Gump, Andy, bank, still, 4⅜" h, cast iron, worn polychrome, newspaper missing 600.00
Howdy Doody
Bank, 4 x 7", china, red and blue stripe shirt, blue neckerchief, rubber trap missing, unmarked, early 1950s 400.00
Mask, 8 x 9", rubber, molded, orig red, white, and blue tag with Howdy, Clarabelle, and Bob Smith copyright, c1948–51 . . . . 75.00
Plaque, Howdy, Clarabelle, Mr. Bluster, multicolored 100.00
Ring, flashlight 95.00
Watch, silvered metal case, plastic crystal over Howdy dial, letters form numerals around face, diecut eyes slowly move clockwise, plaid fabric band, Bob Smith copyright, 1948–51 . . . . 150.00

Jetsons, The
Animation Art, 8½ x 13", gouache on multi–cel, watercolor background, George, Elroy, and Astro in lab, Hanna Barbera Studios, unframed 1,100.00
Lunch Box, Aladdin, 1963 . . . . 65.00
Toy, maid, litho tin windup, bows up and down, Marx 85.00

Jiggs and Maggie
Figure, wood, Jiggs, King Features, 1944 . . . . 25.00
Puzzles, set of 4, 1932 . . . . 40.00

Little Orphan Annie
Mug, 3" h, plastic, Ovaltine premium 30.00
Nodder, 4" h, bisque, Germany 100.00
Pinback Button, 1¼" d, celluloid, "Little Orphan Annie Loves Red Cross Macaroni" 40.00
Watch, brass, compass and sundial combination, Egyptian hieroglyphics on back, Ovaltine, 1938 . . . . . 50.00

Mulligan, bank, still, 5¾" h, cast iron, polychrome 135.00

Nipper, RCA dog
Bank, still, 6" h, white metal, worn flocking, marked "Radio Corporation of America" 135.00
Key Case, emb gold letters, NY Talking Machine, RCA 60.00
Radio, plush, stuffed, vinyl collar, c1950 . . . . 150.00
Salt and Pepper Shakers, pr, Lenox 35.00
Watch Fob, orig strap 75.00

Popeye
Bank, dime register, 1929 . . . . 70.00
Big Little Book, *Popeye,* Saalfield, 1934, Elzie Crisler Segar 35.00
Cereal Bowl, 1935 . . . . 60.00
Egg Cup, figural, china 120.00
Fountain Pen, 1930 . . . . 25.00
Pencil Sharpener, tin, dated 1929 . . 30.00
Pipe, orig card 30.00
Toy, Jitter Bug Band, kazoos, cymbal, orig box, c1930 . . . . 85.00

Reddy Kilowatt
Badge, brass, star shape 12.00

Figure, glow in the dark, electric outlet
  base, orig card 32.00
Magic Gripper 20.00
Pinback Button, 7/8" d, red, white, and
  blue, Reddy wearing army helmet,
  carrying rifle, marching through "V"
  symbol, 1942 . . . .   25.00

Superman
  Animation Art, 9½ x 11½", gouache
    on full celluloid, hand prepared
    background, Superman flies thru
    night sky, Filmation Studios 500.00
  Belt Buckle, 1 x 1½", brass, emb,
    hinged loop, Pioneer, c1940 . . . .   150.00
The Shadow, ring, plastic, white, glows
  in the dark, images of Shadow wearing mask and holding gun forms
  band, 1941 . . . .   375.00

Tom and Jerry
  Animation Art, Metro–Goldwyn–
    Mayer Studios, unframed
    8¾ x 11½", gouache on multi–cel,
      watercolor production back-
      ground, "Just Ducky," Tom, Jerry,
      and the Duck, 1953 . . . . 1,100.00
    8¾ x 11¾", gouache on full cellu-
      loid, colored pencil layout draw-
      ing of book and cup, Jerry stands
      on book 550.00
    9 x 13", gouache on full celluloid,
      colored pencil layout drawing of
      street, Tom and Jerry's mail-
      boxes 1,760.00
  Poster, full length cartoon special, 27
    x 41", 1962, MGM 15.00
  Scarf, silk, Tom and Jerry in pirate
    costumes, multicolored, c1950 . . .   25.00

Tom Corbett
  Badge, 2" d, silvered brass, diecut,
    emb, re-soldered 35.00
  Ring, plastic, blue, inset space suit
    celluloid disk, c1952 . . . .   15.00
Uncle Wiggily, umbrella, black fabric, full
  color Wiggily and pig wearing beret
  under umbrella in downpour decal,
  curved wood hand grip, 24" d opened   75.00
Uneeda Biscuit Slicker Boy, sign, "Spe-
  cial Fresh From The Ovens, Nabisco
  Uneeda Biscuits" 20.00

Yellow Kid
  Movie Flip Book 125.00
  Pinback Button
    No. 4 . . . .   25.00
    No. 12 . . . .   30.00
    No. 70 . . . .   30.00
    No. 125 . . . .   60.00
  Stickpin, ¾" h painted white metal die-
    cut figure, 1¼" stickpin, c1896 . . .   75.00

Yogi Bear
  Animation Art, 9½ x 13½", gouache
    on multi–cel, watercolor production
    background, Yogi and Boo–Boo

**Yellow Kid, pinback button, High Ad-
miral Cigarettes, copyright 1898, policeman, 1¼" d, $40.00.**

    eating watermelon, top sgd by
    Hanna and Barbera, unframed . . .   715.00
  Doll, 27" h, stuffed, plush, vinyl head
    and hands, orig Knickerbocker tag   25.00
  Press Book, 1964, *Hey There, It's
    Yogi Bear* 12.00

Yosemite Sam
  Alarm Clock, 3½" plastic cube, Sam
    on dial face, electric, 1970 . . . . . .   25.00
  Animation Art, 8 x 10", gouache on
    full celluloid, watercolor production
    background, Yosemite Sam in
    Western town, Warner Bros Stu-
    dios, c1970 . . . . 1,450.00

CHELSEA

History: Chelsea is a fine English porcelain designed to compete with Meissen. The factory began operating in the Chelsea area of London, England, in the 1740s. Chelsea products are divided
into four periods: (1) Early period, 1740s, with incised triangle and raised anchor mark; (2) The
1750s, with red raised anchor mark; (3) The
1760s, the gold anchor period; and (4) The Derby
period from 1770–1783. In 1924 a large number
of the molds and models of figurines were found
at the Spode-Copeland Works, and many items
were brought back into circulation.

Reference: Susan and Al Bagdade, *Warman's
English & Continental Pottery & Porcelain, 1st Edition,* Warman Publishing Co., Inc., 1987.

Bowl, 7⅝" d, oval, lotus molded, rose,
  purple, blue, yellow, green, iron–red,
  and gray painted int., insect hovering
  beside floral bouquet, brown edged
  petal molded rim, red anchor mark 1,000.00

Clock, 10⅞" h, molded as flower bouquet, central sunflower enclosing clock, works by Fladgate, scroll molded base, multicolored pastels, c1761, gold anchor mark, some restoration **12,000.00**

Cup and Saucer, striped pink tulip and columbine dec, yellow ground, gilt rim, scroll and puce foliage handle, c1760, gold anchor mark **375.00**

Dish, 12¾" d, center painted with bouquets and scattered flowering branches, wide border with three cartouches of courting couples, molded foliage scrolls alternating with molded diaper and branches, rim chips, c1755, red anchor mark, pr **4,450.00**

Figure, 8¾" h
   Man and Maid, reclining lamb at feet, pr **175.00**
   Peasant Couple, working in garden, man resting on spade, woman using watering can **185.00**

Patch Box, 1¹/₁₆" l, lady's face, black domino mask, rose–cut diamond mounted eyes, mounted pink stone mouth, faceted rock crystal cov, hinged gold mount rim, c1755 ..... **1,100.00**

Plate, multicolored floral dec, white ground, 9⅞" d, $100.00.

Plate
   8⅜" d, rose, iron–red, yellow, brown, blue, and green floral bouquet and sprigs dec, brown edged scalloped rim, red anchor mark, pr **335.00**
   9" d, striated purple blue and gray painted tulip, iron–red dotted center, brown edged scalloped rim, red anchor mark **7,700.00**

Tea Bowl and Saucer, iron–red, gold, and blue, Queen Charlotte pattern, spiral fluted **185.00**

Wax Seal, ¾" h, figural, squirrel, red, mounted on gilt metal ring, c1755 .. **285.00**

"CHELSEA" GRANDMOTHER'S WARE

History: "Chelsea" Grandmother's ware identifies a group of tableware with raised reliefs of either grapes, sprigs of flowers, or thistles on a white ground. Some examples are lustered.

The ware was made in the first half of the 19th century in England's Staffordshire district by a large number of manufacturers. The "Chelsea" label is a misnomer, but commonly accepted in the antiques field.

Plate, Vintage pattern, copper luster dec, 7" d, $20.00.

Bowl, 6½" d, Sprig	20.00
Butter Pat, Thistle	15.00
Coffeepot, Grape	165.00
Creamer, Grape	50.00
Cup and Saucer, handleless	
Grape	35.00
Sprig	40.00
Thistle	35.00
Pitcher, 6¾" h, Scrolls and Medallions	75.00
Plate	
6¾" d, Staffordshire Knot, eagles and nest	20.00
7¼" d, Grape	18.00
8" d, Sprig	25.00
9" d, Grape	25.00
Sauce Boat, Grape	30.00
Sugar, cov, Grape	50.00
Teapot, cov, Sprig	115.00
Vegetable Bowl, cov, Thistle	50.00

CHILDREN'S BOOKS

History: Because there is a bit of the child in all of us, collectors always have been attracted to children's books. In the 19th century books were popular gifts for children, with most of the children's classics written and published during this time. These books were treasured and often kept throughout a lifetime.

Developments in printing made it possible to

include more attractive black and white illustrations and color plates. The work of these artists and illustrators has added value beyond the text itself.

References: Barbara Bader, *American Picture Books From Noah's Ark To The Beast Within,* Macmillan, 1976; Virginia Haviland, *Children's Literature, A Guide To Reference Sources,* Library Of Congress, 1966, first supplement, 1972, second supplement, 1977, third supplement, 1982.

Libraries: Free Library of Philadelphia, PA; Library of Congress, Washington, D.C.; Pierpont Morgan Library, New York, NY; Toronto Public Library, Toronto, Ontario, Canada.

Additional Listings: See *Warman's Americana & Collectibles* for more examples and an extensive listing of collectors' clubs.

Note: dj = dust jacket; wraps = paper covers; pgs = pages; unp = unpaged; n.d. = no date; teg = top edges gilt

The Gingerbread Boy, No. 3100–0, copyright The Platt & Munk Co., Inc., MCMXXXII, $25.00.

Allingham, William, *In Fairy Land,* Richard Doyle, illus, Longmans, Green, 1870, 31 pgs, 1st ed 550.00
Anderson, Anne, *Old French Nursery Songs,* Harrap, n.d., 64 pgs, 1st ed, dj 55.00
Bannerman, Helen, *Little Black Sambo,* Ethel Hay, illus, Saalfield, 1942, unp, wraps 25.00
Baum, L. Frank, *The Magic of Oz,* John R. Neill, illus, Reilly & Lee, 1919, 266 pgs, 1st ed 650.00
Brett, David, *Baby's ABC,* Dean's Rag Books #80, 1949, 16 pgs 30.00
Carroll, Lewis, *Alice's Adventures In Wonderland,* Willy Pogany, illus, Dutton, 1929 .... 125.00
Crane, Walter, *Pothooks & Perseverance: or the ABC-Serpent,* Marcus Ward, 1886, 24 pgs, 1st ed 175.00

Cox, Palmer, *The Brownies Through The Union,* Century, 1895, 144 pgs, 1st ed 75.00
DeBrunhoff, Jean, *Babar en Famille,* Hachette, 1938, 40 pgs, 1st ed 125.00
Fairmont, Ethel, *Rhymes For Kindly Children,* Johnny Gruelle, illus, P.F. Volland, 1916, unp, 1st ed 30.00
Godden, Rumer, *The Dolls House,* Tasha Tudor, illus, Viking, 1962, 136 pgs, dj, 1st ed 45.00
Greenaway, Kate, *Mother Goose or the Old Nursery Rhymes,* Warne, n.d., 52 pgs 100.00
Gruelle, Johnny, *The Magical Land of Noom,* Donohue, n.d., 157 pgs 60.00
Heward, Constance, *Ameliaranne Keeps Shop,* Susan B. Pearse, illus, McKay, 1928, unp, 1st ed, dj 45.00
James, Will, *My First Horse,* Scribner, 1940, unp, 1st ed 45.00
Kingsley, Charles, *The Water-babies,* W. Heath Robinson, illus, Houghton Mifflin, 1915, 320 pgs, 1st ed 225.00
Lear, Edward, *The Nonsense ABC,* Macmillan, 1928, 40 pgs, 1st ed ... 175.00
Lofting, Hugh, *The Story of Doctor Doolittle,* Frederick A. Stokes, 1920, 180 pgs, 1st ed, signed 150.00
May, Robert L., *Rudolph the Red-Nosed Reindeer,* Marion Build, illus, Maxton, 1950, 20 pgs, pop up 40.00
Montgomery, Frances Trego, *Billy Whiskers,* Witt Fry, illus, Saalfield, 1902, 159 pgs, 1st ed 20.00
Moore, Clement C, *The Night Before Christmas,* Arthur Rackham, illus, George C. Harrap, 1931, 36 pgs, dj, 1st ed 275.00
Pardee, L.C., *Folk Of The Woods,* Charles Livingston Bull, illus, Doubleday, 1913, 129 pgs, 1st ed 30.00
Pyle, Howard, *The Story of the Champions of the Roundtable,* Scribner's, 1905, 329 pgs, 1st ed 100.00
Potter, Beatrix, *Appley Dapply's Nursery Rhymes,* Frederick Warne, 1917, 53 pgs, 1st ed 150.00
Scott, Anna M., *A Year With The Fairies,* M. T. Ross, illus, P. F. Volland, 1914, 99 pgs, 1st ed 95.00
Sendak, Maurice, *Higglety Pigglety Pop!,* Harper & Row, 1967, 69 pgs, dj, 1st ed 125.00
Seuss, Dr., *The Cat In the Hat Comes Back,* Random House, 1958, 63 pgs, dj, 1st ed 200.00
Stratton-Porter, Gene, *Laddie,* Herman Pfeifer, illus, Doubleday Page, 1913, 602 pgs, 1st ed 40.00
Thompson, Ruth Plumly, *The Perhappsy Chaps,* Arthur Henderson, il-

lus, P. F. Volland, 1918, 95 pgs, 1st
ed **250.00**
Tucker, Elizabeth S., *Little Rosebuds,*
Maud Humphrey, illus, Stotes, 1898 **90.00**
Ungerer, Tomi, *Crictor,* Harper & Bros,
1958, 32 pgs, dj, 1st ed **50.00**
Upton, Bertha, *The Golliwogg's Fox
Hunt,* Florence Upton, illus, Long-
mans Green, 1905, 66 pgs, stiff wraps **60.00**
Winter, Milo, *The Aesop For Children,*
Rand McNally, 1919, 112 pgs **40.00**

CHILDREN'S FEEDING DISHES

History: Unlike toy dishes meant for play, children's feeding dishes are the items actually used
in the feeding of a child. Their colorful designs of
animals, nursery rhymes, and children's activities
are meant to appeal to the child and make meal
times fun. Many plates have a unit to hold hot
water, thus keeping the food warm.

Although glass and porcelain examples from the
late 19th and early 20th centuries are most popular, collectors are beginning to seek some of the
plastic examples from the 1920s to 40s, especially
those with Disney designs on them.

References: Doris Lechler, *Children's Glass
Dishes, China and Furniture,* Collector Books,
1983; Doris Lechler, *Children's Glass Dishes,
China, Furniture, Volume II,* Collector Books, 1986;
Lorraine May Punchard, *Child's Play,* published
by author, 1982; Margaret & Kenn Whitmyer, *Children's Dishes,* Collector Books, 1984.

**Egg Cup, green base, blue sky, decal
"This Is The Way Policeman Tray Stops
Traffic On A Busy Day," marked "Ger-
many," 2¼" d, 3⅝" h, $75.00.**

Baby Feeding Dish
7⅜" d, decals of cats and rooster,
marked "Roma" **50.00**
8" d, seated dog, gray band, sgd
"Roseville" **75.00**

9" d, three parts, green crystal, See
Saw Margery Daw, scene of chil-
dren, two dogs, cat, and pig on rim **35.00**
Bowl
6¼" d, Nursery Rhyme, cobalt blue **20.00**
7½" d, Dollie Dimples and Sammy,
gold rim, marked "Buffalo Pottery" **75.00**
Cereal Set, cereal bowl, mug, and plate
6" d plate, Nursery Rhyme, Jack and
Jill, marked "Royal Bayreuth" . . . **125.00**
7½" d plate, 5" d bowl, 3⅝" h mug,
sterling silver, wide repousse border, chased farm landscape, each
marked "Tiffany & Co," c1926, 22
oz, 10 dwt **2,100.00**
8" d plate, 2⅜" d bowl, 8¼" l porringer,
sterling silver, sides divided into
four scenic fairy tale panels, Art
Nouveau strapwork, gilt int.,
marked "Tiffany & Co," c1907, 32
oz, 10 dwt **9,350.00**
Creamer, rabbit, red jacket, green band,
marked "Roseville" **45.00**
Mug, Grapevine Ovals **18.00**
Plate
6½" d, Dr Franklin Maxim, "It Is Hard
For An Empty Bag To Stand Free,"
pawn shop scene, black line border **85.00**
7" d, Bo Peep, Roosevelt Bears bor-
der **45.00**
7½" d, Sunbonnet Girl, rolled edge,
Roseville **95.00**

CHILDREN'S NURSERY ITEMS

History: The nursery is a place where children
live in a miniature world. Things come in two sizes.
Child scale designates items actually used for the
care, housing, and feeding of the child. Toy or doll
scale denotes items used by the child in play and
for creating a fantasy environment which copies
that of an adult or his own.

Cheap labor and building costs during the Victorian era enabled the nursery to reach a high level
of popularity. Most collectors focus on items from
the 1880 to 1930 period.

References: Doris Lechler, *Children's Glass
Dishes, China, and Furniture,* Collector Books,
1983; Doris Lechler, *Children's Glass Dishes,
China, Furniture, Volume II,* Collector Books, 1986;
Doris Lechler, *English Toy China,* Antique Publi-
cations, 1989; Doris Lechler, *Toy Glass,* Antique
Publications, 1989; Anthony and Peter Miall, *The
Victorian Nursery Book,* Pantheon Books, 1980;
Lorraine May Punchard, *Child's Play,* published by
author, 1982.

Additional Listings: Children's Books, Children's Feeding Dishes, Children's Toy Dishes,
Dolls, Games, Miniatures, and Toys.

Alphabet and Counting Board, metal and wood, 1917 . . . . 50.00

Baby Cart, wood spoke wheels, iron springs, wicker top, old worn black repaint with red striping, 63" l 300.00

Bed, Sheraton, wooden, turned legs and posts, wooden slat railings, old green paint, 29 x 48 x 30½" 225.00

Bucket, 3¾" h, wooden, stenciled red dec, yellow ground, green metal bands, American, late 19th C 150.00

Car, child's, lever action, wood, wire spoke steel wheels, worn orig red and green paint, yellow striping, "The Irish Mail," 40" l 350.00

Carriage, doll size, 34" l, wood, orig brown and yellow paint, striping, and dec, leatherized cloth top with fringe 450.00

Cart, child's, pedal, steel frame, wire spoke wheels, wooden seat, worn black paint, 36" l 650.00

Chair, Windsor, fan back, labeled "Stickley," 22" h 500.00

Cradle Cover, 15¼ x 34¾", Shaker, narrow rect poplar frame, dovetailed corners, inside chamfer, three arched bentwood hoops, old worn patina . . 35.00

Crib Quilt
24½ x 24", crazy, beaded silk and velvet, echo embroidery, turquoise, marigold, and crimson velvet strips border, American, 1891 . . . . 900.00
60 x 54", cotton, white, stuffed, central diamond medallion of flower basket, diamond quilted background surrounded by double border of inner border with meandering floral vine, outer border of swag and tas-

sel design, ball fringe, American, c1790–1810 . . . . 2,400.00

Handkerchief, 12" sq, cotton, printed scene of Little Red Riding Hood and Wolf 25.00

Pull Toy, 35" l, papier mache sheep, glass eyes, old worn white repaint, replaced leather ears, painted green wood base, red wheels, early 20th C 200.00

Rattle, sterling silver, coral ring 375.00

Rocking Horse
32" l, cut–out wooden silhouette of running horse, orig polychrome paint, upholstered seat 125.00
51" l, 34¼" h, horsehide cov over wood and sawdust body, red and mustard dec rockers, replaced saddle, American, 19th C 500.00

Rug, hooked yarn, 18 x 33½", white cat on blue and pink cushion, two tone brown ground 60.00

Sled
35" l, wood, metal tipped wooden runners, old red and green paint, black striping, painting of running horse on top, homemade, age cracks . . 130.00
37" l, wood, metal trim, cast iron swans heads, work orig green paint, polychrome floral dec 325.00
52¼" l, 13¼" w, 4¾" h, pine, two peaked runners, wrought iron blades, shaped seat, oval American flag flanked by mustard and dark blue diapering, runners inscribed "Village Romp" in gold letters 8,250.00

Stuffed Animal, cat, velvet, painted stripes, 12½" l, 6¾" h, America, late 19th C, eyes missing, old repairs . . 600.00

Sleigh, push, 44" l, wood, steel fittings, bentwood runners, old red and green repaint, worn striping over earlier blue, removable varnished handle, upholstered int. 175.00

Wagon
26½" l, all wood, orig stenciled dec, red trim and varnish, wood spokes with metal rims 850.00
34" l, 14¼" h, Blue Streak Coaster, wooden bed, steel wheels, hard rubber treads, worn alligatored orig paint, hand break 275.00
36" l, Express, name stenciled on each side, attached brass horn, tailgate missing, American, late 19th C 350.00

Father Christmas Teether, Santa Claus head, mother of pearl teether, sterling silver, English, 5¼" l, $300.00.

CHILDREN'S TOY DISHES

History: Dishes made for children often served a dual purpose—play things and a means of learning social graces. Dish sets came in two sizes. The first was for actual use by the child when entertaining her friends. The second, a smaller size than the first, was for use with dolls.

Children's dish sets often were made as a side line to a major manufacturing line either as a complement to the family service or as a way to use up the last of the day's batch of materials. The artwork of famous illustrators, such as Palmer Cox, Kate Greenaway, and Rose O'Neill, can be found on porcelain sets.

References: Doris Lechler, *Children's Glass Dishes, China and Furniture*, Collector Books, 1983; Doris Lechler, *Children's Glass Dishes, China, Furniture, Volume II* Collector Books, 1986; Doris Lechler, *English Toy China*, Antique Publications, 1989; Doris Lechler, *Toy Glass*, Antique Publications, 1989; Lorraine May Punchard, *Child's Play*, published by author, 1982; Margaret & Kenn Whitmyer, *Children's Dishes*, Collector Books, 1984.

Tin, tea set, Dutch boy and girl dec, $35.00.

Akro Agate
Cup and Saucer, Interior Panel, jade	20.00
Tea Set, Raised Daisy, 13 pcs, orig box	210.00

Castor Set, Sandwich, single bottle, salt and pepper shakers, metal frame .. 50.00
China
Creamer and Sugar, cov, Willow Ware, blue and white	30.00

Dinner Set
15 pcs, Noritake, robin's egg blue dec, orig box	120.00
17 pcs, Geisha Girl	85.00
29 pcs, Moss Rose, orig box	115.00
Tea Set, Felix The Cat, pink ground, c1920	300.00

Graniteware
Coffeepot, blue and white	75.00
Plate, gray	15.00
Wash Bowl and Pitcher, Confetti pattern	250.00

Milk Glass
Mug, Gooseberry, 1⅞" h	30.00
Punch Cup, Nursery Rhyme	25.00

Table Set, Thumbelina, cov butter, creamer, and cov sugar 50.00
Pattern Glass
Butter, cov, Pennsylvania, dark green	100.00

Creamer
Drum	65.00
Liberty Bell, clear	65.00
Twist, blue opalescent	80.00
Cup and Saucer, Two Children, amber	60.00
Ice Cream Platter, ABC	125.00
Lemonade Pitcher, Lily Of The Valley	125.00

Lemonade Set, pitcher and tumblers
Frances Ware, amber top, four tumblers	200.00
Hobbs, amber, two tumblers	100.00
Mug, Wee Branches	20.00

Pitcher
Patee Cross, gold trim	48.00
Waffle and Button	30.00
Punch Set, Tulip and Honeycomb, 7 pcs	80.00
Saucer, Cat In Boot	20.00

Spooner
Colonial, green, Cambridge	20.00
Hawaiian Lei	20.00

Sugar, cov
Colonial, green, Cambridge	28.00
Ribbed Forget Me Not	32.00
Tappan, amethyst	45.00

Table Set, cov butter, creamer, sugar, spooner
Lion's Head, clear	375.00
Menagerie, blue	275.00
Nursery Rhyme, clear	250.00
Pennsylvania, clear	170.00
Sweetheart, Cambridge	65.00
Tray, Doyle 500, amber	50.00
Tumbler, Pattee Cross	15.00

Tin
Mug, 2½" h, Little Bo Peep	18.00
Tea Set, dogs and cats, red, blue, and white, marked "Germany," 9 pcs	75.00

CHRISTMAS ITEMS

History: The celebration of Christmas dates back to Roman times. Several customs associated with modern Christmas celebrations are traced back to early pagan rituals.

Father Christmas, believed to have evolved in Europe in the 7th Century, was a combination of the pagan god Thor, who judged both the good and punished the bad, and St. Nicholas, the generous Bishop of Myra. Kris Kringle originated in Germany and was brought to America by the Germans and Swiss who settled in Pennsylvania in the late 18th century.

In 1822 Clement C. Moore wrote "A Visit From St. Nicholas" and developed the character of

Santa Claus into what we know today. Thomas Nast did a series of drawings for *Harper's Weekly* from 1863 until 1886 and further solidified the character and appearance of Santa Claus.

Reference: Robert Brenner, *Christmas Past*, Schiffer Publishing, Ltd., 1986; George Johnson, *Christmas Ornaments, Lights & Decorations*, Collector Books, 1987, 1990 value update; Nancy Schiffer, *Christmas Ornaments: A Festive Study*, Schiffer Publishing, Ltd., 1984; Margaret & Kenn Whitmyer, *Christmas Collectibles*, Collector Books, 1987; 1990 value update.

Periodicals: *Golden Glow of Christmas Past*, P.O. Box 14808, Chicago, IL 60614; *Hearts of Holly, The Holiday Collectors Newsletter*, P.O. Box 105, Amherst, NH 03031; *Ornament Collector*, R. R. #1, Canton, IL 61520.

Additional Listings: See *Warman's Americana & Collectibles* for more examples.

Advisor: Lissa L. Bryan-Smith and Richard M. Smith.

ABC Plate, 7⅛″, Father Christmas opening gate to house, "Merry Christmas" under scene, polychrome enamel, worn gilt trim	70.00
Book	
Santa Claus Comes to America, Caroline Singer and Cyrus Leroy Baldridge, writers and illus, hard cover	18.00
The Christmas Stocking, Charles E. Graham & Co, three children hanging stockings on fireplace	8.00
The Night Before Christmas, Cupples & Leon Co, NY, 1913, hard cover	12.50

Candy Container, Santa Claus, cardboard, natural roping, red suit, plaster face, branches in hand, c1920, 10½″ h, $250.00.

The Romance Of A Christmas Card, Kate Douglas Wiggin, 1st ed, 1916	10.00
Candy Container	
4″ h, Father Christmas, green glass, metal lid on bottom	225.00
8″ h, Santa, red felt suit, pink composition face, cotton beard, feet slide out for candy	90.00
Catalog, *Heathers for Christmas Gifts*	18.00
Christmas Fence	
3″ h, wood, folding, red and green . .	40.00
4″ h	
Cast Iron, 10 sections, dark green, gate	185.00
Wood, 3 sections, unpainted, picket, constructed from cheese boxes	75.00
5″ h, wood, 4 sections, blue, picket, gate	90.00

Ornament, automobile, blue body, gold gilted base, 2⅜ x 1⅜ x 1¾″, $65.00.

Deer	
Art Glass, blown, 5″ h stag, 4″ h doe, silvered, Germany	70.00
Celluloid, 3″ h, white, antlers	7.00
Composition, 4½″ h, brown, wood legs, metal antlers, Germany	45.00
Metal, 5″ h, brown, marked "Germany"	35.00
House	
Cardboard, 4″ h, white mica, cellophane windows	5.00
Log Cabin, 5″ h, white mica roof, marked "Germany"	18.00
Village, 5″ h, lithograph paper, five buildings, USA	25.00
Light Bulbs, Japan	
Clown, 3″ h, blue suit	15.00
House, 2½″ h, pink and blue	10.00
Lantern, 4½″ h, Oriental, red	18.00
Santa, 3″ h, one leg in chimney . . .	25.00
Street Lamp, 2″ h	12.00
Lights	
Bubble, orig box	35.00
Celluloid, assortment of figures on large string	150.00

Ornament
Chromolithograph
Angel
7" h, Dresden wings 80.00
Resting on hands, tinsel trim . . 10.00
Father Christmas
8" h, brown cat, fur hat, toys at
feet 25.00
9" h, cotton batting coat, flat . . . 150.00
Three children, 4" h, winter cloth-
ing, tinsel trim 15.00
Cotton Batting
Bird on clip, 3", white 25.00
Boy, 4" h, white, composition face,
brown cotton shoes, Germany 120.00
Carrot, orange and red, green pa-
per top 17.50
Girl, 4" h, Kewpie type, composition
face, white legs, orange shirt . . 150.00
Santa, 4" h, tomato red suit, black
rim, legs and boots 40.00
Dresden
Dog, 4" h, setter type, silver, stand-
ing in green grass 50.00
Doll Carriage, 3" h, three dimen-
sional, gold 125.00
Rooster, 6" h, flat, gold, red, and
green 48.00
Slipper, 5" h, flat, gold, netting, tin-
sel trim 40.00
Zepplin, 3½" l, three dimensional,
detailed trim 350.00
Glass
Barrel, gold and white, wire wrap,
unsilvered, Victorian 60.00
Basket, art glass, small glass or-
anges 85.00
Bottle
Victorian, red, wire wrap, unsil-
vered 35.00
Wine, red and pink, paper label
"Malaga" 40.00
Clown, head, ruffle 45.00
Fish
5" h, blue, red trim 90.00
Porcupine type, blue and gold 30.00
Goldilocks, blonde hair, red band
and bow 160.00
House, elf peeking out door, gold,
red trim 50.00
Mushroom on clip, red and white,
unsilvered 42.00
Parrot on clip, blue, red, and silver 45.00
Windmill, blue, unsilvered 8.00
Wine Keg, red and silver, flowers 20.00
Kugels
Grapes, purple and blue 85.00
Sphere, green, 4" d 42.00
Metal, basket, metal handle, 3" h . . 35.00
Wax, angel, early
Large 85.00
Small 42.00

Photograph, black and white
3 x 5", three children holding tree,
trimmed tree and toys background,
c1910 . . . . 15.00
5 x 7", girls, group dressed as angels
in church, two ceiling high dec
trees, c1920 . . . . 25.00
Pinback Button
"Health for All," ½" d, Santa head and
National Tuberculosis Assoc sym-
bol 5.00
"Joe, The Motorists Friend," 1½" d,
Santa head, pack of toys, suspending red ribbon and bell 10.00
"Meet Me At Kline, Eppinhimer and
Co," ⅔" d, Santa head, white back-
ground 8.00
"Merry Christmas, Butler Bros, Co,"
1¼" d, Santa head, star back-
ground 8.00
Plaque, 14½" d, papier mache, center
child portrait, holly berry leaf trail rim,
buff ground, artist sgd, dated 1884 90.00
Putz Animal
Camel, 5" l, composition body, hide
covering, wood legs, Germany . . 38.00
Cow, 4" h, celluloid, brown, Japan . . 10.00
Donkey, 3", composition, hide covering wood legs, Germany 20.00
Ram, 2" h, celluloid, tan, USA 7.00
Roly Poly, 6" h, Santa, red, green belt 250.00
Santa
3/4" h, walking with staff in hand, celluloid 20.00
1" h, celluloid, standing in cardboard
sleigh, pulled by two brown rein-
deer 45.00
2" h
Chenille, green, composition face,
Japan 18.00
Cotton batting, standing by paper
house, composition face 65.00
5½", Santa on chimney, red suit, composition face 70.00
8¼" h, standing, composition legs
and boots, felt coat, basket on back 400.00
Tree
2" h, brush, green, snow, Japanese 2.00
8" h, paper, green, USA 15.00
48" h, feather, green, red berries, candle clip, sq white base with holly
stencil, Germany 400.00
Tree Stand, cast iron, painted black and
gold, marked "North Bros, Mfg Co,
Philadelphia, PA" 60.00

CIGAR CUTTERS

History: Counter and pocket cigar cutters were
used at the end of the 19th and the beginning of
the 20th centuries. They were a popular form of

advertising. Pocket-type cigar cutters often were a fine piece of jewelry that was attached to a watch chain.

COUNTER TOP

Advertising
Blackstone Cigars, cast iron, keywind
spring cutter 350.00
Champagne 5¢, cast iron 185.00
Hotel Sherman Co, figural street light,
red globe in ornate base, marked
"Reed & Barton" 250.00
King Alfred 10¢ Cigar, 1901, cast iron,
ornate Waterbury clock on top, me-
chanical 575.00
Peter C Beck Co, Jobbers in Tobacco
& Cigars, Racine, Wisc, 9" h 100.00
Que Placer Superior Quality Havana Ci-
gar, cast iron, man smoking cigar and
drinking wine scene, The Brunhoff
Manufacturing Co, Cincinnati, Ohio,
c1902 . . . . 145.00
Figural
Boy sitting on ornate rock, metal, 7"   400.00
Spearhead, cast iron, orig paint . . .   60.00
Wheel, mariner's, brass and wood,
6½" 125.00

Pocket, metal, man, arm swings to cut cigar, 1⅝" h, $85.00.

POCKET

Advertising
Fifth Ave Cigar, keywind 25.00
Morrel's Fine Hams 25.00
Fob type, silver 25.00
Knife type
Arrowhead, SP, enamel dec 125.00
Trumpet, brass 50.00
Miniature
Clown, leaping, spring action 70.00
Monkey, riding tricycle, swing action   120.00

Victorian Lady, large bust, spring ac-
tion 150.00
Scissor Handle, sterling silver, repousse   40.00

CIGAR STORE FIGURES

History: Cigar store figures were familiar sights in front of cigar stores and tobacco shops from about 1840. Figural themes included Sir Walter Raleigh, sailors, Punch figures, ladies, and Indi-ans, the most popular.

Most figures were carved in wood, although fig-ures also were made in metal and papier mache for a short time. Most carvings were life size or slightly smaller and brightly painted. A coating of tar acted as a preservative against the weather. Of the few surviving figures, only a small number have their original bases. Most replacements are due to years of wear and usage by dogs.

Use of figures declined when local ordinances were passed requiring shop keepers to move the figures inside at night. This soon became too much trouble, and other forms of advertising developed.

Reference: A.W. Pendergast and W. Porter Ware, *Cigar Store Figures*, The Lightner Publish-ing Corp., 1953.

Indian Princess, yellow dress, blue feathers, replaced green base, 56½" h, $4,000.00.

General Butler, 30½" h, counter top
type, pine, painted, carved, cigar
clenched in mouth, navy blue jacket
with gold buttons, red and white
striped trousers and bow tie, mounted
on gray painted base 51,700.00
Indian
Chief
27½" h, counter top type, pine,
holding bunch of cigars in raised
right arm, wearing feathered
headdress, orange costume,
green cloak, leather fringed leggins, mounted on painted sq
base, 19th C 8,250.00

88" h, pine, arm raised shielding eyes, bunch of cigars in other, one foot resting on rock, wearing feathered headdress, feather trimmed costume with leggins, painted green, red, and yellow, orig base inscribed "Ed A Feltham, Cigars and Tobacco," orig bars surrounds top of base, c1880 . . . . **36,300.00**

Princess, 79" h, pine, carved and painted, red gown with navy and gold trim, feathered headdress, feathered girdle, and brown cloak, holding tobacco products, molded and painted composition base, stepped and rolled pedestal inscribed Cigars Tobacco 5¢-10¢, c1890 . . . . **15,400.00**

Squaw, 45½" h, carrying box quiver, applied carved and polychromed arrows, circular bosses, and tomahawk, painted, mounted on metal base, left arm missing, American, c1870 . . . . **26,000.00**

CINNABAR

History: Cinnabar is a ware made of numerous layers of a heavy mercuric sulfide and often referred to as vermillion, the red hue in which it is most commonly found. It was carved into boxes, buttons, snuff bottles, and vases. The best examples were made in China.

Reference: Sandra Andacht, *Oriental Antiques & Art: An Identification And Value Guide,* Wallace-Homestead, 1987.

Box, Chinese figures in garden, 3¾ x 5⅜", $75.00.

Bowl, 8" d, garden scene, blue enamel int. **225.00**
Box, 5" l, dragon design detail, blue enameled metal int. **300.00**
Cup, 4½" d, dragon handles, c1900 . . **200.00**
Dish, 10¾" d, deeply carved, leafy

melon vines int. and ext., black lacquer bottom **880.00**
Incense Burner, pagoda style, Taoist mask design, c1900 . . . . **1,300.00**
Jar, 4", flowering plants, carved floral scrolls, diaper ground, domed cov, gilt metal rim and finial, pr **120.00**
Lamp, 18" h, carved, gilt brass fittings **375.00**
Plate
12¾" d, double dragon design **375.00**
13" d, floral scene, red on green, c1900 . . . . **450.00**
Tray, 15" l, bird and flower scene, reddish brown **625.00**
Sweetmeat, Box, 4½ x 9 x 9", carved, eight Buddhist Emblems, diaper ground, latticework platform galleried base, openwork cov **1,320.00**
Vase
10" h, landscape design **120.00**
10½" h, ovoid, long cylindrical neck, carved lotus flowers and leaves, high foot rim with scrolling floral band, pr **250.00**
11½" h, landscape design, figures, and flowers, wood stands, pr **270.00**

CLAMBROTH GLASS

History: Clambroth glass is a semi-opaque, grayish-white glass which resembles the color of the broth from clams. Pieces are found in both a smooth finish and a rough sandy finish. Sandwich Glass Co. and other manufacturers made clambroth glass.

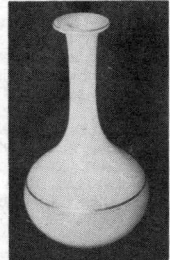

Barber Bottle, gold line dec, 6" h, $40.00.

Box, cov, 5" l, multicolored florals, engraved SP holder **60.00**
Candlestick, dolphin, petal socket **500.00**
Dresser Jar, 4½" h, orig octagonal stopper **225.00**
Egg Cup, cov, Diamond Point **950.00**

Toothpick Holder, basket, Sandwich ..	**200.00**
Vase, 6″ h, emb leaf rim	**15.00**

CLARICE CLIFF

History: Clarice Cliff, born on January 20, 1899, in Tunstall, Staffordshire, England, was one of the major pottery designers of the twentieth century. At the age of thirteen, she left school and went to Lingard, Webster & Company where she learned free hand painting. In 1916 Cliff was employed at A. J. Wilkinson's Royal Staffordshire Pottery, Burslem. She supplemented her in-house training by attending a local school of art in the evening.

In 1927 her employer sent her to study sculpture for a few months at the Royal College of Art in London. Upon returning, she was placed in charge of a small team of paintresses at the Newport Pottery, taken over by Wilkinson in 1920. Cliff designed a series of decorative motifs which were marketed as "Bizarre Ware" at the 1928 British Industries Fair.

Throughout the 1930s Cliff added new shapes and designs to the line. Her inspiration came from art magazines, books on gardening, and plants and flowers. Cliff and her Bizarre Girls gave painting demonstrations in stores of leading English retailers. The popularity of the line increased.

World War II halted production. When the war ended, the hand painting of china was not renewed. In 1964 Midwinter bought the Wilkinson and Newport firms.

The original pattern names for some patterns have not survived. It is safe to rely on the handwritten or transfer printed name on the base. The Newport Pattern books in the Wilkinson's archives at the Hanley Library also are helpful.

Bizarre and Fantasque are not patterns. Rather they are range names, Bizarre being used from 1928 to 1937 and Fantasque used from 1929 to 1934.

References: Leonard R. Griffin and Louis Meisel, *Clarice Cliff & The Bizarre Affair*, Thames and Hudson; Howard Watson, *Collecting Clarice Cliff*, Kevin Francis Publishing Ltd., 1988.

Collector's Club: Clarice Cliff Collectors Club, Fantasque House, Tennis Drive, The Park, Nottingham, NG7 1AE, England.

Reproduction Alert: In 1986 fake *Lotus* vases appeared in London and quickly spread worldwide. Very poor painting and patchy, uneven toffee-colored Honeyglaze are the clues to spotting them. Collectors also must be alert to patterns being added to plain items bearing the "Clarice Cliff" backstamp.

In the summer of 1985, Midwinters produced a series of limited edition reproductions to honor Clarice Cliff. They are clearly dated 1985 and contain a special amalgamated backstamp.

Ashtray	
Crocus pattern	**65.00**
Gay Day pattern	**75.00**
Biscuit Jar, barrel shape, 8″ h	
Celtic Harvest pattern	**200.00**
Geometric pattern	**900.00**
Oriental Garden pattern	**950.00**
Bowl, 5″ d, 2¼″ h, Fantasque Bizarre, compressed spherical form, painted House and Bridge pattern, orange, yellow, brown, and black, printed mark	**225.00**
Candlesticks, pr, Geometric pattern, 3″ h	**475.00**
Charger, 12″ d, Windbells pattern, printed mark "Fantasque Hand-painted, Bizarre by Clarice Cliff, Newport Pottery England"	**425.00**
Coffeepot, cov, 7½″ h, 4″ d, Bizarre, Gay Day pattern, cylindrical, bright orange, purple, blue, and green flowers, yellow, cream, and brown ground ..	**200.00**
Cup and Saucer, Harvest pattern	**12.00**
Demitasse Service, Floral pattern, service for six	**2,500.00**
Dinner Service, Bizarre, Rhodanthe pattern, pastel shades, large bowl, 9⅞″ l platter, six dinner plates, bowls, fruit bowls, bread and butter plates, cups and saucers	**450.00**
Marmalade jar, cov, beehive shape	
Autumn Crocus pattern	**225.00**
Bizarre, orange, thin green and blue bands	**300.00**
Mustard Pot, cov, Bizarre, blue and green	**160.00**

Pitcher, Bizarre Ware, 7⅝″ h, $525.00.

Pitcher	
6″ h, Gay Day pattern	**575.00**
9½″ h, My Garden pattern, streaky yellow and brown glaze, purple flower handle, green leaves	**245.00**
11″ h, Celtic Harvest pattern, honey	

glaze, raised sheaves of wheat, orange flowers, fruited orange, yellow, and green handle, marked "Clarice Cliff" **200.00**

Plate
6½" d
    Autumn Crocus pattern **75.00**
    Spring Crocus pattern **65.00**
10½" d
    Buckingham Palace scene **15.00**
    Queen Elizabeth portrait **25.00**

Salad Bowl, 8" d, Celtic Harvest, metal rim **265.00**

Soup Bowl, Devonshire pattern **12.50**

Sugar Shaker, 5¼" h, cone shape, black, dark green, light green, and white, marked "Bizarre/Clarice Cliff/Newport Pottery" **185.00**

Tea Set, Geometric pattern, service for two **2,400.00**

Teapot, cov, Bonjour pattern, orange and brown bands **525.00**

Vase
  7" h, 5" d, My Garden pattern, salmon pink ground, raised pink, blue, and purple flowers, marked "Newport Pottery, Clarice Cliff" **125.00**
  8½" h, 6½" d, Heavy Raised Florals pattern, blue and cream ground, raised pink, blue, and purple flowers, marked "Newport Pottery, Clarice Cliff" **175.00**
  8⅞" h, Bizarre, cylindrical, everted rim, yellow and orange lotus blossoms above blue–green Delicia patterned body, molded "195" with Cliff stamp, provisional patent number **330.00**
  12½" h, 4¾" d, Raised Parakeets pattern, blue and cream ground, emb green, yellow, and blue parakeets, marked "Newport Pottery, Clarice Cliff" **190.00**

CLEWELL POTTERY

History: Charles Walter Clewell was first a metal worker and second a potter. In the early 1900s he opened a small shop in Canton, Ohio, to produce metal overlay pottery.

Metal on pottery was not a new idea, but Clewell was perhaps the first to completely mask the ceramic body with copper, brass, "silvered" and "bronzed" metals. One result was a product whose patina added to the character of the piece over time.

Most of the wares are marked with a simple incised "CLEWELL" along with a code number. Because Clewell used pottery blanks from other firms, the names "Owens" or "Weller" are sometimes found.

Since Clewell operated on a small scale with little outside assistance, only a limited quantity of his art work exists. He retired at the age of 79 in 1955, choosing not to reveal his technique to anyone else.

References: Paul Evans, *Art Pottery of the United States, 2nd Edition,* Feingold & Lewis Publishing Corp., 1987; Ralph and Terry Kovel, *The Kovels' Collector's Guide To American Art Pottery,* Crown Publishers, Inc., 1974.

Tankard Set, pitcher and mugs, riveted metal design, marked "Clewell, Canton, OH," $650.00.

Ashtray, 3¼" d, copper, circular imp mark "Clewell, Canton, OH," 1922 **175.00**

Bowl, 4½" d, riveted overlay finish, sgd, circular imp mark "Clewell Coppers," seal **200.00**

Candlesticks, pr, 10" h, dark metallic glaze, green base patina, incised "Clewell," numbered **475.00**

Vase
  12¾" h, bulbous shoulder tapering towards foot, long flared neck, blue patinated finish over bronze, incised "Clewell/454026" **900.00**
  14" h, baluster, cased in verdigris metal, engraved "Clewell 303–6," bruised **1,100.00**

CLIFTON POTTERY

History: The Clifton Art Pottery, Newark, New Jersey, was established by William A. Long, once associated with Londhuna Pottery, and Fred Tschirner, a chemist.

Production consisted of two major lines: Crystal Patina, which resembled true porcelain with a subdued crystal-like glaze, and Indian Ware or Western Influence, an adaptation of the American Indians' unglazed and decorated pottery with a high glazed black interior. Other lines included Robin's Egg Blue and Tirrube. Robin's Egg Blue is a variation of the crystal patina line but in blue-green instead of straw colored hues and with a less prominent "crushed crystal" effect in the glaze. Tirrube is on a terra cotta ground, features brightly colored, slip decorated flowers, and is often artist signed.

Marks are incised or impressed. Early pieces may be dated and shape numbers impressed. Indian wares are identified by tribes.

References: Paul Evans, *Art Pottery Of The United States, 2nd Edition,* Feingold & Lewis Publishng Corp, 1987; Ralph and Terry Kovel, *The Kovels' Collector's Guide To American Art Pottery,* Crown Publishers, Inc., 1974.

Humidor, Indian Ware, brown, 4½″ w, 4¼″ h, $65.00.

Biscuit Jar, cov, 7″ h, 4¼″ d, gray–brown ground, enameled running ostrich and stork, florals, bail handle 275.00
Cologne Bottle, 8⅞″ h, white ground, hp butterfly and flowers, Victorian 40.00
Compote, fluted, hp, cat scene, metal base 65.00
Cruet
  5½″ h, yellow over white, floral dec, pint int., applied handle 40.00
  5¾″ h, blue ground, hp swallow, orig stopper 45.00
Decanter, 11½″ h, rose shading to deep rose, purple flowers, gilt butterfly on neck, applied handle, marbleized rose and white stopper 110.00
Flask, 8⅞″ h, moon shape, cream ground, stepped handles, hp birds and flowers, English, late 19th C, pr 325.00
Goblet, 10¾″ h, pedestal base, opaque

blue, polychrome enamel floral dec, gilt trim 85.00
Ring Box, cov, 1¾″ d, 1¾″ h, turquoise, gold flowers and leaves 50.00
Salt, 2⅜″ d, light gray ground, enameled herons and foliage, silverplated rim and handle 40.00
Sweetmeat Jar, 4″ h, hp ducks and cranes, robin egg blue, cow finial . . 350.00
Vase
  6½″ h, baluster, ftd, wide flaring scalloped neck, light gray ground, blue, yellow, and green enameled flowers 30.00
  10″ h, apple green ground, cottage and water scene, gilt scrolling and flowers, deep rust shading on base, neck, and top 80.00
  10½″ h, squatty, long cylindrical neck, ruffled rim, cream shaded to forest green ground, hp mill scene, brown banding, fired gold trim 110.00
  14½″ h, cone shape, folds, blue, white enamel floral dec and beading, Webster Bros silverplate holder . . 275.00
  17¼″ h, baluster, ftd, cut scalloped top, creamy opaque ground, enameled mill scene, enameled pink floral border, gold trim, pr 400.00

CLOCKS

History: The sundial was the first man-made device for measuring time. Its basic disadvantage is well expressed in the saying: "Do like the sundial, count only the sunny days."

With need for greater dependability, man developed the water clock, oil clock, and the sand clock respectively. All these clocks worked on the same principle—time was measured by the amount of material passing from one container to another.

The wheel clock was the next major step. These clocks can be traced back to the 13th century. Many improvements on the basic wheel clock were made and continue to be made. In 1934 the quartz crystal movement was introduced.

Recently an atomic clock has been invented that measures time by the frequency of radiation and only varies one second in a thousand years.

Identifying the proper model name for a clock is critical in establishing price. Condition of works also is a critical factor. Examine the works to see how many original parts remain. If repairs are needed, try to include this in your estimate of purchase price. Few clocks are purchased purely for decorative value.

References: *Collectors Guide To Clocks Price Guide,* L-W Promotions, 1973 (revised 1986 price list); Roy Ehrhardt, *Clock Identification And Price Guide: Book I,* rev. ed., Heart of America Press, 1979; Roy Ehrhardt, *Clock Identification And Price*

Guide: Book II, Heart of America Press, 1979; Roy Ehrhardt, ed., *The Official Price Guide To Antique Clocks,* House of Collectibles, Third Edition, 1985; Rick Ortenburger, *Vienna Regulators And Factory Clocks,* Schiffer Publishing, Ltd., 1990; Robert W. & Harriett Swedberg, *American Clocks and Clockmakers,* Wallace-Homestead, 1989.

Collectors' Club: National Association of Watch and Clock Collectors, Inc., P.O. Box 33, Columbia, PA 17512. Dues: $20.00.

Museums: American Clock & Watch Museum, Bristol, CT; Museum of National Association of Watch and Clock Collectors, Columbia, PA.

Advertising, "True Time Tellers, Octagon Alarms," New Haven Clock Co., Tom–Tom, 8 day, alarm, c1920, $850.00

MISCELLANEOUS

Advertising

Dr. Pepper, Drink & Bite to Eat, wall, Telechron, 15″ 300.00

General Electric, shelf, figural, refrigerator, white heavy metal case, electric, 5¼ x 9″ 100.00

Goulding's Manuers, wall, New Haven Clock Company, New Haven, CT, 1900, 8 day time movement, paper on zinc dial, label on back of case, minor staining on dial, 32″ h 800.00

Jacob Lucks Clothier, Watkins, NY, figural, dog, black man holding sign above 160.00

Lucky Strike Tobacco, 1870–80, regulator, 8 day time movement, black and gold lower glass sgd "Haskell & Adams Boston Mass," replaced paper dial, New Haven Clock Co, 24″ h 225.00

Monells Teething Cordial for Children, 1875, 8 day time movement, gold raised letters, Somers Clock Co, 30½″ h 850.00

Peter's Shoes, New Haven Clock Co., c1930, alarm, Art Deco, 4 x 4″ . . . 50.00

Purina Poultry Chows, electric, three dials, red, white, and blue checkerboard bag 40.00

R C Barstone Co, Jewelers, c1890, sq, oak case, pressed molding and bracket, 30 day double wind time movement, second bit, Waterbury Clock Co. 36″ h 400.00

Weatherbird, rooster in center, 17″ d 550.00

Alarm

Attleboro, 36 hour, nickel plated case, owl dec, 9″ 70.00

Bradley, brass, double bells, Germany 35.00

Champion, 30 hour, American movement, metal frame, ornamental feet, solid back brace, 9″ 70.00

Gilbert, Wm L., Bi-Nite, 4″ black dial, luminous numerals and hands, 6½″ h, 4½″ d 8.00

New Haven, c1900, 30 hour, silver plated case, perfume shape, beveled glass mirror, removable cut glass scent bottle, beaded handle 175.00

Thomas, Seth, 1910–20, one day time and alarm movement, second bit, metal case, 10¼″ h 50.00

Tiger, La Sallita, one day, nickel plated brass case, Ivorine dial, beveled crystal, self-centered wheels, western frictionless pivots 25.00

Waterbury, Kremlin-Moselm, one day, calendar, alarm, 3¾″ dial, hammered gilt case, brass winding and setting parts 50.00

Blinking Eye, figural

Dog, German, patented 1928, carved, dog, eyes revolve independently of each other to indicate time, 30 hour balance wheel movement, 8″ h 200.00

Owl, unknown maker, c1920, nickel plated white metal front, green eyes, 30 hour level movement, hardwood case, paper dial, nickel plated bezel, beveled glass lacks key, 6½″ h 325.00

Boat Clock, Seth Thomas, Thomaston, CT, 1880, nickel plated brass case, painted dial with seconds indicator, 8 day double wind movement with lever escapement, 6¼″ d 90.00

Car, 1930, 8 day time movement, second bit, metal case, 3″ d 35.00

Gaslight, American, 1900, cast brass bezel and feet, 30 hour lever movement, milk glass shade, 5¾″ d 170.00

Glass, Lalique, molded opalescent sq case, medium relief of nude female naiads, long beaded hair, gilt metal clock face with engine turned ground, 4½″ h, case molded "R. Lalique," c1932 . . . . 6,200.00

Gravity

American, c1925, brass case, powered by weight of clock movement descending along two posts, lifting movement back winds the clock for another 24 hours, marked "Patented 8/2/21," 10¼" **175.00**

French, c1940, sold by Shreve, Crump & Low, Boston, 17" h, powered by the fall of the movement along the brass rails, rewinding accomplished by lifting the movement back to the top of rails, mahogany case with turned columns and brass finials, 30 hour movement, porcelain dial, encased in polished stone drum **800.00**

Inkstand, Wm. L. Gilbert, Parlor Ink, bird on branch separates two bottles, 6½" . **150.00**

Kitchen
New Haven Clock Co., c1930, white painted case, 8 day time movement, 11¾" h **60.00**

Marine Lever
D Pratt & Son, c1880, 30 hour time movement, second bit, 8" h **90.00**

Seth Thomas
8 day double wind brass movement, mahogany case, c1910, 8¼" d **100.00**
15 day time movement, two barrels, oak veneered case, c1890, 8½" d **70.00**

Night Light, Standard Novelty Co, New York, nickel plated case, 30 hour lever Ansonia movement, revolving milk glass dome, 6" h **225.00**

Novelty
Birdcage, Japanese, c1940, revolving globe inside birdcage, bird connected to escape shell, marble base, winding key missing, marble base cracked and repaired, 11" h **200.00**

Figural
Intoxicated Man, Germany, 1930, wood, carved, movement turns man's head back and forth and plays tune on bellows, 17½" h **550.00**
Tennis Racket, New Haven, c1900, 1 day time, gold plated finish, thermometer on handle **125.00**

Lamp
Bradley B., Boston, MA, mechanism on top ignites small brass lamp when alarm strikes, solid walnut case, carved dec, 30 hour time and alarm movement, paper on zinc dial, orig brass pendulum, H J Davies, NY, 1865 movement, Bradley illuminating alarm mechanism, orig paper label on back, 14½" **1,100.00**
Unknown Maker, American, c1900, lamp, brass case, revolving glass shade, 30 hour time movement

wound by key on back of lamp, repainted shade, 12½" **350.00**

Paperweight
Ideal Clock Co, New York, c1900, 1 day lever time, imitation black polished marble case **90.00**
Welch, E. N., Bristol, Ct, 1860, Briggs Rotary Patent, rotary escapement mounted on turned wood base, cast feet, orig glass dome, nickel plated pendulum ball, 8" **300.00**

Ship
Chelsea, 1920–30, 8 day time brass movement, second bit, 5¼" d . . . **175.00**
Seth Thomas, 20th C, porcelain dial, nickel-plated case, 8 day time movement, second bit, 5½" d . . . **175.00**
W A Fletcher Co, 20th C, brass, 8 day time movement, second bit, 8½" d **200.00**
Waterbury Clock Co, 20th C, brass, missing minute hand, 5½" d **70.00**

Water, English, oak and brass, marked "B. Kindle-1651-Halifax," 30" **200.00**

Shelf, Connecticut, stencil dec, half columns, crest, 19th C, $325.00.

SHELF CLOCKS

Acorn
Brown, J. C., Bristol, CT, 8 day time and strike, driven by fusee spring, case and sidearms of laminated wood, fine old finish, laminations with alternating light and dark wood, orig glass tablet depicting scene in the city with carriages and buildings, maker's label on back-

board, minor retouching on lower glass **15,000.00**

Forestville Mfg. Co., Bristol, CT, 1847, laminated wood, lyre shape arms, 8 day time and strike lyre fusee movements, pendulum, painted zinc dial, orig upper glass, painted green trim, 24½″ h **700.00**

Balloon, unknown maker, c1880, mahogany case, maple inlay, dish dial, 8 day time and strike fusee brass movement, quarter hour double strike, 18½″ h **700.00**

Beehive

Chelsea, c1900, brass, porcelain dial, 5¼″ h **50.00**

New Haven, Guide, 1 day, strike, castle scene in glass **150.00**

Waterbury Clock Co., c1870, rosewood veneered case, 8 day time, strike, and alarm brass movement, 18¾″ h..................... **75.00**

Welch, E. N., c1875, rosewood veneered case, 8 day time, strike, alarm brass movement, 18½″ h .. **100.00**

Box or Cottage

Ansonia, c1870, rosewood veneered case, 8 day time and strike brass movement, 18¼″ h **85.00**

Brewster & Ingraham, 1845–50, 30 hour time and strike movement, mahogany case, 13¾″ h **150.00**

Gilbert & Co, c1890, rosewood veneered case, orig glass and dial, 8 day time and strike movement, 13½″ h **120.00**

J. C. Brown, 1850–60, 8 day brass time and strike movement, rosewood veneered case, 14¾″ h ... **400.00**

New Haven Clock Co, c1880, rosewood veneered case, 8 day time and strike movement, 13¾″ h ... **125.00**

S. B. Terry, c1840, mahogany case, 30 hour time and alarm ladder brass movement, 11″ h **175.00**

Seth Thomas, c1880

Mahogany veneered case, replaced hands, 30 hour time and strike movement, 9½″ h **150.00**

Rosewood case, orig glass, 30 hour time and strike movement, half lyre movement, patent dated dial, c1860, 14½″ h **125.00**

Walnut veneered case, label, 30 hour time and strike movement, 9½″ h **225.00**

Terry Clock Co, c1870, rosewood case, peak top, 30 hour time and strike movement, 18″ h **375.00**

Unknown Maker, c1880, rosewood veneered case, band inlay, 8 day time movement, 11¼″ h **75.00**

Waterbury Clock Co., c1890, rosewood veneered case, 30 hour time and strike movement, 13½″ h ... **75.00**

Bracket

Bigelow & Kennard, c1875, ornate oak case, brass and silver dial, fretwork, 8 day and Westminster chimes, 14″ h **2,300.00**

Harley, William, Chelsea, mid 18th C, George III, ebonized, arched painted dial, subsidiary date hand and strike silent control, conforming arched hooded case, brass ogee bracket feet, sgd plate, 15″ h **4,100.00**

Loundes, Charles, Pall Mall, London, 4th quarter 17th C, verge movement, fitted engraved backplate, molded ebony case, gilt metal escutcheons, 13″ **10,000.00**

Louis XV, Darville, Paris, mid 18th C, kingwood, balloon form case, asymmetrical ormolu crest, borders, and feet, circular enamel plaquette dial, sgd on dial and movement, 15½ x 35″ **12,000.00**

Quare, Daniel and Stephen Horseman, London, early 18th C, George I, ebony, circular silvered annular ring, Roman hours and Arabic minutes, arched dial with engraved brass containing strike silent control and date aperture, enclosed by conforming glazed door beneath a stepped domed crest, brass bail carry handle, sgd dial, 20″ h **16,000.00**

Roskel, Robert, London, early 19th C, Regency, ebonized, circular silvered dial with Roman numerals, molded brass bezel, arched case, surmounted bail carry handle, brass ogee bracket feet, sgd dial, 15″ h, 10″ w **1,800.00**

Unknown Maker, 1830–50, 8 day brass fusee time and strike movement, brass Gothic grill work, Ogee bracket base, painted cast iron dial, 17″ h **450.00**

Valentine Royston, 19th C, brass sgd and engraved 8 day time and strike fusee movement, brass dial, crotch grain mahogany case with brass feet, 13½″ h **900.00**

Calendar

Davis Clock Co., Columbus, MS, column flat top, 8 day strike, 7″ dial, 25″ **450.00**

Ithaca Clock Co., 1870, 8 day time, strike and calendar movement, club escapement, cottage style case, orig backboard with label, 22¼″ h **600.00**

L. F. & W. W. Carter, c1870, rosewood

veneered case, 8 day time and strike weight driven movement, B B Lewis calendar movement, 36" h 600.00

Seth Thomas, c1880, 8 day time, strike, and calendar movement, veneered walnut case, orig instruction label, 25¾" h 600.00

Welch Spring & Co, c1870, rosewood veneered case, 8 day time and strike, B B Lewis calendar movement, 19¼" h 300.00

Candlestick, S B Terry, c1840, milk glass base, replaced dome, 30 hour time brass movement, 10" h 200.00

Carriage
Dent, E., Paris, mid 19th C, sgd dial, 5¾" 1,200.00

Japy, France, c1840, one piece case, porcelain dial, 8 day time, strike, and alarm, hour repeat, engraved platform and balance cock, movement inscribed by maker, alarm hand replaced, 7½" h 650.00

Sandoz, Gve., Palais Royal, polychrome enamel dec on sides and back, later lever platform, molded sgd oval case 1,500.00

Waterbury Clock Co., Waterbury, CT, 1908, miniature, cast gilded brass case, porcelain dial, maker's trademark, 30 hour time movement, lever escapement 150.00

Crystal Regulator
Bailey, Banks & Biddle, c1880, curved front door, 8 day time and strike brass movement, mercury pendulum, 11" h 325.00

Black, Star & Frost, c1880, 8 day time and strike brass movement, 16" h 1,050.00

Gilbert, Wm. L., Tuscan, 8 day, half hour strike, ivory porcelain dial, visible escapement, Brazilian green onyx columns, ormolu gold finish, urn and wreath finial, 19" 850.00

French, mantel
Louis XV, gilt bronze clock house surmounted with pensive mythological figures, crowned by cupid seated on stylized mollusk, porcelain clock face with painted Arabic and Roman numerals, 26½" h 5,500.00

Napoleon II, 2nd half 19th C, 14½", gilt bronze mounted white marble clock in Louis XVI style, 1¼" white enamel dial with Roman and Arabic numerals, inscribed "L. Leroy Cie. a Paris, 7 Bould. de la Madeleine," hour and half hour striking movement on single bell, modern wood base 900.00

Neveux, Haas & Cie, c1920, molded temple of love, movement con-

Shelf, French, mantel, Louis XVI, Paris, bisque, figural, Perseus freeing Andromeda, enamel dial sgd "Ridel a Paris," oval plinth base, late 18th C, 19" h, $3,500.00.

tained within cornice, diamond studded handles above figure of cupid playing harp, silver gilt case with sky blue enamel, engine turned ground, orig leather carrying case, 11" 7,000.00

Garniture, French, 3 pcs
Louis XVI style, Lesteau Le Jeune, 19th C, Sevres porcelain and gilt bronze, after 18th C example by Kinable, lyre form clock surmounted by Apoline mask, enamel dial with gilt bronze bezel, paste brillians, companion anthenienne form garnitures with satyr mass, holding bouquets of roses as candelabra, 22" h clock, 3 pcs 6,000.00

Louis Philippe, 2nd/3rd quarter 19th C, gilt bronze and verde antico marble, stamped "G. Megnin," columned case surmounted by griffin finials and flower-filled basket, the flanking four light candelabra applied with female therms 1,325.00

Gingerbread (Kitchen)
Ansonia, X–0. 6, 8 day, hour and half hour strike, oak case, 22½" 175.00

F. Kroeber Clock Co., Wanderer, 8 day gong strike, 6" fancy dial, walnut case, elaborate geometric tablet, 23" 290.00

Gilbert, Wm. L., Forest, 8 day strike, 7" dial, oak case, tablet with bird and butterfly in marsh setting, 24½" 200.00

Ingraham, Mt. Vernon, 22", 8 day, half hour strike, highly emb, octagon door, solid oak relief of Mt. Vernon on crest, made for 1904 St. Louis World's Fair, 22" h 300.00

New Haven Clock Co, c1915, pressed oak case, 8 day time, strike and alarm movement, 24½" h 70.00

Thomas, Seth, Ogden, 8 day, spring, strike, alarm, cathedral gong, black walnut case, two finials flanking base, 21½" **200.00**

Waterbury Clock Co, c1880, 8 day time, strike, and calendar brass movement, missing barometer and thermometer, 22" h **175.00**

Welch, Sampson (Admiral), 8 day, half hour strike, cathedral bell, 6" dial, oak case, Sampson bust portrait on crest, ship on tablet, 24" **275.00**

Lyre, gilt bronze and crystal

Charles X, sulphide bust portrait flanked by cut glass columns, elaborately chased with Neo-classical motifs, 25" **7,500.00**

French Empire, mask with crown above lyre strings flanged by pair of facing swan heads holding swag over Roman numeral enamel dial, Baccarat crystal base with center ormolu mounted ribbon tied swag and trumpet, works by Archambult, Paris, 20" **2,250.00**

Shelf, mantel, George III, satinwood and brass, dial sgd "Eardley Norton," plate sgd "Gravell & Tolkein," late 18th C, 13¼" w, 9" d, 18½" h, $8,500.00.

Mantel

A. Stowell & Co., Boston, eight day time and strike movement, engraved face, mahogany arched top, rect cast, key and pendulum, Westminster chimes, 18½" h, 12⅞" w **600.00**

Birge, Mallory & Co., Bristol, CT, second quarter 19th C, Empire, mahogany, enamel dial, eglomise panel with split balusters, surmounted carved eagle **450.00**

Boston Clock Co., c1890, onyx, 8 day, half hour cathedral strike, seven jeweled movement, bronze gilded ornaments, 10" h **275.00**

Caldwell, Edward F. and Co, NY, first quarter 20th C, American Renaissance, drum form marble case resting on cushion of scrolling satyr masks, plinth with angled feet as floral bouquets, gilt bronze mounts, circular enamel dial contained by reeded bezel, sgd on dial "Edward F. Caldwell & Co., New York," 16 x 12" **2,400.00**

Gilbert, William L. & Co, c1903, 8 day time and strike movement, marbleized wood case, black, bell top, 18½" h **200.00**

Gruber, Jacques, c1900, earthenware, arched crest, circular white enameled dial, relief flowers and leafage between molded uprights, iridescent olive-green and pink glaze, inscribed "J. Gruber, Ceramique/Rambervillers" in black enamel, 22¼" h **6,500.00**

New Haven Clock Co, c1920, tambour, mahogany case, 8 day time and strike movement, Westminster chimes, 8¾" h **110.00**

Rehaist, Paris, early 19th C, Empire, gilt bronze, circular engine turned dial, conforming drum form case, surmounted by four Ionic columns with Napolean portrait busts, molded base with cast acanthus and lotus leaf tips, sgd dial, 26" h **5,500.00**

Russell & Jones, wood, 8 day, slow strike, 5" dial, Tennessee marble columns, marble finished wood, 10" h **125.00**

Sessions, c1930, tambour, mahogany case, 8 day time and strike movement, 10" h **60.00**

Terry & Andrews, c1840, iron case, MOP inlay, gold dec, 8 day time and strike lyre movement, 13¾" h **100.00**

Thomire & Cie, early 19th C, Empire, arched case flanked by two gilt bronze figures of Atlanta and Meleager, white marble plinth with hunt trophy, quivers, and arrows, circular enamel dial, sgd on dial "Thomire & Cie," 17½x 28" **8,500.00**

Thomas, Seth, c1890

Beehive, 8 day brass time and strike movement, quarter hour Sonora chimes, inlaid mahogany case, 14½" h **400.00**

Rosewood veneered case, 8 day time and strike brass movement, c1880, 10½" h **75.00**

Victorian, oak case, pressed oak side panels, 8 day time and strike movement, second bit, 18½" h **300.00**

Unknown Maker, c1870, iron case, floral dec, paw feet, 16" h **120.00**

Waterbury Clock Co, c1890, 8 day time and strike movement, 9½" h   **150.00**

Massachusetts Shelf

Mahogany, Balch, Daniel, Jr., Newburyport, MA, c1790, Federal, two sets of reeded pilasters, lower door with keystone and arch, scrolled pediment, plinth with brass urn and flame finials, brass dial, 28½ x 12 × 6" **12,000.00**

Maple, Sherwin, William, Buckland, MA, 1830, time and strike 30 hour wood works movement, shaped crest, turned feet and turned columns flanking glazed door with mirror tablet, paper label, orig wood dial, and weights, stenciling removed from crest and traces can be seen **900.00**

Metal

Brass

Art Deco, Ansonia, c1920, 8 day time and strike movement, 10¾" h **150.00**

Victorian, France, c1880, cornucopia, Bacchus head, and lion's head dec, paw feet, porcelain dial, 8 day time and strike outside escapement movement, 16" h   **150.00**

Bronze

Ansonia, one day time, Art Nouveau case, 4¼" **75.00**

Charles X, 19th C, French gilt bronze, bronze winged maiden clasping torch, drawing back the "Veil of Night," rect base with relief chariot and putti, 20" **1,150.00**

Louis XVI, Louis Berthoud, flower filled urn with satyr mask carry handles, surmounted by snakes, waisted base, foliate cast plinth, circular enamel dial within beaded bezel, 19" **900.00**

Gilt Bronze

Louis Philippe, Poirier and Bouge, Paris, early 19th C, circular engine turned dial within faux stone wall forming seat for figural cupid, green marble base, draped with flowers and ribbons, flower form feet, 12 x 5 x 19" . . **4,500.00**

Louis XV, Ferdinand Berthoud, mid 18th C, block form case surmounted by celestial globe, infant astronomer studying chart leans against case, molded guillouche ornamented base, circular enamel dial contained by guillouche bezel, sgd on dial and movement, 12 x 5 x 12" **6,250.00**

Louis XVI, Lepaute, third quarter 18th C, figural, urn resting on fluted truncated column, draped with laurel and floral swags, surmounted by pine cone, twin annular rings at mid point, coiled serpent pointer, sgd on base "Lepaute," 19" h **28,000.00**

Iron

Pomeroy, N., Bristol, CT, c1865, cast iron case, MOP inlay, gold dec, 30 hour level movement inscribed by maker, painted zinc dial, nickel plated balance wheel visible through opening in dial, orig pendulum, 10¼" **250.00**

Unknown Maker, cast, eagle, shield, and flag dec, metallic finish and dark red paint, paper clock face, 13" h **135.00**

Waterbury, c1910, 8 day time and strike movement, 9½" h **75.00**

Nickel, F. Kroeber Clock Co., NY, 1880, strike, carriage type, gilt front, glass sides, 6½" **275.00**

Ormolu

Freres, Napoleon III, three putti with garlands, black spherical dial, gilt stars, foliate and swag encrusted baroque base, time and strike movement imp "Japy Freres & Co," and "Rollin A Paris," 21" h **4,750.00**

Unknown Maker, lyre form, Charles X, c1825, putti supported by dolphins, rect pedestal base, half hour strike, glass dome, 18" h **1,600.00**

Pot Metal, N. Shure Co., c1934, 30 hour movement, figural knight, silvered finish, 6¼" **75.00**

Mirror Side

Gilbert, Wm. L., 8 day, walnut, cherubs dec **400.00**

Unknown Maker, Austrian, Neoclassical, burl walnut and ebonized wood, circular enameled dial, marble columns, mirror back and sides, parquetry floor, 22" h **1,100.00**

Ogee

Ansonia, c1880, crotch grain mahogany veneered case, orig lower glass, 30 hour time and strike movement, 18¾" h **125.00**

Bristol Brass & Clock Co, c1880, veneered, orig label, 30 hour time and strike movement, 19" h **75.00**

Hill, Goodrich & Co., Plainville, CT, c1850, 8 day brass time and strike movement with a cast iron back plate cased in a brass shell, choice mahogany veneer, glazed door with painted tablet opening to gilted carved crest and columns, gilted columns with mirrors behind, orig dial and paper label, tablet repainted, mirror behind right column partially gone, minor veneer damage, 31″ **700.00**

New Haven, Weight No. 2, one day, strike, zebra wood case, 26″ **200.00**

Thomas, Seth, c1870, 30 hour brass time and strike movement, rosewood veneered case, Empire, 15¾″ h **175.00**

Waterbury Clock Co, c1870, 30 hour time, strike, and alarm movement, mahogany veneered case, 19″ h, Empire **200.00**

Pillar and Scroll

Chelsea, c1930, reverse painted glass, orig instruction booklet, 8 day time and strike balance wheel movement, 24¼″ h **600.00**

Dohenes, Ephraim, Bristol, CT, c1830, Federal, carved mahogany, shaped crest, three brass urn finials above a hinged glazed door, eglomise panel with houses and pond, tapering columns, bracket feet, 31 x 17½″ **750.00**

Ephraim Downes, Bristol, CT, mahogany case, wood works and painted face, printed paper label, orig reverse painted glass with printed message "Take it home to your wife," brass finials, weights and pendulum, brass knob added to door, 31¼″ h **1,350.00**

North, Norris, Wolcottville, CT, swan's neck, three brass urn finials, painted dial with foliate spandrels, cottage in wood scene glass, 30⅜″ **1,400.00**

Terry, Eli and Samuel, CT, 1830, mahogany case, delicate scrolled crest and feet, 30 hour time and strike wood movement, painted wood dial, maker's label, eglomise tablet, three brass finials, old pendulum and weights, 31½″ **1,000.00**

Thomas, Seth

Federal, Plymouth, CT, c1805, swan's neck pediment, three brass urn finials, glazed door, eglomise panel with houses and floral band, white painted wood dial, Roman chapter ring, floral spandrels, flanked by colonettes, shaped apron, bracket feet **3,850.00**

Miniature, c1920, scrolled crest, pillars, finials, 8 day time and strike movement, 17″ h **250.00**

Porcelain or China Case

F. Kroeber, c1880, 8 day time and strike movement, 12″ h **250.00**

Japy Frere, c1880, made for Bailey,

Banks, and Biddle, 8 day time and strike brass movement, 18¼″ h . . **500.00**

New Haven Clock Co, c1890, 8 day time and strike brass movement, 8½″ h **175.00**

Terregina Clock Co., c1870, 30 hour time only movement, architectural case, orig label, repainted, 8¾″ h **80.00**

Unknown, England, mauve, polychrome Middle Eastern transfer scene with gilt, marked "Made in England," 12″ h **55.00**

Shelf

Bartholomew, E. G. & W., c1830, carved pineapple finials and paw feet, refinished case and splat, 30 hour wood time and strike movement, 25½″ h **250.00**

Boardman & Wells, 1830–40, half columns, stenciled, eagle on crest, replaced bell, 30 hour brass bushed time and strike movement, 32″ h **425.00**

Cummens, William, Roxbury, MA, 1800–10, Federal, inlaid mahogany, two parts, upper section with flame and urn finials, pierced fretwork cresting flanked by two similar finials, rect line inlaid plinth, glazed door, white painted bell shaped dial, Arabic chapter ring, inscription "Warranted by Wm Cummens," flanked by gilt ribbon tied floral boughs and arabesques, lower section with box base inlaid with patterned stringing, ogee bracket feet, 36¼″ h, 14″ w, 6¼″ d **17,600.00**

Goodwin, E.O., c1850, brass 8 day time and strike movement, rosewood veneered case, orig label and hands, 15⅛″ h **400.00**

Eli Terry & Sons, c1825, 8 day wood time and strike movement, carved columns, splat, and feet, 37″ h . . . **900.00**

Forestville Mfg. Co

Half column, mahogany veneer case, stencil dec, works stamped "W C Johnson," 8 day brass time and strike movement, c1850, 30″ h **325.00**

Triple Decker, Empire, 8 day brass time and strike weight driven movement, c1840, 36″ h **300.00**

Gilbert, c1880, Victorian, ebonized case, incised Eastlake dec, 8 day brass time and strike movement, 19″ h **200.00**

Hart, Orrin, c1830, 30 hour wood time and strike movement, stenciled columns and splat, mahogany veneer case, 34½″ h **250.00**

Hoadley, Silas, c1830, stenciled columns and splat, 30 hour upside down wood time, strike and alarm movement, 36″ h **700.00**

Ingraham Clock Co, c1870
  Doric Model, 30 hour time, strike, and alarm movement, rosewood veneered case, black and gold eagle dec glass, 16¼″ h **150.00**
  Grecian Model, 30 hour time and strike movement, rosewood case, 15¼″ h **175.00**

Ingraham, E.
  Empire, rosewood case, ripple molded door, label "Late Brewster & Ingraham," 30 hour time, strike and alarm movement, c1850, 17½″ h **200.00**
  Venetian, mahogany case, figure "8" style, orig label, 8 day time and strike movement, c1870, 15¾″ h **150.00**

Jerome & Darrow, c1825, 30 hour wood time and strike movement, 29″ h **1,150.00**

Jones, Edward K., c1835, 30 hour wood time and strike movement, 27″ h **200.00**

Seymour Hall & Co, c1830, 30 hour wood time and strike movement, marbleized columns, eagle splat, turned feet, 34″ h **225.00**

Seymour, William & Porter, c1825, 8 day wood time and strike movement, gilded columns and eagle splat, mahogany plate works, 36″ h **600.00**

Terry & Andrews, Empire, mahogany case, double column, orig label and glass, 30 hour brass time and strike movement, 26½″ h **200.00**

Terry, Eli & Co., Empire, mahogany veneer case with ebonized pilasters, gold stenciled floral dec and eagle crest, paw feet, wood works and painted face, weights and pendulum, 33¾″ h **175.00**

Thayer, E. c1830, 30 hour wood Groaner movement, carved pillars and splat, 35″ h **300.00**

Thomas, Seth
  Empire, c1860, 8 day weight driven brass time and strike movement, perpetual calendar, rosewood case, gilt dec, 33″ h **650.00**
  Lincoln model, c1880, 8 day weight driven brass time and strike movement, walnut Eastlake case, 26½″ h **900.00**

Unknown Maker, c1830, 8 day brass Salem bridge movement, weight driven, second bit, carved fruit crest and paw feet, 30¾″ h **2,300.00**

Waterbury, c1870, Victorian, 8 day

brass time and strike movement, walnut case, 14¼″ h **75.00**

Whiting, Riley, c1830, 30 hour wood time and strike movement, carved columns and splat, 34¾″ h **325.00**

Skeleton
  English, c1870, time fusee movement, fall-off strike, stand and dome, 15½″ h **550.00**
  French, c1840, weight driven, frame stamped "Augt. Moineau Roland Degrege," 23″ **3,500.00**
  Victorian, Gothic Revival, unknown maker, mid 19th C, Gothic style pinnacles with foliate pierced dial, fusee movement, white marble base, glass dome, 16″ h **1,300.00**

Steeple
  Birge & Fuller, c1840, 8 day time and strike wagon spring movement, 20″ h **1,000.00**
  Birch & Fuller, Bristol, CT, double decker, mahogany veneer, orig reverse painted glass door panels, fusee movement, brass works, label, pendulum and key, old dark finish, 26½″ h **2,100.00**
  Boardman, Chauncey, c1840, refinished case, replaced door glass, 30 hour fusee time and strike movement, 20″ h **100.00**
  Brewster & Ingraham
    Mahogany case, brass springs, 30 hour time and strike movement, c1850, 20″ h **350.00**
    Rosewood veneered case, frosted and cut door glass, c1840, 19¼″ h **350.00**
  Gilbert, Wm. L. 8 day movement, mahogany veneer, painted glass with sailing ship, restored dial, 19¾″ . . **250.00**
  Manross, Elisha, Bristol, Ct, 1850, 30 hour time and strike movement, mahogany veneered case, door with orig tablet depicting "Market Place Quebec," orig dial and paper label, movement retains orig brass springs, minor veneer loss, orig tablet cracked **150.00**
  Pratt, Daniel, 1850–60, 8 day time and strike movement, rosewood veneered case, orig glass with St. Louis Courthouse, 19½″ h **250.00**
  Terry & Andrews, c1860, 8 day time and strike lyre movement, orig glass, 25½″ h **600.00**
  Unknown Maker
    Empire, Waterbury brass 8 day time and strike movement, ripple molding, c1840, 14⅛″ h **150.00**
    Rosewood veneered case, London

label, 30 hour time and alarm
movement, c1875, 15¾" h **200.00**
Waterbury Clock Co., Waterbury, CT,
1875, mahogany veneered case,
floral transfer glass, painted zinc
dial, paper label, 30 hour time and
alarm movement, old pendulum,
lacks key, glass tablet background
repainted, replaced minute hand,
15" **250.00**

**Tall Case, Williard, Aaron, Hepple-
white, mahogany, French feet, string
inlay fluted columns, rocking ship
movement, sgd dial, orig paper label,
$30,000.00.**

TALL CASE CLOCKS

Avery, John, Preston, CT, c1770, Chippendale, cherry, hood with three
flame finials, scalloped whale tails
fretwork, arched glazed door, brass
engraved dial, Roman and Arabic
chapter rings, sweep seconds ring,
calendar day aperture, engraved C
scroll spandrels, engraved signature,
fluted colonettes above waisted case,
arched thumb molded cupboard door,
applied scalloped banding, ogee
bracket feet, baseboard replaced,
92¾" h, 17½" w, 9⅞" d **44,000.00**
Bramer, Paulus, Amsterdam, 18th C,
choice walnut veneered slender case
with inlays, engraved brass dial inscribed by maker, 8 day time and

strike movement, hour and half hour
strikes on different bells, old weights
and pendulum, lacks key, replaced
feet, door glass, 79" h **4,250.00**
Christ, Daniel, Kutztown, PA, c1785,
98¾" h, Chippendale carved walnut,
molded swan's neck crest hood, flowerhead carved terminals, three turned
finials, arched glazed door, white
painted dial with moon phases, minute and date registers, inscribed
"Daniel Christ," fluted colonettes,
waisted case with shaped door,
fluted quarter columns, molded
base with stylized leaf carved panel
and fluted quarter columns, ogee
bracket feet **28,600.00**
Cuff, William, Europe, 1800, hood with
molding, carved panel base, carved
oak case, engraved brass dial, three
train musical movement striking on
nest of eight bells, iron weights and
period pendulum, 93" h **1,000.00**
Cummens, William, Roxbury, Massa-
chusetts, c1805, 99" h, mahogany,
pierced fretwork crest hood, three
brass phoenix and urn finials, arched
glazed hinged door, white paint dial
with minute register, painted harbor
scene centers inscription "Arranted
by Wm Cummens," brass stop fluted
colonettes with brass Corinthian capitals, waisted case with cross banded
hinged door, quarter columns, cross
banded base, white painted dial with
minute register, ... **17,600.00**
Duffield, Edward, Philadelphia, c1745,
rect coved cornice and arched glazed
molded door hood, brass dial with Roman and Arabic chapter rings, sweep
second ring, calendar day aperture
surmounted with an engraved disk
marked "Edw Duffield, Philadelphia,"
spandrels embellished with cast eagles and urns, waisted case with
arched thumb molded cupboard door,
box base with bun feet, 88½" h **9,350.00**
Ellicott, Joseph, Buckingham, PA,
c1760, Queen Anne, mahogany,
hood with stepped and molded flat
top, arched and glazed door, brass
dial with silvered Roman and Arabic
chapter rings, day of the month indicator inscribed, C scroll foliate spandrels, polychrome painted scene of
Colonial man in lush landscape with
Indians, hood flanked by colonettes,
waisted case, astragal bead molded
cupboard door, box base, bracket
feet, side pane of hood cracked, 87¾"
h, 19¼" w **24,200.00**
Fessler, John, Fredericktown, MD,

c1810, 99¾" h, Federal inlaid walnut, molded swan's neck pediment hood, fan inlaid terminals, three urn finials, arched hinged door, white painted dial with moon phases, minute and date registers, inscribed "John Fessler Fredericktown," waisted case with hinged door, canted corners, paneled base with inlaid canted corners, splayed bracket feet **8,250.00**

Glinn, George, Boston, c1750, 100" h, walnut, inverted bell form cresting, gilded flaming urn form finials, carved tympanum and fret carved arched frieze, waisted case with arched door and reeded columns, two train movement, strike silent dial, blocked base with carved winged animal paw feet **236,500.00**

Hassam, Stephen, Charlestown, NH, c1780, Chippendale, cherry, hood with three reeded plinths, brass finials, arched molded cornice, glazed door, engraved brass dial inscribed "Stephen Hassam," eight day brass weight driven movement, brass mounted reeded columns, tombstone molded door flanked by brass mounted reeded quarter columns, base with scrolled ogee bracket feet, old finish **5,000.00**

Huston, William, Philadelphia, c1780, Chippendale carved mahogany, molded swan's neck crest, two urn and flame finials, one ball and steeple finial center, tympanum with carved acanthus leaves, arched glazed door, engraved brass dial with moon phases, minute and calendar registers, stop fluted columns with cast metal Corinthian capitals, waisted case with shaped hinged door, fluted quarter columns, paneled base, ogee bracket feet **16,500.00**

Jones & Woods, 1850–60, black walnut case, highly carved Columbus head, mercury cut glass pendulum, Astro regulator, 83" h **14,000.00**

Louis XVI, late 19th C, gilt bronze, spherical, gilt bronze amorini borne upon clouds and holding floral garlands, mounted tapered pedestal sq section with elaborate gilt bronze floral mounts, terminating lion's paw feet, mounted on a shaped plinth raised on four gilt bronze cast acanthus feet, 90½" h **13,500.00**

Mulliken, Samuel, Bradford, Massachusetts, c1755, 85¼" h, Queen Anne, pine, molded cornice hood, two giltwood ball finials, arched glazed door, engraved brass dial above inscription "Samuel Mulliken Bradford," allegorical figural appliquéd spandrels, calendar chapter ring, turned colonettes, waisted case with rect hinged door, molded base **5,775.00**

Nutting, Wallace, case copied from John Goddard, Chippendale, mahogany, 8 day brass time and strike movement with moon phases, two block and shells, broken arch hood with three flame finials, carved rosettes, fluted hood column, fluted quarter column, blocks and shells on waist, door, and base panel **7,250.00**

Owen & Sile, Chester, PA, 1790–1810, Chippendale, carved mahogany, 8 day, white painted dial, sgd "Owen & Sile Chester," painted moon face, hood with scrolled pediment with dentil molding and rosettes, centering an urn and leaf finial above trailing leafage, glazed arch door, and fluted colonettes, waisted case with leaf carved molding over a shaped door flanked by fluted quarter columns, base with shield panel, ogee bracket feet, works may not be orig to case, 97½" h **17,500.00**

Parke, John, Patterson, New Jersey, c1810, 97½" h, Federal inlaid mahogany, molded hood with swan's neck cresting ending with flowerhead pressed gesso caps, brass ball and steeple finials, arched glazed door, white painted dial, minute and calendar date registers, rocking ship mechanism above inscription "John Parke Patterson," oval inlaid door below with fluted quarter columns, molded and cyma shape skirt, bracket feet **29,700.00**

Pearsall & Embree, New York, late 18th C, Federal, mahogany, arched hood surmounted with peaked pediment, brass acorn finials, waisted case with shaped inlaid, brass stop fluted quarter columns, molded base with bracket feet, 96" h **6,500.00**

Peaslee, Robert, Boston, MA, c1730–40, Queen Anne, inlaid walnut, coffered bonnet hood over coved molding above paneled pediment, arched glazed door with cylindrical colonettes, molded capitals and bases, brass dial with Roman and Arabic chapter rings, sweep seconds ring and calendar day aperture, circular engraved convex disk inscribed "Rob. Peaslee, Boston," waisted line inlaid case with arched line inlaid box, line inlaid applied base molding, some repairs to case molding, 91½" h, 18" w, 9¾" d **9,900.00**

Rose, Daniel, Reading, PA, c1805, 122″ h, mahogany, musical, shaped crest and fan centering inlaid conch shell hood, arched hinged door, white painted dial with moon phases, minute and date registers, abbreviated days of week, bright cut dec minute and second hands, inscribed "Daniel Rose," interlaced scrolls and woven fabric on sides of hood, waisted case with oval inlaid door and canted corners, line and bellflower inlaid base, splayed satinwood bracket feet . . . **110,000.00**

Scafe, William, London, early 18th C, George I, walnut case, silvered annular ring, Roman hours and Arabic minutes, maker's signature, day of week, moon phase, arched dial, arched and stepped hood, waisted case, 99″ h **8,000.00**

Seip, David, Bucks County, PA, 19th C, Chippendale style, birch, arched hood with swan's neck and dentilated cornice, waisted case, fluted corner columns, French bracket feet, enamel dial with second hand, lunette dial, 96″ h **13,500.00**

Taber, S., New England, early 19th C, Country Federal, grain painted, arched glazed door flanked by freestanding columns, flat top hood, waisted case with thumb molded door, molded base, short bracket feet, painted dial, 83″ h **1,600.00**

Unknown Maker
Connecticut, c1795, 84½″ h, Chippendale, inlaid cherrywood, pierced crest hood, three brass ball and steeple finials, arched glazed door, white painted dial with moon phases, minute and date registers, waisted case with scalloped oval inlaid door, fluted quarter columns, patarae inlaid base, ogee bracket feet **14,300.00**

Hepplewhite, pine, freestanding columns and high arched gooseneck hood, wood works and painted wood face, pewter hands, orig brown graining weights and pendulum, cut out feet, 82″ h **1,550.00**

Maryland, c1820, 93½″ h, Federal, inlaid mahogany, molded swan's neck pediment hood, flowerhead carved terminals, urn finial, glazed hinged door, white painted dial with moon phases, minute and date registers, fluted colonettes, waisted case with oval and diamond inlaid door, inlaid base, splayed bracket feet **3,025.00**

New England, early 19th C, Federal, mahogany, Roxbury type hood with brass stop fluted colonettes, enamel dial with date ring, waisted case with arched door, brass stop fluted quarter columns, ogee bracket feet, 96″ h **3,750.00**

Pennsylvania, cherry, free standing columns and well shaped broken arch pediment with sunburst rosettes and turned finials on hood, brass works with second hand and calendar movement and moon phases, initialed and label marked "Wilson & Osborn, Birmingham," painted metal face with flowers and strawberries, weights and pendulum, mellow finish, ogee feet, 94½″ h **5,000.00**

Wagstaffe, Thomas, London, c1785, 105″ h, George III, mahogany, pierced fretwork crest hood, three brass ball and steeple finials, glazed hinged door, engraved silvered and brass dial with minute and calendar date registers, inscribed "Tho Wagstaffe, London" hinged shaped door below, brass stop fluted quarter columns, paneled base with brass stop fluted quarter columns, bracket feet, ... **6,325.00**

Wilder, Joshua, Hingham, MA, 1815–20, Federal, mahogany, dwarf, three brass urn finials, pierced fretwork, arched glazed door, white painted dial, Roman chapter ring, sweep seconds, calendar day and day of the week rings, lunar dial, arch inscribed, spandrels embellished with gilt scrolls flanked by turned colonettes, waisted case, rect cross banded door, molded edge, cross banded box base, shaped apron, bracket feet, chalk inscription on reverse with initials "JW" and 1820, 48½″ h, 11″ w, 6⅛″ d . . . **99,000.00**

Willard, Aaron, Jr., Boston, c1810, 99½″ h, Federal, inlaid mahogany, pierced fretwork crest on hood, three brass ball and steeple finials, arched glazed door, white painted dial, polychrome basket of fruit above inscription "Aaron Willard, Jun'r, Boston," minute and calendar date registers, waisted case with hinged molded door, fluted quarter columns with brass capitals, splayed bracket feet **19,800.00**

Willard, Simon, Roxbury, MA, c1805, 95½″ h, Federal, inlaid mahogany, pierced pediment hood, three ball and steeple finials, arched glazed door, white painted dial, minute and date registers, inscribed "S Willard," brass stop fluted colonettes, waisted case, cross banded hinged door, brass stop fluted quarter columns, cross banded base, ogee bracket feet **19,800.00**

WALL

Art Deco, cherry case, 8 day Westminster chimes movement, orig finish, 35″ h **325.00**

Banjo

Chelsea, c1920, mahogany case, 8 day time and strike spring driven movement, marine lever, 33″ h . . . **550.00**

Cummens, William, Boston, MA, c1810, 8 day T-bridge movement, cross banded mahogany frames, paint tablets, sea creatures pulling shell boat with driver, old finish, orig brass finial, 34″ **2,000.00**

Howard & Davis, c1850, #1, grain painted case, 8 day weight driven time movement, second bit, orig painted and sgd dial, replaced glasses, 50″ h **2,100.00**

Howard, E. & Co., c1900, #5, oak case, 8 day time movement, replaced pendulum rod, repainted dial, 30″ h **500.00**

Jones, E., c1825, mahogany and eglomise, giltwood pineapple finial, circular glazed door, white painted dial, throat panel with floral red and gold dec, inscription "E Jones," bottom hinged door with Neptune seated in shell pulled by seahorse panel, spherule mounted gilt acorn pendant below, 43½″ h **6,600.00**

Levi Hutchins, Concord, New Hampshire, 1820, gold front, painted iron dial, 8 day time movement with T-bridge and step train, pendulum, 42″ h **800.00**

New Haven Clock Co, c1920, inlaid mahogany case, eagle finial, dec door, 12-day time movement, 17⅝″ h **150.00**

Plymouth Clock Co, Thomaston, Ct, 1930, mahogany, eagle finial, two glasses with Washington and Mount Vernon dec, painted dial, 8 day time and strike movement, chime rod, 29″ h **120.00**

Thomas, Seth, c1920, mahogany case, 8 day time spring driven movement, 30″ h **250.00**

Tifft, 1830–40, mahogany case, 8 day time movement, replaced finial and glass, 34″ h **700.00**

Unknown Maker, mahogany case, gilded facade, brass works, repainted metal face, gilded finial, replaced reverse painted glass panels, 34″ h **1,800.00**

Unknown Maker, Boston, Massachusetts, c1820, gold stenciled frames, brass eagle finial, two painted tablets, painted iron dial, 8 day time movement with iron weight and pendulum, inscribed "Cleaned by E. Taber, Oct 4, 1836," J. J. Beals paper label, 35″ h **2,700.00**

Waterbury Clock Co, c1912, Willard #3, 8 day time weight driven movement, orig glass, 43½″ h **800.00**

Whiting, Samuel, Concord, Mass, 1820, gilded bracket, painted glasses, painted iron dial, 8 day time movement, step train, T-bridge, period lead weight, touch mark "SW," 41″ h **1,550.00**

Willard, Aaron, Boston, early 19th C, Federal, gilt wood, eglomise panels surrounded by gilt twist frames, enamel dial and finial, 40″ h . . . **9,950.00**

Willard, Aaron, Jr., c1820, painted iron dial, 8 day time movement, step train, lead weight, brass pendulum, orig reverse painted tablets, inscribed "A Willard Jr./No 1860" **7,000.00**

Willard School, Boston, Mass, 1810, cross banded mahogany case, cast brass eagle finial, painted tablets, painted iron dial, 8 day time movement with T-bridge and step train, lead weight and pendulum, 34½″ h **1,500.00**

Boule, made for J.E. Caldwell & Co., Philadelphia, late 19th C, Louis XV style, brass inlaid and dore mounted case, bracket day time and strike movement elaborate porcelain and brass dial, bronze molding, 41¾″ h **3,000.00**

Calendar

Ansonia, drop octagon, 8 day, strike, rosewood veneer, gilt molding, 24″ **300.00**

Carter, L.F. & W., c1860, rosewood veneered case, 8 day time movement, B. B. Lewis calendar, 30¾″ h **500.00**

Ingraham Clock Co, 1870–80, figure "8" rosewood case, 8 day time and strike movement, B. B. Lewis calendar, two labels, 30″ h **650.00**

Ithica, No. 2 Bank, oak case, 8 day, 61″ **2,750.00**

Jerome & Co., Register, 8 day, 33¾″ **1,500.00**

Pretiss, Empire, walnut case, 60 day, two springs **2,000.00**

Thomas, Seth, c1875

Office, rosewood veneered case, 8 day time movement, calendar on bottom, 32½″ h **1,600.00**

Peanut shape, rosewood veneered case, 8 day double wind time movement, hands marked "S.T.," orig dial, refinished case, 23¼″ h **1,900.00**

Cuckoo

German, Black Forest, c1881, one day, quarter hour strike, carved ivy dec, 24" **400.00**

Keebler Clock Co., Philadelphia, PA, 1920, pressed log design, leaves, flowers, nest of birds, brass spring pendulum, 5 x 4 x 1¾" **90.00**

Lux, 1942, hunting scene, synthetic, carved wood deer head with glass eyes, spread antlers, two rifles, quail, and rabbit, half hour strike, 4" dial, white raised Roman numerals, 75" chain, 16" h, 10" w **250.00**

Unknown Maker, c1880, 30 hour pull chain time and strike movement, Black Forest movement, American label, 20" h **150.00**

Gallery

A. Martens & Co, Paris, 1890s, metal case, 8 day time movement, pendulum, dial sgd, French label, worn painted finish, 15¼" d **50.00**

Brewster & Ingraham, c1840, round, 8 day east/west time movement, sgd orig wood dial, 13" d **400.00**

E. Howard, ivory painted case, 8 day time balance wheel movement, 13½" d **200.00**

Seth Thomas, c1890, Arcade model, mahogany finish case, 30 day time movement, orig label, repainted dial, 23" d **350.00**

Unknown Maker, American, c1900, gilt finish, 8 day time movement, replaced paper dial, 26" d **300.00**

Lyre

Bingham, B. D., Nashua, American Empire, mahogany, acanthus carved body, eglomise panel, 32" h **750.00**

Taber, E., Roxbury, Mass, c1810, mahogany case, finial, 8 day weight driven time movement, 41" h **3,750.00**

Unknown Maker, 19th C, mahogany sides and face, eagle finial, lyre throat glass, door glass with eagle and cornucopia dec, 40½" h **4,250.00**

Unknown Maker, MA, 1825, painted iron dial, 8 day brass time movement, true lyre clock without lower door, carved throat with two mahogany panels and carved finial, molded base with a bracket, orig weight, refinished, 40½" **4,250.00**

Mirror

Morrill, Benjamin, New Hampshire, 1810–20, wheelbarrow 8 day time weight driven movement, orig label, 30¼" h **4,500.00**

Unknown Maker, c1820, gilded front, crest and bracket, painted tablet, painted wood dial, 8 day time brass

movement, lead weight and period pendulum, 42" h **650.00**

Miscellaneous

Dutch Friesland, 18th C, crown verge, gilded filigree dec, 26½" h **850.00**

Marble, J. Polsey, c1875, 8 day time weight driven brass movement, 31" h **900.00**

Unknown Maker, Connecticut, 1860, ebonized papier mache case, octagonal, delicate gold dec, MOP inlay, paper on zinc dial, 8 day Seth Thomas lever movement, 12¼" h **90.00**

Wall, Regulator, Seth Thomas #2, walnut case, original dial, restored and refinished, $900.00.

Regulator

Ansonia Clock Co, Ansonia, CT, 1900, rosewood grained poplar case, paper on zinc dial, black and gold tablet, 8 day time and strike movement, pendulum, paper label on case int., 24½" h **375.00**

Atkins Clock Co, c1850, short drop, mahogany veneered case, applied carving, 8 day time movement, 25½" h **350.00**

Boston Clock Co., 1880–90, painted cherry case, 8 day time movement, 34" h **800.00**

Daniel Pratt & Sons, c1870, rosewood veneered case, 8 day time movement, 21½" h **200.00**

E. Ingraham, c1910, pressed oak case, 8 day time and calendar spring driven movement, 36" h . . **400.00**

Gilbert, c1910, pressed oak case, 8 day time and strike movement, refinished, 32½" h **375.00**

Howard, c1880

Keyhole grained case, 8 day weight

driven time movement, sgd dial, label illus ten different Howard clocks, 31″ h 6,000.00

#60, black walnut case, 8 day beat escapement movement, second bit, mercury pendulum, orig and complete, 80″ h 9,000.00

#70, quarter grain carved oak case, 8 day weight driven time movement, 43½″ h 3,500.00

Little & Eastman Co., Boston, Mass, c1890, quarter grain oak case, sgd 8 day time movement, 35¼″ h ... 650.00

Sessions, c1910, Star Pointer, long drop, pressed oak case, 8 day time brass spring driven movement, label, 32¾″ h 325.00

Terry, Silas B., Plymouth, CT, 1830, mahogany veneered case, painted zinc dial, black and gold tablet, solid plate 8 day time piece, replacements and refinishing, 33½″ h 550.00

Thomas, Seth, 1860s, model #1, mahogany case, 8 day weight driven time movement, calendar on bottom, label on back door, orig dial, 41¼″ h 1,500.00

Waltham Clock Co., c1900, quarter grain oak case, 8 day weight driven time movement, 37½″ h 700.00

Waterbury Clock Co., Waterbury, CT, 1910, oak case, Regulator tablet, painted zinc dial, 8 day time and strike movement and half hour strike, pendulum, 32″ h 375.00

School House

Atkins, Whiting & Co., Bristol, CT, c1850–54, 30 day time and strike movement powered by a lever, rosewood veneered case, hexagonal shape top, rippled molding around edge, lower door with orig tablet and opens to expose label from company, minor touch up on dial, minute hand replaced, 25″ h, 17″ w 2,000.00

Ingraham, c1900, pressed oak case, 8 day time, strike, and calendar movement, 18¾″ h 325.00

Jerome, c1850, 8 day, 12″ dial, octagon, mahogany and rosewood case 300.00

New Haven Clock Co., c1870, regulator, mahogany veneered case, 8 day time movement, 24″ h 200.00

Russell & Jones, c1889, 8 day, spring, 12″ dial, gilt glass, walnut and oak case, 26″ 350.00

Sessions Clock Co., 1915–20, oak case, 8 day time, strike, and calendar movement, orig label, 19½″ h 300.00

Seth Thomas, c1920, Globe model, rosewood veneered case, 8 day time movement, long drop, orig label, 31½″ h 650.00

Waterbury Clock Co., c1890, short dew drop, mahogany veneered case, 8 day time and calendar movement, 24″ h 200.00

Wag on Wall

Astragal, English, 19th C, painted wood, painted stag above black painted clock face, gilt corner dec, white ground, 12″ h 200.00

Dutch, 18th C, 30 hour time and strike pull up movement, painted and scroll front, pierced crest of lions and flower vase, standing lions flank face, angel dec at top corners of face, retains old weights, pendulum, and wall bracket, paint touch-up, repairs, 28″ 800.00

CLOISONNÉ

History: Cloisonné is the art of enameling on metal. The design is drawn on the metal body; wires, which follow the design, are glued or soldered on the body. The cells thus created are packed with enamel and fired; this step is repeated several times until the level of enamel is higher than the wires. A buffing and polishing process brings the level of enamels flush to the surface of the wires.

This art form has been practiced in various countries since 1300 B.C. and in the Orient since the early 15th century. Most cloisonné found today is from the late Victorian era, 1870–1900, and was made in China and Japan.

Vase, black ground, metallic base, pastel flowers, Japanese, 5″ h, $175.00.

Bowl
8" d, 2½" h, yellow dragons, flaming pearl around rim and int., black ground, brass stand **130.00**
14 x 4¼", geometric design **150.00**
Box, 4¾" l, bird and flower design, red ground, marked "Made in China" **85.00**
Brush Pot, 5" h, butterfly and asters dec, light blue ground, sgd "Takeuchi," Japanese, c1875 .... **195.00**
Bulb Planter, 11⅞", quatrefoil, landscape medallions, floral dec, iron–red border, lappet band, gilt metal foot **250.00**
Charger, 12" d, pink and rose florals, green leaves, two gray flying birds and one sitting on branch, scalloped edge, turquoise blue ground **400.00**
Cigarette Canister, 3⅛" h, cylindrical; dragon dec **30.00**
Dish, 9", oval, blue lotus, 1880 ...... **90.00**
Figure
Birds, 4" h, removable heads, pr ... **220.00**
Horse, 9", Tang style, c1880 ...... **275.00**
Ginger Jar, 6¾", yellow scaly dragon, dark blue ground, ornate carved wood base, marked "China" **275.00**
Humidor, cov, 8" h, 5¾" d, colorful flowers, double "T" fret cloisonnes, light blue border, brick red ground, brass Foo dog finial, ornate teakwood base **225.00**
Incense Burner
Lion, 10", 1800 .... **400.00**
Multicolored floral dec, brass lid with cut–out butterflies, cobalt blue ground and 3 feet **225.00**
Jar, cov, 4⅛" d, 4½" h, white, blue, green, and rust with flowers and butterflies panels around top, black, gold, blue, and flowers below **290.00**
Jardiniere, 10", multicolored dragon and floral motif, black ground, teakwood base, Chinese **150.00**
Mirror, 17¾", incised birds on flowering branch mirror, pedestal, floral scrolls, blue ground **425.00**
Perfume, 2", oval, red, gold, blue, and white florals, hanging loops **75.00**
Plate
5" d, multicolored, phoenix bird in tree **140.00**
7¼" d, mallard duck, blue ground, Chinese **100.00**
Salt and Pepper Shakers, pr, 2" d, 2½" h, pale blue fishscale ground, one with multicolored dragon, other with cranes, Japanese **225.00**
Sauceboat, turquoise artichoke dec, green handle, marked "China" **110.00**
Teapot, cov, 3½" h, double gourd shape, diagonal flower and butterflies bands, white and green interspersed with black and goldstone, Japanese **245.00**
Tumbler, 3¾" h, beaker shape, flared,

iron–red serpentine dragon, sky blue ground **110.00**
Vase
3½" h, 1¾" d, multicolored peacock, silver wire flowers at bottom, white foil ground, Japanese **650.00**
6", multicolored floral design, yellow ground, multicolored floral design and medallion with dark blue ground **250.00**
9¾" h, 3¾" d, exotic dragons on shield shaped panels, green with goldstone, butterflies around top, blue ground, Japanese **395.00**
10", pottery, 2 blue, turquoise, rust, and black panels, butterfly rim ... **300.00**
18", egg shape body, high flared foot, thin neck, everted scalloped rim, yellow band of stylized dragons, turquoise ground, China, late 18th C **800.00**
18½" h, 7½" d, bird in cherry tree, deep pink and white blossoms, green leaves, pink ground, Japan **12,000.00**

CLOTHING

History: While museums and a few private individuals have collected clothing for decades, it is only recently that collecting clothing has achieved a widespread popularity. Clothing reflects the social attitudes of a historical period.

Christening and wedding gowns abound and hence are not in large demand. Among the hardest items to find are men's clothing from the 19th and early 20th centuries. The most sought after clothing is by designers, such as Fortuny, Poiret, and Vionnet.

Note: Condition, size, age, and completeness are critical factors in purchasing clothing. Collectors divide into two groups: those collecting for aesthetic and historic value and those desiring to wear the garment. Prices are higher on the West coast; major auction houses focus on designer clothes and high fashion items.

References: C. Willett Cunnington, *English Women's Clothing in the Nineteenth Century,* Dover Publications, 1990 (reprint of 1937 book); Maryanne Dolan, *Vintage Clothing 1880–1960,* Second Edition, Books Americana, 1987; Cynthia Giles, *The Official Identification And Price Guide To Vintage Clothing,* House of Collectibles, 1989; Tina Irick-Nauer, *The First Price Guide to Antique and Vintage Clothes,* E.P. Dutton, 1983; Sheila Malouff, *Clothing With Prices,* Wallace-Homestead, 1983; Terry McCormick, *The Consumer's Guide To Vintage Clothing,* Dembner Books, 1987; Diane McGee, *A Passion For Fashion: Antique, Collectible, and Retro Clothes,* Simmons-Boardman Books, 1987.

Periodical: *Vintage Clothing Newsletter*, P.O. Box 1422, Corvallis, OR 97339.

Collectors' Club: The Costume Society of America, P.O. Box 761, Englishtown, NJ 07726.

Museums: Los Angeles County Museum (Costume and Textile Dept.), Los Angeles, CA; Metropolitan Museum of Art, New York, NY; Museum of Costume, Bath, England; Philadelphia Museum of Art, Philadelphia, PA; Smithsonian Institution (Inaugural Gown Collection), Washington, D.C.

Additional Listings: See *Warman's Americana & Collectibles* for more examples.

Bathing Suit, man's, black wool, $40.00.

Baby Christening Outfit, cotton, gown, slip, and matching cap, white, c1920	85.00
Baby Sacque, cotton, embroidered, Victorian	45.00
Bed Jacket, rayon, peach, quilted, c1940	18.00
Blouse	
Cotton, large collar with crocheted accents, white, fitted at waist	35.00
Silk chiffon, beaded front, c1915	25.00
Bodice and Skirt, girl's, gray striped silk, printed black flock, black velvet trim, c1876	65.00
Camisole, cotton, white, lace, Victorian	60.00
Cape	
Net, appliquéd, short, c1840	35.00
Wool, black, ribbons, black beading, c1880	75.00
Chemise, linen, short sleeves, lawn frill trim, monogrammed, c1820	45.00
Doublet, gentleman's, velvet, emerald green, gold sequins and paste jewels, embroidered, hose, late 18th C, 17th C style, European, altered	150.00
Dress	
Chiffon, chemise flapper style, black	

embroidered net, blue and black abstract and foliate motifs, bugle beaded openwork insertions **350.00**

Cotton, white, whitework neckline, short pull sleeve, waist, vandyked hem and front panel, American, c1820	715.00
Crepe, brown, silvered sequined bodice, peplum, matching hat, c1940	65.00
Homespun Linen, child's, blue, yellow, and white plaid, drawstring neck, high waist, long set-in sleeves, American, c1830, minor discoloration	300.00
Muslin, embroidered stripes, long sleeves, tucking edges, c1820	135.00
Silk	
Cream and gray stripes, fitted bodice, geometric and foliate pattern skirt, beads, sequin, and rhinestone trim, designed by Mainbocher	140.00
Olive Green, printed pink chino flowers, labeled "Riley, East Orange, NJ" c1893	85.00
Red, crystal beaded bodice, full skirt, c1950	35.00
Silk Gauze, ivory, posies of pink roses, blue hydrangea, labeled "B Altman & Co, made in Paris," c1914	285.00
Dressing Jacket, muslin, lace trim	465.00
Duster, lawn, white, watteau back, lace trim, handmade, c1880	50.00
Evening Coat, black velvet, ermine trim ties, full length, c1930	75.00
Fur Coat, Persian lamb, black, matching hat, medium, orig Petra Furriers–Waterloo, Iowa label	60.00
Jacket	
Lady's, velvet, mushroom color, cut and embroidered, gold thread, cut steel, scrolling leaves and tassels, attached ivory satin waistcoat bodice, pink watered silk lining, Worth, Paris label, c1900	1,650.00
Man's, suede, brown, all over fringe trim, marked "Berman Buckskin Co"	100.00
Nightgown	
Cotton, white, crocheted bodice	25.00
Lawn, embroidered flowers, valenciennes lace trim, monogrammed, matching chemise and drawers, c1890	100.00
Satin, pink, lace trim, medium	20.00
Nightshirt, man's, cotton, white, long	25.00
Pajamas	
Satin, pink, monogrammed pocket, white piping trim	35.00
Silk, pink, ribbon rosettes, crocheted trim, c1920	90.00

Petticoat, cotton

Lace insert, initials "S D," c1900 ... **40.00**

Tucking trim, inscribed "Kathie Morres," c1860 .... **45.00**

Riding Habit, wool, black, lady's side saddle type, 2 pcs **125.00**

Robe

Cotton, green print, medium, 1893 **40.00**

Indian Blanket, multicolored, c1940 **35.00**

Shirt, man's, homespun linen, natural color, button closure **50.00**

Skirt

Felt, circular, pink, appliquéd poodles, flowers, and beads, c1950 ...... **15.00**

Muslin, white, full length, deep tucks, ruffled flounce, hand embroidered **40.00**

Slip, cotton, white, rows of tucks and lace inserts, crocheted top and flowers **25.00**

Suit, boy's, double breasted, velvet pants, silk shirt, 1907 .... **40.00**

Swimsuit, wool, green and wine, orig Bradley Wool Knitwear label, c1920 **25.00**

Teddy

Batiste, c1920 .... **12.00**

Silk, peach, hairpin lace yoke **30.00**

Wedding Gown, satin, wax flowers, beaded hat, Victorian **185.00**

CLOTHING ACCESSORIES

References: Rod Dyer & Ron Spark, *Fit To Be Tied: Vintage Ties Of The Forties And Early Fifties,* Abbeville, 1987; Evelyn Haetig, *Antique Combs & Purses,* Gallery Graphics Press, 1983; Richard and Teresa Holiner, *Antique Purses,* Second Edition, Collector Books, 1987; Mary Trasko, *Heavenly Soles: Extraordinary Twentieth-Century Shoes,* Abbeville Press, 1989.

Additional Listings: See *Warman's Americana & Collectibles* for more examples.

Handbag, beaded, floral design, crocheted top, green, rose, yellow, and white design, $60.00.

Apron

Cotton, green and white check, hand sewn **40.00**

Linen, Irish, crocheted filet trim, pocket **15.00**

Bonnet

Cotton, baby's, ecru, embroidery, c1870 .... **35.00**

Velvet, black, sequin trimmed multicolored silk band, lace trim, huge bow, feathers, jet beading, c1900 **40.00**

Booties, baby, cream wool, red braid trim, c1850 .... **85.00**

Chasuble

Brocatelle, gold, green and gold orphrey, 16th C **200.00**

Velvet, crimson, orphrey embroidered colored silks, metal thread, roundels of Madonna and Child, four Saints within strapwork, Spanish, 16th C **2,750.00**

Dalmatic, silk, crimson, gold thread embroidered flowers, 18th C **475.00**

Garters, child's, Lord Milford, orig card **18.00**

Gloves, man's, clipped buffalo and leather, medium **50.00**

Handbag

Alligator, marked "Made in Cuba" .. **50.00**

Beaded

Multicolored, 14K gold frame, jeweled clasp, marked "Black Starr & Frost" **375.00**

White, silk, opal beads and sequins **20.00**

Mesh, enameled, gold, black, and white, curved frame, cabochon sapphire thumbpiece, foxtail tassel, seed pearls, mesh strap, enamel slide **1,000.00**

Suede, clutch, flap front with cut out sterling silver plaque at each end with chyrosprase stone and gold wash accents, Austria silver standard mark and makers mark "A. F.," retailers stamp "Spaulding & Co" inside suede **250.00**

Velvet, black, silver Art Deco embroidery, 8" l **50.00**

Hat

Derby, black felt **25.00**

Flapper type, fur, feathers and rhinestones **20.00**

Panama, man's size 7 .... **30.00**

Necktie, Brussels lace, 19th C **45.00**

Parasol

French, lace

Brussels lace over Saxe blue silk, carved ivory handle with bees on tree trunk, entwined ribbon, acorn finial, c1860 .... **125.00**

Chantilly, black lace over black satin, carved ivory chain link handle, c1860 .... **175.00**

Shawl

Silk, Chinese, ivory, embroidered flowering vines, knotted silk fringe **85.00**

Wool, green, beige, and olive green plaid, fringed	**25.00**
Stockings, nylon, orig package	**35.00**
Sweater, child's, sailboat motif, red, white, and blue	**20.00**
Veil, ecru net and lace, full length, 1918	**100.00**

Tureen, cov, handled, Imari type dec, polychromed finial, c1805–10, 9″ d 10½″ h, $1,200.00.

COALPORT

History: In the mid-1750s Ambrose Gallimore established a pottery at Caughley in the Severn Gorge, Shropshire, England. Several other potteries, e.g., Jackfield, developed in the area.

About 1795 John Rose and Edward Blakeway built a pottery at Coalport, a new town founded along the right-of-way of the Shropshire Canal. Other potteries located adjacent to the canal were those of Walter Bradley and Anstice, Horton, and Rose. In 1799 Rose and Blakeway bought the "Royal Salopian China Manufactory" at Caughley. In 1814 this operation was moved to Coalport.

A bankruptcy in 1803 led to refinancing and a new name, John Rose and Company. In 1814 Anstice, Horton, and Rose was acquired. The South Wales potteries at Swansea and Nantgarw were added. The expanded firm made fine quality, highly decorated ware. The plant enjoyed a renaissance in the 1888 to 1900 period.

World War I, decline in trade, and shift of the pottery industry away from the Severn Gorge brought hard times to Coalport. In 1926 the firm, now owned by Cauldon Potteries, moved from Coalport to Shelton. Later owners included Crescent Potteries, Brain & Co., Ltd., and finally, in 1967, Wedgwood.

References: Susan and Al Bagdade, *Warman's English & Continental Pottery & Porcelain, 1st Edition,* Warman Publishing Co., Inc., 1987; Michael Messenger, *Coalport 1795–1926, Antique Collectors' Club,* 1990.

Additional Listings: Indian Tree Pattern.

Creamer and Sugar, Indian Tree pattern, c1920, pr	**65.00**
Dessert Service, partial, assembled, Rock and Tree pattern, Imari palette, gilt edges, c1805–10, 19 pcs	**3,575.00**
Dinner Service, partial, iron–red bellflower vine intertwined with gilt scrolling foliate vine, feather molded gilded rims, c1820, 132 pcs	**17,600.00**
Ink Stand, 6½″ l, crescent shape, yellow foliage scroll border, gilt edged orange band, gold diamond devices border, gilt foliate dec on top, four pen holes, three larger apertures, two ink pots, pounce pot, c1805	**425.00**
Miniature, cup and saucer, 1″ h, cobalt blue, heavy gold trim, gold beading	**100.00**
Plate, 10⅜″ d, green ground, three cartouches with floral bouquets on rim, white center with large floral bouquet, gilt bellflowers border, imp potter's mark, minor damage, set of 12, c1825	**1,200.00**
Platter, 10¾″ l, Tobacco Leaf pattern, Chinese export style, underglaze blue, turquoise, chartreuse, rose, iron–red, yellow, green, salmon, puce, and gold, scalloped rim with underglaze blue band, four underglaze blue flowering branches on underside, c1805, pr	**2,500.00**
Tea Service, cov teapot and stand, creamer, cov sugar, birds perched on branches, gilt scroll, trellis, and foliate borders alternating with panels of reserved flowers, blue ground, gilt line rims, c1820	**660.00**

COCA-COLA ITEMS

History: The originator of Coca-Cola was John Pemberton, a pharmacist from Atlanta, Georgia. In 1886 Dr. Pemberton introduced a patent medicine to relieve headaches, stomach disorders, and other minor maladies. Unfortunately, his failing health and meager finances forced him to sell his interest.

In 1888 Asa G. Candler became the sole owner of Coca-Cola. Candler improved the formula, increased the advertising budget, and widened the distribution. Accidentally, a "patient" was given a dose of the syrup mixed with carbonated water instead of still water. The result was a tastier, more refreshing drink.

As sales increased in the 1890s, Candler recognized that the product was more suitable for the soft drink market and began advertising it as such. From these beginnings a myriad of advertising items have been issued to invite all to "Drink Coca-Cola."

Dates of interest: "Coke" was first used in advertising in 1941. The distinctive shaped bottle was registered as a trademark on April 12, 1960.

References: Deborah Goldstein Hill, *Wallace-Homestead Price Guide to Coca-Cola Collectibles,* Wallace Homestead, 1983; Allan Petretti, *Petretti's Coca-Cola Collectibles Price Guide,* The Nostalgia Company, 1989; Al Wilson, *Collectors Guide To Coca-Cola Items, Volume I,* (revised: 1987) and *Volume II,* (1987), L-W Book Sales.

Collectors' Club: The Coca-Cola Collectors Club International, P.O. Box 546, Holmdel, NJ 07733.

Museum: Schmidt's Coca-Cola Museum, Elizabethtown, KY.

Additional Listings: See *Warman's Americana & Collectibles* for more examples.

Tray, Spring Board Girl, artist Sunblom, 1939, 13 x 10″, $125.00.

Ashtray, aluminum, emb, 1950s	5.00
Banner	
13 x 41″, "Have a Coke Compliments of this Store," 1950s	25.00
19 x 57″, 1939	75.00
Blotter	
1923	35.00
1955, children at party scene	5.00
1956	4.00
Bottle Carrier, six holder	
Cardboard, 1930s	40.00
Metal	25.00

Bottle Opener, eagle head, 1912–20	100.00
Button, uniform, ¾″, c1910	45.00
Calendar	
1917, woman holding glass	900.00
1923, lady holding bottle	375.00
1931, boy and dog	475.00
1942, man, woman, and snowman	75.00
Chalkboard, tin, 1958	95.00
Change Purse, triangle shape, c1908	85.00
Change Receiver, Drink Coca-Cola 5¢, 1911	700.00
Change Tray, 1912	200.00
Cigar Band	35.00
Clock	
Dome, 6 x 9″, 1950s	800.00
Schoolhouse, octagon, Roman numerals, E Ingraham Co, Bristol, Conn, 1903–05	1,750.00
Coaster, aluminum, set of 6	25.00
Cribbage Board, 1940s	45.00
Display, store, bottle, 1930s	250.00
Door Push	
Aluminum, 1905	300.00
Porcelain, bottle shape, 16″, 1950s	145.00
Festoon	
Autumn Leaves, 1922	600.00
Morning Glory, 1932	500.00
Flyswatter, wire mesh, wood handle, 1942	5.00
Glass, bell shape, 1929–40	30.00
Ice Chest, metal	55.00
Ice Scoop, plastic	5.00
Ice Tong, 1920s	150.00
Menu Board	
Cardboard, 1950s	40.00
Tin, 1939	75.00
Wood, metal trim, 1940s	150.00
Mug, ceramic, emb "Coca-Cola," c1920	500.00
Pocket Knife, stainless two blades, marked "Remington," c1930	100.00
Pocket Watch, "Time for a Cold Bottle of Coca-Cola," 1920s	750.00
Pretzel Dish, aluminum, 1930s	195.00
Punch Card, 5¼ x 6½″, 1940s	25.00
Radio	
Bottle shape, 30″, 1933	1,500.00
Cooler shape, 1949	595.00
Ruler, wood, 1940s	5.00
Sign	
6 x 12″, glass, "Drink Coca-Cola, Please Pay When Served," 1932	750.00
10 x 30″, paper, man holding hot dog and bottle, "An Ice Cold with a Red Hot," metal strip top and bottom	275.00
11 x 35″, tin, 1941	175.00
12 x 29″, porcelain, "Coca-Cola Sold Here Ice Cold," 1940s	225.00
12 x 36″, tin, "Drink Coca-Cola In Bottles 5¢," c1908	650.00
14 x 30″, cardboard, oblong, bottle and hamburger, "Tasty together!," 1934	125.00

16 x 27", cardboard, two dancers, "Entertain your thirst," wood frame, 1943 .... **150.00**
18 x 54", tin, "Serve Coca-Cola at Home," 1950 .... **150.00**
20 x 15", tin, emb, 1927 .... **1,400.00**
21 x 38", cardboard, girl seated waving one hand, glass in other, 1931 **375.00**
29 x 56", cardboard, "Mind Reader," c1940 .... **100.00**
36 x 52", man with bicycle, bottle in one hand, "Drink Coca-Cola," late 1940s **125.00**
Syrup Bottle, label under glass, c1920s **300.00**
Thermometer
  1908, 5 x 21", wood **195.00**
  1923, oval, with bottle, pat "Dec 25th, 1923" **50.00**
  1930, 17" l, tin, bottle shape **100.00**
  1941, bottles **125.00**
  1950, 9", tin **140.00**
  1959, 12" d, round, "Drink Coca-Cola, Be Really Refreshed" **100.00**
Toy, truck, 19", wood, Buddy L, c1940 **1,500.00**
Tray
  1905, 10½ x 13", oval **1,800.00**
  1910, 10½ x 13¼" **500.00**
  1913, 12½ x 15¼", oval **500.00**
  1916, 8½ x 19", oblong **200.00**
  1934, Johnny Weissmuller **200.00**
  1938, 10½ x 13¼", seated lady holding bottle **85.00**
  1948, screened background **40.00**
Umbrella, 1920s **750.00**
Vienna Art Plate, topless girl, orig gold frame, 1908 .... **700.00**
Whistle, wood, 1920s **50.00**
YoYo, 1930s **50.00**

COFFEE MILLS

History: Coffee mills or grinders are utilitarian objects designed to grind fresh coffee beans. Before the advent of stay-fresh packaging, coffee mills were a necessity.

The first home size coffee grinders were introduced about 1890. The large commercial grinders designed for use in stores, restaurants, and hotels often bear an earlier patent date.

Reference: Terry Friend, *Coffee Mills,* Collector Books, 1982.

COUNTERTOP (COMMERCIAL)

Enterprise No 3, 15" h, cast iron, two wheel, orig red paint and decals ... **595.00**
Fairbanks-Morse, 38" h, 2 wheels, brass finial, white paint **350.00**
J Wright, cast iron, two wheel **75.00**
Golden Rule, cast iron **195.00**

Imperial No. 1 Mill, 6⅞" sq, 9½" h, manufactured by Arcade Co., Patented June 5, 1894, $85.00.

FLOOR MODEL (COMMERCIAL)

Dell, John C. & Sons, 66" h, sand blasted and primed cast iron, brass hopper, 33" wheels **900.00**
Enterprise, 72" h **400.00**

LAP (DOMESTIC)

De Ve, 4¼" h, wood, copper plated top and crank, drawer **35.00**
Imperial, 5½" sq, dovetailed box **25.00**
Logan & Strobridge, machine dovetailed, cast iron hopper and handle, oak base **70.00**
Rock Hard, Garant-Sewaarborge, maple, aluminum hopper, drawer **25.00**
Unmarked, 5" sq, tin, decorative iron mechanism **55.00**

TABLE (DOMESTIC)

Charles Parker Co, 14¼" h, cast iron handle and crank, tin top and filler **80.00**
Enterprise Mfg Co, No 0, 11½" h, cast iron, clamp on type, stenciled flag dec **160.00**
Peugeot Freres Brevetes, 20" h, cast iron, wood drawer, emb brass label, black paint over green, wood base, France c1900 .... **70.00**
Unmarked, 13" h, emb cast iron top, slide open hopper **70.00**

WALL (DOMESTIC)

Brighton, cast iron, mounted on wood board **65.00**

Koffie, red glass canister, crank handle, measuring cup at base, mounted on board **75.00**

Parker 50, cast iron and tin, emb eagle .. **40.00**

Royal, cast iron **35.00**

Steinfield #17, lacy iron grinder, glass canister **35.00**

COIN OPERATED ITEMS

History: Coin operated items include amusement games, pinball, jukeboxes, slot machines, vending machines, cash registers and other items operated by coins.

The first jukebox was developed about 1934 and played 78 RPM records. Jukeboxes were important parts of teenage life before the advent of portable radios and television.

The first pinball machine was introduced in 1931 by Gottlieb. Pinball machines continued to be popular until the advent of solid state games in 1977 and advanced electronic video games.

The first three-reel slot machine, the Liberty Bell, was invented in 1905 by Charles Fey in San Francisco. In 1910, Mills Novelty Company copyrighted the classic fruit symbols. Improvements and advancements have lead to the sophisticated machines of today.

Vending machines for candy, gum, and peanuts were popular from 1910 until 1940 and can be found in a wide range of sizes and shapes.

Because of the heavy usage these coin operated items received, many are restored and at the very least have been repainted by either the operator or manufacturer. Using reproduced mechanisms to restore pieces is acceptable in many cases, especially when the restoration will be able to perform as originally intended.

References: Jerry Ayliffe, *American Premium Guide To Jukeboxes And Slot Machines, Gumballs, Trade Stimulators, Arcade,* Books Americana, 1985; Richard Bueschel, *Pinball I: Illustrated Historical Guide To Pinball Machines, Volume I,* Hoflin Publishing Ltd., 1988; Richard Bueschel, *Slots 1: Illustrated Guide to 100 Collectible Slot Machines, Volume 1,* Hoflin Publishing Ltd., 1989; Nic Costa, *Automatic Pleasures: The History Of The Coin Machine,* Kevin Francis Publishing Ltd., 1988; Bill Enes, *Silent Salesmen: An Encyclopedia Of Collectible Gum, Candy & Nut Machines,* published by author, 1987; Stephen K. Loots, *"The Official Victory Glass Price Guide To Antique Jukeboxes, 1988 (Third) Edition," Jukebox Collector Newsletter,* 1988.

Periodicals: *Coin-Op Newsletter,* 909 26th Street, N.W., Washington, DC 20037; *Jukebox Collector Newsletter,* 2545 SE 60th Street, Des Moines, IA 50317.

Additional Listings: See *Warman's Americana & Collectibles* for separate categories for Jukeboxes, Pinball Machines, Slot Machines, and Vending Machines.

GAME

Chester Pollard, arcade, derby race, wheel mechanism moves horses around track, c1903 .... **2,000.00**

Contact Junior, pinball, wood case, Pacific Amusement Mfg Co, 1933 .... **750.00**

Iron Claw, arcade, Exhibit Supply Co, 1926 .... **1,250.00**

Kicker & Catcher, Baker Novelty Co, c1935 .... **200.00**

Shoot the Bear, arcade, Seeburg, includes manuals **1,500.00**

Spear the Dragon, arcade, Exhibit Supply Co, restored, c1927 .... **5,500.00**

National Cash Register, Model 422, small crank, bronze, mahogany base, 1912, 20 x 16¾ x 23", $850.00.

JUKEBOX

AMI Hideaway, seven 200 selection wall boxes **2,550.00**

Ristaucrat Inc, countertop selector ... **900.00**

Rockola

Counter type, 12 selection, 1939 ... **750.00**

Floor type, 1428, wood work, ornate trim, lights up **3,250.00**

Seeberg

Model VL **3,200.00**

Symphonola, wood dec, 78 rpm, c1936 .... **1,200.00**

Western Electric Selectraphone, pneumatic driven record selector, 1928 .. **3,000.00**

Wurlitzer

Model 24, 24 selection, 1938 ..... **2,250.00**

Model 800, 20 selection, visible turntable system, 1940 .... **2,750.00**

Model 1700, 45 rpm, 104 selections, orig, 1950s **3,000.00**

SLOT MACHINE

Caille's Bull Frog, upright, 1904 ..... 13,500.00
Jennings
  Improved Century Vender, counter
    top type, 5¢, restored cabinet ... 1,500.00
  Little Duke, counter top type, 1¢ ... 1,950.00
Mills
  Black Cherry, counter top type, 5¢,
    repainted 1,400.00
  Four Bells, console, 5¢, 1939–48 .. 700.00
  Owl, upright, oak cabinet, c1897 ... 6,000.00
Pace, The Kitty, 25¢, countertop 3,500.00
Wattling, Lincoln De Lux, counter top
  type, 5¢, 1926–29 .... 2,000.00

VENDING

Advance Model, gumball, 1¢, restored,
  c1923 .... 200.00
Bull's Head, perfume, 15″ h, cast iron
  and glass, orig paint, paper directions 3,200.00
Clawson Machine Co, 1¢, candy, cast
  iron, tiger striped copper finish, pat
  Oct 24, 1917 .... 1,250.00
Dixie Cups, glass cylinder with cast
  metal mechanism, 1¢ operation ... 120.00
Jacob's, 5¢, cigar, 36″ w, wood, glass,
  and metal, accommodates three
  brands, marked, pat 1907 .... 1,400.00
Master, 16″ h, gumball, 1¢, Norris Mfg
  Co, c1923 .... 190.00
Mabey Electric Eat 'Em Hot, peanut,
  orig cup dispenser, c1934 .... 350.00
National Dispenser Co, 1¢, mints, four
  cylindrical glass columns, rotating
  lazy Susan style, pre 1939 .... 125.00
Northwestern Vending Corp, match,
  cast iron, dolphin design, 1¢, attached cigar cutter 475.00
Silver Comet, 6 x 6½ x 8″, cigarette,
  counter top type, 1¢, Redco Products,
  La Crosse, Wisconsin, c1930 ..... 160.00
Wilbur's Chocolate, glass dome, metal
  base, National Vending Machine Co,
  c1904 .... 2,500.00
Whiffs of Fragrance, perfume, 17″h, 14″
  w, cast aluminum, orig polychrome
  dec, paper instructions, and labels on
  bottles, Mills Novelty Co, c1912 ... 5,700.00

MISCELLANEOUS

Cash Register, National, Model 8, orig
  top and clock, orig delivery sticker
  marked "4/17/1900" 1,800.00
Knotty Peek, 1¢ 450.00
Music Box, 17″ l, 5″ h, Swiss cylinder,
  eight tunes, 6″ cylinder with single
  comb, faux rosewood case 420.00
Postage Stamp, 22″ h, 10″ w, aluminum

and wood, beveled mirror, 2, 4, and
  5¢ stamps 1,700.00
Radio, Kollerola, hotel model, 25¢ for
  two hours, keys, Madison, Wisconsin 225.00
Trade Stimulator, Chicago Club House,
  counter top type, 1¢ gumball, poker
  wheels, Daval 360.00
Weighing, National Automatic, 69″ h,
  cast iron, porcelain dial, ornate, nice
  patina, period repaint in silver, 1¢ .. 1,000.00

COMIC BOOKS

History: Shortly after comics first appeared in
the newspapers of the 1890s, they were reprinted
in book format, often used as promotional giveaways by manufacturers, movie theaters, candy
stores, and stationery stores. The first modern format comic was issued in 1933.

The magic date is June 1938 when DC issued
Action Comics No. 1, marking the first appearance
of Superman. Thus began comics' "Golden Age,"
which lasted until the mid-1950s and witnessed
the birth of the major comic book publishers, titles,
and characters.

In 1954 Fredric Wertham authored *Seduction of
the Innocent*, a book which pointed a guilt-laden
finger at the comic industry for corrupting youth,
causing juvenile delinquency and undermining
American values. Many publishers were forced out
of business, while others established a "comics
code" to assure parents that their comics were
compliant with morality and decency censures up-
held by the code authority.

Comics "Silver Age," mid-1950s through the end
of the 1960s, witnessed the revival of many of the
characters from the Golden Age in new comic formats. The era began with *Showcase No. 4* in
October 1956, which marked the origin and first
appearance of the Silver Age Flash.

While comics survived in the 1970s, it was a low
point for the genre. In the early 1980s a revival
occurred. In 1983 comic book publishers, aside
from Marvel and DC, issued more titles than existed in the past forty years. The mid and late
1980s were a boom time, a trend which appears
to be continuing into the 1990s.

References: Ernst and Mary Gerber (compi-
lers), *Photo-Journal Guide To Comics, Volume
One (A-J)* and *Volume 2 (K-Z)*, Gerber Publishing
Company, 1990; John Hegenberger, *Collector's
Guide To Comic Books*, Wallace-Homestead,
1990; D. W. Howard, *Investing in Comics*, The
World of Yesterday, 1988; Robert Overstreet, *The
Official Overstreet Comic Book Price Guide, No.
20*, House of Collectibles, 1990.

Periodical: *Comic Buyers Guide*, 700 State
Street, Iola, WI 54990.

Museum: Museum of Cartoon Art, Rye, NY.

Reproduction Alert: Publishers frequently reprint popular stories, even complete books, so the

buyer must pay strict attention to the title, not just the portion printed in outsized letters on the front cover. If there is any doubt, look inside at the fine print on the bottom of the inside cover or first page. The correct title will be printed there in capital letters.

Also pay attention to the size of the comic. Reprints often differ in size from the original.

Note: The comics listed below are in fine condition, meaning they have a cover that has almost no wear, is still relatively flat, clean, and shiny, and has no subscription crease, writing, yellowing at margins, or tape repairs. Minor color flaking is permitted at the spine, staples, or corners. Inside, a hint of yellowing is acceptable.

Dell, *Andy Panda,* Feb–April 1958, $1.00.

PRE-GOLDEN AGE

Ace Comics, No. 4, David McKay Publications 125.00
Famous Funnies, No. 3, Buck Rogers strip reprints begin, Eastern Color .. 500.00
King Comics, No. 12, strip reprint, David McKay Publications 80.00
Star Comics, No. 5, Little Nemo, Ultem Publishing 100.00
Western Picture Stories, No. 1, Comics Magazine Company 300.00

GOLDEN AGE

Adventure Comics, No. 271, origin of Luthor, DC 35.00
Adventures of Bob Hope, No. 22, National Periodical Publications 15.00
All Star Western, No. 67, Johnny Thunder begins, National Periodical Publications 27.50
Batman, No. 140, Joker story 30.00
Bride Romances, No. 8, Quality Comics Group 5.00
Cisco Kid Comics, No. 2, Dell Publishing 17.50
Dark Mysteries, No. 20, female bondage and blood drainage story, Master-Merit Publications 25.00
Dennis The Menace, No. 11, Giant Christmas issue, Winter 1962 ..... 10.00
Donald Duck, No. 134, Gold Key 3.50
Falling In Love, No. 22 .... 5.00
Flash Comics, No. 35, origin of Shade, National Periodical Publications ... 150.00
Four Color, No. 88, Bugs Bunny's Great Adventure, Dell 35.00
GI Combat, No. 33, Quality Comics Group 7.00
Gunsmoke, No. 18, Dell 12.50
Howdy Doody, No. 8, Dell 14.00
Jungle Comics, No. 57, Fiction House Magazines 50.00
Little Iodine, No. 9, Dell 4.00
Looney Tunes and Merrie Melodies Comics, No. 80, Dell 7.00
Love Romances, No. 57, Matt Baker artist, Marvel 7.50
The Lucy Show, No. 2, Gold Key 15.00
March of Comics, Western Publishing
No. 95, Oswald Rabbit 8.00
No. 116, Roy Rogers 20.00
No. 166, Santa and His Reindeer .. 4.00
No. 282, Mister Ed 7.00
No. 423, Little Monsters 1.50
Mickey Mouse, No. 68, Dell 2.50
National Velvet, 4-Color 1312, Dell ... 8.00
Perfect Love, No. 7, Ziff-Davis 8.00
Porky Pig, No. 42, Gold Key 2.00
Rawhide Kid, No. 1, Atlas 70.00
Richie Rich, No. 47, Harvey Publications 6.00
Rod Cameron Western, No. 2, Fawcett Publications 45.00
Romantic Love, No. 19, Realistic 15.00
Sheena, Queen of the Jungle, No. 12, Fiction House Magazine 40.00
Smiley Burnette Western, No. 3, Fawcett Publications 30.00
Star Spangled War Stories, No. 22, National Periodical Publications 14.00
77 Sunset Strip, 4-Color 1106, Gold Key 18.00
Space Patrol, No. 2, Ziff-Davis Publishing Co. 100.00
Straight Arrow, No. 33, Magazine Enterprises 8.00
Superboy, No. 122, DC 2.00
Tessie The Typist, No. 3 .... 15.00
Terrors of the Jungle, No. 8, Star Publications 27.50
Uncle Milty, No. 1, Victoria Publications 60.00
Uncle Scrooge, No. 55, Gold Key 12.00
Walt Disney Comics, No. 37, Donald Duck, Dell 65.00
Weird Mysteries, No. 7, used in *Seduction of the Innocent*, Gillmore Publications 75.00
Wonder Woman, No. 35, National Periodical Publications 55.00

SILVER AGE

Action Comics, No. 269, DC	17.50
The Amazing Spiderman, No. 290, Marvel	1.00
Aquaman, No. 2, DC	60.00
Avengers, No. 88, Marvel	4.00
Barry N. Goldwater, Dell	8.00
Captain America, No. 255, 40th Anniversary, Marvel	3.00
Captain Atom, No. 11, Millennium, DC	1.00
Casper, The Friendly Ghost, No. 48, Harvey Publications	7.50
Daredevil, No. 25, Marvel	10.00
Doom Patrol, No. 4, DC	2.00
Fantastic Four, Marvel	
No. 1	3,000.00
No. 23	50.00
No. 198	1.50
No. 320, Thing vs. Hulk	1.50
House of Mystery, No. 180, DC	2.50
Huckleberry Hound, No. 33, Gold Key	2.50
Incredible Hulk, No. 175, Marvel	2.00
Justice League, No. 3, DC	7.50
MAD, No. 105, Batman TV show take-off, EC Comics	2.50
Marvel Team Up, No. 18, Torch and Hulk, Marvel	3.00
New Teen Titans, No. 16, DC	3.00
Strange Tales, No. 128, Marvel	10.00
Thor, No. 185, Marvel	1.75
Top Cat, No. 14, Gold Key	3.00
Warlord, No. 31, DC	3.00
X-Men, No. 39, new costumes, Marvel	12.50

POST-SILVER AGE

Adolescent Radioactive Black Belt Hamsters, No. 1, black and white, Eclipse	2.00
Airboy, No. 8, Rescue Davy, Eclipse ..	3.00
Battlestar Galactica, No. 4, Marvel ...	.30
Blood Sword, No. 7, JAD	1.50
Conan The Barbarian, No. 23, first appearance of Red Sonja, Marvel	6.00
Dagar The Invincible, No. 3, introduces Graylin, Dagar's woman, Gold Key	2.00
Dick Tracy in 3-D, No. 1, Blackthorne	2.00
Dragonforce, No. 3, black and white, Aircel	2.00
Elfquest, No. 2, 2nd printing, $1.25 cover, WARP Graphics	2.50
Further Adventures of Indiana Jones, No. 8, Marvel	.75
Mai, The Psychic Girl, No. 2, 1st printing, Eclipse	2.00
Mighty Mites, No. 2, Batman parody, Eternity	2.00
Omaha The Cat Dancer, No. 2, Steeldragon	2.00
The Saga of the Swamp Thing, No. 27, DC	3.00

Star Trek, No. 5, DC	2.50
Strontium Dog, No. 10, Quagmire	1.50
Sun Runners, No. 1, Pacific	1.50
Teenage Mutant Ninja Turtles, No. 1, Mirage	
1st Printing	125.00
5th Printing	1.00
T.H.U.N.D.E.R. Agents, No. 4, Tower	10.00

COMPACTS

History: In the first quarter of the 20th century attitudes regarding cosmetics changed drastically. The use of make-up during the day was no longer looked upon with disdain. As women became "liberated" and as more and more of them entered the business world the use of cosmetics became a routine and necessary part of a woman's grooming. Portable containers for cosmetics became a necessity.

Compacts were made in a myriad of shapes, styles, combinations and motifs, all reflecting the mood of the times. Every conceivable natural or man-made medium was used in the manufacture of compacts. Commemorative, premium, souvenir, patriotic, figural, combination compacts, Art Deco, and enamel compacts are a few examples of the compacts that were made in the United States and abroad. Compacts combined with cigarette cases, music boxes, watches, hatpins, canes, lighters, etc., also were very popular.

Compacts were made and used until the late 1950s when women opted for the "Au Naturel" look. The term "vintage" is used to distinguish the compacts from the first half of the twentieth century from contemporary examples.

Reference: Roselyn Gerson, *Ladies' Compacts of the 19th and 20th Centuries*, Wallace-Homestead Book Company, 1989.

Collector's Club: The Compact Collectors Club, P.O. Box Letter S, Lynbrook, NY 11563.

Advisor: Roselyn Gerson.

Additional Listings: See *Warman's Americana & Collectibles* for more examples.

Daniel, black leather, portrait of lady encased in plastic dome, Paris	80.00
Evans, goldtone, heart shape, black twisted carrying cord, lipstick concealed in black tassel suspended from bottom	225.00
Fifth Avenue, vanity case, "Cosmetist," aquamarine enamel, powder, rouge, lipstick, cleansing cream, and mascara, England	150.00
Flato, goldtone, jeweled horse and carriage mounted on lid, blue velvet protective case, sleeve for jeweled lipstick	80.00
Foster & Bailey, vanity case, blue cloisonne, suspended from enameled	

Bakelite vanity case, rect, black, rhinestone geometric design on lid, int. mirror, powder and rouge compartments, coin pocket on back, black carrying cord, lipstick concealed in tassel, $250.00.

perfume container, powder and rouge compartments, lipstick attached at base, tassel and black enameled finger carrying ring **900.00**

Gray, Dorothy, engine turned goldtone, hat shape, ribbon and fruit dec **60.00**

Italian, hand mirror shape, sterling silver, stylized floral engraving, lipstick concealed in handle, coral cabochon thumbpiece **300.00**

Japanese, vanity case, ext. and int. gilt inlaid, carrying chain, mirror, coin holder, and powder compartment . . **250.00**

Kigu, compact and cigarette case, silvered and goldtone, tandem lipstick and carrying chain, England **60.00**

Lampl, light blue enamel, five colorful three dimensional scenes from Alice in Wonderland encased in plastic domes on lid **150.00**

Rex Fifth Avenue, vanity–pochette, navy blue, gold polka dots, taffeta drawstring, mirror on outside base **75.00**

R. G. & Co., vanity case, sterling silver, yellow cloisonne enamel, tango chain, painted flowers on lid, lipstick and perfume tube suspended from enameled and silver finger ring chain **250.00**

Unknown Maker

Compact, ebony wood, castanets shape, metal Paris insignia centered on lid, orange tasseled carrying cord **200.00**

Compact, red, white, and blue, telephone dial shape, slogan "I Like Ike" imprinted on lid, red map of USA on lid center **200.00**

Powder Tier, silvertone triple tier vanity case, swivel compartments for powder, rouge, and lipstick **125.00**

Vanity Bag, sterling silver mesh, hallmarked, octagonal, goldtone int. and finger ring carrying chain . . . **450.00**

Vanity Case

Antique goldtone, two sided filigree, red stones set in lids, powder and rouge compartments, lipstick concealed in tassel, carrying chain **225.00**

Bolster shape, rhinestone studded, powder, rouge, and cigarettes compartments, black faille carrying case with sleeves for lipstick and comb **90.00**

Volupte, goldtone, hand shape, faux diamond engagement ring on ring finger **120.00**

Whiting & Davis Co, vanity bag, purple, black, and silver mesh, purple enameled vanity case on outside corner of frame, lined int., powder sifter, metal mirror and rouge compartment on lid, carrying chain **450.00**

CONSOLIDATED GLASS COMPANY

History: The Consolidated Lamp and Glass Company resulted from the 1893 merger of the Wallace and McAfee Company, glass and lamp jobbers of Pittsburgh, and the Fostoria Shade & Lamp Company of Fostoria, Ohio. When the Fostoria, Ohio, plant burned down in 1895, Corapolis, Pennsylvania, donated a seven-acre tract of land near the center of town for a new factory. In 1911 the company was the largest lamp, globe, and shade works in the United States, employing over 400 workers.

In 1925 Reuben Haley, owner of an independent design firm, convinced John Lewis, president of Consolidated, to enter the giftware field utilizing a series of designs inspired by the 1925 Paris Exposition Internationale des Arts Decoratifs et Industriels Modernes and the work of Rene Lalique. Initially, the glass was marketed by Howard Selden through his showroom at 225 Fifth Avenue, New York, New York. The first two lines were Catalonian and Martele.

Additional patterns were added in the late 1920s: Florentine (January 1927), Chintz (January 1927), Ruba Rombic (January 1928), and Line 700 (January 1929). On April 2, 1932, Consolidated closed it doors. Kenneth Harley moved thirty-five to forty moulds to Phoenix. In March 1936 Consolidated reopened under new management. The

"Harley" moulds were returned. During this period the famous Dancing Nymph line, based on an 8" salad plate in the 1926 Martele series, was introduced.

In August 1962 Consolidated was sold to Dietz Brothers. A major fire damaged the plant during a 1963 labor dispute. In 1964 the company closed its doors for good.

References: Ann Gilbert McDonald, *Evolution of the Night Lamp*, Wallace-Homestead Book Co., 1979; Jack D. Wilson, *Phoenix & Consolidated Art Glass, 1926–1980*, Antique Publications, 1989.

Ashtray, Ruba Rombic, crystal	300.00
Basket, Catalonia, green, applied handle	40.00
Berry Bowl, 8" d, Criss Cross, cranberry opalescent	155.00
Box, cov	
Fruit & Leaf, Martele line, scalloped edge, 5 x 7"	60.00
Roses and Bird, blue, round	110.00
Butter Dish, cov, Cone, pink	85.00
Candlesticks, pr	
Dancing Girls, French Crystal	175.00
Hummingbird, Martele line, jade green, 6¾" h	200.00
Celery Tray, Ruba Rombic, smoky topaz	115.00
Cigarette Box, cov, Santa Maria, opaque milk white, gold sailing ship on lid, emb dolphins on sides	125.00
Compote, Ruba Rombic, smoky topaz, 7" d	200.00
Condiment Set, Florette, blue, cased, salt and pepper shakers, cov mustard jar, handled stand	125.00
Cracker Jar, Florette, orig SP rim, lid, and bail handle	
Light green cased glass	200.00
Pink	265.00
Creamer and Sugar	
Catalonia, amethyst	45.00
Ruba Rombic, jungle green	135.00
Cruet, Guttate, cased pink, orig stopper	300.00
Decanter Set, Catalonia line, amber, decanter and three tumblers	120.00
Lamp	
Kerosene, Guttate, cased pink font, clear base	400.00
Table, Cockatoo, blue, bittersweet, tan, and white	275.00
Perfume Bottle, Ruba Rombic, lilac, matching stopper	250.00
Pitcher, water	
Cone, cased pink	200.00
Guttate, cased pink, applied clear handle, 9½" h	200.00
Iris, amethyst	200.00
Plate	
Bird of Paradise, deep amethyst stain, Martele line, 10¼" d	40.00

Catalonia, green	40.00
Ruba Rombic, smoky topaz, 7" d . .	35.00
Salt and Pepper Shakers, pr	
Cone	
Green	70.00
Pink	75.00
Guttate	
Green	80.00
Pink satin	100.00

Salt Shaker, Rib and Scroll pattern, pink cased, orig tin top, $55.00.

Sauce Dish, Criss Cross, cranberry opalescent	60.00
Sherbet, Fruit Fruits, green, ftd	15.00
Spooner	
Criss Cross, cranberry opalescent . .	130.00
Florette, pink, metal rim and handles	70.00
Sugar Bowl, cov, Guttate, pink satin . .	135.00
Sugar Shaker, orig top, Cone, blue . . .	125.00
Syrup Pitcher, Guttate, cased pink, orig top	400.00
Toothpick	
Florette, pink	65.00
Guttate, cranberry	175.00
Tumbler	
Five Fruits, green, ftd	30.00
Guttate, pink satin	50.00
Umbrella Stand, Blackberry	
Amber	375.00
Red Satin	700.00
White ground, gold dec	500.00
Vase, 9½" h, sculptured yellow flowers, green leaves and stems, opaque white ground	75.00

CONTINENTAL CHINA AND PORCELAIN (GENERAL)

History: By 1700 porcelain factories existed in large numbers throughout Europe. In the mid-18th century the German factories at Meissen and Nymphenburg were dominant. As the century ended, French potteries assumed the leadership role. The "golden age" of Continental china and porcelains was from the 1740s to the 1840s.

Americans living in the last half of the 19th century eagerly sought the masterpieces of the European porcelain factories. In the early 20th century this style of china and porcelain was a "blue chip" among the antiques collectors.

References: Susan and Al Bagdade, *Warman's English & Continental Pottery & Porcelain, 1st Edition*, Warman Publishing Co, Inc, 1987; Rachael Feild, *Macdonald Guide To Buying Antique Pottery & Porcelain*, Wallace-Homestead, 1987.

Additional Listings: France—Haviland, Limoges, Old Paris, Sarreguemines, and Sevres; German—Austrian Ware, Bavarian China, Carlsbad China, Dresden/Meissen, Rosenthal, Royal Bayreuth, Royal Bonn, Royal Rudolstadt, Royal Vienna, Schlegelmilch, and Villeroy and Boch; Italy—Capo-di-Monte.

Samson, scent bottle, multicolored, 5″ h, $750.00.

FRENCH

Chantilly
   Dish, 9¾″ l, quatrefoil, Kakiemon palette, chrysanthemum, chocolate rim, c1740 .... 200.00
   Plate, 9½″ d, blue and white, carnations, basketwork border, blue hunting horn mark, c1845, set of 12 750.00
   Sauce Tureen, 10½″ w, oval, multicolored loose spring flower bouquet, scattered flowers, and insects, brown line rims, fixed silver stand with ram's head terminals and reeded band, c1770, blue hunting horn and "F" mark, later silver mounts 300.00
Galle Faience
   Compote, 9″ d, scalloping rim, waisted cylindrical base, dark blue and yellow, blossom sprays, central unicorn and centaur, sgd "E Galle Nancy," pr 990.00
   Figure, 13¼″ h, cat, seated brown tabby, green glass eyes, sgd "Galle Nancy," minor restoration 500.00

Gravy Boat, 10″ l, 4¾″ h, pitcher body, handle, quatrefoil base, pale blue, dark blue and yellow floral borders, blossoms sprays, dragonfly, sgd "E Galle Nancy" 385.00
Niderviller, plate, 13½″ d, multicolored center of four fishermen, large tree and buildings, scattered floral border, interlaced "C" mark under Ducal coronet, c1770 .... 300.00
Paris
   Coffee Service, cov coffeepot, cream jug, cov sugar bowl, twelve cups and saucers, La Fontaine's fables scene, French titles, gilt borders, c1810, 27 pcs 7,700.00
   Dish, 12″ w, oval, multicolored loose bouquets and scattered flowers, gilt rims with molded foliage, c1772, Pierre Anton Hannong, blue script "H" mark, iron–red "R" mark, pr . 900.00
   Ice Pail, 8¼″ h, cov, liner, foliate scroll handles with gilding, all-over painted scattered blue and pink cornflowers, gilt foliage, band of pink and blue cornflower branches, gilt rims, c1785, Locre factory, blue crossed torch mark, pr 2,225.00
Saint Cloud
   Bough Pot, 4¾″ h, white, mask handles, all-over molding of flowering plants and ferns, wide gadroon band, narrow gadroon bands at rim and foot, c1730 .... 1,775.00
   Cup and Saucer, 2¾″ d, white, branches of plum trees, mid 18th C, pr 1,700.00
Samson
   Basket, 10″ w, all-over basketweave pattern, two loop handles, male and female mask terminals, painted loose bouquets and scattered flowers, turquoise and puce chevron border, Hochst and Samson marks 385.00
   Jar, cov, 17″ h, famille verte type dec, baskets of flowers under trailing canopies, late 19th C 800.00
   Urn, 16¼″ h, polychrome, enamel floral dec, red cartouche mark, pr .. 550.00

GERMAN

Ansbach, coffeepot, cov, 8″ h, pear shape, fruit finial, dome cov, scrolling handle, short spout with molded female mask and feathers, loose bouquets and scattered flowers dec, c1765, blue coat of arms and "A" mark, restored finial 1,100.00
Berlin
   Coffee Pot, cov, 10¾″ h, oviform,

berry finial, handle and spout formed as serpent coiled around pot, gilt scales, three biscuit figures of seated winged griffins, circular base, blue scepter mark, c1805 .. **900.00**

Ewer, 8⅞" h, scrolling handle, short spout, all-over yellow and blue marbled glaze, c1720, rim chips **4,000.00**

Hot Milk Jug, cov, oviform, berry finial, handle and spout formed as serpent coiled around pot, gilt scales, three biscuit figures of dolphins, circular base, blue scepter mark, c1805 .... **350.00**

Sweetmeat Dish, 7½" w, three molded yellow fruits and cov, white blossom finials, fixed leaf shaped stand with branch handle, c1765, blue scepter mark, finials restored, minor chips **1,320.00**

Vase, 39" h, portrait, baluster, waisted foliate banded neck, oval reserved with bust length portrait of Kaiser Wilhelm I, painted by H Stadler, blue ground, gilt foliate scrolls, out scroll ringed bird mask handles, lappet trim border on shoulder, base, waisted socle, cylindrical raised plinth, c1870 .... **9,350.00**

Faience

Tankard, pewter mounted hinged cov with ball thumbpiece, cylindrical

9" h, blue, green, yellow, and manganese basket of flowers, blue line borders, cracked urn thumbpiece **650.00**

9½" h, manganese, green, blue, and yellow strutting peacock in landscape, rockwork with flowerheads, black line borders, c1750, attributed to Hannoversch-Munden **675.00**

9¾" h, manganese, green, blue, iron–red, and yellow prancing horse in landscape, palm trees and flowering shrubs, blue line borders, c1750, attributed to Erfurt, inscribed "J. G. Z. 1749" .. **800.00**

Nymphenburg

Cup and Saucer, 3¾" d, bell shaped bowl, Maximillian Joseph Platz, burnished gilt int. and scroll handle, c1835 .... **1,900.00**

Figure, 9½" h, lady attacked by spotted dog, yellow hat, green dress, purple bodice, striped apron, shaped base, imp mark, after Bustelli **880.00**

Sandoz, Gerard, centerpiece, cov, 21½" l, faceted oblong base with two handles, lid molded with classical seated maiden, glazed white, incised artist's

monogram on lid, base imp "Schwartzburger Werkstatten fur Porzellankunst U2135" and monogram **3,100.00**

ITALIAN

Deruta, jar, 7¼" h, majolica, inscribed "Ghoma di Lava," scrollwork, grotesques, and leaf forms **500.00**

Doccia

Coffee Cup and Saucer, flaring cylindrical cup with C scroll handle, purple highlights, c1755, pr **125.00**

Coffeepot, cov, 9½" h, pear shape, blue and puce dragon head spout, scroll handle with key pattern and foliage, flat stepped cov, multicolored floral dec, c1775, restored handle **650.00**

Dish, 9⅝" w, shell shape, central bouquet of purple flowers surrounded by floral sprays, continuous twisting branches of leaves and nuts border, c1780, five point purple star mark **150.00**

Gamboni, vase, 12½" h, inverted baluster, stylized birds and foliage, brown and cream, turquoise ground, painted "Gamboni Italy" with a flower **450.00**

Savona, compote, 14" d, blue and white dec, floral border, pierced, blue lighthouse mark **1,200.00**

COOKIE JARS

History: Cookie jars, colorful and often whimsical, are now an established collecting category in their own right. Do not be misled by the high prices released at the 1988 Andy Warhol auction. Many of the same cookie jars that sold for over one thousand dollars each can be found in the field for less than one hundred dollars.

Many cookie jar forms were manufactured by more than one company and, as a result, can be found with different marks. This resulted from mergers or splits by manufacturers, e.g., Brush-McCoy which is now Nelson McCoy. Molds also were traded and sold among companies.

Cookie jars often were redesigned to reflect newer tastes. Hence, the same jar may be found in several different style variations.

References: Harold Nichols, *McCoy Cookie Jars: From The First To The Latest*, Nichols Publishing, 1987; Fred and Joyce Roerig, *Collector's Encyclopedia of Cookie Jars*, Collector Books, 1991; Ermagene Westfall, *An Illustrated Value Guide To Cookie Jars*, Collector Books, 1983.

Abingdon Pottery

Goldilocks **85.00**

Granny **50.00**

Little Miss Muffet	175.00
Money Sack, yellow, gold trim	45.00
Mother Goose	50.00
Pineapple	25.00

American Bisque

Animal Cookies	15.00
Bear, eyes closed	25.00
Bell, "Ring for Cookies"	15.00
Cat, brown and yellow, pink bow	20.00
Chick, wearing tam	35.00
Clown, painted dots	25.00
Cookie Truck	35.00
Kittens, ball of yarn	25.00
Majorette	40.00
Schoolhouse, bell	25.00
Spaceship	50.00
Wooden Soldier	30.00

California Originals

Bert, Muppet	20.00
Big Bird	55.00
Rabbit, brown	12.00
Goebel, Thumper	75.00

Mammy, McCoy Pottery, $85.00.

McCoy Pottery

Antique Car	35.00
Asparagus	25.00
Covered Wagon	40.00
Girl, praying	40.00
Hen on Nest, white	25.00
Little Boy Blue	45.00
Lollipops	40.00
Old Woman's Shoe	65.00
Picnic Basket	20.00
Pirate Chest	32.00
Teepee	70.00
Windmill, blue	35.00
Wishing Well	35.00
Pee Dee Co, Albert Apple	40.00

Pfaltzgraff

Cookie Cop	35.00
Train	60.00

Red Wing

Monk, blue	48.00
Pierre	65.00
Teapot, round top	125.00

Regal China

Davy Crocket	100.00
Hubert Lion	125.00
Koala Bear	350.00
Quaker Oats	50.00
Snoopy	125.00

Robinson Ransbottom

Chef with bowl of eggs	75.00
Cow Jumped Over The Moon, gold trim	65.00
Peter Peter Pumpkin Eater	50.00
Preacher, black hat, sq glasses	40.00
World War II Soldier	50.00
Tat–L–Tale, voice box in lid	350.00

Twin Winton

Bear on Stump	35.00
Bunny Rabbit Sheriff	18.00
Chicken	20.00
Cottage	35.00
Dutch Girl	25.00
Keystone Cop	100.00
Monk	25.00
Poodle, counter	25.00

COPELAND

COPELAND AND SPODE

History: In 1749 Josiah Spode apprenticed to Thomas Whieldon and in 1754 worked for William Banks in Stoke-on-Trent. In the early 1760s Spode started his own pottery, making cream colored earthenware and blue printed whiteware. In 1770 he returned to Banks' factory as master, purchasing it in 1776.

Spode pioneered the use of steam powered pottery making machinery and mastered the art of transfer printing from copper plates. Spode opened a London shop in 1778 and sent William Copeland there about 1784. A number of larger London locations followed. At the turn of the century Spode introduced bone china. In 1805 Josiah Spode II and William Copeland entered into partnership for the London business. A series of partnerships between Josiah Spode II, Josiah Spode III, and William Taylor Copeland resulted.

In 1833 Copeland acquired Spode's London operations and the Stoke plants seven years later. William Taylor Copeland managed the business until his death in 1868. The business remained in the hands of Copeland heirs. In 1923 the plant was electrified; other modernizations followed.

In 1976 Spode merged with Worcester Royal Porcelain to become Royal Worcester Spode, Ltd.

References: Susan and Al Bagdade, *Warman's English & Continental Pottery & Porcelain, 1st Edition,* Warman Publishing, 1987; D. Drakard & P. Holdway, *Spode Printed Wares,* Longmans, 1983; L. Whiter, *Spode: A History Of The Family, Factory, And Wares, 1733–1833,* Barrie & Jenkins, 1970.

Creamer, blue band, gold trim, ivory ground, No. 893, c1810, 5½" w, 4½" h, $75.00.

Basket, 11 x 8½", white, shaded pink to white int., gold floral and leaf dec, intertwined pink handle, 1851–55 .... **225.00**
Bowl, 8½" d, fruit, Imari type, blue, green, and orange, pedestal base, scalloped edge, c1850 .... **85.00**
Compote, 9½ x 2¾", white, floral dec, turquoise dots, gold trim, lattice sides **225.00**
Creamer and Sugar, 3¼" h, Blue Willow, marked "Copeland's China England" **200.00**
Cup, Red Tower pattern **12.00**
Demitasse Cup and Saucer, Red Tower pattern **15.00**
Dessert Service, pr of oval 9½" l reticulated baskets and stands, three 9½" w shell shaped dishes, 10½" w oval dish, circular 10" w ftd compote, twelve 8" d plates, Tumbledown Dick pattern, Pattern No 3716, iron–red and blue bird perched on multicolored flowering branches, green and brown cracked ice ground, gilding, blue and imp Spode marks, c1825 .... **2,875.00**
Dinner Service
Pattern No. 2038, thirty 9½" d dinner plates, twelve 9¾" d soup plates, 8¼" d dessert plates, oval 14¼" l cov soup tureen, pr 10¼" l cov vegetable dishes, five graduated plat-

ters, Kakiemon palette, iron–red, blue, yellow, and gilt, flowering prunus within blue line and iron–red and gilt scroll and arch, border with four reserves of flowers on gilt scrolling foliage, iron–red edge, undersides with iron–red flowering branches, marked "Spode," c1820, 72 pcs **15,400.00**
Pattern No. 2976, thirty–four 10¼" d dinner plates, sixteen 9½" d dessert plates, eighteen 10½" d soup plates, six graduated platters, pr 7⅜" d cov sauce tureen with stand, 12¾" d cov soup tureen and stand, three 10¼" d cov vegetable dishes, Chinese taste, iron–red, blue, and gilt flowers, blue lines, wide band of iron–red and blue cell pattern, shaped reserved cartouches, gilt lines, gadrooned edge, imp "Spodes New Stone," c1830, 80 pcs **11,000.00**
Wickderdale pattern, service for eight, marked "Copeland and Spode" .. **250.00**
Figure, 12" h, parian, Lady of the Lake, nude figure, loosely draped cloth, seated on bank, molded fish and reeds below, imp marks "Marshall Fect SC, Copeland," mid 19th C ... **400.00**
Game Plate, 12" d, 19th C repro of Chelsea–Derby, sculptured biscuit ware, Chinese style pheasants and butterflies, gilt, claret ground, fake Chelsea marks, initials CAR surround fleur–de–lis, numbered **200.00**
Oyster Plate, hp, insects and flowers **35.00**
Pitcher, 4¾" h, Drabware, Golfing, bulbous, deep green ground, molded golfing subjects, cream leaf border, printed and imp marks, c1900 ..... **425.00**
Plate
6¼" d, Red Tower pattern **8.00**
7¾" d, Red Tower pattern **10.00**
9⅝" d, Pattern No. 2879, Chinese taste, iron–red, green, and gilt central loose bouquets, chrysanthemum and scrolling foliage band, four floral reserves, four scattered flowering branches and diaper rim edge, printed iron–red Spode stone china mark, set of 12 .... **725.00**
Punch Bowl, 12½" d, multicolored, Chinese garden scene, gold trim, c1810 .... **750.00**
Salt and Pepper Shakers, pr, Red Tower pattern **15.00**
Soup Plate, 7¾" d, Red Tower pattern **12.00**
Tea and Coffee Service, cov teapot, cov coffeepot, cream jug, cov sugar, waste bowl, five coffee cans, six teacups, eleven saucers, 7⅛" d plate, pr

8½″ d circular dishes, blue and white, Chinamen in landscape, diaper borders with flowerhead reserves, gilt lines, c1818 . . . . **1,760.00**
Tureen, cov
  7½″ d, blue and white, bridge scene with flowers, matching stand, c1820 . . . . **125.00**
  11 x 9 x 6″, Red Tower pattern **75.00**
Vegetable Dish, cov, 10″ l, Geisha pattern, blue **100.00**

COPPER

History: Copper objects, such as kettles, tea kettles, warming pans, measures, etc., played an important part in the 19th century household. Outdoors, the apple butter kettle and still were the two principal copper items. Copper culinary objects were lined with a thin protective coating of tin to prevent poisoning. They were relined as needed.

Great emphasis is placed by collectors on signed pieces, especially those by American craftsmen. Since copper objects were made abroad as well, it is hard to identify unsigned examples.

References: Mary Frank Gaston, *Antique Copper*, Collector Books, 1985; Henry J. Kauffman, *Early American Copper, Tin, and Brass*, Medill McBride Co., 1950.

Additional Listings: Arts and Crafts Movement and Roycroft.

Reproduction Alert: Many modern reproductions also exist.

Coffee Server, 16½″ h, iron stand, $325.00.

Bed Warmer
  41″ l, engraved bird on lid, orig handle **175.00**
  45″ l, engraved floral and bird, turned wood handle **375.00**
Bowl, 10″ d, hammered, wrought copper handles **65.00**

Box, cov, 9″ l, rect, hammered finish, stylized blossom on cov, imp Craftsman Studios mark **300.00**
Candleholder, four holders, sgd "W L Fletcher" **25.00**
Candy Bowl, 16½″ d, dovetailed, rounded bottom, iron rim handles . . **125.00**
Chafing Dish, 11″ h, dish supported by three realistically modeled rabbits, wooden base, marked "Black, Starr & Forest" **450.00**
Clam Steamer, double **200.00**
Coal Hod
  14¼″ l, double ended **100.00**
  17″ h, brass handles, 19th C **150.00**
Dipper, 80″ l, orig pole with wrought iron **650.00**
Dish, 6″ d, circular, hammered center, Greek key rim, sgd "The Jarvie Shop" **275.00**
Inkwell, 2″ h, tapered cylinder, cov, rivets round edge, glass liner, imp Gustav Stickley mark **385.00**
Jar, 11¼″ d, 9″ h, hammered, dovetailed seams **35.00**
Kettle on Stand, 11¼″ h, sq, scroll cut border, brass stud trim, spout and handles, open sq brass base, scrolled feet and terminals, imp Benham and Froud mark **275.00**
Lamp, 9″ h, 5¾″ w, compressed sq, circular foot rim, beaded mid molding, patinated, applied silver seaweed, fish, seashells, and crab dec, orig wick holder now fitted for electricity, marked "Gorham," c1884 . . . . **3,850.00**
Letter File, 5″ h, hammered copper, imp Gustav Stickley mark **165.00**
Measure
  5″ d, 3⅞″ h, cylindrical, brass rim, labeled "Fairbanks & Co US Standard New York" **295.00**
  6¼″ h, haystack, Continental, 19th C **80.00**
  7½″ h, Fleming Apple Distillery, Fairmount, New Jersey **35.00**
  15″ h, haystack, dovetailed, four gallon, English **85.00**
Pitcher, 9¼″ h, tankard shape, marked "D Bentley & Sons, N 3rd St, Phila" **65.00**
Pot
  8½″ d, dovetailed, cylindrical, cast brass rim handles, marked "V Olac & Sons, Phila" **65.00**
  9 x 18″, oval, dovetailed seams, 12½″ wrought iron handle **65.00**
  10½″ h, dovetailed, cov, iron handle **60.00**
  11½″ d, cast iron handle, marked "D H & M Co, NY" **55.00**
  13¾″ d, dovetailed, cast iron handle, marked "D N" **45.00**
Saucepan
  7″ d, dovetailed, cast iron handle . . **45.00**
  9″ d, dovetailed, wrought copper handle **75.00**

Skimmer, 53" l, iron shaft mount, orig
wood pole **200.00**
Tea Kettle
6" h, dovetailed construction, gooseneck spout, swivel handle **75.00**
7½" h, dovetailed construction,
gooseneck spout, swivel handle,
stamped "W Morrison, NY 6 Q" . . **110.00**
14½" h, dovetailed, attached base . . **65.00**
Vase
7¼" h, cylindrical, applied silver rim
and mid rib, circular silver foot, patinated red colored surface with two
applied silver insects and spider,
monogram, marked "Tiffany & Co,"
dated 1880 . . . . **4,200.00**
7¾" h, cylindrical, patinated red sur-
face, applied silver vines, leaves
and butterfly, silver zipper and ring
handle, marked "Tiffany & Co,"
c1877 . . . . **4,625.00**
9" h, ovoid, hammered, dark patina
with rubs, marked "Dirk Van Erp"
in brown box below windmill motif
and "San Francisco" **850.00**
Wash Boiler, canning rack **75.00**
Weathervane, 30½" h, 34" l, full bodied
ram, standing, orig gilding, American,
late 19th C **4,500.00**

CORALENE

History: Coralene is a glass or china object
which has the design painted on the surface of the
piece and tiny glass colorless beads applied with
a fixative. The piece is placed in a muffle which
fixes the enamel and sets the beads.

Several American and English companies made
glass coralene in the 1880s. Seaweed or coral was
the most common design. Other motifs were
"Wheat Sheaf" and "Fleur-de-Lis." Most of the
base glass was satin finished.

China and pottery coralene, made from the late
1890s to the post WW II era, is referred to as
Japanese coralene. The beading is opaque and
inserted into the soft clay. Hence, it is only half to
three-quarters visible.

Reproduction Alert: Reproductions are on the
market, some using an old glass base. The
beaded decoration on new coralene has been
glued and can be scraped off.

CHINA

Bowl, 8" d, blue matte ground, purple
plums, green leaves, c1910 . . . . . . **175.00**
Box, cov, 1½ x 2 x 3", copper matte
ground, pink, lavender, and green
thistles, marked "Kinran Pat. 16132
Japan" **125.00**

Ewer, 4" h, 3½" d, green and gold
ground, pink and green fruit, green
top and bottom trim, Japanese **200.00**
Sugar Shaker, white ground, orange
coralene seaweed dec, orig top . . . **175.00**
Vase
6½" h, white coralene Japanese
cherry tree dec, deep green satin
ground, Hawkes trefoil mark **215.00**
8¼" h, 3½" d, cylinder, two small handles, coralene beaded pink nastur-
iums, trailing green leaves, brown
ground, Japanese **410.00**

**Vase, dimpled oval, transparent clear
orange glass ground, multicolored floral blossoms and leaf dec, marked
"Patent," 8" h, $200.00.**

GLASS

Bowl, 5½" d, herringbone, MOP, blue,
pink coralene seaweed dec, crimped
top, applied glass rim **615.00**
Pickle Castor, DQ rubina insert, white
coralene flowers and dotting, ornate
Tufts frame, braided handle **235.00**
Pitcher, 7¾" h, sq mouth, shaded pink
satin ground, yellow coralene seaweed dec, applied frosted handle,
Hobbs, Brockunier & Co **750.00**
Sweetmeat, 3½" d, 4¾" h, white Bristol
glass base, orange coral coralene
dec **325.00**
Toothpick Holder, 2½" h, sq raised rim,
bulbous body, glossy peachblow
ground, opaque lining, yellow sea-
weed coralene dec **275.00**
Tumbler, white satin ground, acorns and
leaves dec outlined in coralene **45.00**
Vase
5½" h, 4" d, shaded pink snowflake
MOP satin glass, white lining, white
enameled dot beading around top,
wheat coralene dec **550.00**
7½" h, bulbous, blue, yellow coralene
seaweed dec **265.00**

CORKSCREWS

History: The corkscrew is composed of three parts: (1) handle, (2) shaft, and (3) worm or screw. The earliest known reference to "a Steele Worme used for drawing corks out of bottles" is 1681. Samuel Henshall, an Englishman, was granted the first patent in 1795.

Elaborate mechanisms were invented and patented from the early 1800s onward, especially in England. However, three basic types emerged: "T" handle (the most basic, simple form), lever, and mechanism. Variations on these three types run into the hundreds. Miniature corkscrews, employed for drawing corks from perfume and medicinal bottles between 1750 and 1920, are among the most eagerly sought by collectors.

Nationalistic preferences were found in corkscrews. The English favored the helix worm and tended to coppertone their steel products. By the mid-18th century English and Irish silversmiths were making handles noted for their clean lines and practicality. Most English silver handles were hallmarked.

The Germans preferred the center worm and nickel plate. The Italians used chrome plate or massive solid brass. In the early 1800s the Dutch and French developed elaborately artistic silver handles.

Americans did not begin to manufacture quality corkscrews until the late 19th century. They favored the center worm and specialized in silver mounted tusks and carved staghorn for handles.

Steel, split ring, ball bearings at base of handle, German, 6½" l, $85.00.

LEVER

Bronzed Steel, Heeley A1, double lever patent, helical worm **65.00**
Chrome, zig-zag design, 10½" extended, French **60.00**

Steel, bronzed, helical worm, double lever patent, Heeley "A1" **60.00**

MECHANISM

Brass Case, secondary wood swivel jointed handle, brush, applied Royal supporters, marked "Thomason Patent Ne Plus Ultra" **300.00**
Bone handle, English rack and pinion corkscrew, polished, brush and hanging ring, four plain post open barrel, narrow rack, long wire helix, side handle, sgd "Verinder," c1800 . . . . . .   **400.00**
Cast Iron, clamp on type, lacy openwork, emb "Phoenix," patented 1887   **190.00**
Chrome Frame, cylindrical ebony wood handle, steel, ciphered worm, marked "Swiss Made, 2908A3" **130.00**
Steel Frame, foliate scrolling raising arm, ebony handle, steel ciphered worm, marked "Champion, Made in USA" **100.00**

MINIATURE

Chrome, elephant, corkscrew trunk . . .   **40.00**
Ivory handle, crescent shape, chromed turned steel shaft wire helix, c1790–1820 . . . .   **70.00**
Meissen, porcelain Johann Von Schiller head, center worm, underglaze crossed swords mark, c1870 . . . . .   **375.00**
MOP, carved palmette handle, helical worm **20.00**

NOVELTY

Brass, bullet shape, Lemp Beer, St Louis adv, 3" l, c1897 . . . .   **95.00**
Celluloid, mermaid, bent at waist, marked "Geschutz" **275.00**
Pewter, triton blowing a shell, steel ciphered worm, 19th C **90.00**
Silver, gaucho and horse, oblong platform handle, seal from sheath with scrolling, Archimedean screw **800.00**
Wood, man wearing hat, comical face, 4" l **12.00**

T-HANDLE

Bone handle, Henshall type, incised button, helical worm, c1820 . . . . . .   **125.00**
Staghorn handle, ornate SS cap **100.00**
Steel, "The Surprise," cage frame, marked "Registered by George Willetts, Birmingham, England," 1884 . .   **95.00**
Wood, shaped and turned handle, ciphered center worm, bell and wire cutter, cap lifter, "Williamson" on shaft, marked "Ptd 13 Dec 1898" **30.00**

COSMOS GLASS

History: Cosmos glass is a milk glass pattern made by the Consolidated Lamp and Glass Company, c1900.

Cosmos glass is identified by its distinctive pattern. The ground is a molded cross-cut design. Relief molded flowers are painted in pink, blue, and yellow. Cosmos glass comes in an extended tableware line which includes several sizes and shapes of lamps.

Butter Dish, cov, $200.00.

Butter Dish, cov, pink band	195.00
Cologne Bottle, 4½" h, orig stopper . .	100.00
Creamer	150.00
Miniature Lamp	
7" h, fish net ground	350.00
9" h, pink, yellow, and blue dec, electrified	85.00
Pickle Castor, pink band, ftd, SP frame	385.00
Pitcher, 5" h	175.00
Salt and Pepper Shakers, pr	175.00
Spooner, pink flowers	130.00
Sugar, cov	175.00
Syrup Pitcher, 6½" h, pink and yellow flowers	200.00
Tumbler	85.00

phasis placed on glazes. Lustreware is one of the most common types. Commercial wares marked "Lakeware" were produced from 1927 to 1931.

Early marks include an incised "Cowan Pottery" on the redware (1913–17), an impressed "Cowan," and an impressed "Lakewood." The imprinted stylized semicircle with or without the initials R. G. was later.

References: Paul Evans, *Art Pottery of the United States, 2nd Edition,* Feingold & Lewis Publishing Corp., 1987; Ralph and Terry Kovel, *The Kovels' Collector's Guide to American Art Pottery,* Crown Publishers, Inc., 1974.

Museums: Cowan Pottery Museum, Rocky River Public Library, Rocky River, OH; Everson Museum of Art, Syracuse, NY.

Bookends, pr, polar bears eating fish, ivory glaze	215.00
Bowl	
5" d, 3" h, yellow luster glaze	65.00
8" d, blue luster glaze, marked "R Guy Cowan"	25.00
Candleholder, three lite, vine dec	65.00
Candlesticks, pr, figural	
4½" h, seahorses, green	40.00
12" h, nudes, ivory glaze	250.00
Centerpiece, 6½" h, nude central flower holder, #698	165.00
Figure	
11" h, flamingo, ivory glaze	200.00
11½" h, egret, ivory glaze	125.00
12" h, peacock, turquoise glaze	85.00
Flower Holder, 6½" h, nude, white . . .	85.00
Place Card Holder, 3" h, cream glaze, imp mark	20.00
Strawberry Jar, mint green glaze	75.00
Tile, fish dec	100.00
Vase	
7" h, Chinese orange glaze	60.00

COWAN POTTERY

History: R. Guy Cowan founded the Cowan Pottery in 1913 in Cleveland, Ohio. The establishment remained in almost continuous operation until 1931 when financial difficulties forced closure.

Early production was redware pottery. Later a porcelain-like finish was perfected with special em-

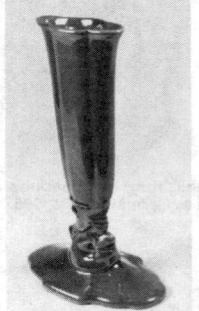

Vase, blue irid, 7¼" h, $25.00.

7½″ h, pillow form, blue luster 85.00
10″ h, handled, deep blue–green glaze 65.00
12″ h, pillow, mythical figures, glossy royal blue crackle glaze 250.00

CRANBERRY GLASS

History: Cranberry glass is transparent and named for its color, achieved by adding powdered gold to a molten batch of amber glass which then is reheated at a low temperature to develop the cranberry or ruby color. The glass color first appeared in the last half of the 17th century, but was not made in American glass factories until the last half of the 19th century.

Cranberry glass was blown, mold blown, or pressed. Examples often are decorated with gold or enamel. Less expensive cranberry glass was made by substituting copper for gold and can be identified by its bluish-purple tint.

Reference: William Heacock and William Gamble, *Encyclopedia Of Victorian Colored Pattern Glass: Book 9, Cranberry Opalescent from A to Z,* Antique Publications, 1987.

Additional Listings: See specific categories, such as Bride's Baskets, Cruets, Jack-in-the-Pulpit Vases, etc.

Reproduction Alert: Reproductions abound. These pieces are heavier, off-color, and lack the quality of older examples.

Cruet, bulbous body, applied clear handle, clear faceted stopper, 6½″ h, $65.00.

Barber Bottle, 6¾″ h, 3½″ d, hobnail, rings of clear hobnails on neck 175.00
Bell, 14″ h, applied clear handle, clapper missing, c1870 . . . . . 350.00
Bowl
5¾″ d, 4¾″ h, three rows of applied clear leaves dec, three applied clear scroll feet 300.00
6¾″ d, applied wide crystal band, berry pontil base 230.00
7 x 9 x 3¾″, pale cranberry body, opalescent ribs, signed by maker, marked "Murano" 100.00
8″ d, 4¾″ h, double row of shell pattern, applied crystal ribbon candy rigaree, three scroll feet, berry pontil 425.00
Box, 3½″ d, 3″ h, hinged lid, round, white and gold lilies dec 165.00
Castor Set, open salt, pepper shaker, and mustard jar, heavy paneled sides, silverplate frame, MOP handle 250.00
Carafe, DQ, threaded, polished pontil . 125.00
Creamer, 5″ h, 4¼″ w, sq top, IVT, applied deep amber thorn handle with four applied amber leaves on branch, light petal flower 335.00
Cruet, 8¾″ h, slightly ribbed, round mouth, applied clear handle, cranberry bubble stopper 120.00
Decanter
9″ h, applied clear handle, cranberry stopper 275.00
9½″ h, Thumbprint, applied clear reeded handle 120.00
9¾″ h, gold floral dec, applied clear handle, clear stopper, c1870 . . . . 300.00
Epergne, 21″ h, three large lilies, applied rigaree, two twisted canes, crimped cranberry bowl base 1,150.00
Jack In The Pulpit Vase, 10″ h, 5½″ d top, lacy gold floral dec, pr 225.00
Jar, cov, 9″ h, 4¾″ d, white, blue, and gold flowers and scrolls dec, applied crystal feet, cov with applied cranberry finial and crystal trim 425.00
Lemonade Set, pitcher and six tumblers, Thumbprint pattern 150.00
Pipe, 14″ l 200.00
Pitcher
4½″ h, Coin Spot 50.00
7½″ h, bulbous, sq mouth, IVT, applied clear handle 150.00
9″ h, bulbous, sq mouth, IVT, applied clear finely ribbed handle 210.00
11″ h, bulbous, applied floral and gold designs, narrow top, clear handle . . 165.00
Salt, master
2⅜″ d, 1⅝″ h, white enameled dot flowers, gold trim, three applied clear feet 60.00
3″ d, 1½″ h, round, white opaque threading 50.00
3¾″ d, 1¾″ h, round, applied clear shell trim 55.00

Sugar Shaker, 6½″ h, cylindrical, bulbous base, SS top **75.00**

Syrup, cranberry to clear, inverted cut design, SS holder **500.00**

Tumbler, set of 8, gold dec **40.00**

Vase

  5″ h, ruffled top, ribbed, small heavy gold rose garlands **150.00**

  6″ h

    Corset shape, Coin Spot, crimped edge **50.00**

    Cylinder, pleated flaring neck, IVT **70.00**

    Egg Shape, crimped top, DQ, gold mica flecks, applied clear rigaree and feet **100.00**

  8″ h, enameled white florals and butterfly, ornate silverplate stand marked "Reed & Barton" **350.00**

  10¼″ h, three petal top, blue enameled flowers, white scrolls, green leaves, gold trim, pr **325.00**

Water Jug, 6½″ h, shaded **65.00**

Witch Ball, 5″ d, opalescent hobnails, pr **210.00**

CROWN MILANO

History: Crown Milano is an American art glass produced by the Mt. Washington Glass Works, New Bedford, Massachusetts. The original patent was issued in 1886 to Frederick Shirley and Albert Steffin.

Normally it is an opaque white satin glass finished with light beige or ivory color ground embellished with fancy florals, decorations, and elaborate heavy raised gold. When marked, pieces carry an entwined CM with crown in purple enamel on the base. Sometimes paper labels were used. The silver plated mounts often have "MW" impressed or a Pairpoint mark as both Mount Washington and Pairpoint supplied mountings.

Advisors: Clarence and Betty Maier.

Biscuit Jar, cov, 6″ h, 5½″ d, barrel shape, pale yellow fading to creamy white ground, deep pink apple blossom clusters and pale pink blossoms, green leaves, gray–green branches extending from tree trunk, floral motif embossed collar and lid marked "P" in diamond **685.00**

Box, cov, 6″ d, round, all-over red blossoms and scrolls dec, emb SP rims, orig velvet lining, sgd **475.00**

Creamer and Sugar, cov, 4″ h, dainty

Syrup Pitcher, melon shaped, pale lemon ground, modified version of Queen's design, raised enamel dots, silverplated lid and handle, 5½″ h, 3¼″ d, $1,250.00.

  multicolored floral dec, gold finial and shell handles, sgd **5,250.00**

Cup and Saucer, glossy finish, slight vertical ribbing, all–over tulip, rose, and cornflower dec, gold edges and highlights, applied handle with scrolls, numbered #605, Mt Washington ... **785.00**

Ewer

  10½″ h, woman and sheep on obverse, birds and roses on reverse, framed with raised laurel leaves, garland, lilac and opal ground, gold rope handle, sgd "Crown Milano" and #504 .... **2,750.00**

  12″ h, white neck and body, overall background shadow dec of sepia colored scrolls and florals, dark blue, light blue, rust, coral, pink, yellow, green, black, and gold enameled hundreds of individual dots form stylized florals and geometric dec, raised gold abstract dec on spout, brushed gold highlights on twisted handle **1,750.00**

Salt and Pepper Shakers, pr, shiny finish, pink florals, gold detail stripes, orig tops, Mt Washington **225.00**

Sweetmeat Jar, 4¼″ h, 4″ d, raised molded in stars, enamel and jewel stylized starfish dec, gold and silver highlights, twig finial, emb crab on lid **850.00**

Urn, 11½″ h, egg shape, overlaid gold roses, leaves, and branches dec, rose branch shadow background, gold neck and lid dec, finial repair, sgd **850.00**

Vase

  10½″ h, cov, heavy enameled green and brown ivy leaves and vines, outlined in gold, lighter swirl design over lid, base, and background .. **2,280.00**

  11¼″ h, court lady and gentleman figures dec, surrounded by gold scrolls, top folds down to form handles, red crown surrounded by laurel leaves mark, sgd "Albertine" .. **850.00**

CRUETS

History: Cruets are small glass bottles used to hold oil, vinegar, wine, etc., for the table. The high point of cruet use was during the Victorian era when a myriad of glass manufacturers made cruets in a wide assortment of patterns, colors, and sizes. All cruets had stoppers; most had handles.

References: Dean L Murray, *More Cruets Only*, Killgore Graphics, Inc., 1973; William Heacock, *Encyclopedia of Victorian Colored Pattern Glass: Book 6, Oil Cruets From A To Z*, Antique Publications, 1981.

Additional Listings: Pattern Glass and specific glass categories such as Amberina, Cranberry, and Satin.

Opalescent, Daisy and Fern, blue ground, parian swirl mold, applied blue handle, clear faceted stopper, 6¼" h, $165.00.

Amberina
   3" h, ball shape, tiny IVT pattern, orig
      stopper, polished pontil **200.00**
   6" h, IVT, rose amber, applied amber
      handle, faceted amber stopper . .   **250.00**
Burmese, 6½" h, satin finish, melon
   ribbed body, orig mushroom stopper,
   undecorated, Mount Washington . . . **1,285.00**
Cranberry, 7½" h, 3¾" d, enameled
   white flowers and leaves, applied
   clear handle, clear bubble stopper . .   **175.00**
Opalescent Glass
   Hobb's Hobnail, white, orig stopper,
      polished pontil **100.00**
   Seaweed, blue **265.00**
Pattern Glass
   Broken Column **45.00**

Daisy and Button, blue, amber stop-
   per **95.00**
Dewey, amber **125.00**
Fancy Loop, Heisey **38.00**
Fandango **35.00**
Keystone **25.00**
Lacy Daisy **25.00**
Opposing Drops **28.00**
Orinda **21.00**
Paneled Diamond Block **25.00**
Paneled Thistle **25.00**
Pineapple and Fan, Heisey **45.00**
Quartered Block **25.00**
Tacoma **24.00**
Peachblow, 6½" h, mahogany shading
   to cherry red to cream, white int., tre-
   foil top, Wheeling **1,285.00**
Satin, 5" h, DQ, MOP, pink, thorn handle
   and stopper **575.00**
Spangle, clear glass, blue at base, sil-
   ver mica flakes, profuse random white
   mottling, clear faceted glass stopper   **235.00**
Spatter, Reverse Swirl, chrysanthemum
   base, blue speckled, applied blue
   handle, orig stopper **225.00**

CUP PLATES

History: Many early cups and saucers were handleless, with deep saucers. The hot liquid was poured into the saucer and sipped from it. This necessitated another plate for the cup, the "cup plate."

The first cup plates made of pottery were of the Staffordshire variety. In the mid-1830s to 40s, glass cup plates were favored. Boston and Sandwich Glass Company was one of the main contributors to the lacy glass type.

It is extremely difficult to find glass cup plates in outstanding (mint) condition. Collectors expect some marks of usage, such as slight rim roughness, minor chipping (best if under rim), and in rarer patterns a portion of a scallop missing.

Reference: Ruth Webb Lee and James H. Rose, *American Glass Cup Plates*, published by author, 1948, reprinted by Charles E. Tuttle Co., Inc. in 1985.

Notes: The numbers used are from the Lee–Rose book in which all plates are illustrated.

Prices are based on plates in "average" condition.

GLASS

LR 3, clear, 3⅞", blown three mold, at-
   tributed to Boston and Sandwich
   Glass Co **175.00**
LR 13, deep blue, 3¾", A-type mold,
   plain rim, New England **60.00**
LR 15, clear, 3⁷⁄₁₆", pontil, seven shallow

rim chips, edge roughage, New England origin **75.00**
LR 22-A, clear, 3 7/16", 15 scallops with shelves, New England or Sandwich origin **85.00**
LR, 36, 3 1/4", opal opaque, 17 even scallops **475.00**
LR 44, 3 1/4", clear, attributed to Sandwich or new England Glass Co, very slight rim roughage **100.00**
LR 46, lavender, 3 1/2", 15 even scallops, strawberry diamond pattern, eastern origin **125.00**
LR 52, opalescent, 3 3/4"; 15 scallops with points between, eastern origin **200.00**
LR 60, clear, 3 3/8", plain rope, cross hatching, eastern origin **200.00**
LR 64A, opaque white, known as Parker White cup plate, ex-William Elsholz and James J. Rose Collections, five small shallow flakes on upper rim . . **3,250.00**
LR 79, pink tint, 3 3/4", rope top and bottom, New England origin **50.00**
LR 82, opaque blue, 3 5/8", plain rim, 5 pointed star center, attributed to New England **275.00**
LR 107, 3 3/8", clear, plain rim, attributed to Philadelphia area, slight underfill, trace of mold roughness **50.00**
LR 120, clear, 3 1/16", 30 even scallops, midwestern origin **165.00**
LR 135, clear, 3 7/16", 24 bull's eyes, points between, attributed to midwestern origin **75.00**
LR 150-B, clear, 2 15/16", plain, robe on bottom, midwest origin **50.00**
LR 163, light green, 3 1/4", 34 scallops, radial lines between, midwest origin **65.00**
LR 179, lavender, 3 7/16", 10 scallop, rope top and bottom, attributed to Philadelphia area **125.00**
LR 183-B, deep blue, 3 1/2", octagonal rim, 7 scallops between corners, midwest origin **90.00**
LR 200, clear, 3 1/8", 96 sawtooth scallops, midwest origin **35.00**
LR 225-A, clear, 3 1/2", 12 large scallops, 4 small scallops between, attributed to Philadelphia area **50.00**
LR 255, amethyst tint, 3 5/8", 24 bold scallops, divided by pairs of small scallops **20.00**
LR 311, 3 5/8", 23 bold scallops, pairs of smaller scallops between each, Sandwich origin, amber stain on center design and border triangles, 2 scallops missing **300.00**
LR 343-B, clear, 3 7/16", plain, dotted below **45.00**
LR 388, opaque white, 3 5/16", plain, central star, attributed to Philadelphia area **35.00**
LR 412, clear, 3 3/16", 10 sided, star center, Sandwich origin **95.00**
LR 425, 3 3/8", deep amethyst, unlisted color, 9 large scallops with hearts between on rim, trace of mold roughness **1,600.00**
LR 430, clear, 3 3/8", 9 large scallops, hearts between diamond diapering, eastern origin **75.00**
LR 455, opal, 3 7/8", 48 even scallops, Sandwich origin **265.00**
LR 465-F, 3 3/8", violet blue, 63 even scallops, Sandwich origin, one scallop missing, 5 tipped **130.00**

Historical Staffordshire, castle Garden Battery, New York, Enoch Wood, dark blue, 3 5/8" d, $300.00

GLASS, HISTORICAL

LR 569, 3 7/16", clear, President Harrison, 67 even scallops, two scallops lightly tipped **40.00**
LR 576, medium blue, 3 9/16", 25 large scallops, 2 smaller scallops between, Sandwich origin **85.00**
LR 580, clear, 3 3/4", Victoria and Albert, 56 even scallops, English origin . . . **250.00**
LR 605-A, clear, 3 1/2", octagonal, ship, 3 scallops lightly tipped **275.00**
LR 643, clear, 3 9/16", Bunker Hill Monument, 53 even scallops, drape pattern shoulders, Sandwich origin **35.00**
LR 653, clear, 3", plain, eagle, laurel wreath, large chip **125.00**
LR 668, clear, 3 1/16", 56 even scallops, attributed to midwestern origin **100.00**
LR 677-E, 3 7/16", clear, octagonal, Midwest, perfect condition **325.00**

PORCELAIN OR POTTERY

English Transferware, 3 3/4", black transfer, Boston Mails...Gentlemen's Cabin **75.00**
Pink Luster **45.00**

Staffordshire, Historical

Hyena, 4¼", quadrupeds series, Hall	75.00
Oak Leaves, 4", Rogers, dark blue, faint hairline	25.00
Valley Of The Sanandoch From Jefferson's Rock, light colors	75.00
Worcester Cathedral, 4", Hall, tiny rub on rim	40.00

Staffordshire, Romantic

Corinth, James Edwards	40.00
Damacus, Wm Adams and Sons, blue and white	50.00
Garden Scenery, Mayer, pink, 12 sided	30.00
Lozere, Edward Challinor	65.00
Tuscan Rose, John and William Ridgway	45.00

CUSTARD GLASS

History: Custard glass was developed in England in the early 1880s. Harry Northwood made the first American custard glass at his Indiana, Pennsylvania, factory in 1898.

From 1898 until 1915, many manufacturers produced custard glass patterns, e.g., Dugan Glass, Fenton, A. H. Heisey Glass Co., Jefferson Glass, Northwood, Tarentum Glass, and U.S. Glass. Cambridge and McKee continued the production of custard glass into the Depression.

The ivory or creamy yellow custard color is achieved by adding uranium salts to the molten hot glass. The chemical content makes the glass glow when held under a black light. The higher the amount of uranium, the more luminous the color. Northwood's custard glass has the smallest amount of uranium, creating an ivory color; Heisey used more, creating a deep yellow color.

Custard glass was made in patterned tableware pieces. It also was made as souvenir items and novelty pieces. Souvenir pieces are marked with place names or hand painted decorations, e.g., flowers. Patterns of custard glass often were highlighted in gold, enamel colors, and stains.

Reference: William Heacock, *Encyclopedia Of Victorian Colored Pattern Glass, Book IV: Custard Glass From A to Z*, Peacock Publications, 1980.

Reproduction Alert: L. G. Wright Glass Co. has reproduced pieces in the Argonaut Shell and Grape and Cable patterns. It also introduced new patterns, such as Floral and Grape and Vintage Band. Moser reproduced toothpicks in Argonaut Shell, Chrysanthemum Sprig, and Inverted Fan & Feather.

Additional Listings: Pattern Glass.

Banana Boat, Geneva, green dec	125.00

Berry, master

Argonaut Shell, 10½" l	140.00
Beaded Circle	185.00
Chrysanthemum Sprig	145.00

Sugar and Creamer, Argonaut Shell, gold details, $225.00.

Fan	200.00
Geneva, green dec, 8½" oval	85.00
Grape and Cable, 7½", ruffled edge	45.00

Berry Set

Argonaut Shell, 7 pcs	500.00
Chrysanthemum Sprig, 11" d x 5" h master oval bowl, six individual bowls, script "Northwood" marks	500.00
Everglades, 7 pcs	725.00
Grape and Gothic Arches, 7 pcs	475.00
Victoria, 7 pcs	625.00

Butter Dish, cov

Argonaut Shell	245.00
Chrysanthemum Sprig	185.00
Geneva, red and green dec	125.00
Grape and Cable	225.00
Intaglio	220.00
Maple Leaf	200.00
Victoria	285.00
Winged Scroll	160.00

Compote, jelly

Chrysanthemum Sprig	70.00
Geneva	100.00
Maple Leaf	375.00
Ring Band	165.00

Creamer

Beaded Circle	125.00
Chrysanthemum Sprig	85.00
Fluted Scrolls	50.00
Grape and Cable	100.00
Intaglio	95.00
Jackson	65.00
Jefferson	110.00
Louis XV	55.00
Vermont	90.00
Wild Bouquet	135.00

Creamer and Sugar, individual size, Heart with Thumbprints, pr	125.00
Dresser Tray, Northwood Grape	225.00

Goblet

Beaded Swag, souvenir	60.00
Grape and Gothic Arches	50.00

Pitcher, water

Beaded Circle	425.00
Cherry and Scale	325.00
Chrysanthemum Sprig	365.00

Diamond with Peg	250.00
Georgia Gem, good dec	310.00
Inverted Fan and Feather	400.00
Louis XV	225.00
Vermont	250.00

Salt and Pepper Shakers, pr, orig top
Argonaut Shell	350.00
Carnelian	450.00
Fluted Scrolls	100.00
Geneva	175.00
Louis XV	215.00
Punty Band, souvenir	80.00
Ring Band, souvenir	115.00

Sauce
Argonaut Shell	67.50
Delaware, rose stain	65.00
Peacock and Urn	40.00

Spooner
Beaded Circle	120.00
Chrysanthemum Sprig	75.00
Georgia Gem, floral dec	55.00
Intaglio	85.00
Louis XV	55.00
Maple Leaf	85.00
Trailing Vine, blue	60.00
Victoria	55.00

Sugar, cov
Chrysanthemum Sprig, blue	325.00
Diamond with Peg	95.00
Georgia Gem	115.00
Jefferson	140.00
Winged Scroll	160.00

Table Set, 4 pcs
Carnelian	850.00
Geneva	500.00
Louis XV, gold dec	450.00
Ring Band	500.00

Toothpick Holder
Chrysanthemum Sprig, sgd "Northwood"	150.00
Georgia Gem, souvenir	35.00
Harvard	35.00
Ivorina Verde	85.00
Tiny Thumbprint	55.00
Vermont, green dec	135.00
Wild Bouquet, blue trim, enameled dec	90.00

Tumbler
Argonaut Shell	85.00
Cherry and Scale	45.00
Chrysanthemum Sprig	20.00
Fluted Scrolls	40.00
Geneva, dec	55.00
Grape and Cable, nutmeg stain	300.00
Intaglio, green trim	40.00
Inverted Fan and Feather	70.00
Louis IV	35.00
Punty Band, souvenir	35.00

Water Set, pitcher and four matching tumblers, Chrysanthemum Sprig, pink and green stain, gold trim | 525.00

Whiskey, Diamond Peg, souvenir | 45.00

Wine
Diamond with Peg	45.00
Punty Band, souvenir	50.00
Tiny Thumbprint	48.00

CUT GLASS, AMERICAN

History: Glass is cut by the process of grinding decoration into the glass by means of abrasive-carrying metal wheels or stone wheels. A very ancient craft, it was revived in 1600 by Bohemians and spread through Europe, to Great Britain, and to America.

American cut glass came of age at the Centennial Exposition in 1876 and the World Columbian Exposition in 1893. The American public recognized American cut glass to be exceptional in quality and workmanship. America's most significant output of this high quality glass occurred from 1880 to 1917, a period now known as the "Brilliant Period."

About the 1890s some companies began adding an acid-etched "signature" to their glass. This signature may be the actual company name, its logo, or chosen symbol. Today, signed pieces can command a premium over unsigned pieces since the signature clearly establishes the origin.

However, caution should be exercised in regard to signature identification. Objects with forged signatures have been in existence for some time. To check for authenticity, run your finger tip or finger nail lightly over the area with the signature. As a general rule, a genuine signature cannot be felt; a forged signature exhibits a raised surface.

Many companies never used the acid-etched signature on the glass and may or may not have affixed paper labels to the items originally. Dorflinger Glass and the Meriden Glass Co. made cut glass of the highest quality, yet never acid-etched a signature on the glass. Furthermore, cut glass made before the 1890s was not signed. Many of these wood polished items, cut on blown blanks, were of excellent quality and often won awards at exhibitions.

Consequently, if collectors restrict themselves to signed pieces only, many beautiful pieces of the highest quality glass and workmanship will be missed.

References: E. S. Farrar & J. S. Spillman, *The Complete Cut & Engraved Glass Of Corning*, Crown Publishers [Corning Museum of Glass monograph], 1979; John Feller, *Dorflinger: America's Finest Glass, 1852–1921*, Antique Publications, 1988; J. Michael Pearson, *Encyclopedia Of American Cut & Engraved Glass*, Volumes I to III, published by author, 1975; Albert C. Revi, *American Cut & Engraved Glass*, Thomas Nelson, Inc., 1965; Martha Louise Swan, *American and Engraved Glass*, Wallace-Homestead, 1986; H. Weiner & F. Lipkowitz, *Rarities In American Cut Glass*, Collectors House of Books, 1975.

Collectors' Club: American Cut Glass Association, 1603 SE 19th, Suite 112, Edmond Professional Bldg., Edmond, OK 73013.

Museums: The Corning Museum of Glass, Corning, NY; High Museum of Art, Atlanta, GA; Huntington Galleries, Huntington, WV; Lightner Museum, St. Augustine, FL; Toledo Museum Of Art, Toledo, OH.

Advertising, display piece, 4″ h, triangular wedge, engraved and cut trademark and "Hawkes Crystal"	425.00
Banana Bowl, 14½″ l, Harvard border, cut florals and leaves, Harvard center, scalloped serrated rim	175.00
Basket	
5½″ d, 8″ h, Berlyn pattern, Quaker City Glass Co, applied twisted handle, three step pedestal base	365.00
6½″ d, Brilliant Period, intaglio cutting, applied twisted handle	145.00
8 x 11¾″, Panel pattern, hobstars and elongated vesicas, flaring scalloped and serrated rim, pointed overall notched handle, sgd "Hawkes"	5,000.00

Bowl, Hunt's Royal pattern, 9″ d, $350.00.

Bowl	
8″ d	
Marseilles pattern, hobstar and star	225.00
Phlox pattern, intaglio cut flowers, hobstar and fan motifs, sgd "Tuthill"	265.00
Pinwheel, fan and notched prism, star cut base, scalloped and serrated rim	125.00
Prima Donna pattern, sgd "Clark"	325.00
Royal pattern, Russian pattern sides, hobstar button, pentagonal strawberry diamond lozenge and large hobstars, sgd "Hunt"	325.00
Venetian pattern, chain of hobstars, fan, star, and strawberry diamond, sgd "Hawkes"	285.00
8½″ d, bars of cane, 32 point hobstars, serrated scalloped rim, sgd "Clark"	200.00
9″ d	
Adonis pattern, cane, fan, hobstar, and strawberry diamond, sgd "Clark"	230.00
Colonna pattern, hobstar, cross—cut diamond, star, and fan, sgd "Libbey"	225.00
Notched prism flares, sgd "Maple City Glass Co,"	225.00
Russian cut sides, floral and leaf wreath center, sawtooth scalloped rim	125.00
10″ d	
Hobstars, prism, relief diamond and fans, scalloped sawtooth rim	250.00
Jubilee pattern, Dorflinger	450.00
10″ d, 3″ h, Brilliant Period, feather wreath centering intaglio shield, American	650.00
Butter Dish, cov	
4¾″ h dome, hobstars and rayed fluted panels, faceted knob, matching 8″ d tray, scalloped cut rim, sgd "Hawkes"	300.00
4¾″ h dome, pinwheel cutting, 5″ d underplate	115.00
7½″ d underplate, hobstars and florals, dome lid	200.00
Butter Tub	
Diamond and fan cutting, cov	225.00
Hobstars, high tub handles	150.00
Calling Card Receiver, 8½″ l, intaglio floral and leaf motifs, scalloped rim, sgd "Tuthill"	200.00
Candelabra, three arm, Brazilian pattern, fan, star, and strawberry diamond, sgd "Hawkes," pr	6,100.00
Candlestick	
2″ h, 3½″ d, cross—cut hobnail and fan, sgd "Libbey"	175.00
8″ h, bull's eyes, knobbed stem, Cutting No. 126, Meriden Cut Glass	250.00
9″ h, inverted bell shaped bowl, hexagonal column, rayed circular base, sgd "Hawkes"	120.00
10″ h, Comet pattern, pr	700.00
11″ h, amber, baluster form hollow stem, engraved vintage pattern on stem and base	100.00
14″ h, blown hollow teardrop stem, star cut bases, Hawkes trademark, pr	450.00
18″ h, Fancy Prism, teardrop in stem, Hawkes, pr	3,000.00
Candy Dish, divided, 8″ d, intaglio floral, twin handles	85.00

Carafe

7" h, notched fluted neck, bulbous body, hobstars and cross–cut diamonds 100.00

7¼" h, 6½" d, hobstars, crosshatching, and fan, notched panel cut neck, rayed base, bulbous 125.00

8½" h, 6¼" d base, Pineapple and Fan pattern, cross–cut diamond and fan, rayed base, notched eight panel neck, horizontal cutting ... 100.00

Celery Tray

8" l, Brilliant Period, sgd "Tuthill" ... 100.00

11" l, hobstars, serrated rim 150.00

12" l, Chrysanthemum pattern 225.00

Centerpiece Bowl, 11½" d, 7½" h, Brilliant Period, squatty, heavy walled, stepped horizontal cutting above multiple hobstar center band, massive star cut base 650.00

Champagne, Monarch pattern variant, Hoare 45.00

Cheese Dish

5½" h, chain of hobstars, arcadia crosshatches, notched prisms, faceted star knob, 8" d scalloped rim underplate 450.00

7½" h, 9" d, Brilliant Period, strawberry and diamond with fan pattern plate, domed cov with faceted knob, minor pattern roughness .. 225.00

Clock

5 x 10", Harvard pattern, horizontal step and line cutting, rect base circular clock enclosure 975.00

11½" h, domed case, ribbed silver thread surface, three floral medallions, iris, roses, and asters, crosshatched border with vintage motif, stepped platform base with ribbing and diamonds, orig Chelsea movement and dial, retailer's mark "Caldwell, Philadelphia," Sinclaire 3,700.00

Cologne Bottle

6½" h, bulbous, all-over cross–cut diamonds, fluted neck, flanked rim, faceted cut bulb stopper 120.00

8" h, round, Brilliant Period, hobstar and fan pattern, faceted stopper 125.00

Compote

8" d, Wreath and Thistle pattern, teardrop in stem 150.00

8" d, 8⅝" h, Buffalo pattern, Buffalo Cut Glass Co, heavy blank 350.00

8½" d, rolled over edge, vintage intaglio, sgd "Tuthill" 400.00

10" d, 7¾" h, Strawberry Diamond and Fan pattern, Bakewell & Pears, small flake inside rim .. 1,200.00

10¼" h, cup shaped body, cut bands and elongated ovals, wide circular foot cut with ovals, collared conical

stem, wide turned out rim cut with thumbprints, sgd "Hawkes" 345.00

Creamer and Sugar

4½" h, diamond point cutting, notched prism handles, pedestal base ... 325.00

5¾" h, Brilliant Period, hobstar, faceted knopped pedestal base, Hawkes trademark, minor pattern roughness 550.00

7" h, intaglio, applied blue handles and base, sgd "Libbey" 275.00

Cruet

Hobstars and fans, orig stopper, notched handle, sgd "Fry" 175.00

Petticoat, strawberry diamond, fan, and stars, hobstar base, triple notched handle, faceted stopper 125.00

Decanter

9½" h, sq, chamfered corners, zipper, fan, vesicas, multifaceted stopper, pr 350.00

12" h, relief diamond cut bulbous body, clear panels, slender honeycomb neck, applied clear handle, matching teardrop stopper 150.00

13½" h, Harvard and Floral pattern, bowling pin shape 425.00

Dresser Box, 4½ x 3 x 3", large hobstar on top with expanding rays, prisms around lid, hinged 175.00

Dresser Tray, 10 x 7", Sheraton pattern, oval, engraved medallions, triple miter–cut bands alternating with strawberry diamond bands, sgd "Hawkes" 200.00

Fernery

7½" d, pinwheels, fans, vesicas with Harvard variant, tri–ftd 70.00

8 x 4", Harvard pattern sides, sgd "Clark" 225.00

Finger Bowl, 4¾" d, Brilliant Period, Lotus pattern, Eggington 90.00

Fruit Compote, 8⅝" h, 8" w, Brilliant Period, Buffalo pattern, extremely clear and heavy blank, Buffalo Cut Glass Co 350.00

Goblet

5½" h, Brilliant Period, Russian cut, cut–button variant, faceted teardrop knopped stem, set of six ... 650.00

6" h, Brunswick pattern 115.00

7" h, Millicent pattern 85.00

Horseradish Jar, cov, Brilliant Period, Pinwheel and Thumbprint pattern, orig stopper 135.00

Ice Bucket, 17 x 10", Marlboro pattern, two handles, matching underplate, Dorflinger 1,500.00

Ice Cream Set, 14¾" d service tray, twelve 7" d plates, cut, engraved, and polished Poppy pattern, marked "Hawkes Gravic Glass," 13 pcs 5,500.00

Ice Cream Tray, 14¼ x 7½", deeply cut
hobstars, prism, and nailhead 375.00
Lamp, 13¾" h, Brilliant Period, dome
top, hobstar and pinwheel cutting,
matching cut standard, prism ring . . 500.00
Lamp Base, 30" h, octagonal faceted
shaft, stepped horizontal cutting,
added vertical faceting, conforming
octagonal platform base, two socket
mounting, Hawkes trademark 650.00
Loving Cup, 8½" h, hobstars, fans, and
strawberry diamonds, hobstar base,
pedestal, three honeycomb handles 3,250.00
Mayonnaise Bowl, 6¾" d, matching 7½"
d underplate, hobstars, hobnail and
crosshatches, scalloped serrated
rims 350.00
Mint Tray, 6" d, hobstars and nailhead,
sawtooth and scalloped edge 115.00
Napkin Ring, Brilliant Period cutting . . 85.00
Nut Dish, 3" d, hobstars and buttons
forming star, Greek key type border,
set of 12 . . . . 150.00
Orange Bowl, 8" deep, Rayed Points
pattern 225.00
Perfume Bottle
4" l, lay down type, curved, int. stopper, ornate SS top 100.00
12" l, Russian pattern, Gorham SS
cap 275.00

**Pitcher, Cluster pattern, O. F. Egging-
ton, Corning NY, c1910, 10" h, $300.00.**

Pitcher, 11" h, tankard, bands of Harvard at rim and base, prism and step
cuttings, fluted spout, serrated rim,
double notched handle 170.00
Presentation Pitcher, 15" h, raised ex-

tended lip, applied handle, heavy
walled teardrop crystal body, carved
portrait of "Thomas G Hawkes," artist
sgd "W H Morse," coat of arms on
reverse, Hawkes tripartite trademark
on handle 4,000.00
Punch Bowl, 14 x 13", two part, hob-
stars, cane, vesica, and fan, scalloped serrated rim and base, sgd with
star in circle 1,400.00
Punch Cup, Russian pattern, hobstar
foot 65.00
Salt, master, 3" d, global, hobstars and
crosshatches, sgd "Hawkes" 230.00

**Scent Bottle, floral motif Sterling silver
cap, orig glass int. stopper, 3½" l,
$150.00.**

Sugar, cov, intaglio cut strawberries, floral, and leaves, applied double handles, cov marked "Sterling" 150.00
Tray
9" l, leaf shape, handled, deeply cut,
Hunt's Royal pattern, scalloped
serrated rim 300.00
11½" d, octagonal, turned up rim,
chain of hobstars, center pinwheels
and cane encircling hobstar, scalloped sawtooth edge 425.00
13½" l, 11½" w, heart shape, hobstars, bars of cane, vesicas with
buttons and crosshatches, scalloped serrated rim, fan in handle 650.00
14" l, rect, hobstars, fans, and
wedges of hobnails, scalloped serrated rim, few polished teeth 145.00
14½" l, 11½" w, oval, Plaid and Thistle pattern, cut and engraved, Sinclaire "S" in wreath trademark . . . 4,200.00
Vase
7½" h, 5" w, amethyst cut to clear,
Diamond Point and Fan pattern . . 160.00
10" h, tapered, hobstars and crosshatches into prism cut bars, pinwheels and fans, scalloped rim,
sgd "Libbey" 100.00
10½" h, corset, band of hobstars at
scalloped serrated rim, bull's eye
and prismatic cut body, hobstar
base 150.00
11¾" h, trumpet, cut and etched
flower garlands, Gravic, Hawkes 260.00

12" h, trumpet, ftd, cross-cut diamond and fan 90.00
13" h, corset, top wreath of florals and leaves, all-over bull's eyes connected with crosshatches, scalloped sawtooth rim 225.00
16" h, cylindrical, scalloped serrated rim, hobstars and crosshatches, slightly flared base 450.00
Water Set, 11" h pitcher, four 6¼" h goblets, Brilliant Period, hobstar and cane cutting, 5 pcs 250.00
Wine
6¾" h, cranberry cut to clear, overall diamond design, tapered bowl . . . 100.00
8¼" h, 3" d, Rhine type, Brilliant Period cutting, amber bowl, stem, and star cut foot 60.00

CUT VELVET

History: Several glass manufacturers made cut velvet during the late Victorian era, c1870–1900. An outer layer of pastel color was applied over a white casing. The piece then was molded or cut in a ribbed or diamond shape in high relief, exposing portions of the casing. The finish had a satin velvety feel, hence the name "cut velvet."

Vase, ribbed, undulating crimped top, pink, white int., 7½" h, $225.00.

Bottle, 8" h, ribbed, shaded blue, white lining 175.00
Bowl, 6" d, 4¼" h, shiny pink, applied crystal rim trip, crystal feet 255.00
Celery Vase, 6½" h, deep blue, DQ, box pleated top 725.00

Creamer, 3¼" h, bulbous, blue, DQ, applied white satin glass handle 200.00
Pitcher, 8½" h, pink, sq mouth, frosted reeded twisted handle, rosettes, and neck ring 425.00
Rose Bowl, 4¼" h, 2⅞" d, egg shape, four crimp top, rose overlay, DQ, white lining 165.00
Tumbler, 3¾" h, medium pink, lighter pink striping, ribbed 85.00
Vase
6½" h, stick, rose, DQ, white lining 225.00
13½" h, double gourd, long neck, pale gold, DQ 650.00

CZECHOSLOVAKIAN ITEMS

History: Objects marked "Made in Czechoslovakia" were produced after 1918 when the country claimed its independence from the Austro-Hungarian Empire. The people became more cosmopolitan, liberated, and expanded their scope of life. Their porcelains, pottery, and glassware reflect many influences.

A specific manufacturer's mark may be identified as being much earlier than 1918, but this only indicates the factory existed in the Bohemian or Austro-Hungarian Empire period.

Reference: Ruth A. Forsythe, *Made in Czechoslovakia*, Richardson Printing Corp., 1982.

Atomizer, clear blue glass stem, gold ground top with enameled floral dec, $125.00.

GLASS

Bowl, 9" d, scalloped rim, irid gold, marked, c1925 . . . . 145.00
Box, cov, 4" h, rect, ruby red faceted body, brass mounts, marked "Made In Czechoslovakia," c1920 . . . . 280.00
Lemonade Set, 10" pitcher, two matching glasses, sapphire blue, green,

and aubergine ground, sapphire blue
threaded shoulder, blue ribbed handles, sgd, c1930 .... **225.00**
Perfume, lovebirds, pink top **135.00**
Pitcher, 10″ h, smoky topaz, green
streaks, cobalt threading **80.00**
Spittoon, 3″ h, lady's, cobalt blue glass,
spattered colors **65.00**
Vase, yellow, black snake, ruffled top **175.00**

POTTERY AND PORCELAIN

Bowl, 4″ d, crackle, hp floral dec **30.00**
Candy Dish, multicolored spatter, black
feet **45.00**
Creamer, gold luster ext, black handles
and trim, marked "Czechoslovakia" **12.00**
Figure, 17″ h, cockatoo, yellow and or-
ange **125.00**
Pin Dish, Pierrot, black and white **80.00**
Seafood Set, figural, crab, 5 pcs **75.00**
Vase, 10½″, applied handles, paper la-
bel, additional orig NY store label .. **225.00**

DAVENPORT

History: John Davenport opened a pottery in
Longport, Staffordshire, England in 1793. His ware
was of high quality, light weight, and cream colored
with a beautiful velvety texture.

The firm made soft-paste (Old Blue), luster
trimmed ware, and pink luster with black transfer.
There have been pieces of Gaudy Dutch and Spatterware found with the Davenport mark. Later Davenport became a leading maker of ironstone and
early flow blue. His famous "Cyprus" pattern in
mulberry became very popular. His heirs continued
the business until the factory closed in 1886.

Reference: Susan and Al Bagdade, *Warman's
English & Continental Pottery & Porcelain, 1st Edition,* Warman Publishing Co., Inc., 1987.

Biscuit Jar, 6½″ h, Imari style dec, SP
cov and bail, c1870 .... **140.00**
Bowl and Underplate, red flowers,
green leaves, c1840 .... **60.00**
Compote, 9″ h, hp, pink flowers, gold
trim, c1830 .... **90.00**
Cup and Saucer
Clifford pattern **95.00**
Green wreath, gold trim **60.00**
Japan pattern, c1870 .... **45.00**

**Pitcher, transfer crackle pattern, tan
ground, serpent handle, 6″ h, $75.00.**

Cup Plate, Friburg pattern **25.00**
Dessert Service
20 pcs, multicolored floral sprays,
scroll surrounds, gilt stylized foliage
on green border, puce printed
mark, c1850 .... **1,000.00**
21 pcs, eleven dessert plates, two
7¼″ sauce boats and stands, six
shaped serving dishes, white
ground, green and white floral dec,
c1825 .... **1,200.00**
Ewer, 9″ h, multicolored, flower dec,
c1830 .... **175.00**
Fruit Bowl, ftd, 2½ x 9½″, hp roses, gold
trim, c1865 .... **135.00**
Gravy Boat, blue and white flowers .. **85.00**
Plate
7½″ d, hexagonal, emb floral border,
green transfer of child and cat ... **85.00**
8¾″ d, earthenware, medium blue
transfer printed English landscape,
ruined abbey, imp "Davenport" .. **50.00**
9″ d, maroon and gold border, gold
medallion center, marked "Davenport," c1850 .... **25.00**
10¾″ d, Cyprus pattern, imp anchor
mark **55.00**
Platter
9 x 12½″, Cyprus, mulberry **100.00**
10 x 9″, blue Oriental scene, c1820 **75.00**
10⅜ x 13⅝″, Amory pattern, flow
blue, rect, chamfered corners, incised "Amory," anchor mark **165.00**
Teapot, Imari design **140.00**
Tray, 11 x 9″, cloverleaf design, c1850 **130.00**
Tureen, 10½″ l, Cyprus pattern, mulberry **100.00**
Urn, 6″ h, white with blue and gold trim,
classic figure, handled **250.00**
Vegetable Dish, ftd, 6½″ d, 5½″ h,
stoneware, loop handles, domed cov,
gilt accents, Imari style dec, matching
underplate, c1840, chipped, pr **450.00**

DECOYS

History: Carved wooden decoys, used to lure
ducks and geese to the hunter, have become

widely recognized as an indigenous American folk art form in the past several years.

Many decoys are from the 1880–1930 period when commercial gunners commonly hunted using rigs of several hundred decoys. Many fine carvers also worked through the 1930s and 1940s.

The value of a decoy is based on several factors: (1) fame of the carver, (2) quality of the carving, (3) species of wild fowl—the most desirable are herons, swans, mergansers, and shorebirds, and (4) condition of the original paint (o.p.).

The inexperienced collector should be aware of several facts. The age of a decoy, per se, is usually of no importance in determining value. Since very few decoys were ever signed, it will be quite difficult to attribute most decoys to known carvers. Anyone who has not examined a known carver's work will be hard pressed to determine if the paint on one of his decoys is indeed original.

Repainting severely decreases a decoy's value. In addition, there are many fakes and reproductions on the market and even experienced collectors are occasionally fooled.

Decoys listed below are of average wear unless otherwise noted (o.p. indicates original paint).

Reference: Joe Engers (general editor), *The Great Book of Wildfowl Decoys*, Thunder Bay Press, 1990; Henry A. Fleckenstein, Jr., *American Factory Decoys*, Schiffer Publishing, Ltd.; Ronald J. Fritz, *Michigan's Master Carver Oscar W. Peterson, 1887–1951*, Aardvark Publications, 1988; Gene and Linda Kangas, *Decoys: A North American Survey*, Hillcrest Publications, 1983; Art, Brad and Scott Kimball, *The Fish Decoy*, Aardvark Publications, Inc., 1986; Carl F. Luckey, *Collecting Antique Bird Decoys: An Identification & Value Guide*, Books Americana, 1983.

Periodicals: *Decoy Hunter Magazine*, 901 North 9th, Clinton, IN 47842; *Decoy Magazine*, P.O. Box 1900, Montego Bay Station, Ocean City, MD 21842; *The Wild Fowl Art Journal*, Ward Foundation, 655 South Salisbury Blvd, Salisbury, MD 21801.

American Merganser Drake, unknown maker, Massachusetts, carved, raised, and crossed wing tips, head turned to right	500.00
Black Duck	
Ben Holmes, Connecticut, hollow carved, repainted body and bill	2,000.00
Ben Schmidt, carved feather detail and wing tips, o.p.	350.00
C. Ralph Wells, Connecticut, hollow carved, o.p.	450.00
Charles Hart, Massachusetts, carved wing tips and diamond shape nostrils, o.p.	400.00
Doug Jester, scratch feather paint	700.00
Mason Factory, Michigan, premier grade, o.p.	550.00

R. Sabatini, hollow carved, o.p.	200.00
Unknown Maker, hollow carved, raised wing tips, old paint	350.00
Black-Breasted Plover, Harry V. Shourds, o.p., replaced bill	250.00
Bluebill, mated pair, Percy Grant, New Jersey, carved heart-shape wings	400.00
Bluebill Drake	
Harry V. Shourds, New Jersey, hollow carved, old repaint	425.00
John McLoughlin, New Jersey, hollow carved, carved tail feathers and raised crossed wing tips, o.p., sgd on bottom	700.00
Mason Factory, Michigan, standard grade, glass eyes, o.p., split bottom	225.00
Ward Brothers, balsa, raised wing tips, head turned to left	1,100.00
Bluebill Hen	
George Robert, New York, balsa body, head turned to back, o.p.	325.00
Ira Hudson, Virginia, painted, reglued bill	1,200.00
Irving Miller, Michigan, glass eyes, o.p. 11½″ l	150.00
Mason Factory, Michigan, standard grade, painted eyes, slight red painted speckled body, split bottom	125.00
Blue-Wing Teal, mated pair, Mason Factory, Michigan, premier grade, o.p.	5,000.00
Blue-Wing Teal Drake, Mason Factory, Michigan, premier grade, o.p.	700.00
Blue-Wing Teal Hen	
George Robert, New York, cork, branded "Manning" on bottom	200.00
James Holly, Maryland, o.p.	3,750.00
Mason Factory, Michigan, premier grade, o.p., average wear	600.00
Brant	
Hurley Conklin, New Jersey, hollow carved, o.p., detail	400.00
Joe Lincoln, Massachusetts, self bailing	1,400.00
Mason Factory, Michigan, challenge grade, hollow carved, orig and old paint, worn	250.00
Miles Hancock, Virginia, o.p.	500.00
Percy Grant, o.p.	225.00
Rhoades Truax, New Jersey, hollow carved, carved eyes, old paint	200.00
Bufflehead, mated pair, Paul Gibson, sgd and dated on bottom	400.00
Bufflehead Drake, John McLoughlin, New Jersey, hollow carved, repainted	350.00
Canada Goose	
Bill Oler, New Jersey, hollow carved, branded "Wm Oler" on bottom	325.00
Harry V. Shourds, hollow carved, old repaint	350.00
Madison Mitchell, Ward style head, o.p.	350.00

R.A. Nickerson, carved, Elmer Crowell repaint, oval brand **1,600.00**

Unknown Maker, balsa body, feeding position, incised feather detail, old paint **375.00**

Ward Brothers, Maryland, carved raised wing tips and back feathers, head turned to right **1,700.00**

Canvasback, mated pair, Ward Brothers, balsa, sgd "Lem and Steve," dated 1948 .... **2,300.00**

Canvasback Drake

Mason Factory, Michigan, standard grade, tack eyes, o.p. **150.00**

Miles Hancock, o.p. **400.00**

Ward Brothers, balsa body, sgd, dated 1948 .... **1,700.00**

Canvasback Hen, Mason Factory, Michigan, premier grade, o.p., minor wear **1,150.00**

Curlew

Harry V. Shourds, o.p. **800.00**

Unknown Maker, Virginia, old paint, replaced bill **900.00**

Eider Drake, unknown maker, hollow carved, head turned to right **1,300.00**

Eider Hen

Pete Mitchell, Maine, carved, preening position, deep inlet neck **1,900.00**

Golden Plover, unknown maker, carved wings, o.p. **500.00**

Goldeneye, mated pair, unknown maker, head slightly turned, o.p., rect brand on bottom **3,000.00**

Goldeneye Drake

Harry V. Shourds, hollow carved, repainted, minor restoration **350.00**

Mason Factory, Michigan, standard grade, tack eyes, repainted **70.00**

Unknown Maker, attributed to James Hurlburt, Connecticut, carved eyes, o.p. **1,700.00**

Green-Wing Teal Drake

Ben Schmidt, Michigan, carved feather detail on back, o.p. **600.00**

Mark McNair, hollow carved, sgd on bottom **525.00**

Ward Brothers, carved, standing position **1,800.00**

Green-Wing Teal Hen, George Robert, cork **200.00**

Mallard, mated pair

Dodge Factory, Michigan, carved graceful body, o.p., restored necks **1,100.00**

Nick Sacchi, hollow carved, raised wing tips, o.p. **350.00**

Tube Dawson, Illinois, hollow carved, o.p. **600.00**

Mallard Drake

Hector Whittington, hollow body, turned head, glass eyes, old repaint, 16¾" l **175.00**

Mason Factory, Michigan, premier grade, o.p., one eye replaced, small chip **400.00**

Ward Brothers, raised wing tips, head turned to right **1,200.00**

Mallard Hen

Hector Whittington, Oglesby, Ill, hollow body, turned head, glass eyes, old repaint, 17¼" l **225.00**

Mason Factory, Michigan, premier grade, o.p., split back and neck .. **375.00**

Merganser Hen

Doug Jester, Virginia, carved, unused **1,750.00**

J. E. Hendrickson, New Jersey, hollow carved, o.p. **225.00**

Miles Hancock, scratch feather paint, sgd on bottom **550.00**

Unknown Maker, balsa body, initialed "HA" on bottom **500.00**

Pintail, Delaware River, Bordentown, N.J. by Black, $450.00.

Pintail Drake

Lloyd Tyler, Maryland, long graceful body, o.p. **500.00**

Mason Factory, Michigan, standard grade, glass eyes, o.p. **1,200.00**

Ward Brothers, balsa body, sleeping position, sgd, dated 1948, o.p. ... **4,300.00**

William Shaw, Illinois, hollow carved, repainted **200.00**

Pintail Hen

Don Zeng, Chicago, carved, o.p., glass eyes, 13½" l **375.00**

Mason Factory, Michigan, standard grade, glass eyes, o.p. **200.00**

Plover

Unknown Maker, New England, painted brown, white speckled breast, peg bill, 9" l, late 19th C .. **225.00**

Redhead, mated pair

Robert Sellers, Maryland, o.p., carved "X" under tail **700.00**

Stevens Factory, New York, o.p. ... **950.00**

Redhead Drake

George Robert, New York, balsa body, head slightly turned to left .. **150.00**

Harry V. Shourds, hollow carved, repainted **200.00**

Mason Factory, Michigan, challenge grade, o.p. **1,150.00**

Ward Borthers, balsa body, sgd
"Lem," dated 1948 . . . . **1,300.00**
Redhead Hen, Ward Brothers, balsa
body, o.p. **1,700.00**
Red-Breasted Merganser, mated pair
Miles Hancock, carved, o.p. **2,200.00**
Unknown Maker, defined carved
wings, o.p. **4,250.00**
Red-Breasted Merganser Drake
Captain Preston Wright, Massachu-
setts, incised wings, maroon, or-
ange, and yellow painted feathered
breast, orig horsehair comb, o.p. . **17,500.00**
Samuel Squires, carved crest on
back, o.p., branded on bottom . . . **5,000.00**
Unknown Maker, New Jersey, hollow
carved, sleeping position, re-
painted **250.00**
Ruddy Duck Drake, Roy Black, raised
wing tips, carved keel and initials
"RWB" **400.00**
Sandpiper, unknown maker, Massachu-
setts, sealing wax eyes, o.p., re-
placed bill **700.00**
Sickle Bill Curlew, Mason Factory, Mich-
igan, carved, minor crazing, o.p. . . . **5,500.00**
Surf Scoter, Gus Wilson, Maine, carved
wing tips, old repaint **175.00**
Squaw, J. E. Hendrickson, hollow
carved, o.p. **200.00**
Widgeon Drake
Miles Pirnie, Michigan, o.p. **275.00**
Unknown Maker, carved wing tips,
branded "Reg Smith" on keel . . . **150.00**
Yellowlegs
A. Elmer Crowell, o.p. **3,750.00**
Mark Holland, carved tail and wing
feathers, sgd on base **275.00**
Unknown Maker, Virginia, o.p. **600.00**
William Mathews, Virginia, carved
wing tips and eyes, old paint **1,500.00**

DEDHAM POTTERY

History: Alexander W. Robertson established
the Chelsea Pottery in Chelsea, Massachusetts,
in 1860. In 1872 it was known as the Chelsea
Keramic Art Works.

In 1895 the pottery moved to Dedham, and the
name was changed to Dedham Pottery. Their prin-

cipal product was gray crackleware dinnerware
with a blue decoration, the rabbit pattern being the
most popular. The factory closed in 1943.

The following marks help determine the approximate age of items: (1) Chelsea Keramic Art
Works, "Robertson" impressed, 1876–1889; (2)
C.P.U.S. impressed in a cloverleaf, 1891–1895; (3)
Foreshortened rabbit, 1895–1896; (4) Conven-
tional rabbit with "Dedham Pottery" stamped in
blue, 1897; (5) Rabbit mark with "Registered,"
1929–1943.

Reference: Lloyd E. Hawes, *The Dedham Pottery And The Earlier Robertson's Chelsea Potteries,* Dedham Historical Society, 1968.

Reproduction Alert: Several rabbit pattern
pieces have been reproduced.

**Plate, Pond Lily, artist Maude Daven-
port's mark, 6¼" d, $200.00.**

Ashtray
4" d, round
Elephant, stamped mark **350.00**
Magnolia, stamped registered . . . **200.00**
4¾" h, standing figure of naughty
Dutch boy, shallow oval form tray,
crackle glaze **600.00**
Bouillon Cup and Plate, 6" d, Duck,
stamped **400.00**
Bowl
7" d, Rabbit, stamped registered . . . **350.00**
7¼" d, 3¾" h, scalloped rim, wide
mouth, squat bulbous base,
striated glossy brown on blue
glaze, imp "CKAW," glaze chips . . **100.00**
Charger, 12" d, Rabbit, imp and
stamped registered **275.00**
Console Set, pr 3½" d candlesticks, 6"
d bowl, Rabbit, stamped, 1931, 3 pcs **650.00**
Creamer, 5⅛" h, Rabbit, stamped reg-
istered **425.00**
Dish, 7" d, five sided, stamped regis-
tered **475.00**
Egg Cup
1½" h, single, Rabbit, unmarked . . . **200.00**

Egg Cup Underplate, 4½″ d
- Duck 140.00
- Elephant 150.00
- Iris 150.00

Flask, 8¾″ h, 7″ w, pillow shape, narrow ring turned neck, scroll shaped handles, flattened round body, four ball feet, striated green and brown glaze, imp mark "CKAW," kiln pulls on feet 375.00

Jar, cov, 5½″ h, paneled urn shape tapering to four cut–out feet, conical cov, glossy olive glaze, imp "CKAW," repaired 200.00

Knife Rest, 3¼″ l, figural, rabbit 425.00

Paperweight, 2½″ l, 1⅝″ h, Rabbit, stamped 300.00

Plate
- 6″ d
  - Azalea, imp and stamped registered marks 125.00
  - Clover, imp and stamped registered marks 500.00
  - Duck, imp rabbit mark, pre 1929 175.00
  - Snow Tree, sgd "Maud Davenport" imp and stamped 225.00
- 6⅛″, Swan, double imp rabbit mark, post 1929 . . . . 200.00
- 6¼″ d, Crab, imp and stamped registered marks 350.00
- 6⅜″ d, Horse Chestnut, double imp rabbit mark, post 1929 . . . . 75.00
- 7½″ d
  - Dolphin, imp and stamped registered marks 650.00
  - Swan, double imp rabbit mark, post 1929 . . . . 150.00
- 8¼″ d
  - Central Poppy, imp and stamped registered marks 650.00
  - Crab, stamped registered, dated 1931 . . . . 425.00
- 8$\frac{5}{16}$″ d, Rabbit, one ear, imp rabbit signature, pre 1929 mark 125.00
- 8½″ d
  - Clover, stamped, nick and minor roughness 100.00
  - Crab, imp and stamped registered marks 375.00
  - Dolphin, imp and stamped registered mark, nick and minor roughness 200.00
  - Duck, stamped mark 300.00
  - Iris, deep blue 180.00
  - Lobster, stamped 1931 mark, imp mark 400.00
  - Tapestry Lion, imp and stamped registered marks, glaze imperfections 250.00
  - Rabbit, deep blue 180.00
  - Snow Tree, post 1929 mark 125.00
  - Turkey, pre 1929 . . . . 175.00
- 8⅝″ d
  - Birds in potted orange tree border, incised rabbit mark 150.00
  - Moth, stamped mark 375.00
  - Pond Lily, incised rabbit mark . . . 175.00
  - Poppy, impressed rabbit and pre 1929 mark 400.00
- 9⅝″ d, Duck, post 1929 mark 275.00
- 9¾″ d, Turkey, stamped mark 275.00
- 10″ d
  - Azalea, imp and stamped registered marks, nick 150.00
  - Bird In The Potted Orange Tree, stamped 600.00
  - Polar Bear, imp and stamped registered marks, small rim repair 425.00
  - Rabbit, imp rabbit mark, pre 1929 mark 200.00
  - Scottie Dog, begging Scottie dogs, imp and stamped registered marks 2,400.00
- 10¼″ d, Rabbit, raised design, imp "USCP" mark 275.00

Platter, 9⅞ x 6⅛″, Rabbit, rect, pre 1929 300.00

Tea Tile, 4⅝″ d, Rabbit, stamped marks, dated 1931 . . . . 300.00

Toothpick Holder, 2¼″ h, cylindrical, mustard glaze, imp "CKAW" 165.00

Tray, 8″ w, 12¾″ l, oval, Rabbit, stamped 425.00

Vase
- 6″ h, Oxblood, squat bulbous body, short neck, sgd "DP97E" 1,600.00
- 6⅛″ h, Crackleware, swollen form, tapering towards base, narrow neck, stylized plant and floral motifs, imp Dedham mark 2,300.00
- 6¼″ h, squatty baluster, mauve dripped high glaze, incised "Dedham Pottery," artist Hugh Cornwall Robertson monogram 1,760.00
- 7″ h, Crackleware, swollen form, tapering towards base, narrow neck, imp "CKAW," kiln pull on side . . . 250.00
- 8¼″ h, Oxblood, cylindrical tapering towards base, elongated neck, irid red glaze, imp "CKAW" 950.00
- 11¾″ h, flared rim, elongated neck, bulbous base and foot, honeycomb texture, stippled floral dec, glossy blue–green glaze, imp "CKAW" . . 550.00

Vegetable Dish, cov, 11″ d, Rabbit, stamped mark 375.00

DELFTWARE

History: Delftware is pottery of a soft red clay body with tin enamel glaze. The white, dense, opaque color came from adding tin ash to lead glaze. The first examples had blue designs on a white ground. Polychrome examples followed.

The name originally applied to pottery made in the region around Delft, Holland, beginning in the 16th century and ending in the late 18th century. Tin came from the Cornish mines in England. By the 17th and 18th centuries English potters in London, Bristol, and Liverpool were copying the glaze and designs. Some designs unique to English potters also developed.

In Germany and France, the ware is known as Faience and in Italy as Majolica.

Reference: Susan and Al Bagdade, *Warman's English & Continental Pottery & Porcelain, 1st Edition,* Warman Publishing Co., Inc., 1987.

Reproduction Alert: Much souvenir Delft-type material has been produced in the late 19th and 20th centuries to appeal to the foreign traveler. Don't confuse these modern pieces with the older examples.

Miniature Lamp, blue dec, white ground, 10½″ h, $275.00.

Bowl, 10¾″ d, manganese, floral spray within diaper border, ochre line rim, Lambeth, c1780 .... **450.00**
Butter Tub, 4½″ h, polychrome, harbor scene on cov and sides, gold finial and handles, marked "VA," Dutch, c1740–80 .... **350.00**
Charger
    13¾″ d, blue and white, central floral panel surrounded by four similar designs, yellow enamel rim, under-glazed sgd initials "HB" for Hugo Brouwer, De Posteleyne Byl, Dutch, late 18th C **250.00**
    15½″ d, circular, lobed curving rim, center with riffed circle, English, late 17th C **1,800.00**
Dish
    11¾″ d, blue and white, center painted with flowering plants and rockwork, wide paneled stylized foliage border, Dutch, mid 18th C .. **225.00**
    12¼″ d, blue and white, Chinaman holding scroll in landscape, half flowerheads and foliage border, yellow line rim, Dutch, c1760, pr **715.00**
Figure, 9″ h, Harlequin, standing, one hand on pillory around neck, hat in other, blue, yellow, iron–red, and green costume, hexagonal base, stylized flowers in blue and green line borders, De Twee Scheepjes, Pennis factory, c1750–60 .... **9,900.00**
Flask, 7″ h, flattened round base, narrow short neck, round foot, blue, white, and black floral dec, windmill landscape scene of man and harp, loops for rope, sgd "AK," Holland, minor edge chips **250.00**
Plaque, 11″ w, shaped, blue and white, oval portrait of lady in center, diaper ground, two putti seated on scrolling flowered foliage, baskets of flowers, border of scrolling flowered foliage with parrots and masks, mid 18th C **450.00**
Plate, 11⅝″ d, circular, center dec of Chinese lady holding fan, seated under tree, man in attendance, bird in flight, diaper border with stylized foliage reserves, attributed to Bristol, England, c1750 .... **385.00**
Punch Bowl, 10¼″ d, 5¼″ h, ftd, dolphins and Chinoiserie border rim int., figured country landscape ext., minor wear and roughness, 18th C **2,860.00**
Puzzle Jug, 6¾″ h, three spouts, white ground, blue dash border above pierced neck, verse, flanked by flowers and blue lines, attributed to Liverpool, England, c1740 .... **935.00**
Tile Picture, 40½ x 50¼″, blue and white, river scene, men fishing, house on far band, figures in teahouse, Dutch, early 18th C, some tiles restored and replaced **7,150.00**
Vase
    6¾″ h, baluster, brown ground, multicolored stylized flowering branches, lobed cartouche reserves, Dutch, c1765, De Porceleyne Claeuw factory mark, minor restorations, pr **440.00**
    11″ h, octagonal oviform, cov, fluted dome cov with Fo dog finial, fluted vases, painted Chinese figures, shaped rect cartouches, blue ground, stiff leaves and floral reserves, Dutch, early 18th C, blue marks, pr **1,870.00**
Wall Pocket, 7¾″ h, blue and white, molded masks, scrolls, and foliage, Liverpool, c1770 .... **375.00**

DEPRESSION GLASS

History: Depression glass is a glassware made during the period of 1920–40. It was an inexpensive machine-made glass, produced by several companies in various patterns and colors. The number of pieces within a pattern also varied.

Depression glass was sold through variety stores, given as premiums, or packaged with certain products. Movie houses gave it away from 1935 until well into the 1940s.

Like pattern glass, knowing the proper name of a pattern is the key to collecting. Collectors should be prepared to do research.

References: Gene Florence, *The Collector's Encyclopedia of Depression Glass, Ninth Edition,* Collector Books, 1990; Gene Florence, *Elegant Glassware of the Depression Era, Fourth Edition,* Collector Books, 1990; Gene Florence, *Very Rare Glassware Of The Depression Years,* Collector Books, 1987; Gene Florence, *Very Rare Glassware of the Depression Years, Second Series,* Collector Books, 1990; Carl F. Luckey and Mary Burris, *An Identification & Value Guide to Depression Era Glassware, Second Edition,* Books Americana, 1986; Mark Schliesmann, *Price Survey, Second Edition,* Park Avenue Publications, Ltd, 1984; Hazel Marie Weatherman, *1984 Supplement & Price Trends for Colored Glassware Of The Depression Era, Book 1,* published by author, 1984.

Periodical: *The Daze,* Box 57, Otisville, MI 48463.

Collectors' Club: National Depression Glass Association, Inc., P.O. Box 11123, Springfield, OH 65808.

Reproduction Alert: Send a self addressed stamped business envelope to *The Daze* and request a copy of their glass reproduction list. It is one of the best bargains in the antiques business.

Additional Listings: See *Warman's Americana & Collectibles* for more examples.

ADAM, Jeannette Glass Company, 1932 through 1934. Made in crystal, delphite blue, green, pink, and yellow. The price for crystal is low because of low demand. Delphite blue and yellow pieces are rare.

	Green	Pink		Green	Pink
Ashtray, 4¼"	18.50	24.00	Plate		
Bowl			6", sherbet	8.00	7.50
4¾", dessert	10.00	9.50	7¾", sq, salad	8.00	7.50
5¾", cereal	30.00	30.00	9", sq, dinner	17.00	20.00
7¾"	15.00	16.00	9", grill	13.25	12.50
9"	30.00	20.00	Platter, 11¾"	15.00	15.00
10", oval	17.50	15.00	Relish Dish, 8", divided	12.00	10.00
Butter Dish	225.00	60.00	Salt and Pepper Shakers, pr	75.00	45.00
Cake Plate, 10", ftd	17.50	14.00	Saucer	6.00	7.50
Candlesticks, pr, 4"	72.00	65.00	Sherbet, 3"	30.00	20.00
Candy Jar, cov, 2½"	80.00	60.00	Sugar, cov	40.00	30.00
Coaster, 3¼"	12.00	14.50	Tumbler		
Creamer	14.00	12.00	4½"	18.00	16.00
Cup	18.00	20.00	5½"	30.00	28.00
Lamp	200.00	200.00	Vase, 7½"	35.00	95.00
Pitcher, 32 oz	30.00	24.50			

ANNIVERSARY, Jeannette Glass Co., 1947–49. Made in crystal and pink.

	Crystal	Pink		Crystal	Pink
Bowl			9", dinner	3.50	5.00
4⅞", berry, small	1.50	3.00	Sandwich Server, 12½" d	5.00	8.50
7⅜", soup, flat	3.50	6.25	Saucer	1.00	1.25
9", fruit	8.00	12.00	Sherbet, ftd	2.50	4.50
Butter Dish	35.00	45.00	Sugar, cov	5.00	6.50
Compote, 3 legs	3.00	7.50	Vase, 6½"	6.00	8.00
Cup	2.50	4.50	Wall Pocket	10.00	15.00
Pickle Dish, 9"	3.50	6.50	Wine, 2½ oz	6.00	10.00
Plate					
6¼"	1.50	2.25			

Left: Adam, plate, pink, 9″ d, $20.00. Center: Columbia, saucer, crystal, $2.00. Right: Florentine No. 2, gravy, underplate, yellow, $80.00.

BLOCK OPTIC, "Block," Hocking Glass Co., 1929–1933. Made in green, pink; limited production in crystal, yellow.

	Crystal	Green	Pink	Yellow
Bowl				
4″, berry	—	4.50	4.50	—
5¼″, cereal	—	8.00	7.50	9.50
8½″, master berry	—	20.00	18.00	—
Butter Dish, cov	—	35.00	35.00	—
Candy Dish	—	30.00	35.00	45.00
Creamer	—	6.50	6.00	8.00
Cup	—	6.00	4.00	6.00
Goblet				
4¾″, champagne	5.50	15.00	—	—
7¼″, 9 oz.	5.50	18.00	16.00	20.00
Ice Tub, 6″	20.00	25.00	—	25.00
Mug	—	35.00	—	—
Pitcher				
8″, 80 oz	—	34.00	36.00	—
8½″, 64 oz	—	32.50	30.00	—
Plate				
6″, bread & butter	1.50	2.00	2.00	3.00
8″, luncheon	2.00	3.00	2.50	3.50
9″, dinner	—	10.00	15.50	13.00
10″, dinner	—	14.00	14.00	—
Salt and Pepper				
Shakers, pr, ftd	—	25.00	45.00	55.00
Sherbet	4.00	4.50	4.00	6.50
Sugar, cone shape	—	7.50	8.00	8.00
Tumbler				
5 oz	—	8.00	10.00	—
9 oz	—	8.50	—	—
10 oz	—	12.00	10.00	—
Tumble-Up Set	—	75.00	—	—
Vase, 5¾″	—	55.00	—	—
Whiskey	4.00	15.00	—	—

COLUMBIA, Federal Glass Company, 1938–1942. Made in crystal and pink.

	Crystal	Pink		Crystal	Pink
Bowl			8½″, salad	12.00	—
5″, cereal	10.00	—	10½″, ruffled	12.50	—
8″, low soup	12.00	—	Butter Dish, cov	14.00	18.00

	Crystal	Pink
Cup	3.50	10.00
Plate		
6", bread and butter	1.50	5.00
9½", luncheon	3.75	14.75
11", chop	6.00	—

	Crystal	Pink
Saucer	2.00	5.00
Snack Plate	20.00	—
Tumbler	10.00	—

CUPID, Paden City Glass Company, 1930s. Made in black, canary yellow, green, light blue, and pink. All colors currently have the same values.

	All Colors
Bowl	
8½", oval, ftd	40.00
9¼", center handle	45.00
Cake Plate, 11¾"	45.00
Cake Stand, 2" h, ftd	40.00
Candlesticks, pr, 5" w	50.00
Candy, cov, ftd, 4¾" h	72.00
Compote, 6¼"	30.00
Console Bow, 11"	48.50
Creamer, 5", ftd	36.00
Ice Bucket, 6"	65.00

	All Colors
Ice Tub, 4¾"	60.00
Lamp, silver overlay	150.00
Mayonnaise, 6" d	40.00
Plate	
8", luncheon	20.00
10½", dinner	30.00
Samovar	185.00
Sugar, 5", ftd	45.00
Tray, 10¾", center handle . .	40.00
Vase, fan shape	75.00

DIANA, Federal Glass Company, 1937–41. Made in amber, crystal, and pink.

	Amber	Crystal	Pink
Ashtray, 3½"	—	2.00	3.00
Bowl			
5", cereal	5.00	3.00	3.75
5½", soup, cream	8.00	6.00	7.75
9", salad	—	—	9.00
11", console	8.00	5.00	7.00
12", scalloped edge	7.50	5.50	6.50
Candy Dish, cov	25.00	20.00	22.50
Coaster, 3½"	—	2.00	3.00
Creamer	4.00	3.00	4.00

Left: New Century, tumbler, blue, 9 oz, $7.00. Center: Royal Ruby, soup bowl, $10.00. Right: Windsor, tumbler, pink, 4" h, $10.00.

	Amber	Crystal	Pink
Cup	3.50	2.00	3.50
Demitasse Set, 2 oz	—	5.00	14.00
Plate			
5½", child's	—	2.00	3.50
6", bread and butter	1.50	1.00	1.50
9½", dinner	4.50	3.75	4.25
11¾", sandwich	6.00	4.50	5.00
Platter, 12", oval	7.50	5.00	6.50
Salt and Pepper Shakers, pr	65.00	20.00	30.00
Saucer	1.25	1.00	1.00

FLORENTINE NO. 2, "Poppy No. 2," Hazel Atlas Glass Company, 1934–37. Made in crystal, green, ice blue, pink, and yellow. Limited production in cobalt blue and amber.

	Crystal	Green	Ice Blue	Pink	Yellow
Ashtray	24.50	24.50	—	—	—
Bowl					
4½", berry, small	10.00	10.00	—	9.00	16.00
4¾", soup, cream	7.50	9.00	30.00	12.00	15.00
5½"	—	—	—	—	35.00
6", cereal	—	—	—	14.50	35.00
8", berry, master	15.00	15.00	—	16.50	16.50
9", flat	10.00	10.00	—	—	—
Butter Dish	115.00	125.00	—	—	125.00
Candlesticks, pr	60.00	60.00	—	—	45.00
Candy Dish	65.00	65.00	—	95.00	—
Coaster, 3¼"	8.00	8.50	—	14.00	17.50
Compote, ruffled, 3½"	16.00	12.00	45.00	6.50	18.00
Creamer	5.50	7.50	—	—	12.00
Cup	5.00	5.00	—	—	7.00
Custard Cup	42.00	42.00	—	—	55.00
Gravy Boat set	—	—	—	—	80.00
Grill, cup ring	—	45.00	—	—	—
Nut Dish, ruffled	—	—	32.00	9.75	—
Parfait, 6"	50.00	50.00	—	—	60.00
Pitcher					
6¼", 24 oz, cone	—	—	—	—	85.00
7½", 28 oz, cone	35.00	35.00	—	—	25.00
7½", 48 oz	42.50	42.50	—	100.00	140.00
8", 76 oz	75.00	75.00	—	200.00	175.00
Plate					
6", sherbet	2.00	2.50	—	—	3.50
6¼", indentation	—	—	—	—	22.00
8½", salad	5.00	5.00	—	6.00	8.00
10", dinner	6.75	10.00	—	12.00	12.00
10¼", grill	7.00	12.00	—	—	12.00
11", oval, gravy	—	—	—	—	42.50
Platter, 11½"	7.00	15.00	—	12.00	14.00
Relish					
10", 3 part	25.00	25.00	—	14.00	15.00
Plain	—	—	—	—	15.00
Salt and Pepper Shakers, pr.	30.00	30.00	—	—	35.00
Saucer	—	2.25	—	—	3.00
Sherbet, ftd	6.00	7.00	—	—	10.00
Sugar, open	5.50	6.50	—	—	9.00
Sugar Lid	18.00	18.00	—	—	23.00
Tray, condiment	—	—	—	—	75.00

	Crystal	Green	Ice Blue	Pink	Yellow
Tumbler					
3½", 5 oz, juice	7.50	10.00	—	8.00	18.00
3½", 5 oz, ftd	6.75	8.75	—	9.00	10.00
4", 5 oz, ftd	7.50	7.75	—	—	15.00
4", 9 oz, water	10.00	10.00	50.00	—	—
4½", 9 oz, ftd	20.00	20.00	—	12.00	25.00
5", 12 oz, iced tea	20.00	20.00	—	25.00	30.00
Vase, 6"	45.00	45.00	—	—	55.00

MAYFAIR, Federal Glass Company, 1934. Made in amber, crystal, and green.

	Amber	Crystal	Green
Bowl			
5", cream soup	12.50	10.00	14.00
5½", sauce	5.00	4.00	5.50
6", cereal.	12.00	8.00	12.50
Creamer, ftd	9.50	7.50	8.50
Cup	5.00	4.00	8.00
Plate			
6¾", salad.	3.50	2.50	4.75
9½", dinner	12.00	8.00	10.00
9½", grill	9.00	7.50	8.00
Platter, 12", oval	12.50	10.00	14.00
Sauce	2.00	1.50	2.00
Sugar, ftd	10.00	8.00	8.50
Tumbler, 4½", 9 oz	10.00	7.00	14.00

NEW CENTURY, Hazel Atlas Company, 1930–35. Made in amethyst, cobalt blue, crystal, green, and pink.

	Amethyst	Cobalt Blue	Crystal	Green	Pink
Ashtray/Coaster, 5⅜"	—	—	25.00	24.00	—
Bowl					
4½", berry	—	—	4.50	4.50	—
4¾", cream, soup	—	—	8.00	8.00	—
8", berry.	—	—	9.25	9.00	—
Butter Dish	—	—	50.00	50.00	—
Casserole, 9", cov	—	—	45.00	45.00	—
Cup	8.50	8.50	5.00	5.00	9.00
Decanter.	—	—	40.00	40.00	—
Goblet					
2½", wine	—	—	12.00	12.00	—
3¼", cocktail	—	—	15.00	15.00	—
Pitcher					
7¾", 60 oz	25.00	25.00	26.00	25.00	—
8", 80 oz	30.00	30.00	30.00	30.00	30.00
Plate					
6", sherbet.	—	—	2.00	2.00	—
7⅛", breakfast	—	—	5.00	5.00	—
8½", salad	—	—	5.50	5.50	—
10", dinner	—	—	10.00	10.00	—
10", grill	—	—	12.00	12.00	—
Platter, 11", oval	—	—	10.00	10.00	—
Salt and Pepper Shakers, pr.	—	—	25.00	25.00	—

	Amethyst	Cobalt Blue	Crystal	Green	Pink
Saucer	4.00	4.00	2.00	2.25	4.00
Sherbet, 3″	—	—	5.00	5.00	—
Sugar	—	—	5.00	5.00	—
Sugar, cov.	—	—	8.00	8.50	—
Tumbler					
3½″, 5 oz.	6.50	6.50	7.50	7.25	6.50
4″, 5 oz, ftd	—	—	8.00	8.00	—
4⅛″, 9 oz.	7.00	7.00	7.50	7.50	7.00
4⅞″, 9 oz, ftd	—	—	10.00	10.00	—
5″, 10 oz	10.00	10.00	10.00	10.00	10.00
5¼″, 12 oz	10.00	10.00	14.00	14.00	10.00
Whiskey, 2½″, 1½ oz	—	—	6.00	6.00	—

PARROT, "Sylvan," Federal Glass Company, 1931–1932. Made in amber and green, with limited production in crystal and blue.

	Amber	Green		Amber	Green
Bowl			9″, dinner	25.00	30.00
5″, berry	10.00	12.00	10½″, grill	20.00	25.00
7″, soup	25.00	28.00	Platter	48.00	30.00
8″, berry	60.00	50.00	Salt and Pepper Shakers, pr	—	195.00
10″, oval, vegetable	45.00	42.00	Saucer	8.00	8.75
Butter Dish, cov	800.00	250.00	Sherbet, cone	18.00	20.00
Creamer, ftd	30.00	20.00	Sugar, cov	325.00	150.00
Cup	20.00	25.00	Trivet	—	500.00
Hot Plate, 5″	—	500.00	Tumbler		
Pitcher, 8½″	—	950.00	4¼″	90.00	90.00
Plate			5½″	95.00	95.00
5¾″, sherbet	12.00	17.50	5¾″	90.00	95.00
7½″, salad	—	17.50			

ROYAL RUBY, Anchor Hocking Glass Company, 1938–60s. Made in ruby red.

	Ruby Red		Ruby Red
Ashtray, 4½″, sq	3.50	3 qt, tilted	30.00
Bowl		3 qt, upright	30.00
4¼″, berry	4.00	Plate	
5¼″	5.00	6½″, sherbet	2.00
7½″, soup	10.00	7″, salad	3.50
8″, veg, oval	12.00	7¾″, luncheon	6.00
8½″, berry	22.00	9″, dinner	8.00
10″	18.00	9¼″, dinner	8.50
11½″, salad	20.00	13¾″, dinner	12.50
Creamer		Punch Bowl Set, 15 pcs.	95.00
Flat	4.50	Saucer	
Ftd	6.50	Round	2.50
Cup		Sq	2.50
Round	5.00	Sherbet	6.50
Square	5.00	Sugar	
Goblet	12.00	Flat	4.00
Lamp	25.00	Ftd	6.00
Pitcher		Sugar Lid	7.50
22 oz, tilted	25.00	Tumbler	
22 oz, upright	25.00	2½ oz, ftd, wine	9.00

	Ruby Red			Ruby Red
3½ oz, cocktail	6.50	Vase		
5 oz, juice	3.00	4", ball		4.50
9 oz, water	6.00	6½", bulbous		7.50
13 oz, iced tea.	8.50	10", bird decal		15.00

STARLIGHT, Hazel, Atlas Glass Company, 1938–40. Made in cobalt blue, crystal, pink, and white.

	Cobalt Blue	Crystal	Pink	White
Bowl				
5½", cereal	3.50	3.00	3.50	3.50
8½", closed handles.	8.50	4.50	8.50	—
11½", salad.	18.00	12.00	18.00	—
Creamer.	—	3.50	—	3.50
Cup	—	4.00	3.50	4.00
Plate				
6", bread and butter	—	2.00	3.00	2.25
8½", luncheon	—	2.50	3.50	2.50
9", dinner	—	3.50	6.00	3.50
13", sandwich	—	4.00	8.00	—
Relish Dish.	—	3.00	5.00	—
Salt and Pepper Shakers, pr	—	20.00	—	—
Saucer.	—	1.25	2.00	1.25
Sherbet	—	3.50	—	—
Sugar.	—	3.50	—	3.50

WATERFORD, "Waffle," Hocking Glass Company, 1938–44. Made in crystal and pink. Limited production in yellow and white. Forest green made in the 1950s.

	Crystal	Forest Green	Pink
Ashtray, 4"	4.00	—	5.75
Bowl			
4¾", berry	4.25	—	6.50
5½", cereal	15.00	—	12.00
8¼", berry	8.00	—	18.00
Butter Dish, cov	20.00	—	180.00
Cake Plate, 10¼", handled.	5.00	—	9.00
Coaster, 4"	2.00	—	4.00
Cup	5.00	—	8.00
Creamer			
Miss America style.	6.50	—	—
Oval	2.50	—	7.50
Goblet			
5¼".	15.00	—	9.50
5½", Miss America style	25.00	—	40.00
Lamp, 4".	25.00	—	—
Pitcher			
42 oz, tilted juice	14.00	—	—
80 oz, tilted ice lip	20.00	—	100.00
Plate			
6", sherbet.	1.50	—	3.50
7⅛", salad.	3.50	—	3.50
9⅝", dinner	7.00	—	10.00
13¾", sandwich	8.00	8.00	8.00
Relish, 13¾", 5 part.	20.00	—	—

	Crystal	Forest Green	Pink
Salad Fork and Spoon, pr	14.00	—	—
Salt and Pepper Shakers, pr	6.00	—	—
Saucer	2.50	—	3.50
Sherbet, ftd.	3.50	—	9.50
Sugar			
Cov.	5.25	—	6.50
Open	2.50	—	10.00
Tray, 14″, handled	4.00	30.00	—
Tumbler			
3½″, 5 oz, juice	—	—	25.00
4⅞″, 10 oz, ftd	8.00	—	15.00

WINDSOR, "Windsor Diamond," Jeannette Glass Co., 1936–46. Made in crystal, green and pink; limited production in amberina and delphite.

	Crystal	Green	Pink
Ashtray, 5¾″	15.00	40.00	35.00
Bowl			
4¾″, berry	2.00	5.50	4.00
5″, cream soup	6.00	16.00	18.00
5½″, cereal	8.00	12.00	13.00
7⅛″, console, 3 legs.	6.00	—	17.50
8″, two handles	6.00	14.00	15.00
8½″, master berry	6.00	12.00	15.00
9½″, vegetable, oval.	8.00	15.00	12.00
12½″, fruit, console	12.00	—	70.00
Butter Dish, cov	22.50	40.00	36.00
Cake Plate			
10¾″, ftd	8.00	12.00	15.00
13½″, thick	8.00	12.00	13.00
Candlesticks, pr, 3″	12.50	—	65.00
Candy Jar, cov	8.00	—	20.00
Coaster, 3¼″.	5.00	15.00	8.00
Compote	10.00	12.00	12.00
Creamer.	2.50	9.50	7.00
Cup	2.00	7.00	5.00
Pitcher			
4½″, 16 oz.	20.00	—	90.00
6¾″, 52 oz.	15.00	55.00	22.50
Plate			
6″, sherbet.	2.50	8.00	6.00
7″, salad	4.00	8.50	14.00
9″, dinner	3.50	9.50	12.50
10¼″, sandwich, handled	4.00	8.00	12.00
13⅝″, chop	9.00	15.00	22.50
Platter, 11½″, oval.	8.00	11.00	12.00
Relish, 11½″, divided.	4.00	9.00	60.00
Salt and Pepper Shakers, pr	15.00	45.00	30.00
Saucer.	3.00	4.00	3.50
Sherbet	3.00	12.50	8.25
Sugar, cov	4.00	20.00	22.00
Tray			
4″, sq	10.00	25.00	30.00
4⅛ × 9″.	12.00	24.00	20.00
Tumbler			
3¼″, 5 oz	6.00	25.00	15.00
4″, 9 oz.	5.00	22.00	10.00

DISNEYANA

History: Walt Disney and the creations of the famous Disney Studios hold a place of fondness and enchantment in the hearts of people throughout the world. The release of "Steamboat Willie" featuring Mickey Mouse in 1928 heralded an entertainment empire.

Walt and his brother, Roy, showed shrewd business acumen. From the beginning they licensed the reproduction of Disney characters in products ranging from wristwatches to clothing. In 1984 Donald Duck celebrated his 50th birthday, and collectors took a renewed interest in material related to him.

The market in Disneyana has been established by a few determined dealers and auction houses. Hake's Americana and Collectibles of York, PA, offers several hundred Disneyana items in each of their bimonthly mail and phone bid auctions. Sotheby's collector carousel auctions often include Disney cels, and Lloyd Ralston Toys auctions include Disney toys.

References: Robert Heide & John Gilman, *Cartoon Collectibles,* 1984 (only covers Disney material); Richard Schickel, *The Disney Version: The Life, Times, Art and Commerce of Walt Disney,* Avon Books, 1968; Michael Stern, *Stern's Guide to Disney Collectibles, First Series,* 1989, *Second Series,* 1990, Collector Books; Tom Tumbusch, *Tomart's Illustrated Disneyana Catalog and Price Guide,* Vols. 1, 2, 3, and 4, Tomart Publications, 1985; Tom Tumbusch, *Tomart's Illustrated Disneyana Catalog and Price Guide, Condensed Edition,* Wallace-Homestead, 1989.

Archives: Walt Disney Archives, 500 South Buena Vista Street, Burbank, CA 91521.

Collectors' Club: Mouse Club, 2056 Cirone Way, San Jose, CA 95124

Additional Listings: See *Warman's Americana & Collectibles* for more examples.

Advisor: Ted Hake.

Alice In Wonderland
    Figure, 5" h, ceramic, 1960 Walt Disney Production label 30.00
    Planter, 3½ x 7 x 7", ceramic, dark rose pastel, Alice in center with planting areas on each side, Disney copyright, c1951 . . . . 30.00
Bambi
    Figure, 7½" h, ceramic, glazed, c1950 50.00
    Rug, 21 x 39", Bambi and Thumper, black border, white fringe, c1960 25.00
    Salt and Pepper Shaker, pr, 2½" h, figural, Thumper, orig sticker on chest and corks, Goebel marks, 1950 . . . . 100.00
Cinderella
    Book, 9 x 12", *Walt Disney's Cinderella,* black, white, and pink cov, 16

pgs, includes music, lyrics, and black and white character pictures, Walt Disney Music Company copyright 1955 . . . . 30.00
    Pitcher, 7" h, figural, Fairy Godmother, pale blue, marked "Cinderella Ware by Permission Walt Disney/England," 100.00
    Record, 78 rpm, purple label, 24 pg storybook, Walt Disney's Cinderella, RCA Victor, Little Nipper Storybook, 1949 copyright 35.00
Davy Crockett
    Record, 45 rpm, "The Ballad Of Davy Crockett" and "Cowboy Favorites," 7 x 7" color sleeve, Cricket Records, copyright 1953 . . . . 15.00
    Stamp Book, 8½ x 11", 32 pgs, 60 stamps, Walt Disney Productions, copyright 1955 . . . . 25.00
    Wallet, vinyl, brown, color Crockett and tepees illus, orig box, copyright Walt Disney, c1955 . . . . 40.00
    Wristwatch, green plastic case, brown leather strap with silver crossed rifles and powder horns, orig box with plastic powder horn used to hold watch, Copyright Walt Disney Productions, c1954 . . 350.00
Donald Duck
    Bank, Donald sitting holding coin in one hand, glazed, c1940 . . . . 65.00
    Book
        Donald Duck and the Hidden Gold, Simon & Schuster, 78 pgs, hardcover, 1951 . . . . 25.00
        Walt Disney's Donald Duck and the Witch, Little Golden Book, Simon & Schuster, 1953, light wear . . . 12.00
    Bubble Gum Wrapper, 4" l, red, white, and blue, inscribed "Three Stix/Three colors," unopened, c1940 100.00
    Planter, 6½" h, ceramic, white, red, blue, and yellow details, glazed, unused, c1940 . . . . 25.00
    Plate, 9" d, flared out edge, recessed Donald image, light green background, Disney copyright on rim edge, c1960 . . . . 25.00
    Watering Can, 5½" h, tin, Donald riding donkey, red and yellow handles, 1938 Enterprises copyright 50.00
Dumbo
    Figure, 4" h, ceramic, wearing yellow hat, glazed, American Pottery label, c1940 . . . . 100.00
    Songbook, *Walt Disney's Dumbo Song Book,* 7½ x 9½", 32 pgs, Whitman copyright 1941 . . . . 25.00
    Toy, squeeze, 5" h, rubber, pink, blue, and yellow accents, Dell, 1950s . . 15.00
Fantasia, souvenir program,*Walt Disney*

Presents *Fantasia*, 9½ x 12½", 28 pgs, 1940 copyright **30.00**

Lady and The Tramp

Belt, 12" l, vinyl metal buckle, red with white, yellow, green, and blue illus, copyright Walt Disney Productions, c1955 . . . . **35.00**

Figure

Lady, 1½" h, plastic, white, Marx, c1955 . . . . **10.00**

Tramp, 2" h, plastic, tan, Marx, c1955 . . . . **10.00**

Doll

Lady, 8½" h, stuffed, tan, burnt orange accents, plastic eyes, white silk ribbon around neck, orig tag, Woolikin, c1955 . . . . **75.00**

Tramp, 8" h, stuffed, brown, plastic eyes and nose, squeaker mechanism, Shuco, c1955 . . . . **150.00**

Mickey Mouse, hand puppet, early pie eye, $20.00.

Mickey Mouse

Bank, 3" h, tin, yellow, beehive shape, Mickey approaches door holding honey jar in one arm and key in other hand, marked "Elbezet" and "Made In Germany," 1934 . . . . . . **450.00**

Better Little Book

Mickey Mouse and the Desert Palace, #1451, c1940 . . . . **20.00**

Mickey Mouse and the Dude Ranch Bandit, #1471, 1943, 430 pgs **50.00**

Mickey Mouse in the Foreign Legion, #1428, 1940, light soiling **25.00**

Big Little Book

Mickey Mouse Runs His Own Newspaper, #1409, 1937 . . . . **35.00**

Mickey Mouse and Bobo the Elephant, #1160, missing title page **15.00**

Mickey Mouse and the Sacred Jewel, 1487, 1936 . . . . **35.00**

Mickey Mouse in Blaggard Castle, #726, 1934, taped repairs **20.00**

Book, *Mickey Mouse & his Friends*, Whitman, 1936, linen **100.00**

Door Knocker, brass, riveted hinge holds oval with full figure Mickey, inscribed "Made Under License" **200.00**

Figure, 10", chalkware **35.00**

Flashlight, 6" l, metal, color illus on side, Usalite, 1930s **75.00**

Guitar, 10 x 30 x 2½", plastic, black, white plastic front with two stickers, one of Mickey, other with "Mouse-getar," "Mouseketeers" logo, Disney copyright, c1960 . . . . **35.00**

Handkerchief, 8 x 8", white, black white, and red cowboy Mickey lassoing Pluto, 1930s **30.00**

Pencil Box, 5 x 8½ x 1¼", cardboard, blue and yellow, tray and drawer, Mickey as ringmaster, Donald riding seal, c1937 . . . . **25.00**

Pitcher, 4½" h, ceramic, figural, beige, dark green base, blue hands, marked "Made In Japan" **25.00**

Planter, 5" h, ceramic, pink, yellow, and tan pastel accents, Disney copyright, c1940s **40.00**

Rug, throw, 21 x 39", Mickey on see-saw with three bunnies, bluish-gray background, c1940 . . . . **75.00**

Sand Pail, 5" h, color scene on side, swivel handle, unused, Ohio Art Co **100.00**

Silverware Set, 3 pcs, stainless, MIB, 1959 . . . . **75.00**

Toy, pull, wood and metal, General Toy, Canada, 1940s **85.00**

Valentine Card, 3½ x 4½", gray, color Mickey on front lifting barbells with red heart shape designs, Mickey and Minnie on park bench inside, c1930 . . . . **30.00**

Minnie Mouse

Figure, 6", ceramic, glazed, leaning on broom wearing blue outfit, American Pottery label, c1940 . . . **100.00**

Toy, wind-up, tin, black rubber ears, wire knitting needles with attached fabric, built-in key, orig box **400.00**

Peter Pan, figure, 6", green and flesh colored beads, plastic head, green plastic hat, red plastic base, spring-loaded button, bends in various positions, Kohner, early 1950s **50.00**

Pinocchio

Better Little Book, *Pinocchio and Jiminy Cricket*, #1435, 1940, light edge wear and taped repair **30.00**

Doll, 9½" h, composition, jointed, movable head and arms, white and green outfit, yellow hat, orig tag marked "Knickerbocker," c1940 . . **500.00**

Figure, 10", chalkware **20.00**

Planter, 4" h, ceramic, glazed, Pin-

occhio and Figaro, marked "Japan," c1940 . . . . **25.00**
Record, set of 4, 78 rpm, Decca Records, includes cover and booklet, 1946 . . . . **75.00**
Toy, wind-up, "Pinocchio The Acrobat," tin, built-in key, 1939 Disney copyright **200.00**
Pluto
Figure, 3½" l, rubber, dark red, black accents, Seiberling, early 1930s **35.00**
Mug, ceramic, 3" h, large color Pluto picture on one side, small Mickey picture on other, marked "Patriot China," 1930s **75.00**
Sleeping Beauty
Filmstrips, 2" w, 22" l, set of 3, paper, titles "Aurora Meets Prince Philip," "Philip Rescues His Princess," and Aurora Returns To The Castle," orig boxes, c1959 . . . . **20.00**
Puppet, pr, King Hubert and King Stefan, molded rubber head, fabric hand cover, Gund, c1956 . . . . . . **40.00**
Record, 78 rpm, "I Wonder," c1959 **10.00**

Snow White, song book, Souvenir Album, black, white, and orange, Bourne, Inc. Music Publishers, $50.00.

Snow White
Book
Dopey, He Don't Talk None, Whitman, 1938, linen **40.00**
Snow White & Rose Red, 1930s **45.00**
Candy Bag, white paper, illus of Snow White holding candy bags ready to pass out to dwarfs with hands extended, marked "Snow White and the Seven Dwarfs Candy/Pure/Delicious," 1938 Disney copyright . . **20.00**
Doll Set, 22" Snow White, 7" h dwarfs, vinyl, washable rooted hair, dwarfs names inscribed on jacket edge, orig box, tag marked "$19.98" and "Deluxe Toy Creations, Inc, NY" **450.00**
Puppet, Dopey, Walt Disney Products **22.00**

Puzzle, 11 x 14", tray, full color, Jaymar, c1960 . . . . **10.00**
Sheet Music, "Heigh-Ho" **15.00**
Tea Set, 3" h teapot, 2" creamer, open sugar, three cups and saucers, white, dark orange accent lines, color transfer scenes, Wadeheath, c1930 . . . . **250.00**
Three Little Pigs
Figure, set of 3, 3½" h, bisque, pigs playing fiddle, horn, and drum, 1930s **90.00**
Puzzle, 14 x 22", orig box, Jaymar, c1940 . . . . **40.00**
Toothbrush Holder, 3½" h, bisque, relief figures of pigs, marked "Made In Japan," 1930s **50.00**
Zorro
Mask, fabric, black, two black and silver plastic eye pieces with one way view lenses, orig unopened card, copyright Westminster and Walt Disney Productions, c1960 . . . . . **40.00**
Rifle, 21" l, plastic, black, black and white Zorro sticker on sock, pr darts with rubber suction cups, unused metal target, orig box, T Cohn, Brooklyn, c1960 . . . . **150.00**

DOLL HOUSES

History: Doll houses date from the 18th century to modern times. Early doll houses often were handmade, sometimes with only one room. The most common type was made for a young girl to fill with replicas of furniture scaled especially to fit into a doll house. Special sized dolls also were made for doll houses. All types of accessories and styles allowed a doll house to portray any historical period.

References: Flora Bill Jacobs, *Dolls' Houses in America: Historic Preservation in Miniature,* Charles Scribner's Sons, 1974; Donald and Helene Mitchell, *Dollhouses, Past and Present,* Collector Books, 1980; Eva Stille, *Doll Kitchens 1800–1980,* Schiffer Publishing, 1988; Blair Whitton (ed.), *Bliss Toys And Dollhouses,* Dover, 1979.

Museums: Margaret Woodbury Strong Museum, Rochester, NY; Washington Dolls' House and Toy Museum, Washington, D.C.

Bliss, four rooms, three story, litho, wood, metal, c1910, 25 x 20" **1,800.00**
Converse, wood, cottage, hinged front, two int. rooms, 12" **250.00**
Hacker, Christian, Nurnberg, Germany, painted, front stucco facade, five rooms, two and one half story, steeple roof, two chimneys, bay window, papered int., FAO Schwarz label, 34" **500.00**
Folk Art, pierced glazed windows, front

McLoughlin Folding Doll House, two rooms, highly dec interiors, orig box, 17″ l, 12″ d, 16″ h, $770.00.

door, pitched roof, pr chimneys, shell dec, mounted on platform, 18 x 18 x 11″, American, early 1900 . . . . **660.00**
Japanese Palace, open room with floral and bird motif dec, red lacquered central stairway, multi level platform, pagoda roof, includes seven festival dolls with painted facial features and ceremonial robes, 27 x 18 x 15″ . . . **880.00**
Marx, metal, orig carton **50.00**
McLoughlin, folding, two rooms, highly dec int., orig box, 16 x 17 x 12″, American **770.00**
Schoenhut
   Two rooms, two story, wood and pressed board, red shingled roof, green shutters, decal on base, 16 x 15 x 11″ **275.00**
   Eight rooms, attic, gray blocks, c1917, 28 x 23 x 23″ **1,200.00**
Schwartz, F. A. O., cottage, five room, pierced multi-pane windows, hinged front door, red painted mansard type roof, includes 1920s furniture, 21 x 34 x 12″, German, 1900 . . . . **990.00**
Tudor, three story, pierced glazed windows, thatched roofs, complete with furniture, 46 x 69 x 30″, c1920 . . . . **1,320.00**
Wood
   Barn, three stalls, lithographed paper sides, painted, two composition nodding pull toy horses, 16 x 20 x 12″, c1900 . . . . **220.00**
   House
      French style, four story, framed pierced glazed and bay arched windows, eight rooms and three attic rooms, salmon pink with white trim, c1890 . . . . **3,850.00**
      New England, two story, pierced glazed windows, front porch with turned columns and hand rails, two hinged entrance ways, roof lifts off, 30 x 21 x 18½″, c1900 **1,760.00**

Oklahoma style, one room, three pierced glazed windows, hinged door, clapboard sides, front porch with two columns, lift-off tiled gabled roof, 31 x 27 x 25″, c1910 . . . . **500.00**
Train Station, elongated and round windows, two central arched entrance ways, gold painted pilasters, balustrade dec roof, maroon, gold, and green finish, 17 x 16½ x 13″, c1900 . . . . **610.00**
Whippany, three story, nine rooms, wood, pierced glazed windows, hinged front door, stairs, lattice work, orig wallpaper, carpets, and lace curtains, includes furniture and accessories, fitted with electricity and doorbell, 45 x 48 x 16″, New Jersey, 1901 **8,250.00**

DOLLS

History: Dolls have been children's play toys for centuries. Dolls also have served other functions. During the 14th through 18th century doll making was centered in Europe, mainly in Germany and France. The French dolls produced in this era represented adults and were dressed in the latest couturier designs. They were not children's toys.

During the mid-19th century, child and baby dolls, made in wax, cloth, bisque, and porcelain, were introduced. Facial features were hand painted; wigs were made of mohair and human hair. They were dressed in baby or children's fashions.

Marks from the various manufacturers are found on the back of the head, neck, or back area. These marks are very important in identifying the doll and date of manufacture.

Doll making in the United States began to flourish in the 1900s with names like Effanbee, Madame Alexander, Ideal, and others.

References: Johana Gast Anderton, *More Twentieth Century Dolls From Bisque to Vinyl, Volume A-H, Volume I-Z, Revised Edition,* Wallace-Homestead, 1974; John Axe, *The Encyclopedia of Celebrity Dolls,* Hobby House Press Inc., 1983; Julie Collier, *The Official Identification And Price Guide To Antique & Modern Dolls, Fourth Edition,* House of Collectibles, 1989; Jan Foulke, *9th Blue Book Dolls and Values,* Hobby House Press Inc. 1989; R. Lane Herron, *Herron's Price Guide To Dolls,* Wallace-Homestead, 1990; Polly Judd, *Cloth Dolls, Identification and Price Guide,* Hobby House Press, 1990; Wendy Lavitt, *American Folk Dolls,* Alfred Knopf, Inc., 1982; Wendy Lavitt, *Dolls,* Alfred A. Knopf, 1983; Lydia and Joachim Richter, *Bru Dolls,* Hobby House Press, 1989; Patricia R. Smith, *Modern Collector's Dolls, Editions 1, 2, 3, 4, 5,* Collector Books, 1973, 1975, 1976, 1979, 1984; Patricia R. Smith, *The World of Alexander-*

kins, Collector Books, 1985; Marjorie Victoria Sturges Uhl, *Madame Alexander, Ladies of Fashion,* Collector Books, 1982; Florence Theriault, *Theriault's Doll Registry Price Guide, Volume III,* published by author, 1988.

Periodicals: *Doll Reader,* Hobby House Press, Inc., 900 Frederick Street, Cumberland, MD 21502; *Dolls The Collector's Magazine,* P.O. Box 1972, Marion, OH 43305.

Collector's Clubs: Madame Alexander Fan Club, P.O. Box 146, New Lenox, IL 60451; United Federation of Doll Clubs, P.O. Box 14146, Parkville, MO 64152.

Museums: Margaret Woodbury Strong Museum, Rochester, NY; Yesteryears Museum, Sandwich, MA.

Additional Listings: See *Warman's Americana & Collectibles* for more examples.

French Fashion, bisque head, shoulder plate, arms, and hands, articulated kid body, orig wig, 17″ h, $1,750.00

Arranbee Doll Co.
  10″, storybook, composition swivel neck, jointed arms and legs, molded and painted hair and eyes, orig costume, c1930 . . . . 150.00
  13″, solid dome bisque head, composition body, painted hair, sleep eyes, recostumed, marks: Arranbee 375.00
Averill, Georgene
  12″, International, cloth, mask face, painted features, yarn hair, orig clothes, wrist tag, and box 60.00
  16″, infant baby, composition head, soft cloth body, composition hands,

flange neck, painted hair, sleep eyes, closed mouth, marks: Genuine/Madame Hendren/Doll/522/ Made in USA 140.00
Bru, Casimir
  11″ h, poured bisque head, six piece composition body, brown glass eyes, closed mouth, cork plate, pierced ears, silk dress, marks: Bru Jne R 2 . . . . 935.00
  14¼″ h, bisque swivel head and shoulder plate, tri-color blue eyes, closed mouth, pierced ears, articulated wood arms jointed at shoulders, elbows, and wrists, leather body, gussets at hips and knees, orig undergarments including corset, marks: E on head and shoulder plate 4,250.00
  17″ h, pressed bisque head, wood jointed body, brown paperweight eyes, outlined open/closed mouth, cork pate, pierced ears, key wound mechanical music box, marks: circle dot, Bte S.G.D.G. 6,600.00
  18″ h, pressed bisque head, kid over wood body, bisque lower arms, blue paperweight eyes, outlined open/closed mouth, brown wig, pierced ears, wearing lacy dress and Jumeau leather shoes, marks: Bru Jne 8, breastplate Bru Jne N.6 7,150.00
  23″ h, bisque swivel head, shoulderplate, kid body, bisque lower arms, repainted wood lower legs, brown paperweight eyes, highlighted lids, outlined open/closed mouth, cork pate, pierced ears, marks: circle dot Bru Jne 19 . . . . 1,320.00
Cameo Doll Co., 17″, Little Annie Rooney, composition jointed arms and legs, yellow yarn braids, painted round eyes, watermelon smile, painted black stocking feet, molded yellow shoes, gray velvet jacket, pink plaid skirt, c1920 . . . . 210.00
Effanbee
  13½″, Suzanne, brown sleep eyes, light hair, orig red and white dress, straw hat, bracelet tags, four outfits and orig suitcase 200.00
  14″, Skippy, composition, jointed at neck, shoulders, and hips, yellow molded and painted hair, blue painted side glancing eyes, closed mouth, redressed, marks: Effanbee Skippy P.L. Crosby 275.00
  16″, Patsy Joan, composition five piece body, straight legs, molded and painted hair, green sleep eyes, real and painted lashes, closed mouth, orig yellow dress, bonnet,

undergarments, shoes, and stockings, orig heart bracelet, orig soiled box, marks: Effanbee Patsy Joan ... **700.00**

Fleischmann & Bloedel, 20" h, bisque head, wood and composition jointed body, blue paperweight eyes, outlined open mouth, upper teeth, cork pate, pierced ears, marks: Eden Bebe Paris 7 .... **1,210.00**

Gaultier, Ferdinand, 29" h, bisque head, wood and composition jointed repainted body, brown paperweight eyes, outlined closed mouth, cork pate, old wig, maroon taffeta coat, marks: F. G. within scroll 13 ...... **4,125.00**

Gaultier, Francois
17" h, bisque poured swivel head, shoulderplate, kid body, blue threaded glass eyes, closed mouth, blonde wig, silk dress, carrying umbrella, marks: F. G. **935.00**
18" h, bisque swivel head, Gesland stockinet body, blue glass eyes, blonde mohair wig, deep mauve velvet dress, straw bonnet, c1870 **2,990.00**
21" h, bisque head, composition jointed body, blue paperweight eyes, open mouth, upper teeth, pierced ears, Mama Papa voice box, cork pate, marks: 8 F.G. within a scroll **1,320.00**
22" h, poured bisque head, wood and composition ball-jointed repainted body, blue paperweight eyes, outlined closed mouth, cork pate, pierced ears, pink silk dress, marks: F. G. within scroll 9 and body stamped Jumeau Medaille d'Or Paris **1,760.00**
23", poured bisque head, wood and composition jointed body, brown paperweight eyes, closed mouth, cork pate, pierced ears, marks: F.G. within a scroll 8 .... **2,310.00**

Handwerck, Heinrich
34" h, bisque head, wood and composition ball-jointed body, brown sleep eyes, open mouth, upper teeth, pierced ears, non-working voice box, marks: W Germany Heinrich Handwerck Simon & Halbig 7½ **550.00**
36" h, bisque head, repainted wood and composition ball-jointed body, brown sleep eyes, open mouth, upper teeth, pierced ears, wearing armor, marks: Germany Heinrich Handwerck Simon & Halbig ... **880.00**

Hertel, Schwab and Co., 15" h, bisque head, repainted wood and composition ball-jointed toddler body, blue glass goggle side glance sleep eyes, watermelon smile, marks: Hertel, Schwab & Co. 165-5 .... **4,620.00**

Heubach, Gebruder
10" h, bisque head, cloth body, leather bellows in torso, intaglio eyes, whistling mouth, molded hair, marks: 2/8774 Heubach in a square **880.00**
14" h, bisque head, wood and composition ball-jointed body, brown sleep eyes, pouty mouth, marks: 8420 5 Heubach Germany 23 ... **1,100.00**

Ideal
13", Shirley Temple, composition head, five piece jointed composition straight limbs, blonde curly mohair wig, brown plastic sleep eyes, open mouth, plastic teeth, pleated organdy dress, pin, marks: Shirley Temple on head and torso, Genuine/Shirley Temple/Doll/Registered Pat. off/Ideal Toy Co. on dress label **175.00**
20", Toni, hard plastic, jointed at neck, shoulders, and hips, dark brown nylon wig, blue sleep eyes, closed mouth, orig dress and box with contents **450.00**
21" h, Deanna Durbin, jointed composition body, sleep eyes, orig clothing and button, c1938, marks: Deanna Durbin Ideal USA **225.00**

Jumeau, Emile
14" h, Bebe, bisque head, composition jointed body, brown paperweight eyes, outlined closed mouth, blonde wig, pierced ears, dress, hat with flowers, and shoes, marks: red Depose Tete Jumeau Bte S.G.D.G. 5, artist's checkmark **2,530.00**
14" h, bisque head, wood and composition jointed body, blue paperweight eyes, outlined open mouth, upper teeth, cork pate, pierced ears, pink silk dress, orig Jumeau bee marked leather shoes, paper label, marks: 1907 5 red Tete Jumeau **1,430.00**
15" h, bisque socket head, jointed composition body, blue glass threaded stationary eyes, closed mouth, pierced ears, dress, high laced French leather boots, marks: Depose Tete Jumeau Bte SGDG 5 **2,800.00**
20" h, bisque swivel head and shoulder plate, stationary blue glass threaded paperweight eyes, closed mouth, pierced ears, leather body, orig blonde wig, gold watch and chain, stanhope and lorgnette, undergarments, 2 piece dress, high button brown shoes, marks: Jumeau MEDALLE D'OR Paris **2,300.00**

21″, bisque head, wood and composition jointed body, brown paperweight eyes, outlined closed mouth, pierced ears, cork pate, dress, hat, and leather shoes, marks: Depose Tete Jumeau Bte S.G.D.G. 10 and artist checkmark ... **3,575.00**

22″ h, bisque head, composition jointed body, blue sleep eyes, outlined open mouth, upper teeth, pierced ears, blue velvet dress, replaced hands, marks: 1907 10 ... **1,210.00**

26″ h, bisque head, wood and composition ball-jointed body, brown paperweight eyes, outlined closed mouth, brown wig, pierced ears, long dress and bonnet, marks: Depose Tete Jumeau 12 and artist's checkmark ... **2,530.00**

35″ h, bisque head, jointed composition body, blue paperweight eyes, outlined open mouth, upper teeth, pierced ears, oval sticker, marks: red Tete Jumeau 16 ... **2,420.00**

Kammer & Reinhardt

7½″ h, bisque head, five piece composition body, blue sleep eyes, closed mouth, blonde wig, orig costume, marks: Kammer & Reinhardt K*R Simon & Halbig 117 A 19 ... **1,540.00**

8½″ h, bisque head, composition ball-jointed body, intaglio eyes, closed pouty mouth brown wig, cotton navy blue skirt with apron, green cotton shirt, marks: K*R/114/23 ... **1,320.00**

12″ h, bisque head, wood and composition jointed body, brown intaglio eyes, pouty mouth, orig blonde wig, orig sailor costume, marks: K * R 107 30 ... **13,200.00**

13″ h, bisque head, wood and composition ball-jointed body, blue intaglio eyes, closed pouty mouth, blonde wig, marks: Kammer & Reinhardt K*R 114 3 ... **1,045.00**

15″ h, bisque head, wood and composition ball-jointed toddler body, blue goggle eyes glancing to one side, watermelon smile, marks: K * R Simon & Halbig 131 ... **6,050.00**

17″ h, boy, bisque head, wood and jointed composition body, brown glass sleep eyes, open/closed mouth, brown wig, wearing striped pants, ruffled shirt, jacket, and hat, marks: V K * R S & H 1151 A 38 ... **1,870.00**

21″ h, bisque head, repainted wood and composition ball-jointed toddler body, blue sleep eyes, open mouth with two upper teeth, painted and molded hair, marks:

Kammer & Reinhardt, Simon & Halbig K*R 127 50 ... **1,100.00**

32″ h, bisque head, wood and composition ball-jointed body, flirty blue glass eyes, open mouth, upper teeth, marks: K & R Simon & Halbig Germany 117n ... **1,650.00**

Kestner

11″ h, bisque head, wood and composition ball-jointed toddler body, glass goggle eyes, watermelon smile, marks: made in C 7 Germany J.D.K. 221 ges. gesch, shoes marked 2 0 C.P. M.R.R. Jr. ... **4,070.00**

15″ h, bisque head, wood and composition ball-jointed toddler body, brown glass goggle eyes glancing to one side, watermelon smile, brown wig, dress, shoes, and straw hat, marks: Germany, J.D.K. 221 ges gesch. made in Germany ... **3,410.00**

15¾″ h, socket head, jointed composition body, blue glass sleep eyes, open mouth with teeth, marks: Made in E Germany 9/129 ... **550.00**

21″ h, bisque head, wood and composition ball-jointed body, brown glass eyes, open mouth with inset upper teeth, marks: E made in Germany 9./Germany/J.D.K./247 ... **990.00**

28″ h, bisque head, wood and composition ball-jointed body, blue threaded glass eyes, open mouth with upper teeth, marks: K made in 14. Germany J.D.K. 1249 ... **880.00**

Kruse, Kathe

15″ h, molded muslin head, cloth jointed body, painted facial features, c1920, marks: 87584 ... **675.00**

16″, molded muslin painted head, cloth body jointed at shoulders and hips, painted short brown hair, brush stroked curls, painted blue-gray eyes, closed pouty mouth, red and white cotton dress, marks: Kathe Kruse and numbers on sole of foot ... **1,750.00**

16½″, molded muslin painted head, cloth body jointed at shoulders and hips, stitched toes and fingers, separate thumbs, light brown brush stroked hair, painted brown eyes, pink romper suit, coat, and matching bonnet, paint flake on tip of nose ... **1,850.00**

19″, molded muslin head, blonde wig, cloth jointed body, painted facial features, c1930, marks: Kathe Kruse/8399 ... **750.00**

Lenci

11″, felt, molded head coated with cellulose covering, cotton torso and

Lenci, Tom, felt, painted facial features, blonde curly hair, blue felt shirt, brown smock, gray shorts, paper label on shirt, riding orig hobby horse, orig box, c1930, 20½" h, $3,300.00.

felt limbs, blonde mohair wig, painted brown eyes, blue dress, purple shawl, wood clogs, yellow felt goose under arm, marks:purple stamp 450.00

12", felt, painted facial features, blonde wig, yellow dress and green coat, matching hat 660.00

15" h, felt, molded and painted facial features, fringe hair under cap, wearing red jacket and green pants with patches, marks: metal button in ear 770.00

19" h, felt, flirty eyes, painted mouth, blonde wig, wearing red coat, maroon skirt, and matching hat with feather 935.00

Madame Alexander, 7" h, Dionne Quintuplets, wearing matching sunsuits with orig tag, bonnets, and pins with names, seated on swing, marks: Alexander c1935 . . . . 1,045.00

Marque, Albert, 22" h, bisque head, composition jointed body, blue wistful glass eyes, closed mouth, replaced arm, 1916, marks: a Marque 22,000.00

Marseille, Armand

7" h, bisque head, composition five piece body, blue glass goggle eyes glancing to one side, watermelon smile, blonde wig, antique white dress, marks: 3223 a.10 0 M 275.00

13" h, Oriental, bisque head, five piece bent limb composition baby body, brown glass eyes, closed mouth, painted hair, marks: A Ellar within star M Germany 3.K 825.00

16½" h, Oriental, bisque head, five piece bent limb composition baby body, brown sleep eyes, closed mouth, painted hair, marks: A.M. Germany 353 3½ K 1,320.00

18¼" h, bisque, socket head, jointed composition body, brown glass sleep eyes, open mouth with teeth, marks: Made in Germany Armand Marseille 390 D.R.G.M. 2426/7/A5M 200.00

19" h, Oriental, bisque head, repainted composition body, five piece bent limb baby body, sleep eyes, closed mouth, painted hair, marks: A.M./Germany/353/4.K . . .   990.00

35" h, bisque head, wood and composition ball-jointed body, brown sleep eyes, open mouth, upper teeth, white cotton dress, restored fingers and neck joint, marks: A. 16 M. D.R.G.M. 374830 374831 . . . .   330.00

37" h, bisque head, repainted wood and composition ball-jointed body, brown sleep eyes, open mouth, upper teeth, sailor outfit, marks: a 16 M D.R.G.M. 374830 374831 . . . .   990.00

42" h, bisque head, repainted wood and composition ball-jointed body, blue sleep eyes, open mouth with upper teeth, wearing military uniform, marks: Armand Marseille, A 20 M 1,870.00

Nancy Ann Story Book Doll, bisque, one pc head, body, moveable arms, painted features, blue gown, $30.00.

Nancy Ann Storybook Doll

3½", Christening Baby, hard plastic, straight baby legs, jointed shoulders and hips, molded painted yellow hair, closed mouth, marks: Storybook Dolls/USA/Trademark/Reg. 1952 . . . .   25.00

5", bisque, one piece body, painted eyes, Cinderella, mark: Story/Book/Doll/USA on back 30.00

5½", bisque, one piece body, painted features, Elsie Marley, 1942 . . . . .   25.00

6", hard plastic, black sleep eyes, Jeannie, marks: Storybook Dolls/USA/Trademark/Reg. 1952 . . . . .   25.00

Nippon, 20", Hilda type, bisque socket head, composition five piece bent limb baby body, brown wig, brown glass sleep eyes, open mouth, teeth, recostumed, marks: B9 RE Nippon incised on head **225.00**

Putnam, Grace S., Bye Lo Baby
13", solid dome bisque head, flange neck, cloth body, celluloid hands, lightly painted brown hair, molded forelock, blue glass sleep eyes, closed mouth, white gown and matching slip, non functioning crier, marks: Copr. by Grace S. Putnam incised on head, Bye-Lo stamped on body **300.00**
16", solid dome bisque head, flange neck, cloth body, celluloid hands, lightly painted brown hair, molded forelock, blue glass sleep eyes, closed mouth, christening gown and matching bonnet, non functioning crier, marks: Copr. by Grace S. Putnam incised on head, Bye-Lo stamped on body **325.00**

Russian, stockinette dolls, Smolensk peasant costumes, 15" h, pr, $250.00.

Schoenhut, 19½" h, boy, deep carved head, blue intaglio eyes, closed mouth, orig wig, wearing baseball outfit **1,000.00**

Simon & Halbig
12" h, bisque shoulder head, brown glass eyes, blonde human hair wig, purple flowered muslin dress, straw bonnet, c1880, marks: S 4 H **770.00**
16" h, Oriental, black, bisque head, wood and composition jointed body, brown sleep eyes, open mouth with upper teeth, wearing orig red and white floral robe, marks: Simon & Halbig S.H. 1129 DEP 7 .... **1,980.00**
19" h, bisque head, wood and composition ball-jointed body, blue glass eyes, open mouth with upper teeth, blonde wig, pierced ears, marks: Simon & Halbig DEP Germany Santa 1249 7½ **770.00**
22" h, bisque head, wood and composition ball-jointed body, blue glass eyes, open mouth, upper teeth, pierced ears, molded bust, repainted hands, marks: 1159 S. & H. DEP 8 Germany **1,210.00**

Societe Francaise de Bebes et Jouets
24", bisque socket head, blue glass sleep eyes, brunette human hair, orig Jumeau flower sprigged frock and leather shoes inscribed "Bebe Jumeau 11," c1990 .... **1,700.00**
29" h, bisque head, wood and composition jointed body, blue sleep eyes, open mouth, upper teeth, brown wig, pierced ears, orig cotton floral chemise with label, orig Jumeau box, marks: Societe Francaise de Fabrication de Bebes & Jouets S.F.B.J. 301 Paris, red Tete Jumeau **1,980.00**

Steiner, Jules Nicholas
8" h, pressed bisque head, composition jointed body, jointed wrists, blue paperweight eyes, open mouth with upper teeth, blonde wig, cork pate, pierced ears, orig chemise, marks: A 3, red Le Parisien .. **1,320.00**
24" h, bisque head, composition jointed body, blue paperweight eyes, pierced ears, closed mouth, brown wig, marks: Steiner/Paris/Fre A.17 .... **4,675.00**
36" h, pressed bisque head, jointed composition body, replaced blue glass eyes, outlined open mouth, brown wig, pierced ears, wearing layered dress and hat, marks: J Steiner Bte S.G.D.G. Paris Fi Re A 21, Le Parisien **2,090.00**

Thuillier, A. 22" h, bisque head, gusset jointed kid body, blue paperweight eyes, light brown mohair wig, French style dress, matching bonnet, pink leather shoes, c1890, marks: A10T **70,000.00**

Unknown Maker
13" h, French, bisque swivel head, gusset kid body, bisque lower arms, blue threaded glass eyes, outlined closed mouth, blonde wig, cork pate, pierced ears, orig tan skirt with matching coat **2,310.00**
16" h, French, bisque swivel head, shoulderplate, gusset kid body,

stitched fingers, blue threaded glass eyes, outlined closed mouth, blonde wig, cork pate, wedding gown, marks: incised 4 .... **1,760.00**
23" h, poured bisque head, French wood and composition jointed body, straight legs, blue glass eyes, open mouth, upper teeth, marks: 5 **1,100.00**
37", German, bisque head, wood and composition ball-jointed repainted body, blue sleep eyes, open mouth, upper teeth, tremble tongue, marks: 4711 105 .... **1,100.00**

DOOR KNOCKERS

History: Before the advent of the mechanical bell or electrical buzzer and chime, a door knocker was considered an essential door ornament to announce the arrival of visitors. Metal was used to cast or forge the various forms; many cast iron examples were painted. Collectors like to find knockers with English registry marks.

Parrot, cast iron, green and yellow paint, $85.00.

BRASS

Cat, arched back	**50.00**
Devil, Belgium	**35.00**
Dog's head, 7"	**65.00**
Eagle, 8½"	**60.00**
Federal Style, 10½" l	**230.00**
Grecian Urn, 7"	**30.00**
Jenny Jones	**75.00**
Lady, hand holds mirror	**35.00**
Lion's head, 4", ring knocker, c1880 ..	**75.00**
Owl, 3½" h	**35.00**
Seahorse and shell	**80.00**

BRONZE

Dolphin, 11" l	**275.00**
Grecian Head, 4½"	**80.00**
Kissing Couple, 10½"	**40.00**
Renaissance Style, open lyre form, maiden center, inverted lion on each side, shell shape basin, green patina, 11½" h, Continental, late 19th C ...	**880.00**

CAST IRON

Amish Man, movable eyes	**25.00**
Butterfly	**65.00**
Fruit Cluster	**22.00**
Lady's hand, holding ball, ruffled cuff, ring on finger, 6"	**70.00**
Parrot, 4½" l, polychrome paint	**65.00**
Spider, hanging from web, bee caught, 3½"	**95.00**

DOORSTOPS

History: Doorstops became popular in the late 19th century. They can be found flat or three dimensional and were made in cast iron, bronze, wood, and other material. Hubley, a leading toy manufacturer, made many examples.

References: Jeanne Bertoia, *Doorstops: Identification And Values*, Collector Books, 1985; Marilyn Hamburger and Beverly Lloyd, *Collecting Figural Doorstops*, A.S. Barnes and Company, 1978.

Reproduction Alert: Reproductions are proliferating as prices on genuine doorstops continue to rise. There is usually a slight reduction in size in a reproduced piece unless an original mold is used at which time original size remains the same. Reproductions have less detail, lack of smoothness to the overall casting, and lack of detail in the paint. If there is any bright orange rusting, this is strongly indicative of a new piece. Beware. If it looks too good to be true, it usually is.

Notes: Pieces described below contain at least 80% or more of the original paint and are in very good condition. Repainting drastically reduces price and desirability. Poor original paint is preferred over repaint.

All listings are cast iron and flatback castings unless otherwise noted.

Doorstops marked with an asterick are currently being reproduced.

B + H = Bradley and Hubbard.

Advisor: Craig Dinner.

Basket
11" h, rose, ivory wicker basket, natural flowers, handle with bow, sgd "Hubley 121" **135.00**

Golfer, light blue coat and hat, red and green trimmed pants, 8″ h, $375.00.

15⅜″ h, fruit, tan wicker basket, blue ribbon and bow, Hubley 260.00

Bellhop, black, 7½″ h, carrying satchel, facing sideways, orange-red uniform and cap 350.00

Bowl, 7 x 7″, green-blue, natural colored fruit, sgd "Hubley, 456" 100.00

Boy
9⅜″, "The Tiger," hands at side, riding outfit, cartoon like eyes, "FISH" on front, sgd "Hubley 269" 650.00
10⅝″ h, wearing diapers directing traffic, police hat, red scarf, brown dog at side 400.00
11″ h, full figure, Dutch, hands in pocket, blue jump suit and hat, red belt and collar, brown shoes, blonde hair 375.00
12¾″ h, native wearing turban and leopard skin, one hand extended . 500.00

* Caddie, 8″ h, carrying brown and tan bag, white, brown knickers, red jacket 375.00

Cat
* 7″, male and female holding each others waist, dressed 235.00
* 8″, black, red ribbon and bow around neck, on pillow 125.00
9½″ h, 7″ w, full figure, Persian, sitting, gray, light markings, sgd "Hubley" inside casting 140.00
10½″ l, fireside, full figure, gray, light markings, sgd "Hubley" inside casting 140.00

Child, 17″ h, reaching, naked, flesh color, short curly brown hair 625.00

Clown, 10″ h, full figure, 2 sided, red suit, white collar, blue hat, black shoes 545.00

Cottage
6⅜″ h, three dimensional garden, tan roof, 3 red chimneys, flowers, 2 pc casting, Ann Hathaway 250.00
8⅝″ l, 5¾″ h, Cape type, blue roof, flowers, fenced garden, path, sgd "Eastern Speciality Mfg Co 14″ . . 125.00

Dancer
8⅞″ h, Art Deco couple doing Charleston, pink dress, black tux, red and black base, "FISH" on front, sgd "Hubley 270" 485.00
11⅛″ h, black woman doing Rhumba, red, yellow, and blue dress, red kerchief 325.00

Dog
Boston Bull
9″ h, full figure, facing left, black, tan markings 110.00
10½″ h, facing right, black, white markings 75.00
Boxer, 8½ x 9″, full figure, facing forward, brown, tan markings 165.00
Pekingese, 14½″ l, 9″ h, full figure, life-like size and color, brown, sgd "Hubley" 500.00
* Puppies, 7″, three puppies in basket, natural colors, sgd "Copyright 1932 M Rosenstein, Lancaster, PA, USA" 275.00
Japanese Spaniel, 9″ h, black and white, long curly hair, sgd "1267" 175.00
Wire Haired Fox Terrier, 9 x 8″, full figure, facing sideways, tan, brown markings 90.00

Drum Major, 12⅝″, full figure, ivory pants, red hat with feather, yellow baton in right hand, left hand on waist, sq base 325.00

Duck, 7½″, white, green bush and grass 225.00

Elephant, 14″, pulling coconut out of palm tree, natural color 165.00

Fisherman, 6¼″ h, standing at wheel, hand blocking sun over eyes, rain gear 140.00

Fish, 9¾″ h, three, fantail, orig paint, sgd "Hubley 464" 135.00

Flower
Goldenrods, 7⅛″ h, natural color, sgd "Hubley 268" 150.00
Jonquil, 7″ yellow flowers, red and orange cups, sgd "Hubley 453" . . . 150.00

Frog, 3″, full figure, sitting, yellow and green 50.00

Girl
9″
French, holding skirt out at sides, hat, sgd "Hubley 23" 125.00
Sunbonnet, blue hat, pink dress . . 215.00
10⅞″, bathing, yellow and red swimsuits, green and yellow bathing caps under umbrella, "FISH" on front, sgd "Hubley 250" 425.00
* 13¾″ h, 9¾″ l, white hat, flowing cape, holding orange jack-o-lantern with red cutout eyes, nose, and mouth 650.00

* Golfer, 10" h, overhead swing, hat and ball on ground, Hubley **300.00**

Horse, 7⅞" h, jumping fence, jockey, sgd "Eastern Spec Co #790" **185.00**

House
5½" h, 8¼" l, 2 story, attic, path to door, shutters, sgd "Sophia Smith House" **225.00**
6" h, woman walking up front stairs, grapevines, sgd "EasternSpec Co" **175.00**

* Kitten, 7" h, 3 kittens in wicker basket, sgd "M Rosenstein, c1932, Lancaster, PA" **325.00**

Lighthouse, 7¾" h, 9" l, three dimensional buildings and light house, base, Highland **275.00**

* Mammy
8½" h, full figure, red dress, white apron, blue kerchief with white spots, sgd inside "Hubley 327" .. **125.00**
12", full figure, blue dress, white apron, red kerchief with white spots, sgd "copyright Hubley" inside **300.00**

Messenger Boy, 10" h, bouquet in hand, cap, rosy checks, front sgd "FISH" **375.00**

Monkey, 8⅜" h, on yellow and black barrel, green, yellow face, ears, tail and paws, sgd "Taylor Cook No 3, 1930" **375.00**

Musician, 6⅞" h
Black man playing saxophone, white pants, red jacket **475.00**
Black man playing drums, black paint **425.00**

Pan, 7" h, with flute, sitting on mushroom, green outfit, red hat and sleeves, green grass base **140.00**

Parrot, 13¾" h, in ring, two sided, heavy gold base, sgd "B & H" **210.00**

Penguin, 10" h, full figure, facing sideways, black, white chest, top hat and bow tie, yellow feet and beak, unsgd Hubley **250.00**

* Pheasant, 8½", brown, bright markings, green grass, sgd "Fred Everett" front, sgd "Hubley" back **200.00**

Policeman, 9½" h, leaning on red fire hydrant, blue uniform and tilted hat, comic character face, tan base, "Safety First" on front **600.00**

Popeye, 9" h, full figure, pipe in mouth, white hat, blue pants, black and red shirt, sgd "Hubley, 1929 King Features Syn, Made in USA" **700.00**

Owl, 9½" h, sits on books, sgd "Eastern Spec Co" **225.00**

* Quail, 7¼" h, 2 brown, tan, and yellow birds, green, white, and yellow grass, Fred Everett on front, sgd "Hubley 459," **225.00**

Rabbit
8⅛" h, eating carrot, red sweater, brown pants **285.00**

15¼" h, sits on hind paws, tan, green grass, detailed casting, sgd "B & H 7800" **400.00**

Ringmaster, 10½" h, full figure, hands clasped behind back, red jacket, green pants, top hat **650.00**

Rooster
7", standing, black, colorful detail .. **135.00**
12", full figure, black, red comb, yellow claws and beak **275.00**
13" h, red comb, black and brown tail and chest, yellow stomach **300.00**

Ship
5¼" h, clipper, full sails, American flag on top mast, wave base, 2 rubber stoppers, sgd "CJO" **55.00**
11¼", three masts, full sail **40.00**

Skier, 12½" h, full figure, woman, red scarf, gloves, and belt, blue ski suit and beret, wood skis at side **375.00**

Squirrel, 9", sitting on stump eating nut, brown and tan **175.00**

Stork, 13¾", white, yellow beak, orange feet, black markings, flowers and grass **265.00**

Storybook
Huckleberry Finn, 12½" h, floppy hat, pail, stick, Littco Products label .. **400.00**
Humpty Dumpty, 4½" h, full figure, sgd "661" inside **275.00**
Little Miss Muffet, 7¾" h, siting on mushroom, blue dress, blonde hair **140.00**
Little Red Riding Hood
7½" h, 9½" w, sgd "NUYDEA" ... **375.00**
9½", basket at side, red cape, tan dress with blue pattern, blonde hair, sgd "Hubley" **350.00**
Mary Quite Contrary, 11⅜" h, blue hat, yellow dress and socks, green watering can, "Littco Products" label **500.00**
Puss in Boots, flat back, head sticking out of boot, sgd "Creations Co 1930" **300.00**

Tiger, 8½" h, tan, black stripes, baseball bat on shoulder, black base **400.00**

* Windmill, 6¾" h, 6⅞" w, ivory, red roof, house at side, green base **90.00**

Woman
8" h, Colonial, sgd "Hubley" **115.00**
8½" h, minuet, one hand on hip ... **160.00**
8¾" h, peasant, blue dress, black hair, fruit basket on head **125.00**
* 11" h, flowers and shawl **135.00**
12" h, carrying parasol and hat box in left hand, satchel with "Phoebe" in right hand, flowered hat **265.00**

Zinnias, 11⅝" h, multicolored flowers, blue and black vase, detailed casting, 2 rubber stoppers, sgd "B & H" ... **175.00**

K.P.M.

1727

Dresden
1883-93

N
Dresden
MODERN MARK

DRESDEN/MEISSEN

History: Augustus II, Elector of Saxony and King of Poland, founded the Royal Saxon Porcelain Manufactory in the Albrechtsburg, Meissen, in 1710. Johann Frederick Boettger, an alchemist, and Tschirnhaus, a nobleman, experimented with kaolin clay from the Dresden area to produce porcelain. By 1720 the factory produced a whiter hard paste porcelain than that from the Far East. The factory experienced its golden age in the 1730–50s period under the leadership of Samuel Stolzel, kiln master, and Johann Gregor Herold, enameler.

Many marks were used by the Meissen factory. The first was a pseudo-oriental mark in a square. The famous crossed swords mark was adopted in 1724. A small dot between the hilts was used from 1763–74 and a star between the hilts from 1774 to 1814. Two modern marks are swords with a hammer and sickle and swords with a crown.

The Meissen factory was destroyed and looted by forces of Frederick the Great during the Seven Years' War (1756–1763). It was reopened, but never achieved its former greatness.

In the 19th century, the factory reissued some of its earlier forms. These later wares are called "Dresden" to differentiate them from the earlier examples. Further, there were several other porcelain factories in the Dresden region, and their products also are grouped under the "Dresden" designation of collectors.

Reference: Susan and Al Bagdade, *Warman's English & Continental Pottery & Porcelain, 1st Edition,* Warman Publishing Co., Inc., 1987.

DRESDEN

Center Bowl, 17″ l, 7½″ w, boat shape, four sq feet, hp, floral int., applied flowers on front and back, sgd "K Frulauf" 325.00
Charger, 18″ d, soldiers receiving provisions, flower garland order, black enamel pseudo AR cipher, 19th C . . 650.00
Figure, 13 x 7½″, man playing piano, woman playing cello, period lace dress, molded base, gilt accents . . . 400.00
Loving Cup, 5½ x 6½″, three gold handles, red ground, ornate gold trim framing scenes of nymphs 325.00
Plate, 8¼″ d, cupids in center, cobalt blue border, raised gold dec and flowers, pr 365.00
Tile, 4″ sq, draped young woman holding lyre, putti in tree playing violin, sgd "H Rock," framed 300.00
Vase, 16″ h, cov, shield shaped body, gilt and puce ground, oval reserve of putti in landscapes, wide gilt band, waisted neck molded with leaves, gadrooned base, waisted socle, sq plinth, wired for electricity, pr 1,320.00

Meissen, coffeepot, European regimental encampments, diapered puce borders, gilding, underglaze blue crossed swords mark, 9½″ h, $2,250.00.

MEISSEN

Bowl, 6⅞″ d, multicolored scattered Deutsche Blumen, brown rim, c1740, blue crossed swords mark 425.00
Candelabra, 19½″ h, four light, flower encrusted scroll molded standard, applied putti as the Seasons, waisted rocaille molded base, scrolled feet, 19th C, blue crossed swords mark, pr 2,420.00
Clock, mantel, 18½″ h, circular enamel dial sgd "Hry MAPC," molded case surmounted by winged female figure, flanked by foliate branches and winged putti with floral garland, tree

trunk base with applied male figure and two floral encrusted candlearms, scroll molded incurved base, blue crossed swords mark, late 19th C **2,000.00**

Coffeepot, cov, multicolored loose floral bouquet, fluted spout and handle with molded acanthus, blue crossed swords and star mark **500.00**

Desk Set, 7 x 10½″ tray, sander, cov inkwell, and bell, gilt trim, framed polychrome dec harbor scenes, puce harbor scene medallions to border, cross swords mark, late 19th C, 4 pcs **900.00**

Ecuelle, cov
6¼″ w, two handles, gilt berry finial, underglaze blue flowers, gilding, multicolored European flowers and woman seated on grassy mount, Hausmalerei, c1750, blue crossed swords mark **1,760.00**

10″ d, matching stand, lemon finial, entwined branch handles, multicolored landscapes in shaped cartouches, blue and yellow scroll work, all—over molded puce flowerheads, pierced border on stand, c1750, blue crossed swords mark **2,650.00**

Figure
6″ h, flutist attending to maiden nursing child, molded gilt lined base, 19th C, blue crossed swords mark **1,225.00**

6½″ h, lovers, seated gentleman offering flowers to maiden, rockwork gilt edged base, 19th C, blue crossed swords mark **1,225.00**

8¾″, tailor, floral patterned costume, riding goat, sq molded gilt edged base, 19th C, blue crossed swords mark **1,150.00**

9¾″ h
Love Letter, lady consoling another lady, standing before flowering garland draped column, molded gilt edged base, 19th C, blue crossed swords mark **2,200.00**

Study of Love, Venus holding globe and writing on tablet, seated on rockwork, attended by putti, oval foliate and scroll molded base, 19th C, blue crossed swords mark **2,860.00**

Swordsman, lady, and drummer, scroll molded base, 19th C, blue crossed swords mark **1,760.00**

13½″ h, Commerce of Cupids, classical maidens inspecting putti in winged cart, oval molded base with gilt edged leaf chain band, 19th C, blue crossed swords mark **6,380.00**

Lamp, 19¾″ h, shade with lithophane medallions and applied flowers, polychrome, gilt, four figures on base,

crown in wreath mark, minor edge damage **650.00**

Pagoda Figure, seated Chinese man
6¾″ h, multicolored flowered robes, nodding heads and hands, 19th C, blue crossed swords mark, pr . . . **9,900.00**

13″ h, multicolored flowered robe, articulated head, hands, and tongue, 19th C, blue crossed swords mark **9,000.00**

Pipe Bowl, 3½″ h, white, figural, Lord Byron, turban, molded leaf tips, blue crossed swords mark **425.00**

Plate, 8¾″ d, Schmetterling pattern, stylized butterfly in central floral spray, chocolate rims, c1735, blue crossed swords mark, set of 3 . . . . **1,650.00**

Tureen, cov, 9¾″ d, circular, Imari pattern, blue, iron—red, and gilt, flower sprays in stylized lappets border, pine cone finial, c1730, blue crossed swords mark **3,350.00**

Vase
20½″ h, baluster, pierced body with applied scrolling flowering forget—me—not branches, pierced cov, bird finial, blue crossed swords mark, late 19th C **1,430.00**

22½″ h, baluster, continuous painted scene of amorous figures, lush landscape, Venus and Cupid cavorting in sky, owls at shoulders, flower encrusted base with pierced acanthus foot, 19th C, blue crossed swords mark **9,900.00**

DUNCAN AND MILLER

History: George Duncan, Harry B. and James B., his sons, and Augustus Heisey, his son-in-law, formed George Duncan & Sons in Pittsburgh, Pennsylvania, in 1865. The factory was located just two blocks from the Monongahela River, providing easy and cheap access by barge for materials needed to produce glass. The men, from Pittsburgh's southside, were descendants of generations of skilled glass makers.

The plant burned to the ground in 1892. James E. Duncan, Sr., selected a site for a new factory in Washington, Pennsylvania, where operations began on February 9, 1893. The plant prospered, producing fine glassware and table services for many years.

John E. Miller, one of the stockholders, was responsible for designing many fine patterns, the most famous being "Three Face." The firm incorporated, using the name The Duncan and Miller Glass Company until its plant closed in 1955. The company's slogan was "The Loveliest Glassware in America." The U.S. Glass Co. purchased the molds, equipment, and machinery in 1956.

References: Gail Krause, *The Encyclopedia Of*

Duncan Glass, published by author, 1984; Gail Krause, *A Pictorial History Of Duncan & Miller Glass,* published by author, 1976; Gail Krause, *The Years Of Duncan,* published by author, 1980.

Collectors' Club: National Duncan Glass Society, P.O. Box 965, Washington, PA 15301.

Additional Listings: Pattern Glass.

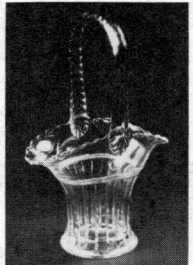

Basket, clear, scalloped rim, applied clear molded handle, $20.00.

Animal
Duck, crystal	55.00
Swan, 12″ h, ruby	50.00
Ashtray, Teardrop, individual size	5.00
Basket, floral etching, 6″, crystal	25.00

Bonbon, Terrace, rolled up handles, cobalt blue 15.00

Bowl
Caribbean, 8½″, blue	100.00
Puritan, console, rolled edge, cutting, crystal	30.00
Sanibel, blue opal	75.00

Candlesticks, pr
First Love, 5¾″, 2 lite, clear	60.00
Language of Flowers, 2 lite, clear . .	68.00
Celery, Canterbury, 11″, crystal	20.00
Champagne, Sandwich, 5¼″, 5 oz . .	20.00
Cheese Dish, Caribbean, blue	30.00
Cigarette Box, cov, Patio, green	40.00
Coaster, Sandwich	10.00

Compote
Buck and doe etching, 10 x 9¼″ . . .	100.00
Puritan, green	15.00
Condiment Set, Teardrop, crystal, 5 pc	65.00

Creamer and Sugar
First Love	35.00
Sandwich	12.00

Cup and Saucer
Canterbury, crystal	14.00
First Love	20.00
Spiral Flutes, amber	7.00
Epergne, 9½ x 4½″, Caribbean, blue	90.00
Finger Bowl, Spiral Flutes, green	7.50

Goblet
First Love, 10 oz	18.00

Theme, cut	15.00
Willow, cut	8.00
Ice Bucket, First Love, orig handle . . .	75.00
Martini Pitcher, First Love	145.00
Mayonnaise, underplate, Teardrop . . .	15.00
Nappy, Sandwich, 5″	5.00
Pitcher, Radiance, ½ gallon, sapphire blue, blown	85.00

Plate
Hostess, 16″	85.00
Nautical, 8½″	15.00
Sandwich, 8″	10.00
Willow, 8¾″	12.00
Punch Set, Caribbean, crystal, ruby handles, 15 pcs	225.00
Relish, First Love, 7″, 3 part	25.00
Salt and Pepper, First Love, pr	25.00

Sherbet
Georgian, green	9.00
Spiral Flutes, 4¾″, pink	10.00
Teardrop, low, ftd	4.50
Sugar, Puritan, green	5.00
Tumbler, Astair, ruby, 10 oz	15.00

Vase
Canterbury, 7¼″, inverted candle . . .	110.00
Cornucopia, 8″, three feathers	75.00

DURAND

History: Victor Durand (1870–1931), born in Baccarat, France, apprenticed at the Baccarat glass works where several generations of his family worked. In 1884 Victor came to America to join his father at the Whitall-Tatum & Co. in New Jersey. In 1897 father and son leased the Vineland Glass Manufacturing Company in Vineland, New Jersey. Products included inexpensive bottles, jars, and glass for scientific and medical purposes. By 1920 four separate companies existed.

When Quezal Art Glass and Decorating Company failed, Victor Durand recruited Martin Bach, Jr., Emil J. Larsen, William Wiedebine, and other Quezal men and opened an art glass shop at Vineland in December, 1924. Quezal style iridescent pieces were made. New innovations included cameo and intaglio designs, geometric Art Deco shapes, Venetian Lace, and oriental style pieces. In 1928 crackled glass, called Moorish Crackle and Egyptian Crackle, was made.

Much of Durand glass is not marked. Some bear a sticker labeled "Durand Art Glass," some have the name "Durand" scratched on the pontil, or "Durand inside a large "V". Etched numbers may be part of the marking.

Durand died in 1931. The Vineland Flint Glass Works was merged with Kimble Glass Company a year later, and the art glass line discontinued.

Ashtray, 5″ d, irid blue and green, center match holder 750.00
Bowl, 8″ d, 6½″ h, orange cased to opal,

Vase, orange ground, blue leaves and vine dec, 7½" h, $800.00.

overall irid green leaf and vine dec, sgd "Durand" in "V" 1,400.00
Candlesticks, pr, 9½" h, clear amber baluster, pulled blue tip feathers, etched wheat and leaves on flanged rim 275.00
Compote, 8" d, white feather design center, blue ground, pale green stem and foot 725.00
Lamp
Floor, 70" h, 12" shade, triparte swan cage, gold threaded vasiform shade, gilt metal twisted shaft, three leaf and scroll dec feet 1,000.00
Table
13" h base, 24" h overall, brilliant blue base with applied threading, orig double socket fittings 800.00
14" h, shade with gold and green hearts and vines, irid opal ground, applied heavy gold threading, yellow int., bronze tree form base 2,100.00
Plate, 8⅝" d, feather pattern, blue, opal, and clear, cross hatched cut center 200.00
Vase
6" h, flared, tapered body, white heart and vine dec, blue ground, sgd . . 1,100.00
7⅛" h, baluster, ftd, King Tut, pale green, gold swirling dec, sgd "Durand" 715.00
7½" h, ovoid form, everted lip, amber, mottled amber irid, inscribed "Durand/1968-6," first quarter 20th C 275.00
7½" h, 10" d, squatty, bulbous, hard ribbed body, bulbous neck, irid light to dark ruby, sgd "Durand #1977–10" 3,950.00

8" h, tapered globe, white gold feather, blue tip, gold threading, irid gold ground, sgd "V Durand" 1,550.00
8⅛" h, bulbous ovoid form, tapered cylindrical mouth, graduated double shoulder, red irid rim at base, silver irid sgd "Durand/1978–8" . . 330.00
9½" h, ovoid, flared rim, transparent amber, opal and green layers of heat reactive glass, crackled, gold irid int. 500.00
9¾" h, flared, irid blue, threaded, minor loss to threads, sgd "V Durand" 325.00
11½" h, classical shape, ftd, white pulled feathers, blue tips, irid gold ground, thin gold threading, script sgd "Durand" 2,100.00
18½" h, bulbous, flared rim, elongated neck, irid blue body, mirror base, sgd "Durand 1974 8" 2,000.00

ENGLISH CHINA AND PORCELAIN (GENERAL)

History: The manufacture of china and porcelain was scattered throughout England, with the majority of the factories located in the Staffordshire district. The number of potteries was over one thousand.

By the 19th century English china and porcelain had achieved a world wide reputation for excellence. American stores imported large amounts for their customers. The special production English pieces of the 18th and early 19th centuries held a position of great importance among early American antiques collectors.

References: Susan and Al Bagdade, *Warman's English & Continental Pottery & Porcelain, 1st Edition,* Warman Publishing, 1987; David Battie and Michael Turner, *The Price Guide to 19th and 20th Century British Porcelain,* Antique Collectors' Club; Peter Bradshaw, *18th Century English Porcelain Figures, 1745–1795,* Antiques Collectors' Club; Geoffrey A. Godden, *Godden's Guide To Mason's China And The Ironstone Wares,* Antique Collectors' Club; Geoffrey A. Godden, *Lowestoft Porcelain,* Antique Collectors' Club; R. K. Henrywood, *Relief Molded Jugs, 1820–1900,* Antique Collectors' Club; Rachael Feild, *Macdonald Guide To Buying Antique Pottery & Porcelain,* Macdonald & Co., Ltd., 1987; Llewellyn Jewitt, *The Ceramic Art of Great Britain,* Sterling Publishing, 1985 (reprint of 1883 classic); Griselda Lewis, *A Collector's History Of English Pottery,* Antique Collectors' Club; Donald C. Peirce, *English Ceramics: The Frances and Emory Cocke Collection,* High Museum of Art, 1988; Simon Spero, *The Price Guide To 18th Century English Porcelain,* Antique Collectors' Club.

Additional Listings: Castleford, Chelsea, Coalport, Copeland and Spode, Liverpool, Royal Crown Derby, Royal Doulton, Royal Worcester, Historical Staffordshire, Romantic Staffordshire, Wedgwood, and Whieldon.

BOW

Candlestick, 7¹⁵⁄₁₆″ h, Autumn, modeled as youthful Bacchus, wearing wreath of grape clusters and lavender nosed yellow leopard skin, standing beside putto, holding end of grapevine entwined around blue edged scroll, maroon and blue rococo scroll candlestick, maroon, puce, and blue edged scrolled molded base, black enamel stroke mark, c1760 . . . . **2,000.00**

Figure, 4¾″ h, white, Winter, old man in hooded coat leaning on stick, seated on pile of logs, warming hands over flaming braizer, from set of The Seasons **880.00**

Plate, 8¼″ d, rose, blue, iron–red, gray, yellow, brown, purple, turquoise and green exotic birds and insects, brown edged scalloped rim, James Giles type painting, c1770 . . . . **400.00**

CAUGHLEY

Dish, 7¾″ l, shell shape, lobed rim, center floral sprig, four floral garlands, double line border, underglaze blue "S" mark, c1780 . . . . **250.00**

Plate, 8¼″ d, blue and white, fluted edge, center with Chinamen in boat on river, house and trees on banks, powder blue ground with four fan shaped Chinese landscapes alternating with circular floral reserves, c1775, mock Oriental character mark, set of 3 . . . . **775.00**

Sauce Boat, 6¼″ w, blue and white, painted flowering branches, molded foliate cartouches, pleated ground, scattered leaves, cell pattern border, c1775, blue crescent marks, pr **350.00**

Tea Service, assembled, two teapots, two waste bowls, cov sugar, cream jug, painted scattered cobalt blue and gilt flowers, band of cobalt blue gilt and stylized flowers, blue crescent marks, c1785 . . . . **275.00**

COALBROOKDALE

Bowl, 3½″ h, cov, ftd, blue encrusted flowers and leaves surrounding enamel dec floral bouquets, gilt accents, branch like handles, mid 19th C **200.00**

Garniture, 8″ and two 7″ vases, handles, cobalt blue ground, encrusted flowers and leaves, gilt accents, mid 19th C . . . **300.00**

Vase, 12¼″ h, flower encrusted body, green trim, flower and bird cartouches, molded leafy handles, gilt trim, mid 19th C, pr **1,000.00**

DERBY

Bough Pot, 7¼″ w, bombe shape, foliage scroll handles, painted "View of Darley near Derby" and "Mattock Church, Derbyshire," titled on base, gilt diaper and foliage borders, bright blue ground, gilt scroll feet, c1825, Robert Bloor & Co, iron–red crown mark, crossed batons and Derby mark, pr **1,870.00**

Cream Jug, Pattern No. 127, tapering cylindrical shape, straight spout, gilt and stylized half flowerheads in arches, blue band edged in gilt, gilt dentil int. rim, puce crown crossed batons and "D" mark, c1800 . . . . **175.00**

Figure, 2¾″ h, pug, red–fawn fur, green collar, yellow bells, puce bow, seated on oval base with green, yellow, and puce molded scrolls, c1770, tail broken **715.00**

Plate, 8⅞″ d, multicolored center of exotic birds in landscape, stiff gilt leaves border on pale blue ground, gilt stylized flowerheads rim band, c1820, iron–red crown mark, crossed batons and "D" mark, gilder's mark attributed to John Moscrop **335.00**

Teapot, cov, 9½″ w, Pattern No. 110, interlaced blue line and gilt foliage, scroll handle, spout molded with wreath of bellflowers, puce crown, crossed batons and "D" mark **165.00**

Vase, 7⅞″ h, flower encrusted, shaped, pierced flaring rim, scroll molded gilt enriched handles, birds perched on branches, insects above pierced skirt and flowers, flaring base, some chips to flowers, c1770 . . . . **225.00**

FLIGHT, BARR AND BARR

Crocus Pot, 9″ w, 4″ h, "D" form, molded pilasters and panels, arcaded base, pale salmon ground, gilded stylized anthemion and foliate, painted still life panel of shells and coral, conforming top pierced panel, Barr Flight and Barr Worcester, early 19th C **8,000.00**

Dinner Service, 36 pcs, 11″ sq bowl, ten dinner plates, twelve dessert plates, ten soup plates, three oval platters, underglaze blue, iron–red, and orange Oriental floral dec, central iron–

red sprig, gilt band border, imp crowned "FBB" marks, c1820 . . . . . **2,250.00**

Urn, 5″ h, topographical, campaniform body, naturalistic shades, two small figures in gilt edged rect view, white beadwork band, gilt foliate border, gilt eagle handles, circular foot with gilt lyre, palmette, and foliage spray border between robin's egg blue bands, flaring rim with gilt banded and foliage borders, gilded sq foot, brown script view Birkleigh Vale near Plymouth inscription, crowned "Barr Flight & Barr Royal Porcelain Works Worcester," c1810 . . . . **2,000.00**

MASON

Dinner Service, partial, 90 pcs, Imari type dec, marked "Masons Patented Ironstone" **2,800.00**

Platter, 18¾″ l, chamfered rect, Willow pattern, underglaze blue transfer print, whorl border, crowned "Patent Ironstone China" mark, c1820 . . . . . **375.00**

Sauce Tureen, 6¾″ w, cov, matching stand, gilt spire finial, melon reeded dome cov, conforming bowl, blue foliage scroll handles, iron–red and blue Imari type pattern, gilding, pierced molded base, c1820, impressed "Mason's Patent Ironstone China" marks, pr **2,000.00**

New Hall, teapot, bulbous, helmet top, oval finial, red and blue floral dec, gold trim, Pattern 422, 1790–1805, $300.00.

NEW HALL

Bowl, 6¼″ d, Pattern No. 1277, printed and colored reserved panels of mother and child, dark blue ground, gilt vines **100.00**

Hot Water Jug, Oriental pattern, pewter lid and spout cov, c1812 . . . . **250.00**

Punch Bowl, 10″ d, puce and magenta enameled flowers, green laves on ext., center puce floral bouquet, gold foot band, c1780 . . . . **250.00**

Tea Service, teapot and stand, cream jug, sugar bowl, six cups and saucers, six teabowls, 7¾″ d plate, Pattern No. 644, blue leaves and berries, gilt branches, center patera, and rims, c1810 . . . . **1,210.00**

WORCESTER

Coffee Cup and Saucer, Kempthorne pattern, Chinese taste dec, iron–red, blue, green, and gilt flowering plants, blue and gilt diaper reserved border with iron–red half flowers, crescent mark, c1770 . . . . **275.00**

Dish
7½″ h, cushion shape, sq rim with gilted cobalt band, painted floral spray, four floral spandrel bouquets, underglaze blue crescent mark, c1770 . . . . **330.00**
8″ w, leaf shape, brown branch handle, green and yellow edge, purple veins, printed bouquet and scattered flowers, c1770 . . . . **1,870.00**

Plate
6⅝″ d, octagonal, center with Chinese man poling river boat, reserved on powder blue ground, fan shaped landscapes alternating with circular floral reserves, c1775, mock Oriental character mark **375.00**
7¾″ d, Blind Earl, scalloped, molded rose bud sprig, green, brown, and pink, painted scattered flowering branches and insects, scalloped border, gilt C–scrolls, c1770, pr . . **2,650.00**

Sauce Boat, Cos–Lettuce, stalk handles, scattered flowers and insects, brown line rims, int. with floral dec, c1760, pr **1,540.00**

Tea Bowl and Saucer
Floral Dec, white ground, painted iron–red, green, yellow, purple, and blue flowering branches, insects, flowerheads, and scrolls, c1765 . . **300.00**
Fruit Dec, green ground, painted fruit, green border within gilt scrolls, c1770 . . . . **235.00**

ENGLISH SOFTPASTE

History: Between 1820 and 1860 a large number of potteries in England's Staffordshire district produced decorative wares with a soft earthenware (creamware) base and a plain white or yellow glazed ground.

Design or "stick" spatterware was created by a cut-sponge (stamp), hand painting, or transfer. Blue was the dominant color. The earliest patterns were carefully arranged geometrics and generally covered the entire piece. Later pieces had a decorative border with a center motif, usually a tulip. In the 1850s Elsmore and Foster developed the Holly Leaf pattern.

King's Rose features a large, cabbage-type rose in red, pale red, or pink. The pink rose often is called "Queen's Rose." Secondary colors are pastels of yellow, pink, and occasionally green. The borders vary: a solid band, vined, lined, or sectional. The King's Rose exists in an oyster motif.

Strawberry China ware comes in three types: strawberries and strawberry leaves (often called strawberry luster), green feather-like leaves with pink flowers (often called cut-strawberry, primrose, or old strawberry), and a third type with the decoration in relief. The first two types are characterized by rust red moldings. Most pieces have a creamware ground. Davenport was one of the many potteries who made this ware.

Yellow-glazed earthenware (canary luster) has a canary yellow ground, transfer design which is usually in black, and occasional luster decoration. The earliest pieces date from the 1780s and have a fine creamware base. A few hand painted pieces are known. Not every piece has luster decoration. Marked pieces are uncommon.

Marked pieces are uncommon. Because the ground is softpaste, the ware is subject to cracking and chipping. Enamel colors and other types of decoration do not hold well. It is not unusual to see a piece with the decoration worn off.

Reference: Susan and Al Bagdade, *Warman's English & Continental Pottery & Porcelain, 1st Edition,* Warman Publishing Co., Inc., 1987.

Additional Listings: Adams Rose, Gaudy Dutch, Salopian Ware, Staffordshire Items.

DESIGN SPATTERWARE

Bowl
7½ x 4", polychrome stripes	75.00
9½, serrated rim, blue, white, and black trim	290.00
Creamer, 4", purple spatter	75.00
Cup and Saucer, floral, blue, green, ochre, and red	135.00
Cuspidor, 7¼ x 5", blue and white dec	75.00
Jug, 7", barrel shape, rosettes, fern prongs, blue	150.00

Mug
4", geometric dec, red, green, and brown	90.00
6", rosettes, blue, green bands	90.00

Plate
8⅜", green stick spatter, gaudy four color floral center, red rim stripes	125.00
8½", black stick spatter border, center red and blue flower, green leaves	175.00
8¾", red concentric center circles, narrow red line border with stars circled in blue	100.00
9", stars in center, pin wheels around narrow red line border	100.00
9¼", green flowers, red stick spatter center	115.00
10½", tulip, purple and blue spatter, marked "Cotton & Barlow"	325.00

Platter
12", red and green	175.00
16", purple and green	230.00
Sugar, cov, 5", white, blue, and red flowers, green leaves, closed ring and shell handles	100.00
Waste Bowl, floral rim, spatter overlay, marked "Adams"	50.00

KING'S ROSE

Coffeepot, 12", pink, green, yellow, and red dec, dome lid, c1825, minor restoration	1,200.00
Creamer, helmet shape, brick red rose	230.00
Cup and Saucer, solid border	170.00
Gravy Ladle, 6¾", deep purple enamel dec	50.00

Plate
6½", vine border, yellow puff balls	140.00
7½", pink border	145.00
Platter, 13"	300.00
Sauce Boat, 6¾"	150.00
Soup Plate, 9"	160.00
Sugar, cov, pink rose	175.00
Tea Set, cov teapot, four handleless cups and saucers, brick red rose, imp "Wood"	600.00
Teapot, Queen Anne shape, minor chips on cov	450.00
Toddy, 5¾", vine border, pink rose	75.00

STRAWBERRY CHINA

Bowl, 6¼", pink luster, red and green enamel, wide strawberry border, c1820	175.00
Coffeepot, 11¼", strawberry luster, dome cov, strawberry finial	465.00
Creamer, 6¼"	175.00
Cup and Saucer, handleless	100.00
Mug, 2½", applied handle	80.00

Plate
6½", strawberries and morning glories, pink luster border	185.00
8¼", Cut Strawberry	185.00
10"	150.00
Relish, 8¾", shell shape	115.00
Soup Plate, 8¼"	175.00

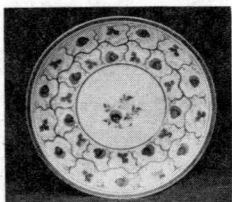

Strawberry, plate, pink luster band and vine dec, 8″ d, $65.00.

Sugar, cov, raised strawberries, strawberry knob	130.00
Teapot, 4¼ x 9½″	375.00

YELLOW GLAZED EARTHENWARE

Cup and Saucer, 3″ d handleless cup, 4¾″ d saucer, brown transfer, couple at tea **300.00**
Jug
  4½″, silver luster border and round medallion of Peace as young girl . **360.00**
  5¾″, black transfer print, silver luster dec, inscribed "Accept this trifle from a friend whose love for thee shall never end" and "George Lawton, 1809" under spout **700.00**
Mug, child's
  1⅞ x 2″, silver luster trim **250.00**
  2″, brown transfer, silver luster rim, boys flying kite, inscribed "For a favorite" **230.00**
Pitcher
  3¾″, red and orange flowers, wine dec on neck **625.00**
  5½″ h, black transfer, Sir Francis Burdett, silver luster roundel, canary ground, c1835 .... **950.00**
Plate
  6¼″, bright green band, sponged border, center inscribed "Thomas," c1820 .... **425.00**
  7⅜″, bright red and green floral dec, emb floral rim **300.00**
  8½″, red transfer center scene, molded acanthus border, imp Wood **275.00**
Potpourri Vase, 7½″, 6 classical figures outlined in black enamel, flaming brazier, inscribed "Sacrifice A L'Hymen," silver luster lion head handles **425.00**

FAIRINGS, MATCH-STRIKERS, AND TRINKET BOXES

History: Fairings are small, charming china objects which were purchased or given away as prizes at English fairs in the 19th century. Although fairings are generally identified with England, they actually were manufactured in Germany by Conte and Boehme of Possneck.

Fairings depicted an amusing scene either of courtship and marriage, politics, war, children, and animals behaving as children. Over four hundred varieties have been identified. Most fairings bore a caption. Early examples, 1860–70, were of better quality than later ones. After 1890 the colors became more garish, and gilding was introduced.

The manufacturers of fairings also made match-strikers and trinket boxes. Some were captioned. The figures on the lids were identical to those of the fairings. The market for the match-strikers and trinket boxes was identical to that for the fairings.

Reference: Susan and Al Bagdade, *Warman's English & Continental Pottery & Porcelain, 1st Edition*, Warman Publishing Co., Inc., 1987.

Advisors: Barbara and Melvin Alpren.

Trinket Box, white ground, blue decoration, girl putting on stockings, imp marks, 3½ x 4 x 2″, $145.00.

FAIRINGS

Baby and Dog, pulling at doll, 2¾ x 2½ x 5″	175.00
Baby's First Step, three children, hand in hand	200.00
O Do Leave Me A Drop, two cats at bowl	225.00
Power of Love, lady with tray, 3¼ x 3½″	185.00
Twelve Months After Marriage	200.00
Will We Sleep First or How, 5½ x 4″	200.00

MATCH–STRIKERS

Crown and scepter, oval, applied flowers on borders	265.00

Drum and drumsticks, red, white, and blue, gilt accents	250.00
Tea Party, three ladies around tea table	300.00

TRINKET BOXES

Boy on bed, putting on pajamas	150.00
Cameo, musical instruments on lid, 3¾"	100.00
Cavalier in canoe	200.00
Chest of Drawers, bombe front, pocket watch on top	175.00
Piano, figural, 2⅜"	75.00

FAIRY LAMPS

History: Fairy lamps, originating in England in the 1840s, are candle burning night lamps. They were used in nurseries, hallways, and dim corners of the home.

Two leading candle manufacturers, the Price Candle Company and the Samuel Clarke Company, promoted fairy lamps as a means to sell candles. Both contracted with other manufacturers of glass, porcelain, and metal to produce the needed shades and cups. For example, Clarke used Worcester Royal Porcelain Company, Stuart & Sons, and Red House Glass Works in England, plus firms in France and Germany. Clarke's trademark was a small fairy with a wand surrounded by the words "Clarke Fairy Pyramid, Trade Mark."

Fittings were produced in a wide variety of styles. Shades ranged from pressed to cut glass, from Burmese to Nailsea. Cups are found in glass, porcelain, brass, nickel, and silver plate.

American firms selling fairy lamps included Diamond Candle Company of Brooklyn, Blue Cross Safety Candle Co., and Hobbs-Brockunier of Wheeling, West Virginia.

Fairy lamps are found in two pieces (cup and shade) and three pieces (cup with matching shade and saucer). Married pieces are common.

References: John F. Solverson, *Those Fascinating Little Lamps*, Antique Publications, 1988; John F. Solverson (comp.), *Those Fascinating Little Lamps, Miniature Lamps Value Guide*, Antique Publications, 1988.

Reproduction Alert: Reproductions abound.

Vaseline ribbed dome, green pressed Clarke base, 2⅞ x 3½", $200.00.

"S. Clarke, Fairy" sgd "Thos. Webb & Sons-Queen's Burmese"	1,550.00
6½" h, 8" d, dome shade dec with red flowers, yellow centers, tapestry flower bowl base with cream ground, pink flowers, aqua and gold trim, base marked "Clarke"	950.00
Frosted, 6½" h, blue to white, molded leaf design, ruffled rims	200.00
Goofus Glass, 7" h, rose dec, flash fired green, three smoke holes on top, wood base	30.00
Mt Washington, 5¼", peachblow, clear glass candle cup	250.00
Nailsea, Verre Moire	
4⅛" x 4", opaque white looping on shade, clear marked "Clarke" base	150.00
5" h, 5½" d, white loopings, frosted cranberry body, dome shaped shade, bowl shaped base with ruffled edge, clear Clarke insert marked "Clarke"	425.00
6½" h, 5¾" d, white loopings, red satin body, dome shaped shade, bowl shaped base with six pinched in pleats, clear Clarke insert marked "Clarke Fairy Patent Trade Mark"	845.00
Opalescent, 3¾ x 2⅞", blue emb rib, pyramid, clear marked "Clarke" base, shade reg #130643	85.00
Opaline, 17", French blue, four large faceted jewels in purple and dark blue, filigree brass mountings	275.00
Peachblow, 6⅜", peachblow shade and base with blue, white, brown and green enamel dec, white int., clear marked "Clarke Cricklite" base	410.00
Satin Glass	
5" h, Diamond Quilted shade, clear pressed Clarke's cricklite base	110.00
5⅛" h, opaque white and frosted loop	

Baccarat, 5¼ x 4", Rose Tiente, Sunburst pattern, saucer base 235.00
Bisque, figural, head
  Monkey, 3½" h, natural coloring, amber eyes 365.00
  Pekingese Pup, blue collar, amber eyes, black nose 485.00
Brass, 5⅜" h, cast, jeweled, handle .. 125.00
Burmese
  5" h, flower and vines dec shade, clear base, sgd "S Clarke/Patent/ Trade Mark/Fairy" 550.00
  6", Burmese candle insert, marked

shade, rose base, clear Clarke
burner 50.00
6¼" h, blue, white loopings 400.00
6¾" h, cranberry, opaque white loopings 700.00
Spatter Glass
4 x 14", Swirl pattern shade, gold,
white, and pink spatter, white int.,
clear marked "Clarke" glass peg
base, brass candlestick 425.00
13¾" d, 17¾" h, double, emb ribbed
overlay shades, SP Cricklite base 450.00
Stevens & Williams, 3⅞ x 4½, pink and
white swirled stripes, clear marked
"Clarke" base 175.00

FAMILLE ROSE

History: Famille Rose is Chinese export enameled porcelain in which the pink color predomi-
nates. It was made primarily in the 18th and 19th
centuries. Other porcelains in the same group are
Famille Jaune (yellow), Famille Noire (black), and
Famille Verte (green).

Decorations include courtyard and home
scenes, birds, and insects. Secondary colors are
yellow, green, blue, aubergine, and black.

Mid to late 19th century Chinese export wares
similar to Famille Rose are identified as Rose Canton, Rose Mandarin, and Rose Medallion.

Reference: Sandra Andacht, *Oriental Antiques
& Art: An Identification And Value Guide,* Wallace-
Homestead, 1987.

**Bowl, Chinese armorial, int. with arms
of Dalling and Foster in pretense beneath underglaze blue Fitzhugh border,
later gilding, rolled lip, arms repeated
on ext., blue enamel floral sprays,
c1785, 13" d, $2,700.00.**

Bowl, 6½" d, central peach medallion
with heron, peaches, symbols of lon-
gevity, and Immortals, gold rim, Tong-
zhi seal mark 225.00
Candleholders, pr, 7¼" l, figural, elephants, standing, heads turned to
side, trunks curled, painted iron–red
bodies, gilt ground cloths with pink

peony dec on backs, baluster holder
in ingot shaped howdahs, 19th C ... 4,000.00
Dish, 12¾" l, scrolled boat shape, waisted, raised spreading oval feet, undulating at upper rims, curled at ends,
painted opaque enamels, bands of
fruit and flowers, circular reserves of
Chinese river landscapes, gilt details,
Qianlong, pr 2,200.00
Garden Stool, 18½" h, barrel shape,
pierced, multicolored enamel dec, pr 2,310.00
Jardiniere, 8½" h, 11¾" w, 8½" d, rect,
multicolored flowering branches, lappet border 1,320.00
Lamp Base
24¾" h baluster form vase, multicolored enamel dec, sq wood base,
pr 1,320.00
32½" h, baluster form Famille Noire
vase, brass standard with hardstone finial, circular Chinese fretwork base 715.00
Punch Bowl
10¼" d, gilt, painted sepia, iron–red
and multicolored enamels, after
"Judgment of Paris" painting on
ext., divided by clusters of peonies,
int. with center peony and gilt spear
headband, base rim repair, c1750 3,000.00
11½" d, gilt, painted, two large
scrolled panels depicting Western
fox hunters in European landscapes, one with meet, other with
chase, small panels of Chinese
families on terraces, reserved
ground of dense iron–red "Y" pattern, int. with central medallion of
sportsman and dogs, scalework
bands, additional landscape
panels, dotted cell pattern, rim
crack, Qianlong 5,280.00
Salt, open, 3¼" l, oblong, armorial,
trencher, painted iron–red, turquoise,
pale green, yellow, and blue opaque
enamels, cartouche shaped coat of
arms below rampant lion crest,
c1750, pr 6,000.00
Taper Holder, 4½" l, figural, recumbent
Buddhistic lion, painted iron–red
body, gilt ground cloth with pink peony
dec on back, baluster holder, 19th C 1,500.00
Teapot, 8¾" h, armorial, globular, angular spout, looped angular handle,
painted iron–red, turquoise, pale
green, yellow, and blue opaque
enamels, cartouche shaped coat of
arms below rampant lion crest, c1750 3,100.00
Tureen, cov, 15" w, armorial, oblong, octagonal, hare's head handles, pomegranate finial, painted iron–red, turquoise, pale green, yellow, and blue
opaque enamels, cartouche shaped

coat of arms below rampant lion crest,
c1750 . . . . **11,000.00**

Vase

10¼″ h, baluster, bright enameled reserves of court scene on one,
equestrian battle scene on other,
green tiger handles, pr **450.00**

11¾″ h, baluster, domed cov, underglaze blue, iron–red, and multicol-
lored enamels, large scrolled
panels of mother and child beside
recumbent water buffalo, couples
at leisure outside rustic retreats,
dense ground of gilt scrolls, enriched floral sprays, gilding worn,
Qianlong, set of 3 . . . .   **2,000.00**

23″ h, baluster, narrow neck, bulbous
mouth, splayed foot, flowers of four
seasons dec **600.00**

Wall Sconce, 7⅜″ h, shaped semi–circular tray, painted peony dec, oblong
pierced bracket terminating in ruyi
lappet, reinforced at angles by three
scrolls, dragon's head at base, detachable cylindrical candleholder
socket emerging from mouth of second dragon, painted iron–red, turquoise, and gilt, painted mother and
child standing in garden painted on
back, Qianlong **3,300.00**

FENTON GLASS

History: The Fenton Art Glass Company began
as a cutting shop in Martins Ferry, Ohio, in 1905.
In 1906 Frank L. Fenton started to build a plant in
Williamstown, West Virginia, and produced the first
piece of glass in 1907. Early production included
carnival, chocolate, custard, and pressed plus
mold blown opalescent glass. In the 1920s stretch
glass, Fenton dolphins, jade green, ruby, and art
glass were added.

In the 1930s boudoir lamps, "Dancing Ladies,"
and various slags were produced. The 1940s saw
crests of different colors being added to each piece
by hand. Hobnail, opalescent, and two-color overlay pieces were popular items. Handles were
added to different shapes, making the baskets
they created as popular today as then.

Through the years Fenton has added beauty to
their glass by decorating it with hand painting, acid
etching, color staining, and copper wheel cutting.
Several different paper labels have been used. In
1970 an oval raised trademark also was adopted.

References: Shirley Griffith, *A Pictorial Review
Of Fenton White Hobnail Milk Glass*, published by
author, 1984; William Heacock, *Fenton Glass: The
First Twenty-Five Years*, O-Val Advertising Corp,
1978; William Heacock, *Fenton Glass: The Second Twenty-Five Years*, O-Val Advertising Corp,
1980.

Collectors' Club: Fenton Art Glass Collectors
Of America, Inc, P. O. Box 384, Williamstown, WV
26187.

Additional Listings: Carnival Glass.

Ashtray, Hobnail, blue opal, fan, 5½″	30.00
Banana Bowl, ftd, Silver Crest	28.00
Basket	
Hobnail, opalescent	
Blue, 4″	45.00
Cranberry, 10″	175.00
Silver Crest, divided, 9″	100.00
Vasa Murrhina, 11″	
Aventurine and green	80.00
Blue, green, and white	120.00
Biscuit Jar, lilac, cov	260.00
Bonbon	
Jade, two dolphin handles, 6″	21.00
Rose Crest	12.50
Bowl	
Crest, emerald green, 5 x 2¾″, heart	37.50
Gold Crest, 6″	10.00
Jade, ftd, rolled edges, dolphin han-
dles	100.00
Jamestown, blue, 5″	55.00
Lily Pad	45.00
Ming Green, 12″, oval	60.00
Cake Plate, Silver Crest, pedestal . . .	27.00
Candlesticks, pr	
Apple Blossom Crest	28.00
Celeste, blue, 8″	66.00
Chinese Coral, trumpet, 6½″	50.00
Flame, red, 8¾″	250.00
Hobnail, cranberry opal	125.00
Peach Crest, 4½″	25.00
Pekin, blue, 8½″ h	125.00
Candy Dish, cov, Cameo	42.00
Claret, Georgian, ruby, 4½ oz	18.00
Cologne Bottle, orig stopper, Ruby Ov-
erlay	40.00
Compote	
Apple Blossom Crest	32.00
Dolphin, pink	40.00
Flame Crest, 6″	90.00
Hobnail, cov, plum opal	70.00
Lincoln Inn, light blue	42.00
Slag, flame, 7″, ftd	30.00
Console Set, Chinese, yellow, oval
bowl, 3″ candlesticks	155.00
Cookie Jar, cov	
Big Cookie, ebony	145.00
Macaroon, jade	110.00
Creamer and Sugar, Georgian, ruby . .	35.00
Cruet, Hobnail, blue	28.00
Fairy Lamp, Burmese, artist sgd	55.00
Flower Pot, attached saucer, Apple
Blossom Crest, 5″ h	70.00
Goblet, Historic American	22.00
Hat	
Hobnail, cranberry opal, 3″	37.50
Peach Crest, 3″	28.00
Rib Optic, French Opalescent, 9″ . .	175.00

Ruby Overlay, 4½"	35.00
Snow Crest, 5½ x 5", green	105.00
Jug, handle	
Moonstone, 8½"	60.00
Mulberry, 4½"	100.00
Rose Crest	45.00
Silver Crest, 8½"	30.00
Lamp, Hobnail, cranberry opal, two light, sgd	585.00
Madonna, candle lamp, frosted blue	55.00
Marmalade Set, Hobnail, blue opal, 3 pcs	100.00
Mayonnaise Set, Hobnail, blue opal, 3 pcs	75.00
Perfume, blue overlay	28.00
Pitcher	
Burmese, 4½" h, hp maple leaves	30.00
Coin Spot, blue	150.00
Optic Spot, lime green	150.00
Vasa Murrhina, Autumn Orange, small	66.00
Plate	
Pekin, blue, 6"	18.50
Rose Crest, 12"	37.00
Silver Crest, 8"	10.00
Powder Jar, cov, milk glass	25.00
Salt and Pepper Shakers, pr	
Hobnail, French opal	35.00
Polka Dot, cranberry opal, 3"	65.00
Sherbet	
Historic American	20.00
Plymouth, cobalt, 4¼"	24.00
Sugar Shaker, Dot Optic, cranberry opal, 4½"	125.00
Tidbit, Silver Crest	
Three tier	45.00
Two tier	35.00
Tumbler	
Diamond Optic, amberina, #1600	40.00
Stars and Stripes, cranberry opal, 3¾"	125.00

Vase, Gold Crest, fan shape, white, ruffled amber rim, 7" h, $25.00.

Vase	
Blue Ridge, 9½"	100.00
Dancing Lady	
Crystal	200.00
Ruby	300.00

Dolphin, pink, fan, cut dec, 6"	65.00
Honeysuckle, hobnail, 6"	30.00
Ivy, cranberry, 7"	65.00
Jamestown, blue, 12"	80.00
Mandarin, fan, 5½"	40.00
Periwinkle, fan, blue, 8½ x 5½"	85.00
Vasa Murrhina	
4", blue, green, and white	55.00
15", pink, green, and white	115.00
Wisteria, fan, orig label, 8"	65.00

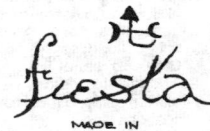

FIESTA

History: The Homer Laughlin China Company introduced Fiesta dinnerware in January, 1936, at the Pottery and Glass Show in Pittsburgh, Pennsylvania. Fredrick Rhead designed the pattern; Arthur Kraft and Bill Bensford molded it. Dr. A. V. Blenininiger and H. W. Thiemecke developed the glazes.

The original five colors were red, dark blue, light green (with a trace of blue), brilliant yellow, and ivory. A vigorous marketing campaign took place between 1939 and 1943. In 1938 turquoise was added; red was removed in 1943 because of the war effort and did not reappear until 1959. In 1951 light green, dark blue, and ivory were retired and forest green, rose, chartreuse, and gray added to the line. Other color changes took place in the late 1950s, including the addition of a medium green.

Fiesta ware was redesigned in 1969 and discontinued in 1972–73. In 1986 Fiesta was reintroduced by Homer Laughlin China Company. The new china body shrinks more than the old semivitreous and ironstone pieces, thus making the new pieces slightly smaller than the earlier pieces. The modern colors are also different in tone or hue. The cobalt blue is darker than the old blue. Other modern colors are black, white, apricot, and rose.

References: Linda D. Farmer, *The Farmer's Wife Fiesta Inventory and Price Guide*, published by author, 1984; Sharon and Bob Huxford, *The Collectors Encyclopedia of Fiesta, Sixth Edition*, Collector Books, 1987.

Reproduction Alert.

Additional Listings: See *Warman's Americana & Collectibles* for more examples.

Ashtray	
Charcoal Gray	70.00
Medium Green	125.00
Red	38.00
Rose	65.00

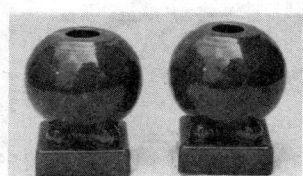

Candleholders, round, orange, pr, $50.00.

Bowl
  4¾"
    Chartreuse 20.00
    Cobalt Blue 16.00
  5½", medium green 50.00
Calendar Plate, 1954, ivory 35.00
Candlesticks, pr
  Bulb
    Cobalt Blue 32.00
    Yellow 25.00
  Tripod
    Ivory 235.00
    Turquoise 225.00
Casserole, cov
  Charcoal Gray 150.00
  Chartreuse 145.00
  Rose 170.00
Chop Plate, 15", cobalt blue 25.00
Coffee Mug
  Medium Green 55.00
  Rose 70.00
Compote, 12", ivory 70.00
Cream Soup, cobalt blue 28.00
Creamer
  Individual, red 80.00
  Regular
    Charcoal Gray 16.00
    Red 16.00
Cup and Saucer
  Charcoal Gray 32.00
  Dark Green 22.00
  Rose 30.00
Deep Dish Plate
  Dark Green 25.00
  Red 30.00
  Rose 35.00
Dessert Dish, 6"
  Charcoal Gray 45.00
  Red 35.00
Egg Cup
  Chartreuse 95.00
  Ivory 34.00
  Turquoise 32.00
  Yellow 32.00
Juice Pitcher
  Red 125.00
  Yellow 25.00
Juice Tumbler
  Cobalt Blue 25.00

  Rose 30.00
  Yellow 13.50
Nappy, handle, 8½"
  Ivory 24.00
  Medium Green 60.00
  Red 32.00
Onion Soup, cov, cobalt blue 325.00
Pitcher, disc
  Charcoal Gray 175.00
  Chartreuse 140.00
  Yellow 60.00
Plate
  9" d
    Cobalt Blue 12.00
    Medium Green 30.00
    Yellow 6.00
  9½" d, rose 14.00
  10" d
    Medium Green 75.00
    Yellow 18.00
Platter, oval
  Chartreuse 25.00
  Medium Green 80.00
  Turquoise 18.00
Salt and Pepper Shakers, pr, yellow .. 15.00
Sauce Boat
  Charcoal Gray 45.00
  Medium Green 115.00
Sugar, cov, red 32.00
Teapot, Rose 210.00
Tray, figure 8
  Cobalt Blue 45.00
  Turquoise 130.00
Vase, 8"
  Ivory 350.00
  Red 400.00

FIGURAL BOTTLES

History: Figural Bottles, made of porcelain either in glaze or bisque form, achieved popularity in the late 1800s and remained popular to the 1930s. The majority of figural bottles were made in Germany, with Austria and Japan accounting for the balance. They averaged in size from three to eight inches.

Figural bottles were shipped to the United States empty and filled upon arrival. They were then given away to customers by brothels, dance halls, hotels, liquor stores, and taverns. Some were lettered with the names and addresses of the establishment; others had paper labels. Many were used for holidays, e.g., Christmas and New Year.

Figural bottles also were made in glass and other materials. The glass bottles held perfumes, foods, or beverages.

References: Ralph & Terry Kovel, *The Kovels' Bottle Price List, 8th Edition,*, Crown Publishers, 1987; Otha D. Wearin, *Statues That Pour*, Wallace-Homestead, 1965.

Periodical: *Antique Bottle And Glass Collector,* P.O. Box 187, East Greenville, PA 18041.

Additional Listings: See *Warman's Americana & Collectibles* for more examples.

Pottery, Bennington, fish-shaped, brown glaze, 9" l, $500.00.

BISQUE

Fox, 6¼", standing, wearing brown suit	**35.00**
Gentleman, 6", Victorian, compliments paper label "Holiday Greetings," cork stopper	**145.00**
Sailor, 6½", cartoon type, high gloss front, white pants, blue blouse and hat, marked "Made in Germany" . . .	**110.00**

GLASS

Bear, 11" h, opaque white	**70.00**
Boot, aqua, emb "Saratoga Dressing," tooled lip, America, 1870—80	**30.00**
Bunker Hill Monument, 12" h, clear, cologne, American, 1870—80	**25.00**
Elk	
Bust, 11¾" h, holding clock in antlers, orig paint, screw threaded wide opening on base	**75.00**
Tooth, milk glass, orig gold paint . . .	**100.00**
Hessian Soldier, 7" h, clear, light inner haze, American, 1890	**45.00**
Moses, 10⅞" h, green, emb "Poland Water," flaring lips	**175.00**
Pig, 6¾" h, clear, slight amethyst tint, emb "Drink While It Lasts From The Hogs," America, 1870—80	**175.00**
Violin, 9" h, light electric blue, pontil scar	**45.00**

PORCELAIN

Bulldog, 8", Majolica type glaze, removable head	**65.00**
Camel, 7½ l, 4" h, mother of pearl glaze, orig stopper, German	**90.00**
Coachman, 10⅜" h, Rockingham glaze, emb "1849" mark	**700.00**
French Priest, 10¼" h, 3⅞" d, orig porcelain hat stopper, black and white, flesh tone face and hand, marked "ROBJ Paris"	**335.00**
My Bootlegger, 9", man carrying	

steamer trunk, upper body form bottle, knee lift to store six shot glasses	**145.00**
Napoleon, 10" h, 3⅜" d, orig porcelain hat stopper, gray, black buttons and cocked hat, flesh tone face and hand, marked "ROBJ Paris"	**335.00**
Sweet Potato, 7" l, int. glazed, Welsh, late 19th C	**65.00**
Toby, 7⅞" h, Rockingham	**45.00**
Tree, 9", Indian Chief head center, brown glaze	**85.00**
Wolf, 4⅞" h, seated, reading book, marked "Germany" on base, late 19th C	**40.00**

FINDLAY ONYX GLASS

History: Findlay onyx glass, produced by Dalzell, Gilmore & Leighton Company, Findlay, Ohio, was patented in 1889 for the firm by George W. Leighton. Due to high production costs resulting from a complex manufacturing process, the glass was made only for a short time.

Layers of glass were plated to a bulb of opalescent glass through repeated dippings into a glass pot. Each layer was cooled and reheated to develop opalescent qualities. A pattern mold then was used to produce raised decorations of flowers and leaves. A second mold gave the glass bulb its full shape and form.

A platinum luster paint, producing pieces identified as silver or platinum onyx, was applied to the raised decorations. The color was fixed in a muffle kiln. Other colors such as cinnamon, cranberry, cream, raspberry, and rose were achieved by using an outer glass plating which reacted strongly to reheating. For example, a purple or orchid color came from the addition of manganese and cobalt to the glass mixture.

Reference: James Measell and Don E. Smith, *Findlay Glass: The Glass Tableware Manufacturers, 1886-1902,* Antique Publications, 1986.

Bowl, 7½" d, cream	**400.00**
Celery, 6" h, cream, rim chips	**200.00**

Mustard Jar, raspberry, silverplated cov, 3⅜" h, $1,400.00.

Creamer, 4½" h, cream	**250.00**
Dresser Box, cov, 5" d, cream, round .	**650.00**
Mustard, cov, cream, hinged metal cov, marked "Sterling" spoon	**550.00**
Pitcher, water, 7½" h, cream, applied opalescent handle, polished chip on rim	**800.00**

Spooner

Cream, 4¼" h, platinum blossoms, rough edge	**245.00**
Raspberry, 4" h	**800.00**
Sugar Bowl, cov, 5½" h, cream	**300.00**

Sugar Shaker, 5½" h, metal top

Raspberry	**350.00**
Silver	**250.00**
Syrup, cov, cream, hinged metal thumb lift lid, applied opalescent handle . . .	**450.00**
Toothpick, 2½" h, cream, minute rim chips	**350.00**

Painting, Walter E. Baum, Perkiomen Mill, Bucks County, PA, $19,250.00.

FINE ARTS

Notes: There is no way a listing of a hundred paintings or less can accurately represent the breadth and depth of the examples sold over the last year. To attempt to make such a list would be ludicrous.

In any calendar year, tens, if not hundreds of thousands of paintings are sold. Prices range from a few dollars to millions. Since each painting is essentially a unique creation, it is difficult to establish comparables.

Since an essential purpose of *Warman's Antiques And Their Prices* is to assist its users in finding information about a category, this "Fine Arts" introduction has been written primarily to identify the reference books that you will need to find out more about a painting in your possession.

Artist Dictionaries: Emmanuel Benezit, *Dictionnaire Critique et Documentaire des Peintres, Sculpteurs, Dessinateurs et Graveurs*, 10 volumes, third edition, Grund, 1976; Mantle Fielding, *Dictionary of American Painters, Sculptors and Engravers*, Apollo Books, 1983; J. Johnson and A. Greutzner, *Dictionary of British Artists, 1880–1940: An Antique Collector's Club Research Project Listing 41,000 Artists*, Antique Collector's Club, 1976; Les Krantz, *American Artists*, Facts on File, 1985.

Introduction: Alan Bamberger, *Buy Art Smart*, Wallace-Homestead Book Company, 1990.

Price Guide References, Basic: William T. Currier (compiler), *Currier's Price Guide To American Artists 1645–1945 at Auction, 1989–1990 Edition*, Currier Publications, 1989; William T. Currier (compiler), *Currier's Price Guide To European Artists 1545–1945 at Auction, 1989–1990 Edition*, Currier Publications, 1989; Huxford's *Fine Art Value Guide, Volume II*, Collector Books, 1991; Susan Theran, *The Official Price Guide To Fine Art*, House of Collectibles, 1987.

Price Guide References, Advanced: Richard Hislop (editor), *The Annual Art Sales Index*, Weybridge, Surrey, England, Art Sales Index, Ltd., since 1969; Enrique Mayer, *International Auction Record: Engravings, Drawings, Watercolors, Paintings, Sculpture*, Paris, Editions Enrique Mayer, since 1967; Susan Theran (editor), *Leonard's Price Index of Art Auctions*, Auction Index, Inc., since 1980.

Museum Directories: *American Art Directory*, R. R. Bowker Co.; American Association of Museum, *The Official Museum Directory: United States and Canada*, updated periodically.

FIREARM ACCESSORIES

History: Muzzle loading weapons of the eighteenth and early nineteenth centuries varied in caliber and required the owner to carry a variety of equipment with him, including a powder horn or flask, patches, flints or percussion caps, bullets, and bullet molds. In addition, military personnel were responsible for bayonets, slings, and miscellaneous cleaning equipment and spare parts.

In the mid-19th century, cartridge weapons replaced their black powder ancestors. Collectors seek anything associated with early ammunition from the cartridges themselves to advertising material. Handling old ammunition can be extremely dangerous due to decomposition of compounds. Seek advice from an experienced collector before becoming involved in this area.

Military related firearm accessories generally are worth more than their civilian counterparts. See "Militaria" for additional listings.

Reproduction Alert: The amount of reproduction and fake powder horns is large. Be very cautious!

Bullet Mold

7½", brass, American, 18th C, sgd "IM" on bottom, cast 4 buttons, 2 thick flat buttons of 21mm and 16mm d, and 2 thick rounded surface ones of 15.5mm d, crude wooden period handles 250.00

9", brass, American, 18th C, casting 6 round buttons with central raised letter "I" for infantry, one 25mm, one 18mm, and four 14.5 mm d, the casting each including the eyelet, wooden handles missing 550.00

Canteen, Painted

Cheesebox style, dark red paint overall, one side painted in gold with a large primitive eagle with shield breast, the top of the shield red with cream lettering "No. 37", the other side painted in gold letters "Lt Rufus Cook", pewter nozzle, square nail construction, 7" d, 2⅝" deep, loops for the strap missing 1,600.00

Cheesebox style, very dark blue paint overall, both sides with large gold sunburst border around an oval, fancy script letters "H.G." within, large initials "A.T." burned into the wood on one side at a later but antique date, 3 leather carrying cord straps that are not the originals, 7½" d, 3" deep, paint one side worn 900.00

Cartridge Belt

Civilian, American, 1st quarter 19th C, 15" long pouch with 25 tin cylinders for paper cartridges, pouch mounted on the inside of the 2½" leather belt, pouch flap fits over the belt when tied, a vent prick and brass chain tied to the small simple buckle 500.00

Military, belt and plate, Kerksis #160, embossed with 5 pointed star, spread winged eagle, etc., on the orig tan morocco leather belt, shoulder strap and frog for sword, strong traces of light gilt finish to plate, forward suspension for the frog restitched, gold embossing at edges of leather very faint 200.00

Cartridge Boxes

Hall & Hubbard, .22 Calibre, box, green and black label, "100 No. ½ 2–100/PISTOL CARTRIDGES," 3⅞ x 2 x 1", cov with molted cream and black paper, empty, missing about half green side label $300.00

Phoenix Metallic Cartridge Co., box, early green and black label, "50 CARTRIDGES/32–100 CALIBRE LONG," 3⅞ x 2⅛ x 1¼", opened but full, three-quarter raised "P" headstamped cartridges 250.00

Smith, Hall & Farmer, .22 Calibre, box, green and black label, large view of Smith & Wesson 1st Model 2nd Issue, "100 No. 1 PISTOL CARTRIDGES...Successors to SMITH & WESSON in the manufacture of Cartridges," 3⅞ x 1⅞ x 13/16", cov with marbled paper, empty, light age 400.00

Union Metallic Cartridge Company

.32 Calibre, box, cream and black label "FIFTY .32 CALIBRE/No. 2/ PISTOL CARTRIDGES," engraving of Smith & Wesson 1st Model 3rd Issue, 4 x 2⅛ x 1¼", checkered covering, orange and black side labels, unopened . . . 200.00

.32 Calibre, box, orange and black label, large picture of Smith & Wesson 1st Model 3rd Issue, 50 .32 calibre short, 3¼ x 1¾ x 1", plaid covered, unopened, orange and black side label 75.00

.32–100 Short, box, orange and black label, "FIFTY No. 2 or 32–100 SHORT", large illus of Smith & Wesson 1st Model 2nd Issue, 4 x 2 x 1", checkered wrapping, opened but full, missing about 20% of the side label 275.00

Winchester, .32 Calibre, box, green and black label, "50 No. 32/Extra Short" and "FOR REMINGTON RIDER PISTOL," opened, missing some cartridges 375.00

Epaulets, military, pr, gilt, officer, large "MASSACHUSETTS" buttons with standing Indian warrior, orig purple carton with green edging, lid with orig label "MILITIA ESTABLISHMENT/ BENT & BUSH/BOSTON" 250.00

Flask, Powder

Brass

8¼", body emb on one side "RIFLE HORN" within a curved panel surrounded with a toothed design, complete with the orig faded green carrying cord, orig lacquer finish 150.00

7⅝", screw-off brass top marked "A.M. FLASK & CAP Co.," fitted with four carrying rings, orig green carrying cord, brass body emb on one side with crossed revolvers, stars, eagel with shield breast, cannon with large American flag to each side, ground with various military weapons and accessories, missing spout

screw, body with 90% orig dark
lacquer **450.00**
Copper
Colt Dragoon flask, emb on both
sides with stand of flags over
crossed rifles and crossed pistols, "COLTS PATENT" in ribbon
below, cover for the balls compartment stamped "COLTS PAT-
ENT", the top inspected "WAT"
and "K", the dispensing nozzle
stamped "35/Grs", missing on of
the three screws that holds the
top to the body, strong traces of
orig gold colored lacquer, retains
40 to 50% of orig dark lacquer
finish **850.00**
7¾", pear shape, emb on both
sides with group of hounds fighting with bear in woods, script in-
itials below, brass top **90.00**
Horn body, brass mounts, top
stamped with number "5" and with
adjustable measuring device, 6¾"
overall, very similar to Model 1839
Colt Patterson shortgun flask but
without serial number and proper
markings **225.00**
Iron, military, 10¼" overall, turned
wooden plug for spout, body made
of molded or stamped sheet iron
with rolled over seam and two steel
carrying rings on each side, orig
black paint, complete with orig carrying cord, early 19th C **75.00**
Flask, Shot, leather
7", black pigskin body stamped
"SYKES/EXTRA/lb/1," fitted with
carrying ring, 2" German silver top
with bright steel dispenser stamped
"SYKES EXTRA" **70.00**
8½", emb on both sides with a Highland scene showing a Scottish
hunter alongside a fallen stag with
2 hounds, brass top . . . .   **50.00.**
Gorget, British, engraved with the Royal
Cipher over large "GR", 1790–1820   **275.00**
Holster, Western, Colt Single Action
Holster, tooled dec along borders on
both sides, brown leather **125.00**
Horn, Powder
10½", orig oak spout plug carved in
the shape of an eagle's head, plain
wood base fitted with a large brass
stud, body with raised carving of a
large eagle, an Indian Head, grape
vines, a flying pheasant, the American shield, flowers, and the name
"Paul/Bohret," late 19th C **300.00**
11", spout carved with a faceted pat-
tern ending in scallops, scalloped
pattern repeated about ⅓ down to-

**Powder Horn, engraved with arch de-
sign, sgd "W. Carr, 1789," 12" l, $650.00.**

wards pine base, body engraved
with 2 pecking chickens and a large
marine scene showing a 3 masted
warship flying the English flag plus
2 smaller large boats and 2 row-
boats with a man in each, the carving primitive but well done, base
with a brass button for carrying
cord, c1800 with nice age patina-
tion **400.00**
14¼", engraved, nearly entire surface
cov with floral designs along with
fish, bird, and animal, long panel
outlined with a rope–like border engraved "JAMES BOUING 1756,"
neat scalloping just before the recessed portion 3½" from the spout,
wooden stopper, flat pine plug with
period brass carrying ring, base rim
originaly drilled with 2 holes for carrying cord, rim of horn and plug
chipped during sue **3,250.00**
16", King George's War style, en-
graved, inscribed "JAMES
WAUGHT/HIS HORN
Sye:11:1748" in two ribbon ban-
ners with fancy shaded letters,
much geometric and flora engraving, stag with "A BU/CK" below, a
doe with "DO" below, the name
"WILLIAM" in shaded letters, also
inscribed "Ebenezer Woods of Gro-
ton October ye 7 1748" all with a
fine line beneath, below this the
numbers 1 through 12, flat pine
plug with copper carrying ring,
raised ring carved 3" from spout,
rim of horn at base drilled with 2
net holes and bottom for a carrying
cord during use **5,500.00**
Powder Keg, wood, standard construc-
tion, 9¼" h, 6¼" d, wooden plugged
end with black painted number 56,
3¼" black and white "ORIENTAL
POWDER MILLS" label, plus 2"
"EASTERN SPORTING FFG GUN-
POWDER," the other end with 5"
"ORIENTAL POWDER MILLS BOS-

TON FF WESTERN SPORTING POWDER G" purple and gold label, orig wooden screw plug with slight chips **500.00**

Target Ball, Bogardus, approx. 2¾" d, molded, amber glass, surface with overall net pattern, bottom with raised sunburst pattern, middle with a ½" band "BOGARDUS GLASS BALL PATd APRIL '10 1877," unusual chips at neck **200.00**

Water Can, military, American, late 19th C, tinned, 13" h with the folding handle upright, 17" overall to tip of spout which has holder for cup or glass on each side, painted a dark maroon overall with tan–yellow striping, one side lettered "N.H.N.G." (New Hampshire National Guard?), the other "Co. H," some chipping of paint, about 80 to 85% remaining **425.00**

Water Keg, wooden, American, late 18th or early 19th C, oval cross section with flattened bottom, held together by two Shaker style wide tongued wooden straps, 9 x 7½ x 9", large hand forged nail on each end for carrying cord, orig wood stopper **350.00**

FIREARMS

History: The 15th century arquebus was the forerunner of the modern firearm. The Germans refined the wheelock firing mechanism during the 16th and 17th centuries. English settlers arrived in America with the smoothbore musket; German settlers had rifled arms. Both used the new flintlock firing mechanism.

A major advance was achieved when Whitney introduced interchangeable parts into the manufacturing of rifles. The warfare of the 19th century brought continued refinements in firearms. The percussion ignition system was developed by the 1840s. Minie, a French military officer, produced a viable projectile. By the end of the 19th century cartridge weapons dominated the field.

Two factors control pricing firearms–condition and rarity. The value of any particular antique firearm covers a very wide range. For instance, a Colt 1849 pocket model revolver with a 5" barrel can be priced from $100.00 to $700.00 depending on whether or not all the component parts are original, whether some are missing, how much of the original finish (bluing) remains on the barrel and frame, how much silver plating remains on the brass trigger guard and back strap, and the condition and finish of the walnut grips. Be careful to note any weapon's negative qualities. A Colt Paterson belt revolver in fair condition will command a much higher price than the Colt pocket model in very

fine condition. Know the production run of a firearm before buying it.

References: Norman Flayderman, *Flayderman's Guide To Antique American Firearms...And Their Values*, 4th ed., DBI Books, 1987; Joseph Kindig, Jr., *Thoughts On The Kentucky Rifle In Its Golden Age*, 1960, available in reprint; Russell and Steve Quetermous, *Modern Guns: Identification & Values, Revised 8th Edition*, Collector Books, 1991.

Periodical: *Gun List,* 700 East State Street, Iola, WI 54990.

Pistol, 36 caliber, Navy Revolver, E. Whitney, New Haven, 6 cyl., $600.00.

FLINTLOCK PISTOLS—SINGLE SHOT

English, East India Co., military, 9" barrel, London proofs, 15¾" overall, captive ramrod, lock stamped "Crown/S" and with standing lion mark of East India Company, walnut full stock with heavy brass mounts, forend missing 1¾ x½" chip of wood broken out by ramrod, tip of forend and brass forend cap repaired **325.00**

English, Officer's pistol, 64 caliber, smoothbore, octagonal barrel with London proofs, 14½" overall, beveled lock with sliding half cock safety, sgd "S. Wallis", lightly engraved steel trigger guard, plain walnut stock with shield shape silver wrist escutcheon, full stock with shield shape silver wrist escutcheon, barrel rebrowned **475.00**

English, pistol, 2½" screw–off barrel with London proofs, 6¾" overall, iron boxlock frame sgd "Saunder" and "Liverpool", typical slab walnut grip **350.00**

Irish, military, unproved 9" barrel, lock marked with Broad Arrow and Crown, large Crown over "GR", and "DUBLIN/CASTLE", full stock with heavy brass mounts, trigger guard engraved "F/2", bottom half of grip an old oak replacement without usual furniture, stock with old repair, c1770 . . . . . . **350.00**

Kentucky, .45 caliber, 9½" octagonal barrel, unmarked, fitted with open sights, 14¼" overall, lockplate with roller frizzen spring and goose neck hammer with some light engraved decoration, sgd "JOHN WALKER/ WARRANTED", full stock with applied trigger strips, orig heavy reddish varnish finish with brass mounts, plain forend cap, 2 faceted ramrod pipes, two engraved escutcheons for the lockplate screws, trigger guard with simple engraved pineapple finial and engraved bow, stock dec with several silver inlays **10,500.00**

Kentucky, 10" octagonal iron barrel, 48 caliber, full curly maple stock with brass forend cap, brass trigger guard and ramrod pipes, lock marked "Ashmore/Warranted" **3,000.00**

New York State Militia, 50 caliber, 9" octagonal Birmingham proved brass barrel, smoothbore, engraved "ALBANY" on top flat, 1" overall, engraved locked sgd "POND & CO.", full stock with lightly engraved brass mounts, barrel key escutcheon possibly old pewter replacement, stock broken from trigger to rear of barrel, poor repair, antique brass tipped ramrod a short replacement **700.00**

U.S. Model 1808, Navy, Simeon North, Berlin, CT, c1808–10, 10½" round barrel, 64 caliber, smoothbore, unmarked barrel, lock marked with spread eagle above U. STATES ahead of hammer and vertically at rear S. NORTH/BERLIN/CON., hickory ramrod with swelled tip, full walnut stock, pin–fastened, iron belt hook attached to left side of stock **3,000.00**

U.S. Model 1813, Army and Navy, Simeon North of Middletown, CT, c1813–15, 9¹/₁₆" round barrel, 69 caliber, smoothbore, breech of barrel marked P/US on left side and inspector marking H.H.P. above touchhole, lock marked ahead of hammer S. NORTH over an American eagle motif with letters U and S at either side over bottom line MIDLN CON., hickory ramrod with swelled tip at one end and metal ferrule at other, iron mountings **2,250.00**

U.S. Model 1819, Simeon North, Middletown, CT, c1819–23, 10" round barrel, 54 caliber, smoothbore, barrel marked at breech J/P/US, lock marked ahead of hammer S. NORTH over American eagle and shield motif with letters U and S at either side over bottom line MIDLTN CONN., date of production marked at rear of lock below safety bolt, swivel type ramrod, iron mountings, sliding safety bolt, brass blade front sight, oval shape rear sight on tang **1,000.00**

PERCUSSION PISTOLS—SINGLE SHOT

Note: Conversion of flintlock pistols to percussion was common practice. Most English and U.S. military flintlock pistols listed above can be found in percussion. Values for these percussion converted pistols are from 40 to 60% of the flintlock values as given.

Blunt & Syms side hammer, Blunt & Syms, New York, NY, c1840s–50s, 6" octagon barrel, 44 caliber, barrel marked "B & S NEW YORK," dec broad scroll engraving on frame, iron forend, ramrod mounted beneath, bag shape handle, walnut grips **300.00**

Clement, underhammer pistol, .36 caliber, 7¾" half round barrel, stamped "Wm T. CLEMENT/GREENFIELD/ MASS./CAST STEEL", Serial No. 12, walnut grip with small silver escutcheon on each side, grip with old glued break (no listing in Flayderman for this maker) **400.00**

Elgin Cutlass Pistol, Morrill, Mosman & Blair, Amherst, MA, 4" round barrel riffled with six grooves, 34 caliber, a bowie blade 11" long and 1½" wide fastened to the barrel and etched with a vase containing fruit surmounted by "ELGIN'S PATENT" in script in a rect and an eagle holding a pennant in his beak (right), vase containing fruit surmounted by "Morill/Mosman/& Blair/ Amherst Mass" and eagle holding pennant in beak (left), leather scabbard **4,500.00**

Elgin Cutlass Pistol, fake, 10" blade with usual etched floral pattern including "Elgin's Patent" and "Merrill, Mosman/&Blair/Amherst, Mass.", 14½" overall, 4" barrel marked "CAST STEEL", frame and hammer with crude floral engraving, well made fake **600.00**

English, pair, 60 caliber, 10" octagonal barrel, smoothbore, 2 gold bands at breach, sunken gold maker's stamp "T. KETLAND/& Co/LONDON", finely engraved lock with same maker's mark, period conversion to percussion, engraved silver forend caps, silver barrel key plates, opposite locks inlaid a small silver rectangle, engraved steel trigger guards, butt caps engraved "J. Read/US Marines" (commissioned a 2nd Lt. in U.S. Marines in 1848, later resigned and became Captain in C.S. Marine Corps), straight walnut stocks, checkered, ramrods replaced **4,500.00**

European, target pistols, pair, 50 caliber,

deeply rifled, 9½" octagonal watered steel barrels, Crown "V" proofed and inlaid in silver "l.h.DAMM in ELBER-FELD", blade front sights, adjustable rear sights on profusely engraved tang, profusely engraved back action locks, engraved steel butt caps and trigger guards, single set trigger, grained burl walnut stocks, checkered wrists, engraved steel sideplate ... **2,000.00**

U.S. Model 1842, Henry Aston, Middletown, CT (also by Ira N. Johnson of Middletown, CT, and Palmeto Armory of Columbia, SC), c1845–52, 8½" round barrel, 54 caliber, smoothbore, proof stamps on breech of barrel beneath which are inspector's initials, date stamping on barrel tang, lockplate marked US/H. ASTON forward of hammer, marked vertically at rear MIDDTN/CONN., swivel type steel ramrod, all brass mountings, brass blade front sight **650.00**

Waters, Single Shot, A. H. Waters & C., Millbury, MA, mid–1840s to 1849, round barrel, 54 caliber, smoothbore, flat flush fitted lockplate, marked "A. H. WATERS & Co./MILLBURY MASS." in center of lock, side lug nipple, iron furniture, brass blade front sight, oval shape rear sight on tang **500.00**

PERCUSSION PISTOLS—MULTI–SHOT

Colt

Dragoon, Second Model, 7½" part round, part octagonal barrel, 44 caliber, 6 shot, barrel stamped "AD-DRESS SAML COLT NEW–YORK. COLT'S/PATENT" with "U.S." centered beneath, one piece walnut grip, squareback trigger guard and rect cylinder stop slots, Texas Ranger and Indian fight scene roll engraved on cylinders **4,500.00**

Navy, Model 1861, 7½" round barrel, 36 caliber, 6 shot, creeping style loading lever, barrel stamped "AD-DRESS COL. SAML COLT NEW–YORK, U.S. AMERICA–.36 CAL," cylinder roll scene depicts battle between Texas Navy and that of Mexico, one piece walnut grip . . . **1,200.00**

Paterson Belt Model, No. 2, 5½" octagonal barrel, 31 caliber, 5 shot, barrel stamped "Patent Arms M'g Co Paterson N:J Colt's Pt.," engraved cylinder, disappearing trigger, no trigger guard, flared walnut grips **4,500.00**

Pocket, Model 1849, barrel lengths of 3", 4", 5" and 6", 31 caliber, 5 or 6 shot, octagon barrel with attached loading lever, barrel stamped "AD-DRESS COL SAML COLT NEW-YORK U.S. AMERICA," cylinder engraved with stagecoach holdup scene, round trigger guard, walnut grips **550.00**

Remington

Belt, New Model, 6½" octagon barrel, 36 caliber, 6 shot, barrel stamped "PATENTED SEPT. 14, 1856/E. REMINGTON 7 SONS, ILION, NEW YORK U.S.A./NEW MODEL," round cylinder, threads visible at breech end, safety notches on cylinder shoulders between nipples **600.00**

Navy, 1861, 7⅜" octagon barrel, 36 caliber, 6 shot, barrel stamped "PATENTED DEC 17, 1861/MAN-UFACTURED BY REMINGTON'S ILION, N.Y.," round cylinder, walnut grips **650.00**

Remington–Beals 3rd Model Pocket Revolver, cased, 4" octagon barrel, 31 caliber, 5 shot, barrel stamped "BEAL'S PATENT 1856 7 57 758/MANUFACTURED BY REMING-TON'S ILION, N.Y.," orig cardboard box with brass bullet mold, quantity of bullets, eagle and shield flask, mushroom shape cleaning rod with screw–in type extension, extra pawl spring, can of Eley percussion caps **2,250.00**

Other

Deringer and Deringer Type

Deringer, Henry, Philadelphia, PA, c1830–60, medium pocket model, 3½" barrel, 41 caliber, barrel stamped "DERINGER/ PHILADELA," identical marking appears on lockplate, checkered walnut stock, German silver trigger guard and butt cap (Flayderman 7D–002) **800.00**

Robertson, Philadelphia, PA, pocket, 4½" barrel, approx. 41 caliber, barrel stamped "ROB-ERTSON, PHILA.," forends have double wedges and escutcheons and double ramrod pipes (Flayderman 7D–022) **550.00**

Pepperboxes

Bacon, Thomas K., Norwich, CT, c1852–58, 4" ribbed barrel, 31 caliber, 6 shot, barrel stamped "BACON & CO., NORWICH, CT" and "CAST STEEL," single action, underhammer, engraved nipple shield, blued finish, walnut grips (Flayderman 7B–001) . . . **350.00**

Pecare & Smith, Ten–Shot, Jacob Pecare and Joseph Smith, NY, late 1840s to early 1850s, 4″ barrel, 28 caliber, 10 shot barrel cluster, dec scroll engraving on frame and barrel shield, semi—concealed hammer visible from top, trigger folds down, brass frame, walnut grips (Flayderman 7B-013) **1,750.00**

Stocking & Co., Worcester, MA, late 1840s to early 1850s, 31 caliber, 6″ barrel cluster, barrel stamped "STOCKING & CO., WORCESTER" and "CAST STEEL WARRANTED," dec scroll engraving on iron frame and nipple shield, trigger spur guard (Flayderman 7B-017) **350.00**

REVOLVERS (CARTRIDGE)

Colt
Bisby, 38 Colt caliber, Serial Number 303447 (1907 production), 7½″ barrel, Rampant Colt checkered grips, 95% orig glassy blue finish on barrel (Flayderman 5B-149) .. **3,200.00**

Border Patrol Revolver, 357 Magnum, Serial Number J85904, 4″ barrel, target sights, over—size checkered walnut "COLT" medallion grips, blued **250.00**

Model 1911, Auto, Serial Number 554379, "UNITED STATES PROPERTY" marking above no., orig commercial style blue finish rather than usual WWI pasty blue finish, checkered walnut grips, with "US" issue holster made by "GRATON & KNIGHT CO./1943" **650.00**

Sheriff's Model, 45 caliber, Serial Number SA40819, orig shipping carton, orig Colt Factory display case for the pistol and extra cylinder, orig tabs and papers **700.00**

Woodsman, caliber 22LR, Serial Number 153549, 4½″ barrel, 99.5% orig pre—War blue finish, orig carton missing one—half of end label ... **550.00**

Harrington & Richardson, blue Jacket No. 2, caliber 32RF, Serial Number 589, full factory engraved, deeper cuts highlighted with black paint or enamel, checkered hard rubber grips with head of dog at top, 99% plus orig nickel finish **175.00**

High Standard, Supermatic Trophy Auto, caliber 22 LR, Serial Number 236994, 7¼″ barrel, spare 5½″ barrel, orig foam plastic carton, blued, 99.9% brand new **400.00**

Hopkins & Allen XL Navy, Serial Number 952, caliber 38RF, 6½″ round barrel, varnished grips, orig brown leather holster, leather flap replace during period with a piece of black oil cloth, cylinder with 80% nickel, blued trigger and case colored hammer (Flayderman 8A-065) **650.00**

Luger, Model S/42, 9mm caliber, chamber date 1937, Serial Number 6660, all matching except the magazine with correct aluminum base, Nazi Eagel proofs **750.00**

Mauser, Banner Luger, 9 mm caliber, 1942 chamber date, Serial Number 3672, all matching, orig issue black leather holster with spare matching magazine, slight wear on holster ... **1,300.00**

Remington, Police Revolver, factor conversion to 38RF, Serial Number 4754, 3½″ barrel, nickel plated brass trigger guard, varnished walnut grips (Flayderman 5E-029) **1,300.00**

Savage, Model 1917 Auto, caliber 32, Serial Number 255730, visible spur type hammer, ten—shot magazine, 3¾″ barrel, dull blue—black finish, later production with model designation on left side of frame, 99% plus dull blue—black finish (Flayderman 8B-019) **200.00**

Smith & Wesson
Model 1½ Old, Serial Number 10322, caliber 32RF, 5—shot non-fluted cylinder, rosewood grips, 80% orig blue, left grip missing a small chip at rim (Flayderman 5G-027) **350.00**

Model 90–1, 32 S & W Long caliber, Serial Number H40754, 3″ barrel, holster **125.00**

32 Safety 1st Model DA, Serial Number 77788, caliber 32 S &W, 3″ barrel, 5—shot fluted cylinder, bottom of left grip stamped with number 6304, black hard rubber "S & W" grips, over 95% orig blue, only hints of bright wear at edge (Flayderman 5G–043) **100.00**

38 Double Action Perfected, Serial Number 9296, caliber 38 S&W, 6″ barrel, 5—shot fluted cylinder, "S&W" checkered hard rubber grips, about mint with bright case colored trigger and hammer, blued release catch at top of frame, balance of steel parts with 99.9% orig nickel plate (Flayderman 5G–080) **300.00**

Stevens Diamond Model, 22 caliber, Serial Number 47867, 6″ barrel, orig cardboard carton, cov with dark brown small diamond pattern lightly embossed in surface, orig black and gold end label (Flayderman 5H–016) **700.00**

FLINTLOCK LONG ARMS

Concord Light Infantry Musket, 75 caliber, 42″ round barrel, stamped with various marks including "7,M,I or JH" plus several others that again were struck at angle, full stocked with brass mounts, a sheet silver Indian, Massassoit, inlaid on right side of butt, left side with silver eagle, both inlays surrounded by silver wire inlay, additional silver wire inlay at barrel tang, tailpiple and sideplate, silver shield to rear of lock screws, trigger guard marked "Concord Lt. Infantry", very good reconversion to flint **3,400.00**

Kentucky, 48 caliber, 40½″ three–inch part round and part octagonal barrel, sgd "JOHN RUP", 55½″ overall, converted to percussion during period of use, engraved and scalloped patchbox with pierced and flowing C–scroll carving on both sides of cheekpiece, inlaid with a stylized engraved silver star, further extensive carving around tang and tailpiple, forward of trigger guard tangs with incised Indian head, engraved trigger guard bow, faceted ramrod pipes, 8 engraved silver pointed oval barrel key plates on each side of forend, engraved silver wrist escutcheon with script initials "H.J.", 1st quarter of 19th C **45,000.00**

Kentucky, 52 caliber, 45″ part round barrel, unmarked, smoothbore, thick walls at muzzle probably rifled, full stock with 3 brass ramrod pipes, brass trigger guard, fine raised sideplate with beveled and scalloped edges, wide brass butplate with faceting at top, brass patchbox, maple stock with simple raised carved area at wrist, simple raised carved scroll at barrel tang, late 18th C, flintlock period but not orig to piece, other minor restorations **1,800.00**

New England Flower, 53″ barrel, unmarked, flat beveled lockplate signed in block letters "WHITE/& ELY", brass mounts including a raised oval wrist escutcheon, early Brown Bess style long tailed sideplate, full cherry stock, reconverted to flint using correct style original hammer, 41″ of forend restored, right side of butt with long grain crack **1,250.00**

New England Flower, 54½″ round barrel, 75 caliber, shallow raised rib running to the front sight and light engraved dec at breech and tang, lightly engraved flat beveled lockplate sgd "T. Earl", full cherry stock with brass

mounts, cloud shape sideplate, ornate buttplate, 4 ramrod pipes, orig flint, broken at wrist, poor repair . . . **4,000.00**

U.S. Model 1803, Harpers Ferry Armory, later production, c1814–20, 54 caliber, single shot, muzzleloader, 33″ part octagon and part round 36″ barrel, blade front sight, open rear sight, lock with integral forged iron flashpan with fence at rear, brass mountings, walnut half stock of 30½″ with small cheekrest, brass patchbox on right side of butt (Flayderman 9A–114) . . **3,500.00**

U.S. Model 1808, Thomas French, Canton, MA, Contract Musket, Harpers Ferry pattern, tail of lock stamped "CANTON/1810", below the pan with the eagle and "US" over "FRENCH" (well struck with no trace of "T."), barrel stamped "US/V" with sunken eagle head CT proof (Flayderman 9A–131) **1,500.00**

U.S. Model 1819, Hall, breech loading, second production type, Harpers Ferry Armory, John Hall's patents, 52 caliber, single shot, 32⅝″ round barrel, three barrel bands, breechblock deeply stamped "J. H. HALL/ H.FERRY/1836" (Flayderman (A–249) **1,250.00**

PERCUSSION LONG ARMS

Note: Conversion of flintlock long arms to percussion was common practice. Most English, French, and U.S. military flintlock model long arms listed in the previous section can be found in percussion. Values for these percussion converted long arms are from 40 to 60% of the flintlock values previously noted.

Kentucky, 40 caliber, 38¼″ rifled octagonal barrel, sgd "G. KOPP", 53″ overall, full stock with applied tiger stripes and brass mounts, forend cap, 3 ramrod pipes, trigger guard with double set triggers, long single screw sideplate with two small retaining screws, buttplate and toeplate, oval patchbox, cheekpiece with 2½″ thin oval German silver inlay engraved with American Eagel, engraved orig percussion lock sgd "THE DAISY" within a banner, ramrod replaced with old cleaning rod **750.00**

Kentucky Rifle, swivel breech, 51″ overall, deeply rifled 38 caliber octagonal barrels, sgd "JOHN . SHULER/LIVERPOOL. PA" on both top flats, one side of the barrel group a flat piece of steel, the other with four brass ramrod pipes, tiger stripped butt stock with engraved brass sideplate, light engraved brass trigger guard with double set triggers, engraved brass patchbox and toe plate, lightly engraved German silver escutcheon at write, 2″ inlay on left side, back action lock sgd "N. ASHMORE," old ramrod probably not orig **1,250.00**

Mississippi Rifle, Robbins, Kendall & Larence, rebored 58 caliber, dated 1850 on lock and barrel tang, fitted for socket bayonet, Model 1861 rear sight, brass tipped ramrod (Flayderman 9A–287) **950.00**

Tennessee Mountain Rifle, 50 caliber, 45½″ heavy octagonal barrel, pinprick marking on top of flat "H 35", right flats cov with old sheet of copper at the nipple drum, old too small percussion lock appears to have been on gun for long time, full stock with pewter forend cap and two simple brass pipes, hand forged trigger guard with double set triggers, iron buttplate with brass toeplate, basic oval patchbox with inlaid German silver arrow in front, check rest with large crudely engraved German silver blossom, replaced ramrod, damage to forend of stock **475.00**

U.S. Model 1842, Springfield Armory, c1844–1855, 69 caliber, single shot, muzzleloader, 42″ round barrel, three barrel bands, lockplate stamped with American eagle motif above "US" forward of hammer, stamped vertically behind hammer "Springfield/1852," inspector initial cartouche stamped on left side of stock, steel ramrod with trumpet head, bayonet lug on bottom of barrel at muzzle, walnut stock with comb (Flayderman 9A–291) **900.00**

Model 1863, Rifle Musket, Type II (a.k.a. Model 1864), Springfield Armory, c1864–65, 58 caliber, single shot, muzzleloader, 40″ round barrel, three barrel bands, lock stamped with eagle motif to right of hammer, "U.S./SPRINGFIELD" beneath nipple bolster, "1864" at angle at rear section of lock, single leaf rear sight, walnut stock (Flayderman 9A–341) **1,000.00**

RIFLES

Garand, Model M–1, made at Springfield Armory, near mint welded receiver, Elmer balance **300.00**

Griffin & Howe Rifle, .416 Rigby caliber, 26″ barrel engraved "No. 1954 GRIFFIN & HOWE INC. NEW YORK", ramp front sight, 3 leaf rear sight (50,

Pennsylvania Long Rifle, Peter Moll, Hellertown, Warranted No. 58, artificially striped stock, c1830, 55½″ l, $3,000.00.

100, and 150 yards), "POLDI ANTI–CORRO" barrel with caliber marking "416 RIGBY", magnum square bridge Mauser action, walnut stock with checkered wrist and forend, large horn forend tip, orig swing swivels, cheekrest, orig rubber recoil pad . . . **5,750.00**

Lee Enfield Carbine, .303 caliber, left side of receiver stamped "No 5MKIROF(F)5/45/N202", good to very good condition **125.00**

Marlin, Model 1893 Carbine, 32 Special caliber, 20″ barrel, 2 barrel bands, carbine style buttplate, no provision for saddle ring (Flayderman 5D–034) **500.00**

Mauser Commercial Sporter, 9.3 x 62 caliber, front of receiver checkered and with "MAUSER" banner, button release floor plate, grained orig Mauser stock missing buttplate **700.00**

Remington

Hepburn, 40–70 caliber, 28″ half round barrel with adjustable wind gauge peep front sight (period, but not Remington), no provision for rear sight, tang with Long Range Remington sight missing the elevation screw, nickel plated Swiss buttplate (Flayderman 5E–105) . . **900.00**

U.S. Model 1917, 30–06 caliber, barrel stamped "R" over Ordnance bomb and "9–18", 99% plus original blue **750.00**

Ruger, No. 1, .308 Winchester caliber, mounted with a scope block, about new **600.00**

Winchester

Model 1892, 25–20 caliber, 23″ round barrel, full magazine, checkered steel shotgun style buttplate, fitted with later sling swivels, barrel and tube with 98% orig blue (Flayderman 5K–075) **650.00**

Model 1894, Sample, Serial No. 128249, 30 caliber, full factory scroll engraved, left side with a large panel showing a ram, the right with a stag, light scroll work at rear of round barrel, bit more on forend cap, deluxe varnished wood, checkered hard rubber shotgun butt plate, first shipped from warehouse on January 4, 1904, exhibited for 24 years 18,000.00

SHOTGUNS

Beretta S–2, 12 gauge, 30″ barrels, vent rib, engraved action, single trigger, 14¼″ pull, rubber pad, Browning trunk case, slight handling marks only . . . 2,400.00

Beretta Silver Snipe, 20 gauge, top lever break open, box lock, hammerless, 30″ barrel, full choke, blued, nickel receiver, checkered walnut pistol grip stock and forearm 350.00

Fox Super Fox, 12 gauge, top lever break open, box lock, hammerless, double trigger, automatic ejector, 32″ double barrel, full choke, blued, checkered walnut pistol grip stock and forearm 450.00

High Standard Flite–King Trophy, 410 gauge, hammerless, slide action, repeating, 5–shot tubular, 27″ barrel, adjustable choke, ventilated rib, blued, checkered wood, plain walnut semi–pistol grip stock and grooved slide handle 150.00

Ithaca Model 37T (Trap), 16 gauge, hammerless, extended slide handle, repeating, 4–shot tubular, 26″ barrel, blued ventilated rib, trap stock, recoil pad 250.00

Mauser Model 620, 12 gauge, top lever break open, box lock, hammerless, automatic ejectors, single trigger, 28″, over and under double barrel, modified and full choke, ribbed, blued, paint walnut pistol grip stock and forearm, recoil pad 750.00

Noble Model 70, 410 gauge, hammerless, slide action, 5–shot tubular, 26″ barrel, full choke, blued, checkered walnut pistol grip stock and slide handle 125.00

Parker Super Grade, 10 gauge, 32″ double barrels with standard address on matted rib, action with very deeply sculpted bolsters and totally covered in extremely fine scroll engraving with two small panel scenes on each side and a small "PARKER BROS." with a ribbon, bottom of action also with two scenes, trigger guard with scene, barrel and water table stamped with "6″, Parker skeleton type buttplate, light pitting from post storage, reblued . . 4,000.00

Remington Model 17, 20 gauge, hammerless, slide action, bottom ejection, repeating, 3–shot tubular, 30″ steel barrel, full bore, matted sighting groove on receive, blued, plain walnut pistol grip stock and forearm 225.00

J. P. Sauer & Sohn, 26″ double barrel, ejector, bored ¾ choke and improved cylinder, rib marked "Abercrombie & Fitch Co., New York, N.Y. U.S. Agents", double trigger, 14½″ pull, pre–War leather trunk case with cleaning tools 1,200.00

Sears Ted Williams 300, 12 gauge, semi–automatic, gas operated, hammerless, 3–shot tubular, 28″ barrel, variable choke, ventilated rib, blued, checkered walnut pistol grip stock and forearm, recoil pad 200.00

FIREHOUSE COLLECTIBLES

History: The volunteer fire company has played a vital role in the protection and social growth of many towns and rural areas. Paid professional firemen usually are found only in large metropolitan areas. Each fire company prided itself on equipment and uniforms. Conventions and parades gave the fire companies a chance to show off their equipment. These events produced a wealth of firehouse related memorabilia.

References: Chuck Deluca, *Firehouse Memorabilia: A Collectors Reference*, Maritime Antique Auctions, 1989; Mary Jane and James Piatti, *Firehouse Collectibles*, The Engine House, 1979.

Periodical: *The Fire Mark Circle of the Americas*, 2859 Marlin Dr., Chamblee, GA 30341.

Museums: Insurance Company of North America (INA) Museum, Philadelphia, PA; Oklahoma State Fireman's Association Museum, Oklahoma City, OK; San Francisco Fire Dept. Memorial Museum, San Francisco, CA.

Additional Listings: See *Warman's Americana & Collectibles* for more examples.

Advisor: H. Thomas Laun.

Alarm Box
  Gamewell Excelsior, cast iron, code wheel and number plate, telegraph door, orig weathered paint 300.00
  Hercucite, quick acting door with glass bulls eye, code wheel and number plate, orig paint 110.00
  L W Bills, Lexington, MA, cast iron, brass tee handle door 350.00
  Utica Fire Alarm and Telegraph, Utica, NY, cast iron
    Quick Acting Door 370.00
    Telegraph Door 500.00
Alarm Gong
  Gamewell
    Excelsior, oak case, orig finish, 6″ 650.00

Indicator, combination, oak case,
15″ 4,500.00
Star Electric, Binghamton, NY, fancy
case with star on top, 12″ 1,800.00
Star Gong, Boston, orig, 10″ 1,000.00
US Fire And Police Telegraph, maple
"Moses Crane" case, fig leaf finial,
8″ 1,200.00
Bell, apparatus style
American La France, 700 series type
base, eagle finial, orig, 12″ 550.00
Nickel and brass, 10″ 350.00
Seagrave, bracket and clapper, orig,
12″ 475.00
Extinguisher
Ahrens Fox, foam type, 2½ gal 210.00
Auto-Shur Stop, glass, SP pendant
with bracket, orig box and packag-
ing 15.00
Building Type, hanging, copper, soda
and acid type, 2½ gal 10.00
Mack, nickel and brass, foam type,
2½ gal 165.00
Fire Bucket, leather, New England, 19th
C
12¾″ h, painted red, black medallion
with eagle on American shield, inscription "Hose 2" in green, yellow,
gold, red, and white 400.00
12⅞″ h, painted green and red, inscribed "F Hooper" in black, paint
loss, imperfections 250.00
Frame, 22¾ x 18⅜″, gilt gesso, decorated with fire fighting devices, pum-
pers, ladders, hoses, American, late
19th C 475.00
Helmet
London Fire Brigade, composition
and plastic, current issue 75.00
Osborne Hose, CFD, Clinton, NY, ea-
gle, orig, Cairns 295.00
Presentation, presented to Chief of
Watertown FD in 1907 by Members
of Engine 31 and Rescue 1, FDNY,
leather, hp front piece, eagle,
Cairns 950.00
Senator, Dewitt Captain Truck 3, De-
witt, NY, red and white, Cairns . . . 75.00
Lantern
Dewey, Mill, tin, lift cage, orig paint 50.00
Dietz
King, brass, nickel plated, bull's
eye globe 250.00
Mill, tin, lift off cage, attached water
shield 80.00
Queen, brass, clear globe 650.00
Eclipse, green over clear globe,
marked "American La France Fire
Engine Company" 1,000.00
Ham's, brass and nickel, wire slide,
water shield, distributed by Boston
Woven Hose Company 265.00

Nozzle, Playpipe
Akron, chrome and brass, 2½″ round
hard rubber handle, three tips . . . 200.00
Callaghan, brass, leather handles,
one tip, 1883 patent, 2½″ 235.00
La France, nickel and brass, leather
handle, three tips, marked 285.00
Underwriters, standard length, one tip 45.00
Print, Currier & Ives, "The Great Fire At
Boston, November 9th & 10th 1872,"
typographical inscription below image,
lithograph, hand coloring, 8 x 12¾″
image size, period carved frame . . . 125.00
Ribbon, 1910 Convention, Syracuse,
NY, brass Franklin Fire Chiefs car
broadside, fire chief photo and pin on
bottom 100.00
Siren
Electric
Sireno, brass, trumpet shape, 6 volt 200.00
Sterling Senior Model 30, red lens,
6 or 12 volt 225.00
Hand Crank, Sterling, bracket 450.00

**Speaking Trumpet, presentation,
brass, engraved, $625.00.**

Trumpet
4th Ass't Engineer, CFD, nickel over
brass 675.00
Miller, brass, nickel plated, marked 400.00
Osborne Hose, Clinton, NY, 1897,
nickel and brass, engraved, flowers
and steamer broadside, crossed
hook's and ladders, helmet type
rings for cord attachment 1,250.00

FIREPLACE EQUIPMENT

History: The fireplace was a gathering point in
the colonial home for heat, meals, and social in-
teraction. It maintained its dominant position until
the introduction of central heating in the mid-19th
century.

Because of the continued popularity of the fireplace, accessories still are manufactured, usually in an early American motif.

Reproduction Alert: Modern blacksmiths are reproducing many old iron implements.

Additional Listings: Brass and Iron.

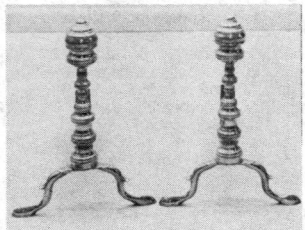

Andirons, pr, brass, acorn finial, 17″ h, $400.00.

Andirons, pr
    12½″ h, cast iron, heart finials **400.00**
    15″, h, brass, Queen Anne, late 18th
      C, banded ball standard, spurred
      arched supports, snake feet **450.00**
    16″ h, brass, Federal, early 19th C,
      urn form standard resting on sq
      plinth, cabriole legs, club feet . . .   **400.00**
    17″ h, brass, Federal, early 19th C,
      banded lemon form standard,
      spurred arched supports, ball feet   **375.00**
    17½″ h, wrought iron, open cage style
      scrolled design, knob feet and fini-
      als **200.00**
    20″ h, cast iron, figural, George Wash-
      ington **250.00**
    22″ h, brass, double lemon tops,
      pierced gallery, ball feet, matching
      double lemon top log stops, pr . . .   **3,500.00**
    35″ h, brass, Aesthetic Movement,
      American **1,500.00**
Bellows
    Papier Mache, spade form, enameled
      spray of flowers, black ground, re-
      verse with gilt C scrolls, diapering
      dec on handles, studded leather
      sides, Victorian, mid 19th C **200.00**
    Wood and brass, fruit and foliate dec,
      painted, 16½″ l **110.00**
Broiler, 26½″ h, wrought iron, tripod
    base, penny feet, adjustable lyre
    shape rack with tines, cast finial . . .   **400.00**
Coal Box, copper, emb laurel wreath
    dec, 12″ w, 12″ d, 13″ h **150.00**
Coal Grate, George III, late 18th C, bell
    metal, rect basket, cast iron back
    plate, dancing maidens ornament,
    pierced front skirt, surmounted by

urns, straight tapered legs, spade
    feet, 32″ w, 17″ d, 38½″ h **300.00**
Dutch Oven, 19″ l, tin, iron spit **200.00**
Fender, brass
    42½″ l **100.00**
    44″ l, late Empire, pierced body, paw
      feet **500.00**
    51½″, D-form, pierced **225.00**
Fire Back
    23″ h, 27″ w, cast iron, relief design,
      classical bust in laurel wreath,
      tools, and "H W Stiegel, Elizabeth
      Furnace, 1769" **6,200.00**
Fire Board, 22¾ x 36¼″, painted, geo-
    metric blue, yellow, green, sienna,
    black, and white pattern, American,
    19th C **2,000.00**
Kindling Tub, Georgian style, coppered
    oak, brass bound, oval, 24″ w, 17″ d,
    16″ h **1,500.00**
Log Basket, 17 x 16 x 12″, brass, turned
    rod spindles, stationary handle **150.00**
Mantel Clock
    Empire style, 10½″ h, Ansonia, black
      enameled metal, gilt incising **100.00**
    Renaissance Revival, 17″ h, bronze,
      urn top, dial with porcelain chap-
      ters, gong **225.00**
Mantel Garniture, 3 pcs, 11″ h Crystal
    Regulator clock, pr 9⅝″ h matching
    candlesticks, cased brass, enamel in-
    lay **1,500.00**
Mantel Mirror, 51 x 53″, Victorian,
    carved, gesso and gold leaf **750.00**
Pole Screen
    Late George III, walnut and satin-
      wood, shield form, fitted embroi-
      dered and painted satin panel, rect
      standard, entwined C scroll base,
      ball feet, pr **8,500.00**
    Regency
      30″ h, 19″ w, brass and mesh, spin-
      dle gallery, arched feet **75.00**
      52″ h, early 19th C, rosewood, cir-
      cular needlework panel, brass
      and rosewood standard, incur-
      vate triangular base, melon
      reeded parcel gilt feet **450.00**
Tongs, 28″ l, iron **18.00**
Trivet, iron and brass, lyre form **70.00**

FISCHER J.
BUDAPEST.

FISCHER CHINA

History: In 1893 Moritz Fischer founded his factory in Herend, Hungary, a center of porcelain production from the 1790s.

Confusion exists about Fischer china because of its resemblance to the wares of Meissen, Sevres, and Oriental export. It often was bought and sold as the product of these firms. Forged marks of other potteries are found on Herend pieces. The mark "MF," often joined, is the mark of Moritz Fischer's pottery.

Fischer's Herend is hard paste ware with luminosity and exquisite decoration. Pieces are designated by pattern names, the best known being Chantilly Fruit, Rothschild Bird, Chinese Bouquet, Victoria Butterfly, and Parsley.

Fischer also made figural birds and animal groups, Magyar figures (individually and in groups), and Herend eagles poised for flight.

Reference: Susan and Al Bagdade, *Warman's English & Continental Pottery & Porcelain, 1st Edition,* Warman Publishing Co., Inc., 1987.

Vase, two-winged serpent handles, reticulated body, base, and neck, blue, pink, gold bands and accents, blue stamped "Fisher, J Budapest," 13″ h, $325.00.

Basket, 9½″, reticulated, multicolored florals, gold trim, twig feet	650.00
Cache Pot, 5″ h, handles, Rotchschild Bird pattern	175.00
Charger, 13″ d, multicolored florals, gold trim	325.00
Ewer, 7½″ h, multicolored enameled florals, gold trim	215.00
Figure, rabbit, marked "Herend"	70.00
Nappy, 4½″, triangular, Victoria Butterfly pattern, gold trim	125.00
Pitcher, 11″ h, bulbous, reticulated lip, dolphin handle	575.00
Plate, 7½″ d, Chantilly Fruit pattern . .	90.00
Sauce Boat, underplate, matching china ladle, Victoria Butterfly pattern, gold trim	265.00
Tureen, cov, lemon wedge finial, marked "Herend, Hungary"	200.00
Urn, 12″ h, reticulated, blue floral dec, shield mark	325.00

Vase	
8″ h, reticulated, gold handles, blue flowers, green leaves, shield mark	250.00
10½″ h, reticulated, pink, blue, green, and white flowers	200.00
12″ h, bulbous, extended neck, cobalt blue reticulated handle, ochre, multicolored flowers, gold accents, deep rose sides	375.00

FITZHUGH

History: Fitzhugh, one of the most recognized Chinese Export porcelain patterns, was named for the Fitzhugh family for whom the first dinner service was made. The peak period of production was from 1780 to 1850.

Fitzhugh features an oval center medallion or monogram surrounded by four groups of flowers or emblems. The border is similar to that on Nanking china. Occasional border variations are found. Butterfly and honeycomb are among the rarest.

Blue is the common color. Color is a key factor in pricing with rarity in ascending order of orange, green, sepia, mulberry, yellow, black, and gold. Combinations of colors are scarce.

Reference: Sandra Andacht, *Oriental Antiques & Art: An Identification And Value Guide,* Wallace-Homestead, 1987.

Reproduction Alert: Spode Porcelain Company, England, and Vista Alegre, Portugal, currently are producing copies of the Fitzhugh pattern. Oriental copies also are available.

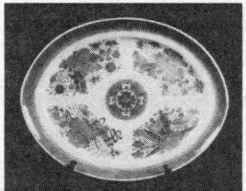

Platter, blue and white, 15¾″ l, $475.00.

Cider Jug, 11½″ h, cov, underglaze blue, 19th C	2,400.00
Hot Water Dish, 10⅝″ d, underglaze blue, center pine cone and beast medallion, four clusters of flowers and precious objects in trellis diaper border, spearhead and dumbbell border, blue spouts, c1840	400.00
Plate	
7⅞″ d, dessert, orange, center floral sprig medallion, border of butterflies, diaper and scale work panels,	

key fret and floral sprigs on gilt edged rim, c1820, pr **350.00**

9¾" d, dinner, orange, floral sprig in medallion of beasts and trellis diaper work, edged in spearheads and dumbbells, 4 clusters of flowers and precious objects, set of 6, minor chips and restoration, c1810 **2,475.00**

Platter and Strainer, 15⅞" l, oval, orange, deep platter, pierced strainer, gilt edged central aperture, three rows of smaller holes, floral sprig in medallion of beasts and trellis diaper work, edged in spearheads and dumbbells, four clusters of flowers and precious objects, c1810 . . . . . . **2,750.00**

Salt, 4" l, oval, underglaze blue, center pine cone and beast medallion, spearhead and dumbbell border, ruffled rim, Mared pattern border, feathered edge, fluted sides, four clusters of flowers and precious objects, c1820, pr **1,430.00**

Serving Dish, 17¼" l, underglaze blue, oval, pierced insert, 19th C **1,400.00**

Tureen, cov, 13" l, underglaze blue, matching underplate, 19th C **3,200.00**

Vase, 13¼" h, orange, Chinese, late 18th C, early 19th C **300.00**

FLASKS

History: A flask is a container for liquids, usually having a narrow neck. Early American glass companies frequently formed them in molds which left a relief design on the front and/or back. Historical flasks with a portrait, building, scene, or name are the most desired.

A chestnut is hand blown, small, and has a flattened bulbous body. The pitkin has a blown globular body with vertical ribs with a spiral rib overlay. Teardrop flasks are generally fiddle shaped and have a scroll or geometric design.

Dimensions can differ for the same flask because of variations in the molding process. Color is important, with scarcer colors demanding more money. Aqua and amber are the most common colors. Bottles with "sickness," an opalescent scaling which eliminates clarity, are worth much less.

Reference: George L. and Helen McKearin, *American Glass*, Crown Publishers, 1941 and 1948.

Collectors' Club: The National Early American Glass Club, 7417 Allison Street, Hyattsville, MD 20784.

Chestnut

5" h, olive green, crude lip, pontil scar, New England, 1790–1830 . . . . . . **150.00**

5¼" h, light olive green, crude lip,

Scroll, McKearin GIX–12, pint, brilliant light teal, open pontil, c1850, $275.00.

pontil scar, New England, 1790–1830 . . . . **135.00**

Historical

Cornucopia–Urn, McKearin GIII–4, pint, teal green, sheared lip, pontil scar, Coventry Glass Works, Coventry, CT, 1820s **225.00**

Double Eagle

McKearin GII–24, pint, sapphire blue, sheared lip, pontil scar, attributed to Kentucky Glassworks, Louisville, KY, 1850–55 . . . . . . **2,500.00**

McKearin GII–26, quart, deep aqua, sheared lip, iron pontil, attributed to Kentucky Glassworks, Louisville, KY, 1850–55 . . . . . . **200.00**

McKearin GII–70, pint, olive–amber, sheared lip, pontil scar, Coventry Glassworks, Coventry, CT, c1820 . . . . **225.00**

McKearin GII–86, half pint, deep olive–amber, sheared lip, pontil scar, New England, 1846–60 . . **75.00**

Eagle, McKearin GII–65, half pint, olive–amber, narrow round collar, lower bevel, smooth base, Westford Glass Works, Westford, CT, 1860–70 . . . . **150.00**

Masonic–Eagle

McKearin GII–7, pint, medium green–aqua, heavy collared lip, pontil scar, thickly made, New England, 1820–30 . . . . **475.00**

McKearin GIV–18, pint, olive–amber, sheared lip, pontil scar, Keene Marlboro Street Glassworks, Keene, NY, c1820 . . . . . **160.00**

McKearin GIV–19, pint, golden amber, sheared lip, pontil scar, Keene Marlboro Street Glassworks, Keene, NH, c1820 . . . . **120.00**

Sailboat–Star, McKearin GX–9, half pint, medium green–aqua, sheared lip, pontil scar, tiny lip flake, attributed to Joel Bodine & Sons, Bridgetown, NJ, 1846–55 . . . . **225.00**

Success to the Railroad, McKearin

GII–5, pint, golden–amber, sheared lip, pontil scar, very bubbly, inner haze **150.00**
Washington–Taylor
McKearin GI–39, qt, medium pink–amethyst, thinly blown, sheared lip, pontil scar, Dyottsville Glassworks, Philadelphia, PA, 1840–50 . . . . **2,700.00**
McKearin GI–51, qt, medium blue–green, double collared lip, iron pontil, Dyottsville Glassworks, Philadelphia, PA, 1855–65 . . . . **225.00**
Pictorial
Fells Point, Baltimore Monument, McKearin GI–20, pint, aqua, sheared lip, pontil scar, Baltimore Glassworks, Baltimore, MD, 1828–29 . . . . **90.00**
Sheaf of Grain, McKearin GXIII–48, qt, aqua, flat collar, iron pontil, Baltimore Glassworks, Baltimore, MD, c1850 . . . . **125.00**
Sheaf of Wheat, McKearin GXIII–36, pint, red–amber, round collar, bevel smooth base, Westford Glassworks, Westford, CT, 1860–70 . . . **150.00**
Summer Tree–Winter Tree, McKearin GX–16, half pint, aqua, round collar, bevel smooth base, America, 1860–70 . . . . **50.00**
Pitkin, pint, 32 ribs, broken swirl, light green, sheared lip, pontil scar, Midwest America, 1820–40 . . . . **180.00**
Sunburst
McKearin GVIII–5a, pint, light olive–amber, sheared lip, pontil scar, attributed to Pitkin Glassworks, East Hartford, CT, 1820–30 . . . . **1,000.00**
McKearin GVIII–26, pint, aqua, thinly blown, sharp impression, sheared lip, pontil scar, America, 1840–50 **325.00**
Teardrop, 7¾″ h, tulip, etched frosted border, wreath on reverse **150.00**

FLOW BLUE

History: Flow blue or flowing blue is the name applied to china of cobalt and white whose color, when fired in a kiln, produced a flowing or smudged effect. The blue varies in color from dark cobalt to a grayish or steel blue. The flow varies from very slight to a heavy blur where the pattern cannot be easily recognized. The blue color does not permeate through the china.

Flow blue was first produced around 1835 in the Staffordshire district of England by a large number of potters including Alcock, Davenport, J. Wedgwood, Grindley, New Wharf, Johnson Brothers, and many others. The early flow blue, 1830s to 1870s, was usually of the ironstone variety. The late patterns, 1880s to 1910s, and modern patterns, after 1910, usually were made of the more delicate semi-porcelain variety. Approximately 95% of the flow blue was made in England, with the remaining 5% made in Germany, Holland, France, and Belgium. A few patterns also were made in the United States by Mercer, Warwick, and Wheeling Pottery companies.

References: Mary F. Gaston, *The Collector's Encyclopedia Of Flow Blue China,* Collector Books, 1983, 1989 value update; Petra Williams, *Flow Blue China—An Aid To Identification, Revised Edition,* Fountain House East, 1981; Petra Williams, *Flow Blue China II, Revised Edition,* Fountain House East, 1981; Petra Williams, *Flow Blue China and Mulberry Ware—Similarity and Value Guide, Revised Edition,* Fountain House East, 1981.

Collectors' Club: Flow Blue International Collectors' Club, P.O. Box 205, Rockford, IL 61105.

Early Pattern, Cashmere, Francis Morley, creamer, 5½″ h, $175.00.

EARLY PATTERNS: c1825–1850

Bowl, Fairy Villas, John Maddock, 1842, 9″ d	**90.00**
Coffeepot, cov, Lobelia, G Phillips, 1845	**275.00**
Creamer	
Amoy, Davenport, 1844	**245.00**
Columbia, Clementson & Young, 1846, 5¾″ h	**135.00**
Flora, Thomas Walker, 1845	**175.00**
Cup and Saucer, handeless	
Indian Jar, Jacob and Thomas Furnival, 1843	**90.00**
Pelew, Edward Challinor, 1840	**100.00**
Cup Plate	
Indian, F & R Pratt, 1840, rim chip	**30.00**
Scinde, J & G Alcock, 1840	**75.00**
Gravy Boat	
Amoy, Davenport, 1844	**275.00**
Lotus, WH Grindley, 1843	**100.00**
Honey Dish, Indian Jar, Jacob and Thomas Furnival, 1843, 5″ d	**75.00**
Pitcher	
Indian Jar, Jacob and Thomas Furnival, 1843	**225.00**

Scinde, J & G Alcock, 1840 . . . . . . **145.00**
Plate
  Amoy, Davenport, 1844, 9½" d **90.00**
  Candia, Cauldon, 1841 . . . . **65.00**
  Fairy Villas, John Maddock, 1842, 9"
    d **50.00**
  Flora, Thomas Walker, 1845, 9½" d **85.00**
  Indian Jar, Jacob and Thomas Furni-
    val, 1843, 7½" d **50.00**
  Manilla, Podmore Walker, 1845, 9" d **90.00**
  Pelew, Edward Challinor, 1840, 10" d **85.00**
Platter
  Heath's Flower, T. Heath, 1830, 13½" **350.00**
  Scinde, J & G Alcock, 1840, 16" . . . **460.00**
Relish, Scinde, J & G Alcock, 1840,
  shell shape **85.00**
Sauce Dish, Indian, F & R Pratt, 1840 **48.00**
Sauce Tureen, cov, attached underplate
  Oregon, T J & J Mayer, 1845, 6" l
    ladle **425.00**
  Scinde, J & G Alcock, 1840 . . . . . . **400.00**
Soup Plate
  Indian, F & R Pratt, 1840, 10½" d . . **110.00**
  Pelew, Edward Challinor, 1840, 10½"
    d **125.00**
Sugar, cov
  Flora, Thomas Walker, 1845 . . . . . . **185.00**
  Scinde, J & G Alcock, 1840 . . . . . . **200.00**
Teapot, Chapoo, John Wedgwood,
  1850 . . . . **600.00**
Vegetable Dish, cov
  Hong Kong, Charles Meigh, 1845 . . **275.00**
  Manilla, Podmore Walker, 1845 . . . **400.00**
  Scinde, J & G Alcock, 1840, 10½" . . **350.00**

MIDDLE PATTERNS: c1850–1870

Candy Compote, cov, Hong, P & G,
  1850 . . . . **350.00**
Charger, Tryolean, Wm Ridgway & Co,
  1850, 12¼" **145.00**
Creamer
  Coburg, John Edwards, 1860 . . . . . **150.00**
  Lozere, Edward Challinor, 1850 . . . **90.00**
Cup Plate, Carlton, Samuel Alcock,
  1850 . . . . **75.00**
Gravy Boat, Delft, Minton, 1870 . . . . . **85.00**
Match Holder, Carlton, Samuel Alcock,
  1850, gold trim, 3½ x 2" **65.00**
Pitcher, Gothic, Jacob Furnival, 1850,
  6½" h **125.00**
Plate
  Formosa, Thomas, John and Joseph
    Mayer, c1850, 9½" d **80.00**
  Monmouth, New Wharf Pottery, 1870 **45.00**
  Rose & Ivy, Brown Westhead Moore
    & Co, 1870, 10½" d **50.00**
Platter
  Belmont Japan, 19¼", well and tree,
    c1850 . . . . **500.00**
  Madras, Samuel Alcock, 1845, 13½" **200.00**

Soup Plate, Gothic, Jacob Furnival,
  1850 . . . . **75.00**
Syllabub Cup, Hindustan, John Mad-
  dock, 1855 . . . . **90.00**
Vegetable Dish, cov, Carlton, Samuel
  Alcock, 1850, rose finial, restorations **400.00**
Waste Bowl, Morning Glory, unknown
  English maker, 1860 . . . . **145.00**

**Late Pattern, Non Pareil, Burgess &
Leigh, Middleport Pottery, plate, 8½" d,
$50.00.**

LATE PATTERNS: c1880–1900s

Berry Bowl
  Hudson, JC Meakin, 1891, 5¼" d . . **30.00**
  Kenworth, Johnson Bros, 1900 . . . . **40.00**
Bowl, Kenworth, Johnson Bros, 1900,
  7½" d **60.00**
Butter Dish, cov, Oxford, Johnson Bros,
  1900, 3 pc **165.00**
Butter Pat
  Argyle, WH Grindley, 1896 . . . . **28.00**
  Byzantine, Wood & Sons, 1900 . . . . **30.00**
  Grace, WH Grindley, 1897 . . . . **30.00**
  Raleigh, Burgess & Leigh, 1906 . . . **18.00**
  Roseville, John Maddock, 1891 . . . . **32.00**
  Touraine, Henry Alcock, c1898 . . . . **28.00**
  Verona, Alfred Meakin Ltd, 1891 . . . **28.00**
Charger, Non–Pareil, Burgess & Leigh,
  1891, 13¼" **350.00**
Chop Plate, La Belle, Wheeling Pottery,
  1900, 11½", deep blue **125.00**
Creamer
  Kelvin, Alfred Meakin, 1891, small
    chip **70.00**
  La Belle, Wheeling Pottery, 1900 . . . **200.00**
  Marchiel Niel, W H Grindley, c1895 **145.00**
Cup and Saucer
  Kenworth, Johnson Bros, 1900 . . . . **60.00**
  La Belle, Wheeling Pottery, 1900 . . . **55.00**
  Navy, Thos. Till & Son, 1891 . . . . . . **55.00**
  Spinach, Libertas, 1900 . . . . **78.00**
  Touraine, Henry Alcock, c1898 . . . . **78.00**
Demitasse Cup and Saucer, Roseville,
  John Maddock, 1891 . . . . **55.00**

Fruit Bowl, La Belle, Wheeling Pottery, 1900, scalloped **275.00**

Gravy Boat
Alaska, WH Grindley, 1891 . . . . **95.00**
Dundee, Ridgways, 1910 . . . . **100.00**
Ebor, Ridgways, 1910 . . . . **100.00**
Kelvin, Alfred Meakin, 1891, matching underplate **150.00**
Kenworth, Johnson Bros, 1900 . . . . **70.00**
Seville, New Wharf Pottery, 1891 . . **95.00**
Milk Pitcher, Le Pavot, WH Grindley, 1896 . . . . **265.00**
Pitcher, La Belle, Wheeling Pottery, 1900
1½" qt **175.00**
2½" qt **350.00**
Plate
Argyle, WH Grindley, c1896, 10", small chip **35.00**
Chinese, Dimmock, 1908, 9" **85.00**
Clytie, Wedgwood, 1908, 10", small chip on back **70.00**
Gironde, WH Grindley, 1891, 6" . . . **30.00**
Ivanhoe, Wedgwood, 1901, 10" d . . **75.00**
Kelvin, Alfred Meakin, 1891
6¾" d **35.00**
8" d **45.00**
9" d **55.00**
10" d **75.00**
Paris, New Wharf Pottery, 1891, 9" d **50.00**
Raleigh, Burgess & Leigh, 1906
8¾" d **30.00**
9" d **50.00**
9¾" d **45.00**
Richmond, Johnson Bros, 1900, 10" d **55.00**
Shanghai, W & E Corn, 1900, 9¾" d **70.00**
Platter
Argyle, WH Grindley, 1896, 8¾ x 12¾" **165.00**
Chinese, Dimmock, 1908, 15½" . . . **300.00**
Kelvin, Alfred Meakin, 1891, 8½ x 12½" **150.00**
Kenworth, Johnson Bros, 1900, 11 x 14" **175.00**
La Belle, Wheeling Pottery, 1900, 12¾ x 9¼" **110.00**
Melbourne, WH Grindley, 1900, 12 x 18" **245.00**
Melrose, Doulton, 1891, 12 x 18" . . **245.00**
Mikado, W & E Corn, 1900, 12 x 16" **250.00**
Oxford, Johnson Bros, 1900, 10¼ x 14" **175.00**
Raleigh, Burgess & Leigh, 1906, 13½ x 17¾" **200.00**
Tokio, Johnson Bros, 1891, 10¾ x 14½" **200.00**
Oyster Bowl, La Belle, Wheeling Pottery, 1900, 9" d **360.00**
Relish
Abbey, G Jones & Sons, 1900, 5½ x 10½" **120.00**

La Belle, Wheeling Pottery, 1900, 4 x 11" **110.00**
Sauce Dish
Argyle, WH Grindley, 1896 . . . . **30.00**
Dundee, Ridgways, 1910 . . . . **30.00**
Sauce Tureen, tray, Fleur–de–Lis, J & G Meakin, 1891 . . . . **225.00**
Saucer
Kelvin, Alfred Meakin, 1891 . . . . . . **15.00**
Raleigh, Burgess & Leigh, 1906 . . . **15.00**
Soup Plate
Conway, New Wharf Pottery, 1891, 9" **60.00**
La Belle, Wheeling Pottery, 1900, 7½" d **35.00**
Raleigh, Burgess & Leigh, 1906, 8¾" **30.00**
Sugar, cov, La Belle, Wheeling Pottery, 1900 . . . . **250.00**
Syrup Pitcher, La Belle, Wheeling Pottery, 1900, silverplated top **165.00**
Tureen, cov, Gironde, Grindley, 1891 **200.00**
Vegetable Dish, cov
Celtic, WH Grindley, 1897 . . . . **225.00**
Kelvin, Alfred Meakin, 1891, 6¾ x 8½" **110.00**
La Belle, Wheeling Pottery, 1900, 10¼ x 8¼" **250.00**
Osborne, Ridgway, 1905, clover shape, matching underplate **500.00**
Raleigh, Burgess & Leigh, 1906 . . . **225.00**
Waste Bowl, La Belle, Wheeling Pottery, 1900, 6" d **50.00**

FOLK ART

History: The definition of what constitutes folk art is still being vigorously debated among collectors, dealers, museum curators, and scholars. Some want to confine folk art to non-academic, hand made objects. Others are willing to include manufactured material. In truth, the term is used to cover objects ranging from crude drawings by obviously untalented children to academically trained artists' paintings of "common" people and scenery.

The folk art market is subject to hype and manipulation. Neophyte collectors are encouraged to read Edie Clark's "What Really Is Folk Art?" in the December 1986 *Yankee*. Clark's article provides a refreshingly honest look at the folk art market.

Finally, the folk art market is extremely trendy and fickle. What is hot today can become cool and passé tomorrow. Collecting folk art is not for the weak–of–heart or the cautious investor.

References: Kenneth L. Ames, *Beyond Necessity: Art In The Folk Tradition,* W. W. Norton, 1978; Robert Bishop and Judith Rieter Weissman, *Folk Art: The Knopf Collectors' Guides To American Antiques*, Alfred A. Knopf, 1983; Henry Niemann and Helaine Fendelman, *The Official Identification and Price Guide To American Folk Art*, House of Collectibles, 1988.

Museum: Museum of American Folk Art, New York, NY; Abby Aldrich Rockefeller Folk Art Center, Williamsburg, VA.

Andirons, pr, cast iron, 20 x 27 x 15", figural, drummer, attached by screw thread to cast iron grate, presented to "Red" Bird Massillon, Ohio, band leader, World War II **750.00**

Bellhop and Ashtray, 37" h, carved and painted pine, black features, gray uniform, red striping and buttons, red socks, black shoes, cap lifts to reveal brass ashtray, black base, American, c1930 . . . . **5,500.00**

Drawing, pen and ink, 30¾" h, 26¾" w, Spencerian calligraphy, cat, brown ink, cream colored paper, titled "M—Meow—W," sgd "E. B.," stains, old frame with white and gold repaint . . **450.00**

Eagle, carved and gilded wood, 36″ wing span, painted shield, $3,500.00.

Figure, carved and painted, early 20th C
Eagle
   5½" h, back to back pair, minor retouch of paint **275.00**
   13¾" h, glass eyes, naturalistic colors, green painted base **1,300.00**
   19¼" h, 36" w, perched on rock, wings spread, brown and green paint over orig gilding, old repaired breaks to beak **2,000.00**
Squirrel, 3½" h, painted cream, black dash highlights, minor paint wear **150.00**
Swan, 3½" h, 5" l, attributed to George Boyd, Seabrook, NH **350.00**
Game Board, checkerboard, wooden, 15⅜ x 24", worn black and white paint **185.00**
Motto, 16¾" h, 14¾" w, "Home Sweet Home, Remember the Giver, Anna Meulford, 1876," bird nest in flowering tree, pen and ink drawing, minor stains, shadow box frame **175.00**
Plaque, 28" l, 9½" h, carved gilt and painted wood, eagle, wings spread, head raised towards banner "Don't Give Up The Ship," shield tucked under wing, attributed to John Haley

Bellamy, Kittery Point, ME, late 19th C **2,800.00**
Quilt, 65½ x 52½", cyanotype on cotton, views of Camden, ME, 1890–1910, forty rect photographic images printed on fabric, late 19th C scenes and occupations, each sq bordered with woven white ribbon, some water stain and discoloration, attributed to Frank Leslie, photographer in Camden, ME, from 1880–1920 . . . **3,650.00**
Sled, painted and dec, two peaked runners with wrought iron blades, shaped seat dec with oval American flag, mustard and dark blue diapering, runners inscribed "Village Romp" in gold letters, 52¼" l, 13¼" w **8,250.00**
Theorem
   11¼ x 8¾", watercolor, pencil, and mica on paper, yellow and red tulips, roses, chrysanthemums, and pansies, glittering bowl, c1830, framed **1,430.00**
   12¼ x 13⅛", watercolor on velvet, buildings, trees, and deer, red, yellow, green, brown and blue, old grained frame **4,800.00**
   14 x 12¼", watercolor on velvet, pot of flowers, sgd "Jessie N. Boyer," gilt frame **500.00**
   18½ x 19½", watercolor on velvet, basket of fruit, label on reverse "By Clarissa (Cummmins) Merriam When A Young Girl. She was born March 17, 1805. Mother of Leander Merriam who gave library to the town of Auburn, Mass," framed . . **3,500.00**
Valentine, Scherensnitte, (cut work), scissored white paper mounted over olive green ground, 13" d, inscribed in pen and ink in 19th C hand, hex sign type cuttings with hearts and other borders **2,000.00**
Watch Hutch, 9⅞" h, New England, early 19th C, tall case clock shape, carved wood, painted brown, brick red highlights, inset inscription "JST 1808" and "Time" **3,250.00**
Whirligig, 12¾" h, policeman, worn and faded black and white paint, modern base **1,200.00**

FOOD BOTTLES

History: Food bottles were made in many sizes, shapes, and colors. Manufacturers tried to make an attractive bottle that would ship well and allow the purchaser to see the product, thus assuring him that the product was as good and as well made as home preserves.

Reference: Ralph & Terry Kovel, *The Kovels' Bottle Price List, 8th Edition,* Crown Publishers, Inc, 1984.

Periodical: *Antique Bottle and Glass Collector,* P.O. Box 187, East Greenville, PA 18041.

Additional Listings: See *Warman's Americana & Collectibles* for more milk bottle listings.

Horseradish, dark green, $50.00.

Baking Powder, Eddy's, tin top	12.00
Gin, 12½″ h, deep olive green, case, crudely applied lip, smooth base, early 19th C	175.00
Horseradish, 5″ h, Heinz Noble & Co, emb, two anchors, horse head on lid, 1873	275.00
Lemonade, 2¾″ h, G. Foster Clark & Co, Eiffel Tower	8.50

Milk

Alta Crest Farms, qt, green	700.00
Big Elm/Dairy/Company, qt, green . .	250.00
Brighton/Place Dairy, qt, green	325.00
Brookfield, half pint, emb, round, clear	60.00
Deluxe Cream Separator, qt, sq, clear, red pyroglazed letters on two sides	350.00
Langs Creamery, Buffalo, NY, qt, green	300.00
NL Martin, Boston, qt, clear, sq, tin top, emb "Climax 107" on base, light haze	375.00
Pure Milk, qt, clear, tin screw top with handle, Adlam patent on base, light haze	850.00
Thatcher's, qt, clear, Absolutely Pure Milk, man milking cow, "The Milk Protector Thatcher Mfg Co." on base	275.00
Uptons Farms, pint, pyroglazed, clear	70.00
Weckerle, qt, green	150.00

Pepper Sauce, 8⅞″ h, Cathedral, six panels, blue-green, applied ring lip, open pontil base, c1850 . . . . | 350.00

Pickle

8″ h, octofoil, dark green, rolled lip, smooth base, attributed to Stoddard, NH, 1860–70	400.00
9¼ h, cathedral, aqua, rolled lip, smooth base, America, 1870–80	70.00
11½″ h, J McCollick & Co, New York, bluish–aqua, applied ring lip, iron pontil base, beaded bands, paneled shoulder, emb, c1850 . . .	900.00
13½″ h, cathedral, sq, emerald green, applied ring lip, iron pontil base, c1850	1,100.00

Vinegar, 10″ h, Whitehouse, jug . . . . . | 20.00

FOOD MOLDS

History: Food molds were used both commercially and in the home. For the most part, pewter ice cream molds and candy molds were used on a commercial basis; pottery and copper molds were used in homes. Today, both types are collected largely for decorative purposes.

Pewter ice cream molds were made primarily by two American companies: Eppelsheimer & Co. [molds marked E & Co., N.Y.] and Schall & Co. [molds marked S & Co.]. Both companies used a numbering system for their molds. The Krauss Co. bought out Schall & Co., removed the S & Co. from some, but not all the molds, and added more designs [marked K or Krauss].

The majority of pewter ice cream molds are individual serving molds. When used, one quart of ice cream would make eight to ten pieces. Scarcer, but still available, are banquet molds which used two to four pints of ice cream per example. European pewter molds [CC is a French mold mark] are available.

Chocolate mold makers are more difficult to determine. Unlike the pewter ice cream molds, maker's marks were not always on the mold or were covered by frames. Eppelsheimer & Co. of New York marked many of their molds, either with their name or with a design resembling a child's toy top with "Trade Mark" and "NY." Many chocolate molds were imported from Germany and Holland and were marked with the country of origin and, in some cases, the mold maker's name.

Reference: Judene Divone, *Chocolate Moulds: A History & Encyclopedia,* Oakton Hills Publications, 1987.

Additional Listings: Butter Prints.

CHOCOLATE MOLDS

Clamp Type, no hinge, two piece

Clown, 9″, numbered "15262"	75.00
Jack-O-Lantern, heavy wire clamp	35.00
Santa and bag, 10⅜″ h, three part, tin	225.00

Chocolate mold, Kewpie, unknown maker, 9¾″ h, $75.00.

Snowman, 4″, wearing hat 50.00
Stocking, 8″, marked "59 4271, Larrosh, Schw Gmund" 125.00
Frame or Book Type (Measurements based on single cavity size)
Car, 3 x 5″, four door sedan 15.00
Cat, bird, and rabbit, 3⅜ x 11¾″, three cavities, relief carved, wood 125.00
Christmas scene, 4½ x 8″ 30.00
Fish, 14½″ l, wood 235.00
Heart, 6½ x 6″, two cavities 60.00
Pencil, 8½″, two cavities 30.00
Rabbit, 8 x 10″, lollipop type, eight cavities 55.00
Santa, 4½″, unmarked 20.00
Tray Type (Measurement is overall tray size)
Candy Bar, each section marked "Hershey" 20.00
Coin, 6 x 15″, Rosemarie de Paris, marked "Eppelsheimer & Co, NY, Feb 1944" 20.00
Rabbit and chicken, 11 x 17″, six rows, marked "2215.s" 100.00
Rooster, 12 x 10″, one cavity 65.00

ICE CREAM MOLDS

Banquet Size
Duck, marked "Krauss #44" 250.00
Log, 10″ 175.00
Sea Shell, marked "Krauss 36B" .. 200.00
Santa Claus, marked "E & Co #194" 350.00
Individual Size
Blimp, 4⅛″ l, pewter 35.00
Boat, 5⅛″ l, pewter, marked "S & Co" 25.00
Chrysanthemum, marked "313" ... 55.00
Cornucopia, tin washed copper, marked "287" 25.00
Eagle, marked "E-655" 90.00

Flower, cluster of three roses, worn number 35.00
Football, 3⅛″ l, pewter 30.00
King of Hearts, marked "E-920" ... 35.00
Morning Glory, marked "S-239" 40.00
Oriental man, 3⅞″ h, pewter, marked "E & Co NY" 25.00
Pumpkin, marked "E-309" 25.00
Sailboat, marked "S-553" 60.00
Santa, in sleigh pulled by reindeer, antlers added 65.00
Soldier, 5⅝″ l, pewter 45.00
Strawberry, marked "503" 65.00
Turkey, worn number, marked "E & Co, NY" 40.00

MISCELLANEOUS

Butter
Cow, round, cased, 4½″ d, refinished 65.00
Pineapple pattern, pat 1866 ...... 125.00
Star flower pattern, 10″ l, lollipop shape, one side round, other square, wood 250.00
Cake, Griswold
Lamb 75.00
Rabbit 175.00
Cookie, 4¼ x 6″, cast iron, oval, basket of fruit pattern, holly border, mid 1800s 165.00
Patty, orig box, Griswold 20.00
Pudding, 8″ w, tin, star with five points 50.00

POTTERY (Center Design Indicated)

Coiled Fish, 10½ x 11¼″, redware, greenish amber glaze 225.00
Lion, ironstone 90.00
Rabbit, 8½″, yellow ware 200.00
Turk's head, 11¾″ d, redware, brown and green, clear glaze 75.00
Turtle, 8½″ l, blue and white, marked "Germany" 80.00

FOSTORIA GLASS   FOSTORIA

History: Fostoria Glass Co. began operations at Fostoria, Ohio, in 1887, and moved to Moundsville, West Virginia, its present location, in 1891. By 1925 Fostoria had five furnaces and a variety of special shops. In 1924 a line of colored tableware was introduced. Fostoria was purchased by Lancaster Colony in 1983, and continues to operate under the Fostoria name.

Reference: Hazel M. Weatherman, *Fostoria, Its First Fifty Years*, published by author, c1972.

Collectors' Club: Fostoria Glass Society of America, P.O. Box 826, Moundsville, WV 26041.

Museum: Huntington Galleries, Huntington, WV.

Baker, Vesper, green, oval, 9" 40.00
Bowl
   Baroque, 10½", handle 12.00
   Chintz, 13" 35.00
   Grape Brocade, emerald green, 13" 100.00
   Vesper, green, berry, 5½" 14.00
Cake Plate, Oak Leaf, green, handles 125.00
Candlesticks, pr, Oak Leaf, black, 3" . . 85.00
Candy, cov, Baroque, Meadow Rose
   etch 90.00
Celery
   American, 10½" 15.00
   Vesper, green, 11" 37.00
Cigarette Box, Coin, gold 120.00
Claret, Heather 30.00
Cocktail, Vesper, amber 20.00
Cologne, Jenny Lind, milk glass, orig
   stopper 70.00
Compote
   Coin, emerald green, 8½" 200.00
   Vesper, green, 6½" 35.00
Console Bowl, Colony, rolled, 9¾" . . . 20.00
Console Set
   June, yellow, 11½" d bowl, 2" candle-
     sticks 65.00
   Versailles, Azure blue, scroll bowl . . 145.00
Cordial
   Heather 34.00
   Navarre, 1 oz 50.00
Cream Soup and Liner
   Fairfax, pink 14.00
   Trojan, topaz 28.00
Creamer and Sugar
   June, yellow 30.00
   Midnight Rose 35.00
   Seascape, opalescent pink 50.00
   Vesper, amber, ftd 35.00
Cruet, Hermitage, topaz 85.00
Cup and Saucer, Vesper, green, ftd . . 16.00
Decanter, American, orig stopper 70.00
Figure, mermaid, crystal 125.00

**American pattern, water pitcher, ice lip,
8¼" h, $125.00.**

Finger Bowl, Trojan, topaz 20.00
Goblet
   June, pink 40.00
   Willowmere 24.00
Ice Bucket, Baroque, crystal 55.00
Ice Cream Dish, Hermitage, Azure blue 15.00
Iced Tea
   American, handle 250.00
   Jamestown, amethyst 11.00
Juice Tumbler, Vesper, amber, ftd 18.00
Mayonnaise, American, orig liner 24.00
Mustard, American, 3¾", cov 22.00
Nappy, Coin, blue frosted, handled . . . 22.00
Pitcher
   Hermitage, 3 pint, topaz 125.00
   Jamestown, amethyst 95.00
   Trojan, topaz 325.00
   Versailles
     Green 360.00
     Pink 335.00
Plate
   Baroque, crystal
     7", salad 5.50
     8", luncheon 8.00
     14", Meadow Rose etch 45.00
   June, yellow
     6", bread and butter 5.50
     9½", dinner 22.00
   Minuet, crystal, dinner 7.00
   Trojan, topaz, 7½", salad 7.50
Platter, Vesper, green, 11" 50.00
Salt and Pepper Shakers, pr, Coin, blue 55.00
Sauce Boat and Liner, Trojan, topaz . . 100.00
Sherbet
   American, handles 115.00
   Jamestown, amethyst 8.00
Sugar Pail, Trojan, topaz 110.00
Torte Plate, Colony, 15" 55.00
Tray, 16", American, pedestal 135.00
Tumbler
   Navarre, blue 20.00
   Versailles, yellow, 5½" h, set of 8 . . 12.00
Vase
   American
     7" 55.00
     12" 100.00
   Grape Brocade, green, 8" 100.00
   Mardi Gras, 7¼", sgd "Fostoria,"
     dated 90.00
   Oakleaf, pink 100.00
Vegetable Bowl, Trojan, topaz, oval . . 55.00
Whip Cream Bowl, Trojan, topaz, two
   handles, 5½" 18.00

FRAKTUR

History: Fraktur, the calligraphy associated with
the Pennsylvania Germans, is named for the elaborate first letter found in many of the hand drawn
examples. Throughout its history printed, partially
printed, hand drawn, and fully hand drawn works

existed side by side. Frakturs often were made by the school teachers or ministers living in rural areas of Pennsylvania, Maryland, and Virginia. Many artists are unknown.

Fraktur exists in several forms—geburts and taufschein (birth and baptismal certificates), vorschrift (writing example, often with alphabet), haus sagen (house blessing), bookplates and marks, rewards of merit, illuminated religious text, valentines, and drawings. Although collected for decoration, the key element in fraktur is the text.

Fraktur prices rise and fall along with the American folk art market. The key market place is Pennsylvania and the Middle Atlantic states.

References: Donald A. Shelley, *The Fraktur-Writings Or Illuminated Manuscripts Of The Pennsylvania Germans,* Pennsylvania German Society, 1961; Frederick S. Weiser and Howell J. Heaney (compilers), *The Pennsylvania German Fraktur Of The Free Library Of Philadelphia,* Pennsylvania German Society, 1976, two volumes.

Museum: The Free Library of Philadelphia, Philadelphia, PA.

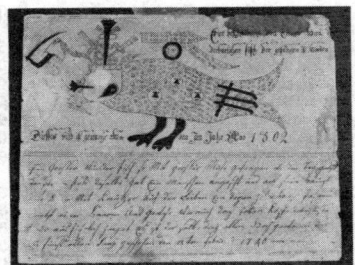

Hand-drawn, fish, religious text, southeastern PA, THS, 1802, 7⅞ x 6⁵⁄₁₆," $450.00.

HAND DRAWN

Brecht, John, double bookplate, each part 4 x 6½", right side: oval with heart top and bottom, left side in shape of tombstone with dome top, two lines of music at top of each page and one line of music at bottom, book: *Harfe Der Kinder Zions,* records birth of Fronica Schimmel to Christain Schimmel and his wife, Maria, on May 10, 1803, in Springfield Township, Bucks County, PA, work dated January 13, 1813, some moisture damage **2,300.00**

Blowsy (Flying) Angel Artist, birth and baptismal certificate, Northampton County, dated 1800, 9½ x 13½", watercolor, pen, and ink on paper, center text block consumes lower two-thirds of paper, flanked by flowers above which are blowsy angels extending into center above text block, birth of Magdelena Gunziger **2,500.00**

Eyer, Johann Adam, religious poem beginning "Jesu Mein Seelen Freund Lass Dich" (Jesus My Soul's Companion), 7¾ x 9¾", top consists of central heart from which radiates floral vines and flowers, a pair of blue birds perched on vines, blowsy angels flank heart, elaborate tulip floral border flanks text, bottom has two red breasted birds enclosing text passage, dated April 10, 1792 . . . . **20,000.00**

Gottshall, M., bookplate, 4¼ x 6½", heart with text, face above heart, tulip growing from heart, leave accents, loose in copy of 1815 Billmeyer *New Testament,* dated November 18, 1835, ex. Levi Yoder collection **22,000.00**

Krebs, Frederick, birth and baptismal certificate, 12¾ x 8", central heart motif containing birth information, flanked on both sides by smiling star at tover over large petal flower from which radiate several smaller petal flowers, records birth of Elizabath Hermann on October 2, 1791, in Berks County, PA **1,150.00**

Krebs, Frederick, series of four watercolor drawings, "The Parable of the Prodigal Son," first drawing shows son on horse leaving home, second drawing shows son being driven from lodging when money is exhausted, third drawing shows son tending pigs, fourth drawing shows son receiving father's forgiveness, 15¼ x 11½", framed in two frames **17,600.00**

Peterman, Daniel, birth and baptismal certificate, 11¾ x 14", central text, small flower vase in center of top from which radiate floral and vine motif concluding with upside-down tulips on sides, two parrots in upper quadrants, a woman flanks text on each side in bottom half, records birth of Catharina Trambach in 1856 . . . . . . **5,000.00**

Souder, John, work book, more than forty works by this 1940 fraktur artist, group of related articles and photographs **1,600.00**

Unknown

Birth and Baptismal Certificate, c1805–1810, 17 x 13¾", "C" sided and topped square outlined with red and green stripe, tulip and stylized floral motifs radiate out from point of square, red and green stripe border, records birth of Daniel Spangler on July 26, 1804, in Northampton County, PA **1,750.00**

Bookplate

Southeastern PA, 1828, 4¼ x 6½", block format, lower third with text message indicating songbook belongs to Susanna Meyers, upper two–thirds consist of large stylized floral tree flanked by a smaller tree on each side, book: 1820 Michael Billmeyer's *Hafe der Kinder Zions* **1,350.00**

Southeastern PA, c1840s, 3 x 4¾", watercolor, pen, and ink on paper lining of cardboard book cover, heart with text from which radiates tulips and stems, bird sits on two of lesser tulips, shades of orange, yellow, lavender, and black, for "Georg Reiff," dated 1844, stains, frame 5 x 6¾" . . . **425.00**

Drawing, southeastern PA, c1820–40, laid paper, horizontal dec bands, top with two facing birds surrounded by flowers, block letters "REBECCA SNYDER," birds and flowers, bottom with man and dog flanking central flower, red, yellow, blue, pale green, and brown, stains and small tears, old black frame 8½ x 9¾" **3,700.00**

Song Book, southeastern PA

1810, manuscript, Abraham Geissinger's *Little Book of Harmonious Melodies*, 7¾ x 4½", bookplate in front consists of large heart with text, tulip and leafy vines begin at point of heart and extend up sides, dated December 22, 1810, songs in alphabetical order, many pages have decorative work, two pages of manuscript text at end **6,000.00**

1821, manuscript, Anna Schimmel, 7⅞ x 4⅜", bookplate, central dominate text block with "A" of Anna illuminated, vertical panel on right with basket of flowers, vertical panel on left with twisted floral vine, fancy border, dated, complete **4,700.00**

HAND DRAWN–PRINTED

Brechall, Martin, birth and baptismal, printed form by Hütter, Easton, 1821, 13 x 16", central heart, borders hand painted with filigrees and flowers in red, yellow, blue, and green, for Lea Schull **950.00**

Dulheur, Henrich, birth and baptismal, 13 x 15¾" **950.00**

Otto, Heinrich, birth and baptismal certificate, parrot facing inward in upper left quadrant, geometric floral and stripe border across top, oval theme floral border across bottom, records birth of Jacob Thomas in 1767 . . . . **3,000.00**

Unknown Artist, birth certificate, Northampton County, 1821, 7¾ x 12", German calligraphy, inscription within a keystone device, hand painted paired birds and large flowering tulip plants, birth of Maria Margaretha Scherner **750.00**

PRINTED

Adam and Eve, Ville, H. W. Lancaster **500.00**

Birth and Baptismal

Baumann and Ruth, Ephrata	**350.00**
Baumann, John, Ephrata	**400.00**
Blumer & Busch, Allentown, PA	**150.00**
Currier & Ives, New York	**40.00**
Dreisbach, Bath	**200.00**
Eagle Bookstore, Reading	**75.00**
Ebner, Henrich, Allentown, PA	**200.00**
Kessler, Charles, Reading, PA	**85.00**
Lange, D. P., Hanover, PA	**200.00**
Lutz & Scheffler, Harrisburg, PA . . .	**40.00**
Mentz, George W., Philadelphia . . .	**100.00**
Peters, G. S., Harrisburg, PA	**100.00**
Ritter, Johann, Reading, late form . .	**75.00**
Sanno, Friederich, Carlisle, PA	**400.00**
Schnee, Joseph, Lebanon, PA	**500.00**

Note: If signed by a scrivener, increase value by 25% to 40%

Haus Sagen

Blummer and Bush, Allentown, PA .	**200.00**
Ritter, Reading	**140.00**

FRANKART

History: Arthur Von Frankenberg, artist and sculptor, founded Frankart, Inc., in New York City in the mid-1920s. Frankart, Inc., mass produced practical "art objects" in the Art Deco style into the 1930s. Pieces include aquariums, ashtrays, bookends, flower vases, lamps, etc. Although Von Frankenberg used live female models as his subjects, his figures are characterized by their form and style rather than specific features. Nudes are the most collectible; caricatured animals and other human figures were also produced, no doubt, to increase sales.

With few exceptions, pieces were marked Frankart, Inc., with a patent number or "pat. appl. for."

Pieces were cast in a white metal composition in the following finishes: cream–a pale iridescent white; bronzoid–oxidized copper, silver, or gold; french–a medium brown with green in the crevices; gun metal–art iridescent gray; jap–a very dark brown, almost black, with green in the crevices;

pearl green—pale iridescent green; and verde—a dull light green. Cream and bronzoid were used primarily in the 1930s.

Note: All pieces listed are all original in very good condition unless otherwise indicated.

Advisor: Walter Glenn.

Ashtray, kneeling female nude, arms extended to left, holding green custard glass ashtray, Roman green finish, 9¼" h, $275.00.

Ashtray
5½" d, seated honey bear, holding honey pot ashtray	125.00
8" d, gaucho on horse, pottery sombrero ashtray	285.00
9" d, ballerina dancing in center, 8" d round onyx tray	275.00

Bookends, pr
5" h, stylized circus ponies	150.00
6" h, lions, seated	125.00
7" h, female heads, long necks	210.00
9½" h, Indian chief and squaw with papoose	175.00
10" h, female nudes on headstand	275.00

Centerpiece Bowl, 15" d dish, 8½" h nude flower frog	275.00
Cigarette Lighter, Shriner's head, Atlantic City, NY, 1927	200.00
Incense Burner, 5", female head on burner base, leaning back to blow smoke through mouth	185.00

Lamp
9" h, two kneeling nudes, embracing 8" d crackle glass globe	485.00
12" h, two nudes standing face to face, amber rods	825.00
23" h, two female figures wearing pajamas and wide brimmed hats, strolling across base, silk shade	400.00
Match Holder, 8" h, burro with pack on back	150.00
Wall Plaque, 6" h, seated nude, floral framework	275.00

FRANKOMA POTTERY

History: John N. Frank founded a ceramic art department at Oklahoma University in Norman and taught there for several years. In 1933 he established his own business and began making Oklahoma's first commercial pottery. Frankoma moved from Norman to Sapulpa, Oklahoma, in 1938.

A fire completely destroyed the new plant later the same year, but rebuilding began almost immediately. The company remained in Sapulpa and continued to grow. Frankoma is the only American pottery to be permanently exhibited at the International Ceramic Museum of Italy.

In September 1983 a disastrous fire struck once again, destroying 97% of Frankoma's facilities. The rebuilt Frankoma Pottery reopened on July 2, 1984. Production has been limited to 1983 production molds only. All other molds were lost in the fire.

Prior to 1954 all Frankoma pottery was made with a honey-tan colored clay from Ada, Oklahoma. Since 1954 Frankoma has used a brick red clay from Sapulpa. During the early 1970s the clay became lighter and is now pink in color.

There were a number of early marks. One most eagerly sought is the leopard pacing on the FRANKOMA name. Since the 1938 fire, all pieces have carried only the name FRANKOMA.

References: Phyllis and Tom Bess, *Frankoma Treasures*, published by authors, 1983; Susan N. Cox, *Collectors Guide To Frankoma Pottery*, Book I, published by author, 1979, and Book II, published by author, 1982.

Additional Listings: See *Warman's Americana & Collectibles* for more examples.

Advisor: Phyllis Bess.

Vase, bulbous, green mottled glaze, cloud—like incised design, impressed mark, 5½", $30.00.

Animal, miniature
Irish Setter, desert sand	60.00
Trojan Horse, blue	60.00
Ashtray, Texas, green, #459	15.00

Baker
Lazybones, Autumn Yellow, 3 qt, orig heater	45.00
Mayan Az, 10 oz, Ada clay	45.00

Plainsman, individual size, Ada clay	40.00
Bank, elephant	10.00
Batter Pitcher	28.00
Bicentennial Plate, 1973	60.00
Bookends, pr, Clydesdale Horse, rearing, 8½"	125.00
Bowl, 9 x 2½", oval, Prairie Green, panther mark	50.00
Casserole, Wagon Wheel, green	35.00

Christmas Card

1957	50.00
1958	50.00
1959	50.00
1968	25.00
1973	15.00
Creamer, Wagon Wheel, brown and cream glaze	8.00

Decanter, orig stopper

#1217, red, sgd "John Frank, #1217"	77.00
#1787, red, sgd "Janice Frank, #1787"	65.00
Dish, leaf shaped, #225	22.50

Figure

Dreamer Girl, black glaze	125.00
Fan Dancer, green and brown	115.00
Indian Bowl Maker, green	25.00
Puma, one sitting, other laying, brown satin glow, pr	38.00
Flower Bowl	22.00
Magazine Rack, Serva–Tray	45.00

Mug

Advertising, American Airlines	30.00

Political

1969, GOP, Nixon/Agnew	45.00
1970, elephant, blue glaze	40.00

Planter

Cactus, oblong, Ada clay	30.00
Mallard, 9½"	8.50
Plaque, Will Rogers, green border, Ada clay, hand sgd "St Clair Homer"	125.00

Salt and Pepper Shakers, pr

First National Bank of Tulsa	25.00
Puma green, Ada clay	40.00
Teapot, Wagon Wheel, 6 cup, Ada clay	45.00

Vase

Black Ball, #55, early clay	25.00
Corkbark, 10" h	28.00
Flying Goose, pillow shape	20.00
Ram's Head, Ada clay	25.00

Wall Pocket

Acorn, green, early clay, #190	30.00
Phoebe, light brown, #730	60.00

FRATERNAL ORGANIZATIONS

History: Benevolent and secret societies played an important part in American society from the late 18th to the mid-20th centuries. Initially the societies were organized to aid members and their families in times of distress or death. They evolved from this purpose into important social clubs by the late 19th century.

In the 1950s, with the arrival of civil rights, an attack occurred on the secretiveness and often discriminatory practices of these societies. The fraternal movement, with the exception of the Masonic organizations, suffered serious membership loss. Many local chapters closed and sold their lodge halls. This resulted in many fraternal items arriving in the antiques market.

Additional Listings: See *Warman's Americana & Collectibles* for more examples.

Masonic, apron tube, celluloid, 16⅜" l, $25.00.

MASONIC

Box, 5" w, 2" h, brass, engraved Masonic symbol above "Work while it is day" inscription, moon and stars, slightly domed octagonal lid, conforming case and base, 19th C	70.00
Firing Glass, 3½" h, copper wheel engraved Masonic square and compass, round base, trumpet bowl	275.00
Goblet, etched "1908 St Paul"	65.00

Plate

6", etched "May 1906 Los Angeles"	45.00
8¼" d, Toledo, 1906, polychrome center scene, fraternal symbols around scalloped rim, inscribed, 64th Annual Conclave of Toledo Commandery, 1906, Knowles, Taylor & Knowles	35.00
Pouch, 1¼ x 2½", leather, black, snap top, gold Masonic symbol with "G" in center, includes silvered metal fold out razor	25.00
Sign, 38" h, 31" l, pine, carved, two crossed gilt tipped standards, left with entwined leaf vine, right with serpent, free carved gilt chain enclosing initials "FT" in center above black hand with relief carved pink heart, trapezoidal facade pierced with open work inscription, two men figures flanked by cane, open book, anvil, pr sandals and Mason and Oddfellows symbols, man standing before fence inscribed "Jerusalem" and "Jarico," initials "MO" on left of scene, crossed hands on right, shaped base, American, late 19th C	9,900.00
Spoon, sterling silver, emb bowl	38.00
Stickpin, 14k gold, pearl setting	30.00

Tumbler, "Landmark Lodge No 127, Baltimore, 1866–1916," milk glass . . **40.00**

OTHERS

Benevolent & Protective Order of the Elks, B.P.O.E.
Calling Card Case, 1½ x 2", sterling silver, inscribed and dated 1913 . . **100.00**
Cigarette Case, brass, Elks emblem **20.00**
Mug, purple, elk's head and clock, silver handle and trim **35.00**
Paperweight, glass, round **15.00**
Pitcher, 12" h, china, purple shaded elk's head and clock emblems, white ground, National Art China, Trenton, NJ **100.00**
Shaving Mug, gold on white, Elk emblem **40.00**
Stein, 10", pottery, hunter sprawled on ground, elk nearby, "We Are Brothers" **75.00**
Eastern Star
Cup and Saucer, emblem **10.00**
Hatpin, silver plated **15.00**
Plate, Indiana Grand Chapter, 1949 **25.00**
Independent Order of Odd Fellows, I.O.O.F.
Book, souvenir, 1922 Convention, paperback **25.00**
Dish, 5¾", pink luster, c1840 . . . . . . **65.00**
Letter Opener, 4¾", ivory color celluloid, black Denver convention 1908 inscription, bronco riding cowboy on reverse, Indiana Chapter, officers listed **25.00**
Mold, cookie, 5 x 6½", oval, cast iron, 3 interlocking links and symbols, heart in hand **220.00**
Trivet, 8¼" l, cast iron, insignia and heart in hand in laurel wreath . . . **25.00**
Knight of Columbus
Sword, dress, detailed blade, scabbard, McLilley Co, Columbus, OH **45.00**
Watch Fob, medallion type **35.00**
Knights of Pythias, goblet, glass, clear, "1900, Rochester" **30.00**
Shrine
Goblet, ruby flashed, St Paul, 1908 **60.00**
Hat, Fez, felt **20.00**
Humidor, paneled clear glass, metal Art Nouveau style cov, various ornate emblems finial, Yaarab Temple, Atlanta **75.00**
Plate, 10½", comic beat up Shriner center, camel border, dessert and palms **55.00**
Shot glass, cranberry, gold sheaf of wheat pattern, Shrine symbol, marked "Syria Temple Pittsburgh 1908, Brown, Motheral, Moore, Robinson" **165.00**

Toothpick Holder, glass, clear, Pittsburgh and New Orleans, 1910 . . . **40.00**

FRUIT JARS

History: Fruit jars are canning jars used to preserve food. Thomas W. Dyott, one of Philadelphia's earliest and most innovative glass makers, was promoting his glass canning jars in 1829. John Landis Mason patented his screw-type canning jar on November 30, 1858. This date refers to the patent date, not the age of the jar. There are thousands of types of jars in many colors, types of closures, sizes, and embossings.

References: Alice M. Creswick, *The Red Book of Fruit Jars No. 5*, published by author, 1987; Bill Schroeder, *1000 Fruit Jars: Priced And Illustrated, Revised 5th Edition*, Collector Books, 1987.

Atlas E-Z Seal, quart, blue glass, raised letters, $5.00.

Acheson Oildag Co Reg Aquadag US Pat Off Port Huron, Mich, clear, smooth lip **15.00**
American Fruit Jar, light green, qt, handmade, glass lid, wire bail **100.00**
Anchor Hocking, clear, qt, machine made, glass lid, wire bail, anchor emb on side, H superimposed on anchor **5.00**
Atlas Mason, aqua, qt, handmade, zinc lid **25.00**
Ball
Aqua, qt, handmade, glass lid, ground top, emb in script "The Ball, Pat. Apl'd For" **45.00**
Blue, Sure Seal, smooth lip, lightning beaded neck seal **4.00**
Green, pt, handmade, zinc lid, ground lip, emb in script "Ball Mason's Patent 1858" **3.25**
Bamberger's Mason Jar, blue, smooth lip **12.00**
Blue Ribbon, clear, qt, glass lid, wire clip **7.50**

Boldt Masom (error) Jar, aqua, smooth
lip **25.00**
Cadiz, aqua, ground lip **450.00**
Clark Fruit Jar Co, blue, qt, handmade,
glass lid emb "Clark Fruit Jar Cleve-
land" **48.00**
Conserve, clear, qt, handmade, glass
lid, wire bail **7.50**
Cunningham & Co, Pittsburgh, sapphire
blue, applied rim lip, iron pontil, orig
cork closure, qt, c1860 . . . . **3,600.00**
Dexter, aqua, ground lip glass insert and
screw band, patd Aug 8th 1865 . . . **35.00**
Doolittle, aqua, qt, handmade, glass lid,
emb "Doolittle The Self Sealer" . . . **60.00**
Double Safety, clear, pt, machine made,
glass lid, wire bail **4.00**
Economy, amber, pt, metal lid, spring
clip **5.00**
Electric, aqua, circle with script writing,
ground lip, wide mouth **12.00**
Empire, aqua, qt, handmade, stopper
neck, name emb in arch **215.00**
F & J Bodine, Philada, aqua, ground,
7¼" h, 1865–70 . . . . **100.00**
Flickinger, aqua, qt, handmade, glass
lid, wire bail **18.00**
Forster Jar, clear, smooth lip, glass in-
sert and screw band **8.00**
G & D, aqua, ground lip, metal push-
down lid **15.00**
Good House Keepers, clear, 2 qt, ma-
chine made, zinc lid **2.00**
H & R, light green, groove ring wax
sealer, pressed laid-on ring **10.00**
Hamilton, clear, qt, handmade, glass lid,
metal clip **45.00**
Hazel Atlas E Z Seal, clear, smooth lip **10.00**
Hoosier, aqua, qt, handmade, threaded
glass lid, emb "Hoosier Jar" **315.00**
Improved Gem, L G Co reverse, aqua,
ground lip, glass insert and screw
band **400.00**
Independent, aqua, qt, handmade,
glass screw lid **40.00**
J. D. Willoughby, blown glass, bulbous,
inverted base, iron pontil, rolled over
rim, 6¾" h **145.00**
Kerr
Economy, clear, smooth lip **4.00**
Self Sealing, Trademark Reg Pat-
ented Mason
Light green, smooth lip, Mason
beaded neck seal, 2 pc lid **6.00**
Sky blue, pt, smooth lip, 2 pc lid **25.00**
Lafayette, aqua, script **90.00**
Lyon Jar, clear, pat Apr 10 1900 . . . . . **2.00**
Mason
Aqua, ground lip, X patent Nov 30th
1858 . . . . **15.00**
Green, qt, hand made, zinc lid, emb
"S Mason's Patent 1858" **4.50**

McDonald Perfect Seal, clear, pt, machine made, glass lid, wire bail, emb
"McDonald Perfect Seal" **5.00**
Myers Pat'd 1869 Test Jar, aqua,
ground lip, metal lid with attached
brass clamp, clamp marked "P M Hin-
man Pat Apl For" **150.00**
Ohio, clear, 2 qt, handmade, zinc lid,
emb "Ohio Quality Mason" **12.00**
Pine Deluxe Jar, clear, pt, machine
made, glass lid, wire bail, emb **5.00**
Regal, clear, qt, handmade, glass lid,
emb "Regal" in oval **3.00**
S. B. Dewey Jr/Rochester/NY, aqua,
smooth base, whittle marked, orig
rusted stopper, America, c1870 . . . . **300.00**
Sure, aqua, qt, handmade, glass lid,
spring wire clip, emb **220.00**
Tropical, clear, qt, machine made, zinc
lid, name emb in script **2.75**
Winslow Jar, aqua, qt, handmade, glass
lid, wire clip, emb **45.00**
Yeoman's Fruit Bottle, aqua, wax cork
closure **45.00**

FRY GLASS

History: The H. C. Fry Glass Co. of Rochester,
Pennsylvania, began operating in 1901 and continued until 1933. Their first products were brilliant
period cut glass. They later produced depression
tablewares. In 1922 they patented heat resisting
ovenware in an opalescent color. This "Pearl Oven
Glass" was produced in a variety of oven and table
pieces including casseroles, meat trays, pie and
cake pans, etc. Most of these pieces are marked
"Fry" with model numbers and sizes.

Fry's beautiful art line, Foval, was produced only
in 1926-27. It is pearly opalescent, with jade green
or delft blue trim. It is rarely signed, except for
occasional silver overlay pieces marked "Rockwell." Foval is always evenly opalescent, never
striped like Fenton's opalescent line.

Reference: Fry Glass Society, *Collector's Encyclopedia of Fry Glass,* Collector Books, 1989.

Collectors' Club: H. C. Fry Glass Society, P.O.
Box 41, Beaver, PA 15009.

Reproduction Alert: In the 1970s, reproductions of Foval were made in abundance in Murano,
Italy. These pieces, including candlesticks, toothpicks, etc., have teal blue transparent trim.

Bean Pot, Ovenware, 1 qt **30.00**
Bouillon Cup and Saucer, Foval, two
Delft handles **85.00**
Candleholder, azure blue **15.00**
Compote, 9" d, jade stem **350.00**
Creamer and Sugar, 3½" h creamer,
2½" h sugar, Foval, Delft blue trim
and handles, pedestal base **325.00**

Lemonade Tumbler, green handle, 5¼"
h, $75.00.

Cup and Saucer, Foval
  Foval handle 50.00
  Jade handle 60.00
Egg Cup, jade base 135.00
Hat, 2⅛" h, opaque white, red trim ... 45.00
Jack In The Pulpit, 10½" h, 3½" w top,
  Foval, jade green trim 785.00
Lemonade, Foval, jade handle
  Flat 90.00
  Footed 75.00
Parfait, 6½" h, Delft stem 175.00
Pie Plate, Ovenware, marked "Kidi-
  bake" 20.00
Pitcher, 9¼" h, Diamond Optic, chrome
  green, ground pontil 85.00
Plate
  7½" d, jade, silver overlay 175.00
  8½" d
    Delft 135.00
    Foval, jade trim 85.00
  10" d, Pearlware, banded sterling sil-
    ver floral pattern 85.00
Platter, Ovenware, etched thistle dec 30.00
Punch Cup, clear, crackle finish, Delft
  blue handle 35.00
Reamer
  Opalescent 25.00
  Pink 40.00
Sherbet, 4¼" d, jade stem 100.00
Tea Set, Foval, 6½" h cov teapot,
  creamer, and sugar bowl, white pearl
  opal, green jade opaline handles,
  spout, and finial 400.00
Teacup and Saucer, azure blue 20.00
Teapot, Foval, blue handle, spout, and
  finial, three cup, #2001 .... 325.00
Toothpick Holder, Foval, Delft blue han-
  dle 80.00
Trivet, Ovenware 12.00
Vase
  9" h, Foval, trumpet shape, jade base 375.00
  10¼" h, black 35.00
Wine, 5" h, Foval 140.00

FULPER POTTERY

History: The American Pottery Company of Flemington, New Jersey, made pottery jugs and hou-
sewares from the early 1800s. They made Fulper
Art Pottery from approximately 1910 to 1930.

Their first line of art pottery was called Vasekraft.
The shapes were primarily either rigid and controlled, being influenced by the arts and crafts
movement, or of Chinese influence. Equal concern
was given to the glazes which showed an incredible diversity.

Pieces made between 1910 and 1920 were of
the best quality, because less emphasis was put
on production output. Almost all pieces are
molded.

Reference: Robert Blassberg, *Fulper Art Pottery: An Aesthetic Appreciation,* Art Lithographers,
1979.

Bowl, 13" d, low form, lobed inverted
  rim, mixed blue glaze, ink stamp mark 350.00
Coffee Set, 7¼" h coffeepot, creamer,
  sugar, cylindrical, vertical lapped dec,
  crystalline green and brown glaze,
  stamped mark 550.00
Console Set, 16" d ribbed bowl, pr
  matching candlesticks, deep rose
  matte, turquoise trim, scalloped rim . 250.00
Flower Bowl, 7¼" h, 10½" d shallow
  bowl, blue, gold, and brown flambe
  glaze on mustard ground, gray and
  yellow int., supported by three effigy
  figures, stepped disc base, stamped
  vertical mark 400.00
Lamp, table, earthenware and leaded
  glass
  14" h, truncated conical shade with
    green and yellow glass geometric
    frieze, light and dark brown glaze,
    cylindrical shaft, conical disc foot,
    ink stamped "Fulper 106" 4,200.00
  21½" h, 17" d shade, mushroom
    shape, heraldic form colored glass
    inserts in shade, matte blue glaze,
    printed logo and number "1" 16,500.00
Vase
  9⅜" h, beehive, heavy crystalline
    aqua to green glaze, imp "Fulper"
    and "88L" 350.00
  11¼" h, flaring cylinder, molded styl-
    ized geometric dec, copper crystal-

Vase, dark olive matte glaze, three feet, stamped mark, 4¾″ d, 4¾″ h, $100.00.

line glaze, raised signature "Fulper" 4,625.00

11½″ h, swollen tapering base, rolled up and narrow neck, matte glaze shaded green to rose, incised vertical mark, partial paper label, chips on base from kiln pull, c1918 .... 400.00

12¼″ h

Exaggerated baluster, brown–black drip glaze, blue ground, molded mark 3,850.00

Ovoid, two ring handles, dark crystalline brown to striated tan glaze, printed mark 550.00

13⅜″ h, cylindrical, triangular cut out motif, four projecting buttresses, matte mocha glaze, partial paper label 2,200.00

13½″ h, cylindrical, heavy periwinkle glaze, metallic gray drips, printed marks 265.00

15″ h, classical urn form, two scrolling handles at shoulder, high crystalline tortoiseshell brown, stamped mark 375.00

29⅛″ h, tapering cylindrical, swollen shoulder, wide mouth, short neck, mottled dark on light green glaze, incised vertical mark, retailer's paper label, base chips from kiln pull, hairline on base 325.00

FURNITURE

History: Two major currents dominate the American furniture marketplace—furniture made in Great Britain and furniture made in the United States. American buyers continue to show a strong prejudice for objects manufactured in the United States. They will pay a premium for such pieces and accept them above technically superior and more aesthetic English examples.

Until the last half of the 19th century formal American styles were dictated by English examples and design books. Regional furniture, such as the Hudson River Valley [Dutch] and the Pennsylvania German styles, did develop. A less formal furniture, often designated as the "country" or vernacular style, developed throughout the 19th and early 20th centuries. These country pieces deviated from the accepted formal styles and have a genre charm that many collectors find irresistible.

America did contribute a number of unique decorative elements to English styles. The American Federal period is a reaction to the English Hepplewhite period. American designers created furniture which influenced, rather than reacted, to world taste in the Gothic Revival style, Arts and Craft Furniture, Art Deco, and Modern International movement.

FURNITURE STYLES [APPROX. DATES]

William and Mary	**1690–1730**
Queen Anne.................	**1720–1760**
Chippendale................	**1755–1790**
Federal [Hepplewhite]	**1790–1815**
Sheraton	**1790–1810**
Empire [Classical]...........	**1805–1830**
Victorian	
French Restauration.........	**1830–1850**
Gothic Revival............	**1840–1860**
Rococo Revival	**1845–1870**
Elizabethan	**1850–1915**
Louis XIV	**1850–1914**
Naturalistic	**1850–1914**
Renaissance Revival	**1850–1880**
Neo-Greek	**1855–1885**
Eastlake	**1870–1890**
Art Furniture	**1880–1914**
Arts and Crafts	**1895–1915**
Art Nouveau................	**1896–1914**
Art Deco..................	**1920–1945**
International Movement	**1940–Present**

In the 1988 auction season, a Newport, Rhode Island, Chippendale desk–bookcase sold for 12.1 million dollars. Many other pieces broke the half million dollar barrier.

Country pieces, with the exception of Windsor chairs, seem to have stabilized and even dropped off slightly in value. The country-designer-look no longer enjoys the popularity it did during the American Bicentennial period.

Furniture is one of the few antiques fields where regional preferences are a factor in pricing. Victorian furniture is popular in New Orleans, and unpopular in New England. Oak is in demand in the Northwest, not so much in the Middle Atlantic states.

Prices vary considerably on furniture. Shop around. Furniture is plentiful unless you are after a truly rare example. Examine all pieces thoroughly. Too many furniture pieces are bought on impulse. Turn furniture upside down; take it apart. The amount of repairs and restoration to a piece has a strong influence on price. Make certain you know about all repairs and changes before buying.

Beware of the large number of reproductions. During the twenty-five years following the American Centennial of 1876, there was a great revival in copying furniture styles and manufacturing techniques of earlier eras. These centennial pieces now are over one hundred years old. They confuse many dealers and collectors.

The prices listed below are "average" prices. They are only a guide. High and low prices are given to show market range.

References: Joseph T. Butler, *Field Guide To American Furniture,* Facts on File Publications, 1985; E & R Dubrow *Furniture, Made In America, 1875–1905,* Schiffer Publishing, Ltd., 1982; Eileen and Richard Dubrow, *American Furniture of the 19th Century, 1840–1880,* Schiffer Publishing, Ltd., 1983; Rachael Feild, *Macdonald Guide To Buying Antique Furniture,* Wallace-Homestead, 1989; Benno M. Forman, *American Seating Furniture, 1630–1730,* Winterthur Museum, W. W. Norton & Company, 1988; Don Fredgant, *American Manufactured Furniture,* Schiffer Publishing, Ltd., 1988; *Furniture Dealers' Reference Book, Zone 3, 1928–29,* reprint by Schiffer Publishing, Ltd., 1988; Phillipe Garner, *Twentieth-Century Furniture,* Van Nostrand Reinhold, 1980; Myrna Kaye, *Fake, Fraud, Or Genuine, Identifying Authentic American Antique Furniture,* New York Graphic Society Book, 1987; William C. Ketchum, Jr., *Furniture, Volume 2: Chests, Cupboards, Desks, & Other Pieces,* Knopf Collectors' Guides To American Antiques, Alfred A. Knopf, 1982; Kathryn McNerney, *Pine Furniture, Our American Heritage,* Collector Books, 1989; Kathryn McNerney, *Victorian Furniture,* Collector Books, 1981, values updated 1988; Milo M. Naeve, *Identifying American Furniture: A Pictorial Guide To Styles and Terms, Colonial to Contemporary, Second Edition,* American Association for State and Local History, 1989; Don & Carol Raycraft, *Collector's Guide To Country Furniture, Book II,* Collector Books, 1988; Charles Santore, *The Windsor Style in America, Volume II,* Running Press Book Publishers, 1987; Tim Scott, *Fine Wicker Furniture, 1870–1930,* Schiffer Publishing, 1990; Marvin D. Schwartz, *Furniture: Volume 1: Chairs, Tables, Sofas & Beds,* Knopf Collector's Guides To American Antiques, Alfred A. Knopf, 1982; Robert W. and Harriett Swedberg, *American Oak Furniture, Style and Prices, Book II,* Wallace-Homestead, 1984; — *Country Furniture and Accessories with Prices, Book 1,* 1983, *Book II,* 1984, Wallace-Homestead; —, *Collector's Encyclopedia of American Furniture,* Collector Books, 1990; — *Country Pine Furniture,* Wallace-Homestead, 1983; —*Furniture of the Depression Era,* Collector Books, 1987; —*Victorian Furniture, Book I,* 1976, *Book II,* 1983, *Book III,* 1985, Wallace-Homestead; —*Wicker Furniture,* Wallace-Homestead, 1983; Gerald W. R. Ward, *American Case Furniture,* Yale University Art Gallery, 1988; Derita Coleman Williams and Nathan Harsh, *The Art and Mystery of Tennessee Furni-*

ture, Tennessee Historical Society, 1988; Lyndon C. Viel, *Antique Ethnic Furniture,* Wallace-Homestead, 1983.

There are hundreds of specialized books on individual furniture forms and styles. Two examples of note are: Monroe H. Fabian, *The Pennsylvania-German Decorated Chest,* Universe Books, 1978, and Charles Santore, *The Windsor Style In America, 1730–1830,* Running Press, 1981.

Additional Listings: Arts and Craft Movement, Art Deco, Art Nouveau, Children's Nursery Items, Orientalia, Shaker Items, and Stickley.

Bed, Victorian, walnut, arched headboard, 88″ h, $1,250.00.

BEDS

Arts and Crafts, Gustav Stickley, double, Model No. 923, c1909, oak, tapered posts and five wide slats across head and foot boards, red decal, 59″ w, 78″ l, 42½″ h **5,000.00**

Baroque, Italian, simulated marble, high scrolling headboard dec in pastiglia with vacant cartouches and foliage, carved scrolled feet, painted, and marbleized in greens and blues, losses to paint and gilt, 45¾″ w, 84″ h, pr **3,575.00**

Chippendale, tall post, curly maple, turned posts, scrolled headboard with poplar panel, orig side rails, old mellow refinishing, minor repairs to posts, 80″ h, 60 x 72″ mattress **3,000.00**

Chippendale Style, mahogany, four posters, carved, Drexel, 65″ w, 86½″ l, 67½″ h **700.00**

Classical, mid–Atlantic states, c1820, post, tall, spiral carved foot posts with classical acanthus leaves and beading above dies and turned feet, red painted head posts flank similarly painted scrolled headboard, orig rails with minor additions, tester missing, 55⅞″ w, 78¼″ l, 81¾″ h **2,400.00**

Directorie, parcel ebonized, painted gray, over scrolled rect headboard and footboard, baluster turned reeded colonettes, paneled side rails, turned tapering feet, horn casters, 51″ w, 70½″ l, 48″ h **1,320.00**

Empire, American
  Birch, high poster, shaped headboard, rope and acanthus carved turned posts, orig rope rails, arched canopy frame, 66¾″ h, 55 x 72″ mattress **1,500.00**
  Mahogany, sleigh, tiger maple, scrolling headboard and footboard **1,000.00**

Federal, pencil post, walnut, scalloped head and footboards, orig rails and canopy frame, 76½″ h, 46½ x 65″ mattress **4,100.00**

George III, four poster
  Mahogany, stop fluted turned tapering foot posts, detachable cartouche shaped knee brackets with carved scrolling foliage and pendant blossoms, hairy paw feet and casters, 39½″ w, 82¼″ l, 93″ h **2,650.00**
  Walnut, carved, brass mounted, circular tapered head posts, shaped mahogany headboard, reeded and acanthus carved foot posts, ring turned feet, casters, 91½″ h **10,000.00**

Queen Anne, PA, early 19th C, low poster, turned and painted pine, head and foot posts with flattened ball finials, shaped head and footboards, tapered feet, orig rope rails, orig green paint, 48½″ w, 73¼″ h **3,500.00**

Rope
  Curly Maple, light natural refinishing, replaced side rails, 54½″ h, 47 x 74″ mattress **1,500.00**
  Painted, American, late 18th or early 19th C, red paint, cylinder turned short headposts, compressed ball turned finials, center triangular arched headboard, tapering turned legs, conforming footposts, molded rails, 73½″ l, 48″ w, 31″ h **6,600.00**
  Poplar, hired man's, old red paint, turned posts, peaked head and footboards, orig rails, minor wear and damage, 25½″ h, 39½ x 69″ mattress **500.00**

Poplar and Curly Maple, poplar headboard and rails, turned curly maple posts, trumpet shaped finials, orig rails, one finial broken and reattached, 54″ h, 52 x 70″ mattress **600.00**

Walnut, PA, late 18th or early 19th C, lowpost, cylindrical turned short headposts, ball turned finials, center arched headboard, turned tapering legs, conforming footposts and footboard, rails, 73¾″ l, 49⅛″ w, 31″ h, later hardware added to support box spring **700.00**

Sheraton, American, tester, cherry, turned posts and foot rail, shaped headboard, orig canopy **1,250.00**

Victorian
  Brass, c1900, straight top rail, curved corners, ring shaped capitals, cast iron side rails, 61″ h, 55 x 94″ mattress **1,200.00**
  Cottage, c1890, bamboo style, maple and bird's eye maple **1,000.00**

Bench, settle, American or English, late 17th C or early 18th C, pine, oak, paneled front, sides, back, lift top seat, 30″ w, $850.00.

BENCHES

Arts and Crafts, American
  Settle, Model No. 265, oak, sixteen vertical slat back, slat sides, leather upholstered seat cushion, white L & J G Stickley decal mark, 75½″ l, 31″ d, 34″ h **800.00**
  Window, Limbert, Grand Rapids, MI,

1907, No. 243, oak, canted flat sides with four sq cut outs each centering seat, leather cushion, branded mark, dark color, shellac finish, 24″ w, 15½″ d, 24″ h **4,500.00**

Baroque Style, hall, walnut, pierced scrolled crest, scrolled arms, hinged seat, 47″ w, 15½″ d, 35¾″ h **300.00**

Chippendale, Philadelphia, settle, orig red and black graining, yellow and green striping and floral dec, turned legs, worn orig rush seat, scrolled arms, slat back, 48″ l **900.00**

Chippendale Style, vanity, walnut, needlepoint seat, refinished, 33″ l, 15″ h **450.00**

Country, American, primitive
Cobbler's, pine, varnished, replaced leather set, replaced case of twelve drawers, under slung drawer missing, fourteen cobbler's tools, 49″ l **600.00**

Settle, pine, dark brown repaint, cut out ends, hinged seat, horizontal board back, top board broken and repaired, 60″, 57″ h **750.00**

Water, pine, old blue and green paint, cut out ends, base shelf, crest, 43 x 18″, 32¼″ h **225.00**

Empire, settle, orig pale green paint, brown and black striping, free hand green and black foliage dec, brown vinegar graining seat, 79¾″ l **2,300.00**

Federal, c1810, window, mahogany, upholstered seat and rolled arms, sq tapering legs, sq H stretchers, refinished, minor repair to one leg, 39½″ l, 16″ w, 29″ h **900.00**

George III, mid 18th C, window, mahogany, rect seat, scrolling arms, later velvet cov, straight legs, blind fret carved, H stretcher, 38″ l, pr **4,250.00**

Georgian, English, settle, country, pine, curved, vertical panels on base and back, cut out ends, hinged seat, high back, worn finish, 63 x 55½″ **600.00**

Louis XV Style, window, fruitwood, scrolled voluted arms, cabriole legs, pale gray and dusty rose striped silk upholstery, 41½″ l **225.00**

Regency, first half 19th C, mahogany, oblong padded top, curule supports, turned stretcher, later green velvet cov, 34″ l **1,800.00**

Windsor, kneeling, country, splayed, bamboo turned legs, reeded edge top, gray over olive green and red paint, 6¾ x 36¾″, 6″ h **325.00**

BENTWOOD

In 1856, Michael Thonet of Vienna perfected the process of bending wood using steam. Shortly after, Bentwood furniture became popular. Other manufacturers of Bentwood furniture were Jacob and Joseph Kohn; Philip Strobel and Son; Sheboygan Chair Co,; and Tidoute Chair Co. Bentwood furniture is still being produced today by the Thonet firm and others.

Box
6¼″ h, round, old green repaint **135.00**

20½″ l, pine, dec, two finger construction, laced lid, handle, sliding wooden bolt, carved scroll ears, orig red and black graining, green semi–circular edging, yellow script name and 1848 . . . . **500.00**

Carrier, 9¼″ d, round, lid, wire bale and wooden handle, orig salmon red paint **300.00**

Chair
Austrian, Vienna Secession Style, c1910, side, back splat with three circular perforations, three slender spindles, painted black, set of 8 . . **5,000.00**

Hoffman, Josef, side, three horizontal turned wood slat back, carved cornice, five turned wood vertical rods, solid seat, stencil dec on four straight legs, paper label, 36″ h . . **300.00**

Thonet, arm, c1935, lacquered, pine frame, upholstered back and seat, 43″ h **400.00**

Rocker
Kohn, J & J, caned seat and back, bentwood loop arms, c1870, 44½″ h **1,320.00**

Thonet, arched twined top rail, cut velvet fabric fitted back, armrests, and seat, elaborate scrolling frame, curved runners, 53″ l **700.00**

Table, Josef Hoffman, c1905, circular top, wood spheres dec below rim, 21¼″ h **400.00**

BLANKET CHESTS

Chippendale, American, c1780
Curly maple, two drawers, lift top, refinished, replaced hardware, 39″ l, 19¼″ d, 41″ h **250.00**

Blanket Chest, champor, dovetailed, brass hardware, 42½″ l, 21½″ h, $250.00.

Walnut, pine and poplar secondary wood, dovetailed case, three dovetailed drawers, apron drop, ogee feet, wrought iron hinges and till, old finish, replaced brasses, minor damage, two board top with minor warp and separation at seam, 50¾" w, 22½" d, 35½" h **2,900.00**

Federal, country, inlaid walnut, dovetailed case, two overlapping dovetailed drawers, dovetailed bracket feet, int. till, repairs, old replacements, refinished, 49¾" w, 18¾" d, 25½" h **1,000.00**

Grain Painted, early 19th C

American, six board chest, pine, old red repaint, one dovetailed overlapping drawer, lift lid with till, scroll cut feet, one foot chipped, replaced whittled pulls on drawer, replaced wing bat brass escutcheons, 37¾" l, 17¾" d, 33½" h **500.00**

New England

Pine, six board, putty painted geometric design, burnt umber on yellow ochre, 41½" l, 16" d, 32¼" h **2,000.00**

Single long base drawer, yellow ochre and burnt umber graining, cov till, replaced brass pulls, 43¾" l, 22" d, 33" h **1,500.00**

New York, ochre and burnt umber graining to simulate mahogany, painted stringing and cross banded veneer in outline, single long base drawer, old brasses, very minor blemishes on top, 45¼" l, 19⅜" d, 34¾" h **900.00**

New York State, pine, six boards, vinegar painted with yellow ochre and burnt umber, minor imperfections, 50½" l, 21½" d, 29⅛" h . . . **1,900.00**

Ohio, Sugarcreek, poplar, worn red, painted olive brown and yellow floral and heart dec, dovetailed, cut out heart apron, int. drawer, bracket feet, repaired, 37½" l, 17½" d, 23½" h **850.00**

Hepplewhite, country, Pennsylvania, pine, orig red paint, grain traces, three dovetailed drawers and case, orig locks, wrought iron strap hinges, brass escutcheons, stenciled initials, "W H G," French feet, 50" l, 23" d, 29¼" h **2,200.00**

Sheraton, country

Pine and poplar, orig red paint, molded edge top, paneled front and ends, sq corner posts, mortised and pinned frame, scalloped apron, turned feet, 44" l, 19½" d, 25½" h **675.00**

Walnut, molded edge lid and till, paneled sides and ends, sq corner posts, turned feet, refinished, 37½" l, 17" d, 21½" h **400.00**

BOOK CASES

Arts and Crafts, American

Lifetime, Grand Rapids, MI, c1912, rect top, three doors each with eight panes, iron pulls, corner posts with through tenons, sgd metal tag, 61⅜" w, 13" d, 49¼" h **4,000.00**

Stickley, L & J G

Model No. 645, oak, three int. shelves, glass paned doors, L & J G Stickley mark, 49" w, 12" d, 55" h **3,200.00**

Model No. 647, c1906, oak, gallery top, exposed key tenons over three doors with twelve panes each, copper swing pulls, straight apron, stenciled number on back, splits in back, metal brace under front, minor nicks, 69¼" w, 12" d, 55" h **5,500.00**

Stickley, Gustav, Model No. 716, c1905, gallery top, two doors with eight panes, V swing pulls, red decal, 42½" w, 13¼" d, 56½" h **4,000.00**

Chippendale

Maryland or Philadelphia, 1765–85, mahogany, three sections, upper: dentil molded triangular pediment, plinth with contemporary bust of William Shakespeare, plain veneered frieze, center: bookcase with double glazed cupboard doors, astragal mullions, Chinoisere pattern, molded base, lower: chest with short thumb molded central drawer flanked by two similar box drawers, two graduated long drawers flanked by fluted quarter columns, ogee bracket feet, 44¾" w, 25¼" d, 106¼" h **16,500.00**

New England, 1770–1800, cherry, two sections, upper: bookcase with ogival molded cornice, double diamond lattice pattern glazed doors, eight adjustable int. shelves, lower: double paneled cupboard doors, compartment and shelved int., two sliding drawers, molded base, minor restoration, 65½" w, 18½" d, 98¾" h **8,800.00**

Edwardian, English

Inlaid, stepped rect breakfront molded cornice, applied dentils, frieze inlaid with drapery, two glazed mullioned doors, flanked by glazed mullioned doors, central fall front secretary drawer over three graduated drawers, flanked by two short drawers over door inlaid with foliate urns, shaped bracket feet, 88" w, 22" d, 86" h **8,000.00**

Painted, arched rect superstructure, center painted medallion and foliate garlands, three graduated shelves, mirrored panels back, lower case with two doors, polychromed foliate swags suspending trophies, sq tapering legs **5,250.00**

Empire, American, mahogany, rect top, cushion molded frieze, three glazed doors enclosing shelves with three quarter columns, shaped feet, electrified, 78" w, 17½" d, 58½" h **525.00**

George I, walnut, projecting molded cornice, glazed doors, shelf int., two short and two long feather banded drawers, bracket feet, 43¾" w, 18¼" d, 74½" h **8,500.00**

George III, third quarter, 18th C, breakfront, mahogany, three sections, upper: dentil molded triangular pediment, urn finial, center: bookcase with double glazed cupboard doors, astragal mullions, Chinoisere pattern, three adjustable shelves, flanked by similar set back glazed cupboard doors, lower: case with two solid cupboard doors, astragal bead molded panel, hollow corners, flanked by similar set back single cupboard doors, molded base, 78" w, 105" h **24,200.00**

Georgian Style, glazed doors, dark gray, gold pressed molding, broken arch pediment, light blue int., 32" w, 11" d, 85" h **450.00**

Regency Style, breakfront, japanned, black, rect molded cornice, outset ends, two glazed mullioned doors flanked by two similar doors, conforming plinth, overall Oriental court scenes dec, 86" w, 19½" d, 88" h . . **3,500.00**

Victorian, walnut, two drawers, two glazed paned doors, orig glass and brasses, 43" w, 15" d, 74½" h **500.00**

BOXES

Band Box, wallpaper cover, American
14½" l, 11" h, squirrel pattern on top, blue, pink, green, and brown floral motif on sides, c1835, wear **950.00**

18¾" l, 12⅛" h, two dogs on top, sides cov with "Walking Beam Side Wheeler" pattern, labeled "Joseph S Tillinghast Band Box Manufacturer and dealer in French and American Paper Hangings, one door west of the Post–Office, Union Street, New Bedford," MA, c1832, minor imperfections, old repairs . . **950.00**

Box, bride's, bentwood, 22" l, 14¾" w, $200.00.

Bible, English, oak, slant top, butterfly hinge, carved foliate dec and date "1674," 28½" w, 21⅓" d, 18¾" h . . . **1,300.00**

Candle Box, PA, early 19th C, painted pine, rect, sliding lid, carved finger hold, painted stylized basket of blossoms and leaves, red, green, and yellow, black ground, 10¼" l, 5½" d, 5¼" h **1,760.00**

Cutlery, PA, mid 19th C, painted pine, rect, molded edge, two sliding lids with finger holds, hand hold, top and sides painted deep yellow, green shaped borders, red outlines, 13¼" l, 10" d, 8¼" h **2,420.00**

Desk

Country, poplar, dovetailed case, slant top lid, scrolled gallery, old dark finish over earlier red, edge damage, holes and deterioration in bottom board, 24¾" w, 15¼" d, 10½" h **90.00**

New England, early 19th C, grain painted, pine, hinged slope lid, three compartments above three drawers, imperfections, 15½" l, 11" d, 7¾" h **750.00**

Document

American, beech, orig polychrome floral dec, bright colors, worm holes, one wooden hinge pin restored, 11¾" l **1,150.00**

American, c1800, paint dec, hinged lid, ivory escutcheon, top dec with houses and rolling landscape, front and side panels dec with marine and pastoral scenes, darkened, minor wear, and abrasions, 9" l, 5½" h **1,600.00**

Queen Anne, English, c1720–40, shagreen, elongated rect, sloping hinged top, silvered bail handle, interlaced and pierced backplate, deep compartment, four silvered ball and claw feet, minor tears to cov, 12¾" l, 5½" d, 8⅜" h **1,450.00**

Dome Top

American, pine, orig salmon paint, yellow and black striping, orig polychrome floral dec on lid and ends, crossed peacock feathers on front, dovetailed, iron lock and hasp, wear and age cracks in top, 28" l **700.00**

Pennsylvania, Lancaster County, c1800, Bucher, painted pine, rect, domed hinged lid, flowing red and yellow feathery tulips and leaves, cream—yellow striping, black ground, orig tin hinges, 6¼" l, 2¾" h **1,760.00**

Goody, Arts and Crafts, Roycroft, c1910, mahogany, rect, imp logo on lid, brass hinges, 22⅞" l, 12¼" w, 9½" h **400.00**

Hat, French, 19th C, metal, chicken dec on front, broken leather strap, 13" l **350.00**

Ice Fishing Box, American, 20th C, painted and dec, yellow heightened green box, naturalistic colored fish, sgd "Fleck" minor wear, 42" l, 13½" w, 14" h **850.00**

Knife, PA, 19th C, painted pine, rect, deep sided, central divider, pierced heart shaped handhold, painted green, black, and yellow striping, 12½" l, 10" h **4,675.00**

Salt, primitive, pine, lollipop crest, layers of flaking paint, 12¾" h **75.00**

Shaving, attributed to German Settlement of Waldoboro, ME, late 18th C, chip carved white birch, long rect, sliding lid carved with diamond, heart, pinwheel, and pot of flowers, sawtooth borders, carved finger holds, side carved with large compass, star, double heart, and pinwheel, int. with two small compartments, curved handle, 11½" l **1,000.00**

Storage, cov, bentwood
  10" d, round, old worn patina **50.00**
  14" l, oval, pine, orig orange paint, polychrome tulips, laced seams, age cracks, re–nailed repairs **250.00**

Wall, American, 19th C
  Pierced and carved side floral medallions, front star devices, painted yellow, red paint highlights, age cracks and losses, 10⅝" w, 12" h **2,500.00**
  Primitive, poplar, old dark patina, 24 pigeonholes, 18½" w, 27" h **100.00**

Writing, George III Style, inlaid mahogany, lift lid, hinged writing surface, fitted int., 15" l, 7½" w, 8¼" h **500.00**

CABINETS

Bar, Art Deco, walnut, sarcophagus form, two doors, sq top with drop front cabinet on left, mirrored bar, small drawer on right between two open bays, 48" w, 21" d, 54½" h **450.00**

China
  Arts and Crafts
    Lifetime Co, 1912, oak, rect top cut around corner posts, two plain glass doors, and sides, adjustable shelves, 43" w, 14½" d, 57" h **650.00**
    Stickley, L & J G, Model No. 746, c1912, oak, overhanging top, two doors, six smaller panes above single glass panels, adjustable shelves, arched toe board, 44" w, 16¼" d, 62" h **3,500.00**
    Stickley Bros, Grand Rapids, MI, c1912, rect top, two doors with gently arched divider, top int. fitted with mirror, branded mark, 46" w, 14½" d, 62¼" h **850.00**

Cabinet, store, Belding Bros & Co, oak, 40" w, 79" h, $2,500.00.

Victorian, Biedermeier, highly figured and burled olive wood veneer, ebonized trim, classical style details, architectural cornice, single glass door, two dovetailed drawers, refinished, 52" w, 32" d, 58" h ... **850.00**

Corner, Continental, oak, carved, raised paneled door, shelf int., shaped apron and feet, 29½" w, 17" d, 37" h **900.00**

Demilune, Georgian Style, shaped back splash, molded edge top, frieze drawer, two doors, acanthus carved cabriole legs, claw and flattened ball feet, painted white, 36" h, 46" w, 23" d **75.00**

Display
   Art Nouveau, French, c1900, carved mahogany, arched crest, carved tendrils and leaf tip lunettes, open platform with pierced undulating foliate frame work, poppy carved stiles, rect beveled and mirrored glass door, short cabriole legs with tendril pierced spandrels, wired for int. lighting, 35¼" w, 98" h **2,750.00**
   Rococo, South German, 18th C, walnut, scrolling heavily molded open pediment, center gilded bronze cartouche plate, two arched doors of fielded panels, marquetry figures of court ladies, basal molded and conforming stand with shaped apron, cabriole legs, 46" w, 19½" d, 71½" h **4,500.00**
   Dressing, George I, c1710, gentleman's, burl walnut, double dome top with two inset beveled mirrored doors fitted with shelves and drawers, brush slide and four graduated feather banded drawers in base, bracket feet, 42½" w, 22½" d, 79½" h **19,000.00**
   Filing, American, c1910, golden oak, plain vertical stack, five drawers, orig brass nameplates and pulls **500.00**
   Kitchen, McDougall, Hoosier type, c1900, oak, two parts, three small cupboard doors with inset glass panels over pr of cupboard doors, white graniteware work surface, inset bread board, base with three graduated drawers, cupboard door, orig hardware and packing label, refinished **600.00**
   Medicine, Victorian, hanging, corner, walnut, applied oak beading, shaped gallery, mirror, single door, one int. shelf, 19" h **200.00**
   Smoking, Arts and Crafts, English, sq top, imp for circular tray, single door, copper strap hinges and lock, fitted int., four splayed legs, old finish, tray missing, 26" h **325.00**
   Vitrine
      Arts and Crafts, K Hpanderez Hollandia, c1910, ebony inlaid oak, arched recessed backboard, central pr of beveled glass cupboard doors over long door, int. shelves, open shelves, drawers, pr of leaded glass cupboard doors, sq legs, stamped maker's mark, 42½" w, 72" h **2,475.00**
      Louis XV Style, slant front, hinged rect lift top, shaped shelf int., carved apron with shell pendant center, cabriole legs with putti dec

at top, scrolled feet, electrified, 57½" w, 29" d, 46" h **1,100.00**
Louis Philippe, Continental, ormolu mounted ebony, rect cove molded top, two glazed paneled doors, shaped apron with scrolling foliage, paneled legs, 30" w, 13" d, 40½" h, pr **1,000.00**
Regency Style, English, japanned, black, molded D shaped top, shaped crest, conforming case, glazed door, cabriole legs, ball and claw feet, Oriental court scenes dec, 39½" w, 18" d, 55½" h **800.00**

CANDLE SHIELDS

Chippendale
   American, 1760–65, carved mahogany, cylindrical turned pole, adjustable cartouche shaped screen, molded and carved frame, clustered column pedestal with leafage carved ball, tripod scrolled legs carved with leafage and trailing pendant vines and fruit, scrolled feet with rect molded base, 61¼" h **39,600.00**
   Philadelphia, c1770, attributed by Thomas Affleck, carving attributed to Bernard and Jugiez, carved mahogany, turned cylindrical pole, adjustable screen with intricately carved frame, tapering fluted shaft, acanthus carved baluster, swirl gadroon carved ball, acanthus carved tripod cabriole legs overlaid with trailing husk and vines, carved hairy paw feet, 60" h **66,000.00**
Georgian Style, mahogany, flame veneer frame, petit point floral design, tapered spool turned stem, turned base, minor veneer loss, 17¼" h . . . **200.00**
Regency, first quarter 19th C
   Chinese lacquer panel, adjustable, brass standard, turned beech stand, incurvate triangular plinth, brass capped ball feet, 55" h, pr **5,500.00**
   Giltwood, rect panel with molded border, scrolling frame, shells and ornaments at corners with volutes, trestle base, 33" w, 48" h **1,400.00**

CANDLESTANDS

Centennial, Hepplewhite style, mahogany, elongated pentagonal top, old base repairs to tripod base **265.00**
Chippendale
   American, country, cherry, dished top, turned column, snake feet, tripod base, worn refinishing, 15" d, 26" h **575.00**
   Massachusetts, mahogany, raised

Candlestand, Chippendale, American, mahogany, serpent feet, 18″ d, 27½″ h, $1,500.00.

dish rim, turned column, spiral fluted urn, tripod base, ribbed pad feet, 18″ d, 27″ h **9,000.00**

Pennsylvania, c1800, mahogany, circular dished tilt top, birdcage support, vase form standard, cabriole legs, snake feet, 23½″ d, 29¼″ h **4,400.00**

Decorated, poplar, round top, orig red and black graining, gilt stenciled compote of fruit dec, turned column, turned base with three feet, 17½″ d, 28¼″ h **250.00**

Federal

American, country

Birch, dish form top, turned urn form standard, cabriole legs, snake feet, 17″ d, 26½″ h **1,800.00**

Birch and Maple, rect tilt top, canted corners, birdcage support, vasiform standard, cabriole legs, club feet, 24″ w, 18″ d, 29″ h **450.00**

New England, c1800, mahogany, oval tilt top, ring turned standard, cabriole legs, snake feet, 28½″ h . . . **1,800.00**

Grain Painted, New England, late 18th C, all–over 19th C red paint, black accents, minor imperfections, 16″ w, 15″ d, 24¾″ h **1,200.00**

Hepplewhite

American, c1790, birch, turned pedestal, tapered spider legs, spade feet, refinished, minor repairs to legs, 27¾″ h **900.00**

American, early 19th C, mahogany, tilt top, spider legs **700.00**

Country

Birch, tilt top, rect one board top, cut corners, well turned column, spider legs, high feet, old varnish finish, dark varnish stain on base, 14½″ w, 21¼″ l, 28″ h . . . **700.00**

Maple, shaped top and column,

spider legs, spade feet, refinished **400.00**

New England, maple, screw type adjustment, branded "A W W" on top, orig paint, 32″ h, 18th C **850.00**

Queen Anne, American, mahogany, tilt top, snake feet **1,500.00**

Chair, side, walnut, stretcher base, upholstered slip seat, set of 4, $4,000.00.

CHAIRS

Art Moderne, American

Laminated Cardboard, designed by Frank O. Gehry, c1970, compressed scroll base, canted back, 33½″ h, pr **5,300.00**

Lucite, designed by Lorin Jackson, c1942, shield back, molded bunting motif, trapezoidal upholstered seat, 36¼″ h **3,500.00**

Arts and Crafts, American

Arm, oak

Harden Co, Camden, NY, c1910, slat back, double crest rail over five vertical slats, curved arms over four vertical slats per side, spring cushion, orig paper label, 30″ w, 38¼″ h **500.00**

Phoenix Furniture Co, Grand Rapids, MI, cc1894–1920, designed by David Wolcott Kendall, caned back and seat, wide flat arms . . **1,500.00**

Stickley, Gustav

Five horizontal slat back, spindled sides, decal mark, 33″ w, 37½″ d, 39½″ h **10,450.00**

Fixed back, No. 324, four horizontal back slats, flat arms over five vertical slats, re–upholstered spring cushion seat, sgd "Gustav Stickley," c1904, 29" h **1,500.00**

Child's, Model No. 342, two horizontal slats, orig leather seat, two side stretchers, dark finish, orig paper label **300.00**

Dining

Indiana Hickory Furniture Co, hickory, log and twig construction, woven seats, branded manufacturer's mark, retailers metal tag "Paine Furniture Boston," set of four **800.00**

Stickley Bros, c1907, Model No. 901 1/2, crest rail bowed vertical back slats, upholstered seats, double side stretchers, stenciled number, damage to seats, minor nicks and scratches, 19¾" w, 38¼" h, set of seven **1,100.00**

Stickley, Gustav, c1910, Model Nos. 353 and 353A, designed by Harvey Ellis, three vertical back slats, arched apron, drop in seats with orig red Fabricoid, set of six, four side chairs, two armchairs, 40" h **8,250.00**

Stickley, L & J G, c1910, Model No. 1340, straight crest over three vertical slats, upholstered seats, double side stretchers, unsigned, varnish, nicks, restoration to seat, set of twelve **1,700.00**

Morris

Limbert, Michigan, c1910, four horizontal back slats, slightly shaped arm over five vertical slats, spring cushion seat, branded, replaced pegs, 34" w, 41" d, 36" h **2,800.00**

Morris, William Co., Model No. 498, oak, four horizontal slat back, five vertical slat sides, 33½" w, 37" d, 35" h **1,540.00**

Stickley, Gustav, Model No. 2342, c1902, oak, flat arms, through tenons, five slats down each side, adjustable back, five horizontal slats, 31¼" w, 35½" d, 44½" h **6,400.00**

Stickley, L & J G, oak

Model No. 412, four horizontal slat back, broad shaped arms, leather upholstered cushions, white L & J G Stickley decal mark, 35" w, 38¼" d, 38½" h . **700.00**

Model No. 471, four horizontal slat back, six slat sides, faux leather upholstered cushions, L & J G Stickley red decal mark **1,870.00**

Side

Model No. 338, three back slats with inlaid copper, pewter, and fruitwood sinuous organic forms, drop in rush seat, red Gustav Stickley decal, designed by Harvey Ellis, c1904, 39" h **3,850.00**

Model No. 808, five vertical slat back, leather upholstered seat, white L & J G Stickley decal mark, 38" h **265.00**

Model No. 1350, three horizontal slats, orig upholstered seat, two lower side stretchers, sgd "The Work of L & J G Stickley," 34½" h, set of four **700.00**

Centennial, Queen Anne style, side, worn orig dark finish, minor damage to Spanish feet, two with replaced rush seats, set of six **1,950.00**

Chippendale

Massachusetts, c1770, corner, arm, rounded top rail, pierced baluster splats, columnar supports, sq drop in seat, front cabriole leg with ball and claw foot, three tapered cylindrical legs with cylindrical feet . . . **8,800.00**

Philadelphia, 1760–80

Arm, walnut, serpentine crest, center carved shell, vertically pierced splat flanked by scrolled and shaped arms, scrolled hand grips over C shaped supports, trapezoid slip seat, shaped apron with center carved shell, cabriole legs, shell carved knees, ball and claw feet, small repair on right stile at juncture with arm, 30½" w, 22¼" d, 40½" h **49,500.00**

Side, walnut, crested back, sq legs with corner brackets, joined by stretchers **600.00**

Empire Style, arm, mahogany, rect padded back, padded arms, ormolu mounted classical busts, bowed padded seat, sq tapered legs with brass caps, white striped fabric upholstery **825.00**

Federal

American, lolling, serpentine rect back, scrolled arms, inlaid downswept supports, flared seat, sq tapering legs with stretcher **1,430.00**

Massachusetts

Arm, shield back carved with bellflower and wheat sheath sprigs, pierced splat, serpentine seat, scrolled arms, sq molded tapered legs with stretcher, c1800 **1,320.00**

Side, Salem, 1800–10, inlaid mahogany, molded and incised shield back, five shaped ribs terminating in inlaid fan above trapezoidal over upholstered seat, serpentine front rail, sq tapering line inlaid legs, H stretcher, minor loss to inlay, 37¼" h, pr **1,320.00**

Side, inlaid mahogany, shield back, arched rail, carved foliate pendant above pierced and fluted splat, flared seat, sq molded legs, c1790 . . . . **935.00**

New York, 1800–10, side, carved mahogany, stepped and molded rect back, center pierced urn form splat, carved with drapery swag, surmounted by Prince of Wales carved plume, flanked by leaf carved vertical slats, over upholstered bow front seat, sq tapering molded legs, spade feet, 35¾" h, set of four . . . **14,300.00**

Philadelphia, 1790–1810, arm, carved mahogany, molded shield shaped and upholstered back, flanked by short shaped arms with carved rosettes over curved and molded supports, over upholstered seat, reeded apron, sq tapering reeded legs with carved rosettes, several old repaired breaks, 35¾" h **12,100.00**

George II, Provincial, c1735, corner, oak, yoke form crest, twin baluster form splats, pillar supports, molded seat frame, upholstered drop in seat, deeply valanced skirt, cabriole and three turned tapering legs **700.00**

George II Style, library, mahogany, serpentine crest rail, acanthus carved arms, carved cabriole legs, pad feet, 37" h **250.00**

George III

Arm, mahogany, waved molded crest rail, center foliage above pierced vase splat, scrolling arms, drop in pad floral needlework upholstered seat, sq fluted legs joined by stretchers **2,200.00**

Dining, two arm chairs, two side chairs, mahogany, molded shield form back, carved crest of wheat sheaves and bellflowers, oval parquetry panel on pierced splat, upholstered seat, serpentine front, straight tapered legs, H stretcher, set of four **3,500.00**

George III Style

Arm, mahogany, oval padded back, padded arms, bowed padded seat, molded frame, turned tapering stop fluted legs, turned feet, painted cream, ivory leather upholstery . . **1,100.00**

Corner, mahogany, tub shaped back, two pierced carved interlacing splats, drop in pad seat, sq cham-

fered molded legs, gold fabric upholstery **500.00**

Hall, mahogany, shield shaped back, bowed plank seat, sq tapering legs, spade feet, pr **825.00**

Wing, Gainsborough, raking sq back, padded arms and sq seat, sq legs with "H" stretcher, mushroom moquette upholstery, pr . . **3,850.00**

Georgian Style, English, 18th C, mahogany

Arm, relief carved arms and legs, casters **500.00**

Side, elaborate carved knees, pierced relief carved back splat, ball and claw feet **550.00**

Hepplewhite, American, side, mahogany, shield back, rush seat **300.00**

Hitchcock, side, orig red and black graining, yellow and green striping, gilded stenciling, black painted balloon rush seat **175.00**

International Movement, Frank Lloyd Wright, for H C Price Co Tower, Bartlesville, OK, 1953–56, aluminum, articulated hexagonal back and seat, pedestal supported by modified hexagonal base, long downward sloping arms, orig fabric, 32⅝" h **26,400.00**

Ladder Back

Arm, four slat back, turned finials, ram's horn scroll arms, replaced rope rush seat, sausage turned legs and posts, worn black paint **600.00**

Child's, high chair, replaced board seat and bottom slat, worn old brown patina, minor damage, 35½" h **700.00**

Side, rabbit ear, orig red and black graining, yellow and black striping and floral design on crest, worn pale green painted rush seats, set of 4 . . . . **900.00**

Louis XV, arm, fruitwood, pastel flame stitch upholstery, set of 4 . . . . **1,100.00**

Queen Anne

Side

American, early 18th C, open splat, rabbit ears, rush seat, Spanish feet, 19th C repaint **650.00**

American, country, hard and soft wood, yoke crest, vase splat, worn rush seat, turned legs, duck feet, bulbous front stretcher, dark brown refinishing **600.00**

New England, 1730–50, all-over old black paint, 19th C gilt scrolling and polychrome floral dec on splat, 39½" h **500.00**

Philadelphia, 1740–60

Carved walnut, incise molded shaped and arched crest rail,

center carved shell, solid spooned vase shaped splat flanked by curved flat stiles, balloon shaped slip seat, shell carved cabriole legs, tongued slipper feet, repairs to stiles, 42" h, pr **44,000.00**

Carved tiger maple, yoke crest, vase shaped splat, drop in seat, cabriole legs, trifid feet, flat shaped stretchers, attributed to Savery School **27,500.00**

Wing, soft pastel flame stitch upholstery **950.00**

Queen Anne Style, 19th C, country, side, yoke shape crest, vase shape splat, replaced rush seat turned legs, duck feet, turned front stretcher, turned posts, dark finish **175.00**

Regency, English, 1820–30, side, mahogany, parcel gilt, incised bowed paneled crest rail, ball finials, sabre front, green upholstered drop in seat, pr **470.00**

Regency Style, English, late 19th C, arm, bamboo, painted, bowed back, bamboo turned spindles, slit cane tilted seat, squab on bamboo turned legs, similar stretchers, pr **1,550.00**

Victorian

Eastlake, PA, side, dec, orig brown paint, white striping, polychrome floral dec on crest, set of 4 . . . . . **300.00**

Renaissance Revival, NY, c1870, parcel gilt, ebonized mahogany and walnut, C scroll and leaf carved crest rail, foliate embroidered upholstered rect back, fluted stiles with acorn finials, shaped arms with ring turned supports, serpentine upholstered seat, trumpet form legs, castors, all–over gilt incised linear dec, pr **1,000.00**

Rococo Revival, NY, John Henry Belter, lady's, arm, laminated rosewood, exaggerated arched crest with applied rose in center, upholstered oval back with a grape, cornucopia, rose, and entwined tendril pierce carved frame, serpentine seat with matching apron, cabriole legs carved with floral pendants at knees, scrolled toes, matching side chair, pr **6,050.00**

William and Mary

Arm, PA, 18th C, walnut, shaped crest rail, three molded vertical slats flanked by shaped stiles, baluster turned supports, solid plank seat, block and cylinder turned legs, box stretcher, rear feet pieced, seat restored, 42½" h **58,300.00**

Side

Oak

American, c1700, scroll carved crest rail flanked by turned stiles, baluster finials, three vertical molded slats, recessed plank seat, short baluster turned and block legs, turned stretchers, 43½" h, pr **6,600.00**

Pennsylvania, c1710–30, shaped crest rail, three molded vertical slats flanked by rect tapering stiles, plank seat, block and short baluster turned legs, baluster and ring turned front stretcher, two flanking balusters replaced, 38¼" h **8,800.00**

Walnut, PA, c1710–30, shaped crest rail, three vertical molded slats flanked by rect tapering stiles, plank seat, block and ball turned legs, paired baluster turned front stretcher, seat restored, 40" h **550.00**

Chair, Windsor, New England, c1800, bow back, arm, hardwoods, pine seat, $2,750.00.

Windsor

Bow Back

Arm

16" h seat, spindle back, turned arm supports, oval shaped seat, splayed base, bulbous turnings, "H" stretcher, old worn black and green paint . . **2,100.00**

16½" h seat, turned arm sup-

ports, wide flat arms, saddle seat, splayed base, bulbous turnings and H stretcher, old refinishing, repairs to seat . . . **575.00**
17¾" h seat, hard and softwood, cherry arms, bamboo turnings, worn green paint **1,300.00**
Side, 7 spindle back, bamboo turning, saddle seat, H stretcher

Red repaint, 18½" h seat **350.00**
Refinished **170.00**
Brace Back, orig natural finish, Wallace Nutting, label **600.00**
Comb Back, York, PA
Arm, Maclow, sgd and dated 1948 **700.00**
Child's, high chair, American, c1790, arched crest, volute carved terminals, six tapered spindles and shaped arms, elliptical seat, turned legs and stretchers, orig worn red and black paint, yellow highlights . . **40,000.00**
Fan Back
Arm, PA, splayed base, bulbous turnings, turned arm supports, crest with carved ears, black repaint **2,000.00**
Side, refinished, saddle seat, turned posts, shaped crest, splayed base, bulbous turnings, H stretcher, well executed repairs, 15¾" h seat **350.00**
Hooped Back, elm and fruitwood, wheel splat, saddle seat, flared ring turned baluster legs, H stretcher, pr **1,100.00**
Rod Back, American, 19th C, orig dark green paint and gold dec . . . **120.00**
Sack Back, PA, c1780, arched top rail, spindle back, horizontal rail forms scrolled arms, canted baluster form supports, oval saddle seat, splayed baluster turned legs with H stretcher, painted dark green **1,430.00**

CHESTS OF DRAWERS

Art Furniture, PA, 1901, maple, painted and decorated, splashboard above two short and four molded and graduated long drawers, front stenciled "E. S. S. Schmucker," dated "A. D. 1901," paneled ends, turned feet, painted red, black outlines, 39½" w, 20¾" d, 56" h **5,775.00**
Arts and Crafts, American, oak
Model No. 622, four long graduated drawers, two short drawers, panel construction sides, large red Gustav Stickley decal with "Stickley" outlined, 41" w, 22½" d, 50" h, c1902 . . . . **4,500.00**
Model No. 902, arched back rail, two

top drawers, four horizontal drawers, oval hammered pulls, red decal in top right drawer, 39¾" w, 22" d, 53½" h **4,200.00**
Model No. 909, oak, two short drawers over three graduated drawers, panel construction sides, red Gustav Stickley decal in top right drawer, paper label, 37¼" w, 19" d, 42" h **2,450.00**
Chippendale
American
Mahogany, four graduated drawers, ogee bracket base, orig hardware, old finish, 35" w, 20¼" d, 39¼" h **2,700.00**
Tiger Maple, projecting cornice top, six graduated drawers, bracket feet, 42" w, 19½" d, 51¾" h . . . **3,000.00**
Massachusetts, Boston area, c1770, mahogany, reverse serpentine, oblong top, thumb molded edge, four graduated long drawers with cockbeaded surrounds, molded base, ball and claw feet, 37¾" w, 20½" d, 33½" h **25,300.00**
Massachusetts, North Shore, 1765–85, mahogany, rect top, molded edge, serpentine front, conforming case, four cockbead molded and graduated long drawers, molded base, center shaped pendant, straight bracket feet, orig brasses, 34⅜" w, 20¼" d, 30" h **33,000.00**
New England, 1770–1790, maple, rect molded edge top, conforming case, four graduated long drawers, molded base, straight bracket feet, orig brasses, 39½" w, 18¼" d, 32⅞" h **4,625.00**
New England, 1780–1800, maple, rect top, reverse serpentine front, conforming case, four graduated long drawers, bracket feet, orig brasses, 39⅜" w, 21¼" d, 34¾" h **3,300.00**
New Hampshire, early 19th C, six graduated drawers
Birch, reddish brown finish, molded cornice with relief carved frieze, dovetailed case, detailed bracket feet, carved sunburst on center drop, replaced brasses, 36" w, 19¾" d, 62¾" h **6,300.00**
Birch, scalloped bracket feet, oval brass escutcheons, orig wooden pulls and surface, minor old repairs, 36¼" w, 16⅝" d, 56¾" h **5,000.00**
Philadelphia, c1780, mahogany, rect molded top, carved fret bands, two small cockbeaded drawers over three graduated cockbeaded long drawers, fluted pilasters, refinished,

replaced brasses, one foot pieced, minor repairs, 35" w, 19½" d, 32¼" h **13,000.00**

Empire, American, country
Cherry and walnut, four dovetailed drawers with applied edge beading, turned feet, refinished, 42" w, 44½" h **850.00**
Cherry, curly maple facade, four dovetailed drawers, applied edge beading, turned and rope carved pilasters and feet, opalescent glass swirled pulls, old dark finish, 41" w, 20½" d, 46½" h **500.00**

Chest of Drawers, Federal, New England, tiger maple, bow front, reeded edge, cock beaded drawers, shaped skirt, French bracket feet, 39½" w, 40" h, $3,600.00.

Federal
American, mahogany, bow front, four graduated drawers, reeded stiles and upper and lower bands, circular carved motifs, inset panel sides, bracket feet, 42½" l, 37¼" h **1,870.00**
Massachusetts, c1800, maple and mahogany veneer, bow front, four long drawers with inlay, orig brass, old refinish, minor cockbeading loss, 39⅝" w, 21¾" d, 35¾" h . . . **2,600.00**
Massachusetts, 1800–1815, inlaid cherrywood, bow front, rect top, center diamond shape and trefoil point inlay, conforming case with four cockbeaded molded and graduated long drawers, inlaid rect line panel with trefoil leaf motifs at each corner, molded base, bracket feet, 37" w, 18¾" d, 33½" h **7,150.00**

New England, 1790–1810
Curly Maple, inlaid mahogany, bow front, oblong top, inlaid edge, four graduated cockbeaded long drawers, shaped skirt, slightly splayed bracket feet, 41¼" w, 20½" d, 37½" h **7,150.00**
Inlaid mahogany, bow front, rect top, patterned inlaid stringing, conforming case, four graduated long drawers with maple banding and stringing, shaped apron, French feet, 38¾" w, 20½" d, 34" h **6,000.00**
Maple, molded cornice, six graduated long drawers, slightly splayed bracket feet, 37¾" w, 20" d, 54½" h **5,225.00**
Pennsylvania, western, c1815, mahogany inlaid, bow front, contrasting cross banded veneer surrounds, four drawers, orig brasses, minor imperfections, 23" w, 43¼" d, 38⅛" h **1,500.00**
George I Style, walnut, molded rect top, two cross banded short drawers over three inlaid long drawers, later bracket feet, 37¼" w, 20" d, 37½" h **1,000.00**
George II, walnut, cross banded top, two short and three long feather banded drawers, bracket feet, 38½" w. 38¾" h **4,675.00**

Hepplewhite, American, country
Birch, orig red and black flame graining, yellow and green striping, four dovetailed drawers in beaded frame, scalloped apron, cut out feet, turned wood pulls, emb brass escutcheons, 36⅜" h **3,400.00**
Cherry, poplar secondary wood, walnut and maple inlay on stiles, top drawer and top edge, four dovetailed drawers with applied edge beading, solid ends, sq tapered feet, old refinishing, dated 1824 inside case, turned replacement knobs, back leg broken and re–attached, 39" w, 20½" d, 40½" h . . . **2,000.00**
Mahogany, four graduated drawers, slightly turned out feet, refinished, replaced hardware, 41" w **1,300.00**
Walnut, inlaid, four graduated dovetailed and cock beaded drawers, scrolled apron, French feet, 36⅜" w, 40½" h **3,000.00**

Sheraton
Birch, bow front, reeded columns, turned feet, refinished, 42" w **825.00**
Maple and cherry, bow front, curly and bird's eye veneer, paneled ends, four dovetailed drawers with applied edge beading, scalloped

apron, turned feet, refinished, 39¾"
w, 44" h **2,400.00**
Walnut, curl, four dovetailed drawers
with applied edge beading, scalloped apron, turned feet, clear lacy
pulls, refinished, 41" w, 39¼" h . . **1,200.00**

Victorian, American
Mahogany, bowed rect molded top,
conforming case, two short drawers
over three graduated drawers,
shaped apron, French feet, resto-
ration, 43½" w, 21" d, 41¼" h . . . **2,750.00**
Rosewood, ivory inlaid, rect top, four
short and four long drawers, free
standing reeded columns, inlaid
base, turned feet, restoration on
lower left base molding, 51½" w,
20¼" d, 45" h **5,775.00**

William and Mary
English, late 17th C, oak, double
fronted frieze drawer, geometrically
paneled deep drawer over two similar shallow drawers, double
paneled sides, stiles continue to
plain sq supports, 36¼" w, 36¼" h **2,200.00**
Pennsylvania, 1720–40, walnut, rect
top, applied cove molding, two
short drawers over three graduated
long drawers, molded base, compressed ball turned feet, 39⅝" w,
21¾" d, 40" h **38,500.00**

CHESTS, OTHER

Apothecary, poplar, eight overlapping
drawers, orig iron pulls and scalloped
gallery, simple feet, old red stain, 18"
w, 6" d, 23" h **750.00**
Carpenter's, pine and oak, old finish,
dovetailed case, fitted int. with six
drawers, sliding lid, 33¾" l **260.00**

Chest On Frame
Chippendale, CT, curly maple, dovetailed case, molded cornice, eight
overlapping dovetailed drawers,
scalloped drop and chip carving,
ogee feet, old worn refinishing, replaced brasses, 40¼" w, 20½" d,
81" h **13,500.00**
George I, walnut, projecting oblong
molded top, conforming recessed
case, two frieze and two full cross
banded drawers, molded and scalloped base, cabriole legs, pad feet,
44" w, 20½" d, 42" h **2,600.00**
George II, walnut, molded cornice top
with two short and two long drawers, one false drawer with fitted int.,
two graduated drawers on bottom,
fluted chamfered corners, bracket
feet, 30" w, 65" h **19,800.00**

Georgian, mahogany, simple band inlay top, string inlay around base,
two short and eight long drawers,
French splayed bracket feet, 42" w,
19½" d, 75¼" h **2,750.00**
Queen Anne, American, country, wal-
nut, dovetailed case, seven dovetailed overlapping drawers, inlaid
initials "M. E." on top drawer, replaced base with scalloped apron,
cabriole legs, duck feet, repairs to
drawers, replaced cornice, replaced brasses, refinished, 39" w,
58½" h **1,150.00**
William and Mary, PA, 1730–60, wal-
nut, rect lift top, deep compartment,
case with two horizontal fielded
panels over two thumb molded
short drawers, inverted baluster
turned legs, ball turned feet joined
by molded box stretcher, 48⅞" w,
24¾" d, 40½" h **5,000.00**

Commode
Federal, Salem, MA, 1800–15, mahogany, demi–lune top, conforming
case, central cockbeaded molded
drawer flanked by similar hinged
compartment drawers, double cupboard doors with molded panels,
three molded trays, flanked by similar cupboard doors, shelves int.,
scalloped apron, French feet, 55"
w, 32" d, 40" h **46,200.00**
George III Style, in the manner of
John Cobb, satinwood and syca-
more, serpentine top banded in
molded bronze, pr of cupboard
doors with marquetry panels and
summer flowers, knife edge corners continuing to gilt bronze sa-
bots, 42" w, 21½" d, 36" h, pr . . . **14,000.00**

Louis XV
Burl wood, gilt metal, marble top,
51¾" l **1,200.00**
Parquetry Kingwood, ormolu
mounted, marble top, serpentine
molded top, two drawers, shaped
apron, cabriole legs with sabots,
21¼" w, 14½" d, 32½" h **700.00**

Louis XVI
Mahogany, eared Ste Anne marble
top, paneled sides, three graduated paneled drawers, fluted column front stiles, pilaster rear
stiles, toupie feet, 45½" l, 33¾"
h, 18th C **4,125.00**
Walnut, three drawers, restored
and refinished, 34¾" w, 17¼" d,
33½" h **450.00**

Regency Style, bombe shape, parquetry kingwood, ormolu, marble
top, 51" w, 25" d, 32½" h **4,500.00**

Highboy

Chippendale, Philadelphia, walnut, swan neck cresting with flowerhead terminals, carved shell and foliate scroll, fluted quarter columns, scroll carved apron, acanthus carved cabriole legs, claw and ball feet, 44" w, 95" h **6,050.00**

Queen Anne

American, maple, flat top, six short and five long drawers, fan carved upper and lower drawer, shaped apron, cabriole legs with duck feet, refinished, replaced hardware, 32" w, 20¼" d, 73½" h . . **14,500.00**

Connecticut, 1750–80, carved cherry, two sections, upper: molded scrolled pediment, pinwheel carved rosettes, center flame and urn finial and pendant shell, case with three short drawers, center carved with convex shell above four thumb molded and graduated long drawers, flanked by fluted pilasters, lower: single thumb molded long drawer over three short drawers, center one with carved convex shell above triple flat arched apron, two urn turned drops, cabriole legs, pad feet, several small drawer lip repairs, rear left leg restored, 39" w, 20¼" d, 86¼" h **38,500.00**

Country, walnut facade, pine sides, molded cornice, dovetailed case, seven molded edge dovetailed drawers, scalloped apron, maple cabriole legs, duck feet, orig base, refinished, replaced cornice, 34" w, 19½" d, 56" h **4,500.00**

New England

Cherry, flat top, replaced molding on top, replaced hardware . . **4,000.00**

Curly Maple, flat top, projecting molding cornice, five short and four long drawers, shaped apron, orig supports extend from bottom to top section on back, 35⅝" w, 19¾" d, 68¼" h **11,000.00**

Tiger Maple, molded flat top, four long and five short walnut drawers, shaped apron, 38¼" w, 21" d, 68⅛" h, c1750 . . . . **13,500.00**

William and Mary, Philadelphia, 1715–30, stained cedar, two sections, upper: elaborate molded cornice, bolection molded frieze drawer over case of three short drawers, three graduated long drawers, double bead molded dividers, lower: mid molding over short central drawer flanked by two short deep drawers, ogival arched apron, short baluster and ring turned legs, molded arched stretcher, 42" w, 23" d, 67¼" h . . . **54,000.00**

Lowboy

Chippendale, PA, c1765, carved and inlaid walnut, oblong quarter veneered top, notched corners, four molded drawers, fluted quarter columns, volute and shell carved shirt, shell carved cabriole legs, ball and claw feet, restorations, stamped "J Hooten" on underside of center drawer, 33¾" w, 21¾" d, 28" h . . . **16,500.00**

Lowboy, Chippendale, PA, walnut, molded top, thumb molded drawers, scalloped apron, cabriole legs, trifid feet, 34" w, 28½" h, $28,000.00.

Chippendale Style, tiger and bird's eye maple, claw and ball feet . . . **1,100.00**

Queen Anne

American, maple, rect top with molded edge, two short and one long drawers, fan carved central drawer, scalloped apron, cabriole legs, pad feet, 31½" w, 36½" h **1,760.00**

American, walnut, satinwood inlay, rect molded edge top, three drawers, scalloped apron, round tapered legs, pad feet, 32" w, 19½" d, 28¾" h **2,400.00**

Massachusetts, 1720–50, walnut, rect top, molded edge, three drawers with molded surrounds, shaped beaded skirt hung with turned pendants, circular tapering legs, pad feet, 33¾" w, 20½" d, 30" h **6,200.00**

Pennsylvania, walnut, molded edge top with notched corners, four overlapping dovetailed drawers, scalloped front and side aprons, cabriole legs, trifid feet, good old dark alligatored finish, replaced bottom drawer, reset top, 33¾" w, 21¾" d, 28⅝" h . . **13,500.00**

Queen Anne Style, walnut, carved shell in skirt, drake feet **1,300.00**

William and Mary Style, walnut faced, turned legs, three drawers, serpentine X stretcher, 33¼" w, 21" d, 29" h **550.00**

Sugar Chest

Hepplewhite, attributed to NC, cherry, dovetailed case, large till, lift off lid, inlaid stars, lines, and circles, frame with single dovetailed drawer, sq tapered legs, cut out leg brackets, old finish, old repairs, replaced moldings, 31¼" w, 15¾" d, 36" h **11,000.00**

Sheraton, walnut, fine turned legs, single drawer in base, int. divided into three sections, fine dovetailed construction, sgd "Read Atlanta GA," old refinish, 29" w, 18¾" d, 39" h **3,000.00**

Wardrobe, Federal, attributed to John Shaw, Annapolis, MD, c1795, mahogany, five sections, breakfront molded cornice with plain frieze, above case with double cupboard doors with applied astragal bead molded panels and hollow corners, five sliding tray shelves, lower case of single long drawer with fold down writing surface flanked by compartments and sliding covers, two bead molded short drawers, two similar graduated long drawers, straight bracket feet, two flanking full length sections with bead molded

panels and cupboard doors, 70" w, 21½" d, 92" h **16,500.00**

CRADLES

Chippendale, birch, canted sides, scalloped headboard, turned posts and rails, refinished, 37½" l **300.00**

Country

Curly Maple, fiddle back figured cherry panels, sq posts, turned finials, mortised and pinned rails, cut out designs in rails, oak rockers, 38¾" l **200.00**

Poplar, old worn green paint, dovetailed, shaped rockers and scalloped ends with heart cutouts, wear and edge damage, 39" l **250.00**

Grain Painted, New England, early 19th C, pine, yellow ochre and burnt umber painting simulating tiger maple, 37½" w, 19¼" d, 25½" h **375.00**

Victorian, walnut, sausage turned spindles **300.00**

Windsor, New England, c1800–20, bamboo turned spindles, worn finish **800.00**

Cupboard, corner, Chippendale, PA, pine, $7,500.00.

CUPBOARDS

Armoire

French Provincial, fruitwood, shaped top, two cupboard doors, int. shelves, shaped apron, scrolled feet, carved, 52" w, 25" d, 84" h . . **2,300.00**

Louis XVI, provincial, walnut and

Cradle, mixed woods, five spindle ends, patent 1869, replaced cushion, 37" l, 31½" h, $350.00.

chestnut, triple panel sides, shaped fielded triple paneled doors, fluted stiles, scalloped scroll bordered apron with stylized flowering tree center, shaped sq feet, step molded cornice, 57½" w, 93" h, ... **3,250.00**

Chimney, pine, dovetailed case, cornice, paneled door, open shelf, green wash repaint, base recut, 14" w, 25½" d, 64¾" h **350.00**

Corner
American, c1800
Cherry, dentil molding, glazed upper section, pr paneled cupboard doors, scalloped apron, refinished with strong traces of orig red paint, some orig glass, 45" w, 25" d, 86" h **4,200.00**

Grain Painted, Chippendale, c1780–1810, molded cornice above arched double glazed cupboard doors, three shaped int. shelves, arched chip carved molding with center cartouche, doors flanked by molded pilasters, two molded edge panel doors, molded base, losses to glass, minor restoration, 58½" w, 98½" h **3,775.00**

Pine and Poplar, 2 pcs, cherry finish, top with single door of twelve panes of old glass, molded cornice, pr paneled cupboard doors, scalloped apron, bracket feet, traces of old paint, replaced hinges and door latches, minor edge damage, refinished, 42" w, 84½" h **4,500.00**

English, 2 pcs, pine, bracket feet, paneled doors with applied moldings, molded cornice, scalloped shelf int., old dark brown finish, 46" w, 80" h **1,900.00**

Pennsylvania, painted
Pine, 18th C, red and black graining, two arched paneled doors with red painted int. on top, two doors on bottom with shelf int., fluted columnar stiles, thumb molded cornice above stylized flowerhead carved dentil frieze, 53" w, 96" h **6,600.00**

Pine and Poplar, first quarter 19th C, 2 pcs, upper sect with molded cornice, arched glazed door opening to shelved int. with plate rails, pierced for spoons, projecting lower sect with two drawers over pr of cupboard doors, turnip feet, painted red, stippled yellow highlights, door painted white, 28" w, 90" h **21,000.00**

Hanging
English, oak, paneled door, triangular ornaments, wrought iron butterfly hinges, old dark finish, 23½ x 12½ x 26¼" **175.00**

Jelly
Cherry and Poplar, paneled ends and doors, applied molding, one dovetailed drawer, sq tapered feet, refinished, 37¾" w, 50½" h **875.00**

Linen Press
Country, cherry, 2 pcs, two dovetailed drawers and turned feet in base, double doors with six panes of glass in top, molded cornice, old refinishing, 44" w, 72" h **1,100.00**

Georgian
Mahogany, fan and string inlay, shell shape dec on corners of doors and drawers, orig finish, replaced hardware, 46¾" w, 20½" d, 81½" h **2,250.00**

Pine, projecting fret carved and dentil molded cornice, arcaded raised panel doors, shelf int., three short and one long drawer, bracket feet, stained, orig brasses, 34¾" w, 20" d, 77" h .. **1,800.00**

Pennsylvania, pine, stained, projecting molded cornice, raised paneled doors, shelf int., three graduated drawers, scrolled bracket feet, 46½" w, 20½" d, 78½" h **2,600.00**

Pine and Walnut, dovetailed case, turned feet, paneled doors, base and cornice molding, two dovetailed drawers in bottom int., orig paint with red wash, 42" w, 75" h **900.00**

Pewter, American, pine, open, one piece
Painted, board and batten door, wrought iron H hinges, blue repaint over traces of earlier red, feet worn down, old replaced hinges, 37¾" w, 14¼" d, 59½" h **1,700.00**

Traces of old reddish brown finish, wide one board ends, board and batten door, slightly truncated top with three shelves, simple cornice, minor edge wear, feet shortened, 37½" w, 22½" d, 81" h **1,200.00**

Pie Safe, country
Painted, front hinged door with pierced rooster, sides pierced with hex signs, corners form feet, painted white, 30" w, 19¾" d, 33¼" h **2,310.00**

Pine and poplar, punched tin circular designs, two dovetailed drawers, sq posts with ruined feet, refinished, 36½ x 22 x 46½" **1,200.00**

Tin, PA, rect molded top, hinged door, pierced animals and figures, sides pierced with animals and hearts, side inscribed "Centennial Safe G H Read 1876," old restoration to back of top, 31" w, 25½" d, 35" h ... **1,650.00**

Walnut, double doors with three punched tin panels with star, circle, and heart designs, two dovetailed drawers cut out feet, refinished, 42¾" w, 48½" h **850.00**

Wall

Canada, 19th C, painted, step back, upper section with pair of paneled cupboard doors, three int. shelves, two drawers, lower section with pair of paneled cupboard doors, two int. shelves, all–over orig blue paint, turned wooden knobs, minor imperfections, 53¾" w, 17¾" d, 86½" h **6,000.00**

Country

Cherry, poplar secondary wood, molded cornice, two top doors each with eight panes of old glass, two dovetailed drawers, raised panel doors, simple cut out feet, orig finish, later brass pulls, minor repairs, 48" w, 13¼" d, 84" h **3,500.00**

Pine, mellow refinishing, step back, bracket feet, paneled doors, two dovetailed drawers with beaded edges, molded cornice, brass thumb latches **1,600.00**

Poplar, two pcs, old red paint, molded cornice, pr doors with glass panes, two dovetailed drawers, paneled doors, simple cut out feet, beaded trim, orig a one pc cupboard, 52" w, 18" d, 82¼" h **1,250.00**

Walnut, paneled doors and two dovetailed drawers in base, double doors with eight panes of glass on top, molded cornice, old red repaint, 49¾" w, 22¼" d, 88" h **1,100.00**

Pennsylvania, 19th C, closed face, poplar, pair of cupboard doors with arched panels, four small drawers over two drawers, paneled lower cupboard doors flanked by turned columns, refinished with traces of orig paint, two drawer pulls missing, replaced hinges and glass, 53" w, 18½" d, 85½" h **2,300.00**

Wardrobe, country, pine, simple detail, raised panel door, beaded edge stiles, molded cornice, shelves and wood hooks int., worn dark brown finish, 75¾" h **510.00**

DAYBEDS

Anglo–Indian, rect over scrolled caned back and seat, plank arms, baluster turned legs, turned feet, 81" l **600.00**

Art Deco, stepped cabinet with drop front above two door bay headboard, 98" l, 32" w, 43½" h **600.00**

Arts and Crafts

Morris, William, oak, rect, angular raised end, green floral fabric upholstered cushions, 85" l, 28¼" w, 24" h **1,100.00**

Stickley, Gustav, Model No. 216, c1904, wide crest rail over five vertical slats, cane seat, large red decal, 79½" l, 31" w, 29¼" h **3,300.00**

Stickley, L & J G, Model No. 291, c1912, slanted head over five vertical slated ends, open sides, spring cushion seat, sgd "The Work of L & J G Stickley," 76" l, 30" w, 26" h **1,200.00**

Charles X, mahogany, slightly bowed rect padded back, padded seat, turned tapering legs, ball feet, crimson silk upholstery **500.00**

Directorie Style, late 19th C, carved beechwood, out scrolled ends carved with reclining swans heads, multicolored pink and ivory striped silk upholstery, 41" w **2,025.00**

Empire, ormolu mounted mahogany, rect back, rect splat applied with ribbon tied wreath and winged eagle, bowed padded seat, sq tapering splayed legs, gray cotton upholstery **700.00**

Jacobean Style, oak, ornately carved, 76" l **750.00**

Louis XV Style, Provincial, oak, ladderback, waved crestrail, horizontal splats carved with foliage, bowed rush seat, turned tapering legs, shaped front stretcher, matched set of six, two matching fauteuils **1,650.00**

Mission, c1910, oak, four shaped pyramidal posts, wide center rail over seven slats per side, slip seat frame, leather cushion, 76" l, 31" w, 27½" h **500.00**

Regency, beechwood, cartouche shaped padded back, carved scrolling leaf tips, serpentine padded seat, cabriole legs carved at knee with acanthus leaves, scrolled feet, blue and white cotton upholstery **935.00**

Victorian, early, mahogany, brass inlaid, over scrolled padded back, rect padded seat, baluster turned leaf tip carved legs, brass casters, green and ivory striped silk upholstery, 81" l ... **4,400.00**

Desk, Chippendale, American, late 18th C, cherry, slant front, 39½" w, 45½" h, $5,000.00.

DESKS

Art Nouveau, Louis Majorelle, French, mahogany, shaped top, out turning, buttressed legs, two long drawers, upper gallery with two pigeonholes, two short drawers, cast floral gilt bronze pulls, sgd "L Majorelle Nancy," 44¼" w, 27" d, 35" h **13,200.00**

Arts and Crafts, American
Stickley, Gustav
  Chalet, c1905, flat sides center shallow gallery top, paneled drop front, exposed key tenons, shoe-foot base, red decal, 22" w, 46" h **1,700.00**
  Drop Front
    Model No. 706. c1904, designed by Harvey Ellis, oak, panel fruit inlaid with three sections of pewter, copper, and fruitwood sinuous bud design, fitted int., large red decal, 30" l, 11¼" d, 44" h **18,700.00**
    Model No. 729, c1910, gallery over lid, two half drawers, three lower long drawers, paper label, int. crack, some veneer chips, 36½" w, 15" d, 45" h **2,700.00**
  Partners, c1902–03, flat rect top, central drawer, pull out writing surface above four drawers on either side, wooden pulls, lower shelf with kneehole, V board sides, prominent key tenons, shoe-foot base, red decal, 22" w, 46" h, mirrored on opposing side, large red signature, retailer's label, minor older surface nicks, waxed finish, 60" l, 40" d, 30" h **7,000.00**

Stickley, L & J G
  Lady's, oak, two drawers, shaped undertier shelf, red decal mark on back, new leather top, 34½" l, 20" d, 34" h, c1901 . . . . **1,650.00**
  Writing, Model No. 612, c1912, oak, two small bands of drawers on writing surface, double drawers center middle drawer and kneehole, varnished, stains, some roughness, 48" l, 30" d, 36½" h **1,400.00**
Wright, Frank Lloyd and George M Niedecken, for Henry J Allen House, Wichita, KS, 1917, walnut, bank of four drawers to right, one long drawer over kneehole, sq pulls, rail and stile construction on sides and back, straight legs with slight turned out foot, matching 36" h chair, 42" w, 24" d, 32" h **17,600.00**

Chippendale
American, country, slant front, cherry, dovetailed case and four drawers, beaded frame, fitted int., bracket feet, 38 x 19 x 42½" h, old refinishing **3,400.00**
Massachusetts, Boston area, c1770, serpentine front, mahogany, rect hinged lid, fitted int. with valanced pigeonholes and small drawers, center document drawers, four blocked and serpentine drawers, orig brasses, molded base with pendant, blocked ogee bracket feet, 41" w, 21½" d, 42½" h **18,700.00**
New England, c1800, slant front
  Birch, wavy, fitted int. with divided pigeonholes, and two tiers of four drawers, four long drawers, orig brasses, old refinish, int. blocks and casters added, 39" w, 18⅜" d, 44¼" h **3,000.00**
  Curly Maple, rect top, four overlapping graduated drawers, molded edge lid, stepped arrangement fitted int., seven dovetailed drawers, pigeon holes, and center door, ogee feet, replaced brasses, old finish, minor damage, 36" w, 18" d, 41⅜" h **10,000.00**
Empire Style, ormolu mounted mahogany, pedestal, rect molded top, inset gilt tooled green leather writing surface, fitted side slides, frieze fitted with central drawer flanked by two drawers over two pedestals containing three drawers, Egyptian terms, conforming plinth, 59½" w, 33½" d, 30" h **7,000.00**
Federal
Connecticut, 1795–1815, slant lid, in-

laid cherry, thumb molded slant lid with line inlay border and quarter fans, fitted int. with central prospect and document drawers, two banks of short drawers over longer drawer above three valanced pigeonholes, case of four cock bead molded line and quarter fan inlaid graduated long drawers, chamfered and fluted corners, modified French feet, some veneer chips, 40" w, 21" d, 42¼" h **4,650.00**

Massachusetts, North Shore, 1800–10, tambour, inlaid mahogany, two parts, upper section: rect top with line inlay, cross banding above hinged line inlaid rect door, int. with stack of two short drawers over valanced compartment flanked by tambour sliding doors, flanked by cross banded and line inlaid pilasters, lower section: line inlaid and cross banded writing flap above two long line inlaid drawers, flanked by line inlaid pilasters, sq tapering line and bell flower inlaid legs, 37" w, 20" d, 44¼" h **8,800.00**

Rhode Island, c1800, mahogany veneer, rect top, four reeded columns, two tambour doors enclosing two pigeonholes and three small drawers, center prospect door, fold out writing surface, slide supports, three graduated long drawers, old finish, replaced brasses, minor surface imperfections, 40" w, 21" d, 51" h **4,750.00**

George II, English, 18th C, slant front, mahogany, cross banded, two short and three long graduated drawers, ogee bracket feet, 35¾" w, 42¼" h **2,475.00**

George III
Butler's, Irish, late 18th C, mahogany, rect molded top, conforming case, secretary drawer with fitted int., three graduated drawers, fluted columns, shaped bracket feet, restorations, 44½" w, 22½" d, 39¾" h **2,860.00**
Kneehole, yew wood, rect molded top, inset tooled leather writing surface, two frieze drawers, kneehole backed by cupboard door flanked by pairs of short drawers, bracket feet, 44½" w, 23" d, 30¼" h **2,350.00**
Pedestal, walnut, rect cross banded top with tooled leather inset, nine cock beaded drawers, bracket feet, 68" w, 26½" d, 30" h **1,400.00**
Slant front, mahogany, rect top, fitted int., four graduated drawers with fluted canted corners, pierced

bracket feet, 42½" w, 20½"d, 42¾" h **5,000.00**

Hepplewhite
Butler's, walnut, inlay, straight feet, scalloped apron, three dovetailed drawers, fitted int., repairs, 43" w, 42" h **1,500.00**
Clerk's, pine, layers of old blue and gray paint, slant top lift lid, int. fitted with eleven pigeonholes, one dovetailed drawer, tall sq tapered legs, damage to top and edge molding, added int. iron brace, 30½" w, 24½" d, 55" h **450.00**
Slant front
American, 1790–1800, cherry, mahogany faced drawers with inlaid flamewood panels, stepped int., 39⅝" w **4,500.00**
English, late 18th C or early 19th C, mahogany, string inlay, fitted int., four drawers, slightly turned out feet, refinished, 36" w **1,750.00**

Louis XV Style, lady's writing, parquetry burl walnut, polychrome dec, cabriole legs, 35½" w, 18¾" d, 49" h **1,700.00**

Neoclassical, Austrian, early 19th C, rosewood, rect top, two writing slides, central long drawer flanked by four short drawers, shaped X supports, carved stretcher, gilded dec, paper label of Rettenmayer, Wiesbadene, 47¼" l, 31" d, 29½" h **9,000.00**

Rococo, South German, mid 18th C, walnut, marquetry, writing, oblong molded top with three quarter gallery, canted lid with sunk marquetry roses panel, stepped drawers int., full serpentine frieze drawer, cabriole legs, 46½" w, 23" d, 41½" h **2,200.00**

Schoolmaster's, 19th C, pine, lift top, tapered legs, refinished, replaced hinges **250.00**

Victorian
Davenport
Inlaid Pollard elm, rect top, fitted compartment above hinged slant lid, two leaf tip carved cabriole supports backed by case fitted with four drawers opposed by four sham drawers, turned feet, wood casters, 20½" w, 21" d, 33¼" h **2,500.00**
Mahogany, rect top, fitted with hinged slant lid, inset green leather writing surface backed by three quarter baluster gallery enclosing compartment, four small drawers above case fitted with small drawer above four graduated drawers opposed by slide

over four sham drawers, reeded bun feet, 23¼" w, 34½" h **3,200.00**
Pedestal, mahogany, rect molded top, inset red leather writing surface, frieze fitted with three drawers over two pedestals with three graduated drawers, conforming plinth, 42½" w, 23½" d, 30" h **4,400.00**

Dough Trough, table top, painted pine, 32 x 16 x 9½", $85.00.

DOUGH TROUGHS

Decorated, pine, one board top, scrolled apron, splat base, turned legs, 25½" x 44¾ x 28¼" **500.00**
Maple, dovetailed, board and batten top, scalloped apron, rect legs, 35 x 22 x 30" **275.00**
Pine
American, dovetailed, canted sides, old green repaint on base, scrubbed two board top, sq legs, one dovetailed overlapping drawer in apron, one corner of top has repair, 23½ x 33½ x 28" h **325.00**
English, old dark finish, minor insect damage, 17½ x 38 x 30" **150.00**
Poplar, orig lid, orig red paint, 34" l . . . **115.00**
Walnut, Louis XV, Provincial, mid 18th C, oblong molded top with serpentine front, canted dough box, conforming valanced skirt carved with flowering urn, turned supports and box stretcher, 40½ x 22 x 37" **2,125.00**

DRY SINKS

Butternut, two doors, one int. shelf, orig stippling and finish, 35 x 20 x 42" . . **500.00**
Curly Maple, rect well, work surface to right with short drawer, two poplar wood cupboard doors, short bracket feet, hardwood edge stripes, minor repairs, refinished, 55" w, 34½" h . . **2,200.00**
Grain Painted, American, mid 19th C, simulated oak graining, cupboard top with two paneled doors, hood opening over dry sink, base with four graduated drawers and two cupboard doors, cast iron hardware, 54" w, 21¼" d, 78" h **1,400.00**

Pine, paneled doors, one drawer, crest, 54 x 17½", 30" h **450.00**
Pine and Poplar, old mustard yellow graining, turned feet, paneled doors with orig cast iron latches, one dovetailed drawer, well with lift lid cov, backboard crest with vertical seam, 49" w, 21½" d, 33" h **1,150.00**
Poplar
Crest, off center door with swing out attached shelf, orig cast iron thumb latch, simple cutout feet, stripped finish, 33 x 18½ x 26" **350.00**
Paneled doors, one small drawer, porcelain pull, simple cut out feet, worn layers of old green paint, plugged hole in side, 42" w, 19¾" d, 34" h **550.00**
Walnut and Poplar, pr of paneled doors, one drawer, old finish, dark green paint on int. of hutch top, orig cast iron latches with brass knobs, bottom end damage on feet, 52" w, 18½" d, 49" h **800.00**

Umbrella Stand, cast iron, $250.00.

HAT RACKS AND HALL TREES

Art Deco, French, c1925, wrought iron, rect, top set with shallow open hat shelf above octagonal mirror, shallow verde antico shelf on angled support wrought with straight bands and coils, two rect sections set with three coat hooks, outset rect umbrella stands, scrolls and imp geometric devices, 51¾" w, 75" h **12,100.00**
Arts and Crafts, Gustav Stickley, c1904, Model No. 53, four iron hooks on two tapering posts, two hooks on rect exposed tenon cross brace, 22" w, 65½" h **1,700.00**

Civil War, American, c1870, cast iron, painted and gilded, cast in half round, uprights formed by bayonets, criss crossed by pr of eagle headed sabres, two other sabres flanking hung with rope twists and tassels, olive branches crossbar hung with rope twists and tassels, small US shield, shield shaped mirror plate, base with US mail pouches, acorns, tassels, and ribbons, rope twist hooks, 26" w, 73" h **5,000.00**

Victorian
  Cast Iron
    Jack and the Bean Stalk, figural, old green and gold repaint, English registry number, 33½" h .. **400.00**
    Vase of flowers, oval mirror, umbrella stand base, old professionally repaired base break, 67½" h **550.00**
  Wrought iron, painted black, 73" h .. **350.00**
  Windsor, pine, bamboo turned, six knob like hooks, orig yellow varnish, black striping, 33¾" l **150.00**

Magazine Rack, American, walnut, single drawer, brass pull, acorn finials, brass casters, 23¼" h, $1,250.00.

MAGAZINE RACKS

Arts and Crafts
  American, early 20th C, four squared posts jointed by inverted V shaped side rail, over two vertical slats, five shelves, 54⅝" **325.00**
  Limbert, MI, c1910, four open shelves centered by flat sides with cut–out circles at base, branded, refinished, 20" w, 14" d, 36½" h **600.00**
  Michigan Chair Co, c1912, panel sided, rect top, five shelves each with six V grooved boards, projecting pins, dark finished, 19¾" w, 11¾" d, 45½" h **700.00**
  Roycroft, c1910, Model No. 078, oak, arched gallery and flat sides, three shelves, logo, refinished, 17¼" w, 37½" h **850.00**
  Stickley, Gustav, Toby, pedestal, sq top, applied corbels on carved flat sides, four open shelves, orig

tacked leather strips, 14" w, 12¾" d, 34½" h **425.00**

George III, early 19th C, mahogany, three compartments, two graduated drawers, turned legs, casters, 20" l, 16" d, 22¼" h **1,000.00**

Regency, mahogany, five open manganese splats, ring turned corner supports, case fitted with drawer, ring turned tapering legs, brass caps and casters, 19¼" w, 14" d, 20" h **1,650.00**

Victorian, c1850
  Mahogany, three sections formed by columnar arcades, basal drawer, turned legs, 19" w, 14" d, 19" h .. **1,100.00**
  Walnut, two handles, four compartments, pierced scrolled ends, turned supports, casters, 23" l, 18" d, 20½" h **550.00**

William IV, early 19th C, rosewood, twin bow form end crest rails, scrolling supports, joined by turned divider rails, two compartments, rect dais, C scroll legs, paw feet, 19½" w, 17½" d, 19" h **1,600.00**

Mirror, George II Style, early 19th C, giltwood, rect two section plate, molded C scroll borders and pilasters, pierced framework of waves, foliage, and flowerheads, everted foliage crest, 61" h, $8,500.00.

MIRRORS

Art Nouveau, wrought iron, octagonal, reticulated internal edge, upper part mounted by stylized fountain and floral ground, beveled edge mirror, stamped "E Brandt" lower right corner, 43" l, 38½" w **63,800.00**

Arts and Crafts

Michigan Chair Co, Grand Rapids, MI, 1915, wall, shaped cut–outs, center rect mirror, scalloped details, orig paper label, 35½" w, 23½" h **100.00**

Stickley, Gustav, c1909, Model No. 910, oak, simple arched frame, hand wrought iron hooks and chain, red decal, brown paper label, 35" w, 23½" h **1,450.00**

Classical, American, 1820–30, girandole, giltwood, circular, surmounted by eagle on rocky plinth, molded frame hung with gilt spherules, applied oak leaf and acorn frieze, convex mirror with ebonized reeded surround flanked by carved acanthus leaves over acanthus carved pendant, carved seahorse on rocky plinth with pineapple drop, small breaks and repairs, 44½" w, 9" d, 64¼" h **14,300.00**

Chippendale, American, 1770–90

Mahogany and giltwood, pierced and scrolled pediment, center carved eagle flanked by shaped ears, rect mirror with gilt molded frame, shaped pendant flanked by shaped ears, minor repairs, 29½ x 15" . . . **2,200.00**

Mahogany and parcel gilt, scrolled crest with flowerhead terminals with center spread winged eagle, mirror plate with leaf tip carved border within egg and dart border, suspended floral vines on sides, scrolled pendant on bottom, 31" w, 61" h **1,430.00**

Mahogany Veneer, gilted phoenix and liner, refinished and re–gilted, repairs, reveneered ears, 24¼" w, 45½" h **800.00**

Walnut and giltwood, shaped crest, pierced shell reserve, rect mirror plate, shaped pendant with center gilt convex shell, 20" w, 38" h . . . **4,000.00**

Empire

Ogee, mahogany, veneered, gilted molding, 41" h **125.00**

Ormolu mounted, mahogany, rect inset plate, conforming paneled frame, arched molded cornice, classical bust in center of foliate wreath, paterae corners, 30" w, 57" h **900.00**

Federal, America, 19th C

Architectural, double spiral columnar sides, flowerheads and ribbon swag with bows on top, gilted, 56½" h **2,900.00**

Eglomise, grain painted, attributed to PA, coved architectural cornice over two upright reeded columnar supports, bases fitted with brass rosettes, center eglomise panel brightly painted farm house and buildings, rect mirror plate, grain painting resembles tiger maple and marbleizing, 16" w, 30" h **1,760.00**

Split baluster, eglomise panel of fruit, orig gilting, one corner block missing, imperfections, paint loss, 30¾" h **300.00**

George I, walnut and parcel gilt, rect, chased gilted slip and shaped walnut border, open pediment and phoenix, 27" w, 60" h **8,000.00**

George III, English, late 18th C

Giltwood, oval, segmented inner frame, gadrooned outer border, foliage arabesque crest, kylix urn with flame and pendant trailing floral vines, small chips, 33¼" w, 69" h **6,000.00**

Inlaid Mahogany, shaving, arched rect plate, two twist and ring turned supports over bowed case, three drawers, ball feet, 21" w, 9" d, 23" h **350.00**

Georgian, English, late 18th C, convex, eagle crest, spiral side arm candleholders, 41" h **3,250.00**

Hepplewhite, shaving, bow front, pine with mahogany veneer, line edge inlay, turned feet and posts, one dovetailed drawer, beveled frame with old glass, 15½" w, 19" h **115.00**

Louis XV Style, over mantel parcel gilt, painted green, shaped rect plate, conforming molded frame, carved scrolling foliage and rocailles, 65" w, 47¾" h **700.00**

Louis XVI, Continental, giltwood, rect plate, conforming beaded frame, pierced scrolling foliate crest, shaped side brackets, 28" w, 45" h **1,875.00**

Queen Anne

American, crest with gilted convex panel, replaced glass, restorations, 32⅛" h **800.00**

Continental, 18th C

Japanned, black and gold, dressing, arched rect beveled plate, conforming molded frame, two turned supports, stepped case with three drawers over long drawer, bun feet, 15" w, 6¾" d, 26" h **700.00**

Walnut veneer, raised gilt ornamentation, 28¾" h **750.00**

English, c1730–40, arched and shaped, center stylized floral dec, bolection molded conforming frame, 17¾" w, 15¾" h **12,100.00**

Regency Style, giltwood
Cartouche form, carved, 38 x 26″ .. **350.00**
Convex, circular plate, reeded ebony
molding, conforming beaded frame
headed by winged eagle flanked by
leaf tips, applied base, 24″ w, 35″ h **1,650.00**
Sheraton, American, 1800–20 architectural, mahogany, rosette dec, 32½″ h **100.00**
Victorian, cast iron, old black repaint,
gold, red, blue, and white painted
shield, eagle, one with printed bust of
Washington, other Franklin, marked
"Design patented Nov 25, 1862,"
11¾″ w, 19½″ h, pr **1,600.00**
William and Mary, English, walnut, rect
plate, quarter–round molded frame **1,325.00**

**Rocker, mixed woods, orig paint and
stencil dec, c1900, $300.00.**

ROCKERS

Arrow Back, orig ink graining, scrolled
arms, widely splayed back **200.00**
Art Deco, Louis Sognot, c1930,
chromed metal, upholstered seat and
back, 36″ h **1,200.00**
Art Furniture, American, c1850, wrought
iron and brass, scrolled stiles form
downward curving arm supports,
joined by transverse at rear, mounted
upholstered leather cushion and arm
pads **4,675.00**
Arts and Crafts, American
Morris, Model No. 413, oak, four horizontal slat back, orig cushions in
poor condition, branded "L & J G
Stickley," 29″ w, 34½″ d, 36″ h **935.00**
Stickley, Gustav
Model No. 303, c1904, sewing,
oak, four horizontal back slats,

canvas seat, wide seat rail, orig
paper label, 14″ w, 16″ d, 33″ h **375.00**
Model No. 323, c1904, oak, four
horizontal back slats, flat arms
over five vertical slats, re–upholstered spring cushion seat, sgd,
36″ h **1,700.00**
Country, decorated, painted
Plank Seat, attributed to NY state,
c1825, crest rail painted with red
flowers, arrow form uprights,
shaped arms and turned legs, light
green ground **2,100.00**
Writing arm, worn orig red and black
paint, white striping, black stenciled
detail, damaged woven splint seat,
wear and minor age cracks in writing arm **200.00**
Grained and Stencil Dec, New England,
c1830, rosewood grained, olive green
stenciled crest, thumb back, yellow
striping, 15¼″ h seat, 32¼″ h **350.00**
Ladder Back, arm, country, turned arms
and posts, rabbit ear back posts, four
slats, paper rush seat, refinished ... **85.00**
Salem, New England, refinished, 19th
C **110.00**
Shaker, black repaint, replaced woven
seat, restoration to front leg, #4 ... **300.00**
Sheraton, country, maple, rush seat, refinished **80.00**
Victorian, quarter saw oak, hand carved
back, upholstered spring seat, French
legs **250.00**
Windsor
Bow Back, saddle seat, seven spindle
back, old finish, repairs **125.00**
Comb back, arrow slats, black re-
paint, gold striping, painted holly
crest **150.00**

SECRETARIES

Art Deco, Rene Drouet, c1925, parchment, fall front, oval top with inset
door, leather lined writing surface,
lighted, shelved int., two short drawers at top, bottom section with single
cupboard door, shelved int., inset oval
base, two ivory mounted keys, 29¼″
w, 49½″ h **8,500.00**
Arts and Crafts, American, Model No.
728, oak, drop front, shallow dish
opening to fitted int., one horizontal
drawer, undertier shelf, red Gustav
Stickley decal mark in drawer, 30¼″
w, 13¾″ d, 43¼″ h **675.00**
Baroque, Italian, 17th C, walnut, two
sections, upper sect: projecting
molded cornice, lifts for storage area,
pr of paneled doors, int. with small
drawers, lower sect: slightly project-

Secretary, Hepplewhite, New England, tiger maple veneer and mahogany, $7,500.00.

ing, pull out writing slide, two paneled doors, heavily molded base, bun feet, 31½" w, 18½" d, 61½" h **7,500.00**

Chippendale, American, cherry, projecting molded cornice, recessed paneled doors fitted with shelves and three drawers, fold out velvet inset writing surface, three graduated drawers, turned feet, 39" w, 20" d, 78" h **1,500.00**

Chippendale Style, hand made, block front, claw and ball feet, fan carved lid, 35½ x 20¼ x 91¾" **2,250.00**

Empire, mahogany, carved, projecting cornice, mullioned glazed doors, shelf int., fall front drawer with fitted int., carved rope turned half columns, front hairy paw carved feet, turned back feet, sgd and dated "Edward West, 1829," 51¾" w, 22" d, 93¾" h **4,850.00**

Federal, lady's, 2 pcs, mahogany, turned feet bottom with three dovetailed drawers with applied beading, hinged writing shelf, double door top with applied molding, fitted int., scrolled crest with reeded posts and brass finials, 18 x 65 x 37½" **2,000.00**

George III, English, 18th C, faded mahogany, three-quarter fret carved superstructure, molded shelf over fitted case, hinged secretary door, eight small int. drawers, over three graduated drawers, shaped bracket feet, 37½" w, 14¾" d, 59¼" h **4,500.00**

Georgian, early, English, japanned, scarlet, upper part with enclosed pr of domed fielded paneled doors, paneled entablature, interrupted scroll cornice, base with sloping fall front, fitted int., four long drawers, bracket feet, raised, gilt, and colored Chinoiseres, 38½" w, 82½" h **14,300.00**

Hepplewhite, New England, late 18th C, mahogany, inlaid, butler style drawer and two long drawers in base, three shelves in cupboard top, 40¾" w, 67¼" h **3,000.00**

Sheraton, country, attributed to East Liverpool, OH, c1880, two pcs, cherry, bookcase top: molded cornice, paneled doors, adjustable shelves, base: dovetailed case, three dovetailed drawers, fold down slant front, fitted int., four pigeon holes, two dovetailed drawers, turned feet, old brown graining, replaced brasses, 34" w, 19¼" d, 76½" h **2,200.00**

Venetian Rococo Style, late 19th C, painted and gilted, broken arch and urn crest, pair of shaped mirrored cabinet doors, serpentine base, hinged slant top, fitted int., three drawers, floral scrolling dec, 46" w, 24" d, 103½" h **9,500.00**

Victorian, Renaissance Revival, walnut, burl veneer, turned and carved ornaments, hand carved bust of Shakespeare finial, three dovetailed drawers, dovetailed upper case with mirrored door, bird's eye maple fitted int., base with turned legs and stretcher, 46½" w, 22" d, 91½" h . . . **3,500.00**

Wooton, American, 1880–84, Queen Anne pattern, walnut and maple, carved turned and incised three-quarter gallery, triangular carved hinged long document door, two carved and paneled bowed doors, incised carved drop front opening to fitted compartments, pigeonholes, and drawers, over numerous vertical and horizontal divided compartments, four center drawers, int. of left door fitted with divided compartments, right door fitted with forty sq storage boxes, sides paneled and incised with ebonized triangles, outstretched molded, canted, and carved legs, casters, two gallery finials missing, minor damage, 42½" w, 71" h **10,000.00**

SETTEES

Arts and Crafts

Limbert, c1912, Model No. 807, drop arm, two concave crest rails over six vertical slats, vertical center post, drop arms, brown simulated leather seat, two lower stretchers, re-upholstered, 40½" l, 20½" d, 37¼" h **275.00**

Stickley, Gustav
Model No. 165, c1902–03, even arm, four tapering posts centering three sets of repeating slightly flared back slats, re–upholstered, red decal, 60" l, 26" d, 40" h 12,000.00
Model No. 208, c1905, straight rail over nine back slats, caned seat frame, 79¾" l, 31½" d, 28¾" h 9,250.00
Model No. 222, c1905–06, even arm, tall tapering posts joined by wide horizontal crest rail, twenty–two vertical slats, red decal on lower leg, newer int. rails, 79⅛" l, 32½" d, 36¼" h 13,000.00
Model No. 286, c1906, tall spindle back, spindles from under flat arm to lower through tenon stretcher, new seat and frame, refinished, 48" l, 24" d, 49" h .. 3,500.00
Stickley, L. & J. G., Fayetteville, NY, c1912, Model No. 220, Prairie style, wide flat arms and crest rail supported by corbels over inset panels, two per side, six across back, spring cushion seat, light refinish, branched "The Work of L & J G Stickley," 84½" l, 36¾" d, 29" h 18,000.00
Charles II Style, 18th C, walnut, carved and parcel gilt, shaped back with finial corners, turned shaped legs, stretcher, Flemish tapestry upholstery, 64" l 2,250.00
Chinese Export, early 19th C, carved hardwood, shaped crest with center carved shell, scrolled lotus petal carved arms, molded seat rail with acanthus carved reserves, scrolled volute carved and ring turned feet, minor repairs to arms, 91" l 11,000.00
Empire, American, mahogany, ivory damask upholstery, carved, 56" l 550.00
Empire Style, gilt metal mounted and mirrored walnut, re–upholstered, columnar arm supports, 57¾" l 1,900.00
Federal, MA, North Shore, 1800–15, inlaid mahogany, gently arched upholstered back, flanked by molded sloping arms, reeded baluster turned supports, bowed upholstered seat, turned and reeded tapering legs, headed by inlaid rect panels outlined with patterned stringing, old break and repair to one leg at frame juncture, 71" w, 26" d, 35¼" h 16,500.00
Neo–Classical, Italian, late 18th C, chair back, four pierced oval chair backs, carved flowerheads, scrolling open arms, padded seat, carved drapery on apron, paterae on baluster turned

leaf tip carved legs, celadon cotton upholstery, restorations, 74" l 3,300.00
Sheraton, white repaint, black, red, and gold dec, turned legs, outward curved feet, balloon shape rush seat, turned arm supports, scrolled arms, pierced rail back, shell and vintage dec crest 2,300.00
Victorian, garden, cast iron, floral and foliate dec, painted white, 45½" l ... 900.00
Windsor, American, country, spindle back, plank seat, refinished, 40" l .. 875.00

Sideboard, Federal, mahogany, bow front, two short drawers, two cupboard drawers, single long drawer, pr of recessed cupboard doors, straight tapered legs, brass caps and casters, 61" w, 39" h, $10,500.00.

SIDEBOARDS

Art Nouveau, French, c1900, walnut, arched and thumb molded cornice, leaded and textured glass door, quarter round platforms on splayed supports, lower section with molded edge over two cupboard doors, rect platform, stylized bracket feet, 59" w, 85" h 2,000.00
Arts and Crafts
American, oak, trapezoidal top, three central drawers with triangular pulls, flanked by cabinets, hammered strap hinges, single long drawer, open angular sides, 77" l, 24" d, 39¼" h 950.00
Stickley Bros, MI, c1910, Model No. 8609, oak, gallery top, two glass doors over overhanging surface, two half drawers, long drawer and two cabinet doors, swing pull handles, stenciled number, minor nicks and scratches, 54" w, 22" d, 62" h 950.00
Stickley, Gustav
Model No. 804, c1912, oak, graduated drawers, two cupboard doors, high arched apron, slab sides, exposed tenons, branded mark, 54" w, 22" d, 42" h 14,300.00

Model No. 818, oak, rect top, horizontal back rail, row of three drawers, undershelf, red Gustav Stickley decal in top right hand drawer, 48″ l, 19½″ d, 39″ h ... **2,100.00**

Stickley, L & J G, Model No. 738, c1912, oak, plate rail, rect top, two center drawers flanked by two cabinet doors, strap hinges, branded mark, minor stains, 60″ l, 20″ d, 46″ h **1,900.00**

Classical, MA, early 19th C, mahogany veneer, ovolo corners, beaded concentric circles, gadrooning in outline, acanthus leaf carving, reeding and carved hairy paw feet, old refinish, replaced brasses, minor imperfections, 60½″ l, 23¾″ d, 41″ h **6,000.00**

Edwardian, inlaid mahogany, three quarter brass gallery, conforming cast, drawer above two tambour doors, flanked by drawer above door on sq tapering legs, spade feet, 85″ w, 26″ d, 36¾″ h **2,325.00**

Federal
American, 1800–10, mahogany, bow front, banded and strung edge, inlaid stiles with pendant bellflowers, tapered sq legs, 40″ h, 53¾″ l ... **23,100.00**

New York, c1805, inlaid mahogany, oblong top, central drawer flanked by two convex drawers, pr of hinged doors flanked by pr of convex doors, oval and carrot inlaid dies, line and bellflower inlaid sq tapering legs, cross banded cuffs, 71½″ l, 27½″ d, 39″ h **38,500.00**

George III, c1800, mahogany, satinwood inlay, cross banded and strung top, six sq tapered legs with bronze capped feet, 78¼″ l, 34¼″ **9,350.00**

George III Style, mahogany, satinwood inlay, two drawers and two doors, sq tapered legs with sq feet, 60″ w, 21″ d, 31″ h **2,200.00**

Georgian Style, mahogany, shaped top, three drawers, two doors, sq tapered legs, spade feet, 48½″ w, 24¾″ d, 35½″ h **800.00**

Hepplewhite, American, mahogany, inlaid, seven drawers, two cupboards, orig finish, replaced hardware, 61¾ x 20½ x 42¼″ **2,300.00**

Hepplewhite Style, American, southern, hunt board, poplar, ash, and birch, brownish stain repaint, two nailed drawers, applied beading, molded top edge, high sq tapered legs, handmade, 49¾″ w, 21½″ d, 48¾″ h **450.00**

Neoclassical, Continental, inlaid yew ormolu, glazed doors above mirrored backsplash, swan form supports, two aligned frieze drawers over cupboard doors in base, raised on tapered feet, 60″ w, 19½″ d, 82″ h **1,700.00**

Regency, inlaid mahogany, serpentine rect top, conforming case, central drawer over two fan inlaid brackets, flanked by deep drawer, shallow drawer above deep drawer, sq tapering legs, spade feet, restorations, 55″ w, 24″ d, 36½″ h **4,200.00**

Rococo Style, carved, marquetry and parquetry, marble top, 77½″ l **1,600.00**

Sheraton, American, country, curly maple, poplar secondary wood, scalloped crest, three dovetailed drawers, base shelf, turned posts and feet, turned curly maple pulls, light natural refinishing, 36½″ w, 36½″ h **3,750.00**

Victorian
Eastlake, rosewood, inlaid ebony door, ebonized and gilted moldings, incised carved leaf dec enhanced with gold, 60 x 22¼ x 51¾″ **3,500.00**

Rococo Revival, walnut, broken arched crest with high relief nut carving, shelf over inset mirror and foliate carved supports, two drawers, four recessed paneled doors with high relief carved fruit, nuts, and game, plinth base, 67½″ w, 21″ d, 82″ h **2,600.00**

Sofa, Federal, NY, 1785–1800, mahogany, maple, beech, pine, American gumwood, orig back burlap, 98½″ l, 39¼″ h, $75,000.00.

SOFAS

Art Nouveau, Carlo Bugatti, c1900, ebonized wood, rect back and mechanical seat, slightly scrolling rect arms, parchment upholstery, painted swallows and leafy branches, hammered brass trim, four block form feet, 66⅜″ l **1,750.00**

Classical
American, mahogany, back scrolled crest rail flanked by scrolled and

leaf carved terminals, upholstered back, out scrolled arm rests with star punch and floral basket carving, scroll carved supports, rect seat, cornucopia carved returns, paw feet, minor wear, 78" l **715.00**

New York, c1820–25, mahogany, concave carved crest rail ending in carved eagle heads, upholstered back and seat, scroll arms extending into convex molded seat rail, carved and applied wing returns, lion's paw feet, 85" l, 37½" h **7,000.00**

Classical Style, Duncan Phyfe style, mahogany, carved, yellow geometric upholstery, 82½" l **300.00**

Empire, American, 1820–30, mahogany, scrolled back, cornucopia legs, paw feet, re–upholstered, 88" l **700.00**

Federal

American, figured mahogany frame, crest and scrolled arms with simple inlay, scrolled legs, brass paw feet, repairs to frame and front legs, old finish, new silk brocade upholstery, 71¼" l **1,000.00**

New York, c1810, mahogany, reeded crest, center panel carved with thunderbolts tied with bow, upholstered back, reeded arm supports, reeded and waterleaf carved uprights, bowed upholstered seat, circular reeded legs, brass castors, legs reduced, repairs to two rear legs, 71¼" l **8,750.00**

George III, c1800, carved mahogany, channel molded frame, arched back, high downswept arms, curved seat rail, four front ring turned tapering supports, outer supports headed by oval carved paterae below stiff leaf carved arm supports, brass caps and casters, striped yellow satin upholstery **3,200.00**

George III Style, Neoclassical taste, carved beech, slightly arched back continuing to rounded downswept sides with centerpad arms, bowed seat, four fluted turned tapering front supports, four molded outset rear supports, flowered gold damask upholstery, pr, one 19th C, other later **13,200.00**

Georgian Style, mahogany, camelback, ivory damask upholstery, Marlborough legs, 84" l **425.00**

Louis XV, transitional style, giltwood, carved, rounded arms, taupe foliate silk damask upholstery, 82" l **1,400.00**

Napoleon III, Aubusson tapestry, giltwood, serpentine crest rail, padded arms, volute supports, cabriole legs, 72" l **2,750.00**

Regency, mahogany, carved, reclining arms form chaise, black and white striped upholstery, 58½" l **1,600.00**

Victorian, Biedermeier, fruitwood and ebonized wood, upholstered central flat top back, rounded corners, cornucopia form scrolled ends with foliated capitals supporting broad flattened domed arm rests, cylindrical bolsters, broad seat rail above reeded flattened triangular frieze, broad sq front supports, bottle green mohair upholstery, 72" l **3,850.00**

SPINNING WHEELS

34½" h, oak and hardwood, turned and chip carved detail, incomplete and mismatched parts **100.00**

36" h, oak, turned legs, chip carved back, marked "A Knox" **200.00**

38" h, maple, flax wheel, orig parts . . . **300.00**

45" h, 30" d wool wheel, oak, cast iron parts **325.00**

48" h, wool, walnut, PA, mid 19th C . . **450.00**

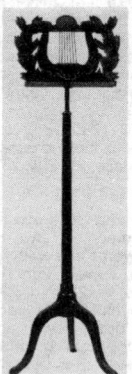

Stand, music, Regency, adjustable lyre form rest, columnar support, tripod base, 54" h, $1,100.00.

STANDS

Bakery Cooling Rack, country, softwood, beveled edge cornice, removable shelves, chamfered edges on shoe feet, old red paint over black, 63½" h **525.00**

Book Stand, Victorian, walnut veneer, end pieces set with pate sur pate plaques of cupids playing badminton, Bettemann's patent, sold by Shreve Crump and Low, 16" l **500.00**

Crock Stand, country, American, primitive, five stepped shelves, old green repaint, late wire nail construction, 38" w, 30" d, 31" h **125.00**

Dressing, Empire, walnut, rect top, frieze drawer, adjustable swing mirror with turned supports, ring turned standard on trefoil base, flat bun feet, 17" w, 13¾" d, 49" h **300.00**

Drink Stand, Arts and Crafts, L & J G Stickley
  Model No. 22, c1910, oak, overhanging round top, wide skirt, four splay legs joined by cross stretchers, Handcraft decal, 18" d, 28¼" h . . **1,300.00**
  Model No. 574, 1912, oak, rect cut–corner top, tall legs, lower shelf on cross stretcher base, branded, 18" d, 29" h **550.00**

Kettle, Federal, CT or northern New England, c1795, birchwood and maple, circular dished top, cyma shaped edge, spirally ribbed standard, cabriole legs, snake feet, minor restoration, 12½" d, 28½" h **2,500.00**

Music, Victorian, oak and mahogany, checkered line inlaid lip, tapered reeded standard, circular platform, four stylized animal legs, 19th C . . . **1,650.00**

Night
  Chippendale, RI, 1780–1800, cherry, top and skirt with molded edge, orig brass, old surface, 21⅛" w, 25¾" d, 28¼" h **1,800.00**
  Country
    Cherry, curly and bird's eye maple veneer, turned legs, two dovetailed drawers, one with ogee, other with curved front, refinished, 17½" w, 22½" d, 28½" h **300.00**
    Walnut, drop leaf, turned legs, two dovetailed drawers with applied pressed edge molding, 16" w, 20" d, 29" h **225.00**
  Federal
    New England, coastal, c1810, cherry, inlaid, top and single drawer outlined with stringing and quarter fan inlays, skirt and legs with stringing, old glass pull, refinished, 18⅛" w, 17" d, 26¾" h **1,900.00**
    New York, 1790–1810, mahogany, thumb molded rect top, plain apron, incised beaded drawer, four thin turned tapering legs, bulbous cuffs, 15" w, 21½" d, 27" h **1,760.00**
  Folk Art, cherry, two board top with

cut out ovolo corners, two dovetailed drawers, turned legs, facade, sides of apron and front legs with relief flower carving, punched designs, old worn finish, 21" w, 21¼" d, 29" h **600.00**

Plant
  Country, American, ash column, burled ash top, three cast iron branch legs, 10½" d, 33¼" h **150.00**
  Chinese Export, late 18th C, lacquer, circular inset porcelain plaque of figures in court setting, molded border, turned support within scrollwork, tripod base with scrolling toes, black ground with stenciled scenes, gilt highlights, 14" d, 30" h, pr **11,000.00**

Reading, Georgian, mahogany, oblong tilting top, turned standard, scrolling tripod base, ball feet, 19½" w, 16" d, 25" h **1,100.00**

Spool, walnut, four tiers, turned column with finials on top, one drawer, refinished, 49¼" h **270.00**

Tray on Stand, George III Style, mahogany, oval, shaped gallery, oval flower filled basket inlay, sq tapering splayed legs, X stretcher, 27½" w, 20½" d, 27½" h **770.00**

Umbrella, Arts and Crafts, Gustav Stickley, c1912, Model No. 54, oak, four sq tapering posts, copper drip pan insert, paper label, 33¼" h **6,000.00**

Urn, George III Style, mahogany, circular top, ivory baluster gallery, spirally turned standard, acanthus carved baluster base, downswept tripod, whorled feet, 11½" d, 47½" h **3,250.00**

Wash
  Country, pine, simple turned feet and pilasters, paneled door, one dovetailed drawer, lift lid top, 29¼" w, 16½" d, 31¼" h **210.00**
  Sheraton
    Country, refinished cherry, turned feet and posts, dovetailed drawer and gallery, 19½" w, 16½" d, 28" h **300.00**
    Decorated, pine, orig white paint, red and green striping, turned legs and posts, dovetailed drawer, crest with corner shelves, hole for bowl, white porcelain knobs, 20¾" w, 16¼" d, 32¾" h **225.00**

STEPS

Bed, English, mahogany, emb leather applied to top of each step, top step

pens to commode, 24¾ x 17¼ x
18½", late 18th C, early 19th C **275.00**

Library

George III, late 18th C, mahogany,
rect molded hinged top, eight
steps, 49½" l, 53½" h extended . . **2,150.00**

Regency, early 19th C, mahogany,
three steps, inset green leather
treads, scrolling banister, sq balusters, castered feet, 46" w, 27" d,
56" h **23,000.00**

**Stool, foot, pine, five board type, 17" l,
9" h, $50.00.**

STOOLS

Broom Maker's, splayed turned legs,
mid shelf, wood and wrought iron
clamps, worn gray paint, 36" h **225.00**

Foot

Arts and Crafts, American, oak

Stickley, L & J G, rect, leather upholstered top, branded "L & J G
Stickley," 16¼ x 19¾ x 13¾" .. **500.00**

Stickley, Gustav, c1906, Model No.
302, leather top, short flaring
feet, red decal and paper label,
12¼" d **425.00**

Decorated, rect top, splayed turned
legs, old dark green paint, yellow
and green "F" and flower, 7½ x
13½" **65.00**

Empire, American, 1830–40, mahogany, needlepoint and burgundy velvet upholstery **125.00**

George I, c1740, walnut

Oval, padded top in later figural petit point, molded frame, angled
cabriole legs with bold paneled C
scroll capitals, ball and claw feet,
20" l **26,000.00**

Rect, needlepoint seat, cabriole
legs, pad feet, 20" l, 17" w, 14¾"
h **1,400.00**

George II Style, English, mahogany,
oval padded seat, conforming
frieze, cabriole legs, acanthus, ball
and claw feet, green and brown
needlepoint **715.00**

Jacobean Style, English, oak, rect
molded top, carved frieze, baluster
turned fluted legs, block feet, box
stretcher, 17½' w, 14" d, 19½" h **535.00**

Louis XV Style, Continental, giltwood,
painted, 25" l, 17" d **500.00**

Mission, oak, rect, arched skirt, four
vertical slats per side, 20¼" l, 14"
d, 16" h **325.00**

Victorian

Adjustable, L Postauka & Co, Cam-
bridgeport, Mass, re–upholstered seat, orig label, patent
date April 4, 1871 .... **375.00**

Walnut, finger carved, green velvet
upholstery **250.00**

Windsor, oval, splayed base, old
green repaint, 10 x 14", 10¾" h .. **225.00**

Piano, adjustable, mahogany, circular
seat, turned legs, worn leather upholstery, 21" h **75.00**

TABLES

Banquet, Queen Anne Style, Eldred
Wheeler, maple, double pedestal, two
additional leaves, 84" l, (extends to
124") 48" w, 29½" h **1,600.00**

Book, Arts and Crafts, L & J G Stickley,
Model No. 516, c1912, oak, sq overhanging top, corresponding base,
each side alternating with open shelf
and slat sides, sgd "The Work of L &
J G Stickley," minor stains, 27" sq, 29"
h **3,250.00**

Breakfast

George III, 18th C, mahogany, circular top, reeded edge, quadruple
scrolled support, brass paw feet
and casters, 47" d, 30" h **6,050.00**

George IV, 1820–30, mahogany, rect
two piece top, molded edge,
rounded corners, shaped platform
with ringed vasiform standard, four
scrolled flat reeded legs with foliate
cast brass caps and casters, 54" l,
28½" h **1,650.00**

Regency, mahogany, tilt-top, rect
rounded corner cross banded and
line inlaid top, vasiform and reeded
standard, shaped base, scrolled
knees, reeded brass caster feet,
48½" w, 36" d, 27½" h **1,500.00**

Card

Chippendale, Philadelphia, 1760–80,
carved mahogany, rect hinged top,
outset rounded corners, recessed
baize cov surface, corner candle
pockets, conforming apron, center
bead molded short drawer, acanthus carved cabriole legs, ball and

Table, card, Federal, Michael Allison School, NY, c1810, mahogany, ovolo corners, oval inlaid reserves, straight tapered legs, banded cuffs, 36″ w, 29½″ h, $4,750.00.

claw feet, minor repairs and restoration, 33¾″ w, 32½″ d, 28⅜″ h . . **71,500.00**
Classical, New York, 1820–30, carved mahogany, D shaped hinged top, cross banded and line inlaid with molded edge, concave apron with center foliate carved reserve over feather and acanthus carved urn shaped pedestal, coved shelf, four lion's paw feet with acanthus carved knees and casters, 37½″ w, 37⅛″ open, 30½″ h **2,000.00**
Federal
  American, mahogany, flame veneer apron, folding top, convoluted apron with conforming reeded edge top, turned and reeded legs, swing leg support, brass acanthus leaf caps and casters, old refinishing, 37¾″ w, 17″ d, 30¼″ h **1,300.00**
  American, mahogany, hinged demi–lune top, green baize surface, arched line inlaid tapered sq legs headed by black terminals with floral medallion inlay, 36″ d, 30″ h **1,210.00**
  Massachusetts, attributed to Jacob Forster, c1790, mahogany, inlaid, D shaped hinged top, cross banded and line inlaid, straight tapering legs, old refinish, 36″ w, 17½″ d, 28¼″ h **2,000.00**
  George I, early 18th C, walnut, fold over, concertina, oblong top, outset corners, conforming frieze, herringbone cross banded drawer, straight tapered legs, lappet collars, pad feet, 31½″ w, 15″ d, 28½″ h **4,500.00**
  George III, mid 18th C, mahogany, oblong fold over top, serpentine sides and front, carved blind fret edge, recessed rect frieze, concer-

tina action with blind fret carved straight tapered supports, 33½″ w, 16″ d, 28½″ h **3,750.00**
Hepplewhite, mahogany
  American, fly leaf, inlaid **1,850.00**
  New England, D shape, string inlay **700.00**
Regency, mahogany, demi–lune top with tooled baize lined int., conforming frieze, rear slide out drawer, sq tapered legs, cuff feet on casters, brass mounted, 45″ w, 22¼″ d, 28¾″ h **3,750.00**
Center
Art Deco, French, c1925, hexagonal walnut top, ebony edge, ebonized hexagonal pedestal with relief carving of trees, vegetation, and tribesman, ivory masks mounted at mid section, three African ivory tusks with relief carving of crocodiles and birds, tapering hexagonal walnut and ebony base, 31″ d, 28″ h . . . **3,850.00**
Arts and Crafts, American
  Limbert, Michigan, c1910, Model No. 120, octagonal, four flat legs with spade cut–outs joined by flat stretchers, branded, refinished, 45¼″ d, 29¾″ h **850.00**
  Oak, round top, four sq legs joined by cross stretchers, exposed tenons, pyramidal center finial, 40″ d, 30″ h **1,550.00**
  Tile top, rect top inlaid with geometric and figural Pewabic tiles, lustered polychrome glazes, 25½″ l, 18¾″ d, 25½″ h **1,100.00**
George III, mid 18th C, mahogany, lozenge form, galleried top, conforming frieze, straight legs pierced to form four columns, joined to frieze by spaced spandrels, stepped block form feet, 19½″ w, 29¾″ d, 27½″ h **1,600.00**
Neoclassical, Italian, marquetry fruitwood, polychrome pietra dura inset top, sq tapered legs, 45½″ w, 22″ d, 20½″ h **1,900.00**
Queen Anne, PA, 1740–1770, walnut, rect top overhangs apron with three short thumb molded drawers, turned tapering legs, pad feet, 62¼″ w, 38″ d, 29½″ h **6,150.00**
Coffee, International Movement, George Nakashima, commissioned by International Paper, c1980, rosewood and walnut, rect top with free edge, four inlaid butterfly keys, cruciform base, marked "IP," 70½″ l, 36½″ w, 20½″ h **6,000.00**
Console
Art Moderne, American, attributed to Lorin Jackson, c1942, horseshoe

shaped mahogany base and rect top, lucite winged torch, medallion on center of mirrored back, two stylized Egyptian columns support mirrored one drawer top, applied lucite Minoan frieze, 48″ w, 20″ d, 33½″ h **7,700.00**

Chippendale Style, mahogany, marble rect top, scroll carved frieze, chamfered sq legs, 48½″ w, 36″ d, 27½″ h **1,500.00**

Empire, c1800–10, mahogany, rect gray flecked marble top, plain frieze, drawer with two stylized swans drinking from fountain, swan within berried laurel wreath mounted on corners, tapered columnar supports with gilt bronze mountings, rear pilasters support mirror, rect plinth, 40″ l, 35¼″ h, pr **6,600.00**

Federal, Salem, MA, 1795–1815, inlaid and carved mahogany, demi–lune, cross banded border, molded edge, conforming veneered apron, three astragal end panels, similar small inlaid panels over each leg, four waterleaf carved turned, tapering, and stop fluted legs, waterleaf carved cuffs, tapering feet, joined by open curved X stretcher, central astragal shaped medial block, repairs to stretchers and one leg, pr **30,800.00**

George III, late 18th C, D form white veined marble top inlaid with trailing husk ornament and urn, molded and carved border, resting on later conforming gilt wood stand in Neoclassical taste, fluted frieze center panels of urns, straight tapered molded legs, 48″ w, 23½″ h, 33″ h **13,000.00**

Couch, Chinese, 19th C, lacquered, top dec of gold and red painted peach branches, sprays of flowers, and bats, black ground, 43″ w, 30″ d, 16″ h . . **7,500.00**

Dining

Arts and Crafts

Indiana Hickory Furniture Co, early 20th C, hickory, circular top, bent and lot wood supports, branded manufacturer's mark, retailers metal tag "Paine Furniture Boston," 47½″ d, 28¾″ h **900.00**

Gustav Stickley, c1910, Model No. 632, oak, round top, five sq tapering post legs, four 12″ w extension leaves, 48″ d, 29¼″ h . . **6,125.00**

Federal, mahogany, inlaid maple oval panel on each end, reeded baluster form legs, plain feet, 78½″ l extended, 29″ h **3,575.00**

George III, 19th C, mahogany

Three pedestals, reeded edge, three tripod sabre supports on ring turned pedestals, brass paw feet and casters, 144″ l, 29″ h **11,000.00**

Twin pedestals, mahogany, oblong molded top, finely figured, turned standard, downswept quatrepod supports, brass castered feet, 72″ l, 51¼″ w, 28¼″ h, extends by two leaves to 111″ **21,000.00**

Georgian Style, carved, walnut, five leaves, 67″ l closed **800.00**

Sheraton, American, first quarter 19th C, curly maple top, turned maple legs, refinished, 35¾″ l, 17″ w closed, 27½″ h **500.00**

Display, American, attributed to Packard Bldg, San Francisco, c1926, wrought iron, inset rect coral American marble top with crystalline deposits, entrelac cast frieze, scrolled wrought iron supports, slightly arched cruciform stretchers, circular feet, 72½″ l, 31½″ h **3,850.00**

Dressing

Queen Anne, oak and elm, rect top with molded edge, three drawers, scalloped apron, sq cabriole legs with sq molded black feet, 29″ l, 28″ h **3,025.00**

Regency, English, 19th C, mahogany, three drawers, backsplash with shelf, 36¾″ l **750.00**

Sheraton, country, attributed to New York state, c1830, cherry, all–over red paint, scalloped back and conforming side panels, rect top varnished, sq legs with ringed capitals over round tapering legs, ball feet, all orig condition, orig brasses, 30¾″ w, 16¼″ d, 32″ h **850.00**

William and Mary, MA, c1720, walnut veneer, two deep drawers, small center drawer, shaped "X" stretcher with finial, replaced brasses, top re–veneered, minor imperfections, 33⅜″ w, 23″ d, 30″ h **4,000.00**

Drop Leaf

Chippendale, mahogany, rect top, molded sq cabriole legs, ball and claw feet, 41¾″ l, 27¼″ h **3,125.00**

Federal

American, cherry and mahogany, rect top and mahogany inlaid panel, fan spandrels, arrow inlaid edge apron, sq tapered legs, 36″ l, 27½″ h **1,650.00**

Massachusetts, 1800–1815, cherry, rect top, two drop leaves, plain apron, turned reeded tapering legs, 48″ l, 47½″ w, 28″ h . . **2,750.00**

New England, 1790–1810, cherry, rect top, two drop leaves, plain apron, sq tapering legs, 42½" l, 41¾" w, 27¾" h **2,860.00**

Hepplewhite, country, maple, sq tapered legs, refinished, 18½" w, 35¾" d, 28" h **425.00**

Jacobean Style, round, turned gate legs, 29" h, 72" d extended **2,500.00**

Queen Anne

American, cherry and maple, swing legs, pad feet, refinished, 47" l, 27½" h **3,500.00**

American, PA, late 18th C, walnut, rect top, two drop leaves, cabriole legs, refinished, repairs to top, 48½" w, 19" d, 28" h **1,500.00**

English, mahogany, tapered legs, duck feet and pads, oval top, restored apron, 46" w, 27½" h ... **400.00**

Sheraton, country, cherry and tiger maple, six legs, refinished, 42" l, 29¼" h **350.00**

Table, game, Regency, rosewood, twin drop leaves, removable panel with inlaid ebony and ivory checkerboard, backgammon well, full frieze drawer, sq tapering standard, incurvate rect base, 20" w, 28½" h, $1,400.00.

Game

Chippendale, American, late 18th C, country, pine and maple, shaped top, single drawer, tapered molded legs, refinished, 36" l, 16" d, 26¼" h **600.00**

George II

Mahogany, oblong fold over top, ovolo corners, leather lined playing surface, candlestick and ticket wells, conforming frieze with full drawer, straight tapering turned legs, pad feet, 32½" w, 16" d, 28½" h **1,400.00**

Walnut, rect eared hinged top, brown leather gilt tooled playing surface, carved chip cups, conforming frieze, cabriole legs, pad feet, 32" w, 15½" d, 29" h **3,300.00**

Victorian, rosewood, hinged rect molded top, opens to inlaid chessboard playing surface, frieze fitted with drawer, shaped wooden basket flanked by S shaped molded supports terminating in single support, circular molded plinth, scrolled feet, 18¼" w, 16" d, 28½" h **1,100.00**

Harvest, country, pine and birch, sq chamfered legs, mortised and pinned stretchers and apron, worn finish, 84" w, 27¾" h **1,000.00**

Hunt, Victorian, Georgian taste, drop leaf, mahogany, oval twin flap top, conforming frieze, sq chamfered molded legs, 98" w, 56½" l extended, 29" h **2,000.00**

Hutch

American

Maple and pine, one dovetailed drawer, turned feet and posts, refinished, 42½" w, 29" h **500.00**

Pine, country

Rect, three board top, cut out feet, lift lid seat, old worn dark patina, age cracks and scorching, 30" w, 60" l, 29" h **850.00**

Simple cutout feet, mortised ends, old worn brown paint, replaced pins, 63½" w, 29½" h **3,700.00**

Pennsylvania, second quarter 19th C, painted and grained, pine and maple, all-over mustard paint, underside of top comb grained and outlined, 17½" h hinged seat, 54" w, 35¾" d, 51⅛" h **1,300.00**

Library

Arts and Crafts

Stickley, Gustav, Model No. 428, oak, arched apron, protruding post legs, medial shelf with keyed tenon below, 49" w, 31½" d, 30" h **1,980.00**

Stickley, L & J G, Model No. 531, oak, rect, one long drawer, undertier shelf joined by through tenons to side stretchers, white "L & J G Stickley" decal in drawer, 49" l, 30" d, 29" h **1,210.00**

Baroque, Italian, 18th C, walnut, rect top, two drawers with lozenge cushion fronts, cylindrical column supports on blocked bases, circular turned feet, molded sq tied stretcher **2,200.00**

George III, mahogany, rect tooled leather inset top, two drawers, sq tapered legs, brass cap caster feet, 29¼" h, 47¾" w, 31½" d **3,250.00**

Pembroke

Federal, NY, c1810, mahogany, rect top, two shaped drop leaves, single

drawer, orig pull, casters, old refinish, shaped leaves extend to 32¾",
30" w, 18¼" d, 27¾" h **1,000.00**

George III, inlaid mahogany, oval cross banded top, cock beaded frieze drawer, sq tapered legs, cuffed feet, 36½" w extended, 32" l, 28½" h **875.00**

Hepplewhite

Country, birch, sq tapered legs with casters, mortised and pinned apron, mellow brown finish, 44" w, 28⅝" h **400.00**

Drop Leaf, mahogany, inlays, refinished, 31¼" l, 21" w closed, 39½" w opened **2,400.00**

Sheraton, country

Cherry, turned legs, shaped leaves, old alligatored varnish on base, rubbed out finish on top, rule joints, repairs, 19 x 40", 28¾" h, 11½" leaves **500.00**

Maple, folding apron wings, turned legs, old finish, 17¼ x 36¼", 28" h, 9" leaves **1,250.00**

Pier

Classical, New York, 1815–25, carved mahogany, rect marble over convex apron with fruit stenciling, flanked by acanthus leaves over stenciled frieze, rect glass plate flanked by mahogany pilasters, free standing mahogany tapering columns with carved giltwood capitals and bases, coved stenciled base, carved lion's paw feet with giltwood acanthus leaf carving and cornucopia carved brackets, 41¼" w, 19" d, 39¼" h **5,000.00**

Empire, Continental, last half 19th C, mahogany, ebony and gilt Egyptian style figural front supports, gray marble top, 38½" w, 32½" h **1,900.00**

Refectory, European, oak, cut out ends, pinned trestle and apron, removable top, old dark finish, 72" l, 30" h **280.00**

Sawbuck, English, oak, dark finish, breadboard top, chamfered sq legs, pinned trestle, 65½" l, 28¾" h **175.00**

Sellette, Art Nouveau, inlaid mahogany, two shelves with marquetry woodbine and butterfly, four carved and buttressed legs, sgd "Galle" in marquetry, 45" h **4,650.00**

Serving

Arts and Crafts, Gustav Stickley, c1912, oak, Model No. 802, two short drawers, four tapering legs, arched apron, branded mark, 41¾" w, 18" d, 39½" h **4,650.00**

Federal, MA, c1810, cherry, inlaid, serpentine top, rounded corners,

maple veneered drawer with flame birch panels, tapered cylindrical legs, 31¾" w, 29⅛" h **880.00**

Sewing

Classical, New England, c1825, mahogany veneer, rect top, two D shaped leaves, two working drawers, compartmented int., replaced bag, orig brasses, minor staining to surface, minor veneer loss, 19½" w, 18" d, 28½" h **900.00**

Federal, MA, cherry, rect top, two cock beaded drawers, out set rounded corners, leaf carved stiles form reeded cylindrical legs, turned feet, 22" w, 27½" h, c1810 ...... **1,430.00**

Napoleon III Style, mother-of-pearl and brass inlaid, shaped lift top, inset mirror back, well and shelf int., cabriole legs with sabots, label "J Clifford, St Louis, MO" **750.00**

Sheraton, country, cherry, bowed drawer, old refinish **250.00**

Side

Art Moderne, American, attributed to Lorin Jackson, c1942, lucite, oval glass top, circular skirt with applied rosettes, four tapering legs, 21¼" d, 25¾" h, pr **4,400.00**

Art Nouveau

Inlaid Mahogany, two tiers, two deep dish shelves with marquetry flowers and vines, three twist carved legs, branded "L Marjorelle Nancy," 18" w, 29" h **4,100.00**

Marquetry, inlaid mahogany, rounded triangular top, marquetry cock and poppies, inscription "Quand Le Coq Chanteaura, Mon Amour Pour Vous Finira," sgd "Galle" in marquetry, 21¼" w, 28½" h **2,640.00**

Arts and Crafts, American

Limbert, Grand Rapids, MI, c1907, oval top, oval lower shelf, cross member base, sq cut–outs, orig dark finish, branded mark, 47½" l, 36" d, 29¼" h **3,750.00**

L & J G Stickley, oak, octagonal, four legs joined by cross stretcher, white L & J G Stickley decal mark, 18" d, 20" h **1,100.00**

Louis XV, Provincial, mid 18th C, walnut, oblong dished top, recessed frieze with two end drawers, shaped apron, cabriole legs, whorled feet, 15" w, 23½" d, 26½" h **3,200.00**

Neo–Classical, Italian, late 18th C, walnut, oblong top with oval marquetry panel of classical figure, multiple marquetry borders, conforming recessed frieze with ornament, full end drawer, straight tapered legs, 22″ w, 17″ d, 27½″ h **2,200.00**

Victorian, Renaissance Revival, American, 1860–70, rosewood, gilt incised, circular black marble top, leaf carved frieze and pedestal with geometric inlay, foliate carved tripod base, tiger paw feet, trefoil base on carved bun feet, losses to two feet, 19″ d, 30¾″ h **6,600.00**

William and Mary, walnut, oblong molded and calamander cross banded top, outset corners, rect frieze with full herringbone cross banded drawer, cup and trumpet legs, X stretcher, compressed ball feet, 26″ w, 17″ d, 27½″ h **1,000.00**

Tavern
 Federal
  Country, hardwood and pine, scrubbed finish, turned legs, mortised and pinned stretcher and apron, repaired, 38¾″ l, 28″ h **250.00**
  Maple and pine, oval pine top, plain apron, block and turned cylindrical legs with cylindrical feet, 32″ l, 27″ h, 18th C **1,980.00**
 Hepplewhite, country
  Maple and cherry, pine one board top with bread board ends, mortised and pinned apron, one dovetailed drawer, sq tapered legs, reattached top, drawer pull missing, 28½″ w, 43″ l, 27½″ h **500.00**
  Maple and pine, sq tapered maple legs, mortised and pinned pine apron, pine breadboard scrubbed top, red traces on base, 37½″ l, 26½″ h **750.00**
 Queen Anne
  Cherry, shaped sides, triangular pad feet, old refinishing, replaced glue blocks, 28¾″ l, 27″ h **2,500.00**
  Pine and maple, mortised and pinned apron, molded edge, one dovetailed drawer, turned tapered legs, duck feet, old dark red repaint, worm holes in base, age cracks, replaced warped top, 26¾″ w, 37⅓″ l, 26″ h **600.00**

Tea
 Arts and Crafts
  American, oak, circular top, sq section legs joined by cross stretcher, 20″ d, 26″ h **900.00**
  Stickley, L & J G, Model No. 577, c1910, oak, circular top, lower round shelf on cross stretchers, sgd "Handcraft," some stains and roughness, 29¾″ w, 29″ h **550.00**

Chippendale
 Mahogany, tilt top, tripod base, claw and elongated ball feet, serpentine top, old finish, 33″ sq, 27″ h **650.00**
 Walnut, dish top, birdcage support, claw and ball feet, 33″ d, 28″ h **675.00**

George III, mahogany, carved, tilt top, pie crust top, birdcage support, acanthus carved urn form standard, acanthus carved cabriole legs, pad feet, 32″ d, 27½″ h **4,750.00**

Queen Anne, English, early 18th C, walnut, dish shaped rect top, conforming frieze, cabriole legs, pointed pad feet, restorations, 34″ w, 21¼″ d, 27¼″ h **3,500.00**

Trestle
 Arts and Crafts, L & J G Stickley,
  Model No. 404, c1904, overhanging rect top, flatboard sides, cut-out base, lower shelf with keyed tenons, unsigned, refinished, 36″ w, 28¼″ h **900.00**
  Model No. 593, double side supports joined by lower shelf, exposed keyed tenons, shaped feet, refinished, 48″ l, 30″ w, 29″ h **600.00**
  Model No. 594, c1910, large overhang above double sides, joined by tenoned flat lower shelf, shaped shoe foot base, unsigned, 72″ l, 45¼″ w, 30½″ h . . **3,700.00**

Work
 Country, cherry, turned legs, one dovetailed drawer, refinished, 27¾″ w, 23½″ d, 29¾″ h **625.00**
 Decorated, Continental, walnut, cartouche satinwood arabesque inlaid border, ebonized top, with floral stenciled reserve above line inlaid fitted frieze drawers, sides and back with pull out inlaid basket with panels, fluted tapered legs, shaped stretcher with center finial, caster feet, 30″ h **2,000.00**
 Empire, American, second quarter 19th C
  Cherry, two drawers, refinished, replaced knobs, 28¾″ h **200.00**
  Mahogany, flame veneer, turned biscuit corners, two dovetailed drawers, top with divided int., rope turned posts, turned and acanthus carved columns on case, pull out work bag frame, carved acanthus and paw feet, old worn refinishing, minor edge damage and veneer repair, replaced brasses, 19″ w, 22¼″ l, 30″ h **1,200.00**

Mahogany, sq top, two drawers, turned legs, medial shelf, hairy paw caster feet, 32½" w, 30¼" h ... **750.00**

Federal

Massachusetts, c1815, cherry, rect top, rounded corners, two drawers, ring turned stiles form tapered cylindrical legs, 19¾" w, 28¾" h **610.00**

New York, mahogany, fold over top, three drawers, pedestal with oval facets, knot and paw feet, foliate carved knees, embellished gold dec with ebony outline, 23½" w, 20⅝" d, 32½" h **3,750.00**

Pennsylvania, pine and poplar, removable three board top, two dovetailed overlapping drawers, turned legs, professional red and black repaint on base, 29½" w, 54½" l, 29½" h **950.00**

Hepplewhite, American

Flame birch top, bird's eye maple drawer face, top sliced to reduce warping, replaced hardware, 38" h **525.00**

Walnut, drop leaves, one drawer ... **250.00**

Sheraton

Tiger Maple, country, one drawer, refinished **850.00**

Walnut, one drawer, refinished ... **325.00**

Writing

Arts and Crafts, oak, rect, two top drawers, four post legs, undershelf stretcher, crown decal mark for Grand Rapids, MI, 56½" l, 34" w, 29¼" h **750.00**

George III, mahogany, carved, tooled leather inset top, center bowed drawer flanked by two deeper drawers, sq tapered legs, spade feet, 53½" w, 26" d, 30½" h ... **3,000.00**

Louis XVI, mahogany, gold tooled tan leather top with molded edge, paneled sides, five projecting paneled drawers, brass inset fluted stiles, sq tapering legs with block feet, 63" l, 31½" h **5,500.00**

Provincial, Continental, fruitwood, shaped thumb molded top, three inlaid frieze drawers, cabriole legs, hoof feet, 72½" w, 28½" d, 29¼" h ... **2,500.00**

TEA WAGONS

Oriental, raised Chinese figures in landscape, D drop leaves, turned legs, two wheels, black lacquer finish ... **300.00**

Victorian, brass, glass **700.00**

Wicker, 1900–20, natural, tight weave design, open top with utensil basket on side, shelf on bottom, wood wheels **500.00**

WAGON SEATS

Wagon seats cannot be classified with seats from a wagon. Early wagon seats were usually constructed with a double frame and a basketry–type seat. They served a dual purpose: in the house and in the family wagon for additional seating.

Country, board along back and sides above seats, trestle feet, board across front below seat, orig black, red, and gold paint, 34½" l, 14" h ... **525.00**

Ladder Back

Three slat back, turned stiles, polychrome floral dec, top slats with oval painted scenes, worn orig red paint with yellow striping, replaced paper rush seat, 34¾" l **375.00**

Two slat back, turned stiles, splint seat, red paint, 35" l **565.00**

Pine, painted and dec, worn old dark gray paint, black, red, and yellow striping, 30" l **150.00**

Wicker, stool, painted white, 13½" h, $150.00.

WICKER

Bench, photographer's, tight weave seat, leaf motif back, rolled arm, stick, ball and curlicue detail, natural and green, c1890 .... **625.00**

Chair

Arm, rattan wrapped, tight weave, geometric diamond shape panel on back, upholstered seat **350.00**

Morris style, adjustable back, white, rolled arms, stick, ball, and scroll detail, blue cushion, c1898 ..... **1,000.00**

Side, shaped woven crest, vase shaped ornate splat, pressed seat, 17½" w, 39" h **175.00**

Chaise Lounge, Wakefield Rattan Co, c1890, rolled arms with scrollwork, continuous and star caned back,

wrapped legs, rolled footrest, yellow floral cushion **800.00**
Desk, natural, gallery wood top, basketweave and openweave design, one drawer, shelf on top with arched front, ball feet, c1900 .... **325.00**
Etagere, rattan wrapped, six tiers, arch rest insert with oval mirror, scrollwork, cabriole legs, X stretcher, 69″ h **1,100.00**
Ferner, cane and wicker, wrapped legs, 31″ h **240.00**
Lectern, tight weave design, rolled edge, shelf, diamond pattern design on front, brown, brass reading lamp, c1910 .... **300.00**
Rocker, platform, rolled edge, high back, patent, 25″ w, 47″ h **450.00**
Sofa, scrolled back, diamond design, upholstered seat, 65″ l, 37″ h **275.00**
Stand

Dressing, Heywood Bros and Wakefield Rattan Co, c1898, oak top, elaborate scrollwork, spindle, wrapped legs and mirror supports, natural, beveled mirror **1,150.00**
Plant, Dryad Works, England, c1915, natural, two tiers, top: two sq and one rect open section; bottom: shelf with small supports separating platform with ball feet, tight weave design, wrapped and braided edges, wrapped supports **425.00**

Table

End, sq top with looped edge, stick, ball, and curlicue detail, small woven tier middle, wrapped legs with stretcher, c1890 .... **375.00**
Tea, natural, oak top and serving shelves, top with rounded corners, stick, ball, and scroll detail, flared wrapped legs and balls, c1890 .. **575.00**

YARN WINDERS

Floor Type, primitive, oak, mortised frame, two reels, one stationary, one adjustable, 51″ h **90.00**
Niddy Noddy, maple, mortised, 17¼″ l **85.00**
Spoke Type

Two Spoke, hardwood, old worn dark green paint, mortised and pinned construction, minor age cracks and edge damage, 24″ h **75.00**
Four Spoke, curly maple, 27″ d, 35½″ h **150.00**
Six Spoke

33″ h, hard and soft wood, old brown patina, turned and chip carved detail, some damage .. **150.00**
40″ h, 28″ w, hickory, walnut, and pine, rect upright with hand hold, incised gauge, carved walnut in-

Yarn Winder, six spokes, poplar, all original, $250.00.

dicator, turned wheel and ears, later pine heart shaped base, angularly set Windsor feet, PA, early 19th C **2,000.00**
41½″ h, turned and chip carved detail, dark green repaint **100.00**
47″ h, 30″ d wheel, pine and hardwoods, old dark cherry colored finish, turned and chip carved detail, age cracks, counting needle missing **50.00**
Winding Reel, mahogany, two adjustable bobbins, quatrefoil base, 47½″ h **175.00**

GAME PLATES

History: Game plates, popular between 1870 and 1915, are specially decorated plates used to serve fish and game. Sets originally included a platter, serving plates, and a sauce or gravy boat. Many sets have been divided. Today, individual plates are used for wall hangings.

Reference: Susan and Al Bagdade, *Warman's English & Continental Pottery & Porcelain, 1st Edition,* Warman Publishing Co., Inc., 1987.

BIRDS

Plate

9″, woodcock, gold trim, green border, marked "Petrus Regout, Maastricht, Holland" **15.00**
9½″, grouse center, five medallions with birds and insects, brown to tan, green border, marked "Z S and Co Bavaria" **45.00**
10″, duck, white, gray, and black body, emerald green head, standing in marsh, gadrooned gilt border within

traditional border, Royal Copenhagen 990.00
12¼", birds in flight, hp gold scalloped edge, marked "Limoges" 190.00
12½" d, quail, hp, natural setting, pink flowers, irregular scalloped heavy gold edge, artist sgd 245.00
13", facing pr, pheasant and quail, cream and green ground, artist sgd "Ch Barbois" 500.00

Bird, plate, scalloped edge, heavy gold trim, sgd "Vitet Limoges," 9½" d, $125.00.

Platter,
13¾ x 9½", duck, oval, hp, natural setting, gold handles, artist sgd, Limoges blank 225.00
14 x 11½", pheasant, cobalt blue and gold border, multicolored center scene, marked "R. K. Beck" 80.00
18" l, pheasants, heavy gold border, artist sgd 500.00
Set, 13 pcs, 20½" l platter with two turkeys, twelve plates with hp designs, artist sgd, marked "Limoges, France" 600.00

DEER

Plate, 13¾", stag in woods, hp, raised enamel dec 200.00
Set, 13 pcs, platter, twelve plates, deer, bear and game birds, yellow ground, scalloped border, marked "Haviland China," sgd "MC Haywood" 3,000.00

ELK

Plate
9", natural colors, scalloped edge .. 40.00
10", multicolored, dark brown and amber scalloped border, Limoges 25.00

FISH

Plate
9", bass, artist sgd "Morley," marked "Lenox" 60.00
9½", different species in center, named on reverse, set of 12, sgd "C Hart," Royal Doulton 1,500.00
10½", trout, cobalt border, marked "M Z Austria" 70.00
Platter, 16½", bass, water lilies, emb, artist sgd "Max," marked "Limoges" 165.00
Set
11 pcs, platter, ten plates, artist sgd "Muville," marked "Limoges" 550.00
13 pcs, 23½" l platter, twelve plates, different species on each plate, yellow border, gold trim, marked "Limoges, France" 400.00

MOOSE

Plate, 9", bull moose and mate, mountain background, marked "R. K. Beck" 40.00

SQUIRREL

Plate, 10" d, perched on tree branch, eating acorn, forest landscape background, beaded border, numbered "239/3549," Royal Copenhagen ... 990.00

WEASEL

Platter, 18" l, carrying red squirrel in mouth, winter scene, sky blue ground, paneled and beaded border, dentil rim, gilt and green highlights, numbered "239/3520," Royal Copenhagen 1,100.00

GAMES

History: Mass production of board games did not take place until after the Civil War. Firms like McLoughlin Brothers, Milton Bradley, and Selchow and Righter were active in the 1860s, followed by Parker Brothers, who began in 1883. Parker Brothers bought out the rights to the W. & S. B. Ives Co., who had produced some very early games in the 1840s, including the "first" American board game, The Mansion of Happiness. All except McLoughlin Brothers are giants in the game industry today.

McLoughlin Brothers's games are a challenge to find. Not only does the company no longer exist [Milton Bradley bought them out in 1920], but the lithography on their games was the best of its era. Most board games are collected because of the bright, colorful lithography on their box covers. In addition to spectacular covers, the large Mc-Loughlin games often had lead playing pieces and fancy block spinners, thus making them even more desirable.

Common games like Anagrams, Authors, Jack-straws, Lotto, Tiddledy Winks, and Peter Coddles do not command high prices, nor do the games of Flinch, Pit, and Rook, which still are being produced.

Games, with the exception of the common ones stated above, generally are rising in price. However, interesting to note is the fact that certain games dealing with good graphics on popular subject matter, e.g. trains, planes, baseball, Christmas and others, often bring higher prices because they are also sought by collectors in those particular fields.

Condition is everything when buying. Do not buy games that have been taped or that have price tags stickered on the face of their covers. Also, beware of buying games at outdoor flea markets where weather elements can cause fading and warping.

References: R. C. Bell, *The Board Game Book*, The Knapp Press, 1979; Lee Dennis, *Warman's Antique American Games, 1840-1940*, Warman Publishing Co., 1986; Brian Love, *Great Board Games*, 1895–1935, Macmillan Publishing Co., 1979; Brian Love, *Play The Game: Over 40 Games From The Golden Age Of Board Games*, Reed Books, 1978.

Collectors' Club: American Game Collectors Association, 4628 Barlow Dr., Bartlesville, OK 74006.

Museum: Washington Dolls' House and Toy Museum, Washington, D.C.

Additional Listings: See *Warman's Americana & Collectibles*.

Ally Sloper Game, Milton Bradley, c1915, 13 x 7", boxed target game, throw wooden balls into clown's mouth **50.00**
American Heritage Battle–Cry Civil War Game, Milton Bradley, boxed board game, 1961, 10 x 20 x 2", multicolored Civil War scene on cov, 22 blue 1" soldiers, 22 gray 1" soldiers, orig instruction book with outline of Civil War history, photos of soldiers, paintings of battles, etc., light general wear **50.00**
American Heritage Dog Fight Game, Milton Bradley, boxed board game, 1963 copyright, 10 x 20 x 2", three sectioned game board, full color aerial battlefield scene, minor damage to box **50.00**
Auto Race, Gorham Pressed Steel Corp, c1930, 10¾ x 22", multicolored litho metal board, five colored metal cars **175.00**
Bagatelle, early push–type, 1⅛ x 9¹⁵⁄₁₆

x 19¼", wooden, multicolored litho pasted to face marking points, wooden stick with wooden block to push ball, one wooden and one clay ball, instructions pasted on back ... **125.00**
Big Trail Game, The, boxed board game, 13½ x 17 x 1½", based on 1930 Movietone picture with John Wayne and Tyrone Power Sr, 14 x 26" multicolored board with wagon train illus, instruction booklet and wooden pawns, metal figures, full color illus box, several pawns and four figures missing **75.00**
Bobsey Twins On The Farm Game, The, Milton Bradley, boxed board game, 1957, 8½ x 16½ x 1", multi-colored 16 x 16" playing board with fruits and vegetables illus, spinner, and eight playing pcs **35.00**
Champion Game of Baseball, The, Proctor Amusement, boxed board game, c1900, 9 x 12", inside cov instructions, unused score card, litho heavy paper gameboard with baseball diamond, attached spinner, bleachers, and stands, paper markers in orig envelope **115.00**
Charlie Chan, Whitman, boxed card game, 1939, 5 x 6 x 1", 35 playing cards, instruction card, black, white, and red crime fighting scenes, multicolored box **60.00**
Comical Tivoli Game, Spear Bavaria, c1900, boxed board game, 11 x 8", litho of early clowns, three diecut clowns attached to box cov, eight orig wooden marbles **135.00**
Diver Dan Tug–O–War Game, Milton Bradley, boxed board game, 1961, 8½ x 16½ x 1½", National Broadcasting Co, 8 x 16" playing board, built in spinner, diecut playing piece of diver and octopus fighting over chest, multicolored box illus of fish, sea shells, and mermaid **20.00**
Excuse Me! Parker Bros, card game, copyright 1923, 7½ x 4¾", 124 printed pink and white cards, instruction sheet **15.00**
Flintstones Stoneage Game, The, Transogram, boxed board game, 1961, 17 x 9", orig gameboard, instructions, and punched out cards **40.00**
Flying The Beam, Parker Bros, boxed board game, c1940, 9½ x 18½ x 1½", 18 x 18" playing board, spinner board, four miniature metal replica transport planes, instructions missing, colored photo type illus on box lid **30.00**
Game of Bang, McLoughlin, boxed board game, 1912, 15 x 8", orig spin-

ner, game board on box bottom, playing pcs **75.00**

Game of Cinderella, Stoll & Edwards, boxed board game, 1923, 17 x 9", multicolored cov with Cinderella and witch, pullout litho board, spinner, handwritten instructions, markers, and heart shaped cards **70.00**

Game of Parlor Baseball, McLoughlin Bros, 1897, boxed board game, 17 x 19", vivid litho cov of early baseball players, outlined in bold, board with playing field and two litho spinners, 18 wooden playing markers **1,500.00**

Game of Snap, Milton Bradley Co, #4073, $35.00.

Great Charlie Chan Detective Mystery Game, The, Milton Bradley, boxed board game, 1937, 11½ x 22½ x 2¼", 22 x 22" playing board with Chan's office as center, three sets of cards, fifty small wooden counter ships, full color lid illus, minor stains and soiling **175.00**

Hop Scotch Tiddledy Winks, Parker Bros, game of skill, 1891, 10¼ x 6¾", one cup, twenty winks, one red and yellow felt pad with bull's eye, one felt hopscotch court pad, advertising sheet, instruction sheet **25.00**

James Bond 007 Thunderball Game, Milton Bradley/Gilrose, boxed board game, 1965, 19 x 9 x 2", photo box from movie, board, agent pcs, and orig cards **35.00**

Klondyke Nugget Game, The, boxed board game, c1890, 4 x 8 x 1", full color illus of mine, miner holding "Boss Nugget," multicolored game board, mine covers, and gold nuggets **75.00**

Leave It To Beaver Money Maker Game, Hassenfield, boxed board game, 1959, 9 x 16", black and white photo of Beaver, pullout board, spinner, money, and orig cards **130.00**

Lee At Havana Game, boxed board game, c1898, 5 x 7 x 1", Spanish—American War, set of 52 cards and instruction sheet, full color paper label on lid **60.00**

Lindy Hop–Off, Parker Bros, boxed board game, c1927, 14½ x 13⅜," two dice cups, two dice, sixteen cards, four painted metal airplanes, instruction sheet, lift out folding multicolored litho board **375.00**

Meet The Presidents Game, Selchow & Righter Co, boxed board game, 1965, 9½ x 19 x 2", unused, mint contents **45.00**

Movie Inn, W. G. Young & Co, Inc., skill game invented by Willis G Young, copyright 1917, 10⅞ x 7¼", multicolored litho board, five steel balls, instructions printed at bottom **40.00**

Northwest Passage, Promotional Laboratories, Inc., boxed board game, 1969, 9 x 17½ x 1½", premium game given away at Esso gas stations, small plastic oil tankers, oil derrick, and oil barrel disks, oil storage tanks, spinner, multicolored 17 x 17" playing board with illus of Alaskan shoreline, "Exploring The Northwest Passage Past And Present" story and photos on back of board, corner box split, light creases on spinner **20.00**

Oriental Color Game, McLoughlin Bros, 1875, wooden box, 7½ x 4½", fifty four multicolored litho cards, litho double arrowed block spinner, instruction booklet **75.00**

Parker Brothers Baseball Game, Parker Bros, boxed board game, 1949, 20 x 13", playing board of baseball diamond with litho players, stand–up scoreboard with names of 16 pro teams, scorecard pads, 48 playing cards, wood playing pcs, orig instructions, unused **125.00**

Popeye's Sliding Boards and Ladders Game, KFS Built–Rite, boxed board game, 1958, 14 x 7", multicolored cover showing characters, unused **75.00**

Strange Game of Forbidding Fruit, The, Parker Bros, boxed card game, c1900, 4 x 5½ x1½", 40 cards, full color paper label on lid of three men stealing apples, charging farm yard dog **55.00**

Tally–Ho, Snow, Woodman & Co, c1880, 11¼ x 11¼", thirty six white wooden pegs, thirty six black wooden pegs, lift out board, instruction sheet, multicolored litho board with red star center **50.00**

Zippy Zeps Air Game, Alderman Fairchild Co, boxed board game, c1925, 18 x 9″, twenty five cards, five colored metal zeppelins, multicolored litho folding board, instructions on back of box cov **85.00**

Zoom, All Fair, boxed board game, late 1930s, 10 x 13½ x 1½″, multicolored 9½ x 23″ topographical playing board, 8 x 9″ black cardboard instrument control panel with silver lettering and features, eight wood playing pieces, metal spinners, very light wear **35.00**

GAUDY DUTCH

History: Gaudy Dutch is an opaque, soft-paste ware made between 1790 and 1825 in England's Staffordshire district. Most pieces are unmarked; marks of various potters, including the impressed marks of Riley and Wood, have been found on pieces.

The pieces first were hand decorated in an underglaze blue, fired, and then received additional decoration over the glaze. Many pieces today have the over glaze decoration extensively worn. Gaudy Dutch found a ready market within the Pennsylvania German community because it was inexpensive and intense with color. It had little appeal in England.

Reference: Eleanor and Edward Fox, *Gaudy Dutch*, published by author, 1970, out-of-print; John A. Shuman, III, *The Collector's Encyclopedia of Gaudy Dutch & Welsh*, Collector Books, 1990.

Reproduction Alert: Cup plates, bearing the impressed mark "CYBRIS," have been reproduced and are collectible in their own right. The Henry Ford Museum has issued pieces in the single rose pattern, although they are of porcelain and not soft-paste.

Advisor: John D. Querry.

Butterfly
Creamer **875.00**

Dove pattern, saucer, 5⅝″ d, $350.00.

Cup Plate **975.00**
Plate, 7¼″ **775.00**
Platter, oval, 14″ **1,800.00**
Sugar Bowl, rect **1,350.00**
Tea Bowl and Saucer, butterfly center position **875.00**

Carnation
Coffeepot, high dome, cov **2,500.00**
Creamer **750.00**
Cup Plate **975.00**
Plate, 9¾″ **725.00**
Soup Plate **775.00**
Sugar Bowl **850.00**
Tea Bowl and Saucer **600.00**
Teapot **850.00**

Dahlia
Creamer **850.00**
Plate, 8⅜″ d, double border **1,200.00**
Sugar Bowl **1,200.00**
Tea Bowl and Saucer **975.00**

Double Rose
Creamer **650.00**
Cup Plate **750.00**
Plate, 8¾″ **775.00**
Tea Bowl and Saucer **600.00**
Toddy Plate **625.00**
Waste Bowl **675.00**

Dove
Creamer **675.00**
Plate, 8¼″ **675.00**
Sugar Bowl **750.00**
Tea Bowl and Saucer **650.00**
Teapot, knop restored on lid **625.00**
Toddy Plate **675.00**

Grape
Creamer **450.00**
Cup Plate **725.00**
Plate, 9¾″ **525.00**
Soup Plate, 8¾″ **675.00**
Teapot **650.00**
Toddy Plate **450.00**

Leaf
Bowl, unusual shape **975.00**
Tea Bowl and Saucer **775.00**

Oyster
Creamer **375.00**
Plate
6½″ **450.00**
8½″ **525.00**
10″ **650.00**
Tea Bowl and Saucer **425.00**
Teapot **625.00**
Toddy Plate **625.00**
Waste Bowl, rim chips **350.00**

Primrose
Plate, 8¾″, imp "Riley" **650.00**
Sugar Bowl **850.00**
Tea Bowl and Saucer **675.00**

Single Rose
Coffeepot, high dome **1,500.00**
Creamer **450.00**
Cup Plate **1,075.00**

Plate
  7½", imp mark 325.00
  9½" 425.00
Sugar Bowl 650.00
Tea Bowl and Saucer 325.00
Waste Bowl 300.00
Straw Flower
  Plate, 9¼" 750.00
  Soup Plate 975.00
Sunflower
  Plate, 6½" 750.00
  Tea Bowl and Saucer 775.00
Urn
  Creamer 375.00
  Cup Plate 1,075.00
  Plate, 5½" 775.00
  Soup Plate 525.00
  Tea Bowl and Saucer 375.00
  Teapot 650.00
  Waste Bowl 350.00
War Bonnet
  Creamer 575.00
  Cup Plate 950.00
  Plate
    6⅜" 575.00
    8¼" 675.00
  Soup Plate 775.00
  Tea Bowl and Saucer 550.00
Water Lily, tea bowl and saucer, pink
  luster border 1,075.00
Zinnia
  Plate
    6⅜" 550.00
    8½" 575.00

GAUDY IRONSTONE

History: Gaudy Ironstone was made in England around 1850. Most pieces are impressed "Ironstone" and bear a registry mark. Ironstone is an opaque, heavy body earthenware which contains large proportions of flint and slag. Gaudy Ironstone is decorated in patterns and colors similar to Gaudy Welsh.

Floral
  Cup and Saucer, handleless, stains,
    one cup chipped, others pinpoints,
    set of six 360.00
  Pitcher, 4¼" h, luster trim, minor chips   65.00
  Plate, 8½" d, underglaze blue, poly-
    chrome and purple luster dec . . .   100.00
  Sugar, cov, 7¼" h, luster trim, mis-
    matched lid 85.00
  Teapot, 9½" h, luster trim, fruit finial,
    marked "Walley," and English re-
    gistery mark 235.00
  Wash Bowl and Pitcher Set, green,
    blue, red, and black, red stick spat-
    ter band on pitcher, marked "Malkin
    & Co" 125.00

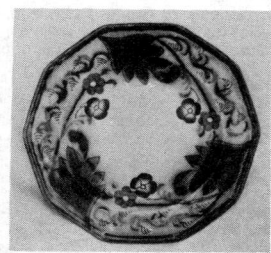

Plate, floral dec, imp "Pearl White," 8½" d, $50.00.

Morning Glory
  Cup and Saucer, handleless 75.00
  Creamer, 6½" h, paneled, foliage
    handle 150.00
  Pitcher, 8" h, paneled, underglaze
    blue 210.00
  Plate, 6¼" d, underglaze blue, poly-
    chrome enamel and luster dec . . .   60.00
  Sugar, cov, 8" h, paneled, underglaze
    blue, foliage handles 150.00
Rose
  Pitcher, 8" h, blue underglaze dec,
    blue, red, and green enamel roses
    and flowers, minor edge flakes . .   225.00
  Plate, 9½" d, red, blue, green, and
    black 85.00
Strawberry
  Coffeepot, 10" h 575.00
  Cup and Saucer, handleless 150.00
  Plate, 8½" d, glaze flakes 230.00
  Platter, 13½" l, underglaze blue
    strawberries, polychrome enamel
    dec, purple luster 220.00
  Sugar, cov, 8½" h 400.00
  Waste Bowl, 5⅜" h 150.00
Urn
  Plate
    7⅛" d 65.00
    9½" d 125.00
  Toddy Plate, 4¾" d 175.00

GAUDY WELSH

History: Gaudy Welsh is a translucent porcelain that was originally made in the Swansea area of England from 1830 to 1845. Although the designs resemble Gaudy Dutch, the body texture and weight differ. One of the characteristics is the gold luster on top of the glaze.

In 1890, Allerton made a similar ware. These wares are heavier opaque porcelain and usually bear the export mark.

References: John A. Shuman, III, *The Collec-*

tor's Encyclopedia of Gaudy Dutch and Welsh,
Collector Books, 1990; Howard Y. Williams, *Gaudy Welsh China,* Wallace-Homestead, out-of-print.

Columbine
Bowl, 10″ d, 5½″ h, ftd, underglaze
blue and polychrome enamel floral
dec 400.00
Plate, 5½″ d 50.00
Tea Set, 17 pcs, c1810 .... 475.00
Daisy and Chain
Creamer 185.00
Cup and Saucer 75.00
Sugar, cov 200.00
Teapot 200.00
Flower Basket
Bowl, 10½″ d 185.00
Mug, 4″ h 85.00
Plate 60.00
Sugar, cov, lion's head handles, luster
trim 150.00
Grape
Bowl, 5¼″ d 50.00
Cup and Saucer 72.00
Mug, 2¼″ h, cobalt blue leaves, rust
colored vine 60.00
Plate, 5¼″ d 55.00
Teapot, boat shaped body, wide flar-
ing rim, dome cov, curved spout,
angular handle, underglaze blue,
polychrome enamels, pink luster
trim, small filled spout flakes 325.00
Grape IV, teapot, bulbous, flaring foot,
wide slanted rim, inset domed cov,
curved spout, C scroll handle, poly-
chrome enamel, purple luster, minor
wear and flakes 400.00
Oyster
Bowl, 6″ d 80.00
Creamer, 3″ h, dark blue wide neck
band, ovoid body 100.00
Cup and Saucer 65.00
Jug, 5¾″ h, c1820 .... 80.00
Soup Plate, 10″ d, flange rim 85.00

Tulip pattern, plate, 6¼″ d, $30.00.

Strawberry
Creamer 85.00
Mug, 4⅛″ h 125.00
Plate, 8¼″ d 140.00
Soup Plate, 9″ d 115.00
Tulip
Bowl, 6¼″ d 45.00
Cake Plate, 10″ d, molded handles . 100.00
Creamer, 5¼″ h 80.00
Sugar, cov, 6¾″ h 115.00
Teapot, 7¼″ h 150.00
Wagon Wheel
Cup 60.00
Mug, 2½″ h 65.00
Pitcher, 8½″ h 175.00
Plate, 8¾″ d 75.00

GEISHA GIRL PORCELAIN

History: Geisha Girl porcelain is a Japanese export ware whose production commenced during the last quarter of the 19th century and continued heavily until WWII. The ware features kimono-clad Japanese ladies and children amidst Japanese gardens and temples. There are over 125 brightly colored scenes depicting the pre-modern Japanese lifestyle. Over 140 marks and almost 200 patterns and variations have been identified on pieces.

Geisha Girl ware may be totally hand painted, hand painted over a stenciled design, or occasionally decaled. The stenciled underlying design is usually red-orange, but also is found in brown, black, and green (rare).

All Geisha Girl items are bordered by one or a combination of blues, reds, greens, rhubarb, yellow, black, browns, or gold. The most common is red-orange. Borders may be wavy, scalloped, or banded and range from 1/16″ to ¼″. The borders themselves often are further decorated with gold, white or yellow lacings, flowers, dots, or stripes. Some examples even display interior frames of butterflies or flowers.

Geisha Girl is found in many forms including tea, cocoa, lunch, and children's sets, dresser items, vases, serving dishes, etc. Large plates or platters, candlesticks, miniatures, and mugs are hardest to locate. Geisha Girl advertising items add to a collection.

Reference: Elyce Litts, *The Collectors Encyclopedia Of Geisha Girl Porcelain,* Collector Books, 1988.

Additional Listings: See *Warman's Americana & Collectibles* for more examples.

Reproduction Alert: Geisha Girl porcelain's popularity continued after WWII and it is being reproduced today. Chief reproduction characteristics are a red-orange border, very white and smooth porcelain, and sparse coloring and detail.

Reproduced items include dresser, tea and sake sets, toothpick holders, small vases, table plates, and salt and pepper shakers.

Advisor: Elyce D. Litts.

Bon Bon Dish, 6", chrysanthemum shape, Battledore pattern, olive green	**22.00**
Bowl	
8¾", Inside The Teahouse, pale green, ftd	**75.00**
10", Chinese Coin motif, ruffled, pierced handle	**85.00**
Calling Card Tray, 8 x 6", Parasol F, free form, cobalt blue with gold	**35.00**
Butter Pat, cherry blossom shape reserve geisha, red line int. frame, flower and butterfly backdrop	**10.00**
Children's Dishes	
Bowl, 2¼ x 1", red, flower gathering	**10.00**
Demitasse Set, 15 pcs, pot, creamer and sugar, six cups and saucer, Parasol C	**65.00**
Cracker Jar, Garden Bench E, wavy red with gold, mint green and gray geometric with gold	**85.00**
Creamer, 4", Feeding The Carp, ribbed, hour glass shape, red with gold	**17.00**
Cup and Saucer	
After Dinner	
Lady In Rickshaw B, ribbed cup, scalloped saucer, red	**18.00**
Pointing D, red	**10.00**
Tea, Garden Bench B, pedestal, lobed, scalloped saucer, red with gold	**25.00**
Dish, 8", red with gold, reserve pattern, butterflies, chrysanthemums, and gold background	**55.00**
Egg Cup, child reaching for butterfly, red with gold	**15.00**
Gravy Boat, underplate, Rice Harvesters A, leaf shape, mint green, deep green, and red, gold border	**25.00**
Hair Receiver, Garden Bench B, red, maple leaf base	**22.00**
Humidor, Battledore pattern, blue scallop, gold line	**70.00**
Mustard Jar	
Circle Dance, red, gold lacing, spoon	**25.00**
Rendevous, apple green with gold	**30.00**
Nappy, Temple A, underlying design, hand fluted edge, sea green border, handle	**45.00**
Plate	
6", boy with scythe, cobalt blue with gold	**10.00**
6⅛", Flag Day, red, yellow lacing	**15.00**
7⅜", Porch, cobalt blue with gold, fluted swirl, scalloped edge	**15.00**
8½", children in boat, swirl, fluted, cobalt blue, gold lacing, scalloped edge	**30.00**

Napkin Ring, River's Edge pattern, pine green border, red-orange border, marked "T" in cherry blossom and "Japan", $35.00.

Relish Dish, Picnic B, red-orange with gold, floret edge, reserves	**25.00**
Salad Set, 7 pcs, master, six individual, red, gold buds	**110.00**
Salt and Pepper Shakers, pr, 2", Garden Bench F, red-orange and gold top, cobalt shoulders	**18.00**
Tea Set, 13 pcs, pot, sugar, creamer, five cups and saucers, Geisha In Sampan B, pink ground	**50.00**
Teapot, melon ribbed, red and cobalt blue	**45.00**
Tray, 5 x 5", heart shape, oversized irises, red	**15.00**

GIRANDOLES AND MANTEL LUSTRES

History: A girandole is a highly elaborate branched candleholder, often featuring cut glass prisms surrounding the mountings. A mantel lustre is a glass vase with attached cut glass prisms.

Girandoles and mantel lustres usually are found in pairs. It is not uncommon for girandoles to be part of a large garniture set. Girandoles and mantel lustres achieved their greatest popularity in the last half of the 19th century both in the United States and Europe.

GIRANDOLES, PR

14", silver plated and cut glass, three tiers hung with faceted drops, scrolled candle arms, c1900	**150.00**
18", courting couple, brass relief, triple branch with prisms, marble base	**100.00**
18½", scrolled leaves, grape leaf bobeches, ornate casting, triangular base, 5 arms, 2 removable	**300.00**
20½" h, pierced and shaped rect frame, orig glass, damaged crest, Italian Rococo, 18th C	**400.00**

Girandoles, brass, eight lusters around each candle section, ten lusters across back, floral motif, 17" h, 10½" w, pr, $375.00.

21" h, gilt metal, faceted glass, 3 light, Louis Philippe style	450.00
24" h, cut glass, carved and gilded, draped white marble bases, Regency	5,500.00
35½", bronze, glass seven light glass drops suspended from pressed glass stars	500.00

MANTEL LUSTRES

10", ruby, overlay with white and gilt foliage, faceted cut glass prisms, c1875	400.00
13" h, gilt bronze and crystal, faceted collar, beaded molded and engine turned base, ball feet, George III, late 18th, early 19th C, pr	22,000.00
14", ruby glass, enamel forget-me-not dec	425.00
14½", pink cased, enamel painted flower swags with gilt scrolls, scalloped bulbous bowl, 2 rows clear prisms	275.00
18¾", white cased, gilted lusters, flaring scalloped rims with line borders, painted figural scenes, overall gilted scrollwork, circular bases	300.00
20" h, gilt bronze and cranberry glass, Napoleon III style, hurricane shades, pr	500.00
Ruby Glass, crown top, enameled white floral and bed dec, painted gold dec, clear hanging prisms	425.00

GLASS ANIMALS

History: It did not take glass manufacturers long to realize that there was a ready market for glass novelties. In the early nineteenth century, walking sticks and witch balls were two dominant forms. As the century ended, glass covered dishes with an animal theme were featured.

In the period between World War I and II, glass manufacturers such as Fostoria Glass Company and A. H. Heisey & Company created a number of glass animal figures for the novelty and decorative accessory markets. In the 1950s and early 1960s a second glass animal craze swept America led by companies such as Duncan & Miller Glass Company and New Martinsville - Viking Glass Company. A third craze struck in the early 1980s when companies such as Boyd Crystal Art Glass, Guernsey Glass, Pisello Art Glass, and Summit Art Glass began offering the same animal figure in a wide variety of collectible glass colors, with some colors in limited production.

There are two major approaches to glass animal collecting: (a) animal type and (b) manufacturer. Most collectors concentrate on one or more manufacturer, grouping their collections accordingly.

References: Everett Grist, *Covered Animal Dishes*, Collector Books, 1988; Evelyn Zemel, *American Glass Animals A to Z*, A to Z Productions, 1978.

Price Note: Prices are for animal figures in clear (crystal) glass unless otherwise noted.

Bear	
Boyd, Balloon Bear, red	6.50
New Martinsville	
Baby	40.00
Mama	175.00
Papa	225.00
Carp, 15¾" h, curved dorsal fin and tail, clear with bronze cast, molded "R Lalique," etched "France," bronze luminaire base cast with stylized aquatic vegetation	9,900.00
Deer	
Baccarat, paperweight, Gridel series, sgd	200.00
Fostoria	
Sitting	45.00
Standing	40.00
Dog	
Barth Art, Fireside series	
Laying	70.00
Sitting	65.00
Boyd, Skippy, sitting, Crown Tuscan	10.00
Heisey, Scottie	125.00
Imperial, Scottie, bookend, caramel slag, Cambridge mold	100.00
New Martinsville	
Police dog	65.00
Wolfhound	65.00
Dolphin	
Baccarat, sgd	75.00
Pisello, carnival, marigold	12.00
Donkey	
Duncan Miller, with peasant	475.00
Imperial, caramel slag	35.00
Dragonfly, 8¼" h, car mascot, frosted, wings closed, engraved and molded "R Lalique France"	5,500.00

Duck	
Duncan Miller, 5″, ashtray	16.00
Fostoria, mama	45.00
Imperial, caramel slag, wings up	25.00
Viking, 15″, orange	50.00
Eagle, bookend	
Cambridge	75.00
Fostoria	85.00
Elephant	
Co–Op, black	125.00
New Martinsville, bookend	100.00
Summit, clown, 4¼″, red	15.00
Frog, Co–Op, green, cov, flint	85.00
Gazelle, Heisey	1,500.00
Giraffe, Heisey, head turned	150.00
Goose	
Duncan Miller, plump type	225.00
Heisey	
Wings half	75.00
Wings Up	85.00
Hen, covered animal dish	
Hazel Atlas, white, nest base	10.00
Westmoreland	
Amberina, 5″, nest base	35.00
Blue opalescent, 5″, nest base	30.00
White hen, wicker basket base, two handles	50.00

Owl, Degenhart Glass Co, jade green, $45.00.

Heron	
Cambridge, 9″	65.00
Duncan Miller	90.00
Horse	
Boyd, Joey, leaping, lavender	12.00
Fostoria, colt,	
Sitting	45.00
Standing	40.00
Guernsey, Rocky, slag	12.00
Heisey	
Filly, forward pose	600.00
Sparky	125.00
New Martinsville, head up	90.00
L. E. Smith, rearing, green	35.00
Lion, white milk glass, picket base	50.00

Monkey, Baccarat, paperweight, black, Gridel series, sgd	200.00
Owl	
Fostoria	200.00
Viking, 8½″, orange	100.00
Pelican	
Baccarat, paperweight, Gridel series, sgd	200.00
Fostoria, pr with clock and night light	250.00
Pheasant	
Baccarat, paperweight, Gridel series, sgd	200.00
Heisey, Ringneck	135.00
Paden City, Chinese	100.00
Piglet, New Martinsville, standing	150.00
Pigeon, Cambridge, Pouter, bookends, pr	145.00
Pony, Imperial, standing, caramel slag	25.00
Porpoise, New Martinsville	450.00
Rabbit, Paden City, cottontail, frosted	60.00
Robin, mug, Imperial	
Purple slag	32.00
Red slag	35.00
Rooster	
Heisey, vase	85.00
Lalique, 18½″ h, life size, strutting, clear, metal luminaire mountings, stenciled "R Lalique France"	8,800.00
Seagull, Cambridge, flower frog, 8½″	50.00
Sparrow, Heisey	150.00
Squirrel	
New Martinsville	35.00
Paden City, on log	35.00
Swan	
Cambridge, 3″, sgd	
Pink	35.00
Topaz	30.00
Duncan Miller	
5″, solid	18.50
6½″, leaf	
Pink	85.00
Vaseline opalescent	185.00
7″, open	12.00
8″, Sylvan, blue opalescent	55.00
Heisey, solid	400.00
Swordfish, blue opalescent, Duncan Miller	400.00
Tropical Fish, Heisey, made into lamp base	1,200.00

GLASS, EARLY AMERICAN

History: Early American glass covers glass made in America from the colonial period through the mid-19th century. As such it includes the early pressed glass and lacy glass made between 1827 and 1840.

Major glass producing centers prior to 1850 were Massachusetts with the New England Glass Company; the Boston and Sandwich Glass Company, South Jersey; Pennsylvania with Stiegel's

Manheim factory at Pittsburgh; and Ohio with Kent, Mantua, and Zanesville.

Early American glass was collected heavily during the 1920 to 1950 period. It has now regained some of its earlier popularity. Leading sources for the sale of early American glass are the mail auctions of David and Linda Arman and the auctions of Richard A. Bourne, Early Auction Company, Garth's, and Skinners.

References: William E. Covill, *Ink Bottles and Inkwells*, 1971; Lowell Inness, *Pittsburgh Glass: 1797–1891*, Houghton Mifflin Company, 1976; George and Helen McKearin, *American Glass*, Crown, 1975; George and Helen McKearin, *Two Hundred Years of American Blown Glass*, Doubleday and Company, 1950; Helen McKearin and Kenneth Wilson, *American Bottles And Flasks*, Crown, 1978; Adeline Pepper, *Glass Gaffers of New Jersey*, Scribners, 1971; Jane S. Spillman, *American and European Pressed Glass*, Corning Museum of Glass, 1981; Kenneth Wilson, *New England Glass And Glassmaking*, Crowell, 1972.

Collectors' Club: The National Early American Glass Club, 7417 Allison Street, Hyattsville, MD 20784.

Additional Listings: Blown Three Mold, Cup Plates, Flasks, Sandwich Glass, and Stiegel Type Glass.

Zanesville, flask, brilliant amber, expanded vertical ribbing, 24 rib mold 8¼″ h, 6⅞″ w, $1,200.00.

Amelung (New Bremen Glass)
  Salt, 2½ x 2¾″, cobalt blue, pattern molded, checkered diamond, applied solid foot 850.00
  Wine, 6⅜″ h, clear, blown, applied dome foot, folded rim, hollow stem, small bubble in thick solid base of bowl 250.00
Boston and Sandwich Glass Co
  Lamp, 11¼″ h, Acanthus Leaf, light peacock blue, sand finish, brass standard, brass collar, marble base, 1850–60 .... 375.00

Salt
  Neal BT–4D, boat, clear, Lafayette, small base chip 300.00
  Neal CT–1, silvery opaque blue, one large chip on corner, several small chips 150.00
  Neal EE–8A, lacy, clear, round, eagles and ships 400.00
Ellenville, NY, creamer, 3¾″ h, brilliant yellow amber, blown, Jacob Relyea 500.00
Freeblown
  Bowl
    4¾″ d, 3⅝″ h, finely blown, blown foot and multiple piece knops in stem, cobalt blue, opaque white rim on lip and foot edge, pontil scar, early 19th C 425.00
    6¼″ w, 3¾″ h, aqua, folded over rim, applied foot, pontil scar, America, 1820–50 .... 550.00
    7″ d, 3½″ h, aqua, folded over rim, pontil scar, America, 1820–50 .. 275.00
    7″ d, 5″ h, amethyst, pontil scar .. 75.00
    10″ d, 4½″ h, greenish aqua, high base kick–up, pontil scar, small outer lip chip 150.00
  Creamer
    3¼″ h, deep blue–purple, applied handle, multiple base crimping, pontil scar, Midwest America, early 19th C 475.00
    4¼″ h, aqua, applied foot, applied handle with crimping, pontil scar, America, 1820–50 .... 300.00
  Miniature, bowl, 1½″ h, 3⅝″ d, light green, thinly blown, folded in rim, pontil scar, America, 1820–40 ... 300.00
  Vase, 9⅜″ h, deep orange–amber, applied foot, pontil scar 1,100.00
Lacy
  Bowl, 7⅜″ d, Princess Feather, small chips 65.00
  Candlestick, 9¼″ h, flint, canary, sq stepped base, fluted column and petal socket, chips 175.00
  Dish, oblong, 7⅛″ l, Gothic, Lee PL 101, small chips 45.00
  Dish, oval
    8⅛″ l, Butterfly, Lee PL 95, small chips 145.00
    8½″ l, Peacock Eye, chips 60.00
  Dish, round, 7⅜″ d, Nectarine, Lee PL 93, chips 110.00
  Plate
    8″ d, Peacock Eye and Thistle, small chips 70.00
    8⅝″ d, Tulip and Acanthus, Lee PL 131 .... 125.00
    9″ d, Oak Leaf, Lee PL 126, small chips 135.00
  Sugar Bowl, 5¼″ h, matching lid, Lee PL 154, chips 175.00

Mantua
- Flask, 6″ h, blown, chestnut, pale green, 16 swirled ribs **165.00**
- Pan, 6″ d, blown, pale green, 16 ribs, folded over rim **375.00**
- Toilet Bottle, 4½″ h, quarter pint, deep purple–amethyst, flared, flanged lip, pontiled base **450.00**

New England Glass Co, Cambridge, MA
- Candlestick, 8½″ h, clear, milky cast, hexagonal, petal socket, wafer attachment, pontil scar **80.00**
- Demijohn, 11¼″ h, blown, crude sloping collar, pontil scar, 1840–60 . . . **30.00**
- Lamp, fluid
  - 11¾″ h, Loop pattern, amethyst, octagonal standard, sq base, wafer attachment, orig double burner, minor base chips, 1840–60 . . . . **1,200.00**
  - 19⅜″ h, pressed and cut, clear, frosted and cut matching shades, minor roughage and small chips, pr **900.00**
- Vase, 7¼″ h, Circle and Ellipse pattern, amethyst, c1840–60 . . . . . . **175.00**

New Jersey, South
- Bank, 10⅜″ h, clear, blown, applied rigaree and prunts, arch of four applied struts, applied chicken finial, solid ball stem attached to thick round base **1,200.00**
- Bottle, 11⅜″ h, clear, blown, powder horn form, opaque white loopings, cobalt blue bands **225.00**
- Bowl, 5¾″ h, clear, blown, opaque white loopings **175.00**
- Cane, 32½″ l, clear, amber center, four applied opaque swirled ribs . **150.00**
- Wine, 4⅜″ h, clear, smokey cast, thick applied base, iron pontil **90.00**

New York
- Bowl, 14 x 4¼″, aqua, folded rim, wear, star in flared rim **225.00**
- Compote, 6⅜ x 6¼″, free blown, clear, thick applied base, polished pontil **75.00**
- Vase, 4½ x 5½″, urn shape, yellow–green, rolled rim, large faint pontil **150.00**

Phoenix Glassworks, Boston, MA, Thomas Cains, 1820–40
- Decanter, qt, clear, broken chain dec, two tripartite neck rings, pontil scar
  - Hollow blown unpatterned stopper **275.00**
  - Waffle stopper **225.00**

Pillar Molded, vase, 16¼″ h, clear, eight pillars, polished pontil **75.00**

Pittsburgh
- Candlestick, 6¾″ h, dolphin, clambroth base, opaque blue socket, McKearin 196–6, minute roughage **700.00**
- Compote
  - 10″ d, 7⅞″ h, blown, flint, cut with star foot, bulbous stem and bowl with cut roundels, strawberry diamonds and fans, minor pinpoint flakes **200.00**
  - 10¼″ d, 8″ h, blown, flint, cut with wide foot, baluster stem, and flared bowl with cut roundels and scallops, minor wear and scratches **150.00**
- Decanter, 12¼″ h, blown, pillar molded, flint, applied collar and lip **175.00**
- Plate, 7″ d, lacy, octagonal, clear, Basket of Flowers pattern, R. B. Curling & Sons, several small chips and edge roughage **300.00**
- Vase, 11″ h, tulip, deep amethyst, opaque white edge bands on octagonal paneled bowl, solid reverse baluster standard, applied foot, polished pontil, c1840–60 . . . . **4,000.00**

Zanesville
- Bottle, blown
  - 7⅝″ h, globular, amber, 24 swirled ribs, minor wear **450.00**
  - 8¾″ h, club shape, aqua, 24 swirled ribs, minor sickness **100.00**
- Cruet, 6⅜″ h, purple–blue, tapered, 24 molded ribs, swirled to the left, slightly flared, rolled lip **2,400.00**
- Salt, 2½ x 3⅛″, ftd, blue–green, 24 vertical ribs, applied irregular solid foot, pontil, slightly ground rim . . . **1,200.00**

GOLDSCHEIDER

History: Friedrich Goldscheider founded a porcelain and faience factory in Vienna, Austria, in 1885. Upon his death, his widow carried on operations. In 1920 Walter and Marcell, Friedrich's sons, gained control. During the Art Deco period, the firm commissioned several artists to create figural statues, among which were Pierrettes and sleek wolfhounds. During the 1930s, the company's products were more traditional.

In the early 1940s, the Goldscheiders fled to the United States and re-established operations in Trenton, New Jersey. The Golscheider Everlast Corporation is listed in Trenton City directories between 1943 and 1950. Goldscheider Ceramics, located at 1441 Heath Avenue, Trenton, New Jersey, was listed in the *1952 Crockery and Glass Journal Directry*. The firm was not listed in 1954.

Bust, 15¼″ h, woman, stylized head, red unglazed earthenware, coiling hair, rose on collar, black painted wood base, imp circular label "Goldscheider/Wien," c1925 . . . . **1,200.00**

Bust, black woman, blue hair, orange highlights, sgd "Goldscheider, Vienna, 1927" on pedestal base, $800.00.

Figure
8" h, young nude, seated, black oval base, stamped "Austrian Goldscheider" and "Lorenzl" 1,650.00
8¾" h, dancer, full yellow dress, imp and stamped marks, inscribed "Latour" 440.00
16¼" h, dancer, one arm extending holding floral skirt, stamped "Lorenzl" and numbered 1,500.00
18½" h
  Butterfly Girl, cape painted to resemble monarch butterfly, imp numbers, painted marks, artist sgd "Lorenzl" 2,310.00
  Dancer, standing nude, plumed headdress, flowering cape, molded artist's name, printed Austrian marks 1,980.00
19" h, dancer, brunette, striding forward, blue floral halter dress, imp marks, artist sgd "Dakon" 1,430.00
20¼" h, Moroccan Woman, bronze, greenish brown patina, inscribed "Celine Lepage," stamped "4" and "Made In France," imp Goldscheider/La Stele exhibition seal 17,600.00
24" h, partially draped maiden, playing flute, leopard at feet, oval base with floral garland, sgd in base "Podola," stamped and imp marks . . . 1,750.00
Lamp Base, porcelain, polychrome
17" h, brunette harem dancer, holding pink flowered skirt out at ends, sq green base with flower filled urns, column standard, sgd "Rosie," printed and imp marks, restoration to hands 750.00
32" h, figural, standing bare breasted female, long lavender gown, holding garland of fruit and grains, stepped base, column standard, printed and imp marks, matching silk beaded shade, minor restoration to base 2,200.00
Plaque, 13½" w, 25⅛" h, earthenware, rect, molded, maiden in profile, garland of blossoms and berries in hair, large blossom and cluster on left, earth tones, designer sgd "Lamassi," Goldscheider mark, c1900 . . . . . . 1,000.00
Wall Mask, 11¼" h, girl, brown curly hair, red lips, aqua scarf 165.00

GONDER POTTERY

History: Lawton Gonder established Gonder Ceramic Arts, Inc., at Zanesville, Ohio, in 1941. He gained experience while working for other factories in the area. Gonder experimented with glazes, including Chinese crackle, gold crackle, and flambé. Lamp bases were manufactured under the name Eglee at a second plant location.

Gonder pieces are clearly marked. The company ceased operation in 1957.

Vase, green–blue, 6½" h, $10.00.

Basket, 6½" h, leaf pattern, turquoise ext., pink coral int., marked "H-39 Gonder USA" 30.00
Bowl, pedestal, gold crackle, marked "H-80" 30.00
Cornucopia, 7" l, turquoise and brown, marked "E5" 15.00
Ewer
  6" h, gray, fluted 10.00
  12" h, figural swan 30.00
Figure
  13" l, horse head, blue and green onyx glaze 40.00
  18¼" l, panther, jade green 90.00
Tea Set, cov teapot, creamer, and cov sugar, brown mottled 25.00
Vase
  9" h, mottled turquoise and brown, pink int. 15.00
  12" h, gray, marked "K-26" 12.00
  Fan, gold and turquoise 24.00

GOOFUS GLASS

History: Goofus glass, also known as Mexican Ware, Hooligan glass, and Pickle glass, is a pressed glass with relief designs. The back or front was painted. The designs are usually in red and green with a metallic gold ground. It was popular from 1890 to 1920 and was used as a premium at carnivals.

It was produced by several companies: Cresent Glass Company, Wellsburg, West Virginia; Imperial Glass Corporation, Bellaire, Ohio; LaBelle Glass Works, Bridgeport, Ohio; and Northwood Glass Co., Indiana, Pennsylvania, Wheeling, West Virginia, and Bridgeport, Ohio. Northwood marks include "N," "N" in one circle, "N" in two circles, and one or two circles without the "N."

Goofus glass lost its popularity when people found the paint tarnished or scaled off after repeated washings and wear. No record of its manufacture has been found after 1920.

Reference: Carolyn McKinley, *Goofus Glass*, Collector Books, 1984.

Additional Listings: See *Warman's Americana & Collectibles* for more examples.

Salt Shaker, Grape and Leaf pattern, 2¼" w, 4" h, $18.00.

Bowl
9½" d, relief molded, red carnations	35.00
10" d, Dogwood, ornate, orig paint	40.00
11" d, Strawberries	35.00
Candy Dish, 5¼" d, 2" h, Grape and Cable	25.00
Coaster, 3" d, gold, red flowers, orig paint, set of 4	40.00
Decanter, LeBelle Rose, orig stopper	50.00
Dresser Tray, 6" sq, Cabbage Rose, flash fired roses, orig paint	30.00
Miniature Lamp, 9" h, oil, Cabbage Rose, milk glass	50.00
Perfume Bottle, 3½" h, painted pink tulips	15.00
Plate, Rose, pine cone border	30.00
Powder Box, Puffy Rose	45.00
Powder Jar, cov, 4½" d, relief molded, white cabbage rose	20.00

Salt Shaker, Grape and Leaf, 2½" d, 4" h	18.00
Syrup, relief molded, red roses, lattice work ground, orig top	45.00
Tray, 8¼" w, 11" l, Chrysanthemum, bronze and red	35.00
Vase	
5" h, Poppy, white	20.00
7" h, Cabbage Rose, white, relief molded	45.00
10½" h, Peacock, relief molded	75.00

MARK

GOSS CHINA AND CRESTED WARE

History: In 1858 William H. Goss opened his Henley factory and produced terra cotta ware. A year later he moved to Stoke-on-Trent and added Parian ware to his line. In 1883 Adolphus, William's son, expanded on his father's idea of decorating small ivory pots and vases, with the coat of arms of schools, hospitals, colleges [especially Oxford and Cambridge], and other motifs to appeal to the souvenir seeking English "day-tripper." The forms used were copied from ancient artifacts in museums.

William died in 1906, his son in 1913. Following business setbacks, the firm was sold in 1929 to Geo. Jones & Sons Ltd., who had previously acquired Arcadian, Swan, and other firms that made crested wares. As late as 1931 the Goss name was still being used. In 1936–37 Cauldon Potteries purchased the Goss assets. Production ceased in 1940. In 1954 Ridgeway and Adderley acquired all Goss assets [molds, patterns, designs, and right to use the Goss name and trademark].

1883 to 1931 pieces carry the mark of GOSHAWK, with W. H. Goss beneath, and "England" on later pieces. Many early examples carry an impressed "W. H. Goss," either with or without the printed mark.

Other manufacturers of crested ware in England were: Arcadian, Carlton China, Grafton China, Savoy China, Shelley, and Willow Art. Gemma in Germany also made crested wares.

Crests are of little value unless they match, e.g., Shakespeare's jug with Shakespeare's crest. Collectors tend to collect one form (vase, ewer, jug, etc.), one particular crest, or one type of object (boat, cat, dog, etc.). Price is determined not by crest, but size, condition, and bottom mark.

References: Sandy Andrews, *Crested China: The History of Heraldic Souvenir Ware*, Milestone

Publications [England]; John Galpin, *A Handbook Of Goss China,* Milestone Publications; Nicholas Pine, *The 1984 Price Guide To Goss China,* Milestone Publications, 1984; Nicholas Pine and Sandy Andrews, *The 1984 Price Guide To Crested China* (including revisions to *Crested China*), Milestone Publications; Roland Ward, *The Price Guide To The Models Of W. H. Goss,* Antiques Collectors' Club.

Collectors' Clubs: The Goss Collectors Club, 3 Carr Hill Gardens, Barrowford, Nelson, Lancashire BB9 6PU; The Crested Circle, 26 Urswick Road, Dagenham, Essex RM9 6EA.

Vase, model of Roman vase found at Walmar Lodge, 2⅝ h, $25.00.

GOSS

Bottle, Swiss Vinegar, Wymondham	20.00
Bucket, Norwegian, Maldon	25.00
Building	
First and Last House	135.00
Huers House	200.00
Look Out House	140.00
Manx cottage	100.00
Shakespeare's house	100.00
St. Nicholas Chapel	200.00
Candle Snuffer, Aseroovy crest, white, 2¼"	50.00
Ewer	
Arundel, 4½"	20.00
Shrewsbury, 4"	20.00
Jug	
Assyrian Armour	20.00
Litchfield, Warwick	30.00
Kettle, Hastings	20.00
Night Light, Robert Burns, 6"	150.00
Plate, 10", Armorial	25.00
Porringer, Deconport	35.00
Pot, Winchester, Lewes	30.00
Tray, 5", crinkle	20.00
Urn, Falmouth	20.00
Vase	
Coronation Amphora	40.00
Doncaster, Seven Oaks	25.00
Pineapple, City of Edinburgh	30.00
Southwold	40.00
Winking Cat, 4"	25.00

OTHER CRESTED WARE MANUFACTURERS

Arcadian	
Bathing Wagon, Stockbridge	30.00
Turtle, Infracombe	25.00
Warming Pan, Tesbury	30.00
Carlton	
Urn, Bourne	20.00
Vase	
Keswick	20.00
Mundesley-On-Sea	10.00
Clifton	
Elephant, Lewisham	20.00
Six sided container, Coventry	15.00
Florentine	
Suitcase, Frome	20.00
Tower, Blackpool	25.00
Gemma	
Coal Hod, Southport	20.00
Teapot, cov, Salesbury	30.00
Shelley	
Fish Basket, Fleetwood	30.00
Headlamp, Cockermouth Cycle Oil	45.00
Olive Jar, Sussex	25.00
Scent Bottle, Richmond Surry	25.00
Tea Caddy	
Abbey of Glastonbury	25.00
Florest Hova	25.00
Seashell, Saltburn-by-the-Sea	30.00
Victoria, watering can, Matlock Bath	30.00
Willow Art, Shakespeare Cottage	150.00

GOUDA POTTERY

History: Gouda and the surrounding areas of Holland have been one of the principle Dutch pottery centers for centuries. Originally the potteries produced a simple utilitarian Delft type earthenware with a tin glaze and the famous clay smoker's pipes.

When the pipe making portion declined in the early 1900s, the Gouda potteries turned to pottery. Influenced by the Art Nouveau and Art Deco movements, artists expressed themselves with free form and stylized designs in bold colors.

Reference: Susan and Al Bagdade, *Warman's English & Continental Pottery & Porcelain, 1st Edition,* Warman Publishing Co., Inc., 1987.

Periodical: *The Dutch Potter,* 47 London Terrace, New Rochelle, NY 10804.

Reproduction Alert: With the Art Nouveau and Art Deco revivals of recent years, modern reproductions of Gouda pottery currently are on the market. They are difficult to distinguish from the originals.

Vase, Phoenix bird, white dec, black ground, 10½" h, $300.00.

Basket, 6" d, 7¾" h, high matte glaze, floral dec 150.00
Biscuit Jar, cov, 8", multicolored 130.00
Bowl
3" d, handles 32.00
5½" d, 3½" h, Damascus mark 50.00
Candlestick
3¾", green, rust, cobalt, ochre, marked "Candis 1137" and house mark 50.00
4⅛" d, 7⅛" h, Spino pattern, yellow flowers, green leaves, black ground, satin finish, house mark, pr 150.00
6½" d, 3" h, circular, handle, matte green, yellow, blue, and cream dec, marked "0139 DAM II Holland," c1885 . . . . 100.00
Charger, 12", multicolored flowers, rope border, black rim 150.00
Compote, 7⅝", black ground, geometric design, multicolored scroll int. 165.00
Dish, 8" d, 4" h, three sections, handle, brick, cream, blue, and gold dec, black ground, satin finish, crown mark and "Regina" 90.00
Ewer, 9½", matte finish, Anjer house mark 125.00
Humidor, 6" h, white high glaze, floral dec, Jilliana Gouda house mark . . . 250.00
Incense Burner, 8" h, Roba, flowers and geometric designs, green ground . . 100.00
Inkwell, 8" w, attached pen tray, matte finish, blue, Purdah Gouda, orange and black house mark 200.00
Jug, 10", orig stopper, multicolored dec, black matte ground 175.00
Planter, 12" l, 7" w, 4" h, rect, Yssel pattern 150.00
Plate, 10½", matte finish, multicolored dec 100.00
Potpourri Jar, 4", high glaze, multicolored dec, black base 85.00

Tobacco Jar, cov, 5", Verona pattern . . 80.00
Tray, 10½", leaf dec, autumn colors . . 150.00
Tumbler, 4⅜" h, 3⅝" d, multicolored flowers, green leaves, black ground, satin finish, marked "Nerf" and house mark 55.00
Vase
10" h, Regina, high gloss, rust, light purple, olive green, and forest green flowers and leaves, black ground, gold dots 125.00
12" h, ovoid, tapering neck, everted rim, painted burgundy and amber blossoms, curving stems, speckled variegated green ground, sgd, small repair on rim 385.00
16½" h, urn form, green, tan, black, and white floral dec, numbered "0123R/0123," sgd "Herat/Gouda/ Holland/AR" 650.00

GRANITEWARE

History: Graniteware is the name commonly given to iron or steel kitchenware covered with enamel coating.

The first graniteware was made in Germany in the 1830s. Graniteware was not produced in the United States until the 1860s. At the start of World War I, when European manufacturers turned to the making of war weapons, American producers took over the market.

Colors commonly marketed were white and gray. Each company made their own special color, including shades of blue, green, brown, violet, cream, and red.

Older graniteware is heavier than new graniteware. Pieces with cast iron handles date from 1870 to 1890; wood handles date from 1900 to 1910. Other dating clues are seams, wood knobs, and tin lids.

References: Vernagene Vogelzang and Evelyn Welch, *Granite Ware, Collector's Guide With Prices,* Wallace-Homestead, 1981; Vernagene Vogelzang and Evelyn Welch, *Granite Ware, Book II,* Wallace-Homestead, 1987.

Collectors' Club: National Graniteware Society, 4818 Reamer Road, Center Point, IA 52213.

Reproduction Alert: Graniteware still is manufactured in many of the traditional forms and colors.

Additional Listings: See *Warman's Americana & Collectibles* for more examples.

Boiler, double, cream, green trim, lid . . 45.00
Bowl, 7", robin's egg blue and white, mottle 25.00
Bread Dough Riser, blue and white, mottle 165.00
Bucket, 2 qt, aqua swirl, bail 20.00
Cake Pan, 10" d, blue and white swirl 25.00

Coffeepot, mottled gray, bail handle with wooden hand grip, $90.00.

Cocoa Dipper, gray, hollow handle ...	225.00
Coffeepot	
Black and white speckle, large	30.00
Blue spatter, six cup	55.00
Blue speckle, replaced hinge	40.00
Gray, V neck, wood handle	75.00
White ground, multicolored bird in flowers, pewter gooseneck spout, handle, and top	200.00
Diaper Pail, gray, wood handle, lid, label	40.00
Dipper, blue	12.00
Flour Canister, blue and white, mottle, lid	170.00
Funnel, gray	25.00
Grater	
Medium blue	115.00
White and gold, German	125.00
Iron, flat, blue	225.00
Loaf Pan, gray	25.00
Lunch Pail, cobalt, 4 pcs	75.00
Measure, gray, 1 cup	95.00
Milk Pan, blue and white	35.00
Mixing Bowl, blue and white, swirl ...	100.00
Mold, fluted, gray	45.00
Muffin Pan	
Blue and white, mottle, eight section	250.00
Gray	25.00
Pan, large, two handles, gray mottle ..	25.00
Pie Baker, white and red	21.00
Pie Pan	
Cobalt, white veins, 6"	25.00
Gray	15.00
Skimmer, blue and white swirl	65.00
Soap Dish, hanging, blue swirl	110.00
Soup Tureen, gray, flat bottom, slot lid for ladle handle	300.00
Stew Pan, red and white swirl, tin lid	40.00
Strainer, gray, octagonal, three legs, side handle, attached drain pan ...	375.00
Tea Strainer, blue and white, mottle, pierced holes	200.00
Teapot	
Ball shape, pink to white ground, flow-	
ers and bullrushes, dec, ornate pewter	170.00
Gray, gooseneck	90.00
Washboard, cobalt blue	60.00

GREENAWAY, KATE   K.G.

History: Kate Greenaway, or "K.G." as she initialed her famous drawings, was born in 1846 in London. Her father was a prominent wood engraver. Kate's natural talent for drawing soon evident, and she began art classes at the age of 12. In 1868 she had her first public exhibition.

Her talents were used primarily in illustrating. She did cards for Marcus Ward, which are largely unsigned. China and pottery companies soon had her drawings of children appearing on many of their wares. By the 1880s she was one of the foremost children's book illustrators in England.

Collectors' Club: Kate Greenaway Society, 10 Felton Avenue, Ridley Park, PA 19078.

Reproduction Alert: Some Greenaway buttons have been reproduced in Europe and sold in the United States.

Almanac, 1883, published by George Routledge & Sons, $100.00.

Biscuit Jar, cov, boy, pastel dec	150.00
Bowl, amber daisy and button pattern, girl and dog on Reed and Barton SP holder	500.00
Bust, 5" h, girl with glasses, frilly bonnet, ribbons, lace	60.00
Children's Book, *Birthday Book*, Warne, color illus	45.00
Children's Feeding Dishes, cup, saucer, and 6" d plate, 3 pcs	100.00
Children's Play Dishes, tea set, 7 pcs, children and dachshund pulling tablecloth, 7 pcs	150.00

Figure

4" h, bisque, child with basket	175.00
9½" h, children jumping rope, pr	600.00
Match Holder, girl helping little sister over log, place for matches and striker	90.00
Match Safe, SP, emb children	50.00
Mug, SS, "Bessie 1882"	60.00
Nodder, bisque, elderly couple, wearing eyeglasses, cloak, bonnet, and high hat	130.00
Picture Frame, 6 x 5", SS, two girls look out window, grandfather clock, blue velvet back, c1885	200.00
Plate, 9" d, children playing, with oversized fruit, birds, and flowers	100.00
Print, 6 x 8", *Outdoor Tea Party,* fifteen girls, sgd	90.00
Salt and Pepper Shakers, pr, 4" h, girl and girl in long coats, girl with muff	80.00
Sugar Shaker, boy in long coat, porcelain	95.00
Thimble Holder, girl holds SS thimble	125.00
Tile	
"May," 6" sq	75.00
"Pipe Thee High," small boy with horn, Wedgwood	75.00
Toothpick Holder, SP, ornate, girl, standing, marked "Tufts"	175.00
Vase, 4" h, figural girl, holder with orig frosted dec bud vase, sq ornate ftd base, marked "Tufts"	145.00

GREENTOWN GLASS

History: The Indiana Tumbler and Goblet Co., Greentown, Indiana, produced its first clear, pressed glass table and bar wares in late 1894. Initial success led to a doubling of plant size in 1895 and other subsequent expansions, one in 1897 to allow for the manufacture of colored glass. In 1899 the firm joined the combine known as the National Glass Company.

In 1900, just before arriving in Greentown, Jacob Rosenthal developed an opaque brown glass, called "chocolate," which ranged in color from a dark, rich chocolate to a lighter "cream" coffee hue. Production of chocolate glass saved the financially pressed Indiana Tumbler and Goblet Works. The Cactus and Leaf Bracket patterns were made almost exclusively in chocolate glass. Other popular chocolate patterns are Austrian, Dewey, Shuttle, and Teardrop and Tassel. In 1902 National Glass Company bought Rosenthal's chocolate glass formula so other plants in the combine could use the color.

In 1902 Rosenthal developed the Golden Agate and Rose Agate colors. All work ceased on June 13, 1903, when a fire of suspicious origin destroyed the Indiana Tumbler and Goblet Company Works.

After the fire, other companies, e.g., McKee and Brothers, produced chocolate glass in the same pattern design used in Greentown. Later reproductions also have taken place, with Cactus among the most heavily copied pattern.

References: Brenda Measell and James Measell, *A Guide To Reproductions of Greentown Glass,* 2nd ed., The Printing Press, 1974; James Measell, *Greentown Glass, The Indiana Tumbler & Goblet Co.,* Grand Rapids Public Museum, 1979.

Collectors' Club: National Greentown Glass Association, 1807 West Madison, Kokomo, IN 46901.

Museums: Greentown Glass Museum, Greentown, IN; Grand Rapids Public Museum [Ruth Herrick Greentown Glass Collection], MI.

Additional Listings: Holly Amber and Pattern Glass.

Nappy, Leaf Bracket pattern, chocolate, tripod feet, $65.00.

Animal Dish, cov	
Cat, hamper base, chocolate, chip on base of basket	200.00
Dolphin, chocolate	
Beaded rim, fish finial lid	300.00
Sawtooth edge	185.00
Berry Set, Leaf & Bracket, chocolate, 7 pcs	245.00
Bowl	
6¼" d, Cactus, chocolate	75.00
8" d, Dewey, amber, ftd	30.00
Butter Dish, cov	
Daisy, milk glass	75.00
Overall Lattice, clear	65.00
Compote, jelly, 5¼" d, Cactus, chocolate	150.00
Cordial, Overall Lattice, clear	35.00
Creamer	
Cactus, chocolate	115.00
Cord Drapery, blue	85.00
Indian Head, Nile green	475.00
Cruet, orig stopper	
Cactus, chocolate	140.00
Chrysanthemum Leaf, chocolate	850.00
Wild Rose and Bowknot, chocolate	325.00
Dresser Tray, Wild Rose and Bowknot, chocolate	310.00
Goblet, Diamond Prisms, clear	65.00
Lemonade, Cactus, chocolate	75.00
Mug, cov, 6½" h, Indoor Drinking Scene, Nile green	100.00

Pitcher, water

Cord Drapery, clear	50.00
Racing Deer and Doe, clear	165.00
Ruffled Eye, chocolate	550.00
Squirrel, clear	165.00
Punch Cup, Shuttle, clear	10.00
Relish, Cord Drapery, amber	90.00
Rose Bowl, Austrian, small	30.00

Salt and Pepper Shakers, pr, Cactus,

chocolate, lids missing	90.00

Sauce

Leaf Bracket, chocolate	35.00
Water Lily and Cattail, chocolate	100.00

Spooner

Austrian, clear	35.00
Cupid, clear	145.00
Wild Rose and Bowknot, chocolate	145.00
Toothpick, Cactus, golden agate	95.00

Tumbler

Cord Drapery, chocolate	200.00
Teardrop and Tassel, cobalt blue	50.00
Wildflower, amber	38.00
Wine, Shuttle, clear	18.00

GRUEBY POTTERY

History: William Grueby was active in the ceramic industry for several years before he developed his own method of producing matte glazed pottery and founded the Grueby Faience Company in Boston, Massachusetts, in 1897.

The art pottery was hand thrown in natural shapes, hand molded, and hand tooled. A variety of colored glazes, singly or in combinations, were produced with green being the most prominent. In 1908 the firm was divided into the Grueby Pottery Company and the Grueby Faience and Tile Co., the latter making art pottery until bankruptcy forced closure shortly after 1908.

References: Paul Evans, *Art Pottery of the United States, 2nd Edition*, Feingold & Lewis Publishing Corp., 1987; Ralph and Terry Kovel, *The Kovels' Collector's Guide to American Art Pottery*, Crown Publishers, Inc., 1974.

Bowl, 11″ d, eleven molded leaves, cucumber green glaze, imp mark, inscribed "RE" for artist Ruth Erickson and "4/4" **1,320.00**

Lamp, 22½″ h, 18⅛″ d shade, geometric green and yellow leaded glass shade with swirling leaf band, marked "Tiffany Studios New York," bronze cap finial, green glazed base imp mark, designer Ruth Erickson monogram **17,600.00**

Lamp Base, 13¼″ pottery base, 24¼″ h overall, elongated neck flaring to bulbous base, dark green patina, tooled repeated three petaled floral dec, stems trailing between alternating broad base leaves, imp mark, "No. 32," artist sgd "A. L." for Annie Lingley, bronze three light standard and font attributed to Tiffany & Co, NY, c1905 .... **3,250.00**

Paperweight, 4″ l, scarab, imp mark, chips **325.00**

Tile, Prancing Horses, white horses, green earth, blue sky, 6¼ x 6″, $600.00.

Tile

5⅝ x 7″, rect, molded white polar bear dec, deep blue ground **350.00**

6″ d, figural, cherub and cornucopia, relief dec, gold and cream, green glaze, artist initials "E. M.," c1910 **225.00**

8″ d, St George slaying the dragon, green and blues, c1905 .... **800.00**

Urn, squat bulbous body, flared lip, wide mouth, angled shoulder, matte green glaze, imp circular mark and number "1," incised artist's initials "M" for Marie A Seaman, c1905 .... **2,700.00**

Vase

4¾″ h, compressed spherical body, cylindrical neck, heavy pale blue–green glaze, imp mark, inscribed "E, W, D" within circle **715.00**

6″ h, compressed spherical body, slightly everted rim, seven broad

molded leaves, cucumber green
glaze, imp mark **825.00**
7⅝″ h, baluster, vertical ribs, thick
cucumber glaze, imp mark, incised
artist Ruth Erickson monogram .. **2,550.00**
8″ h, pear shape, grainy matte green
glaze, molded petals around base,
long stemmed buds ascending
sides, imp "Grueby, Boston, Mass" **1,100.00**
11⅜″ h, cylindrical body, low relief,
rising lappet shape leaves from
base to mouth, yellow tulip buds at
mouth, imp "Grueby Faience Co
Boston USA" **6,050.00**
11½″ h, melon, three groups of white
glazed jonquils, green impasto
glaze body, imp mark, incised artist
Wilhelmina Post mark **31,000.00**
13¼″ h, bulbous body, elongated
neck with molded rim, horizontal
ribbing, veined texture, curdling
foot, imp "Grueby Faience Co Bos-
ton USA" in block letters **1,760.00**
22½″ h, tall baluster, finely carved
stylized leaves, green glaze, imp
mark **16,500.00**

HAIR ORNAMENTS

History: Hair ornaments, one of the first accessories developed by primitive man, were used to
remove tangles and keep hair out of one's face.
Remnants of early combs have been found in
many archaeological excavations.

As fashion styles changed through the centuries, hair ornaments kept pace through design and
use changes. Hair combs and other hair ornaments are made in a wide variety of materials,
e.g., precious metals, ivory, tortoise shell, plastics,
and wood.

Combs were first made in America during the
Revolution when imports from England were restricted. Early American combs were made of horn
and treasured as valued toiletry articles.

Reference: Evelyn Haetig, *Antique Combs and
Purses*, Gallery Graphics Press, 1983.

Back Comb, celluloid, Spanish, Art Nou-
veau, c1910 .... **90.00**
Barrette, 2½″ d, rhinestone dec, 1950s **20.00**
Hairclip, rhinestone dec, c1930, pr ... **15.00**
Comb
Plastic, rhinestone crown accent,
1940s **35.00**
Tortoiseshell, 5½″ w, 4″ l, brass frame
eagle with faceted rhinestones ... **300.00**
Hairpin
Amber, Art Deco, c1925 .... **45.00**
Tortoise, sterling filigree, English, Vic-
torian, c1890 .... **65.00**

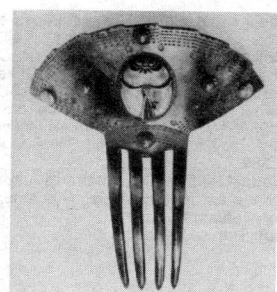

**Comb, Bakelite, fan-shaped, olive
green, black stripes, applied blue and
red plastic ovals, center scarab beetle,
punched line work edge, 5 x 4¼″,
$50.00.**

Ornament
Celluloid, Victorian, c1900 .... **35.00**
Plastic, black, shaft with box shape
dec on top, seven pasted rhine-
stone dec on sides of box, 1960s **20.00**
Tortoiseshell, Art Nouveau style,
c1910 .... **65.00**
Side Comb, plastic
Eighteen rhinestones, 1940s **25.00**
Silver metal and rhinestone tiara
shape dec, hinged **30.00**
Tiara, encircles gathered hair, hand set
rhinestones, 1940s **70.00**
Tuck Comb, etched design with nine
stones **25.00**

HALL CHINA COMPANY

History: Robert Hall founded the Hall China
Company in 1903 in East Liverpool, Ohio. He died
in 1904 and was succeeded by his son, Robert
Taggart Hall. After years of experimentation, Robert T. Hall developed a leadless glaze in 1911,
opening the way for production of glazed household products.

The Hall China Company made many types of
kitchenware, refrigerator sets, and dinnerware in
a wide variety of patterns. Some patterns were
exclusive, such as Heather Rose for Sears.

One of the most popular patterns was Autumn
Leaf, an exclusive premium designed in 1933 for
the Jewel Tea Company by Arden Richards. Still
a Jewel Tea property, Autumn Leaf has not been
listed in catalogs since 1978 but is produced on a

replacement basis with the date stamped on the back.

References: Harvey Duke, *Superior Quality Hall China*, ELO Books, 1977; Harvey Duke, *Hall 2*, ELO Books, 1985; Harvey Duke, *The Official Price Guide To Pottery And Porcelain*, Collector Books, 1989; Margaret and Kenn Whitmyer, *The Collector's Encyclopedia of Hall China*, Collector Books, 1989.

Additional Listings: See *Warman's Americana & Collectibles* for more examples plus a separate section on Autumn Leaf.

Advisor: Harvey Duke.

Teapot, hook cover, blue, gold trim, $30.00.

MISCELLANEOUS

Bowl, Radiance, Chinese Red, 14" . . .	16.00
Irish Coffee Mug, Chinese Red	8.00
Pretzel Jar, Morning Glory	55.00
Vase, bud, yellow	5.00
Water Server, Nora Daffodil	10.00

PATTERNS

Autumn Leaf. Premium for Jewel Tea Co. Produced from 1933 until 1978.

Bowl	
Berry	4.00
Mixing, 3 pcs	38.00
Coffee Pot, 8"	24.00
Coffee Server, 8¼"	30.00
Cream Soup	15.00
Custard Cup	4.00
Iced Tea, frosted	12.50
Jug, ball, #3	15.00
Mustard, 3 pc	40.00
Pitcher, 6"	12.00
Plate	
Bread and butter, 5½"	3.00
Salad, 6"	3.50
Platter	
9"	10.00
13½	15.00

Souffle, large	12.00
Vegetable, oval	14.00

Heather Rose. Produced during the 1940s.

Coffeepot, "Terrace"	30.00
Creamer and Sugar	12.00
Cup and Saucer	4.00
Gravy Boat	10.00
Plate, 10", dinner	5.00
Tureen, cov	18.00

Orange Poppy. Premium for Great American Tea Co. Produced from 1933 through 1950s.

Baker, fluted	12.00
Casserole, cov, oval	30.00
Creamer and Sugar	24.00
Cup and Saucer	7.00
Jug, 6½"	15.00
Plate, 9"	7.50
Salt and Pepper Shaker, handled, pr	18.00

Rose Parade. Kitchenware line introduced in the 1940s.

Bowl, salad	15.00
Casserole, cov, tab handle	30.00
Creamer and Sugar	20.00
Salt and Pepper Shaker, sani-grid, pr	20.00
Teapot, 32 oz	25.00

Springtime. Premium for Standard Tea Co. Limited production.

Batter Bowl, Chinese red	47.00
Bowl, 10", oval	8.50
Cake Plate	15.00
Creamer and Sugar	15.00
Cup and Saucer	8.50
Gravy	10.00
Pie Baker	15.00
Plate	
Bread and butter, 6¼"	4.00
Dinner, 9"	8.00
Platter, 13"	12.50
Soup Plate	5.25
Teapot, cov, 6 cup	40.00

TEAPOTS

Airflow, turquoise, gold dec	30.00
Boston, green, gold dec	24.00
Daffodil, twin spout	50.00
Disreali, pink, gold dec	25.00
Globe, inverted spout, lemon	60. 00
Nautilus, 6 cup, yellow	75.00
New York, brown, gold dec	20.00
Philadelphia, green, gold dec	28.00

HAMPSHIRE POTTERY

History: In 1871 James S. Taft founded the Hampshire Pottery Company in Keene, New Hampshire. Production began with redwares and stonewares, followed by majolica decorated wares in 1879. A semi-porcelain, with the recognizable matte glazes plus the Royal Worcester glaze, was introduced in 1883.

Until World War I the factory made an extensive line of utilitarian and art wares including souvenir items. After the war the firm resumed operations, but only made hotel dinnerware and tiles. The company dissolved in 1923.

Reference: Joan Pappas and A. Harold Kendall, *Hampshire Pottery Manufactured by J. S. Taft & Company, Keene, New Hampshire,* published by author, 1971.

Vase, dark blue, imp mark, 4¼″ h, $175.00.

Bulb Bowl, 9⅞″ d, dark green matte glaze, yellow buds, light green leaves, glossy lime green int., unglazed bisque liner	115.00
Ewer	
6½″, two handles, dark green glaze, sgd "J. S. T. & Co, Keene, NH" . .	100.00
8¼″, striated matte green, fancy looped handle	35.00
Lamp Base, 19″ h, elongated standard, repeating buds flaring to base, stylized leaf dec, green matte glaze, stamped "Hampshire Pottery" and "M", c1910	660.00
Mug, 7″ h, dark green glaze shading to red, relief border top and bottom . . .	60.00
Pitcher, 7½″ h, holly dec	80.00
Tea Set, 3 pcs, olive green gloss, gold "Tampa, Florida"	90.00
Umbrella Stand, 17⅝″ h, deep matte green, high relief trailing ivy, textured ground	85.00
Vase	
5½″ h, molded leaf dec, green matte glaze, two handles, pedestal base	115.00
8¼″ h, bulbous, curled leaf and stem handle, broad leaves dec, artist initials, imp "Hampshire Pottery" . .	320.00
8½″ h, swollen cylindrical, wide mouth, short neck, repeating molded tulip dec, imp Cadmon Robertson mark, c1910	350.00
11″ h, cylindrical, flaring ruffled top, molded, gathered and tied at neck, matte green glaze, imp "Hampshire"	425.00
15½″, six emb long and wide pointed leaves alternating with six buds, matte green finish, paper label "Hampshire Ware, 1871"	600.00

HAND PAINTED CHINA

History: Hand painting on china began in the Victorian era and remained popular through the 1920s. It was considered an accomplished art form for women in the upper and upper middle class households. It developed first in England, but spread rapidly to the Continent and America.

China factories in Europe, America, and the Orient made the blanks. Belleek, Haviland, Limoges, and Rosenthal are among the European firms. American firms include A. H. Hews Co., Cambridge, Massachusetts; Willetts Mfg. Co., Trenton, New Jersey; and Knowles, Taylor and Knowles, East Liverpool, Ohio. Nippon blanks from Japan were used heavily during the early 20th century.

The quality and design of the blank is a key factor in pricing. Some blanks were very elaborate. Many pieces were signed and dated by the artist.

Aesthetics is critical. Value is added to a piece when a decorator goes beyond the standard forms and creates a unique and pleasing design.

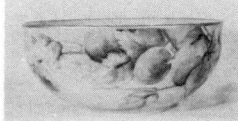

Bowl, Belleek blank, purple plums, green leaves, gold rim, int. painted, marked "LCH, Belleek, 1922," $200.00.

Bowl	
9½″, strawberries, flowers, and leaves, green ground, artist sgd, Bavaria	45.00
10 x 12″, yellow and brown ducklings, ribbed scallop shell, gilt edge, artist sgd "Jean Pouyat," Limoges	100.00
Candlestick, 5¾″, pink roses, shaded yellow and blue ground, gold trim . .	28.00
Cheese Dish, 6¼ x 9″, cov, pink floral sprays, green leaves, pale blue shaded to white, gold trim, applied handles	100.00

Cider Set, pitcher, six handled mugs, blackberries and foliage on pitcher, different fruit on each mug, pastel blue and green ground, 7 pcs	170.00
Compote, 9⅞ x 5¼", multicolored flowers, romantic landscape, matching pr	200.00
Cruet, blue and white flowers, matching stopper	65.00
Cup, yellow, 1½" figural butterfly on handle	20.00
Dresser Tray, 11 x 16", center spray of multicolored flowers, gold flower wreath, white ground, pink border, sgd	80.00
Hatpin, Victorian motif, baroque sleeved dec, gold overlay, 7½" gilt pin, c1890	90.00
Jewelry, brooch, tropical scene	20.00
Pitcher, 6", leaves, gold handle and trim, Limoges blank	90.00
Plate	
Bread and Butter, pink flowers, gold trim	70.00
Dinner, 11", scalloped gold trim border, pastel yellow single rose, green foliage, artist sgd, Haviland blank, 1901	65.00
Platter, 9½ x 14", oval, peasants gathering hay and loading it onto horse drawn wagon, unmarked Faience blank	65.00
Shaving Mug, lady dressed in brown and white, white plumes and red ribbon on hat	65.00
Sugar Shaker, pastel pansies, Bavaria	45.00
Sweetmeat, 9" d, reticulated rim, low pedestal base, deep purple blackberry dec, artist sgd, Haviland blank, 1901	60.00
Tobacco Jar, 7¼" h, multicolored Indian bust, gold trim and finial, artist sgd "Florence Weaver, 1925," initials on finial, blank marked "Favorite, Bavaria"	200.00
Toothpick Holder, 2¼ x 2", shaded pink to blue, pink flowers, gold trim	25.00
Vase	
6¾" h, grapes, moriage, floral, ruffled top, three ftd, Nippon, Royal Moriye mark	265.00
7½", bud, daffodils, Rosenthal blank	45.00

HATPINS AND HATPIN HOLDERS

History: When the vogue for oversized hats developed around 1850, hatpins became popular. Designers used a variety of materials to decorate the pin ends, including china, crystal, enamel, gem stones, precious metals, and shells. Decorative subjects ranged from commemorative designs to insects.

Hatpin holders are porcelain containers set on a dresser to hold these pins. The holders were produced by major manufacturers, among which were Meissen, Nippon, R. S. Germany, R. S. Prussia, and Wedgwood.

Reference: Lillian Baker, *Handbook for Hatpins & Hatpin Holders,* Collector Books, 1983; 1988 value update.

Collectors' Club: International Club for Collectors of Hatpins and Hatpin Holders, 15237 Chanera Avenue, Gardena, CA, 90249.

Museum: Los Angeles Art Museum, Costume Dept., Los Angeles, CA.

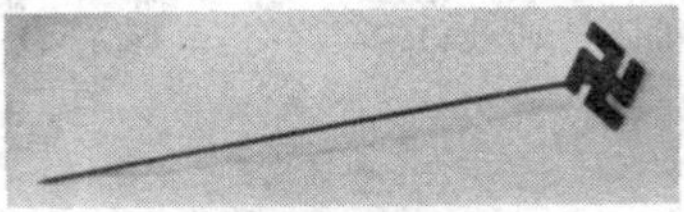

Hatpin, swastika shape, green dec, blue ground, $15.00.

HATPINS

Art Nouveau	
Four sided, sterling silver, 12"	65.00
Lady, opens to mirror	110.00
Brass	
Lacy openwork, 10½" l, large rhinestones on dome top	30.00
Owl, figural	35.00
Carnival Glass, figural, flying bat, black, silver luster	32.00
Crystal, hand cut, blown teardrop shape inside, attached to 10½" brass pin . .	125.00
Cloisonne, Japanese, foil back, marked in Japanese script	75.00
Ivory, 1⅛" elephant, hand carved	90.00
Jet Glass, 3¼", cut and faceted, riveted to wire frame, japanned pin shank . .	175.00
Mosaic, brass button sleeve type metallic mounting, gold wire trim, 8" brass pin, stamped "GS," c1875 . . .	60.00
Mother-of-Pearl, 2" d	15.00
Peacock Eye Glass	
Oval head, 7½" steel pin	40.00
Three sided leaf motif, gilded brass, peacock eye set atop	75.00
Rhinestones, faceted amber, 1½" d, 10" shank	80.00
Silver	
German, beetle, 1½ x 1¼", green enameled wings and body, red eyes	60.00
Sterling	
Purple faceted stone, ornate, 2" d	70.00
Six sided, floral, 7"	55.00

HATPIN HOLDERS

Bisque, 5¼" h, Egyptian motif, pink and
white, c1909 . . . . **130.00**
China
  Belleek, hp "E" and floral dec, Willets **65.00**
  Limoges, gold emb border, cream
    ground **30.00**
  Nippon, 4¾" h, Bleriot Airplane se-
    ries, hp lavender, green, and rust
    airplane crossing channel dec,
    beading and moriage accents . . . **200.00**
  Noritake, Azalea pattern **35.00**
  Royal Bayreuth, 4½" h, Art Nouveau
    Lady, saucer base, blue mark . . . **450.00**
  Royal Doulton, 5" h, hp, Ophelia, lav-
    ender and pink, dark cream
    ground, dark green trim, seven pin
    holes **175.00**
  R.S. Prussia, 4¾" h, roses, luster fin-
    ish, scalloped base **235.00**
  Schafer & Vater, 5" h, pink, cameos
    dec with dark blue frame, pale blue
    trim, Crown and Sunburst mark
    with incised letter "R" **125.00**
Glass
  Carnival, Butterfly and Berry pattern,
    blue, Fenton **700.00**
  Chocolate, 7⅞" h, ftd, c1905 . . . . . . **300.00**
Pottery, 5" h, hp rooster dec, "Keep Me
  on the Dressing Table," ftd, Torquay **85.00**
Silver, 4" h, platform with pin cushion,
  figural cherub holding ring, c1895 . . **145.00**

HAVILAND CHINA

History: In 1842, American china importer
David Haviland moved to Limoges, France, where
he began manufacturing and decorating china
specifically for the U.S. market. Haviland is synonymous with fine, white, translucent porcelain,
although early hand painted patterns were generally larger and darker colored on heavier whiteware blanks than are later ones.

David revolutionized French china factories by
both manufacturing the whiteware blank and decorating it at the same site. In addition, Haviland
and Company pioneered the use of decals in decorating china.

David's sons, Charles Edward and Theodore
split the company in 1892. Theodore opened an
American division in 1936 which continues until
today. In 1941 Theodore bought out Charles Edward's heirs and recombined both companies un-

der the original name of H. and Co. The Haviland
family sold its interests in 1981.

Charles Field Haviland, cousin of Charles Edward and Theodore, worked for, and then ran, the
Casseaux Works after his marriage in 1857 until
1882. Items continued to carry his name as decorator until 1941.

Haviland patterns were not consistently named
until after 1926. Pattern identification is difficult
because of the similarity found in the over 66,000
patterns that have been made. Numbers assigned
by Arlene Schleiger and illustrated in her books
have become the identification standard for matching.

References: Mary Frank Gaston, *Haviland Collectibles & Art Objects*, Collector Books, 1984;
Arlene Schleiger, *Two Hundred Patterns of Haviland China, Books I-V*, published by author, 1950–
1977.

**Bouillon cup and saucer, gold trim,
gold emb fleur–de–lis, marked "G. D.
A. France, G. B. Field, Haviland, Limoges," $30.00.**

Basket, reticulated, rope design, three
  curved feet, marked "Theo Haviland" **135.00**
Bouillon Cup and Saucer, small green
  flowers and leaves **25.00**
Bowl, 5½" d, Greek key dec, black and
  yellow **15.00**
Butter Dish, cov, Wedding Ring **85.00**
Cake Plate, 10" d, blue floral spray, gold
  handles **45.00**
Children's Feeding Dish, plate, Kate
  Greenaway style nursery rhyme dec
  with children and dog **100.00**
Coffee Service, coffeepot, creamer, and
  sugar, Wedding Anniversary, marked
  "H & Co" **125.00**
Compote, 9" d, 2¾" h, blue and pink
  flowers, gold scalloped edge **60.00**
Cup and Saucer, Moss Rose, 1885
  mark **40.00**
Demitasse Cup and Saucer, yellow flo-
  ral spray **30.00**
Dresser Set, hair receiver, cov powder

box, fitted tray with handle, yellow floral, gold borders **135.00**

Foot Bath, 11" h, 13" w, white ground, gold bands, gold trimmed elaborate handles, marked "Haviland" **750.00**

Gravy Boat, cov, attached underplate, oval, green and gold geometric dec . **50.00**

Oyster Plate, cobalt and gold, marked "H & Co" **65.00**

Pitcher, 9" h, pink flowers **85.00**

Plate
  5" d, Arbor pattern **15.00**
  6" d, Autumn Leaf pattern **10.00**
  7½" d, hp, pink roses, gold trim, Diana blank, artist sgd **30.00**
  8½" d
    Baltimore Rose pattern, pink, Ranson blank, marked "Haviland & Co" **20.00**
    Hand Painted
      Butterflies, napkin corners, double mark **20.00**
      Pansies, pastel ground, artist sgd **25.00**
    Silver Anniversary pattern **20.00**
  9½" d, Grand Pacific Hotel, Chicago, Club du Barry shape, gold encrusted cobalt, marked "H & Co" **48.00**
  10³⁄₁₆" d, service, gold swag and scroll design, cobalt blue ground border, 20th C, set of 12 .... **600.00**

Platter
  11¾" l, Arbor pattern **55.00**
  13¾" l, Silver Anniversary pattern . . **65.00**

Powder Box, cov, 5" d, tiny blue florals, gold rims, center portrait of lady in gold frame, inscribed "MMT–1891" on lid int. **100.00**

Ramekin and Saucer, No. 24 pattern, Ranson blank **35.00**

Relish, white, scattered pink flowers, scalloped **30.00**

Sauce, Arbor pattern **12.00**

Soup Plate, apple blossom dec, scalloped edge **15.00**

Soup Tureen, cov, Baltimore Rose pattern **285.00**

Sugar, cov, Wedding Ring **85.00**

Vegetable Dish, cov, 9½" w, Persia pattern, octagonal **200.00**

HEISEY GLASS

History: The A. H. Heisey Glass Co. began producing glasswares in April, 1896, in Newark, Ohio. Heisey was not a newcomer to the field, having been associated with the craft since his youth.

Many blown and molded patterns were produced in crystal, colored, milk (opalescent), and Ivorina Verde (custard) glass. Decorative techniques of cutting, etching, and silver deposit were employed. Glass figurines were introduced in 1933 and continued until 1957 when the factory ceased production. All Heisey glass is notable for its clarity. Not all Heisey glassware is marked with the familiar "H" within a diamond.

References: Neila Bredehoft, *The Collector's Encyclopedia of Heisey Glass, 1925–1938*, Collector Books, 1986; Mary Louise Burns, *Heisey's Glassware of Distinction*, 2nd edition, published by author, 1983; Lyle Conder, *Collector's Guide To Heisey's Glassware for Your Table*, L-W Books, 1984; Tom Felt and Bob O'Grady, *Heisey Candlesticks, Candelabra, and Lamps*, Heisey Collectors of America, Inc, 1984; Sandra Stoudt, *Heisey On Parade*, Wallace-Homestead, 1985.

Collectors' Club: Heisey Collectors of America, P.O. Box 4367, Newark, OH, 43055.

Museum: National Heisey Glass Museum, Newark, OH.

Reproduction Alert: Some Heisey molds were sold to Imperial Glass of Bellaire, Ohio, and certain items were reissued. These pieces may be mistaken for the original Heisey. Some of the reproductions were produced in colors which were never made by Heisey and have become collectible in their own right.

Examples include: the Colt family in Crystal, Carmel Slag, Ultra Blue, and Horizon Blue; the mallard with wings up in Carmel Slag; Whirlpool (Provincial) in crystal and colors; and, Waverly, 7" oval footed compote in Carmel Slag.

Animal
  Giraffe, head back **150.00**
  Goose, wings half up **85.00**
  Ringneck Pheasant **110.00**
  Rooster, fighting **110.00**
  Scottie Dog **85.00**

Ashtray
  Lariat, 3½", round **10.00**
  Orchid, 3" sq **28.00**
  Ridgeleigh, club shape **8.00**

Bookend, Horsehead, frosted, pr **100.00**

Bowl
  Daffodil **90.00**
  Lariat, 8½", clear **35.00**
  Plantation Ivy, 9", fruit **140.00**
  Queen Anne, shallow 9" d, Orchid etch **70.00**

Box, cov, Horsehead
  4" **110.00**
  6" **95.00**

Butter Dish, cov
  Orchid **180.00**
  Provincial **80.00**

Cake Stand, Locket on a Chain **125.00**

Candle Vase, Ridgeleigh, Sahara, #1469 .... **65.00**

Candlesticks, pr
Athena, two light 40.00
Hawthorne Pluto, 3½" 90.00
Heisey Rose, three light, #142 .... 175.00
Lariat, two light 55.00
Old Williamsburg, 11" h 235.00
Orchid, three light 145.00
Rose, 3" 70.00
Tea Rose, trident 65.00
Thumbprint & Panel 40.00
Whirlpool, two light 50.00
Candy Dish, cov
Colonial
Crystolite, 7" 55.00
Empress, silver overlay, ftd 60.00
Rose, finial 65.00
Seahorse, tall, ftd, handles 150.00
Celery Tray
Greek Key, 12", #433 .... 40.00
King Arthur, diamond optic hand dec,
11" 24.00
Champagne, Heisey Minuet, saucer .. 22.00
Cheese and Cracker Set
Heisey Rose, 12" 150.00
Orchid, 12" 125.00
Cigarette Box, crystal, horse head finial,
6 x 4" 75.00
Claret, Jamestown, crystal 25.00
Coaster, Ridgeleigh, Sahara, 3½" 12.00
Cocktail, rooster stem 65.00
Cocktail Shaker, Ispwich 275.00
Cologne Bottle
Seven Circle, duck stopper, moon-
gleam 280.00
Victorian, crystal, orig stopper 50.00
Compote
Greek Key, jelly, handled 21.00
Petticoat Dolphin, flamingo 275.00
Console Bowl, Twist, moongleam, gold
bird border, 12½" d 60.00
Cordial
Colonial, 1½ oz 10.00
Orchid 110.00
Creamer and Sugar
Crystolite, individual 30.00
Hotel, green 45.00
Octagon, moongleam 70.00
Orchid, individual size, ftd 50.00
Ridgeleigh, oval 40.00
Waverly, rose etch 80.00
Cruet
Crystolite 45.00
Empress, moongleam foot and stop-
per 225.00
Provincial 45.00
Ridgeleigh 45.00
Yeoman, Sahara, 2 oz 65.00
Cup and Saucer
Empress, Alexandrite 110.00
Yeoman, flamingo 20.00
Goblet
Orchid 40.00

Old Sandwich, 10 oz 17.00
Rose, 7" 40.00
Spanish Crystal, cut dec, 10 oz 35.00
Yeoman, flamingo, 8 oz 25.00
Ice Tub, dolphin foot, crystal 40.00
Jug, Colonial, 1 pt 155.00
Juice Tumbler
Glenford 22.00
Orchid, ftd 36.00
Jug, Narrow Flute, three pint 70.00
Lemon Dish, Empress, dolphin handles 75.00
Mantel Lusters, pr, Ispwich, cobalt,
prisms, orig inserts 990.00
Marmalade Jar, Plantation, pineapple
shape, cov, sgd spoon 100.00
Mayonnaise, liner
Lariat 38.00
Plantation Ivy, underplate, etched .. 110.00
Mustard
Provincial 45.00
Saturn 28.00
Nappy, Greek Key 8.50
Nut Cup
Empress, crystal 8.00
Twist, flamingo 16.00
Oyster Cocktail, Pied Piper 25.00
Parfait, Albermale, green stem 40.00
Pitcher
Hotel, 1 qt, crystal 45.00
Pied Piper, 54 oz 185.00
Plate
Empress
4½", Sahara 10.00
8" round, Alexandrite 75.00
8" sq, Sahara 25.00
Plantation Ivy, 8½" 22.50
Rose, 8" 20.00
Whirlpool, 12½" 25.00
Yeoman, 6", flamingo 12.00
Punch Set
Victorian, 15" d bowl, twelve cups .. 300.00
Whirlpool, bowl and ten cups 175.00
Relish
Crystolite, four leaf clover shape ... 35.00
Empress, 10", crystal 20.00
Plantation, three section, 11" 35.00

Salt, clear, tub shape, $25.00.

Twist, two sections, cutting dec, Sahara **65.00**
Server, center handle, King Arthur, diamond optic hand dec **40.00**
Sherbet
  Acorn, Flamingo **16.00**
  Empress, Alexandrite **90.00**
  Lariat **10.00**
  Orchid **19.00**
  Ridgeleigh **10.00**
  Yeoman, flamingo **8.00**
Tray, Heisey Rose, 14″ d, dolphin center handle **175.00**
Vase
  Cathedral **85.00**
  Moongleam, 22″ h, 5″ d flared top .. **200.00**
  Ridgeleigh, 8″, Sahara **125.00**
Wine, Orchid **48.00**

HOLLY AMBER

History: Holly Amber, originally called Golden Agate, was produced by the Indiana Tumbler and Goblet Works of the National Glass Co., Greentown, Indiana. Jacob Rosenthal created the color in 1902. Holly Amber is a gold colored glass with a marbleized onyx color on raised parts.

A new pattern, Holly [No. 450], was designed by Frank Jackson for Golden Agate. Between January 1903 and June 1903, more than 35 items were made in this pattern; the factory was destroyed by fire in June.

References: Brenda Measell and James Measell, *A Guide To Reproductions of Greentown Glass, 2nd Edition,* The Printing Press, 1974; James Measell, *Greentown Glass, The Indiana Tumbler & Goblet Co.,* Grand Rapids Public Museum, 1979.

Collectors' Club: National Greentown Glass Association, 1807 West Madison Street, Kokomo, IN 46901. **Museums:** Greentown Glass Museum, Greentown, IN; Grand Rapids Public Museum [Ruth Herrick Greentown Glass Collection], MI.

Additional Listing: Greentown Glass.

Bowl
  7½ x 4½ x 2″, oval **325.00**
  8½″ d **475.00**
Butter Dish, cov, 7¼ x 6¼″ **1,200.00**
Cake Stand **2,000.00**
Compote, cov, 7½″ h, two int. rim chips **800.00**
Creamer, 4½″ h **625.00**
Cruet, 6½″ h, orig stopper **2,100.00**
Honey, cov **750.00**
Match Holder **400.00**
Mug, 4½″ h, handle **550.00**
Nappy, 4½″ d, handle, minute int. rim roughness **425.00**
Parfait **575.00**
Relish, oval **275.00**
Salt and Pepper Shakers, pr **500.00**

Tumbler, 3⅞″ h, $550.00.

Sauce Dish **225.00**
Spooner, 4″ h, 3½″ d top, 2⅝″ d base, small flake at base **485.00**
Sugar, open **500.00**
Syrup, 5¾″ h, SP hinged lid **2,000.00**
Toothpick, 5″ h **625.00**
Tray, water, round **600.00**
Tumbler, 3⅞″ h **550.00**
Vase, 6″ h **425.00**

HORN

History: For centuries horns from animals have been used for various items, e.g., drinking cups, spoons, powder horns, and small dishes. Some pieces of horn have designs scratched in them. Around 1880 furniture made from the horns of Texas longhorn steers was popular in Texas and the southwestern United States.

Additional Listings: Firearm Accessories.

Chair, steer horns, $2,250.00.

Beaker, 6½", scratch carved compass
star 50.00
Box, cov, 2¾", brass hinges 30.00
Chair, arm, longhorn top splat, U
shaped back connected by smaller
horns, twelve horns form legs and
base, cowhide cov seat and back, pr 2,000.00
Cup, 3 x 5", scratch carved hunting
scenes, applied handle 75.00
Ladle, scratch carved reindeer in bowl 100.00
Offering Box, 7¼ x 3½ x 2", hanging
type, slant top, arched back 40.00
Snuff Box, 1¾", wood plug, ring handle 48.00
Spoon, 11¼" l, white glass bead
wrapped crooked handle, carved
bird's head, red pierced dec, oval
bowl 500.00
Stool, foot, velvet upholstered seat,
horn legs 150.00
Tumbler, 2½" h 20.00

HULL POTTERY

History: In 1905 Addis E. Hull purchased the Acme Pottery Company, Crooksville, Ohio. In 1917 the A. E. Hull Pottery Company began making a line of art pottery, novelties, stoneware, and kitchenware, later including the famous Little Red Riding Hood line. Most items had a matte finish with shades of pink and blue or brown predominating.

After a disastrous flood and fire in 1950, J. Brandon Hull reopened the factory in 1952 as the Hull Pottery Company. New, more modern style molds, mostly with glossy finish, were produced. The company currently produces pieces, e.g. the Regal and Floraline lines, for sale to florists.

Hull pottery molds and patterns are easily identified. Pre-1950 vases are marked "Hull USA" or "Hull Art USA" on the bottom. Many also retain their paper labels. Post-1950 pieces are marked "Hull" in large script or "HULL" in block letters.

Each pattern has a distinctive number, e.g., Wildflower with a "W" and number, Waterlily with an "L" and number, Poppy with 600 numbers, Orchid with 300 numbers, etc. Early stone pieces have an H.

References: Brenda Roberts, *The Collectors Encyclopedia Of Hull Pottery,* Collector Books, 1980; Mark E. Supnick, *Collecting Hull Pottery's "Little Red Riding Hood": A Pictorial Reference and Price Guide,* L-W Book Sales, 1989.

Additional Listings: See *Warman's Americana & Collectibles* for more examples.

Advisor: Joan Hull.

PRE-1950 (MATTE)

Bowknot
Candleholder, B-17, 3½", pr 15.00
Ewer, B-1, 5½", green to blue 40.00
Jardiniere, B-15, 5¾", green to blue 45.00

Teapot, B-20, 6" 30.00
Vase, B-8, 8½", pink to blue 175.00
Calla Lily
Cornucopia, 570/33, 8", turquoise
and cream 50.00
Vase, 560/33, 13" 70.00
Dogwood
Basket, 501, 7½", peach 100.00
Jardiniere, 516, 4¾", blue to pink, orig
label 25.00
Vase, 516, 4¾", turquoise to cream 25.00
Iris
Ewer, 13" 150.00
Jardiniere, 413, 5½", blue to pink .. 35.00
Vase, bud, 410, 7½", peach 40.00
Little Red Riding Hood
Cookie Jar, folded basket, 13" 75.00
Creamer, imp "Pat Des-No 135889" 10.00
Mustard, spoon, 5¼" 150.00
Pitcher, open head, 8" 150.00
Salt and Pepper Shaker, pr, imp "Pat
Des-No 135889" 15.00

Vase, White Lily, cream ground, 6½" h, $45.00.

Magnolia
Basket, 10, 10½" 35.00
Candleholder, 27, 4", blue to pink, pr 35.00
Console Set, bowl, 26, 12½", pr
candlesticks, 27-4 .... 90.00
Cornucopia, 6-12, tan 90.00
Creamer and Sugar, 24 and 25, 3¾",
brown to yellow, set 65.00
Lamp Base, 12½" 150.00
Pitcher, H-3, 5½" 12.50
Teapot, H-20, 6½" 30.00
Vase, 2, 8½", blue to pink 40.00
Mardi Gras/Granada
Basket, 65, 8" 40.00
Planter, 204, 6" 30.00
Vase, 216, 9" 45.00
Novelty
Bank, Piggy, emb florals, 14" 40.00
Casserole, Cinderella, 7½" 25.00
Shaving Mug, Old Spice, 3" 25.00
Orchid
Bookends, pr, 316, 7" 400.00
Bowl, 314, 13" 75.00
Candy Dish, cov, 158 .... 15.00
Vase, 308, 4¼" 25.00

Poppy
Basket, 601, 12″		7.50
Bowl, 608, 4¾″		5.00
Ewer, 610, 4¾″		50.00
Wall Pocket, 609, 9″		75.00

Rosella
Cornucopia, R-13, 8½″	35.00
Creamer and Sugar, R-4, 5½″	60.00
Wall Pocket, R-10, 6½″	30.00

Tulip
Vase
6″, 104-33	40.00
10″, 100-33	18.00

Water Lily
Cornucopia, double, L27, 12″, pink	90.00
Jardiniere, L23, 5½″, pink	55.00
Vase, L-12, 10½″, pink and aqua, orig paper label	65.00

Wildflower
Pitcher, W-2, 5½″	10.00
Tea Set, teapot, 72, 8″, creamer, 73, 4¾″, and sugar, 74, 4¾″, 3 pcs	400.00
Vase, W-15, 10½″	40.00

Woodland
Basket, W-9	45.00
Console Bowl, W-29	20.00
Cornucopia, W-10, 11″	35.00

POST-1950

Blossom Flite
Cornucopia, T-6, 10¼″, pink and charcoal	35.00
Planter, T-12, 10½″, pink and charcoal	50.00

Butterfly
Ashtray, 7″	25.00
Bonbon, 6½″	25.00
Honey Jug, T-1	15.00
Pitcher, 8¾″	35.00
Teapot, T-14	15.00

Capri
Pitcher, 6¼″	25.00
Urn, 9″	30.00

Continental
Console Bowl, 51	10.00
Vase, strawberry design, imp "Hull USA 46"	15.00

Ebb Tide
Console Bowl, E-12	12.00
Creamer, E-15	7.50
Sugar, cov, E-16	7.50
Vase, E-6, fish	12.00

Imperial
Madonna, F-7, 7″	25.00
Planter, F-475, praying hands, 6″	25.00

Royal
Basket, W9, 8¾″	25.00
Vase, 10¾″	25.00
Window Box, 82, 12½″	30.00

Serenade
Ashtray, S-23	15.00

Cookie Jar, imp "Hull USA O-18"	20.00
Sugar, cov, S-19	7.50
Planter, S-4	15.00

Tuscany
Candy Dish, 9, 8½″	25.00
Ewer, 13, 12″	50.00
Leaf Dish, 19, 13″	30.00

Woodland, glossy glaze
Candleholder, pr, W-30	12.00
Console Bowl, W-29	15.00
Jardiniere, W-7, 5½″	75.00
Vase, W-6, 6½″, pitcher shape	10.00

HUMMEL ITEMS

History: Hummel items are the original creations of Berta Hummel, born in 1909 in Massing, Bavaria, Germany. At age 18, she was enrolled in the Academy of Fine Arts in Munich to further her mastery of drawing and the palette. Berta entered the Convent of Siessen and became Sister Maria Inconnentia in 1934. In this Franciscan cloister, she continued drawing and painting images of her childhood friends.

In 1935 W. Goebel Co. in Rodental, Germany, began reproducing Sister Berta's sketches into 3 dimensional bisque figurines. The Schmid Brothers of Randolph, Massachusetts, introduced the figurines to America and became Goebel's U.S. distributor.

In 1967 Goebel began distributing Hummel items in the U.S. A controversy developed between the two companies involving the Hummel family and the convent. Law suits and countersuits ensued. The German courts finally effected a compromise. The convent held legal rights to all works produced by Sister Berta from 1934 until her death in 1946 and licensed Goebel to reproduce these works. Schmid was to deal directly with the Hummel family for permission to reproduce any preconvent art.

All authentic Hummels bear both the signature, M.I. Hummel, and a Goebel trademark. Various trademarks were used to identify the year of production. The Crown Mark (CM) was used in 1935, Full Bee (FB) 1940–1959; Small Stylized Bee

(SSB) 1960–1972; Large Stylized Bee (LSB) 1960–1963; Three Line Mark (3L) 1964–1972; Last Bee Mark (LB) 1972–1980, Missing Bee Mark (MB) 1979–Present.

References: John F. Hotchkiss, *Hummel Art II*, Wallace-Homestead, 1981; Carl F. Luckey, *Hummel Figurines and Plates, 7th Edition*, Books Americana, 1984; Lawrence L. Wonsch, *Hummel Copycats With Values*, Wallace-Homestead, 1987.

Collectors' Clubs: Goebel Collectors' Club, 105 White Plains Road, Tarrytown, NY 10591; Hummel Collectors Club, P.O. Box 257, Yardley, PA 19067.

Additional Listings: See *Warman's Americana & Collectibles* for more examples.

Ashtray
　Joyful, #33, FB, 6 x 3½″ 150.00
　Happy Pastime, 62, 3½″ 75.00
　Let's Sing, #114, CM, 3½ x 6¾″ . . . 300.00
Bookends, pr
　Book Worm, #14/A & B, 5½″ 350.00
　Farm Boy and Goose Girl, #60/A & B, CM, 6″ 800.00
　Strolling Along, #5, CM 275.00
Candleholder
　Candlelight, #192, 6¾″, long candle 475.00
　Hearld Angels, #37, SB, 4″ 125.00
　Silent Night, #54, FB, 5½ x 4¾″ . . . 250.00
Candy Box
　Happy Pastime, #III/69, 3L, 6″ 115.00
　Joyful, #III/53, 3L, 6¼″ 110.00
　Let's Sing, #III/110, 6″ 85.00
　Singing Lesson, #III/63, CM, 5¼″ . . 500.00
Dealer Plaque, #187, FB 800.00
Figurine
　Adoration, #23/1, FB 300.00
　Angelic Song, #144, FB 105.00
　Apple Tree Boy, #142-1 . . . . 150.00
　Be Patient, #197/2/0, FB 125.00
　Bird Watcher, #300, LB 65.00
　Busy Student, #367 . . . . 50.00
　Celestrial Musician, #188 . . . . 80.00
　Close Harmony, #336 . . . . 90.00
　Confidentially, #314, LB 70.00
　Coquette, #179, SB 105.00
　Cow, #214-K, LB 45.00
　Crossroads, #331, LB 130.00
　Culprits, #56A, SSB 150.00
　Donkey, #214-J, LB 30.00
　Drummer, #240, FB 90.00
　Easter Time, #384, LB 85.00
　Farewell, #65, LB 80.00
　Feathered Friends, #344 . . . . 80.00
　Flower Madonna, #10/1
　　Color, FB 300.00
　　White, FB 125.00
　Flower Vendor, #381 . . . . 75.00
　Girl With Sheet Music, #389, LB . . . 25.00
　Going to Grandma's, #51/1, SM, 6″ 300.00
　Good Shepherd, #42/1, FB, 7½″ . . . 2,000.00
　Goose Girl, #47/3/0, LB 80.00

Happy Birthday, #176/0, FB, 5½″ . . 200.00
Happy Pastime, #69 . . . . 45.00
Latest News, #184, LB 135.00
Letter to Santa, #340 . . . . 110.00
Little Fiddler, #4, LB 50.00
Little Pharmacist, #332, 3L 90.00
Little Thrifty, #188, LB 132.00
Madonna, #45-I, 12″, FB 150.00
Mail's Here, #126, LB 300.00
Merry Wanderer, #11/0, FB 175.00
Mountaineer, #315, 3L 90.00
On Secret Path, #386, LB 75.00
Out of Danger, #56/B, FB, 6¼″ 2,500.00
Playmates, #58/0, FM, 2″ 150.00

Figure, Postman, #119, marked "Goebel, W. Germany," 5¼″ h, $95.00.

School Girls, #177/I, SM, 7½″ 800.00
Shepherd Boy, #2146, 3L 50.00
Singing Lesson, #63, LB 65.00
Sister, #98, CM, 4¾″ 300.00
Skier, #59 . . . . 80.00
Smart Little Sister, #346, 3L 90.00
Stargazer, #132, LB 110.00
Street Singer, #131, LB 45.00
The Run-A-Way, #327, LB 80.00
Wayside Harmony, #111/3/0, 3¾″, CM 290.00
We Congratulate, #214E, 3½″ 50.00
Font
　Angelic Prayer, #75, white angel, SSB 30.00
　Child Jesus, #26/0, 1½ x 5″, CM . . 90.00
　Child with Flowers, #36/I, 3½ x 4½″, FB 200.00
　Devotion, #147, 5 x 3″, SSB 35.00
　Good Shepherd, #35-1, crown mark 250.00
　Holy Family, #246, SB, 3 x 4″ 60.00
　Seated Angel, #167, FB, 3¼ x 4¼″ 70.00
Lamp, table, Out of Danger, #44/B, 9½″ h, FB 375.00

Nativity Set
- 12 pcs, #214 A-O, current **700.00**
- 16 pcs, #260, A-R, wood stable, current **2,875.00**

Plaque
- Flirting Butterfly, #139, CM, 2½" ... **250.00**
- Mail Coach, #140, LB, 4½ x 6¼" .. **130.00**
- Retreat To Safety, #126, 4¾ x 5", CM **500.00**
- Standing Boy, #168, 4⅛ x 5½", LB **125.00**
- Tuneful Goodnight, #180, 4 x 4¾", SSB **250.00**

IMARI

History: Imari derives its name from a Japanese port city. Although Imari ware was manufactured in the 17th century, the wares most commonly encountered are those made between 1770 and 1900.

Early Imari was decorated simply, quite unlike the later heavily decorated brocade pattern commonly associated with Imari. Most of the decorative patterns are an underglaze blue and overglaze "seal wax" red supported by turquoise and yellow.

The Chinese copied Imari ware. Important differences of the Japanese type include grayer clay, thicker glaze, runny and darker blue, and deep red opaque hues.

The pattern and colors of Imari inspired many English and European potteries, such as Derby and Meissen, to adopt a similar style of decoration for their wares.

Reference: Sandra Andacht, *Oriental Antiques & Art: An Identification And Value Guide,* Wallace-Homestead, 1987.

Reproduction Alert: Reproductions abound, and many manufacturers continue to produce pieces in the traditional style.

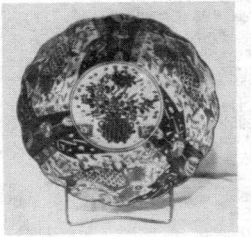

Bowl, blue, orange, and yellow marine motif, 1870, 10" d, $450.00.

Bowl
- 5" d, set of 6, hexagonal, brocade and floral dec, Japanese **300.00**
- 7¼" d, polychrome dec **60.00**

- 9¾" d, two large panels with black ship, two small panels with two Dutchmen, and phoenix medallion int., two roundels with black ship, two panels with two Dutchmen, and floral scrollwork ext., iris spray base, Japanese, c1800 .... **1,400.00**
- 10" d, ribbed body, Japanese **240.00**
- 10¾", oval, fluted **350.00**
- 15½" d, flower filled basket dec int., floral reserves ext., Japanese ... **400.00**

Chamber Set, 14¼" h pitcher, 17¼" d wash bowl, cov chamber pot, cov soap dish, cov toothbrush holder, Japanese, 19th C **1,300.00**

Charger
- 11" d, bird and floral dec, Kangxi Period, pr **1,300.00**
- 12" d, scalloped rim, central floral panel, outer floral and geometric panels, enamel palette, Japanese, late 19th C **325.00**
- 15½" d, Japanese
  - Brocade and floral dec **750.00**
  - Riverscape dec **250.00**
- 16¼" d, polychrome enamel dec ... **325.00**
- 17" d, scalloped rim, underglaze blue, enamel dec paneled scenes of children, overall mountain landscape scene, gilt accents, Japanese, late 19th C **300.00**

Cup, 3½" d, blue iris dec, gold outline, 1860 .... **35.00**

Dish
- 8¼" d, central medallion with three blue underglaze bamboo, pine, and plum trees, Japanese, 18th C ... **150.00**
- 13" l, fish form, Japanese **400.00**

Ginger Jar, 4½" h, Japanese, pr **200.00**

Jar, 24¾", cov, baluster form, phoenix birds in flight and blossoming peony branches rising from open fence, lappet border, blue bud knop, Chinese, Kangxi Period **3,750.00**

Jardiniere
- 9½" h, polychrome and gilt dec, Japanese **200.00**
- 10" d, 8" h, Japanese, 19th C **500.00**

Platter, 10¼" l, ducks amongst lotus dec, scalloped, Chinese Export, c1750, pr **1,500.00**

Sauce Boat
- 8½" l, silver form, floral dec, Chinese Export, c1740 .... **800.00**
- 9½" l, floral dec, Chinese Export, pr **1,400.00**

Server, 4½ x 8", pr **170.00**

Spoon Tray, 7" l, oval, floral dec, Chinese Export **275.00**

Tea Caddy, floral dec, Chinese Export **150.00**

Tray, 5¾", sq, polychrome **140.00**

Trembleuse, 5" d, all-over floral dec, Chinese Export **675.00**

Vase
18½" h, baluster shape, red and blue, tree peonies and flinches dec, flared rim, base and shoulder band dec, gold accents, late 19th C, Japanese 400.00
23" h, ovoid form, two medallions with flower dec, Japanese 1,600.00

IMPERIAL GLASS

History: Imperial Glass Co., Bellaire, Ohio, was organized in 1901. Its primary product was pattern (pressed) glass. Soon other lines were added including carnival glass, NUART, NUCUT, and NEAR CUT. In 1916 the company introduced "Free-Hand," a lustered art glass line, and "Imperial Jewels," an iridescent stretch glass that carried the Imperial cross trademark. In the 1930s the company was reorganized into the Imperial Glass Corporation and continues to produce a great variety of wares.

Imperial recently has acquired the molds and equipment of several other glass companies–Central, Cambridge and Heisey. Many of the "retired" molds of these companies are once again in use. The resulting reissues are marked to distinguish them from the originals.

Reference: Margaret and Douglas Archer, *Imperial Glass*, Collector Books, 1978.

Collectors' Club: National Imperial Glass Collectors Society, P.O. Box 534, Bellaire, OH 43906.

Additional Listings: See Carnival Glass, Pattern Glass, and *Warman's Americana & Collectibles* for more examples of Candlewick.

ENGRAVED OR HAND CUT

Bowl, 9½" d, three sprays of flowers, molded star base 35.00
Celery Vase, three side stars, cut star base 40.00
Pitcher, 6" h, daisies, molded star base 45.00
Tumbler, buzz star dec 20.00

JEWELS

Compote, 7½" d, irid teal blue 60.00
Creamer, amethyst, pearl, and green luster 75.00

Lustered, vase, orange ground, gold swirls, 10½" h, $325.00.

Vase, 8" h, flared rim, irid silver, mulberry ground 125.00

LUSTERED (FREE HAND)

Bowl, 14¾" d, 13½" h, shallow, flared, irid gold, stretched irid, sgd "Lustre Art 114," verdigris metal standard with three caryatids of nude men .. 700.00
Lamp, hall, elaborate scrolled gilt metal platform and chain design, center gold, white, and green irid shade, sgd "Lustre Art" on top rim 500.00
Vase
6" h, flared rim, orange int., opal body, pulled blue and green leaf pad and random vine design, partial label 325.00
6¾" h, flared cylindrical, scalloped rim, dark blue and orange, white heart and vine dec 220.00
10¾" h, baluster, blue, orange trailing heart and vine dec 335.00

NUCUT

Berry Bowl, 7½" d 25.00
Compote, 5½" d 25.00
Creamer 15.00
Fern Dish, 8" d 40.00
Nappy, 6" d, heart shape, handle 25.00
Salad Bowl, 10¾" d 35.00
Tumbler 18.00

PRESSED

Animal Dish, cov, rabbit on nest, milk glass 40.00
Bookends, pr, Cathay Empress, jade green 100.00
Cake Plate
Cape Cod, crystal
Round, ftd 48.00

Square, four small feet	**80.00**
Molly, 12″ d, green opal, ftd	**45.00**
Candlesticks, pr	
Dolphin, blue	**45.00**
Rosette Crystolite, ruby, #1503	**100.00**
Candy Dish, cov, 9¼″ h, ruby, orig paper label	**32.00**
Cologne Bottle, Hobnail, blue milk glass, ruffled, orig stopper, pr	**45.00**
Cruet, Cape Cod, olive green	**35.00**
Figure, Junk, Cathay, sgd	**145.00**
Goblet, Cape Cod, crystal	**8.00**
Parfait, Cape Cod, crystal	**9.00**
Sweets Jar, Sweeney, orig paper storybook	**80.00**
Toothpick, ivory, orig label	**18.00**

Pipe	
8⅜″ l, curved expanding stem, high relief carved sea mammals and kayak figures, engraved banding near mouthpiece	**600.00**
12″ l, curved expanding stem, high relief carved dogs, wolves, walrus, and seal dec, baleen inset features, carved flaring bowl with engraved black pigment dec	**1,000.00**
Presentation Knife, 14″ l, ivory, curved form, incised groove on each side, engraved black pigment animal and figure scenes	**1,700.00**

INDIAN ARTIFACTS, AMERICAN

History: During the historic period there were approximately 350 tribes of Indians grouped into the following regions: Eskimo, Northeast and Woodland, Northwest Coast, Plains, and West and Southwest.

American Indian artifacts are quite popular. Currently the market is in a period of stability following a rapid increase of prices during the 1970s.

References: John W. Barry, *American Indian Pottery, 2nd Edition,* Books Americana, 1984; Robert Edler, *Early Archaic Indian Points & Knives,* Collector Books, 1990; Larry Frank, *Indian Silver Jewelry of the Southwest, 1868–1930,* Schiffer Publishing, Ltd., 1900; Lar Hothem, *Arrowheads & Projectile Points,* Collector Books, 1983; Lar Hothem, *North American Indian Artifacts, 3rd Edition,* Books Americana, 1984; *North American Indian Points,* Books Americana, 1984; Noel D. Justice, *Stone Age Spear And Arrow Points Of the Midcontinental and Eastern United States,* Indiana University Press, 1987; Dawn E. Reno, *The Official Identification and Price Guide To American Indian Collectibles,* House of Collectibles, 1988; Sarah and William Turnbaugh, *Indian Baskets,* Schiffer Publishing, 1986.

Periodical: American Indian Basketry Magazine, P.O. Box 66124, Portland, OR 97266.

Note: American Indian artifacts listed below are objects made on the North American continent during the pre-historic and historic periods.

ESKIMO

Basket, 2¾″ d, 1¼″ h, baleen, coiled, compressed rounded form, fitted lid with carved ivory seal head with baleen inset eyes, pierced ivory disk in base	**475.00**
Hunting Implement, 65″ l, wood shaft, three barbed bone prongs in middle, barbed bone spear point	**475.00**

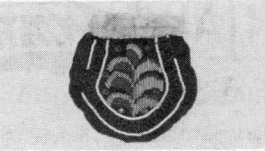

Pouch, leather, beading, drawstring top, 4″ h, $50.00.

NORTHEAST AND WOODLANDS

Cradleboard, 27″ l, wood, polychrome, flaring rect form, bentwood head guard, scalloped foot rest, carved sunk relief flower, bird, and crown motifs, dated "1888" and inscribed, Iroquois	**3,000.00**
Cuffs, pr, 11″ l, beaded, polychrome floral design on black wool, knit ties, Woodlands, pr	**50.00**
Purse, 5 x 5¼″, beaded, polychrome floral beading, black ground, silk red rim binding, Iroquois	**75.00**
Snowshoes, pr, 28″ l, wood and rawhide, beaver tail style, bentwood frame with two crossbars, crosshatch weave mesh with bird track designs, red and green twined cotton tassels, Naspaki/Montagnais	**800.00**

NORTHWEST COAST

Bag	
11½ x 9½″, cornhusk, natural and aniline dyed wool geometric designs, hide edge mouth and thong handles, Nez Perce	**325.00**
13½ x 12″, cornhusk, stepped and serrated geometric devices on one side, banded stepped diagonal bars on other, hide thong handle, Nez Perce	**425.00**

Basket

2⅜" h, key design, red and purple .. **175.00**

5" h, cov, spruce root, cylindrical form, dark brown, and golden yellow dyed grass banded geometric dec, closed and open twined body, Tlingit **325.00**

6" d, sawtooth design, brown **150.00**

6½" d, brown and yellow bands, Modoc **250.00**

7¼" d, two shades of brown design, lid, Athapaskan **85.00**

Pipe, 12" l, wood, carved stylized raven, cylindrical copper pipe, pierced at end **150.00**

Rattle, 10" l, wood, polychrome, cylindrical handle surmounted with carved oval human head with incised facial features, abalone shell dec insets .. **400.00**

Spoon, 12" l, wood, elongated oval bowl, back curved handle with red and black painted totemic device .. **550.00**

Staff, 38" h, wood, cylindrical shaft, finely carved incised and pierced human and animal totemic figures, shiny dark reddish brown patina **1,000.00**

Totem Pole, 108" h, cedar, concave back, high relief carved figures, black, white, vermilion, yellow, orange, blue, and green painted details, Kwakiutl **5,250.00**

PLAINS

Awl Case, 8½", elongated cylindrical form, beaded, yellow twisted fringe, Cheyenne/Kiowa **1,200.00**

Belt, leather, sky blue seed bead and brass tack dec, metal trade buckle **450.00**

Club, war, beaded, 24" l **75.00**

Cradleboard, 24" h, sinew sewn, stitched apple green, white heart, red, yellow, clear green, turquoise, royal, and sky blue stepped and forked geometric designs, white ground, silk ribbon and glass tube bead dec, hide thong suspensions, calico trade cloth lining, hide body, hardwood frame, Cheyenne, c1890 .... **3,250.00**

Doll, 13" h, male figure holding drum, hides face, hands, and costume, trade cloth body, cotton fiber coiffure, glass trade bead adornments, cotton and sinew sewn **200.00**

Moccasins, pr

10" l, beaded, polychrome design .. **275.00**

10½" l, sinew sewn, hard soles, beaded uppers with block and linear bar motif, light turquoise ground, Sioux **475.00**

11" l, sinew sewn, hard soles, beaded uppers with stitched geometric devices, Cheyenne **440.00**

Parfleche Case, 30 x 14¾", lime, purple,

navy, and forest green painted geometric dec, polychrome **1,300.00**

Pipe Bag

15", deerskin, sinew sewn, stitched cross, feather, bar, and triangle designs, teal blue ground, fringed and beaded **1,500.00**

22½" l, geometric devices stitched on both sides, white ground, beaded, quill wrapped parfleche slat panel, hide fringe, Sioux **800.00**

Spoon, 11¼" l, horn, elongated oval bowl, white glass bead wrapped crooked handle with carved bird's head, red pigment carved and pierced dec **500.00**

Tipi Ornament, 9¼" d, hide panel with bead stitched dec, enclosing banded border, beaded edge, yellow fringe, Northern **1,600.00**

Vest, child's, 13½" l, stitched winged and footed geometric designs, hide thong ties, sinew sewn, beaded, Sioux **1,000.00**

WEST AND SOUTHWEST

Basket

6" h, geometric design, faded, Papago **95.00**

6½" d, globular form, coiled, bracken fern root dec, willow ground, Pomo **350.00**

7¾" d, dark brown geometric design, star, Pima **350.00**

8½" d, dark brown geometric design, Maltese cross, Pima **425.00**

10" d, polychrome bands, rawhide trim, tin cones, Apache **400.00**

10 x 12", oval, dark brown geometric design **250.00**

Bowl

4¼" d, blackware, geometric design, sgd "Marie Julian," Santa Clara .. **475.00**

5⅛" h, blackware, black design, sgd "Nita," Santa Clara **85.00**

5¾" d, polychrome design, sgd "B Chino, Acoma, NM" **70.00**

6¼" d, blackware, black design, sgd "Tonita Jaun," Santa Clara **175.00**

7" d, polychrome design, sgd "K Collateta," Hopi **45.00**

7½" d

Hopi, polychrome design, cylindrical mouth, pale yellow, black and red painted dec, dec band **100.00**

Santo Domingo, polychrome design, sgd "Alvina Garcia, Sto Domingo Pueblo, NM" **35.00**

7¾" d, polychrome design, folded rim, sgd "L Negale, Zia" **110.00**

8¼" d, polychrome design, red slip, sgd "L Chino, Acoma NM" **65.00**

Bullet Pouch, leather, beaded and fringed, c1880 .... 275.00
Ceremonial Bowl, 5" d, polychrome design, sgd "MRS San Felipe Pue" .. 65.00
Cuffs, pr, 5¼' l, leather, applied loom beaded cov, polychrome design, yellow ground 100.00
Dish
  5½" d, blackware, matte painted dec, gun metal finish, inscribed "Maria/Popovi," San Ildefonso 800.00
  6¼" d, polychrome flowers, Zia 15.00
Effigy Pot, 7½" l, frog, polished blackware, sgd "Manuel Quesada," Casas Grande 105.00
Jar
  2⅞" h, 4" d, blackware, matte painted shoulder with bear paw motif, gun metal finish, inscribed "Maria & Julian," San Ildefonso 400.00
  4¾" d, brown design, Hopi 85.00
  7⅜" h, polychrome design, sgd "K Collateta," Hopi 85.00
  7¾" h, polychrome design, sgd "Elizabeth Medina, Zia" 305.00
  8" h
    Acoma, polychrome birds and vines 95.00
    Casas Grande, polychrome birds 150.00
  9¾" h, polychrome design, polished red, sgd "Nicolasa, Santa Clara" 55.00
Kachina Doll, 9" h, wood, paint, yarn, feathers, marked "Left hand hunter, Tema Hopi" 55.00
Moccasins, pr, 9½" l, parfleche soles, beaded deerskin uppers, beaded edge ankles 800.00
Pitcher, 6" h, teapot shape, polychrome design, Zia 150.00
Pot
  2⅝" h, blackware, open work design, inset turquoise stone, sgd "Stephen Baca Santa Clara" 55.00
  9" d, 7¼" h, polychrome design, sgd "Sambe," Casas Grande 175.00
Rug
  37 x 48", reservation pattern, woven by Rose Smith, Farmington, New Mexico, Navaho 250.00
  37½ x 67", red, dark brown, and white, Navaho 450.00
  47 x 74", light brown, dark brown, red, white, and gray, Navaho 550.00
  48 x 70", white, red, and black design, gray ground, Navaho 350.00
Saddle Blanket, 22 x 40", tapestry pattern, red, green, and purple, Navaho 425.00
Story Teller Figure, Jemez
  5½" l, sgd "Yoy, Jemez" 50.00
  6" h, polychrome design, sgd "Lucy Tsosio" 85.00

Wedding Jar
  6¼" h, black on red mottled clay, sgd "MRS San Felipe Pueblo" 45.00
  10" h, white slip red and black painted tail bird and hatched geometric designs, red paint indented base, Acoma 600.00
  11" h, polychrome design, marked "FcW," Jemez 35.00

INDIAN TREE PATTERN

History: The Indian Tree pattern is a popular pattern of porcelain made from the last half of the 19th century until the present. The pattern consisting of an Oriental crooked tree branch, landscape, exotic flowers, and foliage is found in predominantly greens, pinks, blues, and oranges on a white ground. Several English potteries, including Burgess and Leigh, Coalport, and Maddock, made wares with the Indian Tree pattern.

Reference: Susan and Al Bagdade, *Warman's English & Continental Pottery & Porcelain, 1st Edition,* Warman Publishing Co., Inc., 1987.

Soup Plate, marked "Maddock/England," 9" d, $25.00.

Bowl
  7¼", handled 15.00
  10 x 5½", fruit, ftd, scalloped, marked "Copeland and Spode" 135.00
Chocolate Set, chocolate pot, six cups and saucers, marked "Copeland and Spode," 14 pcs 180.00
Compote, 8", ftd, marked "Coalport" .. 60.00
Egg Cup, marked "Coalport" 12.00
Pitcher, 6", marked "Maddox & Sons" 40.00
Plate
  8", fluted, marked "Coalport" 15.00
  9", soup, marked "Maddock, England" 20.00
  9½", KPM 15.00
Platter
  11 x 14¼", oval, marked "Maddock, England" 65.00

18½", marked "Spode" 100.00
Salt and Pepper Shakers, beehive shape, pr 50.00
Sauce Boat, 8", 2 pcs, matching underplate, marked "Coalport" 100.00
Soup Tureen, 10", matching cov and ladle, Maddock & Sons 130.00
Sugar, cov, marked "Minton" 50.00
Tea Set, teapot, creamer, sugar, six cups and saucers, six 7" plates, marked "Coalport," 23 pcs 300.00

INK BOTTLES

History: Ink was sold in glass or pottery bottles in the early 1700s in England. Retailers mixed their own formula and bottled it. The commercial production of ink did not begin in England until the late 18th century and in America until the early 19th century.

Initially, ink was supplied in pint or quart bottles, often of poor manufacture, from which smaller bottles could be filled. By the mid-19th century when writing implements were improved, emphasis was placed on making an "untippable" bottle. Shapes ranging from umbrella style to turtles were tried. Since ink bottles were displayed, shaped or molded bottles became popular.

The advent of the fountain pen relegated the ink bottle to the back drawer. Bottles lost their decorative design and became merely functionable items.

References: Ralph & Terry Kovel, *The Kovels' Bottle Price List,* 8th edition, Crown Publishers, 1987; Carlo & Dot Sellari, *The Standard Old Bottle Price Guide,* Collector Books, 1989.

Periodicals: *Antique Bottle and Glass Collector,* P. O. Box 187, East Greenville, PA 18041.

Additional Listings: See *Warman's Americana & Collectibles* for more examples.

Staffords Ink, green glass, 2¼" d, 3" h, $25.00.

Barrel Shape, clear, sq tooled lip, smooth base, emb "Pat March 1st 1870" 80.00
C Chandler & Co, 2⅝" h, cottage shape, greenish aqua, rough sheared lip, smooth base, England, c1880 .... 140.00
Carters Permanent Blue Black Ink, 2⅞" h, six sided, cobalt blue, smooth base, c1910 .... 260.00
Davis, Thaddeus, eight sided umbrella, bluish–green, folded in lip, pontil scar, orig label "Steel Pen Ink, Thaddeus Davis," America, 1845–60 .... 90.00
Davis, William A., 2½" h, Boston, 7⅞", round, aqua, emb 15.00
Harrison's Columbian Ink, 2" h, round, sapphire blue, rolled lip, open pontil base, c1850 .... 325.00
Hover–Phila, 2¼ h, 2⅛" w, light green, umbrella, rolled lip, pontil scar, America, 1850–60 .... 200.00
J. & I. E. M., 1⅝", igloo shape, golden amber 80.00
L. Poingelet, 1⅞" h, eight sided, chocolate amber, flared lip, open pontil base, 1780–1820 .... 1,350.00
Mason, 2½" h, James S. Mason & Co, eight sided umbrella, aqua, rolled lip, pontil scar, 1850–60 .... 150.00
Master, 5" l, 3" w, 6½" h, house shape, aqua, applied lip, smooth base, emb details, American, 1870–80, Covills #694 .... 650.00
Nicholas & Hall, 2⅞", clear 10.00
Standard Brilliant Violet Ink, 2½" h, umbrella style, aqua rolled lip, open pontil base, c1850 .... 75.00
Tetrapledal Ink, cobalt, faceted, ground top, patent 1883 .... 25.00
Thomas Master Ink, aqua 15.00
Umbrella Style, eight sided, 2½" h
  Blue green, open pontil base, c1850 .... 130.00
  Golden amber, crude tooled lip, open pontil base, c1850 .... 170.00

INKWELLS

History: The majority of the commonly found inkwells were produced in the United States and Europe from the early 1800s to the 1930s. The most popular materials were glass and pottery because these substances resisted the corrosive effects of ink.

Inkwells were a sign of the office or a wealthy individual. The common man tended to dip his ink directly from the bottle. The period from 1870 to 1920 represented a "golden age" when inkwells in elaborate designs were produced.

References: William E. Covill, Jr., *Inkbottles and Inkwells,* William S. Sullwold Publishing, 1971; Betty and Ted Rivera, *Inkstands and Inkwells: A Collector's Guide,* 2nd edition, Crown Publishers, Inc., 1973.

Collectors' Club: Society of Inkwell Collectors, 5136 Thomas Avenue, Minneapolis, MN 55410.

Additional Listings: See *Warman's Americana & Collectibles* for more examples.

Porcelain, sq, advertising "Runelle/Nivernaise/C. Dugnas, Nevers," marked "Depost," 3¼" sq, 1⅝" h, $50.00.

CERAMIC

Bisque, figural, owl's head, glass eyes, multicolored enamel dec **225.00**

Ironstone, 5⁷⁄₁₆" h, figural, human head, labeled brain areas, white, blue, and black dec, glazed, impressed "By F Bridges, Phrenologist," 1850–59 .. **1,400.00**

Staffordshire, 4⅝" h, stag and doe, salmon and gray enamel dec, gilt trim **275.00**

Wedgwood, basalt, 1¾" h, vertical engraved sides, center surrounded by three small openings, imp "B" on base, 18th C **150.00**

GLASS

Cut Glass, 13" l, 10½" d, 7½" h, two faceted cut glass wells, twin brass pen channels, scrolling carry handle, brass border, rect case with frieze drawer, engine turned ball feet, Regency, Boulle work, early 19th C ... **4,250.00**

Cranberry Glass, 2¾" h, figural, daisy, hinged pewter lid **235.00**

Loetz type, 3" sq, irid amber, web pattern, hinged brass lid **250.00**

METAL

Brass

2½" h, 12" l, 4" w, brass, coral stone set in acid etched sq top, cube shaped well, rect tray stamped "Forest Craft Guild," Grand Rapids, MI, c1910 .... **125.00**

5¼" l, 9" w, Art Nouveau, hinged well, sides flaring to tray edges, etched stylized tree motifs, sgd "WD," stamped "709" **150.00**

Bronze

5" h, 7" l, gilt, figural, three owls, graduated sizes, perched on owl claw, glass well, minor damage to glass eyes, late 19th C **275.00**

8¾" l, bronze mounted, jeweled blue enamel, oval tray, all-over white enamel studs, two covered urns, mounted with scrolling handle, pierced foliate feet, French **715.00**

Copper, 2" h, tapered cylindrical copper body, cov, rivets around edge, glass liner, imp Gustav Stickley mark **385.00**

Silver, sterling

2½" h, cylindrical body, copper applied threaded cap, copper monogram dated 1895, applied copper sides, brass vines, leaves, and butterfly with mokume wings, int. glass well, marked "Tiffany & Co" **1,760.00**

4⅛" h, 5⅜" w, circular, hinged cov, spherical finial, flaring handles with ring grips, four flaring feet with pendant scallop shells, rect pan with die rolled border, four scrolling feet, inlaid niello Japanese designs, engraved Japanese style monogram, marked "Tiffany & Co," glass liner, c1874, 7 oz, 10 dwt **9,350.00**

6¼" l, rect, fitted well, pounce pot, quill holder, and bell, rect tray repousse, foliage scrolled feet, engraved, crowned "L" in oval mark, maker's mark "VAD" in rect, Lisbon, Portugal, 18th C, 14 troy oz **1,000.00**

IRONS

History: Ironing devices have been used for many centuries, with the earliest references dating from 1100. Irons from the Medieval, Renaissance, and early industrial era can be found in Europe, but are rare. Fine brass engraved irons and hand wrought irons dominated the period prior to 1850. After 1850 irons began a series of rapid evolutionary changes.

Between 1850 and 1910 irons were heated in four ways: 1) a hot metal slug was inserted into the body, 2) a burning solid, e.g., coal or charcoal, was placed in the body, 3) a liquid or gas, e.g., alcohol, gasoline, or natural gas, was fed from an external tank and burned in the body, and 4) conduction heating, usually drawing heat from a stove top.

Electric irons are just beginning to find favor among iron collectors.

References: Esther S. Berney, *A Collectors Guide To Pressing Irons And Trivets,* Crown Publishers, Inc., 1977; A. H. Glissman, *The Evolution Of The Sad Iron,* published by author, 1970; Brian Jewell, *Smoothing Irons, A History And Collector's*

Guide, Wallace-Homestead, 1977; Judy (author) and Frank (illustrator) Politzer, *Early Tuesday Morning: More Little Irons and Trivets*, published by author, 1986; Judy and Frank Politzer, *Tuesday's Children*, published by author, 1977.

Collectors' Clubs: Friends of Ancient Smoothing Irons, Box 215, Carlsbad, CA 92008; Midwest Sad Iron Collectors Club, 3915 Lay Street, Des Moines, IA 50317.

Museums: Henry Ford Museum, Dearborn, MI; Shelburne Museum, Shelburne, VT; Sturbridge Village, Sturbridge, MA.

Additional Listings: See *Warman's Americana & Collectibles* for more examples.

Advisors: David and Sue Irons.

Slug, cast iron, turned and incised wood handle, cast iron slug, c1850, $120.00.

Billiard Table Iron, English, 6 x 12" base	175.00
Charcoal	
Bless/Drake, face of bearded man on rear, damper, high chimney	75.00
Chinese, open pan, ivory handle, bronze engraved	175.00
Double spout, two or more side dampers, 1902	150.00
Electric	
Deco, Sauders, "Silver Streak," pyrex, red or blue	700.00
Universal Travel, curling iron insert	40.00
English Egg or ball iron, wood handle, rod and ball at end, ½ to 2" d ball . .	100.00
Fluter	
Gribs, wrought fluting scissors	200.00
Knox, machine type, oval on base, enclosed picture of Susan R Knox, 1870	225.00
Fluting board with flat steel clips	45.00
Goffering	
Queen Anne style, 3¾" l barrel, all iron, no heater	375.00
Wrought single barrel, 4" l, spider with three or four legs, no heater	400.00
Miniature	
Double point, sad iron, cylinder grip, all iron, 2½" to 3"	40.00
Geneva, hand fluter, 1866	200.00

Kenrick Co, sad iron, 3" l, all iron, oval base	60.00
Polisher Troy, grid design to bottom, round front	45.00

IRONWARE

History: Iron, a metallic element that occurs abundantly in combined forms, has been known for centuries. Items made from iron range from the utilitarian to the decorative. Early hand-forged ironwares are of considerable interest to Americana collectors.

Reference: Kathryn McNerney, *Antique Iron*, Collector Books, 1984; Herbert, Peter, and Nancy Schiffer, *Antique Iron*, Schiffer Publishing Ltd., 1979.

Additional Listings: Banks, Boot Jacks, Doorstops, Fireplace Equipment, Food Molds, Irons, Kitchen Collectibles, Lamps, and Tools.

Andirons, pr	
15¼", wrought, pitted	300.00
17½" h, sunflower finials over smiling serpentine reeded standard, arched foliate feet, cast August 24, 1886 patent mark, American	5,000.00
20" h, Hessian, figural, hand on hip, walking to left, cast	220.00
20¼" h, wrought, knife blade shape, penny feet, brass urn finials	450.00
21" h, Arts and Crafts, domed finial, tapering faceted standard, angular scrolled feet, applied gilt diamond shaped mounts, English, cast . . .	275.00
22" h, wrought, penny feet, brass finials, 18th C	400.00
Anvil, 5½" d, cast, wood base	10.00
Bottle Opener, cast iron	
4⅜" l, black man, old paint	55.00
5", parrot on perch, polychrome paint	55.00
Full set of teeth, orig paint	70.00

Broad Axe, hand-forged, early 1800s, 12¼" wide cutting edge, $85.00.

Candle Stand, wrought iron
   20" h, tripod base, spring clamp for
      splint and candle socket 500.00
   57" h, adjustable arm with rush light,
      candle socket counter balance,
      cast finial, turned wood base 450.00
   58½" h, adjustable arm with gro-
      tesque animal head ornament,
      brass finial, tripod base, penny feet   500.00
Candlestick
   5", hog scraper, hook and lift, c1800   130.00
   5¾" h, hog scraper, pushup, gold re-
      paint 110.00
   6½" h, hog scraper, pushup, lip han-
      ger 115.00
   6¾" h, wrought, spiral pushup, lip
      hanger, turned wood base 225.00
   7⅛" h, hog scraper, pushup, marked
      "Shaw's Birm" 175.00
   7¼" h, wrought, spiral pushup, lip
      hanger, turned wood base 175.00
   7¾", wrought, spiral pushup, wood
      base 200.00
   8" h, hog scraper, pushup and lip han-
      ger 100.00
Cigar Lighter, 7¾" h, cast, sheet metal
   arm, brass trim, "Gretchen Cigars,
   Louis Ash Co Makers, NY" adv and
   "The Brunhoff Mfg Co Cinti, O," pat-
   ent date 1902–06 . . . .   350.00
Coals Carrier, 31" l, wrought, sliding lid   235.00
Coffee Grinder, 9" h, cast, tin collector   115.00
Cresset, 17" h, wrought 150.00
Desk Set, closing ink well, pen rack, and
   candle socket, varnished, 7⅝" h . . .   200.00
Figure, cast
   Boston Bull Dog, 3" h, orig poly-
      chrome paint 55.00
   Boxer, 2⅞" h, orig polychrome paint   55.00
   Cat, 6⅞" l, oval base, orig polychrome
      paint 155.00
   Cocker Spaniel, 3⅜" l, black paint,
      red collar 35.00
   Elephant, 4" h, cast, gold paint 75.00
   Fly, 4½" l, hinged wings, gold traces   55.00
Fire Mark, 7⅜ x 11½", cast, polychrome
   paint, pitted, marked "F A" 210.00
Fork, 17¼" l, wrought, shaped handle
   with tooled ram's horn finial 135.00
Hearth Bar, 54" l, 26" h, free standing,
   wrought 455.00
Hinges, pr, 27" l, wrought, pitted 85.00
Hitching Post, pr, 68" h, cast, horse
   head, steel posts 90.00
Lamp, European
   Crusie, double, pierced wheel finials,
      tin plated, 7½" h 110.00
   Grease, wrought, hanging, large pan
      and spout, 5" h 100.00
Lantern, 17½" h, conical top, arched

vents, cylindrical body, green glass
   bull's-eyes, painted black, 19th C . .   700.00
Light, ornate cast iron wall bracket, clear
   glass fluid lamp, orig dated burner,
   mercury reflector 70.00
Miniature, tea kettle, 3⅝", cast, goose
   neck spout, wire bale, tin lid, black
   paint 155.00
Muffin Pan, 8½ x 12¾", cast, twelve
   heart shape sections 75.00
Paperweight, 5" l, cast, frog, worn black
   paint 45.00
Peel
   42¾" h, wrought, ram's horn handle   95.00
   43¼" l, wrought 60.00
Plate Holder, 59" h, wrought, triangular
   tier, seven graduated shelves 250.00
Roasting Fork, 27½" l, wrought, three
   prongs, heart cut out handle 250.00
Roasting Rack, 30¼" h, wrought, tripod
   base, penny feet 550.00
Sugar Cutter, marked "A R Timmins &
   Sons" 70.00
Tape Dispenser, cast iron, Victorian, or-
   nate 125.00
Taper Jack, 6¼" h, wrought, detailed
   engraving 850.00
Tea Kettle, cast, gooseneck spout,
   wrought handle
   7" h, marked "No 1" 135.00
   7½" h 115.00
   9" h, marked "No 00 4½ Pints" 95.00
Toaster, wrought
   11 x 15" 110.00
   12½" l 225.00
Trade Sign, 20 x 24", butcher's, saw,
   knife, meat cleaver, and bull, gold and
   silver paint 400.00
Trammel, wrought, sawtooth, ram's
   horn finial, scrolled ratchet 225.00
Trivet, 21½" h, wrought, adjustable
   roasting fork, wood handle 200.00
Utensil Holder, 10" d, wrought, crown
   shape, six hooks 75.00
Wafer Iron, 29½" l, wrought, heart
   shaped, waffle pattern 500.00
Waffle Iron, 27¾" l, cast and wrought   55.00
Wash Board, 21 12/" h, cast, star flow-
   ers on crest 475.00
Windmill Weight, cast
   Horse 275.00
   Rooster, 19¼" h, red and white paint   1,200.00

IVORY

History: Ivory, a yellowish-white organic material, comes from the teeth or tusks of animals and
lends itself well to carving. It has been used for
centuries by many cultures for artistic and utilitarian items.

Ivory from elephants shows a reticulated crisscross pattern in a cross section. Hippopotamus teeth, walrus tusks, whale teeth, narwhal tusks, and boar tusks also are ivory sources. Vegetable ivory, bone, stag horn, and plastic are ivory substitutes which often confuse collectors.

For information on how to identify real ivory, see Bernard Rosett's "Is It Genuine Ivory," in Sandra Andacht's *Oriental Antiques & Art: An Identification and Value Guide* (Wallace-Homestead, 1987).

Note: Dealers and collectors should be familiar with The Endangered Species Act of 1973, amended in 1978, which limits the importation and sale of antique ivory and tortoise shell items.

Box, 4¾", cov, carved, Chinese **75.00**
Brush Pot, 6", shepherd boy resting on water buffalo, bamboo forest scene, black picked out dec, carved wood base, Chinese, late 18th C **825.00**
Bust, 4½" h, carved, man wearing double-breasted coat, cravat tied around neck, 19th C **990.00**
Calling Card Case, 4½", carved intricate floral dec **235.00**
Chess Set, 19" l, hinged wood box opens to game board **150.00**
Cigarette Holder, cat chasing ball **100.00**
Fan, 21 elaborate carved ribs connected with white silk ribbon, boxed, late 19th C **50.00**
Figure
  Boy, 7½" h, seated blowing horn, two geese, circular pedestal, Continental **275.00**
  Hunter, 7½" h, prey strapped to back, carved, African **110.00**
  Ruler, 5⅜" h, seated on throne, carved, Oriental **135.00**
  St Peter, 16¾" h, wearing papal tiara, stole and fringed cape, holding key in right hand, open book in other, mounted on oval ivory base, 19th C **4,950.00**
  Shepherd Boy, 6¼" h, playing horn, bag slung over one shoulder, sitting legs crossed on rocky mound, tapered cylindrical base, 19th C . . . **935.00**
  William Tell, 5½" h **90.00**
  Woman
    6" h, carved, dressed in ruffled and flounced gown, flower in one hand, tapered columnar base, brown tinting, 19th C **440.00**
    8½" h, nude, carrying water jugs . . . **110.00**
Goblet, 7⅜" h, tapered cylindrical form, high relief carved deer and two stags walking in forest, baluster stem, quatrefoil base, Continental, 19th C . . . **550.00**
Incense Burner, 5" h, pierced, Foo Dog cov, rings on handles **220.00**
Knife and fork, carved knife handle of bearded Hermes rising from acanthus base with etched foliate scrollwork steel blade, carved conforming female figure handle on two pronged fork, German, 19th C **880.00**
Lamp Screen, carved
  17½" h, relief garden scene of two children playing with angels in background, floral sprays and vine border, adjustable standard, ftd base with grotesque mask on each corner, 19th C **3,300.00**
  18¼" h, relief man and woman standing in garden, shaped rect border of blossoming rose vine, adjustable ribbed standard, mounted on carved wood base, 19th C **3,575.00**
Memo Pad, 1⅝ x 3⅛", silver metal trim, six leaves with days of the week . . . **65.00**
Mirror, 10¾", hand held, young angel figure, carved, c1890 . . . . **1,100.00**
Necklace, 30" l, beads **45.00**
Needle Case, carved, screw top cylinder **100.00**
Night Lamp, 6½", two elephants circling tree, flowers at top, intricate openwork **125.00**
Pen Holder, 4", cylindrical, carved, three monkeys, wood base, ftd **125.00**
Pipe, 14" l, chicken, rock, and floral motif, stained, inscribed, 1800s **250.00**
Ruler, 6", folding, brass fittings **35.00**

Sculpture, French Gothic, carved, Madonna and Child, $17,600.00.

Snuff Bottle, 3" h, figural, polychrome, Chinese **75.00**
Table, Georgian style, sq top, acanthus carved chamfered legs, X-form stretcher, painted **80.00**
Tankard, 16¼", Alexander The Great In Battle **5,500.00**

Thimble, carved, flowers and leaves, 1880s 55.00
Tusk, 20½" l, carved, graduated elephant design 75.00
Vase, 8", birds picking berries 175.00

JACK-IN-THE-PULPIT VASES

History: Jack-in-the-Pulpit glass vases, made in the trumpet form, were in vogue during the late 19th and early 20th centuries. The vases were made in a wide variety of patterns, colors, and sizes.

Additional Listings: See specific glass categories.

Opalescent swirled stripes, cobalt rim, 9" h, $120.00.

Amberina, 13¼" h, IVT 300.00
Burmese
  8" h, 7" w scalloped rim, applied base, Pairpoint 725.00
  9¾" h, crimped edge, acid finish ... 450.00
Cased
  6" h, 6" w, white ext., shaded maroon int., ruffled top 110.00
  15¾" h, blue ext., white int., ruffled, applied crystal spiral trim, clear foot with scalloped shell trim 225.00
Cranberry, 10" h, applied crystal rigaree and feet 200.00
Loetz, 11¾" h, flower form, lusterous stretched and swirled amethyst irid 300.00
Mt Washington, 10" h, 5" w, deep rose shading to pink satin finish ext., white lining, tightly crimped top 474.00
Opalescent, 5⅜" h, flower petal top, pink and yellow stripes 85.00
Opaline, 5" h, ruffled purple top 85.00
Satin
  4" h, squat form, blossom form opening, seven applied and frosted feet, emerald green int. 45.00

5¾" h, ruffled edge, applied and frosted dec at waist and base, rose int. 170.00
6¾" h, pale violet blue ext., white int., pink ruffled rim 275.00
Silver Overlay, 7½" h, shaded purple ground, ruffled top 115.00
Spatter, pink and light green, clear ground, ruffled, pontil mark 150.00

JADE

History: Jade is the generic name for two distinct minerals, nephrite and jadeite. Nephrite, an amphibole mineral from Central Asia and used in pre-18th century pieces, has a waxy surface and ranges in hues from white to almost a black green. Jadeite, a pyroxene mineral found in Burma and used from 1700 to the present, has a glassy appearance and comes in various shades of white, green, yellow-brown, and violet.

Jade cannot be carved because of its hardness. Shapes are achieved through sawing and grinding with wet abrasives, such as quartz, crushed garnets, and carborundum.

Prior to 1800 few pieces are signed or dated. Stylistic considerations are used for dating. The Ch'ien Lung period (1736–95) is considered the "golden age" of Jade.

Reference: Sandra Andacht, *Oriental Antiques & Art: An Identification And Value Guide*, Wallace-Homestead, 1987.

Museum: Avery Brundage Collection, de Young Museum, San Francisco, CA.

Snuff Bottle, mottled brown jade, hand carved animal, green jade stopper, 3" h, $450.00.

Alms Bowl, 5¾" d, patra form, flared, rounded shoulder, four speckled black vertical inclusions, grayish–green, carved Qianlong character seal mark 2,640.00

Brushwasher, 3⅛", peach borne on gnarled branch form, slender leaves encompassing sides, gray with dark brown, calcified to opaque buff base, Ming Dynasty **2,090.00**

Clasp, 3" l, dragon, carved lotus button, 18th C **75.00**

Ewer, cov, 9¾" h, baluster body, six vertical lobes, barbed rim encircled with key fret border, faceted spout and handle carved with clouds and surmounted by chilong, terminating handle with tab, sage figure asleep amidst rocks and pine on conforming cov, mottled gray, Ming Dynasty . . . **3,300.00**

Figure

Horse with monkey clinging to back of neck, fine detailing, translucent white, russet highlight, ⅞" l **550.00**

Maiden, 6⅛" h, holding flute wearing robe, topknot hair style, standing beside phoenix perched on rocks, peony sprouting branch behind, greenish-white mottle **1,870.00**

Squirrel, recumbent position, head resting on outstretched paws, raised ring outline eyes, incised hair on head, bushy tail, white, intense russet mottling, 2⅛" **3,300.00**

Jewelry

Necklace

Carved pea pod pendant, woven green cord with five green jade balls, Chinese **550.00**

Graduated 6.5 mm apple green beads, 14K yellow gold and rect flat jade plaque, 22" l, Chinese **1,100.00**

Pendant, 1⅝" h, cut out and carved, sinuous dragon arched above a human head, coiled horn surmounting dragon's head, grayish–white, velvet stand, Zhou Dynasty **3,300.00**

Plaque, 1¾", long tailed bird form, head turned back to wings, legs stretched forward, incised details on one side, plain on other, dark beige, Shang Dynasty **3,300.00**

Snuff Bottle

2½" l, shell form, white and russet, coral stopper, Chinese **60.00**

3" h, teardrop shape, white, lapis stopper, Chinese **60.00**

Sword Guard, 2¾" l, cloud form, carved shallow relief detached C-scrolls and bosses forming a taotie mask, grayish white, russet veining, other side black, Ming Dynasty **720.00**

Vase

6⅞" h, figural, Buddha's hand, fruited gnarled branch base, polished stone with dark brown veining, gray and brown mottle **1,650.00**

14¼" h, cov, quadrilobed baluster body, two figures on horseback on one side, other with twenty character inscription above two seals encircled with double line elongated heart border, pierced foliate scroll cascading from mouths of monster masks handles, opaque white mottling **8,800.00**

Vessel, 7⅛" d, rounded form, incised key fret border below lipped rim, curved and faceted spout with carved scrolled loop underneath, concave base incised with dragon leaping toward flaming pearl, translucent pale gray, black inclusions, Ming Dynasty **4,620.00**

JAPANESE AND CHINESE CERAMICS

History: The Chinese pottery tradition has existed for thousands of years. By the sixteenth century, Chinese ceramic wares were being exported to India, Persia, and Egypt. The Ming dynasty (1368-1643) saw the strong development of glazed earthenwares and shapes. During the Ch'ing dynasty, the Ch'ien Lung period (1736-95) marked the golden age of interchange with the West.

Trade between China and the West began in the sixteenth century when the Portuguese established Macao. The Dutch entered the trade early in the seventeenth century. With the establishment of the English East India Company, all of Europe was seeking Chinese-made pottery and porcelain. Styles, shapes, and colors were developed to suit Western tastes. The tradition continued until the late nineteenth century.

Like the Chinese, the Japanese spent centuries developing their ceramic arts. Each region established its own forms, designs, and glazes. Individual artists added to the uniqueness.

Japanese ceramics began to be exported to the West in the mid-19th century. Their beauty quickly made them a favorite of the patrician class.

The ceramic tradition continues into the 20th century. Modern artists enjoy equal fame with older counterparts.

Reference: Sandra Andacht, *Oriental Antiques & Art: An Identification And Value Guide,* Wallace-Homestead, 1987.

Periodical: *The Orientalia Journal,* P.O. Box 94P, Little Neck, NY 11363.

Additional Listings: Canton, Fitzhugh, Imari, Kutani, Nanking, Rose Medallion, and Satsuma.

CHINESE

Bowl

3¾" d, iron–red and white enamel, pale blue and lavender shading

Vase, Sumida Guwa, two monkeys, dragon costumes, red ground, crackle glazed top, sgd cartouche, 7" h, $400.00.

with nine fish swimming in various directions around deep rounded sides, iron–red character hallmark, Guang, pr **1,980.00**

5¼" d, ext. with two dragons striding through flames and clouds above tiered band of lotus petals with lingzhi sprigs, inscribed shou and fu character, int. with leaping dragon medallion and double line border, Daoguang seal mark **530.00**

6¾" d, white enamel branches and trunk of blossoming prunus tree below foot, continuing over rim into int., incised details, double sq blue enamel Yongzheng character Yuzhi mark **2,640.00**

Box, cov, 6⅛" d, cushion form, blue and white, cov babao raised on lingzhi sprigs within medallion, continuous scroll on sides and box, double line borders, Jiajing character mark **3,850.00**

Cup

2¼" d, inverted bell shape, two lively iron–red dragons separated by flaming pearls dec on sides, striding above crested wave band, double line borders, Guangxu character mark, pr . . . **4,400.00**

4⅛" d, cov, deep sides sharply angled above foot, flared towards everted rim, painted iron–red wufu in flight, trailing underglaze blue cloud scroll, medallion of bat on int., matching cup stand with everted pinched flower form rim, Guangxu character mark, pr **1,760.00**

Dish, 5¼" d, incised full faced dragon leaping amidst flower sprigs center, body twisted around flaming pearl, scalloped rim, bright transparent green, egg yolk yellow ground, aubergine double line border, Qianlong seal mark **4,400.00**

Ewer, double gourd shape, blue and white, foliate spray below decorative borders, curbed strap handle, bubble suffused glaze, Yuan Dynasty **560.00**

Flask, 19½" h, moon shape, eight petals enclosing bajixiang radiating from a raised boss centered by flowerhead, lotus scroll bands on side below leaf form handles, lingzhi scroll on neck and foot, key fret borders, painted blue wash, pale yellow ground, mouth rim ground, Yongzheng seal mark . . **8,800.00**

Jar, cov, 10½" h, blue and white, landscape dec, jade finial, K'ang Hsi . . . **1,900.00**

Lotus Bowl, 7¾" d, enamel dec, modeled lotus petals over lotus pad base, int. circular panel with carp, character marks, lotus carved wood stand, 19th C **850.00**

Mug, cov, 7" h, blue and white, spiral molded, painted flower sprays, handle with clouds, Kangxi **1,320.00**

Vase

8¼" h, baluster bottle shape, underglaze red and powder blue, tall slender neck with copper-red sinuous four clawed dragon dec, reverse with two small clouds, deep blue glazed body separated with a recessed cafe-au-lait band **4,950.00**

10¼" h, baluster form, two panels with figures in landscape, floral and scrollwork dec, blue and white, Kangxi mark **250.00**

11¼" h, tapered globular body, tall neck molded with all–over dragons crawling amidst and dissolving into leafy vines design, lappet border below, key fret border encircling white glazed mouth, celadon glaze, molded Qianlong seal mark **1,100.00**

CHINESE EXPORT

Bowl, 10", armorial, circular form, coat-of-arms and floral bouquets dec, blue geometric and fleur-de-lis bands . . . **660.00**

Creamer, helmet shape, circular polychrome scene of gos attacking birds in garden, 18th C **800.00**

Dish, 10¾" d, center painted flowerhead form panel, enclosing flowering foliate spray issuing from rockwork, surrounded by four reserves with floral sprays, famille verte powder blue ground, Kangxi, c1710 . . . . **575.00**

Miniature Cup and Saucer, blue and white, "Cuckoo over the House" pattern, for Dutch market, c1720, pr . . . **500.00**

Pitcher, 6⅜" h, polychrome, raised leaf and children at play design, raised mask spout, 18th C **950.00**

Platter

13″, octagonal shape, ribbons suspending central medallion with initials "JWS," thistle and floral gar-
land borders, pr 610.00

16″, blue and white, leaf form, figures
and quail amongst trees dec, Kak-
iemon style 1,500.00

Sauce Boat, 8½″ l, armorial, famille rose
floral dec, scalloped rim, pr 1,250.00

Tankard, 5½″ h, Masonic, double entwined handle terminating in molded
florets, enamel dec symbols with central pillar, globes, and pavement
within circular panel, rain clouds
above, surrounded by moon, sun,
workbench, tools, square, and compasses, level, plumb, and beehives,
c1800, handle and rim repairs 500.00

Teapot, 5″ h, elaborate coat-of-arms
dec, 19th C 300.00

Vase, 11½″ h, baluster form, medallion
with sepia and gilt landscape dec . . 350.00

JAPANESE

Bowl

4″, shallow, molded figure with sack
of belongings and rocky landscape
dec, red-orange glaze, Sumida
Gawa, late 19th C 440.00

6″, wide crescent body, cloud, diaper,
and floral reserves, beige ground
surrounded with green glaze, three
mushroom form feet, wood box, Or-
ibe 700.00

7″ d, iron–red and green floral and
foliate dec, beige ground, Banko,
Edo period 375.00

Charger, 16″ d, crane and floral dec,
Yatsushiro 400.00

Dish

12″, boat form, stern with notch, wave
ornaments on ext., floral motifs and
diaper dec int., Sansei, Meiji Period 1,100.00

14″ d, fluted well, flat rim, egg and
spinach splash glazed pattern, 19th
C 720.00

Ewer, 9″ h, two panels with foliage and
figure dec, one panel with herons on
plum branches, band of stylized
flower heads on neck, loop handle,
underglaze blue and white, Arita, late
17th C 1,400.00

Jardiniere, 14″ d, globular form, ribbed,
peony and sparrow in shaped reserves, blue, red, and gilt, marked
"Fukagawa sei," late 19th C 1,000.00

Planter, 8½″ h, rabbit form, creamy
crackled white glaze, 19th C 825.00

Teabowl, 4¾″ d, brown and green floral

dec, circular floral geometric reserves, mottled glaze, sgd 200.00

Water Pitcher, 4″ h, globe form, applied
scholar gazing at bowl of food, mottled red and green flambe glaze . . . 330.00

Vase

7″ h, globular form, red-orange phoenix and butterflies above clouds
dec, Eiraku seal, Meiji Period . . . 1,600.00

9½″, ovoid form, three figures playing
tag, elephant form handles, brown
splash glaze, Sumida Gawa, late
19th C 880.00

10½″ h, stoneware, silvered dragon
dec, oily black-brown glaze, imp
mark, 19th C 500.00

12½″ h, pear shape, ribbed body, applied with frolicking monkeys, red
glaze, brown, blue, and beige accents, Sumida Gawa, late 19th C 1,650.00

Vessel, 6″ h, blue dec, crackle glaze,
Kyoto 275.00

JASPERWARE

History: Jasperware is a hard, unglazed porcelain with a colored ground, varying from the most
common blues and greens to lavender, yellow, red,
or black. The white designs are applied in relief
and often reflect a classical motif. Jasperware was
first produced at Wedgwood's Etruria Works in
1775. Josiah Wedgwood described it as "a fine
Terra Cotta of great beauty and delicacy proper
for cameos."

Many other English potters, in addition to Wedgwood, produced jasperware. Two of the leaders
were Adams and Copeland and Spode. Several
continental potters, e.g., Heubach, also produced
the ware.

Reference: Susan and Al Bagdade, *Warman's
English & Continental Pottery & Porcelain, 1st Edition,* Warman Publishing Co., Inc., 1987.

Reproduction Alert: Jasperware still is made
today, especially by Wedgwood.

Note: This category includes all pieces of jasperware which were made by companies other
than Wedgwood. Wedgwood jasperware is found
in the Wedgwood listing.

Biscuit Jar

5⅜ x 6¾″, deep blue, white classical
ladies with cupid, SP rim, lid, handle, and ball feet, marked "Wedg-
wood" 150.00

6 x 6″, bulbous, dark blue, white
hunting scene, SP cover, rim, and
handle, marked "Adams, England" 135.00

Bowl, 7″, dark blue, white relief classical
figures 225.00

Box, cov

3⅞ x 2½ x 2⅛″, blue, white relief

winged lady, flowers, garlands and
cherubs, marked "Germany" 60.00
5", oval, blue, white relief cherub and
nymph, marked "Schafer & Vater,
Germany" 40.00
Chamberstick, black and white, snuffer 265.00
Clock, 9⅛" h, sage green, white relief
cherubs, foliage and flowers, clock
not working 150.00
Coffeepot, 10", green, white relief classical figures 185.00
Creamer, blue, Kewpie, sgd 165.00
Cup and Saucer, blue, white relief classical figures, formal foliage and engine turning, marked "Turner, England," c1800 .... 175.00
Doorknobs, green ground, white cherubs dec, pr 100.00
Hair Brush, lady's, lavender, white relief
lady and cupid, brass rim and handle 100.00
Hair Receiver, 3⅜ x 3½", blue, white
relief classical ladies and flowers,
cupids on lid, marked "Germany" .. 65.00
Jardiniere, 7½", light blue, white relief
of Columbus landing, marked "Copeland" 175.00
Jug, 8", green, white relief fox hunting
scene, c1820 .... 175.00
Match Box, cov
Blue and white 90.00
Lilac Dip 115.00
Perfume Bottle, blue and white, hallmarked SS top 275.00
Pin Dish, green, white Indian Chief dec,
holding bow and arrow, marked "Heubach" 65.00

**Pitcher, brown ground, marked "Cope-
land, Football/JMSD & S/1895, Reg.
180288," 5⅜" h, $300.00.**

Plaque
5½", green, white relief of two children climbing on heron, two children in water, lilies of the valley border, marked "Germany" 70.00
6½ x 5", green, white relief Indian
Chief, marked "Germany" 200.00

Plate, 9", white, shell 200.00
Salt Shaker, dark blue, white relief classical figures 60.00
Sugar, cov, 6", blue, two handles, white
relief sacrifice scene, swan finial,
marked "Adams," c1800 .... 1,150.00
Urn, 8" h, cobalt blue, white relief hunting scene, marked "Adams, Tunstall,
England" 200.00
Vase
7¾", lilac, two green topiary tree handles, white relief of Art Nouveau
woman's face, flowing hair, two
white swans, marked "A Radford
Pottery, Ohio" 850.00
8¼", light blue, white classical figures
cameos, white handles, bolted pedestal base with white scrolling vine
dec 375.00

JEWEL BOXES

History: The evolution of jewelry was paralleled
by the development of boxes in which to store it.
Jewel box design followed the fashion trends dictated by furniture styles. Many jewel boxes are
lined.

**Amethyst glass, enameled florals and
central diamond motif with child, silver
rim and base, 6" d, 4⅞" h, $125.00.**

Bella Ware, 4½" w, pale lavender
ground, violets bunches within scroll,
orig brass hardware, sgd on base,
Helmschmied Manufacturing Co,
Meriden, CT 235.00
Jasperware, 3⅞" d, crimson and white,
classical figures on lid, white raised
cherubs around sides, marked
"Wedgwood," c1920 .... 500.00
Mary Gregory, 4½ x 5½", sapphire blue,
white enamel boy and girl, brass
mounts and handles 575.00
Micro–mosaic and bronze, 8⅜" sq, 4¼"
h, sq, shaped corners, scrolled feet,
Roman scenes on sides, pigeons
drinking from basin on cov, Italian,
19th C 11,000.00

Moser, 5" h, 5" l, rect, cranberry, enamel birds and floral dec, brass mounts and handles, orig key **1,500.00**

Mt Washington, 3¼" h, 4½" d top, 5¼" d base, portrait of monk drinking glass of red wine, solid shaded green opal glass ground, gold washed silverplated rim and hinge, orig satin lining, artist sgd "Schindler" **550.00**

Pairpoint, robin's egg blue opal glass ground, six scalloped medallions of pink, yellow, and coral roses, green leaves, brown traceries, fancy gold wash, silverplated base, four ball feet, sgd and numbered **325.00**

Wavecrest, 8" d, ormolu raised design color, mottled green, pink and white flowers, blue and beige leaves, pink silk lining, hinged lid, c1904 . . . . . . **675.00**

JEWELRY

History: Jewelry has been a part of every culture. It was a way of displaying wealth, power, or love of beauty. In the current antiques marketplace, it is easiest to find jewelry dating between 1800 to 1950.

Jewelry items were treasured and handed down as heirlooms from generation to generation. In the United States, antique jewelry is any jewelry one hundred or more years old, a definition linked to U.S. Customs law. "Heirloom/estate" jewelry, i.e., jewelry at least twenty-five years old and acquired new, used, or through inheritance, is used for old jewelry that does not meet the "antique" definition.

The jewelry found in this listing fits either the antique or "heirloom/estate" definition. The list contains no new reproduction pieces. The jewelry is made of metals and gemstones proven to endure over time. Inexpensive and mass-produced costume jewelry is covered in *Warman's Americana & Collectibles.*

Several major auction houses, especially Christie's, Doyle's, and Sotheby's in New York City, hold specialized jewelry auctions several times each year.

Note: The first step in determining the value of a piece of old jewelry is to correctly identify the metal and gemstones. Take into account the current value of the metal and gemstones plus the piece's age, identifying marks, quality, condition, construction, etc.

References: Lillian Baker, *Fifty Years of Collectible Fashion Jewelry, 1925–1975,* Collector Books, 1986, 1989 value update; Vivienne Becker, *Antique and 20th Century Jewelry,* Van Nostrand Reinhold; David Bennett and Daniela Mascetti, *Understanding Jewellery,* Antique Collectors' Club, 1989; Roseann Ettinger, *Popular Jewelry, 1840–1940,* Schiffer Publishing Co., 1990; Rose

L. Goldemberg, *Antique Jewelry: A Practical And Passionate Guide,* Crown Publishers, Inc., 1976; Arthur Guy Kaplan, *The Official Identification Price Guide To Antique Jewelry, Sixth Edition,* House of Collectibles, 1990; Antoinette Matlins and A. C. Bonanno, *Gem Identification Made Easy,* Gemstone Press, 1988; Antoinette Matlins and A. C. Bonanno, *Jewelry & Gems: The Buying Guide,* Gemstone Press, 1987; Harrice Miller, *The Official Identification and Price Guide To Costume Jewelry,* House of Collectibles, 1990; Michael Poynder, *The Price guide to Jewellery 3000BC–1950AD,* Antique Collectors' Club, 1990 reprint; Dorothy T. Rainwater, *American Jewelry Manufacturers,* Schiffer Publishing Ltd., 1988.

Advisor: Elaine J. Luartes.

Dates:

Georgian	**1714–1837**
Victorian.	**1837–1865**
Edwardian	**1885–1910**
Art Nouveau.	**1880–1920**
Arts and Crafts.	**1895–1915**
Art Deco.	**1920–1930**
Art Retro	**1940–1950**

Bar Pin, Edwardian

Platinum, horizontal axis set, 15 assorted old mine diamonds **1,050.00**

Platinum top, yg base, center axis defined by slightly graduated diamonds, 27 old mine diamonds, c1890 . . . . **3,400.00**

Belt Buckle, Arts and Crafts, 2⅞" w, 1⅞" h, symmetrical, two shield form motifs with double spiral designs, three round chyrosprase stones accented by gold wash, marked with designer (Patriz Huber) monograms and "900/Depouse," Germany, c1901 . . . . **2,100.00**

Bracelet

Art Deco, platinum, flexible band of oval links, center cabochon sapphires alternating with straight line links, 183 round single cut diamonds, c1925 . . . . **4,500.00**

Art Retro, bangle, two sculpted 18K yg feathers, rib set with alternating sections of circular cut rubies and diamonds, 18K yellow and white gold mountings **4,400.00**

Arts and Crafts

7" l, sterling silver, 7 oval cabochon carnelians set in rect linked openwork stylized floral motif plaques, Germany, early 20th C **100.00**

7¼" l, Georg Jensen, Copenhagen, sterling silver, links of alternating linear design, imp marks "Georg Jensen" in beaded oval and "Sterling/Denmark/103" **450.00**

7¾" l, 14 kt gold, 5 oval cabochon

turquoise stones, framed by separate stylized plant form dec, linked by two strands of gold chain, marked "Lebolt 14 k," Chicago, early 20th C **2,000.00**

Victorian, 15 kt yg, scrolling textured crescent form graduated links, flower clasp with one round old mine cut diamond, 11.5 dwt **600.00**

Brooch

Art Deco

Bottle shape, openwork design, old European cut diamonds, calibre cut black onyx, platinum mounting **2,200.00**

Navette shape outline and openwork, oval cut sapphire within round and rose cut diamond, calibre cut sapphire and platinum frame **2,880.00**

Art Nouveau, 2 joined natural scallop shells, openwork yellow gold foliate frame, 8 pearls, sgd "Tiffany & Co" **2,420.00**

Art Retro

Ballerina, dancing yg figure, pear shaped ruby head, yg tutu with circular cut rubies and sapphires, sleeves set with circular cabochon sapphires, 14K yg mounting, sgd "John Rubel" **1,650.00**

Lily shape, circular cut diamond pistil, surrounded by circular cut ruby petals, pave set diamond stem, circular cut emerald and round diamond leaf, rose and white gold mountings **4,180.00**

Arts and Crafts

1½" w, 2" l, open work leaf and floral design, gold setting, surmounted by zircon, central large amethyst surrounded by demantoid garnet, aquamarines, citrines, and tourmalines **2,300.00**

2⅛" l,⅝" h, sterling silver, faceted oval citrine centered by 2 cabochon moonstones, openwork grape and leaf dec **550.00**

Edwardian

Flower, yg, round faceted pink topaz pistil and petals, foiled, framed gold borders, c1875 . . . **700.00**

Shield, platinum, center axis set with 9 natural pearls, 146 assorted old mine single cut and full cut diamonds, c1900 . . . . **3,700.00**

Georgian, French, c1835, platinum top, white gold base, green heart composed of 2 pear shaped 3.00 cts emeralds, foiled, border of diamonds, surmounted by bow set with 65 small round old mine full cut diamonds **9,500.00**

Chateline

7¼" l, sterling silver, spherical perfume bottle, circular threaded cap, suspended from belt clip by two chains, both chased and engraved with maple leaves, applied brass insets and foliage, marked "Dominick & Haff," c1880 . . . . **1,760.00**

10¼" l, 2¾" d circular flask, spot hammered sterling silver, applied Japanese figure holding mokume parasol, silver foliage, trimmed in bamboo form moldings, bamboo form bail handle suspended from chain of disks attached to matching belt clip, American, c1880 . . . . . . **1,100.00**

Choker, Art Retro, c1940, 14 kt yg, flexible band of 13 mm melon reeded spheres, 16" l, 31 dwt **1,600.00**

Dress Clip, Art Deco, platinum, stylized bow tie, center knot with feathered ends, 2 half moon shaped diamonds, 10 marquise, 50 round, 16 baguette cut diamonds, c1925 . . . . **12,000.00**

Earrings, Art Retro, c1945, ruby and diamond, 14K yg, star burst, ruby cluster centers, rays containing tiny diamonds, terminating in rubies, alternating fluted gold rays, sgd "Tiffany & Company" **4,000.00**

Jabot, Art Deco, platinum and white gold, two apple and emerald green carved jade gourds, 14 small round diamonds, c1925 . . . . **3,400.00**

Kilt Pin, sterling silver, arched, pierced crest with applied beads, oval lapis stone, long stem, English, early 20th C **110.00**

Lavaliere, Art Deco, diamond and olivine, platinum and yg, banderole, single fresh water pearl center, 11 old mine diamonds, single pear shaped

Locket, Victorian, yellow gold, center architectural motif micro mosaic, $250.00.

brown diamond, emerald pendant, c1925 .... **4,600.00**

Locket

Art Nouveau, 18K yg, oval, sculpted foliate design, French hallmarks .. **1,210.00**

Edwardian, 14 kt yg and platinum, shield form body, light blue enamel ground, small pierced basket of flowers, set with assorted small round diamonds, double picture openings, c1885 .... **800.00**

Locket and Chain

Art Nouveau, sculpted yellow gold topped rose gold locket, head of Medusa, hair enhanced by diamond collets, reverse monogrammed "EUC," 54" l yellow gold fancy link chain with pear, oval, and circular cut sapphires, peridots, pink tourmalines, zircons, and citrines **10,450.00**

Edwardian, circular 14 kt yg, center diamond floral motif, white enamel bands with ribbon scrolls, engine turned blue gray enamel ground, gold link chain with blue and white enamel arrow motif dividers, c1900 **1,400.00**

Lorgnette

Art Nouveau, yg, sculpted foliate motif handle, oval lenses in rose gold frames **1,870.00**

Victorian, yg, oblong chased case, one side with maiden within scrolling borders, obverse with multicolored enameled flowers, black and gold border, French, c1875 ..... **950.00**

Necklace

Art Deco, line of graduated black onyx and pave set diamond triangular plaques, alternating with diamond collets, platinum mounting, 17½" l platinum oval link chain ... **2,650.00**

Art Nouveau, yg, flexible chain of pierced cylinder form links with carved geometric coral cylinder and bead dividers, 60" l **475.00**

Arts and Crafts

14 kt gold, stylized design, geometric cut outs and curvilinear textured pattern, solitaire diamond over 3 lapis lazuli stones above corresponding lapis lazuli drop, double strand chain spaced with 6 matching lapis lazuli stones, imp marks "K14/Arthur and Bond," early 20th C .. **2,100.00**

Gold, 16" l, floral design plaque set with amethyst, aquamarines, and baroque pearls, alternating smaller plaques with corresponding stone, attributed to Margaret Rogers, Boston **2,500.00**

Necklace and Earrings Set, Victorian, flexible lozenge form enamel links, gold scrolled wire frames, faceted emeralds, cabochon rubies, and rose diamonds, ornamented center bow, pendant drops, fitted red leather box, c1875 ....**18,000.00**

Pearls, cultured

16" l, uniform 9 mm baroque pearls, 14 kt white gold clasp **250.00**

28" l, graduated 7.5–3.5 mm beads, 12 round diamonds set on platinum clasp **350.00**

Pendant

Art Deco, platinum frame, 14 kt white gold, center synthetic green stone, diamond accents, gold and diamond link chain **500.00**

Art Nouveau, c1850, silver top, yg base, circle set with small natural pearl clusters and pairs of diamonds, pearl drop **1,700.00**

Arts and Crafts

18½" l, oval cabochon coral stone set in sterling silver geometric pendant, cut out accents, coral drop, paper clip chain, marked "Handmade/Sterling," logo "T. H. S." **600.00**

22" l, sterling silver, vertical leaf and peridot motif, hammered teardrop shaped plaque, sgd "Plantagenet Handwrought" **225.00**

33" l, Georg Jensen, sterling silver, overlapping flower and swag dec, 5 bezel set lapis lazuli stones, 3 suspended lapis lazuli drops, paper clip chain, imp marks "GJ," "830" in raised beaded ' ovals, and "Denmark/ 33," **1,400.00**

Edwardian

Fleur–De–Lis, platinum top, yg base, 69 assorted old mine diamonds, 8.25 cts, c1875 ...... **1,900.00**

Lozenge, platinum filigree frame, 39 round diamonds, c1910 .... **950.00**

Shield, scrolling, center carved moonstone face, diamond and pearl two strand tassel, 18 small diamonds, white gold top, yg base, c1875 .... **700.00**

Pin

Art Deco, snake, 18 kt yg, red, black, and white enamel snake coiled around arrow, c1920 .... **1,100.00**

Art Retro

Bow, 14 kt red and yg, octagonal cut aquamarine center with six round ruby knots, 8 dwt **400.00**

Floral, 18 kt yg, two stylized blossoms, swirled ribbed petal apron,

clustered pistil, sgd "Yard", 10 dwt **375.00**
Floral Bouquet, 14 kt white gold, scrolling bouquet, 7 baguettes and 56 round diamonds, c1940 **450.00**

Arts and Crafts

1⅝" w,⅞" h, Georg Jensen, sterling silver, oval green onyx cabochon vertically centered by corresponding round stones, framed with openwork bead and bellflower design, imp marks "Georg Jensen" in beaded oval and "Sterling/Denmark/236A" **425.00**

2⅛" d, Georg Jensen, sterling, round, openwork with two butterflies sitting on floral stems, stamped "Georg Jensen" in beaded oval **425.00**

2¼" w,¾" h, oval, rose quartz plaque framed by sterling silver openwork leaf and ball design, marked "Sterling/Germany," early 20th C **75.00**

2½" l, sterling silver, faceted amethyst centered by two baroque pearls, oval openwork leaf setting, gold washed highlights, marked "Sterling" **450.00**

Edwardian, platinum, modified cartouche, 2 old mine 1.00 cts diamond center, flanking center old mine .50 ct center, surrounded by 48 round diamonds **2,000.00**

Ring, Victorian, 14K yellow gold, elongated style, straight row set turquoise surrounded by rose cut diamonds, $375.00.

Ring

Art Deco, platinum, c1920

Black onyx and diamond, oval high dome cabochon onyx within canted onyx bezel centered on diamond shank set with 22 round single cut diamonds, sgd "Black, Starr & Frost" **4,000.00**
Diamond and synthetic sapphires, old mine round diamond, 6 synthetic sapphire trapezoids, flaked by 8 diamonds **700.00**

Art Retro

Diamond, buckle, platinum, one .65 ct diamond, twenty-one round full cut and nine baguette cut diamonds, sgd "Yard," c1950 . . . . **2,000.00**
Diamond, old mine and old European cut diamond plaque, white gold setting **550.00**

Ruby and Diamond

Circular cut ruby hemisphere, flanked on each side by pave set diamond rays, rose and white gold mountings, sgd "T & HM" for Trabert & Hoeffer—Mauboussin **6,600.00**
Three channels of calibre cut rubies, pave set diamond, platinum and yg mounting **1,870.00**

Arts and Crafts, gold

Moonstone, 3 round bezel set moonstones spaced with beads, incised marks "Georg Jensen" in beaded oval, "Denmark" and "925 S" **200.00**
Pearls, 3 graduated baroque pearls, set vertically crossed by 2 sapphires, overall leaf and floral design, early 20th C **800.00**
Star Sapphire, yellow and white gold openwork leaf and flower design, star sapphire center, accented to two diamonds **550.00**

Edwardian

Diamond, platinum, one old mine round diamond, field of 22 assorted single cut round diamonds, c1915 . . . . **3,600.00**
Diamond and blue sapphire, 18 kt white gold, domed geometric field of 38 assorted rose cut diamonds, cabochon sapphire, c1900 . . . . **450.00**

Stick Pin, Victorian, scarf, silver gilt, pietra dura, lapis, coral, and jade flowers and leaves, cable twist frame, $100.00.

Stickpin, Art Nouveau, 18K yg, two sculpted female heads, openwork shield shaped frame, sgd green leather fitted case, sgd "Lalique" . . . **4,450.00**

JUDAICA

History: Throughout history, Jews have expressed themselves artistically in both the religious and secular spheres. Most Jewish art objects were created as part of the concept of "Hiddur Mitzva," i.e., adornment of implements involved in performing rituals both in the synagogue and home.

For almost 2,000 years, since the destruction of the Jerusalem Temple in 70 A.D., Jews have lived in many lands. The widely differing environments gave traditional Jewish life and art a multifaceted character. Unlike Greek, Byzantine, or Roman art which have definite territorial and historical boundaries, Jewish art is found throughout Europe, the Middle East, North Africa, and other areas.

Ceremonial objects incorporated not only liturgical appurtenances, but also ethnographic artifacts such as amulets and ritual costumes. The style of each ceremonial object responded to the artistic and cultural milieu in which it was created. Although diverse stylistically, ceremonial objects, whether for Sabbath, holidays, or the life cycle, still possess a unity of purpose.

Judaica has been crafted in all media, though silver is the most collectible. Sotheby's, Christie's, and Swann's hold several Judaica auctions in the United States, England, Amsterdam, and Israel.

References: Abraham Kanof, *Jewish Ceremonial Art*, Harry N. Abrams, n.d.; Cecil Roth, *Jewish Art—An Illustrated History*, Graphic Society of New York, 1971; Geoffrey Wigoder, (ed.), *Jewish Art and Civilization*, Chartwell Books, 1972.

Museums: B'nai B'rith Klutznick Museum, Washington, DC; H.U.C., Skirball Museum, Los Angeles, CA; Jewish Museum, New York, NY; Judah L. Magnes Museum, Berkeley, CA; Maurice Spertus Museum of Judaica, Chicago, IL; National Museum of American Jewish History, Philadelphia, PA; Yeshiva University Museum, New York, NY.

Advisor: Arthur M. Feldman.

Aspergillum, 11½" h, silver, cylindrical stem with three molded bands, loop handle, engraved inscription dated 1922, Maltese, 4 oz, wood and glass case **500.00**

Beaker, 2½" h, Russian silver, incised shetel scenes, c1870 . . . . **265.00**

Breast Plate, 13½" h, silver, hinged tablet form cover with Hebrew inscription, openwork frame below, applied openwork dec, chased floral and scrolling foliage border, scroll and rocaille rim, chain on reverse, marked "Sterling," 29.5 oz **800.00**

Etrog Container, 4 x 7" box, olivewood, octagonal, hinged lid, attached carved etrog on top, Palestine, c1940 **600.00**

Hanukah Lamp, 10 x 10", Polish silvered brass, Baroque foliate design on back plates, surmounted by repousse crown, two rampant lions on either side of menorah, sgd "Warsaw," mid 19th C **1,200.00**

Megillah
  7" h, silver, cylinder, chased flowers and inscription on reserve, crown form ends with bud finial, parchment scroll of the Book of Esther, 19th C **385.00**
  17½" h, sterling silver, cylinder pierced with banded design of flora and fauna, various semi–precious stones, bird finial, parchment scroll of the Book of Esther, marked "Silver 925," 20th C **850.00**

Kiddush Cup, engraved dec, Russian hallmarks, 1888, 2⅛" h, $75.00.

Menorah
  11½" h, silver filigree, nine candle-sockets over series of triangular panels of filigree rosettes, 12½" troy oz **275.00**
  21½" h, silver, knopped baluster stem, six multi–scroll branches, three scroll branches, circular wax pans, urn form sockets, cast and engraved spread eagle finial, double domed base with band of rose-heads and foliage, four talon feet, detachable oil pitcher, Portuguese, 66.5 troy oz **9,000.00**

Mezuzah, 5½ x 1½", replicated Chagall lithograph, 24 karat yellow gold plated over bronze, 20th C **600.00**

Mug Frames with Tray, 24½" l, silver, filigree, oblong two handled tray with rosettes and overall foliate dec, cylindrical mug frames with similar dec, 74½" troy oz, 20th C **1,600.00**

Rosewater Spice Container, 11½", Middle Eastern silver, rounded bulbous container, incised foliage dec, long tapering top, ftd base **350.00**

Seder Plate, 12 x 10", ceramic, luster finish, Hebrew calligraphy in re-

cessed compartments, Czechlosvak-
ian, c1920 . . . . **1,500.00**
Torah Crown, parcel gilt, plain top, sides
of alternating silver openwork vertical
bands scrolling foliage with eagle,
punched bead border, silver gilt
bands, openwork arabesque Star of
David with hanging bell, body with
similar flowerheads, two gilt lions supporting tablet finial, Star of David
above, cylindrical base, openwork engraved scrolling foliage centering two
Hebrew inscriptions, marked "Ster-
ling" by Klatzk, 66.5 oz **1,250.00**
Torah Pointer, Russian silver, sq ta-
pered handle, two knops and engraved design, hand marked "84"
partial assay mark of 1876, late 19th
C, 4 troy oz **950.00**
Tzadaka, 7″ h, silver, inverted bud
shape, repousse foliage, angled stem
form spout, spout and base with He-
brew inscriptions, 12 troy oz **1,900.00**
Wine Cup, 5¾″, American silver, tulip
form, stemmed, presentation, inscrip-
tion, dated 1866 . . . . **475.00**

JUGTOWN POTTERY

History: In 1920 Jacques and Julianna Busbee
left their cosmopolitan environs and returned to
North Carolina to revive the state's dying craft of
pottery making. Jugtown Pottery, a colorful and
somewhat off-beat operation, was located in
Moore County, miles away from any large city and
accessible only "if mud permits."

Ben Owens, a talented young potter, turned the
wares. Jacques Busbee did most of the designing
and glazing. Julianna handled promotion.

Utilitarian and decorative items were produced.
Although many colorful glazes were used, orange
predominated. A Chinese blue glaze that ranged
from light blue to deep turquoise was a prized
glaze reserved for the very finest pieces.

Jacques Busbee died in 1947. Julianna, with the
help of Owens, ran the pottery until 1958 when it
was closed. After long legal battles, the pottery
was reopened in 1960. It now is owned by Country
Roads, Inc., a non-profit organization. The pottery
still is operating and using the old mark.

**Pitcher, tan, incised ground, 7″ w, 6¼″
h, $100.00.**

Bean Pot, cov, orange, late **40.00**
Bowl, 10⅝″ d, Chinese blue glaze,
honey brown stain, marked **175.00**
Candlesticks, pr, 7″ h, orange glaze . . **50.00**
Creamer, orange glaze **45.00**
Jardiniere, 13″ h, Chinese blue over red
glaze **385.00**
Pitcher, 6½″ h, incised dec **60.00**
Soup Tureen, cov, 7″ h, orange glaze . **45.00**
Teapot, cov, 6½″ h, Chinese blue glaze **95.00**
Vase
6½″ h, bulbous ovoid body, tapering
to rolled rim, sprayed gold and
khaki glaze, imp mark **150.00**
8″ h, Chinese blue glaze, emb han-
dles **225.00**
9½″ h, bulbous tapering towards
base, flaring mouth, narrow neck,
red and blue glaze, gray stone-
ware, imp mark **350.00**

KPM

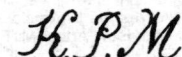

History: The mark, KPM, has been used separately and in conjunction with other symbols by
many German porcelain manufacturers, among
whom are the Königliche Porzellan Manufactur in
Meissen, 1720s; Königliche Porzellan Manufactur
in Berlin, 1832–1847; and Krister Porzellan Manufactur in Waldenburg, mid-19th century.

Collectors now use the term "KPM" to refer to
the high quality porcelain produced in the Berlin
area in the 18th and 19th centuries.

Reference: Susan and Al Bagdade, *Warman's
English & Continental Pottery & Porcelain, 1st Edition*, Warman Publishing Co., Inc., 1987.

Chocolate Pot, blue floral with gold dec **125.00**
Cup and Saucer, painted black Iron
Cross, dated 1914 in gilt laurel
branches, blue ground, continuous
oak branches, yellow band, figural

swan's head handle and neck, blue scepter, iron–red KPM and orb, black cross marks **225.00**

Dessert Plate, 8¾" d, reticulated, gilt border, enamel painted flowers, floral garlands, set of 6 . . . . **450.00**

Ewer, 9" h, hunter and stag cartouche, yellow ground **600.00**

Figure, 6½" h, classical goddess holding fruit, polychrome enameling with gilt, marked "KPM" **175.00**

Jar, cov, 13¾" h, baluster, multicolored oval reserve of classical landscape, gilt foliate border, iron–red branch sprinkled ground, domed cov, pinecone finial, blue scepter and iron–red globe mark **275.00**

Portrait, Renaissance lady, bronze rococo frame, 9 x 6¾", $2,500.00.

Plaque

5" h, Lorelei, multicolored painted oval, nude reclining on rockwork by sea, holding white drape, sgd "Wagner," imp mark **1,100.00**

7¾" h, 5⅞" w, monk, wine cellar scene, one barrel sgd and dated 1865, imp "KPM" and scepter marks, framed **2,750.00**

8⅜" h, 6⅛" w, bust portrait of Christ, crowned with thorns, imp marks and numerals **400.00**

10" h, 7½" w, Psyche, winged maiden in diaphanous drapery seated on grassy mound at edge of cliff, imp marks and numerals **5,720.00**

10" l, Magdelene, scantily draped reclining maiden reading, landscape background, painted after Corregio, sgd "Wagner," imp marks, incised numerals **2,860.00**

10½" h, 8" w, lovesick young girl in bed, roses by her side, imp marks and numerals **8,800.00**

10½" h, 8½" w, Reapers, multicolored, painted after Millet, three central figures picking crops, imp marks and numerals, framed **4,180.00**

11⅛" h, 9" w, two ladies reading letter, dec after Deffregger, sgd "Fleish...," imp marks and numerals **4,625.00**

12½" h, 8" w, Ruth, posed with sheaf of wheat in her hand, brown gown, white head scarf, standing by water, imp marks **4,400.00**

12½" h, 10¼" w, monk, holding tankard, standing in front of keg, painted by L Schnizel, sgd, after E Grutzner, imp marks, incised numerals **3,300.00**

12¾" h, 10½" w, Madonna and child, painted after Raphael, late 19th C, imp marks, framed **3,520.00**

13¼" h, 11¼" w, Sistine Madonna, flanked by saints, two putti at feet, after Raphael, imp mark **2,750.00**

Soup Tureen, cov, 14" h, figural finial **475.00**

Vase, 26" h, all-over children frolicking in garden scene **6,250.00**

KAUFFMANN, ANGELICA

History: Marie Angelique Catherine Kauffmann was a Swiss artist who lived from 1741 until 1807. Her paintings were copied by many artists who hand decorated porcelain during the 19th century. The majority of the paintings are neo-classical in style.

Reference: Susan and Al Bagdade, *Warman's English & Continental Pottery & Porcelain, 1st Edition,* Warman Publishing Co., Inc., 1987.

Biscuit Jar, 5" d, 7" h, scenic panel of three ladies and gentleman, pastels, alternating green and maroon panels, gold trim, SP rim, cov, and handle . . **150.00**

Bowl, 9½" d, two maidens and child . . **65.00**

Condensed Milk Can Holder, cov, matching underplate, classical maiden, green ground, gold tracery . **100.00**

Cup and Saucer, classical scene, royal blue ground, beehive mark **100.00**

Demitasse Set, 3" d, 5¼" h pot, cov sugar, and four demitasse cups and saucers, matching 12" d tray, royal blue band trim, gold band trim, classical scenes with women, men, and cupids **700.00**

Marmalade jar, cov, Three Graces scene **85.00**

Tobacco Jar, portrait front, muted dark green, hints of orange and yellow, silverplated rim and lid, pipe finial, $300.00.

Plate

8" d, three maidens and cupid, gold trim, beehive mark 75.00

9½" d, multicolored scene, Venus reclining, attended by Cupid, tooled gilt band and gilt embellished border, polychrome scroll and urn panels, sgd "Forster," late 19th C 600.00

Tobacco Jar, 7½" h, dark green muted with orange and yellow, SP rim and lid 325.00

Vase, 20" h, classical scene, four maidens, cobalt blue ground, sgd 400.00

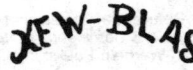

KEW BLAS

History: Amory and Francis Houghton established the Union Glass Company, Somerville, Massachusetts, in 1851. The company went bankrupt in 1860, but was reorganized. Between 1870 and 1885 the Union Glass Company made pressed glass and blanks for cut glass.

Art glass production began in 1893 under the direction of William S. Blake and Julian de Cordova. Two styles were introduced. A Venetian style consisted of graceful shapes in colored glass, often flecked with gold. An iridescent glass, labeled Kew Blas, was made in plain and decorated forms. The pieces are close in design and form to Quezel products, but lack the subtlety of Tiffany items.

The company ceased production in 1924.

Candlestick, pr, 8½", twisted stem, irid gold 725.00

Cuspidor, 5¾" d, 2½" h, squatty, flattened flared rim, amber ground, gold irid, sgd "Kew Blas" 275.00

Decanter, 14", green-gold irid, spherical long stemmed stopper, sgd 275.00

Pitcher, 5", King Tut, white, green, and gold, blue handle, irid blue lining, sgd 1,900.00

Rose Bowl, 3½", green and gold hooked dec, butterscotch ground, gold lining, sgd 525.00

Salt, open, irid gold 225.00

Vase, King Tut variation, white opal, gold irid, scalloped top, 10" h, $1,500.00.

Vase

4" h, ovoid, ivory, gold rim, gold pulled feather dec, engraved "Kew–Blas" 275.00

4½" h, green allover snake skin pattern, gold irid, scalloped rim 650.00

7½" h, baluster form, green pulled wave pattern, white gound, amber irid border, scalloped everted mouth, iridesncent amber int., inscribed "Kew Blas," first quarter 20th C 275.00

12½" h, baluster form, waisted, gold, blue, and pink irid 750.00

KITCHEN COLLECTIBLES

History: The kitchen was a central focal point in a family's environment until the 1960s. Many early kitchen utensils were handmade and prized by their owners. Next came a period of utilitarian products made of tin and other metals. When the housewife no longer wished to work in a sterile environment, color was added through enamel and plastic and design served both an aesthetic and functional purpose.

The advent of home electricity changed the type and style of kitchen products. Many items went through fads. The high technology field already has made inroads into the kitchen, and another revolution seems at hand.

References: Jane H. Celehar, *Kitchens and Gadgets, 1920 to 1950*, Wallace-Homestead, 1982; Linda Campbell Franklin, *300 Hundred Years of Kitchen Collectibles, Second Edition*,, Books Americana, 1982; Glydon Shirley, *The Miracle in Grandmother's Kitchen*, published by author, 1983.

Additional Listings: Baskets, Brass, Butter Prints, Copper, Fruit Jars, Food Molds, Graniteware, Ironware, Tinware, and Woodenware. See *Warman's Americana & Collectibles* for more examples including electrical appliances.

Butter paddle, wooden, 9¼″ l, 5″ d, $25.00.

Apple Peeler
Cast iron, Hudson Co, Leominster, Mass, pat 1882 . . . . **55.00**
Wood, 20½″ l, walnut, patina **105.00**
Beater, two pc, glass and iron
Hutchinson S. & S. **90.00**
Whippo Super Whipper **50.00**
Biscuit Pricker, wood, cross pattern, turned post, mushroom handle **220.00**
Bowl, turned wood
13½ x 14¼″, brown ext., dark patina int. **45.00**
18 x 19½″, worn green paint ext., worn patina int. **275.00**
20″ d, red ext., scrubbed int., two hanging holes on rim **250.00**
Bread Cutter, painted grain trough, cast iron handle, marked "RAADVAD" . . **145.00**
Butter Churn, Dazey
No. 4, St. Louis, Dazey Corp, wooden paddles **110.00**
No. 8 . . . . **75.00**
No. 20 . . . . **100.00**
No. 40 . . . . **40.00**
No. 80 . . . . **100.00**
Butter Paddle
9″ l, maple, rim hook on handle **45.00**
9¼″ l, maple, cherry finish **35.00**
Coffee Grinder, tin, Goldenberg **50.00**
Cook Pot, 12″ d, lid, wrought iron handles, dovetailed seam **45.00**
Cookie Board, 8¾ x 20¼″, wood, carved, two hearts on one side, one on other **485.00**
Cookie Cutter
Fish, 7″ l, tin, strap handle **200.00**

Heart in hand, 3 x 5½″, tin, strap handle, 1830 . . . . **525.00**
Cookie Peel, 21″, pine, hand carved, beveled edge, rect, tapered, paddle end, patina, c1820 . . . . **85.00**
Cranberry Scoop
15″, wood and tin, varnished, branded "Budd & Co" **85.00**
43½″ l, wood, long handle **125.00**
Dough Bowl, hand carved
19½ x 9½″, rect **65.00**
25 x 13″, oval **125.00**
Dough Box
19¼ x 41″, 28″ h, poplar, Hepplewhite style, splayed base with sq tapered legs, dovetailed box, cherry finish **450.00**
22 x 40½″, 29″ h, poplar, dovetailed, splayed base, tapered legs, lid . . **275.00**
Dough Scraper, 4½″ w, wrought iron . . **45.00**
Dutch Oven, Griswold, #8 . . . . **35.00**
Egg Fryer, Griswold, sq **30.00**
Flour Scoop, 14″ l, maple, Shaker style, carved, shaped handle, finger grip **160.00**
Food Chopper, 10¼″ l, two blades, wood handles, marked "P L Schmitt" **65.00**
Food Grinder, Griswold #10 . . . . **35.00**
Fruit Press, 4 qt, Griswold **85.00**
Kraut Cutter
7½ x 17″, curly maple, curved crest with cut out heart, worn finish . . . **200.00**
13 x 41″, ash, cherry dovetailed hopper, refinished **75.00**
Nutmeg Grater, 5¼″ l, tin, wood handle **50.00**
Pie Crimper, 7⅝″ l, brass and wrought iron **325.00**
Pie Lifter
Brass ferrule, turned wood handle, 18th C **75.00**
Wire, wood handle, 13½″ l, Shaker **55.00**
Potato Masher, wood **10.00**
Raisin Seeder, Everett, orig instructions **70.00**
Rolling Pin
18½″ l, curly maple, light finish **55.00**
19¾″ l, turned **25.00**
Salt Box, 8 x 8½″, 9¾″ h, poplar, dovetailed case and drawer with divided int., shaped crest, lift lid, dark finish **100.00**
Toaster, 6 x 8¾″, wire, folds over, twisted handle **75.00**
Vegetable Chopper, 8″, wood handle, six ball shaped blades, Keen Kutter **45.00**
Utensils, fork and brass bowl dipper, wrought iron, shaped handles, engraved initials "LC," 21″ l **170.00**
Waffle Iron
Keen Kutter, four sections, logo . . . **160.00**
Stratton Junior 8, wood handles, stand **110.00**
Wagner, cast iron, wood handle, stand, marked "Wagner, Sidney, OH, pat Feb 22, 1910" **135.00**

KUTANI

History: In the mid 1600s Kutani originated in the Kaga province of Japan. Kutani comes in a variety of color patterns, one of the most popular being Ao Kutani, a green glaze with colors such as green, yellow, and purple enclosed in a black outline. Wares made since the 1870s for export are enameled in a wide variety of colors and styles.

Reference: Sandra Andacht, *Oriental Antiques & Art: An Identification And Value Guide,* Wallace-Homestead, 1987.

Vases, left: two men and flowers, red, 5¾" h, $125.00; right: flowers and birds, red, 7" h, $100.00.

Berry Set, master bowl, six serving bowls, multicolored enamel floral dec, red border, 7 pcs 175.00
Bowl
  4⅜", sq, polychrome, gold flowers, unglazed foot, sgd gold seal form ... 300.00
  7½" d, orange–red and green glaze, gold highlights, unglazed rim and foot, sgd "Dai Ni–pon Ku–tani tus–kuru" 175.00
  8½" d, octagonal, floral and foliate dec, marked "AO Kutani" 200.00
  9½" d, Kaga Ware, all over red enamel, gilt accents, int. with paneled figural, floral, and animal scenes, diaper, scroll, and geometric ground, ext. continuous dragons with clouds, geometric and leaf borders, character mark, Japan, mid 19th C 400.00
Charger, 14" d, figural landscape, multicolored, gilt border 225.00
Chocolate Pot, 8½" h, red, orange, and gold, reserve panels of peonies and birds, people in gardens with peonies, Japanese 150.00
Compote, 8¾" h, enamel dec garden scenes, birds in flight, character marks, Japan, late 19th C, pr 300.00
Creamer and Sugar, cov, 5 x 5¼" creamer, 7½ x 7" ftd sugar, burnt orange

ground, hp scenes, gold tracery, bamboo handles, sgd Oriental character, 19th C 265.00
Dinner Service, 121 pcs, twelve dinner plates, salad plates, soup bowls, butter plates, dessert plates, cups and saucers, and demitasse cups and saucers, coffee pot, creamer and sugar, teapot, gravy boat, cov soup tureen, two platters, vegetable bowl, and salt and pepper shakers, figural and landscape scene, Japanese ... 650.00
Ewer, 8¼" h, duck on floral base, key fret band, green, yellow, aubergine, and blue enamel 175.00
Ginger Jar, cov, 5" h, blue, green, and carmine enamel dec, fu dog finial .. 125.00
Incense Burner, cov, 9" h, squatty, pierced cov, loop finial, enamel dec rust ground, paneled birds in garden setting, gilt accents, three feet, character marks, Japan, 19th C 800.00
Pitcher, 12¼", bottle form, elongated neck, cranes and landscape dec, Meiji period 275.00
Sake Cup, 1⅞", floriform rim, short ring foot, enamel and gilt dec, patterned rim band, gilt scrolling flower and trellis dec 115.00
Umbrella Stand, 28" h, multicolored butterflies, flowers, foliage, and medallions 500.00
Vase
  9¼" h, octagonal form, Japanese .. 200.00
  17" h, lotus leaf and bird dec, mounted as lamp, sgd "AO Kutani" 190.00
  18" h, cov, gourd shape, twisted vine handles, molded leaves and gourds, enameled dec rust ground, paneled scene of peacocks in flower garden, cranes in flight, smaller panel of dragons among clouds, gilt accents, three molded gourd and leaf dec feet, character marks, 19th C 1,000.00

LALIQUE

History: Rene Lalique (1860–1945) first gained prominence as a jewelry designer. Around 1900 he began experimenting with molded glass brooches and pendants, often embellishing them with semiprecious stones. By 1905 he was devoting himself exclusively to the manufacture of glass articles.

In 1908 Lalique began designing packaging for the French cosmetic houses. He also produced many objects, especially vases, bowls, and figurines, in the Art Noveau style in the 1910s. The full scope of Lalique's genius was seen at the 1925 Paris International Exhibition of Decorative Arts. He later moved to the Art Deco form.

The mark "R. LALIQUE FRANCE" in block letters is found on pressed articles, tableware, vases, paperweights, and mascots. The script signature, with or without "France," is found on hand blown objects. Occasionally a design number is included. The word "France" in any form indicates a piece made after 1926.

The post–1945 mark is "Lalique France" without the "R"; there are exceptions to this rule.

References: Katherine Morrison McClinton, *Introduction to Lalique Glass*, Wallace-Homestead, 1978; Tony L. Mortimer, *Lalique*, Chartwell Books, 1989.

Reproduction Alert: Much faking of the Lalique signature occurs, the most common being the addition of an "R" to the post–1945 mark.

Animal
  Fish, 7", sgd "Lalique, France," orig
    paper label 500.00
  Rooster, 9", numbered, sgd "R Lalique, France," orig paper label . .   2,000.00
Atomizer, 3¾" h, figural, cylindrical, procession of female nudes joined by garlands, Le Provencal fragrance, molded "R Lalique, Made In France"   250.00
Bowl
  9½" d, Chicoree, clear and frosted, molded Verrerie d'Alsace mark . .   375.00
  10" d, Nemours, clear and frosted, molded all-over blossoms with black enameled centers, engraved "Lalique France" 600.00
Box, cov, 2¹⁵⁄₁₆" d, circular, opalescent, Coquilles, molded stylized shells, engraved "R Lalique France" 330.00
Candlestick, 3½" h, sgd "R Lalique" . .   600.00
Centerpiece Bowl, 18" l, frosted oak leaves, clear base 700.00
Champagne, 6½" h, clear, engraved "R Lalique, France" 880.00
Charger, 14¼" d, Malines, opalescent, molded "R Lalique," wheel carved "France" 2,970.00
Cigarette Box, 5½" l, rect, hinged top, trimmed in silver, lid molded with heads of wheat, inscribed "Lalique, France" 2,200.00
Dish, 11⅝" d, Gazelles, clear and frosted 375.00
Figure, nude with goose, 6" h, sgd "Lalique," orig paper label 500.00
Pendant, 2⅛" d, oval, clear and frosted, molded with two female nudes, engraved "R Lalique" 770.00

Perfume Bottle
  5¼" h, Ambre D'Orsay, clear and frosted, molded "Lalique" and "Ambre D'Orsay" 2,200.00
Placecard Holder, 1⅝" h, demilune form, clear and frosted, molded baskets of flowers and fruit, engraved "R Lalique," set of 8 . . . .   800.00

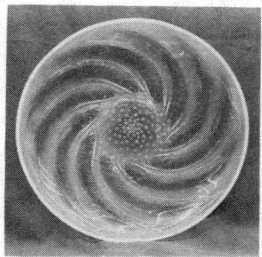

Plate, fish, 10¼" d, $400.00.

Powder Box, 4" d, circular, Emilane, clear and frosted, floral molded lid, molded "R Lalique France" 300.00
Scent Bottle
  3⅜" h, Epines, molded briars, green patina in recesses, engraved "R Lalique France" and molded "R Lalique" 550.00
  4½" h, Palerme, clear, molded "R Lalique," engraved "France" 725.00
  5½" h, Helene, four panels of classical maidens, brown patina, etched "Lalique, France" 750.00
Toothpick, 3½" h, sgd "R Lalique" . . .   600.00
Vase
  4¾" h, Tournesol, clear and frosted, engraved "R Lalique, France, No. 1007" 660.00
  5" h, Dahlias, enameled, molded "R Lalique" 2,530.00
  5½" h, Camaret, frosted, engraved "R Lalique France, No. 1010" 800.00
  5¾" h, Avallon, clear and frosted, birds among berried branches, traces of amber patina, wheel carved "R Lalique, France," engraved "No. 986" 600.00
  6" h, Boulouris, flared cylinder, opalescent band of sparrows on shoulders, vertical ribbing, stamped "R Lalique" 1,760.00
  6¼" h, Meander, clear and frosted, c1935, engraved "R Lalique, France" 1,145.00
  6⅝" h, Ormeaux, clear and frosted,

engraved "R Lalique France No.
984" **385.00**
6¾" h
Formose, clear and frosted glass,
molded "R Lalique" **1,325.00**
Gui, cased, yellow, molded "R La-
lique" **2,200.00**
7" h
Druides, blue patina, engraved and
molded marks **990.00**
Saint Francois, opalescent,
stamped "R Lalique France" . . **900.00**
7⅜" h, Chardons, butterscotch cased
over opal, molded "R Lalique," en-
graved "France" **2,860.00**
7½" h
Coquilles, blue patina, molded
marks **900.00**
Dentele, gray, engraved "R La-
lique, France, No. 943" **1,100.00**
8⅛" h, Tristan, clear and frosted,
wheel carved "R Lalique, France" **3,200.00**
9¼" h, Monnaie Du Pape, clear and
frosted, traces of amber patina,
molded "R Lalique," engraved
"France" **1,760.00**
10¼" h, Archers, clear and frosted,
engraved "R Lalique France No.
893" **3,000.00**

LAMP SHADES

History: Lamp shades were made to diffuse the
harsh light produced by early gas lighting fixtures.
These early shades were made by popular Art
Nouveau manufacturers including Durand, Quezal, Steuben, Tiffany, and others. Many shades
are not marked.

References: Dr. Larry Freeman, *New Lights on
Old Lamps*, American Life Foundation, 1984; Jo
Ann Thomas, *Early Twentieth Century Lighting
Fixtures*, Collector Books, 1980.

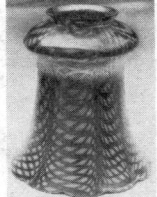

**Steuben, green, purple, and gold irid
fish net pattern, opal ground, gold irid
int., 2½" d fitter ring, 5½" h, $200.00.**

Acid Etched
7" d, multiple leaf pattern, clear
ground, 1870–80 . . . . **45.00**
8" d, hummingbirds and leaves, clear
and frosted, pr, c1870 . . . . **150.00**
8⅜" d, 3¾" h, key like double band,
clear and frosted, late 19th C . . . **20.00**
Burmese, 8¾" d, gas, birds, butterflies,
and floral dec **265.00**
Cameo Glass, 5½" h, 7" d, deep pink
ground, layered white, acid cut blackberry leaves and berry clusters,
crimped edge **325.00**
Durand
3½", candle lamp, gold irid **125.00**
8", King Tut, orange irid ext., opal int. **275.00**
Fostoria, 5" h, gold, green leaves and
vines, white luster ground **125.00**
Imperial, ruffled blue and white double
hooked feather dec, matched set of 3 **325.00**
Hobbs Bruckunier, Coinspot, opalescent and amber optic, 4½" h, 7" d,
c1880 . . . . **50.00**
Jefferson, 9¼" h, 16" d, angular six
sided molded glass panels, alternating Art Deco stylized flame, mottled
orange, amber, brown, and yellow,
sgd "Jefferson" on gilt metal top rim **400.00**
Lalique, 12" d, dome, amber, molded
shells, sgd **500.00**
Northwood, 8¼", light pink, etched flow-
ers, frosted, ruffled **115.00**
Pairpoint, candle lamp, cut and frosted
amethyst glass **125.00**
Quezal
4½" h, lily, gold irid, ten ribbed blossom form, sgd "Quezal," four
matching sgd shades, one unsgd,
one faux sgd, set of 6 . . . . **850.00**
5" h, gold irid, five pulled feather designs outlined in green, luster int.,
sgd, matching set of 4 . . . . **650.00**
5⅛" h, pulled feather, gold irid int.,
applied webbing **175.00**
5¼" h, 12" d, flared aperture on domical shade, heavy walled opal
glass, opal irid coiled vertical zipper
pattern, sgd on inside collet **1,100.00**
7¾" h, 15" d, slightly ribbed half round
dome, cased, amber, opal white,
and gold–amber, irid, sgd on collet
edge **750.00**
Sandwich, 8½" h, 8¾" d, Gothic pattern,
frosted and cut **400.00**
Steuben
6" h, gas, ten ribs, opal ground, green
and gold pulled dec, irid gold int.,
fleur-de-lis mark on collet edge, pr **400.00**
7" h, swirled oval, gold aurene, flared
ruffled rim, fleur-de-lis mark **250.00**
10" d, dome, cased gold, applied gold
aurene rim border, amber and white

zigzag medial band, fleur-de-lis
mark on rim **1,800.00**
Tiffany Studio
3½", candle lamp, ruffled, Favrile . . . **300.00**
16" d, leaded, acorn, green, mottled
green–white, and white tiles, green
acorn border, metal label "Tiffany
Studios New York" **4,500.00**

LAMPS AND LIGHTING

History: Lighting devices have evolved from
simple stone age oil lamps to the popular electrified models of today. Aimé Argand patented the
first oil lamp in 1784. Around 1850 kerosene became a popular lamp burning fluid, replacing
whale oil and other fluids. In 1879 Thomas A.
Edison invented the electric light bulb, causing
fluid lamps to lose favor and creating a new field
for lamp manufacturers to develop. Companies
like Tiffany and Handel developed skills in the
manufacture of electric lamps, having their decorators produce beautiful aesthetic bases and
shades.

References: J. W. Courter, *Aladdin, The Magic
Name in Lamps,* Wallace-Homestead, 1980; J. W.
Courter, *Aladdin Collectors Manual & Price Guide
#13,* published by author, 1990; J. W. Courter,
Aladdin Electric Lamps, published by author,
1987; Robert De Falco, Carole Goldman Hibel,
John Hibel, *Handel Lamps,* H & D Press, Inc.,
1986; Dr. Larry Freeman, *New Light on Old
Lamps,* American Life Foundation, 1984; Nadja
Maril, *American Lighting: 1840–1940,* Schiffer
Publishing, 1989; Leland & Crystal Payton, *Turned
On: Decorative Lamps of the 'Fifties,* Abbeville
Press, 1989; Jo Ann Thomas, *Early Twentieth
Century Lighting Fixtures,* Collector Books, 1980;
Catherine M. V. Thuro, *Oil Lamps,* Wallace-Home-
stead, 1976; Catherine M. V. Thuro, *Oil Lamps II,*
Thorncliffe House, Inc., 1983.

Collectors' Club: The Mystic Light of the Alad-
din Knights, R.D. #1, Simpson, IL 62985; Histori-
cal Lighting Society of Canada, P.O. Box 561,
Postal Station R, Toronto, ON M4G 4E1; Rushlight
Club, Old Academy Library, 150 Main Street,
Wethersfield, CT 06109.

Museum: Winchester Center Kerosene Lamp
Museum, Winchester Center, CT.

Additional Listings: See specific makers and
Pattern Glass.

AMERICAN, EARLY

Betty Lamp
4¼" h, wrought, pitted, missing han-
ger **65.00**
4⅜" h, iron, black repaint, brass finial
plate, heart shaped thumb twist
latch, hanger, stamped crossed
hammer mark **125.00**

**Early American, pewter, brass cap, sin-
gle camphene burner, 8⅜" h, $250.00.**

4½" h, iron, brass heart finial, hanger,
stamped "1848" **375.00**
Crusie, 6½" h, wrought iron, double,
ram's horn finial, hanger, pitted **325.00**
Grease
5" h, wrought, sq pan, corner spouts,
twisted stem with swivel eye **75.00**
6¼" h, cast iron **375.00**
Hand, 2¾" h, pewter, marked "Wm
McQuilkin, Philada" **65.00**
Kettle, 8¾" h, wrought iron, cylindrical
font **225.00**
Lacemaker's, 10" h, blown, clear, cut
circles ring font **325.00**
Petticoat
3⅞" h, pewter, whale oil burner, cast
ear handle, marked "Morey &
Smith, warranted Boston" **155.00**
6¾" h, clear glass, Lyre and Star pattern, applied handle, pewter collar,
pewter and brass burning fluid
burner, snuffer cap **285.00**
Rushlight Holder, wrought iron
8¼" h, candle socket counter bal-
ance, wood base **300.00**
8¾" h, twisted stem, wood base . . . **125.00**
Wall, wrought iron, 20" h, circular back
plate, mounted with scrolling leaf tips,
central support with three scrolling
candle arms, mounted for electricity,
pr **1,760.00**
Whale Oil
8¼" h, pewter, double Bull's-eye lens **450.00**
8¾" h, pewter, applied handle, saucer
base **175.00**
10¼" h, pewter, Roswell Gleason, pr **850.00**

BOUDOIR

Handel, 14¼" h, circular top, sq shade with scalloped edge, sgd "Brown Handel 6034," riveted strapwork standard flaring to circular base, copper finish, imp "Handel" **750.00**

Victorian, blue, pink, yellow, and white mother of pearl satin glass shade, diamond quilted pattern, ruffled, silverplate and brass base **2,550.00**

CHANDELIERS

American

Art Deco

25" h, 34" d, silvered metal, molded and frosted shade, c1925, pr . . **2,500.00**

31¾" h, silvered metal framework, central six sided shade, molded stylized blossoms, six glass panels molded with basket of blossoms around sides **1,210.00**

Arts and Crafts

16¼" d, leaded glass, flared rect form, stylized sunray motif, yellow, aqua, and lavender slag glass, rim imp several times "Pat'd Oct 20 08," Prairie School, attributed to Bradley & Hubbard **275.00**

49" l, three heart cut out lanterns, cylindrical yellow glass liners, hammered copper frame and fluted edge, suspended by three chains **1,500.00**

Bradley & Hubbard, 58" h, 40" d, cast iron, twelve arms, clear fonts, burners, and crimped top chimneys, ceiling fitting marked "Patent date May 26, 1868" **1,100.00**

Gaslight, 43" h, brass, four arms, eight star shape ornaments, four orig acid-cut back and frosted shade with flowers and dragonflies design, 110 prisms, c1880 . . . . . . **1,500.00**

Tiffany

22¼" h, 13⅝" d, leaded glass, hexagonal bronze framework cast with iris leaves, bottom cast as roots, blue and green shaded glass set as Japanese iris, mottled pale peach ground, unsigned **9,900.00**

30" h, 20" d, gilt bronze Moorish style crown ring, twelve irid Favrile glass turtle back tiles, twelve hanging caged gold Favrile balls alternating with beaded and link chain dec, six lamp sockets . . . **23,000.00**

Venetian Glass, blown, eight scrolling arms, opalescent, applied colored floral dec, 23½" h **1,000.00**

FLOOR

Art Nouveau

62" h, gilt bronze serpent standard, basket weave base, Daum Nancy shade, titled "La Tentation," c1925, stamped "E Brandt" **10,000.00**

74" h, bronze, Greek style, four scrolled candle arms, central nozzle, reeded shaft, four paw feet, shaped sq base, mottled green and dark brown patina, sgd "Oscar B Bach," early 20th C, pr **4,000.00**

Arts and Crafts, 57" h, wrought iron, three part columnar shaft, double strap base, double, graduated sq collar, attributed to Frank Lloyd Wright for Arizona Biltmore Hotel, c1927 . . **1,760.00**

Bridge

54½" h **55.00**

61" h **135.00**

62" h, brass trim **175.00**

63½" h, handmade crewel shade . . **75.00**

Durand, 69" h, gilt metal, onyx, and brass standard, flared oval amber, opal, white, and blue crackle glass shade **650.00**

FLUID

Adams & Co, 12" h, clear and frosted font, clear and stippled four column base, flower display under glass in center with orig label, base can be inverted to serving bowl **900.00**

Atterbury & Co

7½" h, Gem pattern, clear font, amber pressed base with textured match striker panels on stem **100.00**

8¼"

Chapman pattern, clear **40.00**

Scroll, clear font, Gem pattern milk glass base **70.00**

9¼", Wave pattern, panel base, clear, marked "October 7th 1873" **50.00**

9½" h, Cottage pattern, panel base, clear, marked "Pat Oct 7th 1873" **45.00**

Beaumont Glass Co, 8½" h, Optic pattern, silver stained band with frosted leaves and flowers **275.00**

Belmont Glass Works, Bellaire, OH, 8⅞" h, clear font, canary yellow base . . . **175.00**

Boston Silver Glass Co, 12½" h, engraved pear shape font, pewter collar, marble base **550.00**

Central Glass Co, 9½" h, Columbian Coin pattern, milk glass **100.00**

Dalzell, Gilmore & Leighton, Findlay, Ohio, 8" h, Queen Heart pattern, clear font, medium green base **250.00**

Hobbs Glass Co.
Coin Dot pattern, blue and opalescent font, clear base, 8¾" h 600.00
Snowflake pattern, hand, cranberry and opalescent, clear applied handle, 2⅞" h 550.00
Limoges, 16¾" h, pale yellow and gold dec, colorful flower garlands, clear floral engraved chimney, marked under base "D & C/France," c1890 ... 175.00
McKee Glass Co, 9½" h, Ribbed Tulip pattern, clear font, milk glass base 125.00
Richards & Hartley, 8½" h, Three Panel pattern, apple green 175.00
Ripley, 12⅝" h, marriage, clear, brass collar and connector, kerosene burners and chimneys, marked "D.C. Ripley & Co, Patented Sept 28, 1870" 800.00
Riverside Glass Co, Findlay, OH, 9¼" h, Empress pattern, olive green, c1900 .... 150.00

HANGING

Adams & Westlake, double railway, cast bronze and brass, orig white enamel metal shades, 32" h, 30" w 1,200.00
American, 19½ h, 11" d, clear glass with engraved heart and thistle dec, baluster form, flaring lip, die rolled metal band and pendant, domed molded circular cov, three suspension chains, 19th C 2,650.00
Bradley & Hubbard, 52" h, store, emb brass font, opaque white shade, filler cap 550.00
Cast Iron, two arms, frosted and etched shades with flowers and butterflies, orig black and gold finish, 32" h, 26" w, c1870 .... 750.00
Galle, French, cameo glass
13½" d, spherical cameo shade, peach frosted ground, salmon red and umber overlay, etched nasturtiums, cameo sgd "Galle" 33,000.00
21½" d circular cameo glass shade, amber and white frosted ground, brown and green overlay, etched blossoms, three additional hanging shades, cameo sgd "Galle" on each, bronze ceiling cap with acanthus dec, suspending chains 44,000.00
Library, brass, cut and frosted glass font, brass shoulder and drip trough, conical shaped opaque white shade, hanger and chain, 25" h, c1880 ... 550.00
Peachblow, mother of pearl shade, deep pink to light pink shading, brass, 12½" h, orig chain and ceiling bracket 300.00
Victorian, brass, hall, deep ruby hobnail cylindrical shade, stamped brass fittings, 31" h, 1870–80 .... 250.00

STUDENT

Bridgeport Brass Co, nickel plated, opaque white shade, clear chimney, 14¾" h 325.00
Mercury, 22" h, brass, opaque white Vienna shade, font higher than reservoir, burner marked "Waterbury" ... 450.00
Nickel plated brass
20¼" h, opaque white cased shade, orig kerosene burner with tubular wick, chimney ring marked "Manhattan Brass Co" 200.00
31½" h, green shade cased in white, Welsbach gasoline mantle burner, marked "Pat Mar 20, 1900" 350.00

Table, Gone With The Wind style, hand painted dec, green ground, artist sgd, Fostoria burner, 31" h, $700.00.

TABLE

Adams & Co, 12⅞" h, Bradford pattern, clear and frosted font, black glass base with foliate engraved panels, c1880 .... 400.00
Art Glass, 14" h, sgd "Phoenix Studios" 200.00
Arts and Crafts, 10" h, wrought iron, three part columnar shaft, double strap base, double, graduated sq collar, attributed to Frank Lloyd Wright for Arizona Biltmore Hotel, c1927 .. 770.00
Cheuret, Albert, 15" h, three carved alabaster tulip shades, slender gilt bronze stems, sinuous leaf form base, inscribed "Albert Cheuret, Made in France," pr 17,600.00
Durand, 14" h, 9" d shallow domical

shade, bright green cased to opal white, gold irid leaf and vine dec, matching base, socket fixture **4,000.00**

Handel
18" d domed frosted glass shade, 23½" h base, reverse painted int. of country landscape, light brown patinated urn form vase, stepped circular foot, shade sgd "Handel," ring stamped "Handel Lamps," and patent no. **9,000.00**

18¼" d domed octagonal finely leaded shade, 23" h base, stylized green and white blossoms and leaves, mottled green, amber, and white ground, ring stamped "Handel Pat'd No. 979684," paneled standard and circular foot, brown patinated base cast "Handel" ... **10,000.00**

23" h, octagonal leaded reverse painted shade, lemon yellow int., four central panels with painted multicolored bouquets, light brown patinated drip pan base, four claw feet **4,000.00**

Heintz Co, Buffalo, NY, c1912, 15" h, 9½" d, patinated copper domical shade, silver overlay, angled arms, matching cylindrical base, socket replaced **750.00**

Jefferson, 10" d hemispherical reverse painted shade, 23" h base, int. lake scene, patinated bronze base, cast stylized dec, shade numbered and inscribed "Jefferson" **2,000.00**

Kuegler, George, American, 20th C, 29¼" h, 23" d amber, mauve, and green glass shade, leaded stylized foliate motif, geometric ground, three light brown patinated bronze base, cast scrolling foliage, masks, and strapwork imp "Gorham Co 094" .. **5,500.00**

Pairpoint
17½" d shade, 23½" h, sharply shouldered circular translucent glass shade, int. painted blossoms, leaves, and birds, deep green ground, stamped "The Pairpoint Corp," silvered bronze base, cast "Pairpoint D307" **6,000.00**

Subes, Raymond, 23½" h, 12½" domed alabaster shade, wrought iron base with foliate design **9,900.00**

Van Erp, Dirk
16" d shade, 15½" h, copper and mica shade, bullet form cap, four sinuous arm supports, copper melon form base, stamped windmill mark and "Dirk Van Erp" in broken box, c1912 .... **46,200.00**

16½" d shade, 8¼" h, conical shade, four mica panels, flaring battens,

reticulated heat cap, four scrolling arms, copper baluster base, stamped windmill mark and "Dirk Van Erp" in unbroken box, c1911 **15,400.00**

23½" d shade, 27" h, broadly sweeping shade with four mica panels, spade form battens, vented cap and collar base, four sinuous arm supports, copper ginger jar base, stamped windmill mark and "Dirk Van Erp" in broken box, c1911 .. **60,500.00**

LANTERNS

History: A lantern is an enclosed, portable light source, hand carried or attached to a bracket or pole to illuminate an area. Many lanterns can be used both indoors and outdoors and have a protected flame. Fuels used in early lanterns included candles, kerosene, whale oil, coal oil, and later gasoline, natural gas, and batteries.

Kerosene, tin, orig flue, "Harr's Cold Blast," C. T. Ham Co, Rochester, NY, 16½" h, $100.00.

Architectural
18" d, 9½" d, ext., Arts and Crafts style, domical copper cov over cylindrical shade, lattice banding, textured amber glass lamber supported by rect wall bracket, c1905 ..... **300.00**

18½", Diamond, three cornered shape, turret top, rear hanger, tin back, two glass front sides, iron candle socket **225.00**

Bicycle
6", nickel plated, marked "Hawthorne Mfg Co, Old Sol Pat USA" **50.00**

7¾' h, Majestic model, nickel plated, clear lens, faceted red and green side lights, c1900 .... **160.00**

Buggy, E. T. Wright & Co, 9" h, orig black paint, late 19th C **75.00**

Candle, 11" h, tin, clear pressed globe, black paint, ring handle **275.00**

Darkroom, 8¾" h, triangular, tin, ruby
glass panels, outside filler cap, brass
label marked "The Challenge" **35.00**
Dashboard, 15" h, spring clips, reflector,
orig red paint, sgd brass label, Kemp
Mfg Co, c1900 .... **150.00**
Dietz
Inspector's, globe marked New York
Central System logo, pressed mark
on back "Ideal Inspector Lamp,"
late 19th C **65.00**
Kerosene, US Navy, brass, marked
"US Navy" **75.00**
Tubular Jr, brass **80.00**
Hall, 29" h, Georgian style, brass plated,
three light **200.00**
Marine
8⅛" h, brass, Fresnel shade, late 19th
C **30.00**
10½" h, brass, Wilcox, Crittendon &
Co, Inc, late 19th C **200.00**
Miner
Galvanized
9½" h, wire hanger, late 19th C .. **25.00**
16¼" h, green paint, label "N L
Piper Co, Toronto," late 19th C **150.00**
Iron, 8" h, iron, chicken finial, wick
pick **250.00**
Sheet metal, 11" h, curved cobalt blue
glass, int. reflector, orig gray paint,
made by Metal Industries Ltd,
Hamilton, Canada, c1900 ...... **200.00**
Tin, marked "Gateshead on Tyne,"
Patterson Lames, Ltd **50.00**
Pierced Tin, 12", New England Glass
Co, patent Oct 24, 1854 .... **175.00**
Pocket, 5¾" h, folding, black and gold
lithograph of man seated on train,
ruby glass panel, c1870 .... **200.00**
Political, voting booth, marked "Ham's" **75.00**
Railroad
7" h, bracket, brass, Williams & Page
Co, Boston, Mass, 1870–80 .... **125.00**
10" h, calcium carbide operated,
marked "The Oxweld Railroad
Lamp," late 19th C **30.00**
11⅛" h, N L Piper Railway Supply Co
Ltd, bulls-eye front lens, orig red
and green sides glasses, corru-
gated reflector lined door, Simplex
burner **200.00**
Rayo
No. 60 CB **90.00**
Pony #15 .... **90.00**
Reflector, 15½" h, Dietz & Co, Model
No 30, sgd, late 19th C **110.00**
Skater's
6½" h, brass, clear globe **45.00**
7" h, brass, bail, kerosene burner,
clear globe **130.00**
7¼" h, tin, clear globe **55.00**

LEEDS CHINA

History: The Leeds Pottery in Yorkshire, England, began production about 1758. Among its
products was creamware that was competitive with
that of Wedgwood. The initial factory closed in
1820, but various subsequent owners continued
until 1880. They made exceptional cream colored
ware, either plain, salt-glazed, or painted with colored enamels, and glazed and unglazed redware.

Early wares are unmarked. Later pieces bear
marks of "Leeds Pottery," sometimes followed by
"Hartley-Green and Co." or the letters "LP". Reproductions also have these marks.

Reference: Susan and Al Bagdade, *Warman's
English & Continental Pottery & Porcelain, 1st Edition,* Warman Publishing Co., Inc., 1987.

Platter, 18th century, $900.00.

Bowl, oval, ftd, reticulated **175.00**
Charger, 15½" d, five color urn, floral
spray, blue feathered edge **450.00**
Chestnut Bowl, cov, reticulated band,
twisted rope handles, 1790–1800 .. **775.00**
Creamer, 3⅜" h, brown, yellow dec .. **125.00**
Cup and Saucer, five color, floral and
cross hatched dec **125.00**
Cup Plate, 3¾" d, Gaudy, blue floral dec **245.00**
Figure, 17" h, stallion, creamware, black
mane and tail, halter and lead, green,
blue, and black sponged base, restored chip on base, c1800 ....**27,500.00**
Jug, 4½" h, baluster, transfer print, underglaze blue, iron–red, yellow,
green, and brown enameled scene of
hunter and two hounds, silver resist
border, blue floral garland, c1815 .. **285.00**
Loving Cup, 4⅞" h, two handles ending

in leaf terminals, three color flowers, inscribed "Robert Hill 1791" 400.00

Plate

7¼" d, eagle dec, underglaze blue, brown, yellow, and green 240.00

8¾" d, creamware, blue flowers and leaves, scalloped blue border . . . 125.00

9½" d, Chinese landscape, underglaze blue, c1780 . . . . 450.00

Platter, 16½" l, creamware, blue feather edge 200.00

Snuff Box, cov, 2¾" d, waisted cylindrical, iron–red, puce, yellow, and green painted floral sprays, floral wreath, inscribed "When This You See, Remember Me, W. G. 1779," and "A Pinch Of This Deserv's A Kiss" 585.00

Sugar, cov, multicolored dec, shell handles, button finial 265.00

Teapot, 7¼" h, Gaudy, blue and white floral dec, repairs to spout and lid . . 265.00

Toddy Plate, 5½" d, peafowl in tree, five color dec 275.00

LENOX   SELLER.

LENOX CHINA

History: In 1889 Jonathan Cox and Walter Scott Lenox established The Ceramic Art Co. at Trenton, New Jersey. By 1906 Lenox formed his own company, Lenox, Inc. Using potters lured from Belleek, Lenox began making an American version of this famous ware.

Older Lenox china has two marks: a green wreath and a palette. The palette mark appears on blanks supplied to amateurs who hand painted china as a hobby. The Lenox Company still exists and currently uses a gold stamped mark.

Reference: Mary Frank Gaston, *American Belleek,* Collector Books, 1984.

Additional Listings: Belleek.

Bouillon Cup, ivory ground, gold rim, sterling silver ftd holder, green wreath mark, set of 10 . . . . 375.00

Bowl, Patriots 150.00

Box, cov, 3¾ x 4¾", spray of flowers in relief, green wreath mark 45.00

Cake Set, 10½" d low pedestal plate, six 7½" d plates, Mimosa pattern, green wreath mark, 7 pcs 185.00

Children's Feeding Dishes, mug and bowl, roosters and chickens dec, green wreath mark 100.00

Compote, Autumn pattern 45.00

Creamer and Sugar, Wheat pattern . . 40.00

Cup and Saucer, Wheat pattern 18.00

Decanter Set, decanter, five shot glasses, ivory, gold trim, green wreath mark 115.00

Dinnerware, Kingsley pattern, service for eight, 40 pcs 600.00

Figure

Bird, 3¼" h, white, green wreath USA mark

Tail turned down 40.00

Tail turned up 40.00

Penguin, black, white, and red, green wreath mark 175.00

Seal, bisque 135.00

Swan, 5" l, gold mark 50.00

Mug, cobalt blue, sterling silver overlay bands 75.00

Plate

9" d, Neoclassical urn and swag border, gilt and blue enamel dec, white ground, retailed by Tiffany & Co, set of 12 . . . . 275.00

10" d, ivory, gold and black floral rims, marked "Lenox, Tiffany & Co," set of 6 . . . . 150.00

Salt and Pepper Shakers, pr, figural, yellow birds, green wreath mark . . . 35.00

Teapot, 3¾", brown glaze, sterling silver overlay, green wreath and unicorn mark 165.00

Toby Jug, William Penn 165.00

Vase, At The Fountain, green top and bottom bands, green wreath mark, c1915–30, 10½" h, $225.00.

Vase

8½" h, Acanthus Leaf pattern, green mark, pr 165.00

9¼" h, pate–sur–pate, white prunus blossoms, birds, and trees, celadon ground, green wreath mark 175.00

LIBBEY GLASS

History: In 1888 Edward Libbey established the Libbey Glass Company in Toledo, Ohio, after the closing of the New England Glass Works of W. L. Libbey and Son in East Cambridge, Massachusetts. The new Libbey company produced quality cut glass for the "Brilliant Period."

In 1930 Libbey's interest in art glass production was renewed. A. Douglas Nash was employed as a designer in 1931.

The factory continues production today as Libbey Glass Co.

Reference: Carl U. Fauster, *Libbey Glass Since 1818—Pictorial History & Collector's Guide,* Len Beach Press, 1979.

Additional Listings: Amberina Glass and Cut Glass.

Candlestick, acid marked "Libbey," 6" h, $400.00.

Bon Bon, amberina, shape #3029, six pointed 1½" fuchsia rim, shallow pale amber bowl, 1½" h, 7" d, sgd	585.00
Bowl, 7" d, amberina, ruffled flared rim, sgd	350.00
Compote, 11" d, 7½" h, clear crystal bowl, fiery opalescent figural elephant stem and platform base, Libbey trademark, designed by Douglas Nash	550.00
Goblet, 7" h, clear, opal cat silhouette stem, sgd	125.00
Pickle Castor, amberina, Swirled Rib pattern, ftd Meriden frame	450.00
Pitcher, 8¾" h, Maize, amber irid, blue husks, applied strap handle, Joseph Locke patent	590.00
Punch Bowl, 14" d, cut, American Brilliant Period, stenciled "Libbey"	700.00
Salt Shaker, Maize, creamy opaque, yellow husks, orig top	90.00
Sherbet	
Cut Glass, set of 12, underplate, American Brilliant Period	900.00
Figural opalescent rabbit stem, sgd	70.00

Vase	
9" h, lily, vertical ribbing pattern, amber to fuchsia	400.00
11¼" h, 4" d deep red ball shaped bowl, 7½" l hollow amber stem, 4" d circular base, sgd	1,000.00
12" h, baluster, etched	250.00
Water Carafe, maize custard, yellow husks outlined in gold	300.00

LIMITED EDITION COLLECTOR PLATES

History: Bing and Grondahl made the first collector plate in 1895. Royal Copenhagen issued their first Christmas plate in 1908.

In the late 1960s and early 1970s, several potteries, glass factories, mints, and artists began issuing plates commemorating people, animals, events, etc. Christmas plates were supplemented by Mother's Day plates, Easter plates, etc. A sense of speculation swept the field, fostered in part by flamboyant ads in newspapers and flashy direct mail promotions.

Collectors often favor the first plate issued in a series above all others. Condition is a prime factor. Having the original box also increases price.

Limited edition collector plates, more than any other object in this guide, should be collected for design and pleasure and only secondarily as an investment.

References: *The Bradford Book of Collector Plates, 12th Edition,* published by Bradford Exchange, 1987; Diane Carnevale, exec. ed., *Collectibles Market Guide & Price Index To Limited Edition Plates, Figurines, Bells, Graphics, Christmas Ornaments, and Dolls, Seventh Edition,* Collectors' Information Bureau, 1990; Gene Ehlert, *The Official Price Guide To Collector Plates, Fifth Edition,* House of Collectibles, 1988; Paul Stark, *Limited Edition Collectibles, Everything You May Ever Need To Know,* New Gallery Press, 1988.

Periodicals: Collector Editions, 170 Fifth Ave, New York, NY 10010; Collectors Mart, Inc. 15100 W. Kellogg, Wichita, KS 67235; Plate World Publication, 9200 N. Maryland Ave., Niles, IL 60648.

Collectors' Club: International Plate Collectors Guild, P.O. Box 487, Artesia, CA 90701.

Museum: Bradford Museum, Niles, IL.

Additional Listings: See *Warman's Americana & Collectibles* for more examples of collector plates plus many other limited edition collectibles.

BAREUTHER (Germany)

Christmas Plates, Hans Mueller artist, 8" d	
1967 Stiftskirche, FE	100.00
1968 Kapplkirche	35.00
1970 Chapel in Oberndorf	18.00

1972 Christmas in Munich	35.00
1974 Church In The Black Forest . .	20.00
1976 Chapel in the Hills	25.00
1978 Mittenwald	30.00
1980 Miltenberg	38.00
1982 Bad Wimpfen	40.00
1984 Zeil on the River Main	42.50
1986 Christmas in Forchhe	42.50

Father's Day Series, Hans Mueller artist, 8″ d

1969 Castle Neuschwanstein	48.00
1970 Castle Pfalz	15.00
1972 Castle Hohenschwangau	30.00
1974 Wurzburg Castle	45.00
1976 Castle Hohenzollern	25.00
1978 Castle Falkenstein	30.00
1980 Castle Cochum	35.00
1982 Castle Zwingenberg	40.00
1984 Castle Neuenstein	42.50

Mother's Day

1969 Mother & Children, FE	75.00
1970 Mother & Children	30.00
1972 Mother & Children	22.00
1974 Musical Children	35.00
1976 Rocking The Cradle	28.00
1978 Blind Man's Bluff	28.00
1980 The First Cherries	35.00
1982 Suppertime	40.00
1984 Village Children	42.50

BERLIN (Germany)

Christmas Plates, various artists, 7¾″ d

1970 Christmas In Bernkastel	130.00
1972 Christmas In Michelstadt	50.00
1974 Christmas In Bremen	25.00
1976 Christmas Eve In Augsburg . .	30.00
1978 Christmas Market At The Berlin Cathedral	55.00
1980 Christmas Eve in Mittenberg . .	55.00
1982 Christmas Eve In Wasserburg .	55.00
1984 Christmas in Ramsau	50.00
1986 Christmas Eve in Gelnhaus . .	65.00

Bing and Grondahl, Christmas, 1954, $100.00.

BING AND GRONDAHL (Denmark)

Christmas Plates, various artists, 7″ d

1895 Behind The Frozen Window . .	3,600.00
1896 New Moon Over Snow Covered Trees	1,475.00
1897 Christmas Meal Of The Sparrows	1,100.00
1898 Christmas Roses And Christmas Star	600.00
1899 The Crows Enjoying Christmas	900.00
1900 Church Bells Chiming In Christmas	800.00
1901 The Three Wise Men From The East	485.00
1902 Interior Of A Gothic Church . .	285.00
1903 Happy Expectation of Children	150.00
1904 View of Copenhagen From Frederiksberg Hill	125.00
1905 Anxiety Of The Coming Christmas Night	130.00
1906 Sleighing To Church On Christmas Eve	100.00
1907 The Little Match Girl	125.00
1908 St. Petri Church of Copenhagen	85.00
1909 Happiness Over The Yule Tree	100.00
1910 The Old Organist	90.00
1911 First It Was Sung By Angels To Shepherds In The Fields	80.00
1912 Going To Church On Christmas Eve	80.00
1913 Bringing Home The Yule Tree	85.00
1914 Royal Castle of Amalienborg, Copenhagen	75.00
1915 Chained Dog Getting Double Meal On Christmas Eve	120.00
1916 Christmas Prayer of the Sparrows	85.00
1917 Arrival Of The Christmas Boat	75.00
1918 Fishing Boat Returning Home For Christmas	85.00
1919 Outside The Lighted Window	80.00
1920 Hare In The Snow	75.00
1921 Pigeons In The Castle Court	55.00
1922 Star Of Bethlehem	60.00
1923 Royal Hunting Castle, The Hermitage	55.00
1924 Lighthouse In Danish Waters	65.00
1925 The Child's Christmas	70.00
1926 Churchgoers On Christmas Day	65.00
1927 Skating Couple	110.00
1928 Eskimo Looking At Village Church In Greenland	60.00
1929 Fox Outside Farm On Christmas Eve	75.00
1930 Yule Tree In Town Hall Square Of Copenhagen	85.00
1932 Lifeboat At Work	90.00
1934 Church Bell In Tower	75.00
1936 Royal Guard Outside Amalienborg Castle In Copenhagen	70.00

1938 Lighting The Candles	110.00
1940 Delivering Christmas Letters	170.00
1942 Danish Farm On Christmas Night	150.00
1944 Sorgenfri Castle	120.00
1946 Commemoration Cross In Honor Of Danish Sailors Who Lost Their Lives In World War II	85.00
1948 Watchman, Sculpture Of Town Hall, Copenhagen	80.00
1950 Kronborg Castle At Elsinore	150.00
1952 Old Copenhagen Canals At Wintertime With Thorvaldsen Museum In Background	85.00
1954 Birthplace Of Hans Christian Andersen, With Snowman	100.00
1956 Christmas In Copenhagen	140.00
1958 Santa Claus	100.00
1960 Danish Village Church	180.00
1962 Winter Night	80.00
1964 The Fir Tree And Hare	50.00
1966 Home For Christmas	50.00
1968 Christmas In Church	45.00
1970 Pheasants In The Snow At Christmas	20.00
1972 Christmas In Greenland	20.00
1974 Christmas In The Village	20.00
1976 Christmas Welcome	25.00
1978 A Christmas Tale	30.00
1980 Christmas In The Woods	42.50
1982 The Christmas Tree	55.00
1984 Christmas Letter	55.00
1986 Silent Night, Holy Night	55.00

Jubilee, various artists

1915 Frozen Window	225.00
1920 Church Bells	65.00
1925 Dog Outside Window	285.00
1930 The Old Organist	225.00
1935 Little Match Girl	900.00
1940 Three Wise Men	1,950.00
1945 Amalienborg Castle	150.00
1950 Eskimos	175.00
1955 Dybbol Mill	200.00
1960 Kronborg Castle	100.00
1965 Churchgoers	40.00
1970 Amalienborg Castle	35.00
1975 Horses Enjoying Meal	50.00
1980 Yule Tree	60.00
1985 Lifeboat at Work	65.00

HAVILAND & PARLON (France)

Christmas Series, various artists, 10″ d

1972 Madonna And Child, Raphael, FE	80.00
1973 Madonnina, Feruzzi	100.00
1975 Madonna And Child, Murillo	45.00
1977 Madonna And Child, Bellini	40.00
1979 Madonna Of The Eucharist, Botticelli	150.00

Haviland Parlon, 1975, Unicorn Surrounded, $75.00.

Lady And The Unicorn Series, artist unknown, 10″ d

1977 To My Only Desire, FE	60.00
1979 Sound	50.00
1981 Scent	60.00

Tapestry Series, artist unknown, 10″ d

1971 The Unicorn In Captivity	145.00
1973 Chase Of The Unicorn	120.00
1975 The Unicorn Surrounded	75.00

LALIQUE (France)

Annual Series, lead crystal, Marie-Claude Lalique, artist, 8½″ d

1965 Deux Oiseaux (Two Birds), FE	800.00
1967 Ballet de Poisson (Fish Ballet)	200.00
1969 Papillon (Butterfly)	80.00
1971 Hibou (Owl)	60.00
1973 Petit Geai (Jayling)	60.00
1975 Due de Poisson (Fish Duet)	75.00

LENOX (United States)

Boehm Bird Series, Edward Marshall Boehm, artist, 10½″ d

1970 Wood Thrush, FE	225.00
1971 Goldfinch	65.00
1973 Meadowlark	60.00
1975 American Redstart	50.00
1977 Robins	55.00
1979 Golden-Crowned Kinglets	65.00
1981 Eastern Phoebes	100.00

Boehm Woodland Wildlife Series, Edward Marshall Boehm, artist, 10½″ d

1973 Raccoons, FE	80.00
1975 Cottontail Rabbits	60.00

1977 Beaver	60.00
1979 Squirrels	75.00
1981 Martens	100.00

LLARDO (Spain)

Christmas, 8″ d, undisclosed artists

1971 Caroling	30.00
1972 Carolers	35.00
1974 Carolers	75.00
1976 Christ Child	50.00
1978 Caroling Child	50.00

Mother's Day, undisclosed artists

1971 Kiss of the Child	75.00
1972 Birds & Chicks	30.00
1974 Nursing Mother	135.00
1976 Vigil	50.00
1978 New Arrival	55.00

RECO INTERNATIONAL (United States)

Christmas Series, Royale, various artists

1969 Christmas Fair, FE	125.00
1970 Vigil Mass	100.00
1971 Christmas Night	50.00
1972 Elks	40.00
1973 Christmas Down	35.00
1974 Village Christmas	60.00
1975 Feeding Time	35.00
1976 Seaport Christmas	30.00
1977 Sledding	30.00

REED & BARTON (United States)

Audubon Serioes, various artists

1970 Pine Siskin, FE	175.00
1971 Red-Shouldered Hawk	75.00
1972 Stilt Sandpiper	70.00
1973 Red Cardinal	70.00
1974 Boreal Chickadee	60.00
1975 Yellow Breasted Chat	60.00
1976 Bay-Breasted Warbler	60.00
1977 Purple Finch	65.00

ROSENTHAL (Germany)

Christmas Plates, various artists, 8½″ d

1910 Winter Peace	550.00
1911 The Three Wise Men	325.00
1912 Shooting Stars	250.00
1913 Christmas Lights	235.00
1914 Christmas Song	350.00
1915 Walking To Church	180.00
1916 Christmas During War	235.00
1918 Peace On Earth	210.00
1920 The Manger In Bethlehem	325.00
1922 Advent Branch	200.00
1924 Deer In The Woods	200.00
1926 Christmas In The Mountains	175.00
1928 Chalet Christmas	175.00

1930 Group Of Deer Under The Pines	225.00
1932 Christ Child	200.00
1934 Christmas Peace	200.00
1936 Núrnberg Angel	185.00
1938 Christmas In The Alps	190.00
1940 Marien Church in Danzig	250.00
1942 Marianburg Castle	300.00
1944 Wood Scape	275.00
1946 Christmas In An Alpine Valley	250.00
1948 Message To The Shepherds	875.00
1950 Christmas In The Forest	185.00
1952 Christmas In The Alps	190.00
1954 Christmas Eve	185.00
1956 Christmas In The Alps	190.00
1958 Christmas Eve	190.00
1960 Christmas In Small Village	200.00
1962 Christmas Eve	185.00
1964 Christmas Market In Núrnberg	225.00
1966 Christmas In Ulm	250.00
1968 Christmas In Bremen	195.00
1970 Christmas In Cologne	165.00
1972 Christmas Celebration In Franconia	90.00
1974 Christmas In Wurzburg	100.00

Royal Copenhagen, 1963, Hojsager Mill, $80.00.

ROYAL COPENHAGEN

Christmas Plates, various artists, 6″ d 1908, 1909, 1910; 7″ 1911 to present

1908 Madonna And Child	1,775.00
1909 Danish Landscape	150.00
1910 The Magi	120.00
1911 Danish Landscape	135.00
1912 Elderly Couple By Christmas Tree	120.00
1913 Spire Of Frederik's Church, Copenhagen	125.00
1914 Sparrows In Tree At Church Of The Holy Spirit, Copenhagen	100.00
1915 Danish Landscape	150.00
1916 Shepherd In The Field On Christmas Night	85.00

1917 Tower Of Our Savior's Church, Copenhagen	90.00
1918 Sheep and Shepherds	80.00
1919 In The Park	80.00
1920 Mary With The Child Jesus	75.00
1921 Aabenraa Marketplace	75.00
1922 Three Singing Angels	70.00
1923 Danish Landscape	70.00
1924 Christmas Star Over The Sea And Sailing Ship	100.00
1925 Street Scene From Christianshavn, Copenhagen	85.00
1926 View of Christmas Canal, Copenhagen	75.00
1927 Ship's Boy At The Tiller On Christmas Night	140.00
1928 Vicar's Family On Way To Church	75.00
1929 Grundtvig Church, Copenhagen	100.00
1930 Fishing Boats On The Way To The Harbor	80.00
1932 Frederiksberg Gardens With Statue Of Frederik VI	90.00
1934 The Hermitage Castle	115.00
1936 Roskilde Cathedral	130.00
1938 Round Church In Osterlars On Bornholm	200.00
1940 The Good Shepherd	300.00
1942 Bell Tower of Old Church In Jutland	300.00
1944 Typical Danish Winter Scene	160.00
1946 Zealand Village Church	150.00
1948 Nodebo Church At Christmastime	150.00
1950 Boeslunde Church, Zealand	175.00
1952 Christmas In The Forest	120.00
1954 Amalienborg Palace, Copenhagen	150.00
1956 Rosenborg Castle, Copenhagen	160.00
1958 Sunshine Over Greenland	140.00
1960 The Stag	140.00
1962 The Little Mermaid At Wintertime	200.00
1964 Fetching The Christmas Tree	75.00
1966 Blackbird At Christmastime	55.00
1968 The Last Umiak	40.00
1970 Christmas Rose And Cat	100.00
1972 In The Desert	85.00
1974 Winter Twilight	80.00
1976 Danish Watermill	80.00
1978 Greenland Scenery	80.00
1980 Bringing Home The Christmas Tree	60.00
1982 Waiting For Christmas	65.00
1984 Jingle Bells	55.00
1986 Wait for Me	55.00

Mother's Day Plates, various artists, 6¼″ d

1971 American Mother	125.00
1972 Oriental Mother	60.00
1974 Greenland Mother	55.00
1976 Mermaids	50.00
1978 Mother And Child	25.00
1980 An Outing With Mother	35.00
1982 The Children's Hour	45.00

ROYAL DOULTON (Great Britain)

Beswick Christmas Series, various artists, earthenware in hand-cast bas-relief, 8″ sq

1972 Christmas In England, FE	40.00
1974 Christmas In Bulgaria	40.00
1976 Christmas In Holland	45.00
1978 Christmas In America	45.00

Mother And Child Series, Edna Hibel artist, 8¼″ d

1973 Colette And Child, FE	450.00
1974 Sayuri And Child	150.00
1976 Marilyn And Child	120.00
1978 Kathleen And Child	100.00

Valentine's Day Series, artists unknown, 8¼″ d

1976 Victorian Boy And Girl	60.00
1978 If I Loved You	40.00
1980 On A Swing	40.00
1982 From My Heart	40.00
1984 Love In Bloom	40.00

Wedgwood (Great Britain)

Christmas Series, jasper stoneware, 8″ d

1969 Windsor Castle, FE	225.00
1971 Piccadilly Circus, London	40.00
1973 The Tower Of London	45.00
1975 Tower Bridge	40.00
1977 Westminster Abbey	48.00
1979 Buckingham Palace	55.00
1981 Marble Arch	75.00
1983 All Souls, Langham Palace	80.00
1985 The Tate Gallery	80.00
1987 Guildhall	80.00

Mother's Day, jasper stoneware, 6½″ d

1971 Sportive Love, FE	25.00
1973 The Baptism Of Achilles	20.00
1975 Mother And Child	35.00
1977 Leisure Time	30.00
1979 Deer and Fawn	35.00
1981 Mare And Foal	50.00
1983 Cupid And Butterfly	55.00
1985 Cupids and Doves	55.00
1987 Anemones	55.00

LIMOGES

History: Limoges porcelain has been produced in Limoges, France, for over a century by numerous factories other than the famed Haviland. One of the most frequently encountered marks is "T. & V. Limoges" which is the ware made by Tressman and Vought. Other identifiable Limoges marks are A. L. (A. Lanternier), J. P. L (J. Pouyat, Limoges), M. R. (M. Reddon), Elite and Coronet.

References: Susan and Al Bagdade, *Warman's English & Continental Pottery & Porcelain, 1st Edition,* Warman Publishing Co., Inc., 1987; Mary Frank Gaston, *The Collector's Encyclopedia Of Limoges Porcelain,* Collector Books, 1980.

Additional Listings: Haviland China.

Biscuit Jar, cov, multicolored flowers, artist sgd	75.00
Bowl, 12″, oval, holly dec, marked "T & V"	100.00
Butter Dish, cov, floral and gold dec	100.00
Cake Plate, 12″ d, open handles, grapes dec, gold trim	75.00
Candlesticks, pr, 5″ h, handled, gold and pastel Art Deco dec	100.00
Celery Dish, 6½ x 13½″, gold scalloped border, green and gray floral border, pink floral center, green marked "GDA/France"	45.00

Chocolate Pot, carnation dec, white ground, gold trim, marked "T & V," 9¼″ h, $125.00.

Chocolate Pot, 9½″ h, melon ribbed, burgundy and gold top and handle, pink and yellow floral dec	185.00
Creamer and Sugar, pink flowers, gold trim, marked "Haviland & Co, Limoges"	70.00
Demitasse Cup and Saucers, floral dec, marked green and red "Theo Haviland, Limoges," set of 6	90.00
Ewer, 6″ h, 8½″ d, royal blue, gold dec and handle, marked "Jacob Petit"	225.00
Fish Set, ten 9½″ d plates, oval sauce boat with underplate, ruffled edges, wide gold rim, central enameled fish portrait, sgd "J Golse," printed marks, early 20th C	650.00
Hair Receiver, hp, bluebirds, gold trim, three small feet	100.00
Game Plaque, 13¼″ l, bird dec, scal-	

loped gold rococo border, sgd "Dubois"	300.00
Game Plate, 10½″ d, hp, facing pair, multicolored pheasants on one, quail on other, natural woodland setting, heavy gold rococo border, pierced for hanging, pr	350.00
Humidor, shaded brown ground, gnomes smoking long Meerschaum pipes, artist sgd "Holmes, Dec 25, 1909," marked "GDA Limoges"	150.00
Jardiniere, 7½″ h, 11″ d, hp, yellow, white, and mulberry roses, enamel highlights, white enamel scroll rim dec, marked "Limoges, France"	300.00
Mug, 6″ h, burgundy and green, grapes, leaves, and vines, arched female figural handle	150.00
Nappy, 10″ d, handle, maple leaf shape, large pink roses dec, marked "Elite, Limoges, France"	65.00
Oyster Plate, 9″, marked "Limoges" and "Tiffany & Co, NY"	85.00
Pitcher	
8½″ h, milk, white, rope and anchor handle	85.00
12″ h, tankard, hp, three color grape cluster dec, emb handle and base, marked "T & V"	150.00
14¾″ h, tankard, gooseberries, artist sgd "Le Roy, H W Guerin, Limoges, France"	290.00
Plaque, 8 x 11″, underglaze blue dec, open seascape with icebergs and sailing vessels, wood frame, printed "D & Co" mark, late 19th C	425.00
Plate	
7″ d, hp, pink and white chrysanthemums, green, and yellow ground, scalloped gold trim, artist sgd	85.00
9″ d, fisherman on riverbank, formal black framed gold border, 1878	50.00
Platter	
13¾″ l, yellow and orange roses	145.00
16½″ l, pink flowers, white ground, dated January 1911, marked "T & V Limoges, Depose"	85.00
Presidential Plate, 8⅝″ d, service of William Henry Harrison, scalloped out rim, outer gilt cornstalk border, inner underglaze blue banding dec with stars, central polychrome dec eagle, marked "T & V France" and "Harrison 1892"	850.00
Punch Bowl, 9½″ d, 4½″ h, three colored grape cluster and foliage, pink int., pink and yellow ext., scalloped edge, gold trim, marked "TV"	200.00
Sardine Set, 5½ x 4½″ cov box, 10 x 9″ tray, swimming fish, starfish, shells and seaweed, pink and blue, marked "TV"	250.00

Vase

9″ h, scenic dec, gold dragon handles and collar, artist sgd "Jean Pouyat" — **90.00**

12½″ h, hp, yellow and brown birds, flowering trees, artist sgd — **125.00**

12½″ h, 9″ l, hp, oval cylinder, white yellow, and ruby roses, multicolored ground, two attached gold ring handles, four gold ball feet, artist "M Perl," marked "Limoges, France" — **550.00**

13¾″ h, baluster form, polychrome floral dec — **50.00**

14¼″ h, hp, ovoid form, chestnut branch dec — **90.00**

Vegetable Dish, 9″ l, cov, oval, blue flowers, marked "Theo Haviland, Limoges" — **50.00**

LINENS

History: The term linen now has become a generic designation for household dressings for table, bed, or bath, whether made of linen, cotton, lace, or other fabrics.

Linen, as a table cover, is mentioned in the Bible and other writings of an early age. We see "borde cloths" in early drawings and paintings with their creases pressed in sharply. It was a sign of wealth and social standing to present such elegance.

During the period before the general use of forks when fingers were the accepted means of dining, napkins were important. They usually were rectangular and large in size. In the early 18th century, napkins lost their popularity. The fork had become the tool of the upper classes who apparently wished to show off their new found expertise in the use of the fork. After diners did much damage to tablecloths, finicky hostesses decided that the napkin was a necessity. It soon reappeared on the table.

The Victorian era gave us the greatest variety of household linens. The lady of the house had time to sit and sew a fine seam. Sewing became a social activity. Afternoon callers brought their handwork with them when they came to gossip and take tea. Every young girl was expected to fill her hope chest with fine examples of her prowess. In the late 19th century these ladies made some very beautiful "white work," using white embroidery of delicate stitchery, lace insertions, and ruffles on white fabrics. These pieces are highly sought after today.

The 20th century saw a decline in that type of fine stitchery. The social pace quickened. Household linens of that period show more bright colors in the embroidery, the designs become more lighthearted and frivolous, and inexpensive machine made lace was used. Kitchen towels were decorated with animals or pots and pans. Vanity sets dominated the bedroom; the Bridge craze put emphasis on tablecloths and napkin sets. To fill the desire for less expensive lace cloths and bedspreads, women of the Depression started crocheting. Many examples of this craft are available.

With the advent of World War II, more women went to work. The last remnant of fine stitchery quickly diminished. Technological advances in production and fibers lessened the interest in hand made linens.

Collecting And Use Tips: Most old linens are fragile, some are age stained from being stored improperly for years. Unless you have a secret for removing these stains without damaging the fabric, look for those items in very good or better condition.

Linens which are not used frequently are best stored unpressed, rolled Boy Scout style, and tucked away in an old pillowcase out of bright light. Be sure the linens and pillowcases have been rinsed several times to remove all residue of detergent.

For laundered pieces which are used often, wrap in acid free white tissue or muslin folders. If the tissue is not acid free, it will cause the folded edges to discolor. If possible, store on rollers to prevent creasing. Creased areas become weak and disintegrate in laundering. Acid-free wrapping material can be purchased from Talas, 104 Fifth Avenue, New York, NY 10011.

References: Virginia Churchill Bath, *Lace*, Henry Regnery Co., 1974; Lois Markrich and Heinz Edgar Kiewe, *Victorian Fancywork*, Henry Regnery Co., 1974; *McCall's Needlework Treasury*, Random House, 1963; Francis M. Montgomery, *Textiles In America, 1650–1870*, W. W. Norton & C. (A Winterthur/Barra Book); Patricia Esterbrook Roberts, *Table Settings. Entertaining And Etiquette. A History And Guide*, Viking Press, 1967.

Collectors' Club: International Old Lacers, Box 1029, West Minster, CO 80030.

Museums: Metropolitan Museum of Art, New York, NY; Museum of Early Southern Decorative Arts (MESDA) Winston-Salem, NC; Museum Of Fine Arts, Boston, MA; Rockwood Museum, Wilmington, DE; Shelburne Museum, Shelburne, VT; Smithsonian Institution, Washington, D.C.

Antimacassar Set, linen, white, satin stitch monogram center, scalloped edges, c1890 — **35.00**

Bedspread

Battenberg, white, all-over design, double size, c1890–1900 — **375.00**

Crocheted, white cotton, overall floral motif pattern, double size, instructions designed and furnished by Grace Coolidge (Mrs. Calvin Coolidge) — **750.00**

Muslin, bleached, two green bower peacock design, motif bolster end, twin size, 1930s kit — **85.00**

Crochet Filet Picture, woodland scene, children on swing, 29 x 22", $75.00.

Rayon satin, pink, plain top, ruffled fall, double size, c1940 . . . .   **45.00**

Blanket Cover, seersucker, white, machine bound, double size, c1935 . . .   **18.00**

Bolster Cover, pr
    Button back, linen, white, small tuck edge ruffles, heavy satin stitch floral design center **95.00**
    Throw type, cotton, white, lace edges ruffles around sides, center of one red embroidery "Sweet," other "Dreams," Pennsylvania, c1880–90 . . . .   **85.00**

Boudoir Pillow Case, pr, 15" d, floral motif machine tape lace, pink satin backing, c1920 . . . .   **25.00**

Bridge Set
    34 x 34"
      Linen, damask, pale pink, chrysanthemum pattern, four matching napkins **25.00**
      Organdy, light yellow, linen appliqued flowers outer edge, hemstitched around appliques and border, four matching napkins . .   **50.00**
    35 x 35", linen, white, rose motif filet crocheted inserts on corners, crocheted edge, four matching napkins **35.00**

Curtain Panel, pr, 36" w, 108" l, white net, overall floral design, machine tambour stitch, scalloped edges, pocket top, c1920 . . . .   **85.00**

Doily
    28" d, Battenberg lace, white linen center, c1900 . . . .   **45.00**
    25" d, two hand tatted rows of medallions, white linen center, c1920   **35.00**
    24" d, linen, white, heavy padded satin-stitch butterflies and flowers, machine made Cluny lace border, c1900 . . . .   **25.00**

Set, six 15" d and 12" d, machine filet lace, cream, c1940 . . . .   **40.00**

Dresser Scarf
    Alencon lace, 14" w, 48" l, floral and medallion designs, ecru, machine made, c1930 . . . .   **40.00**
    Chantilly lace, 15" w, 40" l, white, floral design, machine made **15.00**

Handkerchief
    Chantilly Lace, 14 x 14", black center, 4" white organdy border, c1920 . .   **35.00**
    Cotton, white, bright colored printed flowers, set of 3, c1935 . . . .   **10.00**
    Linen, 12 x 12", white, Apenzell embroidery and drawn work, c1920   **20.00**
    Swiss embroidery, 12½ x 12½", white, delicate lace border, maple framed under glass, early 20th C   **65.00**

Napkins
    Cocktail, 6 x 8", linen, lavender and green, bunch of grapes form, handmade, set of 6 . . . .   **30.00**
    Dinner
      24" sq, linen, double damask, white, chrysanthemum pattern, hand rolled edges, set of 6 . . . .   **25.00**
      28 x 29", linen, damask, white, satin stripe design, satin stitch "E" center, hand rolled edges, set of 8 . . . .   **80.00**
    Luncheon, 15" sq, Madeira, linen, white, pale blue embroidery and cut work corner, set of 8 . . . .   **45.00**

Pillow Cases, pr
    Linen, white, satin stitch monogram, hem stitched, c1900 . . . .   **45.00**
    Muslin, white, embroidered girl with full skirt and flowers, crocheted edge, made from stamped kit, c1930 . . . .   **18.50**
    Percale, French blue, satin stitch "L," wide white crocheted border, c1935–40 . . . .   **22.50**

Place Mat, child's high chair tray, embroidered brown dog diving from board, crocheted edge, made from stamped kit, c1935 . . . .   **12.00**

Sheet
    Linen, matching pillow case, both embroidered "Maria" **60.00**
    Muslin, white, 3" w filet crochet rose motif insert, double size, c1920 . .   **15.00**

Table Cloth
    54 x 54", tea cloth, linen, natural, Battenberg lace center motif and corners, four matching napkins, set   **45.00**
    54 x 56", luncheon, cotton, white, colorful linen flower appliques, crochet edges, six matching napkins, c1930-35, set **35.00**
    68 x 86", all-over machine made lace,

natural, sq motif designs with floral centers, merrow edges **45.00**

68 x 98", dinner, linen, natural, cut work and embroidered floral and leaf pattern center and border, 8 matching napkins, set **200.00**

72" d, rayon, double damask, yellow, floral design, machine turned edges, four napkins, set **15.00**

72 x 98", linen, double damask, chrysanthemum pattern, hand turned hem, 20th C **85.00**

72 x 101", Chinese rice cloth, white, four sections hemstitched together, drawn work and embroidered floral design, deep borders **65.00**

88" d, linen, lace dec **75.00**

102½ x 79", cut work linen, embroidered, twelve matching napkins . . **325.00**

144 x 86", banquet size, Pointe de Venise, ecru, all-over cupids, urns and floral spray design, 12 linen napkins with lace border and corner motif, handmade in China, orig wrapping, unused, c1935–40, set **1,200.00**

Tête-A-Tête Set, 1 mat, 2 matching napkins, linen, light blue, two corners with embroidered pink roses and vines, c1940 . . . . **25.00**

Towel, linen

Damask, pr, woven cobalt blue floral design border, hem stitched, c1900 **65.00**

Hand loomed, 18" w, 36" l, each end with crocheted lace, finely stitched side hems, dated and sgd in black ink "1830" **65.00**

Hand tatted edges and one end c1930 . . . . **15.00**

Woven, red and blue Oriental design and fringe on each end, c1920 . . **18.00**

LITHOPHANES

History: Lithophanes are highly translucent porcelain panels with impressed designs. The design is formed by the difference in thickness of the plaque. Thin parts transmit an abundance of light while thicker parts represent shadows.

Lithophanes were first made by the Royal Berlin Porcelain Works in 1828. Other factories in Germany, France, and England later produced them. The majority of lithophanes on the market today were made between 1850 and 1900.

Collectors' Club: Lithophane Collectors Club, P.O. Box 4557, Toledo, OH 43620.

Museum: Blair Museum of Lithophanes and Carved Waxes, Toledo, OH.

Cup and Saucer, nude, lady, moriage and dragon dec **45.00**

Fairy Lamp, 4" h, white lithophane

Plaque, Suitor, imp "PPM, 1122," c1860, 5¼ x 4⅜", $145.00.

newel post shade, clear base marked "Clarke Cricklite" **450.00**

Lamp

Student, 23½", double type, four scenes, brass base, marked "Germany" **1,850.00**

Wall, brass frame, 2½" h conical four panel shade, woodland scenes, electrified **300.00**

Lamp Shade

10" d, 5¼" h, five panels, childhood scenes, emb brass frame, marked "PPM" **550.00**

13" d, seven panels, European and American scenic views, panel of woman carrying mousetrap upstairs, copper frame **700.00**

Mug, 4¾" h, alpine couple in landscape bottom, blue riverscape with windmills dec, white ground, German **100.00**

Panel

KK, 8 x 16", General Zachary Taylor, holding telescope in left arm, men fighting battle in background, wreath, eagle, and two flags above, leaded frame, ruby flashed **675.00**

PPM

4½ x 5¼", hunters in forest, marked **100.00**

6½ x 8", elderly lady teaching girl to knit, lead mounted edge **150.00**

PR Sickle, 4⅛ x 5", cupid and girl fishing **150.00**

Unknown Maker, 6½ x 8", Christ holding orb with cross, incised "Inri/Die" **185.00**

Portrait, 7⅛ x 5¾", oval, Samuel Colt, sitting at table, revolver in right hand, pair of dividers in left hand, unmounted **875.00**

Stein, dancing couple, transfer of deer,
half liter **100.00**
Tea Set, teapot, creamer, cov sugar, six
cups and saucers **150.00**
Tea Warmer, 6 x 6", four panels
Romantic, Sheffield SS holder, orig
burner **275.00**
Scenic, pierced top, metal frame,
molded ftd base, Germany **165.00**

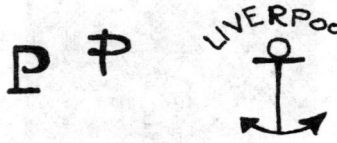

LIVERPOOL CHINA

History: Liverpool is the name given to products
made at several potteries in Liverpool, England,
between 1750 and 1840. Among the early potters
who made tin enameled earthenwares were Seth
and James Pennington and Richard Chaffers.

By the 1780s tin glazed earthenware gave way
to cream colored wares decorated with cobalt,
enamel colors, and blue or black transfers.

The Liverpool glaze is characterized by bubbles
and most often there is clouding under the foot
rims. By 1800 about 80 potteries were working in
the town producing not only creamware, but soft
paste, soapstone, and bone porcelain.

Reference: Susan and Al Bagdade, *Warman's
English & Continental Pottery & Porcelain, 1st Edition*, Warman Publishing Co., Inc., 1987.

Bowl, 9" d, Delft, painted yellow, blue,
green, and manganese, house landscape with fence and bamboo trees,
c1760 . . . . **950.00**

Jug, Commodore Pribler Squadron Attacking the City of Tripoli, Aug 3, 1804, 6⅝" h, $600.00.

Jug
5¼" h, three violet transfers, "Charity"
and two Masonic symbols, small
chips, minor transfer wear **250.00**
6¾" h, black and white transfer "Success to the Farmer," twelve line
verse cartouche on opposite side,
pink luster bands, pink luster "Alice
Davies/Ashton   Upon/Mersey/
Cheshire" under spout, minute age
crack **250.00**
7" h, creamware, polychrome transfer
titled "East View of Liverpool Light
House & Signals on Bidston Hill"
over scene of lighthouse, reverse
with black transfer of British sailing
ship, hairlines, chips, glaze imper-
fections **850.00**
7½" h, three Masonrie transfers, two
embellished with green, age crack
on bottom **200.00**
7⅝" h, creamware, black transfer,
American eagle within chain of sixteen links with states names, reverse with list of population of US,
banner inscribed "Prosperity To
The United States of America," applied strap handle, molded spout,
hairline cracks, restoration **4,100.00**
7¾" h, "Arms of the United States"
transfer on one side, angel addressing seated lady amid ruins
with scroll declaring date of American Independence, crack and
small chips **3,400.00**
9¾" h, three transfers, American ship
with banner "Success to Trade,"
couple in landscape titled "Abbas
and Abra," Great Seal of the US
and date 1804, age cracks and chip
on spout tip **1,100.00**
10½" h, four transfers, American ship
with trophy of arms beneath entitled "The Catharine," black and
white Masonic symbols, wreath
with "Samuel/Ca-neau" (third letter
ground off) under spout, and figure
of Hope leaning on anchor looking
at departing ship, gold and black
leaf band on bottom, age crack and
severe chip on spout **1,600.00**
Miniature, cup and saucer, blue and
white, painted V shaped flock of birds
in flight, two rocky islands, loop handle, Richard Chaffers' factory, c1762 **1,210.00**
Mug
4⅝" h, creamware, brown transfer,
eagle with shield, grasping banner
in beak, laurel branch and arrow in
talons, sixteen stars, linked rings
border with state names, c1800 . . **2,000.00**
4¾" h, pink luster band, three lines

encircled in flowers, "The Watchful Eye/The Silent Tongue/and the Secret Heart," 2½" l crack **125.00**

5⅞" h, black transfer, "An East View of the Iron Bridge Over the Wear Near Sunderland....," "Augusta Wilelmina Charlotta Weyda 1797," old rim repair, stains, hairlines, and chips on base **125.00**

6¼" h, black transfer, ship with American flag, "The True Blooded Yankee," chips and hairline **800.00**

Pitcher

8¼" h, black transfer, "Peace and Prosperity to America," old yellowed repairs **300.00**

9¼" h, creamware, black transfer, Washington portrait surrounded by names of states to one side, Washington standing with Liberty and viewing map of US on reverse, American Eagle titled below "Herculaneum Pottery" under spout, c1800 .... **1,300.00**

10" h, creamware, black transfer, "Poll and my partner Joe" on one side, sailing ship with British flag on reverse, crazed, stained, and chips **450.00**

Plate, 9¾" d, polychrome transfer, titled "Aurora of Newport John Cahoone," imp "Wilson," by Robert Wilson, c1800, restored **360.00**

Puzzle Jug, 6¾" h, Delft, white ground, blue dash border above pierced neck, verse, flanked by flowers and blue lines, three spouts, c1740 .... **935.00**

LOETZ

History: Loetz is a type of iridescent art glass made in Austria by J. Loetz Witwe in the late 1890s. Loetz was a contemporary of L. C. Tiffany and worked in the Tiffany factory before establishing his own operation; therefore, much of the wares are similar in appearance to Tiffany. Some pieces are signed "Loetz," "Loetz, Austria," or "Austria." The Loetz factory also produced ware with fine cameos on cased glass.

Bottle

11½" h, oviform, pinched sides, four upturned and crimped handles, rose gold irid ground, rainbow irid oil spot dec **6,600.00**

11¾" h, bulbous, extended neck, everted rim, four upturned handles, rose gold irid ground, rainbow irid oil spot dec **19,800.00**

Bowl

5½" d, 3¾" h, silver and emerald green layered between crystal, center opal layer, polished pontil **1,700.00**

Vase, irid purple, unsigned, 7⅝" h, $150.00.

14" d, internally dec, large green, white, and claret center blossom, claret border, c1930 .... **2,000.00**

Candlesticks, pr, 7¼", opal, amber streaks, irid threading on base, SS rim **650.00**

Chalice, 5½" h, blue green irid, tear drop motif, engraved "Loetz, Austria," c1900 .... **2,425.00**

Compote

10" d

Dimpled, pink, brass stand **400.00**

Ruffled, silver base, glass scarabs, sgd **600.00**

12" d, 12" h, scarab design, silver base, sgd **550.00**

Dish, 12½" l, leaf form, channel molded S curve, pinched ruffled rim, honeycombed textured ext., yellow ground, pink irid, sgd "Loetz Austria" **825.00**

Loving Cup, 4⅛" h, beaker form, red, green, and orange streaks, silver overlay flowers and trailing vines, three applied silver cased handles, c1900 **1,450.00**

Vase

4¾" h, double gourd, everted rim, swirled maroon, salmon, cream, and gold irid designs, engraved "Loetz, Austria" **2,450.00**

5" h

Bud, stick, platinum and black pulled feather dec, slender stem with small lip **625.00**

Spherical, inverted pinched rim, ring foot, red crackled glass over clear glass, inscribed "Loetz/Austria" **385.00**

6" h
Baluster, waisted, oil spot irid, florals and foliage, gold tracery . . **525.00**
Oviform, pinched, everted rim, oil spot irid, deep turquoise, sgd "Loetz, Austria" **950.00**
6¾" h, triangular, pinched and everted rim, all-over random lozenge form indentations, blue silver irid over emerald green ground **600.00**
8" h, swelling oviform, textured, overall gold irid, applied pendent trailings, inscribed "Loetz, Austria" . . **600.00**
8¼" h
Baluster, cobalt blue, zigzag irid, three applied threads with pad prunts, sgd "Loetz Austria" across polished pontil **5,500.00**
Cylindrical, amethyst, green, and silver, layered between crystal, polished base **1,900.00**
9½" h, mollusk shape, stylized, sinuous marine plant stem with applied tendrils on sides, splayed foot, overall silvery irid **800.00**

LOTUS WARE CHINA

History: Knowles, Taylor and Knowles Co., East Liverpool, Ohio, made a translucent, thinly potted china between 1891 and 1898. It compared favorably to Belleek. It first was marked "KTK." After being exhibited at the 1893 Columbian Exposition in Chicago, Col. John T. Taylor, company president, changed the marking to Lotus Ware because the body resembled the petals of the lotus blossom.

Blanks also were sold to amateurs who hand painted them. Most artist-signed pieces fit this category.

Bowl
3¾" d, wreath of pink roses, blue rim, gold scrolls, marked "Lotus Ware" **150.00**
4" h, tapered globe, white, beaded netting, beaded ruffled rim, one bead missing, marked "Lotus Ware" **60.00**
9" d, white, twig handles, encrusted porcelain particles, leaf designs, irregular scalloped rim **700.00**
Cream Pitcher, white enamel daisies on rim, pale green ground green twig handle with gold trim, marked "Lotus Ware" **275.00**
Creamer and Sugar, cov, ovoid, arched panels with leaves, marked "K. T. & K." **100.00**
Ewer, 6" h, white, emb floral rim, marked "K. T. & K." **80.00**

Jug, gold neck, floral dec, white ground, $325.00.

Pitcher, 5" h, squatty, pink and white apple blossoms, gold tied twig handle, marked "Lotus Ware" **300.00**
Punch Bowl, 16" d, gold painted elks, wreath of forget–me–nots, peach ground, attached mulberry base, int. with ear of corn, wheat, peaches, and grape pods on pale blue ground, presentation piece by East Liverpool Lodge #258, marked "K. T. & K." . . **350.00**
Shell Dish, 5" d, gold enameling and monogram **125.00**
Teapot, cov, individual, ovoid, red line emb flowers, gold and blue handle and spout, marked "Lotus Ware" . . . **200.00**
Vase, 9" h, white, leaves forming base, gold highlights, marked "K. T. & K," professionally repaired floral tips . . . **225.00**
Whiskey Jug, 7½" h, encrusted shells and glass bits, marked "K. T. & K." **800.00**

LUSTER WARE

History: Lustering on a piece of pottery creates a metallic, sometimes iridescent, appearance. Josiah Wedgwood experimented with the technique in the 1790s. Between 1805 and 1840 luster earthenware pieces were created in England by makers such as Adams, Bailey and Batkin, Copeland and Garrett, Wedgwood, and Enoch Wood.

Luster decorations often were used in conjunction with enamels and transfers. Transfers used for luster decoration covered a wide range of public and domestic subjects. They frequently were accompanied by pious or sentimental doggerel as well as the humors of everyday life.

Copper luster was created by the addition of a copper compound to the glaze. It was very popular in America during the 19th century and experienced a collecting vogue from the 1920s to the 1950s. Today it has a limited market. The market stagnation can partially be attributed to the large number of reproductions, especially creamers and the "polka" jug, which fool many new buyers. Reproductions are heavier in appearance and weight than the earlier pieces.

Pink luster was made by using a gold mixture. Silver luster was first covered completely with a thin coating of a "steel luster" mixture, containing a small quantity of platinum oxide. An additional coating of platinum, worked in water, was applied before firing.

Sunderland is a coarse type of cream colored earthenware with a marbled or spotted pink luster decoration which shades from pink to purple. A solution of gold compound applied to the white body developed the many shades of pink.

The development of electroplating in 1840 created a sharp decline in the demands for metal-surfaced earthenware.

Reference: Susan and Al Bagdade, *Warman's English & Continental Pottery & Porcelain, 1st Edition,* Warman Publishing Co., Inc., 1987.

Additional Listings: English Softpaste.

Pink Luster, pitcher, curlicue and leaf pattern, sawtooth int. rim dec, marked "Wedgwood Eturia, Barlaston, Made In England," 3¾" h, $75.00.

COPPER

Bowl
5¾" d, emb, green band, copper luster body	75.00
6¾" d, cov, deep waisted, ftd, matching waisted domed cov, knob finial, white orange band with copper luster scrolling leafy band	200.00
Bust, 8½" h, Pluto, bearded, four sided flaring pedestal base, overall copper luster glaze	75.00
Creamer, 4½" h, General Lafayette and	

surrender of Cornwallis commemoration transfer, canary luster band	175.00
Crocus Pot, enameled blue, green, and white floral dec	175.00
Cup and Saucer, stylized floral dec, highlighted copper luster body	65.00
Goblet, 4½" h, wide white center band with pink transfer printed Faith and Hope, copper luster rim and base bands, knobbed stem, round flaring foot	100.00

Pitcher
5" h, bulbous, blue band	70.00
6" h	
Raised enamel basket of multicolored flowers, bearded man spout	100.00
Sq panels, pink and green enameled flowers	85.00
Puzzle Jug, 8⅞" h, ironstone, dancers and clowns transfer, lion and unicorn mark, Elsmore and Forster	125.00
Spill Vase, 4⅜" h, trumpet form, flared rim, wide canary center band with two white reserves, transfer printed scenes of mother and child, polychrome enamel trim, copper luster rim and base band, small base repair	135.00
Tumbler, 2⅝" h, blue floral band	35.00

PINK

Bowl, 6½" d, House pattern	100.00
Chamber Pot, 8½" d, 5½" h, black transfer print of comic verse, int. with applied frog, pink luster and polychrome enamel trim, chip on handle	700.00
Chocolate Pot, heavy emb, ornate gold trim	100.00
Cup and Saucer, orange–red Cadmus, American eagle and Fulton's steamboat transfer, pink luster rim	100.00
Mug, 2½" h, red man and woman transfer, pink luster bands	50.00
Pepper Pot, 4½" h	85.00

Plaque, pierced for hanging
6¾" h, circular, "Prepare to Meet Thy God," floral and leaf garland, black transfer printed verse, ornate border, imp "C. C. & Co," small edge flakes	175.00
8⅝" l, oval, molded putti holding flower garlands, molded goats and procession, trailing foliage border, pink luster edge, Staffordshire, c1795	575.00
Punch Bowl, 12" d, hunting scenes	675.00
Tea Bowl and Saucer, white ground, pink florals, leaves, and trim	85.00
Vase, 6¾" h, ruffled, sq foot, emb, pink luster and polychrome enamel	175.00

SILVER

Bowl, 8⅜″ d, all-over leaf dec **50.00**
Creamer, 3½″ h, bulbous, cream colored, silver luster grapes and leaves, marked "Lawley, England" **35.00**
Jug, 4½″ h, round medallion of Peace, silver luster border **365.00**
Pitcher, 6⅞″ h, silver luster body, polychrome florals and birds, minor wear and stains **300.00**
Salt Shaker, 4″ h, bulbous, beaded dec, ftd pedestal **75.00**
Teapot, 6″ h, ribbed design, ftd **125.00**
Toby Jug, 5¼″ h, seated, wearing tricorn hat **100.00**

SUNDERLAND

Bowl, 8¼″ d, water drop pink luster ground, polychrome dec, black transfer ship and verse panels, hairline . .   **150.00**
Cup and Saucer, pink splash luster int., copper luster ext. **65.00**
Humidor, cov, black transfer print, Parliament building, pewter lock **225.00**
Jug, 7¾″ h, orange luster trim, polychrome transfer ship scenes, view of Sunderland Bridge, verse, rim lines, spout lip wear **125.00**
Mustard Pot, cov, 3½″ h, cylindrical, molded base, applied ribbed double twist handle, all-over pink splash luster dec **125.00**
Pitcher
  4¾″ h, pink luster, paneled black transfers of "Sailors' Farewell" and female surrounded by agricultural symbols **100.00**
  7⅛″ h, pink luster, hexagonal, black transfers of Reverend John Wesley and verse **125.00**
Plaque, 7⅝ x 8½″, rect, scroll molded rim, black transfer printed center scene of sailing ship and verse, "May Peace and Plenty...," copper luster edge trim **250.00**
Plate, 9½″ d, polychrome titled scene "An East View of the New Bridge, Sunderland," white center, brown highlights, pink border **185.00**
Punch Bowl, 11½″ d, zig–zag pink luster ground, polychrome dec, black transfer panels of nautical and Masonic themes **200.00**
Toothpick Holder, mottled pink, enameled white daisies, canary luster base band and leaves **75.00**
Waste Bowl, ftd **75.00**

LUTZ TYPE GLASS

History: Lutz type glass is an art glass attributed to Nicholas Lutz. He made this type of glass while at the Boston and Sandwich Glass Co. from 1869 until 1888. Since Lutz type glass was popular, copied by many capable glass makers, and unsigned, it is nearly impossible to distinguish genuine Lutz products.

Lutz is believed to have made two distinct types of glass, striped and threaded glass. This style often is confused with a similar style Venetian glass. The striped glass was made by using threaded glass rods in the Venetian manner. Threaded glass was blown and decorated by winding threads of glass around the piece.

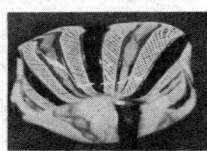

Bowl, white, amethyst, and yellow stripes, goldstone edges, 3 x 3¼″, $35.00.

Compote, 7″ h, lavender, pink, and opalescent swirls, entwined serpent stem   **250.00**
Lemonade, 5½″, cranberry, threaded, clear applied handle, engraved dec   **120.00**
Plate, 6¼″, goldstone, threaded, rose center shading into amber body, ruffled **90.00**
Scent Bottle, sea horse
  2⅛″ l, blown, clear, opaque white spiral ribs, applied blue rigaree **75.00**
  2¾″ l, opaque white, ribbed **50.00**
Tumbler, ftd, 3″ h, gold and white latticino, threaded, six applied strawberries **90.00**

MAASTRICHT WARE

History: Maastricht, Holland, is where Petrus Regout founded the De Sphinx Pottery in 1836. The firm specialized in transfer printed earthenwares. Other factories also were established in the area, many employing English workmen and their techniques. Maastricht china was exported to the United States in competition with English products.

Reference: Susan and Al Bagdade, *Warman's English & Continental Pottery & Porcelain, 1st Edition,* Warman Publishing Co., Inc., 1987.
Periodical: *The Dutch Potter,* 47 London Terrace, New Rochelle, NY 10804.

Bowl, Vlinder pattern, 6″ d, 3″ h, $35.00.

Bowl
4½″ d, Abbey pattern, dark blue transfer, marked "Petrus Regout"	12.00
7½″ d, Timor pattern	30.00
8¼″ d, gaudy floral spatter, blue, green, and yellow, marked "Maastricht"	25.00
Cake Plate, 12″ d, orange and blue flowers, marked "Societe Ceramic Maastricht, Made in Holland"	65.00
Compote, 8¼″ d, 4½″ h, Pajong pattern, Oriental scene, gold border, marked "Petrus Regout & Co"	60.00
Cup and Saucer	
Abbey pattern, blue transfer	20.00
Oriental pattern, dark red transfer . .	35.00
Mug, 3″ h, gaudy floral spatter, polychrome, marked "Maastricht"	75.00
Plaque, 10″ d, portrait of Franklin Roosevelt, green wreath	30.00
Plate	
5⅞″ d, gaudy floral spatter, polychrome, marked "Maastricht" . . .	15.00
7½″ d, Castillo pattern, blue transfer, marked "Petrus Regout"	10.00
8″ d, Abbey pattern, luster trim	15.00
9″ d, blue and white gaudy spatter, floral design, marked "Maastricht"	25.00
Porringer, 3½″ d, Pompeii pattern, marked "Petrus Regout"	65.00
Soup Plate, 10″ d, Abbey pattern, purple transfer	12.00
Waste Bowl, 4⅜″ d, gaudy floral spatter, polychrome, marked "Maastricht" . .	15.00

MAJOLICA

History: Majolica, an opaque, tin glazed pottery, has been produced by many countries for centuries. It originally took its name from the Spanish Island of Majorca, where figuline (a potter's clay) is found. Today majolica denotes a type of pottery which was made during the last half of the 19th century in Europe and America.

Majolica frequently depicted elements in nature: leaves, flowers, birds, and fish. Human figures were rare. Designs were painted on the soft clay body using vitreous colors and fired under a clear lead glaze to impart the rich color and brilliance characteristic of majolica.

Among English majolica manufacturers who marked their works were: Wedgwood, George Jones, Holdcraft, and Minton. Most of their pieces can be identified through the English Registry mark and/or the potter-designer's mark. Sarreguemines in France and Villeroy and Boch in Baden, Germany, produced majolica that compared favorably with the finer English majolica. Most Continental pieces had an incised number on the base.

Although 600 plus American potteries produced majolica between 1850 and 1900, only a handful chose to identify their wares. Among these manufacturers were George Morely, Edwin Bennett, the Chesapeake Pottery Company, the New Milford-Wannoppee Pottery Company, and the firm of Griffen, Smith, and Hill. The others hoped their unmarked pieces would be taken for English examples.

References: Susan and Al Bagdade, *Warman's English & Continental Pottery & Porcelain, 1st Edition,* Warman Publishing Co., Inc., 1987; Marilyn G. Karmason with Joan B. Stacke, *Majolica: A Complete History And Illustrated Survey,* Abrams, 1989; Mariann K. Marks, *Majolica Pottery: An Identification And Value Guide,* Collector Books, 1983; M. Charles Rebert, *American Majolica 1850–1900,* Wallace-Homestead, 1981; Mike Schneider, *Majolica,* Schiffer Publishing, 1990.

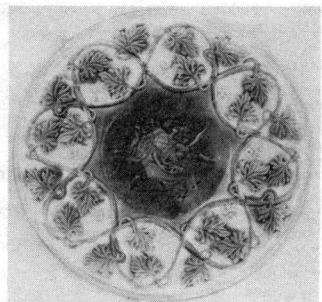

Bowl, low, classical dec on green center, white ground, green leaves, pink flowers, 9½″ d, $120.00.

Bottle, 16″ h, figural, stork, rumpled top, hat stopper, 4″ l beak with spectacles, umbrella under arm, English **825.00**

Bowl

2¾″ d, 3¼″ h, raised basket design, green shading to brown **50.00**

9½″ d, green glazed agate ware, three olive shells, imp Holdcroft, England marks, c1870 . . . . **325.00**

Bread Plate, 12¼″ l, Oak Leaf with Acorns pattern **115.00**

Butter Pat, Shell and Seaweed pattern **145.00**

Cake Plate, pedestal, blue, green, and white, rose buds, Germany **150.00**

Candlestick, 7″ h, figural, Happy Hooligan standing by lamp post **115.00**

Cheese Dish, 10 x 8″, fern and flowers, stippled blue ground, glazed pink int., twig handle, marked "George Jones," English **785.00**

Compote

9″ d, 3½″ h, blue ground, int. relief white flowers, pink berries, green leaves, marked "Zells/Germany" **125.00**

9″ d, 5¼″ h, Daisy pattern, light pink int., Griffin, Smith, & Hill, imp GSH monogram **375.00**

Cup and Saucer, Shell and Seaweed pattern **345.00**

Dish

7″ l, Begonia Leaf, Griffin, Smith, & Hill, imp GSH monogram **185.00**

11¼″ d, 1¼″ h, wide molded rim, variegated light green–blue scrolls and flowers, variegated olive center, scene of gnomes and leaves, bird in flight **125.00**

Inkwell, 10¼″ l, 5″ h, mahogany color, floral enameling, four gold feet **300.00**

Jardiniere, stand

37″ h, glazed and painted, Continental **300.00**

40″ h, glazed and painted, Continental **400.00**

Match Holder, 4 x 5″, Janus type double classical heads, striker side, marked "Wedgwood," registry marks **175.00**

Mush Bowl, Shell and Seaweed **350.00**

Oyster Plate

Deep pink and turquoise, marked "Minton" **650.00**

Turquoise and green, marked "Minton" **375.00**

Turquoise ground, Shell pattern, 9″ d, marked "Minton" **300.00**

Paperweight, 4″ h, figural, owl, pebbled ivory ground, brown trim, pink stars and flowers, marked "Mayer" **115.00**

Pitcher

4½″ h, Hawthorne pattern, mottled colors, Etruscan **125.00**

5½″ h, squatty, mottled browns and yellows, raised flowers and leaves **125.00**

7″ h, figural, fish **155.00**

8″ h, triangular, multicolored fans dec, late 19th C **250.00**

11″ h, figural, owl, c1900 . . . . **275.00**

Plate

6½″ d, Grape Cluster pattern, marked "Germany" **25.00**

8¼″, Shell and Seaweed pattern . . . **325.00**

9″, fan border, Wedgwood **325.00**

Platter, 11″ l, Wild Rose and Rope pattern, aqua ground, cobalt center . . . **115.00**

Sardine Box, turquoise and pink, G Jones **600.00**

Teapot, Shell and Seaweed pattern, albino, Etruscan **350.00**

Tray, 20″ l, figural, fish **110.00**

Umbrella Stand, 24″ h, cobalt blue ground, six panels with leaf dec, central raised putti, minor restoration to base **750.00**

Water Set, Pineapple pattern, 9½″ h water pitcher, four matching tumblers **300.00**

MAPS

History: Maps provide one of the best ways to study the growth of a country or region. From the 16th to the early 20th century, maps were both informative and decorative. Engravers provided ornamental detailing which often took the form of bird's eye views, city maps and ornate calligraphy and scrolling. Many maps were hand colored to enhance their beauty.

Maps generally were published in plate books. Many of the maps available today result from these books being cut apart and sheets sold separately.

In the last quarter of the 19th century, representatives from firms in Philadelphia, Chicago, and elsewhere traveled the United States preparing county atlases, often with a sheet for each township and a sheet for each major city or town. Although mass produced, they are eagerly sought by collectors. Individual sheets sell for $25 to $75. The atlases themselves can usually be purchased in the $200 to $400 range. Individual sheets should be viewed solely as decorative and not as investment material.

Collectors' Club: The Association of Map Memorabilia, 8 Amherst Road, Pelham, MA 01002.

Africa, "Map of Tripoli & Tunis," 1816, Colburn, few minor folds, 10 x 16″ . . **35.00**

Canada, "British America," London/New York, Tallis, 1851, engraved, outline color, 12¾ x 9½″ **75.00**

England, southern England including

Devonshire, aquatint, dated 1693, well preserved, framed, 24¼ x 38¼" 125.00

Mexico, "Mexico Or New Spain In Which The Motions Of Cortes May Be Traced," London, W Stratchan & T Cadell, 1795, engraving, 11⅜ x 15¼" 225.00

United States

"A Map Of Proposed Chesapeake–Delaware Canal Routes," Philadelphia, American Philosophical Society, 1771, J. Smithers after W. Thomas Fisher, engraving 12⅝ x 17" 950.00

Florida, "US Dept of War, Topographical Study of Florida," Washington, DC, 1891, chromolithograph, three colors, 16⅜ x 27½" 75.00

Georgia, "A New And Accurate Map Of The Province Of Georgia In North America," London, J Hinton, 1779, engraving, published in *The Universal Magazine*, 12¾ x 10¾" 300.00

"Map Showing The Proposed Rail Roads From Boston To Burlington From Hale's Map of New England," Boston, JH Bufford, c1845, 20 x 25", four alternative routes with mileage charts 50.00

"Message From The President. . . To The Two Houses Of Congress. . . Maps And Other Illustrations Belonging To Reports Accompanying The Message," Washington, folio, cloth

Part III, Dec 2, 1856, twelve maps and plans, survey maps of Michigan, Wisconsin and Minnesota, Iowa, Arkansas, Louisiana, Florida, California, Washington Territory, New Mexico, Kansas and Nebraska, and Utah, as well as plan and elevation for prison in Washington, DC 115.00

Part IV, Dec 6, 1853, forty-two maps, plans, diagrams, and plates, survey maps of Michigan, Wisconsin and Minnesota, Iowa, Louisiana, Arkansas, and Florida, two maps and five plates of Liberia 120.00

Part IV, 1856, thirty-five maps, plans, and diagrams, survey maps of Michigan, Wisconsin & Minnesota, Iowa, Arkansas, Louisiana, Florida, California, Oregon, Washington Territory, New Mexico, Kansas, and Nebraska, as well as overland routes from Salt Lake City to San Francisco, two charts of Artic expeditions of EK Kane, plan of buildings for Government Hospital for the In-

sane, two plans of buildings for the Naval Academy, 2 volumes of maps 360.00

New York, "Westchester County," Stone and Clark, Ithaca, NY, 1839, framed, 18½ x 13" 350.00

Ohio, "Map of Ohio," engraving, hand colored, published in Columbus, 1822, John Kilborne, barn siding frame, 31 x 32" 650.00

Pennsylvania, "Map of Carlisle," 1867, dowels for hanging at top and bottom, adv in corners, lists of merchants in lower and upper right quadrants, overall browning, 36 x 44" 50.00

Texas, "Map Of The State Of Texas From The Latest Authorities," JH Young, published by Thomas, Cowperthwait, Philadelphia, c1852, multicolored, inset of Galveston City and Northern Texas, 17 x 14" 150.00

MARBLEHEAD POTTERY

History: This hand thrown pottery had its beginning in 1905 as a therapeutic program introduced by Dr. J. Hall for the patients confined to a sanitarium located in Marblehead, Massachusetts. In 1916 production was removed from the hospital to another site. The factory continued under the directorship of Arthur E. Baggs until it closed in 1936.

Most pieces found today are glazed with a smooth, porous, even finish in a single color. The most desirable pieces are decorated with conventionalized design in one or more subordinate colors.

Chamberstick, 4" h, rose matte glaze 85.00

Pitcher, 8¼" h, bulging cylindrical, angular handle, incised scenic band, dark brown trees, sage green ground, robin's egg blue int., incised ship mark and "AB" 850.00

Tile, 6" sq, column of oaks reflected in tidal pools, brown, tan, green, and yellow, incised mark 3,100.00

Vase

4¼" h, cylindrical, stylized dec of two trees, tan, green, and brown, yellow ground, incised mark, painted mark "B I," designed by Arthur Baggs and Hannah Tutt 3,850.00

Rose Bowl, gray ground, leaf and fruit motif, 4⅛″ d, 3⅛″ h, $575.00.

4½″ h, ovoid, swelling towards base, wide mouth, repeating blue, brown, and beige stylized branches, pale slate gray ground, imp mark, artist's initials "HT" for Hanna Tutt, c1915 — **800.00**

4½″ h, 3½″ d, cylindrical, wide mouth, brown and green trees, pale yellow ground, imp mark, artist's initials for Arthur Baggs, 1913 . . . . **2,700.00**

5¼ h, swollen cylindrical tapering towards base, wide mouth, stylized slate and blue floral dec, speckled gray–green ground, imp mark, painted initials "BT" **650.00**

7″ h, swollen cylindrical, shoulder tapering towards base, wide mouth

Stylized brown yellow, and black floral dec, green matte glaze, imp logo, artist initialed "HT" for Hanna Tuff, c1908–10 . . . . . . **10,000.00**

Stylized charcoal gray trees, blue–gray ground, imp logo, artist initials "HT" for Hannah Tutt, c1905 **1,700.00**

Stylized gray floral dec, speckled gray–green ground, imp mark, incised artist's initial "W" **1,600.00**

MARY GREGORY TYPE GLASS

History: The use of enameled decoration on glass, an inexpensive imitation of cameo glass, developed in Bohemia in the late 19th century. The Boston and Sandwich Glass Co. copied this process in the late 1880s.

Mary Gregory (1856–1908) was employed for two years at the Boston and Sandwich Glass Co. factory when the enameled decorated glass was being manufactured. Some collectors argue that Gregory was inspired to paint her white enamel figures on glass by the work of Kate Greenaway and a desire to imitate pate-sur-pate. However, evidence for these assertions is very weak. Further, a question can be raised whether or not Mary Gregory even decorated glass as part of her job at Sandwich.

The result is that "Mary Gregory Type" is a better term to describe this glass. Collectors should recognize that most examples are either European or modern reproductions.

Atomizer, 5¼″ h, cranberry, white enamel young girl, orig bulb and tassel **225.00**

Barber Bottle, 8″ h, cobalt blue, white enamel young girl with tennis racquet, gold trim **375.00**

Butter Dish, 7¾″ w, 4¾″ h, satin finish, dome cov, cranberry, white enamel young boy riding tricycle, painted foliate, clear crystal knob **575.00**

Cruet, green, white enamel young girl carrying flowers, applied clear handle and stopper **90.00**

Decanter

9″ h, green, white enamel young boy chasing a butterfly, clear blown stopper **250.00**

9½″ h, green, white enamel seated girl, applied clear handle, clear blown stopper, c1870 . . . . **300.00**

Dresser Bottle, 7½″ h, 5″ w, 2¾″ d, young girl flying a kite, wreath of morning glories, lilies of the valley, and bearded wheat, nosegay on back, gold tinted embellishments, four

Perfume Bottle, royal blue ground, white enamel girl, gold edging, silver plated stand, marked "Middletown Plate Co," 11¾″ h, $950.00.

tiny feet, lid with gold finial, cased,
mottled pink glass, white lining **685.00**
Heater Lamp, rect side panels with four
different scenes, white enamel figures, ornate metal frame **450.00**
Jewel Box, cov
5½" d, cranberry, white enamel young
girl blowing bubbles, ftd ormolu
base **285.00**
6" d, amber, two white enamel children playing **300.00**
Match Holder, 2¼" h, cranberry, white
enamel young boy **90.00**
Patch Box, 2⅜" d, lime green, white
enamel young girl **175.00**
Perfume, 8½" h, 5½" d, teal blue, white
enamel young boy flying kite, cattail
dec, matching tulip shaped stopper **450.00**
Pin Tray, 4½" l, oval, cranberry, white
enamel young girl holding flower ... **100.00**
Pitcher, 10" h, tankard, bright green,
white enamel young boy with staff,
applied green handle **375.00**
Tumbler, 3¾" h, blue, white enamel
young girl **85.00**
Vase
6" h, fan, deep forest green, white
enamel young boy carrying flower,
walking through woods **285.00**
7" h, baluster, ruffled top, cobalt blue,
white enamel young girl **150.00**
8" h, cylindrical vase, cranberry, SP
holder marked "William Rogers" **250.00**
9⅛" h, 4½" d, facing pair, cylindrical,
slight optic ribbing, cranberry, white
enamel girl holding open umbrella,
boy holding blanket and oars, pr **500.00**
9½" h, 4½" d, facing pair, baluster,
scalloped tops, cranberry, white
enamel girl holding flower, other
with boy holding flower, pr **500.00**
12" h, facing pair, crown tops, gold
rim, white fleur–de–lis dec, mottled
blue ground, white enamel boy
blowing bubble, girl waiting on
other, pr **675.00**
13⅜" h, 4½" d, facing pair, crown tops
with white beaded band, cobalt
blue, white enamel of young ladies
in hats and long dresses, pr **575.00**
Whiskey Glass, 2¼" h, cranberry, white
enamel young girl **90.00**

MATCH HOLDERS

History: After 1850 the friction match achieved
popular usage. The early matches were packaged
and sold in sliding cardboard boxes. To facilitate
storage and to eliminate the clumsiness of using
the box, match holders were developed.

The first examples were cast iron or tin, the latter
often having advertising on them. A patent for a
wall hanging match holder was issued in 1849. By
1880 match holders also were being made from
glass and china. Match holders lost popularity in
the late 1930s and 1940s with the advent of gas
and electric heat and ranges.

**Advertising, Dr Shoop's Health Coffee,
red, blue, white, and orange, 3⅜ x 5",
$125.00.**

Advertising
Bliss Native Herbs, wall type, tin,
Capitol **190.00**
Cochran's Ginger Ale, table type, re-
lief white enamel lettering **45.00**
Dr Shoop's Laxettes, wall type, tin **90.00**
Fuller & Johnson Mfg Farm Imple-
ments & Gasoline Engines, wall
type, tin **125.00**
La Confesion Cuban Cigar, gentle-
man holding cigar, dark blue metal
finish on tin, hinged lid **75.00**
Schlitz Beer, litho, cardboard **325.00**
Brass, figural, pig, pocket type **110.00**
Cast Iron
Figural
Friar, chubby face, church window
background, 6" h, marked "293–
A" **60.00**
Lady's Shoe
Amber, Daisy & Button pattern,
striking surface on sole, 2 x 3
x 6" **50.00**
Red, mounted on gild leaf, 4½ x
5" **100.00**
Hunting scene, Germany **60.00**
Open scrollwork, dated 1867 ..... **55.00**
Glass
Amber, witches kettle, wire bail **40.00**
Clear, lady's head, striking surface,
4¼" h, marked "Columbia," dated
1876 .... **75.00**
Custard, Winged Scroll pattern,
Heisey **100.00**

Milk Glass, Indian, gold dec, 3¼" h	**175.00**
Opaque, white, hand and fan	**20.00**
Nippon, table type, horse head dec each side	**90.00**
Pottery, cannon, Niloak	**40.00**
Royal Bayreuth, wall type, Rose Tapestry, blue mark	**500.00**
Wood, 5¼" h, heart shape, angled pocket, chip carved edges, white sanded paint, gold trim	**60.00**

MATCH SAFES

History: Match safes are small containers used to safely carry matches in one's pocket. They were first used in the 1850s. Match safes are often figural with a hinged lid and striking surface.

Reference: Audrey G. Sullivan, *A History of Match Safes In The United States,* published by author, 1978.

Note: While not all match safes have a striking surface, this is one test, besides size, to distinguish a match safe from a calling card case.

Brass, owl's head, green glass eyes, flattened motif, 2 x 1⅝", $250.00.

Advertising

A. E. Sonnedecker Coal Dealer & Livery & 10¢ Barn, tin, hanging	**70.00**
Dockash Stove Factory, tin, hanging	**55.00**
Fairy Soap, metal	**12.00**
Number Five Cigar, brass, engraved floral pattern, lid	**75.00**
Park Sherman Co, Ever Dry, Springfield, IL	**45.00**
Red Top Rye Distillers, gutta percha	**75.00**
Souvenir 1st National Bank, Fond Du Lac, Wis 1908, celluloid over metal	**30.00**
Art Nouveau style, brass, raised relief lady in pearl panel on one side, raised hunting dog and rider's crop on other, late 1890, early 1900	**75.00**

Glass

Amber, boot shape, hanging	**20.00**
Clear, Miss Liberty's head, hanging, 4½" h	**80.00**
Milk Glass, blue, mottled, flag shield form, hanging, 3⅞" h, marked "America" and "1492/1892"	**175.00**
Russian Enamel, 2" h, stylized cloisonne enamel flowers and scroll dec, blue, white, and translucent red, stip-	

pled gilt ground, striking teeth at base, turquoise dot border, S D Kalashnikov, Moscow, Russia, 1880–90	**440.00**
Souvenir, Mount Vernon, silvered brass, Washington's Mansion and Tomb photos	**45.00**

Sterling Silver

Art Nouveau, floral dec, inscribed "Jack, Nov 12, 1898"	**65.00**
Figural, forearm and clenched fist, hinged cap with striker, inscribed "In This You'll Find a Match," 3" l, late 19th C	**275.00**
Tiffany & Co, rect, engraved diapering, diagonally hinged, 2½" l, late 19th C	**170.00**

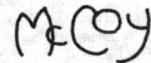

McCOY POTTERY

History: The J. W. McCoy Pottery Co. was established in Roseville, Ohio, in September, 1899. The early McCoy Co. produced both stoneware and some art pottery lines, including Rosewood. In October, 1911, three potteries merged creating the Brush-McCoy Pottery Co. This company continued to produce the original McCoy lines and added several new art lines. Much early pottery is not marked.

In 1910, Nelson McCoy and his father, J. W. McCoy, founded the Nelson McCoy Sanitary Stoneware Co. In 1925, the McCoy family sold their interest in the Brush-McCoy Pottery Co. and started to expand and improve the Nelson McCoy Co. The new company produced stoneware, earthenware specialities, and artware. Most of the pottery marked McCoy was made by the Nelson McCoy Co.

References: Sharon and Bob Huxford, *The Collectors Encyclopedia of McCoy Pottery,* Collector Books, 1980; Harold Nichols, *McCoy Cookie Jars: From The First To The Latest,* Nichols Publishing, 1987.

Additional Listings: *See Warman's Americana & Collectibles* for more examples.

Basket, green, basketweave	**25.00**
Bird Bath, 27" h, Greystone finish	**65.00**
Bowl, Amaryllis pattern, pastel	**24.00**
Cookie Jar	
Bobby Baker	**28.00**
Cookie Safe, sheriff on cov	**28.00**
Cookstove, black	**25.00**
Monk, brown	**16.00**
Owl, brown	**18.00**
Thinking Puppy	**28.00**
Touring Car	**50.00**
Wishing Well	**25.00**

Vase, turquoise ground, pink bead dec, marked "Brush–McCoy," 6" h, $85.00.

Cuspidor, 3½" h, mottled yellow and brown Rockingham glaze, Nurock, 1916	30.00
Ewer, 10" h, emb grapes and leaves, dark brown glaze, marked "Rosewood, McCoy," c1905	200.00
Jardiniere, 11¾" d, 9" h, hp, tulip dec, marked "Loy–Nel–Art"	165.00
Mug	
Corn pattern, pale yellow kernels, green husk, c1910	65.00
Little Red Riding Hood, marked "Brush–McCoy"	45.00
Planter	
Blossom Time, yellow	5.00
Turtle	15.00
Pretzel Jar, cov, emb buccaneer and parrot, green glaze, marked "Nelson McCoy Sanitary Stoneware Co," c1920	75.00
Punch Bowl, pedestal base, emb grapes and leaves, dark brown glaze, marked "Olympia J W McCoy"	375.00
Teapot, Pinecone	20.00
Urn, 6" h, onyx glaze, marked "Nelson–McCoy"	40.00
Vase	
10" h, Springwood pattern, pink glaze, 1961	20.00
13" h, hp, wild roses dec, artist sgd, marked "Loy–Nel–Art"	325.00
14½" h, brown glaze, yellow flowers, marked "Loy–Nel–Art"	100.00
Wall Pocket, figural, mailbox, emb "Letters," green glaze	25.00

McKEE GLASS

History: The McKee Glass Co. was established in 1843 in Pittsburgh, Pennsylvania. In 1852 they opened a factory to produce pattern glass. In 1888 the factory was relocated to Jeannette, Pennsylvania, and began to produce many types of glass kitchenwares, including several patterns of Depression Glass. The factory continued until 1951 when it was sold to the Thatcher Manufacturing Co.

McKee named its colors Chalaine Blue, Custard, Seville Yellow, and Skokie Green. McKee glass may also be found with painted patterns, e.g., dots and ships. A few items were decaled. Many of the canisters and shakers were lettered in black to show the purpose for which they were intended.

References: Gene Florence, *Kitchen Glassware of the Depression Years, 4th Edition*, Collector Books, 1990; Lowell Innes and Jane Shadel Spillman, *M'Kee Victorian Glass*, Dover Publications, 1981.

Additional Listings: See *Warman's Americana & Collectibles* for more examples.

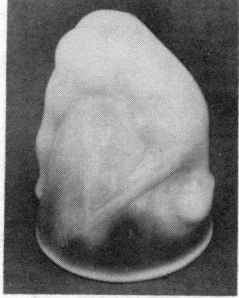

Tumbler, Bottoms Up, caramel opalescent, marked "Patent No. 77726," 3¼" h, $80.00.

Animal, horse, milk glass, base sgd	300.00
Baker, 5 x 7", oval, Skokie Green	15.00
Butter Dish, cov, rect, Seville Yellow	65.00
Canister	
Caramel, 48 oz, marked "Sugar"	75.00
Custard, marked "Coffee"	42.00
Delphite Blue, 48 oz, round	60.00
Children's Toy Dishes, Laurel, Scottie dec	
Cup	40.00
Plate	25.00
Saucer, 2" d	45.00
Clock, peacock blue, tambour shape, not working	250.00
Decanter, pinched sides, Seville Yellow	75.00
Egg Beater Bowl, pouring spout, Skokie Green	10.00
Egg Cup	
Rock Crystal	15.00
Skokie Green	4.50

Flour Shaker, Seville Yellow	20.00
Grease Jar, cov, Seville Yellow	36.00
Juice Tumbler, ftd, Skokie Green, 4½″ h	8.00
Lamp, Dance de Lumierre, green	750.00

Measuring Cup
Seville Yellow	335.00
Ships	25.00
Mixing Bowls, nested set, Ships, set of 3	35.00

Reamer
Grapefruit, Seville Yellow	175.00
Orange, Sunkist, white	12.00

Refrigerator Dish, cov, 5 x 8″
Clear	13.00
Cobalt Blue	28.00
Rolling Pin, Seville Yellow	200.00
Salt and Pepper Shakers, pr, Roman Arches, white	16.00
Sugar Shaker, green transparent, bullet shape	85.00
Tumbler and Coaster, Bottoms Up, Skokie Green	125.00

Wine
Colonial, green	40.00
Rock Crystal	15.00
Sunk Buttons, blue	38.00

MEDICAL AND PHARMACEUTICAL ITEMS

History: Medicine and medical instruments are well documented for the modern period. Some instruments are virtually unchanged since their invention. Others have changed drastically.

The concept of sterilization phased out decorative handles. Early handles of instruments were often carved and can be found in mother-of-pearl, ebony, and ivory. Today's sleekly designed instruments are not as desirable to collectors.

Pharmaceutical items include items commonly found in a drug store and pertain to the items used to store or prepare medications.

References: Bill Carter, Bernard Butterworth, Joseph Carter, and John Carter, *Dental Collectibles & Antiques*, Dental Folklore Books of K.C., 1984; Don Fredgant, *Medical, Dental & Pharmaceutical Collectibles*, Books Americana, 1981; Keith Wilbur, *Antique Medical Instruments*, Schiffer Publishing, 1987.

Museums: National Museum of History and Technology, Smithsonian Institution, Washington, DC; Waring Historical Library, Medical University of South Carolina, Charleston, SC.

APOTHECARY

Advertising
Sign, Smith Bros Cough Drops, 29½ x 11½″, tin	425.00

Advertising Glass, Drink Ferro–Phos, 4¼″ h, $30.00.

Trade Card, Dr Harter's Iron Tonic, Confederate President Jefferson Davis, 1888	30.00

Bottle
7″ h, cylindrical, cobalt blue, ground stopper, marked "TR Iodine," c1850	140.00
12″ h, flared lip, ground stopper, pontil, label, marked "PJ Gentian," c1850	325.00
13″ h, amethyst, tooled lip, ground pontil, painted black, gold, and red label "PULV:MARANT:O:/POT: BROMID," c1800	550.00
Cabinet, pine, lift top, thirty-four bottles int., drawer holds mortar and pestle, cased scales, and utensils, late 19th C	315.00

Jar
11″ h, cov, porcelain, white, gold hp label, fruit border, gold bands, marked "Bals Nervinum," c1870	230.00
11½″ h, sq, brown, metal screw top, paper label "Compressed Lozenges etc. H K Mulford Co, Phila; Chicago," c1880	65.00
16″ h, clear, flared lip, hollow stopper, label "Dr King's New Life Pills Always Satisfy," c1890	325.00
Cabinet, mahogany facade, pine, dovetailed, 46 drawers, wood button knobs, four base paneled doors, old finish, gilt and black labels, new plywood back, orig built-in, 73¾″ w, 50¼″ h	1,650.00
Medicine Dispenser, 10 x 16″, vaseline glass, cylinder shape, blown mold with texture, metal spigot and lid, emb on front "Radium Vitalizer," marked "Radium Assn - Chicago, Ill"	420.00

DENTAL

Advertising Sign, Sozodont Dentifrice, 22 x 16", tin, emb **1,200.00**
Chair, oak, early **170.00**
Display Case, Dr West's Toothbrush, counter, glass **375.00**
Drill, Electro Dental Mfg Co, patent Nov 3, 1903, foot control patent Sept 9, 1911 .... **60.00**
Instrument
  Set of 6, ebony handles, c1860 .... **160.00**
  Tooth Extractor **90.00**

MEDICAL

Advertising Mirror, Frank Mollema, Chiropractor, pocket type **20.00**
Bedpan, miniature, 4¼ x 3¼", porcelain, marked "Popular Perfection Bedpan, Maw-London" **110.00**
Book
  Gunn's Domestic Medicine, 1838 .. **25.00**
  Practice of Obstetrics, 1916, 1,000 pgs **15.00**
Chair, examination, cast iron, nickel plated rim, pin striped dec, orig green paint, sgd "Betz" **100.00**
Dilator, "Dr Young's Rectal Dialtors", boxed, 1920s **30.00**
Doctor's Case, leather, pocket type, four 3¼" glass vials with screw caps, 4¼ x 4½" **15.00**
Ear Speculum, 3 pc, silver, cased horn, American, c1860 .... **90.00**
Fleem knife, three blades, brass holder **55.00**
Inhaler, Vapo-Cresolene, orig parts and box including bottle of medicine, c1895 .... **325.00**
Inkwell, porcelain, head, labeled brain areas, white, blue and black dec, glazed, impressed "By F Bridges, Phrenologist," 5⁷⁄₁₆" h, 1850–59 .... **1,400.00**
Instrument
  Gynocological, 3¼" l, leather case inscribed "Its The Little Things That Count," inside "Compliments of J Sklar Mfg Co, Brooklyn, NY ASTA Convention, Chicago, June, 1914" **725.00**
  Surgical, rosewood case, brass inlay, ebony handles, brass plate on lid engraved "Dr T Brackin, Warren, O," label marked "Max Wocher Y Son, Manufactures of Surgical Instruments, 105 W 6th St Cincinnati, O" **300.00**
Machine
  Davis & Kidders Magneto-Electric Machine, hand crank, orig box, patented Aug 1, 1854, sgd by proprietor "W H Burnap of NYC" **475.00**

Electromedical Shock Box, oak box, c1900 .... **260.00**
Master Violet Ray No 11, orig box and instructions **40.00**
Voltamp Battery No 3, electric shock type, attachments, wood box **45.00**
Surgical Knife, sterling silver, Gorham **60.00**
Table, examination, oak, top folds for body contours, door and four drawers on bottom, wheels, refinished **1,100.00**

OPTICAL

Cabinet, 13 x 22 x 19", oak, toll top, includes test lenses and frames ... **950.00**
Eye Cup
  Amber, 1½" h, c1860 .... **190.00**
  Cobalt Blue, polished pontil, 3" h, c1840 .... **190.00**
Lens Set, lenses and testing frame, 23 x 12" black leather case, Limeburner and Co, Philadelphia **800.00**
Retinascope, ivory handle, English, c1880 .... **25.00**
Schematic Eye, 8" h, circular base, baluster column, alternative lenses **920.00**

MEDICINE BOTTLES

History: The local apothecary and his book of formulas played a major role in early America. In 1796 the first patent for a medicine was issued by the United States Patent Office. Anyone could apply for a patent. As long as the dosage was not poisonous, the patent was granted.

Patent medicines were advertised in newspapers and magazines and sold through the general store and by "medicine" shows. In 1907 the Pure Food and Drug Act, requiring an accurate description of contents of medicine on the label, put an end to the patent medicine industry. Not all medicines were patented.

Most medicines were sold in distinctive bottles, often with the name of the medicine and location in relief. Many early bottles were made in the glass manufacturing area of southern New Jersey. Later companies in western Pennsylvania and Ohio manufactured bottles.

References: Joseph K. Baldwin, *A Collector's Guide To Patent And Proprietary Medicine Bottles Of The Nineteenth Century,* Thomas Nelson, Inc., 1973; Ralph & Terry Kovel, *The Kovels' Bottle Price List, 8th Edition,* Crown Publishers, 1987; Carlo & Dot Sellari, *The Standard Old Bottle Price Guide,* Collector Books, 1989.

Periodicals: *Antique Bottle And Glass Collector,* P.O. Box 187, East Greenville, PA 18041.

Alternative Syrup, Pike & Osgood, rect, olive amber, applied tapered lip, pontil

base, 8¾″ h, Stoddard N H Glass-
works, c1850 . . . . **2,000.00**
Bennet's Magic Cure, sq, beveled
edges, deep blue, applied sq collar
lip, smooth base, 5⅛″ h, 1865–75 . . **375.00**
Billing's Rheumatic Liniment, aqua, sq
collar lip, open pontil, 6″ h, c1850 . . **20.00**
Brant's Purifying Extract, rect, indented
panels, aqua, applied double collar
lip, open pontil base, 10⅛″ h, c1850 **200.00**

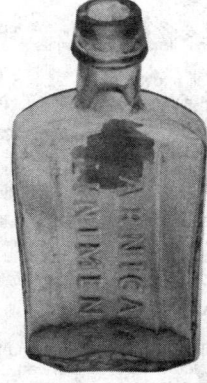

**J. R. Burdsell's Arnira Liniment, NY,
aqua, open pontil, 5⅜″ h, $25.00.**

Cellinian Balm, round, aqua, rolled lip,
open pontil base, 4⅜″ h, c1850 . . . . **50.00**
Clarkes–Lincoln–World Famed Blood
Mixture, gray–blue, 7¼″ h, America,
1870–80 . . . . **30.00**
Craig Kidney Cure Company, The, oval
shape, golden amber, applied lip,
smooth base, emb, 9½″ h, 1870–80 **140.00**
Dr Davis Depurative, sq, beveled
edges, medium yellow–green, applied tapered lip, iron pontil base, 9¾″
h, c1850 . . . . **1,450.00**
Dr H W Jackson, Druggist, Vegetable
Home Syrup, round, olive green, applied tapered lip, iron pontil base, 5¾″
h, c1850 . . . . **650.00**
Dr Ivans & Hart, eight sided, aqua, ap-
plied tapered lip, open pontil base,
7⅝″ h, c1850 . . . . **95.00**
Dr J A Sherman's/Rupture Curative
Compound, rect, indented panels, cobalt blue, blue striations, tooled applied sq collar, smooth base, 8¼″ h,
1870–80 . . . . **1,000.00**
Dr Leroy's Mixture, round, aqua, applied
tapered lip, pontil base, 7½″ h, 1850–
60 . . . . **160.00**
Dr Weaver's Canker Cure, oval shape,
aqua, rolled lip, open pontil base,
emb, 5¼″ h, c1850 . . . . **340.00**
From The Laboratory of G. W. Mer-
chant, rect, emerald green, applied
tapered lip, iron pontil base, 5⅝″ h,
1860 . . . . **120.00**
Gregory's Instant Cure, sq, indented
panels, bluish–aqua, applied tapered
lip, open pontil base, 6⅜″ h, c1850 **725.00**
H K Root's German Ointment, aqua,
flair lip, open pontil, 3⅜″ h, c1850 . . **25.00**
Howards Vegetable Cancer and Canker
Syrup, rect, beveled edges, olive yellow, applied sq collar lip, open pontil
base, 7⅜″ h, c1850 . . . . **2,500.00**
I Covert's Balm of Life, rect, beveled
corners, olive green, applied tapered
lip, open pontil base, 6″ h, c1840 . . **600.00**
C Jillson's Compound Vegetable Syrup,
oval shape, aqua, sq collar lip, open
pontil, 9¼″ h, c1850 . . . . **55.00**
Mrs S A Allen's World's Hair Restorer,
rect, indented panels, purplish–amethyst, sq tooled lip, 7¼″ h, c1870 . . **125.00**
Robert Gibson & Sons/Lozenge/Mak-
ers, English, canister type, aqua,
tooled smooth lip, 13″ h, c1870 . . . . **30.00**
Smith's Green Mountain Renovator,
rect, beveled edges, olive amber, applied double ring lip, pontil base, 7″ h,
c1850 . . . . **675.00**
Swaim's Genuine Panacea, rect, bev-
eled edges, aqua, applied tapered lip,
open pontil base, 7¾″ h, 1830–40 . . **240.00**
Swift's Syphilitic Specific, oval, deep
blue, applied sq collar lip, smooth
base, side strap, 8⅞″ h, c1870 . . . . **240.00**
T J Dunbar & Co, black glass, olive
green, applied inverted tapered lip,
iron pontil, 9⅜″ h, 1850–60 . . . . **150.00**
True Daffy's Elixir, rect, beveled edges,
yellow–green, applied ring lip, ball
pontil base, 4⅞″ h, England, 1830–
50 . . . . **350.00**
USA Hosp Dept, round, aqua, sq tooled
lip, smooth base, 9⅛″ h, c1865 . . . . **250.00**
Ward's Antiseptic Fluid, rect, concave
panels, candy apple green, tooled sq
collar lip, smooth base, 7⅝″ h, c1870 **150.00**
Warner's Safe Cure, oval shape, golden
amber, applied lip, smooth base, 9½″
h, 1870–90 . . . . **160.00**

MERCURY GLASS

History: Mercury glass is a light bodied, double
walled glass that was "silvered" by applying a so-

lution of silver nitrate to the inside of the object through a hole in the base of the formed object.

F. Hale Thomas, London, patented the method in 1849. In 1855 the New England Glass Co. filed a patent for the same type of process. Other American glass makers soon followed. The glass reached the height of its popularity in the early 20th century.

Compote, etched birds and leaves, 5¾″ d, 2¾″ h, $80.00.

Candlesticks, pr	
8″ h	**130.00**
11″ h, enameled floral dec	**120.00**
Candy Dish, 4¼ x 8¼″, clear glass domed dec, pedestal base	**30.00**
Carafe, 5½″ d, 12″ h, mushroom stopper, dated 1909	**50.00**
Compote, 6½ x 7″, enameled white floral dec, gold int.	**65.00**
Creamer, etched grapevine dec, applied clear handle	
6½″ h	**125.00**
6¾″ h, Sandwich Glass Co	**120.00**
Curtain Tiebacks, pr, 2½″ d	**25.00**
Pitcher, 6″ h, etched fern dec	**140.00**
Salt	
1¾″ d, 1¼″ h, silver, three applied clear feet	**35.00**
2⅞″ d, 2½″ h, master, silver ext., gold int., pedestal foot, initials on plug	**90.00**
3″ d, urn shape, ftd	**35.00**
Sweetmeat Dish, 4″ d, 7½″ h, clear cov, pedestal base	**40.00**
Toothpick, white enameled floral dec, gold int.	**40.00**
Urn, 13″ h, baluster shape, marked "Harnish & Co, London"	**250.00**
Vases, pr	
8¾″ h, emerald green, hp floral dec, c1890	**175.00**
10½″ h, cylindrical body, hp flower and leaf band around center	**100.00**
12″ h, ribbed, green, enameled floral and bird dec	**125.00**
Wig Stand, 10¼″ h, discolored stem . .	**90.00**

METTLACH

History: In 1809 Jean Francis Boch established a pottery at Mettlach in Germany's Moselle Valley. His father had started a pottery at Septfontaines in 1767. Nicholas Villeroy began his pottery career at Wallerfanger in 1789.

In 1841 these three factories merged. They pioneered in underglaze printing on earthenware, using transfers from copper plates, and in using coal fired kilns. Other factories were developed at Dresden, Wadgassen, and Danischburg.

The castle and Mercury emblems are the two chief marks. Secondary marks are known. The base also contains a shape mark and usually a decor mark. Pieces are found in relief, etched, prints under the glaze, and cameo.

Prices are for print under glaze unless otherwise specified.

References: Susan and Al Bagdade, *Warman's English & Continental Pottery & Porcelain, 1st Edition,* Warman Publishing Co., Inc., 1987; Gary Kirsner, *The Mettlach Book, Second Edition,* published by author, 1987, R. H. Mohr, *Mettlach Steins, Ninth Edition,* published by author, 1982.

Additional Listings: Villeroy & Boch.

Beaker	
#1134/2327, ¼ L, couple at feast	**110.00**
#1135/2327, ¼ L, Alpine couple . .	**125.00**
#2327/1290C, ¼ L, Bavarian crest	**85.00**
#2815, ¼ L, cameo, dancers	**325.00**
#2842/1175, ¼ L, old dwarf, cane at feet, broken wine goblet	**90.00**
Bowl, #1322, silver rim band, dated 1885 in base, castle mark, 9″ d	**350.00**
Coaster, #2818, etched, smoker toasting, 4½″ d, set of six	**250.00**
Pitcher, #7012, Phanolith dancing, white, matte, blue ground, 12″ h . . .	**650.00**
Plaque	
#1044/95, print under glaze, Burg Eltz, chip on rear inner ring edge	**185.00**
#1044/190, print under glaze, Schlossplatz, Stuttgart, 12″	**265.00**
#1769, 14½″ d, incised battle scene, polychrome enamel, marked "Arnold von Winkelried/Mettlach/1769"	**650.00**
#2623, etched, Quindenus, 7½″ d . .	**150.00**
#2080, etched, four Kurassiers, sgd "Stocke," 15″ d	**1,375.00**
#2875, cameo	**900.00**

#2997, etched, Fall, minor wear to
gold, 17½" d **2,100.00**
#2998, etched, Winter, 17½" d **4,200.00**
Plate, #2960, etched, Art Nouveau, 15"
d **90.00**
Punch Bowl, cov, 2 L, print under glaze
#2226/1062, tavern scenes with sol-
diers on both sides, Schlitt **275.00**
#2280/1005, gnomes at wine press,
other side with King Gnome shar-
ing brew with wine cellar keeper,
Schlitt **375.00**

**Stein, #2090II/10/94, matte finish,
$625.00.**

Stein
#961/2179, 1/4 L, print under glaze,
gnome spilling pitcher of beer on
himself and Prosit, gnome's head
thumb lift, sgd "HS" **250.00**
#1005, 1 L **275.00**
#1028, 2/3 L, relief, hay scene with
man **275.00**
#1102/1909, 1/2 L, print under glaze,
comical scene at Hofbrau, pewter
lid with relief detail of Munich Child **350.00**
#1394, 1/2 L, etched, French card **425.00**
#1520, 1/2 L, etched, Prussian eagle **525.00**
#1526, 1/2 L, print over glaze, comi-
cal map, Munich as beer center of
Europe, pewter lid **300.00**
#1786, 1/2 L, etched, St Florian put-
ting fire out **650.00**
#1909, 1/2 L, print under glaze, man
playing harp to moon with cat and
monkey **200.00**
#1997, 1/2 L, etched and print under
glaze, George Ehret Brewer, inlaid
lid **275.00**
#2077, 1/2 L, raised design, owl

reading book, white lining, pewter
top **250.00**
#2184, 3/10 L, print under glaze,
gnomes and beavers design, pot-
tery insert on lid **325.00**
#2348/1022, 3.3 L, print under glaze,
musician, man, and woman **350.00**
#2373, 1/2 L, etched, St Augustine,
FL, alligator handle, castle mark **675.00**
#2520, 1 L, etched, student and bar-
maid, sgd "HS" **900.00**
#2721, etched and print under glaze,
cabinet maker, castle mark **850.00**
#5013/965, 1/2 L, Faience, print un-
der glaze, "In Arte Libertas," pewter
lid **550.00**
#5022, 1 L, Faience, two scenes, left
oval cartouche of ocean boat
scene, other scene of small farm-
house **1,250.00**
Vase, #3358, Art Nouveau, 12" h **250.00**

MILITARIA

History: Wars always have been part of history.
Until the mid-19th century, soldiers often had to fill
their own needs, including weapons. Even in the
20th century a soldier's uniform and some of his
gear are viewed as his personal property, even
though issued by a military agency.

Conquering armed forces made a habit of acquiring souvenirs from their vanquished foes. They
brought their own uniforms and accessories home
as badges of triumph and service.

Saving militaria may be one of the oldest collecting traditions. Militaria collectors tend to have
their own special shows and view themselves outside the normal antiques channels. However, they
haunt small indoor shows and flea markets in
hopes of finding additional materials.

References: Ray A. Bows, *Vietnam Military
Lore 1959–1973,* Bows & Sons, 1988; Robert
Fisch, *Field Equipment of the Infantry 1914–1945,*
Greenberg Publication, 1989; *North South Trad-
er's Civil War Price Guide, 4th Edition,* North South
Trader, 1988; *Official Price Guide To Military Col-
lectibles,* House of Collectibles, 1985; Jack H.
Smith, *Military Postcards 1870–1945,* Wallace-
Homestead, 1988; Sydney B. Vernon, *Vernon's
Collectors' Guide To Orders, Medals, and Deco-
rations,* published by author, 1986.

Periodicals: *Military Collectors' News,* P.O.
Box 702073, Tulsa, OK 74170; *North South
Trader,* 724 Caroline Street, Fredericksburg, VA
22401.

Collectors' Clubs: American Society of Military
Insignia Collectors, 1331 Bradley Avenue, Hum-
melstown, PA 17036; Association of American Mil-
itary Uniform Collectors, 446 Berkshire Rd, Elyria,
OH 44035; Company of Military Historians, North
Main Street, Westbrook, CT 06498; Imperial Ger-

man Military Collectors Association, Box 38, Keyport, NJ 07735.

Reproduction Alert: Pay special attention to Civil War and Nazi material.

Additional Listings: Firearms and Swords. See World War I and World War II in *Warman's Americana & Collectibles* for more examples.

REVOLUTIONARY

Bayonet, scabbard and over-shoulder sling, "Hauger" 100.00
Book, *Military Journal During The American Revolutionary War...To Which Is Added, An Appendix Containing Biographical Sketches Of Several General Officers,* James Thacher, Boston, 1827, 2nd edition, full leather, worn 75.00

WAR OF 1812

Book, *A Narrative Of Events In The South Of France And Of The Attack On New Orleans in 1814 and 1815,* Capt. John Henry Cooke, London, 1835, 12 mo, worn leather backed boards 60.00
Broadside, Canadian Courant Extra, Montreal, August 12, 1912, text of British Revocation of the Orders in Council, comments about American government declaring war, mounted on heavy paper, somewhat soiled, edges frayed 375.00

CIVIL WAR

Bed, camp, trestle type, wood, folding   300.00

Civil War, daguerreotype, soldier, gutta percha case, gold trim and mountings, 2½ x 2", $100.00.

Blanket, mixed tan wool, brown stripe, US woven in center 500.00
Book
 Berdan's United States Sharpshooters In The Army Of The Potomac 1861-1865, Capt. C.A. Stevens, St. Paul, 1892, 1st edition, orig cloth, illus with plates, faded spine, broken inner front hinge 120.00
 History Of The Fiftieth Regiment Of Infantry Massachusetts Volunteer Militia In The Late War Of The Rebellion, William B Stevens, Boston, 1907, cloth 65.00
 Narrative Of The Campaign In The Valley Of The Shenandoah In 1861, Robert Patterson, Philadelphia, 1865, 128 pgs, 1st edition, sgd presentation copy from author, orig cloth, spine ends chipped, good condition 60.00
Booklet, water-color sketches by Ed S Fuller, dated 1865, cov with pencil medallions, portraits of Union soldiers, patriotic shields, artist's name and date, seven page int. with watercolor sketches of homes, military buildings, logging camp, and church, 4¾ x 3½" 650.00
Bullet Mold, 52 caliber 40.00
Button, officer, Alabama Volunteer Corps, 2 pcs, marked "AVC" between eagle wings 135.00
Canteen, tin, drum shape, red cloth cov, leather strap 85.00
Cartridge Box Plate, oval, marked "US"   30.00
Document Box, 6 x 9 x 3½", painted scene, steam paddle boat, fort on hill, banner reads "April, 1863, USS Benton, Porters Flagship, Bald Head" . . 500.00
Drum, 13 x 17½", painted eagle dec, US shield, sgd "135th New York Volunteers," two walnut drumsticks . . . 1,980.00
Hat, Naval, straw 200.00
Muster roll, 20th Regt Illinois, August to October, 1863, folds out to 20 x 30", document entries 100.00
Saddle, Confederate, C.S. saddle shield 500.00
Stirrups, artillery, brass, marked "US"   40.00
Sword, brass, hand guard with rope twist design grip, knuckle guard stamped "DFM," blade stamped "Empson & Silver, Trenton, NJ" and "US DPM, 1865" 440.00
Tintype, full length, unidentified Federal Cavalry man, gear, sword, and carbine 375.00
Uniform, Federal, enlisted infantry, frock coat, blue piping on collar and cuffs, nine button front, maker and inspector marks in sleeve 1,900.00

Watch Fob, 2″ h, scrimshaw, polychromed red, blue, and green highlights, inscribed "Union/J. C./9/Mass" ... **350.00**

INDIAN WARS

Belt
  Prairie, saber straps, M-85 .... **130.00**
  Saber, officer's, spun metal, buckle and straps **100.00**
Belt and Buckle, eagle dec **45.00**
Cape, dress, artillery officer's **160.00**
Powder Horn, 13″ w, Jos. Colton, Roxbury, 1764, map of Hudson River area, river scene **1,000.00**
Scabbard, 18″ l, blued metal, for 43/70 Springfield bayonet, state of MA, brass device **15.00**
Spurs, cavalry trooper's, nickel plated, orig leather strap **30.00**

FRANCO-PRUSSIAN WAR

Helmet
  Pickelhaube style, brass **200.00**
  Officer's, silver garde star, black eagle on breast of heraldic eagle, plain spike, gilt, chin strap, silk lining **1,500.00**
Medal, French, veteran, black and green ribbon, 1870–71 .... **20.00**

SPANISH-AMERICAN WAR

Button, 1¼″, Veterans Encampment, brown veterans symbol, white ground, blue rim lettering, attached red and yellow ribbons inscribed in silver **12.00**
Flag, Cuban, red, white, and blue, glazed muslin **250.00**
Gloves, officer's **125.00**
Pin, 2″ h, figural, Uncle Sam marching to Cuba, bayonet rifle over shoulder, brass, diecut, emb, c1898 .... **50.00**
Spoon, 16″ l, pine, carved cannons, soldier with gun, initials, marked "July 8, 1899" **400.00**

WORLD WAR I

Bayonet, Remington, case, 1917 .... **90.00**
Buckle, US Balloon Corps, emb hot air balloon **25.00**
Canteen, medic, German, cup, marked "HSD Argonne Nov 1," screw top wood cov, leather harness, 1914 ... **35.00**
Compass, US Army, brass, dated 1918 **50.00**
Dog Tag Stamping Kit, orig wood box **100.00**
Flare Pistol, French, marked "Modele 1918" **125.00**

Hat, US Army, doughboy style **25.00**
Heater, foot, portable, marked "Glogou" **30.00**
Jacket, US Army Medical Corps, insignia **60.00**
Map Case, leather, strap, nine orig tour maps of France **35.00**
Measure, angle, US Army Engineer's Corps, case, 1916 .... **45.00**
Shaving Kit, field, strop and safety razor, blades **40.00**
Trench Knife, Austrian, scabbard, leather carrying thong **50.00**
Uniform, US Army, includes helmet, campaign hat, overseas cap, leggins, and puttees **160.00**

WORLD WAR II

Badge
  Pilot's Wings, snap on back **25.00**
  Wound, German, silver, orig box, unissued **55.00**
Belt and Buckle, German, Luftwaffe, brass with silver wash, 1942 ..... **35.00**
Button, Royal Air Force, brass, emb wings and king's crown **4.00**
Compass
  Gyro, US battleship, electric components and six brass slave compasses, Sperry **900.00**
  Wrist type, Japanese Army **20.00**
Flyers Goggles, Japanese, gray fur lined cups, yellow lenses, boxed ... **15.00**
Hat, parade, Italian black Fascist, long tassel, orig hat badge **50.00**
Helmet, Nazi, decal on both sides, orig chin strap, pre 1945 .... **135.00**
Map, escape, 20 x 24″, Royal Air force, north Italy, black and white **25.00**
Tunic, flight, German Luftwaffe **200.00**
Uniform, WAVES, white sharkskin **50.00**

KOREA

Jacket and Cap, sergeant's OD, Ike style, pile lined cap with ear flaps .. **15.00**
Photo Album, 11 x 15″, troops, guard duty, and USO photos, 2nd Division insignia, inscribed "Soul Patrol, Co B 2nd BN 23rd Inf, APW" **25.00**

VIETNAM

Flag, Viet Cong, 16 x 23″, gold star, squad level **30.00**
Helmet, Navy, patrol pilot's, Fiberglas, white, ear phones, chin strap, gold visor with decal, dated "8–65" **25.00**
Medal, US Service, ribbon with bronze battle star **12.00**

MILK GLASS

History: Opaque white glass attained its greatest popularity at the end of the 19th century. American glass manufacturers made opaque white tablewares as a substitute for costly European china and glass. Other opaque colors, e.g., blue and green, were made. As the Edwardian era began, milk glass expanded into the novelty field.

The surge of popularity in milk glass subsided after World War I. However, milk glass continues to be made in the 20th century. Some modern products are reissues and reproductions of early forms. This presents a significant problem for collectors, although it is partially obviated by patent dates or company markings on the originals and by the telltale signs of age.

Collectors favor milk glass from the pre–World War I era, especially animal covered dishes. The most prolific manufacturers of these animal covers were Atterbury, Challinor–Taylor, Flaccus, and McKee.

References: E. McCamley Belknap, *Milk Glass*, Crown Publishers, 1949, out–of–print; Regis F. and Mary F. Ferson, *Yesterday's Milk Glass Today*, privately printed, 1981; Regis F. and Mary F. Ferson, *Today's Prices For Yesterday's Milk Glass*, privately printed, 1985; S. T. Millard, *Opaque Glass*, Wallace–Homestead, 1975, 4th edition.

Collectors' Club: National Milk Glass Collectors Society, P. O. Box 402, Northfield, MN 55057.

Museum: Houston Antique Museum, Chattanooga, TN.

Notes: There are many so–called McKee animal covered dishes. Caution must be exercised in evaluating pieces because some authentic covers were not signed. Further, many factories have made, and many still are making, split rib bases with McKee–like animal covers or with different animal covers. There is also disagreement among collectors on the issue of flared vs. unflared bases. The prices for McKee pieces as given are for authentic items with either the cover or base signed.

Pieces are cross referenced to the Ferson's and Belknap's books by the (F—) or (B—) marking at the end of a listing.

Animal
Dog, Scottie, 6″ l, sitting, L. E. Smith ... 80.00
Horse, base sgd "McKee" 300.00
Animal Dish, cov
American Hen on Nest, (F567) 65.00
Hen on Nest, blue head, matched numbered top and base, (F12) .. 50.00
Robin with Berry, (F217) 40.00
Rooster, ribbed base, numbered, (F11) 45.00
Squirrel, acorn base, (F15) 125.00
Swan, closed neck, basketweave base, (M278) 65.00
Turkey, nest base, (F62) 75.00

Animal Dish, cov, reclining cat, ribbed base, imp "3" on base int., 5⅜″ w, $65.00.

Bird House, 5¼″ d, "Wren's Honeymoon Hut," marked "Mfg by McKee & Co, Pat Appl'd For" on rim, green roof, white sides, metal base (F223) ... 65.00
Bon Bon, scoop shape, Eagle Glass Co, 1899 (F597) 25.00
Bowl, 8″ d
Arch Border, alternating wide curved arches and interlocking narrow pointed arches, Challinor-Taylor (B100a) 35.00
King's Crown, figural, basketweave pattern on slanted sides, vertical bar pattern on base, eight triangular points forming crown (B1078b) ... 50.00
Candlestick, 3⅜″ h, clown, bust rises from wide curved neck ruff (F129) .. 60.00
Celery, Burred Hobnail 35.00
Compote, lattice edge, hp center, (F175) 25.00
Creamer, Blackberry 40.00
Dish, cov
Hand and dove, patent date, (F52) 120.00
Snare Drum Cannon, (F561) 65.00
Dresser Set, dresser tray, cov puff box, two bottles with stoppers, painted dec ... 60.00
Fish Set, fish platter, four serving dishes, patent date, Atterbury ... 200.00
Fruit Immerser, 1½″ h, scalloped circular disc, small pedestal, used for home canning, four patent dates on base, latest July 20, 1886 (F334) .. 15.00
Match Holder
Indian Head, (B219) 110.00
Minstrel Boy 75.00
Mustard, cov, bull's head, (F14) 125.00
Pickle Dish, 9¾″ l, figural, fish, base imp "Patented June 4, 1872" (F332b) .. 25.00
Plaque, Abraham Lincoln, (F560) 150.00
Plate
7½″ d, Contrary Mule, mule pulling back on rein, Westmoreland, (B271, row 5a) 30.00

8" d, Eagle, stars border, Fenton . . . **35.00**
9" d, Serenade, Greentown, (F41) . . **35.00**
Platter, 13¾", figural, fish, Atterbury, patent date June 4, 1872 (F337c) . . **50.00**
Sugar, Sunflower, row of paneled sunflowers above row of paneled lilies of the valley (B82b) **50.00**
Syrup, French Primrose **50.00**
Toothpick Holder, Tramp Shoe, (F194) **40.00**

MILLEFIORI

History: Millefiori (thousand flowers) is an ornamental glass composed of bundles of colored glass rods fused to become canes. The canes were pulled while still ductile to the desired length, sliced, arranged in a pattern and again fused together. The Egyptians developed this technique in the first century B.C.; it was revived in the 1880s.

Reproduction Alert: Millefiori items, such as paperweights, cruets, toothpicks, etc., are being made by many modern companies.

Box, cov, royal blue and white, 2¾" d, 2½" h, $250.00.

Bowl, 2", pink, green, and white canes, applied handles **40.00**
Cruet, camphor handle **85.00**
Dish, 5" d, octagonal, blue and white canes **125.00**
Goblet, 7½" h, deeply rounded bowl, everted rim, multicolored floral canes, hollow gilt speckled baluster stem, circular foot, Venetian, set of 6 . . . . **1,100.00**
Inkwell, 4½" h, sgd "Paul Ysart" **175.00**
Paperweight, Clichy, 1½" d, central pink cane surrounded by pale, yellow, and white circles, five large pink and white roses outer garland alternating with green and pink pairs of canes **125.00**
Perfume Bottle, round body, seven por-

trait canes, orig metal mountings, Venetian, c1830–40 . . . . **425.00**
Slipper, 5" l, multicolored canes, applied camphor glass ruffle and heel **100.00**
Sugar, cov, 3½ x 4", cobalt blue, white flowers **110.00**
Toothpick Holder, ruffled top, c1890 . . **200.00**
Vase
5½" h, purple bands, white oval lines, white bands, red flowers, yellow centers **150.00**
11" h, bulbous, yellow and green, red dots **115.00**

MINIATURE LAMPS

History: Miniature oil and kerosene lamps, often called "night lamps," are diminutive replicas of larger lamps. Simple and utilitarian in design, miniature lamps found a place in the parlor (as "courting" lamps), hallway, children's rooms, and sickrooms.

Miniature lamps are found in many glass types from amberina to satin glass. Miniature lamps measure 2½ to 12 inches in height with the principle parts being the base, collar, burner, chimney, and shade. In 1877 both L. J. Atwood and L. H. Olmsted patented burners for miniature lamps. Their burners made the lamps into a popular household accessory.

Study a lamp carefully to make certain all parts are original; married pieces are common. Reproductions abound.

References: Ann Gilbert McDonald, *Evolution of the Night Lamp*, Wallace-Homestead, 1979; Frank R. & Ruth E. Smith, *Miniature Lamps,* Schiffer Publishing Ltd., 1981, 6th printing; Ruth E. Smith, *Miniature Lamps - II,* Schiffer Publishing Ltd., 1982; John F. Solverson, *Those Fascinating Little Lamps,* Antique Publications, 1988; John F. Solverson (comp.), *"Those Fascinating Little Lamps"/Miniature Lamps,* (includes prices for Smith numbers) *Value Guide,* Antique Publications, 1988.

Note: The numbers given below refer to the figure numbers found in the Smith books.

Figure III–I, Artichoke, nutmeg burner, 7¾"
Milk glass, white, yellow and green fired–on paint, minor flaking at top of shade **250.00**
Satin glass, red, minor flakes on top edge of shade **725.00**
Figure XVIII–II, overshot, frosted, house scene, 5½" **750.00**
#20–II, blue, Aladdin type **290.00**
#23–I, Time, clear, emb "Time & Light, Pride of America, Grand Vals Perfect Time Indicating Lamp," white beehive chimney, 6⅝" **250.00**

#278–I, milk glass, green basket pattern, $190.00.

#32–I, Little Duchess, cobalt blue, brass saucer, nutmeg burner, 2⅝" .. 115.00

#36–I, Little Buttercup, amethyst, applied handle, nutmeg burner, 2¾" .. 100.00

#106–I, Block House, blue, acorn burner, 5½" 110.00

#109–I, Beaded Heart, green, six toed foot, acorn burner, 5⅜" 310.00

#111–I, Bull's Eye, teal, acorn burner, 5" 150.00

#112–I, Bull's Eye, emerald green, acorn burner, 4⅞" 100.00

#160–I, white milk glass, emb scrolling, green and gold painted dec, hornet burner, 7¼" 200.00

#161–II, Prism, emb, Atterbury 145.00

#179–I, blue milk glass, emb beaded panels, acorn burner, 6⅝", worn paint 125.00

#201–I, Swirl, white milk glass, emb flowers, scrolling highlighted in blue and gold, pink and green painted flowers, hornet burner, 10½" 200.00

#209–I, white milk glass, emb design and flowers, multicolored paint, nutmeg burner, 9½" 150.00

#213–I, Chrysanthemum, white milk glass, pink and yellow dec, hornet burner, 8½" 275.00

#228–II, amber, 5⅞" 125.00

#229–I, green milk glass, emb fishnet and florals, nutmeg burner, 7½" ... 350.00

#276–I, Pineapple in the Basket, white milk glass, fired–on brown paint, nutmeg burner, 7⅜" 175.00

#288–I, red satin glass, emb designs, P & A Victor burner, 11½", crack in shade 175.00

#292–I, white milk glass, emb flowers and scrolls, burgundy ground, burgundy, orange, and green flowers, nutmeg burner, 8" 350.00

#317–I, white milk glass base and shade, green ground, pink and yellow daisy dec, nutmeg burner, 8½" 325.00

#338–I, Florette, green cased glass, nutmeg burner, 6¾" 650.00

#348–I, white milk glass shade, painted naturalistic colored owl, yellow moon, gray–tan ground, brass base and font, acorn burner, 8⅜" 650.00

#385–I, pink cased satin glass, nutmeg burner, 6¾" 375.00

#390–I, bright yellow, melon ribbed shade and base, glossy finish, nutmeg burner, 7", three small flakes on base of shade 475.00

#400–I, Beaded Drape, cherry red satin glass, acorn burner, 9" 150.00

#425–I, irid green, emb dec, nutmeg burner, 9¾" 450.00

#432–I, Twinkle, blue, acorn burner, 6⅞" 225.00

#458–II, white milk glass, heavily emb daisies and leaves, large white milk glass balls around base 400.00

#467–II, blue opal, applied clear feet, foreign burner, 7¾" 1,900.00

#482–I, Daisy and Cube, amber, nutmeg burner, 7¾" 325.00

#509–I, Reverse Swirl, blue opal, acorn burner, 4¼" 200.00

#513–I, Swirl, blue opal, acorn burner, 4¾" 150.00

#531–I, cut velvet, yellow shading to light and back to dark, applied clear frosted feet, acorn burner, 7¾" 3,300.00

MINIATURES

History: There are three sizes of miniatures: doll house scale (ranging from ½ to 1"), sample size, and child's size. Since most earlier material is in museums or extremely expensive, the most common examples are 20th century.

Many mediums were used for miniatures: silver, copper, tin, wood, glass, and ivory. Even books were printed in miniature. Prices are broad ranged, depending on scarcity and quality of workmanship.

The collecting of miniatures dates back to the 18th century. It remains one of the world's leading hobbies.

References: Lillian Baker, *Creative and Collectible Miniatures*, Collector Books, 1984; Flora Gill Jacobs, *Dolls Houses in America: Historic Preservation in Miniature*, Charles Scribner's Sons, 1974; Flora Gill Jacobs, *History of Dolls Houses*, Charles Scribner's Sons; Constance Eileen King, *Dolls and Dolls Houses*, Hamlyn; Eva Stille, *Doll Kitchens, 1800–1980*, Schiffer Publishing, Ltd., 1988; Von Wilckens, *Mansions in Miniature*, Tuttle.

Periodicals: *Miniature Collector,* Collector Communications Corp., 170 Fifth. Ave, New York, NY 10010; *Nutshell News,* Clifton House, Clifton, VA 22024.

Collectors' Clubs: International Guild Miniature Artisans, P.O. Box 842, Summit, NJ 07901; National Association of Miniature Enthusiasts, 123 N. Lemon St., Fullerton, CA 92632.

Museums: Kansas City Doll House Museum, Kansas City, MO; Margaret Woodbury Strong Museum, Rochester, NY; Mildred Mahoney Jubilee Doll House Museum, Fort Erie, Canada; Toy Museum of Atlanta, Atlanta, GA; Washington Dolls House and Toy Museum, Washington, DC.

Additional Listings: See Doll House Furnishings in *Warman's Americana & Collectibles* for more examples.

Sofa, china, hp pastel floral motif, gold trim, French or German, late 19th C, 4⅛″ l, $90.00.

DOLL HOUSE SIZE

Armoire, oak, golden finish, 1″ scale, c1900	115.00
Bathroom Set, Tootsietoy, metal, c1920, 8 pcs	100.00
Bed, maple, honey finish, scalloped head and foot boards, c1900, 6¼″ l	100.00
Chair, carved wood, scrolled arms and back, blue velvet seat, pr	65.00
Desk, Biedermeier, marble top, stencil dec, black ground, c1890	125.00

Dining Room Suite

Tin, 3½″ h oval drop leaf table, five 2″ h side chairs, one 2″ h armchair	90.00
Wood, Strombecker, walnut, table and two chairs	25.00
Dressing Table, maple, rect table, carved legs, scrolled apron, white marble top, mirrored cupboard, drawers, silver knobs, marbleized litho paper on back	150.00
Living Room Suite, Viennese ormolu mounted enamel, loveseat, two arm chairs, two chaises, table, firescreen, grand piano with stool, couples in landscape on each pc, 9 pcs	6,000.00

Piano, 3½″ h, upright, tin, brown painted ground, gilt trim, scrolled crest, emb back, scrolled swivel candle arms, hinged keyboard cov, three legged stool with painted red seat, 19th C	85.00
Settee, 6″ l, maple, Gothic style, carved back with three panels, curved arms, wicker seat	80.00

Table

3¼″ h, brass, tilt top	85.00
5″ w, carved wood, painted scene on top	60.00

ACCESSORIES

Baby Buggy, 4″ h, metal, scrolled, four working wheels	75.00
Bath Tub, 5½″ l, tin, lavender, gold stripes and faucet, tall legs, lower shelf, small matching pail, marked "Made In Germany"	65.00
Bird Cage, 2⅛″ h, brass, parrot	125.00
Candelabra, Petite Princess	20.00
Candlesticks, pr, 4⅜″ h, brass, Queen Anne	200.00
Castor Set, 4⅝″ h, pewter frame, four clear pressed glass bottles	125.00
Chamber Pot, 2⅛″ d, yellow ware, white band, applied handle	45.00
Christmas Tree, undecorated	25.00
Creamer, 3½″ h, blue spatterware, paneled, minor stains, rim chip	125.00
Cup, spatterware, handleless, black and green spatter, stains and edge wear	75.00
Fireplace, Regency style, Petite Princess	12.00
Kettle Stand, 3¼″ h, brass	155.00
Kitchen Stove, Petite Princess	70.00

Lamp

2″ h, tole ware, worn orig red paint	100.00
4″ h, banquet, gilt metal, urn shaped emb base, circular blown glass shade	175.00
Medicine Chest, 2½″ h, gilt metal, rect, hinged front door, shaped crest rail, one shelf int., glass medicine type bottles, 19th C	125.00
Mirror, 1″ h, brass, ormolu, turned columns support oval mirror, 19th C	100.00
Pail, 2⅜″ h, copper, cylindrical	60.00
Refrigerator, Petite Princess	75.00
Sewing Machine, tin, painted, c1920	45.00
Sugar Bucket, 2¼″ h, wooden, stave construction, damage, lid missing	40.00
Tea Cart, Petite Princess	20.00

Tea Kettle

4¼″ h, copper	125.00
4¾″ h, brass, worn lacquer	135.00
Towel Rack, Victorian, wood	35.00
Vase, 1½″, Jasperware, tree trunk shape, Art Nouveau dec	35.00

SAMPLE SIZE

Blanket Chest, 16¼" l, poplar, decorated, heavily alligatored brown graining, green trim, molded edge lid, bracket feet 875.00

Chair, Centennial, Chippendale style, mahogany, modified lyre back, upholstered slip seat, cabriole legs, ball and claw feet, ornately carved stretcher 300.00

Chest of Drawers

13½" w, 9¾" d, 17" h, cherry and walnut, orig two tone varnish finish, four beveled edge overlapping drawers, orig porcelain pulls, darker stained end and front panels, cut–out feet, late wire nail construction, attributed to Ohio Mennonites, alligatored worn varnish, minor edge damage 300.00

13¾" h, Empire, butternut, scrolled crest, four drawers, raised panel ends, scrolled feet, Rockingham glazed knobs, refinished 450.00

15" w, 7" d, 16¾" h, walnut, gallery top with semi–circular cut–out between top drawers, dovetailed case, molded trim, six dovetailed drawers, clear lacy glass pulls, brass casters, old finish, minor damage to knobs 350.00

15½" w, 10¾" d, 16¾" h, Empire, refinished mahogany, four dovetailed drawers with cross banded veneer and applied edge molding, top drawer divided into three false fronts, wide molded pilasters with acanthus carved capitals, carved paw feet, minor veneer repair, replaced glass pulls 2,800.00

Desk, 7" w, 5" d, 10" h, Hepplewhite, walnut and cherry, dovetailed, slant front, three drawers with inlay, fitted int., leather writing surface, scrolled legs, brass knobs 400.00

Furnace, Mueller 425.00

Linen Press, 12⅝" w, 7½" d, 21½" h, pine, rect molded cornice, two doors, int. shelf, lower case fitted with three graduated drawers, shaped bracket feet, Victorian 225.00

Rocker, adv for PA furniture store, painted red, gold stenciled letters, turned spindles back, plank seat, c1900 . . . . 125.00

Settee, 23" l, painted and carved wood, shaped back with three arched crests, vase form splats, scrolled arms, plank seat, ring turned legs and stretchers, polychrome painted yellow and brown flowers, brown ground, PA, c1845 . . 2,000.00

Stand, 15⅞" w, 15⅝" d, 24" h, Sheraton, stripped walnut, applied gallery, one board top with age cracks, single dovetailed drawer with applied edge beading, turned legs 450.00

Wash Stand, 9" w, 5½" d, 14" h, Hepplewhite, walnut, rect, finely turned pencil point bracketed mirror, two drawers, inlay shelf, towel bar, NY, c1852 . . . . 850.00

CHILD SIZE

Bed

10" w, 16¼" l, maple, scrolled head and foot boards, old natural finish, modern counterpane and bolster, heavily played with condition 75.00

21" l, spool, walnut, rockers, old worn finish, one rocker replaced, one rail loose 200.00

Chair

Adirondack, arm, 7½" h, some damage, rockers missing 35.00

Arrowback, side, rabbit ears, worn seat branded "M Davis," bamboo turned legs, old red repaint with traces of green on seat, 28¾" h . . 150.00

Chest of Drawers

9¾" w, 5½" d, 11½" h, Empire, pine and poplar, orig red paint, black vinegar graining, four drawers . . . 625.00

15½" w, 8¼" d, 22½" h, pine, orig red flame graining, two small step back drawers, three large drawers, orig porcelain pulls 550.00

Cradle, 25¾" l, poplar, dovetailed scrolled ends, old dark brown alligatored finish 125.00

Cupboard, wall, 19½" w, 9½" d, 26" h, poplar, old worn brown paint, sq nail construction, age cracks and wear 300.00

Dressing Table, 8 x 15", metal, painted white, wooden table top, floral design, cotton and lace ruffle, celluloid box, mirror, comb, and brush 375.00

Herb Drying Rack, wood, 7" w, 6" h . . 90.00

Quilt, doll size

17 x 25", Four Patch, blues and other prints, pieced and knotted 20.00

20½ x 20½", Nine Patch, pink prints, red sq, machine sewn and quilted, faded, minor repairs 35.00

21½ x 26", Flying Geese, pieced orange and white, machine sewn, over all wear and fading 60.00

Table, drop leaf, 8¼" w, 14" w, 5½" l leaves, 12" h, pine and poplar, sq nail construction, old repairs, old finish 100.00

Trunk, dome top, wood cov paper, separate tray, locks, matched set of four 200.00

MINTON CHINA

History: In 1793 Thomas Minton and others formed a partnership and built a small pottery at Stoke–on–Trent, Staffordshire, England. Production began in 1798 with blue printed earthenware, mostly in the Willow pattern. In 1798 cream colored earthenware and bone china wares were introduced.

A wide range of styles and wares was produced. Minton introduced porcelain figures in 1826, Parian wares in 1846, encaustic tiles in the late 1840s, and Majolica wares in 1850. Many famous designers and artists in the English pottery industry worked for Minton.

Many early pieces are unmarked or have a Sevres type marking. The "ermine" mark was used in the early 19th century. Date codes can be found on tableware and Majolica. Between 1873 and 1911 a small globe signed Minton with a crown on top was used.

In 1883 the modern company was formed and called Mintons Limited. The "s" was dropped in 1968. Minton still produces bone china tablewares and some ornamental pieces.

References: Paul Atterbury and Maureen Batkin, *The Dictionary of Minton*, Antique Collectors' Club; Susan and Al Bagdade, *Warman's English & Continental Pottery & Porcelain, 1st Edition*, Warman Publishing Co., Inc., 1987.

Teapot, gray, blossom dec, 7″ l, 2¾″ h, $175.00.

Asparagus Plate, majolica, shaped rect, molded asparagus flanking well, black printed mark, set of twelve ... **1,045.00**
Bowl, 11″ d, flowerheads, leaves, and scrolls in red, gilt trim, green ground, c1805 .... **1,200.00**
Breakfast Set, plate with attached toast rack, salt and pepper shakers, Dejeuneau, green mark **165.00**
Bulb Planter, 10¾″ l, majolica, emb brown fence, green leaves, turquoise int., marked **145.00**
Cake Stand, hp, roses, green ground, c1877 .... **100.00**
Centerpiece Bowl, 24″ l, oval, turquoise ground, multicolored painted butterfly and geometric patterned reserve, flowerhead medallions against ground of perched birds, lappet pierced waisted rim, out scrolled handles, stylized mask and ball feet, black printed globe mark of 1893 Chicago World's Fair **9,900.00**
Centerpiece Set, 12″ h candlesticks, pedestal center bowl, hp cartouche on each side with Napoleon and Josephine, ram's head dec, deep aquamarine and white ground, gold trim, sgd **1,375.00**
Charger, 15½″ d, circular, concave, painted blossoms, stems, and leaves, two hovering butterflies, lavender, green, brown, yellow, red, and blue, white ground, clear overglaze, earthenware, underglaze and imp marks, c1872 .... **1,700.00**
Cup and Saucer, ribbon swags, rose, c1805 .... **120.00**
Dresser Set, 12 x 9″ tray, cov box, ring tree, gold and green flowers, white ground **225.00**
Ewer, 8½″ h, turquoise, raised putti holding swags leading to Neptune seated under spout, mermaid handle, c1868 .... **600.00**
Jug, 6¼″ h, applied hops and vine dec, 1848 .... **265.00**
Oyster Plate, emb fish, gilt trim, white ground **65.00**
Plate
8″ d, hp, large pink roses, scalloped gold edge, made for Soane & Smith, London, imp mark **100.00**
10″ d, brown glazed, acid etched, eagle grasping rabbit, imp mark, c1875 .... **250.00**
Soup Tureen, cov, underplate, 12¼″ d Hawthorne dec, all–over blue transfer, gilt highlights, molded leaf design handles and finial, imp and printed marks, late 19th C **150.00**
Tile, 6″ h, King Henry **65.00**
Vase, 11″ h, burnt amber, pink, and blue flowers, c1875 .... **165.00**
Wash Bowl and Pitcher, amethyst, ruby, and yellow floral dec **190.00**

MOCHA

History: Mocha decoration usually is found on utilitarian creamware and stoneware pieces and is produced through a simple chemical action. A color pigment of brown, blue, green, or black is made acidic by an infusion of tobacco or hops. When the acidic colorant is applied in blobs to an alkaline ground, it reacts by spreading in feathery, seaplant-like designs. This type of decoration usually is supplemented with bands of light colored slip.

Types of decoration vary greatly, from those done in a combination of motifs, such as "Cat's Eye" and "Earthworm," to a plain pink mug decorated with green ribbed bands. Most forms of mocha are hollow, e.g., mugs, jugs, bowls, and shakers.

English potters made the vast majority of the pieces. Marked pieces are extremely rare. Collectors group the ware into three chronological periods: 1780–1820, 1820–1840, and 1840–1880.

Reference: Susan and Al Bagdade, *Warman's English & Continental Pottery & Porcelain, 1st Edition,* Warman Publishing Co., Inc., 1987.

Cream Pitcher, white ground, narrow black bands, wide blue bands, 3¾" h, $170.00.

Bowl, 9½" d, vibrant agate dec, engine turned brown, blue, and tan border   **1,600.00**
Humidor, 7" h, black, tan, and white checkerboard dec, narrow chocolate, blue, and white bands, acorn finial, orig inner weight, three shallow base chips **2,500.00**
Mug
  4¼" h, agate, blue, white, and brown engined turned rim dec, light brown ground **1,000.00**
  4½" h
    Blue and brown horizontal sausage linked geometric pattern **1,100.00**
    Blue, brown, and mustard twig dec, matching banding **850.00**
    Marbleized blue, brown, and gold, incised green Leeds border ...   **950.00**
  4⅞" h, blue bands, black stripe, and seaweed dec, applied emb seal "Pint" **175.00**

5", olive band with blue stripe and seaweed dec, applied emb seal "Imperial" **150.00**
5½" h
  Black and white combed dec, gold bands top and bottom **2,200.00**
  Bright blue, gold, and dark brown banded geometric pattern, old handwritten note inside with Litchfield, NH provenance **1,000.00**
  Combed black and white dec, gold bands at top and bottom **2,200.00**
5¾" h, pale yellow, blue, white, and dark brown triple vertical earthworm dec, small hairline in bottom   **1,500.00**
6" h
  Black and blue repeated twig dec, pale green ground, blue and dark brown banding, tiny nick on inner rim **1,000.00**
  Black repeated wave lines, black banding, pale blue ground, blue wavy bands at top and bottom   **600.00**
6⅛" h, dark brown seaweed dec, tan band with blue and black striping   **250.00**
6¼" h, gold, brown, and blue earthworm dec, blue and brown banding   **800.00**
Pepper Pot
  3½" h, pale blue, brown, and yellow scroddled pattern, white ground ..   **525.00**
  4" h, brown, black, and cream engine turned geometric pattern **650.00**
  4¾" h, medium blue and brown incised geometric dec, minute flaking around shaker holes **700.00**
Pitcher
  5⅞" h, blue, brown, and dark brown earthworm dec, purple rimmed band, small chip, slight discoloration **600.00**
  6¼" h, black seaweed dec, blue band with blue and black striping **300.00**
  6½" h
    Circular brown and white dots with green incised loop band, slight discoloration, small chip on inner handle **800.00**
    Incised green Leeds band over combed bands around body, molded acanthus leaf spout, pale gray–green and cream dec   ...   **800.00**
  7" h, tobacco, dark brown, and tan twig dec **800.00**
  7¼" h
    Blue, brown, and white earthworm dec, gray–green ground, blue bands, slight loss of glaze, minor wear **500.00**
    Bright blue and brown cat's eye and earthworm dec, blue and dark brown bands, age crack under spout **650.00**

8¼" h, brown, blue, and gold cat's eye and earthworm dec, minor inner rim wear **1,300.00**
Tea Caddy, 5¼" h, marbleized brown, sienna, and white, orig lid, small nicks **1,600.00**
Teapot, 4½" h, marbleized brown sienna and white, green Leeds rim, minor nicks on cov and base **2,000.00**
Water Jug, 10" h, 14½" w, double jugs, white center handle, blue, brown, mustard, and black earthworm, cat's eye, and twig dec, minor rim and base chips, 1" hairline crack in rim **8,000.00**

MONART GLASS

History: Monart glass is a heavy, simple shaped art glass in which colored enamels are suspended in the glass during the glass making process. This technique was originally developed by the Ysart family in Spain in 1923. John Moncrief, a Scottish glassmaker, discovered the glass while vacationing in Spain, recognized the beauty and potential market, and began production in his Perth glassworks in 1924.

The name "Monart" is derived from the surnames Moncrief and Ysart. Two types of Monart were manufactured: a "commercial" line which incorporated colored enamels and a touch of aventurine in crystal, and the "art" line in which the suspended enamels formed designs such as feathers or scrolls. Monart glass, in most instances, is not marked. The factory used paper labels.

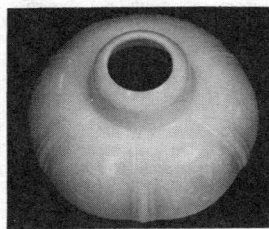

Lamp Shade, white, opal finish, 6¼" d, $75.00.

Basket, 4" h, mottled orange and green **100.00**
Bowl
  9" d, Aventurine, blue, mottled brown and goldstone, pebbled **135.00**
  10½" d, white, gray crackle, yellow and green flecks, oxblood red base and rim **150.00**
Candlesticks, pr, 3" h, mottled blue shading to lavender **75.00**

Vase
8½" h, green rim shaded to clear to brown, green pedestal **60.00**
14" h, bulbous, tapered, extended neck, flared rim, blue shaded to pink, gold highlights, Cluthra **625.00**

MONT JOYE GLASS

History: Mont Joye is a type of glass produced by Saint-Hilaire, Touvier, de Varreaux & Company at their glassworks in Pantin, France. Most pieces were lightly acid etched to give them a frosted appearance and decorated with enameled floral decorations. All pieces listed are frosted, unless otherwise noted.

Vase, light turquoise ground, acid etched frosting, iris dec, gold highlights on flower and leaves, gold band around crimped top, 8" h, $450.00.

Bowl, 3¾" d, enameled floral dec, sgd **265.00**
Pitcher, cameo cutting, crystal, green and gold, brass spout and handle, removable cov, artist sgd "Cristalle Rie Depantin" **500.00**
Rose Bowl, 4¼" d, enameled purple violets, gold stems, gold dec, pinched sides **150.00**
Vase
  5⅛" h, spherical, cylindrical neck and foot, etched and gilt oak leaves and acorns, gilt signature **150.00**
  5½" h, Nile green, gold enameled leaves and enameled lilies of the valley **375.00**
  7½" h, dark green satin ground, enameled pink iris dec **400.00**

10" h
Amber ground, enameled silver
and gold flowers 275.00
Crystal ground, gold leaves, enameled purple violets 350.00

MOORCROFT

History: William Moorcroft was first employed as a potter by James Macintyre & Co., Ltd. of Burslem in 1897. He established the Moorcroft pottery in 1913. The company initially used an impressed mark, "Moorcroft, Burslem"; a signature mark, "W. Moorcroft," followed.

The majority of the art pottery wares were hand thrown, resulting in a great variation among similarly styled pieces. Color and marks are keys to determining age.

Walker, William's son, continued the business upon his father's death and made the same style wares. Modern pieces are marked simply "Moorcroft" with export pieces also marked "Made in England."

Reference: Susan and Al Bagdade, *Warman's English & Continental Pottery & Porcelain, 1st Edition,* Warman Publishing Co., Inc., 1987.

Bowl
7" d, pomegranate and grape ext. and int., blue ground 475.00

Vase, Florian Ware, Lilac pattern, light blue ground, violet and dark blue flowers, marked in green script and brown stamp, 11¾" h, $650.00.

7⅜" d, blue ext. red, yellow, green orchids and white flowers int. 375.00
10½" d, Anemone, sgd, paper label 500.00
Box, cov, Spring Flowers pattern, round 290.00
Bulb Bowl, 6½ x 2¼", white and purple Narcissus, dark blue and green ground, "Potter to the Queen" mark 130.00
Candlesticks, pr
6½" h, Flambe, trees motif 475.00
7⅛" h, Pomegranate, c1918–29 . . . 675.00
Dish
7" l, Aurelian 265.00
7⅜" l, Eventide 1,150.00
Ginger Jar, 7", marked "Walter Moorcroft, 1960" 100.00
Humidor, cov, cornflower dec, brown ground 1,295.00
Jardiniere, 7" h, cylindrical, ftd, pink and purple poppies, blue ground, imp and painted marks, pr 275.00
Match Holder, 2¾" h, pink thistle flowers, mottled green ground, coat of arms, Macintyre mark, green painted initials "WM," printed "Redley Hall," c1897 . . . . 325.00
Plate, 7¼" d, pansy dec 400.00
Vase
3" h, bulbous, pomegranates and grapes dec, blue ground, 1940s . . 125.00
4½" h, green, pink flowers, paper label 100.00
6¼", pink and purple poppies, blue ground, imp and painted marks . . 125.00
7⅞" h, Florian, cylindrical, flaring bulbous, slightly scalloped rim, shaded blue ground, poppies dec, printed Florian mark, green signature "W Moorcroft, des," c1900 . . 1,100.00
8" h, Pomegranate, c1913–25 . . . . . 325.00
9" h, baluster, lavender poppies shoulder dec, pale blue ground, imp Royal mark, 1930, blue painted signature, marked "W Moorcroft" 275.00
15½" h, Flambe, trumpet, red irid glaze, flowering Japanese cherry blossoms, sgd "Moorcroft" 1,650.00

MORIAGE, JAPANESE

History: Moriage refers to applied clay (slip) relief motifs and decorations used on certain classes of Japanese pottery and porcelain.

This decorating was done by three methods: 1) handrolling and shaping, which was applied by hand to the biscuit in one or more layers; the design and effect required determined thickness and shape, 2) tubing or slip trailing, which applied decoration from a tube, like decorating a cake, and 3) hakeme, which is reducing the slip to a liquid and decorating the object with a brush. Color was applied either before or after the process.

Vase, handles, crown top, violets, gold trim, 9½″ h, $250.00.

Bowl, ftd
  6″, pink and green on lavender, floral
    medallions, raised dots 100.00
  7½″, green, floral center, intricate
    white slip work, scalloped edge . . 145.00
Demitasse Cup and Saucer, purple, burgundy, lavender, and pink flowers,
  gold and dotted dec, marked 48.00
Ewer, 7″, lacy dec, floral on green
  ground 85.00
Hatpin Holder, 4¾″, green beading, red
  flowers 60.00
Incense Burner, 3″, gray, slip dragon,
  finial, gold foo dog handles 25.00
Mug, 5½″, pink roses, lacy slip work . . 85.00
Pitcher, 6″, pink on white, floral, green
  slip netting 85.00
Plate, 7½″, blue and white, slip dragon,
  set of 6 . . . . 85.00
Sugar Shaker, pink, applied flowers . . 75.00
Tea Set, 27 pcs, dragon dec, brown,
  green, and white, raised star mark 250.00
Vase
  7½″, white on dark green, floral med-
    allion, handled 200.00
  10½″, pink and orange on rose, floral
    cartouche 225.00
  11½″, multicolored, slip flowers and
    fronds, marble ground, Nippon . . . 175.00

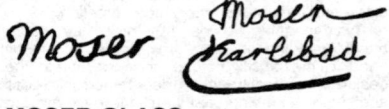

MOSER GLASS

History: Ludwig Moser (1833–1916) founded
his polishing and engraving workshop in 1857 in

Karlsbad (Karlovy Vary), Czechoslovakia. He employed many famous glass designers, e.g., Johann
Hoffmann, Josef Urban, and Rudolf Miller. In 1900
Moser and his sons, Rudolf and Gustav, incorporated Ludwig Moser & Söhne.

Moser art glass included clear pieces with inserted blobs of colored glass, cut colored glass
with classical scenes, cameo glass, and intaglio
cut. Many inexpensive enameled pieces also were
made.

In 1922 Leo and Richard Moser bought Meyr's
Neffe, their biggest Bohemian rival in art glass.
Moser executed many pieces for the Wiener Work-
stätte in the 1920s. The Moser glass factory continues to produce new items.

References: Gary Baldwin and Lee Carno,
Moser–Artistry In Glass: 1857–1938, Antique Publications, 1988; Mural K. Charon and John Ma-
reska, *Ludvik Moser, King of Glass: A Treasure
Chest of Photographs And History,* published by
author, 1984.

**Vase, Art Deco, diagonal cut swirls,
sgd "Alexandrite/Moser/Karlsbad," 6⅛″
h, $300.00.**

Box, 4½ d, amethyst, enameled flowers
  and gold trim, amber applied glass
  salamander on lid, three salamanders
  form feet 610.00
Centerpiece Bowl, oval, scalloped, ftd,
  opaque green slag shading to blue–
  aqua, cased in clear, heavy gold floral
  and scroll dec, ground pontil script
  sgd "Moser Karlsbad" 750.00
Cordial, 1⅜″ h, cranberry cup, clear
  stem, flowers, bee, and bug dec on
  base 60.00
Decanter Set, 10½″ h, 4½″ d, cranberry,
  gold and silver scene of girl and boy
  lovers beside lake and hills, sgd
  "L'Orrenkono" and "Moser," 7 pcs . . 550.00
Finger Bowl, 6″ d, matching 7″ underplate, gold, silver, and blue enamel
  arabesque dec, white petit–point dec,

scalloped shaded pink and lavender
glass **975.00**
Flask, 7½" l, powder horn shape, deep
cranberry, multicolored fern enamel
dec, brass spigot, fittings, and chain **775.00**
Pin Tray, deep red enameled figure,
gold trim **65.00**
Pitcher, 11¾" h, bright transparent blue
ground, applied salamander handle,
heavy gild, enameled fern fronds,
bird, and insects **2,300.00**
Sherry, 4¼" h, gold and white beading,
knobbed stem, wafer base **200.00**
Tumbler, 3¾" h, cranberry, gold enameled flowers and bees dec **80.00**
Vase
4" h, barrel shape, cameo, cobalt blue
ground, carved elephants and jungle scene with bright gold overlay,
traces of green foliage, birds in sky,
grooved cuts base, sgd "Made In
Czechoslovakia–Moser Karlsbad" **1,550.00**
7" h
Cameo, pumpkin ground, green
carved ivy leaves and vines,
marked "Moser Karlsbad" **1,600.00**
Marquetry, emerald green shading
to clear, padded dark green and
orange cameo flowers, ground
pontil marked "Moser Karlsbad" **1,900.00**
10" h, 7" d, malachite, four sided, polished ribbed panels, four semi–
nude woman at each corner **750.00**
11¼" h, trumpet, applied prunts, rubena verde, gilt, polychrome enamel
oak leaf and acorn dec, sgd on
base "Moser No 606, D180" **2,300.00**
12" h, cranberry glass, enameled
paisley dec, sgd on body **1,000.00**
12½" h, 5" d, white spatter, cased
smoky–gray glass, aqua glass rim
pulled into points, applied aqua
plant stems, enameled flowers and
flying insects **700.00**
13½" h, intaglio cut, green to clear **200.00**
14" h, gold intaglio warriors, paneled **450.00**
15½" h, elongated cylinder, flaring towards base, intaglio iris blossoms,
lavender shading to clear, sgd
"Moser, Karlsbad" **425.00**
17" h, trumpet, clear shading to light
green, gold enamel florals **275.00**
Wine Glass, 5" h, light ruby, elaborate
dec **150.00**

MOSS ROSE PATTERN CHINA

History: Several English potteries manufactured china with a Moss Rose pattern in the mid-

1800s. Knowles, Taylor and Knowles, an American firm, began production of a Moss Rose pattern
in the 1880s.

The moss rose was a common garden flower
grown in English gardens. When American consumers tired of English china with oriental themes,
they purchased the Moss Rose pattern as a substitute.

Bowl, 6" d, 3½" h, ftd, marked "Havi-
land" **28.00**
Brush Holder, marked "Shaw" **100.00**
Butter Pat, sq, marked "Meakin," set of
six **115.00**
Cake Plate, ftd, marked "Haviland" **75.00**
Creamer **40.00**
Cup and Saucer, marked "Haviland &
Co, Limoges" **20.00**
Dish, sq, 4¼" w, marked "Meakin" ... **12.00**
Gravy Boat and Underplate **75.00**
Mug, 3" h **10.00**

Plate, 7½" d, $7.50.

Plate
7" d, gold trim, marked "Haviland" **15.00**
8" d, marked "KTK" **30.00**
9½" d **15.00**
Platter
12 x 18", rect **50.00**
15½ x 10½", marked "CFH" **35.00**
Sauce Dish, 5" d, marked "SB & Sons" **8.00**
Shaving Mug, marked "Maddock" ... **45.00**
Spooner, marked "Meakin" **65.00**
Sugar, cov, 7" h **35.00**
Syrup, 8½" h, pewter top, marked
"KTK", c1872 .... **175.00**
Tray, 11 x 7½", marked "JM Co" **22.00**
Tureen, cov, 12½" h, staple repair to lid,
marked "H & L Co" **70.00**
Vegetable Dish, cov, marked "Edward
Bros, England" **100.00**

MOUNT WASHINGTON GLASS COMPANY

History: In 1837 Deming Jarves, founder of the Boston and Sandwich Glass Company, established for George D. Jarves, his son, the Mount Washington Glass Company in Boston, Massachusetts. In the following years the leadership and the name of the company changed several times as George Jarves formed different associations.

In the 1860s the company was owned and operated by Timothy Howe and William L. Libbey. In 1869 Libbey bought a new factory in New Bedford, Massachusetts. The Mount Washington Glass Company began operating again there under its original name. Henry Libbey became associated with the company early in 1871. He resigned in 1874 during the general depression, and the glass works was closed. William Libbey had resigned in 1872 to work for the New England Glass Company.

The Mount Washington Glass Company opened again in the fall of 1874 under the presidency of A. H. Seabury and the management of Frederick S. Shirley. In 1894 the glass works became a part of the Pairpoint Manufacturing Company.

Throughout its history the Mount Washington Glass Company made a great variety of glass including pressed glass, blown glass and art glass, lava glass, Napoli, cameo, cut glass, Albertine, and Verona.

References: George C. Avila, *The Pairpoint Glass Story,* Reynolds-DeWalt Printing, Inc., 1968; Leonard E. Padgett, *Pairpoint Glass,* Wallace-Homestead, 1979; John A. Shuman III, *The Collector's Encyclopedia of American Art Glass,* Collector Books, 1988.

Museum: The New Bedford Glass Museum, New Bedford, MA.

Additional Listings: Burmese, Crown Milano, Peachblow, and Royal Flemish.

Biscuit Jar, 6½" d, melon ribbed, hp gold daisies, shaded blue ground, SP lid, handle, and rim **1,200.00**

Rose Bowl, white ground, yellow scissor cut top, hp violets, 3¾" d, 2¾" h, $200.00.

Bowl, 10½" d, blue satin int., chrysanthemums and leaves ext., ruffled . . **225.00**
Bride's Basket, 11" d, pink ext., peachblow int., gold stylized flowers dec, ornate SP holder with aquatic marine motif, marked "Pairpoint Mfg Co" . . **825.00**
Creamer, tomato shape, hp, floral and leaf dec, light green to white ground, SP handle and spout **275.00**
Creamer and Sugar, Burmese, 3¾" h creamer with applied natural yellow handle, 2" h x 3½" d open sugar . . . **750.00**
Cruet, Burmese, shiny finish, ribbed, deep color, orig hollow blown stopper, applied loop handle **975.00**
Cup, 2¼" h, Burmese, butterflies and fern leaf dec, satin finish **30.00**
Ewer, 13" h, MOP, shaded blue, white lining, applied frosted and twisted rope handle, white pedestal base . . **775.00**
Flower Frog, mushroom dec **245.00**
Lamp, oil, 17¼" h, cameo, rose cut to opaque white, birds, leaves, and designs, wrought iron base, orig Meridan burner and reservoir **1,000.00**
Mustard, cov, Burmese, barrel shaped, vertical ribbed, shiny metal collar and hinged lid, inscribed "1334" **285.00**
Pickle Castor, deep cranberry satin, Optic Diamond and IVT pattern insert, gold spider chrysanthemum dec, ftd Simpson Hall frame, ornate engraved cov, orig silvering **600.00**
Pitcher
  5" h, 5" w, Verona, central motif of gold fish swimming among coral, rust, purple, and green sea plants, green sea plants on handle, gold trimmed spout and rim **950.00**
  6" h, 5½" w, Verona, four yellow, gold, and purple spider mums, six buds, green leaves **425.00**
Rose Bowl, 3" d, scalloped rim, lusterless white ground, hp, Shasta daisy dec **85.00**
Salt Shaker
  2" h, squatty, ribbed body, leaf and flower dec, metal top with seven prongs **100.00**
  4" h, Burmese, painted branch and leaf dec, metal top **60.00**
Sugar Shaker, egg shape, Burmese, deep salmon shading to yellow, all-over beaded white and blue flowers, Timothy Canty style, orig top **1,285.00**
Vase
  3¾" h, lava glass, jet black ground, multicolored flecks outlined in white **1,750.00**
  5" h, Albertine, bulbous, short flared neck, two shell form handles, pink and green oak leaf and flower dec,

raised gold edge outlines, creamy
shadowed background **275.00**
8″ h, 5″ w, double gourd, four naturalistic barn swallows, yellow shad-
ing to pink ground **1,200.00**
10″ h, 5″ d, stick, Burmese, acid finish,
deep color, oak leaf and blue dot
dec, traceries of natural fall color,
c1880 . . . . **1,750.00**
Whiskey Glass, 2¾″ h, Burmese, Optic
Diamond Quilt pattern **385.00**

MULBERRY CHINA

History: Mulberry china, made primarily in the
Staffordshire district of England between 1830 and
1850, is porcelain whose transfer pattern is the
color of mulberry juice. The potters that manufactured flow blue also made Mulberry china; the ware
often has a flowing effect similar to flow blue.

References: Susan and Al Bagdade, *Warman's
English & Continental Pottery & Porcelain, 1st Edition,* Warman Publishing Co., Inc., 1987; Petra Williams, *Flow Blue China and Mulberry Ware-Simi-
larity and Value Guide,* Fountain House East,
Revised Edition, 1981.

**Platter, Cyprus pattern, c1850, 13½ x
10¼″, $100.00.**

Bowl, Japan, Thomas Fell & Co **40.00**
Butter Dish, cov, Coburg, John Edwards **125.00**
Creamer, Washington Vase, Podmore,
Walker & Co **200.00**
Cup and Saucer, handleless cup
Chusan, Thomas Fell **55.00**
Pelew, Edward Challinor & Co **55.00**
Rose, Thomas Walker **55.00**
Scinde, Thomas Walker **55.00**
Wreath, Thomas Furnival & Co **55.00**
Fruit Bowl, Rhone Scenery, T. J. & J.
Mayer, 10¼″ d, handles, ftd **45.00**
Pitcher, Schenectady On The Mohawk,
unknown maker, 8″ h **165.00**
Plate
Flora, Hulme & Booth, 8¾″ d **40.00**

Rhone Scenery, T. J. & J. Mayer, 7¼″
d **30.00**
Washington Vase, Podmore, Walker
& Co, 8¾″ d **45.00**
Platter
American Marine, Mason **80.00**
Chusan, Thomas Fell, 17″ l **185.00**
Scinde, Thomas Walker, 15½″ l **150.00**
Vincennes, Samuel Alcock, 15½″ l **165.00**
Relish, Washington Vase, Podmore,
Walker & Co. **85.00**
Soap Dish, Flora, Hulme & Booth, 3 pcs **150.00**
Soup Tureen, Rhone Scenery, T. J. & J.
Mayer, open **300.00**
Sugar, cov
Corea, J. Clementson **175.00**
Hyson, J. Clementson **150.00**
Teapot
Corea, J. Clementson, minor rough-
ness on spout **275.00**
Cyprus, Davenport **350.00**
Vegetable, Washington Vase, Podmore,
Walker & Co., 8″ d, open **100.00**

MUSIC BOXES

History: Music boxes were invented in Switzerland around 1825 and include a broad field of
automatic musical instruments from a small box to
a huge circus calliope.

A cylinder box consists of a comb with teeth
which vibrate when striking a pin in the cylinder
and produce music from light tunes to opera and
overtures.

The first disc music box was invented by Paul
Lochmann of Leipzig, Germany, in 1886. It used
an interchangeable steel disc with pierced holes
bent to a point which hit the star-wheel as the disc
revolved, and thus produced the tune. Discs were
easily stamped out of metal, allowing a single music box to play an endless variety of tunes. It
reached the height of its popularity from 1890 to
1910. The phonograph replaced it.

Music boxes also were put into many items, e.g.,
clocks, sewing and jewelry boxes, steins, plates,
toys, perfume bottles, and furniture.

Reference: H. A. V. Bulleid, *Cylinder Musical
Box Design and Repair,* Almar Press, 1987.

Collectors' Club: Musical Box Society, International, Rt. 3, Box 205, Morgantown, IN, 46160.

Museums: Bellms Cars and Music of Yesterday,
Sarasota, FL; Lockwood Matthews Mansion, Nor-
walk, CT.

Additional Listings: See *Warman's Americana
& Collectibles* for more examples.

CYLINDER–TYPE

14″ l, simulated rosewood grained case,
applied dec, six tunes **400.00**

15″ l, walnut case, burl walnut facings, missing four teeth **200.00**

15½″ l, inlaid walnut and simulated rosewood case, zither attachment, lever wind, 11″ cylinder, 30 tunes, marked "1735," Switzerland, c1900 **880.00**

17″ l, 5½″ h, inlaid walnut case, eight tune, 6″ cylinder, Duck Son & Pinker, c1900 . . . . **360.00**

18″ l, rosewood case, marquetry inlaid musical instruments on cov, plays ten tunes, Swiss **500.00**

18″ l, 11″ w, 8½″ h, plays six tunes enhanced with three bells and drum, inlaid rosewood veneered case, orig handwritten label **1,000.00**

20″ l, rosewood case, floral inlaid design on lid, orig tune sheet, stop/start and change repeat levers, four tune, Mandoline, late 19th C **2,475.00**

20½″ l, rosewood case, floral inlay on cov and front panel, plays eight tunes **750.00**

24″ l, plays ten tunes, inlaid rosewood case, Swiss **1,050.00**

26″, rosewood case, fruitwood banding, orig tune sheet, side lever wind, zither attachment, stop/start and change repeat levers, eight tune, Bremond Sublime Harmony Piccolo, late 19th C **2,750.00**

28″ l, rosewood, musical motif marquetry inlay on cov, plays ten tunes . . . **2,100.00**

31″, walnut case, fruitwood banding, side lever wind, zither attachment, stop/start and change repeat levers, twelve tune, comb plate emb "AK KI," Jaccard, late 19th C **1,100.00**

43½″ l, Louis XV style, carved, burlwood and kingwood, veneered, mounted on table with one fitted drawer **2,400.00**

DISC–TYPE

9½″ disc, Stella Grand, table model, stained mahogany case, coffered lid, seven discs, c1900 . . . . **1,600.00**

14½″ disc, Polyphon, walnut case, double comb with twelve bells, sepia litho inlaid lid, crank handle, bracket feet, twelve discs, restored, Germany, c1900 . . . . **5,200.00**

17¼″ disc, Stella, table model, mahogany case, drawer **4,200.00**

19″ disc, Symphonion, Penny In Slot, rounded arched pediment, walnut case, split baluster moldings, ten discs **3,000.00**

21″ disc, Olympia, table model, mahogany case, peripheral driven movement, double comb, stop/start lever, 23 x 27″, sixteen discs, c1900 . . . . . **3,850.00**

27″ disc, Regina Orchestral, floor model, oak case, double comb, 78″ h . . **12,750.00**

MISCELLANEOUS

Automation, Singing Bird, 1 x 3 x 2″, SS, enamel dec, blue and black panel ext., oval lid with courtier playing flute to maiden scene with French lake setting, floral dec on lid int., base imp "Sterling Silver, Swiss, 787, D 935," last half 19th C **2,970.00**

Coin Operated

25″ disc, Polyphon, coin–operated, wood case, glazed front door, peripheral drive movement, double comb, 45″ h, ten discs, Germany, c1900 . . **3,850.00**

19⅛″ disc, Symphonion, Style 106NS, coin operated, floor model, walnut case, arched fret carved crest supporting three vasiform finials, glazed arched door with ball and baluster turnings, molded base, bun feet, duplex comb, 51½″ h, ten discs, c1900 **3,850.00**

Organ, Paillard, St. Croix, ten Chinese

Regina, Style 8, automatic changer, coin operated, twelve 27″ discs, peripheral driven movement, double comb, spring barrel, rack, disc selector, crank wound at side, mahogany case, dragon spandrels, spooled railing, 76″ h, $17,600.00.

tunes, eleven keys, seventeen tooth comb, inlaid musical trophies, rosewood lid and box **2,900.00**
Organette
    Automatic, medlodista, 13 x 36 x 12", stencil dec, G W Bates & Co, Boston, MA **2,500.00**
    Mechanical Orguimette Co, five rolls, stained floor cabinet, roll storage drawer, musical boudoir **375.00**
Roller Organ, Mascotte, walnut case, four 2½" rolls, Gately Mfg Co **250.00**
Wood, Swiss Chalet, 8¼ x 11", carved, two German tunes, orig paper label, lists names of tunes **130.00**

MUSICAL INSTRUMENTS

History: From the first beat of the prehistoric drum to the very latest in electronic music makers, musical instruments have provided popular modes of communication and relaxation.

The most popular antique instruments are violins, flutes, oboes, and other instruments associated with the classical music period of 1650 to 1900. Many of the modern instruments, such as trumpets, guitars, drums, etc., have value on the "used," rather than antiques market.

The collecting of musical instruments is in its infancy. The field is growing very rapidly. Investors and speculators have played a role since the 1930s, especially in early string instruments. Sotheby's and Christie's hold annual auctions of fine musical instruments.

References: Tom and Mary Anne Evans, *Guitars: From the Renaissance To Rock; The Official Price Guide To Music Collectibles, Sixth Edition,* House of Collectibles, 1986.

Collectors' Club: Fretted Instrument Guild of America, 2344 South Oakley Avenue, Chicago, IL 60608.

Accordion, Empress, good bellows, Germany, c1890 . . . . **65.00**
Banjo, American
    Edwon C Dobson, New York City, c1900 . . . . **125.00**
    Gibson, five string, resonator, case **110.00**
Bassoon, Heckel, Biebrich, 20th C . . . **1,600.00**
Cello, Sigfried Finkel, German, ivory frog and adjuster, pearl dots, octagonal stick mounted with gold and ivory **1,750.00**
Clarinet, Martin, silver ext., gold int., mother–of–pearl keys, carrying case, Elkhart, IN **250.00**
Cornet
    Concertone, brass, nickel silver mouthpiece, pearl buttons, one water key, 16½" l, c1920 . . . . **150.00**
    Leaders' B–Flat, brass, polished double water key, 1905–10 . . . . **275.00**

Cymbal, 13" d, American, leather handles, c1900 . . . . **160.00**
Drum
    Acme, Professional, bass, 26" d, c1900 . . . . **225.00**
    Military, parade type, cylindrical body, American flag and insignia, rope lacing around sides, orig red paint, 16¼" **450.00**
Flute
    American, eight key, c1920 . . . . . . **125.00**
    Flemish, walnut, 18th C **2,250.00**
    Meyer, ten key, c1900 . . . . **300.00**
Guitar
    American, The Seroco, standard size, c1900 . . . . **325.00**
    Italian, five course, lavish ivory dec, arched back, 38", Matteo Sellas, Venice, 1920–40 . . . . **12,000.00**
Guitar Harp, Gibson Co, inlaid ivory, 27½" l, c1905 . . . . **900.00**
Harmonica
    Hohner's Best, orig box **20.00**
    Opera, US Zone Germany, litho tin box **25.00**
Harp, English, polished walnut, late 18th C **1,250.00**
Mandolin
    Gibson, Style A **600.00**
    The Royal, eleven rosewood ribs, inlaid white holly, inlaid guard plate, early 1900 . . . . **450.00**
Organ
    Prescott Bros, walnut case, two sets of reeds, five stops, c1867 . . . . . **450.00**
    Williams Organ Co, Epworth, oak case, back grill, two and three–fifths ranks of reeds and octave coupler, thirteen stops, c1890 . . . **575.00**
Piano
    Brambach, baby grand, stained mahogany case, sq tapered legs, in-

Piano, Clementi & Co, London, England, c1800, needs restoration, $1,500.00.

cludes bench, 57" l, Serial No 56109 .... **940.00**

Fischer, J.G.L., New York, Ampico Model B Grand Player Piano, mahogany, matching bench and twelve music rolls **13,000.00**

John Player, London, spinet, walnut body, oak trestle stand, inscribed "Johannes Player, Londini fecit," 61½", 17th C **25,000.00**

K Bord, upright, carved mahogany frame, inset marquetry poppies, hollyhocks, and flowering vines, 59¾" w, 48½" h, Paris, France .. **8, 250.00**

Kirkman & Sons, grand, burl maple, adjustable stool, 75" l, London, c1865 .... **6,200.00**

Monarch, baby grand, mahogany case, sq tapered legs, spade feet on casters, 55" l **1,650.00**

Steinway & Sons, baby grand, ebonized, serial #54676, late 19th C .. **3,750.00**

Wm. Knabe & Co, baby grand
Mahogany **800.00**
Walnut **1,600.00**

Pianoforte, upright, Empire style, rosewood and mahogany veneer case, inlaid floral and foliate motifs, hinged rect top with projecting corners, scrolled legs joined by cylindrical cross bar, stool, 70" w, 33½" h, J. Osborne, New York, NY, 1815–29 .. **550.00**

Piccolo, Atlas, cast metal, c1900 .... **55.00**

Saxophone
Dupont, B–Flat Tenor, burnished nickel plate **250.00**
Rushworth & Dreaper, Liverpool, F–Sharp, silverplated **250.00**

Trombone, Dupont
B–Flat, tenor slide, burnished nickel plate **450.00**
E–Flat, alto slide, polished brass ... **650.00**

Tuba, Sousaphone, B–Flat, brass, lacquer bore **2,500.00**

Ukulele, mahogany body, brass peds, block inlay around hole **60.00**

Violin, 23¼" l, lion's head form carved scroll, case and bow, label "Antonius Stradivarius Cremonensis Faceibat Anno 1736," Continental **350.00**

Xylophone, Deayon No 1729, twenty-six bars **60.00**

MUSIC RELATED

Advertising Trade Card, Emerson Piano Co, black on green **3.00**

Bank, piano, musical, clockwork, 7¾" l, 5¾" h, E M Roche Novelty Co, Newark NJ, c1900 .... **7,700.00**

Book
Harmonia Festi, John Alcock, pri-

vately printed, Lichfield, 1791 oblong folio, 59 pgs **175.00**

The Story of British Music, Crowest, F, London, 1896 .... **30.00**

Counter Display, Hohner Harmonicas, four sided, tapered, mounted on clockwork base, revolves, red, silver and gilt lettering, 32" h **130.00**

Music Stand, bronze, tapered neck, French, last quarter 18th C **3,000.00**

Piano Stool, cast iron claw and ball feet, glass ball **125.00**

Sheet Music, *Normandy Chimes,* Powell, 1913 .... **3.00**

MUSTACHE CUPS AND SAUCERS

History: Mustache cups and saucers were popular in the late Victorian era, 1880–1900. They were made by many companies in porcelain and silver plate. The cups have a ledge across the top of the bowl of the cup to protect a gentleman's mustache from becoming soiled while drinking.

Reference: Susan and Al Bagdade, *Warman's English & Continental Pottery & Porcelain, 1st Edition,* Warman Publishing Co., Inc., 1987.

Porcelain, white ground, gold dec, bottom of letters accented with blue, marked "B.S./C & M," $45.00.

PORCELAIN

Bavarian, transfer print, yellow and pink chrysanthemums, shaded white to pink ground **35.00**

Belleek, basketweave, green trim, Irish, second black mark **425.00**

German
Floral design, white ground, marked **35.00**
Pears and foliage, gold trim, light green ground, marked **15.00**
Tassels, gold dec, pink ground, marked **15.00**

Hand Painted
 Birds on branch, pink and brown, gold
  and blue flowers 10.00
 Butterfly on poppy branch, orange
  and blue dec 10.00
 Festooned flowers, gold trim, white
  ground 25.00
 Limoges, floral design, c1880 . . . . 50.00
 Motto, unknown maker
  "For A Gift," band of applied florals,
   gold letters 100.00
  "Merry Christmas," floral ground, gold
   script letters 65.00
  "Think of Me," pink luster 45.00

SILVER PLATED

Left handed, engraved name and date   175.00
Relief scroll work center band, monogram, Gorham, 1896 . . . . 40.00

NAILSEA TYPE GLASS

History: Nailsea type glass is characterized by
swirls and loopings, usually white, on a clear or
colored ground. One of the first areas where this
glass was made was Nailsea, England, 1788–
1873, hence the name. Several other glass
houses, including American factories, made this
type of glass.

**Fairy Lamp, rose, white loopings,
frosted, sgd "S. Clarke" clear glass
base, 4" d, 4¾" h, $325.00.**

Bellows Bottle, 9¼" h, clear, white looping, applied collared mouth, pontil . .   80.00
Bowl, 7⅝" d, sapphire blue, opaque
 white looping, applied clear trim, feet,
 and handles 175.00
Epergne, 15½", green white looping . .   275.00

Flask
 7¼" h, teardrop shape, clear, white
  looping, tooled mouth, pontil 65.00
 Ovoid form, white, pink looping 120.00
Flip, 8¼" h, 6¼" d, light green, milky
 green looping, plain sheared mouth,
 pontil 150.00
Gemel Bottle
 7¾" l, clear, white looping, amethyst
  applied lip, two applied wafers foot,
  applied clear rigaree 25.00
 7⅞" l, clear, white looping, clear ap-
  plied rigaree 30.00
 8½" l, clear, white looping, cobalt blue
  applied lip 35.00
 9½" l, clear, cranberry and white loop-
  ing 55.00
Lamp Shade, 4" h, 7" d, cranberry, white
 pulled ribbon pattern, ruffled edge . .   40.00
Pitcher, 9½" h, deep greenish–aqua,
 white looping, applied solid curled
 end handle and base, sheared
 mouth, ftd 600.00
Rolling Pin, 19¼" l, cylindrical, clear,
 pink looping, 19th C 110.00
Rose Bowl, 4" d, egg shape, frosted
 blue white opaque looping, crimped
 top 175.00
Sugar Shaker, 5" h, pear shape, blue,
 white looping, ftd, orig top 100.00
Vase
 6" h, trumpet form, cased white, pink
  and white looping, two applied
  clear ridged handles 170.00
 9½" h, double ogee form, light green,
  white looping, folded rim, applied
  solid stem and base, tubular pontil   275.00

NANKING

History: Nanking is a type of Chinese porcelain
made in Canton, China, from the early 1800s into
the 20th century for export to America and England. It is often confused with the Canton pattern.
 Three elements help distinguish Nanking from
Canton. Nanking has a spear and post border, as
opposed to the scalloped line style of Canton. The
blues may tend to be darker on the Nanking ware.
Second, in the water's edge or Willow pattern,
Canton usually has no figures. Nanking features a
standing figure with open umbrella on the bridge.
Finally, Nanking wares often are embellished with
gold.
 Green and orange variations of Nanking survive,
although scarce.
 Reference: Sandra Andacht, *Oriental Antiques
& Art: An Identification And Value Guide,* Wallace-
Homestead, 1987.
 Reproduction Alert: Copies of Nanking ware
currently are being produced in China. They are

of inferior quality and decorated in lighter rather than the darker blues.

Bowl, 15" l, oval, flat octagonal rim, c1800 .... 750.00
Chocolate Pot, 9" h, pear shape, Buddhistic lion finial 775.00
Cider Jug, 7¾" h, blue and white, spearhead and lattice borders, coastal village scene, double entwined handle, molded flowers and leaves terminal, base rim chip, early 19th C 400.00
Flagon, 11½" h, orange peel glaze, Buddhistic lion finial 2,000.00
Lamp, wedding, 6¼ x 8¼", overall floral dec, blue and white, vertical reticulation 500.00
Mug, 6⅛" h, water's edge scene 350.00

Plate, water's edge scene, 1780–1800, 9½" d, $125.00.

Platter, 17⅜ x 20", oval, blue and white, coastal village scene, spearhead and lattice borders, minor glaze wear, early 19th C 850.00
Tea Caddy, 5" h, blue and white, gilt trim 750.00
Vegetable Dish, 8¼ x 10", oval, blue and white, spearhead and lattice borders, central coastal village scene, early 19th C 200.00

NAPKIN RINGS, FIGURAL

History: Gracious home dining during the Victorian era meant each household member had their personal napkin ring. Figural napkin rings were first patented in 1869. The remainder of the 19th century saw most plating companies, e.g., Cromwell, Eureka, Meriden, Reed and Barton, etc., manufacturing figural rings, many copying

with slight variations the designs of other companies.

Values are determined today by the subject matter of the ring, the quality of the workmanship, and the condition.

Reference: Victor K. Schnadig, *American Victorian Figural Napkin Rings*, Wallace–Homestead, 1971, out–of–print.

Reproduction Alert: Quality reproductions do exist.

Additional Listings: See *Warman's Americana & Collectibles* for a listing of non–figural napkin rings.

Swans, swimming, individual oval bases, $250.00.

Baseball Player, standing next to ring, bat on shoulder, rect base 250.00
Bird, perched on top of ring, long tail, elaborately scrolled base, Apollo Silver Plate Co 150.00
Boy with begging dog, Kate Greenaway–type figure 260.00
Bull, standing, fancy oval base next to flower etched ring, Knickerbocker Silver Co, 3½ x 2¼" 185.00
Cat
  Crouched beside ring 150.00
  Standing beside ring, full figure, Eureka Silver Plate Co 175.00
Cap beneath ring, horns and swords at sides 330.00
Cherub, pulling cart, movable wheels 225.00
Chick, standing guard over ring, oval base, ball feet, portion of orig label, Meriden 200.00
Cleopatra, kneeling in front of ring, Southington C. Co 350.00
Dog
  Poodle, standing, front paws on round fern etched ring 165.00
  Shepherd, full figure, sitting on round base next to barrel shaped ring, Tufts 165.00
Fans, two on each side of ring 130.00
Fox, sitting, oval ring on back, rect base 165.00
Girl, muff, playful dog, Kate Greenaway–type figure 200.00

Horse, prancing, ring on back, sq base, ball feet	175.00
Little Red Riding Hood, holding basket, Reed & Barton	225.00
Lion, standing, leaning against ring, rect base	175.00
Monkey, standing, oval base, Derby Silver Co	275.00
Owl, perched on leaf shaped base, Van Bergh Co	165.00
Squirrel, sitting on log with acorns	300.00
Turtle Doves, spread wings support ring, Middletown Plate	125.00

NASH GLASS

History: Nash glass is a type of art glass attributed to Arthur John Nash and his sons, Leslie H. and A. Douglas. Arthur John Nash, originally employed by Webb in Stourbridge, England, came to America and was employed in 1889 by Tiffany Furnaces at its Corona, Long Island, plant.

While managing the plant for Tiffany, Nash designed and produced iridescent glass. In 1928 A. Douglas Nash purchased the physical facilities of Tiffany Furnaces. The A. Douglas Nash Corporation firm remained in operation until 1931.

Bowl	
13" d, wide rim, Diamond Optic pattern, cranberry threads, clear ground	275.00

Vase, blue irid, marked "R526," 5½" h, $600.00.

15½" d, Chintz pattern, amber, blue, and green opal, turned down rim	300.00
Candlesticks, pr, 5" h, Chintz pattern, blood red, silver dec	750.00
Creamer, 4¼" h, pale orchid and green design, applied clear handle	315.00
Finger Bowl, 4¾" d, matching underplate, opal rays, cranberry rim, sgd	200.00
Perfume, 7⅞" h, blue and lilac rays, pale blue foot, orig pointed amber stopper, silver blue irid	700.00
Sherbet, 3½" d, 2¼" h, vein textured, gold rainbow irid, sgd	100.00
Stemware, Chintz pattern, blue and green	
Cordial, 4" h	85.00
Goblet, 6½" h	75.00
Vase	
4¾" h, pedestal, bluish gold, inscribed "Nash 644"	325.00
6½" h, bulbous, feathery blue strokes, bubbly lime green streaks, sgd	400.00
9½" h, green and gold irid body, clear irid circular base	275.00

NAUTICAL ITEMS

History: The seas that surround us have fascinated man since time began. The artifacts of sailors have been collected and treasured for years. Because of their environment, merchant and naval items, whether factory or handmade, must be of quality construction and long lasting. Many of these items are aesthetically designed as well.

Richard Bourne, Hyannis, Massachusetts, and Chuck DeLuca, York, Maine, regularly hold auctions of marine items.

References: Alan P. Major, *Maritime Antiques,* A. S. Barnes & Co., 1981; Jean Randier, *Nautical Antiques,* Doubleday and Co., 1977.

Periodical: *Conklin's Guide: Maritime Auction Annual,* Leeward Shore Press, P.O. Box 838-20, Brisbane, CA 94005; *Nautical Brass etc.,* Box 744, Montrose, CA 91020.

Museums: Burgess Mariner's Museum, Newport News, VA; Museum of Science and Industry, Chicago, IL; Mystic Seaport Museum, Mystic, CT; National Maritime Museum, San Francisco, CA.

Advertising Card, "John Kehew Nautical Instruments, New Bedford"	55.00
Backstaff, wood, inlaid label "Made by William Hart in Portsmouth NE/for 1767," 18th C	8,000.00
Barometer	
Mahogany, ivory scales, Spencer & Co, London, 19th C	900.00
Walnut, thermometer and weather chamber, Admiral Fitzroy, 19th C	200.00
Basket, 7½" d, Nantucket, lightship, swing handle, 19th C	250.00

Bell, brass
  8" d, inscribed *Sunek 1958* **150.00**
  9" d, inscribed *SS U Chicago* **300.00**
  14" d, inscribed *SS Pacific Prince* . . **500.00**
Bell Clock, ship's, 6¼" d, brass, Seth
  Thomas **450.00**
Binnacle
  15¼" h, polished brass, Negus, NY **625.00**
  56" h, brass, mahogany base, com-
  plete **700.00**
Block, ship's, 13½" l, wood, one lignum
  vitae, one metal pulley **100.00**
Book
  Marine Navigational Instruments,
  Jean Randier, London, 1980 . . . . **170.00**
  Ships of Kingston, Henry M Jones **30.00**
Certificate
  Authorization, brig *Leonidas* to operate in international trade, framed,
  sgd "James Taylor," dated "1845" **400.00**
  Membership, New York Marine Soci-
  ety, issued to Captain Edward Abel,
  June 14, 1842, oak leaf carved
  frame **200.00**
Chest
  Chart, 48" l, pine, dovetailed, orig
  beckets, contains nine navigational
  charts, 19th C **450.00**
  Sea
  37" l, orig green and brown paint
  and ropework beckets, 19th C **550.00**
  42" l, dovetailed, green paint, 19th
  C **450.00**
Chronometer
  4¾" d, cased, Ulysse Nardin **1,300.00**
  6¼", brass bound case, clock num-
  bered "1774," Made by Charles
  Frodsham, London **3,500.00**
Compass
  Pocket, engraved brass sundial,
  boxed **250.00**
  Sighting, brass, cased, Lilley, London **175.00**
Deck Chair, walnut, late 19th C **350.00**
Ditty Box, 7½" l, panbone, oval, 19th C **290.00**
Document Box, ship's, 18¾ x 11¼ x
  9½", *Peri*, orig paint **150.00**
Harpoon, 33¼" l, double flue, 19th C **250.00**
Helmet, diver's
  Brass, Galeazzi **800.00**
  Copper and brass, labeled "US Navy
  Mark V Model 1" **900.00**
Journal, navigational, Ensign W J Sims,
  200 pgs, orig cov **100.00**
Lamp, cabin, 7½" h, pr, brass, orig gim-
  bals, 19th C **650.00**
Lantern, ship's, copper, clear lens
  21¼" h, orig burner, emb brass label
  "Wm Harvie, Glasgow" **65.00**
  21¾" h, emb brass label "Seahorse" **75.00**
Liquor Chest, captain's, oak case, gold
  dec, ten bottles, pr cut glass tumblers,
  two wine glasses, English **1,000.00**

Model
  Diorama, clipper ship, *Sea Witch*,
  simulated active ocean, wood
  frame glass case **600.00**
Scale
  America's Cup challenger, *Sham-
  rock II*, cased **1,800.00**
  Schooner yacht *America*, planked
  dec, skylights, companionways,
  and sunken cockpit, inlaid ma-
  hogany base, glass case **1,000.00**
Octant
  Ebony, sgd "Geo Buchanan 1778,"
  Joshua Springer, Bristol **800.00**
  Mahogany, boxwood scale, claw type
  radial, ivory nameplate, sgd "Made
  by Thos Howard Liverpool/Elijah
  Tower," 18th C **2,100.00**
  Rosewood, brass mounted radial
  arm, ivory scales and nameplate,
  marked "William Fuss" and "Lev-
  erton Liverpool," 18th C **500.00**
Painting
  Adam, Edouard, (German, 19th C),
  *Portrait of the British Steam/Sail
  Ship Charles Howard Steaming
  Through Rough Seas*, 24 x 36", oil
  on canvas, bird's eye maple frame,
  sgd "Ed Adam 1879/Harve" **1,000.00**
  British School, *Portrait of a British
  Armed Brig*, 12 x 15⅛", watercolor
  on paper, inlaid pine frame, sgd
  "LAC 1825" **1,200.00**
  Cozzens, Fred S., (American, 1856–
  1928), *Tug with a Schooner in Tow*,
  13 x 20¾", watercolor on paper,
  matted and framed, sgd "Fred S
  Cozzens/06" **1,400.00**

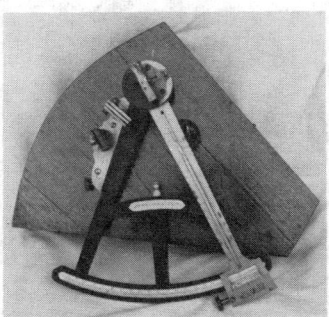

**Quadrant, I. J. Messer, London, import-
er's label Charles Tabor & Co, New
Bedford, cased, 12 x 13 x 3⅝",
$1,000.00.**

Jacobsen, Antonio, (American, 1850–1921), *Pilot Boat Edward F. Williams,* 22 x 36″, oil on canvas, modern frame, sgd "A Jacobsen 1892/705 Palisade Av West Hoboken NJ" **8,000.00**

Otto Fischer, Anton, (American, 1882–1962), *Ship in Moonlight,* 24 x 34″, oil on canvas, framed, sgd "Anton Otto Fischer" **3,200.00**

Pierce, Joseph W., (American, 19th C), *Schooner Yacht America,* 10 x 21½″, oil on artist's panel, gilt frame, sgd "JW Pierce" **1,500.00**

Portholes, ship's, pr, 15″ d, brass, storm cov **200.00**

Quadrant, ebony, ivory inlays **550.00**

Quarterboard, 96″ l, *Aransas,* repainted **300.00**

Scribe, rosewood and mahogany, adjustable, 15¾″ l, 19th C **65.00**

Sextant, 17″ l, mahogany, engraved brass radial arm, ivory nameplate engraved "H Duren New York", Gregory & Wright, London, 18th C **1,100.00**

Speaking Trumpet, captain's, 15½″ l, brass, 19th C **300.00**

Steering Station, orig brass binnacle, compass, and lamps, marked "Negus, New York" **1,700.00**

Sternboard, 54″ w, mahogany, carved, gilded eagle, P Libbey, Maine, sgd on back **1,400.00**

Telegraph
38¼″ h, brass, marked "Made by Chadburns, Liverpool" **800.00**
44¾″ h, brass, Swan, Hunter & Wingham Richardson Ltd, Neptune Works #1858, dated 1840 ...... **700.00**

Telescope, 13¼″ l, pasteboard and red vellum, three draw, horn mounts, screw end caps, sgd "Leonardo Semitecolo" **1,300.00**

Tool Box, sailmaker's, open front, rockers on bottom, canvas seat, marked on bottom, "Mr Will Snowman/Bucksport/Maine," 19th C **100.00**

Trailboard, 58½″ l, gilded, foliate scroll carving, black ground, 19th C **400.00**

Valentine, 9⅛″ d, sailor's, double, set in card on left side, tugboat print on other, 19th C **1,100.00**

NAZI ITEMS

History: The National Socialist Party came to power in the 1920s during a period of severe economic depression in Germany. Under the leadership of Adolf Hitler, the party assumed first political control and then social control over Germany. National socialism dominated all aspects of German life. World War II was launched in 1939 to achieve

a military conquest of Europe. The Nazi era ended in 1945 when Germany surrendered.

References: John M. Kaduck, *World War II German Collectibles,* published by author, 1978, 1983 price update; *The Official Price Guide To Military Collectibles, Fifth Edition,* House of Collectibles, 1985; Sydney B. Vernon, *Vernon's Collectors' Guide To Orders, Medals, and Decorations (With Valuations),* published by author, 1986.

Periodicals: *Military Collectors News,* P.O. Box 702073, Tulsa, OK, 74170; *The MX Exchange,* P.O. Box 3, Torrington, CT 06790.

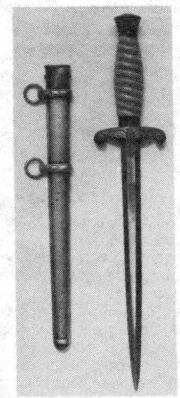

Dagger, officer's, dress, 15″ l, $225.00.

Backpack, Army, horsehair, leather straps, maker's mark, 1936 .... **40.00**

Badge, General Assault, silver, c1940 **30.00**

Banner, 29 x 70″, swastika in center .. **65.00**

Belt Buckle, DAF Labor Front, swastika in wheel **20.00**

Book
Mein Kampf, by A. Hitler, 1933, 407 pgs, orig dust cov **15.00**
Schlag Auf Schlag Battle for Poland, German text, uniform and airplane photos **20.00**

Boots, leather, felt wool tops, Russian front style, reinforcement straps ... **30.00**

Breast Badge, Luftwaffe, pilot's, observer's, gold wreath, silver eagle holds swastika, orig blue case **250.00**

Brooch, large floral swastika, rect back, gilt, 1936 .... **15.00**

Currency, concentration camp, Flossenburg **65.00**

Dagger, Army officer, orange handle, silvered fittings, full eagle's breast, scabbard **140.00**

Dagger Holder, SS, black leather, buckle cross strap, RZM/SS mark 85.00

Desk Plaque, Imperial German Hunting Assoc, stag head, crown, inscribed medal, marble base 90.00

Document, Army "Kriegs–Chronik," service award 40.00

First Aid Case, German Red Cross, leather, 1935, orig contents 20.00

Flag

Army, Regimental Battle, 84 x 144", double sided, eagle, swastika, tricolor 75.00

Parade, NSDAP, 45½" l, hp black swastika on white, double sided, c1920 . . . . 30.00

Flag Pole Top, "Wird Waffe," Bakelite spearhead and oak leaves, cross guard dated 1940, iron cross dated 1939 . . . . 40.00

Funeral Sash, SS, fabric and paper, silver lettering, white fringe, large silver SS Runes 125.00

Hat

Panzer Officer, black wool, silver piping, silver eagle, two silver buttons on ear flaps, maker mark 300.00

R.R. Supervisor, red wool, black velvet band, two gold eagles, rosettes, black visor, orig maker label 200.00

SS, rabbit fur, quilted int., black ties at ear flaps, olive green wool body, RZM/SS, skull and eagle devices 265.00

Lamp, table, 16" h, gold leaf, plaster, eagle, marbleized base, from Munich party headquarters 70.00

Medal, German Red Cross, 1937, black enameled eagle and red cross, red and white ribbon 80.00

Mittens, wool, Luftwaffe, gray wool, blue gray lining, leather tags, pr 15.00

Pennant

Car, 1936 Berlin Olympics, eternal flame, olympic symbol and date, tie ropes 75.00

Parade, 22 x 38", triangular, sewn on swastika on both sides, District No. 16–246 . . . . 85.00

Podium, NSDAP, white border and bottom fringe, large swastika 35.00

Photo Album, 1942–43, official "Reichs–Autobahnen," 21 photos . . 85.00

Pillowcase, 15 x 18", NSDAP eagle and swastika, inscribed "Deutschland Erwacht" 50.00

Pinback Button, ⅝", "Halt Hitler," blue and white, Star of David symbol, 1930–40 . . . . 15.00

Plaque

6 x 8", bronze, Hitler's profile, dark brown patina 175.00

6¾ x 9", Ex–Pres Von Hindenburg, copper plate, facial view, civilian dress 25.00

Plate

7½", white porcelain, DAF insignia 12.00

9", green and white porcelain, green Luftwaffe eagle, Unit #O–H–2 . . . 18.00

Print

8 x 11", Luftwaffe crew, preparing bomber for strike, marked "Berlin, 1940" 15.00

8 x 11½", Rescue at Sea, bomber crew rescued by Pantoon plane, German, sgd, 1941 . . . . 15.00

Ring, silver, crossed swords, helmet, and swastika 50.00

Sheet Music, "In Anticipation Of That Great Day," 9 x 12", black and white, caricature portrait of Hitler on front cov, copyright 1943, Lincoln Music Corp 25.00

Shirt, brown, S.A., black collar tabs, black piping, eagle buttons, c1933 125.00

Snowsuit, mountain troops, white jacket, white painted buttons, attached hood, trousers, Gebirgsjager sleeve patch, 1943 . . . . 200.00

Soup Bowl, NSDAP, 9", large black eagle on bottom, 1938 . . . . 15.00

Sword, police, scabbard 145.00

NETSUKES

History: The traditional Japanese kimono has no pockets. Daily necessities such as money, tobacco supplies, etc., were carried in leather pouches or *inros* which hung from a cord with a netsuke toggle. Netsuke comes from "ne" (to root) and "tsuke" (to fasten).

Netsukes originated in the 14th century and initially were associated with the middle class. By the mid-18th century all levels of Japanese society used them. Some of the most famous artists, e.g., Shuzan and Yamada Hojitsu, worked in the netsuke form.

Netsukes average 1 to 2 inches and are made from wood, ivory, bone, ceramics, metal, horn, nutshells, etc. The subject matter is broad based, but always portrayed in a lighthearted, humorous manner. A netsuke must have no sharp edges. It must be balanced so it hangs correctly on the sash.

Value depends on artist, region, material, and skill of craftsmanship. Western collectors favor *katabori*, pieces which represent an identifiable object.

Reference: Sandra Andacht, *Oriental Antiques & Art: An Identification And Value Guide,* Wallace-Homestead, 1987.

Collectors' Club: Netsuke Kenkyukai Society, Box 11248, Torrance, CA 90510.

Reproduction Alert: Recent reproductions are on the market. Many are carved from African ivory.

Turtle, on lily pad, ivory, carved, sgd . . **45.00**
Zodiac group, ivory **350.00**

NEWCOMB POTTERY

History: William and Ellsworth Woodward, two brothers, were the founders of a series of businesses which eventually merged into the Newcomb pottery effort. In 1885 Ellsworth Woodward, a proponent of vocational training for women, organized a school from which emerged the Ladies Decorative Art League. In 1886 the brothers founded the New Orleans Art Pottery Company with the ladies of the league serving as decorators. The first two potters were Joseph Meyer and George Ohr. The pottery closed in 1891.

William Woodward was on the faculty at Tulane. Ellsworth taught fine arts at the Sophie Newcomb College, a women's school which eventually merged with Tulane. In 1895 Newcomb College developed a pottery course in which the wares could be sold. Some of the equipment came from the old New Orleans Art Pottery.

Mary G. Sheerer joined the staff to teach decoration. In 1910 Paul E. Cox solved many of the technical problems connected with making pottery in a southern environment. Other leading figures were Sadie Irvine, Professor Lota Lee Troy, and Kathrine Choi. Pottery was made until the early 1950s.

Students painted a quality art pottery with a distinctive high glaze. Designs have a decidedly southern flavor, e.g., myrtle, jasmine, sugar cane, moss, cypress, dogwood, and magnolia motifs. Later matte glazed pieces usually are decorated with carved back floral designs. Pieces depicting murky, bayou scenes are most desirable.

References: Suzanne Ormond and Mary E. Irvine, *Louisiana's Art Nouveau: The Crafts Of The Newcomb Style*, Pelican Publishing Company, 1976; Jessie Poesch, *Newcomb Pottery: An Enterprise for Southern Women*, Schiffer Publishing, Ltd, 1984.

Collectors' Club: American Art Pottery Association, 9825 Upton Circle, Bloomington, MN 55431.

Museum: Newcomb College, Tulane University, New Orleans, LA.

Carved ivory, popping eyes, $225.00.

Badger, wrapped in fuki leaf, wood . . . **70.00**
Bird, catching monkey and pig, ivory,
Japanese **150.00**
Boar on rope, ivory, Japanese **40.00**
Clam, group, ivory **70.00**
Dragon, 2″, ivory, coiled tail, sgd **50.00**
Fish with rat, ivory, 3″ **150.00**
Frog, resting on lotus pod, wood, sgd
"Masanao" **190.00**
Foo Dog, ivory, 1½″, 18th C **175.00**
Fukurokuju, standing, white beard,
ivory, 1⅞″, sgd "Mitsugetsu" **100.00**
Geisha, ivory, kneeling, white and red **150.00**
Horse and monkey, ivory, Japanese . . **45.00**
Hotei, wood, sgd **275.00**
Kappa on lily pad, ivory, Japanese . . . **70.00**
Maiden and octopus, ivory, sgd "Kosho" **100.00**
Man
 In barrel, ivory, 1½″, sgd **525.00**
 With octopus coming out of basket,
 ivory, 2″ h **250.00**
 With scroll, ivory **50.00**
Man and child with badger, ivory **70.00**
Merchant, seated, ox with firewood bundles, ivory, 1½″ h, sgd **400.00**
Ojime, buffalo horn, three pc, carved **75.00**
Oni
 Subduing laughing man, staghorn . . **275.00**
 With mask, okame on back, wood . . **80.00**
Ox and frog, ivory, ox with arched back,
sgd "Gyoku," Japanese **80.00**
Rat, group, ivory **125.00**
Rice Cake shape, ivory, 2¾″ d, Japanese, 18th C **60.00**
Sage and deer, seated, ivory **130.00**
Samurai, seated, wood **90.00**
See no evil, hear no evil, speak no evil,
ivory, carved, 3″ h **130.00**
Shell, man nestled inside blowing
conch, ivory tip, 2¾″ l **225.00**
Ship, ivory **150.00**
Study of ear of corn, ivory **90.00**
Study of recumbant puppy, wood **40.00**
Tiger, ivory, Japanese **55.00**

Bowl
 4¼″ d, 4½″ h, flaring sides, white
 Cherokee rose motif, green, white,
 yellow, and blue matte glaze, artist
 Hilda Blank, c1919 . . . . **900.00**

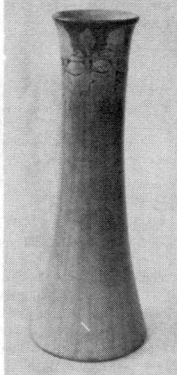

Vase, rose buds alternating with rose leaves, green and blue, marked, 12¼" h, $600.00.

8½" d, 3¼" h, irises and entwined vine, soft blue–green and dark blue ground, matte glaze, artist sgd "Sadie Irvine," c1914 . . . . 950.00

Jar, cov, low relief oak trees, blue and green matte glaze, "Fortitier et Recte" incised on reverse, "1914" in relief on lid, artist Francis Simpson, orig paper label 3,100.00

Pitcher, 5½" h, bulbous, short neck, angled handle, redware, gunmetal matte drip glaze, imp "NC, GM" . . . 375.00

Plaque, 10" w, 6" h, rect, scenic, tree laden with Spanish moss, boat in foreground, matte blue and green glazes, artist initial sgd "HDB" for Henrietta Davidson Bailey 2,700.00

Pot
2½" h, Ali Baba, blue matte glaze . . 80.00
4¼" h, scenic, two live oaks, full moon, blue matte glaze, artist sgd "Henrietta Bailey, 1921" 1,500.00

Vase
5¾" h, flaring rim, undecorated green matte glaze, c1902 . . . . 250.00
6½" h, bud, incised stylized irises, blue green ground, high glaze, artist sgd "HB" for Henrietta Bailey, c1908 . . . . 2,150.00
7¼" h, bulbous, tapering towards ftd base, white, yellow, and green floral dec, blue ground, imp marks, artist sgd "HB" for Henrietta Bailey, c1910 . . . . 1,300.00
7½" h, trailing pink morning glories,

green leaves, blue matte glaze, artist Anna Frances Simpson, 1923 1,500.00
8¼" h, baluster, carved clusters of light blue daffodils, long green stems, medium blue ground, artist sgd "SI" for Sadie Irvine, imp "JM, 250, JE8" 1,000.00
8½" h
Baluster, lavender Louisiana iris dec, yellow highlights, green leaves, blue matte glaze, Henrietta Bailey, 1919 . . . . 3,700.00
Tapering neck, vertically and horizontally narcissus dec, blue and white matte glaze, artist sgd "Sadie Irvine," 1918, orig paper label 2,500.00
17½" h, exaggerated two handle baluster, incised line dec, shaded olive green, imp mark, designer Juanita Mauras monogram 2,650.00

NILOAK POTTERY, MISSION WARE

History: Niloak Pottery was made near Benton, Arkansas. Charles Dean Hyten experimented with native clay, trying to preserve its natural colors. By 1911 he perfected Mission Ware, a marbleized pottery in which the cream and brown colors predominate. The pieces were marked Niloak (kaolin spelled backwards).

After a devastating fire, the pottery was rebuilt and named Eagle Pottery. This factory included the space to add a novelty pottery line which was introduced in 1929. This line usually was marked Hywood-Niloak until 1934 when the name Hywood was dropped from the mark. Mr. Hyten left the pottery in 1941. In 1946 operations ceased.

Additional Listings: See *Warman's Americana & Collectibles* for more examples, especially the novelty pieces.

Note: Prices listed below are for Mission Ware pieces.

Ashtray, 4" d, swirled tan, cream, and brown 25.00
Bowl, 5" d, 2" h, swirled tan, cream, and blue 48.00
Candlestick, 9" h 125.00
Jar, cov, 4¾" h, swirled tan, cream, and blue, imp mark 115.00
Mug, 4" h, swirled tan, cream, and blue, imp mark 125.00
Pitcher, 10" h, strap handle, swirled tan, cream, and blue, imp mark 350.00
Vase
8" h, 3¼" d, cylindrical, swirled pink and burgundy, incised mark 110.00

Lamp Base, swirled tan, cream, and brown, $150.00.

8¼" h
Baluster, swirled tan, cream, and blue, imp mark	125.00
Waisted cylindrical, swirled tan, cream, and blue, imp mark	115.00
10½" h, rolled rim, swirled red, burgundy, and beige	175.00

NIPPON CHINA, 1891–1921

History: Nippon, Japanese hand painted porcelain, was made for export between 1891 and 1921. In 1891, when the McKinley tariff act proclaimed that all items of foreign manufacture be stamped with their country of origin, Japan chose to use "Nippon." In 1921 the United States decided the word "Nippon" no longer was acceptable and required that all Japanese wares be marked with "Japan." The Nippon era ended.

There are over 220 recorded Nippon backstamps or marks. The three most popular are the wreath, maple leaf, and rising sun marks. Wares with variations of all three marks are being reproduced today. A knowledgeable collector can easily spot the reproductions by the mark variances.

The majority of the marks are found in three different colors: green, blue, and magenta. Colors indicate the quality of the porcelain used: green for first grade porcelain, blue for second grade, and magenta for third grade. Marks were applied by two methods, decal stickers under glaze and imprinting directly on the porcelain.

References: Gene Loendorf, *Nippon Hand Painted China*, McGrew Color Graphics, 1975; Joan Van Patten, *The Collector's Encyclopedia of Nippon Porcelain, Series One,* Collector Books, 1979; Joan Van Patten, *The Collector's Encyclopedia Of Nippon Porcelain, Series Two,* Collector Books, 1982; Joan Van Patten, *The Collector's*

Encyclopedia Of Nippon Porcelain, Series Three, Collector Books, 1986.

Collectors' Clubs: Great Lakes Nippon Collectors Club, Rt. 2, Box 81, Peotone, IL 60468; International Nippon Collectors Club, P.O. Box 88, Jericho, NY 11753; Long Island Nippon Collectors Club, P.O. Box 88, Jericho, NY 11753; New England Nippon Collectors Club, 22 Mill Pond, North Andover, MA 01845.

Additional Listings: See *Warman's Americana & Collectibles*.

Advisor: Kathy Wojciechowski.

Vase, handles, roses, gold trim, 7" h, $145.00.

Asparagus Set, 12 x 7½" tray, six matching 7½" plates, green M mark	350.00
Basket	
4", pale blue tiny flowers outlined in gold, gold handle, Rising Sun mark	50.00
6 x 9 x 5", hp int., dogwood blossoms, gold trim	45.00
7", cobalt ground, gold trim, portrait medallion	225.00
Berry Set, large master bowl, seven matching small bowls, large traced pink and blue flowers, green leaves, fancy scalloped edges, Shinzo Nippon mark	100.00
Biscuit Jar, cov, English fox hunt scene	300.00
Bowl	
7", woodland scene, scalloped rim, blue maple leaf mark	175.00
8½", crimped edge, pierced handles, woodland stream scene, green M in wreath mark	90.00
9", handles, hp int., yellow and purple flowers	65.00
10"d, 2½" h, deep red ground, yellow and pink flowers, all over gold dot, scalloped edge, Royal Kinran mark	75.00
11½" d, hp, chrysanthemums, raised beading, cobalt blue ground, gold, single handle	175.00

Cake Set, 10¾″ d master plate with pierced handles, five small serving plates, swans swimming in lake, cobalt, heavy gold trim, maple leaf mark, 6 pcs **350.00**

Calling Card Tray, 7½″, cobalt, pink and red roses, gold trim, green M in wreath mark **125.00**

Candlestick, 8″, woman walking dog on leash, purple and black, gold tracings **115.00**

Candy Dish, 7″, ftd, large red roses with gold tracings, cobalt and gold trim, wreath mark **75.00**

Celery Dish, gold beaded **30.00**

Celery Set, 13½″ master celery dish, six salts, hp stalk of celery in center, wreath mark **175.00**

Child's Feeding Dish, 8″, child playing with dog, Rising Sun mark **85.00**

Chocolate Set, 9½″ h, chocolate pot, four cups and saucers, man on camel scene, green mark 47 . . . . **675.00**

Cigarette Box, 4½″, farm scene on cov, floral dec on base, wreath mark . . . **225.00**

Compote, 7¾″, floral center, Wedgwood style border, three griffins base **450.00**

Condensed Milk Container, 6″, tiny pink and white roses, white beaded scrolling, mauve shaded ground, RC mark **140.00**

Cracker Jar, 9″ w, floral dec, two handles, green mark 47 . . . . **75.00**

Cup and Saucer, cottage and forest scene, bisque, Shinzo mark **40.00**

Ewer
9″, ftd, moriage bird in flight and flowers, hp Nippon mark **250.00**
10¾″, Halloween scene, tapestry, maple leaf mark **700.00**

Ferner, 8¼″, ftd, two handles, lake shore scene, cobalt blue, gold crisscross trim, green M in wreath mark **325.00**

Hair Receiver, ftd
Black and gold, three feet **50.00**
Hand Painted, pink flowers, gold banding, Rising Sun mark **30.00**

Hatpin Holder, 5″, gold scrolled design, portrait of young lady in oval medallion, attached underplate, blue maple leaf mark **190.00**

Humidor
5¼″, scenic, sgd **175.00**
6″, Indian chief on horseback, blown out dec, tortoise shell ground, green M in wreath mark **950.00**
7″, jockey on race horse, moriage dec, green M in wreath mark **475.00**
7¼″, crouching lion, blown out dec, green M in wreath mark **850.00**

Inkwell, 4 x 4″, bisque, bird design, beaded, colorful **150.00**

Jam Jar, 5½″ h, matching 6⅛″ under-

plate, cream ground, pink apple blossoms, green leaves, cobalt borders, gold trim, green M in wreath mark . . **70.00**

Lemonade Set, pitcher and five 3″ mugs, hp, sunset with sailboat **185.00**

Mayonnaise Set, ftd bowl, underplate, ladle, cream ground, orange poppies outlined in gold, RC mark, 3 pcs . . . **75.00**

Mug, 5½″, moriage dragon, gray ground, artist sgd, green M in wreath mark **125.00**

Napkin Ring, holly berries dec **35.00**

Nappy, 6¼″, shaded pink roses, gold dec, beaded, blue TS mark **125.00**

Pin Tray, relief molded flowers, earth tones, bisque finish **45.00**

Pitcher, 11″, pagoda and bridge, yellow ground, enamel flowers, gold rim, base, and handle, blue maple leaf mark **250.00**

Plaque
7¾″, bust of Indian chief, full headdress, moriage border, beading, blue enameled flowers with red jeweled center, pierced for hanging, sgd **275.00**
8¾″, mountain and lake scene, blue and purple flower border, green M in wreath mark **125.00**
10″
Fox Hunt, green M in wreath mark **175.00**
Indian on galloping horse, blown out dec, green M in wreath mark **850.00**
11¼″, Egyptian scene, people in sailboat, orange, brown, and lavender, green M in wreath mark **125.00**
12½″ d, St Bernard, green wreath mark 47 . . . . **550.00**

Plate
9″, heavy red florals, wreath mark . . **75.00**
9½″, hp, pink, castle, yellow trees and water, green M in wreath mark . . **95.00**

Powder Box, cov, 3¾″, ftd, hp, small pink flowers, blue Rising Sun mark **35.00**

Punch Bowl, 10″, cobalt and floral dec, ftd stand, green maple leaf mark, 2 pcs **450.00**

Ring Tree, shallow dish base, gold band, purple violets, gold trim, maple leaf mark **75.00**

Stamp Box, geometric black stripes, int. tray with two compartments, wreath mark **90.00**

Stein, 7″, Galle scene with brown moriage trees, pale orange ground, white enamel flowers, maple leaf mark . . . **400.00**

Sugar Shaker
4¼″, cobalt, flower dec, matching cov, blue maple leaf mark **150.00**
5″, bisque, boat scene, cobalt, gold handle **55.00**

Tankard, 10″, pink floral panels, cobalt, yellow, and green moriage 325.00

Teapot, butterflies 48.00

Tea Strainer, 6″, single handle, cobalt, flowers, heavy gold rim, blue maple leaf mark 100.00

Tea Tile, 5½″, Dutch windmill scene, green M in wreath mark 40.00

Toast Rack, sections for 3 slices of toast, white ground, gold raised bunches of grapes and grape leaves, spoke mark 125.00

Toothpick Holder, three handles, hp, pyramids and palm tree scene, green M in wreath mark 40.00

Tray, 12 x 9″, bisque, water scene, heavy gold trim 100.00

Urn, 18″, portrait, heavy gold trim 850.00

Vase

6″, pale yellow floral and green leaf dec, tan and brown, gold trim and handles, green mark 47 .... 65.00

7″, acorns and leaves, blown out dec, blue maple leaf mark 450.00

7¼″, portrait, lady in pastel colors, cream ground, all over gold designs and flowers, back panel of red and pink roses, maple leaf mark 195.00

7¾″, matte finish, cream ground, peach and yellow roses, green leaves, green M in wreath mark .. 100.00

9″, Art Nouveau style, orange poppies, blue maple leaf mark 135.00

11½″, Art Nouveau style, woodland scene, stylized dec, ram's head handles 325.00

12″, cowboy on horse, desert background, gold handles, Imperial Nippon blue mark 375.00

12½″, cream ground, crisscross gold bands, purple and gold fruit, gold handles, Royal Nishike mark 125.00

13″, handled, black border with gold phoenix bird, green M in wreath mark 235.00

NODDERS

History: Nodders are figurines with heads and/or arms attached to the body with wires to enable them to move. They are made in a variety of materials—bisque, celluloid, papier mache, porcelain, and wood.

Most nodders date from the late 19th century with Germany being the principal source of supply. Among the American made nodders, those of Disney and cartoon characters are most eagerly sought.

Black Woman, seated, holds, removable watermelon, gray hair, head nods, salt shaker type 60.00

Bull Dog Terrier, articulated head, papier mache, minor losses to paint .. 400.00

Cat, 5″ h, composition, black 60.00

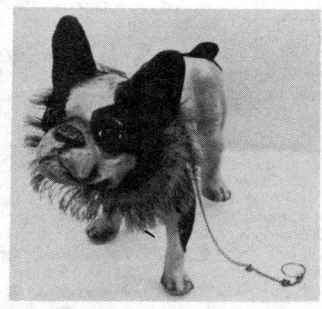

Dog, papier mache, black and white, barks when chain pulled, $400.00.

Dog, 9″ h, sitting, glazed bisque, marked "Staffordshire" 125.00

Donkey, 3″ h, celluloid 30.00

Elephant, 12″ h, composition, head and tail nod 125.00

Goose, celluloid, marked "US Zone, Germany" 30.00

Hobo, 3½″ h, 2¼″ w, green coat, bottle in pocket, tan pants and hat, sitting in chair, holding stick 225.00

Little Orphan Annie, bisque, marked "Germany" 100.00

Man and woman, green and red Alpine costumes, marked "Germany" 150.00

Monkey, 6½″ h, celluloid 65.00

Oriental Man, 4½″ h, 2″ d, standing, aqua robe and hat, carrying two pink baskets 150.00

Oriental Woman, sitting

4¼″ h, 2¼″ w, blond, white and turquoise robe, hat, gold trim, fan in one hand 150.00

5¼″ h, 3″ d, blond, Oriental yellow and white robe, blue trim, pink fan ... 165.00

Rabbit, 7″ h, papier mache, glass eyes 75.00

NORITAKE CHINA

History: Morimura Brothers founded Noritake China in 1904 in Nagoya, Japan. They made high quality chinaware for export to the United States and also produced a line of china blanks for hand painting. In 1910 the company perfected a technique for the production of high quality dinnerware and introduced streamlined production.

During the 1920s Larkin Company, Buffalo, New York, was a prime distributor of Noritake China. Larkin offered Azalea, Briarcliff, Linden, Modjeska, Savory, Sheridan, and Tree In The Meadow patterns as part of their premium line.

The factory was heavily damaged during World War II; production was reduced. Between 1946 and 1948 the company sold their china under the "Rose China" mark, since the quality of production did not match the earlier Noritake China. An 1948 expansion saw the resumption of quality production and the use of the Noritake name once again.

There are close to 100 different marks for Noritake, the careful study of which can determine the date of production. Most pieces are marked "Noritake" and have a wreath, "M," "N," or "Nippon." The use of the letter "N" was registered in 1953.

References: Aimee Neff Alden and Marian Kinney Richardson, *Early Noritake China: An Identification And Value Guide To Tableware Patterns,* Wallace-Homestead, 1987; Joan Van Patten, *Collector's Encyclopedia of Noritake,* Collector Books, 1984.

Additional Listings: See *Warman's Americana & Collectibles* for price listings of the Azalea pattern.

Cup and Saucer, white ground, pink and blue flowers, gold trim, 3″ h cup, 5″ d saucer, $27.50.

Ashtray
3″ d, figural, cat, luster	110.00
4¾″ w, tree trunk, relief molded raccoon, green M in wreath mark . . .	225.00

Bowl
Bird dec, 8″ l, green mark #27, Plate 386	70.00
Iris pattern, ftd	18.00
Red floral border	18.00

Bread Plate, 12″ l, ear of corn dec . . .	50.00
Butter Tub, Azalea pattern	45.00
Cake Plate, Baroda pattern	20.00
Candlesticks, pr, 3½″ h, 4½″ d, tan luster, blue roses, black handle and trim, three ftd base	75.00
Candy Dish, 15″ d, orange and pearl luster, black trim, green mark	35.00

Celery Tray, 12″ l, Azalea pattern	45.00
Chocolate Set, cov chocolate pot, six cups and saucers, white and cobalt blue dec, gold trim	250.00
Compote, blue, gold and white, all–over fruit dec, 2 pcs	175.00
Creamer and Sugar, cov, butterfly and orange flower dec, irid blue ground	35.00
Cup and Saucer, Bahama pattern	24.00
Demitasse Set, cov demitasse pot, creamer, cov sugar, six cups and saucers and 12″ d tray, yellow, white center band, multicolored hp delicate flowers outlined in black, black handles	400.00
Lemon Plate, star shape, center handle	20.00
Mayonnaise, cov, matching underplate, yellow and pink flowers, green foliage, red and gold border	30.00
Napkin Ring, Art Deco, man and woman, pr	100.00

Nut Bowl
6½″ l, molded relief peanuts, Plate 418	90.00
7″ d, relief molded figural owls perched on edge, Plate 356	175.00

Potpourri Jar, 6″ h, blue and white, pierced cov with red and yellow rosebud finial	75.00
Sandwich Server, 8″ d, pearlized center, fruit dec, bird finial	165.00
Sugar Shaker, 6½″ h, scenic	35.00
Tobacco Humidor, collie dog, blown out	550.00

Vase
10″ h, Art Nouveau landscape, handles	200.00
11½″ h, baluster, two gold handles, light and dark blue floral dec, blue and yellow Phoenix Bird, green wreath mark	185.00

Wall Pocket, Art Deco sailing ship scene, red mark	65.00

NORITAKE: TREE IN THE MEADOW PATTERN

History: Tree In The Meadow is one of the most popular patterns of Noritake china. Since the design is hand painted, there are numerous variations of the scene. The basic scene features a large tree (usually in the foreground), a meandering stream or lake, and a peasant cottage in the distance. Principal colors are muted tones of brown and yellow.

The pattern is found with a variety of backstamps and appears to have been imported into the United States beginning in the early 1920s. The Larkin Company distributed this pattern through its catalog sales in the 1920–1930 period.

Reference: Joan Van Patten, *Collector's Encyclopedia of Noritake,* Collector Books, 1984.

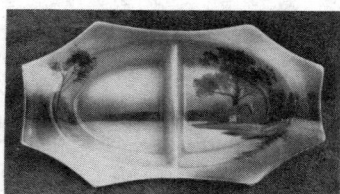

Relish Dish, divided, $45.00.

Ashtray, hp, green M in wreath mark	50.00
Bowl, 7" d	25.00
Bread Tray	45.00
Butter Dish, cov, insert	60.00
Cake Plate, open handles	26.00
Celery Dish, 12" l	40.00
Chocolate Pot, cov	200.00
Compote, cov	100.00
Cracker Jar, cov, melon ribbed	125.00
Creamer and Sugar, cov	60.00
Cruet Set, oil and vinegar, orig stoppers	125.00
Cup and Saucer	20.00
Demitasse Cup and Saucer	18.00
Demitasse Pot, cov	325.00
Hair Receiver	30.00
Lemon Dish, 5½" d, handle	35.00
Mayonnaise, underplate and orig spoon	20.00
Plate	
6½" d	12.00
8½" d	18.00
Platter, 10" l	75.00
Salt and Pepper Shakers, pr	30.00
Sugar Shaker	35.00
Syrup	50.00
Teapot, cov	100.00
Toothpick, 2½" h	50.00
Vegetable Dish, 8" d, octagonal, divided	20.00
Waffle Set	75.00

NORTH DAKOTA SCHOOL OF MINES

History: The North Dakota School of Mines was established in 1890. Earle J. Babcock, an instructor in chemistry, was impressed with the high purity of North Dakota potter's clay. In 1898 Babcock received funds to develop his finds. He tried to interest commercial potteries in North Dakota clay, but had limited success.

In 1910 Babcock persuaded the school to establish a Ceramics Department. Margaret Cable, who studied under Charles Binns and Frederick H. Rhead, was appointed head. She remained until her retirement in 1949.

Decorative emphasis was placed on native themes, e.g., flowers and animals. Art Nouveau, Art Deco, and fairly plain pieces were made.

The pottery is marked in cobalt blue underglaze with "University of North Dakota/Grand Forks, N.D./Made at School of Mines/N.D. Clay" in a circle. Some earlier pieces only are marked "U.N.D." or "U.N.D./Grand Forks, N.D." Most pieces are numbered (they can be dated with University records) and signed by both the instructor and student. Cable signed pieces are most desirable.

Reference: *University Of North Dakota Pottery, The Cable Years,* Knight Publishing Company, 1977.

Vase, dark purple, blue flecks, stamped "U. N. D.," 2¾" h, $100.00.

Ashtray, KEM design, seal 1930	150.00
Bowl, Bentonite, roadrunners dec, sgd "J Mattson"	450.00
Cookie Jar, 9½" h, 6½" d, figural, Black woman, matte chocolate brown glaze, factory ink stamp "Aunt Susan/dht/M Cable"	1,250.00
Figure, donkey, pale gray glaze	75.00
Paperweight, Rebekah	75.00
Pitcher, thick red glaze over green	65.00
Tumbler, 5¼" h, cylindrical, green, marked "University of North Dakota, Grand Forks, ND, Made of School of Mines ND Clay"	60.00
Vase	
4 x 4½", shaded white to light green ground, imp circular and foliage dec, stamped mark, inscribed "95A Huck"	185.00
6½ x 4", squatty, cut back panel dec, ox pulling covered wagon, green, brown ground, circular ink mark, incised "JH"	400.00

NUTTING, WALLACE

History: Wallace Nutting (1861–1941) was one of America's foremost photographers in the first third of the twentieth century. Between 1897 and his death, he took over 50,000 pictures, kept approximately 10,000, destroyed the rest because they did not meet his standards, and commercially marketed over 2,500 of the 10,000. The rest he retained. Of the remaining 7,500 views, some were sold in limited numbers and the others used personally for lectures, research, or simply entertaining friends.

Millions of Nutting's hand–colored platinotype pictures were sold. Nutting opened his first studio in New York City in 1904. In 1905 he moved to a larger studio in Southbury, Connecticut. A Toronto branch office followed in 1907. In 1911–12 Nutting sold his business and house, Nuttinghame, in Southbury. The person who purchased the business backed out, leaving Nutting without a home.

Nutting moved his entire operation, including twenty employees, to Framingham, Massachusetts. His business blossomed. At its peak, it provided employment for over two hundred people in positions ranging from colorists and support staff to salesmen and framers.

Wallace Nutting began actively collecting antiques sometime around 1912. In 1917 he published his first book on furniture, *American Windsor*. In 1928 the first two volumes of *The Furniture Treasury* appeared. Volume 3 followed in 1933.

In 1917–18 Wallace Nutting began offering reproduction furniture for sale. During the early 1920s the business prospered. However, by 1927–28 the business was in decline. The Depression brought further decline. Nutting laid off employees, but refused to allow the business to fold. It was operating on a very limited basis at the time of his death.

During his lifetime Nutting had a close relationship with Berea College in Kentucky. Upon his wife's death, Berea was given the remains of the furniture business. After copying the blueprints and patterns at the Framingham factory for their records, Berea sold the business to Drexel Furniture Company.

References: Michael Ivankovich, *The Alphabetical & Numerical Index to Wallace Nutting Pictures*, Diamond Press, 1988; Michael Ivankovich, *The Guide To Wallace Nutting Furniture*, Diamond Press, 1990; Michael Ivankovich, *The Price Guide To Wallace Nutting Pictures*, Diamond Press, 1989; Wallace Nutting, *The Wallace Nutting Expansible Catalog* (reprint of 1915 catalog), Diamond Press; Wallace Nutting, *Wallace Nutting General Catalog, Supreme Edition* (reprint of 1930 catalog), Schiffer Publishing.

BOOKS

Album, *Up At Vilas Farm,* 22 pgs, mounted, colored, and sgd pictures, leather bound, taken at Charles Nathaniel Vilas Estate in Alstead, NH, one of three known copies **2,850.00**
Furniture Treasury, Volumes I and II, 1948 edition **55.00**
Photographic Art Secrets, 1st edition **135.00**

States Beautiful Series
   Connecticut Beautiful, 2nd edition, sgd by Wallace Nutting, orig dj . . . **75.00**
   Maine Beautiful, 1st edition, green cover **50.00**
   Massachusetts Beautiful, 1st edition, green cover **50.00**
   New Hampshire Beautiful, 1st edition, green cover **60.00**
   New York Beautiful, 2nd edition, tan cover, dj **65.00**
   Virginia Beautiful, 1st edition, green cover, sgd by Wallace Nutting . . . **60.00**

Table, tavern, pine top, maple legs, block branded signature, $1,250.00.

FURNITURE

Chair
   Arm, ladderback, five back slats, bulbous turned front stretchers, sausage turned side stretchers, NE . . **525.00**
   Side, ladderback, five back slats, bulbous turned front stretchers, sausage turned side stretchers, NE, maple finish, Block brand **325.00**
Table, library, maple, single drawer, paper label, light maple finish **750.00**

PICTURES

Anno 1820, black and white, girl climbing stairs of large home, 13 x 16″ . . **200.00**
Announcing The Engagement, #403, three girls at table, wallpapered room, 11 x 14″ **165.00**
Autumn Ripples, #5442, ext. VT river scene, 10 x 12″ **85.00**
Colorist's Coloring Instructions, #228, set of orig colorist's instructions, complete color specifications attached to model picture, 15 x 18″ **200.00**
Comfort And A Cat, #545, girl sewing near Nuttinghame fireplace, cat sleeps in basket on Windsor chair, 13 x 15″ **185.00**

Picture, On The Slope, #312, Rhode Island, 11 x 17″, $225.00.

Cottages On The Old Sod, #9850, Irish scene of two mothers and four young children, thatch roof cottages, 11 x 14″ 675.00

Cypress Heights, #2276, CA seascape, single cypress tree on rocky hilltop, 18 x 22″ 725.00

Dog–On–It, #2739, eight puppies sitting on green garden bench, 7 x 11″ 1,150.00

Drying Apples, #429, Uncle Sam and Granny core apples, fireplace, 10 x 12″ 325.00

Four O'Clock, #633, sixteen cows standing in green field, blue stream, 14 x 17″ 1,150.00

Goose Chase Quilt, The, #2353, blue settle, girl sewing quilt by fireplace, 13 x 22″ 250.00

Grandmother's China, #2366, girl sitting beside corner cupboard filled with china, 11 x 17″ 125.00

Graves–Redfield House, Madison, CT, black and white, front view, brown clapboard house, snow scene, 13 x 16″ 525.00

Guardian Mother, The, #1043, little blond girl, standing to the left of her mother, flowing dresses, 9 x 14″ ... 2,200.00

Hollyhock Cottage, #6414, pink flowers, green garden border English cottage, 10 x 12″ 85.00

Housatonic Blossoms, #980, blossoming trees by rushing Housatonic River, CT, 10 x 16″ 170.00

Ivy and Rose Cloister, #2197, ivy covered red brick CA mission, 13 x 16″ 375.00

June Joy, #6796, road with blossoming trees and bridge, 13 x 17″ 50.00

Litchfield Minster, #5845, English cathedral, 14 x 17″ 150.00

Sunshine and Music, #1340, girl playing piano, formal int. setting, orange dress, 10 x 16″ 210.00

Sylvan Dell, #8129, tall elm tree by stream, 10 x 20″ 115.00

Where Trout Lie, #8645, rippling stream, 13 x 16″ 120.00

Winding The Tall Clock, #3302, girl, formal bedroom, winding tall case clock, 14 x 17″ 165.00

SILHOUETTES

Girl

Looking into mirror, 5 x 5″, round frame 60.00

Sitting at vanity, powder puff, 7 x 8″ 70.00

Sitting on garden bench, 7 x 8″ 80.00

With parasol, garden, 5 x 5″, orig label on back, round frame 125.00

Washington, George, orig label on back, 4 x 5″ 75.00

Washington, Martha, orig label on back, 4 x 5″ 45.00

OCCUPIED JAPAN

History: At the end of World War II, the Japanese economy was devastated. To secure needed hard currency, the Japanese pottery industry produced thousands of figurines and other knickknacks for export. From the beginning of the American occupation until April 28, 1952, these objects were marked "Japan," "Made in Japan," "Occupied Japan," and "Made in Occupied Japan." Only pieces marked with the last two designations are of strong interest to Occupied Japan collectors. The first two marks also were used at other time periods.

The variety of products is endless—ashtrays, dinnerware, lamps, planters, souvenir items, toys, vases, etc. Initially it was the figurines which attracted the largest number of collectors; today many collectors focus on non-figurine material.

References: Gene Florence, *The Collector's Encyclopedia Of Occupied Japan Collectibles, 1st Series* (1976, 1982 revision), *2nd Series* (1979, 1982 revision), *Third Series* (1987), *4th Series* (1970), Collector Books.

Collectors' Clubs: Occupied Japan Collectors Club, 18309 Faysmith Avenue, Torrance, CA 90504; O.J. Club, 29 Freeborn Street, Newport, RI 02840.

Additional Listings: See *Warman's Americana & Collectibles* for more examples.

Ashtray, matching Aladdin lighter 8.00

Bookends, pr, Scottie dog, ceramic ... 25.00

Canister Set, blue flowers and birds, set of four jars 65.00

Cigarette Box, cov, dog's head, red ground, metal 12.00

Cigarette Lighter, figural

Radio, movable dial 45.00

Pistol 25.00

Teapot, silver colored metal, wooden

handle, matching undertray, orig box 25.00

Condiment Set, figural, rooster and hen, creamer, cov sugar, pr salt and pepper shakers 75.00

Cornucopia, 7 x 8", chariot, rearing horse and two cherubs, multicolored beading, gold trim, unglazed bisque .. 75.00

Creamer, 3¼" h, bird on bamboo plant, multicolored flowers, brown and gold border 12.00

Demitasse Set, Willow Ware, blue and white, marked "Maruta" 225.00

Fan, paper, Oriental dec 8.00

Figure, three tan and gray puppies, brown basket, marked, 2⅞" w, 2⅝" h, $12.50.

Figure

6" h, Shoeshine Man, black 38.00

7" h, Mexican girl, marked "Ucagco" 40.00

8" h, Hummel type boy 40.00

Fish Bowl Ornament, mermaid, bisque, blue tail 25.00

Flower Frog, 6" h, figural, girl with bird on shoulder, pastel highlights, gold trim, bisque 45.00

Holy Font, Hummel type 75.00

Incense Burner, figural, American Indian headdress 35.00

Match Holder, 7 x 4½", Colonial couple, each holding basket, striker on side, bisque 45.00

Mug, 4½" h, figural, lean cowboy 30.00

Planter
5¾" l, Gingham Cat 25.00
6" l, duck, bisque 25.00

Platter, 16" l, Courtley pattern, heavy gold trim, marked "Meito Norleans China" 30.00

Salad Set, salad bowl, serving fork and spoon, lacquer ware 20.00

Salt and Pepper Shakers, pr
Frogs, matching tray, 3 pcs 30.00
Hummel type boy and girl 20.00
Windmills, movable blades 25.00

Tape Measure, pig, celluloid, green .. 35.00

Toothpick Holder, little girl pushing baby carriage 12.00

Tray
8¼ x 5", papier mache, hp, roses, marked "Alcohol Proof/SS/Made in Occupied Japan" 20.00
14 x 12", wood, hp, floral 35.00

Wall Pocket, 4" l, Colonial woman on balcony, bisque 30.00

Wind Chimes, 10½" h, 3¾" w, glass, multicolored, orig paper wrapping .. 15.00

G.E. OHR, BILOXI.

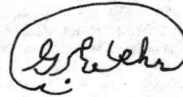

OHR POTTERY

History: Ohr pottery was produced by George E. Ohr in Biloxi, Mississippi. There is some discrepancy as to when he actually established his pottery. Some suggest 1878, but Ohr's autobiography indicates 1883. In 1884 Ohr exhibited 600 pieces of his work, indicating that he had been working for some time.

Ohr's techniques included twisting, crushing, folding, denting, and crinkling thin walled clay into odd, grotesque, and sometimes graceful forms. Much of his early work is signed with an impressed stamp of his name and location in block letters. His later work, often marked with the flowing script designation "G E Ohr," was usually left unglazed.

In 1906, Ohr closed the pottery and stored over 6,000 pieces as his legacy to his family. He hoped it would be purchased by the U.S. Government, which never happened. The entire collection remained in storage until it was rediscovered in 1972.

Today Ohr is recognized as one of the leading potters in the American Art Pottery movement. Some greedy individuals have taken the later unglazed pieces and covered them with poor quality glazes, in hopes of making them more valuable. These pieces, usually with the flowing script mark, do not have "stilt marks" on the bottom.

Reference: Garth Clark, Robert Ellison, Jr., and Eugene Hecht, *The Mad Potter of Biloxi: The Art & Life of George Ohr,* Abbeville Press, 1989.

Bank, 8¼" l, lip shaped, coin slot on top, green and pink mottled glaze, imp "Geo. E. Ohr Biloxi, Miss" 1,980.00

Bowl

3″ h, crumpled conical body, oxblood, malachite green, and blue mottled glaze, int. glazed mustard and green, imp "Geo. E. Ohr, Biloxi, Miss" 13,200.00

3¼″ h, pushed down body, twisted shoulder, pinched and ruffled rim, gunmetal glaze, imp "G. E. Ohr, Biloxi, Miss" 1,980.00

3½″ h, bulbous, boldly folded and ruffled edge, lavender, olive green, and blue glaze, blue and brown dapples, imp "Biloxi, Miss, Geo. E. Ohr" 13,200.00

Pitcher

4⅞″ h, cylindrical, folded cut–out handle, undulating mouth, blue–green glaze, mauve highlights, script incised "G. E. Ohr" 2,860.00

6″ h, squatty, crumpled, folded cut–out handle, gunmetal dripping glaze over moss green, script incised "G. E. Ohr" 3,300.00

Puzzle Mug, high glaze, mottled green, pressed rope and leaf handle, screw under handle, script sgd "G. E. Ohr," 3⅛″ d, 3½″ h, $375.00.

Vase

2½″ h, egg cup shape, chipped edge rim and foot, high glaze Charleston green, stamped "Geo. E. Ohr Biloxi, Miss," minor glaze flakes . . . 180.00

2⅝″ h

Cylindrical body, inverted rim, bulbous shoulder, ftd, matte, grainy gray and green glaze, sgd "GE Ohr" in script 250.00

Spinning Top shape, spotty gray–green semi–matte glaze, script sgd 350.00

2¾″ h, squat angular baluster, fluid pinched handles on both sides, semi–matte green–brown glaze, imp "Geo. E. Ohr, Biloxi, Miss," restoration to one handle 715.00

3⅓″ h, squat angular baluster, high glazed pink, white, blue, and green,

imp "Geo. E. Ohr, Biloxi, Miss," patch of glaze retouched 935.00

3⅜″ h, bulbous, cylindrical neck, everted rim, high blue and brown mottled glazes, green splashed int., imp "G. E. Ohr, Biloxi, Miss," hairline 225.00

3½″ h, baluster, inverted rim, periwinkle blue, splashes of black over body, imp "G. E. Ohr, Biloxi, Miss" 550.00

5¾″ h, bulbous, cylindrical neck, crimped rim, mustard and brown dappled glaze, script incised "G. E. Ohr" 2,650.00

6⅞″ h, flared cylindrical, ruffled neck, bright pink, garnet red and cobalt blue dappled glaze, imp "G. E. Ohr, Biloxi, Miss" 11,000.00

8¼″ h, bulbous, inverted bell shaped neck, mottled olive green and purple rim with dappled gunpowder spots, claret glazed neck with random beige splotches, several burst surfaces showing gray cellular int., malachite green and gunpowder glazed waisted middle, brown, purple and green dappled glazed base, script incised "G. E. Ohr" . . 19,800.00

13″ h, conical, twisted and waisted neck, crimped ruffled rim, hematite metal luster glaze, imp "G. E. Ohr, Biloxi, Miss" 22,000.00

OLD IVORY
84

OLD IVORY CHINA

History: Old Ivory derives its name from the background color of the china. It was made in Silesia, Germany, during the second half of the 19th century. Marked pieces usually have a pattern number (pattern names are not common) and the crown Silesia mark.

Reference: Susan and Al Bagdade, *Warman's English & Continental Pottery & Porcelain, 1st Edition,* Warman Publishing Co., Inc., 1987.

Berry Set, master bowl and four serving bowls, 5 pcs

#11	135.00
#69	150.00
#84	200.00

Biscuit Jar, cov
  #15 .... 350.00
  #16 .... 375.00
Bowl
  6½" d, #16 .... 30.00
  9½" d, #10, scalloped, two handles ... 60.00
Cake Plate, 10" d, pierced handles
  #6 .... 100.00
  #121 .... 95.00
Cake Set, 10" d cake plate with pierced
  handles, six 6¼" d serving plates
  #16 .... 250.00
  #84 .... 225.00
Celery Tray, #84 .... 150.00
Creamer, #32 .... 45.00
Cup and Saucer
  #15 .... 45.00
  #202 .... 35.00
Mustard Pot, cov, #16 .... 100.00
Oyster Bowl, #11 .... 175.00

Plate, Pattern VIII, floral dec, 8" d, $45.00.

Plate
  6" d, #75 .... 18.00
  8½" d, #16 .... 25.00
Platter, #22, 11½" l, holly dec 100.00
Sugar, cov, #84 .... 50.00
Toothpick, #75 .... 85.00

OLD PARIS CHINA

History: Old Paris china is fine quality porcelain made by various French factories located in and about Paris during the 18th and 19th centuries. Some pieces were marked, but the majority was not. Characteristics of this type of china include fine porcelain, beautiful decorations and gilding. Favorite colors were dark maroon, deep cobalt blue, and a deep green.

Reference: Susan and Al Bagdade, *Warman's English & Continental Pottery & Porcelain, 1st Edition*, Warman Publishing Co., Inc., 1987.

Additional Listing: Continental China and Porcelain (General).

Basket, reticulated, white and gold dec, c1825 .... **1,350.00**
Cake Stand, Honore style, green border, 1840–50 .... **185.00**
Clock, mantel, 13¾" h, figural, lyre, central enamel faced clock with French movement, flanked by paneled scenes of a lady on one side, man posed as archer on other, enamel dec, pink ground, gilt trim and beading, hairline, gilt wear, 19th C **350.00**

Compote, white ground, scalloped top, reticulated edge, gold trim, hp fruit dec on standard, 9¼" d, 6¾" h, $65.00.

Dessert Service, cov coffeepot, cov sugar, creamer, eight cups and saucers, eight fruit plates, serving plate, and waste bowl, floral dec, c1850–60 **175.00**
Figure, 18¾" h, Napoleon, standing, one arm tucked behind his back, other tucked into shirt, full military dress, gilt dec, low sq base, inscribed "Roussel–Bardell," late 19th C **600.00**
Inkstand, floral, orig inkwell and sander, 1850–60 .... **650.00**
Mantel Vase, bell like flowered handles, blue ground, paneled enamel portraits of lovers, gilt trim, minor flower damage, pr **300.00**
Plate, 9¼" d, flower basket center, gilt line and borders, ochre ground, c1830, pr **225.00**
Soup Plate, gold and white dec, 1865–70, set of 12 .... **225.00**
Urn, cov, 14½" h, painted hunting scenes, molded acanthus and palmette scrolled double handle, gilt border, sq plinth base, pr **1,000.00**

Vase

17½" h, cov, ormolu mounting, mint green ground, enamel floral bouquet panel, center scene of children riding goat, molded handles and leafy garlands, gilt wear, late 19th C **550.00**

18¼" h, leafy shaped tops, heavily raised molded bellflowers to sides, enamel cartouches of male and female figures, chips, hairlines, late 19th C, pr **225.00**

OLD SLEEPY EYE

History: Sleepy Eye, a Sioux Indian chief who reportedly had a droopy eye, gave his name to Sleepy Eye, Minnesota, and one of its leading flour mills. In the early 1900s Old Sleepy Eye Flour offered four Flemish gray heavy stoneware premiums, decorated in cobalt blue: a straight-sided butter crock, curved salt bowl, stein, and vase. The premiums were made by Weir Pottery Company, later to become Monmouth Pottery Company, and finally to emerge as the present-day Western Stoneware Company of Monmouth, Illinois.

Additional pottery and stoneware pieces were issued. Forms included five sizes of pitchers (4, 5½, 6½, 8, and 9 inches), mugs, steins, sugar bowls, and tea tiles (hot plates). Most were cobalt blue on white, but other glaze hues, such as browns, golds, and greens, were used.

Old Sleepy Eye also issued many other items, including bakers' caps, lithographed barrel covers, beanies, fans, multicolored pillow tops, postcards, trade cards, etc. Production of Old Sleepy Eye stoneware ended in 1937.

In 1952 Western Stoneware Company made a 22 and 40 ounce stein in chestnut brown glaze with a redesigned Indianhead. From 1961 to 1972 gift editions, dated and signed with a Maple Leaf mark, were made for the Board of Directors and others within the company. Beginning in 1973, Western Stoneware Company issued an annual limited edition stein, marked and dated, for collectors.

Reference: Elinor Meugnoit, *Old Sleepy Eye*, published by author, 1979.

Collectors' Club: Old Sleepy Eye Collectors Club, Box 12, Monmouth, IL 61462.

Reproduction Alert: Blue and white pitchers, crazed, weighted, and often with a stamp or the word "Ironstone" are the most copied. The stein and salt bowl also have been made. Many reproductions come from Taiwan.

A line of fantasy items, new items which never existed, includes an advertising pocket mirror with miniature flour barrel label, small glass plates, fruit jars, toothpick holders, glass and pottery miniature pitchers, and salt and pepper shakers. One mill item has been made, a sack marked as though it

were old but of a size that could not possibly hold the amount of flour indicated.

MILL ITEMS

Advertising Premium Cards, set of ten, 5½ x 9", full color Indian lore illus, text, Old Sleepy Eye Indian character trademark **850.00**

Cookbook, "Sleepy Eye Milling Co," loaf of bread shape, chief portrait **135.00**

Dough Scraper, tin blade, wood handle with "Sleepy Eye Flour" **250.00**

Letter Opener, bronze, Indian head on handle, marked "Sleepy Eye Milling Co, Sleepy Eye, MN" **750.00**

Pinback Button, "Old Sleepy Eye For Me," chief bust portrait **150.00**

Spoon

Demitasse, roses in bowl **135.00**

Teaspoon, silverplated, Indian on handle, Unity **90.00**

Mug, 7½" h, Indian head on handle, Indian and Indian village scenes, $400.00.

POTTERY AND STONEWARE

Mug, cobalt blue on white, Indian head on handle, 1906–37 . . . . **235.00**

Pitcher

5¼" h, blue on yellow Indian head on handle **700.00**

6¼" h, cobalt blue on white, Indian head on handle, 1906–37 . . . . . . **225.00**

8" h, blue on cream **275.00**

9" h, blue and white **230.00**

Stein
Brown on yellow, 7¾" h 920.00
Chestnut brown, 1952 . . . .   450.00
Flemish blue on gray, 1903 . . . .   550.00
Sugar Bowl, 4" h, cobalt blue on white,
1906–37 . . . .   360.00
Tile, cobalt blue and white 1,000.00
Vase, 9" h, Flemish blue on gray, dra-
gonfly, frog, and bulrushes on re-
verse, 1903 . . . .   325.00

ONION MEISSEN

History: The blue onion or bulb pattern is of
Chinese origin and depicts peaches and pomegranates, not onions. It was first made in the 18th
century by Meissen, hence the name Onion Meissen.

Factories in Europe, Japan, and elsewhere copied the pattern. Many still have the pattern in production, including the Meissen factory in Germany.

Note: Prices given are for pieces produced between 1870 and 1930. Many pieces are marked
with a company's logo; after 1891 the country of
origin is indicated on imported pieces. Early Meissen examples bring a high premium.

Bowl, 11" d, gold edge, pre 1900 . . . .   170.00
Box, cov, 4 x 4½", round, rose finial . .   70.00
Candlestick, 7" h, pr 75.00
Creamer and Sugar, gold edge, cov
sugar, c1900 . . . .   175.00
Cup and Saucer 65.00
Demitasse Cup and Saucer, blue, gilt
dec, underglaze crossed swords
mark, set of 4 . . . .   275.00
Dinner Service, 65 pcs, includes service
for six, serving dishes, candlesticks,
coffeepot, and teapot 3,000.00
Dish, 7¾" l, oval, marked 70.00
Fruit Knives, set of 6 . . . .   75.00
Funnel 50.00
Meat Pounder 75.00
Mold, melon, handled 30.00
Mustard Pot, 4¾", underplate and ladle   50.00
Pie Crimper, wood handle 25.00
Plate
8½", marked 25.00
9", leaf shape 75.00
9¾", marked 40.00
10" 75.00
Platter
12", oval, marked 65.00
17", marked 225.00

**Platter, Meissen crossed swords mark
and imp marks, 12½ x 25", $500.00.**

20½" l, oval, blue 425.00
21", oval, mid 19th C 425.00
25" l, imp and crossed swords mark   500.00
Pot de Creme 45.00
Salt and Pepper Shaker, pr 40.00
Serving Dish, two sections, butterfly
shape, handle in center 225.00
Skimmer, curve shape, reticulated . . .   60.00
Soup Tureen, marked 170.00
Tea Strainer, wood handle 20.00
Teabowl and Saucer, underglaze blue
crossed swords and dot, 19th C 300.00
Teapot, 10", mid 20th C 325.00
Tray, 15 x 9", rect, flat, mid 20th C . . .   170.00
Vase, 6½", bud 65.00
Vegetable Dish, cov
10", sq 125.00
12½" l, blue 175.00

OPALESCENT GLASS

History: Opalescent glass is a clear or colored
glass with milky white decorations which shows a
fiery or opalescent quality when held to light. The
effect was achieved by applying bone ash chemi-
cals to designated areas while a piece was still hot
and then refiring it at tremendous heat.

There are three basic categories of opalescent
glass: (1) Blown (or mold blown) patterns, e.g.,
Daisy & Fern and Spanish Lace; (2) Novelties,
pressed glass patterns made in limited pieces
which often included unusual shapes such as Corn
or Trough; and (3) Pattern (pressed) glass.

Opalescent glass was produced in England in
the 1870s. Northwood began the American production in 1897 at its Indiana, Pennsylvania, plant.
Jefferson, National Glass, Hobbs, and Fenton
soon followed.

References: William Heacock, *Encyclopedia of
Victorian Colored Pattern Glass, Book II, Opalescent Glass from A to Z, Second Edition*, Antique
Publications, 1977; William Heacock and William
Gamble, *Encyclopedia of Victorian Colored Pattern Glass, Book 9, Cranberry Opalescent from A
to Z*, Antique Publications, 1987.

Barber Bottle, Stars and Stripes, blue   165.00
Berry Bowl, master, Beatty Rib, white   40.00

Pitcher, tankard, Poinsettia pattern, blue ground, Hobbs, Brockunier & Co, 13⅜″ h, $225.00.

Berry Set, Alaska, blue, 7 pcs	385.00
Bowl	
Iris with Meander, vaseline, 8″ d	125.00
Jeweled Heart, green, crimped, 6″ d	20.00
Wreath and Shell, vaseline, 8″ d	95.00
Bride's Basket, Bubble Lattice, cranberry	165.00
Butter, cov	
Beatty Rib, white	65.00
Idyll, green	350.00
Stippled Leaf and Basketweave, blue	235.00
Celery	
Diamond Spearhead, cobalt	110.00
Regal, blue	85.00
Cheese Dish, Hobb's Swirl, cranberry	350.00
Compote, Squirrel & Acorn, green	100.00
Creamer	
Alaska, yellow	55.00
Palm Beach, blue	45.00
Wreath and Shell, vaseline	55.00
Cruet	
Daisy and Fern, blue, faceted stopper	110.00
Hobb's Hobnail, orig faceted stopper	
Blue	225.00
Cranberry	300.00
Spanish Lace, white opal dec, clear ground, applied handle	85.00
Stripe, blue, applied blue handle, cut faceted blue stopper	135.00
Curtain Tiebacks, pr, pewter posts, white	90.00
Finger Bowl, Buckeye Lattice, cranberry	90.00
Jack In The Pulpit Vase, 13½″ h, blue, eight petal top, yellow enameled inside of top and down front	260.00
Jelly Compote	
Diamond Spearhead, vaseline	75.00
Everglades, blue	95.00
Iris with Meander, vaseline	90.00
Swag with Brackets, blue	48.00
Miniature Lamp, Snowflake, cranberry, Smith #186	850.00
Mustard, Striped Opalescent, yellow, 4″ h, orig hinged top	55.00
Pitcher, water	
Buttons and Braids, cranberry	300.00
Diamond Spearhead, cobalt, 7″ h	235.00
Hobnail, cranberry, clear applied handle, 10″ h	150.00
Poinsettia, blue, tankard, bulbous base	175.00
Spanish Lace, blue	110.00
Plate, Wishbone and Drape, green	20.00
Punch Cup, Chrysanthemum Base Swirl, cranberry	40.00
Salt Shaker	
Daisy and Fern, cranberry, orig top, Northwood	85.00
Reverse Swirl, blue	30.00
Striped Opalescent	
Cranberry, 4½″ h, replaced top	35.00
Yellow, 2½″ h, orig oxidized top	35.00
Salt, open, Beatty Rib, white	22.00
Sauce, Alaska, vaseline	45.00
Spooner	
Bubble Lattice, cranberry	135.00
Stippled Leaf and Basketweave, blue	75.00
Wreath and Shell, vaseline	55.00
Sugar Bowl, cov	
Spanish Lace, blue	75.00
Wreath and Shell, vaseline	75.00
Sugar Shaker	
Bubble Lattice, rubina	250.00
Daisy and Fern, netted apple blossom mold, cranberry	245.00
Paneled Sprig, cranberry	185.00
Syrup	
Coin Spot, orig top, blue	125.00
Opal Lattice, cranberry, SP spring lid, "Pat Apr 28, 81" and "Mar 28, 82," applied clear handle	265.00
Table Set, cov butter, creamer, sugar, spooner	
Circled Scroll, green	550.00
Everglades	
Clear	410.00
Vaseline	600.00
Jeweled Heart, green	600.00
Swag with Brackets	
Blue	475.00
Green	475.00
Wreath and Shell, vaseline, dec	600.00
Toothpick	
Iris with Meander, green	75.00
Ribbed Lattice, blue	135.00
Tumbler	
Beatty Rib, white	32.00

Circled Scroll, blue	85.00
Poinsettia, cranberry	85.00
Stars and Stripes, cranberry	75.00
Vase, Hobnail, cranberry	245.00
Water Set, water pitcher and tumblers	
Everglades, blue, 7 pcs	700.00
Iris with Meander	
Blue	650.00
Vaseline	275.00
Jeweled Heart, blue	625.00
Regal, green	565.00
Swag with Brackets, vaseline	575.00
Tokyo, green	675.00

OPALINE GLASS

History: Opaline glass was a popular mid- to late-19th century European glass. The glass has a certain amount of translucency and often is found decorated in enamel designs and trimmed in gold.

Box, cov, pale green, gold enameling, cut dec, French, 4″ d, 2½″ h, $145.00.

Basket, 6″ h, white, gold trim, blue snake encircles handle, shiny ext., satin int.	180.00
Bowl, 9″ d, cov, ftd, enameled floral dec	65.00
Box, cov	
1½″ d, 1½″ h, blue, gold prunus blossoms and leaves	50.00
4″ d, French green, hinged lid, gilt metal mountings	65.00
Creamer, Wheat and Rushes pattern, green	45.00
Epergne, three trumpet vases, blue	200.00
Figure, bird, pink	45.00
Finger Bowl, matching underplate, blue	70.00
Goblet, 5″ h, white	35.00
Mug, 4″ h, white ground, cobalt blue trim, French	100.00
Mustard, drum shape, pink, sgd "Portieux Pig"	35.00
Perfume Bottle, 4⅜″ h, gold bronze filigree overlay collar and hinged cap, French, pr	225.00

Pickle Castor, cov, green insert, SP ormolu frame, c1880	175.00
Relish, pink, Proeger Bird pattern, minor roughness	20.00
Ring Tree, 2½″ d, round dished base, center column, blue, gold and white trim	50.00
Salt and Pepper Shakers, pr, enameled dec, pink ground, orig tops	65.00
Soap Dish, cov, blue, hp, floral dec	75.00
Tumbler, 4½″ h, white, equestrian figure dec, gilt trim	40.00
Vase	
9″ h, bulbous, slender neck, dark green enameled floral dec, mint green ground, pr	180.00
12½″ h, folded handkerchief shape, chain dec, enamel blue and pink flowers, green leaves and branches, bee dec on int., facing pr	450.00

ORIENTAL RUGS

History: The history of oriental rugs or carpets dates back to 3,000 B.C., but it was in the 16th century that they became prevalent. The rugs originated in the regions of Central Asia, Iran (Persia), Caucasus, and Anatolia. Early rugs can be classified into basic categories: Iranian, Caucasian, Turkoman, Turkish, and Chinese. Later India, Pakistan, and Iraq produced rugs in the oriental style.

The pattern name is derived from the tribe which produced the rug, e.g., Iran is the source for Hamadan, Herez, Sarouk, Tabriz, and others.

When evaluating an oriental rug, age, design, color, weave, knots per square inch, and condition determine the final value. Silk rugs and prayer rugs bring higher prices.

References: Murray Eiland, *Oriental Rugs: A New Comprehensive Guide,* Little, Brown and Company, 1981; Linda Kline, *Beginner's Guide To Oriental Rugs,* Ross Books, 1980; Ivan C. Neff and Carol V. Maggs, *Dictionary of Oriental Rugs,* Van Nostrand Reinhold Company, 1979.

Periodical: *Oriental Rug Review,* Beech Hill Road, R.F.D. 2, Meredith, NH 03253.

Reproduction Alert: Beware! There are repainted rugs on the market.

Abadeh, Persia, c1925, 4′ 11″ × 3′ 10″, ivory ground, sil-i-sultan pattern, medium chocolate polygon lozenge border, hooked motifs, decorative guards	1,100.00
Afshar, Persia, c1925, 6′ × 4′ 3″, three elongated tree forms with pr polychrome chickens, ivory and red meander and striped borders	1,650.00
Agra, India, c1925, 12′ 8″ × 7′ 5″, soft grape field, all—over herati pattern	

within red palmette, vine and leaf border, five narrow guard stripes **4,125.00**

Akstafa, Caucasus, runner, c1900, 11' 2" × 4' 3", indigo field, mid-blue, rust, and ivory angular medallions, animals and geometric devices myriad, ivory crab border, three twin guards **4,400.00**

Aubusson, France, c1875, 16' × 12' 6", dark brown field, ivory medallion with floral bouquet, pale green acanthus leaf frame, undulating ivory and pale green border, dark rust outer border **13,200.00**

Bidjar, Persia
Rug, c1910, 7' 5" × 4' 10", red field, repeated floral sprays, lattice arabesque vinery, two birds and leaping stags pattern, indigo foliate border, ivory guards **2,750.00**
Runner, c1875, 10' 3" × 3' 6", cornflower blue medallion on red cartouche, polychrome blossom field and indigo spandrels, ivory floral meander border, five narrow guard stripes **1,540.00**

Hereke, Turkey, c1875, 7' 4" × 3' 10", silk, red violet scrolling vines and animals field, ivory arabesque medallion, ivory arabesque spandrels, gray-

Heriz, midnight blue water bug, palmette, and vine border, red field, large angular medallion anchored in fan palmettes, extending to stylized flowers, leaves, ivory and red spandrels, 8' 4" x 11' 1", $3,500.00.

green calligraphic cartouche border, ivory and red violet floral meander guards **5,225.00**

Heriz, Persia
10' 8" × 7' 2", foliate ivory field, concentric medallions, tri-color spandrels, indigo turtle border, three narrow guards **3,575.00**
11' 8" × 8' 7", c1925, rust-red field, diamond flower head medallions rows, serrated leaf pairs and multiple floral forms, indigo floral meander border, three narrow guards **4,950.00**
12' 3" × 8' 7", c1925, mid-blue field, all-over floral pattern, red central medallion, pale rose turtle border, three dec guard stripes **7,150.00**

Isphahan, Persia, c1950, ivory field, all-over scrolling vines, leaves, and polychrome flower heads, red floral border, ivory and indigo guards **3,300.00**

Karabagh, Caucasus, 1909, 6' 8" × 4' 5", flowering tree with two lions and leaping stags, red floral primary border and two gray guards **1,320.00**

Kashan, Persia, c1925, 6' 3" × 4' 6", ivory field, vases, palmettes, animals, floriforms, helmet, and sword, light beige cup and flower border, pale blue and beige guards **1,430.00**

Kerman, Persia
11' 10" × 8' 11", c1930, ivory field, all-over palmettes, flower head and blossoming vines pattern, dust rose foliate border, four guards . . **6,600.00**
13' 8" × 10', c1925, gold field, oblong floral medallion, conforming sky blue floral spray border, navy ring and ivory, celadon and rose corner devices **1,650.00**
17' 6" × 9' 9", c1925, pale rose field, floral sprays and blossoming branches pattern, mid-blue foliate border, dec guards **8,250.00**

Lori Pambak Kazak, Caucasus, c1875, 7' 1" × 5' 6", red field, two ivory Lori Pambak medallions, concentric hooked diamonds, and geometric designs, ivory hooked lozenge border, reciprocal and checkered guard stripes **2,200.00**

Mahal, Persia, c1925, 22' 7" × 12' 3", indigo field, all-over flower head and cloud bands pattern, red rendered floriform border, five dec guard stripes **5,500.00**

Oushak, Turkey
14' 2" × 9' 11", c1925, mustard gold field, oblong red medallion and vinery, red and gold spandrels, ivory floral primary border, three pairs guard stripes **4,125.00**

16' 8" × 13' 4", c1925, soft red field, green tracery medallion, green spandrels, mid–blue floral meander border, four dec guard stripes . . . **8,800.00**

Sarouk, Persia

6' 6" × 4' 4", c1930, deep wine field, floral composite medallion surrounded by bouquets, midnight floral repeat border, two twin guards **2,200.00**

20' 10" × 12' 3", c1925, deep burgundy ground, all–over floral spray pattern, dark indigo palmette and flower head border, brown and burgundy guard stripes **6,000.00**

Senneh, Persia, c1925, 14' 4" × 10' 7", indigo field, all–over herati pattern, repeated red floriforms border, three twin guards **22,000.00**

Serab, Persia, runner, c1900, 14' 6" × 3' 2", foliate lattice pattern, spaced ivory medallion and medallion halves, camel stylized flower head border, reciprocal and floral meander guard stripes, wide camel outer frame . . . **2,100.00**

Shirvan Kilim, Caucasus, c1875, 9' 1" × 3' 6", banded pattern, alternating latch hook red or indigo lozenges panels and polychrome zig-zag and ivory cross motif panels **1,210.00**

Soumak, Caucasus, c1910, 10' 9" × 8' 1", red field, three large indigo diamond medallions with smaller diamond form medallions in blue and brown, geometric and sylized lozenges, indigo zig-zag border, five dec guard stripes **3,300.00**

Tabriz, Persia, c1925, 11' 4" × 7' 1" **1,760.00**

Talish, Caucasus, c1875, 8' × 3' 9", green field, ascending stylized floral motif, human and animal figures, and geometric patterns, ivory stepped diamond and triangle border, reciprocal, striped and flower head guards **3,850.00**

Veramin, Persia, c1925, 11' 6" × 7' 4", mid–blue field, diamond lattice pattern, with blossoms and birds, red flower head and bird primary border, ivory and mid–blue floral guard stripes **3,575.00**

ORIENTALIA

History: Orientalia is a term applied to objects made in the Orient, which encompasses the Far East, Asia, China, and Japan. The diversity of cultures produced a variety of objects and styles.

References: Sandra Andacht, *Oriental Antiques & Art: An Identification And Value Guide,* Wallace-Homestead, 1987; Lea Baten, *Japanese Animal Art: Antique & Contemporary,* Charles Tuttle, 1989; John Esten (editor), *Blue and White China,* Little, Brown, and Company, 1987.

Periodical: *The Orientalia Journal,* P.O. Box 94, Little Neck, NY 11363.

Additional Listings: Canton, Celadon, Cloisonne, Fitzhugh, Nanking, Netsukes, Rose Medallion, Japanese Prints, and other categories.

Basin, bronze, circular form, loose ring handles, tripod mask feet, 17" d . . . **880.00**

Bowl

Japanese

Bronze, curled lotus leaf form, three raised pod feet, 3¾" h . . . **935.00**

Silver, bulbous body, relief dragon dec, 4⅓" d, Meiji period, sgd "Kanoiche" **250.00**

Korean

Koryo Dynasty, incised celadon, flared lip, gold lacquer, restoration, 7¼" d **225.00**

Yi Dynasty, cov, Korean, plain domed form, 6¾" d **300.00**

Box, cov, Japanese, lacquer

Drum form, black, gilt metal mounts, gilt mon on cov, 9¼" h, 19th C . . . **165.00**

Metal and mother-of-pearl inlay, grid pattern design enclosing shell florets, brown lacquer int., 14½" l . . . **770.00**

Brushpot, powder blue glaze, gilt dec, 5¾" h, 19th C **500.00**

Bucket, Japanese, bronze, copper and gilt colors, 8½" h **130.00**

Candlestick

Chinese, altar, pewter, lotus form bobeches, character form standards, 23½" h, pr **350.00**

Japanese, stag antlers, carved pomegranate, monkey holding lotus form nozzle, 19th C, 9½" h, pr . . . **2,860.00**

Censer

Chinese, cov, rect, bronze, swing handle, 5¼" l, 19th C **880.00**

Ming style, bronze, archaic style dec bands, 10", six character Xuande mark, 19th C **1,650.00**

Japanese, bronze, frog form, pierced cov on back, 13½" l, 19th C **1,760.00**

Ceremonial Set, gilt copper 19" l ladle and 4¼" h waterpot, 16½" l bamboo scripture case, chased flowering foliage, cranes, and turtles, partially rubbed gilt, 18th C **3,520.00**

Clothing

Kimono, Japanese, stitched bats and waves dec, blue, green, and orange, black ground, 61" **250.00**

Jacket, Chinese, 19th C, silk, coral, counted stitch dec on gauze, pavilion and landscape scenes, embroidered white silk sleeve borders with figures, garden setting, 34½" **825.00**

Robe, Chinese, ceremonial, silk and brocaded, elaborate animals in landscape dec, 51½" l **550.00**

Cup, Chinese, hardstone, green, bird and peony band dec, 2" h, pr **45.00**

Dish, Korean, beige floral dec, celadon ground, 6½" d **150.00**

Figure

Buddha guardian, Japanese, Edo period, wood, polychrome traces, 11" h **600.00**

Cockerel, Japanese, bronze, Verdigris patina, 12" l **80.00**

Lion, Chinese, 19th C, head turned back, 5¼" h **525.00**

Old man, Japanese, ivory, carved, 6" h **150.00**

Woman Chinese, late 18th C

8½" h, holding scepter, wearing green robe with multicolor dec **110.00**

9¾" h, standing with hands together at waist, wearing long shawl over full length robe, hair in double chignon, red pigments **500.00**

Furniture

Bench, Chinese, Hongmu, bamboo, rect top, slatted, sq legs, hoof feet, stretchers set with upright struts, 19½" h, 16¾" d, 59½" l **1,980.00**

Bookcase, Japanese, Keaki, wood, out–scrolled end top, asymmetrical arrangement of sliding doors, small drawers, and open shelves, 33" h, 15½" d, 40" w **1,980.00**

Cabinet

Japanese, 19th C, bamboo, galleried top, semicircular front with two cupboard door, five tripod feet, 26¼" h, 15½" d, 15¾" w . . **440.00**

Korean, late 19th C, elmwood, four doors with stringing border, figured front, pierced brass mounts, 32¼" h **850.00**

Chair, Chinese, side, teakwood, oval relief carved back panel, 19th C **200.00**

Chest, Japanese, small drawers above sliding doors, slat sides, iron mounts, 19th C, 29" h, 20¾" d, 30" w **3,300.00**

Etagere, Chinese, rosewood, carved, rect top, sliding doors, multilevel shelves, two base drawers, 40½" h, 32¾" w, 11½" d **425.00**

Screen, Hong Mu, four fold, semicircular outline, leaf paneled, beaded molding, short legs, 70" h, 20" w each panel **1,980.00**

Settee, Chinese, Hongmu, 19th C, rect spindle back with three circular entwined dragon medallions, solid panel seat, cylindrical legs, box stretcher, 35" w **4,675.00**

Stand, red and black lacquer, hexagonal, inset top with latticework, six slender legs joined by latticework stretcher, 30" h 19⅛" w **550.00**

Stool, pr, Chinese, 19th C, barrel form, gray beige, and white marble top encircled with row of bosses, oval reserves on sides, 17¾" h . . **1,760.00**

Table

Chinese, Huanghuali, 17th C, rect top, bird wing spandrels, legs joined by floor stretchers, 16½" h, 20½" d, 35" l **1,760.00**

Japanese, 19th C, black lacquer, scattered mother-of-pearl inlaid top, sq flaring legs with negoro lacquer, 12" h, 30" d, 3⅓" l **1,320.00**

Ginger Jar, Chinese, blue and white, floral dec, ice crackle ground, mounted as lamp, 15½" h **140.00**

Incense Burner, Japanese, bronze

Cylindrical form, domed cov, swing handle, 8½" h, 19th C **935.00**

Elaborate bird and tree relief dec, 22¼" h, mounted as lamps, pr . . . **1,100.00**

Jar

Chinese, Kangxi period, Famille Verte, ovoid form, underglaze blue and enamel dec, children and ladies, garden and palace scene, pierced wood lid, jade inset, 8" h **6,000.00**

Japanese, 19th C, bronze, wide mouth, ovoid body, inset oval handles **550.00**

Korean, Yi Dynasty, ovoid form, narrow mouth, short rim, cream glaze **1,430.00**

Jardiniere, Chinese

Bronze, cast bosses and lion mask handles, 15½" h **420.00**

Rosewood, carved, 35½" h, pr **275.00**

Jewelry Cabinet, Japanese, lacquer floral dec, 11" h **375.00**

Lantern, Japanese, bronze

Cylindrical, slight dome top, pierced mon and cloud shape dec, 16½" h, 18th C **1,100.00**

Ovoid form, pierced bamboo and iris panels, 9¾" h, 19th C **220.00**

Libation Cup, 18th C, carved rhinoceros horn, ruyi fungus, bamboo stalks, and leaves, light honey color, 3⅝" h **1,800.00**

Mask, Japanese, mounted on stand

Demon, cream, black, and gilt details, 12¼" h **1,210.00**

Mythical beast, horned, dragon snout, lacquered, 27½" h **2,640.00**

Warrior, jaw guard piece, 10½" h, 19th C **1,870.00**

Medicine Chest, Japanese, red lacquer, sixty-six small drawers, loose ring pulls, carrying handles on ends, 19th C, 25" h, 9¼" d, 42¼" l **880.00**

Picnic Set, 7 pcs, large container, three cov pouring vessels, two cov bowls, and stand with bowed legs, black lacquer, gilt dec, 18th C **1,980.00**

Planter, Japanese
Lacquer, cylindrical, copper liners, 9¾" h, pr **550.00**
Wood, oval outline, loop handles, copper liner, 28" l, 19th C **310.00**

Roof Tile, Chinese, Ming Dynasty, pottery, scholar wearing turquoise robe, holding open book, aubergine border, glazed, 14" h **1,000.00**

Saki Bottle, Japanese, polychrome dec, 9" h **150.00**

Scroll, Qianlong, silk, embroidered, satin stitch, bird and flowering prunus tree, sewn seed pearls blossoms, peach, white, ream, blue, and green, framed, 35 x 17½" **1,650.00**

Snuff Bottle, Chinese, brass gilded, coral and turquoise beads, 6" h **100.00**

Tea Bowl, Japanese, stoneware, buff, beige glaze dec, stylized brown dec, 4" d **150.00**

Tea Caddy, Japanese, wood, inlaid landscape scene, 4" h **100.00**

Teapot, Japanese, iron
Edo Period, chased cherry blossom motif, stippled surface, sgd, 9½" h **100.00**
Meiji period, Hoo bird, magatama, cloud, and inscription, chased dark patina, sgd, 5½" h **225.00**

Tray, Paktong, overlapping auspicious motif medallions dec, 18¼" l, late 19th C **715.00**

Trunk
Chinese, pigskin Chinoiserie dec, brass mounts, 28" h, 33" w, 28½" d **625.00**
Japanese, 19th C, rect, raised gold and brown lacquer, three friends, pine, bamboo, and flowering prunus designs, brown ground, black lacquer int., 16" h, 23" w, 13½" d **7,500.00**

Urn
Chinese, bronze, baluster form, relief birds in flight dec, two handles, 25" h **350.00**
Japanese, Jomon period, conical body, buff clay, imp rope dec, three twisted peak grooved rim, four vertical carved grooves, 15" h **800.00**

Vase
Chinese
Bronze, raised and enamel inlaid dec, 14" h, late 19th C **150.00**
Powder Blue, ovoid form, waisted neck, glazed, 18th C **550.00**
Japanese, bronze, baluster body, cast demon emptying flask from clouds dec, 12⅛" h **880.00**
Korean, Koryo Dynasty, bronze, bottle type, pear shape, trumpet neck, 13" h **840.00**
Yenyen, Kangxi style, blue and white, shaped panels of immortals, diaper ground, 18" h, 18th C **2,200.00**

Waterpot, Japanese, copper, lappet border bands, heavy patina, 10" h, 19th C **220.00**

OVERSHOT GLASS

History: Overshot glass was developed in the mid-1800s. A gather of molten glass was rolled over the marver upon which had been placed crushed glass to produce overshot glass. The piece then was blown into the desired shape. The finished effect was a glass that was frosted or iced in appearance.

Early pieces were mainly made in clear. As the demand for colored glass increased, color was added to the base piece and occasionally to the crushed glass.

Pieces of overshot generally are attributed to the Boston and Sandwich Glass Co., although many other companies also made it as it grew in popularity.

Basket, 6" d, 7½" h, octagonal, orange shaded to vaseline, emb nubs on sides, applied vaseline handle **200.00**

Compote, open, 8⅜" d, 6⅜" h, scalloped and ruffled, cranberry shaded to clear bowl, applied clear edging, fancy brass dome ftd pedestal base **100.00**

Finger Bowl, fluted and swirled, pink . . **100.00**

Vase, Mandarin Export, 1790–1800, 3⅞" h, $125.00.

Pitcher, light blue ground, applied light amber handle, attributed to Boston & Sandwich Glass Co, 7¾" h, $275.00.

Marmalade Jar, cov and underplate, green, gold snake entwined on cov, attributed to Boston and Sandwich	275.00
Pitcher	
5½" h, clear, applied clear reeded handle	85.00
8" h, ovoid, swirled melon ribbed body, cylindrical neck, pinched spout, cranberry, applied clear reeded handle	200.00
Punch Cup, pink, applied clear handle, attributed to Boston and Sandwich, set of 8	245.00
Rose Bowl, 3¾" d, rubena, applied flowers and pale green leaves	145.00
Vase	
8¼" h, fluted, pink, opal, applied clear handle	100.00
11" h, 3½" d, cranberry, two pink applied flowers, green branch and leaves, applied amber feet, clear edge ruffle	300.00

OWENS POTTERY

History: J. B. Owens began making pottery in 1885 near Roseville, Ohio. In 1891 he built a plant in Zanesville and in 1897 began producing art pottery. Not much art pottery was produced by Owens after 1907, when most of their production centered on tiles.

Owens Pottery, employing many of the same artists and designs of its two crosstown rivals, Roseville and Weller, can appear very similar to that of its competitors (i.e. Utopian—brown glaze; Lotus—light glaze; Aqua Verde—green glaze, etc.).

There were a few techniques used exclusively at Owens. These included Red Flame ware (slip decoration under a high red glaze) and Mission (over-glaze, slip decorations in mineral colors) depicting Spanish Mission scenes. Other specialities included Opalesce (semi-gloss designs in lustred gold and orange) and Coralene (small beads affixed to the surface of the decorated vases).

References: Paul Evans, *Art Pottery of the United States, 2nd Edition,* Feingold & Lewis Publishing Corp., 1987; Ralph and Terry Kovel, *The Kovels' Collector's Guide to American Art Pottery,* Crown Publishers, Inc., 1974.

Vase, Aborigine pattern, 6" h, $250.00.

Ewer, 7" h, early standard glaze, Art Nouveau sterling silver overlay, cluster of yellow leaves and blackberries, brown ground, incised "1773," die stamped "O"	900.00
Jardiniere, 24" h, matching pedestal base, Utopian, matte, tulips, ruffled	325.00
Lamp, 13½" h, red flowers, gold dec, gold bands at top and base, black high glaze, Sudanese	250.00
Umbrella Stand, 20½" h, large brown iris dec, brown and green leaves, matte finish	275.00
Vase	
3" h, two handled bulbous body, short neck, high gloss finish, painted and slip yellow, green, and brown rosebuds and leaves, shaded brown ground, silver cased handles, silver overlay scrolling vines, imp "Utopian J B Owens 896"	220.00
4½" h, 2" d, bulbous, rolled rim, fine, sprayed, semi–matte khaki glaze, incised mark	75.00
8¼" h, dark brown, woman's face, red roses, marked "Owens/Henri Deaux"	350.00

10" h, satiny blue, emb cattails, dark
metallic, gold and pink irid finish ... **300.00**
10½" h, ovoid, Utopian, wild rose dec ... **250.00**

PAIRPOINT

History: The Pairpoint Manufacturing Co. was
organized in 1880 as a silverplating firm in New
Bedford, Massachusetts. The company merged
with Mount Washington Glass Co. in 1894 and
became the Pairpoint Corporation. The new company produced speciality glass items, often accented with metal frames.

Pairpoint Corp. was sold in 1938 and Robert
Gunderson became manager. He operated it as
the Gunderson Glass Works until his death in
1952. From 1952 until the plant closed in 1956,
operations were maintained under the name Gun-
derson-Pairpoint. Robert Bryden reopened the
glass manufacturing business in 1970, moving it
back to the New Bedford area.

References: Leonard E. Padgett, *Pairpoint
Glass,* Wallace-Homestead, 1979; John A. Shu-
mann III, *The Collector's Encyclopedia of American Art Glass,* Collector Books, 1988.

Collectors' Club: Pairpoint Cup Plate Collectors, Box 52D, East Weymouth, MA 02189.

**Wine, Flambé, Rockwell silver design,
black stem, red bowl, marked "Rockwell," 5⅛" h, $150.00.**

Biscuit Jar, 7" h, hp, daisy dec, bulbous
apricot base, sgd and numbered ... **300.00**
Cologne Bottle, 7" h, green, clear foot,
faceted paperweight stopper **200.00**
Compote
  8" d, bubble stem, engraved top and
  base **75.00**
  8½" d, 7½" h, clear, engraved Gainsborough pattern **135.00**
Console Bowl, 12" d, 6¾" h, apple
green, bubble ball connector, engraved Vintage pattern **155.00**
Creamer, opal glass, Delft blue windmill

and landscape, five sailing ships on
reverse, painted blue blown—out
scrolls encircle base, SP handle, rim,
and spout **325.00**
Ice Bucket, 4¾" w, 5½" h, clear, engraved polar bear and sunrise over
icebergs, nickel silver rim and drain
plate **175.00**
Ice Pail, 6" d, 7½" h, clear, engraved
Vintage pattern, nickel silver rim and
drain plate **175.00**
Jewel Box, 7" l, 4" w, 3¾" h, cov, hinged,
pale ivory ground, gold enameled rococo scrolling on lid, large central
medallion, Dresden style roses, wild
roses, pink, yellow, and purple asters,
gold scroll work base, gold washed,
SP rim, base sgd "Pairpoint Corporation" **985.00**
Lamp
  Boudoir, 8¾" h, 4½" d shade, two
  blown—out multicolored sgd pansy
  shades, SP urn form holder sgd
  "Pairpoint Mfg Co" trademark ... **1,200.00**
  Table, 22" h, 16" d reverse painted
  ribbed quatrefoil blown out shade,
  gold and black striped butterflies at
  each corner, blue and pink floral
  dec, white ground, sgd "The Pairpoint Corp," fitted gilt metal two
  socket conforming base sgd "Pairpoint," company trademark **3,000.00**
Lamp Shade
  5½" d, 3½" h, puffy, dark red and
  green reverse painted grape and
  vineyard dec, sgd in gold "Pat. Applied for," pr **500.00**
  9½" d, reverse painted blossoms, butterflies, and trellis dec, sgd "The
  Pairpoint Co" **950.00**
Perfume Bottle, 6" h, octagonal, ribbed
stopper **120.00**
Smoking Stand, three opal glass bowls
mounted in shield shaped maple
wood stand, brass trim and feet,
brass cigar holder, Delft dec of windmills, houses, people, and sailing
ships **550.00**
Toothpick Holder, SP, figural, bear
standing by barrel **120.00**
Vase
  8⅛" h, bud, irid amber, SP holder, sgd **275.00**
  11" h, green luster, engraved vintage
  dec, ten prisms, white bubble ball **150.00**
  12" h, opaque white, oval landscape,
  fruit blossoms and snowbirds dec **500.00**

PAPER EPHEMERA

History: Maurice Rickards, author of *Collecting
Paper Ephemera*, suggests that ephemera are the

"minor transient documents of everyday life"—material destined for the wastebasket but never quite making it. This definition is more fitting than traditional dictionary definitions that stress length of time, e.g., "lasting a very short time." A driver's license, which is used for a year or longer, is as much a piece of ephemera as a ticket to a sporting event or music concert. The transient nature of the object is the key.

Collecting ephemera has a long and distinguished history. Among the English pioneers were John Seldon (1584–1654), Samuel Pepys (1633–1703), and John Bagford (1650–1716). Large American collections can be found at historical societies, libraries, and museums (e.g., Wadsworth Antheneum, Hartford, CT, and Museum of the City of New York) across the country.

When used by collectors, "ephemera" usually means paper objects, e.g., billheads and letterheads, book plates, documents, labels, stocks and bonds, tickets, valentines, etc. However, more and more ephemera collectors are recognizing the transient nature of some three dimensional material, e.g., advertising tins and pinback buttons. Today's specialized paper shows include dealers selling both two and three dimensional material.

References: Anne F. Clapp, *Curatorial Care of Works of Art on Paper*, Nick Lyons Books, 1987; Maurice Rickards, *Collecting Paper Ephemera*, Abbeville Press, 1988; Demaris C. Smith, *Preserving Your Paper Collectibles*, Betterway Publications, 1989.

Collectors' Club: Ephemera Society of America, Inc., P.O. Box 37, Schoharie, NY 12157.

Checks

Adams and Co., San Francisco, 1850s, unused, light blue, vignettes, approx. 8½″ x 4¼″ **50.00**
Illinois Central Railroad, 1853, vignettes **30.00**
I. H. Hershfield, Helena, MT, 1884, vignette, "Pay to order of Fong Foo, San Francisco," slash cancel **25.00**

Clipper Ship Cards, Passage to California

Aspasi, vignette of Roman orator addressing crowd **475.00**
Golden Fleece, Coleman's California Line, vignette of three masted sailing ship at full sail **940.00**
Guardian, C. Comstock & Co.'s Regular Line of Clipper Ships, vignette of company flag **250.00**
Mastiff, John I. Earle & Co., vignette of dog carrying baby in mouth as they flee from Indians on horseback **825.00**
Sam. G. Glover, Comstock's Clipper Line, elaborate Spencerian name . . **250.00**
Sea Serpent, Sutton & Co., vignette of coiled sea serpent holding banner in

Check, sailing ship vignette, dated Aug 2, 1899, 8¼ x 3¾″, $10.00.

mouth, three masted sailing ship at full sail beneath banner **1,375.00**

Fruit Crate Labels

Grape
American Beauty, big red rose, dark green ground **2.00**
Corsair, handsome galleon sailing on rough seas, clouds and sky ground . . **.25**
Moose, very dignified brown moose, yellow lettering, green ground . . . . **.25**
Roseville Belle, 1930s lady, big bell, pink rose, purple grapes, scenic ground . . . . **.50**
Lemon
Cub, cute brown bear cub eating lemons, red ground, Upland, CA **4.00**
Exposition, certificate of Alaska Yukon Pacific Exposition in Seattle in 1909 showing diploma for grand prize won for lemon exhibit, black ground, Santa Barbara, CA **2.00**
Meteor, meteor streaking through evening sky, San Fernando, CA . . **3.00**
Tom Cat, hugh black and white cat lying on a red cushion, orange ground, Orosi, CA **35.00**
Orange
Airship, old four prop commercial plane, royal blue ground, Fillmore, CA **10.00**
Coed, smiling girl graduate, purple ground, Claremont, CA **2.50**
Esperanza, pretty senorita wearing a lace mantilla holding a fancy lace fan, carnation in hair, blue ground, Placentia, CA **1.00**
Lochinvar, brave Lochinvar and fair damsel, black horse, red ground, East Highlands, CA **6.00**
Mammy, black lady eating an orange, yellow ground, FL **2.50**
Orbit, meteor in shape of orange, streaking through starry evening skies, royal blue ground, Exeter, CA **2.50**

Scotch Lassie Jean, Scottish Lassie in kilts, castle, thistle, blue, green, and black ground, Strathmore, CA ... 1.00
Unicorn, galloping buckskin and white pinto unicorn, blue ground, East Highlands, CA 10.00

Pear

Camel, camel and his master at sunrise in desert 2.00
Old Orchard, two young girls in orchard, glitzy 1.00
Round Robin, saucy wide–eyed robin, blue ground 3.00

Letters

Civil War, Surrender of Richmond, letter from Wm. Pershing, 85th Penna. Vol., 1st Brigade, 1st Div., Jones Landing, VA, October 10, 1864, 4 pgs, excellent content 75.00
Medicine, Charles M. Best, letterhead of University of Toronto, Jan. 29, 1975, comments about selection of term insulin and related matters 200.00
Student–Teacher, collection of 58 letter from a Quaker Girl, Sallie Bolton, student–teacher at Lancaster County Normal School, Millersville, PA, 1850s 300.00
Yale Student, collection of 14 letters, 13 from J. H. Bissell to his parents and brother, 1817–18 .... 150.00

Stocks and Bonds

American Express Co., stock certificate, issued and canceled, 1860s, bulldog vignette, sgd Henry Wells and William Fargo 750.00
Central New York & Western RR, issued and canceled, $1,000, 1892, old train vignette, fancy borders, green, pages of coupons 75.00
H. J. Heinz, Co., stock certificate, issued, red 4.00
Hornell Airways, Inc., stock certificate, issued and canceled, vignette of two women and sun rising over mountains, 1920s 75.00
Lincoln Motor Company, stock certificate, issued, 1920s, sgd by W. C. Leland, solid orange 20.00
Pennsylvania Canal Company, bond, issued and canceled, $1,000, 1870, vignette of canal and surrounding area, 2 first issue revenue stamps 85.00
Pittsburg, McKeesport & Youghiogheny RR, issued, train vignette, sgd by Cornelius Vanderbilt for Lake Shore & Michigan Southern RR which guaranteed stock, purple 250.00

Real Estate Association, The, Petaluma, CA, stock certificate, 1876, small size, black and white
Issued, 1890s 25.00
Unissued 4.00
Sovereign Gold Mining, bond, issued and canceled, $5,000, Canadian, 1903, peach borders, coupons 15.00
F. W. Woolworth Co., stock certificate, vignette of eagle over two hemispheres, brown 3.00

White House and Executive Mansion Cards, Signed

Chester A. Arthur, Executive Mansion card, vignette, strong signature 350.00
William H. Taft, White House card, signed "Sincerely Yours, Wm. H. Taft" 250.00
Lyndon B. Johnson, White House card 300.00

PAPERWEIGHTS

History: Although paperweights had their origin in ancient Egypt, it was in the mid-19th century that this art form reached its zenith. The classic period for paperweights was 1845–55 in France where the Clichy, Baccarat, and Saint Louis factories produced the finest examples of this art. Other weights made in England, Italy, and Bohemia during this period rarely matched the quality of the French weights.

In the early 1850s New England Glass Co. in Cambridge, Massachusetts, and the Boston and Sandwich Glass Co. in Sandwich, Massachusetts, became the first American factories to make paperweights.

Popularity peaked during the classic period and faded toward the end of the 19th century. Paperweights were rediscovered nearly a century later in the mid-1900s. Contemporary weights still are made by Baccarat, Saint Louis, Perthshire, and by many studio craftsmen in the U.S. and Europe.

References: Paul Hollister, Jr., *The Encyclopedia of Glass Paperweights,* Paperweight Press, 1969; Leo Kaplan, *Paperweights,* published by author, 1985; George N. Kulles, *Identifying Antique Paperweights-Lampwork,* Paperweight Press, 1987; James Mackay, *Glass Paperweights,* Facts on File, 1973; Edith Mannoni, *Classic French Paperweights,* Paperweight Press, 1984; L. H. Selman Ltd, *Collector's Paperweights: Price Guide and Catalogue,* Paperweight Press, 1986.

Collectors' Club: Paperweight Collectors, P.O. Box 468, Garden City Park, NY 11010.

Periodicals: *Paperweight Gaffer,* 35 Williamstown Circle, York, PA 17404; *Paperweight News,* 761 Chestnut Street, Santa Cruz, CA 95060.

Additional Listings: See *Warman's Americana*

& *Collectibles* for examples of advertising paperweights.

ANTIQUE

Baccarat
   Garland, blue, white, and red cane garland, white and green cane central circle, coral and green star center, 2⅞″ d **600.00**
   Pansy, violet and yellow, stem with eleven leaves, star cut base, 3″ d **475.00**
   Triple cut, six facets, mushroom shape concentric canes, light blue to white to clear overlay, 3″ d **50.00**
Boston and Sandwich, diamond rows, bubble indents, deep green over white, 2¾″ d **675.00**
Clichy
   Daisy, five petals, pink, green stem, swirling latticinio cushion, c1845, 2¾″ d **1,200.00**
   Miniature, four concentric rings of various colors, surrounding six-pointed star cane, 1¾″ d **350.00**
   Multicolored, set up canes, 2½″ d .. **60.00**
   Pink, white, and green rose center cane, enclosed with meandering chain of blue and white canes, five red, white, and green canes around perimeter, white muslin ground, 3¼″ d **2,400.00**
Commemorative, unknown maker
   Abe Lincoln, rect, frosted bust, 4½ x 3″ **25.00**
   General John J Pershing, circular, bust, reverse painted gold, 1917, 3⅞″ d **160.00**

Baccarat, Zodiac, Aquarius, light blue, white figures, sgd, modern, $175.00.

The Grand Army of the Republic, white and clear, 2½″ d **40.00**
Mt Washington, poinsettia, pink, green leaves, multicolored swirled mound, 3½″ d **200.00**
New England
   Apple, red and green, clear circular foot, 2⅜″ h **900.00**
   Fruit, five pears, four cherries, and four leaves, white latticinio bowl, 2¼″ d **300.00**
   Pear, orange and yellow, stem, clear circular base, 2⅜″ h **900.00**
Pairpoint, faceted, diamond cut, upright pink roses, green foliage, 2¾″ d ... **120.00**
Sandwich
   Broken cane, uneven surface, 2½″ d **45.00**
   Poinsettia, pink jeweled flower, two green leaves and stem, 2½″ d ... **400.00**
   Stacked cannonball form, amethyst, 3⅛″ h **200.00**
Val St. Lambert, cut star design, ruby flash overlay, flowers and vines sides **350.00**

MODERN

Ayotte, Rick
   Cardinal, orange and white carnations, sgd and dated 1985 ...... **160.00**
   Hummingbird, green, red throat, white belly, orange trumpet flower, sgd and dated 1985, 2″ d **145.00**
   Magpie bird, blue and white belly, pink rhododendron, sgd and dated 1985, 2″ d **180.00**
   Vermilion Fly Catcher, clear trailing arbutus branch, sgd and dated 1985, 2″ d **130.00**
Baccarat
   Andrew Jackson, emerald base, sgd "M Perry A Jackson, 1971," 2¾″ d **200.00**
   Evangeline Bergstrom, faceted top, amethyst ground, inscribed "R Cochet, 1973, In Memory 1973 Evangeline Bergstrom, 1872–1958," 2¾″ d **250.00**
Banford, Ray, faceted, pink rose, leaves and buds, star cut base, sgd, c1980, 2⅞″ d **500.00**
Hacker, Harold J., green salamander with black feet, color flecked gray–green ground, 2¾″ d **350.00**
Kaziun, Charles
   Button, one red, one yellow, and one blue rose, green swirls separated by three gathering goldstones ground, encircled "K" signature cane, ⅞″ d **250.00**
   Cameo silhouette, lady, black and white, surrounded by six green, white, and pink floral canes, pink

ground, six side facets, circular facet on top, sgd gold "K," 1⅜" d ... **600.00**

Flower, yellow and red, four green and white leaves, light blue ground shot with gold,⅝" d,⅞" h ... **400.00**

Pedestal

Rose, red, seven red heart canes surrounds leaves and signature, c1960, 2⅛" d ... **730.00**

Spider Lily, pink, yellow stardust cane center, translucent aqua gold flecked ground, sgd gold "K," 1⅜" d ... **230.00**

Lewis, Pete, purple and yellow pansy, leaf and bud, sgd and dated 1973, 2⁵⁄₁₆" d ... **100.00**

Lundberg Studios

Butterfly and flowers, lavender and orange, tan and green swirled iridescent ground, sgd and dated 1980, Buzzini 3186, 2¹¹⁄₁₆" ... **120.00**

Fish, yellow stripe, dark millefiori sea plants ground, sgd and dated 1980, D Salazar 111031, 2¾" d ... **100.00**

Spider, black, yellow outline, iridescent gold and smoky blue ground, sgd and dated 1980, Buzzini S675, 2¾" d ... **210.00**

Perthshire

Crocus, lavender, upright pistil, 2¾" d ... **100.00**

Dahlia, pink, faceted, sgd and dated "P 1972," 3¼" d ... **440.00**

Dragonfly, three flowers with yellow ribbon, etched cross hatch base, dated 1974, 3⅜" d ... **500.00**

Rosefeld, Ken, carrots, radishes, asparagus, and beets, cane signature, dated 1985, 2¾" d ... **190.00**

Saint Louis, faceted

Bouquet, faceted, latticinio basket, sgd and dated "SL 1977", 3" d ... **800.00**

Canes, faceted, white, blue, pistachio, and red, sgd and dated "SL 1973," 2⅞" d ... **300.00**

Cherries and leaves, faceted, swirling latticinio cushion, sgd and dated "SL 1975," 3¹⁄₁₆" d ... **525.00**

Fruit, faceted, latticinio cushion, sgd and dated "SL 1979," 3¹⁄₁₆" d ... **400.00**

Garland, star cut base, sgd and dated "SL 1979," 2¹³⁄₁₆" d ... **160.00**

Honeycomb, faceted, millefiori cane signature, sgd and dated "SL 1974," 2¹³⁄₁₆" d ... **650.00**

Stankard, Paul

Bicentennial, St Anthony's Fire Flower, inscribed "2/12" and "00826," cane signature, 3⅛" d ... **2,100.00**

Cayenne pepper plant, red and black peppers, pistachio ground, cane signature, inscribed "50/50 1974 C B617," 2⅛" d ... **700.00**

Chokeberry blossom and berries, cane signature, inscribed "33376," 2¹⁵⁄₁₆" d ... **680.00**

Floral

Mixed bouquet of multicolored flowers with buds and green leaves, "Natures Splendor," red signature cane with black "S," numbered "A 210," dated 1978, 3⅛" d ... **1,800.00**

Multilayered bouquet, red, white, blue, yellow, and orange flowers, green leaves, yellow "S" signature cane, engraved number "45077," 3" d ... **2,700.00**

Orchid, pink, opaque emerald ground, faceted, sgd and dated 1974, 2⁹⁄₁₆" ... **230.00**

Slipper, pink, leaves, transparent cobalt ground, cane signature, inscribed "AP-3 1973C," 2⅛" d ... **700.00**

Tarsitano, Debbie, flowers, blue, three pussy willow sprigs, star cut base, cane signature, c1984, 3¼" d ... **550.00**

Whittemore, Francis

Clematis, blue, white jack-in-the-pulpit, and yellow flower sprig, transparent wine ground, 2⅜" d ... **250.00**

Faceted, yellow flower and bud, green leaves, purple carpet ground, five vertical side flutes, top printie, signature cane on base, inscribed "19" ... **90.00**

Rose, pink, bud and leaves, transparent cobalt ground, sgd, c1975, 2½" d ... **245.00**

Sunflower, blue and white, faceted, transparent wine ground, 2⅜" d ... **250.00**

Ysart, Paul

Dragonfly, ruby, green wings, latticinio stave basket, cane signature, c1960, 2¹³⁄₁₆" d ... **475.00**

Snake, coiled, green ground, cane signature, c1960, 2¹¹⁄₁₆" d ... **560.00**

PAPIER MACHE

History: Papier Mache is made from a mixture of wood pulp, glue, resin, and fine sand which is subject to great pressure and then dried. The finished product is tough, durable, and heat resistant. Various finishing treatments are used, such as enameling, japanning, lacquering, mother-of-pearl inlaying, and painting.

During the Victorian era Papier Mache articles such as boxes, trays, and tables were in high fashion. Papier Mache also found use in the production of banks, candy containers, masks, toys, and other children's articles.

Advertising
Figure, Poll Parrot, 36", movable
head 950.00
Snuff Box, Dr. Syntax The Shooting
Pony, round, yellow and brown
transfer 130.00
Box, 5" w, 4½" h, sq, mother of pearl
Chinese landscapes dec, fitted with
four glass perfume bottles, Victorian 335.00
Bread Tray, 14¼" l, cartouche shape,
blood red, floral spray and butterfly
dec, cavetto and shaped border, gilt
edge, black under surface, England,
c1820 . . . . 500.00
Candy Container
Easter Bunny, 7" h, orig polychrome
paint, marked "Germany" 65.00
Pumpkin 20.00
Santa, 9", wearing white suit 50.00
Snowman 35.00

**Cup, gold ground, black on base, red
band at top, floral dec, marked "Made
in USSR," 2½" h, $35.00.**

Decoy, 16¼" l, crow, orig black paint,
glass eyes 15.00
Fan, Troubadour scene, decoupaged
and painted, reticulated, tassels, mid
19th C 120.00
Figure
23¼" h, man, high wheel bicycle,
comic papier mache figure, brightly
colored polychrome paint, spot
welded metal bicycle, repaired
break at elbow, 20th C 1,600.00
32", workman carrying lunch pail,
wearing overalls 700.00
Lantern, 10½" w, owl, extended wings 190.00
Nodder
Rabbit, 7", glass eyes 70.00
Turkey, 3¾" h, pr, male and female,
orig black paint, polychrome trim,
pewter feet 100.00
Pip-squeak, rooster, 6½" h, spring legs,

wood bellows base, orig polychrome
paint 75.00
Snuff box, 3" d, engraved painted
woman and parrot 85.00
Tea Caddy, 5¾" h, 7⅔" w, MOP inlay,
English 200.00
Toy, pull, 15½" l, tiger, painted cloth cov,
glass eyes, cast iron wheel feet, repainted mouth, worn fur trim, teeth
missing 90.00
Tray
24" l, 19" w, rect, polychrome and gilt
rococo foliate dec, two handles,
stamped "Jennens and Bettridge,
London," 1830–40 . . . . 800.00
32" l, 23" w, black and gold Chinoiserie landscape and figural dec,
red ground, japanned, English . . . 2,700.00

PARIAN WARE

History: Parian ware is a creamy white, translucent, marble-like porcelain. It originated in England in 1842 and was first known as "Statuary
Porcelain." Minton and Copeland have been credited with its development. Wedgwood also made
it. In America, parian ware was manufactured by
Chistopher Fenton in Bennington, Vermont.

At first parian ware was used only for figures
and figural groups. By the 1850s it became so
popular that a vast range of wares were manufactured.

Bust
8" h, Ulysses S Grant, c1860 . . . . . 60.00
11¾" h
Alexandra, pedestal base, imp
"Crystal Palace Art Union, F M
Miller Sculpt, Pub'd Feb 11,
1863, Copeland" 225.00
Shakespeare, pedestal base, imp
"F M Miller, SC" and "Wedgwood
and Sons," back printed "The
Shakespeare Memorial Bust
published Under The Special
Sanction of the National Shake-
speare and Stratford–on–Avon
Tercentenary Committees, by
Howell James and Co., London,
April 23, 1864" 800.00
12¼" h, Alexandra, imp "Art Union of
London, Mary Thornycroft SC,
Copeland, 84", sgd "W T Cope-
land" 250.00
16" h, maiden, garland of flowers in
hair, black pedestal base 150.00
Compote, 10¼" h, low relief grapes and
vines, English 275.00
Ewer, raised scrollwork, glazed green
and pink roping, c1853, Copeland,
one handle damaged, pr 400.00

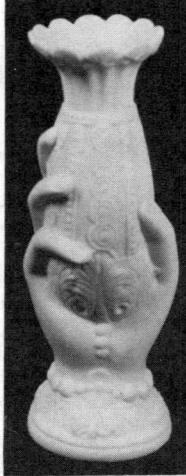

Vase, figural, hand holding bud vase, scalloped top, 8″ h, $150.00.

Figure

5¾″ h, Queen Victoria, biscuit, seated on throne, wood base, hand repaired, c1937 .... 400.00

10¼″ h, group, titled "The Death," dog attacking stag, rocky molded base, horn chips 175.00

12″ h, group, Ariadne, nude female seated on panther, rect base, chips, mid 19th C 250.00

13″ l, Clorinda, wearing armor, imp marks "John Bell Feb 1848," "Minton," and ciphers 500.00

13½″ l, Dorothea, classical female seated on rock, modeler John Bell, registry mark for 1847, imp "Minton" and cipher marks, chips, restoration 175.00

14″ l, Dying Gladiator, classical figure, sword by side, laying wounded, raised oval base, attributed to Bates, Brown–Westhead, Moore and Co., c1860 .... 350.00

14¼″ h, group, nude female seated on panther, rect base, imp "Minton" and 1857 year mark, ear chip ... 700.00

15¼″, group, titled "The Lion in Love," simply draped female pulling thorn from paw of lion, glazed base, imp "Minton" and cipher 1,400.00

15½ and 15¾″, boy and girl, flower

vendors, period attire, nicks, attributed to Robinson & Leadbeater, pr 550.00

21½″ h, Beatrice, standing female, classical style, imp mark "Copeland, Pub March 1, 1860, Edgar Papworth Jun SC" 400.00

21¾″ h, Maiden Hood, standing female, classical style, imp marks "Pub Sept 2, 1861 Copeland" ... 550.00

Pitcher, 10½″ h, deep relief witches and peasants pattern, Jones and Wally, dated 1842 .... 225.00

PATE-DE-VERRE

History: Pate-de-Verre can be translated simply as glass paste. It is manufactured by grinding lead glass into a powder or crystal form, making it into a paste by adding a 2% or 3% solution of sodium silicate, molding, firing, and carving. The Egyptians discovered the process as early as 1500 B.C.

In the late 19th century, the process was rediscovered by a group of French glassmakers. Amalric Walter, Henri Cros, Georges Despret, and the Daum brothers were leading manufacturers.

Contemporary sculptors are creating a second renaissance, lead by the technical research of Jacques Daum.

Bowl, yellow leaves and purple vines, marked "Argy–Rousseau," 3¾″ d, 2″ h, $900.00.

Atomizer, 4¾″ h, cylindrical, dark orange rose blossoms on green vine band at top, mottled orange splashed base, gilt bronze mount imp "EFDE/Ste SOG/Made In France," etched "A Walter/Nancy" on side, c1900 ..... 660.00

Bowl, 4¼″ h, domical, molded central flowerhead, tiers of overlapping feathers, pink, peach, and purple, scrolling wing form handles, conical foot, molded low relief stylized feathers, intaglio sgd "G. ARGY ROUSSEAU," c1926 .... 8,800.00

Box, cov, 4″ l, irregular shaped oviform,

pale yellow, rust, mustard, brown, and
slate blue crab in surf, sgd in mold "A
WALTER NANCY" **2,200.00**
Dish, 6¾" d, irregular shaped, yellow
ground, black and slate blue salamander among green ivy leaves,
small pink blossoms, sgd in mold "A
WALTER NANCY & BERGES" **7,700.00**
Figure
5" h
Mermaid, rising from water, coved
rect base, tinged brown hair, pale
green shading to dark green
body, turquoise water, intaglio
sgd "A WALTER NANCY" and
"JD," designed by Jean Bernard
Descomps **3,250.00**
Parakeet, green, blue, and purple,
sq base, molded "G Argy–Rous-
seau" **1,900.00**
7⅞" h, woman, enveloped in sheer
blown drapery, head tilted and bent
forward slightly, lemon yellow,
streak of orange from hips to toes,
dark green streaked yellow rect
stepped base, incised "A WALTER/
NANCY," c1920 . . . . **1,500.00**
8" h, woman, upswept hair, yellow
classical robes, sitting on green
and brown striated yellow plinth
seat, intaglio sgd "A WALTER
NANCY," c1920 . . . . **2,750.00**
Jewelry, pendant, Amalric Walter
15½" l, bouquet of roses, pale yellow
ground, brown stems, rust colored
buds, green leaves, silk cord . . . **1,100.00**
17¼" l, scarab, green, rust, and turquoise, blue and green silk cord
with turquoise wooden beads, sgd
"AWN" in mold **1,980.00**
Night Light (Veilleuse), 5⅛" h, spherical
molded shade, ochre, burnt orange,
and purple marguerites dec, chan-
neled slightly tapering cylindrical
lower section of shaded purple, intaglio sgd "G ARGY–ROUSSEAU," circular textured wrought iron ring, three
ball feet, c1926 . . . . **13,200.00**
Paperweight
5¼" l, wasp, open wings, brown and
green, yellow centered flower, sgd
in mold "A WALTER NANCY" . . . **6,400.00**
6¾ l, molded sea nymph, mottled
green leaf, sgd in mold "DAUM
NANCY" **4,400.00**
Vase
4¾" h, ovoid, ftd, soft turquoise, lime
green blossoms on shoulder band,
sgd in mold "A WALTER NANCY"
and "GJ sc" **3,850.00**
7¾" h, mottled green and gray,
molded rim frieze of jockeys and

horses, sgd in mold "DECOUR-
CHEMONT" **14,500.00**
9¼" h, ovoid, everted neck, turquoise
and black mottled, carved horizontal bands of berries, sgd in mold
"DECOURCHEMONT" **12,650.00**

PATE-SUR-PATE

History: Pate-sur-Pate, paste on paste, is a
19th century porcelain form featuring relief designs
achieved by painting successive layers of thin pottery paste one on top of the other.

About 1880 Marc Solon and other Sevres artists,
inspired by a Chinese celadon vase in the Ceramic
Museum at Sevres, experimented with this process of porcelain decoration. Solon migrated to
England at the outbreak of the Franco-Prussian
War and worked at Minton, where he perfected the
pate-sur-pate process.

**Box, cov, blue ground, white classical
dec, imp "Limoges," 4⅞" sq, 2⅛" h,
$150.00.**

Book Stand, 16" l, walnut veneer, pate
sur pate end panels with cupids playing badminton, Bettemann's patent,
sold by Shreve Crump and Low . . . **500.00**
Bowl, 7" d, 3½" h, mermaids, green and
white lid, marked "Heubach" **375.00**
Box, cov, triangular, blue ground, white
nude seated on stream bank, gold
trim, sgd "Gol" in design, base
marked "F.M. Barbotine/Limoges,
France" **1,500.00**
Centerpiece, 11" l, pate–sur–pate, car-
touches with putti, ivory and gilt reserves, brown ground, imp and
printed Minton factory marks, dec by
H Holls, c1872 . . . . **1,450.00**
Cup, green, gold dragonflies, white
leaves **100.00**
Lamp Base, 18¾" h vase, shield shaped
body, celadon green ground, allegorical maiden dec, reverse with flower

filled urn, wreath ring handles, gilt metal circular base, fitted for electricity, pr **1,220.00**
Plaque, 10¼″ h, 6¼″ d,
Plate, service, enameled Neoclassical dec, three senic reserves dec in pate sure pate on light blue ground, sgd "AB" for Albione Birks decorator, c1895, Minton, set of twelve **3,250.00**
Urn, 10″ h, slate blue ground, white floral dec **475.00**
Vase
   6″ h, pillow shape, double handles, black ground, white relief cupid chasing butterfly, George Jones . . **525.00**
   16¾″ h, brown and green glazed body, cream dec, dancing nudes and satyrs among waves, marked "HCB France," sgd "A Doux" . . . **825.00**
   18″ h, deep green ground, white classical figure and cupid, woodland setting, white holly neck band, gold trim, sgd "Schenk" **1,250.00**

PATTERN GLASS

History: Pattern glass is clear or colored glass pressed into one of hundreds of patterns. Deming Jarves of the Boston and Sandwich Glass Co. invented the first successful pressing machine in 1828. By the 1860s glass pressing machinery had been improved, and mass production of good quality matched tableware sets began. The idea of a matched glassware table service (including goblets, tumblers, creamers, sugars, compotes, cruets, etc.) quickly caught on in America. Many pattern glass table services had numerous accessory pieces among which were banana stands, molasses cans, water bottles, etc.

Early pattern glass (flint) was made with a lead formula, giving it a ringing quality. During the Civil War lead became too valuable to be used in glass manufacturing. In 1864 Hobbs, Bruckunier & Co., West Virginia, developed a soda lime (non–flint) formula. Pattern glass also was produced in colors, milk glass, opalescent glass, slag glass, and custard glass.

The hundreds of companies which produced pattern glass have involved histories of development, expansions, personnel problems, material and supply demands, fires, and mergers. In 1899 the National Glass Co. was formed as a combine of nineteen glass companies in Pennsylvania, Ohio, Indiana, West Virginia, and Maryland. U. S. Glass, another consortium, was founded in 1891. These combines resulted as attempts to save small companies by pooling talents, resources, and patterns. Because of this pooling, the same pattern can be attributed to several companies.

Sometimes the pattern name of a piece was changed from one company to the next to reflect current fashion trends. U. S. Glass created the States series by issuing patterns named for a particular state. Several of these patterns were new issues, others were former patterns renamed.

References: E. M. Belnap, *Milk Glass,* Crown Publishers, Inc., 1949; Regis F. and Mary F. Ferson, *Yesterday's Milk Glass Today,* privately printed, 1981; William Heacock, *Toothpick Holders from A to Z, Book 1, Encyclopedia of Victorian Colored Pattern Glass,* Antique Publications, 1981; William Heacock, *Opalescent Glass from A to Z, Book 2,* Antique Publications, 1981; William Heacock, *Syrups, Sugar Shakers & Cruets, Book 3,* Antique Publications, 1981; William Heacock, *Custard Glass From A to Z, Book 4,* Antique Publications, 1980; William Heacock, *U. S. Glass From A to Z, Book 5,* Antique Publications, Inc. 1980; William Heacock, *Oil Cruets From A to Z, Book 6,* Antique Publications, 1981; William Heacock, *Ruby Stained Glass From A To Z, Book 7* Antique Publications, Inc., 1986; William Heacock, *More Ruby Stained Glass, Book 8,* Antique Publications, 1987; William Heacock and William Gamble, *Cranberry Opalescent From A to Z, Book 9* Antique Publications, 1987; William Heacock, *Old Pattern Glass,* Antique Publications, 1981; William Heacock, *1000 Toothpick Holders: A Collector's Guide,* Antique Publications, 1977; William Heacock, *Rare and Unlisted Toothpick Holders,* Antique Publications, 1984.

Bill Jenks and Jerry Luna, *Early American Pattern Glass–1850 to 1910: Major Collectible Table Settings with Prices,* Wallace–Homestead Book Co, 1990; Minnie Watson Kamm, *Pattern Glass Pitchers, Books 1 through 8,* privately printed, 1970, 4th printing; Ruth Webb Lee, *Early American Pressed Glass,* Lee Publications, 1966, 36th edition; Ruth Webb Lee, *Victorian Glass,* Lee Publications, 1944, 13th edition; Bessie M. Lindsey, *American Historical Glass,* Charles E. Tuttle Co., 1967; Robert Irwin Lucas, *Tarentum Pattern Glass,* privately printed, 1981; Mollie H. McCain, *Pattern Glass Primer,* Lamplighter Books, 1979; Mollie H. McCain, *The Collector's Encyclopedia of Pattern Glass,* Collector Books, 1982; George P. and Helen McKearin, *American Glass,* Grown Publishers, 1941; James Measell, *Greentown Glass,* Grand Rapids Public Museum Association, 1979; James Measell and Don E. Smith, *Findlay Glass: The Glass Tableware Manufacturers, 1886–1902,* Antique Publications, Inc, 1986; Alice Hulett Metz, *Early American Pattern Glass,* published by author, 1958; Alice Hulett Metz, *Much More Early American Pattern Glass,* published by author, 1965.

Dori Miles and Robert W. Miller, *Wallace-Homestead Price Guide To Pattern Glass, 11th Edition,* Wallace-Homestead, 1986; S. T. Millard, *Goblets I,* privately printed, 1938, reprinted Wallace-Homestead, 1975; S. T. Millard, *Goblets II,* privately printed, 1940, reprinted Wallace-Homestead, 1975; Arthur G. Peterson, *Glass Salt Shak-*

ers: *1,000 Patterns,* Wallace-Homestead, 1970; Jane Shadel Spillman, *American and European Pressed Glass in the Corning Museum of Glass,* Corning Museum of Glass, 1981; Jane Shadel Spillman, *The Knopf Collectors Guides to American Antiques, Glass Volumes 1 and 2,* Alfred A. Knopf, Inc., 1982, 1983; Doris and Peter Unitt, *American and Canadian Goblets,* Clock House, 1970; Doris and Peter Unitt, *Treasury of Canadian Glass,* Clock House, 1969, 2nd edition; Peter Unitt and Anne Worrall, *Canadian Handbook, Pressed Glass Tableware,* Clock House Productions, 1983; Dina von Zweck, *The Woman's Day Dictionary of Glass,* The Main Street Press, 1983.

Museums: Corning Museum of Glass, Corning, NY. National Museum of Man, Ottawa, Ontario, Canada.

Periodical: *Glass Collector's Digest,* Richardson Printing Corp., P.O. Box 663, Marietta, OH 45750.

Additional Listings: Bread Plates, Children's Toy Dishes, Cruets, Custard Glass, Milk Glass, Sugar Shakers, Toothpicks, and specific companies.

Abbreviations:
ah—applied handle

GUTDOBD—Give Us This Day Our Daily Bread
hs—high standard
ls—low standard
os—original stopper

We continue to be fortunate in assembling a panel of prestigious pattern glass dealers to serve as advisors in reviewing the pattern glass listings found in this edition. Their dedication is symbolic of those dealers and collectors who view price guides as useful market tools and contribute their expertise and time to make them better.

Research in pattern glass is continuing. As in the past, we have tried to present patterns with correct names, histories, and pieces. Categories have been changed to reflect the most current thinking of all patterns alphabetically. Colored, opalescent, and clear patterns now are included in one listing, avoiding duplication of patterns and colors.

Pattern glass has been widely reproduced. We have listed reproductions with an *. These markings are given only as a guide and clue to the collector that some reproductions may exist in a given pattern.

Advisors: John and Alice Ahlfeld, Mike Anderton, William Jenks, and Darryl K. Reilly.

ACTRESS (Theatrical)

Made by LaBelle Glass Co., Bridgeport, Ohio, and Crystal Glass Co., c1870. All clear 20% less. Some items have been reproduced in clear and color by Imperial Glass Co.

	Clear and Frosted		Clear and Frosted
Bowl		Open, ls, 5" d	45.00
6", ftd	45.00	Open, ls, 6" d	50.00
7", ftd	50.00	Open, ls, 7" d	65.00
9½", ftd	85.00	Creamer	75.00
8", Miss Neilson	85.00	Dresser Tray	60.00
Bread Plate		Goblet, Kate Claxton (2	
7 x 12", HMS Pinafore	90.00	portraits)	80.00
9 x 13", Miss Neilson	72.00	Marmalade Jar, cov	125.00
Butter, cov	90.00	Mug, HMS Pinafore	50.00
Cake Stand, 10"	150.00	Pickle Dish, Love's Request	
Candlesticks, pr	250.00	is Pickles	45.00
Celery Vase		Pickle Relish, different actresses	
Actress Head	130.00	4½ x 7"	35.00
HMS Pinafore, pedestal	145.00	5 x 8"	35.00
Cheese Dish, cov, The Lone		5½ x 9"	35.00
Fisherman on cov, Two		Pitcher	
Dromios on base	250.00	Milk, 6½", HMS Pinafore,	
Compote		Fanny Davenport and	
Cov, hs, 8" d	225.00	Miss Neilson	275.00
Cov, hs, 10" d	250.00	Water, 9", Romeo & Juliet,	
Cov, hs, 12" d	300.00	balcony scene	250.00
Open, hs, 10" d	90.00	Salt, master	70.00
Open, hs, 12" d	120.00		

	Clear and Frosted		Clear and Frosted
Salt Shaker, orig pewter top	42.50	Spooner	60.00
Sauce		Sugar, cov	100.00
Flat	15.00		
Footed	20.00		

ADONIS (Pleat and Tuck, Washboard)

Pattern made by McKee Bros. of Pittsburgh, Pennsylvania in 1897.

	Canary	Clear	Deep Blue
Bowl, 5″, berry	15.00	10.00	20.00
Butter, cov	70.00	48.00	80.00
Cake Plate, 11″	25.00	20.00	32.00
Cake Stand, 10½″	45.00	30.00	50.00
Celery Vase	35.00	25.00	40.00
Compote,			
Cov, hs	65.00	40.00	75.00
Open, hs, 8″	45.00	30.00	50.00
Open, jelly, 4½″	28.00	18.00	32.00
Creamer	28.00	22.50	32.00
Pitcher, water	55.00	35.00	60.00
Plate, 10″	25.00	18.00	32.00
Relish	18.00	15.00	20.00
Salt and Pepper pr	40.00	35.00	45.00
Sauce, flat, 4″	10.00	8.50	12.00
Spooner	35.00	20.00	38.00
Sugar, cov	40.00	35.00	45.00
Syrup	150.00	50.00	150.00
Tumbler	20.00	16.00	20.00

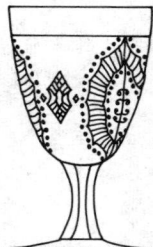

AEGIS (Bead & Bar Medallion, Swiss)

Non-flint pattern made by McKee and Brothers of Pittsburgh, Pennsylvania, in the 1880's. Shards have also been found at the site of the Burlington Glass Works, Hamilton, Ontario.

	Clear		Clear
Bowl, oval	15.00	Pickle, 5 x 7″	15.00
Butter, cov	35.00	Pitcher, water	55.00
Compote		Salt	15.00
Cov, hs	50.00	Sauce	
Open, hs	25.00	Flat	7.50
Creamer	25.00	Footed	10.00
Egg Cup	25.00	Spooner	15.00
Goblet	30.00	Sugar, cov	35.00

ALABAMA (Beaded Bull's Eye and Drape)

Made by U. S. Glass Co., c1898. One of the States patterns. Also found in green (rare).

	Clear	Ruby Stained		Clear	Ruby Stained
Bowl, berry, master .	30.00	—	Nappy	25.00	—
Butter, cov	50.00	150.00	Pitcher, water	72.00	—
Cake Stand	55.00	—	Relish.	24.00	35.00
Castor Set, 4 bottles,			Salt & Pepper	65.00	—
glass frame	125.00	—	Sauce	18.00	—
Celery Vase	35.00	110.00	Spooner	30.00	—
Compote, open, 5",			Sugar, cov	48.00	—
jelly	65.00	—	Syrup	125.00	250.00
Creamer	45.00	60.00	Toothpick	60.00	150.00
Cruet, os	65.00	—	Tray, water, 10½" . .	50.00	—
Dish, rect	20.00	—	Tumbler	45.00	—
Honey Dish, cov . . .	60.00	—			

ALL-OVER DIAMOND (Diamond Splendor, Diamond Block #3)

Made by George Duncan and Sons, Pittsburgh, Pennsylvania, c1891 and continued by U.S. Glass Co. It was occasionally trimmed with gold, and had at least 65 pieces in the pattern. Biscuit jars are found in three sizes; bowls are both crimped and non-crimped; and nappies are also found crimped and non-crimped in fifteen sizes. Also made in ruby stained.

	Clear		Clear
Biscuit Jar, cov	60.00	Ice Tub, handles	35.00
Bitters Bottle	30.00	Lamp, Banquet, tall stem . . .	150.00
Bowl		Nappy	
7"	20.00	4"	15.00
11"	35.00	9"	35.00
Cake Stand	35.00	Plate	
Candelabrum, very ornate, 4		6"	15.00
arm with lusters	175.00	7"	15.00
Celery Tray, crimped or		Pickle Dish, long	15.00
straight	20.00	Pitcher, water, bulbous, 6	
Claret Jug	50.00	sizes	45–60.00
Compote, cov	40.00	Punch Bowl	50.00
Condensed Milk Jar, cov . . .	25.00	Salt Shaker	15.00
Cordial	35.00	Spooner	20.00
Creamer	20.00	Sugar	
Cruet, patterned stopper		Cov	35.00
1 oz	50.00	Open	18.00
2 oz	45.00	Syrup	55.00
4 oz	45.00	Tray	
6 oz	25.00	Ice Cream	30.00
Decanter		Water	30.00
Pint	45.00	Wine	30.00
Quart	45.00	Tumbler	15.00
Egg Cup	20.00	Water Bottle	35.00
Goblet	25.00	Wine	15.00

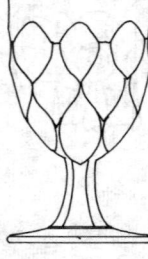

ALMOND THUMBPRINT (Pointed Thumbprint, Finger Print)

An early flint glass pattern with variants in flint and non-flint. Pattern has been attributed to Bryce, Bakewell, and U. S. Glass. Sometimes found in milk glass.

	Flint	Non-Flint		Flint	Non-Flint
Bowl, 4½" d, ftd . . .	—	20.00	Decanter	70.00	—
Butter, cov	80.00	40.00	Egg Cup.	45.00	25.00
Celery Vase	50.00	25.00	Goblet	28.00	12.00
Champagne	60.00	35.00	Punch Bowl	—	75.00
Compote			Salt		
Cov, hs, 4¾", jelly	60.00	40.00	Flat, large	25.00	15.00
Cov, hs, 10".	80.00	45.00	Ftd, cov.	45.00	25.00
Cov, ls, 4¾".	55.00	30.00	Ftd, open	25.00	10.00
Cov, ls, 7"	45.00	25.00	Spooner	20.00	15.00
Open, hs, 10½" . .	65.00	—	Sugar, cov	60.00	40.00
Cordial	40.00	30.00	Sweetmeat Jar, cov.	65.00	45.00
Creamer.	60.00	40.00	Tumbler	45.00	20.00
Cruet, ftd, os.	55.00	—	Wine	28.00	12.00

AMAZON (Sawtooth Band)

Non-flint; made by Bryce Brothers, Pittsburgh, Pennsylvania, late 1870s–1880 and also by the U. S. Glass Co., c1890. Mostly found in clear, either etched or plain. Heacock notes pieces in amber, blue, vaseline, and ruby stained. Over 65 pieces made in this pattern, including a toy set. Add 200% for color, e.g., pedestalled amber cruet with maltese cross stopper ($165.00) and pedestalled blue cruet with hand and bar stopper ($200.00). An amethyst cruet with a hand-bar stopper ($275.00) also is known.

	Etched	Plain		Etched	Plain
Banana Stand.	95.00	65.00	Cordial	40.00	25.00
Bowl			Creamer.	30.00	28.00
4", scalloped	—	10.00	Cruet, os	50.00	45.00
4½", scalloped. . .	—	10.00	Egg Cup.	—	14.00
5", scalloped	—	15.00	Goblet		
6", scalloped	—	25.00	4½".	30.00	—
6½", cov, oval . . .	—	50.00	5"	25.00	—
7", scalloped	—	20.00	6"	30.00	—
8", scalloped	—	25.00	Pitcher, water	60.00	55.00
9", cov	30.00	25.00	Relish.	28.00	25.00
Butter, cov	65.00	50.00	Salt & Pepper, pr. . .	50.00	40.00
Cake Stand			Salt		
Large	—	50.00	Individual.	—	15.00
Small	—	40.00	Master	—	18.00
Celery Vase	35.00	30.00	Sauce, ftd.	10.00	10.00
Champagne	—	35.00	Spooner	25.00	20.00
Claret.	35.00	30.00	Sugar, cov	55.00	45.00
Compote			Syrup.	50.00	42.50
Cov, hs. 7"	—	65.00	Tumbler	25.00	20.00
Open, 4½", jelly . .	45.00	35.00	Wine	25.00	20.00
Open, hs, 9½", sawtooth edge	—	45.00			

ANTHEMION (Albany)

Non-flint made by Model Flint Glass Co., Findlay, Ohio, c1890–1900, and by Albany Glass Co. Also found in amber and blue.

	Clear		Clear
Bowl, 7", sq, turned-in edge	20.00	Pitcher, water	50.00
Butter, cov	65.00	Plate, 10"	20.00
Cake Plate, 9½"	35.00	Sauce	10.00
Cake Stand	40.00	Spooner	25.00
Celery Vase	35.00	Sugar, cov	35.00
Creamer	30.00	Tumbler	25.00
Marmalade Jar, cov	45.00		

APOLLO

Non-flint, first made by Adams and Co., Pittsburgh, Pennsylvania, c1870, and later by U. S. Glass Co., c1891. Frosted increases price 20%. Also found in ruby stained and engraved.

	Clear		Clear
Bowl		Egg Cup	30.00
4"	10.00	Goblet	35.00
5"	10.00	Lamp, 10"	125.00
6"	12.00	Pickle Dish	15.00
7"	15.00	Pitcher, water	65.00
8"	22.50	Plate, 9½", sq	28.00
Butter, cov	55.00	Salt	20.00
Cake Stand		Salt Shaker	25.00
8"	35.00	Sauce	
9"	40.00	Flat	10.00
10"	50.00	Ftd, 5"	12.00
Celery Tray, rect	22.50	Spooner	28.50
Celery Vase	35.00	Sugar, cov	45.00
Compote		Sugar Shaker	45.00
Cov, hs	65.00	Syrup	110.00
Open, hs	35.00	Tray, water	45.00
Open, ls, 7"	25.00	Tumbler	30.00
Creamer	35.00	Wine	35.00
Cruet	60.00		

ARCHED FLEUR-DE-LIS (Late Fleur-De-Lis)

Made by Bryce, Higbee and Co., in 1897–1898. Also gilded.

	Clear	Ruby Stained		Clear	Ruby Stained
Banana Stand	35.00	150.00	Olive, handled	15.00	—
Bowl, 9", oval	18.00	—	Pitcher, water	125.00	300.00
Butter, cov	40.00	135.00	Plate, 7", sq	12.00	45.00
Cake Stand	35.00	—	Relish, 8"	15.00	—
Compote, jelly, cov	18.00	—	Salt Shaker	16.00	45.00
Creamer	30.00	60.00	Sauce	8.00	20.00
Dish, shallow, 7" . . .	12.50	25.00	Spooner, double		
Mug, 3¼"	20.00	30.00	handled	20.00	65.00

	Clear	Ruby Stained		Clear	Ruby Stained
Sugar, cov, double handled	35.00	100.00	Tumbler	15.00	45.00
Toothpick	30.00	300.00	Vase, 10"	35.00	75.00
			Wine	25.00	65.00

ARCHED GRAPE

Flint and non-flint made by Boston and Sandwich Glass Co., c1880.

	Non-Flint		Non-Flint
Butter, cov	45.00	Pitcher, water, ah	60.00
Celery Vase	35.00	Sauce, flat	8.00
Champagne	35.00	Spooner	30.00
Compote, cov, hs	50.00	Sugar, cov	45.00
Creamer	40.00	Wine	35.00
Goblet	25.00		

ARCHED OVALS

Made by U. S. Glass Co., c1908. Found in gilt, ruby stained, green, and rarely in cobalt blue. Popular pattern for souvenir wares.

	Clear	Cobalt	Green	Ruby Stained
Bowl, berry	12.50	—	18.00	—
Bowl, cov, 7"	40.00	—	—	—
Butter, cov	45.00	—	50.00	80.00
Cake Stand	35.00	—	—	—
Celery Vase	15.00	40.00	20.00	—
Compote				
Cov, hs, 8", belled	42.00	—	—	—
Open, hs, 8"	30.00	—	—	—
Open, hs, 9"	35.00	—	—	—
Creamer				
Ind	20.00	—	—	—
Regular	30.00	—	—	25.00
Cruet	35.00	—	45.00	—
Goblet	20.00	—	30.00	35.00
Mug	18.00	30.00	20.00	25.00
Pitcher, water	30.00	—	40.00	—
Plate, 9"	20.00	—	25.00	—
Punch Cup	8.00	—	—	—
Relish, oval, 9"	20.00	—	—	—
Salt & Pepper, pr	45.00	—	50.00	—
Sauce	7.50	—	—	—
Saucer	—	—	—	30.00
Syrup	35.00	—	—	—
Spooner	20.00	—	25.00	35.00
Sugar, cov	35.00	—	40.00	—
Toothpick	18.00	50.00	25.00	35.00
Tumbler	12.00	25.00	18.00	30.00
Wine	15.00	—	20.00	30.00

ARGUS

Flint, thumbprint type pattern made by Bakewell Pears & Co. in Pittsburgh, Pennsylvania, in the early 1870s. Copiously reproduced, some by Fostoria with raised "HFM" trademark for Henry Ford Museum.

	Clear		Clear
Ale Glass	75.00	Goblet	40.00
Bitters Bottle	60.00	Lamp, ftd	75.00
Bowl, 5½"	50.00	Mug, ah	65.00
Butter, cov	85.00	Pitcher, water, ah	225.00
Celery Vase	90.00	Salt, master, open	30.00
Champagne	65.00	Spooner	48.50
Compote, open, 6" d, 4½" h	50.00	Sugar, cov	65.00
Creamer, applied handle	100.00	Tumbler, bar	65.00
Decanter, qt	70.00	Whiskey, ah	75.00
Egg Cup	30.00	Wine	45.00

ART (Job's Tears)

Non-flint produced by Adams and Co., Pittsburgh, Pennsylvania, in the 1870s. Reissued by U. S. Glass Co. in the early 1890s. A milk glass covered compote is known.

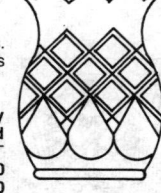

	Clear	Ruby Stained		Clear	Ruby Stained
Banana Stand	95.00	175.00	Regular	55.00	60.00
Biscuit Jar	135.00	175.00	Cruet, os	125.00	250.00
Bowl			Goblet	58.00	—
6" d, 3¼" h, ftd	30.00	—	Mug	35.00	50.00
7", low, collar			Pitcher		
base	35.00	—	Milk	115.00	150.00
8", berry, one end			Water, 2½ qt	85.00	—
pointed	50.00	55.00	Plate, 10"	40.00	—
Butter, cov	60.00	100.00	Relish	20.00	65.00
Cake Stand			Sauce		
9"	55.00	—	Flat, round, 4"	15.00	—
10¼"	65.00	—	Pointed end	18.50	—
Celery Vase	42.50	65.00	Spooner	25.00	55.00
Compote			Sugar, cov	45.00	85.00
Cov, hs, 7"	55.00	185.00	Tumbler	45.00	—
Open, hs, 9"	50.00	—	Vinegar Jug, 3 pt	75.00	—
Open, hs, 9½" d	60.00	—			
Open, hs, 10"	65.00	—			
Creamer					
Hotel, large, round shape	45.00	55.00			

ASHBURTON

A popular pattern produced by Boston and Sandwich Glass Co. and McKee Brothers from the 1850s to the late 1870s with many variations. Originally made in flint by New England Glass Co. and others and later in non-flint. Prices are for flint. Also reported is an amber handled whiskey mug and a scarce emerald green wine glass ($200.00). Some items known in fiery opalescent.

	Clear		Clear
Ale Glass, 5″	90.00	Honey Dish.	15.00
Bar Bottle		* Jug, qt	90.00
Pint.	55.00	Lamp	75.00
Quart	75.00	* Lemonade Glass.	55.00
Bitters Bottle.	55.00	Mug, 7″	100.00
Bowl, 6½″.	75.00	Pitcher, water	450.00
Carafe	175.00	Plate, 6⅝″	75.00
Celery Vase, scalloped top. .	125.00	Sauce	15.00
Champagne, cut	75.00	Spooner	40.00
Claret, 5¼″ h	50.00	* Sugar, cov	90.00
Compote, open, ls, 7½″	65.00	Toddy Jar, cov	375.00
Cordial, 4¼″ h.	75.00	Tumbler	
Creamer, ah	210.00	Bar.	75.00
Decanter, qt, cut and		Water	75.00
pressed, os	250.00	Whiskey	60.00
Egg Cup		Whiskey, ah	125.00
Double	95.00	Water Bottle, tumble up	95.00
Single	30.00	* Wine	
Flip Glass, handled	140.00	Cut	65.00
* Goblet	40.00	Pressed	40.00

ASHMAN

Non-flint, c1880. Pieces are square in shape. There are frequent variations within pieces. Also made in blue.

	Amber	Clear		Amber	Clear
Bread Tray, motto . .	—	55.00	Open hs	—	37.50
Bowl.	—	20.00	Creamer.	45.00	35.00
Butter, cov			Goblet	—	35.00
Conventional final	50.00	38.00	Pitcher, water	—	65.00
Large ball-type fi-			Relish.	—	15.00
nial, sometimes			Spooner	—	40.00
with flowers			Sugar, cov	—	45.00
within the ball . .	—	50.00	Tray, water	50.00	40.00
Cake Stand, 9″	—	40.00	Tumbler	—	25.00
Compotes			Wine	—	25.00
Cov, hs, 12″	—	95.00			

ATLANTA (Square Lion, Clear Lion Head)

Produced by Fostoria Glass Co., Moundsville, West Virginia, c1895. Pieces are usually square in shape. Also found in milk glass, ruby and amber stain.

	Clear	Frosted		Clear	Frosted
Bowl			Cov, hs, 8″ d,		
7″, scallop rim . . .	60.00	75.00	9½″ h.	110.00	150.00
8″, low collar			Open, hs, 5″, jelly	55.00	65.00
base	55.00	85.00	Creamer.	50.00	65.00
Butter, cov	85.00	125.00	Cruet	125.00	150.00
Cake Stand, 10″	95.00	110.00	Goblet	50.00	60.00
Celery Vase	45.00	75.00	Marmalade Jar	75.00	85.00
Compote			Pitcher, water	125.00	175.00
Cov, hs, 7″.	90.00	125.00	Relish, oval.	35.00	40.00

	Clear	Frosted		Clear	Frosted
Salt & Pepper, pr. . .	100.00	125.00	Spooner	50.00	60.00
Salt			Sugar, cov	85.00	100.00
Individual.	30.00	40.00	Toothpick	55.00	60.00
Master	50.00	70.00	Tumbler	45.00	55.00
Sauce, 4"	22.00	25.00	Wine	40.00	65.00

ATLAS

Non-flint glass pattern occasionally ruby stained and etched. Made by Adams and Co., U. S. Glass Co. in 1891, and Bryce Brothers, Mt. Pleasant, Pennsylvania, in 1889.

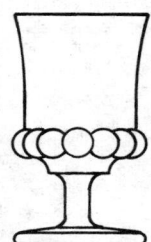

	Clear	Ruby Stained		Clear	Ruby Stained
Bowl, 9"	20.00	—	Pitcher, water	50.00	—
Butter, cov, regular	45.00	75.00	Salt		
Cake Stand			Master	20.00	—
8"	35.00	—	Individual.	15.00	—
9"	40.00	95.00	Salt & Pepper, pr. . .	20.00	—
Celery Vase	28.00	—	Sauce		
Champagne, 5½" h	35.00	45.00	Flat.	10.00	—
Compote			Footed	15.00	20.00
Cov, hs, 8".	65.00	—	Spooner	30.00	35.00
Cov, hs, 5", jelly . .	50.00	65.00	Sugar, cov	40.00	65.00
Open, ls, 7"	40.00	—	Syrup, molasses		
Cordial	35.00	—	can	65.00	—
Creamer			Toothpick	20.00	45.00
Table, ah.	30.00	55.00	Tray, water	75.00	—
Tankard	25.00	—	Tumbler	28.00	—
Goblet	38.00	52.00	Whiskey	20.00	45.00
Marmalade Jar	45.00	—	Wine	25.00	—

AURORA (Diamond Horseshoe)

Made in 1888 by the Brilliant Glass Works, which only existed for a short time. Taken over by the Greensburg Glass Co. who continued the pattern. Also found etched.

	Clear	Ruby Stained		Clear	Ruby Stained
Bread Plate, 10", round, large star in			Relish Scoop, handle.	10.00	25.00
center	30.00	35.00	Salt & Pepper, pr. . .	45.00	80.00
Butter, cov	45.00	90.00	Sauce, flat	8.00	18.00
Cake Stand	35.00	85.00	Spooner	25.00	48.00
Celery Vase	32.50	42.50	Sugar, cov	45.00	65.00
Compote, cov, hs . .	65.00	110.00	Tray, water	45.00	60.00
Creamer.	35.00	50.00	Tray, wine.	35.00	60.00
Goblet	30.00	45.00	Tumbler	25.00	45.00
Mug, handle	50.00	65.00	Waste Bowl.	30.00	45.00
Olive, oval	18.00	35.00	Wine	25.00	35.00
Pitcher, water	40.00	100.00	Wine Decanter, os. .	75.00	150.00

AUSTRIAN (Finecut Medallion)

Made by Indiana Tumbler and Goblet Co., Greentown, Indiana, 1897. Experimental pieces were made in cobalt blue, nile green, and opaque colors.

	Amber	Canary	Clear	Emerald Green
Bowl				
8", round	—	150.00	55.00	—
8¼", rect	—	145.00	50.00	—
Butter, cov	185.00	300.00	90.00	—
Compote, open, ls . .	—	150.00	75.00	—
Cordial	145.00	150.00	50.00	150.00
Creamer	120.00	125.00	40.00	120.00
Goblet	—	150.00	40.00	—
Nappy, cov	—	135.00	55.00	—
Pitcher, water	—	350.00	100.00	—
Plate, 10"	—	—	40.00	—
Punch Cup	150.00	150.00	18.00	125.00
Rose Bowl	—	150.00	50.00	—
Sauce, 4⅝" d	—	50.00	20.00	—
Spooner	—	100.00	40.00	—
Sugar, cov	—	175.00	45.00	—
Tumbler	175.00	85.00	25.00	—
Wine	175.00	150.00	30.00	150.00

BALTIMORE PEAR (Gipsy)

Non-flint, originally made by Adams and Company, Pittsburgh, Pennsylvania, in 1874. Also made by U. S. Glass Company in 1890s. There are 18 different size compotes. Given as premiums by different manufacturers and organizations. Heavily reproduced. Reproduced in cobalt blue.

	Clear		Clear
Bowl		Pickle	20.00
6"	30.00	* Pitcher	
9"	35.00	Milk	80.00
Bread Plate, 12½"	70.00	Water	95.00
* Butter, cov	75.00	Plate	
* Cake Stand, 9"	65.00	8½"	30.00
* Celery Vase	50.00	10"	40.00
Compote		Relish	25.00
Cov, hs, 7"	80.00	* Sauce	
Cov, ls, 8½"	45.00	Flat	15.00
Open, hs	30.00	Footed	20.00
Open, jelly	28.50	Spooner	40.00
* Creamer	30.00	* Sugar, cov	50.00
* Goblet	35.00	Tray, 10½"	35.00

BANDED PORTLAND (Virginia #1, Maiden's Blush)

States pattern, originally named Virginia, by Portland Glass Co. Painted and fired green, yellow, blue, and possibly pink; ruby stained, and rose-flashed (which Lee notes is Maiden's Blush referring to the color, rather than the pattern, as Metz lists it). Double flashed refers to color above and below the band, single flashed refers to color above or below band only.

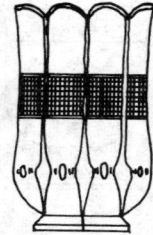

	Clear	Color Flashed	Maiden's Blush Pink
Bowl, 9″	30.00	—	40.00
Butter, cov	50.00	165.00	85.00
Cake Stand	55.00	—	90.00
Candlesticks, pr . . .	80.00	—	125.00
Carafe	80.00	—	90.00
Celery Tray.	25.00	—	40.00
Celery Vase	35.00	—	45.00
Cologne Bottle	50.00	65.00	85.00
Compote			
Cov, hs, 7″.	95.00	—	125.00
Cov, jelly, 6″.	40.00	65.00	90.00
Creamer			
Individual, oval. . .	25.00	35.00	38.00
Regular, 6 oz. . . .	35.00	45.00	50.00
Cruet, os	60.00	90.00	125.00
Decanter, handled. .	50.00	—	100.00
Dresser Tray.	50.00	—	65.00
Goblet	40.00	55.00	65.00
Lamp			
Flat.	45.00	—	—
Tall.	50.00	—	—
Nappy	15.00	55.00	65.00
Olive	18.00	—	35.00
Pin Tray	16.00	—	25.00
Pitcher, tankard. . . .	75.00	95.00	240.00
Pomade Jar, cov . . .	35.00	45.00	65.00
Punch Bowl, hs. . . .	110.00	—	300.00
Punch Cup	20.00	—	30.00
Relish			
6½″.	25.00	30.00	20.00
8¼″.	20.00	35.00	40.00
Ring Holder	75.00	—	125.00
Salt & Pepper, pr. . .	45.00	75.00	75.00
Sardine Box	55.00	—	90.00
Sauce, round, flat,			
4 or 4½″	12.00	—	20.00
Spooner	28.00	—	45.00
Sugar, cov	48.00	75.00	75.00
Sugar Shaker, orig			
top	45.00	—	85.00
Syrup.	50.00	—	135.00
Toothpick	40.00	45.00	45.00
Tumbler	25.00	—	45.00
Vase			
6″	20.00	—	38.00
9″	35.00	—	50.00
Wine	35.00	—	75.00

BARBERRY (Berry)

Non-flint made by McKee Glass Co. and the Boston and Sandwich Glass Co. in the 1860s and 1880s. 6″ plates are found in amber, canary, pale green, and pale blue; they are considered scarce. Also alleged to have been made at Iowa City. Pattern comes in "9 berry bunch" and "12 berry bunch" varieties.

	Clear
Bowl	
6", oval	20.00
7", oval	25.00
8", oval	28.00
8", round, flat	30.00
9", oval	32.00
Butter	
Cov.	50.00
Cov, flange, pattern on edge	100.00
Cake Stand	125.00
Celery Vase	40.00
Compote	
Cov, hs, 8", shell finial	85.00
Cov, ls, 8", shell finial	75.00
Open, hs, 8"	35.00

	Clear
Creamer	30.00
Cup Plate	15.00
Egg Cup	18.00
Goblet	25.00
Pickle	10.00
Pitcher, water, ah	100.00
Plate, 6"	20.00
Salt, master, ftd	25.00
Sauce	
Flat	10.00
Footed	15.00
Spooner, ftd	30.00
Sugar, cov	45.00
Syrup	150.00
Tumbler, ftd	25.00
Wine	30.00

BARLEY

Non-flint, originally made by Campbell, Jones and Co., c1882, in clear; possibly by others in varied quality. Add 100% for color which is hard to find.

	Clear
Bowl	
8", berry	15.00
10", oval	20.00
Bread Tray	30.00
Butter, cov	42.50
Cake Stand	
8"	28.00
10"	32.00
Celery Vase	25.00
Compote	
Cov, hs, 6"	45.00
Cov, hs, 8½"	60.00
Open, hs, 8½"	35.00
Cordial	50.00
Creamer	30.00
Goblet	28.00
Honey, ftd, 3½"	8.00
Marmalade Jar	65.00
Pickle Castor, SP frame	85.00

	Clear
Pitcher, water	
Applied handle	100.00
Pressed handle	65.00
Plate, 6"	35.00
Platter, 13" l, 8" w	30.00
Relish	
Flat, 8" l, 6" w	18.00
Wheelbarrow, 8", pewter wheels	75.00
Salt, master, wheelbarrow, pewter wheels	75.00
Sauce	
Flat	8.50
Footed	10.00
Spooner	21.50
Sugar, cov	35.00
Vegetable Dish, oval	15.00
Wine	30.00

BASKETWEAVE

Non-flint, c1880. Some covered pieces have a stippled cat's head finial.

	Amber or Canary	Apple Green	Blue	Clear	Vaseline
Bowl	22.00	—	25.00	18.00	—
Bread Plate, 11"	35.00	—	35.00	10.00	—
Butter, cov	35.00	60.00	40.00	30.00	40.00
Compote, cov, 7"	—	—	—	35.00	—

	Amber or Canary	Apple Green	Blue	Clear	Vaseline
Cordial	25.00	40.00	28.00	20.00	30.00
Creamer.	30.00	50.00	35.00	28.00	36.00
Cup & Saucer.	35.00	60.00	35.00	30.00	38.00
Dish, oval	12.00	20.00	15.00	10.00	16.00
Egg Cup.	18.00	30.00	20.00	15.00	25.00
* Goblet	28.00	50.00	35.00	20.00	30.00
Mug	25.00	40.00	25.00	15.00	30.00
Pickle.	18.00	30.00	20.00	15.00	22.00
Pitcher					
Milk.	40.00	60.00	45.00	35.00	50.00
* Water	60.00	75.00	80.00	45.00	85.00
Plate, 11", handled .	25.00	38.00	25.00	20.00	30.00
Sauce	10.00	10.00	12.00	8.00	12.00
Spooner	30.00	36.00	30.00	20.00	30.00
Sugar, cov	35.00	60.00	35.00	30.00	40.00
Syrup	50.00	75.00	50.00	45.00	55.00
* Tray, water, scenic center	35.00	45.00	40.00	30.00	55.00
Tumbler, ftd	18.00	30.00	20.00	15.00	20.00
Waste Bowl.	20.00	36.00	25.00	18.00	25.00
Wine	30.00	50.00	30.00	25.00	30.00

BEADED ACORN MEDALLION (Beaded Acorn)

Made by the Boston Silver Glass Co., East Cambridge, Massachusetts, c1869.

	Clear		Clear
Butter, cov, acorn finial.	65.00	Plate, 6"	30.00
Champagne	65.00	Relish.	15.00
Compote, cov, hs	50.00	Salt, master	30.00
Creamer.	40.00	Sauce, flat	15.00
Egg Cup.	25.00	Spooner	25.00
Goblet	30.00	Sugar, cov	45.00
Pitcher, water	90.00	Wine	45.00

BEADED BAND

Attributed to Burlington Glass Co., Hamilton, Ontario, Canada, c1884. Limited production and scarce pattern. May have been made in light amber and other colors.

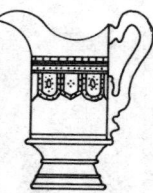

	Clear		Clear
Butter, cov	35.00	Relish	
Cake Stand, 7⅝"	25.00	Double	30.00
Compote, cov		Single	15.00
hs, 8"	55.00	Sauce, ftd.	10.00
ls, 9"	50.00	Spooner	25.00
Creamer.	30.00	Sugar, cov	40.00
Goblet	25.00	Syrup	95.00
Pickle, cov	45.00	Wine	30.00
Pitcher, water, applied strap handle.	100.00		

BEADED GRAPE MEDALLION

Non-flint made by Boston Silver Glass Co., Cambridge, Massachusetts, c1868. Also found in flint; add 40%.

	Clear		Clear
Bowl, 7″	25.00	Honey Dish, 3½″	10.00
Butter, cov, acorn finial	45.00	Pitcher, water, ah	115.00
Cake Stand, 11″	150.00	Plate, 6″	30.00
Celery Vase	50.00	Relish	
Castor Set, 4 bottles	110.00	Cov	140.00
Compote		Open, mkd "Mould Pat'd	
Cov, collared base	85.00	May 11, 1868"	40.00
Cov, hs	75.00	Salt	
Open, hs, 8″	35.00	Individual, flat	20.00
Creamer, ah	48.00	Master, ftd	25.00
Egg Cup	30.00	Spooner	40.00
Goblet		Sugar, cov, acorn finial	60.00
Buttermilk	30.00	Vegetable, cov, ftd	75.00
Lady's	30.00	Wine	55.00

BEADED SWIRL (Swirled Column)

Made by George Duncan & Sons, c1890. The dual names are for the two forms of the pattern. Beaded Swirl stands on flat bases and is solid in shape. Swirled Column stands on scrolled (sometimes gilded) feet, and the shape tapered towards the base. Some pieces trimmed in gold and also in milk white.

	Clear	Emerald Green		Clear	Emerald Green
Bowl			Goblet	35.00	40.00
Berry, 7″	10.00	20.00	Mug	10.00	12.00
Flat	15.00	25.00	Pitcher, water	40.00	85.00
Footed, oval	18.00	24.00	Sauce		
Footed, round	18.00	24.00	Flat	8.00	12.00
Butter, cov	35.00	45.00	Footed	10.00	14.00
Cake Stand	35.00	45.00	Spooner		
Celery Vase	30.00	55.00	Flat	25.00	40.00
Compote			Footed	30.00	45.00
Cov, hs	40.00	50.00	Sugar, cov		
Open, hs	35.00	45.00	Flat	35.00	45.00
Creamer			Footed	35.00	45.00
Flat	25.00	35.00	Sugar Shaker	35.00	60.00
Footed	30.00	40.00	Syrup	48.00	100.00
Dish	10.00	15.00	Tumbler	20.00	30.00
Egg Cup	14.00	15.00	Wine	25.00	35.00

BEAUTIFUL LADY

Made by Bryce, Higbee and Co. in 1905.

	Clear		Clear
Banana stand, hs	30.00	9″, flat	18.00
Bowl		Bread Plate	15.00
8″, low collared base	15.00	Cake Plate, 9″	25.00

	Clear		Clear
Cake Stand, hs	35.00	8″	18.00
Compote		9″	25.00
Cov, hs	35.00	11″	27.50
Open, hs	25.00	Salt and Pepper, pr	60.00
Open, jelly	15.00	Spooner	15.00
Creamer	25.00	Sugar, cov	25.00
Cruet	30.00	Tumbler	15.00
Goblet	35.00	Vase, 6½″	15.00
Pitcher, water	45.00	Wine	20.00
Plate			
7″, sq	15.00		

BELLFLOWER

A fine flint glass pattern first made in the 1830s and attributed to Boston and Sandwich. Later produced by McKee Glass Co. and other firms for many years. There are many variations of this pattern - single vine and double vine, fine and coarse rib, knob and plain stems, and rayed and plain bases. Type and quality must be considered when evaluating. Very rare in color. Prices are for high quality flint. Reproductions have been made by the Metropolitan Museum of Art. Abbreviations: DV - double vine; SV - single vine; FR - fine rib; CR - coarse rib.

	Clear		Clear
Bowl		Dish, SV-FR, 8″, round, flat,	
6″ d, 1¾″ h, SV	75.00	scalloped top	65.00
8″, all types	75.00	Egg Cup	
Butter, cov, SV-FR	100.00	CR	35.00
Castor Set, 5 bottle, pewter		SV-FR	40.00
stand	225.00	Goblet	
Celery Vase, SV-FR	165.00	DV-FR, cut bellflowers	230.00
Champagne		SV-CR, barrel shape	45.00
DV-FR, cut bellflowers	225.00	SV-CR, straight sides	40.00
SV-FR, knob stem, rayed		SV-FR, knob stem, barrel	
base, barrel shape	100.00	shape	55.00
Compote		* SV-FR, plain stem, rayed	
Cov, hs, 8″ d, SV-FR	375.00	base, barrel shape	30.00
Cov, ls, 7″ d, SV	200.00	Hat, SV-FR, made from tum-	
Cov, ls, 8″ d, SV	225.00	bler mold, rare	350.00
Open, hs, 8″, SV	225.00	Honey Dish, SV-FR, 3″	35.00
Open, ls, 7″, DV-FR	90.00	Lamp, whale oil, SV-FR,	
Open, ls, 7″, SV	100.00	brass stem, marble base	175.00
Open, ls, 8″, SV	100.00	Mug, SV-FR	250.00
Open, ls, 9″, SV-CR	125.00	Pitcher	
Cordial, SV-FR, knob stem,		Milk, DV-FR	500.00
rayed base, barrel shape	115.00	Milk, DV, pint	175.00
Creamer, DV-FR	135.00	Milk, SV-CR, quart	175.00
Creamer, SV-FR	135.00	Water, DV-CR	350.00
Decanter		* Water, SV-FR	250.00
Pint, DV-FR, bar top	225.00	Plate, 6″, SV-FR	125.00
Quart		Salt, master	
DV-FR, orig patterned		SV-FR, ftd	60.00
stopper	275.00	DV-FR	35.00
SV-FR, bar top	185.00	Sauce, flat, SV-FR	15.00

	Clear			Clear
Spooner			SV-FR, ftd	90.00
DV	45.00		* SV-FR, cut bellflowers	250.00
SV-FR	35.00		Whiskey, 3½", SV-FR	150.00
Sugar			Wine	
Cov, DV	100.00		DV-FR, cut bellflowers,	
Cov, SV-CR	95.00		barrel shape	250.00
Open, DV-CR	45.00		SV-FR, knob stem, rayed	
Sweetmeat, cov, hs, 6", SV	300.00		base, barrel shape	90.00
Syrup, ah			SV-FR, plain stem, rayed	
Ftd, 10 sides	750.00		base, straight sides	75.00
SV-FR	550.00			
Tumbler				
DV-CR	95.00			

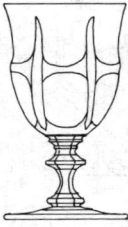

BIGLER

Flint, made by Boston and Sandwich Glass Co. and by other early factories. A scarce pattern in which goblets are most common and vary in height, shape and flare. Rare in color.

	Clear			Clear
Ale Glass	65.00		Goblet	
Bar Bottle, qt	80.00		Regular	48.00
Bowl, 10" d	40.00		Short Stem	50.00
Butter, cov	125.00		Lamp, whale oil, monument	
Celery Vase	100.00		base	155.00
Champagne	95.00		Mug, applied handle	60.00
Compote, 7"	40.00		Plate, 6"	32.00
Cordial	65.00		Salt, master	20.00
Creamer	75.00		Tumbler, water	65.00
Cup Plate	30.00		Whiskey, handled	100.00
Egg Cup, double	50.00		Wine	65.00

BIRD AND STRAWBERRY (Bluebird)

Non-flint, c1890. Made by Beatty and Indiana Glass Co., Dunkirk, IN. Pieces occasionally highlighted by the coloring of birds blue, strawberries pink, and leaves green, plus the addition of gilding.

	Clear	Colors		Clear	Colors
Bowl			Cup	25.00	35.00
5"	25.00	45.00	Goblet	200.00	300.00
9½", ftd	50.00	85.00	Nappy	40.00	65.00
10½"	55.00	95.00	Pitcher, water	235.00	350.00
Butter, cov	100.00	175.00	Plate, 12"	125.00	175.00
Cake Stand	65.00	125.00	Punch Cup	25.00	35.00
Celery Vase	45.00	85.00	Relish	20.00	45.00
Compote			Spooner	50.00	120.00
Cov, hs	125.00	200.00	Sugar, cov	65.00	125.00
Open, ls, ruffled	65.00	125.00	Tumbler	45.00	75.00
Jelly, cov, hs	150.00	225.00	Wine	70.00	100.00
Creamer	55.00	135.00			

BLEEDING HEART

Non-flint, originally made by King & Son, Pittsburgh, PA, c1870, and by U. S. Glass Co., c1898. Also found in milk glass. Goblets are found in six variations. Note: A goblet with a tin lid, containing a condiment (mustard, jelly, or baking powder) was made. It is of inferior quality compared to the original goblet.

	Clear		Clear
Bowl		Dish, cov, 7″	55.00
7¼″, oval.	30.00	Egg Cup.	45.00
8″	35.00	Egg Rack, cov, 3 eggs.	350.00
9¼″, oval, cov	65.00	Goblet, knob stem	35.00
Butter, cov	75.00	Honey Dish	15.00
Cake Stand		Mug, 3¼″	40.00
9″	60.00	Pickle, 8¾″ l, 5″ w	30.00
10″	85.00	Pitcher, water, ah	150.00
11″	90.00	Plate	75.00
Dessert slots	125.00	Platter, oval.	65.00
Compote		Relish, oval, 5½ x 3⅝″.	35.00
Cov, hs, 8″.	75.00	Salt, master, ftd.	60.00
Cov, hs, 9″.	95.00	Salt, oval, flat	20.00
Cov, ls, 7″	60.00	Sauce, flat	15.00
Cov, ls, 7½″	60.00	Spooner	25.00
Cov, ls, 8″	75.00	Sugar, cov	60.00
Open, ls, 8½″	30.00	Tumbler, ftd	80.00
Creamer		Wine	165.00
Applied Handle	60.00		
Molded Handle	30.00		

BLOCK AND FAN

Non-flint made by Richard and Hartley Glass Co., Tarentum, PA, late 1880s. Continued by U. S. Glass Co. after 1891.

	Clear	Ruby Stained		Clear	Ruby Stained
Biscuit Jar, cov	65.00	150.00	Open, ls, 7″	25.00	—
Bowl			Open, ls, 8″	30.00	—
4″, flat	15.00	—	Condiment Set, salt,		
8″, flat	25.00	—	pepper & cruet on		
8″, ftd	20.00	—	tray	75.00	—
9½″.	30.00	—	Creamer		
10 x 6″, rect.	50.00	—	Individual.	—	35.00
Butter, cov	50.00	85.00	Regular	25.00	45.00
Cake Stand			Large	30.00	100.00
9″	35.00	—	Small	35.00	75.00
10″	42.00	—	Cruet, os	40.00	—
Carafe	50.00	95.00	Dish, large, rect. . . .	25.00	—
Celery Tray	30.00	—	Finger Bowl	55.00	—
Celery Vase	35.00	75.00	Goblet	48.00	120.00
Compote			Ice Tub	45.00	50.00
Open, hs, 8″	40.00	165.00	Orange Bowl.	50.00	—
Open, ls, 4″	10.00	—	Pickle Dish	20.00	—

	Clear	Ruby Stained		Clear	Ruby Stained
Pitcher			Ftd, 3¾"	12.00	25.00
Milk	35.00	—	Spooner	25.00	—
Water	48.00	125.00	Sugar, cov	50.00	—
Plate			Sugar Shaker	40.00	—
6"	20.00	—	Syrup	75.00	95.00
10"	22.00	—	Tray, ice cream, rect	75.00	—
Relish, rect	25.00	—	Tumbler	30.00	40.00
Rose Bowl	25.00	—	Waste Bowl	30.00	—
Salt & Pepper	30.00	—	Wine	45.00	80.00
Sauce					
Flat, 5	8.00	—			

BOW TIE

Non-flint made by Thompson Glass Co., Uniontown, PA, c1889.

	Clear		Clear
Bowl		Pitcher	
7"	30.00	Milk	
8"	40.00	5½"	45.00
10¼ d, 5" h	65.00	8"	80.00
Butter, cov	72.50	9"	90.00
Butter Pat	30.00	Water	75.00
Cake Stand, large, 9" d	60.00	Punch Bowl	100.00
Compote, open		Relish, rect	25.00
hs, 5½"	60.00	Salt	
hs, 9¼"	65.00	Individual	25.00
ls, 6½"	45.00	Master	40.00
ls, 8"	55.00	Salt Shaker	65.00
Creamer	60.00	Sauce, flat	18.00
Goblet	65.00	Spooner	35.00
Honey, cov	55.00	Sugar, cov	65.00
Marmalade Jar	65.00	Tumbler	50.00
Orange Bowl, ftd, hs, 10" . . .	75.00		

BROKEN COLUMN (Irish Column, Notched Rib, Rattan)

Made in Findlay, Ohio, c1891, by Columbia Glass Co., c1892, and later made by U. S. Glass Co. May also have been made at Portland, ME. Notches may be ruby stained. A cobalt blue cup is known. The square covered compote has been reproduced. Some items have been reproduced for the Metropolitan Museum of Art. Some items are reproduced by the Smithsonian Institution with a raised "SI" trademark.

	Clear	Ruby Stained		Clear	Ruby Stained
Banana Stand	110.00	—	8"	35.00	—
Basket, applied han-			9"	40.00	—
dle, 12" h, 15" l . .	125.00	—	Bread Plate	60.00	125.00
Biscuit Jar	85.00	165.00	Butter, cov	85.00	175.00
Bowl			Cake Stand		
4", berry	15.00	20.00	9"	70.00	225.00
6", berry	20.00	45.00	10"	80.00	245.00

	Clear	Ruby Stained		Clear	Ruby Stained
Carafe, water	75.00	150.00	Marmalade Jar	85.00	—
Celery Tray, oval . . .	35.00	85.00	Pickle Castor, sp		
Celery Vase	50.00	135.00	frame	150.00	450.00
Champagne	100.00	—	Pitcher, water	90.00	230.00
Claret	75.00	—	Plate		
Compote			4"	25.00	40.00
Cov, hs, 5¼" d,			5"	35.00	—
10¼" h.	90.00	200.00	7½"	40.00	95.00
Cov, hs, 7" d,			Punch Cup	15.00	—
12"h.	85.00	—	Relish	25.00	—
Cov, hs, 10"	110.00	350.00	Salt Shaker	45.00	65.00
Open, hs, 7" d . . .	—	150.00	* Sauce, flat	15.00	20.00
Open, hs, 8" d . . .	75.00	175.00	* Spooner	35.00	85.00
Open, ls, 5" d, 6"			Sugar Shaker	85.00	200.00
h, flared	65.00	135.00	Sugar, cov	70.00	135.00
Creamer	42.50	125.00	Syrup	130.00	400.00
Cruet, os	85.00	150.00	Tumbler	40.00	50.00
Decanter	85.00	—	Vegetable, cov	90.00	—
Finger Bowl	30.00	—	Wine	80.00	125.00
* Goblet	50.00	100.00			

BUCKLE

Flint and non-flint pattern. Sandwich Glass Co. in Massachusetts is attributed to the flint production. The non-flint production was made by Gillinder and Sons in Philadelphia, PA, in the late 1870s.

	Flint	Non-Flint		Flint	Non-Flint
Bowl			Egg Cup	38.00	28.00
8"	60.00	50.00	Goblet	40.00	25.00
10"	65.00	50.00	Pickle	40.00	15.00
Butter, cov	65.00	60.00	Pitcher, water, ah . .	500.00	85.00
Cake Stand, 9¾" . . .	—	30.00	Salt, flat, oval	30.00	15.00
Champagne	60.00	—	Salt, footed	20.00	18.00
Compote			Sauce, flat	10.00	8.00
Cov, hs, 6" d	95.00	40.00	Spooner	35.00	27.50
Open, hs, 8½" . . .	40.00	35.00	Sugar, cov	75.00	55.00
Open, ls	40.00	35.00	Tumbler	55.00	30.00
Creamer, ah	110.00	40.00	Wine	75.00	32.00

BUCKLE WITH STAR (Orient)

Non-flint made by Bryce, Walker and Co. in 1875, U. S. Glass Co. in 1891. Finials are shaped like Maltese crosses.

	Clear		Clear
Bowl		Butter, cov	40.00
6", cov	25.00	Cake Stand, 9"	35.00
7", oval	15.00	Celery Vase	30.00
8", oval	15.00	Compote	
9", oval	15.00	Cov, hs, 7"	60.00
10", oval	18.00	Open, hs, 9½"	30.00

	Clear		Clear
Creamer	35.00	Spooner	25.00
Goblet	30.00	Sugar	
Mug	60.00	Cov.	45.00
Mustard, cov.	75.00	Open	25.00
Pickle	15.00	Syrup	
Pitcher, water, applied		Applied handle, pewter or	
handle	70.00	Brittania top, man's head	
Relish	15.00	finial	80.00
Salt, master, ftd.	20.00	Molded handle, plain tin	
Sauce		top.	60.00
Flat	8.00	Tumbler	55.00
Footed	10.00	Wine	35.00
Spill holder	55.00		

BULL'S EYE

Flint made by the New England Glass Co. in the 1850s. Also found in colors and milk glass, which doubles the price.

	Clear		Clear
Bitters Bottle	80.00	Lamp	100.00
Butter, cov	150.00	Mug, 3½", ah	110.00
Carafe	45.00	Pitcher, water	285.00
Castor Bottle	35.00	Relish, oval	25.00
Celery Vase	85.00	Salt	
Champagne	95.00	Individual	40.00
Cologne Bottle	85.00	Master, ftd	100.00
Cordial	75.00	Spill holder	85.00
Creamer, ah	125.00	Spooner	40.00
Cruet, os	125.00	Sugar, cov	125.00
Decanter, qt, bar lip	120.00	Tumbler	85.00
Egg Cup		Water Bottle, tumble up	125.00
Cov.	165.00	Whiskey	70.00
Open	48.00	Wine	50.00
Goblet	65.00		

BULL'S EYE AND DAISY

Made by U. S. Glass Co., 1909. Also made with amethyst, blue, green, and pink stains in eyes.

	Clear	Emerald Green	Ruby Stained
Bowl	12.00	16.00	30.00
Butter, cov	25.00	28.00	90.00
Celery Vase	20.00	25.00	40.00
Creamer	25.00	28.00	50.00
Decanter	—	110.00	—
Goblet	25.00	28.00	50.00
Pitcher, water	35.00	40.00	95.00
Salt Shaker	20.00	20.00	35.00
Sauce	7.50	10.00	20.00
Spooner	20.00	25.00	40.00
Sugar, open	22.00	30.00	45.00

	Clear	Emerald Green	Ruby Stained
Tumbler	15.00	18.00	35.00
Wine	20.00	25.00	40.00

BULL'S EYE AND FAN (Daisies in Oval Panels)

Made by U.S. Glass, c1910. Also made in blue; prices same as emerald green.

	Amethyst Stain	Clear	Emerald Green	Pink Stain	Sapphire Blue Stain
Bowl					
5", pinched ends	—	—	18.00	—	—
8", berry	—	15.00	20.00	—	30.00
Butter, cov	—	45.00	65.00	—	—
Cake Stand	—	25.00	—	—	—
Creamer					
Individual.	—	10.00	—	—	—
Regular.	—	25.00	30.00	—	35.00
Custard Cup	—	10.00	—	—	—
Goblet	25.00	22.50	45.00	25.00	45.00
Lemonade Mug. 5"	—	20.00	—	—	—
Pitcher					
Lemonade, ftd . . .	—	55.00	—	—	—
Water, tankard . . .	55.00	40.00	100.00	50.00	100.00
Relish.	20.00	15.00	35.00	20.00	35.00
Sauce	25.00	10.00	20.00	25.00	30.00
Spooner	25.00	21.50	45.00	25.00	45.00
Sugar, cov	40.00	35.00	60.00	30.00	35.00
Toothpick	—	35.00	40.00	65.00	—
Tumbler	55.00	15.00	45.00	40.00	35.00
Wine	22.00	20.00	40.00	40.00	25.00

BULL'S EYE WITH DIAMOND POINT (Union)

Made in flint by New England Glass Co., c1869.

	Clear		Clear
Butter, cov	250.00	Salt, master, cov	100.00
Celery Vase	150.00	Sauce	20.00
Champagne	145.00	Spill	75.00
Cologne Bottle, os.	90.00	Spooner	125.00
Creamer.	200.00	Sugar, cov	175.00
Cruet, os	225.00	Syrup	175.00
Decanter, qt, os.	200.00	Tumbler	145.00
Egg Cup.	90.00	Tumble-Up	165.00
Goblet	120.00	Whiskey	150.00
Honey Dish, flat	25.00	Wine	135.00
Lamp, finger, ah	165.00		
Pitcher, water, 10¼", tankard	275.00		

BUTTERFLY & FAN (Grace, Japanese)

Non-flint pattern made by Duncan, Pittsburgh, PA, c1880.

	Clear		Clear
Bread Plate	80.00	Creamer, ftd	45.00
Butter, cov		Goblet	50.00
Flat.	100.00	Marmalade Jar	75.00
Footed	75.00	Pitcher, water	115.00
Celery Vase	75.00	Sauce, ftd.	15.00
Compote		Spooner	30.00
Cov, hs, 8″ d	95.00	Sugar cov, ftd	68.00
Cov, hs, 7″ d	95.00		
Open, hs.	30.00		

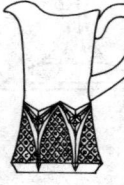

BUTTON ARCHES

Non-flint, made by Duncan and Miller Glass Co. in 1885. Pieces have frosted band. Some pieces, known as "Koral," usually souvenir type, are also seen in clambroth, trimmed in gold. The toothpick holder comes in both a smooth scallop and beaded scallop variety. They have the same value. In the early 1970s souvenir ruby stained pieces, including a goblet and table set, were reproduced.

	Clambroth	Clear	Ruby Stained
Bowl, 8″	—	20.00	50.00
Butter, cov	—	48.00	100.00
Cake Stand, 9″	—	35.00	180.00
Compote, jelly.	—	48.00	50.00
Creamer.	25.00	20.00	45.00
Cruet, os	—	55.00	175.00
* Goblet	40.00	25.00	40.00
Mug	30.00	25.00	30.00
Mustard, cov,			
underplate.	—	—	100.00
Pitcher			
Milk.	—	35.00	100.00
Water, tankard . . .	—	75.00	125.00
Plate, 7″	—	10.00	25.00
Punch Cup	—	15.00	25.00
Salt, ind	—	15.00	—
Salt Shaker, three			
types.	—	15.00	30.00
Sauce, flat	—	8.00	22.00
Spooner	—	25.00	40.00
Sugar, cov	—	35.00	75.00
Syrup.	—	75.00	175.00
Toothpick	30.00	20.00	35.00
Tumbler	20.00	24.00	35.00
Wine	25.00	15.00	35.00

BUTTON BAND (Umbilicated Hobnail, Wyandotte)

Non-flint made by Ripley and Co. in 1880s and U. S. Glass Co. in 1890s. Can often be found engraved, priced the same.

	Clear		Clear
Bowl, 10″	30.00	Goblet	40.00
Butter, cov	45.00	Pitcher	
Cake Stand, 10″	70.00	Milk...............	40.00
Castor Set, 5 bottles in glass		Water, tankard	50.00
stand	135.00	Spooner	28.00
Compote		Sugar, cov	35.00
Cov, hs, 9″...........	120.00	Tray, water	40.00
Open, ls	65.00	Tumbler	25.00
Cordial	35.00	Wine	35.00
Creamer..............	30.00		

CABBAGE ROSE

Non-flint made by Central Glass Co, Wheeling, WV, c1870. Reproduced in colors.

	Clear		Clear
Basket, handled, 12″	125.00	Cov, ls, 7½″...........	100.00
Bitters Bottle, 6½″ h	125.00	Cov, ls, 8½″...........	110.00
Bowl, Oval		Open, hs, 7½″	75.00
7½″................	32.50	Open, hs, 9½″	100.00
8½″................	38.00	Creamer, applied handle ...	55.00
9½″................	40.00	Egg Cup.............	45.00
Bowl, Round		* Goblet	42.50
6″.................	25.00	Mug................	60.00
7½″, cov	65.00	Pitcher	
7½″, open	35.00	Milk...............	150.00
Butter, cov	60.00	Water	125.00
Cake Stand		Relish, 8½″ l, 5″ w, rose-filled	
11″................	40.00	horn of plenty center	38.00
12½″...............	50.00	Salt, master, ftd........	25.00
Celery Vase	48.00	Sauces, six sizes	10–20.00
Champagne	50.00	Spooner	25.00
Compote		Sugar, cov	55.00
Cov, hs, 7½″	110.00	Tumbler	40.00
Cov, hs, 8½″	120.00	Wine	40.00
Cov, ls, 6″	95.00		

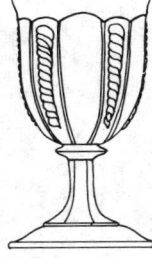

CABLE

Flint, c1850. Made by Boston and Sandwich Glass Co. to commemorate the laying of Atlantic Cable. Also found with amber stained panels and in opaque colors (rare).

	Clear		Clear
Bowl		ls, 7″	50.00
8″, ftd	45.00	ls, 9″	55.00
9″	70.00	ls, 11″	75.00
Butter, cov	100.00	Creamer..............	200.00
Cake Stand, 9″	100.00	Decanter, qt, ground stopper	295.00
Celery Vase	70.00	Egg Cup	
Champagne	250.00	Cov................	225.00
Compote, open		Open	60.00
hs, 5½″	65.00	Goblet	70.00

	Clear			Clear
Honey Dish	15.00	Sauce, flat		20.00
Lamp, 8¾"		Spooner		40.00
Glass Base	135.00	Sugar, cov		120.00
Marble Base	100.00	Syrup		225.00
Pitcher, water, rare	500.00	Tumbler, ftd		200.00
Plate, 6"	75.00	Wine		175.00
Salt, ind, flat	35.00			

CADMUS

Non-flint made by Beaumont Glass Co., Grafton, WV, in mid-1880s.

	Clear		Clear
Bowl	15.00	Goblet	20.00
Butter, cov	35.00	Sauce	8.00
Compote, open		Spooner	15.00
High std	25.00	Sugar, cov	25.00
Jelly	20.00	Tumbler	20.00
Creamer	25.00	Wine	18.00

CALIFORNIA (Beaded Grape)

Non-flint made by U. S. Glass Co., Pittsburgh, PA, c1890. Also with gold trim. Many pieces reproduced.

	Clear	Emerald Green		Clear	Emerald Green
Bowl			Cruet, os	65.00	125.00
5½", sq	17.50	20.00	* Goblet	35.00	50.00
5½ x 8"	—	30.00	Olive, handle	20.00	35.00
6" sq	—	25.00	Pickle	20.00	30.00
7½", sq	25.00	35.00	Pitcher		
8", round	28.00	35.00	Milk	75.00	—
Bread Plate	25.00	45.00	Water	85.00	120.00
Butter, cov	65.00	85.00	* Plate, 8¼", sq	28.00	40.00
Cake Stand, 9"	65.00	85.00	Salt & Pepper	45.00	65.00
Celery Tray	30.00	45.00	* Sauce, 4"	15.00	18.00
Celery Vase	40.00	60.00	Spooner	35.00	45.00
Compote			Sugar, cov	45.00	55.00
Cov, hs, 6½"	65.00	95.00	Sugar Shaker	75.00	85.00
Open, hs, 5", sq	55.00	75.00	Toothpick	40.00	65.00
Open, hs, 7"	45.00	80.00	* Tumbler	32.50	45.00
Open, hs, jelly	55.00	75.00	* Wine	35.00	65.00
Creamer	40.00	50.00			

CANADIAN

Non-flint, made by Burlington Glass Works, Hamilton, Ontario, Canada, c1870.

	Clear		Clear
Bowl, 7" d, 4½" h, ftd	65.00	Butter, cov	85.00
Bread Plate, 10"	45.00	Cake Stand, 9¼"	85.00

	Clear
Celery Vase	65.00
Compote	
Cov, hs, 6"	90.00
Cov, hs, 7"	100.00
Cov, hs, 8"	110.00
Cov, ls, 6"	50.00
Open, ls, 7"	35.00
Creamer	65.00
Goblet	45.00
Mug, small	45.00

	Clear
Pitcher	
Milk	90.00
Water	125.00
Plate, 6", handles	32.50
Sauce	
Flat	15.00
Footed	20.00
Spooner	45.00
Sugar, cov	90.00
Wine	45.00

CANE

Non-flint made by Gillinder Glass Co. and McKee Glass Co., c1885. Goblets and toddy plates with inverted "buttons" known.

	Amber	Apple Green	Blue	Clear	Vaseline
Bowl, 9½", oval	15.00	—	—	—	—
Butter, cov	45.00	60.00	75.00	40.00	60.00
Celery Vase	38.00	40.00	50.00	32.50	40.00
Compote, open, ls, 5¾"	28.00	30.00	35.00	25.00	35.00
Cordial	—	—	—	25.00	—
Creamer	35.00	40.00	50.00	25.00	30.00
Finger Bowl	20.00	30.00	35.00	15.00	30.00
Goblet	25.00	40.00	35.00	20.00	37.50
Honey Dish	—	—	—	15.00	—
Match holder, kettle	18.00	—	35.00	30.00	35.00
Pickle	25.00	20.00	25.00	15.00	20.00
Pitcher, milk	60.00	55.00	65.00	40.00	55.00
Pitcher, water	80.00	85.00	80.00	48.00	85.00
Plate, toddy, 4½"	20.00	25.00	30.00	16.50	20.00
Salt & Pepper	60.00	50.00	80.00	30.00	70.00
Sauce, flat	—	9.50	—	7.00	—
Slipper	30.00	—	25.00	15.00	30.00
Spooner	42.00	35.00	30.00	20.00	30.00
Sugar, cov	45.00	45.00	45.00	25.00	45.00
Tray, water	35.00	40.00	50.00	30.00	45.00
Tumbler	24.00	30.00	35.00	20.00	25.00
Waste Bowl, 7½"	32.50	30.00	35.00	20.00	30.00
Wine	35.00	40.00	35.00	20.00	35.00

CAPE COD

Non-flint, attributed to Boston and Sandwich Glass Co., c1870.

	Clear
Bowl, 6", handled	30.00
Bread Plate	45.00
Butter, cov	65.00
Celery Vase	45.00
Compote	
Cov, hs, 6" d	50.00

	Clear
Cov, hs, 8"	100.00
Cov, hs, 12"	175.00
Cov, ls, 6"	50.00
Open, hs, 7"	50.00
Creamer	45.00
Decanter	160.00

	Clear		Clear
Goblet	45.00	Platter, open handles	45.00
Marmalade Jar, cov	85.00	Sauce, ftd	17.50
Pitcher		Spooner	35.00
Milk	65.00	Sugar, cov	55.00
Water	90.00	Wine	35.00
Plate			
5", handles	30.00		
10"	45.00		

CARDINAL

Non-flint, c1875, attributed to Ohio Flint Glass Co., Lancaster, OH. There were two butter dishes made, one in the regular pattern and one with three birds in the base—labeled in script Red Bird (cardinal), Pewit, and Titmouse. The latter is less common. Goblet and creamer reproduced.

	Clear		Clear
Butter, cov		Pitcher, water	150.00
Regular	65.00	Sauce	
Three birds in base	100.00	Flat, 4"	10.00
Cake Stand	75.00	Footed, 4½" or 5½"	15.00
* Creamer	40.00	Spooner	38.00
* Goblet	30.00	Sugar, cov	60.00
Honey Dish, 3½"			
Cov	45.00		
Open	20.00		

CAROLINA (Inverness)

Made by Bryce Brothers and later by U. S. Glass Co., as part of the States series, c1903. Ruby stained pieces often are souvenir marked. Some clear pieces found with gilt or purple stain.

	Clear	Ruby Stained		Clear	Ruby Stained
Bowl, berry	15.00	—	Plate, 7½"	10.00	—
Butter, cov	35.00	—	Relish	10.00	—
Cake Stand	35.00	—	Salt Shaker	15.00	35.00
Compote			Sauce		
Open, hs, 8"	38.50	—	Flat	8.00	—
Open, hs, 9½"	20.00	—	Footed	10.00	—
Open, jelly	10.00	—	Spooner	20.00	—
Creamer	20.00	—	Sugar, cov	25.00	—
Goblet	25.00	45.00	Tumbler	10.00	—
Mug	20.00	35.00	Wine	20.00	35.00
Pitcher, milk	45.00	—			

CATHEDRAL (Orion)

Non-flint pattern made by Bryce Bros., Pittsburgh, PA., in the 1880s and by U. S. Glass Co. in 1891. Also found in ruby stained, add 50% to clear prices.

	Amber	Amethyst	Blue	Clear	Vaseline
Bowl, berry, 8″	48.00	60.00	50.00	25.00	42.50
Butter, cov	60.00	110.00	62.00	45.00	60.00
Cake Stand	50.00	75.00	60.00	40.00	68.00
Celery Vase	35.00	60.00	40.00	30.00	38.00
Compote					
Cov, hs, 8″	80.00	125.00	100.00	70.00	90.00
Open, hs, 9½″ . . .	50.00	85.00	65.00	55.00	—
Open, ls, 7″	45.00	80.00	35.00	25.00	48.00
Open, jelly	—	—	—	25.00	—
Creamer					
Flat, sq	50.00	82.00	—	35.00	48.00
Tall	45.00	80.00	50.00	30.00	45.00
Cruet, os	80.00	—	—	45.00	—
Goblet	48.00	70.00	50.00	40.00	60.00
Lamp, 12¾″ h	—	—	185.00	—	—
Pitcher, water	75.00	110.00	75.00	60.00	100.00
Relish, fish shape . .	40.00	50.00	50.00	—	45.00
Salt, boat shape . . .	20.00	30.00	24.00	15.00	24.00
Sauce					
Flat	16.00	30.00	20.00	12.00	16.00
Footed	18.00	35.00	22.00	15.00	20.00
Spooner	40.00	65.00	50.00	35.00	45.00
Sugar, cov	70.00	100.00	60.00	50.00	60.00
Tumbler	32.50	40.00	35.00	25.00	40.00
Wine	40.00	60.00	55.00	28.00	50.00

CHAIN WITH STAR

Non-flint, made by Portland Glass Co, Portland, ME, and U. S. Glass Co., c1890.

	Clear		Clear
Bread Plate, 11″, handles . .	30.00	Pickle, oval	12.50
Butter, cov	35.00	Pitcher, water	55.00
Cake Stand		Plate, 7″	25.00
8¾″	30.00	Relish	10.00
10½″	35.00	Salt Shaker	25.00
Compote		Sauce	
Cov, hs	50.00	Flat	10.00
Cov, ls	45.00	Footed	12.00
Open, hs	30.00	Spooner	24.00
Open, ls	30.00	Sugar, cov	35.00
Creamer	25.00	Syrup	45.00
Goblet	25.00	Wine	25.00

CHANDELIER (Crown Jewel)

Non-flint, O'Hara Glass Co., Pittsburgh, PA, c1880, continued by U. S. Glass Co. Also attributed to Canadian manufacturer. Sauce bowls made in amber, $35.00.

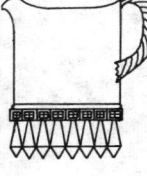

	Etched	Plain		Etched	Plain
Banana Stand	—	100.00	Celery Vase	40.00	40.00
Bowl, 8″ d, 3¼″ h . .	35.00	37.50	Compote		
Butter, cov	85.00	65.00	Cov, hs	80.00	75.00
Cake Stand, 10″ . . .	85.00	65.00	Open, hs, 9½″ . . .	70.00	68.00

	Etched	Plain		Etched	Plain
Creamer	60.00	45.00	Sauce, flat	—	15.00
Finger Bowl	40.00	30.00	Sponge Dish	—	30.00
Goblet	60.00	65.00	Spooner	30.00	35.00
Inkwell, dated hard			Sugar, cov	75.00	85.00
rubber top	—	85.00	Sugar Shaker	125.00	110.00
Pitcher, water	125.00	115.00	Tray, water	70.00	50.00
Salt, Master	—	40.00	Tumbler	45.00	35.00
Salt & Pepper	75.00	65.00	Violet Bowl	—	40.00

CHECKERBOARD (Bridal Rosette)

Made by Westmoreland Glass Co., early 1900s. Reproduced since the 1950s in milk glass and in recent years with pink stain. The Cambridge "Ribbon" pattern, usually marked Nearcut, is similar.

	Clear		Clear
Bowl, 9", shallow	20.00	Plate	
Butter, cov	40.00	7"	15.00
Celery Tray	20.00	10"	20.00
Celery Vase	30.00	Punch Cup	5.00
Compote, open, ls, 8"	25.00	Salt and Pepper	40.00
Creamer	25.00	Sauce, flat	5.00
Cruet, os	40.00	Spooner	20.00
Cup	8.00	Sugar, cov	35.00
Goblet	28.00	Tumbler	
Honey, cov, sq, pedestal	45.00	Iced Tea	15.00
Pitcher		Water	18.00
Milk	40.00	Wine	18.00
Water	35.00		

COLORADO (Lacy Medallion)

Non-flint States pattern made by U. S. Glass Co. in 1898. Made in amethyst stained, ruby stained, and opaque white with enamel floral trim, all of which are scarce. Some pieces found with ornate silver frames or feet. Purists consider these two are separate patterns, with the Lacy Medallion restricted to souvenir pieces. Reproductions have been made.

	Blue	Clear	Green
Banana Stand	45.00	25.00	40.00
Bowl			
6"	35.00	25.00	30.00
7½", ftd	40.00	25.00	35.00
8½", ftd	65.00	45.00	60.00
Butter, cov	200.00	60.00	125.00
Cake Stand	70.00	55.00	65.00
Celery Vase	65.00	35.00	75.00
Compote			
Open, ls, 6"	45.00	20.00	42.00
Open, ls, 9¼"	95.00	35.00	65.00
Creamer			
Individual	45.00	30.00	40.00
Regular	95.00	45.00	70.00
Mug	40.00	20.00	30.00

	Blue	Clear	Green
Nappy	40.00	20.00	35.00
Pitcher			
Milk	145.00	—	100.00
Water	375.00	125.00	185.00
Plate			
6"	50.00	18.00	45.00
8"	65.00	20.00	60.00
Punch Cup	30.00	18.00	25.00
Salt Shaker	65.00	30.00	40.00
Sauce, ruffled	30.00	15.00	25.00
Sherbet	50.00	25.00	45.00
Spooner	65.00	40.00	60.00
Sugar			
Cov, regular	75.00	60.00	70.00
Open, individual	35.00	24.00	30.00
Toothpick	60.00	30.00	45.00
Tray, Calling Card	45.00	25.00	35.00
Tumbler	35.00	18.00	30.00
Vase, 12"	85.00	35.00	60.00
Violet Bowl	60.00	—	—
Wine	—	25.00	40.00

COMET

Flint made by Boston and Sandwich Glass Co in the late 1840s and early 1850s.

	Clear		Clear
Butter, cov	200.00	Pitcher, water	500.00
Compote, open, ls	140.00	Spooner	95.00
Creamer	175.00	Sugar, cov	175.00
Goblet	135.00	Tumbler	110.00
Mug	135.00	Whiskey	165.00

CONNECTICUT

Non-flint. One of the States patterns made by U. S. Glass Co., c1900. Found in plain and engraved. Two varieties of ruby stained toothpicks ($90.00) have been identified.

	Clear		Clear
Biscuit Jar	25.00	Dish, 8", oblong	20.00
Bowl		Lamp, enamel dec	85.00
4"	10.00	Lemonade, handled	20.00
8"	15.00	Pitcher, water	40.00
Butter, cov	35.00	Relish	12.00
Cake Stand	40.00	Salt & Pepper	35.00
Celery Tray	20.00	Spooner	25.00
Celery Vase	25.00	Sugar, cov	35.00
Compote		Sugar Shaker	35.00
Cov, hs	40.00	Toothpick	40.00
Open, hs, 7"	25.00	Tumbler, water	18.00
Creamer	28.00	Wine	35.00

CORDOVA

Non-flint made by the O'Hara Glass Co., Pittsburgh, Pa. It was exhibited for the first time at the Pittsburgh Glass Show, December 16, 1890. Toothpick has been found in ruby stained, valued at $35.00.

	Clear	Emerald Green		Clear	Emerald Green
Bowl, Berry, cov . . .	30.00	—	Punch Bowl	87.50	—
Butter, cov, handled	50.00	—	Punch Cup	15.00	30.00
Cake Stand	45.00	—	Nappy, handled, 6"d	12.00	—
Celery Vase	45.00	—	Salt Shaker.	20.00	—
Cologne Bottle	20.00	—	Spooner.	35.00	45.00
Compote			Sugar, cov	40.00	80.00
Cov, hs	40.00	—	Syrup	125.00	40.00
Open, hs.	35.00	—	Toothpick	20.00	27.50
Creamer.	35.00	45.00	Tumbler	18.00	—
Finger Bowl	16.00	—	Vase	12.00	—
Inkwell, metal lid . . .	80.00	—			
Mug, handled	17.50	30.00			
Pitcher					
Milk.	30.00	—			
Water	48.00	—			

CROESUS

Made in clear by Riverside Glass Works, Wheeling, WV, in 1897. Produced in amethyst and green by McKee Glass in 1899. Some pieces trimmed in gold; prices are for examples with gold in very good condition. Reproduced.

	Amethyst	Clear	Green
Bowl			
4", ftd	65.00	10.00	30.00
6¼", ftd	200.00	65.00	115.00
8", flat	165.00	—	120.00
8", ftd	115.00	25.00	115.00
8", ftd, cov	145.00	35.00	115.00
10", ftd	165.00	—	120.00
* Butter, cov	175.00	85.00	170.00
Cake Stand, 10" . . .	175.00	40.00	140.00
Celery Vase	275.00	65.00	135.00
Compote			
Cov, hs, 5".	115.00	28.00	115.00
Cov, hs, 6".	115.00	28.00	115.00
Cov, hs, 7".	135.00	30.00	125.00
Open, hs, 5"	65.00	18.00	60.00
Open, hs, 6"	75.00	18.00	60.00
Open, hs, 7"	80.00	20.00	75.00
Compote, jelly.	225.00	20.00	185.00
Condiment Set (cruet, salt & pepper on small tray). . . .	225.00	185.00	185.00
Creamer			
Individual.	185.00	60.00	100.00
Regular.	150.00	55.00	120.00
Cruet, os	325.00	135.00	185.00
Pitcher, water	350.00	80.00	235.00
Plate, 8", ftd	75.00	20.00	65.00

	Amethyst	Clear	Green
Relish, boat shaped	70.00	30.00	60.00
Salt & Pepper	135.00	40.00	125.00
Sauce			
Flat	40.00	15.00	37.50
Footed	45.00	18.00	40.00
Spooner	80.00	60.00	70.00
Sugar, cov	175.00	85.00	150.00
*Toothpick	100.00	25.00	85.00
Tray, condiment . . .	75.00	25.00	30.00
*Tumbler	65.00	20.00	50.00

CRYSTAL WEDDING

Non-flint made by Adams Glass Co., Pittsburgh, PA, in the late 1880s and U. S. Glass Co. in 1891. Also found in frosted, amber stained, and cobalt blue (rare). Heavily reproduced in clear, ruby stained, and milk with enamel trim.

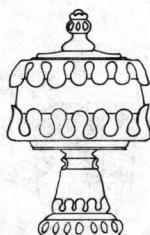

	Clear	Ruby Stained		Clear	Ruby Stained
Banana Stand	95.00	—	Pitcher		
Bowl			Milk, round	110.00	125.00
4½", ind berry . . .	15.00	—	Milk, sq	125.00	200.00
6", sq, cov	65.00	75.00	Water, round	110.00	210.00
7", sq, cov	75.00	85.00	Water, sq	165.00	225.00
8", sq, master			Plate, 10"	25.00	40.00
berry	50.00	85.00	Relish.	20.00	40.00
8", sq, cov	60.00	95.00	Salt		
Butter, cov	75.00	125.00	Individual.	25.00	40.00
Cake Plate, sq	45.00	85.00	Master	35.00	65.00
Cake Stand, 10" . . .	65.00	—	Salt Shaker.	65.00	75.00
Celery Vase	45.00	75.00	Sauce	15.00	20.00
Compote			Spooner	30.00	60.00
Cov, hs, 7 x 13" . .	100.00	110.00	Sugar, cov	70.00	85.00
Open, hs, 7", sq . .	60.00	65.00	Syrup	150.00	200.00
Open, ls, 5", sq . .	50.00	55.00	Tumbler	35.00	45.00
Creamer.	50.00	75.00	Vase		
Cruet	125.00	200.00	Footed, twisted . .	25.00	—
Goblet	55.00	85.00	Swung	25.00	—
Nappy, handle	25.00	—	Wine	45.00	70.00
Pickle.	25.00	40.00			

CUPID AND VENUS

Non-flint made by Richards and Hartley Glass Co., Tarentum, PA, in the late 1870s. Also made in vaseline, rare.

	Amber	Clear		Amber	Clear
Bowl			Butter, cov	—	55.00
8", cov, ftd	—	35.00	Cake Plate	—	45.00
9", oval	—	32.00	Cake Stand	—	60.00
Bread Plate	75.00	40.00	Celery Vase	—	40.00

	Amber	Clear		Amber	Clear
Champagne	—	90.00	Medium, 2½"....	—	35.00
Compote			Large, 3½".....	—	40.00
Cov, hs, 8".....	—	100.00	Pitcher		
Cov, ls, 7"......	—	90.00	Milk.........	175.00	75.00
Cov, ls, 9"......	—	100.00	Water	195.00	65.00
Open, ls, 8½", scalloped.....	135.00	35.00	Plate, 10", round...	75.00	40.00
Open, hs, 9¼"...	—	45.00	Sauce		
Cordial, 3½"......	—	85.00	Flat........	—	10.00
Creamer.........	—	36.50	Footed, 3½", 4" and 4½"......	—	15.00
Cruet, os	—	135.00	Spooner........	—	35.00
Goblet	—	75.00	Sugar, cov	—	65.00
Marmalade Jar, cov	—	85.00	Wine, 3¾"........	—	85.00
Mug					
Miniature.......	—	40.00			

CURRIER AND IVES

Non-flint made by Bellaire Glass Co. in Findlay, OH, in 1890. Known to have been made in colors, but rarely found. A decanter is known in ruby stained.

	Clear		Clear
Bowl, oval, 10", canoe shaped	30.00	Plate, 10"	20.00
		Relish..............	18.00
Butter, cov	50.00	Salt Shaker..........	30.00
Compote		Sauce, oval	12.00
Cov, hs, 7½"	95.00	Spooner.............	30.00
Open, hs, 7½", scalloped	50.00	Sugar, cov	45.00
Creamer..............	30.00	Syrup...............	75.00
Cup and saucer	30.00	Tray	
Decanter.............	35.00	Water, Balky Mule	65.00
Dish, oval, boat shaped, 8"	27.50	Wine, Balky Mule.......	50.00
Goblet, knob stem........	25.00	Tumbler.............	45.00
Lamp, 9½", hs	75.00	Water Bottle, 12" h, os.....	55.00
Pitcher		Wine, 3¼"............	18.00
Milk.................	65.00		
Water	70.00		

DAHLIA

Non-flint, made by Portland Glass Co, Portland, ME, c1865, and Canton Glass Co., c1880. Also attributed to a Canadian manufacturer.

	Amber	Apple Green	Blue	Clear	Vaseline
Bowl............	30.00	25.00	25.00	18.00	30.00
Bread Plate	55.00	50.00	60.00	45.00	55.00
Butter, cov	80.00	70.00	85.00	40.00	80.00
Cake Plate	60.00	45.00	60.00	24.00	60.00
Cake Stand, 9"	72.50	50.00	50.00	25.00	72.50
Champagne	65.00	85.00	75.00	55.00	75.00
Compote					
Cov, hs, 7"......	100.00	85.00	85.00	55.00	80.00
Open, hs, 8"	60.00	45.00	45.00	30.00	60.00

	Amber	Apple Green	Blue	Clear	Vaseline
Cordial	55.00	50.00	50.00	35.00	55.00
Creamer	40.00	35.00	35.00	25.00	40.00
Egg Cup					
Double	80.00	65.00	65.00	50.00	80.00
Single	55.00	40.00	40.00	25.00	55.00
Goblet	55.00	85.00	75.00	40.00	65.00
Mug					
Large	55.00	55.00	55.00	35.00	55.00
Small	50.00	45.00	40.00	30.00	50.00
Pickle	35.00	30.00	30.00	20.00	35.00
Pitcher					
Milk	70.00	55.00	55.00	50.00	70.00
Water	100.00	90.00	90.00	55.00	90.00
Plate					
7″	45.00	40.00	40.00	20.00	45.00
9″, handles	35.00	45.00	50.00	18.00	50.00
Platter	50.00	45.00	45.00	30.00	50.00
Relish, 9½″ l	20.00	20.00	20.00	15.00	25.00
Salt, ind, ftd	35.00	30.00	30.00	5.00	35.00
Sauce					
Flat	15.00	12.00	15.00	10.00	15.00
Footed	20.00	15.00	15.00	10.00	20.00
Spooner	50.00	45.00	50.00	35.00	50.00
Sugar, cov	75.00	60.00	60.00	40.00	75.00
Syrup	75.00	—	—	55.00	—
Wine	45.00	40.00	45.00	25.00	45.00

DAISY AND BUTTON

Non-flint pattern made in the 1870s by several companies in many different forms. In continuous production since inception. Also found in amberina, amber stain, and ruby stained.

	Amber	Apple Green	Blue	Clear	Vaseline
Bowl, triangular	40.00	45.00	45.00	25.00	65.00
Bread Plate, 13″ . . .	35.00	60.00	35.00	20.00	40.00
Butter, cov					
Round	70.00	90.00	70.00	65.00	95.00
Square	110.00	115.00	110.00	100.00	120.00
Butter Pat	30.00	40.00	35.00	25.00	35.00
Canoe					
4″	12.00	24.00	15.00	10.00	24.00
8½″	30.00	35.00	30.00	25.00	35.00
12″	60.00	35.00	28.00	20.00	40.00
14″	30.00	40.00	35.00	25.00	40.00
Castor Set					
4 bottle, glass std	90.00	85.00	95.00	80.00	75.00
5 bottle, metal std	105.00	100.00	110.00	100.00	95.00
Celery Vase	48.00	55.00	40.00	30.00	55.00
Compote					
Cov, hs, 6″	35.00	50.00	45.00	25.00	50.00
Open, hs, 8″	75.00	65.00	60.00	40.00	65.00
Creamer	35.00	40.00	40.00	18.00	35.00
Cruet, os	100.00	80.00	75.00	45.00	80.00
Egg Cup	20.00	30.00	25.00	15.00	30.00

	Amber	Apple Green	Blue	Clear	Vaseline
Finger Bowl	30.00	50.00	35.00	30.00	42.00
Goblet	40.00	50.00	40.00	25.00	40.00
Hat, 2½"	30.00	35.00	40.00	20.00	40.00
Ice Tub	—	—	—	—	75.00
Inkwell	40.00	50.00	45.00	30.00	45.00
Parfait	25.00	35.00	30.00	20.00	35.00
Pickle Castor	125.00	90.00	150.00	75.00	150.00
Pitcher, water					
Bulbous, reed					
handle	125.00	95.00	90.00	75.00	90.00
Tankard	62.00	65.00	62.00	60.00	65.00
Plate					
5", leaf shape . . .	20.00	24.00	16.00	18.00	25.00
6", round	10.00	22.00	15.00	6.50	24.00
7", square	24.00	35.00	25.00	15.00	35.00
Punch Bowl, stand	90.00	100.00	95.00	85.00	100.00
Salt & Pepper	30.00	40.00	30.00	20.00	35.00
Sauce, 4"	18.00	25.00	18.00	15.00	25.00
Slipper					
5"	45.00	48.00	50.00	45.00	50.00
11½"	40.00	50.00	30.00	35.00	50.00
Spooner	40.00	40.00	45.00	35.00	45.00
Sugar, cov	45.00	50.00	45.00	35.00	50.00
Syrup	45.00	50.00	45.00	30.00	45.00
Toothpick					
Round	40.00	55.00	25.00	40.00	45.00
Urn	25.00	30.00	25.00	15.00	30.00
Tray	65.00	65.00	60.00	35.00	60.00
Tumbler	18.00	30.00	35.00	15.00	25.00
Vase, wall pocket . .	125.00	—	—	—	—
Wine	15.00	25.00	20.00	10.00	45.00

DAISY AND BUTTON WITH CROSSBARS (Mikado)

Non-flint pattern made by Richards and Hartley, Tarentum, PA, c1888.

	Amber	Blue	Clear	Vaseline
Bowl				
6"	20.00	30.00	15.00	25.00
9"	40.00	40.00	25.00	35.00
Bread Plate	30.00	45.00	25.00	35.00
Butter, cov				
Flat	55.00	55.00	45.00	55.00
Footed	—	75.00	25.00	60.00
Celery Vase	36.00	40.00	30.00	50.00
Compote				
Cov, hs, 8"	55.00	65.00	45.00	55.00
Open, hs, 8"	45.00	50.00	30.00	45.00
Open, ls, 7"	30.00	—	20.00	45.00
Creamer				
Individual	25.00	30.00	18.00	30.00
Regular	42.50	45.00	35.00	40.00
Cruet, os	75.00	85.00	35.00	100.00
Goblet	40.00	40.00	25.00	48.00
Mug, 3" h	15.00	18.00	12.50	20.00

	Amber	Blue	Clear	Vaseline
Pitcher				
Milk.	65.00	80.00	45.00	90.00
Water	95.00	85.00	65.00	125.00
Salt & Pepper	40.00	50.00	30.00	45.00
Sauce				
Flat.	15.00	18.00	10.00	15.00
Footed	18.00	25.00	15.00	24.00
Spooner	35.00	35.00	25.00	35.00
Sugar, cov				
Individual.	25.00	35.00	10.00	25.00
Regular.	50.00	60.00	25.00	55.00
Syrup.	100.00	125.00	65.00	125.00
Toothpick	40.00	40.00	28.00	35.00
Tumbler	20.00	25.00	18.00	25.00
Wine	30.00	35.00	25.00	30.00

DAISY AND BUTTON WITH V ORNAMENT (Van Dyke)

Made by A. J. Beatty & Co., 1886–1887.

	Amber	Blue	Clear	Vaseline
Bowl				
9″	30.00	40.00	25.00	35.00
10″	30.00	40.00	25.00	35.00
Butter, cov	75.00	95.00	65.00	85.00
Celery Vase	50.00	55.00	30.00	55.00
Creamer.	30.00	50.00	30.00	50.00
Finger Bowl	28.50	45.00	22.50	55.00
Goblet	35.00	45.00	25.00	50.00
Mug	20.00	30.00	20.00	35.00
Pickle Castor	120.00	120.00	85.00	100.00
Pitcher, water	65.00	90.00	48.00	60.00
Punch Cup	12.00	20.00	12.50	25.00
Sauce, flat	20.00	20.00	12.00	30.00
Spooner	40.00	38.50	35.00	45.00
Sugar, cov	50.00	75.00	45.00	65.00
Toothpick	32.50	40.00	28.50	35.00
Tray, water	55.00	65.00	35.00	55.00
Tumbler	25.00	28.00	15.00	35.00

DAKOTA (Baby Thumbprint, Thumbprint Band)

Non-flint made by Ripley and Co., Pittsburgh, PA, in the late 1880s and early 1890s. Later reissued by U. S. Glass Co. as one of the States patterns. Prices listed are for etched fern and berry pattern; also found with fern and no berry, and oak leaf etching, and scarcer grape etching. Other etchings known include fish, swan, peacock, bird and insect, bird and flowers, ivy and berry, stag, spider and insect in web, buzzard on dead tree, and crane catching fish. Sometimes ruby stained with or without souvenir markings. There is a four piece table set available in a "hotel" variant, prices are about 20% more than the regular type.

	Clear Etched	Clear Plain	Ruby Stained
Basket, 10 x 2″	250.00	225.00	275.00
Bottle, 5½″	45.00	35.00	—

	Clear Etched	Clear Plain	Ruby Stained
Bowl, berry	45.00	30.00	—
Butter, cov	65.00	40.00	125.00
Cake Cover, 8″	300.00	200.00	—
Cake Stand			
9½″.	58.00	35.00	—
10½″.	65.00	45.00	—
Celery Tray	35.00	25.00	—
Celery Vase	40.00	30.00	—
Compote			
Cov, hs, 5″	60.00	—	—
Cov, hs, 7″	65.00	—	—
Cov, hs, 8″	75.00	—	—
Cov, hs, 9″	75.00	—	—
Cov, hs, 12″	95.00	75.00	—
Cov, 6″, jelly	65.00	50.00	—
Open, hs, 7″	55.00	40.00	—
Open, hs, 10″ . . .	75.00	60.00	—
Condiment Tray . . .	—	72.00	—
Creamer.	55.00	30.00	60.00
Cruet	90.00	55.00	135.00
Goblet	35.00	28.00	75.00
Pitcher			
Milk.	100.00	80.00	200.00
Tankard	125.00	95.00	225.00
Water	95.00	75.00	190.00
Plate, 10″	85.00	—	—
Salt Shaker.	65.00	50.00	125.00
Sauce			
Flat.	20.00	18.00	—
Footed	25.00	20.00	—
Spooner	30.00	25.00	65.00
Sugar, cov	65.00	55.00	85.00
Tray, water	100.00	75.00	—
Tumbler	35.00	30.00	55.00
Waste Bowl.	75.00	45.00	—
Wine	30.00	20.00	55.00

DEER AND PINE TREE (Deer and Doe)

Non-flint pattern, made by Belmont Glass Co., and McKee Glass Co. 1883. Souvenir mugs with gilt found in clear and olive green. Also made in canary (vaseline). The goblet has been reproduced.

	Amber	Apple Green	Blue	Clear
Bread Plate	100.00	125.00	125.00	75.00
Butter, cov	125.00	425.00	125.00	95.00
Cake Stand	—	—	—	75.00
Celery Vase	—	—	—	75.00
Compote				
Cov, hs, 8″, sq . . .	—	—	—	100.00
Open, hs, 7″	—	—	—	45.00
Open, hs, 9″	—	—	—	55.00
Creamer.	95.00	85.00	90.00	65.00

	Amber	Apple Green	Blue	Clear
Finger Bowl	—	—	—	55.00
* Goblet	—	—	—	55.00
Marmalade Jar	—	—	—	90.00
Mug	40.00	45.00	50.00	40.00
Pickle	—	—	—	24.00
Pitcher				
Milk	—	—	—	90.00
Water	125.00	125.00	125.00	125.00
Platter, 8 x 13"	—	—	80.00	60.00
Sauce				
Flat	—	—	—	18.50
Footed	—	—	—	25.00
Spooner	—	—	—	65.00
Sugar, cov	—	—	—	85.00
Tray, water	100.00	—	90.00	60.00

DELAWARE (Four Petal Flower)

Non-flint pattern made by U. S. Glass Co. c1899. Also found in amethyst (scarce), clear with rose trim, custard, and milk glass. Prices are for pieces with perfect gold trim.

	Clear	Green w/gold	Rose w/gold
Banana Bowl	50.00	55.00	65.00
Bowl			
8"	30.00	40.00	50.00
9"	25.00	60.00	75.00
Bottle, os	90.00	150.00	185.00
Bride's Basket, SP frame	—	115.00	165.00
Butter, cov	60.00	115.00	150.00
Claret Jug, tankard shape	110.00	195.00	200.00
Celery Vase, flat . . .	75.00	90.00	95.00
Creamer	45.00	65.00	70.00
Cruet, os	90.00	200.00	250.00
Finger Bowl	25.00	50.00	75.00
Lamp Shade, round .	—	—	75.00
Pin Tray	30.00	55.00	95.00
Pitcher, water	50.00	150.00	125.00
Pomade Box, jeweled	—	250.00	350.00
Puff Box, bulbous, jeweled	—	200.00	315.00
Punch Cup	18.00	30.00	35.00
Sauce, 5½", boat . .	15.00	35.00	30.00
Spooner	45.00	50.00	55.00
Sugar, cov	65.00	85.00	100.00
Toothpick	40.00	125.00	150.00
Tumbler	20.00	40.00	45.00
Vase			
6"	—	45.00	70.00
8"	—	55.00	75.00
9½"	—	80.00	85.00

DIAMOND POINT

Flint, originally made by Boston and Sandwich Glass Co., in the 1830-1840 period, and by the New England Glass Co. Many other companies manufactured this pattern throughout the 19th century.

	Flint	Non-Flint		Flint	Non-Flint
Bowl			Egg Cup	40.00	20.00
7", cov	60.00	20.00	Goblet	45.00	35.00
8", cov	60.00	20.00	Honey	15.00	—
8", open	45.00	15.00	Mustard, cov	28.50	—
Butter, cov	95.00	50.00	Pitcher		
Cake Stand, 14"	185.00	—	Pint	185.00	—
Candlesticks, pr	145.00	—	Quart	275.00	—
Celery Vase	75.00	30.00	Plate		
Champagne	85.00	—	6"	30.00	—
Claret	90.00	—	8"	50.00	—
Compote			Salt, master, cov	75.00	—
Cov, hs, 8"	135.00	—	Sauce, flat	14.00	—
Open, hs 10½", flared	100.00	—	Spillholder	45.00	—
Open, hs, 11", scalloped rim	110.00	—	Spooner	45.00	25.00
Open, ls, 7½"	50.00	40.00	Sugar, cov	65.00	—
Cordial	165.00	—	Syrup	150.00	—
Creamer, ah	115.00	—	Tumbler, bar	65.00	35.00
Decanter, qt, os	165.00	—	Whiskey, ah	85.00	—
			Wine	75.00	30.00

DIAMOND THUMBPRINT

Flint, attributed to Boston and Sandwich Glass Co., and other factories from 1840 to 1850s. Compotes are being reproduced for Sandwich Glass Museum.

	Clear		Clear
Bitters Bottle, orig pewter pourer, applied lip, polished pontil	450.00	Finger Bowl	100.00
		* Goblet	350.00
Butter, cov	200.00	Honey Dish	25.00
Celery Vase, scalloped top	185.00	Pitcher, water	650.00
Champagne	285.00	Sauce, flat	25.00
Compote		* Spooner	85.00
Cov, hs, 8"	150.00	* Sugar, cov	150.00
Open, ls, scalloped, 8"	50.00	Tumbler, bar	125.00
Cordial	325.00	Whiskey, ah	300.00
Creamer	225.00	* Wine	250.00
Decanter			
Pint, ns	175.00		
Quart, os	225.00		

EGG IN SAND (Bean)

Non-flint, c1880. Has been reported in colors, but rare.

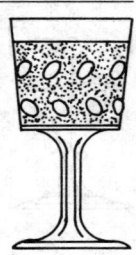

	Clear			Clear
Bread Plate, octagonal	25.00		Salt and Pepper	65.00
Butter, cov	40.00		Sauce	5.00
Compote, cov, jelly	45.00		Spooner, flat rim	30.00
Creamer................	30.00		Sugar, cov	35.00
Dish, swan center	40.00		Tray, water	40.00
Goblet	35.00		Tumbler	33.00
Pitcher, water	45.00		Wine	35.00
Relish.	12.00			

EMPRESS

Made by Riverside Glass Works, Wellsburg, WV, c1898. Also found in amethyst (rare). Clear and emerald green pieces trimmed in gold; prices are for pieces with gold in very good condition.

	Clear	Emerald Green		Clear	Emerald Green
Bowl, 8½″........	—	45.00	Pitcher, water	65.00	150.00
Breakfast Set, ind creamer and			Punch Cup, ftd	20.00	35.00
			Salt Shaker.......	30.00	50.00
sugar	40.00	85.00	Spooner	40.00	70.00
Butter, cov	50.00	100.00	Sugar, cov	45.00	125.00
Celery Vase	55.00	—	Sugar Shaker	55.00	110.00
Creamer.........	40.00	80.00	Syrup...........	60.00	350.00
Cruet	50.00	175.00	Toothpick	—	150.00
Oil Lamp, atypical ..	60.00	225.00	Tumbler	32.50	55.00

ESTHER (Tooth and Claw)

Non-flint made by Riverside Glass Works, Wellsburg, WV, c1896. The green has gold trim. Also found in ruby stained and amber stained with enamel decoration.

	Clear	Green	Ruby Stained
Bowl, 8″	25.00	50.00	—
Butter, cov	65.00	100.00	150.00
Cake Stand, 10½″..	60.00	80.00	—
Celery Vase	40.00	90.00	—
Compote, jelly, hs ..	30.00	75.00	—
Cracker Jar.......	—	—	200.00
Creamer.........	45.00	70.00	75.00
Cruet, os	45.00	245.00	—
Goblet	40.00	95.00	75.00
Pitcher, water	65.00	165.00	250.00
Plate, 10″	—	60.00	—
Relish...........	20.00	25.00	40.00
Salt & Pepper.....	50.00	100.00	—
Spooner.........	35.00	50.00	60.00
Sugar, cov	55.00	70.00	100.00
Syrup...........	—	200.00	—
Toothpick	48.00	85.00	—
Tumbler	25.00	48.50	55.00
Wine	35.00	—	—

EXCELSIOR

Flint made by several firms, including Sandwich and McKee, from 1850s-1860s. Quality and design vary. Prices are for high quality flint.

	Clear		Clear
Bar Bottle	85.00	Goblet, Maltese Cross	50.00
Bowl, 10", open	125.00	Lamp, hand	95.00
Bitters bottle	95.00	Mug	30.00
Butter, cov	100.00	Pickle Jar, cov	45.00
Candlestick	125.00	Pitcher, water	350.00
Celery Vase, scalloped top	85.00	Salt, master	30.00
Champagne	60.00	Spillholder	75.00
Claret	45.00	Spooner	60.00
Compote		Sugar, cov	90.00
Cov, ls	125.00	Syrup	125.00
Open, hs	85.00	Tumbler, bar	50.00
Cordial	40.00	Whiskey, Maltese Cross	65.00
Creamer	85.00	Wine	45.00
Egg Cup			
Double	55.00		
Single	40.00		

EYEWINKER

Non-flint made in Findlay, OH, in 1889. Reportedly made by Dalzell, Gilmore and Leighton Glass Co., who were organized in 1883 in West Virginia, moved to Findlay in 1888. Made only in clear glass; colors have been reproduced. A goblet and toothpick were not originally made in this pattern.

	Clear		Clear
Banana Stand, hs	135.00	Lamp, kerosene	125.00
Bowl		Nappy, folded sides, 7¼"	30.00
6½"	25.00	Pitcher, water	95.00
9", cov	75.00	Plate	
* Butter, cov	70.00	7"	30.00
Cake Stand, 8"	55.00	9", sq, upturned sides	65.00
Celery Vase	45.00	10", upturned sides	85.00
Compote		Salt Shaker	35.00
Cov, hs, 6½"	60.00	Spooner	35.00
Cov, hs, 9½"	90.00	Sauce	15.00
Open, 7¼", fluted	65.00	Sugar, cov	55.00
Open, 4½", jelly	45.00	Syrup, pewter top	125.00
Creamer	65.00	Tumbler	45.00
Cruet	65.00		

FEATHER (Doric)

Non-flint made in Indiana in 1896 and by McKee Glass. Later the pattern was reissued with variations and quality differences. Also found in amber stain (rare).

	Clear	Emerald Green
Banana Boat, ftd . . .	75.00	175.00
Bowl, oval		
8½"	25.00	—
9¼"	18.00	75.00
Bowl, round		
4"	15.00	—
4½"	15.00	—
6"	20.00	—
7"	25.00	75.00
8"	30.00	85.00
Bowl, sq		
4½"	15.00	—
8"	30.00	—
Butter, cov	55.00	150.00
Cake Plate	65.00	—
Cake Stand		
8"	40.00	125.00
9½"	50.00	125.00
11"	70.00	175.00
Celery Vase	35.00	85.00
Champagne	65.00	—
Compote		
Cov, hs, 8½"	125.00	250.00
Cov, ls, 4¼", jelly	100.00	150.00
Cov, ls, 8¼"	150.00	—
Open, ls, 4"	15.00	—

	Clear	Emerald Green
Open, ls, 6"	20.00	—
Open, ls, 7"	30.00	—
Open, ls, 8"	35.00	—
Cordial	125.00	—
Creamer.	40.00	85.00
Cruet, os	45.00	250.00
Dishes, nest of 3: 7", 8", and 9"	40.00	—
Goblet	55.00	150.00
Honey Dish.	15.00	—
Marmalade Jar	125.00	—
Pickle Castor	145.00	—
Pitcher		
Milk.	50.00	165.00
Water	75.00	250.00
Plate, 10"	35.00	—
Relish.	18.00	—
Salt Shaker.	35.00	70.00
Sauce	12.00	—
Spooner.	25.00	60.00
Sugar, cov	45.00	80.00
Syrup	125.00	300.00
Toothpick	85.00	165.00
Tumbler	45.00	85.00
Wine		
Scalloped border	40.00	—
Straight border. . .	25.00	—

FINECUT

Non-flint made by Bryce Bros., Pittsburgh, PA, c1879, and by U. S. Glass Co. in 1891.

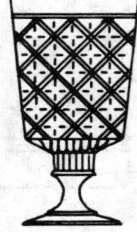

	Amber	Blue	Clear	Vaseline
Bowl, 8¼".	15.00	20.00	10.00	15.00
Bread Plate	50.00	60.00	25.00	50.00
Butter, cov	55.00	75.00	45.00	60.00
Cake Stand	—	—	35.00	—
Celery Tray.	—	45.00	25.00	40.00
Celery Vase, SP holder	—	—	—	115.00
Creamer.	38.00	40.00	35.00	75.00
Goblet	45.00	55.00	22.00	42.00
Pitcher, water	100.00	100.00	60.00	115.00
Plate				
6"	—	20.00	8.00	—
7"	25.00	40.00	15.00	20.00
10"	30.00	50.00	21.00	45.00
Relish.	15.00	25.00	10.00	20.00
Sauce, flat	14.00	15.00	10.00	14.00
Spooner.	30.00	45.00	18.00	40.00
Sugar, cov	45.00	55.00	35.00	45.00
Tray, water	50.00	55.00	25.00	50.00
Tumbler	—	—	18.00	28.00
Wine	—	—	24.00	30.00

FINECUT AND PANEL

Non-flint pattern made by many Pittsburgh factories in the 1880s. Reissued in the early 1890s by U. S. Glass Co. An aqua wine is known.

	Amber	Blue	Clear	Vaseline
Bowl				
7"	28.00	35.00	15.00	30.00
8", oval	40.00	—	18.00	30.00
Bread Plate	50.00	45.00	30.00	—
Butter, cov	65.00	75.00	40.00	60.00
Cake Stand, 10" . . .	50.00	75.00	30.00	50.00
Compote				
Cov, hs	125.00	135.00	75.00	130.00
Open, hs	65.00	65.00	35.00	60.00
Creamer	35.00	50.00	25.00	40.00
Goblet	40.00	48.00	20.00	35.00
Pitcher				
Milk	65.00	—	—	50.00
Water	85.00	85.00	40.00	45.00
Plate				
6"	25.00	30.00	15.00	25.00
7¼"	25.00	30.00	15.00	25.00
Platter	30.00	50.00	25.00	30.00
Relish	20.00	25.00	15.00	20.00
Sauce, ftd	15.00	25.00	8.00	15.00
Spooner	35.00	45.00	20.00	30.00
Sugar, cov	37.50	42.50	30.00	32.50
Tray, water	60.00	55.00	50.00	60.00
Tumbler	25.00	30.00	20.00	38.00
Waste Bowl	30.00	35.00	20.00	35.00
Wine	30.00	35.00	20.00	35.00

FLAMINGO HABITAT

Maker unknown, etched pattern.

	Clear		Clear
Bowl, 10", oval	35.00	Creamer	40.00
Celery Vase	45.00	Goblet	45.00
Champagne	45.00	Sauce, ftd	15.00
Cheese Dish, blown	110.00	Spooner	25.00
Compote		Sugar, cov	50.00
Cov, 4½"	75.00	Tumbler	30.00
Cov, 6½"	95.00	Wine	42.50
Open, 5", jelly	35.00		
Open, 6"	40.00		

FLORIDA (Emerald Green Herringbone, Paneled Herringbone)

Non-flint made by U. S. Glass Co., late 1880s-1890s. One of States patterns. Reproduced in green and other colors.

	Clear	Emerald Green		Clear	Emerald Green
Berry Set	75.00	110.00	Nappy	15.00	25.00
Bowl			Pitcher, water	50.00	75.00
7¾″	20.00	25.00	Plate		
9″	20.00	25.00	7½″	12.00	18.00
Butter, cov	50.00	85.00	9¼″	15.00	25.00
Cake Stand			Relish		
Large	60.00	75.00	6″, sq	10.00	15.00
Small	30.00	40.00	8½″, sq	15.00	22.00
Celery Vase	30.00	35.00	Salt Shaker	25.00	50.00
Compote, open, hs,			Sauce	8.00	15.00
6½″, sq	—	40.00	Spooner	20.00	35.00
Creamer	30.00	45.00	Sugar, cov	32.00	50.00
Cruet, os	40.00	110.00	Syrup	60.00	175.00
* Goblet	25.00	40.00	Table set	125.00	185.00
Mustard Pot, attach-			Tumbler	20.00	30.00
ed underplate, cov	25.00	45.00	Wine	25.00	50.00

GALLOWAY

Non-flint made by U. S. Glass Co., 1904. Clear glass with and without gold trim; also known with rose stain and ruby stain.

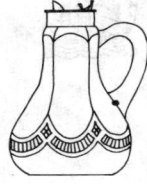

	Clear w/gold	Rose Stained		Clear w/gold	Rose Stained
Basket, no gold	75.00	—	Pitcher		
Bowl			Milk	60.00	—
6½″	25.00	—	Tankard	75.00	—
8½″, oval	25.00	—	Water, ice lip	65.00	175.00
8½″, round	25.00	—	Plate, 8″, round	40.00	65.00
9¾″	35.00	50.00	Punch Bowl	160.00	—
11″ d, 3″ h	45.00	—	Punch Bowl Plate,		
Butter, cov	65.00	125.00	20″	80.00	—
Cake Stand	65.00	90.00	Punch Cup	10.00	15.00
Carafe, water	55.00	85.00	Relish	20.00	30.00
Celery Vase	35.00	75.00	Rose Bowl	25.00	—
Champagne	65.00	—	Salt Dip	25.00	—
Compote			Salt & Pepper, pr.	35.00	—
Open, hs, 4¼″	35.00	—	Sauce		
Open, hs, 10″,			Flat	10.00	—
scalloped	85.00	—	Footed	12.00	—
Creamer	30.00	50.00	Sherbet	25.00	—
Cruet	45.00	—	Spooner	30.00	80.00
Egg Cup	35.00	—	Sugar, cov	55.00	75.00
Finger Bowl	40.00	—	Sugar Shaker	40.00	—
Goblet	80.00	—	Syrup	65.00	135.00
Lemonade	35.00	—	Toothpick	30.00	55.00
Mug	38.00	50.00	Tumbler	25.00	—
Nappy, tricorn	—	50.00	Vase, swung	30.00	—
Olive, 6″	20.00	30.00	Waste Bowl	38.00	—
Pickle Castor, sp			Water Bottle	40.00	—
holder and lid	65.00	—	Wine	45.00	—

GARFIELD DRAPE

Non-flint pattern issued in 1881 by Adams & Co., Pittsburgh, Pennsylvania, after the assassination of President Garfield.

	Clear		Clear
Bread Plate		Honey Dish.	15.00
Memorial, portrait of		Goblet	40.00
Garfield	65.00	Pitcher	
"We Mourn Our Nation's		Milk.	70.00
Loss", portrait	75.00	Water, ah.	75.00
Butter, cov	60.00	Water, strap	100.00
Cake Stand, 9½".	75.00	Relish, oval.	20.00
Celery Vase	45.00	Sauce	
Compote		Flat.	8.50
Cov, hs, 8".	100.00	Footed	12.00
Cov, ls, 6"	85.00	Spooner	35.00
Open, hs, 8½"	40.00	Sugar, cov	60.00
Creamer.	40.00	Tumbler	35.00

GEORGIA (Peacock Feather)

Probably Richards and Hartley, but reissued by several glass companies, including U. S. Glass Co. in 1902 as part of their States series. Rare in blue. (Chamber lamp, pedestal base, $275.00). No goblet known in pattern.

	Clear		Clear
Bon bon, ftd	25.00	Decanter	70.00
Bowl, 8"	25.00	Lamp	
Butter, cov	45.00	Chamber, pedestal	85.00
Cake Stand, 10"	50.00	Hand, oil, 7"	80.00
Celery Tray, 11¾"	35.00	Mug	22.50
Compote		Nappy	28.00
Cov, hs, 8".	50.00	Pitcher, water	70.00
Open, hs, 7"	30.00	Plate, 5¼".	15.00
Open, hs, 8"	42.50	Relish.	15.00
Open, ls, 10"	30.00	Salt Shaker.	40.00
Open, jelly.	20.00	Sauce	12.50
Condiment Set, tray, oil cruet,		Spooner	35.00
salt and pepper	75.00	Sugar, cov	45.00
Creamer.	35.00	Syrup, metal lid.	65.00
Cruet, os	55.00	Tumbler	35.00

HAND (Pennsylvania #2)

Made by O'Hara Glass Co., Pittsburgh, Pennsylvania, c1880. Covered pieces have a hand holding bar finial, hence the name.

	Clear		Clear
Bowl		Compote	
9"	37.50	Cov, hs, 7".	60.00
10"	40.00	Cov, hs, 8".	95.00
Butter, cov	85.00	Open, hs, 7¾"	45.00
Cake Stand	55.00	Open, ls, 9"	20.00
Celery Vase	48.00	Cordial, 3½"	85.00

	Clear		Clear
Creamer	40.00	Spooner	30.00
Goblet	45.00	Sugar, cov	75.00
Marmalade Jar, cov	90.00	Syrup	125.00
Pickle	20.00	Tumbler	85.00
Pitcher, water	75.00	Wine	55.00
Sauce			
Flat	12.00		
Footed	15.00		

HEART WITH THUMBPRINT (Bull's Eye in Heart)

Non-flint, made by Tarentum Glass Co. 1898. Some emerald green pieces have gold trim. Made experimentally in custard, blue custard, opaque nile green and cobalt. Some pieces are found with ruby stain. (Creamer $175.00)

	Clear	Emerald Green		Clear	Emerald Green
Banana Boat	75.00	—	Mustard, SP cov	95.00	100.00
Barber Bottle	115.00	—	Nappy	30.00	60.00
Bowl			Pitcher, water	200.00	—
7" sq.	35.00	—	Plate		
9"	42.00	—	6"	25.00	75.00
9½" sq	35.00	—	10"	35.00	—
10" scalloped	45.00	—	Powder Jar, SP cov	65.00	—
Butter, cov	125.00	175.00	Punch Cup	20.00	35.00
Cake Stand, 9"	150.00	—	Rose Bowl		
Carafe, water	100.00	—	Large	60.00	—
Card Tray	20.00	45.00	Small	30.00	—
Celery Vase	65.00	—	Salt & Pepper, pr.	95.00	—
Compote			Sauce, 5"	20.00	35.00
Open, hs, 7½",			Spooner	50.00	—
scalloped	150.00	—	Sugar		
Open, hs, 8½"	100.00	—	Ind	28.00	35.00
Cordial, 3" h	125.00	—	Regular, cov	85.00	90.00
Creamer			Syrup	95.00	—
Ind	30.00	45.00	Tray, 8¼" l, 4¼" w	30.00	—
Regular	60.00	110.00	Tumbler	45.00	—
Cruet	75.00	—	Vase		
Finger Bowl	45.00	—	6"	35.00	65.00
Goblet	58.00	125.00	10"	65.00	—
Hair Receiver, lid	60.00	—	Wine	45.00	—
Ice Bucket	60.00	—			
Lamp					
Finger	65.00	115.00			
Oil, 8"	50.00	160.00			

HOLLY

Non-flint made by Boston and Sandwich Glass Co., late 1860s, early 1870s.

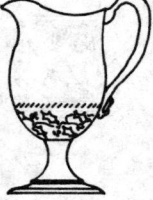

	Clear		Clear
Butter, cov	150.00	Compote, cov, hs	165.00
Cake Stand, 11"	135.00	Creamer, ah	125.00
Celery Vase	85.00	Egg Cup	65.00

	Clear		Clear
Goblet	100.00	Sauce, flat	20.00
Pitcher, water, ah	225.00	Spooner	60.00
Salt		Sugar, cov	125.00
Flat, oval	65.00	Tumbler	125.00
Ftd	60.00	Wine	125.00

HONEYCOMB

A popular pattern made in flint and non-flint glass by numerous firms, c1850–1900, resulting in many minor pattern variations. Rare in color.

	Flint	Non-Flint		Flint	Non-Flint
Ale Glass	50.00	25.00	Honey, cov	—	25.00
Barber Bottle	45.00	25.00	Lamp		
Bowl, cov, 7¼" pat'd			All Glass	—	45.00
1869, acorn finial	100.00	45.00	Marble base	—	40.00
10"	—	40.00	Lemonade	40.00	20.00
Butter, cov	65.00	45.00	Mug, half pint	25.00	15.00
Cake Stand	55.00	35.00	Pitcher, water, ah	165.00	60.00
Castor Bottle	25.00	18.00	Plate, 6"	—	12.50
Celery Vase	45.00	20.00	Pomade Jar, cov	48.00	20.00
Champagne	50.00	—	Relish	30.00	—
Claret	35.00	—	Salt, master, cov,		
Compote, cov, hs			ftd	35.00	30.00
6½" x 8½"h	100.00	50.00	Salt & Pepper	—	40.00
9¼ x 11½"h	110.00	65.00	Sauce	12.00	7.50
Compote, open, hs			Spillholder	24.00	—
7 x 5"h	35.00	25.00	Spooner	65.00	35.00
7 x 7"h	60.00	40.00	Sugar		
7½", scalloped	42.00	—	Frosted rosebud		
8 x 6¼"h	65.00	—	finial	—	50.00
11 x 8"h	135.00	—	Regular	75.00	45.00
Compote, open, ls,			Tumbler		
7½", scalloped	40.00	—	Bar	35.00	—
Cordial, 3½"	25.00	—	Flat	—	12.50
Creamer, ah	35.00	20.00	Footed	—	15.00
Decanter			Vase		
Pint	55.00	18.50	7½"	45.00	—
Quart, os	70.00	65.00	10½"	75.00	—
Egg Cup	20.00	15.00	Whiskey, handled	125.00	—
Finger Bowl	48.00	—	Wine	35.00	15.00
Goblet	25.00	15.00			

HORN OF PLENTY

A fine flint glass pattern reputed to have been first made by Boston and Sandwich Glass Co. in the 1850s. Later made in flint and non-flint by other firms.

	Clear Flint		Clear Flint
Bar Bottle, pewter spout, 8"	135.00	Shape of Acorn	130.00
Bowl, 8½"	145.00	Butter Pat	20.00
Butter, cov		Cake Stand	350.00
Conventional finial	125.00	Celery Vase	150.00

	Clear Flint		Clear Flint
Champagne	145.00	Mug, small, applied handle	150.00
Compote		Pepper Sauce Bottle, pewter	
Cov, hs, 6¼"	175.00	top	200.00
Cov, hs, 8¼" d, 5¾" h,		Pitcher, water	600.00
oval	350.00	Plate, 6"	100.00
Open, hs, 7"	130.00	Relish, 7" l, 5" w	45.00
Open, hs, 8"	125.00	Salt, master, oval, flat	75.00
Open, hs, 9¼"	200.00	Sauce	
Open, hs, 10½"	140.00	4½"	20.00
Open, ls, 8"	55.00	5¼"	25.00
Open, ls, 9"	85.00	Spillholder	65.00
Cordial	150.00	Spooner	45.00
Creamer, ah		Sugar, cov	175.00
5½"	225.00	Tumbler	
7"	175.00	Bar	85.00
Decanter, os		Water	75.00
Pint	150.00	Whiskey	
Quart	165.00	Applied handle	235.00
Egg Cup	45.00	Shot glass, 3"	100.00
* Goblet	75.00	Wine	125.00
* Lamp	200.00		

HORSESHOE (Good Luck, Prayer Rug)

Non-flint made by Adams & Co. and others in the 1880s.

	Clear		Clear
Bowl, cov, oval		Goblet	
7"	150.00	Knob Stem	40.00
8"	195.00	Plain Stem	38.00
Bread Plate, 14 x 10"		Marmalade Jar, cov	110.00
Double horseshoe handles	65.00	Pitcher	
Single horseshoe handles	40.00	Milk	110.00
Butter, cov	95.00	Water	85.00
Cake Plate	40.00	Plate	
Cake Stand		7"	45.00
9"	70.00	10"	55.00
10"	80.00	Relish, 5 x 7"	20.00
Celery Vase, knob stem	40.00	Salt	
Cheese, cov, woman		Ind, horseshoe shape	20.00
churning	275.00	Master, horseshoe shape	100.00
Compote		Sauce	
Cov, hs, 7", horseshoe		Flat	10.00
finial	95.00	Footed	15.00
Cov, hs, 8 x 12¼"	125.00	Spooner	35.00
Cov, hs, 11"	135.00	Sugar, cov	65.00
Creamer, 6½"	55.00	Vegetable Dish, oblong	35.00
Doughnut Stand	75.00	Waste Bowl	45.00
Finger Bowl	80.00	Wine	150.00

ILLINOIS

Non-flint. One of the States patterns made by U. S. Glass Co., c1897. Most forms are square. A few items are known in ruby stained, including a salt, $50.00, and a lidless straw holder with the stain in the inside, $95.00.

	Clear	Emerald Green		Clear	Emerald Green
Basket, ah, 11½"	100.00	—	Salt		
Bowl, 8"	35.00	—	Ind	15.00	—
Butter, cov	60.00	—	Master	25.00	—
Candlesticks, pr	80.00	—	Salt and Pepper, pr	40.00	—
Celery Tray, 11"	40.00	—	Sauce	20.00	—
Cheese, cov	75.00	—	Spooner	35.00	—
Creamer			Straw Holder, cov	175.00	400.00
Ind	30.00	—	Sugar		
Regular	40.00	—	Ind	30.00	—
Cruet	65.00	—	Regular, cov	55.00	—
Marmalade Jar	135.00	—	Sugar Shaker	65.00	—
Olive	18.00	—	Syrup, pewter top	95.00	—
Pitcher, milk, round,			Toothpick		
SP rim	175.00	—	Adv emb in base	45.00	—
Pitcher, water			Plain	30.00	—
Square	65.00	—	Tray, 12 x 8", turned		
Tankard, round,			up sides	50.00	—
SP rim	75.00	135.00	Tumbler	30.00	40.00
Plate, 7", sq	25.00	—	Vase, 6", sq	35.00	45.00
Relish			Vase, 9½"	—	125.00
7½" x 4"	18.00	—			
8½" x 3"	18.00	—			

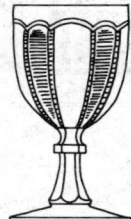

IOWA (Paneled Zipper)

Non-flint made by U. S. Glass Co. c1902. Part of the States pattern series. Available in clear glass with gold trim (add 20%) and ruby or cranberry stained. Also found in amber (goblet $65.00), green, canary, and blue. Add 50% to 100% for color and amber stained.

	Clear		Clear
Bowl, berry	12.00	Olive	15.00
Bread Plate, motto	80.00	Pitcher, water	50.00
Butter, cov	40.00	Punch Cup	15.00
Cake Stand	35.00	Salt Shaker, single	24.00
Carafe	35.00	Sauce, 4½"	6.50
Compote, cov, 8"	40.00	Spooner	30.00
Corn Liquor Jug, os	60.00	Sugar, cov	35.00
Creamer	30.00	Table Set, 4 pc	125.00
Cruet, os	30.00	Toothpick	20.00
Cup	15.00	Tumbler	25.00
Goblet	28.00	Wine	32.50
Lamp	125.00		

JACOB'S LADDER (Maltese)

Non-flint made by Portland Glass Co, Portland, ME, and Bryce Bros, Pittsburgh, PA, in 1876, and U. S. Glass Co in 1891. A few pieces found in amber, yellow, blue, pale blue, and pale green.

	Clear		Clear
Bowl		6¾" x 9¾"	20.00
6" x 8¾"	15.00	7½" x 10¾"	20.00

	Clear			Clear
9", berry, ornate SP holder, ftd	**125.00**	Cruet, os, ftd		**85.00**
Butter, cov	**65.00**	Goblet		**60.00**
Cake Stand		Honey, 3½"		**10.00**
8" or 9"	**50.00**	Marmalade Jar		**75.00**
11" or 12"	**60.00**	Mug		**100.00**
Castor Bottle	**18.00**	Pitcher, water		**150.00**
Castor Set, 4 bottles	**100.00**	Plate, 6¼"		**20.00**
Celery Vase	**45.00**	Relish, 9½ x 5½"		**15.00**
Cologne Bottle, Maltese cross stopper, ftd	**85.00**	Salt, master, ftd		**20.00**
Compote		Sauce		
Cov, hs, 6"	**60.00**	Flat, 4", or 5"		**8.00**
Cov, hs 7½"	**60.00**	Footed, 4"		**12.00**
Cov, hs, 9½"	**125.00**	Spooner		**35.00**
Open, hs, 7½"	**35.00**	Sugar, cov		**60.00**
Open, hs, 8½", scalloped	**30.00**	Syrup		
Open, hs, 9½", scalloped	**38.00**	Knight's Head finial		**125.00**
Open, hs, 10"	**40.00**	Plain top		**100.00**
Creamer	**35.00**	Tumbler, bar		**85.00**
		Wine		**35.00**

JERSEY SWIRL (Swirl)

Non-flint pattern made by Windsor Glass Co., Pittsburgh, Pennsylvania, c1887. Heavily reproduced in color. The clear goblet also reproduced.

	Amber	Blue	Canary	Clear
Bowl, 9¼"	**55.00**	**55.00**	**45.00**	**35.00**
Butter, cov	**55.00**	**55.00**	**50.00**	**40.00**
Cake Stand, 9"	**75.00**	**70.00**	**45.00**	**30.00**
* Celery Vase	**42.00**	**42.00**	**35.00**	**30.00**
* Compote, hs, 8"	**50.00**	**50.00**	**45.00**	**35.00**
Creamer	**45.00**	**45.00**	**40.00**	**30.00**
Cruet, os	—	—	—	**25.00**
* Goblet				
Buttermilk	**40.00**	**40.00**	**35.00**	**30.00**
Water	**40.00**	**40.00**	**35.00**	**30.00**
Marmalade Jar	—	—	—	**50.00**
Pickle Castor, SP frame and lid	—	—	—	**125.00**
Pitcher, water	**50.00**	**50.00**	**45.00**	**35.00**
Plate, round				
6"	**25.00**	**25.00**	**20.00**	**15.00**
8"	**30.00**	**30.00**	**25.00**	**20.00**
10"	**38.00**	**38.00**	**35.00**	**30.00**
Salt, Ind	**20.00**	**20.00**	**18.00**	**15.00**
Sauce, 4½", flat	**20.00**	**20.00**	**15.00**	**10.00**
Spooner	**30.00**	**30.00**	**25.00**	**20.00**
Sugar, cov	**40.00**	**40.00**	**35.00**	**30.00**
Tumbler	**30.00**	**30.00**	**25.00**	**20.00**
Wine	**50.00**	**50.00**	**40.00**	**15.00**

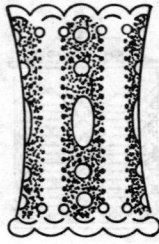

KANSAS (Jewel With Dewdrop)

Non-flint originally produced by Co-Operative Flint Glass Co., Beaver Falls, Pennsylvania. Later produced as part of the States pattern series by U. S. Glass Co. in 1901. Also known with jewels stained in pink or gold. Mugs have been reproduced in vaseline, amber, and blue.

	Clear		Clear
Banana Stand	90.00	Creamer	40.00
Bowl		Goblet	55.00
7", oval	35.00	Mug, regular	45.00
8½"	45.00	Pitcher	
Bread Plate, ODB	45.00	Milk	50.00
Butter, cov	65.00	Water	60.00
Cake Plate	45.00	Relish, 8½", oval	20.00
Cake Stand		Salt Shaker	50.00
7⅝"	45.00	Sauce, flat, 4"	15.00
9"	50.00	Sugar, cov	65.00
10"	85.00	Syrup	125.00
Celery Vase	45.00	Toothpick	65.00
Compote		Tumbler	45.00
Cov, hs, 7"	80.00	Whiskey	15.00
Cov, hs, 8"	125.00	Wine	65.00
Open, hs, 6½", jelly	50.00		
Open, hs, 9½"	60.00		
Open, ls, 6½"	45.00		

KENTUCKY

Non-flint made by U. S. Glass Co., c1897, as part of the States pattern series. The goblet is found in ruby stained ($50.00). A footed, square sauce ($30.00) is known in cobalt blue with gold. A toothpick holder is also known in ruby stained, $150.00.

	Clear	Emerald Green		Clear	Emerald Green
Butter, cov	50.00	—	Plate, 7", sq	15.00	—
Cake Stand, 9½"	40.00	—	Punch Cup	10.00	15.00
Creamer	25.00	—	Salt & Pepper, pr.	50.00	—
Cruet, os	45.00	—	Sauce, ftd, sq	8.00	12.00
Cup	10.00	20.00	Spooner	35.00	—
Goblet	20.00	50.00	Sugar, cov	30.00	—
Nappy	10.00	15.00	Toothpick, sq	35.00	85.00
Olive, handle	25.00	—	Tumbler	20.00	30.00
Pitcher, water	55.00	—	Wine	28.00	38.00

KING'S CROWN (Ruby Thumbprint; X.L.C.R.)

Known as Ruby Thumbprint when pieces are ruby stained. A non-flint pattern made by Adams and Co., Pittsburgh, Pennsylvania, in the 1890s and later. Made in clear and with the thumbprints stained amethyst, gold, green, and yellow, and in clear with etching and trimmed in gold. It became very popular after 1891 as ruby stained souvenir ware. Cobalt blue pieces reported as very rare. Approximately 87 pieces documented. NOTE: Pattern has been copiously reproduced for the gift-trade market. New pieces are easily distinguished: in the case of Ruby Thumbprint, the color is a very pale pinkish red; green and blue pieces have an off-color. Reproduced in milk glass. Available in amethyst stained in goblet ($30.00) and wine ($10.00) and in green stained in goblet ($25.00) and wine ($15.00). Add 30% for engraved pieces.

	Clear	Ruby Stained		Clear	Ruby Stained
Banana Stand, ftd . .	85.00	135.00	Cup & Saucer	55.00	70.00
Bowl			Custard Cup	15.00	25.00
9¼", pointed	35.00	90.00	Honey, cov, sq	100.00	175.00
10", scalloped . . .	45.00	95.00	Goblet	30.00	45.00
Butter, cov	50.00	90.00	Lamp, oil, 10"	135.00	—
Cake Stand			Mustard, cov	35.00	75.00
9"	68.00	125.00	Pickle, lobed	18.00	40.00
10"	75.00	125.00	Pitcher		
Castor Bottle	45.00	70.00	Milk, tankard	75.00	100.00
Castor Set, glass			Water, bulbous . . .	95.00	225.00
stand, 4 bottles . .	175.00	325.00	Water, tankard . . .	110.00	200.00
Celery Vase	40.00	60.00	Plate, 7"	20.00	45.00
Claret	35.00	50.00	Punch Bowl, ftd	275.00	300.00
Compote			Punch Cup	15.00	30.00
Cov, hs, 6"	85.00	150.00	Salt, master, sq	25.00	60.00
Cov, hs, 7"	45.00	195.00	Salt, ind, oblong . . .	16.00	30.00
Cov, hs, 8"	55.00	245.00	Salt & Pepper	40.00	70.00
Cov, ls, 12"	90.00	225.00	Sauce, 4"	15.00	20.00
Open, hs, 5½" . . .	55.00	65.00	Spooner	45.00	50.00
Open, hs, 7½" . . .	45.00	65.00	Sugar, cov	50.00	85.00
Open, hs, 8¼" . . .	75.00	95.00	Toothpick	20.00	35.00
Open, ls, 5¼"	30.00	45.00	Tumbler	20.00	35.00
Open, ls, 9"	40.00	85.00	Wine	25.00	40.00
Cordial	45.00	—			
Creamer					
Ind	30.00	35.00			
Regular	50.00	65.00			

KING'S #500

Made by King Glass Co. of Pittsburgh, Pennsylvania in 1899. It was made in clear, frosted, and a rich, deep blue, known as Dewey Blue, both trimmed in gold. Continued by U. S. Glass Co. in 1891 and made in a great number of pieces. A clear goblet with frosted stem ($50.00) is known. Also known in dark green and a ruby stained sugar is reported ($95.00).

	Clear w/gold	Dewey Blue w/gold		Clear w/gold	Dewey Blue w/gold
Bowl			Creamer	30.00	50.00
7"	10.00	30.00	Cruet	45.00	175.00
8"	12.00	35.00	Cup	15.00	15.00
9"	14.00	45.00	Decanter, locking		
Butter, cov	65.00	125.00	top	100.00	—
Cake Stand	40.00	60.00	Lamp		
Celery Vase	20.00	—	Hand	45.00	—
Compote			Stand	65.00	—
Covered	45.00	—	Pitcher, water	55.00	200.00
Open	30.00	—	Relish	20.00	30.00

	Clear w/gold	Dewey Blue w/gold		Clear w/gold	Dewey Blue w/gold
Rose Bowl	20.00	45.00	Sugar, cov	45.00	75.00
Salt Shaker, single	15.00	40.00	Syrup.	55.00	225.00
Sauce	15.00	35.00	Tumbler	25.00	35.00
Spooner	30.00	70.00			

KOKOMO (Bar and Diamond, R and H Swirl Band)

Made in clear glass by Richards & Hartley, Tarentum, Pennsylvania in the late 1880s to 1891. Found in ruby stained and etched. About 54 pieces manufactured.

	Clear	Ruby Stained		Clear	Ruby Stained
Bowl, 8½", ftd	24.00	—	Cruet	35.00	—
Bread Tray	30.00	45.00	Decanter, 9¾", wine	55.00	95.00
Butter, cov	35.00	—	Finger Bowl	25.00	35.00
Cake Stand	45.00	165.00	Goblet	25.00	45.00
Celery Vase	30.00	45.00	Lamp, hand, atypi-		
Compote			cal—has no dia-		
Cov, hs, 7½"	35.00	165.00	monds.	50.00	100.00
Open, hs, 5"	20.00	—	Pitcher, tankard	55.00	100.00
Open, hs, 6"	25.00	—	Sauce, ftd, 5"	8.00	10.00
Open, hs, 7"	30.00	—	Spooner	25.00	45.00
Open, hs, 8"	35.00	—	Sugar, cov	45.00	65.00
Open, ls, 7½" . . .	20.00	—	Sugar Shaker	35.00	75.00
Condiment Set, ob-			Syrup	45.00	130.00
long tray, shakers,			Tray, water	35.00	90.00
cruet	80.00	195.00	Tumbler	20.00	35.00
Creamer, ah	35.00	50.00	Wine	20.00	35.00

LILY OF THE VALLEY

Non-flint pattern made by Boston & Sandwich, Sandwich, Massachusetts, in the 1870s. Shards have also been found at Burlington Glass Works, Hamilton, Ontario. Lily of the Valley on Legs is a name frequently given to those pieces having three tall legs. Legged pieces include a covered butter, covered sugar, creamer and spooner. Add 25% for this type.

	Clear		Clear
Butter, cov	70.00	Goblet	55.00
Buttermilk Goblet	35.00	Honey	12.00
Cake Stand	65.00	Nappy, 4"	20.00
Celery Tray	40.00	Pickle, scoop shape	20.00
Celery Vase	55.00	Pitcher	
Champagne	80.00	Milk	125.00
Compote		Water	135.00
Cov, hs, 8½"	85.00	Relish	15.00
Open, hs	50.00	Salt, master	
Creamer, ah	65.00	Cov	125.00
Cruet, os	110.00	Open	50.00
Egg Cup	40.00	Sauce, flat	12.00

	Clear			Clear
Spooner	35.00		Footed	65.00
Sugar, cov	75.00		Vegetable Dish, oval	30.00
Tumbler			Wine	100.00
Flat	50.00			

LION

Made by Gillinder and Sons, Philadelphia, Pennsylvania, in 1876. Available in clear (20% less). Many reproductions.

	Frosted			Frosted
Bowl, oblong			Cordial	175.00
6½ x 4¼"	55.00		* Creamer	75.00
8 x 5"	50.00		Egg Cup, 3½" h	65.00
Bread Plate, 12"	90.00		* Goblet	70.00
Butter, cov			Marmalade Jar, rampant	
Lion's head finial	90.00		finial	85.00
Rampant finial	125.00		Pitcher	
Cake Stand	85.00		Milk	450.00
Celery Vase	85.00		Water	350.00
Champagne	175.00		Relish, lion handles	38.00
Cheese, cov, rampant lion			Salt, master, rect lid	250.00
finial	400.00		* Sauce, 4", ftd	25.00
Compote			* Spooner	75.00
Cov, hs, 7", rampant finial	150.00		Sugar, cov	
* Cov, hs, 9", rampant finial,			Lion head finial	90.00
oval, collared base	150.00		Rampant finial	110.00
Cov, 9", hs	185.00		Syrup, orig top	400.00
Open, ls, 8"	75.00		Wine	250.00

LOG CABIN

Non-flint made by Central Glass Co. Wheeling, West Virginia, c1875. Also available in color, but rare. Creamer, spooner, and covered sugar reproduced in clear and cobalt blue.

	Clear			Clear
Bowl, cov, 8 x 5¼ x 3⅝" . . .	400.00		Pitcher, water	300.00
Butter, cov	300.00		Sauce, flat	75.00
Compote, hs, 10½"	275.00		* Spooner	120.00
* Creamer	100.00		* Sugar, cov	275.00
Marmalade Jar, cov	275.00			

LOOP AND DART

Clear and stippled non-flint pattern of the late 1860s and early 1870s. Made by Boston & Sandwich, Sandwich, Massachusetts, and Richards & Hartley, Tarentum, Pennsylvania. Pattern related to Loop and Dart with Diamond Ornament and Loop and Dart with Round Ornament. Flint add 25%.

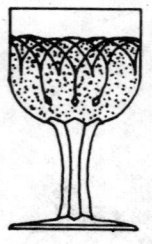

	Clear		Clear
Bowl, 9″, oval	25.00	Pitcher, water	75.00
Butter, cov	45.00	Plate, 6″	35.00
Cake Stand, 10″	40.00	Relish	18.00
Celery Vase	35.00	Salt, master	50.00
Compote		Sauce	5.00
Cov, hs, 8″	85.00	Spooner	25.00
Cov, ls, 8″	65.00	Sugar, cov	50.00
Creamer	35.00	Tumbler	
Cruet, os	95.00	Footed	30.00
Egg Cup	25.00	Water	25.00
Goblet	25.00	Wine	35.00
Lamp, oil	85.00		

LOUISIANA (Sharp Oval and Diamond, Granby)

Made by Bryce Bros., Pittsburgh, Pennsylvania in 1870s, continued later (about 1892) by U. S. Glass Co. as one of the States patterns. Also available with gold and also comes frosted.

	Clear		Clear
Bowl, 9″, berry	20.00	Matchholder	35.00
Butter, cov	65.00	Mug, handled, gold top	25.00
Cake Stand	45.00	Nappy, 4″, cov	30.00
Celery Vase	30.00	Pitcher, water	65.00
Compote		Relish	15.00
Cov, hs, 8″	75.00	Spooner	30.00
Open, hs, 5″, jelly	40.00	Sugar, cov	45.00
Creamer	30.00	Tumbler	25.00
Goblet	30.00	Wine	35.00

MAGNET AND GRAPE (Magnet and Grape with Stippled Leaf)

Flint first made by Boston and Sandwich Glass Co., c1860. Later non-flint versions have grape leaf in either clear or stippled. Reproduced by Metropolitan Museum, New York with frosted leaf.

	Flint Frosted Leaf	Non-Flint Stippled or Clear Leaf		Flint Frosted Leaf	Non-Flint Stippled or Clear Leaf
Bowl, cov, 8″	175.00	75.00	Compote		
Butter, cov	185.00	40.00	Cov, hs, 4½″	125.00	—
Celery Vase	150.00	25.00	Open, hs, 7½″	110.00	65.00
Champagne	135.00	45.00	Cordial, 4″	125.00	—

	Flint Frosted Leaf	Non-Flint Stippled or Clear Leaf		Flint Frosted Leaf	Non-Flint Stippled or Clear Leaf
* Creamer	175.00	40.00	Relish, oval	35.00	15.00
Decanter, os			Salt, ftd	50.00	25.00
Pint	150.00	75.00	Sauce, 4″	20.00	7.50
Quart	200.00	85.00	Spill	65.00	—
Egg Cup	80.00	20.00	Spooner	95.00	30.00
* Goblet			* Sugar, cov,	125.00	80.00
American Shield	300.00	—	Syrup	125.00	55.00
Low Stem	75.00	—	* Tumbler, water	110.00	30.00
Regular stem	70.00	30.00	Whiskey	140.00	25.00
Pitcher			* Wine	90.00	50.00
Milk, ah	—	75.00			
Water, ah	350.00	75.00			

MAINE (Paneled Stippled Flower)

Non-flint made by U. S. Glass Co., Pittsburgh, Pennsylvania c1890. Researchers dispute if goblet was made originally. Sometimes found with enamel trim or overall turquoise stain.

	Clear	Emerald Green		Clear	Emerald Green
Bowl, 8″	30.00	40.00	Mug	35.00	—
Bread Plate, oval, 10			Pitcher		
× 7¾″	30.00	—	Milk	65.00	85.00
Butter, cov	48.00	—	Water	50.00	125.00
Cake Stand	40.00	60.00	Relish	15.00	—
Compote,			Salt Shaker, single	30.00	—
Cov, jelly	50.00	75.00	Sauce	15.00	—
Open, hs, 7″	20.00	30.00	Sugar, cov	45.00	75.00
Open, ls, 8″	38.00	55.00	Syrup	75.00	225.00
Open, ls, 9″	30.00	35.00	Toothpick	125.00	—
Creamer	30.00	—	Tumbler	30.00	45.00
Cruet, os	80.00	—	Wine	50.00	75.00

MANHATTAN

Non-flint with gold, made by U. S. Glass Co., c1902. A depression glass pattern also has the "Manhattan" name. A table sized creamer and covered sugar are known in true ruby stained, and a goblet is known in old marigold carnival glass. Heavily reproduced.

	Clear	Rose Stained		Clear	Rose Stained
Biscuit Jar, cov	60.00	85.00	Butter, cov	55.00	—
Bowl			Cake Stand, 8″	45.00	55.00
6″	18.00	—	Carafe, water	40.00	65.00
8¼″, scalloped	20.00	—	Celery Vase	25.00	—
9½″	20.00	—	Cheese, cov, 8⅜″ d	—	115.00
10″	22.00	—	Compote, cov, hs,		
12½″	25.00	—	9½″	45.00	—

	Clear	Rose Stained		Clear	Rose Stained
Creamer			Relish, 6"	12.00	—
Individual.	20.00	—	Salt Shaker, single	20.00	35.00
Regular.	30.00	60.00	Sauce	14.00	20.00
Cruet			Spooner	20.00	—
Large	65.00	115.00	Straw Holder, cov . .	65.00	—
Small	50.00	—	Sugar		
* Goblet	25.00		Individual, open . .	15.00	—
Ice Bucket	—	65.00	Regular, cov	40.00	65.00
Olive, Gainsborough	30.00	—	Syrup.	48.00	175.00
Pitcher, water, tank-			Toothpick	30.00	—
ard, ½ gal	60.00	125.00	Tumblers		
Plate			Ice Tea	30.00	—
6"	6.50	30.00	Water	20.00	—
8"	15.00	—	Vase, 6"	18.00	—
10¾".	20.00	—	Violet Bowl	20.00	—
Punch Bowl	125.00	—	Water Bottle	40.00	—
Punch Cup	10.00	—	Wine	20.00	—

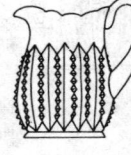

MARDI GRAS (Duncan and Miller #42, Paneled English Hobnail with Prisms)

Made by Duncan and Miller Glass Co., c1898. Available in gold trim and ruby stained.

	Clear	Ruby Stained		Clear	Ruby Stained
Bowl, 8", berry	18.00	—	Plate, 6"	10.00	—
Butter, cov	65.00	145.00	Punch Bowl	225.00	—
Cake Stand, 10" . . .	65.00	—	Punch Cup	10.00	—
Celery Tray, curled			Relish.	12.50	—
edges	25.00	—	Sherry, flared or		
Champagne, saucer	32.00	—	straight	35.00	—
Claret.	35.00	—	Spooner	25.00	—
Compote			Sugar, cov	35.00	65.00
Cov, hs	55.00	—	Syrup, metal lid. . . .	65.00	—
Open, jelly, 4½" . .	30.00	55.00	Toothpick	35.00	125.00
Cordial	35.00	—	Tumbler		
Creamer			Bar	25.00	—
Ind, oval	20.00	—	Champagne.	20.00	—
Regular.	35.00	60.00	Water	30.00	40.00
Finger Bowl	25.00	—	Vase, trumpet shape,		
Goblet	35.00	—	3 sizes	20.00	—
Lamp Shade.	35.00	—	Wine	30.00	65.00
Pitcher					
Milk.	50.00	—			
Water	75.00	200.00			

MARYLAND (Inverted Loop and Fan; Loop and Diamond)

Made originally by Bryce Brothers, Pittsburgh, Pennsylvania. Continued by U. S. Glass Co. as one of their States patterns.

	Clear w/gold	Ruby Stained		Clear w/gold	Ruby Stained
Banana Dish......	35.00	85.00	Olive, handled.....	15.00	—
Bowl, berry......	15.00	35.00	Pitcher		
Bread Plate	25.00	—	Milk...........	42.50	135.00
Butter, cov	65.00	95.00	Water	50.00	100.00
Cake Stand, 8"....	40.00	—	Plate, 7", round....	25.00	—
Celery Tray.......	20.00	35.00	Relish, oval......	15.00	55.00
Celery Vase	28.00	65.00	Salt Shaker, single	30.00	—
Compote			Sauce, flat	14.00	20.00
Cov, hs	65.00	100.00	Spooner.........	30.00	55.00
Open, hs, 7½"...	40.00	—	Sugar, cov	45.00	60.00
Open, jelly......	25.00	45.00	Toothpick........	125.00	175.00
Creamer.........	25.00	55.00	Tumbler	25.00	50.00
Goblet	30.00	48.00	Wine	40.00	75.00

MASCOTTE (Minor Block)

Non-flint made by Ripley and Co., Pittsburgh, Pennsylvania, in the 1870s. Reissued by U. S. Glass Co. in 1898. The butter dish shown on Plate 77 of Ruth Webb Lee's *Victorian Glass* is said to go with this pattern. It has a horseshoe finial and was named for the famous "Maude S," "Queen of the Turf" trotting horse during the 1880s. Apothecary jar and pyramid jars made by Tiffin Glass Co. in the 1950s.

	Clear	Etched		Clear	Etched
Bowl			Open, hs, 9"	—	35.00
Cov, 5"	—	35.00	Open, ls, 8".....	30.00	45.00
Cov, 6"	—	35.00	Creamer.........	30.00	45.00
Cov, 7"	—	45.00	Goblet	40.00	45.00
Cov, 8"	—	50.00	Pitcher, water	55.00	65.00
Cov, 9"	—	55.00	Plate, turned in		
Open 9"	35.00	40.00	sides..........	38.00	—
Butter Pat........	10.00	15.00	Pyramid Jar, 7" d,		
Butter, cov			one fits into other		
"Maude S"	100.00	—	and forms tall jar-		
Regular.........	50.00	65.00	type container with		
Cake Basket, handle	80.00	65.00	lid, three sizes		
Cake Stand	35.00	50.00	with flat sepa-		
Celery Vase	35.00	40.00	rators	40.00	—
Cheese, cov	70.00	80.00	Salt Dip	25.00	—
Compote			Salt Shaker, single	25.00	25.00
Cov, hs, 5".....	—	40.00	Sauce		
Cov, hs, 6".....	—	45.00	Flat...........	8.00	15.00
Cov, hs, 7".....	—	55.00	Footed	12.00	16.00
Cov, hs, 8".....	75.00	85.00	Spooner........	30.00	35.00
Cov, hs, 9".....	—	90.00	Sugar, cov	40.00	45.00
Open, hs, 5"	—	25.00	Tray, water	40.00	55.00
Open, hs, 6"	—	25.00	Tumbler	20.00	35.00
Open, hs, 7"	—	30.00	Wine	25.00	30.00
Open, hs, 8"	—	35.00			

MASSACHUSETTS (Geneva #2, M2-131)

Made in 1880s, maker unknown, and continued in 1898 by U. S. Glass Co. as one of the States series. The vase ($45.00) and wine ($45.00) are known in emerald green. Some pieces reported in cobalt blue and marigold carnival glass. Reproduced in clear and colors.

	Clear		Clear
Bar Bottle, metal shot glass for cover	75.00	Plate, 8"	32.00
Basket, 4½", ah	50.00	Punch Cup	15.00
Bowl		Relish, 8½"	25.00
6", sq	17.50	Rum Jug	110.00
9", sq	20.00	Spooner	22.00
* Butter, cov	70.00	Sugar, cov	40.00
Celery Tray.	28.00	Toothpick	40.00
Cologne Bottle, os	37.50	Tumbler	
Compote, open	35.00	Champagne or Juice	25.00
Cordial	55.00	Water	30.00
Creamer	28.00	Whiskey (shot).	15.00
Cruet, os	45.00	Vase	
Goblet	45.00	6½", trumpet	25.00
Mug	20.00	7"	25.00
Olive	8.50	9", trumpet	35.00
Pitcher, water	75.00	Wine	40.00

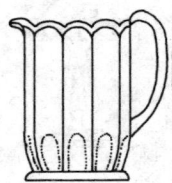

MICHIGAN (Loop & Pillar)

Non-flint made by U. S. Glass Co., c1893. One of the States pattern series. The 10¼" bowl ($42.00) and punch cup ($12.00) are found with yellow or blue stain. Also found with painted carnations. Other colors include "Sunrise," gold, and ruby stained.

	Clear	Rose Stained		Clear	Rose Stained
Bowl			Olive, two handles. .	10.00	25.00
7½"	15.00	30.00	Pickle	12.00	20.00
9"	35.00	60.00	Pitcher		
10¼"	35.00	62.00	8"	50.00	—
Butter, cov	60.00	125.00	12"	70.00	150.00
Celery Vase	40.00	85.00	Punch Bowl, 8"	50.00	—
Compote			Punch Cup	8.00	—
Jelly, 4½"	45.00	75.00	Relish.	20.00	35.00
Open, hs, 9¼" . . .	65.00	85.00	Salt Shaker, single, 3		
Creamer			types.	20.00	30.00
Ind, 602 tankard. .	20.00	65.00	Sauce	12.00	22.00
Regular.	30.00	50.00	Sherbet cup, handled	12.00	15.00
Cruet, os	60.00	225.00	Spooner	50.00	72.00
Crushed Fruit Bowl	75.00	—	Sugar, cov	50.00	75.00
Finger Bowl	15.00	—	Syrup	95.00	175.00
Goblet	35.00	65.00	* Toothpick	45.00	100.00
Honey Dish.	10.00	—	Tumbler	30.00	40.00
Lemonade Mug. . . .	24.00	40.00	Vase, bud	35.00	35.00
Nappy, Gainsborough handle	35.00	—	Wine	35.00	50.00

MINERVA

Non-flint made in the United States and probably in Canada in the 1870s. There are two forms.

	Clear			Clear
Bowl			**Creamer**	45.00
Footed	40.00		Goblet	80.00
Rectangular			Marmalade Jar, cov	150.00
7"	25.00		Pickle	25.00
8 x 5"	30.00		**Pitcher**	
9"	45.00		Milk	75.00
Bread Plate	65.00		Water	185.00
Butter, cov	75.00		**Plate**	
Cake Stand			8"	55.00
8"	95.00		10", handled	60.00
9 x 6½"	100.00		Platter, oval, 13"	65.00
10½"	120.00		**Sauce**	
13"	145.00		Flat	18.50
Champagne	85.00		Footed, 4"	20.00
Compote			Spooner	50.00
Cov, hs, 7"	90.00		Sugar, cov	65.00
Cov, ls, 8"	85.00		Waste Bowl	50.00
Open, hs, 10"	60.00			
Open, hs, octagonal ftd	95.00			

MINNESOTA

Non-flint made by U. S. Glass Co., late 1890s. One of the States patterns. A two-piece flower frog has been found in emerald green ($46.00).

	Clear	Ruby Stained		Clear	Ruby Stained
Basket	65.00	—	Mug	25.00	—
Biscuit Jar, cov	55.00	150.00	Olive	15.00	25.00
Bowl, 8½", flared	30.00	100.00	Pitcher, water, tankard	85.00	200.00
Butter, cov	55.00	—	**Plate**		
Carafe	35.00	—	5", turned up edges	25.00	—
Celery Tray, 13"	25.00	—	7⅜" d	15.00	—
Compote			Relish	20.00	—
Open, hs, 10", flared	60.00	—	Sauce, boat shape	15.00	35.00
Open, ls, 9", sq	55.00	—	Spooner	25.00	—
Creamer			Sugar, cov	40.00	—
Individual	20.00	—	Syrup	65.00	—
Regular	30.00	—	Toothpick, 3 handles	35.00	150.00
Cruet	35.00	—	Tumbler	20.00	—
Cup	18.00	—	Wine	40.00	—
Goblet	35.00	50.00			
Hair Receiver	30.00	—			

MISSOURI (Palm and Scroll)

Non-flint made by U. S. Glass Co. c1899, one of the States pattern series. Also made in amethyst and canary.

	Clear	Emerald Green		Clear	Emerald Green
Bowl, berry, 8"	15.00	35.00	Cake Stand, 9"	35.00	45.00
Butter, cov	45.00	65.00	Celery Vase	30.00	—

	Clear	Emerald Green		Clear	Emerald Green
Cordial	55.00	—	Relish	10.00	12.50
Creamer	25.00	40.00	Salt Shaker, single	35.00	45.00
Cruet	55.00	130.00	Sauce, flat, 4″	10.00	16.00
Dish, cov 6″	65.00	—	Spooner	25.00	48.00
Doughnut stand, 6″	40.00	—	Sugar, cov	50.00	65.00
Goblet	50.00	60.00	Syrup	85.00	—
Mug	35.00	45.00	Tumbler	30.00	38.00
Pickle Dish, rectangular	18.00	27.50	Wine	40.00	45.00
Pitcher					
Milk	40.00	85.00			
Water	75.00	85.00			

MOON AND STAR (Palace)

Non-flint and frosted (add 30%). First made by Adams & Co., Pittsburgh, Pennsylvania, in 1874 and later by several manufacturers, including Pioneer Glass who probably decorated ruby stained examples. Six different compotes documented. Also found with frosted highlights. Heavily reproduced in clear and color.

	Clear		Clear
Bowl		Cruet	125.00
6″	25.00	Egg Cup	35.00
8″, Berry	30.00	Goblet	45.00
12½″, Round	42.00	Lamp	140.00
Bread Plate, rect	45.00	Pickle, oval	20.00
Butter, cov	70.00	Pitcher, water, ah	175.00
Cake Stand, 10″	50.00	Relish	20.00
Carafe	42.50	Salt, ind	10.00
Celery Vase	35.00	Salt & Pepper, pr.	70.00
Champagne	75.00	Sauce	
Claret	47.50	Flat	8.50
Compote		Footed	12.00
Cov, hs, 8″	75.00	Spooner	45.00
Cov, hs, 10″	68.00	Sugar, cov	65.00
Cov, ls, 6½″	55.00	Syrup	150.00
Cov, ls, 10″	68.00	Tray, water	65.00
Open, hs, 9″	40.00	Tumbler, ftd	60.00
Open, ls, 7½″	25.00	Wine	60.00
Creamer, ah	55.00		

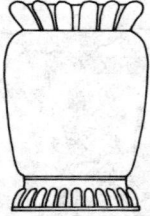

NEVADA

Non-flint made by U. S. Glass Co. as a States Pattern. Pieces are sometimes partly frosted and have enamel decoration. Add 20% for frosted.

	Clear		Clear
Biscuit Jar	45.00	Compote, cov, 8″, hs	45.00
Butter, cov	68.00	Creamer	30.00
Cake Stand, 10″	35.00	Cruet	35.00
Celery	25.00	Cup, custard	12.00

	Clear		Clear
Pickle, oval	10.00	Sauce	10.00
Pitcher, water, tankard, ½ gal	40.00	Spooner	35.00
Salt		Sugar, cov	35.00
Ind	15.00	Syrup, tin top	45.00
Master	20.00	Toothpick	38.00
Salt Shaker, single, two types	20.00	Tumbler	15.00

NEW HAMPSHIRE (Bent Buckle, Modiste)

Non-flint made by U. S. Glass Co. in the States Pattern series. There is a large ruby mug ($50.00), 5½" bowl ($25.00), syrup ($48.00), toothpick ($40.00), and tumbler ($40.00). A vase is known in green stain ($30.00).

	Clear w/gold	Rose Stained		Clear w/gold	Rose Stained
Bowl			Goblet	25.00	45.00
Flared, 8½"	15.00	25.00	Mug, large	20.00	45.00
Round, 8½"	18.00	30.00	Pitcher, water, tankard	70.00	90.00
Square, 8½"	25.00	35.00	Relish	18.00	—
Butter, cov	45.00	70.00	Sugar		
Cake Stand, 8¼"	30.00	—	Cov	45.00	60.00
Carafe	60.00	—	Ind, open	20.00	25.00
Celery Vase	35.00	50.00	Syrup	75.00	—
Compote, open	38.00	55.00	Toothpick	25.00	40.00
Creamer			Tumbler	20.00	35.00
Ind	20.00	30.00	Vase	35.00	50.00
Regular	30.00	45.00	Wine	30.00	50.00
Cruet	55.00	135.00			

NEW JERSEY (Loops and Drops)

Non-flint made by U. S. Glass Co. in States Pattern Series. Items with perfect gold are worth more than those with worn gold. An emerald green 11" vase is known, value $75.00.

	Clear w/gold	Ruby Stained		Clear w/gold	Ruby Stained
Bowl			Creamer	35.00	60.00
8", flared	25.00	50.00	Cruet	50.00	—
9"	32.50	65.00	Goblet	40.00	—
10", oval	30.00	—	Olive	18.50	—
Bread Plate	30.00	—	Pickle, rect	15.00	—
Flat	75.00	100.00	Pitcher		
Footed	125.00	—	Milk, ah	75.00	—
Cake Stand, 8"	65.00	—	Water		
Celery Tray, rect	25.00	—	Applied handle	80.00	210.00
Compote			Pressed handle	50.00	185.00
Cov, hs, 5", jelly	45.00	55.00	Plate, 12"	30.00	—
Cov, hs, 8"	75.00	—	Salt & Pepper		
Open, hs, 6¾"	30.00	—	Hotel	50.00	—
Open, hs, 8"	60.00	—	Small	35.00	55.00

	Clear w/gold	Ruby Stained		Clear w/gold	Ruby Stained
Sauce	14.00	30.00	Syrup, no gold	90.00	—
Spooner	27.00	75.00	Toothpick	55.00	225.00
Sugar, cov	60.00	80.00	Tumbler	30.00	50.00
Sweetmeat, 8"	45.00	—	Wine	40.00	60.00

O'HARA DIAMOND (Sawtooth and Star)

Non-flint, made by O'Hara Glass Co. in 1928 and by U. S. Glass Co. in 1898.

	Clear	Ruby Stained		Clear	Ruby Stained
Bowl, berry			Lamp, Oil	50.00	—
Individual	—	25.00	Pitcher, water,		
Master	25.00	75.00	tankard	—	165.00
Butter, cov, ruffled			Plate		
base	45.00	125.00	7"	20.00	—
Compote			8"	30.00	—
Cov, hs	40.00	185.00	10"	40.00	—
Open, hs, jelly	48.00	145.00	Salt, master	15.00	35.00
Condiment Set, pr			Salt Shaker	20.00	35.00
salt and pepper,			Spooner	20.00	55.00
sugar shaker, tray	—	250.00	Sugar, cov	35.00	90.00
Creamer	30.00	60.00	Sugar Shaker	55.00	150.00
Cruet	55.00	150.00	Syrup	55.00	200.00
Cup and Saucer	40.00	60.00	Tumbler	30.00	45.00
Goblet	25.00	50.00			

ONE HUNDRED ONE

Non-flint made by the Bellaire Goblet Co., Findlay, Ohio, in the late 1870s.

	Clear		Clear
Bread Plate, 101 border, Farm implement center, 11"	75.00	Pitcher, water, ah	125.00
		Plate	
Butter, cov	40.00	6"	15.00
Cake Stand, 9"	65.00	7"	15.00
Celery Vase	50.00	8"	15.00
Compote		Relish	15.00
Cov, hs, 7"	60.00	Sauce	
Cov, ls	60.00	Flat	10.00
Creamer	45.00	Footed	15.00
Goblet	50.00	Spooner	25.00
Lamp, hand, oil, 10"	80.00	Sugar, cov	45.00
		Wine	60.00

OREGON #1 (Beaded Loop)

Non-flint. First made in the 1880s. Reissued in 1907 as one of the States series. Reproduced in clear and color by Imperial.

	Clear		Clear
Berry Set, master, 6 sauces	**72.00**	Honey Dish	**10.00**
Bowl		Mug	**35.00**
7"	**15.00**	Pickle Dish, boat shape	**15.00**
8"	**15.00**	Pitcher	
9", berry, cov	**25.00**	Milk	**40.00**
Bread Plate	**35.00**	Water	**60.00**
Butter, cov		Relish	**15.00**
English	**65.00**	Salt, master	**20.00**
Flanged	**50.00**	Sauce	
Flat	**40.00**	Flat, 3½ to 4"	**10.00**
Cake Stand	**35.00**	Footed, 3½"	**15.00**
Carafe, water	**35.00**	Spooner	
Celery Vase	**30.00**	Flat	**24.00**
Compote		Footed	**26.00**
Open, hs, 8"	**50.00**	Sugar, cov	
Open, ls, 9"	**40.00**	Flat	**25.00**
Creamer		Footed	**30.00**
Flat	**30.00**	Syrup	**55.00**
Footed	**35.00**	Toothpick	**55.00**
Cruet	**50.00**	Tumbler	**25.00**
Goblet	**35.00**	Wine	**40.00**

PALMETTE

Non-flint, late 1870s. Syrup known in milk glass.

	Clear		Clear
Bowl		Cup Plate	**55.00**
8"	**25.00**	Egg Cup	**40.00**
9"	**15.00**	Goblet	**35.00**
Bread Plate, handled, 9"	**30.00**	Lamp, 8½", all glass	**95.00**
Butter Dish, cov	**60.00**	Pickle, scoop shape	**20.00**
Butter Pat	**35.00**	Pitcher, water, ah	**120.00**
Cake Stand	**80.00**	Relish	**18.00**
Castor Bottle	**20.00**	Salt, master, ftd	**22.00**
Castor Set, 5 bottles	**125.00**	Salt Shaker	**55.00**
Celery Vase	**55.00**	Sauce, flat, 6"	**10.00**
Champagne	**75.00**	Shaker, saloon, oversize	**80.00**
Compote		Spooner	**35.00**
Cov, hs, 7"	**65.00**	Sugar, cov	**55.00**
Cov, hs, 8½"	**75.00**	Syrup, ah	**125.00**
Cov, hs, 9¾"	**85.00**	Tumbler	
Open, ls, 5½"	**25.00**	Bar	**75.00**
Open, ls, 7"	**30.00**	Water, ftd	**40.00**
Creamer, ah	**65.00**	Wine	**110.00**

PANELED FORGET-ME-NOT (Regal)

Non-flint, made by Bryce Bros., Pittsburgh, Pennsylvania, c1870. Made in limited
production in amethyst and green.

	Amber	Blue	Clear
Bread Plate	—	—	**30.00**
Butter, cov	**50.00**	**60.00**	**45.00**

	Amber	Blue	Clear
Cake Stand, 10″ . . .	70.00	90.00	45.00
Celery Vase	45.00	70.00	36.00
Compote			
Cov, hs, 7″.	90.00	110.00	65.00
Cov, hs, 8″.	80.00	100.00	68.00
Open, hs, 8½″ . . .	60.00	75.00	50.00
Open, hs, 10″ . . .	60.00	80.00	40.00
Creamer.	45.00	60.00	35.00
Cruet, os	—	—	45.00
Goblet	50.00	65.00	32.00
Marmalade Jar, cov	60.00	80.00	50.00
Pickle, boat shape. .	25.00	35.00	15.00
Pitcher			
Milk.	90.00	110.00	50.00
Water	90.00	110.00	75.00
Relish, scoop shape	55.00	55.00	65.00
Salt & Pepper, pr. . .	—	—	65.00
Sauce, ftd.	18.00	25.00	12.00
Spooner	40.00	50.00	25.00
Sugar, cov	60.00	80.00	40.00
Wine	55.00	70.00	60.00

PANELED THISTLE (Delta)

Non-flint made by J. P. Higbee Glass Co., Bridgeville, Pennsylvania, in the early 1900s. The Higbee Glass Co. often used a bee as a trademark. This pattern has been heavily reproduced with a similar mark. Occasionally found with gilt. A covered sugar in ruby stained is known.

	Clear		Clear
Basket, small size	65.00	Plate	
Bowl		7″.	20.00
8″, bee mark	25.00	10″, bee mark	30.00
9″, bee mark	30.00	Punch Cup, bee mark	20.00
Bread Plate	40.00	Relish, bee mark.	24.00
Butter, cov, ...	60.00	Rose Bowl, 5″.	50.00
Cake Stand, 9″	35.00	Salt, ind	20.00
Candy Dish, cov, ftd	30.00	Sauce	
Celery Tray.	20.00	Flared, bee mark	14.00
Celery Vase	40.00	Footed	20.00
Champagne, bee mark	40.00	Spooner	25.00
Compote		Sugar, cov	45.00
Open, hs, 8″	30.00	Toothpick, bee mark	45.00
Open, hs, 9″	35.00	Tumbler	25.00
Open, ls, 5″, jelly	30.00	Vase	
Creamer, bee mark	40.00	5″.	25.00
Cruet, os	50.00	9¼″.	25.00
Doughnut Stand, 6″.	25.00	Wine, bee mark.	30.00
Goblet	35.00		
Honey, cov, sq, bee mark. . .	80.00		
Pitcher			
Milk.	60.00		
Water	70.00		

PAVONIA (Pineapple Stem)

Non-flint made by Ripley and Co. in 1885 and by U. S. Glass Co. in 1891. This pattern comes plain and etched.

	Clear	Ruby Stained		Clear	Ruby Stained
Bowl, 9″	20.00	—	Plate, 6½″, etched	17.50	—
Butter, cov, flat	75.00	125.00	Salt		
Cake Stand, large,			Ind	15.00	50.00
etched.	55.00	—	Master	28.00	50.00
Celery Vase, etched	45.00	75.00	Salt Shaker.	25.00	—
Compote			Sauce, ftd, 3½″ or		
Cov, hs, 6″	65.00	—	4″	15.00	—
Cov, hs, 8″	75.00	—	Spooner, pedestal . .	45.00	50.00
Open, jelly, etched	38.00	—	Sugar, cov, flat	55.00	75.00
Creamer, etched . . .	48.00	65.00	Tray, water, etched	75.00	—
Cup and Saucer . . .	35.00	—	Tumbler, etched		
Finger Bowl, ruffled			bellflowers	35.00	50.00
underplate	48.00	110.00	Waste Bowl.	70.00	—
Goblet, etched	35.00	60.00	Water Set, tankard, 6		
Mug	—	50.00	tumblers	285.00	325.00
Pitcher			Wine, etched	35.00	40.00
Lemonade.	125.00	135.00			
Water	75.00	195.00			

PENNSYLVANIA (Balder)

Non-flint issued by U. S. Glass Co., 1898. Also known in ruby stained. A ruffled jelly compote documented in orange carnival.

	Clear w/gold	Emerald Green		Clear w/gold	Emerald Green
Biscuit Jar, cov	65.00	100.00	Goblet	24.00	—
Bowl			Juice Tumbler.	10.00	20.00
8″, berry	25.00	35.00	Pitcher, water	60.00	—
8″, sq	20.00	40.00	Punch Bowl	175.00	—
Butter, cov	60.00	85.00	Punch Cup	10.00	—
Carafe	45.00	—	Salt Shaker.	10.00	—
Celery Vase	45.00	—	Sauce	10.00	—
Cheese Dish, cov . .	65.00	—	Spooner	24.00	35.00
Compote, hs, jelly . .	50.00	—	Sugar, cov	40.00	55.00
Creamer			Syrup	50.00	—
Ind	15.00	35.00	Toothpick	35.00	90.00
Regular.	25.00	50.00	Tumbler	28.00	40.00
Cruet, os	41.00	—	Whiskey	15.00	—
Decanter, os	100.00	—	Wine	15.00	40.00

PICKET

Non-flint made by the King Glass Co., Pittsburgh, Pennsylvania in the 1870s. Pattern has five different size compotes. Toothpick holders are known in apple green, vaseline, and purple slag.

	Clear		Clear
Bowl, 9½", sq	30.00	Goblet	30.00
Bread Plate	70.00	Pitcher, water	75.00
Butter, cov	45.00	Salt	
Celery Vase	40.00	Ind	10.00
Compote		Master	35.00
Cov, hs, 6"	65.00	Sauce	
Cov, hs, 8"	85.00	Flat	15.00
Cov, ls, 8"	95.00	Footed	20.00
Open, hs, 6"	30.00	Spooner	30.00
Open, hs, 7", sq	35.00	Sugar, cov	45.00
Open, hs, 8"	35.00	Toothpick	35.00
Open, hs, 10", sq	70.00	Tray, water	65.00
Open, ls, 7"	50.00	Waste Bowl	40.00
Creamer	48.00	Wine	85.00

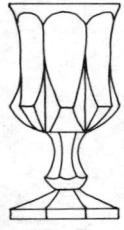

PORTLAND

Non-flint pattern made by several companies c1880–1900. An oval pintray in ruby souvenir ($20.00) is known, and a flat sauce ($25.00).

	Clear w/gold		Clear w/gold
Basket, handled	85.00	Lamp base, 9"	75.00
Biscuit Jar, cov	90.00	Pitcher, water, straight sides	55.00
Bowl		Pomade Jar, SP top	30.00
Berry	20.00	Puff Box, glass lid	35.00
Small, flat, cov	30.00	Punch Bowl, 13⅝", ftd	150.00
Butter, cov	50.00	Punch Cup	10.00
Cake Stand, 10½"	45.00	Relish	15.00
Carafe, water	45.00	Salt Shaker	16.00
Celery Tray	25.00	Sauce	8.00
Compote		Spooner	30.00
Cov, hs, 6"	60.00	Sugar, cov	45.00
Open, hs, 8¼"	40.00	Sugar Shaker	40.00
Open, hs, 9½"	45.00	Syrup	50.00
Open, ls, 7"	45.00	Toothpick	25.00
Creamer	30.00	Tumbler	18.00
Cruet, os	48.00	Vase	25.00
Decanter, qt, handled	50.00	Water Bottle	40.00
Goblet	35.00	Wine	30.00

PRINCESS FEATHER (Rochelle)

Non-flint made by Bakewell, Pears & Co. in the late 1870s. Occasional pieces made in flint. Later by U. S. Glass Co. in the 1890s. Also made in milk glass. A rare blue opaque tumbler has been reported.

	Clear		Clear
Bowl		Cake Plate, handled	35.00
7", cov, pedestal	35.00	Celery Vase	40.00
7", oval	20.00	Compote	
8", oval	25.00	Cov, hs, 7"	50.00
9", oval	30.00	Cov, hs, 8"	50.00
Butter, cov	50.00	Open, ls, 8"	35.00

	Clear		Clear
Creamer, ah	55.00	Relish	20.00
Dish, oval	20.00	Sauce	8.00
Egg Cup	40.00	Spooner	30.00
Goblet	45.00	Sugar	
Pitcher, water	75.00	Cov	55.00
Plate		Open	25.00
6"	30.00	Wine	45.00
7"	35.00		
8"	40.00		
9"	45.00		

QUEEN ANNE (Bearded Man)

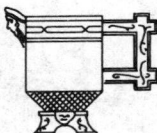

Non-flint made by LaBelle Glass Co., Bridgeport, Ohio, c1879. Finials are Maltese cross. At least 28 pieces documented. A table set and water pitcher are known in amber.

	Clear		Clear
Bowl, cov		Egg Cup	45.00
8", oval	45.00	Pitcher	
9", oval	55.00	Milk	75.00
Bread Plate	50.00	Water	85.00
Butter, cov	65.00	Spooner	40.00
Celery Vase	35.00	Sugar, cov	55.00
Compote, cov, ls, 9"	75.00	Syrup	100.00
Creamer	40.00		

QUESTION MARK (Oval Loop)

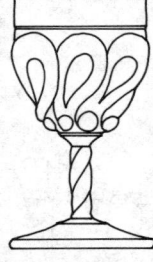

Made by Richards and Hartley in 1895 and later by U. S. Glass Co., 1891. An 1888 catalog lists 32 pieces. Scarce in ruby stained.

	Clear		Clear
Bowl		Cordial	20.00
4", round, ftd	15.00	Creamer	30.00
7", oblong	18.00	Goblet	25.00
7", round, ftd	20.00	Nappy, ftd	20.00
8", oblong	25.00	Pitcher	
8", round, ftd	25.00	Milk, bulbous	40.00
9", oblong	30.00	Milk, tankard	45.00
10", oblong	25.00	Water, bulbous	50.00
Butter, cov	30.00	Water, tankard	55.00
Candlestick, chamber, finger		Salt Shaker	15.00
loop	45.00	Sauce, 4", collared	10.00
Celery Vase	28.00	Spooner	20.00
Compote		Sugar Shaker	35.00
Cov, hs, 7"	50.00	Sugar, cov	25.00
Cov, hs, 8"	65.00	Tumbler	20.00
Open, hs, 7"	25.00	Wine	20.00
Open, ls	15.00		

RED BLOCK (Late Block)

Non-flint with red stain made by Doyle and Co.; later made by five companies plus U. S. Glass Co. in 1892. Prices for clear 50% less.

	Ruby Stained		Ruby Stained
Bowl, 8″	75.00	Rose Bowl	75.00
Butter, cov	110.00	Sauce, flat, 4½″	20.00
Celery Vase, 6½″	85.00	Salt Dip, ind	50.00
Creamer		Salt Shaker, single	60.00
Individual	45.00	Spooner	45.00
Regular	70.00	Sugar, cov	90.00
Decanter, 12″, os, variant	175.00	Tumbler	45.00
*Goblet	45.00	Water Set, pitcher, 6	
Mug	50.00	tumblers	285.00
Pitcher, water, 8″ h	175.00	*Wine	45.00

REVERSE TORPEDO (Bull's Eye Band, Bull's Eye with Diamond Point #2, Pointed Bull's Eye)

Made by Dalzell, Gilmore & Leighton Glass Co., Findlay, Ohio, c1888–1890. Also attributed to Canadian factories. Sometimes found with etching.

	Clear		Clear
Banana Stand, 9¾″	100.00	Open, hs, 7″	65.00
Biscuit Jar, cov	135.00	Open, hs, 8⅜″ d	45.00
Bowl		Open, hs, jelly	50.00
8½″, shallow	30.00	Open, ls, 9¼″, ruffled	85.00
9″, fruit, pie crust rim	70.00	Goblet	85.00
10½″, pie crust rim	75.00	Honey Dish, sq, cov	145.00
Butter, cov	75.00	Pitcher, tankard, 10¼″	160.00
Cake Stand	85.00	Sauce, flat, 3¾″	20.00
Celery Vase	55.00	Spooner	30.00
Compote		Sugar, cov	85.00
Cov, hs, 7″	80.00	Syrup	165.00
Cov, hs, 10″	125.00	Tumbler	30.00
Cov, hs, 6″	80.00		
Open, hs, 10½″ d, V shape			
bowl	90.00		

ROMAN ROSETTE

Non-flint made by Bryce, Walker and Co. 1875–1885. Reissued by U. S. Glass Co. in 1892 and 1898. Attributed to Portland Glass Co. Also seen with English registry mark. Also known in amber stained.

	Clear	Ruby Stained		Clear	Ruby Stained
Bowl			Celery Vase	30.00	95.00
6″	12.00	—	Compote		
8½″	15.00	50.00	Cov, hs, 4½″, jelly	50.00	—
Bread Plate	30.00	75.00	Cov, hs, 6″	65.00	—
Butter, cov	50.00	125.00	Creamer	32.00	45.00
Cake Stand, 9″	45.00	—	Cordial	50.00	—

	Clear	Ruby Stained		Clear	Ruby Stained
*Goblet	40.00	—	Salt & Pepper, glass		
Lemonade Mug. . . .	35.00	—	tray.	40.00	100.00
Mug.	35.00	—	Sauce	15.00	20.00
Pitcher			Spooner	25.00	45.00
Milk.	45.00	150.00	Sugar, cov	40.00	80.00
Water	50.00	140.00	Syrup	85.00	125.00
Plate, 7½".	35.00	65.00	Wine	45.00	65.00
Relish, oval, 9"	20.00	40.00			

ROSE-IN-SNOW

Non-flint made by Bryce Bros., Pittsburgh, Pennsylvania in the square form, c1880. Also made in the more common round form by Ohio Flint Glass Co. and after 1891 by U. S. Glass Co.

	Amber and Canary	Blue	Clear
Butter, cov			
Round.	50.00	125.00	45.00
Square	60.00	150.00	50.00
Cake Stand, 9"	85.00	175.00	90.00
Compote			
Cov, hs, 8".	125.00	175.00	80.00
Cov, ls, 7"	100.00	150.00	75.00
Open, ls, 5¾" . . .	40.00	120.00	35.00
Creamer			
Round.	60.00	100.00	45.00
Square	65.00	120.00	45.00
* Goblet	40.00	55.00	35.00
* Mug, "In Fond Remembrance" . .	45.00	110.00	32.00
* Pickle Dish			
Double, 8½" x 7"	45.00	110.00	100.00
Single, oval, handles at end. . . .	25.00	95.00	20.00
Pitcher, water, ah . .	175.00	200.00	125.00
Plate			
5".	40.00	40.00	35.00
6".	30.00	80.00	18.00
7".	30.00	82.00	20.00
Platter, oval.	—	—	125.00
Sauce			
Flat.	15.00	20.00	12.00
Footed	8.00	48.00	18.00
Spooner			
Round.	30.00	80.00	25.00
Square	38.50	100.00	35.00
Sugar, cov			
Round.	55.00	120.00	50.00
Square	50.00	140.00	45.00
Tumbler, bar	60.00	100.00	50.00

SAWTOOTH (Mitre Diamond)

An early clear flint-glass pattern made in the late 1850s by the New England Glass Co., Boston and Sandwich Glass Co., and others. Later made in non-flint by Bryce Brothers and U. S. Glass Co. Also known in milk glass, clear deep blue, and canary yellow.

	Flint	Non-Flint		Flint	Non-Flint
Butter, cov	75.00	45.00	Pitcher, water		
Cake Stand, 10″ . . .	85.00	55.00	Applied handle. . .	150.00	95.00
Celery Vase, 10″ . . .	60.00	30.00	Pressed handle . .	—	55.00
Champagne	65.00	30.00	Plate, 6½″.	45.00	30.00
Compote			Pomade Jar, cov . . .	50.00	35.00
Cov, hs, 9½″	85.00	48.00	Salt		
Open, ls, 8″, saw-			Cov, ftd	65.00	40.00
tooth edge	50.00	30.00	Open, smooth		
Cordial	50.00	30.00	edge	25.00	20.00
Creamer			Spooner	70.00	30.00
Applied handle. .	75.00	40.00	Sugar, cov	65.00	35.00
Pressed handle . .	—	30.00	Tumbler, bar	50.00	25.00
Cruet, acorn stopper	100.00	—	Wine, knob stem . . .	35.00	20.00
Egg Cup.	45.00	25.00			
Knob Stem	45.00	25.00			
Plain Stem	—	20.00			

SKILTON (Oregon #2)

Made by Richards & Hartley of Tarentum, Pennsylvania in 1888 and by U. S. Glass after 1891. This is not one of the U. S. Glass States pattern series and should not be confused with Beaded Loop, which is Oregon #1, named by U. S. Glass Co. It is better known as Skilton (named by Millard) to avoid confusion with Beaded Loop.

	Clear	Ruby Stained		Clear	Ruby Stained
Bowl			Creamer.	30.00	55.00
4″, round	10.00	—	Dish, oblong, sq . . .	25.00	—
5″, round	15.00	—	Goblet	35.00	50.00
6″, round	20.00	—	Olive, handled.	20.00	—
7″, rect	20.00	—	Pickle	15.00	—
8″, rect	25.00	—	Pitcher		
9″, rect	30.00	—	Milk.	45.00	125.00
Butter, cov	45.00	110.00	Water	50.00	125.00
Cake Stand	35.00	—	Salt & Pepper, pr. . .	45.00	—
Celery Vase	35.00	95.00	Sauce, ftd	12.00	20.00
Compote			Spooner, flat	28.00	55.00
Cov, hs, 7″.	45.00	—	Sugar, cov	35.00	85.00
Cov, hs, 8″.	45.00	—	Tray, water	45.00	—
Open, ls, 4″.	10.00	—	Tumbler	25.00	40.00
Open, ls, 7″.	25.00	—	Wine	30.00	45.00
Open, ls, 8″.	30.00	75.00			

SNAIL (Compact, Idaho, Double Snail)

Non-flint made by George Duncan & Sons, Pittsburgh, Pennsylvania, c1880, and by U. S. Glass Co. in the States Pattern series. Ruby stained pieces date after 1891. Add 30% for engraved pieces.

	Clear	Ruby Stained
Banana Stand.....	145.00	225.00
Basket, cake or fruit		
9"	85.00	—
10"	95.00	—
Bowl		
4"	20.00	90.00
4½"	20.00	—
7", cov	60.00	45.00
7", oval	28.00	45.00
7", round	28.00	45.00
8", cov	60.00	45.00
8", oval	28.00	45.00
8", round	28.00	45.00
9", oval	30.00	—
9", round	30.00	—
10"	35.00	45.00
Butter, cov	75.00	160.00
Cake Stand		
9"	85.00	—
10"	95.00	—
Celery Vase	35.00	85.00
Cheese, cov	95.00	—
Compote		
Cov, hs, 6".....	50.00	—
Cov, hs, 7".....	50.00	100.00
Cov, hs, 8".....	80.00	135.00
Cov, hs, 10"....	125.00	—
Open, hs, 6"	30.00	—
Open, hs, 7"	45.00	—
Open, hs, 8"	35.00	—
Open, hs, 9", twisted stem, scalloped	75.00	—
Cracker Jar, cov ...	85.00	—
Creamer.........	65.00	75.00
Cup, Custard	30.00	—

	Clear	Ruby Stained
Cruet, os	100.00	275.00
Finger Bowl	50.00	—
Goblet	65.00	95.00
Marmalade, cov ...	90.00	125.00
Pitcher		
Milk, tankard	100.00	—
Water, bulbous...	125.00	—
Water, tankard...	135.00	250.00
Plate		
5"	35.00	—
6"	35.00	—
7"	40.00	—
Punch Cup........	35.00	—
Relish, 7", oval	25.00	—
Rose Bowl		
3"	50.00	—
5"	45.00	—
6"	45.00	—
7"	50.00	—
Salt		
Ind	35.00	—
Master	35.00	75.00
Salt Shaker		
Bulbous........	65.00	90.00
Straight sides....	60.00	90.00
Sauce	25.00	45.00
Spooner.........	45.00	75.00
Sugar		
Ind, cov........	50.00	—
Regular, cov	60.00	100.00
Sugar Shaker	85.00	200.00
Syrup...........	125.00	225.00
Tumbler	55.00	65.00
Vase	50.00	—
Violet Bowl, 3"	50.00	—
Wine	65.00	—

SPIREA BAND

Non-flint made by Bryce, Higbee & Co., Pittsburgh, Pennsylvania, c1885.

	Amber	Blue	Clear	Vaseline
Bowl, 8"	25.00	40.00	20.00	30.00
Butter, cov	50.00	55.00	35.00	45.00
Cake Stand, 11" ...	45.00	55.00	40.00	45.00
Celery Vase	40.00	50.00	25.00	40.00
Compote, cov, hs, 7"	44.00	65.00	40.00	44.00
Cordial	38.00	42.00	20.00	38.00
Creamer..........	32.50	44.00	35.00	35.00
Goblet	30.00	35.00	25.00	35.00
Pitcher, water	65.00	80.00	35.00	60.00
Platter, 10½"......	32.00	42.00	20.00	32.00
Relish...........	30.00	35.00	18.00	30.00

	Amber	Blue	Clear	Vaseline
Sauce				
Flat...........	10.00	12.00	5.00	9.00
Ftd	15.00	18.00	8.00	14.00
Spooner.........	30.00	35.00	20.00	35.00
Sugar, open	32.00	40.00	25.00	32.00
Tumbler	24.00	35.00	20.00	30.00
Wine	30.00	35.00	20.00	30.00

SPRIG

Non-flint made by Bryce, Higbee & Co., Pittsburgh, Pennsylvania, mid-1880s.

	Clear		Clear
Bowl, 10", scalloped	35.00	Pitcher,. water	50.00
Bread Plate	40.00	Relish..............	12.00
Butter, cov	65.00	Salt, master	55.00
Cake Stand, 8"	35.00	Sauce	
Celery Vase	40.00	Flat	12.00
Compote		Ftd	15.00
Cov, hs..............	60.00	Spooner	25.00
Open, hs.............	45.00	Sugar, cov	40.00
Creamer...............	30.00	Wine	40.00
Goblet	30.00		

STATES, THE (Cane and Star Medallion)

Non-flint made by the U. S. Glass Co. in 1908. Also found in emerald green; add 50%.

	Clear w/ gold		Clear w/gold
Bowl		Plate, 10"	25.00
7", round, 3 handles.....	25.00	Punch Bowl, 13" d........	75.00
9¼", round	30.00	Punch Cup	8.00
Butter, cov	65.00	Relish, diamond shape	35.00
Celery Tray.............	20.00	Salt & Pepper	40.00
Cocktail	25.00	Sauce, flat, 4", tub shape...	10.00
Compote		Spooner...............	25.00
Open, hs, 7"	30.00	Sugar, cov	45.00
Open, hs, 9"	40.00	Syrup................	65.00
Creamer		Toothpick, flat, rectangular,	
Ind, oval	18.00	curled lip	45.00
Regular, round.........	30.00	Tray, 7¼" l, 5½" w........	18.00
Goblet	35.00	Tumbler	22.00
Pitcher, water	45.00	Wine	30.00

TENNESSEE (Jewel and Crescent; Jeweled Rosette)

Made by King Glass Co., Pittsburgh, Pennsylvania, and continued by U. S. Glass Co., in 1899, as part of the States series.

	Clear	Colored Jewels		Clear	Colored Jewels
Bowl, berry	20.00	30.00	Creamer	30.00	—
Bread Plate	40.00	75.00	Goblet	40.00	—
Butter, cov	55.00	—	Mug	40.00	—
Cake Stand			Pitcher		
9½"	38.00	—	Milk	55.00	—
10½"	45.00	—	Water	65.00	—
Celery Vase	35.00	—	Relish	20.00	—
Compote			Spooner	35.00	—
Cov, 5", jelly	40.00	55.00	Sugar, cov	45.00	—
Open, hs, 8"	45.00	—	Syrup	90.00	—
Open, hs, 9"	45.00	—	Toothpick	75.00	85.00
Open, hs, 10"	45.00	—	Tumbler	35.00	—
Open, ls, 7"	35.00	—	Wine	65.00	85.00

TEXAS (Loop with Stippled Panels)

Non-flint made by U. S. Glass Co., c1900, in the States Pattern series. Occasionally pieces found in ruby stained. Reproduced in solid colors.

	Clear w/gold	Rose Stained		Clear w/gold	Rose Stained
Bowl			Pickle, 8½"	25.00	—
7"	20.00	40.00	Pitcher, water	125.00	—
9", scalloped	35.00	50.00	Plate, 9"	35.00	60.00
Butter, cov	75.00	125.00	Sauce		
Cake Stand, 9½"	60.00	80.00	Flat	10.00	18.00
Celery Tray	30.00	—	Footed	20.00	—
Celery Vase	40.00	—	Spooner	35.00	—
Compote			Sugar		
Cov, hs, 6"	60.00	—	Individual, cov	45.00	—
Cov, hs, 8"	75.00	—	Regular, cov	65.00	—
Open, hs, 5"	40.00	—	Toothpick	25.00	95.00
Creamer			Tumbler	25.00	—
Individual	20.00	—	Vase		
Regular	40.00	—	6½"	25.00	—
Cruet, os	60.00	165.00	9"	35.00	—
Goblet	85.00	95.00	Wine	50.00	100.00

THOUSAND EYE

The original pattern was non-flint made by Adams Glass Co, Tarentum, PA, 1875, and by Richards and Hartley, 1888. (Their Pattern No. 103). It was made in two forms: Adams with a three knob stem finial, and Richards and Hartley with a plain stem with a scalloped bottom. Several glass companies made variations of the original pattern and reproductions were made as late as 1981. Crystal Opalescent was produced by Richards and Hartley only in the original pattern. (Opalescent celery vase $70.00; open compote, 8", $115.00; 6" creamer, $85.00; ¼ gallon water pitcher, $140.00; ½ gallon water pitcher, $180.00; 4" footed sauce, $40.00; spooner, $60.00; and 5" covered sugar, $80.00). Covered compotes are rare and would command 40% more than open compotes. A 2" mug in blue is known.

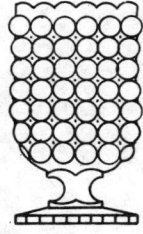

	Amber	Apple Green	Blue	Clear	Vaseline
ABC Plate, 6", clock center	50.00	55.00	52.00	45.00	52.00
Bowl, large, carriage shape	—	—	85.00	—	85.00
Butter, cov					
6¼"	65.00	75.00	70.00	45.00	90.00
7½"	65.00	75.00	70.00	45.00	90.00
Cake Stand					
10"	50.00	78.00	55.00	30.00	84.00
11"	50.00	78.00	55.00	30.00	84.00
Celery, hat shape . .	50.00	65.00	60.00	35.00	55.00
Celery Vase, 7"	50.00	60.00	52.00	45.00	55.00
Christmas Light	27.00	45.00	35.00	25.00	40.00
Cologne Bottle	25.00	45.00	35.00	20.00	45.00
Compote, cov, ls, 8", sq.	—	100.00	100.00	—	—
Compote, open					
6"	35.00	40.00	38.00	25.00	38.00
7"	38.00	44.00	40.00	30.00	40.00
8", round	40.00	50.00	44.00	35.00	48.00
8", sq, hs.	39.00	50.00	48.00	38.00	55.00
9"	48.00	56.00	52.00	40.00	52.00
10"	55.00	65.00	60.00	45.00	60.00
Cordial	35.00	52.00	40.00	25.00	58.00
Creamer					
4"	32.00	40.00	36.00	25.00	38.00
6"	38.00	75.00	55.00	35.00	72.00
Creamer & Sugar Set	—	—	—	100.00	—
*Cruet, 6"	40.00	58.00	47.00	35.00	60.00
Egg Cup.	65.00	85.00	70.00	45.00	90.00
*Goblet	37.00	42.00	38.00	35.00	45.00
Honey Dish, cov, 6 × 7¼"	85.00	95.00	90.00	70.00	92.00
Inkwell	45.00	—	75.00	35.00	80.00
Jelly Glass	20.00	25.00	22.00	15.00	23.00
Lamp, Kerosene					
hs, 12"	120.00	150.00	130.00	100.00	140.00
hs, 15"	125.00	155.00	135.00	110.00	150.00
ls, handled	110.00	115.00	110.00	90.00	120.00
Mug					
2½"	23.00	30.00	25.00	20.00	32.00
3½"	23.00	30.00	25.00	20.00	32.00
Nappy					
5"	34.00	—	39.00	30.00	45.00
6"	39.00	—	44.00	35.00	52.00
8"	45.00	—	50.00	42.00	60.00
Pickle.	25.00	30.00	27.00	20.00	29.00
Pitcher					
Milk, cov, 7"	85.00	110.00	105.00	70.00	105.00
Water, ¼ gal	70.00	85.00	80.00	55.00	80.00
Water, ½ gal	80.00	92.00	84.00	65.00	85.00
Water, 1 gal	90.00	100.00	95.00	85.00	95.00
*Plate, sq, folded corners					
6"	24.00	28.00	26.00	20.00	26.00
8"	26.00	30.00	28.00	22.00	30.00
10"	34.00	50.00	36.00	25.00	34.00

	Amber	Apple Green	Blue	Clear	Vaseline
Platter					
8 × 11″, oblong..	40.00	48.00	42.00	38.00	45.00
11″, oval	75.00	80.00	55.00	40.00	75.00
Salt Shaker, pr					
Banded	60.00	68.00	62.00	58.00	62.00
Plain	50.00	60.00	55.00	40.00	56.00
Salt, ind	80.00	95.00	90.00	50.00	90.00
Salt, open, carriage					
shape	—	—	—	50.00	—
Sauce					
Flat, 4″	10.00	22.00	12.00	8.00	15.00
Footed, 4″	12.00	25.00	15.00	10.00	20.00
Spooner	32.00	48.00	40.00	27.00	45.00
*String Holder	35.00	60.00	45.00	30.00	42.00
Sugar, cov, 5″	52.00	70.00	54.00	45.00	55.00
Syrup, pewter top . .	80.00	100.00	70.00	55.00	70.00
Toothpick					
Hat	35.00	52.00	58.00	30.00	45.00
Plain	35.00	50.00	55.00	25.00	40.00
Thimble.	55.00	—	—	—	—
Tray, water					
12½ ″, round	64.00	78.00	65.00	55.00	60.00
14″, oval	65.00	80.00	75.00	60.00	74.00
*Tumbler	26.00	62.00	34.00	21.00	30.00
*Wine	35.00	50.00	40.00	20.00	40.00

THREE-FACE

Non-flint made by George E. Duncan & Son, Pittsburgh, Pennsylvania, c1872. Designed by John E. Miller, a designer with Duncan, who later became a member of the firm. Companies in the Pittsburgh area produced many patterns in expectation of the 1876 Philadelphia Centennial Exposition. It has been heavily reproduced.

	Clear		Clear
Biscuit Jar, cov	300.00	Cov, ls, 4″	150.00
Butter, cov	140.00	Open, hs, 7″	75.00
Cake Stand		Open, hs, 8″	85.00
9″	150.00	Open, hs, 9″	135.00
10″	160.00	Open, ls, 6″	75.00
11″	165.00	Open, jelly, paneled	
Celery Vase		"Huber" top	85.00
Plain	95.00	Creamer.	135.00
Scalloped	95.00	Goblet	85.00
Champagne		Lamp, Oil	150.00
Hollow stem.	250.00	Marmalade Jar	200.00
Saucer type.	150.00	Pitcher, water	375.00
Claret.	100.00	Salt Dip	35.00
Compote		Salt & Pepper.	75.00
Cov, hs, 7″.	165.00	Sauce, ftd.	25.00
Cov, hs, 8″.	175.00	Spooner	80.00
Cov, hs, 9″.	190.00	Sugar, cov	125.00
Cov, hs, 10″.	225.00	Wine	150.00
Cov, ls, 6″	160.00		

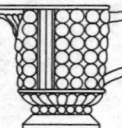

THREE PANEL

Non-flint made by Richards & Hartley Co., Tarentum, Pennsylvania, c1888, and by U. S. Glass Co. in 1891.

	Amber	Blue	Clear	Vaseline
Bowl				
7″	25.00	40.00	20.00	45.00
8½″.	25.00	40.00	20.00	45.00
10″	40.00	50.00	35.00	48.00
Butter, cov	45.00	50.00	40.00	50.00
Celery Vase, ruffled top	55.00	65.00	35.00	55.00
Compote, open, ls, 7″	35.00	55.00	25.00	40.00
Creamer.	40.00	45.00	25.00	40.00
Cruet	250.00	—	—	—
Goblet	30.00	40.00	25.00	35.00
Mug	35.00	45.00	25.00	35.00
Pitcher, water	100.00	125.00	40.00	110.00
Sauce, ftd.	15.00	15.00	10.00	15.00
Spooner.	42.50	45.00	30.00	40.00
Sugar, cov	55.00	60.00	48.00	70.00
Tumbler	35.00	40.00	20.00	30.00

TORPEDO (Pigmy)

Non-flint made by Thompson Glass Co., Uniontown, Pennsylvania, c1889. A black amethyst master salt ($150.00) also known.

	Clear	Ruby Stained		Clear	Ruby Stained
Banana Stand.	75.00	—	8″, plain base, pattern on bowl . . .	85.00	—
Bowl			Marmalade Jar, cov	85.00	—
Cov, 7″ d, 7¼″ h. .	65.00	—	Pickle Castor, sp holder	125.00	—
Cov, 8″	40.00	—	Pitcher		
Open, 4″	—	20.00	Milk, 8½″.	75.00	150.00
Open, 7″	18.00	—	Water, 10½″.	85.00	175.00
Open, 8″	20.00	—	Punch Cup	25.00	—
Open, 9″	20.00	45.00	Salt		
Open, 9½″, flared rim.	38.00	—	Ind	20.00	—
Butter, cov	85.00	—	Master	35.00	—
Cake Stand, 10″ . . .	85.00	—	Salt Shaker, single, 2 types.	50.00	—
Celery Vase, scalloped top	40.00	—	Sauce, 4½″, collared base	15.00	—
Compote			Spooner, scalloped top	45.00	—
Cov, hs, 13¾″ . . .	165.00	—	Sugar, cov	65.00	—
Cov, hs, 4″, jelly. .	65.00	—	Syrup	95.00	175.00
Open, jelly.	48.00	—	Tray, water		
Creamer.	50.00	—	10″, round	85.00	—
Cruet, os, ah.	80.00	—	11¾″, clover shaped	75.00	—
Cup and Saucer . . .	60.00	—	Tumbler	45.00	55.00
Decanter, os, 8″ . . .	85.00	—	Wine	90.00	—
Finger Bowl	55.00	—			
Goblet	45.00	85.00			
Lamp					
3″, handled	75.00	—			

TRUNCATED CUBE (Thompson's #77)

Non-flint made by Thompson Glass Co., Uniontown, Pennsylvania, c1892. Also found with engraving.

	Clear	Ruby Stained		Clear	Ruby Stained
Bowl			Pitcher, water, tank-		
4", berry	—	15.00	ard	50.00	110.00
8"	—	40.00	Spooner	30.00	50.00
Butter, cov	50.00	90.00	Salt Shaker, single	15.00	30.00
Celery Vase	40.00	55.00	Sugar, cov	30.00	70.00
Creamer			Syrup	40.00	100.00
Ind	20.00	30.00	Table Set, 5 pcs	135.00	200.00
Regular	35.00	65.00	Toothpick	30.00	40.00
Decanter, os, 12" h	60.00	150.00	Tumbler	22.50	35.00
Goblet	30.00	50.00	Wine	25.00	40.00

U. S. COIN

Non-flint frosted, clear, and gilted pattern made by U. S. Glass Co. in 1892 for three or four months. Production was stopped by U. S. Treasury because real coins, dated as early as 1878, were used in the molds. 1892 coin date is the most common.

	Clear	Frosted		Clear	Frosted
Bowl			Cruet, os	375.00	500.00
6"	170.00	220.00	Epergne	—	1,000.00
9"	215.00	325.00	Goblet	250.00	400.00
Bread Plate	175.00	325.00	Goblet, dimes	—	550.00
Butter, cov, dollars			Lamp		
and halves	250.00	450.00	Round font	275.00	450.00
Cake Stand, 10"	225.00	400.00	Square font	300.00	—
Celery			Mug, handled	185.00	300.00
Tray	200.00	—	Pickle	200.00	—
Vase, quarters	135.00	350.00	Pitcher, water, dol-		
Champagne	—	400.00	lars	400.00	800.00
Compote			Sauce, ftd, 4", quar-		
Cov, hs, 7"	300.00	500.00	ters	100.00	185.00
Cov, hs, 8", quar-			Spooner, quarters	225.00	325.00
ters and dimes	—	415.00	Sugar, cov	225.00	350.00
Open, hs, 7", quar-			Syrup, dated pewter		
ters and dimes	200.00	300.00	lid	—	525.00
Open, hs, 7", quar-			* Toothpick	180.00	275.00
ters and halves	225.00	350.00	Tray, water, 8", rect	275.00	—
Open, 8⅜" d,			Tumbler	135.00	235.00
6½" h	—	240.00	Waste Bowl	225.00	—
Creamer	350.00	500.00	Wine	225.00	375.00

U. S. SHERATON (Greek Key)

Made by U. S. Glass Co in 1912. This pattern was made only in clear, but can be found trimmed with gold or platinum. Some pieces are marked with the intertwined U. S. Glass trademark.

	Clear		Clear
Bon Bon, 6″, ftd	15.00	Squat, medium	30.00
Bowl		Tankard	35.00
6″, ftd, sq	15.00	Plate, sq	
8″, flat	12.00	4½″	8.00
8″, ftd, sq	14.00	9″	12.00
Bureau Tray	30.00	Pomade Jar	14.00
Butter, cov	35.00	Puff Box	14.00
Celery Tray	30.00	Punch Bowl, cov, 14″	90.00
Compote		Ring Tree	25.00
Open, 4″, jelly	12.00	Salt Shaker	
Open, 6″	14.00	Squat	12.00
Creamer		Tall	15.00
After dinner, tall, sq ft	12.00	Salt, ind	17.00
Berry, bulbous, sq ft	15.00	Sardine Box	35.00
Large	18.00	Spooner	
Cruet, os	25.00	Handled	15.00
Finger Bowl, underplate	24.00	Tray	12.00
Goblet	18.00	Sugar, cov	
Lamp, miniature	50.00	Individual	15.00
Marmalade Jar	35.00	Regular	20.00
Mug	15.00	Sundae Dish	10.00
Mustard Jar, cov	30.00	Syrup, glass lid	35.00
Pickle	10.00	Tumbler	
Pin Tray	12.00	Iced Tea	15.00
Pitcher, water		Water	12.00
One half gallon	30.00		

UTAH (Frost Flower, Twinkle Star)

Non-flint made by U. S. Glass Co. in 1901 in the States Pattern series. Add 25% for frosting.

	Clear		Clear
Bowl		Creamer	30.00
Cov, 6″	20.00	Goblet	25.00
Open, 8″	18.00	Pickle	12.00
Butter, cov	35.00	Pitcher, water	45.00
Cake Plate, 9″	20.00	Salt & Pepper, in holder	45.00
Cake Stand		Sauce, 4″	8.50
8″	20.00	Spooner	15.00
10″	30.00	Sugar, cov	35.00
Celery Vase	20.00	Tumbler	15.00
Compote		Wine	25.00
Cov, ls, 6″, jelly	25.00		
Open, ls, 6″, jelly	18.00		

VERMONT (Honeycomb with Flower Rim; Inverted Thumbprint with Daisy Band)

Non-flint made by U. S. Glass Co., 1899–1903. Also made in custard (usually decorated), chocolate, caramel, and novelty slag, milk glass, and blue. Toothpick has been reproduced in clear and opaque colors.

	Clear w/gold	Green w/gold		Clear w/gold	Green w/gold
Basket, handle	30.00	45.00	Pitcher, water	50.00	125.00
Bowl, berry	25.00	45.00	Sauce	15.00	20.00
Butter, cov	40.00	75.00	Spooner	25.00	75.00
Celery Tray.......	30.00	35.00	Sugar, cov	35.00	80.00
Creamer.........	30.00	55.00	*Toothpick	35.00	60.00
Goblet	40.00	50.00	Tumbler	20.00	40.00

VIKING (Bearded Head)

Non-flint, made by Hobbs, Brockunier, and Co. in 1876 as their centennial pattern. No tumbler or goblet originally made.

	Clear		Clear
Apothecary Jar, cov.	55.00	Creamer, 2 types.	50.00
Bowl		Cup, ftd	35.00
Cov, 8″, oval	55.00	Egg Cup..............	40.00
Cov, 9″, oval	65.00	Marmalade Jar	85.00
Bread Plate	70.00	Mug, ah	50.00
Butter, cov	75.00	Pitcher, water	100.00
Celery Vase	45.00	Relish...............	20.00
Compote		Salt, master	40.00
Cov, hs, 9″.........	95.00	Sauce	15.00
Cov, ls, 8″, oval	75.00	Spooner..............	35.00
Open, hs............	60.00	Sugar, cov	65.00

WAFFLE AND THUMBPRINT

Flint made by the New England Glass Co. and Boston & Sandwich Glass Co., c1850. Later by Bryce, Walker & Co., Pittsburgh, Pennsylvania.

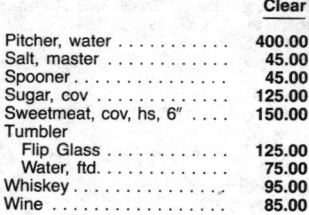

	Clear		Clear
Bowl, 5 x 7″	30.00	Pitcher, water	400.00
Butter, cov	95.00	Salt, master	45.00
Celery Vase	105.00	Spooner..............	45.00
Champagne	90.00	Sugar, cov	125.00
Claret................	110.00	Sweetmeat, cov, hs, 6″	150.00
Compote, cov, hs	150.00	Tumbler	
Creamer..............	125.00	Flip Glass	125.00
Decanter, os		Water, ftd.	75.00
Pint................	100.00	Whiskey..............	95.00
Quart	145.00	Wine	85.00
Egg Cup..............	45.00		
Goblet, knob stem........	65.00		
Lamp			
9½″................	115.00		
11″, whale oil..........	175.00		

WASHINGTON (Early)

Flint made by New England Glass Co., c1869.

	Clear		Clear
Ale Glass	125.00	Egg Cup.	75.00
Bowl, 6 x 9″, oval	45.00	Goblet	110.00
Bottle, bitters	85.00	Honey Dish, 3½″.	30.00
Butter, cov	175.00	Lamp	150.00
Celery Vase	95.00	Pitcher, water	375.00
Champagne	125.00	Plate, 6″	60.00
Compote		Salt, master	55.00
Cov, hs, 6″.	125.00	Sauce	25.00
Cov, hs, 10″.	175.00	Spooner.	75.00
Cordial.	150.00	Sugar, cov	125.00
Creamer.	200.00	Tumbler	85.00
Decanter, os	150.00	Wine	125.00

WESTWARD HO! (Pioneer)

Non-flint, usually frosted, made by Gillinder & Sons, Philadelphia, Pennsylvania, late 1870s. Molds made by Jacobus who also made Classic. Has been reproduced.

	Clear		Clear
Bread Plate	175.00	Marmalade Jar, cov.	200.00
Butter, cov	185.00	Mug	
Celery Vase	125.00	2″	225.00
Compote		3½″.	175.00
Cov, hs, 5″.	225.00	Pitcher, water	250.00
Cov, hs, 9″.	275.00	Sauce, ftd, 4½″.	35.00
Cov, ls, 5″	150.00	Spooner.	85.00
Open, hs, 8″	125.00	Sugar, cov	185.00
Creamer.	95.00	Wine	200.00
Goblet	90.00		

WHEAT AND BARLEY (Duquesne)

Non-flint made by Bryce Bros., Pittsburgh, Pennsylvania, in the late 1870s. Later made by U. S. Glass Co., 1891.

	Amber	Blue	Clear	Vaseline
Bowl, 8″, cov.	35.00	40.00	25.00	35.00
Butter, cov	45.00	60.00	35.00	55.00
Cake Stand				
8″	30.00	45.00	20.00	30.00
10″.	40.00	50.00	30.00	40.00
Compote				
Cov, hs, 7″.	45.00	55.00	40.00	45.00
Cov, hs, 8″.	50.00	55.00	45.00	50.00
Open, hs, jelly . . .	32.50	40.00	30.00	35.00
Creamer.	30.00	40.00	28.00	35.00
Goblet	35.00	47.50	25.00	40.00
Mug	30.00	40.00	20.00	35.00
Pitcher				
Milk.	70.00	85.00	40.00	95.00
Water	85.00	95.00	45.00	100.00
Plate				
7″	20.00	30.00	15.00	25.00
9″, closed handles	25.00	35.00	20.00	40.00

	Amber	Blue	Clear	Vaseline
Salt & Pepper	45.00	55.00	35.00	45.00
Sauce				
Flat, handle	12.00	15.00	10.00	15.00
Footed	15.00	15.00	10.00	15.00
Spooner	30.00	40.00	24.00	30.00
Sugar, cov	40.00	50.00	35.00	40.00
Syrup	175.00	195.00	85.00	—
Tumbler	30.00	35.00	18.00	30.00

WILDFLOWER

Non-flint made by Adams & Co., Pittsburgh, Pennsylvania, c1874, and by U. S. Glass Co., c1898. This pattern has been heavily reproduced.

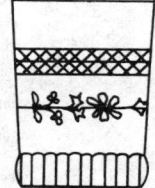

	Amber	Apple Green	Blue	Clear	Vaseline
Bowl, 8″, sq	25.00	35.00	35.00	18.00	20.00
Butter, cov					
Collared base . . .	40.00	50.00	50.00	35.00	45.00
Flat	35.00	45.00	45.00	30.00	40.00
Cake Stand, 10½″. .	50.00	80.00	75.00	45.00	50.00
Champagne	40.00	55.00	50.00	25.00	45.00
Celery Vase	55.00	60.00	55.00	35.00	55.00
Compote					
Cov, hs, 8″,					
oblong	80.00	85.00	85.00	50.00	75.00
Cov, ls, 7″	—	—	70.00	—	—
Open, hs	80.00	—	—	—	—
Creamer	35.00	50.00	45.00	40.00	48.00
* Goblet	30.00	40.00	40.00	25.00	40.00
Pitcher, water	55.00	95.00	65.00	40.00	70.00
Plate, 10″, sq	30.00	30.00	45.00	25.00	30.00
Platter					
10″, oblong	40.00	45.00	40.00	30.00	30.00
11 x 8″, deep scal-					
loped edges . . .	—	—	45.00	—	—
Relish	20.00	22.00	20.00	18.00	20.00
* Salt, turtle	45.00	50.00	50.00	30.00	40.00
Salt Shaker	35.00	55.00	40.00	20.00	45.00
Sauce, ftd, 4″,					
round	17.50	18.00	18.00	15.00	17.50
Spooner	30.00	35.00	30.00	20.00	40.00
Sugar, cov	45.00	45.00	50.00	30.00	45.00
Syrup	125.00	150.00	140.00	65.00	150.00
Tray, water, oval . . .	50.00	60.00	60.00	40.00	55.00
Tumbler	40.00	35.00	35.00	25.00	35.00
Wine	45.00	45.00	45.00	25.00	45.00

WILLOW OAK (Wreath)

Non-flint made by Bryce Bros. Pittsburgh, Pennsylvania, c1880, and by U. S. Glass Company in 1891.

	Amber	Blue	Canary	Clear
Bowl, 8″	25.00	40.00	48.00	20.00
Butter, cov	55.00	65.00	80.00	40.00
Cake Stand, 8½″. . .	60.00	65.00	70.00	45.00
Celery Vase	45.00	60.00	75.00	35.00
Compote				
Cov, hs, 7½″	50.00	65.00	80.00	40.00
Open, 7″	30.00	40.00	48.00	25.00
Creamer.	40.00	50.00	60.00	30.00
Goblet	40.00	50.00	60.00	30.00
Mug	35.00	45.00	54.00	30.00
Pitcher				
Milk.	50.00	60.00	72.00	45.00
Water	55.00	60.00	72.00	50.00
Plate				
7″	35.00	45.00	50.00	25.00
9″	32.50	35.00	40.00	25.00
Salt Shaker.	25.00	40.00	55.00	20.00
Sauce				
Flat, handle, sq . .	15.00	20.00	24.00	10.00
Footed, 4″	20.00	25.00	30.00	15.00
Spooner.	35.00	40.00	48.00	30.00
Sugar, cov	68.50	70.00	75.00	40.00
Tray, water, 10½″ . .	35.00	50.00	60.00	30.00
Tumbler	30.00	35.00	45.00	25.00
Waste Bowl.	35.00	40.00	40.00	30.00

WISCONSIN (Beaded Dewdrop)

Non-flint made in Pittsburgh, Pennsylvania, in the 1880s. Later made by U. S. Glass Co. in Indiana, 1903. One of States patterns. Toothpick reproduced in colors.

	Clear		Clear
Banana Stand.	75.00	Cruet, os	80.00
Bowl		Cup & Saucer.	50.00
4½ x 6½″	28.00	Goblet	65.00
6″, oval, handled, cov	40.00	Marmalade Jar, straight	
7″, round	42.00	sides, glass lid.	125.00
8″, oblong, preserve	42.00	Mug	35.00
Butter, flat flange.	75.00	Pitcher	
Cake Stand		Milk.	55.00
8½″.	45.00	Water	70.00
9½″.	55.00	Plate, 6¾″.	25.00
Celery Tray.	45.00	Punch Cup	12.00
Celery Vase	45.00	Relish.	25.00
Compote		Salt Shaker, single	30.00
Cov, hs, 6″.	45.00	Spooner.	30.00
Cov, hs, 7″.	55.00	Sugar, cov	55.00
Cov, hs, 8″.	65.00	Sugar Shaker	90.00
Open, hs, 9½″	35.00	Sweetmeat, 5″, ftd, cov	35.00
Open, hs, 10½″	35.00	Syrup	110.00
Open, jelly.	20.00	*Toothpick	55.00
Condiment Set, SP, horse-		Tumbler	40.00
radish on tray	100:00	Wine	75.00
Creamer.	50.00		

WYOMING (Enigma)

Made by U. S. Glass Co., in the States Pattern series, 1903.

	Clear		Clear
Bowl, 8″	15.00	Goblet	65.00
Butter, cov	50.00	Mug	40.00
Cake Plate	55.00	Pitcher, water	75.00
Cake Stand	70.00	Relish	15.00
Compote, cov, hs, 8″ d.	85.00	Spooner	30.00
Creamer		Sugar, cov	45.00
Covered	50.00	Syrup, small	65.00
Open	35.00	Wine	85.00

X-RAY

Non-flint made by Riverside Glass Works, Wellsburgh, West Virginia, 1896 to 1898. Prices are for pieces with gold trim. A toothpick holder is known in amethyst ($125.00). Also, a toothpick holder with marigold iridescence is known ($35.00).

	Clear	Emerald Green		Clear	Emerald Green
Bowl, berry, 8″, beaded rim	25.00	45.00	Goblet	20.00	35.00
Butter, cov	40.00	75.00	Pitcher, water	40.00	75.00
Celery Vase	—	50.00	Salt & Pepper, pr.	25.00	45.00
Compote			Sauce, flat	8.00	10.00
Cov, hs	40.00	65.00	Spooner	25.00	40.00
Jelly	—	40.00	Sugar		
Creamer			Ind, open	20.00	32.50
Individual	15.00	30.00	Regular, cov	35.00	45.00
Regular	30.00	60.00	Syrup	—	265.00
Cruet	—	140.00	Toothpick	30.00	60.00
Cruet Set, 4 leaf clover tray	125.00	350.00	Tumbler	12.00	25.00

YALE (Crow-foot, Turkey Track)

Non-flint made by McKee and Brothers Glass Co., Jeannette, Pennsylvania, patented, 1887.

	Clear		Clear
Butter, cov	45.00	Pitcher, water	65.00
Bowl, berry, 10½″	20.00	Relish, oval	10.00
Cake Stand	55.00	Salt Shaker, single	30.00
Celery Vase	35.00	Sauce, flat	10.00
Compote		Spooner	20.00
Cov, hs	50.00	Sugar, cov	35.00
Open, scalloped rim	25.00	Syrup	65.00
Creamer	30.00	Tumbler	20.00
Goblet	30.00		

ZIPPER (Cobb)

Non-flint made by Richards & Hartley, Tarentum, Pennsylvania, c1880.

	Clear		Clear
Bowl, 7″	15.00	Pitcher, water, ½ gal	40.00
Butter, cov	40.00	Relish, 10″	15.00
Celery Vase	25.00	Salt Dip	5.00
Cheese, cov	55.00	Sauce	
Compote, cov, ls, 8″	45.00	Flat	7.50
Creamer	35.00	Footed	12.00
Cruet, os	45.00	Spooner	25.00
Goblet	20.00	Sugar, cov	35.00

S.E.G.

PAUL REVERE POTTERY

History: Paul Revere Pottery, Boston, Massachusetts, was an outgrowth of a club known as "The Saturday Evening Girls." The S.E.G. was a group of young female immigrants who met on Saturday nights for reading and crafts such as ceramics.

Regular production began in 1908. The name Paul Revere was adopted because the pottery was located near the Old North Church. In 1915 the firm moved to Brighton, Massachusetts. Known as the "Bowl Shop," the pottery grew steadily. In spite of popular acceptance and technical advancements, the pottery required continual subsidies. It finally closed in January, 1942.

Items produced range from plain and decorated vases to tablewares to illustrated tiles. Many decorated wares were designed and glazed either in an Art Nouveau matte finish or an occasional high glaze.

In addition to the impressed mark, paper "Bowl Shop" labels were used prior to 1915. Pieces also can be found dated with P.R.P. or S.E.G. painted on the base.

References: Paul Evans, *Art Pottery of the United States, Second Edition,* Feingold & Lewis Publishing Corp, 1987; Ralph and Terry Kovel, *The Kovels' Collector's Guide to American Art Pottery,* Crown Publishers, Inc., 1974.

Collectors' Club: American Art Pottery Association, 9825 Upton Circle, Bloomington, MN 55431.

Bowl	
4¾″ d, green and beige landscape border, blue ground, indistinctly sgd "S. E. G....17..."	150.00
6½″ d, rolled rim, shallow body, matte slate blue glaze, faintly sgd	165.00
8½″ d, white incised band of flowers, yellow ground, sgd "SEG 4–16," artist initials "FL" for Fanny Levine, rim repaired	275.00
9″ d, flared rim, matte turquoise glaze, sgd, dated, artist's initials	175.00
Cup and Plate, 3¼″ h cup, 7¾″ d plate, yellow–green and blue landscape with center yellow chick, turquoise ground, imp, sgd "016," artist's initials "E. M.," Edith Brown monogram	375.00
Mug, 5″ h, motto, flaring cylindrical, applied loop handle, incised and painted red, yellow, blue, green, and black roosters and motto, teal ground, sgd, paper label, chip	550.00

Vase, tapered cylinder, rim band, light blue, high glaze, 5¾″ h, $45.00.

Mush Set, 5½" d bowl, matching pitcher, green and yellow highlights, central goose medallion, medium blue ground, Brighton, MA, c1925 . . . . . **400.00**

Plate, 8½" d, brown and white landscape border, sgd "S. E. G. 10–13," artist's initials "FL" **200.00**

Vase

8½" h, swollen cylindrical, tapering towards base, wide mouth, imp mark, sgd "E 6–24" **600.00**

10" h, swollen cylindrical, wide mouth, rolled lip, sea blue glaze, painted mark "S. E. G. 1–2. . .," initial "P" **250.00**

PEACHBLOW

History: Peachblow, an art glass which derives its name from a fine Chinese glazed porcelain, resembles a peach or crushed strawberry in color. Three American glass manufacturers and two English firms produced peachblow glass in the late 1880s. A fourth American firm renewed the process in the 1950s. The glass from each firm has its own identifying characteristics.

Hobbs, Brockunier & Co., Wheeling peachblow: Opalescent glass, plated or cased with a transparent amber glass; shading from yellow at the base to a deep red at top; glossy or satin finish.

Mt. Washington "Peach Blow": A homogeneous glass, shading from a pale gray-blue to a soft rose color. Pieces may be enhanced with glass appliqués, enameling, and gilding.

New England Glass Works, New England peachblow [advertised as "Wild Rose," but called "Peach Blow" at the plant]: Translucent, shading from rose to white; acid or glossy finish. Some pieces enameled and gilded.

Thomas Webb & Sons and Stevens and Williams, England: Around 1888 these two firms made a peachblow style art glass marked "Peach Blow" or "Peach Bloom." A cased glass, shading from yellow to red. Occasionally found with cameotype designs in relief.

Gunderson Glass Co.: About 1950 produced peachblow type art glass to order; shades from an opaque faint tint of pink, which is almost white, to a deep rose.

Reference: John A. Shuman III, *The Collector's Encyclopedia of American Glass,* Collector Books, 1988.

Note: All pieces listed below are satin finish unless otherwise noted.

GUNDERSON

Compote, 5" h, 5½" d, acid finish, morning glory shape, pink shading to lavender to white baluster stem, 3¼" d base **375.00**

Creamer and Sugar, 3½" h, 5¾" w, acid finish, deep pink, vertical stripes, applied reeded handles **485.00**

Cup and Saucer, 2¾" h, 3½" w cup, 5" d saucer, acid finish, deep pink shading to white, applied white reeded handle, applied foot on cup **265.00**

Decanter, 10" h, bulbous, ftd, pouring lip, deep raspberry shaded to pale pink to white, orig peachblow stopper, reeded shell applied peachblow handle **775.00**

Goblet, acid finish, deep raspberry, applied peachblow foot **275.00**

Sugar, 3½" h, ftd, baluster stem, deep raspberry **275.00**

Toothpick **50.00**

Tumbler **100.00**

Vase, 6½" h, 3¾" d shoulder tapering to 2½" d base, rose pink shoulder band, white rim shading **150.00**

MT WASHINGTON

Creamer, 5¼" h, ribbon edge, applied handle, orig paper label "Patented/Peach/Mt W G Co/Blow/Dec 15 '85" **2,600.00**

Cruet, 5½" h, cylindrical ribbed body, blackberry vine dec, orig white faceted molded stopper with blue–gray tint, two small foot flakes on base . . **1,000.00**

Pitcher, 7¾" h, overshot, applied clear handle **285.00**

Sugar, cov, orig paper label **1,750.00**

NEW ENGLAND

Bowl, 5½" d, ruffled rim **375.00**

Celery Vase **875.00**

Creamer, 3" h, bulbous, ribbed, deep raspberry to white, white violets, leaves, and buds dec, gold trimmed handle and rim **550.00**

Pitcher, 6¼" h, crimped top, applied handle **1,300.00**

Punch Cup, acid finish, deep rose shading to white, applied white handle . . **425.00**

Rose Bowl, 4" h, 4" d, acid finish, deep color shading **485.00**

Salt Shaker, 3¾" h, acid finish, deep color, orig SP top **525.00**

Spooner, 4⅝" h **400.00**

Sweetmeat Jar, acid finish, SP cov with peach knob, SP handled frame sgd "Pairpoint Mfg Co, Quadruple Plate," c1900 . . . . **325.00**

Toothpick Holder, 2⅜" h, Wild Rose, ruffled top, orig paper label "NEGW/Wild Rose/Patd March 2, 1886" **525.00**

Tumbler, 3¾" h, velvety satin finish, deep raspberry–red fading to½" band of blush white base **445.00**

Vase, 6⅛" h, acid finish, Wild Rose, ruffled top edge 450.00

WEBB

Bowl, 3¾" d, folded and pinched rim, stamped on bottom "Queen's Burmese Ware Patented/Thos/Webb/&/Sons" 375.00

Finger Bowl, 5" d, acid finish, crimped top, applied clear rigaree, creamy white int. 200.00

Scent Bottle, 2¾" d, acid finish, enameled blue, white, and yellow forget—me—nots, green leaves, creamy white lining, hallmarked SS screw on dome top 675.00

Vase, 8½" h, butterfly hovering near tree, gold flowers and buds, deep pink shading to white, creamy lining 785.00

Pitcher, Wheeling, Hobbs, Brockunier, glossy, quadrafoil top, applied amber handle, c1883, 7½" h, $650.00.

WHEELING

Creamer, 3½" h, bulbous, fuchsia shading to amber, applied amber handle 1,150.00

Decanter, 9¼" h, flattened globular body, cylindrical neck, glossy finish, applied amber handle with swirled ribbing, faceted spherical amber stopper, Hobbs, Brockunier & Co 470.00

Finger Bowl, 4¾" d, cased, yellow shading to deep red, opaque white int. . . 400.00

Mustard Pot, 3" h, orig top 600.00

Pear, 6¾" h, red and amber, white lining 485.00

Tumbler 485.00

Vase, 7" h, cylindrical, flared, ruffled top, narrow amber border, Drape pattern 650.00

PEKING GLASS

History: Peking glass is a type of cameo glass of Chinese origin. Its production began in the 1700s and continued well into the 19th century. The background color of Peking glass may be a delicate shade of yellow, green, or white. One style of white background is so delicate and transparent that it often is referred to as the "snowflake" ground. The overlay colors include a rich garnet red, deep blue, and emerald green.

Box, cov, turquoise, Oriental figures and dog, 4⅝" d, $200.00.

Bowl
  6", cobalt, two etched lotus reserves, diaper border 150.00
  7" d, blue overlay flowers, butterfly, and foliage dec, white ground, teakwood stand 250.00
  11½" d, flaring rim, blue 350.00

Cup and Saucer, blue overlay dragons and clouds, white ground, sterling silver saucer 190.00

Jar, 5¾", cov, urn shape, cobalt, geometric pattern 600.00

Snuff Bottle
  All—over dec, wild geese and riverscape dec, painted int., c1900 . . . 100.00
  Figural and riverscape dec, painted 80.00
  Lotus dec, Jadeite stopper, painted 100.00

Vase
  4", blue on white, lotus leaves and flowers dec 125.00
  8½" h, 5½" d, bulbous, flaring top, double ring neck, cameo, red cut to white, Peking ducks and lotus dec, pr 550.00
  9" h, Chinese bright red dec, milk white ground, c1920 . . . . 290.00

10″, baluster shape, yellow overlay monkey and pine tree dec, white ground, early 20th C, pr **300.00**

12″, yellow overlay fish dec, white ground **375.00**

13″ h, baluster, deep crimson red tropical fish and lotus dec, milk white ground **750.00**

PELOTON

History: Wilhelm Kralik of Bohemia patented Peloton art glass in 1880. Later it was also patented in America and England.

Peloton glass is found with both transparent and opaque grounds with opaque being more common. Opaque colored glass filaments (strings) are applied by dipping or rolling the hot glass. Generally, the filaments (threads) are pink, blue, yellow, and white (rainbow colors) or a single color. Items also may have a satin finish and enamel decorations.

Cruet, light blue, multicolored strings, clear stopper, 7″ h, $265.00.

Biscuit Jar, 5¼″ h, melon ribbed, multi-colored strings, cased, white lining, silverplated top **550.00**

Bowl, boat shape, rainbow strings ... **325.00**

Pitcher

9¾″ h, clear, swirled body, red, yellow, blue, and white strings, applied clear reeded handle **250.00**

11″, multicolored strings, clear applied reeded handle, amber ground **550.00**

Plate, 7¾″, blue strings, clear ground, enamel floral dec **100.00**

Rose Bowl, multicolored strings, applied crystal shell feet, opaque white ground **310.00**

Vase

4¼″ h, fan, satin, ribbed frosted body, yellow, red, and blue filaments, frosted floral base **80.00**

4¼″ h, 4¾″ d, squatty, ribbed, tricorn folded over top, rose, yellow, blue, and white strings, white lining **300.00**

6″ h, 4½″ w, corset, shaded lavender to off white opaque ground cased in crystal, vertical ribs, all over pink, white, yellow, blue, and red strings, tightly crimped top **450.00**

6½″ h, 4″ w, vertical ribs, ruffled top, white ground, pink, yellow, and blue strings, five wishbone feet **400.00**

9″ h, baluster, sapphire blue ground, white strings, double handles **200.00**

PERFUME, COLOGNE, AND SCENT BOTTLES

History: Decorative bottles to hold scents have been made in various shapes and sizes. They reached a "golden age" during the second half of the 19th century.

An atomizer is a perfume bottle with a spray mechanism. Cologne bottles usually are larger and have stoppers which also may be used as applicators. A perfume bottle has a stopper that often is elongated and designed as an applicator.

Scent bottles are small bottles used to hold a scent or smelling salts. A vinaigrette is an ornamental box or bottle with a perforated top used to hold aromatic vinegars or smelling salts. Fashionable women of the late 18th and 19th centuries carried them in purses or slipped them into gloves in case of a sudden fainting spell.

Reference: Hazel Martin, *A Collection Of Figural Perfume & Scent Bottles*, published by author, 1982; Jacquelyne Jones–North, *Commercial Perfume Bottles*, Schiffer Publishing, 1987; Jacquelyne Jones–North, *Czechoslovakian Perfume Bottles & Boudoir Accessories*, Antique Publications, 1991; Jacquelyne North, *Perfume, Cologne, and Scent Bottles*, Schiffer Publishing, 1987; Jean Sloan, *Perfume and Scent Bottle Collecting With Prices, Second Edition*, Wallace–Homestead, 1989.

Collectors' Club: Perfume and Scent Bottle Collectors, 2022 East Charleston Blvd., Las Vegas, NV 89104.

ATOMIZERS

Baccarat

5″ h, 3½″ l, oval, etched crystal body, metal chrome top, marked **90.00**

6" h, amberina 75.00
Cambridge Glass, 6¼", gold stippled,
opaque jade, silk lined box 140.00
Opalescent, 5½" h, cranberry striped 90.00

COLOGNES

Blown Three-Mold, 6", purple, tooled
flared lip, pontil, ribbed 650.00
Bohemian Glass
2½ x 7⅜", ruby circles and medallion
with etched deer scene, cut scalloped base, ruby frosted, and clear,
ruby cut stopper 140.00
3 x 6¾", Vintage Pattern, ruby and
clear, orig steeple stopper 125.00
Cameo, 7⅝", white grapes and leaves,
raspberry red drapery ground, spring
hinged repousse silver stopper,
Thomas Webb and Sons 4,200.00
Cut, 5⅛" h, double cut, overlay, ruby to
clear, cut glass stopper 125.00
Opalescent, tooled eight panels, 4⅝" h,
c1860 .... 400.00
Pairpoint, paperweight stopper
7" h, clear, elaborate floral engraving,
orig open red rose in stopper,
Charles Kaziun signature cane .. 750.00
8¾", floral engraving, open red rose
in stopper with Charles Kaziun signature cane, sgd by maker "Otto C
Banks" 750.00
Paperweight, 5¼" h, concave facet cut,
blue and white concentric rings, red
and white canes, French 125.00
Sandwich, 9" h, opaque, white, elaborate dec, satin finish, pr 175.00

PERFUMES

Cameo
4", bulbous, white trailing fuchsias,
red ground, hinged spherical silvered metal cap, Stevens and Williams, c1900 .... 370.00
4⅜" h, bulbous, band of rust, deep
mauve, and white florals enameled
on neck, carved wildflowers, apricot, olive green, and gray streaked
ground, flattened bulbous carved
stopper, Daum Nancy, c1900 .... 4,500.00
Cranberry
2¼ x 5¾", sanded gold enameled
leaves, white enameled flowers,
clear ball stopper, gold trim 120.00
3⅜" l, oval, lacy filigree openwork ormolu, gilt collar, engraved, hinged
lid, inner stopper, attached chains
and finger ring 240.00
Cut Glass
4" l, lay down type, curved, int. stopper, ornate SS top 90.00

6" h, green cut to clear, prism and
mirror cut, clear cut faceted stopper 140.00
12" l, Russian pattern, Gorham SS
cap 265.00
Czechoslovakian
5½", cut, pink, frosted floral stopper 50.00
8½", amber, eight panel cut, waisted,
stopper 110.00
Lalique, 4", heart shape, Farouche
Ricci, sgd, red plush box 300.00
Moser, 4½" lay down type, cranberry,
white overlay, gold holly leaves and
thistles 235.00
Opaline, 8½", pink, cream, and gold
fleur-de-lis, matching stopper 150.00
Paperweight
3½" h, open red rose in base and
stopper, blue and white signature
cane under rose, Charles Kaziun 950.00
4" h, lavender crocus in base and
stopper, green leaves, yellow "W"
signature cane under leaves,
Whittemore 250.00
Porcelain, floral dec, Germany 40.00
Staffordshire, 2¾", pillow type, hp, garlands, gold dec, corner tassels, pr .. 200.00

SCENTS

Amethyst, 2½" h, pewter cap 120.00
Blown 3-mold, Sunburst pattern, cobalt
blue 75.00
Camphor Glass, 8", gold motif 45.00
Clear, 2⅜" h, blown, white looping, applied cobalt blue rigaree 85.00
Early American, 3" h, ovoid, peacock
blue, twenty-six vertical rib pattern,
sheared mouth and pontil, attributed
to Kent, OH 250.00
Northwood, 1¾" h, pull-up design, eight
horizontal bands, alternating stripes
of rust, chartreuse, and white, SS cap 390.00
Opalescent
2½" h, two part mold, Baroque pattern, hinged lid 75.00
3¼" l, horizontal and vertical ribs ... 25.00
3⅛" h, Diamond panels, threaded
pewter cap 35.00

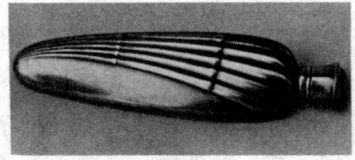

**Vinaigrette, Sterling silver, Art Nou-
veau, 3¼" l, $150.00.**

VINAIGRETTES

Cranberry, 2¼ x 1″, rect, cut, enameled
  pink roses, green leaves, gold dec
  hinged lid, stopper, finger chain **170.00**
German, 1″ h, silver, stein shape, enam-
  eled, marked "Gruss a München" . . **500.00**
Sterling Silver, 2 x 1½″, engraved scrolling, hinged lid with scene on top,
  pierced gold inner lid, Nathaniel Mills,
  Birmingham, 1849 . . . . **275.00**

PERSONALITY COLLECTIBLES

History: While a host of fictional characters orig-
inate from the comics, movies, radio, and television, a group of "stars" who retained their own
identity are also a by–product. Hopalong Cassidy
is a fictional character; Gene Autry and Roy Rogers are real life personalities. Real life drama also
produces "heroes" honored for an act of bravery
or a unique personal achievement.

The fame achieved by stars and heroes has
attracted the attention of promoters and manufacturers for over a century. From Buffalo Bill's Wild
West Show to Michael Jackson's Coca–Cola commercial, star power has shown itself to be a proven
value. Little wonder the advertising and toy industry has produced so many products featuring stars
and heroes.

This category includes only objects related to
real life personalities. Sometimes the line can become very blurred. Do Edgar Bergen and Charlie
McCarthy belong under character Items or personality collectibles? We have chosen to list them in
this category.

References: Richard DeThuin, *The Official
Identification and Price Guide To Movie Memorabilia*, House of Collectibles, 1990; Ted Hake,
Hake's Guide To TV Collectibles, Wallace–Home-
stead, 1990; John Hegenberger, *A Collector's
Guide To Movie Memorabilia*, Wallace–Home-
stead, 1991; Jefferson Graham, *Come On Down
!!! – The TV Game Show Book*, Abbeville Press,
1988; Richard O'Brien, Collecting Toys, A Collec-
tor's Identification & Value Guide, No. 5*, Books
Americana, 1990; Anthony Slide, *A Collector's
Guide To TV Memorabilia*, Wallace–Homestead,
1985; John R. Warren, *Warren's Movie Poster
Price Guide*, Overstreet Publications, 1986.

Periodicals: *Big Reel*, P.O. Box 83, Madison,
NC 27025; *Movie Collectors' World*, P.O. Box 309,
Fraser, MI 48026.

Additional Listings: See Character Items in
Warman's Antiques and Their Prices and Cowboy
Collectibles, Movie Personalities, Radio Charac-
ters and Personalities, Shirley Temple, and TV
Personalities & Memorabilia in *Warman's Ameri-
cana & Collectibles*.

Allen, Jimmie
  Booklet, "Jimmie Allen Air Battle,"
    Skelly Gas premium, 1935 . . . . . **30.00**
  Bracelet, secret message **15.00**
  Member Certificate, 8 x 11″, parch-
    ment paper, green border, red seal,
    "Full Fledged Pilot Member," Rich-
    field Oil issue, c1934 . . . . **45.00**
  Whistle, secret signal **20.00**
  Wings, brass, imprinted "Betsy Ross
    Bread" **40.00**
Allyson, June, coloring book, 1952 . . . **24.00**
Andrew Sisters, record set, Decca, five
  78 rpm records **22.00**
Autry, Gene, big little book, *Law of the
  Range* **10.00**
Bergan, Edgar and Charlie McCarthy
  Bank, still, 7½″ h, white metal, poly-
    chrome, missing monocle **65.00**
  Radio Show Ticket, 1½ x 3½″, tan
    and black, from "Edgar Bergen
    With Charlie McCarthy" March,
    1951 show, Columbia Broadcasting
    System, Coca–Cola sponsor **20.00**
  Sheet Music, *Love Walked In,* 1938
    musical film "The Goldwyn Follies,"
    9 x 12″ **85.00**
Berle, Milton, beer coaster, Balletine, ra-
  dio show **15.00**
Boyd, William as Cassidy, Hopalong
  Gun, Zoomerang, red **80.00**
  Napkins, unopened **42.00**
  Pencil Sharpener, yellow **30.00**
  Radio, black, mint condition **600.00**
  Stationary, orig box, cards, and en-
    velopes, marked "Buzza Cardoza
    Hoppy" **175.00**
  Wrist Watch, 1958, working **85.00**
  Wrist Watch Box, cardboard saddle **200.00**
Chaplin, Charlie
  Advertising Pinback Button, 1¼″ d,
    black and white, Chaplin laughing,
    Sampeck/Triple Service Suit,
    c1920 . . . . **40.00**
  Mirror, 1¾ x 2¾″, celluloid, pocket,
    black and white photo, inscribed
    "Hartsook Photo/S. F.–L.A." **100.00**
  Pinback Button,⅝″ d, black and white,
    late 1920s **25.00**
Coogan, Jackie
  Pencil Box **35.00**
  Pinback Button,⅝″ d, black and white,
    late 1920s **25.00**
Davis, Bette, magazine cover, *Photo-
  play*, Oct 1938, full color portrait cov,
  10½ x 14″ **12.00**
Dionne Quintuplets
  Booklet, Lysol, "Country Doctor Talks
    to Women," 32 pgs **20.00**
  Doll, 7½″ h, composition, jointed,
    brown molded hair, orig pink dress

and hat, Yvonne pin, Madame Alexander **150.00**
Fan, 8 x 14", cardboard, babies playing in sand, 1936 .... **20.00**
Poster, 14½ x 32", full color, Quaker Oats adv, 1935 .... **75.00**
Garland, Judy
Magazine Cover
Life, 1944 .... **7.00**
People Today, 1950 .... **12.00**
Mask, 7 x 9", face, diecut paper, "Dorothy from Wizard of Oz, 1939," on back **20.00**
Jolson, Al, orig movie program with ticket stub, Jazz Singer, Warner Theater, NY **850.00**
Karloff, Boris, movie poster, "Ghost in the Invisible Bikini" **75.00**

Laurel and Hardy
Figure, 2" h, 1¼" w, flat metal, painted, finely detailed, oval base, Mignot **20.00**
Mask, 9 x 9", paper, printed caricature face, marked "Laurel & Hardy's Laughing 20's," c1966, pr **40.00**
Pinback Button,¾" d, dark blue and white litho, Western Theater Premium Co, c1930 .... **35.00**
Planter, china, 3½ x 3½ x 4¼", full dimensioned caricature portraits, fleshtones, black, and white, glossy brown and black derbies, marked "Japan" **125.00**
Lindbergh, Charles
Game, Lucky Lindbergh, orig instructions **35.00**
Photograph, 8 x 10", brown tone, standing by plane, wearing dress suit, c1927 .... **25.00**
Pinback Button
1" d, "Welcome Home Lindy," black and white, photo, bottom rim inscription "Capt C A Lindbergh," attached red, white, and blue ribbons, detailed aluminum diecut of plane **70.00**
1¼" d, "Plucky Lindy," black and white, photo, gold horseshoe, red, white, and blue ribbon **35.00**

Marx Brothers
Program, Curtain Time Variety Show, 8½ x 11", 16 pgs, c1945, features Chico and Connee Boswell, black, white, and maroon cov **65.00**
Publicity Folder, 5¼ x 8½", "Double Dynamite", RKO Radio Pictures, 1951, features Groucho, Jane Russell, and Frank Sinatra, black, white, and red cov **50.00**
Sheet Music, *Alone,* 1935 MGM film, "A Night At The Opera", 9¼ x

12¼", blue photo of Brothers, orange, blue, and white cov **35.00**
McNeill, Don, Breakfast Club, yearbook, 1954 .... **8.00**
Monroe, Marilyn
Magazine
Gala, Vol 1, May–June 1960, 62 pgs, pin–up photos with captions, full color cover of Marilyn in pink swimsuit **80.00**
Marilyn Monroe Pin–Ups, 8½ x 11" folio, Maco Magazine Corp, 1953 copyright, 32 pgs **60.00**
Record, "The River of No Return," promotional, 78 rpm, RCA Victor label, black and white label with photo portrait, c1954 .... **75.00**

Marilyn Monroe, black silk and rhinestone evening hat, black netted veil, letter of authenticity, $1,650.00.

Pickford, Mary, pinback button,⅝" d, black and white, late 1920s **25.00**
Ranger, Lone, drinking glass, dated 1938 .... **25.00**
Rogers, Will
Poster, 27 x 41", "County Chairman", Fox, 1935, portrait, coral background **600.00**
Teaspoon, figural handle, SS **35.00**
Temple, Shirley
Book, *How I Raised Shirley Temple,* Screenland, 1935, photobook ... **18.00**
Children's Books
Birthday Book, 6th birthday, unused **65.00**
Five Books About Me, orig box, marked "No. 1730" **70.00**
Doll
12" h, composition, jointed, replaced curly blond and navy and white sailor dress, Ideal **45.00**
17" h, composition, jointed, replaced blond wig, replaced pink cotton dress, Ideal **75.00**
Paper Doll, ten outfits, cut out, marked "1719", orig box **39.00**

Statue, 6½" h, composition, frilly red
trimmed dress **50.00**
Sheet Music, *Animal Crackers In My
Soup* **14.00**
Wynn, Ed, figure, 10" h, cardboard,
bright paper label, Fire Chief outfit,
movable arms, legs, and head, c1930 **60.00**

PETERS AND REED POTTERY

History: J. D. Peters and Adam Reed founded
their pottery company in South Zanesville, Ohio,
in 1900. Common flowerpots, jardinieres, and
cooking wares comprised their early major output.
Occasionally art pottery was attempted, but it was
not until 1912 that their Moss Aztec line was introduced and widely accepted. Other art wares included Chromal, Landsun, Montene, Pereco, and
Persian.

Peters retired in 1921 and Reed changed the
name of the firm to Zane Pottery Company.
Marked pieces of Peters and Reed Pottery are
unknown.

Bowl, Pereco, 5½" d, 3¼" h, $65.00.

Bowl, 5" w, 4" h, Moss Aztec **140.00**
Bookends, pr, 5" h, Pereco, stylized dec,
matte green glaze **45.00**
Jug
4½" d, 4" h, high glaze, applied gold
lion's head and grapevines, dark
brown glaze **65.00**
8" h, mottled blue, traces of tan and
blue drip **25.00**
Mug, 5¾" h, high glaze, floral sprigs . . **35.00**
Nursing Feeder, grape and leaf garland
dec around spout, glossy brown glaze **30.00**
Pitcher, 6½" h, tankard, Moss Aztec, art-
ist sgd **65.00**
Vase
3½" h, Zane Ware, squatty, blue and
brown **25.00**
6½" h, Zane Ware, squatty, brown,
drip effect **35.00**
7¾" h, blackberry dec **45.00**
9¾" h, Moss Aztec, pine cone dec **75.00**
12" h, Landsun, blue glaze **90.00**

Wall Pocket
7¾" l, Pereco, Egyptian dec **85.00**
9" l, Moss Aztec, Art Nouveau figural
nude **175.00**

PEWTER

History: Pewter is a metal alloy, consisting
mostly of tin with small amounts of lead, copper,
antimony, and bismuth added to improve forma-
bility and hardness. The metal can be cast, formed
around a mold, spun, easily cut, and soldered to
form a wide variety of utilitarian articles.

Pewter ware was known to the ancient Chinese,
Egyptians, and Romans. English pewter supplied
the major portion of the needs of the American
colonies for nearly 150 years before the American
Revolution. The Revolution ended the embargo on
raw tin and allowed the small American pewter
industry to flourish. This period lasted until the Civil
War.

The listing concentrates on the American and
English pewter forms most often encountered by
the collector.

Reference: Donald L. Fennimore, *The Knopf
Collectors' Guides to American Antiques, Silver &
Pewter,* Alfred A. Knopf, Inc., 1984.

Collectors' Club: Pewter Collector's Club of
America, 29 Chesterfield Road, Scarsdale, NY
10583.

**Coffeepot, Savage, Middletown, CT, 10"
h, $425.00.**

Basin
Belcher, Joseph, faint touchmark, pit-
ting, and scratches, 8" d **650.00**
Boardman, Thomas Danforth, faint
eagle touch, 8" d **210.00**
Danforth, Samuel, Hartford, CT,
c1800, very faint mark, 6⅝" d . . . **400.00**
Ellis, Samuel, London, 18th C, 9⅛" d **200.00**
Hamlin, Samuel, pitted, faint touch-
mark, 7¾" d **100.00**
Jones, Gershom, Providence, RI,

1774–1809, minor pitting on inside, worn touch mark, 7¾″ d **1,250.00**

Lee, Richard, Springfield, VT, 1795–1815, 5¾″ d **300.00**

Rust, H N, 8″ d **650.00**

Stafford, Spencer, Albany, NY, c1820, 7¾″ d **300.00**

Townsend, Thomas, London, England, touchmarks, 13″ d **225.00**

Beaker

Woodbury, J. B., Beverly, MA, and Philadelphia, PA, 1830–38, handle, good mark, 3″ **400.00**

Yale, Hiram, Wallingford, CT, 1822–31, cast dec handle, 2¾″ h **150.00**

Bedpan, Thomas Danforth Boardman, Hartford, CT, c1820, 10½″ l, triple touch marks **400.00**

Bowl, unmarked, American, ftd, 6″ d . . **250.00**

Candlestick

Calder, William, Providence, RI, 1817–56, minor pitting on base, 10″ h **325.00**

Dunham, Rufus, Westbrook, ME, c1840, straight line touch, 6″ h, pr **900.00**

Endicott & Sumner, New York City, 1846–51, 8⅜″ h **350.00**

Gleason, Roswell, Dorchester, MA, c1840, 6½″ h **250.00**

Hopper, Henry, NY, straight line touch, 10″ h **275.00**

Ostrander & Norris, New York City, 1848–50, saucer base, resoldered, 4″ h **150.00**

Smith & Co, Boston, MA, mid 19th C, curved line touch, 6⅛″ h **150.00**

Unmarked, American, trumpet shape, c1810, 5¾″ h **200.00**

Wildes, Thomas, Philadelphia, PA and New York City, 1829–40, straight line touch, complete with bobeche, 10″ h **200.00**

Castor Set

Dunham, Rufus, Westbrook, ME, five clear cut bottles, frame marked "R Dunham 200," 13¼″ h **85.00**

Smith, Eben, Beverly, MA, 1813–56, four clear bottles **375.00**

Trask, Israel, Beverly, MA, 1807–56, five clear Sandwich Glass "Gothic Arch" pattern bottles, three with orig pewter tops, 9½″ h **250.00**

Chamberstick, Meriden Britannia Co., 1850, saucer base, gadroon molding, 4¼″ h **225.00**

Charger

Austin, Nathaniel, Charleston, MA, 13½″ d **450.00**

Badger, Thomas, Boston, MA, eagle touch, 13⅜″ d **650.00**

Cloudsley, Nehemigh, English, c1690, multiple reed rim, 18¼″ d **600.00**

Eadem, Semper, Boston, MA, 12⅛″ d **600.00**

Hamlin, Samuel, worn and pitted, knife scratches, touchmark, 11½″ d **300.00**

King, Richard, London, England, 16½″ d **375.00**

Langworthy, Lawrence, Devonshire, England and Newport, RI, 15″ d . . **400.00**

Leapidge, Thomas, London, 1673–1725, 15″ d **200.00**

Leigh, Charles White, London, England, 14¾″ d **300.00**

Pierce, Samuel, Springfield, MA, pitting, knife marks, dent in rim, 11¼″ d **210.00**

Coffeepot

Boardman & Hart, NY, repair in bottom, touchmark, 10½″ h **200.00**

Calder, William, Providence, RI, c1839, lighthouse, 11″ h **650.00**

Dunham, Rufus, Westbrook, ME, 1837–61, straight line touch mark, crude repair on bottom affecting small portion of mark, 11″ h **275.00**

Gleason, Roswell, Dorchester, MA, 19th C, straight line touch mark, 11″ h **250.00**

Griswold, Ashbill, Meriden, CT, pyriform, 10½″ **350.00**

Homan & Co, Cincinnati, OH, cast foliage finial, engraved floral design, marked "H Homan," 10¼″ h **235.00**

Porter, Freeman, Westbrook, ME, c1840, pear shape, marked "F Porter No. 2/Westbrook," 10¾″ h **250.00**

Richardson, George, Boston & Cranston, RI, 1818–45, 11″ h, "G Richardson, Warranted" touch **525.00**

Trask, Israel, Beverly, MA, c1830, lighthouse, bright cut engraved band, 11″ h **350.00**

Lamp, double font, American, unknown maker, 12″ h, $400.00.

Whitlock, John H, Troy, NY, marked "Whitlock, Troy, NY," 11½" h 325.00

Communion Bowl, Hiram Yale & Co, Yalesville, CT, 1824–35, ftd, 10¼" d, 5¾" h 600.00

Communion Flagon
Kirchen, Georg, German, 1763, hinged cov, oval finial, heart motifs dec 725.00
Smith, Eben, Beverly, MA, 1814–56, 10½", lighthouse shape, straight line touch 425.00

Communion Plate, Thomas Boardman, Hartford, CT, 1805–50, eagle touch mark, 13⅛" d 550.00

Creamer, Joseph, Henry, English export, London, 1740–85, three small feet, marked "HJ" 2,500.00

Cup, Birch & Villers, England, 1775–1820, double handles 325.00

Dish, deep
Calder, William, Providence, RI, c1830, 10⅜" d 450.00
Derby, Thomas, S., Middletown, CT, c1840, Derby's General Jackson touch mark, 13¼" d 600.00
Hamlin, Samuel, Hartford, CT, late 18th C, normal wear 600.00
Roos, Sven Bengtsson, Goteborg, Sweden, 1768–1802, hammered surface, 13" d 250.00

Egg Cup, unmarked, American 50.00

Flagon, Smith & Fletman, Albany, marked, 12" h 350.00

Flower Pot Jardiniere, James Putnam, Malden, MA, c1840, three paw feet stand horizontally from the bottom, 7¾" d, pr 350.00

Funnel, unmarked, American, ring hanger, 4⅜" d, 6⅜" l 125.00

Inkwell, unmarked, American, five quills, 6⅞" d 150.00

Jardiniere, James Putnam, Malden, MA, c1840, three paw feet, 7¾" d, pr ... 350.00

Ladle
Danforth, Josiah, Middletown, CT, 13¼" l 600.00
Unmarked, American, engraved handle, 13¾" l 225.00
Yates, John, Birmingham, England, c1835, minor pitting on bowl int., 13½" l 80.00

Lamp
Camphene
Gleason, Roswell, Dorchester, MA, c1830, acorn font, 7¾" h 275.00
Ostrander & Noyes, New York City, 1848–50, resoldered handle, saucer base, 8½" h 400.00
Unmarked, bell shape, 2" h 100.00
Chamber
Gleason, Roswell, Dorchester, MA,

c1845, saucer base, lemon font, orig whale oil burner, 4½" h ... 325.00
Porter, Freeman, Westbrook, MA, brass and tin whale oil burner, ring handle, 6" h 425.00
Taunton Britannia Mfg Co., Taunton, MA, 1830–35, marked "T.B.M. Co/ 24," 3¾" h, pr 650.00
Gimbal, Dunham & Sons, Portland, ME, 1861–82, arched touch, 4½" h 600.00
Grease, Continental, 18th or early 19th C, 9" h 150.00
Petticoat, Morey & Smith, cast ear handle, fluid burner missing snuff caps, marked "Morey & Smith, warranted, Boston," 3⅛" h 175.00
Whale Oil
Gleason, Roswell, Dorchester, MA, c1840, lemon fonts, period whale oil burners, 8" h, pr 500.00
Hopper, Henry, New York City, 1842–47, orig whale oil burners, straight line touch on bottom, 7" h, pr 750.00
Smith & Co, orig double drop whale oil burner, 5⅝" h 375.00
Unmarked, saucer base, ring handle, 2¼" h 200.00

Measure
English, one half pint, Channel Island Jersey type, 1750–1800 ...... 375.00
Unmarked, attributed to Thomas Danforth III, tankard shape, 6" h 325.00

Mug
Eddon, William, London, c1750, pint, tulip shape 150.00
Unmarked, tankard, tulip shape, 3¾" h 55.00
Whitmore, Jacob, Middletown, CT, 1758–90, qt, fair mark 1,750.00

Pitcher
Dunham, Rufus, Westbrook, ME, c1845, two quart size, cider type, 6½" h 350.00
Gleason, Roswell, Dorchester, MA, c1840, lid, 12" h 650.00
Homan & Co, Cincinnati, hinged lid, resoldered finial, marked, 12" h .. 110.00
Richardson, George, Sr., Boston, MA, 1818–28, cov, 10" h 750.00
Unmarked, American, pigeon breasted, reverse "C" handle, removable lid, 5½" h 300.00

Plate
Austin, Nathaniel, Charlestown, MA, eagle touchmark, 8" d 250.00
Badger, Thomas, Boston, MA
7¾", stamped initials on rim 300.00
8½" d, touchmark 325.00
Barnes, Blakeslee, Philadelphia, PA, rect touchmark and B Barnes with eagle, 7⅞" d 235.00

Billings, William, Providence, RI, rim
engraved "B W," 7⅞" d **350.00**
Calder, William, Providence, RI,
c1840
8⅜" d, eagle touch **375.00**
10⅝" d **250.00**
Compton, Thomas, English export,
1802–17, single reed, 7⅝" d **150.00**
Danforth, Samuel, Hartford, CT,
touchmarks, 7⅞" d **325.00**
Danforth, Thomas I, lion touchmark,
8" d **350.00**
Danforth, William, Middletown, CT, 8"
d **325.00**
Havelin, Samuel, Hartford, CT, int.
touchmark, 8⅛" d **375.00**
Jones, Gershom, Providence, RI,
1774–1908, single reed, 8⅜" **550.00**
Kilbourn, Samuel, Baltimore, MD,
7¾" d **325.00**
Lightner, George, Baltimore, MD, "G
Lightner, Baltimore" touchmark,
7⅞" d **225.00**
Swanson, Thomas, c1770, Ellis and
Swanson marks, 7⅞" d, pr **150.00**
Unmarked, American, 8" d **150.00**
Porringer
Boardman, Thomas D and Sherman
Boardman, Hartford, CT, c1810–
30, keyhole type crown handle, tri-
angular bracket, 5" d **325.00**
Green, Samuel, Boston, MA, cast
crown handle, 5½" d **550.00**
Hamlin, Samuel, Providence, RI,
c1790, flowered handle, minor int.
pitting, good touch mark, 5½" d . . . **500.00**
Unmarked, attributed to David Mel-
ville, Newport, RI, c1780–90, flow-
ered handle initialed "FGW," 5" d **150.00**
Salt
Boyd, Parks, Philadelphia, PA, 1795–
1819, beaded rim and base, ftd . . **950.00**
Unmarked, 18th C, molded leaf de-
sign, 2¼" h **30.00**
Soap Box, unmarked, American, circu-
lar, hinged lid, 4⅜" **125.00**
Soup Plate, Swanson, Thomas, En-
glish, circular, hinged lid **125.00**
Sugar Bowl
Boardman & Hart, NY, c1835, orig lid,
little minor denting, 8" h **350.00**
Hiram Yale & Co, Yalesville, CT,
1824–35, 5½" h **50.00**
Richardson, George, Boston and
Cranston, RI, 1818–45, fine condi-
tion **3,000.00**
Unmarked, attributed to Boyd Parks,
Philadelphia, PA, 1795–1819,
beaded lid, rim, and foot **7,500.00**
Spoon, William Bradford, New York City,
1719–85, round bowl, 6⅝" l **1,600.00**
Syrup, unmarked, American, miniature,

lighthouse coffeepot shape, resold-
ered lid to hinge, 5½" h **225.00**
Tea Set, Flag & Homan Pewter, Cin-
cinnati, OH, 3 pcs, 9⅝" h teapot,
creamer, and sugar, marked **75.00**
Teapot
Boardman, Thomas D and Samuel,
Hartford, CT, cast acorn finial, copper bottom marked "TD & SB," 8⅜"
h **100.00**
Gleason, Roswell, Dorchester, MA,
c1840, inverted mold, minor pitting,
12" h **650.00**
Smith, Eben, Beverly, MA, c1830,
bright cut engraved band, straight
line touch, 7½" h **500.00**
Warming Dish, Griffin, Thomas, London,
c1760, two handles, 12⅜" d **300.00**

PHOENIX BIRD CHINA

History: Phoenix Bird pattern is a blue and
white china exported from Japan during the 1920s
to 1940s. A limited amount was made during the
"Occupied Japan" period.

Initially it was available at Woolworth's 5 & 10,
through two wholesale catalog companies, or by
selling subscriptions to needlecraft magazines.
Myott Son & Co., England, also produced this pattern under the name "Satsuma," c1936. These
earthenware items were for export only.

Once known as "Blue Howo Bird China," the
Phoenix Bird pattern is the most sought after of
seven similar patterns in the Hō-ō bird series.
Other patterns are: Flying Turkey (head faces forward with heart-like border); Howo (only pattern
with name on base); and Twin Phoenix (border
pattern only, center white). The Howo and Twin
Phoenix patterns are by Noritake and are occasionally marked "Noritake." Flying Dragon (bird-
like), an earlier pattern, comes in green and white
as well as the traditional blue and white and is
marked with six oriental characters. A variation of
Phoenix Bird pattern has a heart-like border and
is called Hō-ō.

Phoenix Bird pattern has over 500 different
shapes and sizes. Also varying is the quality found
in the execution of design, shades of blue, and
shape of the ware itself. All these factors must be
considered in pricing. The maker's mark tends to
add value; over 90 marks have been cataloged.

Post 1970 pieces were produced in limited
shapes with precise detail, but are on a milk white
ground and usually don't have a maker's mark.
When a mark does appear on a modern piece, it
appears stamped in place.

Reference: Joan Collett Oates, *Phoenix Bird
Chinaware*, published by author, *Book One*, 1984,
Book Two (A through M), 1985, *Book Three (N
through Z and post 1970)*, 1986; *Book Four (with
a section On Flying Turkey)*, 1989.

Collectors' Club: Phoenix Bird Collectors of America, 5912 Kingsfield Drive, West Bloomfield, MI 48233.

Additional Listings: See *Warman's Americana & Collectibles* for more examples.

Advisor: Joan Oates.

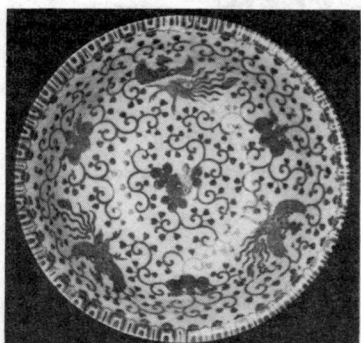

Bowl, marked "Japan/T" in flower, 10" d, 2⅝" h, $35.00.

Bowl
5" d	10.00
5¾" d	12.00
8¼" d, soup	40.00
10" d, fruit	45.00
Butter Pat	8.00
Cake Tray, cut out handles	40.00
Dish, 8⅞" d	30.00
Ginger Jar, 5⅛" h	10.00
Hot Water Pot, cov	35.00
Jar, cov, bath salts	35.00
Matchbox Holder, Ho–O, stand	75.00
Nut Cup, three feet	15.00
Pie Plate, 6¾" d, plain edge	10.00

Plate
6" d, bread and butter	5.00
8½" d, luncheon, marked "Nippon"	25.00
11¼" d, chop	55.00

Platter
10" l, oval	25.00
13½" l, 9" w, scalloped	45.00
15½" l	75.00
Reamer, pitcher base	55.00
Rice Tureen, 6½" h, "S" style handles, #1	80.00
Salt and Pepper Shaker, pr	20.00
Sauce Boat, 3½" h, #3	30.00
Sherbet, Ho–O	20.00
Soap Dish, 7½"	25.00
Sugar Bowl, cov, 3½" h	20.00
Syrup, Ho–O, #12	20.00

Tankard, water, 6½" h	75.00
Tea Strainer	15.00
Teapot, #11–B	45.00

PHOENIX GLASS

History: Phoenix Glass Company, Beaver, Pennsylvania, was established in 1880. Known primarily for commercial glassware, the firm also produced a molded, sculptured, cameo–type line from the 1930s until the 1950s.

Reference: Jack D. Wilson, *Phoenix & Consolidated Art Glass, 1926–1980,* Antique Publications, 1989.

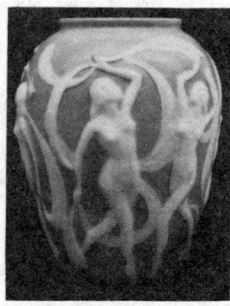

Vase, sculpted nudes, light blue ground, cream figures, orig paper label, 11½" h, $500.00.

Ashtray, Praying Mantis, triangular	45.00

Bowl
8" l, boat shape, sculptured green lemons and foliage, white ground	85.00
14" d, sculptured diving nudes, three colors	200.00
Cigarette Box, cov, 4½" d, 3½" h, sculptured white flowers, blue ground	65.00
Creamer and Sugar, Catalonia pattern, yellow	45.00

Lamp, table
6½" h, sculptured lavender peonies, white ground	100.00
11" h, sculptured yellow ferns and foliage, gray ground	150.00
28" h, Gone with the Wind style, double oil burner, cameo cut, raised orchid design, green opal ground, brass mounts, sgd "Phoenix," converted to electric	3,000.00
Planter, 8½" l, sculptured green lion, white ground	65.00

Plate
8¼" d, dancing nudes, yellow **60.00**
8½" d, kumquats, green **50.00**
Vase
6¼" h, sculptured pink peonies, green
    leaves, white ground **90.00**
8½" h, sculptured white dancing
    nudes, light green ground **150.00**
9" h, pillow shape, sculptured deep
    blue fish, white ground **200.00**
10" h, Wild Rose, white pearlized rus-
    set **125.00**
11" h, 7" d, baluster, frosted ground,
    large blue flowers, tan stems,
    green leaves **350.00**
18", Thistle, MOP flowers
    Pale blue ground **225.00**
    Slate ground, orig label **500.00**

Victor, 78 RPM, Charles Ross Taggart, black label, 12" d, $7.50.

PHONOGRAPH RECORDS

History: With the advent of the more sophisticated recording materials, such as 33⅓ RPM long playing records, 8–track tapes, cassettes, and compact discs, earlier phonograph records became collectors' items. Most have little value. The higher priced examples are rare (limited production) recordings. Condition is critical.

References: L. R. Docks, *1915–1965 American Premium Record Guide, 3rd Edition,*, Books Americana, 1986; Fred Heggeness, *Country Western Price Guide,* FH Publishing, 1990; Jerry Osborne, *The Official Price Guide To Records, Ninth Edition,* House of Collectibles, 1990; Fred Heggeness, *Country Western Price Guide,* FH Publishing, 1990; Neal Umphred, *Goldmine's Price Guide To Collectible Record Albums,* Krause Publications, 1989.

Collectors' Club: Association For Recorded Sound Collectors, P.O. Box 75082, Washington, DC 20013; International Association of Jazz Record Collectors, Box 10208, Oakland, CA 94610.

Periodicals: *Discoveries,* P.O. Box 255, Port Townsend, WA 98368; *Goldmine,* 700 E. State Street, Iola, WI 54990.

Additional Listings: See "Records" in *Warman's Americana & Collectibles* for those recordings in price range from $5.00 to $25.00.

Note: Most records, especially popular recordings, have a value of less than $3.00 per disc. *The records listed here are classic recordings of their type and are in demand by collectors.*

Lee Andrews & The Hearts, White Cliffs
   Of Dover, red plastic, Rainbow 250   **90.00**
Frank Blevins' Tar Heel Rattlers, I've
   Got No Honey Babe Now, Columbia
   15765-D **90.00**
The Buccaneers, The Stars Will Re-
   member, Rama 21 . . . .   **125.00**

Cannon's Jug Stompers, Wolf River
   Blues, Victor 23272 . . . .   **85.00**
George Castelle & The Castelles, Over
   A Cup Of Coffee, Grand 109 . . . . .   **80.00**
Darby & Tarlton, Going Back To My
   Texas Home, Columbia 15715–D . .   **50.00**
Cecil Gant, The Incomparable Cecil
   Gant, Sound LP 601 . . . .   **45.00**
Jay Garber & His (Greater Columbia
   Recording) Orchestra, How Could
   Red Riding Hood?, Victor 20322 . . .   **20.00**
Gay Notes, For Only A Moment, Drexel
   905 . . . .   **65.00**
Harris & Harris, Teasing Brown, Victor
   3859 . . . .   **70.00**
King Solomon Hill, The Gone Dead
   Train, Paramount 13129 . . . .   **225.00**
Hornets, I Can't Believe, States 127 . .   **70.00**
Johnny Howard, Hastings Street Jump,
   De Luxe 6044 . . . .   **60.00**
George E Lee & His (Novelty Singing)
   Orchestra, Down Home Syncopated
   Blues, Merritt 2206 . . . .   **250.00**
Fate Morable's Society Syncopators,
   Frankie and Johnny, Okeh 40113 . .   **75.00**
Original Memphis Five, Kansas City
   Kitty, Vocalion 15810 . . . .   **35.00**
Paramount Pickers, Salty Dog, Para-
   mount 12779 . . . .   **90.00**
Parham's Black Patti Band, Um–Te–
   Da–Da–Da, Black Patti 8038 . . . . .   **60.00**
Parrots, Please Don't Leave Me,
   Checker 772 . . . .   **110.00**
Patton And Lee, Troubled 'Bout My
   Mother, Vocalion 02904 . . . .   **115.00**
Pelicans, Aurelia, red plastic, Parrot 793   **175.00**
Jim Reeves, Teardrops Of Regret, Ma-
   cy's 115 . . . .   **45.00**
Posey Rorer & The North Carolina
   Ramblers, As We Sat Beneath The
   Maple On The Hill, Edison 52414 . .   **40.00**

Sonny Boy Williamson, Skinny Woman, Bluebird 7012 .... **25.00**
Willie Mae, I'd Rather Drink Muddy Water, Vocalion 03404 .... **20.00**
Wrens, I Won't Come To Your Wedding, Rama 184 .... **85.00**
Malcolm Yelvington, Drinkin' Wine Spodee–O–Dee, Sun 211 .... **35.00**

PHONOGRAPHS

History: Early phonographs were commonly called "talking machines." Thomas A. Edison invented the first successful phonograph in 1877. Other manufacturers followed with their variations.

Collectors' Club: Antique Phonograph Collectors Club, 502 E. 17th Street, Brooklyn, NY 11226.

Periodical: *Horn Speaker*, Box 53012, Dallas, TX 75253.

Victor #1, early 19th C, $650.00.

American Graphophone Co, Graphophone Type Q, c1897 .... **275.00**
Brunswick, Parisiane, collapsible cardboard horn **400.00**
Columbia
   Disc Graphophone, 1902 .... **1,000.00**
   Grafanola Baby Regent **400.00**
   Graphophone, oak dome cov and cabinet **550.00**
Edison
   Amberola 30 .... **325.00**
   Diamond Disc Model No S19 ..... **150.00**
   Gem, Model C **300.00**
   Model 50 .... **275.00**
   Triumph, Model H **500.00**
Garrard, hand crafted snakeskin horn, 1920 .... **1,250.00**

Harmony, oak case, painted morning glory horn **400.00**
Junophone, table model, oak case, metal wood grain finish horn **250.00**
Kalamazoo Duplex **1,350.00**
McDonald Graphophone, oak case, open works **800.00**
Regina Reginaphone Disc Musical Box and Phonograph, oak case, MOP inlay, five 15½" discs, c1904 .... **2,100.00**
Sears Roebuck & Co, Silvertone, 1914 **150.00**
Victor
   Model 1050, record changer **450.00**
   V, oak horn, 1905–1914 .... **1,375.00**
   V–II, wood horn **1,250.00**
Victrola
   Model VI, table type, oak **150.00**
   Model XI **100.00**
Zonophone, Champion, table model, oak case, ribbed brass horn **750.00**

PICKARD CHINA

History: The Pickard China Company was founded by Wilder Pickard in Chicago, Illinois, in 1897. Originally the company imported European china blanks, principally from the Havilands at Limoges, which they then hand painted. The firm presently is located in Antioch, Illinois.

Bowl
   5" d, gooseberry dec **75.00**
   7" d, strawberries dec, artist sgd ... **85.00**
Cake Plate, 10" d, basket with fruit and flower dec, gold etched edges, artist's initials, 1912 mark **125.00**
Candlesticks, pr, 4½" h, etched gold .. **45.00**
Celery Tray, 13½" l, gold band, grape dec, creamy ground, sgd "Challinor" **85.00**
Chocolate Pot, 11½" h, white MOP ground, orchids and foliage dec ... **165.00**
Creamer and Sugar, gold peacock medallions, blue and white floral etched ground **170.00**
Demitasse Pot, poinsettia dec, artist sgd, dated 1910 .... **200.00**
Dinner Service, service for six, serving pcs, heavy gold border, c1925, marked "Pickard, Rosenthal," 52 pcs **5,200.00**
Ewer, 6½" h, bulbous, tricorn, deep sea green matte ground, gold blueberries and leaves, heavy gold spout, handle, and neck, gold swirls, artist sgd "Coufall," 1905 mark **325.00**

Mug, gold banding and trim, poinsettia, panel form, oil style glaze, white ground, artist sgd, 6⅞″ h, $200.00.

Marmalade, cov, cream ground, orange water lilies, green lily pads, scalloped gold trim and outlines, artist sgd "Tolpin," 1898 mark 175.00
Mustard, cov, attached underplate, hp, green and gold Art Deco design, marked "Pickard" 125.00
Pitcher, 8″ h, 5⅝″ d, six sided, gold ground, 1½″ band of blue, green, white, and gold water lilies, gold int., artist sgd "James," etched 1912 to 1922 mark 275.00
Plate
  6″ d, hp, poppies, rococo gilt scallops, artist sgd "Leach," 1905 mark . . . 50.00
  8″ d, waterfall, river, trees, gold trim, matte finish, artist sgd "Marker" . . 175.00
  9″ d, carnations, gold 100.00
Powder Box, cov, 4″ d, hp, roses, sgd "A. K. France/Wall" 125.00
Salt Shaker, Tolpin pattern, lemon dec 40.00
Tea Set, cov teapot, creamer, cov sugar, etched gold, pink roses on black band, artist sgd 300.00
Tray, 15½″ l, scenic, pierced handle, gold rim, artist sgd "Gasper" 150.00
Vase
  6½″ h, stylized lavender flowers, trailing leaves, cream ground, gold trim 150.00
  9″ h, water scene, trees, and foliage, matte ground, artist sgd 445.00
  9¼″ h, scenic, matte finish, sgd "Challinor" 400.00
  11″ h, cylindrical, hp, maiden, partially clad, long red hair, butterfly in hand, white ground, artist sgd "M" 250.00
Wine Set, decanter, orig stopper, eight wine glasses, matching tray, black ground, gold grapes, sgd "Hess" . . 625.00

PICKLE CASTORS

History: A pickle castor is a table accessory used to serve pickles. It generally consists of a silver plated frame fitted with a glass insert, matching silver plated lid, and matching tongs. Pickle castors were very popular during the Victorian era. Inserts are found in pattern glass and colored art glass.

Clear, Swirl pattern insert, begging dog finial, orig tongs, Hartford Quadplate, 10″ h, $175.00.

Amethyst, applied floral dec, SP frame and lid 275.00
Cranberry
  Barrel insert, multicolored enamel floral dec, figural frame with acorns and dog's feet 400.00
  Decorated, IVT pattern insert, ornate Meridian frame, orig tongs 300.00
Craquelle, gargoyles on top, satin pewter silver–look Pairpoint frame, acorn finial on engraved lid 235.00
Green Glass, enameled florals, ornate SP frame 225.00
Pattern Glass
  Currier & Ives, blue 145.00
  Daisy and Button, bird's nest on top, orig tongs, minor damage to silver 185.00
  Sprig, blue, Reed and Barton frame, orig fork, fancy lid 150.00
  Opalescent, Daisy and Fern, blue apple blossom mold, ornate ftd SP frame, orig tongs 265.00
  Pomona, second grind, blue cornflower dec, all orig 500.00
  Rubena, quilted, decorated insert, ftd, fancy frame, orig tongs 275.00
Satin Glass
  Cranberry, Optic Diamond and IVT pattern insert, gold spider chrysan-

themum dec, ftd Simpson Hall frame, ornate engraved cov, orig silvering 600.00

Yellow barrel shaped insert, flowers and butterfly dec, lid slides on handle, cherubs on front and back corners of frame, marked "Rogers," 11" h 735.00

PIGEON BLOOD GLASS

History: Pigeon blood refers to the deep orangish-red colored glass ware produced around the turn of the century. Do not confuse it with the many other red glass wares of that period. Pigeon blood has a very definite orange glow.

Tumbler, alternating panel and rib, 3½" h, $65.00.

Biscuit jar, Beaded Drapery pattern, ornate SP rim, cov, and handle 200.00
Bowl, 9" d, c1880 .... 150.00
Bride's Basket, 9½" d, enamel floral dec, SP holder 200.00
Creamer, Torquay pattern, SP rim and handle 125.00
Cruet, IVT, orig stopper 225.00
Pickle Castor, Bulging Loops pattern, 8" h SP ftd frame, marked "Empire Mfg Co" 285.00
Pitcher, Torquay pattern 320.00
Salt Shaker, Bulging Three Petal 25.00
Sugar Shaker, Bulging Loop 250.00
Syrup, Scroll and Net pattern, satin finish, applied frosted handle, orig top 575.00
Table Set, cov butter, creamer, cov sugar, and spooner, Torquay pattern, orig SP rims and lids 575.00
Vase, 10½" h, enameled flowers 185.00

PINK SLAG

History: True pink slag is found only in the molded Inverted Fan and Feather pattern. Quality pieces shade from pink at the top to white at the bottom.

Reproduction Alert: Recently pieces of pink slag, made from molds of the now defunct Cambridge Glass Company, have been found in the Inverted Strawberry and Inverted Thistle pattern. This is not considered "true" pink slag and brings only a fraction of the Inverted Fan and Feather pattern prices.

Tumbler, Inverted Fan and Feather, 4" h, $450.00.

Butter, cov 650.00
Creamer 450.00
Cruet, 6½" h, orig stopper 1,300.00
Jelly Compote 375.00
Marmalade Jar, cov 875.00
Punch Cup
  Feather pattern, 2¼" h 40.00
  Fiery opalescent shading to pale pink 265.00
Sauce 225.00
Spooner 350.00
Toothpick Holder 850.00
Tumbler 485.00
Water Pitcher 775.00

PIPES

History: The history of pipe making dates as early as 1575. Almost all types of natural and manmade materials, some which retained smoke and some that did not, were used to make pipes. Among the materials were amber, base metals, clay, cloisonné, glass, horn, ivory, jade, meerschaum, parian, porcelain, pottery, precious metals, precious stones, semi–precious stones, assorted woods, *inter alia*. Chronologically the four most popular materials and their generally accepted introduction dates are: clay, c1575; woods, c1700; porcelain, c1710; and meerschaum, c1725.

National pipe styles exist around the globe wherever tobacco smoking is custom or habit. Pipes reflect a broad range of themes and messages, e.g., figurals, important personages, commemoration of historical events, mythological characters, erotica and pornographica, the bucolic, the bizarre, the grotesque, and the graceful.

Pipe collecting began in the mid-1880s; William Bragge, F.S.A., Birmingham, England, was an early collector. Although firmly established through the efforts of free-lance writers, auction houses, and museums (but not the tobacco industry), the collecting of antique pipes is an amorphous, maligned, and misunderstood hobby. It is amorphous because there are no defined collecting bounds; maligned because it is conceived as an extension of pipe smoking, now socially unacceptable [many pipe collectors are avid non-smokers]; and misunderstood because of its association with the "collectibles" field.

References: R. Fresco-Corbu, *European Pipes*, Lutterworth Press, 1982; E. Ramazzotti and B. Mamy, *Pipes et Fumeurs des Pipes. Un Art, des Collections, Sous le Vent,* 1981; Benjamin Rapaport, *A Complete Guide To Collecting Antique Pipes*, Schiffer Publishing, 1979.

Collectors' Club: Pipe Collectors International, Inc., P.O. Box 22085, Chattanooga, TN 37422.

Periodicals: *Pipe Collectors Of The World,* Box 11652, Houston, TX 77293; *Universal Coterie of Pipe Smokers,* 20-37 120th Street, College Point, NY 11356.

Museums: Museum of Tobacco Art and History, Nashville, TN; National Tobacco-Textile Museum, Danville, VA; U.S. Tobacco Museum, Greenwich, CT.

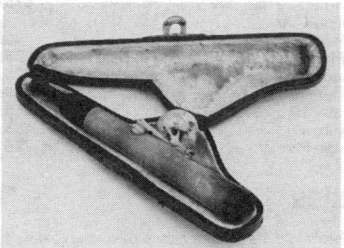

Skull, amber stem, cheroot holder, orig case, 3¹³⁄₁₆″, $200.00.

Briar, 11″ l, carved bearded man bowl, horn stem	**165.00**
Clay, 4¼″, blue and white bowl, brown stem, Ohio	**160.00**
Ivory, angel with wings, amber stem	**150.00**
Meerschaum, carved	
6⅛″ l, St George and the Dragon, cheroot holder	**450.00**
6¼″ l, Girl with spinning wheel, cheroot holder, cracked amber stem, fitted case	**550.00**

6⅝″ l, head of Pan, amber stem, fitted case	**375.00**
6⅞″ l, tavern scene, maid serving hunter, cheroot holder, amber stem, fitted case	**425.00**
7¼″ l, horse head, agitated expression, gold ferule, cheroot holder, amber stem, fitted case	**475.00**
8″ l, 6″ h, laughing bearded soldier, map of France engraved on helmet and tunic, silver fitting set with turquoise, orig stem and case missing	**2,600.00**
8¼″ l, Indian head, chief in full head dress, 14 carat ferule marked "Shreve & Co," composition stem, fitted case marked "C. P. F."	**650.00**
10½″ l, hunting, maidens with wolves chase stag around rose, amber stem, fitted case	**1,300.00**
Porcelain	
3½″ h, Turkish gentleman bowl, bust head, jeweled and beaded turban, underglaze enamels, metal stem mount, hinged bowl cov, German, 19th C	**1,500.00**
19″ l, twig stem, brass fittings, Bavarian	**50.00**
Silver, sterling, boatswain, macrame cord	**40.00**
Wood, hand holding bowl	**80.00**

POCKET KNIVES

History: Alcas, Case, Colonial, Ka-Bar, Queen, and Schrade are the best of the modern pocket knife manufacturers, with top positions enjoyed by Case and Ka-Bar. Knives by Remington and Winchester, firms no longer in production, are eagerly sought.

Form is a critical collecting element. The most desirable forms are folding hunters (1 and 2 blades), trappers, peanuts, Barlows, elephant toes, canoes, Texas toothpicks, Coke bottles, gun stocks, and Daddy Barlows. The decorative aspect also heavily influences prices. Values are for pocket knives in mint condition.

References: James F. Parker, *The Official Price Guide to Collector Pocket Knives, 9th Edition,* House of Collectibles, 1987; Jim Sargent, *Sargent's American Premium Guide To Pocket Knives: Identification and Values,* Books Americana, 1986; Ron Stewart and Roy Ritchie, *The Standard Knife Collector's Guide,* Collector Books, 1986.

Periodical: *Knife World,* P.O. Box 3395, Knoxville, TN 37917.

Collectors' Clubs: American Blade Collectors, P.O. Box 22007, Chattanooga, TN 37422; Canadian Knife Collectors Club, 3141 Jessuca Court, Mississauga, ON L5C1X7; The National Knife Collectors Association, P.O. Box 21070, Chattanooga, TN 37421.

Museum: National Knife Museum, Chattanooga, TN.

Additional Listings: See *Warman's Americana & Collectibles* for more examples.

Case, scrimshaw handle, Nantucket, whaling scene, $150.00.

CASE

Case uses a numbering code for its knives. The first number (1–9) is the handle material; the second number (1–5) designates the number of blades; the third and fourth number (0–99) the knife pattern. Stage (5), pearl (8 or 9), and bone (6) are most sought in handle materials. The most desirable patterns are 5165—folding hunters, 6185—doctors, 6445—scout, muskrat—marked muskrat with no number, and 6254—trappers.

In the Case XX series a symbol and dot code is used to designate a year.

1920–40

5111½ blade, lock	600.00
53131, canoe	1,000.00
5452	300.00
6245, dog groomer	200.00
6261	120.00
8265	1,000.00

1940–65

4200, melon taster, serrated blade	150.00
42507, "Office Knife" on handle	100.00
5265	200.00
61093	175.00
62009, Barlow	100.00
6214, with shield	65.00
640045R, scout	25.00
Muskrat	90.00

1965–70, XX series

5254	85.00
5172, bulldog	150.00
6111½	100.00
6143, Daddy Barlow	40.00
92042	100.00

1970–80 (number of dots indicates year)

2137, sod buster	25.00
52131, canoe	100.00
5375, stag	70.00
6246R, rigger	45.00
P13755, stag, Kentucky Bicentennial	50.00

KA-BAR (Union Cutlery Co., Olean, NY)

The company was founded by Wallace Brown at Tidioute, PA in 1892. It was relocated in Olean, NY, in 1912. The products have many stampings including Union [inside shield], U-R Co. Tidioute [variations], Union Cutlery Co. Olean, NY, Alcut Olean, NY, Keenwell, Olean, NY, and Ka-Bar. The larger knives with a profile of a dog's head on the handle are most desirable. Pattern numbers rarely appear on a knife prior to the 1940's.

21107, Grizzly	2,000.00
2217, rigger	70.00
61161, composition handle	125.00
6191, knife, fork, spoon	625.00
6250, elephant toe	300.00
6260, KF	100.00
Cigar Cutter	150.00

KEEN KUTTER (Simons Hardware, St. Louis, MO)

K1771¾, Daddy Barlow	150.00
K1898¾, toothpick	100.00
K8464¼, Kattle	50.00

REMINGTON, last made in 1940

R1273, bullet	1,500.00
R1535, florist	80.00
32373, cattle	250.00
R273, Texas Jack	190.00
3335, scout, red, white, and blue	285.00
4235, red, white, and blue	200.00
Bullet, authorized reproduction	60.00

WINCHESTER

1701, Barlow	100.00
1920, hunter	1,100.00
2070, office knife	75.00
2380, doctor's	350.00
3022, whittler	250.00
3376	250.00

OTHER MANUFACTURERS

Elephant Toe

Cattaraugus Cutlery Co.	300.00
Ibberson, pearl work back	300.00
New York Knife Co.	350.00

Folding Hunter

Bower, Atlanta, GA	85.00
C. Platts & Sons, Eldred, PA	100.00
Cattarangus Cutlery Co.	350.00
George Wosterholm & Son Cutlery Co., General Taylor	1,500.00
Marbles Arms Co.	350.00
New York Knife Co.	500.00
Queen Cutlery Co., Titusville, PA	100.00
Schrade Walden, Walden, NY	150.00

Union Razor Co., Titusville, PA	**100.00**
Valley Forge Cutlery Co., NJ	**200.00**
Western States Cutlery Co., Boulder, CO, buffalo skull mark	**300.00**

POISON BOTTLES

History: Poison bottles were designed to warn and prevent accidental intake or misuse of their poisonous substances, especially in the dark. Poison bottles generally were made of colored glass, embossed with "Poison" or a skull and crossbones, and sometimes were coffin-shaped.

John H. B. Howell of Newton, New Jersey, designed the first safety closure in 1866. The idea did not become popular until the 1930s when bottle designs became simpler and the user had to read the label to identify the contents.

References: Ralph and Terry Kovel, *The Kovels' Bottle Price List, 8th Edition,* Crown Publishers, Inc., 1987; Carlo and Dorothy Sellari, *The Standard Old Bottle Price Guide,* Collector Books, 1989.

Periodical: *Antique Bottle and Glass Collector,* P.O. Box 187, East Greenville, PA 18041.

Amber, embossed "POISON," triangular front, ribbed corners, blown, 3⁹⁄₁₆" h, $6.00.

Chester A. Baker, Boston, cobalt	**50.00**
Dicks Ant Destroyer, Finlay Dicks & Co, New Orleans	**30.00**
Figural, skull, 4⅛" h, crossed bones on base, cobalt blue, tooled lip, smooth base, light inner haze	**1,300.00**
Kilner Bros, Makers Made in England, round, fluted panels, topaz, emb "POISON" on two shoulders, 8¾" h, 1900–20	**75.00**
Leavin's English Vermin Destroyer, aqua, oval, open pontil, 9"	**175.00**

Martin Poison Bottle, aqua, tooled ring lip, 4⁹⁄₁₆" h, England, c1902	**350.00**
Owl Drug Co, triangular, owl sitting on mortar and pestle, cobalt blue, tooled lip, 4⅜" h	**170.00**
Trilets, Poison, triangular, blue, 3⁵⁄₁₆" h, 1900–30	**25.00**
Triloids, Poison, triangular, blue, 3⁵⁄₁₆" h, 1900–30	**25.00**
W T & Co, round, cobalt blue, tooled lip, lattice and diamond pattern, 7¼" h, c1890	**70.00**

POLITICAL ITEMS

History: Since 1800 the American presidency has always been a contest between two or more candidates. Initially souvenirs were issued to celebrate victories. Items issued during a campaign to show support for a candidate were actively being distributed in the William Henry Harrison election of 1840.

Campaign items cover a wide variety of materials—buttons, bandannas, tokens, pins, etc. The only limiting factor has been the promoter's imagination. The advent of television campaigning has reduced the emphasis on individual items. Modern campaigns do not seem to have the variety of materials which were issued earlier.

References: Herbert Collins, *Threads of History,* Smithsonian Institution Press, 1979; Stan Gores, *Presidential and Campaign Memorabilia With Prices, Second Edition,* Wallace-Homestead, 1988; Theodore L. Hake, *Encyclopedia of Political Buttons, United States, 1896–1972,* Americana & Collectibles Press, 1985; Theodore L. Hake, *Political Buttons, Book II, 1920–1976,* Americana & Collectibles Press, 1977; Theodore L. Hake, *Political Buttons, Book III, 1789–1916,* Americana & Collectibles Press, 1978; Edmund B. Sullivan, *American Political Badges and Medalets, 1789–1892,* Quarterman Publications, Inc., 1981. (Note: Theodore L. Hake issued a revised set of prices for his three books in 1984.)

Collectors' Club: American Political Items Collectors, P.O. Box 340339, San Antonio, TX 78234.

Periodical: *Political Collector,* 444 Lincoln Street, York, PA 17404.

Museum: Smithsonian Museum, Washington, D.C.

Note: The abbreviation "h/s" is used to identify a head and shoulder photo or etching of a person.

Additional Listings: See *Warman's Americana & Collectibles* for more examples.

Advisor: Theodore L. Hake.

Advertising Card
  Greeley, Horace, 2½ x 4", sepia paper, image of Greeley surrounded by slogan "What I Know About Charter Oak Stoves/Is, That They

Are Always The Cheapest To Buy!
Best To Use!," blank reverse **75.00**

Harrison, 3½ x 5", inscribed "We Advocate Iron–Clad Clothing For Working Men/Benjamin Harrison," issued by Quincy Shirt and Overall Co, Quincy, Il, c1888 . . . . **25.00**

Ashtray, Dewey, 4" d,¾" h, brass, "Dewey Headquarters/Hotel Walton/Phila 1940" **15.00**

Badge, Franklin D. Roosevelt, 1934, $35.00.

Badge, Harrison, 1888, 1½ x 2½" diecut and emb brass shell, three prongs, log cabin, animal skin on front wall, barrel of hard cider **150.00**

Bandanna
Eisenhower, 26" sq, red, white, and blue, shield and star design, "Win With Ike For President," inscription above large blue and white portrait **65.00**
Carter/Mondale, 1980, 28" sq, bright green and white polyester **20.00**

Banner, 7 x 7½", red, white, and blue, wooden rod, gold cord at top, inscribed "America's Choice/Keep America Strong/Make America Safe/Re–Elect Roosevelt For Freedom–Humanity–Democracy" **30.00**

Bowtie, 1960, 4¼ x 6½", clip–on, bright yellow, gold sparkles, hp, black and red design, "I'm For Kennedy" **65.00**

Bumper Sticker, 4 x 18", black, white, blue, and orange, inscribed "Kennedy For President," issued by "Massachusetts Committee For John F Kennedy For President" **18.00**

Button
1896, Bryan, ⅞", brown rooster, silver and gold tail feathers, stepping on gold thorn branch, 16 silver wheat stalks, inscribed "Bryan and Sewall", "16 to 1" **85.00**
1901, 1¼", "In Memoriam President Wm. McKinley," closed back, St. Louis Button Company **18.00**
1904, ⅞", TR/Lincoln, brown and white photos, light blue ground, blue stars, gold eagle and rim, inscribed "50th Anniversary Of The Republican Party/1854 Lincoln/Roosevelt 1904" **35.00**
1924, ⅞", Davis/Smith, dark blue on white, John W Davis 1924 campaign **160.00**
1940, 1¼", Roosevelt/Wallace, jugate, brown photos, bright red, white, and blue rim **40.00**
1944, 1¼", blue on white, inscribed "Dewey/The Racket Buster/New Deal Buster" **15.00**
1956, 1⅛", red, white, and blue, inscribed "I Like Ike And Clyde" . . . **24.00**
1960, 1¾ x 2¾" rect, Nixon/Lodge, red, white, and blue, light pink faces **10.00**
1968, 1¼", Nixon/Agnew, jugate, black and white ovals, red, white, and blue designs, white ground . . **8.00**
1980, 1¾", Reagan/Bush, jugate, black and white center, red, white, and blue edge, "Let's Make America Great Again" **5.00**

Calendar
FDR, 16 x 34", paper sheet for calendar, full color portrait surrounded by Art–Deco border in gold, green, blue, and brown, c1930 . . . . **20.00**
Wilkie/McNary, 12 x 15", cardboard, dark green and gold borders, color photo of US Capitol, inset black and white photos of Wilkie and McNary, inscribed "President Wendell Wilkie," "Vice–President Charles L McNary," and "Greetings And Good Wishes," c1940 . . . . . . **45.00**

Car Attachment, 4½ x 12", "Rise With Roosevelt," dark blue, red, and white lettering, copyright 1932 . . . . **75.00**

Change Tray, Taft/Sherman, 4½", jugate, "Grand Old Party," tin, colored litho, names of Republican presidents from 1856 to 1908 printed around raised rim, color scene of candidates, American flags, and White House . . **70.00**

Cigar, bubble gum, Reagan, orig cellophane wrapper, inscribed "Reagan Is Right" **8.00**

Cigar Band Set, twenty five 1 x 3" bands, emb color designs, color portraits of presidents Washington through T Roosevelt, c1904 ...... **30.00**

Cigar Box, 8½ x 9½ x 1½", "True Yankee," portrait of T Roosevelt surrounded by pair of eagles holding the constitution and a big stick, label inside lid, c1920 .... **50.00**

Cigar Box Cover, 5½ x 8", "10¢ Al Smith 10¢", litho tin frame, clear glass center, beige, dark brown lettering, slips over cigar box lid, c1928 .... **40.00**

Clicker, Nixon, 2½", blue and white litho tin, "Click With Dick" **15.00**

Clock, 4 x 9 x 14", electric, white metal, gold, FDR at ship's wheel which surrounds clock dial, United Clock Corp, Bklyn, NY, c1930 .... **125.00**

Doll Head, 6", donkey or elephant, three–dimensional, light gray plush, red, white, and blue fabric striped ears, black and white cardboard eyes, ribbon tags on red, white, and blue neckties inscribed "Dem" and "GOP," gold elastic cord, black yarn mane, Gund, c1960–64 .... **20.00**

Elephants Hoover/Curtis, 1½ x 4 x 2½", celluloid, beige, three–dimensional, name painted on side in black, pr .. **125.00**

Fan, Dewey, 10 x 10½", cardboard, die-cut, white, dark blue **30.00**

Figure, Caroline and John–John, 6", hp, ceramic, copyright 1963, black and gold foil sticker marked "Inarco/Japan," inscribed "Cleveland, Ohio" and "E1844/E1845" **75.00**

Game, Meet The Presidents, 9½ x 19 x 2" box, unused, coin holder, presidential coins from Washington through Nixon, spinner, diecut circles for coins on gameboard, 1965, Selchow & Righter Co **20.00**

Glass, Bryan and Sewall, 3½", jugate, 1896 campaign, clear glass, frosted white portraits surrounded by stars, inscribed "Sixteen To One/Free Coinage Of Silver" **85.00**

Harmonica, By Jiminy Peanut Harmonica, three–dimensional, peanut shape, raised dec, 6 x 7" card inscribed "The Big Happy Smile That Everybody Knows," "Giftco, Inc," 1977 .... **8.00**

Jug, ⅞" h, Harrison and Morton, miniature, brown pottery, small handle, black paper label **85.00**

Key Ring

1960 Democratic Convention, three–dimensional white metal donkey, painted brown, brass link chain, brass key ring holding large, heavy, brass key, one side of key shows smiling donkey standing on roof of jet plane, inscribed "Delegate Los Angeles 1960," reverse inscribed "Air Transport Association/Flying Donkey Club/National Democratic Convention" **10.00**

Nixon, key ring/pocket knife, red, white, and blue plastic disk inscribed "President Nixon, Now More Than Ever," pair of knife blades inside disk, brass key chain, orig gold box **15.00**

License Plate

Hoover, 3½ x 12", red, white, and blue, embossed letters, c1928 ... **30.00**

Dewey, 6 x 10", fiberboard, dark blue ground, yellow inscription "Harrisburg Republican Club With Dewey–Bricker," 1944 .... **25.00**

Carter, 6 x 12", Inauguration, beige background, dark blue and red, set of 2 .... **25.00**

Magazine, 8½ x 11", "This Is Ike/A Picture Story Of The Man," soft cover, 96 pgs, Holt & Co, 1952, 1st edition ... **5.00**

Matchbook, 1½ x 2", "New York/We Like Ike!," red, white, and blue, unused, cardboard diecut of Ike inside cover, each individual match is lettered either "New York State" or "We Like Ike!" **15.00**

Necktie, Dewey, full–size, rust color, silkscreen, black, white, and yellow, image of Capitol dome above Dewey, "Abraham & Strauss/Brooklyn," c1948 .... **20.00**

Pen, 5", Goldwater, brass, black inscription, "Let's Win With Goldwater" ... **10.00**

Pencil, 4", "Landon & Knox 1936," jugate, pencil stub in pull–out metal tube **175.00**

Pennant, "Wallace/Taylor," white, dark blue ground and lettering **25.00**

Photo Card, 3½ x 5¾", "John F Kennedy And His Family," pictorial biography, black and white photos, caption on reverse, boyhood to presidency, no mention of assassination, 6 x 7½ x 1" box, "Ed–Un-Cards," c1964, boxed, set of 42 ... **40.00**

Pipe, 6", "Dewey" green and white sticker on bowl, Missouri Meerschaum Co, c1948 .... **50.00**

Plate

9", Benjamin Harrison, glazed, beige, dark brown portrait, leaf designs on rim, reverse has pressed–in mark "BM & Co Extra Quality," c1888 .. **30.00**

6", "For President William H Taft,"

white china, center brown photo image, marked "National China Co" 20.00

Playing Cards, 2½ x 3½", "Politicards," boxed deck, full color caricatures of Democrats, Republicans, and other political figures from 1980 .... 20.00

Poster

12½ x 18", For President Warren G Harding, large sepia photo, Edmonston Studio, Washington 70.00

11 x 15", Franklin D Roosevelt, gray and white photo, bright red inscription, small caption "Photo August 1944" 25.00

14 x 20", Welcome President Nixon to Pekin, stiff cardboard, dark blue and orange, white ground, c1970 20.00

18 x 27", Reagan satire, color, designed to resemble movie poster, Free Enterprise Films Presents Ronald Reagan In 'Bedtime For Brezhnev', two large scenes, six inset pictures, political figures in western outfits, Oh Dawn, N.Y. distributors, copyright 1981 .... 25.00

Puppet

Johnson, 10", donkey, dark blue fabric, white mouth, dark maroon lettering, button eyes, 1964 .... 10.00

Nixon/Agnew, 12", caricature, fabric, large thick latex rubber head, Nixon with blue fabric, white felt collar, light blue felt tie, Agnew with black and white check fabric, red collar and red felt bow tie, c1970. pr ... 80.00

Radio, Carter, 3 x 3 x 7½", figural, peanut, Carter's head at top, black plastic wrist strap, c1976 .... 35.00

Ribbon, 2½ x 6", Press, President Truman, Philadelphia, Oct. 6, 1948, red, white, and blue fabric, gold letters, 1½" metal stickpin 40.00

Ring, flasher

Kennedy, John, silver plastic base, color insert portrait of JFK and American flag, "35th President/ John F Kennedy/1917–1963" ... 20.00

Nixon, gold plastic base, light blue plastic disk inset, black and white picture of Nixon and Agnew, "President Nixon's Visit to Peking 21st Feb 1972" 15.00

Serving Tray, 10 x 13 x 1", "Compliments of Cigar Makers' Union No 236 Reading, PA," litho metal, raised edge, dark green background, gold designs and lettering, black and light blue Union's paper stamp cigar box seal "Look For The Blue Label On Every Box" and "Smoke Only Union Made Cigars" inscriptions on edge, c1900 .... 135.00

Booklet, Al Smith, *National Life Magazine*, Volume 1, No. 1, 1928, 45 pgs, 8⅜ x 10½", $25.00.

Sheet Music, 8½ x 11", *Thomas E Dewey March*, 4 pgs, red, white, and blue, caption "Dedicated To A Great Governor Of New York State," includes photos of Dewey and the National Championship American Legion Band–Syracuse Post No 41, 1952 .... 10.00

Stickpin, 1", "Four Years More," emb tin, lunch pail, drinking cup, and carrying handle, soldered straight pin on reverse, 1900 .... 50.00

Stovepipe Hole Cover, 8" d, flat, "Hoover For President," litho tin, white and black, metal fastener riveted to reverse, c1928 .... 30.00

Stud

Cox, lapel, small white metal rooster, name at center 25.00

Democratic 100 Club, brass, blue enamel circle, FDR at center 5.00

Tie Clip, 2", exact replica of a "Yale" key, gold plating, "The Yale & Towne Mfg Co" inscribed on round end, "First For Ike" stamped on shaft, issued by Yale Ike Club, 1952 ...... 90.00

Tile, JFK, 6 x 6", white, full color illus of Pres And Mrs. John F Kennedy, fabric covering and wall hanger on back .. 25.00

Tin Can, 2½" d x 4½" h, I Like Ike, elephant holding flag, red, white, and blue 25.00

Tintype

Lincoln, ⅞ x 1¹⁄₁₆" brass frame 300.00

George McClellan, 7/8 x 1 1/16" brass
frame **125.00**
Token
Lincoln, 3/4", 1864 campaign, copper,
bust of Lincoln and "1864" on front,
linked chain surrounding "O.K." on
reverse **50.00**
Garfield/Arthur, 1", 1880 campaign,
brass, jugate busts on front, names
and "Union" on reverse **25.00**
Blaine/Logan, 1", 1884 campaign,
brass, jugate busts on front,
"Union" and slogans on reverse **35.00**
Watch Fob
1 1/2", brass, black lettering, "To Wash-
ington/Roosevelt And Fairbanks/
1904" **20.00**
Taft, 1 5/8", celluloid, portrait **50.00**
Wooden Nickel, Goldwater, 1964, re-
verse slogan "A Choice Not An Echo" **8.00**

POMONA GLASS

History: Pomona glass, produced only by the
New England Glass Works and named for the
Roman goddess of fruit and trees, was patented
in 1885 by Joseph Locke. It is a delicate lead,
blown art glass which has a pale, soft beige ground
and a top one–inch band of honey amber.

There are two distinct types of backgrounds.
First ground, made only from late 1884 to June
1886, was produced by fine cuttings through a wax
coating followed by an acid bath. Second ground
was made by rolling the piece in acid resisting
particles and acid etching. Second ground was
made in Cambridge until 1888 and until the early
1900s in Toledo where Libbey moved the firm after
purchasing New England Glass works. Both methods produced a soft frosted appearance, with fine
curlicue lines more visible on first ground pieces.
Designs are used on some pieces, which were
etched and then stained in color. The most familiar
design is blue cornflowers.

Do not confuse Pomona with "Midwestern Pomona," a pressed glass with a frosted body and
amber band.

Reference: Joseph and Jane Locke, *Locke Art
Glass: A Guide For Collectors,* Dover Publications,
1987.

Bowl
5" d, Rivulet pattern, second grind,
fluted, blue stain **80.00**
5 1/4" d, second grind, fluted, cornflower dec **30.00**
Creamer, 6" d, 3" h, second grind, fair
staining, ruffled top, applied crystal
crimped base **225.00**
Creamer and Sugar, first grind
Amber stained handles and wide ruffled upper border **585.00**

**Mustard, Flower and Pleat, washed
color, SP top, 3 1/8" h, $40.00.**

New England Glass Co **425.00**
Lemonade, pr, leaf design, first grind,
handle, one with crack under handle **110.00**
Nappy, 5 1/4" d, Cornflower dec, blue, first
grind, applied handle, ... **125.00**
Pitcher, 4 1/2" h, milk, first grind, Thumbprint pattern, sq top, stained rim and
handle **350.00**
Punch Cup
Amber leaf design, first grind **35.00**
Cornflower dec, blue, first grind **60.00**
Set of 12 .... **240.00**
Spooner, 5" h, IVT, second grind, red
stemmed blueberry dec and crimped
base **125.00**
Tumbler
3 3/4", first grind, pansy spray on one
side, butterfly on other **135.00**
4", second grind, DQ, blue cornflower
dec **100.00**
Vase, 5" h, second grind, Blueberry pattern, ruffled, applied crimped base **550.00**

PORTRAIT WARE

History: Plates, vases, and other articles with
portraits on them were popular in the second half
of the 19th century. Although male subjects, such
as Napoleon or Louis XVI, were used, the ware
usually depicted a beautiful woman, often unidentified.

A large number of English and Continental
China manufacturers made portrait ware. Because
most ware was hand painted, an artist's signature
often is found.

Additional Listings: KPM and Royal Vienna.

Cabinet Plate, 9 1/3" d, painted portrait of
Mme De Genlis, cobalt and gilt geometric dec concentric bands, four
painted floral reserves on rim,
Sevres, 18th C **425.00**

Cup and Saucer
  2½" h, cup with Marie Antoinette portrait in gilt medallion, cobalt blue ground, polychrome pastoral scene on saucer, Sevres, 18th C 300.00
  3" h cup with polychrome portrait of Louis XVI in gilt medallion, celeste blue ground, central polychrome floral monogram on saucer, celeste blue border with gilt trim, Sevres, 18th C 300.00
Dresser Tray, 12" l, two portrait medallions, four floral medallions, gold design, white ground, marked "Nippon"   225.00
Jewel Box, 10½ x 5", blown—out florals, ribbons on cov, center multicolored portrait of seated woman, 18th C attire, beige ground, gold highlights, marked "Mt Washington" 950.00
Plaque, pierced for hanging
  9¾", cavalier, hp, artist sgd, marked "Coronet" 165.00
  10", Lund, hp, artist sgd "F Tenner," beehive mark 350.00
  10¼", bust of beautiful lady, green ground, gold rococo border, artist sgd, marked "Coronet" 165.00

Plate, woman with flowing brown hair, maroon border, gold dec, green mark "Johnson Bros, England," 8¾" d, $50.00.

Plate
  8" d, bust length portrait of Anmuth, Vienna style, gilt scroll, diaper and foliate pattern border, sgd "Wagner," framed 825.00
  8½" d, lady with dark hair, gray scarf, shaded ochre rim, marked "TVL, Franzant Mehlem" 50.00
  9½" d
    Josephine, bust length portrait, Vi-

enna style, blue ground, wide border with gilt foliate scrolls, sgd "Wagner" 715.00
    La Marquise de Venneuil, painted portrait, three floral reserves on enamel jewel rim, cobalt ground, Sevres 400.00
    Maiden, bust length portrait, Vienna style, brown hair, off the shoulder shift, holding pink roses, metallic burgundy ground rim, framed 1,760.00
  9¾" h, bust length portrait of Ariadne, Vienna style, border of gilt foliage, metallic red ground, lobed rim, sgd "Wagner" 1,220.00
  10"
    American Indian, hp, artist sgd "Coronet" 65.00
    Queen Louise, beehive mark 110.00
  11¾", five portraits of Louis XV, Marie Theresa, and Marie Antoninette, gold trim, blue ground, pierced for hanging 140.00
  17", woman, jade green border, gold trim, marked "Victoria, Austria" . .   150.00
Shaving Mug, woman, dressed in brown and white, white plumes and red ribbon on hat 65.00
Tile, lady wearing large hat, round . . .   45.00
Vase
  9½" h, burgundy ground, portrait of maiden, gold framed cartouche, artist sgd, Vienna shield mark, numbered 1,275.00
  10", blonde lady, daisies in hair, multicolored flowers, gold scroll handles 250.00

POSTERS

History: The poster was an extremely effective and critical means of mass communication, especially in the period before 1920. Enormous quantities were produced, helped in part by the propaganda role posters played in World War I.

Print runs of two million were not unknown. Posters were not meant to be saved. Once they served their purpose, they tended to be destroyed. The paradox of high production and low survival is one of the fascinating aspects of poster history.

The posters of the late 19th century and early 20th century represent the pinnacle of American lithography printing. The advertising posters of firms such as Strobridge or Courier are true classics. Philadelphia was one center for the poster industry.

Europe pioneered in posters with high artistic and aesthetic content. Many major artists of the 20th century designed posters. Poster art still plays a key role throughout Europe today.

References: John Barnicoat, *A Concise History of Posters*, Harry Abrams, Inc., 1976; George Theofiles, *American Posters of World War I: A Price and Collector's Guide*, Dafram House Publishers, Inc.; Walton Rawls, *Wake Up, America!: World War I and The American Poster*, Abbeville Press, 1988; Stephen Rebello and Richard Allen, *Reel Art: Great Posters From The Golden Age of The Silver Screen*, Abbeville Press, 1988.

Collectors' Club: Poster Society, Inc., P.O. Box 43171, Montclair, NJ 07043.

Additional Listings: See *Warman's Americana & Collectibles* for more examples.

Advisor: George Theofiles.

Broadside, Reward Poster, Abraham Lincoln's assassins, carte–de–visite photographs of John Wilkes Booth, John H. Surratt, and David E. Harold, issued in 1865 by Edwin Stanton, Secretary of War, $18,700.00.

ADVERTISING

Arrow Shirts, 22 x 28″, c1925, litho, young couple in sailboat, blue water ground, orig frame 450.00

Cocomalt, 10 x 16″, full color, features premium book "Walt Disney's Pinocchio," 1939 .... 150.00

Frigidaire, We Cool Our Milk With Frigidaire, 19 x 14″, c1935, enameled dairy sign, white cow, blue ground, minor chipping 110.00

Heinz Baked Beans, 24 x 31″, c1915, vivid colors 325.00

Lux Radio Theater, 15 x 23″, full color, advertising Broadway hits broadcast through Columbia network, sponsored by Lux Toilet Soap, c1930 ... 40.00

Moxie, Drink Moxie, 19 x 19″, c1920, diecut head of soda fountain jockey 210.00

Nivea, 44 x 60″, Farago, 1938, bathing beauty, dark bronze suntan, gold and yellow background, floating tube holding bottle of Nivea suntan oil .. 550.00

Prince Albert, The National Joy Smoke, 21 x 27″, c1925, Chief Lean Wolf, bright colors 325.00

Wrigleys Gum–Enjoy Daily–Chewing Helps You On The Job, 45 x 40″, Otis Shepard, c1943, airbrushed design, workers welding, sparks flying in unison in front of repeated design of Wrigley's Gum, deep blues, greens, reds, and yellows 500.00

MOVIE

One Sheet, silent

All Of A Sudden Norma, 41 x 81″, BB Features, c1914, Bessie Barriscale, Ritchey stone litho, beautiful woman in front of moonlit window 550.00

Charlie Chaplin In The Thief Catcher, 28 x 41″, c1920, Chaplin with cigar leaning amid title, orange, brown, grays, red, and green, red borders 900.00

Half Way To Heaven, 27 x 41″, Paramount, c1925, Charles Buddy Rogers, Jean Arthur, bright blue and purple ground 275.00

Story Seas, 27 x 41″, Pathe, c1920, JP McGowan, Helen Holmes, litho of stars in front of burning and sinking steamship 350.00

One Sheet, 27 x 41″

Adventure In Diamonds, Paramount, 1939, George Brent, Isa Miranda, starlet looking through jeweled facets, black ground 225.00

Beyond Bengal, Showmen's Pictures, Harry Schenks, c1933, stone litho, boa constrictor attacking screaming native, lurid multicolor, cobalt blue ground **300.00**

Charlie's Aunt, Fox, 1941, Jack Benny, Kay Francis, Anne Baxter **275.00**

Daytime Wife, Fox, 1939, Tyrone Power, Linda Darnell, leggy secretary taking dictation at left, portrait close–ups of stars **475.00**

Gentlemen After Dark, United Artists, 1942, Brian Donlevy, Miriam Hopkins, Preston Foster, looming portrait of Donlevy **150.00**

Invisible Menace, Warner Bros, 1937, Boris Karloff, Marie Wilson, litho, yellows, browns, and burnt oranges **425.00**

Madame X, MGM, 1937, Gladys George, John Beal, litho 1930's image **225.00**

Navy Spy, Grand National, 1937, Conrad Nagel, Eleanor Hunt, pulp cover like artwork of Nagel, flaming biplanes and dogfight **275.00**

Rebecca Of Sunnybrook Farms, Fox, 1938, Shirley Temple, Randolph Scott, bright Tooker litho, Temple in overalls and straw hat **975.00**

Something For The Boys, 20th Century Fox, 1944, Carmen Miranda, Michael O'Shea, Phil Silvers, Earl Moran pin–up art of Vivian Blaine in leggy pose **325.00**

Two Fisted Gentleman, Columbia, 1936, James Dunn, June Clayworth, boxing theme **225.00**

World And The Flesh, Paramount, 1932, George Bancroft, Miriam Hopkins, silk screen like design of Hopkins against black background, smiling Bancroft as Russian sailor **425.00**

Three Sheets, 41 x 81″

Abraham Lincoln, Feature Productions, 1930, Walter Huston, Una Merkel, D W Griffith production, image of Lincoln, white and blue foggy montage of other characters, Civil War battle **550.00**

Hoosier Schoolmaster, Monogram Pictures, 1935, Charlotte Henry, Norman Foster, litho portrait against book motif, full color, bright red ground **325.00**

Vertigo, Paramount, 1958, James Stewart, Kim Novak, Alfred Hitchcock film **650.00**

TRANSPORTATION

All Weather Fleet Goes Through, 25 x 40″, PA Railroad–Stormy or Starry The Night...Low Fares To All Points, full color, Loewy designed streamlined engine **500.00**

American–Hawaiian Steamship Company, 34 x 22″, Fred Pansing, c1900, chromolithograph, single stack steamer **975.00**

Fly To America By Clipper–Pan American World Airways, 28 x 42″, Von Arenburg, c1947, silk screen, Clipper in front of ghostly image of charging Indian chieftain, NY skyline **575.00**

In Old Kentucky, 27 x 40″, N C Wyeth, c1921, Modern Kentucky Is Served By The PA Railroad," Daniel Boone hunting **625.00**

Tahiti–Fly Teal, 24 x 38″, c1952, exotic, Australian, offset litho, stylized nude Tahitian maiden bathing, deep green ground, one of 7,000 copies **475.00**

United Air Lines–Colorado, 25 x 40″, c1953, Joseph Binder, fisherman, casting under shooting airliner **325.00**

United States Lines To America, 25 x 40″, c1935, US liner, unfurled American banner, reds, white, blues, black, yellows, upper right margin expertly rebuilt **675.00**

WORLD WAR I

Americans All, 27 x 40″, Howard Chandler Christy, 1919, Columbia holds wreath above honor roll of ethnic names **225.00**

Columbia Calls, Enlist In The Army, 28 x 40″, Francis A Halstead, kromolithograph of Columbia with banner and sword, atop globe, sky blue ground **200.00**

Enlist Now And Go With Your Friends, 28 x 40″, Arthur N Edrop, issued by Mayor's Committee NYC, silhouettes of doughboys against American flag stripes ground **275.00**

Go Over The Top–US Marines, 21 x 28″, John A Coughlin, 1917, Marine leaps from trenches carrying Lewis gun **275.00**

Our American Boys In The European War, silent movie, Triangle Film, 27 x 41″, 1916, litho of wounded soldier being attended to in front of American ambulance **375.00**

Pull Together Men–The Navy Needs Us, 14 x 22″, Paul R Bloomhower, c1917, Boston Committee on Public Safety window card, sailors rowing lifeboat, dark green and orange sea **150.00**

You Can Help–American Red Cross, 20 x 30″, W T Benda, litho, lady knitting **150.00**

WORLD WAR II

Arise Americans–Your Country And Your Liberty Are In Grave Danger, 28 x 41", McClelland Barclay, 1941, sailor preparing deck gun **150.00**

Become A Paratrooper–Jump Into The Fight, 17 x 25", Steve Savage, paratrooper and M–1 carbine **350.00**

Hit Back–Enlist In The Coast Guard–Remember Pearl Harbor, 22 x 28", 1943, silk screen, Coast Guard ensign, yellow ground **110.00**

If You Must Talk–Tell It To The Marines, 19 x 28", 1942, Marine talking to factory worker, bright orange ground . . **125.00**

United Nations Fight For Freedom, 29 x 40", Broder, 1942, flags of all nations, silver Statue of Liberty **100.00**

We Clear The Way–The Corps Of Engineers, 19 x 25", Schlikjer, 1942, engineer holds sledge hammer and rifle, battle panorama **250.00**

POT LIDS

History: Pot lids are the lids from pots or small containers which originally held ointments, pomades, or soap. Although a complete set of pot and lid is desirable to some collectors, lids are the most collectible. The lids frequently were decorated with multicolored underglaze transfers of rural and domestic scenes, portraits, florals, and landmarks.

The majority of the containers with lids were made between 1845–1920 by F. & R. Pratt, Fenton, Staffordshire, England. In 1920, F. & R. Pratt merged with Cauldon Ltd. Several lids were reissued by the firm using the original copper engraving plates. They were used for decoration and never served as actual lids. Reissues by Kirkhams Pottery, England, generally have two holes for hanging and often are marked as reissues. Cauldon, Coalport, and Wedgwood were other firms making reissues.

References: Susan and Al Bagdade, *Warman's English & Continental Pottery & Porcelain, 1st Edition,* Warman Publishing Co., Inc., 1987; A. Ball, *The Price Guide to Pot-Lids And Other Underglaze Multicolor Prints On Ware, Second Edition,* Antique Collectors' Club, 1980; Ronald Dale, *The Price Guide To Black and White Pot–Lids,* Antique Collectors' Club; Barbara and Sonny Jackson, *American Pot Lids,* published by authors, 1987.

Note: Sizes are given for actual pot lids; size of any framing not included.

Alexandra Toothpaste/Dr. Ziemer's/ Matchless For Beautifying And Preserving The Teeth & Gums/London, portrait of Queen Alexandra, facing left, black and gray on white, outer gold band, 3½" d **220.00**

Areca Nut Tooth Paste
Army and Navy Co–Operative Soci-

Pratt, titled "Pretty Kettle of Fish," 4⅛", $300.00.

ety Limited, two military men shaking hands and holding flags, black on white, 3¹⁄₁₆" d, rust stains **85.00**

Barclay and Sons, Farringdon St. London/A Fleet Marriage Party From A Print Of The Time, gold border, black on white, 3½" d, stable hairline across lower left **1,900.00**

Cleansing Preserving And Beautifying The Teeth/Lewis and Burrows Ltd. London, roses, black on white, 2¾" d **80.00**

For Cleansing And Whitening The Teeth And Gums/Timothy White Company Chemists, Portsmouth, geometric center, black on brown, 2¹⁵⁄₁₆" d **85.00**

Bazin's Ambrosial Shaving Cream/X. Bazin, Philadelphia/Premium Perfumery, American eagle center, flower assortment below, blue on white, 3¹⁄₁₆" d **700.00**

Cherry Tooth Paste
B & Co. T, cherry cluster on leafy branch, black on white, 2⁹⁄₁₆" d . . **300.00**

Patronized By The Queen/For Beautifying and Preserving The Teeth, Prepared By John Gosnell & Co. London, young head profile of Queen Victoria facing left, shades of blue and black on white, gold band, 3³⁄₁₆" d **110.00**

Cold Cream/R. Lemmon, Chemist, The, The Pharmacy Hythe, geometric border, gray on white, 2½" d, light rust stain **70.00**

Donald's Magic Razor Sharpener, razor

in bottom center, stars on left, right, and top, black on white, 2" d **180.00**

Huggin's Cherry Tooth Paste/For Cleansing Beautifying and Preserving The Teeth & Gums/Trademark R. Higgins, Chemist 235 Strand Next Temple Bar London, street scene, black on white, 2¾" d **180.00**

Napoleon Price & Cos. Cherry Toothpaste/For Beautifying & Preserving The Teeth & Gums 27 Bond St. London, bust of Queen Victoria and Prince Albert, shades of yellow, black on white, 3³⁄₁₆" d **800.00**

Otto Of Rose Cold Cream/S. F. Goss Chemist, 460 Oxford St, red rose center, green leaves, black letters, white ground, 2⅝" d **110.00**

Rimmels Cherry Tooth Paste, cherry bunch, deep yellow and pink cherries, green leaves, yellow–orange black band on white, 3" d, professional repairs **550.00**

Saponaceous Shaving Compound/Prepared By X. Bazin, Perfumer, Philadelphia, geometric stars border, black on white, 4⅜" d **245.00**

Senior's Carbolic Tooth Paste For Preserving & Beautifying The Teeth & Gums Trademark, kiwi feeding, outer geometric border, black on white, 2⁵⁄₁₆" d **135.00**

Victoria Carbolic Toothpaste/For Preserving And Beautifying The Teeth/Perfumes The Breath. Strengthens The Gums/A. B., warrior with shield lying against lion, black on white, sq with rounded corners, 2½" l **150.00**

Worsley Wholesale Perfumer/Philadelphia/Capitol at Washington, linear border, view of Old Capitol Building, violet on white, 3½" d **475.00**

PRATT

PRATT FENTON

PRATT WARE

History: The earliest Pratt earthenware was made in the late 18th century by William Pratt, Lane Delph, Staffordshire, England. In 1810–1818, Felix and Robert Pratt, William's sons, established their own firm, F. & R. Pratt, in Fenton in the Staffordshire district. Potters in Yorkshire, Liv-

erpool, Sunderland, Tyneside, and Scotland copied the ware.

The wares consisted of relief molded jugs, commercial pots and tablewares with transfer decoration, commemorative pieces, and figure and animal groups.

Much of the early ware is unmarked. The mid-19th century wares bear several different marks in conjunction with the name Pratt, including "& Co."

References: Susan and Al Bagdade, *Warman's English & Continental Pottery & Porcelain, 1st Edition*, Warman Publishing Co., Inc., 1987; John and Griselda Lewis, *Pratt Ware 1780–1840*, Antique Collectors' Club, 1984.

Additional Listing: Pot Lids.

Plaque, Christ in the Wheat Field, multicolored, sgd "J Austin," c1851, 13" d, $125.00.

Bank, 5" h, house shape, coin slot in roof, open chimney, two figures, faces in windows, professional repair **600.00**

Creamer, 4¾" h, children at play, heart shaped cartouche, underglaze blue, green, and brown **200.00**

Money Box, 5" h, modeled as house, two children peering from windows, flanked by man and woman, blue, ochre, brown, and green, base and chimney restored, c1820 . . . . **600.00**

Pipe

8" l, looped snake like stem, bowl modeled as half figure of Admiral Nelson, military coat and tall hat, molded ribbons titled "Nelson" and "Forever," clasped hands, blue, yellow, orange, and brown underglazed enamels, c1800 . . . . **1,300.00**

8¼" l, coiled and twisted stem, bowl modeled with bust of woman's head, blue, yellow, and orange underglaze enamels, slight glaze wear, c1800 . . . . **1,400.00**

8½" l, snake, coiled stem, molded scale body, head with open mouth holding bowl, all–over brown, green, blue, and yellow underglazed enamel cross and line dec, stained mouthpiece wear, c1800 **750.00**

10" l, snake, scaled body, head with open mouth holding bowl, double loop form and molded cottage figure to stem, blue, yellow, brown, and orange underglazed enamels, slight staining, nicks, c1800 . . . . . **2,600.00**

12¾" l, elongated, molded fluted bowl, green, orange, and blue underglazed enamel dot and dash dec, stem damage, c1800 . . . . . . **1,300.00**

Pitcher

7¼" h, relief scenes of children, heart shaped medallions, titled "Sportive Innocence" and "Mischievous Sport," rim hairlines, chip on base **250.00**

7½" h, relief busts and floral dec, six colors, minor glaze wear and stains **400.00**

Platter, 12" l, Blind Fiddler **100.00**

Sugar, cov, 5¾" h, almond shaped relief medallion of woman and child, figural swan finial, stains, minor wear, and chips **400.00**

Tea Bowl and Saucer, 5¼" d, peafowl perched on leafy branch, blue, yellow, green, and ochre **275.00**

Vase, 7" h, finger, four colors, leaves and flowers, minor wear, slight hairline, pr **950.00**

PRINTS

History: Prints serve many purposes. They can be a reproduction of an artist's paintings, drawings, or designs. Prints themselves often are an original art form. Finally, prints can be developed for mass appeal as opposed to aesthetic statement. Much of the production of Currier & Ives fits this latter category. Currier & Ives concentrated on genre, urban, patriotic, and nostalgia scenes.

Prints are beginning to attract a wide following. This is partially because prices have not matched the rapid rise in oil and other paintings.

References: Frederic A. Conningham and Colin Simkin, *Currier & Ives Prints, Revised Edition*, Crown Publishers, Inc., 1970; Denis C. Jackson, *The Price & Identification Guide to J. C. Leyendecker & F. X. Leyendecker*, published by author, 1983; Carl F. Luckey, *Collector Prints Old and New*, Books Americana, 1982; Craig McClain, *Currier & Ives: An Illustrated Value Guide*, Wallace-Homestead, 1987; Ruth M. Pollard, *The Official Price Guide To Collector Prints, 7th Edition*, House Of Collectibles, 1986.

Collectors' Clubs: American Historical Print Collectors Society, Inc., 25 West 43rd St., Suite 711, New York, NY 10036. *Imprint*; Prang-Mark Society, Century House, Old Irelandville, Watkins Glen, NY 14891.

Reproduction Alert: Reproductions are a problem, especially Currier & Ives prints. Check the dimensions before buying any print.

Additional Listing: See Wallace Nutting.

Grant Wood, Seed Time & Harvest, artist sgd, dated 1937, $1,900.00.

Albee, Grace Thurston Arnold, American, Nayatt, etching, sgd in pencil across lower margin "ED 35, Nayatt, Grace A. Albee, N. A./1954", full margins, 6¼ x 7½", good condition mat and frame **290.00**

Arms, John Taylor, The Sarah Jane, etching and drypoint, sgd in pencil, numbered 62/78, titled, 1920, 10½ x 7⅛" **850.00**

Audubon, John James

Blue Gray Flycatcher, Havell edition, etching, engraving, aquatint and hand colored, wove paper, "J. Whatman" watermark, full typographical inscription, 19⅜ x 12¼" plate size, good condition, taped edge tears, mount staining, scattering foxing and tape residue, creasing, 1830 . . . . **300.00**

Canada Otter, litho, hand colored, printed by J. T. Bowen, Phila, 27 x 32", damage to top right corner, matted and framed, 1844 . . . . . . **200.00**

Canvas–backed Duck...View of Baltimore, Havell edition, Plate CCCI, engraving, aquatint, hand colored, wove paper, full sheet, pale mat and light staining, other minor defects, 25⅜ x 38⅛", framed **9,900.00**

Long–billed Curlew...City of Charleston, Havell edition, Plate CCXXI, engraving, aquatint, hand colored, wove paper, full sheet, pale mat and light staining, 25⅜ x 35⅜", . . **20,900.00**

Mallard Duck, Havell edition, Plate CCXXI, engraving, aquatint, hand colored, wove paper, full sheet, small tear into border at top edge, mat, light, and time staining, minor defects, 25⅝ x 38⅛", framed **26,500.00**

Bartlett, William Henry, View from Mt. Holyoke, hand colored litho, 6 x 8" **65.00**

Baumann, Gustave, Mountain Pool, color woodblock on wove paper, sgd "Gustave Baumann" in pencil on lower right, titled in pencil lower left, hand and heart stamp in orange ink lower right, identified on William MacBeth Inc. label on reverse, sheet size 13½ x 16⅞", image size 11¼ x 9¾", framed, light stained, adhesive residue on right margin **2,600.00**

Beal, Reynolds, American, 1867–1951
Cape Cod, etching, sgd and dated in pencil lower left "Reynolds Beal/ 1915," full margins, 7¾ x 9¾", good condition mat and frame **275.00**

Gloucester, etching, sgd and dated in pencil lower left "Reynolds Beal/ 1929," full margins, 6⅛ x 10", good condition mat and frame **225.00**

Benson, Frank Weston, The Alarm, etching, artist's proof, label on reverse "Arthur Harlow and Co., Inc., NY," sgd in pencil lower left "Frank W Benson," titled on reverse, full margins, 7¾ x 9¾", good condition mat and frame, 1917 . . . . **950.00**

Birch, William Russell, High Street from the Country Marketplace, Philadelphia–Procession of the Death of George Washington, engraving, 8¼ x 11" **225.00**

Bowen, John T., after John Woodhouse Audubon, ...Missouri Mouse, 1846, litho, hand colored, typographical inscription below and above image, 21 x 27¼" sheet, unframed, very minor soiling, nicks along edges **150.00**

Calder, Alexander, American, 1898–1976
Potpourri, serigraph, colored, pencil sgd, initialed "S A," 29 x 21¾" . . . **600.00**

Sun and Moon, litho, hand colored, pencil sgd, inscribed "E A," 29¾ x 22" **450.00**

Casimer, Luigi, Berlin, etching, hand colored, pencil sgd, 13¾ x 16¾", English, 19th C **350.00**

Chagall, Marc, Solomon, sgd in pencil, color litho, numbered 34/75, 1956, cream wove paper, full sheet printed to edges, 14 x 10¼" **1,500.00**

Cook, Howard, Under the El, crayon and pencil drawing, sgd, 18¾ x 13¾", American, 1901–80 . . . . **1,500.00**

Currier and Ives, publisher
American Field Sports, A Chance For Both Barrels, after A. F. Tait, litho, hand colored, wove paper, fine impression, trimmed margins, scattered pale foxing, pale staining in margins, 18⁵⁄₁₆ x 26⅝", 1857, framed **1,870.00**

American Field Sports, Retrieving, after A. F. Tait, litho, hand colored, wove paper, fine impression, trimmed margins, scattered foxing, very pale staining, 18⅜ x 26¾", 1857, framed **2,200.00**

Celebrated Stallions, The, litho, hand colored, margins slightly trimmed, minor stains, 7" crease, mounted and unframed, 20¼ x 28¾", 1866 **750.00**

Flora Temple, litho, hand colored, stains, wear, and minor damage, mounted and unframed, 20¾ x 28", 1860 . . . . **550.00**

Hung up–With the Starch Out, stains, matted and framed, 14½ x 18¾", 1878 **300.00**

Little Snowbird, litho, hand colored, inscribed "Presented by M. W. Buckingham," minor stains, refinished poplar frame, 16½" x 12½" w **175.00**

Scene of the Wissahickon/near Philadelphia, litho, hand colored, titled in stone lower corner, 8½ x 12½" image, considerable foxing, framed **175.00**

Trotting Cracks on the Snow, litho, hand colored, stains, wear, and small edge tears, mounted and unframed, 19½" h, 29¾" h, 1858 . . . **1,900.00**

Western Farmer's Home, The, litho, hand colored, stains, 13½ x 17½" w, framed **375.00**

Currier, Nathaniel, publisher
American Country Life, Pleasures of Winter, litho, hand colored, typographical inscription below image, 16¾ x 24" image, period style burl frame, minor paper discoloration, framed **1,200.00**

American Winter Scenes, Evening, litho, hand colored, 21 x 28", minor water stains along left margin, framed, 1854 . . . . **200.00**

American Winter Sports, Deer Shooting On The Shattagee, after L. Mauer, litho, hand colored, wove paper, margins, pale foxing showing through at bottom margin, pale mat staining, 17⅝ x 25¾", 1855, framed **4,400.00**

Dali, Salvador, Lovers, etching and aquatint, gold glitter added, impression #160 of 250, pencil sgd, numbered in margin, 22½ x 15¼" **300.00**

Eldred, Lemuel D.
Fishing Village, etching, sgd in etching and in pencil lower right "L. D. Eldred," minor wrinkles, full margins, 4 x 6½", matted and framed **375.00**
Low Tide, etching, etd in etching lower right, sgd in pencil in margin lower right, paper toned to woody brown, full margins, 4⅛ x 6¾", good mat and frame **485.00**

Fox, R. Atkinson
Approaching Storm **70.00**
Poppies **50.00**
Spirit of Youth **85.00**

Gardiner, Eliza Draper, Lady Among Poppies, color woodblock on paper, sgd in pencil in the image, upper left, 10½ x 10⅛" image, framed **2,500.00**

Gearhart, Francis, Rain Tomorrow, color woodblock, wove paper, sgd "Francis H. Gearhart" in pencil lower right, titled in pencil lower left, 10 x 11" image, framed, light mat staining **1,100.00**

Gifford, Robert Swain, Windblown Trees, etching, sgd and dated in etching "R. Swain Gifford/1868," sgd below etching "Drawn and etched by R. Swain Gifford," full margins, 4¾ x 7", good condition mat and frame **300.00**

Gutmann, Bessie Pease
An Anxious Momemt, litho, hand colored, 18½ x 16", orig mat and frame **70.00**
Wedding March, litho, hand colored, 16 x 21", orig frame **100.00**

Haehnlen, J., Philadelphia, Publisher, Funeral Car, Used at the Obsequies of President Lincoln..., litho on paper, full typographical inscription below image, identified in letter on reverse from Edwin Wolf II, image 19 x 26½", good condition, discoloration, scattered punctures, framed **800.00**

Havell, Robert Jr., American, 1793–1878
Bermaculated Duck, engraving, aquatint, hand colored, dated 1836 on plate, 20⅝ x 25⅞" **1,200.00**
Great Northern Diver or Loon, engraving, aquatint, hand colored, dated 1836 on plate, 22½ x 34¾" **1,500.00**
Sharp–tailed Grouse, engraving, aquatint, hand colored, dated 1837 on plate, 23⅝ x 33½" **550.00**

Hazen, Bessie Ella, Ship of Fortune, color woodblock on laid tissue, sgd in pencil lower right, titled in pencil on reverse, 4¼ x 3¼" image, framed, tape on reverse upper left margin . . **125.00**

Hockney, David
Blue Guitar–A Tune, The, etching and aquatint, impression #158 of 200, plate 3, pencil sgd and numbered in margin, 15½ x 19½" **1,600.00**
Portrait of Mother II, litho, four color, impression #3 of 20, pencil sgd and dated, 20 x 17" **2,700.00**

Hollar, Wenceslaus, The Seasons, etchings, laid paper, final states, trimmed to platemarks, pale staining, 9½ x 6⅞", 1641, framed set of four **9,350.00**

Hyde, Helen, Cherry Blossoms Overhead, etching on paper, monogrammed in plate, laid down, 5 x 3⅞", framed **100.00**

Icart, Louis, French, US copyrights after 1920
Belle Rose, color etching and drypoint, wove paper, sgd in pencil, artist's blindstamp, margins, slightly toned, 16½ x 21¼", c1933 . . . . . **880.00**
Girl In Crinoline, color etching and drypoint, sgd in pencil and titled, artist's blindstamp, margin, framed, 22½ x 19", c1937 . . . . **1,980.00**
Parrot, color etching and drypoint, cream wove paper, sgd in pencil, artist's blindstamp, margins, framed, 11¼ x 9", 1928 . . . . **990.00**
Pink Slip, color etching and drypoint, cream wove paper, sgd in pencil, artist's blindstamp, margin, framed, 19½ x 11½", c1928 . . . . **2,100.00**
Sous La Lampe, color etching and drypoint, cream wove paper, sgd in pencil and titled, artist's blindstamp, margin, framed, 15 x 19", c1928 **1,430.00**
Spilled Peaches, color etching and drypoint, wove paper, sgd in pencil, artist's blindstamp, margin, slightly toned, framed, 18¼ x 14", c1928 **1,320.00**
Untitled, color etching and drypoint, cream wove paper, sgd in pencil, artist's blindstamp, margin, framed, 11⅜ x 9", c1928 . . . . **825.00**

Kellogg
Battle of Champion Hills, MS, Mat 16, 1863, litho **125.00**
Double Fishing, litho, small folio . . . **165.00**
Rural Sweets, litho **75.00**

Levine, Jack, Gangster's Funeral, etching, pencil sgd lower right, numberd 101/120, 19½ x 25½" **265.00**

Lieberman, Max, German, 1847–1935, Landscape Study, pencil drawing, 6½ x 9" **550.00**

Morland, George, The History of Laetitia by John Raphael Smith, stipple engravings, hand finished in color, wove paper, trimmed to platemark, minor staining, 17½ x 12¼", 1789, 18th C gilded Hogarth frames, framed set of six 6,000.00

Mucha, Alphonse

Emerald, color litho, sgd in tone lower right, 38 x 15¼", c1900, framed . . 5,280.00

Eveil Du Matin and Repos De La Nuit, two Panneaux Decoratifs, color litho, sgd in stone, 16 x 43", 1899, pr mounted in floral and tracery framework, pr 12,100.00

Four Seasons, Spring, Summer, Fall, and Winter, color litho, sgd in stone, 1896, framed, set of 4 . . . . 52,800.00

Gismonda, color litho, Plate 27 from Les Maitres de L'Affiche, 14 x 15½", framed 1,100.00

Le Lierre, litho, printed in colors, wove paper, sgd in stone, printed by F. Champenois, trimmed margins, framed, 14½ x 14½", 1901 . . . . . 770.00

Monaco–Monte Carlo, color litho, sgd in the stone, 28 x 43", 1897 . . . . . 9,900.00

Salon des Cent, color litho, sgd in stone lower right, 24 x 16", 1896, framed 3,300.00

Norton, Elizabeth, Library Step, Stanford University, 1922, color woodblock on Japan paper, sgd and dated "E. Norton 1922" in pencil lower right, monogrammed in block lower right, annotated "del. sc. et imp" in pencil lower left, 5½ x 4½", framed 500.00

Parrish, Maxfield

Garden of Opportunity, litho, triptych, 1925, 25 x 24" 275.00

Jason and the Talking Oak, litho, 1908, 11 x 9" 80.00

New Moon, litho, hand colored, 12 x 16" 45.00

Valley of Enchantment, litho, 1946, medium folio 70.00

Richert, Charles H., Manset Fish Wharf, color woodblock, wove paper, sgd in pencil lower right, titled in pencil lower left, annotated in pencil on reverse, 4⅞ x 7" image, framed 450.00

Roybet, Ferdinand, French, 1840–1920, The Procession, charcoal drawing, blue, orange and white pastel highlights, sgd and dated, stamped "Vente F Roybet," 11¼ x 16½" 400.00

Soyer, Raphael, American, 1899–1987, Portrait of a Standing Nude, black ink drawing, sgd in sepia ink, numbered "164," 7 7/16 x 12⅜" 950.00

Steinlin, Theophile, Cat, litho, wove paper, sgd in stone, faint buckling, few minor handling creases, 10 x 8", framed 385.00

Taber, Charles & Co., Sperm Whaling No. 2, The Conflict, from painting by J. Cole, printed by Prang & Mayers Lithography, Boston, MA, 1858, litho, large folio, orig gold leafed frame . . 3,600.00

Thayer & Co, Boston, Lithographers, View of the Grand Mass Washingtonian Convention on Boston Common, on the 30th of May, 1844, litho, hand colored on paper, full typographical inscription below image, 8½ x 13⅓" h image, period burl frame, staining and fading 150.00

Toulouse Lautrec, Henri De, May Belfort, color litho, sgd in stone, 31¼ x 24¼", foxing, framed 8,250.00

Wade, F. J., Philadelphia, Lithographer, Philadelphia in the Olden Time, litho, hand colored on paper, initialed "SSS & DC" in stone lower right, full typographical inscription below image, three vignettes below, primary image 13¾ x 24", period gold leafed frame, 1875 . . . . 900.00

Walker, W B, Death of Admiral Lord Nelson, mezzotint, published for Knot Co, London, Jan 20, 1806, 9⅞ x 13½", Hogarth type frame 600.00

Waltner, Charles, Return from Harvesting, after Jules Adolphe Breton, etching, proof on parchment, pencil sgd by both artists, 16¼ x 32½", antique frame 200.00

Whistler, James Abbott McNeill, Little Salute, etching, 2nd state, laid paper, 3¼ x 8½", framed 600.00

Zorn, Anders, Sweden, 1860–1920

Against the Current, etching, sgd in pencil, 1919, 4½ x 6⅜" 350.00

Madonna, etching, sgd and dated plate, pencil sgd in margin, 9¾ x 7¾" 950.00

PRINTS—JAPANESE

History: Buying Japanese woodblock prints requires attention to detail and skilled knowledge of the subject. The quality of the impression (good, moderate, or weak), the color, and condition are critical. Various states and strikes of the same print cause the price to fluctuate. Knowing the proper publisher and censor's seals are helpful in identifying an original print.

Most prints were recopied and issued in popular versions. These represent the vast majority of the prints found in the marketplace. These popular versions should be viewed solely as decorative since they have little value.

A novice buyer should seek expert advice before buying. Talk with a specialized dealer, museum curator, or auction division head.

The listings below concentrate on details to show the depth of data needed for adequate pricing. Condition and impression are good, unless indicated otherwise.

O = Oban, 10 x 15"   C = Chuban, 7 x 10"
t = tat-e,   H = Hosoban, 5½ x
   large in width   13"
y = yoke-e,   T = Triptyck
   large in length

Reference: Sandra Andacht, *Oriental Antiques & Art: An Identification And Value Guide,* Wallace-Homestead, 1987.

Eisen

Imayo jibin sankumimai, high ranking courtesan, sgd *Keisai Eisen–ga,* with *kiwame* and publisher's seals, fair impression and color, center crease, fair state **175.00**

Ukiyo nijuyonko series, Yang Hsiang shown teasing cat, sgd *Keisai Eisen–ga,* with kiwame and publisher's seal, good impression, slight wrinkling, Ot **725.00**

Eizan, Kakemono–E, humorous tiger emerging from behind large stalk of bamboo, sgd *Kikugama Eizan hitsu,* good impression, fair color, good condition **375.00**

Gakutei, seated geisha playing the *biwa,* from *Hanazo bantsuki* series, sgd *Gakutei,* color slightly faded, C   **950.00**

Harunobo, courtesan showing the neck

Hiroshinge, water fall, 1825–60, late strike, Cy, $150.00.

of her kamoro before a screen dec with farmers harvesting rice, entitled *Jin, Virtue,* from *The Five Cardinal Virtues* series, sgd *Suzuki Harunobo ga,* Ct **7,750.00**

Hiroshige

Mishima asagiri, "Morning Mist, Mishima," from *Toto meisho* series, "Famous Places of the Eastern Capital," sgd *Hiroshige ga,* with *Hoseido/Senkakudo,* publisher's seals, margins trimmed, slightly rubbed, and soiled, Oy **675.00**

Night View, c1820, wood block, matted and unframed, 9¼" h, 14¼" w   **250.00**

Raining View of Ohashi, from 100 Views of Yedo, wood block, matted and unframed, 11¼" h, 7½" w . . .   **250.00**

Hiroshige II, Chuban Album, complete set of series *Edo meisho yonju hakkei/Forty–eight famous Sights of Edo,* each sgd *Hiroshige–ga,* some margins with *aratame/negetsu* (c1860) and publisher *Tsuta–ya Kichizo* seals, good states, laid down, Ct . . .   **1,350.00**

Hokuji, *Omocha–e* with inset *okubi–e* portrait of *IChimura Kakitsu* next to eight scappered depictions of various hair styles and hats, individual label cartouches, sgd *Shunkosai Hokushu–ga* with artist, carver, and publisher *Toshijura–ya Shinbei* seals, fair impression, Ot **325.00**

Hokusai

Aoyama enza matsu, "The cushion pine at Aoyama," from *Fugaku sanjurokkei* series, "Thirty–six views of Mt Fuji," sgd *Hokusai Iitsui hitsu,* slightly faded, center fold, Oy . . .   **2,650.00**

Sinsho Suwa–ko, "Lake Suma in Shinano Province," from *Fugaku sanjurokkei* series, "Thirty–six views of Mt Fuji," sgd *Zen Hokusai litsui hitsu,* publisher's seal *Eijudo,* Oy **4,250.00**

Uki–e depicting the Oji Inari Shrine, sgd *Hokusai ga,* slightly faded and trimmed, Oy **300.00**

Kawase Hasui

Ebisu Harbor, Sado Island in Winter, Tabi miyage dinishi series, sgd *Hasui,* seated *Kawase,* dated Taishi 10 (1921), *Watanabe* publisher's seal, Oy **1,200.00**

Okayamajo no Asahi/Dawn at Okayama Castle, dated Showa 30 (1955), misty view of castle, sgd *Hasui,* circular *Watanabe Shosaburo* seal, good impression, color, and state, Ot **350.00**

Kikumaro, courtesan seated by hibachi, surrounded by female attendants, blossoming prunus and sparrow, sgd *Kikumaro hitsu*, fair impression, poor color, stained, Ot **275.00**

Kunisada

Kakemono–e, high ranging courtesan walking in elaborate kimono, sgd *Kochoro Kunisada hitsu*, with *Aratame/negetsu* seal, c1865, good impression, fair color, faded, toned, trimmed, backed **225.00**

Three bijin walking with long sword and flute under flowering cherry trees at night, sgd *Kochoro/Ichiyosai Toyokuni ga*, two *nanushi* and publisher seals, good impression, toned, backed, Ot **200.00**

Kotondo, Beauty in sudden shower, sgd *Genjin ga,*, dated Showa 4 (1929), numbered 84/200, published by Sakai– Kawaguchi, large Ot **1,000.00**

Kuniyoshi

Giyu hakken–den series, depicting *Inyuama Dosetsu*, sgd *Ichiyasi Kuniyoshi–ga*, two *naushi* and publisher seals, fair impression and color, faded, fair state, Ot **100.00**

Tanuki print showing four drunken badgers dancing and singing, illus text passage, sgd *Ichiyusai Kuniyoshi– giga*, and one *Nanushi* and anonymous publisher's seal, fair impression and color, slightly faded, Ot **150.00**

Oda Kazuma, entitled *Matsue Ohashi/The Great Bridge of Matsue*, group of figures crossing bridge in snow storm, sgd *Kazuma hitsu*, red artist's seal, right margin with title and dated Taisho 13 (1924), very good impression and color, Oy **850.00**

Ohayagashi, Kuniyoshi, Fisherman, c1830, wood block, matted and unframed, 10½ x 15″ w **175.00**

Tori Kyonagi, from series *Hinagata wakana no hatsumoyo*, sgd *Kiyonaga ga*, fair impression and color, faded, rough margins, Ot **750.00**

Toyokuni I, three courtesans and their attendants strolling on busy street, sgd *Toyokuni–ga, kiwame* and *Iwato–ya Kisaburo* publisher's seal, fair impression, pool color, faded, fair state, Ot **400.00**

Utamaro, one courtesan standing over another in front, sgd *Utamaro hitsu*, with *kiwame, negetsu, (1806)* and publisher's seals, fair impression, poor color, faded, wrinkled, Ot **300.00**

Utamaro II, Beauty, half length, holding up her baby who plays with ball, sgd *Utamaro hitsu, kiwame* seal, publish-

er's seal *Iwatoya Kisaburo*, and censor's seal of Kisabura, Ot **2,000.00**

Yakamura Koko (Toyonari), three quarter view of actor *Matsumoto Koshiro* as *Sekibei*, sgd *Koka– ga*, publisher's seal and blind printed date Taisho 8 (1919), good impression and color, Ot **900.00**

Yoshikawa Kampo, actor *Nakamura Ganjiro* as *Kamiya Jihei* (c1922), sgd, publisher *Sato Shotaro*, reverse with additional publisher cartouche, edition 51/200, good impression and color, foxed, slightly toned, Ot **375.00**

Yoshitoshi

Diptych Set, from series *Shinsen Azuma Nishiki– e/Newly Selected Edo Color Prints*, entitled *Tamiya Botaro no Hanashi/the Story of Tamiya Botaro*, sgd *Yoshitoshi*, one seal reading *Taiso*, left margin dated Meiji 19 (1886) and publisher *Tsunanshima Kamekichi* cartouche, good impression and colors, margins partially trimmed, Ot **650.00**

Triptych Set, entitled *Taiheiki 'Sengatake' honjun no zu*, showing samurai *Takuma Morimasa* bound in ropes held by warriors, sgd *Ikahaisai Yoshitoshi hutsu* with *Aratame/negetsu (c1867)* and publisher *Tsunajima Kamekuchi* seals, fair impression and color, fair state, Ot **310.00**

PURPLE SLAG (MARBLE GLASS)

History: Challinor, Taylor & Co., Tarantum, Pennsylvania, c1870s–80s, was the largest producer of purple slag in the United States. Since the quality of pieces varies considerably, there is no doubt other American firms made it as well.

Purple slag also was made in England. English pieces are marked with British Registry marks.

Other color combinations, such as blue, green, or orange, were made, but are rarely found.

Additional Listings: Greentown Glass (chocolate slag) and Pink Slag.

Reproduction Alert: Purple slag has been heavily reproduced over the years and still is reproduced at present.

Bowl, 8″, Dart Bar pattern	**50.00**
Butter Dish, cow finial on cov	**35.00**
Cake Stand, plain	**120.00**
Celery Vase, Fluted	**80.00**
Compote, 5″ d	
Beaded Hearts pattern, 4½″ h	**70.00**
Scroll with Acanthus pattern	**40.00**
Jack-In-The-Pulpit Vase, 6″	**30.00**

Cruet, Imperial Glass Co, 7″ h, $45.00.

Match Holder, 5″, dolphin head	**65.00**
Plate, 10″, Lattice edge	**75.00**
Spooner, Scroll with Acanthus pattern	**120.00**
Sugar, cov, Fluted	**165.00**
Toothpick, Scroll with Acanthus pattern	**115.00**
Vase, 10″ h, wispy purple swirls, cloudy and clear body	**100.00**

PUZZLES

History: The jigsaw puzzle originated in the mid-18th century in Europe. John Silsbury, a London map maker, was selling dissected map jigsaw puzzles by the early 1760s. The first jigsaw puzzles in America were English and European imports and aimed primarily at children.

Prior to the Civil War, several manufacturers, e.g., Samuel L. Hill, W. and S. B. Ives, and McLoughlin Brothers included puzzle offerings as part of their line. However, it was the post-Civil War period that saw the jigsaw puzzle gain a strong foothold among the children of America.

In the late 1890s and first decade of the twentieth century, puzzles designed specifically for adults first appeared. Both forms have existed side by side ever since. Adult puzzlers were responsible for two twentieth century puzzle crazes: 1908–09 and 1932–33.

Prior to the mid-1920s the vast majority of jigsaw puzzles were cut using wood for the adult market and composition material for the children's market. In the 1920s the die-cut, cardboard jigsaw puzzle evolved. By the time of the puzzle craze of 1932–33, it was the dominant puzzle medium.

Jigsaw puzzle interest has cycled between peaks and valleys several times since 1933. Mini-revivals occurred during World War II and in the mid-1960s when Springbok entered the American market.

References: Linda Hannas, *The Jigsaw Book*, Dial Press, 1981, out of print; Anne D. Williams, *Jigsaw Puzzles: An Illustrated History and Price Guide*, Wallace-Homestead, 1990.

Additional Listings: See *Warman's Americana & Collectibles* for an expanded listing.

Collectors' Club: American Game Collectors Association, 4628 Barlow Drive, Bartlesville, OK 74006.

Adult, hand cut, Parker Brothers, Pastime Picture Puzzle, "Visiting the Invalid Dog," $35.00.

ADULT

Wood

Milton Bradley, Premier Jigsaw Puzzles, 15 x 11″, 300 pcs, "Tyrolean Waters," interlocking cut, some figural pieces, minor cutting along color lines, 1937	**30.00**
Detroit Publishing Company, Library Picture Puzzle, 8 x 10″, 150 pcs, "Dickens Studies: Bill Sykes," J. Barnhard print of Sykes glowering at cowering mastiff, non–interlocking, c1930s, cardboard box	**30.00**
Friss, George W., 13 x 9″, 238 pcs, "For Weal or Woe," wedding reception in country Victorian setting, non–interlocking, cut on color lines, c1910s or 20s, old candy box with Fiss label . .	**40.00**
Gleason, H. A., Cheerio Jig Saw Puzzles, 16″ x 20″, 535 pcs, "A Scout Is Friendly," picture of boy scout assisting elderly couple to read time table, interlocking, 12 figural pieces, cardboard box	**50.00**

Gencraft/Glendex, 14 x 10", 304 pcs, "Tree Island," New England landscape scene, interlocking, 1960s, cardboard box **20.00**

Little Cut–Up Jigsaw Puzzle, Chicopee, MA, 9 x 7", 110 pcs, "Elysian Fields," R. A. Box print of woman reclining by mountain lake, interlocking, 1932, cardboard box **30.00**

Madmar Interlox Puzzle, Blue Ribbon, 20 x 16", 755 pieces, "Spoils of War," Prussian officers enjoying leisurely evening of music and relaxation in European parlor, interlocking, c1920s **55.00**

Parker Brothers, Pastime Picture Puzzle, 7 x 9", 105 pcs, "The Jade Parure," Whitman Addett picture of woman seated at her vanity, curlicued interlocking cut, 12 figural pieces, 1930, cardboard box **25.00**

Parker Brothers, Pastime Picture Puzzle, 20" x 15", 471 pcs, "An Old Fashioned Farm," pastoral summer scene of Tudor cottage by stream, interlocking and color line cutting, 50 figural pcs, c1920s, box missing **50.00**

Picture Puzzle Exchange (Washington Street, Boston), 10 x 14", 255 pcs, "Rouen," merchants selling wares in old section of town, non–interlocking, 1934, cardboard box with wreath design **40.00**

Straus, Joseph K., 16 x 12", 288 pcs, "Anne Hathaway's Cottage," interlocking, early Straus, cardboard box **20.00**

Unknown cutter, 13 x 10", 125 pcs, "U.S.S. Saratoga at Sea," aircraft carrier and escorting ships with biplanes in sunset sky, interlocking, c1940, blue and yellow box **25.00**

Unknown cutter, 10 x 7", 160 pcs, "Song of Victory," native Americans on victorious horseback ride through central American plains, non–interlocking, early 1900s, box missing **35.00**

Unknown cutter, 12 x 9", 222 pcs, untitled, autumn landscape of stream and forest, combination of interlocking and non–interlocking, box missing .. **25.00**

Die–cut, Cardboard

Note: Cardboard puzzles from the post–1945 period sell between fifty cents and two dollars depending on company and subject matter.

Milton Bradley, Mayfair Jig Picture Puzzle, "Winter Moonlight," over 200 pcs, cardboard box **3.00**

J. R. Brundage, Woozy–Jig Picture Puzzle, untitled (Venetian scene), approx.

250 pcs, cardboard box has art work of two dancing Blacks **20.00**

Consolidated Paper Box, Picture Perfect Puzzle, 19½ x 15½", approx. 375 pcs, "Mountain Warfare," WWII battle scene, cardboard box **20.00**

Dolly Folding Kite and Toy Co. (Dayton, OH), Jig–O–Lox, 15 x 11", over 200 pcs, untitled, pointers and setters, cardboard box **4.00**

Einson–Freeman, Every Week Jig–Saw Puzzle, No. 19, "The Conquerors," illus. by Albin Henning, 1933, cardboard box **10.00**

Einson-Freeman, Radio Stars Series, RS-3, "Rudy Vallee," 1933, cardboard box **30.00**

Regent Specialties, Inc., DeLuxe Picture Puzzle, approx. 16 x 20", approx. 400 pcs, "Silver Moon," 1930s, cardboard box **12.50**

Santway Photo–Craft Company, Muddle Puzzles, Fine Art Series J, "Yosemite Falls," cardboard box **12.00**

Tuco Picture Puzzle, "The Star of Bethlehem," over 350 pcs, miniature guide picture on cover of cardboard box .. **5.00**

Viking, Picture Puzzle Weekly, A–6, "The Cardinal's Portrait," 1932, cardboard box **10.00**

Viking, Picture Puzzle Weekly, C–8, "Women and Children First," 1933, cardboard box **20.00**

University Distributing Company, Jig of the Week, No. 18, "Charging Elephant," 1933, cardboard box **6.00**

CHILDREN

Composition

Milton Bradley, Santa Claus Puzzle Box, three puzzle set, 13" x 9", c1924–26, box with lithographed cover of one of puzzles **250.00**

McLoughlin Brothers, Picnic Party Scroll Puzzle, children preparing for picnic by lakeside, box with lithographed cover of puzzle **125.00**

Die–cut, Cardboard

Built–Rite, Junior Picture Puzzle, Famous TV Stars, "Broken Arrow," approx. 100 pcs, cardboard box with guide picture **20.00**

Consolidated Paper Box, set, Children of All Nations, Set No. 2, three puzzles, approx. 50 pcs each, cardboard box with children's parade theme .. **4.00**

Jaymar, Playland Child's Picture Puzzle, Series No. 1, "Organ Grinder," large size pcs, box with guide picture 5.00

Jaymar, Walt Disney Jig Saw Puzzle, Series 4, "Three Caballeros," approx. 22" x 14", over 300 pcs, cardboard box with guide picture and three caballeros in lower right quadrant 30.00

3 Perfect Children's Puzzles, set, approx. 50 pieces each, box cover with illus of children putting together puzzles 8.00

Transogram, Funny Page Jig–Saw Puzzle, Series No. 6, "Fritzi Ritz in Mistaken Identity," approx. 10 x 14", late 1930s, box cover features cartoon characters 40.00

Frame Tray

Built-Rite, Sta–N–Place Puzzles, No. 1229, "Buffalo Bill Jr.," Bill swinging a rope, 1956 .... 20.00

Saalfield, No. 7339, "Boots And Her Buddies," Boots on tree swing while rest of friends picnic 12.00

Whitman, No. 4428, "Bugs Bunny," Bugs escaping into hole ahead of Elmer Fudd 8.00

ADVERTISING

Black Jack Gum, cardboard, 7 x 10½", wife giving husband who holds packages a stick of gum, "Aw Kitty, you know I like licorice!," contains coupon for additional puzzles on puzzle, 1933, envelope 40.00

Creo-Dipt Company, Inc., cardboard, 10 x 5⅝", shows interior of railroad car loaded with Creo–Dipt products, 1932–33, plain cardboard mailing box with company address 35.00

Fisk Tire Company, cardboard, 8½ x 11", No. 5 "Baseball" from Time to Re–tire series, policeman approach two boys watching baseball game through fence, 1933, envelope 35.00

Fisher's Vitamin "D" Bread, cardboard, 7¼ x 9⅜", No. 3 in a series of 6, children seated at table while mother serves lunch, 1932–33, envelope features guide picture 20.00

Lackawanna Railroad, wood, 8½ x 6¾", Phoebe Snow Picture Puzzle No. 1, Phoebe Snow standing on back platform of passenger car traveling through countryside, c1910s, cardboard mailing box 75.00

Lucas Paints and Varnishes, cardboard, 5½ x 7", Giant Painter Puzzle, painter kneeling in miniature village, can of paint by right knee, holding house in left hand, 1920s, original box (2¼ x 4 x⅞") duplicated puzzle picture on lid ... 100.00

Rinso, cardboard, 9⅛" x 5¾", "No wonder the little girl is proud - SHE is wearing a Rinso-washed dress!," boy and girl on tricycles peddle toward Rinso billboard, 1932–33, envelope features guide picture 25.00

Sloan's Liniment, cardboard, 10 x 8", Aerial View of Sing Sing Prison, insert of Warden Lewis Lawes in upper right corner, 1933, envelope 25.00

Southern Ambulance Builders, cardboard, puzzle pictures three types of ambulances on orange ground, original cellophane wrap on box 5.00

Standard Oil Company of New Jersey, cardboard, 7⅞ x 9½", show Christmas Tree flanked by Santa and gas station attendant, packaging unknown 50.00

Sundial Bonnie Laddie Shoes, 10¾ x 8¾", Sundial "Lucky Pup" Jig Saw Puzzle, frame tray type with Bonnie Laddie on the right, features characters from Lucky Pup television show, 1948, envelope with guide picture .. 40.00

White Rose Tea, cardboard, 7 x 9", Puzzle No. 2, "Doggone Lucky," young boy holds cat from attacking dog, figural pieces, 1932–33, envelope with guide picture 15.00

MULTIPURPOSE PUZZLES

Christmas card, cardboard, 9 x 7", The Zahoriks, cartoon characters walking toward tree in front of fireplace, 26 pcs, 6 figural pieces, 1949, canvas mailing sack 17.50

Contest/Advertising, Bay State Brush, cardboard, 8½ x 6½", Limerick Jig–Saw Puzzle, picture shows Chinese origin of roast pig, part of limerick on puzzle, 1932–33, envelope 35.00

Post Card Souvenir, wood, 5½ x 3¾", "71 Chelsea Park Boulevard, Atlantic City, N.J.," 1930s, cardboard mailing box 12.50

Quezal

QUEZAL

History: The Quezal Art Glass Decorating Company, named for the "quetzal," a bird with brilliant colored feathers, was organized in 1901 in Brooklyn, New York, by two disgruntled Tiffany workers, Martin Bach and Thomas Johnson. They soon hired two more Tiffany workers, Percy Britton and William Wiedebine.

The first products, unmarked, were exact Tiffany imitations. In 1902 the "Quezal" trademark was first used. Quezal pieces differ from Tiffany pieces in that they are more defined and the decorations more visible and brightly colored. No new techniques came from Quezal.

Johnson left in 1905. T. Conrad Vahlsing, Bach's son-in-law, joined the firm in 1918, but left with Paul Frank in 1920 to form Lustre Art Glass Company which copied Quezal pieces. Martin Bach died in 1924; by 1925 Quezal ceased operations.

Wares are signed "Quezal" on the base of vases and bowls and rims of shades. The acid-etched or engraved letters vary in size and may be found in amber, black, or gold. A printed label of a quetzal bird was used briefly in 1907.

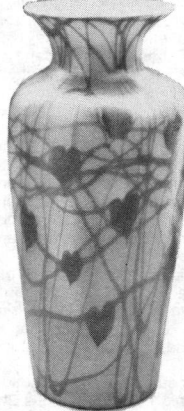

Vase, gold Aurene ground, light green draping vines, heart shaped leaves, 12″ h, $1,400.00.

Bowl, 12″ d, peacock blue, hammered
  silver base, marked "Oscar B Bach,
  NY" 500.00
Candlesticks, pr, 6½″ h, flared bobeche
  rim, ringed hollow baluster opal body,
  overall orange–green King Tut irid
  dec, sgd 950.00
Jack In The Pulpit Vase, 11½″ h, gold
  face, stem and back with gold and
  green leaf pulls and hooked waves,
  ivory ground, sgd "Quezal R 84" . . . 6,000.00
Lamp Shade
  4″ h, floriform, bright irid amber,

ribbed, waisted and everted edge,
  sgd "Quezal," pr 275.00
5″ h, pulled feather, gold irid int., applied webbing 175.00
5¼″ h, bell form, ribbed, gold, irid, sgd
  inside top rim, set of three 450.00
Nut Dish, triangular rim, gently rounded
  body, gold irid, inscribed "Quezal" . . 100.00
Toasting Goblet, 4″ h, opal bowl, fiery
  gold irid int., gold and green pulled
  feather dec, gold chain border, sgd
  "Quezal" inside applied hollow stem
  pedestal, pr 1,500.00
Vase
  6½″ h, vasiform, gold swirls, opal over
    green ribbed body, irid pulled and
    hooked feather dec, Martin Bach
    design, sgd "Quezal" 2,200.00
  8″ h, ovoid, flared rim, applied gold
    disk base, opal glass, gold int.,
    broad random gold irid linear dec,
    sgd "Quezal" 1,100.00
  8½″ h, flask form, brilliant rainbow irid,
    finely chased silver overlay carna-
    tion blossoms, stems, and leaves,
    inscribed "Quezal," Alvin Corp
    mark stamped on silver 1,100.00
  9¾″ h, waisted cylinder, ivory ground,
    gold and green hooked feather dec,
    engraved "Quezal A394" 1,550.00

QUILTS

History: Quilts have been passed down as family heirlooms for many generations. Each is an individual expression. The same pattern may have hundreds of variations in both color and design.

The advent of the sewing machine increased, not decreased the number of quilts which were made. Quilts still are being sewn today.

The key considerations for price are age, condition, aesthetic beauty, and design. Prices are now at a level position. The exception is the very finest examples which continue to bring record prices.

References: American Quilter's Society, *Gallery of American Quilts, 1849–1988,* Collector Books, 1988; Barbara Brackman, *Clues in the Calico: A Guide To Identifying and Dating Antique Quilts,* EPM Publications, 1989; Barbara Brackman, *Encyclopedia of Pieced Patterns, Volume I,* Prairie Flower Publications, 1984; Cathy Florence, *Collecting Quilts: Investments In America's Heritage,* Collector Books, 1985; William C. Ketchum, Jr., *The Knopf Collectors' Guides to American Antiques: Quilts,* Alfred A. Knopf, Inc., 1982; Jean Ray Laury and California Heritage Quilt Project, *Ho For California: Pioneer Women and Their Quilts,* E. P. Dutton, 1990; Lisa Turner Oshins, *Quilt Collections: A Directory For The United States And Canada,* Acropolis Books, Ltd., 1987;

Rachel and Kenneth Pellman, *The World of Amish Quilts,* Good Books, 1984; Schnuppe von Gwinner, *The History of the Patchwork Quilt,* Schiffer Publishing Ltd, 1988.

Collectors' Club: The American Quilter's Society, P.O. Box 3290, Paducah, KY 42002.

Periodical: *Quilter's Newsletter Magazines,* Box 394, Wheat Ridge, CO 80033.

Log Cabin, pieced, cotton, 82 x 82", $350.00.

35 x 34", crib, pieced cotton, New England, c1875, five blocks of red appliqued stars centering green appliqued star, alternating with four blocks of quilted wreaths, red appliqued sawtooth border, quilted meandering vine, red binding 825.00

36 x 35", crib, pieced cotton, American, c1863, four blocks, Snowflake variation, appliqued blue patterned fabric, double sawtooth border, blue binding 1,870.00

42 x 36", crib, pieced cotton, Amish, c1875, Sawtooth pattern, printed red cotton border surrounded by similar blue printed cotton border, red printed cotton edging 4,200.00

58 x 58", pieced and appliqued cotton, American, 19th C, album, nine squares of trees, birds, flowers, and wreaths, floral and vine border, some fading and staining 2,100.00

74 x 82", pieced cotton, Lancaster County, PA, c1910, Diamond–in–the–Square pattern, slate blue diamond with foliate wreath stitching, maroon inner border with grapevine stitching, four slate blue corner squares with tulip stitching, olive green spandrels, second maroon border, slate blue outer border with maroon binding . . 7,500.00

77 x 77", pieced cotton and wool, Amish, Lancaster County, PA, c1925, Sunshine and Shadow pattern, blue, tan, green, red, purple, and black quilted diamonds, sq pink inner border with interlocking ovoid stitching, slate blue border and maroon corner squares with meandering vine stitching, maroon binding, reverse side of binding initialed 7,150.00

78 x 78", pieced wool, eastern PA, c1890, Fan pattern, briar embroidery, center circular fan, semi–circle and quarter–circle fan designs, black wool ground, double border of red wool with interlocking ovoid stitching, outer border of various fabrics, red binding 3,200.00

81 x 82", pieced cotton and flannel, PA, c1900, Pineapple variation pattern, black, lavender, wine, tan, olive, gray, and brown stripes alternating with red diamond blocks, black binding 2,350.00

85 x 72", pieced and embroidered silk and velvet, American, late 19th C, Crazy pattern, echo embroidery, souvenir ribbon of New Orleans 1884 Centennial Exposition, American flag, Chinese pagoda, peacock, elephant, birds, butterflies, and flowers, jade blue velvet border with embroidered flowers 7,500.00

86 x 72", pieced cotton, Amish, Ohio, c1920, Roman Stripes pattern, 56 squares of rose, brown, navy, and red, rose inner border, serpentine chain quilting, lavender outer border, meandering princess feather and sawtooth quilting, red binding 2,650.00

87 x 83", appliqued cotton, Hawaii, mid 19th C, central organic medallion radiating outwards, surrounded by similar border, apricot colored fabric, cream ground, echo stitching, apricot binding 2,100.00

100 x 86", pieced and appliqued cotton, American, mid 19th C, Mariner's Star pattern, twelve squares alternating with sixteen Mariner's Stars, blue calico star and fish scale stitching, border of half Mariner's Stars and half squares with small stars, blue binding, some staining 2,425.00

106 x 106", pieced and appliqued cotton, Springfield, IL, 1850, Friendship, central diamond with organic medallion, ink stamped "Eliza Horne, Springfield, IL, 1850," multiple appliqued calico diamonds with various organic motifs, additional stamped family names, uniform red and green border, red and white edge tassels, minor tears to applique, minor loss of stitching 3,300.00

109 x 91", Broderie Perse, pieced and appliqued cotton, trapunto stitching,

American, 1844, central sq depicting Queen Victoria surrounded by column, balustrade, and urn with flowers, remaining squares of multiple floral designs, five squares stamped with names and dated 1844, inner border of floral fabric strips, outer border of continuous swirling floral and grape vine applique, floral binding . . **11,000.00**

QUIMPER

History: Quimper faience, dating back to the 17th century, is named for Quimper, a French town where numerous potteries were located. Several mergers resulted in the evolution of two major houses—the Jules Henriot and Hubaudiébre–Bousquet factories.

The peasant design first appeared in the 1860s, and many variations exist. Florals and geometrics, equally popular, also were produced in large quantities. During the 1920s the Hubaudiébre–Bousquet factory introduced the Odetta line which utilized a stone body and Art Deco decorations.

The two major houses merged in 1968, each retaining its individual characteristics and marks. The concern suffered from labor problems in the 1980s and recently was purchased by an American group.

Marks: The HR and HR Quimper marks are found on Henriot pieces prior to 1922. The HenRoit Quimper mark was used after 1922. The HB mark covers a long span of time. The addition of numbers or dots and dashes refers to inventory numbers and are found on later pieces. Most marks are in blue or black. Pieces ordered by department stores, such as Macy's and Carson Pirie Scott, carry the store mark along with the factory mark, making them less desirable to collectors. A comprehensive list of marks is found in Bondhus's book.

References: Susan and Al Bagdade, *Warman's English & Continental Pottery & Porcelain, 1st Edition,* Warman Publishing Co., Inc., 1987; Sandra V. Bondhus, *Quimper Pottery: A French Folk Art Faience,* published by author, 1981; Millicent Mali, *Quimper Faience,* Airon, Inc., 1979; Marjatta Taburet, *La Faience de Quimper,* Editions Sous le Vent, 1979, French text.

Museums: Musee des Faiences de Quimper, Quimper, France; Victoria and Albert Museum, French Ceramic Dept., London, England.

Advisors: Susan and Al Bagdade.

Ashtray, 4″ h, 5½″ l, 4″ w, figural male and female peasant standing on back, light brown base, marked "J E Sevellec–Henriot Quimper" **230.00**
Bank, 8″ l, 4″ h, figural, pig, pink face, white body, peasant woman on side with stylized flowers, blue outlined slot, marked "HB Quimper" **385.00**
Bell, 4½″ h, male peasant, rose pantaloons, blue jacket, blue and tan border bands, blue figural fleur-de-lis handle, marked "Henriot Quimper France" **82.00**
Bookends, pr, 6½″ h, one with boy playing bagpipe, black jacket, light blue pants, other with seated girl, orchid shirt, black vest, yellow dress, cream bases, marked "HB Quimper France" **325.00**
Bowl
  7½″ d, cov, iron–red, green, and blue floral chains, blue and yellow banded borders, marked "Henriot Quimper, France" **175.00**
  10″ d, fluted body, peasant lady carrying basket, green blouse, terra cotta apron, blue skirt, ring of florals and blue band on border, pierced for hanging, chips on foot rim, marked "HR Quimper" **295.00**
  14¼″, Art Deco style, blue, white, black, yellow, and orange center scene of two peasant women, geometric int., orange, yellow, and black ext. and handles, cream ground, hairline, marked "Henriot Quimper Sevellec" **190.00**
Box, 4½″ d, decor riche body with dark green dec, black ermine tails, green, blue, and seated male peasant on cov, cov and base marked "HR Quimper" **360.00**
Bulb Pot, 4″ h, 6″ d, decor riche panels with vertical green dec, painted old woman and child on front panel, village background, blue sponged scalloped rim, Porquier–Beau mark **660.00**
Cheese Dish, cov, 10″ l, 8¼″ w, figural bagpipe, seated peasant woman with egg basket on cov, dark blue decor riche border, molded pink and yellow bows, brown pipes, marked "Henriot Quimper" **605.00**
Cider Jug, 7½″ h, male peasant, green, orange, and blue florals, blue sponged handles, marked "HR" . . . **265.00**
Cider Set, 12″ d, tray, 8″ h pitcher, six 3¾″ h mugs, stoneware, stylized overlapping gray–green geometric design outlined in black, soft brown ground, marked "HB Quimper Odetta" **265.00**
Cigarette Holder, 3″ h, 3½″ d, octagonal,

Candlesticks, pr, lighthouse shape, red, green, blue, and yellow peasant and floral design, white ground, chips, marked "Henriot Quimper France," 7¾" h, $350.00.

seated male peasant with pipe on front, female peasant with distaff on reverse cross hatch panels, raised rust dot panels outlined with orange, blue rims, marked "Henriot Quimper France" 100.00

Creamer, 3⅜" h, male peasant under spout, orange shirt, blue pants, blue, yellow, green, and terra cotta floral sprays, green figural dragon handle, marked "Henriot Quimper France" .. 200.00

Cup, 3¼" h, 4" d, female peasant, formal attire, pink ribbons stream from hat, mustard, rose, and green florals, decor riche border around top, blue striped handle, orange rim, marked "HB Quimper" 85.00

Cup and Saucer
Female peasant, four panels of Rouen type florals in rose, green, blue, and cross hatches, marked "HB Quimper" 110.00

Hex Shape
Female peasant, blue, rust, and yellow florals, blue border, striped handle, marked "HR Quimper" 125.00
Three rose, blue, and orange geometric panels, tan ground, marked "Henriot Quimper" 85.00

Dish, 14½" d, 7" h, three molded shells, busts of male and female peasants, center figural handle of fisherman in brown suit holding green fish, white ground, marked "HB Quimper" 250.00

Figure
10" h, fisherman, standing, dark blue hat and shirt, yellow pants, burnt orange net over shoulder, sq base, marked "EJB Henriot Quimper" .. 295.00
12" h, male peasant, standing with arms folded, green shirt, blue jacket, orange pants and shoes, green and yellow stump base, marked "YANN" on front 225.00

Gravy Boat, 7½" l, 4" h, male peasant, scattered florals, emb spouts marked "G" and "M" outlined in blue, blue sponged middle handles, marked "Henriot Quimper France" 245.00

Inkwell, 3½" h, 5" d, attached scalloped blue sponged underplate, cov with seated male peasant and scattered florals, marked "Henriot Quimper France" 415.00

Mug, 3½" h, male peasant on one, female on other, multicolored florals, blue banded rim, marked "Henriot Quimper France," pr 110.00

Mustard Pot, cov, 3¼" h, 4" d, rust, green, and blue florals, blue and gold geometric design on attached underplate, male peasant on lid, two ear handles, marked "HR Quimper" ... 175.00

Nut Dish, 5" d, 2¼" h, trefoil shape, female peasant, scattered florals, blue sponged three pc twisted rope handle with yellow and black knots, marked "Henriot Quimper France" 100.00

Oyster Plate
9" d, six oyster panels with rose, green, and blue florals, blue, green, and mustard center, blue border, marked "HB Quimper France" ... 85.00
9¼" d, six oyster panels with rose and green florals, yellow ringed center, four dots between oysters, blue border, marked "HB Quimper" ... 75.00

Pitcher, 4½" h, Art Deco panels with sailor and peasant woman, blue and gold bands on neck and foot, horizontal and vertical blue and green geometric bands, marked "HB Quimper" 385.00

Plate
5½" d, female peasant, blue striped skirt, white apron, scalloped edge, blue rim, gray ground, marked "Henriot Quimper France" 130.00
6⅞" d, basket with multicolored flowers, rose sponged border, flaking, marked "Henriot Quimper France" 90.00
8" d, geometric designs, cross hatch circles, yellow and blue bands, chipped edges, marked "HR Quimper" 110.00
8½" d, male peasant, holding pipe, blue shirt, rust pants, purple hat, three blue bands, green ground and borders, marked "HB Quimper France" 85.00

Plate, square on square shape, multi-colored center scene, dark blue decor riche on yellow border, Brittany crest on top, pierced for hanging, marked "HR Quimper" on front, 13½" w, $525.00.

8⅞" l, octagonal, female peasant, green blouse, orange apron, and blue skirt, band of simple florals and blue dots on border, blue outlined rim, marked "Henriot Quimper France" 170.00

9" d, dark pink, light purple, white, and yellow open iris, green leaves, white rim, black ground, pierced for hanging, marked "Henriot Quimper" 230.00

9⅛" d, female peasant with cane, blue skirt, pink apron, Rouen type florals, cross hatch panels, scalloped edge, blue rim, marked "HB Quimper" 175.00

9½" d, scalloped, man with bagpipe, rust, green, and blue florals, white ground, marked "Henriot Quimper" 185.00

Platter

13¼" l, peasant man, blue, red, and green florals, ring of florals on border, shaped rim outlined in blue, marked "HR Quimper France" . . . 185.00

14½" l, 11" w, center cartouche of old woman in Art Deco colors, six panels of rose, gold, and blue geometric design, blue sponged and shape rim, tan ground, marked "Lourdes" 375.00

Quintal

5½" h, center cartouche of man playing flute outlined in mustard, blue cross hatch band, green sponge trim inside quintals, rust, green, and blue florals, four dots, marked "Henriot Quimper France Fireside" 230.00

6¼" h, pr, one of male peasant with arms folded, other of peasant woman, scattered flowers on both, cream ground, marked "Henriot Quimper France" 370.00

Salt, 3½" d, geometric yellow circles, panel with circles, blue sponge border, tan ground, marked "Henriot Quimper" 85.00

Sauce Boat, 8" h, 6" l, figural, duck, green and orange sponging on breast, terra cotta, green, and blue feathers, marked "HB Quimper France" 210.00

Serving Dish, 13½" l, 8½" w, 5" h, female peasant, yellow apron, blue bodice, garnet skirt, blue and yellow leaf molded border, blue leaf molded handle, marked "HB Quimper France" 330.00

Serving Plate, 9¾" d, female peasant, shaped rim, sgd "H B Quimper France" 145.00

Snuff Bottle, 2⅞" h, 2¼" w, book shape, blue, yellow, orange, and green rooster, French saying, reverse with Breton woman, "Souvenir" on spine . . . 150.00

Sugar Bowl, 4½" h, cov, female peasant, light blue and rust florals, florals on reverse, pale blue border, two handles, marked "HR Quimper" on front 150.00

Teapot, 8½" h

Hexagonal, pink, green, yellow, and blue peasant woman and florals, yellow ground, marked "HB Quimper France" 75.00

Peasant woman on side in pink, yellow, and blue, single stroke scattered flowers, blue and yellow banded border, blue sponged handle and knob, marked "Henriot Quimper France" 360.00

Tray

13½" l, 9" w, rect, male and female peasants, rust, orange, green, and blue florals, four dots, blue rim with cut corners, marked "HR Quimper on front, "France" on reverse . . . 375.00

15¼" l, rect, blue, green, orange, and pink radiating flowers, blue and yellow banded border, white ground, marked "Henriot Quimper" 165.00

Vase

4½" h, female peasant, yellow lined umbrella, yellow apron, purple skirt, blue bodice, flanked by rust and blue–green florals, florals on reverse, blue borders, two handles, marked "HR Quimper" 150.00

5⅞" h, 11½" w, yellow, aqua, and blue

long necked bird, scattered stylized florals, small blue handles, cream ground, marked "HB Quimper" .. **240.00**

7¼" h, 5½" w, gold, blue, green, and pink peasant couple on front, framed in criss–cross design, single stroke flowers on reverse, six raised finger flutes on top, yellow ground, glaze flakes **187.00**

7½" l, 5" h, fan shape, male peasant, mustard, orange, and rose geometric design, marked "Lannion" **245.00**

8½" h, bust of male peasant, blue–green Breton hat with streamers, brown and tan coat, boat on reverse with rose sails, blue and green striped sea background, sgd "Kervella," marked "HB Quimper" **160.00**

Wall Pocket, 11¼" h, cone shape, peasant woman, florals, yellow and black sponged edge, open blossom around hanging hole, marked "HB" **275.00**

RADIOS

History: The radio was invented over 100 years ago. Marconi was the first to assemble and employ the transmission and reception instruments that permitted sending electric messages without the use of direct connections. Between 1905 and the end of World War I many technical advances were made to the "wireless," including the invention of the vacuum tube by DeForest. By 1920 technology progressed. Radios filled the entertainment needs of the average family.

Changes in design, style, and technology brought the radio from the black boxes of the 1920s to the styled furniture pieces and console models of the 1930s and 1940s, to midget models of the 1950s, and finally to the high–tech radios of the 1980s.

References: Marty & Sue Bunis, *Collector's Guide To Antique Radios,* Collector Books, 1990; Philip Collins, *Radios: The Golden Age,* Chronicle Books, 1987; Alan Douglas, *Radio Manufacturers of the 1920s, Volume 1,* Vestal Press Ltd., 1988; Robert Grinder and George Fathauger, *Radio Collectors Directory And Price Guide,* Ironwood Publishing, 1986; David and Betty Johnson, *Guide To Old Radios, Pointers, Pictures, And Prices,* Wallace-Homestead, 1989.

Periodicals: *Antique Radio Classified,* 9511 Sunrise Boulevard, Cleveland, OH 44133; *Antique Radio Topics & The Classic Radio Newsletter,* Box 28572, Dallas, TX 75228; *Radio Age,* 636 Cambridge Road, Augusta, GA 30909.

Collectors' Clubs: Antique Radio Club of America, 81 Steeplechase Road, Devon, PA 19333; Antique Wireless Association, Box 22E, Breesport, NY 14816.

Museums: Antique Wireless Museum, East Bloomfield, NY; Caperton's Radio Museum, Louisville, KY; Muchow's Historical Radio Museum, Elgin, IL; Museum of Wonderful Miracles, Minneapolis, MN; New England Museum of Wireless and Steam, East Greenwich, RI; Voice of the Twenties, Orient, NY.

Additional Listings: See *Warman's Americana & Collectibles* for more examples.

Fada, 1930–40, $50.00.

Adams–Morgan, Model III Paragon, battery operated, table type, 1924 ..	**250.00**
Advance Electric, Model 88, cathedral type	**150.00**
Bremer Tully, Model 6–35, table type, 1927	**110.00**
Buckingham, Model 30, speaker inside	**120.00**
Capehart, Model 17–K–3, console, 1940	**60.00**
Crosley	
Bandbox	**60.00**
Model 51, 1924	**90.00**
DeForest Radio, Radiocraft, table type, 1920	**700.00**
Edison, Model R–1, dial, 1928	**300.00**
Federal, crystal set, Buffalo, NY, patented 1917	**200.00**
General Electric	
Model A–53, table type, 1936	**75.00**
Model E–68, console, 1936	**90.00**
Model H–520, mantle, plastic, 1939	**25.00**
Grebe, Model CR–9, 1921	**525.00**
Hartman Electric, Jr Upright, console, battery operated, 1926	**125.00**
Kennedy, Colin B, Jacobean, console, battery operated, 1923	**1,100.00**
Metro, Super 7, tubes, gold silk screen, 1926	**125.00**
Montgomery Ward, Model 448, console, 1938	**50.00**

Precision Products, Arborphone, table type, battery operated, 1926	**125.00**
RCA, Radiola 60, No 103 speaker, 9 tube, 1928	**500.00**
Sears Manfacturing, T Torodyne, table type, battery operated	**90.00**
Sears, Roebuck, Model 107A, console, battery operated, 1931	**60.00**
Sonora Phonograph, Model TZ–56, console	**125.00**
Stromberg–Carlson, Model 420–F, console, 1939	**100.00**
Westinghouse	
Model WR–14, cathedral style, 1931	**150.00**
Model WR–166, mantle, plastic	**30.00**

RAILROAD ITEMS

History: Railroad collectors have existed for decades. The merger of the rail systems and the end of passenger service made many objects available to private collections. The Pennsylvania Railroad sold its archives at public sale.

Railroad enthusiasts have organized into regional and local clubs. Join one if interested. Your local hobby store can probably point you to the right person. The best pieces pass between collectors and rarely enter the general marketplace.

References: Stanley L. Baker, *Railroad Collectibles: An Illustrated Value Guide, 4th Edition*, Collector Books, 1990; Phil Bollhagen, *The Pictorial Value Guide to Railroad Playing Cards*, published by author, 1987; Arthur Dominy and Rudolph A. Morgenfruh, *Silver At Your Service*, published by authors, 1987; Richard Luckin, *Dining On Rails*, published by author, 1983, out-of-print.

Collectors' Clubs: Railroad Enthusiasts, 456 Main Street, West Townsend, MA 01474; Railroadiana Collectors Association, 795 Aspen Drive, Buffalo Grove, IL 60089; Railway and Locomotive Historical Society, 3363 Riviera West Drive, Kelseyville, CA 95451.

Periodicals: *Key, Lock and Lantern*, P.O. Box 15, Spencerport, NY 14559; *U.S. Rail News*, P.O. Box 7007, Huntington Woods, MI 48070-7007.

Museums: Baltimore and Ohio Railroad, Baltimore, MD; Museum of Transportation, Boston, MA; New York Museum of Transportation, Albany, NY; California State Railroad Museum, Sacramento, CA.

Additional Listings: See *Warman's Americana & Collectibles* for more examples.

Advisor: Alan H. Altman.

Belt Buckle, Union Pacific, Smith & Wesson insignia on reverse, #J–36, 1866	**75.00**
China	
Ashtray, Great Northern, Mountains &	

Lamp, Club Car, NY Central, tin, repainted base, $50.00.

Flowers, 4″ d, backstamp, Syracuse China	**85.00**
Butter Pat, Atlantic Coast Line, Flora of the South, 3½″ d, backstamp, Syracuse China	**95.00**
Celery Tray, Grand Trunk Western, City of Grand Rapids, 11 x 6″, top logo, Rosenthal China	**185.00**
Cereal Bowl, Baltimore & Ohio, Capitol, 6¼″ d, top logo, Shenango China	**45.00**
Cup and Saucer	
Delaware & Hudson, Canterbury, cup with side logo, Syracuse China	**450.00**
Union Pacific, Desert Flower, backstamp, Syracuse China	**95.00**
Gravy Boat, New York, New Haven & Hartford, Platinum Blue, side marked, backstamp, Buffalo China	**125.00**
Mustard Pot, lid, Chesapeake & Ohio, Staffordshire, backstamp, Shenango China	**175.00**
Pickle Tray, Northern Pacific, Monad, 7¾ x 3¾″, top logo, Shenango China	**200.00**
Plate	
Minneapolis, St Paul & Sault Saint Marie, Logan, 9¾″ d, backstamp, Mayer China	**250.00**
Missouri Pacific, Eagle, 6¼″ d, top logo, backstamp, Syracuse China	**38.00**
9¾″ d, Minneapolis, St Paul & Sault Saint Marie, Logan, backstamp, Mayer China	**250.00**

Platter

Chicago, Milwaukee & Puget Sound, Puget, oval, 12¼ x 8½", top logo, Maddock **200.00**

New York Central, Dewitt Clinton, rect, 8½ x 5¼", top marked, backstamp, Syracuse China . . . **48.00**

Sauce Dish, Reading, Stotesbury, 4¼" sq, backstamp, Scammell China **165.00**

Soup

Norfolk & Western, Cavalier, 8¾" d, top logo, Scammell China **75.00**

Seaboard, Miami, 8" d, top marked, Syracuse China **250.00**

Fire Grenades, Chicago & Northwestern RR, cast iron wall mount, emb "C&NW RR" **115.00**

Glassware

Highball, Pennsylvania, 4½" h, maroon and white train, Washington, DC and New York City skylines . . **25.00**

Water, Nickel Plate Road, 3¾" h, white and blue logo, "NICKEL PLATE ROAD" inside **25.00**

Wine, Canadian National System, 4½" h, 2½" d, stemmed, etched logo **45.00**

Hat

Missouri Pacific, two silver bands, silver "MISSOURI PACIFIC LINES" buttons on each side, cap badge with red Buzzsaw logo, "MISSOURI PACIFIC LINES" inside, "TRAINMAN" below **150.00**

New York Central, two gold bands, two gold "NYC" buttons, "NEW YORK CENTRAL CONDUCTOR" cap badge, blue enamel oval logo, "New York Central System" inside **85.00**

Headlight, 14", marked "Imperial Incandescent Headlight" **250.00**

Lantern

Kansas City Southern Railway, Adams & Westlake Co, Adlake Reliable, single horiz wire guard bellbottom frame, 5⅜" clear globe etched "KCSRY," patent date May 9, 1922, frame marked "KCSRY" **160.00**

New York Philadelphia & Norfolk Railroad, Keystone Lantern Co, The Casey, single horiz wire guard, twist wick raiser, 5⅜" amber globe, patent date Dec 30, 1902, frame marked "NYP&N R CO" **850.00**

Lantern Globe

Pennsylvania Lines, 5⅜", red cast, extended base **150.00**

Rutland, 6", green, etched "Rutland RR Co," manufactured by Macbeth Pearl Glass 227 . . . . **200.00**

Santa Fe, 5⅜", aqua, etched cross logo, "Santa Fe" logo **325.00**

Western Maryland Railroad, 5⅜", clear cast, extended base, rect panel marked "WMRR" **250.00**

Lock, Soo Line, heart shape, brass, chain, Hansl Mfg Co **100.00**

Map, US, railways in service, 1906 . . . **50.00**

Oil Can, emb "NY, NH, & HRR," long spout **70.00**

Plaque, 9¼", copper, builder's, "The Baldwin Locomotive Works/Philadelphia/USA/October 1912" **330.00**

Postcard

Hatfield Station, Fort Meyer, VA, divided back, photo, unused **60.00**

Waiting for the Train, Egypt, Mass, depot, black and white, divided back, July 8, 1913 . . . . **7.00**

Silver, Flatware

Fork, cocktail, Louisville & Nashville, Cromwell, International Silver . . . **22.00**

Knife

Santa Fe #22, Priscilla, large, Rogers Brothers **22.00**

Atlantic Coast Line, Zephyr, small, International Silver **16.00**

Spoon

Serving, Lehigh Valley, Rex, flag logo, Reed & Barton **85.00**

Teaspoon, Northern Pacific, Savoy, Victor **18.00**

Tablespoon, Santa Fe, Albany, Gorham **12.00**

Silver, Holloware

Coffee Pot, New York Central, 8 oz, #070, incised side mark, backstamp, International Silver **85.00**

Cornholder, Pennsylvania, incised PRR Keystone, logo on top, International Silver, pr. **85.00**

Creamer, Southern, 10 oz, #1332, hinged lid, incised SR arrow on side, Reed & Barton **265.00**

Sugar Tongs, Frisco Lines, Dartmouth, 4¼" l, backstamp, Wallace **125.00**

Tureen, cov, Atchison, Topeka & Santa Fe, 6½", double handles, side and top logo, Harrison Brothers **165.00**

Switch Key

L&N RR, 9639 . . . . **15.00**

MK&T RY, Slaymaker, football hallmark **25.00**

NPRR, Fraim, keystone hallmark . . **15.00**

Switch Lock

Boston & Maine Railroad, brass, early style, marked "B&M RR LS S, Sherburne & Co, Boston, MA" . . . **125.00**

Erie Railroad Co, six lever, round . . **200.00**

Water Pail, Soo Line, 13 x 10", emb metal, wide collar on bottom **45.00**

RAZORS

History: Razors date back several thousand years. Early man used sharpened stones. The Egyptians, Greeks, and Romans had metal razors.

Razors made prior to 1800 generally were crudely stamped WARRANTED or CAST STEEL, with the maker's mark on the tang. Until 1870 almost all razors for the American market were manufactured in Sheffield, England. Most blades were wedge shaped; many were etched with slogans or scenes. Handles were made of natural materials: various horns, tortoiseshell, bone, ivory, stag, silver, and pearl. All razors were handmade.

After 1870 razors were machine made with hollow ground blades and synthetic handle materials. Razors of this period usually were manufactured in Germany (Solingen) or in American cutlery factories. Hundreds of molded celluloid handle patterns were produced.

Cutlery firms produced boxed sets of two, four, and seven razors. Complete and undamaged sets are very desirable. Most popular are the 7-Day sets with each razor etched with a day of the week.

The fancier the handle or more intricately etched the blade, the higher the price. Rarest handle materials are pearl, stag, sterling silver, pressed horn, and carved ivory. Rarest blades are those with scenes etched across the entire front. Value is increased by certain manufacturer's names, e.g., H. Boker, Case, M. Price, Joseph Rogers, Simmons Hardware, Will & Finck, Winchester, and George Wostenholm.

    hgb: hollow ground blade
    wb: wedge blade

References: Robert A. Doyle, *Straight Razor Collecting, An Illustrated Price Guide*, Collector Books, 1980, out-of-print; Phillip L. Krumholz, *Value Guide For Barberiana & Shaving Collectibles*, Ad Libs Publishing Co., 1988.

Periodical: *Blade Magazine*, P.O. Box 22007, Chattanooga, TN 37422.

Additional Listings: See *Warman's Americana & Collectibles* for more examples.

AMERICAN BLADES

Challenge Cutlery Co, Bridgeport, Conn, blade etched "Rince," black peacock pattern	55.00
Novelty Cutlery Co, Canton, OH, USA, rounded point blade, handle with cow, horse, train, and owner's name and address, front dated "1921," German Silver ends	80.00
Saffa, John J, St. Louis, two gold camels and scroll scene on blade with "Silver Steel," ivory colored handle	25.00
Schumates Shuraco, blade etched with gold open razor and gentleman's head and "Shumate Registered	

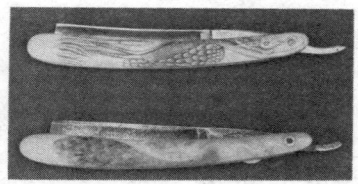

Raised celluloid handles, top: heron eating fish, $70.00; bottom: peacock, $65.00.

Trade Mark," celluloid handle with orange front and green back, MOP tang	65.00
Union Razor Cutlery Co, Union City, GA, banded tobacco pattern handle	40.00

ENGLISH BLADES, SHEFFIELD

Etched "Ask For Wade & Butcher's Hollow Ground Razor," picked bone pattern handle	100.00
Turniss Cutler & Stacey Sheffield, unusual shaped point blade, tang stamped "For Use," two pressed intertwined snakes on mottled horn handle	620.00
Wade & Butcher, hgb, engraved and ornate escutcheon plate with two inlaid engraved star shape metal dec, mottled horn handle, blade etched "The Celebrated Hollow Ground Razor," c1850	70.00

GERMAN BLADES

Boker, H & Co, etched blade with American Lines SS St Louis Ship scene, black celluloid handle	125.00
Eyre, B J, Germany, hgb, blade etched "Extra Hollow Ground" in gold, imitation ivory handle with light blue peacock feather pattern	75.00
Morley, W H & Co, blade etched "Real Hollow Ground," imitation ivory handle with raised orange flower and ribbon dec	55.00
Westfield Mfg Co, hgb, ivory handle with checkered raised shield	50.00

SWISS BLADES

John Engstrom Eskilstuna, frameback, wafer blade, tang with dates up to 1881, ivory handle	50.00

SETS OF RAZORS

7–Day Set, A J Jordan Sheffield, Eng, blades engraved with days of week, tangs etched "Old Faithful," ivory handles with pointed ends, peeled perimeter and inlaid brass escutcheon plate on oak case, purple lining ... **245.00**

7–Day Set, Sheffield Steel Warranted, rounded point hgb, imitation ivory handles, tangs stamped "K" in a circle, leather cov wood case, burgundy velvet lined slotted int. **130.00**

7–Day Set, Taylor Eye–Witness Sheffield, semi–wedge blades with engraved days on top, ivory handle, leather cov wood case with German silver escutcheon plate, blue lining with gold adv, lock, and key **240.00**

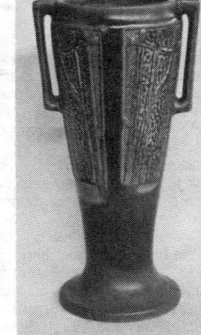

RED WING POTTERY

History: The Red Wing pottery category covers several potteries from Red Wing, Minnesota. In 1868 David Hallem started Red Wing Stoneware Co., the first pottery, with stoneware as its primary product and with a red wing stamped under the glaze as its mark. The Minnesota Stoneware Co. started in 1883. The North Star Stoneware Co., 1892–1896, used a raised star and the words "Red Wing" as its mark.

The Red Wing Stoneware Co. and the Minnesota Stoneware Co. merged in 1892. The new company, the Red Wing Union Stoneware Co., made stoneware until 1920, when it introduced a pottery line which it continued until the 1940s. In 1936 the name was changed to Red Wing Potteries, Inc. During the 1930s it introduced several popular lines of hand-painted pattern dinnerware which were distributed through department stores, Sears, and gift stamp centers. Dinnerware declined in the 1950s, being replaced with hotel and restaurant china in the early 1960s. The plant closed in 1967.

References: Dan and Gail DePasquale and Larry Peterson, *Red Wing Collectibles,* Collector Books, 1985; David A. Newkirk, *A Guide To Red Wing Markings,* Monticello Printing, 1979; Dolores Simon, *Red Wing Pottery With Rumrill,* Collector Books, 1980; Gary and Bonnie Tefft, *Red Wing Potters and Their Wares, Second Edition,* Locust Enterprises, 1987; Lyndon C. Viel, *The Clay Giants, The Stoneware of Red Wing, Goodhue County, Minnesota, Book 2* 1980, *Book 3,* 1987, Wallace-Homestead.

Collectors' Club: Red Wing Collectors Society, Route 3, Box 146, Monticello, MN 55362.

Additional Listings: See *Warman's Americana & Collectibles* for more examples.

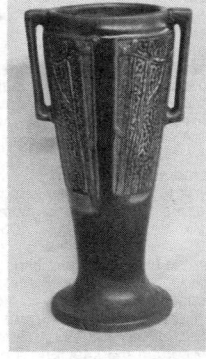

Vase, trumpet, disc base, two handles, four relief panels of brown semi-glaze trees, gray matte ground, marked "Red Wing/Union/Stoneware/Co./Red Wing/Minn," 9¾" h, $45.00.

Ashtray, Minnesota Twins World Series, 1965	60.00
Baking Dish, round, ribbed bands, red and blue sponge dec	55.00
Bean Pot, cov, 1 qt, white ribbed base, brown glazed top, marked "Red Wing Union Stoneware Co," wire bail handle	80.00
Beater Jar, adv, Strawberry Point, Iowa	100.00
Bird Feeder, stoneware, orig tray	45.00
Bowl	
5½" d, double blue band, wide rim, ribbed base	40.00
6½" d, Saffron Ware	60.00
7" d, rust, blue, and cream sponge dec	75.00
11" d, paneled, blue and rust sponge dec	90.00
Butter Churn, 5 gal, large red wing decal, orig lid	225.00
Butter Crock, white, blue adv, two pounds, marked "Red Wing"	90.00
Casserole, cov, 7" d, Grey Line	150.00
Coffee Server, 15" h, Village Brown, metal stand	40.00

Cookie Jar
    Cattails, brown tones 125.00
    Chef, yellow glaze 45.00
    Rooster, green semi–gloss glaze, imp
      "Red Wing USA, #249" 40.00
Crock, 3 gallon, brown salt glaze, cobalt
  blue floral dec 135.00
Custard Cup, Grey Line, sponge dec 185.00
Flower Pot, 10" d, ribbons and berries,
  Brushware 60.00
Jug
    Gallon, beehive shape, turkey eye
      drippings 285.00
    Pint, adv, Connell, Washington 300.00
Pantry Jar, cov, Grey Line, bail handle 425.00
Pitcher, 6" h
    Cherry Band, blue and white 150.00
    Grey Line 175.00
Reamer, yellow 75.00
Sewer Tile Sample, salt glaze, marked
  "Union Stoneware, Red Wing Minn" 125.00
Sign, 6½" h, wing shape, "Red Wing
  Pottery 75th, 1878–1953" 35.00
Slop Jar, cov, blue stripe, lily dec 135.00
Umbrella Stand, florals, Brushware . . . 145.00
Vase
    8½" h, light blue glaze, emb woman
      and florals, imp mark 65.00
    12½" h, Bamboo pattern, green and
      yellow 60.00
Wall Pocket, Gardenia, ivory glaze . . . 40.00
Water Cooler, stoneware, white, red
  wing, oval "Red Wing Union Stone-
  ware" mark 375.00

REDWARE

History: The availability of clay, the same used to make bricks and roof tiles, accounted for the great production of red earthenware pottery in the American colonies. Redware pieces are mainly utilitarian—bowls, crocks, jugs, etc.

Lead-glazed redware retained its reddish color, but a variety of colored glazes were obtained by the addition of metals to the basic glaze. Streaks and mottled splotches in redware items resulted from impurities in the clay and/or uneven firing temperatures.

"Slipware" is a term used to describe redwares decorated by the application of slip, a semi-liquid paste made of clay. Slipwares were made in England, Germany, and elsewhere in Europe for decades before becoming popular in the Pennsylvania German region and elsewhere in colonial America.

Reference: Kevin McConnell, *Redware: America's Folk Art Pottery,* Schiffer Publishing Ltd.

Apple Butter Jar
    4¾" h, glazed int. 30.00
    5¾" h, glazed int. 60.00

Bank
    4⅞" h, green glaze 100.00
    5" h, ovoid, knob handle, two tone
      yellow slip, sgraffito inscription "A
      Present from Sod Hill," clear glaze
      with brown flecks 15.00
    6" h, mottled brown glaze, black
      slashes, knob finial 145.00
Bean Pot, cov, 7" h 45.00
Bowl
    6⅛" d, dark brown sponging, ftd . . . 75.00
    7¼" d
      Brown glaze, open rim handles . . 50.00
      White slip stripes, green and run-
        ning brown glaze 425.00
      Yellow slip dec, wavy lines and
        dots, reddish glaze 325.00
    8½" d, yellow slip dec 30.00
    9½" d, tooled band, dark brown
      sponging, deep orange ground, rim
      spout, ribbed handle 175.00
    9¾" d, orange glazed int. 25.00
    10¼" d, glaze int. 45.00
    15½" d, wheel turned, length wise cut,
      glazed int. 50.00
Bust, 4¾" h, black man, dark brown
  glaze, beaded necklace, yarn hair
  and beard 200.00
Candle Sconce, 6½" h, wheel turned,
  socket in base 350.00
Charger, 12¼" d, coggeled rim, yellow
  slip dec 700.00
Coffeepot, 11¼" h, dome top, tooled
  dec, emb leaf handle, mismatched lid,
  English 150.00
Cup, 2¾" h, brown splotches 50.00
Dish
    6¼" d, 3" h, applied rim handles,
      brown splotched glaze, edge chips 325.00
    7⅜" d, yellow slip wavy line dec . . . 175.00
Figure, 8¾" h, dog, seated, tooled coat
  and detail 450.00
Flask, 4⅛" h, commemorative, yellow
  slip stenciled inscription "The Best is
  not to good for you, Job Funnel
  1774," and impressed mark "The
  Dicker, UC & N Sussex" 175.00
    Flower Pot, 5¾" h, unmatched under
    tray 200.00
Food Mold
    6½" d, 2⅝" h, hexagonal, mottled am-
      ber glaze, chips 40.00
    7" d, turk's head, two–tone green
      glaze, emb ribs and handle, rim
      chips 65.00
    9" d, turk's head, brown sponging,
      chips 25.00
    10½ x 11¼", coiled fish, greenish am-
      ber glaze 225.00
    11¾" d, turk's head, clear glaze,
      brown and green 75.00
Food Storage Jar, 10" h, rare mottled

green glaze, American, early 19th C, one small chip on cov, minor chips in jar **2,600.00**

Jar
  3½" h, brown fleck glaze **55.00**
  5" h, dark sponged dec, tooled line around middle **125.00**
  6¾" h, ovoid, side spout, tooled line on shoulder, strap handle **225.00**
  10" h, ovoid, brownish amber flecks, glazed **300.00**
  10⅝" h, ovoid, strap handle, glazed int. **25.00**

Jug
  6½" h, amber, greenish glaze, oversize strap handle **35.00**
  7¼" h, brown Albany slip, stenciled label "S T Suit, Suitland, My Little Brown Jug, The Whiskey in this jug was made 1869 and jugged by me 1880" **325.00**
  7¾" h, mottled brown glaze, ribbed strap handle **155.00**
  11" h, brown glaze **50.00**

Lamp, 3⅜" h, flared base, open font with wick support, clear glaze with running brown **1,000.00**

Loaf Pan, 12 x 14¾", white slip dec, dark glaze, chip and wear **40.00**

Milk Bowl
  11½" d, brown spots, ext. glaze ... **125.00**
  12¼" d, brown sponged int. glaze .. **55.00**
  12½" d, white and bluish green combed slip dec **60.00**

Mug, 6½" h, sponged brown, ribbed strap handle **800.00**

Pan, 10 x 20", rect **85.00**

Pie Plate
  7¾" d, coggeled rim, three line yellow slip crow's foot design **100.00**
  8" d, three line yellow slip dec, coggeled rim, edge and surface chips **350.00**

8⅞" d, three line yellow slip dec, coggeled rim, hairline crack **55.00**

9" d, coggeled edge **65.00**

9½" d, yellow slip wavy line dec, coggeled rim, old chips **625.00**

Pitcher
  5½" h, brown splotched glaze, strap handle, old glaze chips **225.00**
  7⅜" h, glaze int., white slip rim, English **35.00**
  8" h, brown fleck glaze, ribbed strap handle **90.00**
  10¼" h, thick bluish green mottled glaze **150.00**
  10½" h, Shenandoah, white slip, clear glaze, running green and brown, strap handle, applied ornaments, minor edge chips **1,350.00**

Plate
  8⅜" d, coggeled rim, sixteen dot yellow slip **250.00**
  11" d, PA, slipware dec, initials "NP," upper edge chips **210.00**
  13¾" d, sgraffito, polychrome glaze, marked "Pisa Italy" **35.00**
  14¼" d, PA, yellow slipware dec "St Justin the Apologist," scattered chips, rim flakes **800.00**

Pot, 4½" h, ruffled rim, strap handles, attributed to Schofield Potteryworks, Chester County, PA, early 20th C .. **175.00**

Rundlet, 7½" l, spotted green glaze, attributed to Moravian Potters, NC, early 19th C **300.00**

Salt, 11¾" h, white slip floral dec, "Salt" on rim opening, dark green glaze ... **65.00**

Wash Bowl, 16" d, Shenandoah, white slip, clear glaze, running green and brown, applied handles and soap dish, broken in several pcs and glued **800.00**

Washboard, 7 x 13½", poplar frame, small **325.00**

Plate, four slip cup creating waves and straight lines, crimped edges, 9½" d, $625.00.

RELIGIOUS ITEMS

History: Objects for the worshipping or expression of man's belief in a superhuman power are collected by many people for many reasons.

Icons are included since they are religious mementos, usually paintings with a brass encasement. Collecting icons dates from the earliest period of Christianity. Most antique icons in today's market were made in the late 19th century.

Reproduction Alert: Icons are heavily reproduced.

Altarsticks, pr, 19½" h, giltwood, mounted as lamps, Continental **375.00**

Baptismal Font, 55½" h, oak, octagonal,

Icon

7¾ x 6½", Jesus entering Jerusalem **275.00**

10⅓ x 8½", Virgin Mother and Child, silver on copper oklad, chased scrolls and flowerheads, gilded halo **575.00**

20 x 14", two registers, diocese on upper, lower in three panels with sacrifice of Abraham, flanked by two pairs of saints, gilt ground, crazing, cracks, framed, Greek, early 19th C **750.00**

Painting

8¼ x 11½", Madonna and child, oil on canvas, Spanish, 17th C **650.00**

14 x 12", Our Lady of Smolensk, tempera on panel, Russian, 18th C . . **950.00**

17½ x 15", Christ with Archangel and St Gregory, Moscow **850.00**

Sampler, 13" h, 9¾" w, homespun, Psalm 118, alphabets, multicolored design, Sarah Blatchfoord 1756, framed **725.00**

REVERSE PAINTING ON GLASS

History: The earliest examples of reverse painting on glass were produced in 13th-century Italy. By the 17th century the technique had spread to Central and Eastern Europe. It spread westward as the glass industry center moved to Germany in the late 17th century.

The Alsace and Black Forest regions developed a unique portraiture style. The half and three-quarter portraits often were titled below the portrait. Women tend to have general names. Most male paintings are of famous men.

The English used a mezzotint method, rather than free-style, to create their reverse paintings. Landscapes and allegorical figures were popular. The Chinese began working in the medium in the 17th century, eventually favoring marine and patriotic scenes.

Reverse painting was done in America. Most were by folk artists who favored portraits, patriotic and mourning scenes, floral compositions, landscapes, and buildings. Most folk artists did not sign their work. Known American artists include Benjamin Greenleaf, A. Cranfield, and Rowley Jacobs.

In the late 19th century commercially produced reverse paintings, often decorated with mother-of-pearl, became popular. Themes included the Statue of Liberty, the capitol in Washington, D.C., and various world fairs and expositions.

PORTRAITS

7¾ x 10½", Sylvia, woman in red dress, blue ground, orig frame **125.00**

9½ x 12", Emilie, balloon sleeve dress, large collar **500.00**

Figures, wooden, polychrome, Italian, 18th C, 14¼" h, pr, $1,200.00.

paneled conical top and base, pair of doors, Italian, 18th C **1,100.00**

Bible Box, oak, dark finish, English

15¾ x 22", relief carved semicircular designs, replaced lock and hinges **135.00**

24" l, geometric carved design on front, iron lock and hasp, English **250.00**

Communion Items

Bowl, 10¼" d, ftd, Hiram Yale & Co **600.00**

Chalice, 7" h, pewter, marked "Reed & Barton" **125.00**

Flagon, 11" h, pewter, marked "Taunton Brita Manfg Co" **175.00**

Plate, 13⅛" d, pewter, Thomas Boardman, Hartford, Conn, c1825 **550.00**

Tray, 11⅛" d, pewter, marked "Reed & Barton" **55.00**

Figure

Bishop, 9½" h, ivory, carved, holding crosier in right hand, miniature cathedral in left, opens to seated Virgin and Child with adoring saints, mounted on octagonal wood base, 19th C **1,100.00**

Madonna, 14" h, holding child, wood, carved, polychromed, Spanish . . . **900.00**

St Francis, 16½" h, bronze, blackish brown patina, arms crossed, leaning on two man saw, wood base, inscribed "L Rucki," French, 20th C **5,500.00**

Virgin Mary, 8¾" h, ivory, carved, standing with praying hands, rosary draped over one arm, skirt opens to Christ Resurrection scene, recessed black staining, 19th C . . . **1,320.00**

10 x 8″, woman, plumed hat, seated by column, orig frame 375.00
11⅞ x 9½″, bride, orig frame 550.00
12¼ x 14½″, Napoleon, white uniform, green oval, black rect, gilt flowers in spandrels, beveled frame 1,000.00
14½ x 11½″, George Washington and family, Chinese Export, 19th C, molded wood frame 3,750.00

Cottage scene, MOP on house, green frame with gilt pilaster end pieces, 12 x 24″, $75.00.

SCENES

9″, advertising, Evan's Westbrook Mercantile Co, Lorena, TX, girl in field with pitch fork, orig chain 200.00
9⅜ x 11⅜″, church, wooded landscape, bright colors, framed 300.00
10 x 6½″, battleship, *USS Maine* 75.00
14¼ x 10¼″, winter landscape, Currier and Ives type, inscribed "American Farm Scene," orig frame 125.00
18½ x 16½″, country scene stone bridge, half timber cottage, ogee bird's eye maple veneer frame 125.00
20 x 27″, Blarney Castle, forest scene, mica and abalone highlights 145.00
22 x 21½″, Sorrow of Werter, one with scene of Charlotte at the piano singing, other with Charlotte and Werter grieving, circular panels within star studded border, carved giltwood frame, Chinese Export, early 19th C, pr 3,575.00

RIDGWAY

History: Throughout the 19th century the Ridgway family, through a series of partnerships, held a position of importance in Shelton and Hanley, Staffordshire, England. The connection began with Job and George, two brothers, and Job's two sons, John and William. In 1830 John and William separated, with John retaining the Cauldon Place factory and William the Bell Works. By 1862 the porcelain division of Cauldon was carried on by Coalport China Ltd. William and his heirs continued at the Bell Works and the Church [Hanley] and Bedford [Shelton] works until the end of the 19th century.

Many early pieces are unmarked. Later marks include the initials of the many partnerships.

References: Susan and Al Bagdade, *Warman's English & Continental Pottery & Porcelain, 1st Edition,* Warman Publishing Co., Inc., 1987; G. A. Godden, *Ridgway Porcelains,* Antique Collectors' Club.

Additional Listings: Staffordshire, Historical; and Staffordshire, Romantic.

Pitcher, blue Oriental scene, c1814–30, marked "John & William Ridgway," 7½″ h, $125.00.

Biscuit jar, 6½″ h, Coaching Days and Ways, caramel ground, rattan handle 245.00
Cheese Dish, cov, light brown floral transfer print 85.00
Cup and Saucer, fishing scene 25.00
Cup Plate, Marmora 48.00
Mug, silver luster trim
  3⅞″ h, Coaching Days and Ways . . 40.00
  4″ h, Shakespeare 40.00
  4½″ h, polar bear and cat 45.00
Pitcher, Chester pattern, blue and white 50.00
Plaque
  9½″ d, Robert Burns cottage, caramel glaze, gold luster trim 70.00
  12″ d, In A Snow Drift, Coaching Days and Ways 125.00
Plate
  8″ d, Coaching Days and Ways 40.00
  10″ d, Washington's Headquarters, flow blue 45.00
Platter
  16″ l, oval, Villa pattern, light blue transfer print 80.00
  21⅝″ l, well and tree, blue, green, iron–red, puce, and yellow dec, center stylized flowers and rockwork, griffins, stylized flowerheads, and scrolls against blue diaper ground border, green mark "Imperial Stone China Belisarius," c1835 350.00

Tea Tile, 6″ d, round, Coaching Days and Ways	100.00
Teapot, 6″ h, gooseneck spout, whooping cranes and foliage dec, brown transfer print, white ground, English 1877 registration mark	65.00
Tray, 8¼″ l, Bank of Savannah, handles	175.00
Vase, 4⅞″ h, Coaching Days and Ways, egg shape, caramel ground, black scenes, silver luster band and handle	75.00

RING TREES

History: A ring tree is a small, generally saucer-shaped object made of glass, porcelain, metal, or wood with a center post in the shape of a hand, branches, or cylinder for hanging or storing finger rings.

Bear, standing, holding gun, guarding tree, oval base, Pairpoint, 3¼ x 2⅛ x 3¼″, $125.00.

Bronze, 5″ h, figural, parrot	45.00
Glass	
Cameo, 3¼″ h, acid cut, red flowers, leaves, and stems, leaf ground, St Louis	150.00
Cranberry, 3¼″ h, multicolored flowers, gold leaves	115.00
Cut, 3″ h, clear, flowers and leaves, black enamel bands	55.00
Lalique, 5″ h, figural, Madonna, frosted, marked "R Lalique, France 288"	200.00
Opaline	
2½″ d, column center, round dish, blue, gold and white trim	50.00
3¼″ h, hp, blue, orange and gold dec, ftd	45.00
Porcelain	
Hand Painted, hand and dish, rose dec, gilting, maple leaf mark, marked "Hand Painted"	50.00
Wedgwood, Jasperware	
Cobalt blue, white relief figures, 2¾″ h, marked	120.00
Dark blue, rose border, classical scenes, unmarked	175.00
Dark blue and white, classical figures	180.00
Nippon, hand shape, floral dec, gold ground	45.00
Royal Worcester, 2¾″ h, three prongs, pink and yellow flower dec, beige ground, oval dish, c1898	145.00
Scrimshaw, 5¾″ h, bone, harp shape, Prisoner–of–War	100.00
Sterling Silver, figural, angel, Tiffany & Co	450.00
Tramp Art, fruitwood, hand shape, carved	25.00

ROCK 'N' ROLL

History: Rock music can be traced back to early rhythm and blues music. It progressed and reached its golden age in the 1950s and 1960s. Attention and most of the memorabilia issued during that period focused on individual singers and groups. The two largest sources of collectibles are items associated with Elvis Presley and The Beatles.

In the 1980s two areas—clothing and guitars—associated with key Rock 'n' Roll personalities received special collector attention. Sotheby's and Christie's East regularly feature Rock 'n' Roll memorabilia as part of their collectibles sales. At the moment, the market is highly speculative and nostalgia-driven.

It is important to identify memorabilia issued during the lifetime of an artist or performing group as opposed to material issued after they died or disbanded. This latter material is identified as "fantasy" items and will never achieve the same degree of collectibility as its period counterparts.

References: Jeff Augsburger, Marty Eck, and Rich Rann, *The Beatles Memorabilia Price Guide*, Branyan Press, 1988; *Rosalind Cranor, Elvis Collectibles*, Collector Books, 1983; L. R. Docks, *1915–1965 American Premium Record Guide*, *Third Edition*, Books Americana, 1986; Barbara Penick, *Collecting The Beatles: An Introduction and Price Guide To Fab Four Collectibles, Records and Memorabilia, Volume 1* (1984) and *Volume 2*, Perian Press; Alison Fox, *Rock & Pop*, Boxtree Ltd. (London), 1988; Paul Grushkin, *The Art of Rock—Posters From Presley To Punk*, Abbeville Press, 1986; Jerry Osborne, Perry Cox, and Joe Lindsay, *The Official Price Guide to Memorabilia of Elvis Presley And The Beatles*, House of Collectibles, 1988.

Collectors' Club: Beatles Fan Club of Great Britain, Superstore Productions, 123 Marina St.,

Leonards on Sea, East Sussex, England TN 38 OBN.

Periodicals: Beatlefan, P. O. Box 33515, Decatur, GA 30033; Good Day Sunshine, Liverpool Productions, 397 Edgewood Avenue, New Haven, CT 06511.

Reproduction Alert: Records, picture sleeves, and album jackets, especially for The Beatles, have been counterfeited. Sound may be inferior. Printing on labels and picture jackets usually is inferior to the original. Many pieces of memorabilia also have been reproduced, often with some change in size, color, and design.

Additional Listings: See The Beatles, Elvis Presley, and Rock 'n' Roll in *Warman's Americana & Collectibles*.

Shoes, bright red suede, black laces and soles, worn by Buddy Holly on various tours, late 1950s, $3,850.00.

Bank, Beatles, 10" h, bobbing head, unauthorized, composition, coin slot in back, black hair, pink jacket, black shoes, yellow base, "Yea, Yea, Yea" decal, brown guitar, marked "Hand Painted World Gift Japan," c1960 .. **200.00**

Bicycle Seat, Yellow Submarine, 9 x 10", vinyl, connected to spring frame and post, off–white ground, yellow accents at top and bottom, 5" l yellow sub illus below two groups of tiny bubbles, Huffy, c1968 .... **150.00**

Book, *The Kingston Trio*, 8 x 11", hard cover, black and white and full–color photos, published by Random House, copyright 1960 Highridge Music Inc, 36 pgs **20.00**

Bracelet, Tiger Beat, subscription premium, metallic gold, 1¼"d medallion with raised picture of tiger under Tiger Beat, c1968–70 .... **20.00**

Bust, Elvis, 7" h, plaster, painted, thin glaze, facsimile signature on rect base, c1950 .... **600.00**

Button

James Dean, 2½" d, color photo, issued before his death, mid–1950 **65.00**

I Love Freddy And The Dreamers, 3½" d, red and white lettering, black and white photo of five band members, copyright Premier Talent Associates Inc, c1960 .... **40.00**

Greeting Card

Musical, Beatles, 3½ x 9 x 1", unauthorized, plays "Happy Birthday To You", glued to red box with crank on side, card has full color illustration of four band members who resemble the Beatles, message inside is "Do I Wish You A Happy Birthday? Yea! Yea! Yea! Yea!", c late 1960s **65.00**

Photo

Rock And Roll Stars, 3¼ x 5¼", thirty–six unopened packages, three cards per package, sepia photos, includes Everly Bros, Chuck Berry, Frankie Avalon, Paul Anka and sixty others, orig box, Nu Trading Cards, late 1950s **90.00**

Monkees, playing, fifty–two cards, forty different black and white photos, orig full color box, copyright 1966 Rayburn Production Inc **35.00**

Coloring Book, Beatles, 8½ x 11", 124 pgs, ten black and white photo pgs, Saalfield Publishing Co, copyright 1964 Nems Enterprises Ltd **50.00**

Doll

Boy George, 15" h, plush body, molded vinyl head, red and white outfit, white shoes, red tie, black hat, red yarn hair with beads and bows, yellow and purple make-up, bright red lips, LJN, copyright 1984 Sharpegrade Ltd, orig box marked "The Huggable, Cute, Cuddly Doll" **65.00**

Dave Clark, 4½" h, hard plastic, soft vinyl head, black hair, small drum with facsimile signature, black base, Remco, copyright 1964 ... **70.00**

Ringo Starr, 15" h, plastic, inflatable, black hair, purple suit, black shoes, holding orange and white drum, facsimile signature on drum, copyright 1966 Nems Ltd **60.00**

Figure, Paul McCartney, 4½" h, plastic body, soft vinyl head, life–like hair, black outfit, white shirt, black necktie, removable diecut plastic black guitar, gold trim and facsimile signature on guitar, orig box copyright 1964 .... **150.00**

Hanger, Jimmi Hendrix, 15 x 17", cardboard, black and white photo on both sides, punch–out center, marked "Manufactured Exclusively By Sunders Enterprises/Jimmi Hendrix" ... **170.00**

Lunch Box

Kiss, 7 x 9 x 4", metal, color photos, King–Seeley, copyright 1977 Aucoin Management Inc **60.00**

Bobby Sherman, 7 x 9 x 4", metal, color photos and illus, 6½" h metal thermos with color photo and white plastic cup, King–Seeley, copyright 1972 Bobby Sherman Enterprises Inc **60.00**

The Osmonds, 7 x 9 x 4", metal, full color illus, front with name decal, Aladdin Industries, copyright 1973 Osbro Productions **35.00**

Magazine

Life, 10½ x 13½", Vol 67 #9, Aug 29, 1969, ten page article on Woodstock, color photos **20.00**

Rock–N Roll Stars, 8½ x 11", published by Fawcett Publications, copyright 1956 .... **70.00**

Model Kit, Monkeemobile, partially assembled body, instruction sheet, unused decals orig box, MPC copyright 1967 Raybert Productions Inc, ... **85.00**

Necklace

Brenda Lee, gold chain with cultured pearl pendant, mounted on orig sealed card designed like a record, copyright Brenda Lee, 1950–60 .. **40.00**

Fave!, gold metal, 1¼" medallion with raised flower surrounded by "Fave! Peace And Love", subscription premium, 1968–70 .... **20.00**

Pen, Beatles, 5½" l, plastic, green, 2" clear plastic section with paper photo of band members, facsimile signatures, instrument illus, marked "The Beatles", c1960 .... **60.00**

Plate, James Dean, 10" d, commemorative, white china, green illus and text, five portraits, biography sketch, birth and death dates, back with eulogy text, Kettlesprings Kilns signature, and registration number S846, c1955 .... **160.00**

Poster

Family Dog, 14 x 20", paper, June 1–4, 1967 Concert at Avalon Ballroom, featuring Miller Blues Band and The Doors, #64–1, Victor Moscoso artist, blue, red, and green ... **85.00**

The James Gang, 14 x 22", cardboard, Oct 2, 1971 at Curtis Hixon Hall, Tampa, FL, featuring James Gang and Country Joe McDonald, "Wanted" poster design **20.00**

Yard Birds, 14½ x 23½", paper, 1967 concert at Civic Auditorium, Santa

Monica, featuring Yard Birds, Moby Grape, Iron Butterfly, and Captain Beefheart, red, white, and blue, R. Tolmach artist **65.00**

Puzzle, The Beatles Yellow Submarine, 650 pcs, 19 x 19" completed, titled "Sgt Pepper Band", unopened box, Jaymar copyright 1968 King Features Syndicate **90.00**

Record Album

Chubby Checker Your Twist Party, 12¼ x 12¼" cardboard cov, 33⅓ rpm, Parkway Records label, copyright 1961 .... **20.00**

God Bless Tiny Tim, includes "Tip–Toe Thru' The Tulips With Me", 12¼ x 12¼" cov with photos front and back, paper sleeve missing .. **20.00**

Grateful Dead, 33⅓ rpm, "Sampler For Deadheads" on both sides, one side with "Robert Hunter Tales Of The Great Rum Runners", photo of Garcia on label reverse, mailing address upper left corner orig mailing envelope, San Raphael, CA label, copyright 1974 .... **50.00**

Record Case, Dick Clark, 5 x 8 x 8", cardboard, red, white plastic handle, full color photo, white paper label with facsimile signature, c1950 .... **75.00**

Sheet Music

Tab Hunter, "Young Love", 9 x 12", browntone photo, 2 pgs with words and music, copyright 1956 Stars Inc **10.00**

Monkees, "Mary, Mary" and "She", 8 x 11", paper, 3 pgs with music, color photos on front, copyright 1967 Screen Gems–Columbia Music Inc **10.00**

Songbook

The Doors, 8½ x 11", copyright 1967 Nipper Music Co Inc, 32 pgs, eleven songs including "Light My Fire" and "Break On Through," black and white photos and text .. **20.00**

James Taylor, 8½ x 11", published Nichion Inc, copyright 1971, 72 pgs, includes "Fire And Rain" and "You've Got A Friend," black and white photos, English and Japanese writing **20.00**

Stickers, Peter Criss, Kiss Rockstics, two–dimensional, puffy, orig card, unused, set of six, Dimension Weld, copyright 1978 Aucoin **40.00**

Switchplate Cover, The Yellow Submarine, 6 x 12", cardboard, day–glo colored, copyright 1968 King Features Syndicate **35.00**

Tab, 2" d, I Love Elvis, litho tin, blue and gold lettering, silver ground, c1970 **20.00**

Tile, Elvis, 6" sq, glazed ceramic, cork

backing, cloth hanging loop, Elvis leaning back, marked "Best Wishes Elvis Presley," copyright 1956 Elvis Presley Enterprises 300.00

Travel Case, Beatles, 5 x 13 x 12", vinyl, zippered front, handle, group illus, facsimile signatures on front, Air Flite, copyright Nems Enterprises Ltd, c1960 . . . . 550.00

Viewmaster Reels, Kiss, 4½" envelope, full color photos, set of 3, copyright 1979 Aucoin Management 18.00

Wallet, Elvis, 3 x 4½", vinyl, red, attached keychain, coin purse on back, illus on front, black and white paper photo center, copyright 1956 Elvis Presley Enterprises 400.00

ROCKINGHAM AND ROCKINGHAM BROWN GLAZED WARES

History: Rockingham ware can be divided into two categories. The first consists of the fine china and porcelain pieces made between 1826 and 1842 by the Rockingham Company of Swinton, Yorkshire, England, and its predecessor firms: Swinton, Bingley, Don, Leeds, and Brameld. The Bramelds developed the cadogan, a lidless teapot. Between 1826 and 1842 a quality soft paste body with a warm, silken feel was developed by the Bramelds. Elaborate specialty pieces were made. By 1830 the company employed 600 workers and listed 400 designs for dessert sets and 1,000 designs for tea and coffee services in their catalog. Unable to meet its payroll, the company closed in 1842.

The second category of Rockingham ware includes pieces produced in the famous Rockingham brown glaze, that became an intense and vivid purple-brown when fired. It had a dark, tortoiseshell mottled appearance. The glaze was copied by many English and American potteries. American manufacturers who used Rockingham glaze include D. & J. Henderson of Jersey City, New Jersey; United States Pottery in Bennington, Vermont; potteries in East Liverpool, Ohio; and several potteries in Indiana and Illinois.

Reference: Susan and Al Bagdade, *Warman's English & Continental Pottery & Porcelain, 1st Edition,* Warman Publishing Co., Inc., 1987.

Additional Listings: Bennington and Bennington-type.

Bottle
  5" h, bureau shape, corked hole . . . 85.00
  8½" h, Toby 150.00
Bowl
  8¼" d 25.00
  9½" d 75.00
  13" d, 5¾" h, small base flakes 175.00
Creamer, 3⅞" h, glued handle 25.00
Crock, 6½" d, 5" h, cov, emb peacocks 65.00
Cuspidor
  8¼" d, emb rib dec 10.00
  18" d, shell shape 25.00
Dish
  8" sq, glazed 125.00
  9" sq, emb rim 45.00

Figure, puce and green florals, iron–red and gold trim, 4" h, $120.00.

Figure
  9" h, dog, seated, pr 330.00
  10½" h, dog, seated 325.00
Flask, 7¼" h, emb morning glory, eagle, and flag 100.00
Foot Warmer, brown glaze 70.00
Frame, 8¼ x 9½", cherubs, naked ladies, and foliage scrolls dec 850.00
Jar, 9¼" h, 8" d, cov 150.00
Pie Plate
  9½" d 50.00
  10" d 65.00
Pitcher
  7" h, Toby 110.00
  7⅝" h, emb Cupid and Psyche scene 75.00
  8" h, wreath with Washington bust . . 90.00
  8⅝" h, emb hunt scene, hairlines . . . 45.00
  9¼" h, emb hunt scene 145.00
  9¾" h, emb hunting scene and vintage, dog handle, marked "Made by J B Claire Co, Po'keepsie, NY" 750.00
  9⅞", paneled, leaf design 65.00
  10½" h, emb classical foliage, cov, chips and hairline 75.00

Plate, 8¾", pr, octagonal shape **130.00**
Presentation Pitcher, 10" h, medallion
  portraits on sides, glazed frog figure
  on bottom int., marked "Mrs. John
  Webb" **225.00**
Punch Pot, 7½" h, brown and yellow
  glaze, inset lid, knob finial, 2 qt **230.00**
Salt, 6" d, emb peacocks, crest, hanging
  hole **45.00**
Soap Dish, 4 x 5½", emb foliage dec,
  chip on base **175.00**
Teapot
  6" h, marked "Rebekah at the Well" **65.00**
  7¾" h, emb ribs and acanthus leaves **120.00**
Tray, 8½ x 11", scalloped rim **100.00**
Window Props, 4½" h, female busts, pr **390.00**

ROCKWELL, NORMAN

History: Norman Rockwell (February 3, 1894–
November, 1978) was a famous American artist
and illustrator. During the time he painted, from
age 18 until his death, he created over 2,000
works.

His first professional efforts were illustrations for
a children's book. He next worked for *Boy's Life*,
the Boy Scout magazine. His most famous works
were used by *Saturday Evening Post* for their
cover illustrations.

Norman Rockwell painted everyday people in
everyday situations, mixing a little humor with sentiment. His paintings and illustrations are treasured
because of this sensitive approach. Rockwell
painted people he knew and places with which he
was familiar. New England landscapes are found
in many of his illustrations.

References: Denis C. Jackson, *The Norman
Rockwell Identification And Value Guide To: Mag-
azines, Posters, Calendars, Books, 2nd Edition*,
published by author, 1985; Mary Moline, *Norman
Rockwell Collectibles, Sixth Edition*, Green Valley
World, 1988.

Museums: Corner House, Stockbridge, MA;
Norman Rockwell Museum, Northbrook, IL.

Reproduction Alert: Because of the popularity
of his works, they have been reproduced on many
objects. These new collectibles should not be confused with original artwork and illustrations. However, they do allow a collector more range in collecting interests and prices.

Additional Listings: See *Warman's Americana
& Collectibles* for more examples.

HISTORIC

Advertising Tray, Coca–Cola, Tom Saw-
  yer Eating, 10½ x 13¼", 1931 . . . . . **285.00**
Painting, "Petticoats And Pants," oil on
  canvas, signed "Norman Rockwell,
  l.l.," 26¼ x 22" **33,000.00**

**Bell, Norman Rockwell Museum, Inc.,
Bride and Groom, 1982, $48.00.**

Poster
  "Save Freedom Of Speech/Buy War
    Bonds," town meeting, 28 x 40",
    1943 . . . . **125.00**
  "Let's Give Him Enough And On
    Time," machine gunner, 40 x 28",
    1942 . . . . **950.00**
Window Card, Schmidt's Beer, 24 x 36",
  four men playing cards, 1935 . . . . . **50.00**

MODERN

Bell
  Gorham Fine China, Snow Sculptur-
    ing, 1976 . . . . **45.00**
  Lincoln Mint, Downhill Daring, 1975 **80.00**
Christmas Ornament, Gorham Fine
  China, Tiny Tim, 1980 . . . . **20.00**
Coin, Hamilton Mint, The Four Seasons,
  1½" d, set of four **90.00**
Figure
  Gorham Fine China
    Four Seasons, Grandpa and Me,
      1975, series No. 4, set of four **600.00**
    Missing Tooth **50.00**
    Saying Grace **120.00**
  Grossman Designs, Inc.
    Leapfrog, 1979 . . . . **700.00**
    Schoolmaster, 1973 . . . . **150.00**
Ingot, Franklin Mint, Norman Rockwell's
  Fondest Memories, Playing Hookey,
  1973 . . . . **35.00**
Plate
  Franklin Mint, etched crystal, Ameri-

can Sweethearts, 1977–78, set of 6 .... 170.00
Gorham Fine China, Four Seasons, A Boy and His Dog, 1971, Series No. 1, set of 4 .... 375.00
Gorham Fine China, The Marriage License, 1976 .... 45.00
Rockwell Society of America, A Mother's Love, 1976 .... 98.00
Puzzle, Parker Brothers 533, Happy Birthday Miss Jones, 11 x 14", 1973 15.00
Thimble, Grossman Designs, Inc, Day In The Life Of A Boy, 1980, set of 6 100.00
Toby Mug, Grossman Designs, Inc, Merrie Christmas, 1979 .... 40.00

ROGERS AND SIMILAR STATUARY

History: John Rogers, born in America in 1829, studied sculpture in Europe and produced the first plaster-of-paris statue, "The Checker Players," in 1859. It was followed by "The Slave Auction" in 1860.

His works were popular parlor pieces of the Victorian era. He produced at least 80 different subjects, and the total number of groups made from the originals is estimated to be over 100,000.

Casper Hennecke, one of Rogers's contemporaries, operated C. Hennecke & Company from 1881 until 1896 in Milwaukee, Wisconsin. His statuary often is confused with Rogers's work since both are very similar.

It is difficult to find a statue in undamaged condition and with original paint. Use the following conversions: 10% minor flaking; 10% chips; 10–20% piece or pieces broken and reglued; 20% flaking; 50% repainting.

References: Paul and Meta Bieier, *John Rogers' Groups of Statuary*, published by author, 1971; Betty C. Haverly, *Hennecke's Florentine Statuary*, published by author, 1972; David H. Wallace, *John Rogers: The People's Sculptor*, Wesleyan Univ., 1976.

Periodical: *Rogers Group*, 4932 Prince George Avenue, Beltsville, MD 20705.

ROGERS

Bath, 27" h, sgd **2,000.00**
Charity Patient, 22" h, 1866 .... 650.00
Courtship In Sleepy Hollow, 16½" h, 1870 .... 750.00
Elder's Daughter, 21½" h, 1887 ..... 800.00
Favored Scholar, 21" h, 1873 .... 425.00
First Ride, 18" h, 1888 .... 750.00
Is It So Nominated In The Bond?, 23" h, 1880 .... 375.00
Picket Guard, 1861 .... 750.00

Checkers Up At The Farm, $600.00.

Private Theatricals, 24" h, 1871 ..... 725.00
Returned Volunteer, How The Fort Was Taken, 20" h, 1864 .... 600.00
Rip Van Winkle On The Mountain, 21" h, 1871 .... 550.00
School Examination, 20" h, 1867 .... 500.00
Taking The Oath And Drawing Rations 425.00
Weighing The Baby, 21" h, 1876 ..... 450.00

ROGERS TYPE

Croquet Player, 18" h 225.00
Evening Devotion, 21" h 250.00
First Love, 13½" h, Hennecke 215.00
Lost & Found, 19" h 125.00
Red Riding Hood, 11½" h 325.00
Welcome, 32" h, alabaster 300.00

ROOKWOOD POTTERY

History: Mrs. Marie Longworth Nicholas Storer, of Cincinnati, Ohio, founded Rookwood Pottery in 1880. The name of this outstanding American art pottery came from her family estate "Rookwood," named for the rooks (crows) which inhabited the wooded grounds.

There are five elements to the Rookwood marking system—the clay or body mark, the size mark, the decorator mark, the date mark, and the factory mark. Rookwood art pottery can best be dated from factory marks.

In 1880–1882 the factory mark was the name "Rookwood" incised or painted on the base. Between 1881 and 1886 the firm name, address, and year appeared in an oval frame. Beginning in 1886, the impressed "RP" monogram appeared and a flamemark was added for each year until 1900. After 1900 a Roman numeral, indicating the last two digits of the year of production, was added at the bottom of the "RP" flamemark monogram. This last mark is the one most often found on Rookwood pottery today.

Though the Rookwood Pottery filed for bankruptcy in 1941, it was soon reorganized under new management. Efforts at maintaining the pottery proved futile, and it again was sold in 1956 and in 1959. The pottery was moved to Starkville, Mississippi, in conjunction with the Herschede Clock Co. It finally ceased operation in 1967.

Rookwood wares changed with the times. The variety is endless, in part because of the great variations in glazes and designs due to the creativity of the many talented artists.

References: Herbert Peck, *The Book of Rookwood Pottery*, Crown Publishers, Inc., 1968; Herbert Peck, *The Second Book of Rookwood Pottery*, published by author, 1985.

Collectors' Club: American Art Pottery Association, 9825 Upton Circle, Bloomington, MN 55431.

Basket, 9" h, 20¼" l, folded bowl, two applied handles, four applied lion heads feet, one side dec with alligators, palms, and Nile pyramids, other dec with spider web, copper luster highlights, imp "Rookwood, 1883" **5,000.00**
Bookends, pr
5¼" h, little girl sitting on bench, semi–matte gray blue glaze, imp mark, 1919 . . . . **220.00**
5½" h
Crystalline brown hare's fur glaze, imp mark, artist's monogram, model by William McDonald, 1936 **365.00**
Rook against berried branches, semi–matte tan and dusky blue glaze, imp mark and artist's monogram of Helen Nourse, 1925 **335.00**
Box, cov, 5¼" h, triangular, ftd, abstract molded dec, triangular finial, high powder blue glaze, imp mark and artist's monogram of Louise Abel, 1931 **225.00**
Ewer
6¾" h, four cherries and leaf dec, Eliza C Lawrence, c1900 . . . . **90.00**

8¼" h, rose jar form, mustard yellow, wax matte dec of fruiting branches, imp mark, "1342" above triangle, painted artist's monogram for Catherine Covaleno, 1925 . . . . **600.00**
10" h, standard glaze, bulbous body, long neck, trefoil mouth, paint and slip dec, flowering apple blossoms, yellow, peach, green, green, and brown, shaded brown and green ground, silver cased loop handle and lip, engraved monogram, silver overlay poppies, scrolling foliage, and latticework, marked "Gorham Mfg Co," incised artist's cipher of Emma D Foertmeyer, imp factory mark, 1893 date mark **1,200.00**
Flower Holder, 6½" h, Rook on stump, #2710, blue, c1928 . . . . **75.00**
Inkwell, 8½" l, 8¼" w, 9" h, figural, sphinx, fitted with inkwell, molded pen tray, variegated straw colors, gray matte glaze, artist's mark of Louise Abel, imp pottery mark, 1920 . . . . . **250.00**
Lamp
11¼" h, Aladdin's lamp shape, oblong, loop handle, small pewter cov, black floral and stork outlines, white ground, imp "Rookwood 1882, Hanna Plant, Box Tree," spout chip **150.00**
14" h baluster base, ivory ground, underglaze dec of lavender and pink magnolias, orig fittings, orig medallion label **625.00**
Lamp Base, 23" h, standard glaze, wide mouth fitted with Bradley and Hubbard font, body with angled shoulder dec with leaves and berries, tapering bulbous base, circular patinated brass base, four gargoyle shaped feet **375.00**
Pitcher, 7" h, standard glaze, inverted baluster, painted and slip yellow and brown pansies dec, shaded brown ground, silver cased handle and rim, silver overlaid scrolling acanthus, flowers, and latticework, marked "Gorham Mfg Co," incised artist's cipher of Mary Nourse, imp factory mark, 1892 date mark **1,800.00**
Plaque
4¼" h, 8½" w, incised rook perched on branch, incised name "Rookwood," green tones, imp mark, c1925 . . . . **1,300.00**
8" h, 6" w
San Pan harbor scene, sgd "C Schmidt" on lower left, imp firm mark and "XX," 1920 . . . . **2,650.00**
Woodland river scene, artist's monogram sgd on lower left, imp firm mark and "XXII," designed by Fred Rothenbusch, 1922 . . . . . **2,650.00**

Rose Jar, 5½" h, powder pink, plum blossoms around shoulder, imp mark, "2831, V," and artist's monogram for E. T. Hurley, 1925 .... **350.00**

Tankard, 17½" h, cylinder, standard glaze, painted barn swallows in flight, imp mark, artist's monogram for Albert R Valentien, 1893, hairline **600.00**

Tiles, three 11¾" woodland scenic tiles with raised outline details, blue, pale green, and dark green, twenty 6" surround matte green tiles, imp "Rookwood Faience" **3,850.00**

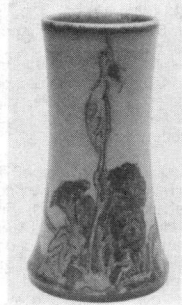

Vase, matte finish, artist sgd "C Crabtree," 1923, 5⅞" h, $600.00.

Vase
4¾" h, white flower dec, blue background, glazed, sgd, numbered "915F" on base **210.00**

5" h, ovoid, standard glaze, apple blossoms, imp marks, incised artist's monogram for Jeanette Swing, 1904 .... **315.00**

5¼" h, standard overglaze, bulbous, pinched sq walls and waisted neck, poppies in green and orange slip, dark brown grown, imp marks, designer Edward Dier's monogram, c1898 .... **450.00**

5½" h, bud, elongated neck, bulbous base, cherry branch, burnt orange and green dec, shaded yellow to brown ground, imp mark and artist sgd "HBS" for Harriet Rosemary Strafer, hairline on base **135.00**

6" h, ovoid, violets and green leaves, gray ground, imp mark, "X," and artist's monogram for Fred Rothenbusch, 1907 .... **330.00**

6¼" h, inverted baluster, standard glaze, holly dec, imp mark, incised artist's monogram for Sara Sax, 1899 .... **300.00**

6¾" h, vellum glaze
Baluster, pale pink, blue, and green bleeding hearts, imp mark, incised "V" and artist's monogram for Edward Diers, 1931 ...... **800.00**

Tapered cylindrical form, waisted neck, everted mouth, painted pink blossom branches, blue ground, "Carolyn Stegner," number "1658F," and other marks, 1917 .... **250.00**

7¼" h, standard overglaze, shouldered oviform, short neck, painted and slipped red, yellow, and green, brown and green shaded ground, silver overlay of engraved scrolling and angular vines and foliage, marked "Gorham Mfg Co," maker "EHW," incised artist's cipher of Sallie Toohey, imp factory and 1902 date mark **2,200.00**

7⅜" h, flared cylinder, inverted rim, vellum glaze, muscadine dec, pale blue and yellow ground, imp mark, artist's monogram for Margaret H McDonald, 1914 .... **550.00**

7½" h
Standard overglaze, baluster, waisted neck, earth tones, poppies slip dec, imp marks, designer Amelia Sprague's monogram, c1892 .... **400.00**

Vellum glaze, scenic, trees in shades of blue and green, pink and yellow sunset, artist's monogram for C McLaughlin, 1915, crazed **1,100.00**

8" h, swollen cylindrical form, sailing galleon in sunset silhouette, light blue, rose, and cream ground, artist sgd Edward Diers, number "2032E," and other marks, 1918 **880.00**

8⅛" h
Baluster, standard glaze, branch of orange nasturtiums, imp mark, artist's monogram for Lenore Asbury, 1903 .... **465.00**

Ovoid, incised curvilinear motif around shoulder, matte blue and burgundy glaze, imp mark and artist's monogram for Charles Todd, 1913 .... **425.00**

8¼" h, standard overglaze, ovoid form, tapered neck, earth tones, painted slip blossoms underglaze dec, imp marks, designer O. Geneva Reed's initials, c1897 ..... **400.00**

8½" h, slender baluster, pale green body, gray neck, shoulder painted with oak leaves and acorns, imp mark and artist's monogram for Lenore Asbury, 1911 . . . . 450.00

9", vellum, scenic, wide mouth, cylindrical, flaring towards base, landscape band in green, blue, peach, and yellow, light gray–blue ground, imp marks and incised artist's signature Kataro Shirayamadani, 1912 . . . . 1,400.00

9⅛" h, matte glaze, wide mouth, angled shoulder and swollen cylindrical, shaded lavender glaze, rose and midnight blue floral dec, artist sgd Sara Sax, 1918 . . . . 750.00

9⅜" h, oviform, flaring mouth, roosters dec, tiger's eye glaze, imp mark, artist's monogram of Harriet E Wilcox, c1894 . . . . 2,100.00

9½" h, vellum glaze, shouldered baluster body, everted rim, painted pink blossom border highlighted in blue below shoulder, medium blue ground within green borders, inscribed Frederick Rothenbusch and other marks, 1924 . . . . 470.00

10" h, vellum, short flared neck, angled shoulder, cylindrical tapering towards foot, pink neck and shoulder, stylized pink, blue, and black floral dec, ivory ground, pink foot, artist sgd Arthur Conant, c1915–20 370.00

10¼" h, tapered cylinder, molded dandelion under blue–green glaze, imp mark, artist's monogram for Anna Marie Valentien, 1904 . . . . . 1,430.00

13" h, flared mouth, tapering toward foot, molded classical dancing women, deep mauve ext. glaze, turquoise int., artist sgd Louise Abel, c1920–32 . . . . 200.00

13½" h, matte glaze, swollen cylindrical body, incised and modeled low relief upright iris, dark red touched blossoms, artist sgd Charles Stewart Todd and other marks, c1914 330.00

13⅝" h, vellum, scenic, cylindrical, flaring towards base, gray–blue landscape scene, shaded yellow to peach ground, imp marks, incised artist's initials E. T. H. for Edward Timothy Hurley, 1913 . . . . 2,000.00

14¾" h, bulbous oviform, peony blossoms dec, amber, yellow, and deep green, slip painted underglaze, radiating brown ground, standard clear overglaze, overlaid ornately chased scrolling silver, stamped logo, decorator's incised signature Kataro Shkrayamadani, c1899 . . . 7,500.00

ROSE BOWLS

History: A rose bowl, a decorative open bowl with a crimped, pinched, or petal top, held fragrant rose petals or potpourri which served as an air freshener in the late Victorian period. Practically every glass manufacturer made rose bowls in a variety of patterns and glass types, including fine art glass.

Additional Listings: See specific glass categories.

Satin glass, yellow, white lining, relief molded metals, 4½" d, 4" h, $70.00.

Cased Glass, 6" h, robin's egg blue ext., white int., applied crystal swag trim, crystal rosettes and scroll feet 255.00

Mount Washington, 3¼" h, wild rose, crimped edge 50.00

Opalescent, Stripe, blue 85.00

Peach Blow

2½" d, 2⅜" h, DQ, MOP, eight crimp top, deep red shaded to amber pink, Webb 300.00

4" d, 3¼" h, Wild Rose pattern, eight crimp top, deep raspberry shading to white, matte acid finish, elaborate lettering and scroll dec, made by Mt Washington for 1893 World's Fair 675.00

Satin Glass

2¼" h, rose, gold enameled flower and bee dec, ruffled top, cased, Webb 125.00

3⅞" h, green to light green cabbage leaf form, crimped edge 100.00

4¼" d, 3½" h, rainbow, DQ, MOP, alternating deep pink, yellow, and blue stripes, applied clear feet, applied berry pontil, marked "Patent" 1,400.00

5⅜" d, 4" h, rose overlay, multicolored petit point enamel, gold dots, white lining 325.00

5½" d, white shading to blue, molded shell body, enamel floral dec 150.00

Spangle Glass, 4″ h, egg shape, crimped top, one yellow, other red, satin finish, pr **100.00**

ROSE CANTON, ROSE MANDARIN, ROSE MEDALLION

History: The pink rose color has given its name to three related groups of Chinese export porcelain. Rose Mandarin was produced from the late 18th century to approximately 1840. Rose Canton began somewhat later and extended through the first half of the 19th century. Rose Medallion originated in the early 19th century and was made through the early 20th century.

Rose Mandarin derives its name from the Mandarin figure(s) found in garden scenes with women and children. The women often feature gold decorations in their hair. Polychrome enamels and birds separate the scenes.

Rose Medallion has alternating panels of figures and birds and flowers. The elements are four in number, separated evenly around the center medallion. Peonies and foliage fill voids.

Rose Canton is similar to Rose Medallion except the figure panels are replaced by flowers. People are present only if the medallion partitions are absent. Some patterns have been named—Butterfly and Cabbage, Rooster, etc. The category actually is a catchall for all pink enamel ware not fitting into the first two groups.

Reference: Sandra Andacht, *Oriental Antiques & Art: An Identification And Value Guide,* Wallace-Homestead, 1987.

Reproduction Alert: Rose Medallion is still made, although the quality does not match the earlier examples.

ROSE CANTON

Bowl, 10″ d, gold trim, scalloped **265.00**
Brush Pot, 4¾″ h, ladies in pavilion, reticulated, relief molded, gilt trim, c1850 . . . . **300.00**
Creamer, 4″ h, double twisted handle, gilt trim **200.00**
Demitasse Cup and Saucer, floral panels, c1860 . . . . **75.00**
Plate, 8½″ d, floral, insects on border **95.00**
Vase, 10½″ h, medallions with flowers, butterflies, and birds, floral borders, mid 19th C **425.00**

ROSE MANDARIN

Bowl, 6″ d, Canton, Chinese, 19th C . . **50.00**
Candlestick, 6″ h, Canton, Chinese, 19th C **200.00**
Dish, 11½″ h, shaped, varying central panels of courtyard figures, wide flo-

Rose Mandarin, plate, 9⅞″ d, $75.00.

ral and butterfly borders, one restored, c1830, pr **950.00**
Fruit Basket and Underdish, 8¼″ w, raised shell handles, pierced sides and rim, central figural courtyard scenes, rose floral and blue key borders, handles restored, c1830 . . . . . **1,300.00**
Hot Water Platter, cov, 10¾ x 13¾″ oval, large central figural courtyard scenes, bird and floral border, acorn finial, c1840 . . . . **2,400.00**
Mug, 4¾″ h, molded spearhead border, double twist handle, c1840, rim nicks **350.00**
Platter, 14⅜ x 17¾″, oval, alternating figural and precious ornaments dec, border of ornaments, traces of central monogram, orange and brown enamel, gilt palette, repair and wear, mid 19th C **200.00**
Pitcher, 8½″ h, scalloped rim, paneled, molded spearhead border, handle repair, c1840 . . . . **650.00**
Shrimp Dish, 10″ w, central courtyard figures panel, wide border of flowers and precious ornaments, c1830 . . . **750.00**
Soup Plate, 9¾″ d, armorial, arms of Grand, ribbed motto "Craigelachie" and "Standfast," varying central figural courtyard scenes, wide floral and butterfly borders, set of 6, c1810 **2,800.00**
Spill Vase, 4¾ h, all–over molded and enamel dec figural courtyard, pierced ground, gilt and floral borders, hairline, restoration, c1840 . . . . **300.00**
Vase
9½″ h, elongated panels of figural courtyard scenes, separated by butterfly and floral dec, gilt field, figural and bird dec borders, rim restored, c1830 . . . . **350.00**
14½″ h, baluster, figural courtyard scenes, fields of birds, butterflies, flowers, and fruit, enamel palette, gilding, c1830, pr **600.00**

Vegetable Dish, cov, 8 x 9½″, oblong, simulated bamboo handle on cov, int. and cov with central courtyard and figural panels, bird and floral borders, slight gilt wear, c1840 . . . . **1,200.00**

ROSE MEDALLION

Brush Box, cov, 7″ l, 3½″ w, 2½″ h, rect, floral and figural panels, leafy floral ground, c1880 . . . . **350.00**
Candlesticks, pr, 9¼″ h, marked "China," c1900 . . . . **900.00**
Canister, cov, set of 5, graduating sizes, 3″, 3¾″, 4″, 5″, and 5¾″, sq, slightly domed cov, alternating floral and figural panels, rim chips, late 19th C **2,100.00**
Chamber Bowl, 16¼″ d, Canton, flaring rim, Chinese, 19th C **1,000.00**
Fruit Platter, 11 x 14¾″, oval, ftd, shaped rim, worn gilt, mid 19th C . . **600.00**
Punch Bowl, 23½″ d, 9″ h, household scenes, butterflies, birds, orange peel glaze, small flakes on table ring, wooden stand **5,400.00**
Shrimp Dish, 10¼″ l, shaped rim, rim nicks, mid 19th C **550.00**
Umbrella Stand, 23¹/₂″ h, cylindrical, hairlines, late 19th C **850.00**
Urn, cov, 15″ h, low domed cov, onion finial, int. rim chip **650.00**
Vase
 15¼″ h, bulbous, mid 19th C **400.00**
 15½″ h, baluster, bulbous center, flaring top and base, top rim repair . . **450.00**
Vegetable Dish, cov, 9½ x 11¾″, shaped oval, acorn finial, rim flake, late 19th C **450.00**

MARKE

ROSENTHAL

History: Rosenthal Porcelain Manufactory began operating at Selb, Bavaria, in 1880. Specialties were tablewares and figurines. The firm is still in operation.
Reference: Susan and Al Bagdade, *Warman's English & Continental Pottery & Porcelain, 1st Edition,* Warman Publishing Co., Inc., 1987.

Bon Bon, 2½ x 5¼″, Winifred pattern, pink Moss Rose dec, SS base **35.00**
Bowl
 5¼″ d, black basalt, emb floral dec **20.00**

Figure, little girl holding floral bouquet in one arm, basket of flowers over other arm, 8½″ h, $125.00.

9″ d, hp, clusters of cherries, green ext., gold trim, double handles, artist sgd **85.00**
Cake Plate, 10″ d, portrait of Mercury, violet ground, gold trim **50.00**
Charger, 15″ d, blue and white Dutch scene **150.00**
Coffee Set, Classic Rose pattern, 5 pcs **135.00**
Cup and Saucer
 Antoinette pattern **15.00**
 Empress Flower pattern **25.00**
Demitasse Cup and Saucer, portrait medallion **50.00**
Figure
 Butterfly, peacock eyes on wings . . . **65.00**
 Dachshund, 7″ h, standing on hind legs **150.00**
 Deer, sitting, 4″ l, 3½″ h **135.00**
 Fairy Queen, 10½″, L. Friedrich–Granau **325.00**
 Girl, 5¼″ h, kissing baby chick **90.00**
 Owl, 18⅞″ h, natural colors, shaped stepped base, marked "Rosenthal Kunst–Abteilung" **250.00**
 Pierrot, 11⅝″ l, reclining, white costume, multicolored accents, c1920, sgd "C Holzer Defanti, Rosenthal Selb Bavaria" **625.00**
 Poodle, white, Prof Karner artist . . . **295.00**
 Princess and Frog, 11″ h, white, gold, and pastel colors **350.00**
 Rabbit, 6½″ h, white, laughing **100.00**
 Turtle, 2½″ l, natural colors **50.00**
Gravy Boat and Tray, Aida pattern, gold trim, c1920 . . . . **30.00**

Hatpin Holder, 5½" h, figural, stylized
bust **35.00**
Mug, 4¾" h, hp, red cherries, leaves,
and vines, shaded green ground ... **75.00**
Plate
  5¾" d, hp, pink flowers, bold rim,
  pierced for hanging **20.00**
  9" d, Madeleine **17.50**
  10" d, portrait, young woman, multicolored, cobalt rim, gold tracery .. **100.00**
Platter, 10" l, 13" w, two fish and snails
center, cream ground, gold trim **60.00**
Soup Plate, pink floral pattern, matching
saucers, set of 10 .... **75.00**
Tea Service, Magic Flute pattern, broad
gold border, relief figures, white
ground, 27 pcs **425.00**
Urn, cov, 10½" h, portrait, woman in garden, multicolored **250.00**
Vase
  3" h, seashell, white satin finish ... **35.00**
  9½" h, tulip, multicolored floral dec,
  double handles, sgd "Walter" ... **150.00**

Roseville
U. S. A.

ROSEVILLE POTTERY

History: In the late 1880s a group of investors purchased the J. B. Owens Pottery in Roseville, Ohio, and made utilitarian stoneware items. In 1892 the firm was incorporated and joined by George F. Young, who became general manager. Four generations of Youngs controlled Roseville until the early 1950s.

A series of acquisitions began: Midland Pottery of Roseville in 1898, Clark Stoneware Plant in Zanesville (formerly used by Peters and Reed), and Muskingum Stoneware (Mosaic Tile Company) in Zanesville. In 1898 the offices also moved from Roseville to Zanesville.

In 1900 Roseville introduced its art pottery: Rozane. Rozane became a trade name to cover a large series of lines. The art lines were made in limited amounts after 1919.

The success of Roseville depended on its commercial lines, first developed by John J. Herald and Frederick Rhead in the first decades of the 1900s. In 1918 Frank Ferrell became art director and developed over 80 lines of pottery. The economic depression of the 1930s brought more lines, including Pine Cone.

In the 1940s a series of high gloss glazes were tried to revive certain lines. In 1952 Raymor dinnerware was produced. None of these changes brought economic success. In November 1954 Roseville was bought by the Mosaic Tile Company.

References: Sharon and Bob Huxford, *The Collector's Encyclopedia Of Roseville Pottery,* Collector Books, 1976; Sharon and Bob Huxford, *The Collector's Encyclopedia Of Roseville Pottery, Second Series,* Collector Books, 1980.

Collectors' Club: American Art Pottery Association, 9825 Upton; Circle, Bloomington, MN 55431.

Additional Listings: See *Warman's Americana & Collectibles* for more examples.

Basket
  Bushberry, brown, #370-8 .... **90.00**
  Columbine, 10", brown **145.00**
  Foxglove **85.00**
  Imperial, 8" **65.00**
  Magnolia, brown, #384-8 .... **75.00**
  Vista, hanging **425.00**
  Zephyr Lily, brown, hanging **95.00**
Bookends, pr
  Freesia
    Blue **110.00**
    Green **70.00**
  Wincraft, blue **45.00**
Bowl
  Bleeding Heart, pink, #380-8 ..... **60.00**
  Bushberry, green, 3" **95.00**
  Freesia, brown, handles, #465-8 .. **75.00**
  Jonquil, #621 .... **55.00**
  Pine Cone, brown, twig handles,
  #354-6 .... **85.00**
  Tuscany, pink, 4 x 10" **135.00**
Candleholders pr
  Cosmos **55.00**
  Lily, #1162-2 .... **40.00**
  Snowberry, green, 5" **50.00**
Candlesticks, pr
  Magnolia, brown, 5" h, #1157 ..... **55.00**
  Zephyr Lily, blue **35.00**
Children's Dish, baby's, rabbits, rolled
edge **45.00**
Console Bowl
  Bittersweet, green, #830-14 ...... **50.00**
  Ferrella, rose, frogs, 9½" **350.00**
Cookie Jar, Magnolia, blue, lid **165.00**
Cornucopia
  Bushberry, brown, #155-8 .... **70.00**
  Pinecone, green, #126-6 .... **50.00**
Ewer
  Magnolia, 6" **40.00**
  Peony **80.00**
  Wincraft, blue, #217-6 .... **30.00**
Flower Frog, Imperial II **32.00**
Flower Pot and Saucer
  Bushberry, blue **125.00**
  Donatello, 4½" **75.00**
  Pine Cone, brown **125.00**
Ginger Jar, Rosecraft, 8", black **150.00**
Jardiniere
  Futura, 8", aqua, pink leaves **600.00**
  Imperial I, 8½" **100.00**
  LaRose, 6½", ... **35.00**

Normandy, 8″	85.00
Pine Cone, brown, #632-5	100.00
Loving Cup, Crystalis, orange matte	1,950.00
Mug, Magnolia #3	45.00
Pitcher, Pine Cone, brown, 10″	400.00
Planter, Earlam, strawberry	95.00
Tea Set, 3 pcs, Snowberry, teapot, creamer, and sugar	135.00
Tray	
Peony, pink and green	50.00
Pine Cone, brown, double handle, 13″	225.00
Urn	
Pine Cone, green, #498	100.00
Sunflower	180.00
Wisteria, blue, 5″	195.00

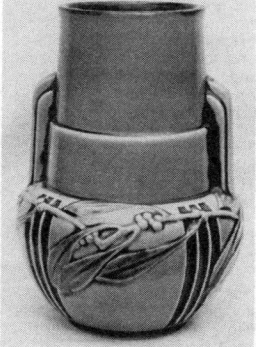

Vase, Laurel, stamped "S," 9³⁄₁₆″ h, $165.00.

Vase	
Apple Blossom, pink, #3889-10	85.00
Bleeding Heart, pink, 9″	65.00
Bushberry	
Brown, 6″	125.00
Green, 7″	60.00
Carnelian II, blue green, 10″	200.00
Columbine, pink, #16-7	50.00
Donatello, 6″	45.00
Florane, brown, 8½″	155.00
Freesia	
7″, handles	50.00
18″, green, #129	255.00
Futura, #433, 10″	110.00
Gardenia, brown, #683-8	60.00
Iris, 7″, pink	90.00
Jonquil, 6½″	85.00
Lotus Trial, blue, #L3-10	165.00
Luffa, brown, bowling ball shape, 6½″	110.00

Magnolia, blue, #99-16	225.00
Monticello, 5″	125.00
Morning Glory, white, handled, 10″	500.00
Moss, pink and green, 13″	245.00
Pauleo, green matte, 18½″	500.00
Peony, 6″, handled	48.00
Pine Cone, blue	85.00
Primrose, pink, #763-7	65.00
Sunflower, 6″	210.00
Vista, floor type, 15″	450.00
White Rose, pink, #984-8	70.00
Zephyr Lily, bud, brown, #201-7	35.00
Wall Pocket	
Carnelian II	150.00
Fuchsia, blue	250.00
Peony	100.00
Pine Cone, double, blue	200.00
Wall Shelf, Pine Cone, brown	280.00
Window Bow, Bushberry, green, #383-6	45.00
Window Box	
Apple Blossom, green, 4 x 13″	145.00
Dahlrose, 16″	225.00

BAVARIA

ROYAL BAYREUTH

History: In 1794 the Royal Bayreuth factory was founded in Tettau, Bavaria. Royal Bayreuth introduced their figural patterns in 1885. Designs of animals, people, fruits, and vegetables decorated a wide array of tablewares and inexpensive souvenir items.

Tapestry ware, rose and other patterns, were made in the late 19th century. The surface of the ware feels and looks like woven cloth. Tapestry ware was made by covering the porcelain with a piece of fabric tightly stretched over the surface, decorating the fabric, glazing the piece, and firing.

The Royal Bayreuth crest mark varied in design and color. Many wares were unmarked. It is difficult to verify the chronological years of production due to the lack of records.

Royal Bayreuth still manufactures dinnerware. It has not maintained production of earlier wares, particularly the figural items.

Reference: Susan and Al Bagdade, *Warman's English & Continental Pottery & Porcelain, 1st Edition,* Warman Publishing Co., Inc., 1987.

Sunbonnet Babies, plate, babies ironing, blue mark, 6½″ d, $65.00.

Art Nouveau
Dresser Tray, blue mark 1,400.00
Pitcher, water, blue mark 1,300.00
Corinthian
Ashtray 35.00
Chamberstick, large, green, serpentine handle 125.00
Creamer, blue mark 100.00
Jardiniere, 7 x 8″ 125.00
Pitcher, 8½″ h 145.00
Toothpick, three handles 100.00
Devil and Cards
Ashtray 200.00
Candy Dish 165.00
Demitasse Cup and Saucer 80.00
Dresser Tray 200.00
Match Holder, hanging 400.00
Pitcher, 7½″ h 485.00
Salt, master 165.00
Wall Pocket, figural, Devil 900.00
Grape Cluster
Creamer, white MOP 125.00
Demitasse Cup and Saucer, MOP,
cerise shading 85.00
Marmalade, cov, green 150.00
Mustard Jar, cov, white MOP 85.00
Wall Pocket
White 250.00
Yellow 225.00
Lobster
Ashtray 50.00
Creamer 50.00
Pitcher, milk 125.00
Salt and Pepper Shakers, pr 125.00
Miscellaneous Patterns
Ashtray, scenic, men fishing, wishbone handle, gold trim 60.00
Biscuit Jar, cov, figural, strawberry .. 125.00
Cake Plate, 10½″ d, open handles,
pink and green cherries, blossoms,
and leaves, satin finish 50.00
Chocolate Pot, cov, boy seated on log 250.00

Creamer, figural
Alligator 300.00
Bell Ringer 235.00
Bull's Head, black 165.00
Butterfly, open wings 275.00
Cat, calico 220.00
Chimpanzee, gray 500.00
Cockatoo 300.00
Dachshund 185.00
Melon, morning glory 175.00
Oak Leaf 125.00
Owl 350.00
Parakeet 225.00
Penguin 325.00
Rooster 200.00
St Bernard Dog 185.00
Strawberry, 4″ h 165.00
Trout, 4″ h 175.00
Creamer and Sugar, cov, turtle, blue
mark 900.00
Hatpin Holder, farmer holding reins of
two horses, farm house in background, scalloped saucer base,
blue mark 245.00
Match Holder, stork, enamel dec,
green and yellow ground 250.00
Mug, 5¾″, tavern scene 125.00
Pitcher, milk
Elk Head, 5½″ h 210.00
Mouse 1,400.00
Plate, 9″ d, girl with basket of flowers,
gold scrolled edge 400.00
Stein, elk dec 400.00
String Holder, rooster, multicolored 225.00
Toothpick
Hunter on horse, dogs dec, kettle
shape, three feet, handle 110.00
Pastoral scene, coal hod shape .. 175.00
Vase
3″ h, two cows, brown and gold
ground, two handles 50.00
3¼″ h, baluster, lady carrying basket, boats and water, blue and
gray ground 50.00
4¾″ h, baluster, hunt scene, horses
and dogs, green and cream
ground 65.00
6½″ h, tavern scene, two handles 210.00
7″ h, bulbous, soccer scene, blue
mark 300.00
Nursery Rhyme
Basket, girl and dog playing 200.00
Bowl, 9½″ d, Goose Girl 145.00
Children's Feeding Dish, Jack and
the Beanstalk 85.00
Salt and Pepper Shakers, pr, Little
Boy Blue 200.00
Poppy
Cake Plate, MOP, open handles ... 200.00
Candy Dish, 5½″ d, MOP 90.00
Nut Dish, red 60.00
Plate, 9″ d, MOP 90.00

Sandbabies
Bell 300.00
Box, cov 85.00
Children's Feeding Dish, 7¼" d 150.00
Match Holder 150.00
Plate, 7½" d 60.00
Snowbabies
Cereal Set, children on sled 150.00
Creamer, squatty 90.00
Inkwell, 4" w, sq base, children on
sled 135.00
Tea Set, teapot, creamer, two cups
and saucers, children on sleds .. 200.00
Sunbonnet Babies
Chamberstick, shield back, babies
fishing, blue mark 500.00
Creamer, 4" h, tankard, babies clean-
ing 200.00
Cup and Saucer, babies sewing ... 150.00
Hatpin Holder 225.00
Mug, sewing 165.00
Plate, 6½" d, babies washing 125.00
Tomato
Biscuit Jar, cov 125.00
Creamer and Sugar, cov 200.00
Cup and Saucer 85.00
Pitcher, milk 175.00
Plate, 9" d 35.00
Salt and Pepper Shakers, pr 75.00
Teapot 150.00

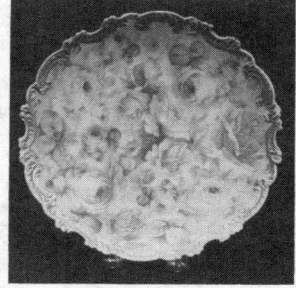

**Rose Tapestry, plate, three color roses,
blue mark, 9½" d, $185.00.**

ROSE TAPESTRY

Basket
3¾" h, multicolored roses, green
mark 400.00
6" h, ftd, oval, multicolored roses .. 125.00
Creamer, 4" h, three color roses, blue
mark 200.00
Cup, 3" h, three color roses 135.00
Dish, leaf shape, three color roses ... 175.00

Dresser Tray
10" l, 7⅜" w, rect, blue mark 175.00
11¼" l, 8" w, rect, blue mark 225.00
Ferner, gold handle, three color roses 225.00
Hair Receiver, ftd 225.00
Hat Pin Holder, three color roses,
pierced base, blue mark 325.00
Match safe, hanging 350.00
Nappy, clover shape, three color roses,
gold ring handle, blue mark 300.00
Pitcher, milk, pinched spout, three color
roses 226.00
Plate
5⅞" d, blue mark 60.00
6" d, raised foliate border design, blue
mark, set of 6 .... 250.00
7⅞" d, raised foliate border design,
green marks, set of 6 .... 275.00
Relish Dish, 8⅛" l, rose dec, blue mark 190.00
Tankard, 4", pink roses, yellow ferns,
beaded, gold handle, blue mark ... 165.00
Toothpick, ftd, blue mark 500.00

TAPESTRY, MISCELLANEOUS

Clock, Christmas cactus, blue mark .. 485.00
Creamer, 3¼" h, woman, mule, and
landscape dec, blue mark 170.00
Dresser Tray, Japanese chrysanthemums, leaf shape 200.00
Match Holder, tavern scene, gold trim,
blue mark 225.00
Miniature, sofa, 4⅞" l, Mountain Goat
dec, blue mark 350.00
Powder Dish, cov, 5½" d, Colonial couple dancing 475.00
String Holder, hanging, rooster 200.00
Vase
4" h, ovoid, scenic, deer and trees,
gold trim, blue mark 225.00
5¼" h, fighting rooster and turkey .. 260.00

ROYAL BONN

History: In 1836 Franz Anton Mehlem founded
a Rhineland factory that produced earthenware
and porcelain, including household, decorative,
technical, and sanitary items. In 1890 the name
"Royal" was added to the mark. All items made
after 1890 include the name "Royal Bonn." The

firm reproduced Hochst figures between 1887 and 1903. These figures, produced in both porcelain and earthenware, were made from the original molds from the defunct Prince-Electoral Mayence Manufactory in Hochst. The factory was purchased by Villeroy and Boch in 1921 and closed in 1931.

Reference: Susan and Al Bagdade, *Warman's English & Continental Pottery & Porcelain, 1st Edition,* Warman Publishing Co., Inc., 1987.

Cake Plate, dark blue transfer print, 10¼″ w handle to handle, $20.00.

Bottle 9″ h, vine and flower dec, brown mark	110.00
Bowl, 9½″ d, cream, floral dec, metal rim, c1760	190.00
Charger, 20″ d, blue Rembrandt portrait transfer center, fruit border	165.00
Cheese Dish, cov, pink floral design	100.00
Cracker Jar, cov, 7½″ h, ovoid, pink, blue, rose, and orange flower dec outlined with gold, beige and cream ground, emb swirls with gold trim, SP rim, cov, and bail handle	125.00
Ewer, 12½″, hp, bird, orchids, and dragonfly, encircling gold lizard handle	175.00
Mug, 4″ h, blackberries and flower dec, shaded green ground	50.00
Portrait Vase, 9¼″ h, bulbous, molded scalloped rim, shaped handles, enamel portraits of young woman, gilt trim, sgd "Dingendorf," printed marks, c1900, pr	700.00
Urn, cov, 24″ h, Rococo style, elaborately painted and enameled, marked	650.00
Vase	
6½″ h, Flamand pattern, blue scenic design, white ground	60.00
9¼″ h, bulbous, enameled portraits of young woman, gilt trim, scalloped rim, short neck, scrolled handles, artist sgd, marked, c1900, pr	700.00
12″ h, hp, floral dec outlined in gold enamel	70.00

12¼″ h

Art Nouveau style, glazed flowers, textured black matte finish	450.00
Shaded green, gold trim, imp and stamped Crown mark, pr	290.00

ROYAL COPENHAGEN

History: Franz Mueller established a porcelain factory at Copenhagen in 1775. When bankruptcy threatened in 1779, the Danish king acquired ownership, appointing Mueller manager and adopting the name "Royal Copenhagen." The crown sold its interest in 1867; the company remains privately owned today.

Blue Fluted, Royal Copenhagen's most famous pattern, was created in 1780. It is of Chinese origin and comes in three styles: smooth edge, closed lace edge, and perforated lace edge (full lace). Many other factories copied it. Flora Danica, named for a famous botanical work, was introduced in 1789 and remained exclusive to Royal Copenhagen. Botanical illustrations were done freehand; all edges and perforations were cut by hand.

Royal Copenhagen porcelain is marked with three wavy lines which signify ancient waterways and a crown, the latter added in 1889. Stoneware does not have the crown mark.

Reference: Susan and Al Bagdade, *Warman's English & Continental Pottery & Porcelain, 1st Edition,* Warman Publishing Co., Inc., 1987.

Additional Listing: Limited Edition Collectors' Plates.

Cup and Saucer, blue flower dec, basketweave border	40.00
Dinner Service, 105 pcs, polychrome floral spray dec, molded basket weave, gilt borders, twelve dinner plates, salad plates, and bread and butter plates, ten soup plates	2,100.00
Dinnerware, Flora Danica pattern, botanical specimen	
Demitasse Cup and Saucer, underglaze blue triple wave mark, green factory mark, #20/3618, set of 8	3,300.00
Plate	
Bread and Butter, 5½″ d, under-	

glaze blue triple wave mark, green factory mark, black title, set of 8 . . . . **1,540.00**

Dinner, 10¼" d, pink and gold molded beadwork border, gilt dentil rim, underglaze blue triple wave mark, #20/3519 and #20/3549, green factory mark and artist's initials, black botanical title, set of 8 . . . . **3,300.00**

Fish, 10" d, reticulated, painted with different fish, green and gold molded beadwork borders, gilt dentil rims, underglaze blue triple wave mark, green factory mark, #19/3549, black title, set of 12 **8,800.00**

Salad

7½" d, paneled and molded beaded border, dentil rim, gilt and pink highlights, pr **550.00**

7⅝" d, underglaze blue triple wave mark, green printed factory mark, #20/3573, black title, set of 8 . . . . **2,200.00**

Platter

11½", reticulated, underglaze blue triple wave mark, #20/3574, green factory mark, black botanical inscription **660.00**

13" d, purple, puce, and green painted dec, gilt highlighted scalloped reticulated border, molded beading and dentil rim, #20/3528 . . . . **770.00**

Soup Tureen, 9" h, 13¼" l, oval, pink and gold molded beadwork border, applied split twig handle with flowerhead terminals on cov, underglaze blue triple wave mark, #20/3559, painters marks and printed crown factory mark, green "Royal Copenhagen/Denmark", black botanical inscriptions **3,300.00**

Sugar, cov, 5½" h, 6" l, oval, molded pink and gilt border and edge, applied entwined twig form handle with flower head and leaf terminals on cov, underglaze blue triple wave and green crown factory mark, inscribed #20/3582 . . . . **935.00**

Wine Cooler, 4¾" h, cylindrical sides, painted, pink and gold molded beadwork border, applied split twig molded handles with flowerhead and leaf terminals, underglaze blue triple wave mark, green painter's and printed mark, #20/3570, black botanical inscription **935.00**

Figure, 8" h, Fairytale III, young lovers kissing, orange, gray, and blue paint, gilding, artist Gerhard Henning, printed and painted marks, c1914 . . **1,100.00**

Gravy Boat, white, blue morning glories, underplate **50.00**

Mug, 4½" h, Christmas, floral dec, c1905 . . . . **140.00**

Salt and Pepper Shaker, pr, 2½" h, Fluted Lace pattern, blue and white **70.00**

Vase, green and black, gold accents, crackle ground, blue three wave mark, 8¼" h, $350.00.

Vase

6" h, orange, gray, and gold crackle, #212/3033 . . . . **90.00**

17" h, baluster, two masted sailing ships dec, pastel blue ground, marked **400.00**

ROYAL CROWN DERBY

History: Derby Crown Porcelain Co., established in 1875 in Derby, England, had no connection with earlier Derby factories which operated in the late 18th and early 19th centuries. In 1890 the company was appointed "Manufacturers of Porcelain to Her Majesty" (Queen Victoria) and from that date has been known as "Royal Crown Derby."

Derby porcelains from 1878 to 1890 carry only the standard crown printed mark. After 1891 the mark carries the "Royal Crown Derby" wording; and, in the 20th century "Made in England" and "English Bone China" were added to the mark.

A majority of these porcelains, both tableware and figures, were hand-decorated. A variety of printing processes were used for additional adornment. Today, Royal Crown Derby is a part of Royal Doulton Tableware, Ltd.

References: Susan and Al Bagdade, *Warman's English & Continental Pottery & Porcelain, 1st Edition*, Warman Publishing Co., Inc., 1987; John Twitchett and Betty Bailey, *Royal Crown Derby*, Antique Collectors' Club.

Cup and Saucer, gray pattern, yellow ground, gold rim, $25.00.

Bowl, Chinoiserie dec, four feet	125.00
Coffee Set, 15 pcs, coffeepot, creamer, sugar, six cups and saucers	950.00
Cup, tapered, pheasant dec, pr	80.00
Cup and Saucer, Imari pattern, 1907	95.00
Dinner Service, 8 pcs, painted and enamel	800.00
Dish, 10½" sq, handle, Imari pattern, marked "Made In England"	50.00
Ewer, 7½", enameled flowers, gold ground, reticulated cobalt blue neck and handle with raised gold dec	650.00
Jar, cov, 6" h, red ground, molded and gilt dec flowers, red printed marks, late 19th C	400.00

Plate

8¾" d, red and green enamel, underglaze blue oak leaf and acorn border, gilt trim, red crown mark and "D"	85.00
9" d, Imari pattern, gilt and painted foliage, ftd, imp and painted marks, 1887, pr	330.00
Potpourri, cov, 11½" h, lobed bulbous body, gilt leafy ground, enamel floral dec, cranberry ground and gilt neck and pierced cov, red mark, year cypher	1,700.00
Urn, cov, 19" h, white blossoms and gilt leaf dec, yellow ground	1,300.00

Vase

6½" h, gilt enriched yellow ground,

all–over butterflies, foliage, and flowerheads dec, iron–red printed marks, 1883 registration mark, pr ... **350.00**

8" h, globular, enameled leaves and jeweled flower dec, eggshell ground, jeweled collar, late 19th C ... **400.00**

10" h, hp, one blossom, pink ground ... **425.00**

ROYAL DOULTON FLAMBE

ROYAL DOULTON

History: Doulton pottery began in 1815 under the direction of John Doulton at the Doulton and Watts pottery in Lambeth, England. Early output was limited to salt-glazed industrial stoneware. John Watts retired in 1854. The firm became Doulton and Company, and production was expanded to include hand-decorated stoneware such as figurines, vases, dinnerware, and flasks. In 1872 the firm began marking their ware "Royal Doulton."

In 1878, John's son, Sir Henry Doulton, purchased Pinder Bourne and Co. in Burslem and the companies became Doulton and Co., Ltd. in 1882. Decorated porcelain was added to Doulton's earthenware production in 1884. The Royal Doulton mark was used on both wares.

Most Doulton figurines were produced at the Burslem plants from 1890 until 1978, when they were discontinued. A new line of Doulton figurines was introduced in 1979.

Beginning in 1913, an "HN" number was assigned to each new Doulton figurine design. The "HN" numbers refer to Harry Nixon, a Doulton artist. "HN" numbers were chronological until 1940, after which blocks of numbers were assigned to each modeler. From 1928 until 1954, a small number appeared to the right of the crown mark; this number added to 1927 gives the year of manufacture of the figurines.

Dickens ware, in earthenware and porcelain, was introduced in 1908. The ware was decorated with characters from Dickens's novels. The line was withdrawn in the 1940s, except for plates, which continued until 1974.

Character jugs, a 20th-century revival of early Toby models, were designed by Charles J. Noke for Doulton in the 1930s. They come in 4 major sizes and feature fictional characters from Dickens, Shakespeare and other English and American novelists, and historical heroes.

Doulton's Rouge Flambee (also Veined Sung) is a highly glazed, strong-colored ware noted most for the fine modeling and exquisite colorings, especially in the animal items. The process used to produce the vibrant colors in this ware is a Doulton secret.

Production of stoneware at Lambeth ceased in 1956; production of porcelain continues today at Burslem.

References: Susan and Al Bagdade, *Warman's English & Continental Pottery & Porcelain, 1st Edition*, Warman Publishing Co., Inc., 1987; Ralph and Terry Kovel, *The Kovels' Illustrated Price Guide to Royal Doulton*, Crown Publishers, Inc., 1980; Jocelyn Lukins, *Collecting Royal Doulton Character & Toby Jugs*, Venta Books, 1985; Kevin Pearson, *The Character Jug Collector's Handbook, 3rd Edition*, Kevin Francis Publishing Ltd, 1986; Kevin Pearson, *The Doulton Figure Collector's Handbook*, Kevin Francis Publishing Ltd, 1986; Ruth M. Pollard, *The Official Price Guide To Royal Doulton, Fifth Edition*, House of Collectibles, 1986; Princess and Barry Weiss, *The Original Price Guide to Royal Doulton Discontinued Character Jugs, Sixth Edition*, Harmony Books, 1987.

Periodicals: *Collecting Doulton*, BBR Publishing, 2, Strattford Avenue, Elsecar, Barnsley, S. Yorkshire, S74 8AA, England; *Jug Collector*, P.O. Box 91748, Long Beach, CA 90809.

Collectors' Club: Royal Doulton International Collectors' Club, P.O. Box 1815, Somerset, NJ 08873.

Animal Mold	
Airedale with Pheasant, HN1022 . . .	400.00
Cat, HN2539, 5″ h, white	125.00
Mountain Sheep, HN2661	175.00
Biscuit Jar, 7¾″ h, cream ribbed ground, band of turquoise, birds and animals on band, SP top, rim, and handle, marked "Doulton, Burslem Pottery"	200.00
Bowl	
3½″ h, Chang, heavy crazed, dripping deep red, cream, and ochre glazes, marked "Chang, Royal Doulton, Noke" and Nixon mark, pr	1,870.00
8⅛″ d, 4¼″ h, blue, brown geometric borders, cows and horses grazing, sgd "Hannah Barlow, 1885"	650.00
Character Jug, miniature, 2¼ to 2½″	
'Ard 'Earing	900.00
Bacchus, bone china	45.00
Fortune Teller	295.00
Gladiator	350.00
Hook	300.00
Mikado	300.00
Old Charlie	45.00
Punch	350.00
Sairey Gump	45.00
Sancho Panza	60.00
Teller	300.00
Character Jug, small, 3½ to 4″	
'Ard 'Earing	735.00

Arriet	100.00
Gondolier	375.00
Character Jug, large, 5¼ to 7″	
Arriet	200.00
Beau	945.00
Clown	865.00
Dick Whittington	375.00
Duchess	400.00
Gulliver	575.00
Henry V, raise flag	175.00
Jockey Johnson	300.00
Mr Pickwick	150.00
Pied Piper	110.00
Regency Beau	575.00
Sam Johnson	325.00
Scaramouche	625.00
Simple Simon	525.00
St George	310.00
Tony Weller	150.00

Figure, Autumn Breezes, HN 1954, $100.00.

Figure	
Antionette	125.00
Afternoon Tea	255.00
Ala Mode	165.00
All Aboard	140.00
Ballerina, HN2116, 7½″ h, lavender and white gown	300.00
Beat You To It	265.00
Bess, HN2002	250.00
Boy Evacuee, HN3202	275.00
Bride, HN2166	170.00
Bridesmaid, HN2874	85.00
Bridget, HN2070	280.00
Cavalier	175.00
Christine, HN2792	265.00
Christmas Parcels	180.00
Clarinda	150.00
Clemency, HN1643	800.00
Coralie, HN2307	180.00
Cup of Tea	135.00

Dream Weaver	180.00
Enchantment, HN2178	140.00
Fiona, HN2694	125.00
First Waltz	200.00
Genevieve, HN1962	190.00
Girl Evacuee, HN3203	275.00
Grand Manner	225.00
Gypsy Dance, HN2230	250.00
Innocence, HN2842	100.00
Karen, HN1994	400.00
Khayyam, Omar, HN2247	150.00
Koko	475.00
Lady Anne Nevill, HN2006, 10¼" h, blue gown, fur trim	650.00
Leading Lady, HN2269	150.00
Leisure Hour, HN2055	275.00
Little Boy blue, HN2062	110.00
Lydia, HN1908	120.00
Make Believe, HN2225	120.00
Master Sweep, HN2205, 8⅝" h	500.00
Matilda, HN2011, 9¾" h, mottled blue gown, red robe	550.00
Maureen, HN1770	275.00
Meditation	185.00
Melanie, HN2261	125.00
Midinette, HN2090	260.00
Miss Muffet, HN1937	235.00
Nina	140.00
Noelle, HN2179	375.00
Old Balloon Seller, HN1315	175.00
Parisian	155.00
Persian Cat, white, HN 2539	150.00
Pride & Joy, HN2945	275.00
Professor	140.00
Reverie	225.00
Royal Governor's Cook, HN2233	400.00
Silversmith	160.00
Solitude	180.00
Stephanie, HN 2807	145.00
Suzette, HN2026	250.00
Sweet Suzie, HN 1918	750.00
Taking Things Easy	155.00
Thank You	130.00
Toothless Granny	1,200.00
Vanessa, HN1836	750.00
Votes for Women	185.00
Veronica, HN1517	255.00
Victoria, HN2471	175.00
Young Master, HN2872	195.00

Flambe

Animal Mold

Cat	85.00
Elephant	125.00
Bowl, 9¾" d, Oriental style	225.00
Vase, 9" h, Veined Sung, bulbous	250.00

Gibson Girl Plate

Miss Babbles, The Authoress, Calls, Reads Aloud	95.00
She Decides To Die In Spite Of Dr Bottles	115.00

Jardiniere, Shakespeare Ware, 9" h, 10" d, cream ground, forest scene with

figures of Ophelia and Hamlet, marked "Royal Doulton"	325.00
Lemonade Set, Chang, 7⅜" h pitcher, six cylindrical cups, heavy red, yellow, blue, green, and cream glaze, lustered plum body, printed marks, 7 pcs	2,200.00

Lighter

Fuzz	255.00
Porthos	645.00
Winkle	585.00

Mug, large

Captain Ahab, D6500	75.00
Granny, D5521	75.00
Long John Silver, D6335	75.00
Old Salt, D6551	75.00
The Trapper, D6609	75.00
Pitcher, Old Curiosity Shop	135.00

Stoneware

Biscuit Jar, 5" d, 6¾" h, cobalt blue borders, tan ground, emb blue flowers, brown leaves, hallmarked SS rim and handle, stoneware lid	175.00
Mug, 4⅜" d, 6" h, tan panels, emb off–white figures of Victorian man and woman riding bicycles, soldier standing by bicycle, brown handle and edging, marked "Doulton Lambeth Stoneware"	285,00
Tankard, 6" h, Queen Elizabeth at Old Moreton Hall, c1920	35.00
Teapot, 9½" h, Gold Lace pattern, H4989	100.00
Toby, 5½" h, Happy John, #6070, c1939	65.00

Vase

7½" h, goat scene, sgd "Florence Barlow," c1878	215.00
12" h, urn shape, all–over autumn maple leaf dec, incised veins, blue–green ground, cobalt blue int. and base, pr	465.00
16" h, bulbous, tapering neck, stylized floral reserve, blue ground, pr	400.00

ROYAL DUX

History: Royal Dux porcelain was made in Dux, Bohemia (Czechoslovakia), by E. Eichler at the Duxer Porzellan-Manufaktur, established in 1860. Many items were exported to the United States. By the turn of the century Royal Dux figurines, vases, and accessories were captivating consumers, especially Art Nouveau designs.

A raised triangle with an acorn and the letter "E" plus Dux, Bohemia, was used as a mark between 1900 and 1914.

Reference: Susan and Al Bagdade, *Warman's English & Continental Pottery & Porcelain, 1st Edition,* Warman Publishing Co., Inc., 1987.

Figure, elephant, brown and gray, marked "Royal Dux," and raised pink triangle mark, 14″ l, 10½″ h, $150.00.

Bowl, 13½″ l, 7″ w, ovoid, woman holding flower, lavender, green, and gold 675.00
Bust
  9″ h, Caesar, gold shirt, floral pink toga over shoulder, green laurel wreath spray on head, floral relief base, pink triangle mark 350.00
  14″ h, woman, green scarf, open pink vest, green bodice, scrolled gold base, matte finish 365.00
Chess Set, 4½″ h king, each pc marked 900.00
Figure
  4″ h, bear with guitar 85.00
  6″ h, peasant girl, hands folded at waist, matte green, pale pink clothes, pink triangle mark 200.00
  8″ h, Greek potter, seated, multicolored, c1900 .... 215.00
  10″ h, lady, peach, #15386 .... 200.00
  12″ l, tiger, pink triangle mark 200.00
  18″ h, pr, man and woman, polychromed earthenware, Biblical attire 700.00
  20″ h, water carrier, male, triangle mark 975.00
Jar, 9″ h, molded, Art Nouveau, woman's face, multicolored 400.00
Lamp, 9″ h, Art Deco, woman spreading edges of cobalt blue gown, flesh tones, brass base 400.00
Powder Jar, 6½″, cobalt and gold, seated lady figure on top, pink triangle mark 600.00
Urn, 12¼″ h, cov, baluster, three rams heads, three scroll and hooved feet, molded shaped trefoil base, royal

blue and cream, gilt trim, ovoid finial, domed cov, pink mark 325.00
Vase
  7¼″ h, muted orange flowers, green leaves, cream ground, black mark 60.00
  8″ h, flowers and cherries, orange and green, pr 90.00
  10″ h, Art Nouveau, matte colors, applied handles 125.00
  14″ h, heavy relief of leaves and open work, soft earth colors, c1900 ... 200.00
  14½″ h, figural, lady emerging from vase playing harp, pink triangle mark 450.00
  14¾″ h, Art Deco, woman draped over vase, cream, bronze, and gold, pink triangle mark 400.00
  15½″ h, shell form, inward curling rim, side with Art Nouveau nymph, cream and gray, gilt accents, triangular mark 900.00

ROYAL FLEMISH

History: Royal Flemish was produced by the Mount Washington Glass Co., New Bedford, Massachusetts. The process was patented by Albert Steffin in 1894.

Royal Flemish has heavy, raised gold enamel lines on frosted transparent glass that separates areas into sections, often colored in russet tones. It gives the appearance of stained glass windows with elaborate floral or coin medallions in the design.

Advisors: Clarence and Betty Maier.

Ewer, Cupid slaying dragon, raised gold, mythological fish in medallions, paste blue and violet blossoms within typical side panels, gold tracery on extended neck, twisted rope handle, 9½″ h, $4,500.00.

Ewer, 12″ h, gold and silver rampant lion and shield, raised gold borders, pastel blue cross with raised gold borders on reverse, applied twisted rope handle 3,250.00

Pitcher, 7¼″ h, tan panels, five silver blossoms and foliage dec, clear glass handle 2,250.00

Rose Jar, 9″ h, ball shape, roses dec, pastel blue and mauve panel ground, ball shape lid, gold embellished finial 2,750.00

Vase
7½″ h, squatty round body, raised bulbed trefoil rim, frosted ground, gilt bordered panels of amber, brown, and rust, classical coin medallions, orig label on base "Mt. W. G. Co. Royal Flemish" 3,000.00

8½″ h, globular, tapered neck, shaped rim turned out with two scroll handles, puce, pink, and blue enameling with gilt highlights, shaded branches of blossoming fruit tree with pendant leaves and applied jeweled berries with gilding, frosted gray ground, diagonal inscribed square and number 593, Mount Washington, late 19th C 1,045.00

GERMANY

RUDOLSTADT

ROYAL RUDOLSTADT

History: Johann Fredrich von Schwarzburg-Rudolstadt was the patron of a faience factory located in Rudolstadt, Thuringen, East Germany, from 1720 to c1790. The pottery's mark was a hayfork and later crossed two-prong hayforks in imitation of the Meissen mark.

In 1854 Ernst Bohne established a factory in Rudolstadt. His pieces are marked "EB."

The "Royal Rudolstadt" designation originated with wares imported by Lewis Straus and Sons (later Nathan Straus and Sons) of New York from the New York and Rudolstadt Pottery between 1887 and 1918. The factory's mark was a diamond enclosing the initials "RW" and which was surmounted by a crown. The factory manufactured several of the Rose O'Neill (Kewpie) items.

Reference: Susan and Al Bagdade, *Warman's English & Continental Pottery & Porcelain, 1st Edition,* Warman Publishing Co., Inc., 1987.

Busts, polychrome bisque finish, 12½″ h, pr, $850.00.

Bon Bon, ring handle, pink roses, green foliage, gold trim, white ground ... 65.00

Bowl, 10″ d, pink, green, and white flowers, gold band 75.00

Celery Tray, 10″ l, hp, large pink and white flowers, white ground 48.00

Creamer, feathered gold over drapery, gold handle 48.00

Cup and Saucer
Happifats dec 35.00
Kewpies, multicolored, sgd "Rose O'Neill Wilson" 100.00
Pastel flowers, gold trim 35.00

Dresser Set, hair receiver, cov powder jar, open handled tray, pastel roses, white ground 60.00

Ewer
11¾″ h, hp, bird, butterfly, ferns, and grasses, ivory ground, gold trim, green serpentine spout, brown handle 150.00
13¾″ h, cream and light pink shell body, pebbled ground, brown worm type handle 175.00

Figure, girl and boy sitting on bench, cream, beige, and gold 200.00

Hatpin Holder, poppies, green and white ground, sgd "Hahn" 50.00

Mug, 3¾″ h, Kewpies, decals, sgd "O'Neill" 125.00

Pitcher
9½″ h, multicolored florals, gilt trim, long thin neck, raised mark 175.00
15½″ h, jeweled, inlaid gold leaves 300.00

Plate
7½″ d, Kewpies, multicolored 110.00
8″ d, open red poppies, green foliage, gold rim 40.00
9⅝″ h, purple flowers, gold highlights 65.00
10½″ d, old mill scene, blue transfer 85.00

Sweetmeat Jar, 5½″ h, cov, pink florals, green and rust leaves, cream ground, SP holder, marked "Middletown" 135.00

Urn, 10″ h, cov, double gold handles,

mythological scene, Hector and Andro crowning maiden, cobalt ground ... **125.00**

Vase

  5¾" h, figural, peacock, open wings, multicolored **65.00**

  10½" h, double handles, multicolored flowers, beige and yellow ground ... **125.00**

ROYAL VIENNA

History: Production of hard paste porcelain in Vienna began in 1720 with Claude Innocentius du Paquier, a runaway employee of the Meissen factory. In 1744 Empress Maria Theresa brought the factory under royal patronage; subsequently the ware became known as Royal Vienna. The firm went through many administrative changes until it closed in 1864. The quality of its workmanship always was maintained.

Many other Austrian and German firms copied the Royal Vienna products, including the use of the "Beehive" mark. Many of the pieces on today's market are from these firms.

Reference: Susan and Al Bagdade, *Warman's English & Continental Pottery & Porcelain, 1st Edition,* Warman Publishing Co., Inc., 1987.

Plate, multicolored portrait center, raised gold and red border, 9½" d, $575.00.

Bowl, 5" d, portrait of woman with cupid, maroon panels, pink and gold int., gold sq handles, bronze dore trim, beehive mark, c1860 .... **525.00**

Box, cov, 6¼" d, 4½" h, round, red ground, center scene of lady on lavender couch, cherub and three attendants, alternating border panels of scenes and flowers, beehive mark ... **350.00**

Charger, 12" d, portrait of three ladies holding globes in garden, artist sgd ... **175.00**

Creamer, 3⅛" h, landscape scenes, figures, harbor, gilt scroll rim band and handle, blue shield mark, c1770 ... **250.00**

Ewer, 15½" h, painted continuous scene of Hector and military, enameled panels, gilt ground, sgd "Bauer," blue beehive mark, late 19th C **1,760.00**

Figure, 7" h, young boy, period costume, enameled, imp beehive mark **300.00**

Jardiniere, 12½" d, transfer printed, two classical maidens in oval panel, cobalt ground, gilt trim, multicolored paneled borders, blue shield mark .. **350.00**

Plaque, 9½ x 12", rect, three women in draped classical garb, pedestal altar, blue shield mark and title **2,750.00**

Plate

  9" d, hp, semi-nude goddess Diana petting reclining lion, wide gold band, royal blue reserves, marked "Kraft de Liebe," blue beehive mark, giltwood frame **1,200.00**

  10¼" d, hp, scene of two seated musicians, heavy gilt scrollwork, cobalt blue border, artist sgd, framed ... **750.00**

Urn, 11" h, scenes of Romans and ladies, molded heads and headdress, gold trim, cube base, beehive marks, pr **950.00**

Vase

  7½" h, 3½" d, two gold trimmed handles, white ground, portrait medallion encircled in gold, lady in purple gown, green leaf wreath, brown hair, gold flowers on reverse, beehive mark **375.00**

  12" h, cov, ovoid, ladies and cherubs in garden, maroon and green neck, gold florals, beehive marks, pr ... **500.00**

ROYAL WORCESTER

History: In 1751 the Worcester Porcelain Company, led by Dr. John Wall and William Davis, acquired the Bristol pottery of Benjamin Lund and moved it to Worcester. The first wares were painted blue under the glaze, followed closely by painting on the glaze in enamel colors. Among the most famous 18th century decorators were James Giles and Jefferys Hamet O'Neale. Transfer-print decoration was developed by the 1760s.

A series of partnerships took over upon Davis's death in 1783: Flight (1783–93), Flight and Barr (1793–1807), Barr, Flight and Barr (1807–13), and Flight, Barr and Barr (1813–40). In 1840 the factory was moved to Chamberlain and Co. in Diglis. Decorative wares were discontinued. In 1852 W. H. Kerr and R. W. Binns formed a new company and revived the ornamental wares.

In 1862 the firm became the Royal Worcester Porcelain Co. Among the key modelers of the late 19th century were James Hadley and his three sons and George Owen, expert at pierced clay pieces. Royal Worcester absorbed the Grainger factory in 1889 and the James Hadley factory in 1905. Modern designers include Dorothy Boughty and Doris Lindner.

References: Susan and Al Bagdade, *Warman's English & Continental Pottery & Porcelain, 1st Edition,* Warman Publishing Co., Inc., 1987; David, John, and Henry Sandon, *The Sandon Guide To Royal Worcester Figures, 1900–1970,* The Alderman Press, 1987.

Museum: Charles William Dyson Perrins Museum, Worcester, England.

Basket, woven white body, gold edge,
  raised mark, c1884 . . . . **350.00**
Biscuit Jar, 9″ h, floral design, gold handles, base, and finial, c1890 . . . . . . **1,150.00**
Bowl, 9″ d, emb grape leaves, beige
  satin finish, gold trimmed openwork,
  c1896 . . . . **325.00**
Candleholder, 5″ h, child leaning against
  large white dog, arms wrapped
  around turquoise candleholder, gold
  trim, turquoise base, c1876 . . . . **375.00**
Cologne Bottle, 3¾″ h , lavender, rust,
  yellow, and green pansies and foliage, SP cap, 1887 date code **225.00**
Cup and Saucer, heart form, beige satin
  finish, bow on handle, gold trim,
  c1896 . . . . **125.00**
Dinner Service, blue floral calico pattern, gilt elephant handles on serving
  pcs, service for 12 plus serving pcs **500.00**
Dish, 7½ l, leaf form, pink daisies, gold
  outlined border **25.00**
Egg Coddle Cup, three birds dec **20.00**
Ewer
  8″ h, flowers, beige ground, four lobed
    shape, gold applied thorn handle,
    c1896 . . . . **275.00**
  8¾″ h, blue flowers, tan leaves, gold
    outlines, cream satin ground,
    dragon twist handle, c1887 . . . . . **450.00**
  17″ h, seventeen emb figures, lions,
    cherubs, dolphins, satyr, and lady's
    face, beige ground, gilt trim, c1894 **1,400.00**
Fairy Lamp, 17″ h, figural, water carriers, gilding, Clarke insert, pr **2,000.00**
Figure
  4¾″ h, rabbit, basket on back, satin
    finish, c1911 . . . . **450.00**
  6½″ h, girl, pink dress, holding flowers
    in folds of skirt, sgd "F G Doughty" **225.00**
  8″ h, Peter Pan, seated, holding bird **175.00**
  9″ h, Kate Greenaway style boy with
    basket, cream and beige satin finish, 1893 date code **550.00**
  11″ h, pr of Eastern water carriers,

man and woman emptying amphora into wells, molded rockwork
    bases, one with printed mark, other
    with imp mark, c1900 . . . . **800.00**
  21″ h, pr, man and woman, polychrome, Biblical dress, overglaze
    mark, stamped mark **1,300.00**

Fruit Bowl, multicolored florals, tan ground, gold elephant heads, 11″ l, $750.00.

Pitcher, 10″ h, 5½″ d, bulbous base,
  cream ground, purple and gold flowers, green and gold leaves, gold neck
  bands and handle, crown mark **250.00**
Plate
  9″ d, Silver Chantilly **25.00**
  10″ d, multicolored wildflowers center,
    etched light green border, purple
    mark **65.00**
  10½″ d, Rosemary pattern **25.00**
Ring Tree, maroon and yellow florals,
  beige satin finish, gold trim, c1912 **115.00**
Rose Bowl, 3″ h, flowers, beige ground,
  pr **200.00**
Tea Caddy, 4″ h, gilded leaf and floral
  dec, ivory ground, green mark **100.00**
Teapot, cov, double spout, Imari pattern, compressed circular body,
  swirled alternating panels of flower
  chains and foliate scrolls, basketweave molded base, four compressed feet, arched handle, iron–red
  printed mark, date "N" letter, 1878 registry mark **335.00**
Tureen, 14½″ l, cov, orig ladle, brown
  ivy dec, brown and gold elephant
  head handles, crow's feet finial, 1880
  date code **265.00**
Urn, 15¼″ h, cov, flying fish shaped handles, hp, rose dec, sgd "W E Jarman,"
  c1910 . . . . **1,300.00**
Vase
  8½″ h, shape #636, elephant handles, dry ivory ground, white
    enamel geometric dec, scene of
    frog hanging from branch, polychrome enamel, gilt highlights,
    wide top border in all–over dull

gold, lustered gold floral dec, printed and imp wheel marks, 1879 ... **650.00**

9¼" h, shape #1938, pink, maroon, and yellow flowers, beige satin ground, gold trim, ftd fluted tops, c1902, pr **600.00**

10" h, spiral form, floral bouquets, pink highlights, white ground **625.00**

10½" h, bamboo form, bamboo handle, relief fern dec **90.00**

12" h, elephant form, howdah, supporting trunk form vase, later entwined log laden molded base, c1900, attributed to James Hadley **2,865.00**

14" h

Pear form, enameled wildflowers, gilt lotus neck, two pierced angular scrolling handles, circular foot, printed registration No. 23321, 1890 date code, pr **715.00**

Tapering form, Persian taste dec, painted peacocks on foliage, pierced angular scrolling handles, printed and imp marks, 1887 date code **1,150.00**

Paperweight, Rochester Ad Club Outing to the Roycrofters, June 10th and 11th, 1911, portrait of Elbert Hubbard, 2¾" d, $150.00.

ROYCROFT

History: Elbert Hubbard, founder of the Roycrofters in East Aurora, New York, during the turn of the 19th and 20th centuries, was considered a genius in his day. He was an author, lecturer, manufacturer, salesman, and philosopher.

Hubbard established a campus which included a printing plant where he published *The Philistine*, *The Fra*, and *The Roycrofter*. His most famous book was *A Message to Garcia*, published in 1899. His "community" also included a furniture manufacturing plant, a metal shop, and a leather shop.

References: Nancy Hubbard Brady, *The Book of The Roycrofters*, House of Hubbard, 1977; Nancy Hubbard Brady, *Roycroft Handmade Furniture*, House of Hubbard, 1973; Charles F. Hamilton, *Roycroft Collectibles*, A. S. Barnes & Company, Inc., 1980; Kevin McConnell, *Roycroft Art Metal*, Schiffer Publishing Ltd, 1990; Paul McKenna, *A New Pricing Guide For Materials Produced by The Roycroft Printing Shop*, Tona Graphics, 2nd edition, 1982.

Additional Listings: Arts and Crafts Movement and Copper.

Bookends, pr, copper

4½ x 4⅞" arched brass washed copper, round leather medallions of ship at sea, stamped logo, c1910 ... **325.00**

6¼ x 4", rect, central stylized owl medallion, sgd logo **150.00**

8½ x 6", dark patina, hammered background, flower, cutout center **200.00**

Candelabra

20" h, SP, wide rimmed socket, slender twisted standard with two shorter curved arms, corresponding rims, flattened disc base, logo, No. 419, c1905, pr **1,200.00**

20½" l, hammered metal, low, horizontal arms, eight bobeches, curled feet, scrolling ends, imp marks, pr **1,250.00**

Centerpiece, 10¾" d, hammered copper, rolled rim, three dimple feet, stamped orb mark **1,450.00**

Chandelier

17¼" d, 26" l, copper, three glass diffusion shades, three chains terminating in rounded conical ceiling cap, stamped orb mark **7,500.00**

48" d, 60" l, wrought iron, two tiered open octagonal form, pierced quatrefoil motif, sixteen candlearms on bottom tier, eight on top, joined by scrolling arms, tassel drop dec, made by Toothacre for Hubbard Hill, c1919 .... **3,850.00**

Clock, desk, 4⅞" h, brass plated, domed rest, orb mark **450.00**

Clothes Tree, 70" h, oak, sq section standard, cruciform foot, four upper and four lower coat hooks, carved orb mark, hardware with imp marks ... **1,320.00**

Goody Box, 23″ w, 12¼″ l, 9″ h, mahogany, rect, imp logo on lid, hammered brass hinges, c1910 . . . . 400.00

Motto, 18 x 17″, "Blessed is that man who has found his work," illuminated, multicolored, paper, period oak frame 385.00

Vase, 12⅛″ h, long cylindrical neck, ftd hemispherical base, hammered copper, American Beauty, imp mark . . . 715.00

Walking Stick, 35″ l, branded date "July 4, 1903," tapering form, imp logo, leather thong 275.00

RUBENA GLASS

History: Rubena crystal is a transparent blown glass which shades from clear to red. It also is found as the background for frosted and overshot glass. It was made in the late 1800s by several glass companies, including Northwood and Hobbs, Brockunier and Co. of Wheeling, West Virginia.

Rubena was used for several patterns of pattern glass including Royal Ivy and Royal Oak.

Pitcher, enameled apple blossoms, applied handle, 7½″ h, $465.00.

Atomizer, 6¾″ h, incised floral dec . . . 150.00
Biscuit Jar, 7 x 9″, melon ribbed body 175.00
Castor Set, Venecia pattern, salt and pepper shakers, cov mustard, and cruet, orig glass handled frame 250.00
Celery, IVT, ruffled rim 85.00
Cruet
  Coin Spot, 6″ h, trefoil rim, applied clear handle, pressed clear faceted stopper 150.00
  Medallion Sprig, orig stopper 200.00
Pitcher, 8″ h, IVT, ruffled top, applied clear handle 135.00
Sugar Shaker, 5½″ h, Coin Spot 300.00

Table Set, 4 pcs
  Royal Ivy, frosted 600.00
  Royal Oak 645.00
Toothpick, 3″ h, ruffled rim, pedestal foot, enameled orange flowers and gold trim 350.00
Vase, 10½″ h, four lobed straight sides, enamel dec and gold trim on upper body, threading on lower body, applied crystal feet, pr 455.00
Water Set, Royal Ivy, frosted, 7 pcs . . 600.00

RUBENA VERDE GLASS

History: Rubena Verde, a transparent glass that shades from red in the upper section to yellow-green in the lower, was made by Hobbs, Brockunier and Co. of Wheeling, West Virginia, in the late 1880s. It often is found in the inverted thumbprint (IVT) pattern, termed "Polka Dot" by Hobbs.

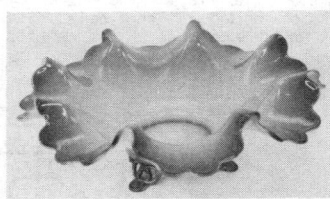

Bride's Bowl, ruffled, red rim shading to green center, cast white metal holder, 9½″ d, $175.00.

Bowl, 9½″ d, Hobnail pattern, crimped rim 175.00
Butter Dish, cov 375.00
Compote, 8″ d 75.00
Epergne, 16″ h, one center lily, applied rigaree, pr 500.00
Finger Bowl, IVT, matching underplate 70.00
Jack In The Pulpit Vase, 13¾″ h, applied crimped clear rigaree spirals 265.00
Pitcher
  7¾″ h, IVT, sq top, top of handle cracked 75.00
  8″ h, Hobnail pattern, applied canary yellow handle 325.00
Syrup, IVT, applied handle, pewter lid, marked "Pat March 29, '83" 335.00
Tumbler, Hobnail pattern 135.00
Vase
  6½″ h, cylindrical, Hobnail pattern . . 275.00
  9½″ h, enameled flowers, gold jewels dec, pr 220.00
  10¼″ h, sq mouth, applied clear edge, foot and rigaree spiraling band . . 185.00

RUBY-STAINED GLASS, SOUVENIR TYPE

History: Ruby-stained glass was produced in the late 1880s and 1890s by several glass manufacturers, primarily in the area of Pittsburgh, Pennsylvania.

Ruby-stained items were made from pressed clear glass which was stained with a ruby red material. Pieces often were etched with the name of a person, place, date, or event and sold as souvenirs at fairs and expositions.

In many cases one company produced the pressed glass blanks; a second company stained and etched them. Many patterns were used, but the three most popular were Button Arches, Heart Band, and Thumbprint.

Reference: William Heacock, *Encyclopedia of Victorian Colored Pattern Glass, Book 7: Ruby-Stained Glass From A to Z*, Antique Publications, Inc., 1986.

Reproduction Alert: Ruby staining is being added to many pieces through the use of modern stain glass coloring kits. A rash of fake souvenir ruby-stained pieces was made in the 1960s, the best-known example is the "bad" button arches toothpick.

Tumbler, Button Arches, Carnival, July 29, 1904, J. M. Craig on reverse, 3⁷⁄₈" h, 2⁷⁄₈" d, $25.00.

Bell, etched holly and berries, clear handle and clapper	85.00
Butter Dish, cov, Button Arches, Lancaster Fair, 1916	150.00
Cordial, Syracuse Fair, 1905	45.00
Creamer, Star of David pattern, St Louis World's Fair, 1904	125.00
Goblet, Glencoe, MN, gold trim	35.00
Mug, Button Band, 1900, etched leaf	35.00

Napkin Ring, Diamond with Peg, etched Bisbee, Ariz, Dec 25, 1908, pr	125.00
Pitcher, Ocean City, NJ, 1908	40.00
Punch Cup, Button Arches, Paducah, VT	25.00
Toothpick	
Beaded Swag, Bucyrus, OH	45.00
Button Arches, etched Carnival July 29, 1904, name J M Craig etched on reverse	30.00
Rib and Bead, etched Naomi	60.00
Tumbler	
Diamond Peg, Indiana, 1910	30.00
Heart Band, Chicago	35.00
Wine	
Thumbprint, etched holly and berries	40.00
Zipper Slash	35.00

RUSSIAN ITEMS

History: During the late 19th and early 20th centuries Russia contained skilled craftsmen in lacquer, silver, and enamel wares. Located mainly in Moscow during the Czarist era (1880–1917), were a group of master craftsmen, led by Faberge, who created exquisite enamel pieces. Faberge also had an establishment in St. Petersburg and enjoyed the patronage of the Russian Imperial family and the royalty and nobility throughout Europe.

Almost all enameling was done on silver. Pieces are signed by the artist and the government assayer.

The Russian Revolution in 1917 brought an abrupt end to the century of Russian craftsmanship. The modern Soviet government has exported some inferior enamel and lacquer work, usually lacking in artistic merit. Modern pieces are not collectible.

ENAMELS

Badge, Imperial Order of St Anne, First Class, translucent red enameling between crossed swords center, St Anne figure on one side, monogram on other, ribbon	250.00
Belt, 27½" l, silver gilt scroll sections, flowers and scrolling leaves, stippled ground, stylized rosette clasp with sky blue central roundel, white dot border, N N Zverev, Moscow, 1899–1908	1,100.00
Belt Buckle, 2¾" l, arabesque outline, cobalt blue, royal blue, turquoise, and translucent red and green scrolling tendrils, oval blue medallion center, dagger clasp of flowers and leaves, white ground, Henrik Tallberg, 19th C	220.00
Bonbon Basket, 4¼" d, silver gilt, champleve enamel, gilt swing handle, three	

Figure, green jacket, purple cape, gilt dec, Popov, mid 19th C, 7½" h, $750.00.

gilt ball feet, gilt int. monogrammed, Moscow, 1891 . . . . **880.00**

Charkahs, 2¼" l, Pan Slavic enameling, clover shape, fitted holly wood box, stylized bird handles, A Lubavin, Moscow, 1895, pr **500.00**

Cigarette Case, 4¾" l, 3⅜" w, diagonal flowering foliage band, cobalt blue ground, silver gilt edges with geometric designs, gilt int., marked "H U," Moscow, 1908–17 . . . . **440.00**

Condiment, Kovsh shape, marked "84" and "EP," enamel loss **200.00**

Demitasse Spoon, silver gilt, flower and leaf dec, pastel green ground, twisted handles, crown finials, set of 6, N Zverev, Moscow, 1899–1908 . . . . . . **1,210.00**

Easter Egg, 1¼" l, blue enamel, striated ground, mounted silver flowers with amethyst and ruby centers, 1908–17 **600.00**

Kovsh, 5¾" l, enameled colorful stylized buds, black and yellow ground **1,500.00**

Salt, 1¾" h, 2½" d, silver gilt, pinched waist, sky blue enamel ground, gilt scrolling cloisonnes, three gilt ball feet, N Zverev, Moscow, 1899–1908 **385.00**

Spoon
  Caviar, 7" l, Art Nouveau style, gilded silver, dark blue champleve enamel, right angle bowl, Anton Kuzmichev, Moscow, 1900 . . . . . . **900.00**
  Serving
    6¾" l, cloisonne enamel stylized foliage bowl, silver gilt stippled ground, handle with heart, teardrop, and animal segments, Sazikov, Moscow, c1890 . . . . **385.00**

7¾" l, Pan Slavic enameling, mythical birds dec, silver gilt ground, twisted stem handle, crown knop, Nemirov–Kolodkin, Moscow, c1886 . . . . **720.00**

Sugar Scoop, 4⅞" l, silver gilt, cloisonne enameled dec, A Kuzmichev, Moscow, 1889 . . . . **660.00**

MISCELLANEOUS

Bowl, 7¼" d, medallion with floral dec, dark rose ground, ... **125.00**

Cigarette Case, 3¾" l, 2¾" w, gold, chased diamond shape lozenges and triangles, silvered int., blue stone clasp **1,430.00**

Icon
  12" h, 10" w, St Sergie of Randonez, scroll and blessing gesture, raised border, ivory ground, restoration, early 19th C **850.00**
  13" h, 10" w, Virgin Vladimirskaya, red robe, red ground, ochre border, ribbed, retouched, worming, giltwood frame, early 19th C **900.00**
  13" h, 11" w, Entry into Jerusalem, Christ riding on donkey, surrounded by followers, gilt ground, restoration and retouching, gilt frame, Moscow School, 18th C **1,400.00**

Medallion, Alexander II, pewter **50.00**

Painting, oil on canvas
  David Burliuk, Russia, 1882–1967, Floral Abstractions, sgd, 26 x 31" **2,100.00**
  Radish Tordia, Russia, 1936, Circus, sgd, titled, dated, and inscribed on reverse, 31½ x 35½" **2,800.00**

Plate, 9½" d, porcelain, polychrome floral nosegay and gilt grape leaf dec, blue ground, 19th C **90.00**

Samovar, 17" h, brass **140.00**

Samovar Set, 3pcs, 18" h samovar, tray, and drip bowl, brass, imperial stamp **280.00**

Teapot, 5" h, porcelain, polychrome, medallion with floral dec, dark rose ground, Dimitrieff **275.00**

SILVER

Beaker
  2¾" h, 2 oz 12 dwt, circular repousse body, chased birds and rocaille dec, three ball feet, marked "T G Assay Master, Fedor Petrov, Moscow, 1765" **575.00**
  3" h, bust figures, holding sword and morning star, gilt details, cyrillic letter slogan on base, pricked ground, MT, Moscow, 1908–17 . . . . **360.00**
  4¼" h, niello entwined foliate spirals

and strapwork, matte ground, gilt int., lobed base, Moscow, 1852–62 — **770.00**

Box, 3½″ l, 2″ w, rounded corners, Russian merchant, niello diaperwork ground, silver hexafoil mounted base, engraved "R," gilt int., Moscow, 1882 — **610.00**

Charger, presentation, 16″ d, circular shaped rim, engraved foliage and mythical beasts, four inscribed roundels, one reading "From the Romanovs to Count Potocki, Dec 16, 1898," int. with crowned five–armed cross of Potocki family, Moscow, 1888–99, maker's mark Cyrillic K Faberge, 33 oz **4,000.00**

Cigar Case, 5⅜″ l, niello dec, Kremlin scene, foliate border, mounted clasp, silver gilt int., Moscow, 1859 . . . . . . **660.00**

Cigarette Case, rect, turquoise enamel cloisonne, arabesques, white beaded enamel border, Gustav Klingert, Moscow, 1892 . . . . **800.00**

Cup, 2 oz, 10 dwt, engraved floral and architectural dec, Vaisily Semenov, Moscow, 1873 . . . . **110.00**

Mirror, 13″ l, hand, lady's, incised tongue ornament, engraved monogram, Moscow **275.00**

Salt, 3⅓″ h, 1 oz 18 dwt, pierced foliage and bird dec, marked "AIM" **220.00**

Snuff Box, 4¾″ l, rect, all–over diaper pattern dec, hinged to, circular monogrammed cartouche **125.00**

Sugar Bowl, 5¾″ h, globe form, lobed sides, circular domed platform base, domed lobed top, knop finial, palmette band on neck and base, gilt int., Assayer A Yashinov, c1825 . . . . **660.00**

Vodka Cup, cylindrical, turquoise enamel cloisonne, arabesques, white beaded enamel border, Gustav Klingert, Moscow, 1893 . . . . **250.00**

SABINO GLASS

History: Sabino glass, named for its creator, Ernest Marius Sabino, originated in France in the 1920s and is an art glass which was produced in a wide range of decorative glassware: frosted, clear, opalescent, and colored glass. Both blown and pressed moldings were used. Hand-sculpted wooden molds that were cast in iron were used and are still in use at the present time.

In 1960 the company introduced a line of figurines, one- to eight-inches high, plus other items in a fiery opalescent glass in the Art Deco style. Gold was added to the batch to give the fiery glow. These pieces are the Sabino that is most commonly found today. Sabino is marked with the name in the mold, an etched signature, or both.

Dragonfly, 6″ h, $85.00.

Ashtray		
	Round	65.00
	Swallow, large	45.00
Bird		
	Feeding, small	20.00
	Nesting, small	20.00
Bowl		
	Berry	50.00
	Fish	50.00
	Shell	45.00
Box, Petalia		90.00
Butterfly, 2¾″, wings open		30.00
Dog		
	Pekingese, small	20.00
	Poodle, 1¾″	20.00
	Scottie	65.00
Elephant		25.00
Lamp		
	Chandelier, 24″ d, 25″ h, central shaft, flared chrome corona, eight down-swept arms in two registers, cylindrical shades, relief molded overlapping leaves flanked by wings, c1925	2,100.00
	Table, 7½″ h, domed, three tiered shade, irregular edge, circular molded foot, fan shaped panels and triangles, shade molded "Sabino 4640 Paris Depose"	735.00
Napkin Ring, birds, marked "Sabino"		35.00
Scent Bottle, Pineapple, 5″		165.00
Snail, 3″		25.00
Statue, 6½″ h, woman, nude, long flowing hair		125.00
Vase		
	11″ h, 7″ w, six lobes, Art Deco geometric dec, royal blue, satin finished, polished highlights, sgd	575.00
	14″ h, ovoid, flared rim, heavy walls, frosted opalescent, molded frieze of partially draped nude women, La Danse poses, sgd "Sabino France," crack on base	500.00

ℂ 𝒮 SALOPIAN

SALOPIAN WARE

History: Salopian ware was made at Caughley Pot Works, Salop, Stropshire, England, in the 18th century by Thomas Turner. The ware is polychrome on transfer. One time classified as Polychrome Transfer, it retains the more popular name of Salopian. Wares are marked with an "S" or "Salopian" impressed or painted under the glaze. Much of it was sold through Turner's Salopian warehouse in London.

Cup and Saucer, handleless, bird on branch, 1¾" x 2⅞" cup, 4¾" d saucer, $145.00.

Bowl, 6½" d, polychrome, classical figures within ovals, brown transfer florals, ochre, pink and green highlights 85.00
Creamer and Sugar, man and woman having tea in garden, black and white transfer 450.00
Cup and Saucer, handleless, soft paste
  Black floral transfer, polychrome enamel dec, hairline and chips on table ring, stains on saucer back .. 75.00
  Brown transfer scene of Britannia, Columbia, floral borders, polychrome enamel, emb ribs, scalloped edge, stains, set of six 450.00
Cup Plate, 4½" d, Deer pattern, polychrome dec 425.00
Dish, 10¾" w, oval, white ground, bright blue scattered flowering branches, shaped blue rim, imp "Salopian," c1780, pr 425.00
Miniature, cup and saucer, handleless, brown transfer, polychrome enamel, pinpoint flakes, repair to table ring .. 150.00
Mug, 4" h, Bird on Branch pattern ... 250.00
Plate
  6" d, Deer, green, yellow, black, and white 200.00
  8" d, white ground, blue scattered flowers, gilt foliage, gilt beads border, blue and gilt banding, imp "Salopian," c1780, set of 14 .... 400.00
  8¾" d, octagonal, Oriental scene ... 185.00
Teapot, Birds and Flowers pattern ... 500.00

SALT AND PEPPER SHAKERS

History: Collecting salt and pepper shakers, whether late 19th century glass forms or the contemporary figural and souvenir types, is becoming more and more popular. The supply and variety is practically unlimited; the price for most sets is within the budget of cost-conscious young collectors. Finally, their size offers an opportunity to assemble a large collection in a small amount of space.

One can specialize in types, forms, or makers. Great art glass artisans such as Joseph Locke and Nicholas Kopp designed salt and pepper shakers in the normal course of their work. Arthur Goodwin Peterson's *Glass Salt Shakers: 1,000 Patterns* provides the following reference numbers. Peterson made a beginning; there are hundreds, perhaps thousands, of patterns still to be cataloged.

The clear colored and colored opaque sets command the highest prices; clear and white sets the lowest. Although some shakers, e.g., the tomato or fig, have a special patented top and need it to hold value, it is not detrimental to the price to replace the top of a shaker.

The figural and souvenir types are often looked down upon by collectors. Sentiment and whimsy are prime collecting motivations. The large variety and current low prices indicate a potential for long-term price growth.

Generally older shakers are priced by the piece; figural and souvenir types by the set. The pricing method is indicated at each division. All shakers are assumed to have original tops unless noted. Identification numbers are from Peterson's book.

References: Gideon Bosker, *Great Shakes: Salt and Pepper For All Tastes*, Abbeville Press, 1986; Melva Davern, *The Collector's Encyclopedia of Salt & Pepper Shakers: Figural And Novelty*, Collector Books, 1985; Melva Davern, *The Collector's Encyclopedia of Salt and Pepper Shakers, Second Series*, Collector Books, 1990; Helene Guarnaccia, *Salt & Pepper Shakers*, Collector Books, 1984; Helene Guarnaccia, *Salt & Pepper Shakers II: Identification & Values*, Collector Books, 1989; Mildred and Ralph Lechner, *The World of Salt Shakers*, Collector Books, 1976; Arthur G. Peterson, *Glass Salt Shakers: 1000 Patterns*, Wallace-Homestead, 1970.

Collectors' Clubs: Antique and Art Glass Salt Shaker Collectors Society, 348 N. Hamilton Street, Painted Post, NY 14807; Novelty Salt and Pepper Shakers Club, 581 Joy Road, Battle Creek, MI 49017; Salt Shaker Collectors Club, 2832 Rapidan Trail, Maitland, FL 32751.

Additional Listings: See *Warman's Americana & Collectibles* for more examples.

ART GLASS (PRICED INDIVIDUALLY)

Erie Twist, white stain glass, hp, delicate pink flowers, shaded buff leaves, 2 pc pewter top, patent 1892, 28–B	65.00
Inverted Fan and Feather, pink slag, 31–O	250.00
Mt Washington	
Egg, flat end	70.00
Tomato	60.00
Peachblow, Wheeling, orig top	300.00
Rubena, enameled dec, pewter top, 175–O	190.00
Satin, Raindrop, MOP, royal blue shading, pastel blue base	235.00

FIGURAL AND SOUVENIR TYPES (PRICED BY SET)

Billiken, white, opaque, and crystal, gilt, Buddha shape, tin top, inscribed on base "The God of things as they out to be," patent 1908, 22–U	55.00
Dutch Boy and Girl, white metal figural top, clear base	90.00
Farmer Pig, gold trim, marked "Shawnee"	25.00
Poppy, orange, green leaves, marked "Royal Bayreuth"	40.00

OPALESCENT GLASS (PRICED INDIVIDUALLY)

Argonaut Shell, blue, 153–K	50.00
Beatty Honeycomb, white, 22–Q	25.00
Ribbons Short, cranberry	40.00
Ribbon Vertical	35.00

OPAQUE GLASS (PRICED INDIVIDUALLY)

Acorn, pink	40.00

Milk Glass, ribbed base, white ground, hp floral vine, orig top, P-36V, $30.00.

Cone, Consolidated, pink	35.00
Double Deck, green opaque	30.00
Egg Shape, Brownie dancing with Golliwog, fan on back, orig pewter lid	100.00
Guttate, green	40.00
Paneled Sprig, milk glass, green dec	32.00
Scrolled Panel, green	35.00

PATTERN GLASS (PRICED INDIVIDUALLY)

Banded Portland, maiden's blush	35.00
Cane, apple green, 156–H	25.00
Dew and Raindrop, 158–O	20.00
Eyewinker, orig top	65.00
Feather, 28–N	18.00
Heart with Thumbprint, gold trim, 30–P	48.00
Maine, 22–M	20.00
New Jersey, hotel size, 34–E	25.00
O'Hara Diamond, ruby stained	35.00
Priscilla #2, emerald green, 169–G	30.00
Red Block, 169–R	60.00
Shell Triple	14.00
Stars and Stripes, 173–S	15.00
Thousand Eye, vaseline	30.00
Wheat and Barley, blue	35.00

SALTGLAZED WARES

History: Saltglazed wares have a distinctive "pitted" surface texture made by throwing salt into the hot kiln during the final firing process. The salt vapors produce sodium oxide and hydrochloric acid, which react on the glaze.

Many Staffordshire potters produced large quantities of this type of ware during the 18th and 19th centuries. A relatively small quantity was produced in the United States. Saltglazed wares still are made today.

Reference: Susan and Al Bagdade, *Warman's English & Continental Pottery & Porcelain, 1st Edition,* Warman Publishing Co., Inc., 1987.

Bottle, 9¼" h, globular, applied foliage, c1755	400.00
Dish, 10" d, lobed, pierced, all–over herringbone, basketweave, and diaper panels, c1760	450.00
Flask, 7" h, figural, reclining pig, cobalt blue eyes, inscribed "Fine Old Bourbon in a Hop...Cairo Mounds, Chicago, St Louis, Cincinnati," c1860	1,400.00
Mug, child's, 2½" h, polychrome red, blue, green, iron–red, and sepia, insect crawling on thorny rose stem, iron–red trellis diaper pattern, three panels of flowerheads, blue and green foliate sprig int. dec, reeded strap handle, Staffordshire, c1780	2,100.00
Pitcher	
8⅛" h, brown and white, emb scenes, Flastaff in laundry basket, trees,	

**Pitcher, tan, English registry marks, 7"
h, $100.00.**

imp "Turner," chips on base and spout	150.00
8⅜" h, blue and white, marked "Chicago pitcher designed by Frank E Burley..., Copeland Spode, England"	300.00
Sauce Boat, 5⅝" l, oval, wide long spout, strap handle, molded diapered cartouches, basketweave, blue scrollwork edges, Staffordshire, c1765	1,540.00
Soup Plate, 9¼" d, polychrome, flowers and vase, molded basketweave and diaper border, c1755	475.00
Teapot	
3¾" h, slightly oval, polychrome rose, pale pink, green, yellow, and black, rose sprig dec, blue ground, crabstock spout and handle, Staffordshire, c1760, chips to spout and flange cov	2,100.00
4⅜" h, English, King of Prussia, all-over ermine field, polychrome enamel panels with bust portrait of king titled "Fred, Prussia Rex" on one side, Prussian eagle with emblematic shield and ribbon on reverse, c1760	1,300.00
Tureen, cov, oval, compressed baluster form, duplessis form finial, C scroll legs with ornamental masks, English, c1775	950.00

SALTS, OPEN

History: When salt was first mined, the supply was limited and expensive. The necessity for a receptacle in which to serve the salt resulted in the first open salt, a crude, hand-carved, wooden trencher.

As time passed salt receptacles were refined in style and materials. In the 1500s both master and individual salts existed. By the 1700s firms such as Meissen, Waterford, and Wedgwood were making glass, china, and porcelain salts. Leading manufacturers in the 1800s included Libbey Glass Co.; Mount Washington; New England Glass Company; Smith Bros.; Vallerysthal; Wavecrest; Webb; and many outstanding silversmiths in England, France, and Germany.

Open salts were used as the only means of serving salt until the appearance of the shaker in the late 1800s. The ease of procuring salt from a shaker greatly reduced the use and need for the open salts.

References: William Heacock and Patricia Johnson, *5,000 Open Salts: A Collector's Guide*, Richardson Printing Corporation, 1982; L. W. and D. B. Neal, *Pressed Glass Dishes Of The Lacy Period 1825–1850*, published by the author, 1962; Allan B. and Helen B. Smith have authored and published ten books on open salts beginning with *One Thousand Individual Open Salts Illustrated* (1972) and ending with *1,334 Open Salts Illustrated: The Tenth Book* (1984). Daniel Snyder did the master salt sections in Volumes 8 and 9. In 1987 Mimi Rudnick compiled a revised price list for the ten Smith books.

Collectors' Club: New England Society of Open Salt Collectors, 587 Dutton Road, Sudbury, MA 01776.

Note: The numbers in parentheses refer to plate numbers in the Smith's publications.

CONDIMENT SETS WITH OPEN SALTS

Porcelain, light pink with gold trim on leaf shaped holder, marked "Made in Bavaria" (388)	125.00
Silver Plated, 3 pcs, emb pattern around bowls, Oriental (461)	50.00

INDIVIDUALS

China	
Dresden Saxony, lily dec on one side (434)	45.00
Majolica, flower shape, overlapping leaves, marked "No 35" (439)	60.00
Unknown Maker, Viking ship, complete plique–a–jour in blue, red, and vaseline, very unusual (455)	1,000.00
Colored Glass	
Cameo, Webb, red ground, white lacy dec around bowl, sgd, matching spoon (137)	600.00
Cobalt Blue, pedestal, sgd "Steuben" (485)	225.00
Irid Gold, sgd "Quezal" (92)	200.00

Lavender, pedestal, frosted (373) .. **75.00**
Ruby, blown, white lace trim (447) .. **95.00**
Sapphire blue, white enamel stylized
  leaves, blossoms, and scrolls,
  touches of pink, green, blue, and yellow, gold rim and wafer foot, 3⅛" d,
  1½" h **285.00**

**Individual, Limoges, green int., scal-
loped edge, white ground, gold trim,
marked "D & C/France," 1⅝" d, 1¾" h,
$10.00.**

Cut Glass
  Pedestal, faceted base (118) **52.00**
  Round, alternating zippered and
    starred panels (361) **25.00**
  Triangular, Star and Diamond, sgd
    "Hawkes" (466) **65.00**
  Tub, tab handles, Diamond and Fan
    (361) **55.00**
Double Salts
  China, Meissen, floral dec int. and
    ext., crossed swords and crown
    mark (460) **75.00**
  Glass
    Blue, silver frames, four ribbed paw
      feet (460) **80.00**
    Milk Glass, turquoise, sgd "Valler-
      ystahl" and "Made In France"
      (460) **35.00**
    Vaseline, ten panels, tall handle
      (460) **50.00**
In Metal Frames
  Clear, ftd SS holder with four pea-
    cocks around outside, marked
    "Sterling" (411) **45.00**
  Cobalt blue liner, basket, pierced rib-
    bon handles, marked "E.P.N.S."
    (413) **35.00**
Metal, copper, heavy, pedestal, deep
  maroon enamel (414) **25.00**
Pressed Glass
  Elliptical, round, rayed bottom (362) **18.00**
  Heisey, octagonal paneled bowl, slop-
    ing octagonal base, marked with
    Heisey "H" in diamond (475) **35.00**
  Liberty Bell, clear, oval, 2¼" **20.00**
  Thumbprint, pedestal, double round
    base, wide top rim, round thumb-
    prints around bowl (362) **30.00**
Wood, Sandalwood, spoon (233) **25.00**

FIGURALS

Donkey, painted, pulling colorful painted
  cart (458) **30.00**
Lafayette Boat, deep cobalt blue, emb
  "Lafayet, [sic] Sandwich, B & S Glass
  Co," c1830, several chips **725.00**
Sleigh with Cupid driving reindeer, SS,
  made in Germany (352) **400.00**

MASTERS

China
  Belleek, shell shape (314) **40.00**
  Leeds, boat shape, pedestal (313) **65.00**
  Minton, ftd, #57957 (314) **47.50**
  Unknown Maker, round, subtly ribbed,
    floral dec, gold and green border
    (384) **45.00**
Colored Glass
  Aventurine, narrow base (316) **55.00**
  Cranberry, horizontal colored ribs
    (316) **65.00**
  Fiery Opalescent, white, baskets of
    fruit and floral designs, emb on
    base "N. E. Glass Company Bos-
    ton," 2⅞" l **275.00**
  Olive–green, beaded scroll and
    scrolled leaf design, attributed to Mt
    Vernon, NY, Glassworks, 2⅞" l,
    c1840 .... **1,200.00**
Cut Glass, round, diamond pattern on
  top of bowl, ribbed base (404) **30.00**

Master, Lusterware, 3" d, 2¼" h, $55.00.

Lacy
  Clear
    Horn of Plenty (329) **60.00**
    Oval Diamond on Pedestal
      (OP3:407) **150.00**
  Colored
    Basket of Flowers, opaque blue
      (BF1C:324) **350.00**
    Eagle, fiery milky opal, American
      eagle on corners, shield center,
      Sandwich Glassworks, c1840,
      3" l **650.00**
    Scrolled Heart, green, (SC7:324) **270.00**

Metal
Pewter, pedestal, cobalt blue liner
(349) **60.00**
Sterling Silver, ftd, rams' heads, Gorham (281) **80.00**
Pressed Glass
Hobnail, round (407) **30.00**
Palmette (471) **57.50**
Square Pillared (341) **25.00**
Vintage (340) **30.00**
Pressed Glass, pedestal
Eyewinker (346) **80.00**
Hamilton (344) **35.00**
Paneled Diamond (331) **45.00**

SAMPLERS

History: Samplers served many purposes. For a young child they were a practice exercise and permanent reminder of stitches and patterns. For a young woman they demonstrated her skills in a "gentle" art and preserved key elements of family genealogy. For the mature woman they were a useful occupation and functioned as gifts or remembrances, e.g., mourning pieces.

Schools for young ladies of the early 19th century prided themselves on the needlework skills they taught. The Westtown School in Chester County, Pennsylvania, and the Young Ladies Seminary in Bethlehem, Pennsylvania, are two examples. These schools changed their teaching as styles changed. Berlin work was introduced by the mid-19th century.

Examples of samplers date back to the 1700s. The earliest ones were long and narrow, usually done only with the alphabet and numerals. Later examples were square. At the end of the 19th century, the shape tended to be rectangular.

The same motifs were used throughout the country. The name is a key element in determining the region. Samplers are assumed to be on linen unless otherwise indicated.

References: Glee Krueger, *A Gallery of American Samplers: The Theodore H. Kapnek Collection*, Bonanza Books, 1984 edition; Betty Ring, *American Needlework Treasures; Samplers and Silk Embroideries From The Collection of Betty Ring*, E. P. Dutton, 1987; Anne Sebba, *Samplers: Five Centuries of a Gentle Craft*, Thames and Hudson, 1979.

1773, Hannah Eelss, age 12, photocopy of family history on reverse, 15¾ x 10", framed **450.00**
1776, Elizabeth Shillaber, alphabets and "Elizabeth Shillaber her Sampler Aged 13, 1776," green, blue, gold, yellow, and bittersweet silk threads, framed, 14½ x 12½" **6,500.00**
1783, Mary Bowles, alphabets, verse, woman, and landscape scene, "Mary

1862, cross stitched, homespun linen, 16 x 20½", $550.00.

Bowles Aged 12, 1783," Essex County, MA, green, blue, lavender, salmon, and pink silk threads, unframed, 16 x 48" **13,000.00**
1786, Margaret Wall, linen, inscription "Margaret Wall her work wrought in the 14 year of her age 1786," silk stitches, 17½ x 13½" **2,000.00**
1793, Lydia Fitch, Suffield, CT, rose and shades of green silk threads, natural linen ground with black stitches, bands of alphabets and numerals, inscribed name and age above vase and flowers flanked by flowers and trees, shaped border, 11½" sq **8,250.00**
1795
Chenery, Phebe, polychrome threads, linen ground, alphabet, inscribed verse above scene of brick building, woman and child surrounded by flowers, birds, and trees, inner sawtooth border enclosed by outer border, outer chain and floral border enclosed by continuous scroll border, 21½ x 17" .. **4,400.00**
Cook, Sally, lines of verse, five alphabets, "Sally Cook's Sampler, aged 14 years, who was born January 28, 1795," 15¼ x 13", framed ... **650.00**
1798, Helena Scyler, two renditions of alphabet, four lines of verse, dated May 14, 1798, several fancy dec designs, 16 x 8¾", framed **350.00**
1799, Mary Day, homespun, Adam & Eve, angels, flowers, verse, and "Mary Day work this sampler in the year of our Lord 1799, 8 yrs," vining border, 18½" h, 14¾" w, framed ... **300.00**
1803, Eliza Thurstanss, cotton homespun, blue floss, alphabets, verse, and "Eliza Thurstanss work, Novbr 4th 1803," maple ogee frame, 8¾" h, 8" w **1,025.00**

1808

Isabella Brooks, religious verse, potted flower, flowering and pine trees, birds, and house chairs, inscripton "Isabella Brooks age 14 years Badminton School 1808," meandering floral border, 12¼ x 10⅞" 750.00

Margaret Tyson Ham, two religious verses, bells and flowers, lady with parasol, roosters, stylized trees and potted flowers, inscription "Margaret Tyson Ham work'd this sampler in the year of our Lord 1808 and in the ninth year of her age," meandering floral border, mahogany veneered frame, 15¼ x 15" . . 700.00

1820, Harriet Benis, linen, alphabets and numerals above urn and verse, inscribed "Sacred to the Memory of Hiram Bemis who was born July 20, 1806 died May 20 1809" and "Wrought by Harriet Bemis Aged 11 years Southborough June 26, 1820," wreaths with family names and dates, houses, trees and picket fence, floral border, blue, cream, and gold threads, framed, 17 x 21½" 900.00

1822, Clarissa Taylor, homespun, alphabet rows and "Clarissa Taylor sampler age 10, 1822," color bleeding, framed, 10¾ x 14" 275.00

1823

Amorena D T Roberts, homespun, alphabets, house and flowers, verse, "Amorena D T Roberts, born 8th month 29th, 1813, wrought 1823," mahogany veneer frame with brass corner rosettes, 20½" h, 20¼" w . 650.00

Cyntha Ray, linen, alphabets and flowers, and verse, "Cyntha Ray, 7 years old the 15th day of February 1823," green, blue, white, yellow and brown, framed, 16" h, 17½" w 1,025.00

1826

Jane Darrah, inscribed "Jane Darrah wrought this in 1826," alphabet, numbers, flower, poem, gilded frame, 18 x 17" 400.00

Hannah W Woodruff, linen, alphabets, four stanza song written for Lafayette's arrival in Newark, bower inscribed "Lafayette whom the nation honors" with American eagle and La Fayette seated with two dignitaries, running vine with carnation blossoms and buds border, "Hannah W Woodruff's work aged 11 years and 5 months Newark May 19th 1826," green, pink, yellow, and black silk stitches, 16 x 16", framed 25,300.00

1830

Sarah Carmack, homespun, alphabets, "Sarah Carmack's work done in the 14th year of her age, 1830," floral border, 18 x 8½", framed . . . 450.00

Martha Tyler, age 11, Portland, Maine, September 6, 1830, alphabets, numbers encircled by vine border, 16½" sq, framed 600.00

1834, Martha Young, Northampton, MA, polychrome threads, linen ground, alphabetic and numeric lines, inscribed verse, meandering floral and vine border, 15½ x 12½" 1,650.00

1836

Isabella Marion Espy, linen, seven rows of alphabets and numerals, four line religious verse, inscription "Isabella Marion Espy Columbus Ohio 1836," solid line embroidery border, 13⅛ x 8" 375.00

Sarah G Vail, homespun, alphabets, verse, and "Sarah G Vail, aged 9 years 1836" and "Miss Elizabeth Houston, Middletown," red, blue, white, and yellow, grained frame, 28¼" h, 22⅝" w 1,750.00

1837

Elizabeth Armstrong, linen, four bands of alphabets and numerals, religious verse, inscription "Elizabeth Armstrong wrought this sampler in the 11th year of her age February 1837," narrow border, 12¼ x 10⅞" 200.00

Marriot Jefferson, English, four lines of verse, overall figures of birds, animals, trees, flowers and abstract designs, dated May 12, 1837, fabric faded, colors bright, 17½ x 12¼", framed 300.00

1838, Jane Harris, linen, silk stitches, stylized trees, potted flowers, animals, and birds, "This I have done for you to see, the care my parents took of me. Jane Harris, August 8, 1838, aged 12 years," floral border, framed, 15 x 12½" 750.00

1839, Catharine Booth, ladies, birds, flowers, and angels, verse "Can a woman's tender care cease toward the child she bare yes she may forgetful be yet will I remember thee" and "Watch and Pray," sgd and dated 1839, framed, 23½" sq 300.00

1840, Mary Hoskins, homespun, alphabets and "Mary Hoskins August 13, 1840," 18½ x 21¼", framed, stained, faded colors 165.00

1841, Emily Brown, NY, polychrome threads, linen ground, alphabets, inscribed name and date over scene of building and garden, flower and vine border enclosed by cross stitched border, color loss, 17 x 16½" **1,320.00**

1856, Mary Ann Pirt, Catgill Hall Near Whitehaven, Cumberland, linen panel, verse, birds, animals, pots and basket, three story brick house, picket fence, trees, plants, and stag, floral vine border, brown, red, green, blue, pink, and white threads, 23½ x 25", carved wood frame **935.00**

SANDWICH GLASS

History: In 1818 Deming Jarves was listed in the Boston Directory as a glass factor. The same year he was appointed general manager of the newly formed New England Glass Company. In 1824 Jarves toured the glass-making factories in Pittsburgh, left New England Glass Company, and founded a glass factory in Sandwich.

Originally called the Sandwich Manufacturing Company, it was incorporated in April 1826 as the Boston and Sandwich Glass Company. From 1826 to 1858 Jarves served as general manager. The Boston and Sandwich Glass Company produced a wide variety and quality of wares. The factory used the free-blown, blown three-mold, and pressed glass manufacturing techniques. Clear and colored glass both were used.

Competition in the American glass industry in the mid-1850s forced a lowering of quality of the glass wares. Jarves left in 1858, founded the Cape Cod Glass Company, and tried to maintain the high quality of the earlier glass. At the Boston and Sandwich Glass Company emphasis was placed on mass production. The development of a lime glass (non-flint) led to lower costs for pressed glass. Some free-blown and blown-and-molded pieces, mostly in color, were made. Most of this Victorian era glass was enameled, painted, or acid etched.

By the 1880s the Boston and Sandwich Glass Company was operating at a loss. Labor difficulties finally resulted in the factory closing on January 1, 1888.

References: Raymond E. Barlow and Joan E. Kaiser, *The Glass Industry In Sandwich*, Vol. 2, Vol. 3 and Vol. 4, distributed by Schiffer Publishing, Ltd.; George S. and Helen McKearin, *American Glass*, Crown Publishers, Inc., 1941 and 1948; Ruth Webb Lee, *Sandwich Glass: The History Of The Sandwich Glass Company*, Charles E. Tuttle, 1966; Ruth Webb Lee, *Sandwich Glass Handbook*, Charles E. Tuttle, 1966; L. W. and D. B. Neal, *Pressed Glass Dishes Of The Lacy Period 1825–1850*, published by author, 1962; Catherine M. V. Thuro, *Oil Lamps II: Glass Kerosene Lamps*, Wallace-Homestead, 1983.

Periodical: *The Sandwich Collector*, McCue Publications, P. O. Box 340, East Sandwich, MA 02537.

Museum: Sandwich Glass Museum, Sandwich, Mass.

Additional Listings: Blown Three Mold and Cup Plates.

Toilet Bottle, clear, ribbed, c1820, 5¼" h, $75.00.

Bowl, 7½" d, Tulip and Acanthus, clear lacy **35.00**
Butter Dish, cov, 6" d, 5¼" h, Horn of Plenty, flint, bust of George Washington finial, small chip on one scallop **1,600.00**
Candlestick, 9" h, columnar, opaque, powdery purple–blue, rough sandy finish **450.00**
Champagne Glass, Sandwich Star, clear **300.00**
Claret, 4½" h, Horn of Plenty, flint, set of 8, one with ground top, two with minute rim flakes, rest undamaged **450.00**
Compote, Horn of Plenty, flint
    6" d, 5⅞" h, Waffle pattern base, minor chips and roughage, pr **100.00**
    7" d, 5⅞" h, Waffle pattern base, minor roughage to base, chips **50.00**
    7" d, 7" h, minute roughage to base **90.00**
    8" d, 6½" h, minor roughage to base **80.00**
Egg Cup, 3¾" h, Horn of Plenty, flint, pr **85.00**
Goblet
    Bull's Eye and Fleur–de–Lis, clear **72.00**
    Comet, clear **75.00**
    Horn of Plenty, clear **50.00**
Ink Bottle, 2¼" h, barrel, tea kettle spout, deep amethyst, ground lip . . **800.00**
Miniature
    Creamer, flint, lacy, clear **55.00**

Tureen, oval, paneled, handles, slotted handled cov, opal, flint 200.00
Vegetable Dish, flint, oval, clear . . . 70.00
Paperweight, 5 x 3¼ x 1⅛", book
shape, vaseline, cut all–over, medal-
lion on fruit, monogrammed "E C G" 300.00
Plate, 6⅜" d, dessert, Horn of Plenty,
flint, set of 15, minor chips and rough-
age 500.00
Pomade, bear, 5¼" h, white, sitting,
base emb "R & C A Wright, Philada,"
cooling flaw on back of head 900.00
Relish, 8" l, oval, lacy, clear 60.00
Salt, 3¼" l, Horn of Plenty, flint 20.00
Salt and Pepper Shakers, pr
Amberina, 4" h 160.00
Christmas, one amber, other blue, ag-
itator 200.00
Sauce Bottle, 5⅞" h, Horn of Plenty,
flint, arched panel marked "Heswan,"
two small annealing lines 100.00
Sauce Dish, Horn of Plenty, flint
3¼" d, minor roughage 20.00
4½" d 30.00
5¼" d, minor roughage and chips . . 18.00
Sugar, cov
Four Petal, flint, globular 30.00
Horn of Plenty, 7½" h, flint 165.00
Star, flint, minute rim roughage to lid 60.00
Vegetable Dish, 11⅛" l, Horn of Plenty,
flint, oval, six chips on scalloped edge 70.00
Whimsey
Flat–Iron, amethyst, three minor
flakes on edges, handle check . . . 650.00
Whiskey Taster, cobalt blue, nine
panels 125.00
Wine, 5¼" h, Horn of Plenty, flint, set of
8 . . . . 650.00

SARREGUEMINES CHINA

History: Sarreguemines ware is a faience porcelain, i.e., tin-glazed earthenware. The factory
was established in Lorraine, France, in 1770, under the supervision of Utzcheider and Fabry. The
factory was regarded as one of the three most
prominent manufacturers of French Faience. Most
of the wares found today were made in the 19th
century. Later wares are impressed Sarreguemines and Germany due to a change of boundaries
and location of the factory.

Reference: Susan and Al Bagdade, *Warman's
English & Continental Pottery & Porcelain, 1st Edition,* Warman Publishing Co., Inc., 1987.

Animal Covered Dish, 5¾" h, hen and
chicks 125.00
Bowl, 8" d, figural, fish, molded scales
and details 65.00

**Plate, black transfer hunting scene, 7"
d, $28.00.**

Character Jug, lawyer, marked "French
Majolica" 125.00
Jug, 6" h, pinched form, free hand
brushed dec, ochre ground 60.00
Oyster Plate, six shells, white ground,
blue trim 65.00
Plate
7½" d, transfer print
Mars 45.00
November 45.00
8½" d, majolica, strawberries and floral trim, aqua ground 75.00
9" d, transfer print, Oriental man . . . 20.00
Rose Bowl, 4" d, majolica, multicolored
floral dec 80.00
Tobacco Jar, cov, relief masks, brown,
yellow trim 85.00
Vase
7" h, tapered, silver crystals, blue–
gray glaze 100.00
8½" h, majolica, gargoyles and lizards 125.00
Wall Pocket, 9½" l, beetle dec, blue,
green, and brown irid glaze 200.00

SARSAPARILLA BOTTLES

History: "Sarsaparilla" refers to a number of
tropical American, spiny, woody vines of the lily
family whose roots are fragrant. An extract was
obtained from these dried roots and used for medicinal purposes. The first appearance in bottle
form dates from the 1840s. The earliest bottles
were stoneware, later followed by glass.

Carbonated water often was added to sarsaparilla to make a soft drink or to make consuming it
more pleasurable. For this reason, sarsaparilla
and soda became synonymous even though they
were two different entities.

References: Ralph & Terry Kovel, *The Kovels'
Bottle Price List, 8th Edition,* Crown Publishers,

Inc., 1987; Carlo & Dot Sellari, *The Standard Old Bottle Price Guide,* Collector Books, 1989.

Periodical: *Antique Bottle and Glass Collector,* P. O. Box 187, East Greenville, PA 18041.

Additional Listings: See *Warman's Americana & Collectibles* for a list of soda bottles.

Mission Beverage, Pioneer Beverages/ San Francisco—Oakland, CA, clear, 7 oz, 8¼″ h, $215.00.

Bristol–Extract of Sarsaparilla, Buffalo, 5½″ h, aqua, rect, sloping collar, pontil scar, c1850	60.00
Bush's Smilax Sarsaparilla, 9¾″ h, aqua, inverted collar, c1850	350.00
Dalton's Sarsaparilla and Nerve Tonic, blue label	40.00
Dr Martins Compound/Syrup of Snake Root/Sarsaparilla & Burdock, 8¾″ h, aqua, tapered lip, c1870	625.00
Dr Townsends/Sarsaparilla/New York, 9½″ h, light to medium green, open pontil and graphite pontil, sloping collared top, sq, beveled corners, c1850	250.00
Hoods & Ayers	12.00
John Bulls–Extract of Sarsaparilla, Louisville, KY, 8¾″ h, aqua, rect, sloping collar, smooth base, c1870	55.00
Merchants, green, iron pontil	150.00
Recamier, amber	30.00
Sand's Genuine, rect, qt	85.00
Wetherell's, aqua	42.00

SATIN GLASS

History: Satin glass, produced in the late 19th century, is an opaque art glass with a velvety matte (satin) finish, achieved through treatment with hydrofluoric acid. A large majority of the pieces were cased or had a white lining.

While working at the Phoenix Glass Company, Beaver, Pennsylvania, Joseph Webb perfected Mother-of-Pearl (MOP) satin glass in 1885. Similar to plain satin glass in respect to casing, MOP satin glass has a distinctive surface finish and an integral or indented design, the most common being diamond quilted (DQ).

The most common colors are yellow, rose, or blue. Rainbow coloring is considered choice. Satin glass, both plain and MOP, has been widely reproduced.

Additional Listings: Cruets, Fairy Lamps, Miniature Lamps, and Rose Bowls.

Fairy Lamp, rainbow, DQ, MOP, 5″ h, $700.00.

Basket, 6¾″ h, white satin ext., pink int., ruffled edge, frosted applied base and twisted handle, ftd	75.00
Bowl	
11½″ h, 9½″ d, white swirl ext., rich pink lining, box pleated top, re–silvered stand with figural birds on base	350.00
Center Bowl, 11½″ l, 5½″ h, raspberry pink satin cased to herringbone patterned amber glass, crimped and folded camphor rim, enameled blossoms and butterflies, marked "Patent"	550.00
Dresser Jar, 2½″ h, rose, floral dec . . .	60.00
Ewer	
9⅞″ h, blue to white, enameled dec, pinched and ruffled edge, frosted applied handle	75.00
10½″ h, dark blue shading to light blue, herringbone pattern, frosted thorn handle, ring foot and neck	250.00
Pitcher, 5¾″ h, wild rose, applied and frosted handle	100.00
Rose Bowl	
5½″ d, 6″ h, pale blue shaded to dark blue, yellow enamel flowers, leaves, and stems, eight crimp top	225.00
Salt, melon ribbed, worn floral dec . . .	30.00
Toothpick, 2¾″ h, hat shape, yellow, floral dec, ruffled edge	70.00
Vase	
3⅛″ h, rose, enameled flowers and bug dec, ruffled edge	50.00

6" h, 4" d, flattened hobnail, MOP, shaded rose, white lining, four petal fold over top 550.00

8" h, red frosted glass, English cameo glass style white enameled classical robed figures, attributed to Gillinder, base marked in white "Cameo" 550.00

10¼" h, 5½" d, DQ, MOP, pink, white lining, pr 550.00

10½" h, vasiform, opal cased to yellow satin, two brown elongated four legged dragons, intricate gold accents, attributed to Thomas Webb & Sons 550.00

11½" h, MOP, swirl pattern, pink, ruffled top, reeded handles 355.00

Water Set, 9½" h water pitcher and six matching 4" h tumblers, Diamond Quilt pattern, mother of pearl, deep raspberry shading to pink, ground pontil 1,550.00

SATSUMA

History: Satsuma, named for a war lord who brought skilled Korean potters to Japan in the early 1600s, was a hand-crafted Japanese faience glazed pottery. It is finely crackled, has a cream, yellow-cream, or gray-cream color, and is decorated with raised enamels in floral geometric and figural motifs.

Figural satsuma was made specifically for export in the 19th century. Later satsuma, referred to as satsuma-style ware, is Japanese porcelain also hand-decorated in raised enamels. From 1912 to the present, satsuma-style ware has been mass-produced. Much of the ware on today's market is of this later period.

References: Sandra Andacht, *Oriental Antiques & Art: An Identification And Value Guide,* Wallace-Homestead, 1987; Sandra Andacht, *Treasury of Satsuma,* Wallace-Homestead, 1981.

Bowl

5½" d, cov, drum form finial 700.00

7" d, children playing dec 2,800.00

Box, cov, 2¾ x 3⅝", rect, gilt and enamel dec, bird, floral, and pagoda scene, Japan, early 20th C 110.00

Charger, 12⅞" d, red and black flowers and birds, white ground, gold trim . . 120.00

Dish, 9⅞" d, Kannon, arhats, and dragon, int. dec, scalloped, gilt ground, c1900 . . . . 265.00

Ginger Jar, cov, 4" h, baluster form, figural dec, shaped reserves, dragon on lid 275.00

Jar

6½" h, octagonal, domed lid, figures in landscape dec, fitted on carved wood base, Meiji period 2,100.00

16¼" h, cov, foo dog finial 300.00

Miniature

Bowl, 3" d, green and nd gold dec, impressed signature 50.00

Jar, 2¼" h, six panels, Geisha and Samurai warrior dec 100.00

Teapot, cov, 2¾" h, shaped reserves around body 425.00

Vase

2¼" h, two panels with figure dec 100.00

3½" h, four panel with figure and landscape dec 160.00

Napkin Ring, Myriad butterflies 285.00

Pitcher, 4½" h, warrior scene, gold scrolled handle, c1920 . . . . 230.00

Planter, 11" w, rect, figural dec 250.00

Plate, 9¾" d, wisteria, peonies, and waterfowl, c1900 . . . . 225.00

Tea Set, 12 pcs, teapot, cov sugar, four teacups, and six saucers, figural dec, stylized snake handles, dragon finials 375.00

Tile, 3¾ x 5½", women and children crossing bridge to crowded country inn, polychrome and gilt dec 300.00

Urn

13" h, ceremonial, raised arcaded base enclosing rooster 525.00

16" h, cov, tripod, foo dog finial and handles 260.00

Vase

3¾" h

All–over floral dec, globular form 325.00

Samuarai dec 100.00

Vase, Mandarin Duck, Kinkozan, 5¾" h, $300.00.

5", gilt, blue and red Rakan and Kannon figures, gold relief dragon black matte ground **275.00**

6¼" h, baluster form, waisted neck, shaped reserves with figural, floral, and landscape dec **300.00**

7¾" h, two figural panels, mountainous landscape, one with scholars, other with geishas, pr **575.00**

8¾" h, sq, enamel dec wheel like flowers, stylized leaf border, paneled domestic scenes of female figures, character mark, Kinkozan School, Japan, late 19th C **800.00**

11¼" h, Samurai and Daimyo dec . . **650.00**

11½" h, cranes and floral dec **600.00**

13" h, lilies before rattan fence enclosing flowering peony dec, blue enamel crest and gilt signature on base, 19th C **1,600.00**

14⅜" h, baluster form, figural and raised dragon dec **500.00**

16" h, ovoid form, Samurai dec **550.00**

18½" h, baluster, enamel and gilt dec, central floral panels, geometric borders, heavily raised and molded birds, flowers, and branches, Japan, late 19th C **1,500.00**

23" h, royal blue, elaborated figural dec, Japan **1,500.00**

27½" h, foo dog handles **900.00**

SCALES

History: Prior to 1900 the simple balance scale commonly was used for measuring weights. Since then scales have become more sophisticated in design and more accurate. A variety of styles and types include beam, platform, postal, and pharmaceutical.

Collectors' Club: International Society of Antique Scale Collectors, 111 N. Canal St., Chicago, IL 60606.

Apothecary, brass and mahogany, rect base fitted with two drawers, 18¾" h **990.00**

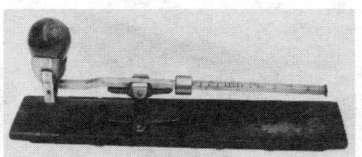

Egg Scale, brass and cast iron, divides into weight by ounces, salesman's sample, c1880, 2⅝ x 13", $115.00.

Baby, tin, dressed bunnies, ducks and mice dec **45.00**

Balance

Countertop

Detecto—Gram, cast iron **75.00**

Henry Troemner, brass, cast iron and wood, weights **200.00**

Spring, hanging type, brass, marked "Forschner" **65.00**

Bushel, brass, hanging, Winchester . . **200.00**

Candy

Dayton—Hobart, Model 100, countertop type **135.00**

National, decal, restored **350.00**

Triner, countertop type, scoop **35.00**

Coin Operated Sidewalk Scale

Jennings, O D, porcelain, white **1,000.00**

Peerless, lollipop type, porcelain, blue, marked **850.00**

Egg Grading, brass, graduated, mounted on rect board, label and instructions **130.00**

Gold Coin, brass, fitted box, orig weights, 8½" l **50.00**

Grain, brass, marked "Ohaus" **250.00**

Grocery Store, hanging type **45.00**

Household, marked "Landers Fary & Clark" **15.00**

Market, cast iron, double beams, scoop and weights, marked "Fairbanks" . . **60.00**

Postal

Hanson Bros Scale Co, c1925 . . . . **40.00**

Pelouze, patent 1895, nickel plated, scroll panels, 5½" h **35.00**

Pelouze Victor, brass and steel, 4½" h, dated 1898 . . . . **30.00**

Steelyard, wrought iron, brass inlay, fig shape, pitted, 32" l **25.00**

SCHLEGELMILCH PORCELAINS

History: Erdmann Schlegelmilch founded his porcelain factory in Suhl in the Thuringia region (in Germany) in 1861. Reinhold, his brother, established a porcelain factory at Tillowitz in Upper Silesia in 1869. In the 1860s Prussia controlled Thuringia and Upper Silesia, both rich in the natural ingredients needed for porcelain.

By the late 19th century an active export business was conducted with the United States and Canada due to a large supply of porcelain at reasonable costs achieved through industrialization and cheap labor. Both brothers marked their pieces with the RSP mark, a designation honoring Rudolph Schlegelmilch, their father. Over 30 mark variations have been discovered.

The Suhl factory ceased production in 1920, unable to recover from the effects of World War I. The Tillowitz plant, located in an area of changing international boundaries, finally came under Polish socialist government control in 1956.

References: Susan and Al Bagdade, *Warman's English & Continental Pottery & Porcelain, 1st Edition,* Warman Publishing Co., Inc., 1987; Mary Frank Gaston, *The Collector's Encyclopedia Of R.S. Prussia and Other R.S. and E.S. Porcelain*, Collector Books, 1982; George W. Terrell, Jr., *Collecting R.S. Prussia Identification and Values*, Books Americana, 1982; Clifford S. Schlegelmilch, *Handbook Of Erdmann And Reinhold Schlegelmilch, Prussia-Germany And Oscar Schlegelmilch, Germany, 3rd Edition*, published by author, 1973.

Reproduction Alert: Many "fake" Schlegelmilch pieces are appearing on the market. These reproductions have new decal marks, transfers, or recently hand-painted animals on old, authentic R.S. Prussia pieces.

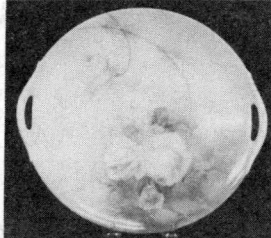

R. S. Germany, cake plate, pink roses, green and cream ground, green mark, 10″ w handle to handle, $40.00.

R. S. GERMANY

Basket, 4¼″ l, 3″ h, three yellow roses, pink shading, scalloped rim and handle, steeple mark	65.00
Berry Set, pink and white roses, 7 pcs	100.00
Bone Dish, cherubs, multicolored, blue mark	25.00
Bowl	
9″ d, morning glories, pastels, scalloped edge	60.00
9½″ d, cotton plant dec	100.00
10″ d, orange and yellow tiger lilies, gray, blue, and lime green ground, gold outlined scalloped edge	75.00
Cake Plate, 9¾″ d, cotton plant dec, open handles	85.00
Candy Dish, 7″ sq, orange roses, gray–green ground, scalloped rim	35.00
Celery Dish, hp, florals	35.00
Chocolate Pot, 6″ h, white rose, green tints, gold trim, green mark	75.00
Creamer and Sugar, cov, pink roses, green ground, gold trim, green marks	100.00

Cup and Saucer, 3½″ d, white roses, pale green ground	50.00
Demitasse Pot, cov, Art Deco mold, cream and tan, large poppy flowers	75.00
Dresser Tray, 10¼″ l, multicolored florals, blue shaded to white ground, gold ruffled border	85.00
Hatpin Holder, pastels	85.00
Nappy, 6½″ d, poppy dec, handle	50.00
Nut Set, master bowl, four serving bowls, open white poppies, light green ground	100.00
Pin Tray, 8″ l, orange and white poppies, gray ground, open double handles, blue mark	45.00
Plate	
8″ d, maroon ground, dogwood blossoms dec	25.00
9″ d, gold roses, white leaves	40.00
Relish, 12½″ l, floral dec	60.00
Sugar, cov, peonies, gold trim, pale green shading to brown ground	40.00
Tankard, 11″ h, poppy and berry dec, sgd	185.00
Tray, 15¼″ l, snowbirds dec, open handles	325.00
Trivet, 6¼″ d, white and pink flowers, green leaves, cream shaded to blue ground, gold tracery, blue mark	45.00

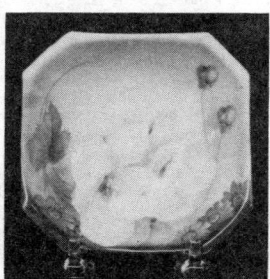

R. S. Poland, berry bowl, white and pale orange flowers, green leaves, small orange–gold border flowers, marked, 4½″ sq, $45.00.

R. S. POLAND

Berry Set, master bowl and six serving bowls, pink and red carnations, red marks	500.00
Box, cov, 3½″ d, pink and white flowers, gray and green luster, gold trim and knob	85.00
Cake Plate, 10″ d, white and pink roses, green, tan, and cream ground, gold trim, open handles	75.00

Candlesticks, pr, 6¼″ h, pink and white flowers, gray and green luster ground, ruffled bases and drip pans 150.00
Creamer, multicolored fuchsia flowers 25.00
Dresser Tray, 12¾″ l, pink and white flowers, green leaves, cream ground, gold rim 115.00
Hair Receiver, cov, violets and lilies of the valley dec 100.00
Hatpin Holder, shaded pink rosebuds, shaded rust ground 85.00
Powder Jar, cov, violets and lilies of the valley dec 100.00
Ring Tree, violets dec, pearlized finish 100.00
Sugar, cov, pink roses, shaded lavender ground, gilt trim 125.00
Vase
  4″ h, 5″ w, multicolored Chinese pheasants, red mark 200.00
  8″ h, gold grapes and leaves, cobalt base, yellow and white roses on tan shaded top, double handles 175.00
  8¾″ h, pink and white roses, cream ground, gold band around top, garlands of gold roses and leaves .. 175.00
  12″ h, peach anemones, white ground, double handles 145.00
Shaving Mug, white florals, gold tracery, steeple mark 75.00
Vase, 12″ h, handles, dark puke and beige flowers 185.00

R. S. Prussia, plate, The Melon Boys, green border, red mark, 8½″ d, $925.00.

R. S. PRUSSIA

Berry Set, Snowballs and Roses, 7 pcs 350.00
Bowl
  6″ d, Carnation mold, roses, ftd, red mark 165.00
  10″ d
    Cattail mold, floral dec 440.00

Fleur–de–lis mold, pink poppies, green ground 135.00
10½″ d
  Grape mold variation 285.00
  Iris mold, pink poppies, yellow shading to dark green ground .. 300.00
11″ d
  Icicle mold, poppy dec 175.00
  Medallion mold, five cupped medallions, tapestry like stippled grounds, profuse florals, center scene of florals reflected in water 325.00
12½″ d, Scalloped mold, swan scene, red mark 400.00
Bread Plate, 13½″ l, gold beading, pink flowers on water, open handles, red mark 135.00
Cake Plate
  10″ d, Carnation mold, pink poppies, pearl border, open handles, red mark 175.00
  12″ d, lilies of the valley dec, satin finish, open handle 250.00
Celery Tray
  13½″ l, Mold 30, Melon Eaters, brown ground 650.00
  14″ l, Mold 252, pink roses, satin finish 175.00
Chocolate Pot, cov, 9″ h, Raspberry mold, swans dec, satin finish 500.00
Creamer and Sugar, cov
  Dogwood Blossoms, pink and white flowers, green tinted ground, gold trim, mold marked #14 .... 90.00
  Mill scene, red marks 300.00
Cup and Saucer, pedestal, floral, red mark 50.00
Hair Receiver, jonquils 155.00
Lemonade Pitcher, 8″ h, pink roses, shaded green to cream ground, red mark 325.00
Mustard Pot, white flowers, soft green ground, orig ladle, satin finish 185.00
Nappy, bud festooned handle, sapphire blue, raised flowers, red steeple mark 85.00
Nut Dish, deep burgundy rim, gold dec, pink roses, light blue flowers, pedestal base, handles, matching underplate 65.00
Pitcher, 10½″ h, tankard, poppies, foliage, and cherries, blown out base, red mark 675.00
Plate
  9″ d, Dice Players, maroon edge, raised gold beads, alternating cream and dark green border with lacy gold flowers, pierced back, marked "R. S." and beehive mark 400.00
  11″ d, light pink roses, beige shading to brown ground, red mark 175.00
Relish, scattered flowers, jewels, red mark 60.00

Sugar Shaker, 4¾" h, roses, luster finish, scalloped base, red mark **225.00**
Vase
4½" h, castle scene **300.00**
6¾" h, lavender violets, red mark .. **175.00**

R. S. SUHL

Bowl, 10" d, sheep herder scene, cottage, red mark **500.00**
Compote, 4½" h, ftd, creamy roses, gold stencil design, green mark **220.00**
Pitcher, 5½" h, red roses, white ground **125.00**
Vase, mill scene, double handles **400.00**

R. S. Tillowitz, stacking teapot, creamer, and sugar, ivory ground, yellow, rust, and blue flowers, gold trim, marked "Royal Silesia," green wreath mark, 7½" d, $85.00.

R. S. TILLOWITZ

Bowl, 10" l, oval, hp, pr of pheasants, blue mark **275.00**
Cheese and Cracker Dish, 8½" d, 2¼" h, open rose and foliage dec, blue mark **50.00**
Marmalade Jar, floral dec, matching underplate **60.00**
Plate, 6" d, lilies of the valley dec **8.00**
Tray, red roses, green leaves, white ground **40.00**
Vase, 7¼" h, owl dec **120.00**

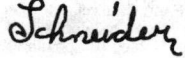

SCHNEIDER GLASS

History: Brothers Ernest and Charles Schneider founded a glassworks at Epiney-sur-Seine, France, in 1913. Charles, the artistic designer, previously had worked for Daum and Galle.

Although Schneider art glass is best known, the firm also made table glass, stained glass, and lighting fixtures. The art glass exhibits simplicity of design; bubbles and streaking often are found in larger pieces. Other wares include cameo-cut and hydrofluoric acid-etched designs.

Schneider signed their pieces with a variety of script and block signatures, "Le Verre Francais," or "Charder." Robert, son of Charles, assumed art direction in 1948. Schneider moved to Loris in 1962.

Vase, globular, fluted, light amber, sgd, 7" d, 7½" h, $125.00.

Charger, 14" d, frosted glass ground, mottled orange overlay, cameo carved stylized fanning foliage, sgd in cameo **3,520.00**
Christmas Tree, 8" h, solid, clear, sgd "Schneider, France" **50.00**
Compote, 10⅜" d, 12½" h, large champagne glass shape, pink opalescent bowl with mottled apple green, mottled cranberry foot and stem, sgd .. **375.00**
Ewer, 12¼" h, ovoid, peaked spout, applied handle, mottled pink body, purple overlay, cameo carved stylized swags, cameo sgd "Charder" and "Le Verre Francais" **1,750.00**
Night Light, 7⅜" h, tangerine ground, red overlay, cameo carved clusters of stylized blossoms and slender curled leaves, sgd "Charder" in cameo, engraved "Le Verre Francais," wrought iron base with three leaf form feet .. **1,450.00**
Vase
10½" h, conical shape, circular cushion foot, translucent blue, applied vertical yellow bands **1,500.00**
11¾" h, spherical body, cylindrical neck with two applied purple handles, mottled burgundy and tomato red, engraved "Schneider" **900.00**
12¼" h, gourd, partially frosted, inter-

nally dec with air bubbles, everted black rim, orange and black organic appliques around shoulder, engraved "Schneider" **15,400.00**

14⅞" h, hexagonal, knopped stem, circular foot, white ground, orange overlay, cameo carved stripes and rectangles, engraved "Charder, Le Verre Francais" **1,760.00**

16½" h, baluster, cushion foot, pink and orange mottled ground, purple shading to lavender ground, cameo carved floral bowers and thorny vines, cameo sgd "Charder," engraved "Le Verre Francais" **1,750.00**

16¾" h, pear shape, everted rim, circular foot, jade green glass with multiple bubble inclusions, applied four vertical crimped glass strips, acid stamped "Schneider" **1,550.00**

23" h, cylinder, ftd, tangerine ground, bright orange shading to brown overlay, cameo carved three striped vertical panels enclosing stylized blossoms, cameo sgd "Charder," engraved "Le Verre Francais" ... **2,420.00**

SCHOENHUT TOYS

History: Albert Schoenhut, son of a toymaker, was born in Germany in 1849. In 1866 he ventured to the United States to work as a repairman of toy pianos for Wanamaker's in Philadelphia, Pennsylvania. Finding the glass sounding bars inadequate, he perfected a toy piano with metal sounding bars. His piano was an instant success, and the A. Schoenhut Company had its beginning.

From that point, toys seemed to flow out of the factory. Each of his six sons entered the business. The business prospered until 1934 when misfortune forced the company into bankruptcy. In 1935 Otto and George Schoenhut contracted to produce the Pinn Family Dolls.

At the same time, the Schoenhut Manufacturing Company was formed by two other Schoenhuts. Both companies operated under a partnership agreement that eventually led to O. Schoenhut, Inc., which continues today.

Some dates of interest: 1872—toy piano invented; 1903—Humpty and Dumpty and Circus patented; 1911–1924—wooden doll production; 1928–1934—composition dolls.

Reference: Richard O'Brien, *Collecting Toys, 5th Edition,* Books Americana, 1990.

Animal
Billy Goat, 9" l	75.00
Donkey, 10" l, laughing	50.00
Elephant, 7" l, tin, 3 pcs	60.00

Gazelle, glass eyes, c1910	500.00
Horse, 10" l, Appaloosa	75.00
Kangaroo, painted eyes, Style II ...	300.00
Leopard, glass eyes	225.00
Poodle, painted eyes	120.00
Rhinoceros, jointed	90.00
Building Toy, Little Village Builder, orig box	75.00

Tiger, circus figure, painted wood, 7½" l, 5¼" h, $175.00.

Circus
Accessory	
Chair	20.00
Platform	15.00
Tent, side show	1,800.00
Horse, jointed, circus rider saddle ..	70.00
Humpty Dumpty Set, performers with glass eyes, accessories, tent with wood base, Humpty Dumpty Circus box top, damaged	600.00
Performer	
Clown, 9" h, wood	30.00
Lion Tamer, wood head	170.00
Ringmaster	75.00
Doll	
11½", blue decal eyes, single stroke brows, closed mouth, jointed body, orig brown wig, redressed in modern clothes, marked "C HE Schoenhut" on head and "Schoenhut Doll/Pat Jan 17th 1911/USA" on body	450.00
14" h, baby, bald head, blue decal eyes, closed mouth, curved limb body, knitted outfit dressed	275.00
19½" h, boy, blue intaglio eyes, closed mouth, orig wig, baseball outfit	1,000.00
Farm Character	
Goat, painted eyes	150.00
Horse, 10", painted eyes	150.00
Milkmaid	75.00
Piano, 19½ x 20 x 10", upright, wood, stool, 18 keys	155.00
Roly Poly, 5" h, papier mache, chubby man with mustache, painted facial features, molded dunce hat, marked "Schoenhut Rolly Dolly, Patent Dec 15, 1908"	100.00

SCIENTIFIC INSTRUMENTS

History: Chemists, doctors, geologists, navigators, and surveyors used precision instruments as tools of their trade. Such objects are well designed and beautifully crafted. The principal medium is brass. Fancy hardwood cases also are common.

References: Crystal Payton, *Scientific Collectibles Identification & Price Guide*, published by author, 1978; Anthony Turner, *Early Scientific Instruments, Europe 1400–1780*, Sotheby's Publications, 1987.

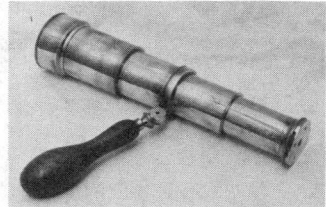

Telescope, hand held, two draw, marked "Plöss in Wien," 9″ l, $275.00.

Astrolabe, mahogany, simulated ivory
  scale, 8″ d 70.00
Barometer
  Aneroid, brass, orig felt lined cased,
    includes thermometer 200.00
  J Lizars, Glasgow and Edinburgh,
    Scotland, cased, 14½ x 9 x 8¾″   800.00
Chronometer, 3″ d, frame holds gimbal,
  Waltham Watch Co 250.00
Circumferenter, marked "Grilite, Paris,
  France," orig case 350.00
Compass, surveyor's, cased
  Charles Helffricht, Philadelphia, PA,
    orig label, walnut case 450.00
  J P Endeen, Truro, England 225.00
Computing Sector, 6½″ l, brass, sgd
  "Buterfield/A Paris," 18th C 450.00
Depth Sounding Instrument, orig box,
  marked "Bassnett's Patent Sounder,"
  19th C 200.00
Microscope
  Binocular, R & J Beck, marked "London and Philadelphia No 11665,"
    19th C 1,000.00
  Monocular
    E Leitz Wetzlar, brass, three turret
      objective, labeled case, marked
      "E Leitz Wetzlar/No 38643/Filiete
      New York," 19th C 300.00
    J B Dancer, Manchester, England,
      brass, iron base, orig case and
      accessories, 19th C 500.00

Octant
  15⅝″ l, brass radial arm, ivory scale
    with engraved anchor, ivory nameplate sgd "Brown & Bristol,"
    stepped case with "Robert King,
    New York" label, 18th C 500.00
  20″ l, ebony, brass mounted radial
    arm, engraved signature, Sterrop,
    London 1,600.00
Quadrant, ebony and brass, incised
  holly wood scale, whale ivory nameplate 1,100.00
Reflecting Circle, brass, sgd "Schwartz
  dil Lencir a Paris," 19th C 1,600.00
Sextant
  3″ d, inlaid silver scales, cased,
    Troughton & Simms, London, 19th
    C 450.00
  10½″ l, brass, double frame, sgd
    "Berge, London, late Ramsden,"
    serial No 1432 . . . .   900.00
Telescope, library, brass
  Charles Chevalier, spotting scope . .   1,400.00
  Ramsden, c1790 . . . .   1,900.00

SCRIMSHAW

History: Norman Flayderman defined scrimshaw as "the art of carving or otherwise fashioning useful or decorative articles as practiced primarily by whalemen, sailors, or others associated with nautical pursuits." Many collectors expand this to include the work of Eskimos and War of 1812 French POWs.

Collecting scrimshaw was popularized during the presidency of John F. Kennedy.

References: E. Norman Flayderman, *Scrimshaw, Scrimshanders, Whales And Whalemen*, N. Flayderman & Co., 1972, out-of-print; Richard C. Malley, *Graven By The Fishermen Themselves*, Mystic Seaport Museum, Inc., 1983.

Periodical: *Whalebone*, P. O. Box 2834, Fairfax, VA 22031.

Museums: Cold Spring Harbor Museum, Long Island, N.Y.; Kendall Whaling Museum, Sharon, Mass.; Mystic Seaport Museum, Mystic, Conn.; National Maritime Museum, San Francisco, Calif.; Old Dartmouth Historical Society, New Bedford, Mass.; Whaling Museum, Nantucket, Mass.

Reproduction Alert: The biggest problem in the field is fakes. A very hot needle will penetrate the common plastics used in reproductions. Ivory will not generate static electricity when rubbed, plastic will. Patina is not a good indicator; it has been faked with tea, tobacco juice, burying in raw rabbit hide, and other ingenious ways. Usually an old design will not be of consistent depth of cut as the ship rocked and tools dulled; however, skilled forgers have even copied this.

Bodkin, 5⅝" l, open carved handle with
baleen inlays, 19th C **225.00**

Cane

33" l, whalebone shaft, paneled whale
ivory knob, 19th C **175.00**

34" l, lady's, tapered rope carved
whalebone shaft, turk's head knot
whale ivory handle, 19th C **900.00**

35" l, tapered whale bone shaft,
carved whale ivory clenched hand
and cuff knob, 19th C **700.00**

36¾" l, shark vertebrae, horn handle,
19th C **250.00**

Clock, miniature, 18¼" h, walnut case,
whale ivory heart, star, and diamond
inlays, three fitted shelves int., brass
engraved dial, 19th C **800.00**

Corset Busk

12½" l, engraved panel portraits of
various people, 19th C **2,700.00**

14" l, engraved in color, Gabriel angel,
sunset, pigeon carrying message,
urn of flowers, and US emblem with
pair of cornucopias, 19th C **600.00**

Cribbage Board, 19¼" l, walrus tusk,
engraved Eskimo life scenes on
ends, reverse with two walrus carv-
ings, c1900 . . . . **300.00**

Dipper, 7½" l, hook shaped whalebone
handle, incised "H," coconut shell
bowl, 19th C **425.00**

Ditty Box, 6" d, baleen, cutout geometric
designs, animal and bird figures, sgd
"Nancy Cummins," dated March 14,
1819, carved "NC" on pine cover . . **400.00**

Drill, hand, 3⅜" l, whalebone handle,
19th C **50.00**

Jagging Wheel

6" l, whale ivory, 19th C **650.00**

8¼" l, unicorn shape, 19th C **450.00**

Handle, 4¾" l, whale ivory sections alternating with metal rings, 19th C . . **60.00**

Knife Box

14" l, crotch grain mahogany, whalebone, baleen, and wood inlays, burl
wood banding around foot, whale-
bone banded handle, 19th C **2,250.00**

15" l, walnut, whalebone moldings,
whalebone flatware inlays on dou-
ble lid **1,250.00**

Model, 19" l, whaleboat, whalebone,
planked hull, raised sails, mounted on
cradle, sgd on whale figure "Luz" . . **1,200.00**

Nutcracker, 6¾" l, black man in shirt and
jacket, jaw holds and cracks nut, 19th
C **800.00**

Plane

9¼" l, semicircular, walrus ivory parts,
19th C **125.00**

13½" l, flat, whalebone parts, 19th C **130.00**

Puzzle, whale ivory, jeweler's loupe
form, missing locking device, 19th C **130.00**

Rolling Pin, 14½" l, wood, two whalebone separators, 19th C **300.00**

Sewing Box, 10⅛ x 5¾ x 10½", abalone
shell, whalebone inlays, two horn outlined drawers, mounted swift on top,
19th C **1,250.00**

Sewing Stand, 10¼ x 9¼ x 11½", inlaid
wood with geometric designs, turned
standard, mounted box with blue velvet pincushion, holds up to 32 spools
around sides, whalebone columns on
each corner, sq base with turned
whalebone feet and one drawer with
whalebone knob, 19th C **350.00**

Shaving Stand, 9 x 3¾ x 9", whalebone
gallery and ornamentation, one
drawer, mirror, 19th C **550.00**

Swift, 19" h, 19th C **1,300.00**

**Tooth, sperm whale, sailor with faded
red British flag, schooner Phoebe, 3¼"
h, $200.00.**

Whale's Tooth

3⅞", pr, engraved in color, one ballerina figure, other seated Liberty **500.00**

6¾" l, engraved in color, Naval battle
on one side, whale ship on other **350.00**

8½" l, engraved, anchored American
warship, fort flying American flag,
and lighthouse, 19th C **2,750.00**

SEBASTIAN MINIATURES

History: Sebastians are hand-painted, lightly
glazed figurines of characters from literature and
history. They range in size from 3 to 4 inches.

Each figurine is made in limited numbers. Other series include children and scenes from family life.

Prescott W. Baston, the originator and designer of Sebastian figures, began production in 1938 in Marblehead, Massachusetts. Sebastian Studios are located in Hudson, Massachusetts. Prescott Baston died on May 25, 1984.

Each year a Sebastian Auction is held in Boxborough, Massachusetts, at the Sebastian Collector's Society meeting. Prices are determined from this source plus the work of the Sebastian Exchange Board, which develops a price list that is the standard reference for the field.

Reference: Dr. Glenn S. Johnson, *The Sebastian Miniature Collection & A Guide To Identifying, Understanding, and Enjoying Sebastian Miniatures,* Lance Corp., 1982.

Collectors' Club: Sebastian Collector's Society, 321 Central Street, Hudson, MA 01749. *Sebastian Miniature Collectors Society News* (quarterly) and *The Sebastian Exchange.*

Priscilla, woman sitting at spinning wheel, $200.00.

Aunt Betzy Trotwood, Marblehead label	50.00
Benjamin Franklin Printing Press	60.00
Cleopatra, version I, 1950–62	200.00
Colonial Kitchen	35.00
Colonial Lacemaker, blue label	25.00
Daniel Boone, 1940–45	140.00
Gathering Tulips	125.00
George Washington, cannon, sgd, 1947	80.00
In The Candy Store, (Necco Candy), 1947	160.00

James Monroe and Elizabeth Monroe, Marblehead mark, pr	200.00
John and Priscilla Alden, green label	30.00
John Smith and Pocahontas, orig Marblehead mark, pr	200.00
Lion, c1947	25.00
Little Mother	50.00
Mr. Beacon Hill	60.00
Parade Rest, green label	25.00
Pilgrims, Marblehead label, MIB	65.00
Santa Claus, 1980	80.00
Sidewalk Days, pr, MIB	120.00
Stagecoach	60.00
Uncle Sam, green label	40.00
Victorian Couple, Marblehead label ..	50.00

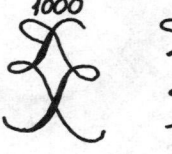 

SEVRES

History: The principal patron of the French porcelain industry in early 18th-century France was Jeanne Antonette Poisson, Marquise de Pompadour. She supported the Vincennes factory of Gilles and Robert Dubois and their successors in its attempt to make soft paste porcelain in the 1740s. In 1753 she moved the porcelain operations to Sevres near her home, Chateau de Bellevue.

The Sevres soft paste formula used sand from Fontainbleau, salt and saltpeter, soda of alicante, powdered alabaster, clay, and soap. Louis XV allowed the firm to use the "double Ls." Many famous colors were developed, including a cobalt blue. The great scenic designs on the ware were painted by such famous decorators as Watteau, La Tour, and Boucher. In the 18th century, Sevres porcelain was the world's foremost diplomatic gift.

In 1769 kaolin was discovered in France, and a hard paste formula developed. The baroque gave way to rococo, a style favored by Jeanne du Barry, Louis XV's next mistress. Louis XVI took little interest in Sevres. Many factories began to turn out counterfeit copies. In 1876 the factory was moved to St. Cloud and was eventually nationalized.

Reference: Susan and Al Bagdade, *Warman's English & Continental Pottery & Porcelain, 1st Edition,* Warman Publishing Co., Inc., 1987.

Reproduction Alert.

Centerpiece, 17½" w, 6" h, 14" d portrait plate set in elaborate brass ftd and handled frame, pink rim, portrait of lady sgd "D Calliana," Serves marks and "Dubarry" on back **1,400.00**

Dessert Service, eighteen dessert plates, two compotes, four cake trays, one cov sauce boat and stand, pink ground, laurel ringed medallion with bust portrait of court figure, floral sprig and scroll border, late 19th C, 25 pcs **7,700.00**

Portrait Plate, multicolored center, cobalt blue border, gold tracery, sgd "Debrie," Chateau Du Tuilleries mark, 9¾" d, $125.00.

Jardiniere
11¼" w, tapering cylindrical shape, shell and scroll handles, multicolored loose bouquets and fruits, gilt scrolling foliate and flowers, turquoise ground, c1763, blue interlaced "L" marks, date letter "K," painter's mark, pr **1,100.00**

12" h, oval, gilt bronze, painted couple with three young women, still life scene on reverse, gilt foliate borders, blue celeste ground with gilt highlights, pierced interlaced strapwork border with flowerheads, two foliate scroll handles, ribbed leaf garland base with beaded bands over oblong base with shaped borders, late 19th C **2,750.00**

Plate, 15½" d, center gilt radiating medallion, five circular medallions on border, painted trophies with inter–red reserves, five lozenge panels enclosing crowned LP initials, arabesque motifs and animals, from Fontainebleau service, c1846, printed "Serves" and "Chateau De F Bleau" marks, date code **1,550.00**

Sugar, cov, fixed stand, 9½" w, oval, interlaced blue and gilt handles, multicolored scattered loose bouquets, blue line and gilt dash borders, gilt dentil rims, palm foliage molded stand, c1769, blue interlaced "L's," date letter Q and painter's mark . . . **825.00**

Urn
22½" h, gilt bronze, drum form body, two panels of lovers and landscape scene within gilt borders, blue celeste reserve ground, waisted cylindrical neck with gilt foliate scrollwork dec embellished with red jewels and white enamel, scrolling handles cast with foliate forms, applied laurel garlands and Cacchus mask terminals at neck, sq shape base with laurel wreath and paneled sides, late 19th C, pr . . . **3,300.00**

28" h, gilt bronze, painted oval panel of Duchess of Devonshire within gilt border, white ground reserve with enameled colors with floral garlands and sprays, gilt scrolling ribbons and festoons, shaped sq base, domed cov mounted with pineapple knop, inscribed blue pseudo crossed L's mark, black title, c1900 . . . . **4, 675.00**

28½" h, ovoid body, gilt with silver highlights crown and shield embellished with fleur–de–lis, laurel garlands, and palms dec, interlaced foliate scrolls reverse, bleu–du–roi ground, all–over gilt fleur–de–lis, applied ram's head handles, acanthus bud knop cov, shaped sq base, inscribed "Sevres, 1786" in gilt overglaze, late 19th C, pr **4,675.00**

37½" h, ovoid body, couple and landscape scene with classical buildings and monuments, elaborate scrollwork border enriched with diapering, entwined sprigs, and floral garlands, bleu–du–roi reserve ground, riverscape and ruins on reverse, mounted winged handles, domed cov with leafy berry knops, swelling cylindrical base with trophies within husk wreathes dec, coved rect base with bracket feet, sgd "L Bertren," cov marked with crossed feathers and CD in blue overglaze, c1900 . . . . **7,700.00**

Vase
19½" h, cov, oval landscape and maiden reserves, cobalt blue and gold field, ormolu handles, base, finial on cov, sgd "Rolli," 19th C, pr **3,000.00**

23½" h, cupids, flower, and mandolin dec, two handles with maiden and garland, Collet, 19th C **1,500.00**

SEWING ITEMS

History: As late as 50 years ago, a wide variety of sewing items were found in almost every home in America. Women of every economic and social status were skilled in sewing and dressmaking. Even the most elegant ladies practiced the art of embroidery with the aid of jeweled gold and silver thimbles. Sewing birds, an interesting convenience item, were used to hold cloth (in the bird's beak) while sewing. Made of iron or brass, they could be attached to table or shelf with a screw-type fixture. Later models featured a pincushion.

References: Joyce Clement, *The Official Price Guide To Sewing Collectibles,* House of Collectibles, 1987; Victor Houart, *Sewing Accessories: An Illustrated History,* Souvenir Press (London), 1984; Gay Ann Rogers, *American Silver Thimbles,* Haggerston Press, 1989; Gay Ann Rogers, *An Illustrated History of Needlework Tools,* John Murray (London), 1983; Estelle Zalkin, *Zalkin's Handbook Of Thimbles & Sewing Implements, First Edition,* Warman Publishing Co., 1988.

Collectors' Club: Thimble Collectors International, P. O. Box 2311, Des Moines, IA 50310.

Periodical: *Thimbletter,* 93 Walnut Hill Road, Highlands, MA 02161.

Museums: Fabric Hall, Historic Deerfield, Deerfield, Mass.; Museum of American History, Smithsonian Institution, Washington, D.C.; Shelburne Museum, Shelburne, Vt.

Additional Listings: See *Warman's Americana & Collectibles* for more examples.

Tape measure, Pug, brass relief, glass eyes, base metal container, 1³⁄₁₆″ d, $50.00.

Bodkin, SS, emb Greek Key type design	40.00
Book, sampler, child's, 18 pgs, dated 1901	150.00
Box	
6½″ h, hardwood, mahogany veneer, ivory eyelets	65.00
9⅞″ h, walnut and pine, dark finish, tambour door, spool rack int., base with drawer	80.00
14¼″ l, inlaid, worn inscription on lid, tray int.	175.00
15 x 9½″, mahogany, rosewood veneer, geometric inlay, turned detail, one large dovetailed drawer, three small glued drawers, quilted satin drawer linings	225.00
Catalog	
Montgomery Ward, Sewing Machines, 1910, 44 pgs	35.00
Structo Weaving Looms, c1920, 42 pgs	25.00
Chatelaine, SS, ring top, chains connect to note pad, thimble, thimble case, and buttonhook, English	500.00
Darner, ebony, emb floral handle marked "Sterling"	40.00
Dress Form, black velvet	35.00
Embroidery Stamp, 1½ x 2 x 4″, wood, hand carved semi-circles, 18th C, American	130.00
Hem Gauge, ornate bands, dated "Oct 2, '94"	50.00
Needle Case, 4″ l, hand covered wood plug, knob finial	25.00
Pin Cushion	
2⅜″ l, heart shape, rosewood, replaced red velvet insert	35.00
4½″ h, cast iron base, red wood covering	20.00
7½″ l, pewter, lady's shoe	20.00
Scissors, silver	
Coin, Victorian, hand wrought, emb grapes and vine handles, hallmarked "E L"	60.00
Sterling, cupids	45.00
Seam Rubber, 6¾″ l, whalebone, mid 19th C	500.00
Sewing Basket, 10″ d, 9½″ h, divided, polychrome painted floral dec, cloth lining, lid, Chinese	55.00
Sewing Bird	
4″ h, cast and wrought iron, heart shape thumb screw	150.00
4¼″ h, iron, heart shape thumb screw	135.00
5¼″ h, brass, pin cushion, table clamp	55.00
Dated "Feb 15, 1853" twice	130.00
Sewing Box, 11¼″ l, inlaid, wallpaper and cloth lined fitted int., lift out tray, made by Sabbeth Day Lake Shakers	115.00
Table Clamp, 3½″ l, sewing aide, cast bronze	35.00
Tape Measure	
Advertising	
H. H. Babcock Co. Carriage & Auto Builders, Watertown, NY, pretty woman on front	25.00
Silks From Loom To You, Watertown NY, Syracuse, NY	20.00
Fish, celluloid	30.00
Hat shape, brass	145.00
Pig in red shoe, celluloid	35.00

Tatting Shuttle, SS, marked "1912" .. **65.00**
Thimble Holder, 3" l, Victorian, ivory, acorn shape, all—over sinuous leaf carving **85.00**
Thread Caddy, 9½" h, turned hardwood, ebonized trim, flanged base **90.00**

SHAKER

History: The Shakers, so named because of a dance used in worship, are one of the oldest communal organizations in the United States. This religious group was founded by Mother Ann Lee, who emigrated from England and established the first Shaker community near Albany, New York, in 1784. The Shakers reached their peak in 1850 with 6,000 members.

Shakers lived celibate and self-sufficient lives. Their philosophy stressed cleanliness, order, simplicity, and economy. Highly inventive and motivated, the Shakers created many utilitarian household forms and objects. Their furniture reflected a striving for quality and purity in design.

In the early 19th century, the Shakers produced many items for commercial purposes. Chairmaking and the packaged herb and seed business thrived. In every endeavor and enterprise, the members followed Mother Ann's advice: "Put your hands to work and give your heart to God."

References: Charles R. Muller and Timothy D. Rieman, *The Shaker Chair,* The Canal Press, 1984; Don and Carol Raycraft, *Shaker, A Collector's Source Book II,* Wallace—Homestead, 1985; June Sprigg and David Larkin, *Shaker Life, Work, and Art,* Stewart, Tabori & Chang, 1987.

Periodical: *The Shaker Messenger,* P.O. Box 45, Holland, MI 49423.

Basket
  6½ x 3¼", berry, wood, Sabbathday Lake Community **150.00**
  10" l, faded pink ribbon **35.00**
Bonnet Mold, poplar, woven, white glaze ext., paper label "8" **135.00**
Box, cov, 11½" l, 4¼" h, five tapering fingers, painted yellow **7,500.00**
Brush, 14", dusting, worn gray paint .. **75.00**
Bucket, 9½ x 10", lid, four laps, copper tacks, wood pins and handle **200.00**
Cheese Drainer, 18 x 6", tin, pierced sides and bottom **325.00**
Coffeepot, 11" h, tin, handle at right angle, Sabbathday Lake **250.00**
Cradle Cover, 15¼ x 34¾", rect, poplar frame, dovetailed corners, inside chamfer, three arched bentwood hoops **25.00**
Cupboard, hanging, 6½" d, 29" w, 62½" h, pine, brown patina, paneled door, orig brass thumb latch, porcelain knob, pigeon hole int. **110.00**

Butter Churn, strap hinges, old red paint, $365.00.

Furniture
Bench, 72" l, meetinghouse, pine, red stain, Canterbury **850.00**
Candlestand, New Lebanon, NY, mid 19th C, cherry, orig finish, 19" l, 18¼" w, 26" h **14,000.00**
Chair
  Arm, No. 7, four shaped vertical slats form tapered backrest, cylindrical stiles with acorn finials, curved armrests, flattened mushroom handrests, trapezoidal woven replaced seat, cylindrical legs joined by box stretcher, stamped mark, Mount Lebanon, 19th C, 41" h **1,100.00**
  Side, spindle back, splint seat, mellow finish, reduced in height ... **50.00**
Rocker
  No. 1, child's, orig dark surface, old red and olive tape seat, trademark "Shakers No 1 Mt. Lebanon, NY" imprinted on reverse of slat, 1880–1920, 29¾" h **1,500.00**
  No. 3, replaced seat, orig finish, New Lebanon, NY **500.00**
  No. 7, birch, four shaped vertical slats form tapered backrest, cylindrical stiles with acorn finials, curved armrests, flattened mushroom handrests, trapezoidal woven replaced seat, cylindrical

legs joined by box stretcher,
rockers, stamped mark, Mount
Lebanon, 19th C, 42" h **1,100.00**
Settee, 58" l, 38" h, birch and pine,
nineteen spindles, varnished, Enfield **5,000.00**
Hanger, 13" l, wood, carved design, paper printed label "EJ" **150.00**
Knife Tray, two section, tiger stripe maple **140.00**
Mail Box, 20 x 24 x 11", pine natural
finish, hinged lid, Enfield **500.00**
Medicine Bottle, clear glass, yellow label "Shaker's Extract of Poke Root,
Mt Lebanon, NY" **60.00**
Rack, pegboard, pine and maple, holds
12 x 16¾" mirror, hardwood framed,
orig red satin finish **435.00**
Seed Box, 38¼" l, curly maple, two dividers, hinged lid, old finish, dovetailed case, screw construction **750.00**
Seeder, 93" l, wood and sheet metal,
handle **75.00**
Sewing Basket, curved handles, cur-
lique trim, pocket with strawberry .. **190.00**
Sewing Box, 7" l, 3" h, grain painted,
orig mounted pin cushion, c1835 ... **750.00**
Spice Chest, 7 x 13 x 6", poplar, nine
drawers, walnut pulls, natural finish **300.00**

SHAVING MUGS

History: Shaving mugs hold the soap, brush,
and hot water used to prepare a beard for shaving.
They come in a variety of materials including tin,
silver, glass, and pottery. One style is the scuttle,
so called because of its "coal scuttle" shape, with
separate compartments for water and soap.

Shaving mugs were popular between 1880 and
1925, the period of the great immigration to the
United States. At first barber shops used a common mug for all customers. This led to an epidemic
of a type of eczema, known as barber itch.

Laws were passed requiring each individual to
have his own mug. Initially names and numbers
were used. This did not work well for those who
could not read. The occupational mug developed
because illiterate workers could identify a picture
of their trade or an emblem of its tools. Fraternal
emblems also were used and were the most popular of the decorative forms. Immigrants especially
liked the heraldry of the fraternal emblems since
it reminded them of what they knew in Europe.

European porcelain blanks were decorated by
American barber supply houses. Prices ranged
from fifty cents for a gold name mug to two dollars
and fifty cents for an elaborate occupational design. Most of the art work was done by German
artists who had emigrated to America.

The invention of the safety razor by King C.

Gillette that was issued to three and one-half million servicemen during World War I brought an end
to the shaving mug era.

References: Susan and Al Bagdade, *Warman's
English & Continental Pottery & Porcelain, 1st Edi-
tion,* Warman Publishing Co., Inc., 1987; Phillip L.
Krumholz, *Value Guide For Barberiana & Shaving
Collectibles,* published by author, 1988; Robert
Blake Powell, *Occupational & Fraternal Shaving
Mugs of The United States,* published by author,
1978.

Collectors' Club: National Shaving Mug Collectors Association, 818 South Knight Avenue,
Park Ridge, IL 60068.

Advisor: Edward W. Leach.

Fraternal, B. P. O. E., elk, gold trim,
marked "T & V Limoges/France,"
$175.00.

BARBER SHOP: FRATERNAL

Ancient Order United Workmen, anchor
shield, A.O.U.W. initials **250.00**
Grand Army of the Republic, American
spread eagle over cannon and American flag above star shape medal in
center, pink and blue floral design
with gold highlights on sides, marked
"D & Co France" **150.00**
Knights of Columbus, blue wrap, gold
trim, black "F.D. Conner" with gold
highlighting, red, white, and blue symbol with gold highlights, gold raised
enamel flowers, green stamped "Germany" on bottom **40.00**
Knights of Pythias, F.C.B. on shield, suit
of armor, crossed halberds **125.00**
Oddfellows, "H.S. Evans" and three
loops across center with "F.L.T" in
gold, marked "Royal China International" on bottom **45.00**
United Mine Workers Of America, flowers around rim, bottom marked "C.T.
Germany" **50.00**
Woodman of the World, blue maple leaf,
stump, axe, bird, and logging tools **150.00**

BARBER SHOP: OCCUPATIONAL

Baker, putting bread in oven, dough
  box, work bench 375.00
Baseball Player, player batting, catcher,
  2 men in field 750.00
Blacksmith, horseshoe, flowers, and
  leaves, blue ribbon, bottom marked
  "MEW Barber Supply Utica, NY, V&D
  Austria" 200.00
Brewery, T. Helb Brewery, buildings,
  horse, and wagon 700.00
Butcher, skinning steer, other steer
  hanging on rack 450.00
Carpenter, sawing board, house frame,
  pile of lumber 425.00
Cyclist, man riding bike on dirt road,
  wearing blue outfit, trees, grass,
  fence, and house 525.00
Delivery Wagon, two horses pulling wa-
  gon full of watermelons, driver with
  whip, tan ground, gold scroll each
  side, "1256 H" on bottom 275.00
Doctor, Dr. E.L. Woodford, gold dec, top
  and bottom bands, dane across center, marked "Limoges, France, 772"   60.00
Electrician, electric generator 275.00
Farmer, 2 horses pulling plow, farm
  house 250.00
Fireman, helmet, axes, ladder, and noz-
  zles 400.00
Hardware Clerk, clerk showing cus-
  tomer saw, barrels, shelves, mer-
  chandise 450.00
Hatmaker, derby, gold trim 275.00
Moving and Hauling, two brown horses,
  pulling wagon, gold rim, dated 1924,
  marked "Royal China International"   235.00
Musician, piano player, upright piano   350.00
Painter, on scaffold, painting building   500.00
Pharmacist, yellow mortar and pestle,
  black highlighting, gold floral design
  on each side, name "W. F. Dodson,"
  gold "4017" on bottom 175.00
Photographer, taking picture of woman
  in chair 1,575.00
Policeman, blue uniform, badge, and
  nightstick 675.00
Restaurant, restaurant int., waiter and
  customers, yellow floor and ceiling,
  blue background hanging light fix-
  tures, wall pictures 820.00
Tinsmith, gray tools with orange,
  marked "7168, 303, TK, 50, Vienna
  Austria" on bottom 190.00

BARBER SHOP: OTHER

American Eagle, perched on American
  shield clutching arrows, gold trimmed
  banner in beak with name in black,

hp, dark blue wrap, white and rouge
  highlights, marked "V.D. Austria" . . .   125.00
Hunter, shooting bird, brown and white
  dog, sunset background, marked
  "Koken Barbers' Supply Co St. Louis,
  USA" 165.00
Liberty Bell, "1776" scroll on each side   200.00
Locomotive and coal car dec 50.00
Man in black carriage, wearing derby
  and lap robe, brown trotting horse,
  green stamped "KPM Germany" on
  bottom 80.00
Pennsylvania, Seal of, "Virtue, Liberty
  & Independence" 190.00
Personalized
  Barr, Clyde, winter scene, raised
    enamel highlights, marked "Koken
    St. Louis, The World's Our Field,
    and W.G. & Co, Limoges France"   65.00
  Schmidt, H.C., hp, flowering lily
    scene, top and bottom gold bands,
    marked "Vienna, Austria" and red
    "2857" on bottom 30.00
Seashore scene, gold highlighted pyr-
  amid shape scene with two blue
  bands on sides, purple mountain
  background, c1885 . . . .   50.00
Shield, compass, arm with hammer, and
  square, emb scroll on both sides . . .   85.00

Scuttle, multicolored florals, white
ground, $45.00.

SCUTTLES

Eagle holding arrow on flag shield . . .   75.00
Floral Spray 40.00
Gambling, Lucky Spots, shows spread
  of aces, flowers on back 125.00
Horses in field 50.00

SHAWNEE POTTERY

History: The Shawnee Pottery Co. was founded
in 1937 in Zanesville, Ohio. The company acquired
a 650,000 square foot plant that formerly housed
the American Encaustic Tiling Company and pro-

duced there as many as 100,000 pieces of pottery per day until 1961, when the plant closed.

Shawnee limited its chief production to kitchenware, decorative art pottery, and dinnerware. Distribution was primarily through jobbers and chain stores.

Shawnee can be marked "Shawnee," "Shawnee U.S.A.," "USA #—," "Kenwood," or with character names, e.g., "Pat. Smiley," "Pat. Winnie," etc.

Reference: Mark Supnick, *Collecting Shawnee Pottery: A Pictorial Reference And Price Guide*, L-W Book Sales, 1989.

Advisor: Mark Supnick.

Planter, Wishing Well, green, marked "710," 8½ x 5¼", $20.00.

Ashtray, squirrel, marked "USA"	10.00
Candle Holder, 6½" h, hand dec gold trim, pr	12.00
Casserole, cov, Corn King	50.00
Cookie Jar	
Corn King, No 66	65.00
Dutch Girl, marked "USA"	50.00
Mugsy	130.00
Smiley Pig, gold trim, flower decal, flowers on bib, marked "USA"	130.00
Creamer	
Corn King, No 70	18.00
Puss 'n Boots	15.00
Cup and Saucer, corn, cup marked "90," saucer marked "91"	30.00
Darning Egg, figure	20.00
Mixing Bowl, Corn King, 6" d	25.00
Pitcher	
Bo Peep	38.00
Charlicleer, gold, red glaze, decal	75.00
Planter	
Birdhouse	8.00
Elf on shoe	8.00
Girl playing mandolin	12.00
Windmill, gold trim, marked "Shawnee 715"	22.00
Platter, 12", corn, marked "Shawnee 96"	20.00
Relish Tray, Corn King, marked "Shawnee 79"	15.00

Salt and Pepper Shakers, pr	
Corn King	25.00
Mugsy	30.00
Smiley Pig, red collar	20.00
Sugar, cov, corn pattern, white and green glaze	20.00
Teapot	
Granny Anne, gold dec	165.00
Rose	20.00
Tom the Piper's son	40.00
Vase	
Bow Knot, marked "USA 819"	12.00
Cornucopia, 5", green	10.00
Fan, 4¼" h, yellow and green, blue flower, marked "USA"	8.00
Hand, marked "USA"	18.00
Vegetable Dish, 9", corn, marked "Shawnee 95"	18.00

SILHOUETTES

History: Silhouettes (shades) are shadow profiles produced by hollow cutting, mechanical tracing, or painting. They were popular in the 18th and 19th centuries.

The name came from Etienne de Silhouette, a French Minister of Finance, who tended to be tight with money and cut "shades" as a pastime. In America the Peale family was one of the leading silhouette makers. An impressed stamp marked "PEALE" or "Peale Museum" identifies their work.

Silhouette portraiture lost popularity with the introduction of daguerreotype prior to the Civil War. In the 1920s and 1930s a brief revival occurred when tourists to Atlantic City and Paris had their profiles cut as souvenirs.

Reference: Blume J. Rifken, *Silhouettes in America, 1790–1840, A Collectors' Guide,* Paradigm Press, 1987.

Couple	
6½" h, 6" w, mother and daughter, painted, sgd "Adolphe," worn printed label "Mons Adolphe, Brighton," daughter identified as "S A Whitmore 1840 at 11 years old," orig frames, pr	400.00
14¼" h, 12¼" w, man and woman, Edwards, orig labels "Mr. James Bruce Wallace" and "Mrs. Ths. Wharton, Birmingham, Coventry Road," dated 1838, oval pine frames, pr	350.00
Girl	
4⅞" h, 4⅛" w, hollow cut, young girl, pencil detail, emb battered brass frame, frame backing marked "Aliranda Hansing 1820"	425.00
11⅜" h, 9¼" w, standing, holding book, simple gilded detail, soiled	

Woman, hollow cut, sgd "Elizabeth Baker, Boston, 1824," 6 x 5", $200.00.

and stained background, old gilt frame	250.00
Gentlemen	
2¾" d, miniature, hollow cut, round emb brass frame, labeled "K... Bowen 1810"	300.00
4¾" h, 3¾" w	
Elderly, bearded, eglomise, flaked black ground, tarnished emb brass frame	200.00
Young man, cut, sgd diagonally under bust and on back, "J. T. Nov 1844," old reeded black frame	200.00
5¼" h, 4⅞" w, hollow cut, labeled "Jas B Ardery," modern frame, family lineage on back	125.00
5⅜" h, 4⅝" w, eglomise, wooden frame, gilded liner	275.00
5⅞" h, 4⅞" w, reverse painted on convex glass, labeled "Striking likenesses in profile shade by H Gibbs," orig black lacquered frame with gilded liner	125.00
8¼" h, 6⅛" w, hollow cut, young man in sailor suit, hair in queue, in detail, imp "Williams" (Henry Williams, Boston 1787–1830), ink inscription "Thomas Scott, the Frigate Niagara 1813," silver gilt frame	975.00
14⅞" h, 12⅜" w, printed textile, DeWitt Clinton, matted and framed	65.00
Group, 16" h, 19¼" w, seven full figure cut outs, watercolor int. background, sgd "Sam'l Brooks family by John Sartain 1864, New York," old gilt frame	1,400.00
Scene, stable, pencil sketch, cut and applied figures, two gentlemen viewing pr of gray hounds held by groom, 17 x 21½", framed, English, 19th C	400.00

Women	
4⅞" h, 4⅛" w, young, hollow cut, pencil and ink detail, emb brass frame	425.00
5⅝" h, 4¾" w, wearing bonnet, hollow cut, worn gilt frame	185.00
11⅝" h, 9⅝" w, young woman, ink wash garden ground, full length, marked "Abigail Good 1846," modern frame	250.00
12" h, 9¾" w, full length, woman with umbrella, sgd "Aug Edouart fecit, 1840," backing cut out showing label "Miss Francis E. Ferrell of Natchez at Saratoga Springs Aug 25, 1840," old grained frame, gilded liner	1,000.00

SILVER

History: The natural beauty of silver lends itself to the designs of artists and craftsmen. It has been mined and worked into an endless variety of useful and decorative items. Pure silver is too soft to be fashioned into strong, durable, and serviceable utensils. Therefore, a way was found to give silver the required degree of hardness by adding alloys of copper and nickel.

Silversmithing in America goes back to the early 17th century in Boston and New York. It began in the early 18th century in Philadelphia. Boston was influenced by the English styles, New York by the Dutch.

References: Frederick Bradbury, *Bradbury's Book of Hallmarks*, J. W. Northend, Ltd, 1987; Louise Bilden, *Marks Of American Silversmiths In the Ineson-Bissell Collection*, Univ. of Virginia Press, 1980; Rachael Feild, *Macdonald Guide To Buying Antique Silver and Sheffield Plate*, Macdonald & Co., 1988; Donald L. Fennimore, *Silver & Pewter*, Alfred A. Knopf *Knopf Collector's Guides To American Antiques*, 1984; *Jewelers' Circular Keystone Sterling Flatware Pattern Index, 2nd Edition*, Chilton Book Company, 1989; Dorothy T. Rainwater, *Encyclopedia of American Silver Manufacturers, 3rd Edition*, Schiffer Publishing Ltd., 1986; Dorothy T. and H. Ivan Rainwater, *American Silverplate*, Schiffer Publishing, Ltd., 1988; Jeri Schwartz, *The Official Identification And Price Guide To Silver and Silver-Plate, Sixth Edition*, House of Collectibles, 1989; Peter Waldon, *The Price Guide To Antique Silver, 2nd Edition*, Antique Collectors' Club, 1982 (price revision list 1988); Seymour B. Wyler, *The Book Of Old Silver, English, American, Foreign*, Crown Publishers, Inc., 1937 (available in reprint).

Periodicals: *Silver*, P. O. Box 1243, Whittier, CA 90609; *Silver Collector*, 170 Fifth Avenue, 12th Floor, New York, NY 10010.

Additional Listing: See Silver Flatware in *Warman's Americana & Collectibles* for more examples in this area.

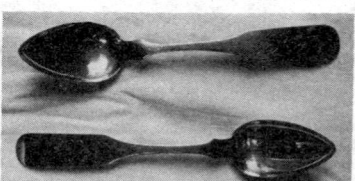

American, Coin, teaspoons, J. M. Mitksch, Bethlehem, PA, two from set of six, set $250.00.

AMERICAN, 1790–1840
Mostly Coin

Coin silver is slightly less pure than sterling silver. Coin silver has 900 parts silver to 100 parts alloy. Sterling silver has 925 parts silver. American silversmiths followed the coin standards. Coin silver also is called Pure Coin, Dollar, Standard, or Premium.

Aiken, George, Baltimore, MD, 1790–1810
  Sugar Urn, 10¼" h, urn shape, tapering cylindrical lid, urn shaped finial, beaded borders, spreading circular foot, sq base, one side with engraved script initials, marked twice on base, 14 oz **2,650.00**
  Teapot, 6¾" h, oval, domed lid, urn shaped finial, S scrolled spout, borders on lid and body, engraved shield in wreath, script monogram, marked on base, 29 oz, 10 dwt . . **1,650.00**
Anthony, Joseph, Jr, Phila, PA, 1784–1814, beaker, 1⅝" h, tapering cylindrical, double incised rim band, engraved script initials, marked twice on base, 2 oz, pr **3,525.00**
Ball, Wm, Phila, PA, c1760, sauceboat, 4⅛" h, 7½" l, oval, scalloped rim, scroll handle, acanthus grip, three scroll legs, shell dec, scalloped pad feet, marked twice on base, 11 oz . . **9,900.00**
Barnet, Archibald, Baltimore, MD, c1790, teapot, 6½" h, oval, domed lid, acorn finial, molded shoulder, pierced gallery, straight spout, wood C scroll handle, applied footrim, engraved script initial "F", marked four times on base, 29 oz, 10 dwt **4,500.00**
Boehme, Charles L, Baltimore, MD, 1799–1812
  Cream Jug and Sugar Urn, 7" helmet shaped creamer, beaded borders, spreading cylindrical foot, sq base, script mark on base, 10½" h sugar urn, tapering cylindrical lid, urn shaped finial, beaded borders, spreading cylindrical foot, sq base, engraved script monogram, eagle base mark, 21 oz, 10 dwt, pr **4,500.00**
  Sugar Sifter, 7" l, pierced oval bowl, rounded end handle, engraved script monogram, 2 oz **825.00**
Boelen, Henricus, New York, NY, 1661–91, porringer, 5" d, 7⅝" l, circular bowl, everted rim, pierced handle, marked on base with conjoined "HB" struck over center punch, 7 oz, 10 dwt **3,850.00**
Chaundrons & Rasch, Phila, PA, early 19th C, salver, 8" d, molded border, band of cast anthemia centering plain surface, three tapering legs, leaf dec, stippled ground, 11.2 oz **600.00**
Cooney, John, Boston, MA, c1700–1720, pepper box, 2½" h, cylindrical, low domed pierced lid, double molded rim, double scrolled and beaded handle, bottom engraved with contemporary initials, marked on side and base, repair to handle joins, 2 oz, 10 dwt **9,350.00**
Cowell, Wm, Boston, MA, 1740–60, cann, 5⅜" h, baluster, molded rim, S scroll handle, drop at upper join, base engraved, marked on base, minor repairs at handle joins, 12 oz **3,300.00**
David, John, Phila, PA, c1800, pap boat, 5" l, oval, everted brim with engraved border, marked twice on base, 1 oz, 10 dwt **825.00**
Dupuy, Daniel, Phila, PA, 1785–1810, sugar urn, 10¾" h, urn shape, tapering cylindrical lid, urn shaped finial, beaded borders, pierced gallery, flaring cylindrical stem, sq base, four ball feet, engraved foliate script initials within bright cut reverse flanked by ribbons and wheat, marked twice on base **10,500.00**
Gorham, Providence, RI, 1848–65, water pitcher, 10⅛" h, baluster, chased medallion, floral and shell design, 33 oz **1,000.00**
Holland, Litteton, Baltimore, MD, c1805, sauceboat, 5½" h, 6½" l, oval, strap handle with bifurcated leaf terminal, oval molded foot, rim and foot with reeded molding, engraved monogram, marked on foot, 7 oz **3,520.00**
Hollingshead, Wm, Phila, PA, 1760–85
  Coffeepot, 12½" h, inverted pyriform, domed, hinged lid, gadrooned finial and molding, carved wooden handle with foliate scrolled terminals, cast S scrolled spout with ruffled cartouche, domed and molded circular foot, engraved foliate script initials "LP" within rococo car-

touche, marked three times on base, 33 oz, 10 dwt **52,800.00**

Teapot, 6¾" h, inverted pyriform, domed lid, baluster finial, S scroll spout, cast cartouche, acanthus leaf terminal, molded circular base, engraved foliate initials, marked three times on base, repair to base and rim, 22 oz **9,900.00**

Hurd, Jacob, Boston, MA, 1740–58

Brazier, 4" h, 12" l, circular, everted brim mounted with three scrolls, pierced foliate sides, circular pierced grate, turned wood handle, three scrolled legs, turned wooden ball feet, side engraved crest, initials engraved on base, marked on base and grate, 16 oz, 10 dwt . . . **71,500.00**

Teapot, 5½" h, pyriform, domed hinged lid, wooden ball finial set in silver moldings, faceted S scroll spout, wooden handle, molded foot rim, marked on cov and body, repair to handle joins, 16 oz **16,500.00**

Lynch, John, Baltimore, c1790, sugar urn, 10½" h, urn shaped, tapering cylindrical lid, urn shaped finial, applied beaded borders, spreading cylindrical foot, beaded border, sq base, body engraved with bright cut shield enclosing script monogram, marked on base, 16 oz, 10 dwt **2,750.00**

Milne, Edmund, Phila, PA, c1760, sauceboat, 4⅝" h, 8⅛" l, oval, scalloped rim, scroll handle, acanthus grip, three scroll legs, shell dec, shell feet, marked twice on base, 12 oz, 10 dwt **7,700.00**

Myers, Myer, New York, NY, 1760–80, teaspoons, 4⅞" l, oval bowl, down turned rounded end handle, midrib on back, front engraved "ICW," each marked "Myers," 2 oz, set of 4 . . . . **3,500.00**

Mytinger, Jacob, Newtown, VA, c1827, chatelaine hook, 2" l, heart shaped, roulettework border, engraved script initials, marked "J Mytinger," 10 dwt **1,100.00**

Owen, John, Jr, Phila, PA, 1804–31, spectacles, 4⅝" w, oval lens frame, hinged and sliding temple pieces, marked on one arm, 1 oz **550.00**

Pancoast, Samuel, Phila, PA, 1785–1795, sugar urn, 8" h, urn shape, tapering cylindrical lid, urn shaped finial, beaded borders, spreading cylindrical foot, sq base, rim and base with engraved borders, marked four times on base, 10 oz, 10 dwt **2,420.00**

Parker, Daniel, Boston, MA, 1755–75, punch strainer, 10⅜" l, circular bowl, dec piercing, molded rim, flanked by two open handles with stylized leaf-

age and terminals, engraved on back, marked on back of handle, 4 oz, 10 dwt **6,600.00**

Pelletreau, Elias, Southampton, NY, c1760, pepper box, 3⅞" h, octagonal, faceted domed pierced lid, baluster finial, S scrolled handle, contemporary engraved initials on base, marked on base, 3 oz, 10 dwt **13,200.00**

Revere, Paul, II, Boston, 1760–1780, 6⅛" h, cann, baluster, double scroll handle, acanthus grip, molded circular foot, front engraved foliate script initials in wreath, marked near rim, 18 oz **38,500.00**

Richards, Thomas, New York, NY, c1810, water pitcher, 9¼" h, baluster, squared handle, gadroon moldings at rim, shoulder, and footrim, engraved with later coat of arms, marked on base, 31 oz, 10 dwt **3,850.00**

Richardson, Joseph, Jr, Phila, PA, 1790–1810

Coffeepot, 13" h, urn shape, tapering cylindrical cov, pineapple finial, S scroll spout, beaded moldings, carved wooden handle with acanthus grip, spreading oval foot, sq base, marked four times, 38 oz, 10 dwt **6,000.00**

Cream Pitcher, 6¼" h, urn shape, strap handle spurred and reeded, spreading cylindrical foot, beaded rim and stem borders, sq base, body engraved with foliage script monogram in wreath, marked on base, repair to rim, 5 oz **725.00**

Tea Caddy, 4¼" h, 5½" w, oval, flat hinged lid, urn finial, beaded borders, center keyhole, engraved oval cartouche with script initials, int. with later brass lock, marked on base, 12 oz, 10 dwt **18,700.00**

Richardson, Joseph, Sr, Phila, PA, 1740–1775

Bowl, 6¾" d, 3⅜" h, circular, flaring sides, molded rim, molded circular foot, base engraved "IM," marked twice on base, 17 oz **27,500.00**

Mote Spoon, 7⅜" l, fig shaped bowl, dec piercing, handle marked twice, 1 oz **3,550.00**

Waiter, 7⅛" d, shaped circular, molded brim, cast applied scroll and foliate rim with chased details, three cabriole legs, stepped slipper feet, center engraved foliage script initials "AR," back engraved initials "R" and "C," marked near brim, 8 oz **41,800.00**

Sayre, Joel, NY, early 19th C

Ladle, 14½" l, tip handled engraved,

canoe form bright cut reserve panel of initials **900.00**

Tea Service, 7" h teapot, stand, cov sugar, creamer, waste bowl, Neoclassical style, canoe form cross section, molded lid and cavetto engraved with bright cut floral bands, monogrammed wreath **6,500.00**

Schanck, Garrett, NY, c1790–95, sugar urn, 9" h, urn shaped, tapering cylindrical lid, cast pineapple finial, beaded borders, spreading cylindrical foot, sq base, engraved script initials, marked on base with maker's name, eagle pseudo hallmark and letter "m", 10 oz, 10 dwt **3,300.00**

Syng, Philip, Jr, Phila, PA, 1740–1771, punch strainer, 5¾" l, circular bowl, concentric ring piercing, scrollwork handle, clip on reverse, bowl with engraved initials, marked twice and leaf pseudo hallmark, 2 oz, 10 dwt **8,250.00**

Warner, A E, Baltimore, MD, 1805–15, punch strainer, 6" l, circular pierced bowl, pierced scrollwork handle, marked on back of handle **2,860.00**

Warner, Thomas, Baltimore, MD, 1803–14, butter dish and stand, 5¾" l, rounded rect dish, flaring straight sides, everted gadrooned rim, molded footrim, gilt int., matching stand with flat brim, gadrooned edge, molded footrim, each marked with marker's mark, eagle's head, and sterling standard mark, 11 oz, 10 dwt **2,650.00**

Winslow, Edward, Boston, MA, 1725–53, porringer, 5" d, 7⅝" l, circular, everted brim, pierced keyhole handle engraved "DRW," date "1760" engraved later in bowl, marked near rim, minor repairs to rim and base, 8 oz, 10 dwt **1,750.00**

Wishart, Hugh, NY, 1793–1824, pap boat, 5" l, oval, curving spout, marked on base, 2 oz **725.00**

American, Sterling, ring tree, saucer base, repousse, three wire extensions, marked "RW & S," 3" d base, 2" h, $145.00.

SILVER, AMERICAN, 1840–1920
Mostly Sterling

There are two possible sources for the origin of the word sterling. The first is that it is a corruption of the name Easterling. Easterlings were German silversmiths who came to England in the Middle Ages. The second is that it is named for the starling (little star) used to mark much of the early English silver.

Sterling silver has 925/1000 parts pure silver. Copper comprises most of the remaining alloy. American manufacturers began to switch to the sterling standard about the time of the Civil War.

Adelphi, NY, punch bowl, 13½" d, 6½" h, cut glass bowl, cut in star and crosshatch design, everted, beaded, and engraved silver rim, c1905 .... **1,000.00**

Black, Starr & Frost, NY
Bowl, 5" h, molded rim, fruiting urn motif, reticulated trellis sides, scrolled feet, polished out monogram, 33 oz **1,100.00**

Coffee and Tea Service, kettle on stand, coffeepot, teapot, creamer, cov sugar, waste bowl, and waiter, classical revival urn shape, chased and engraved classical foliage dec, monogram, 131½ oz **4,000.00**

Fruit Bowl, 12¾" d, shaped and dec everted rim, low foot, 24 oz **450.00**

Punch Bowl, 10¾" d, 7⁵⁄₁₆" h, round, chased classical revival dec, c1900, 34 oz **1,000.00**

Blanchard, Porter, tray, 11" d, shallow round form, flared scalloped edge, stamped logo and "Sterling/Porter Blanchard" **250.00**

Caldwell, J E, Phila, PA, late 19th C
Cake Stand, 15" l, oval, scrolling branch form loop handles, center molded cavetto, repoussed continuous band of summer flowers enclosing diapered ground, monogrammed, 43 ozs, pr **1,500.00**

Compote, 9¾" d, 7" h, crenelated border of stylized shells, heavily cast bellied body, continuous border of mallow and leaves, stippled ground, conforming foot, 79 ozs, pr **4,000.00**

Cracker Scoop, foliate chased scrolled handle, bright cut scoop, 5 oz **300.00**

Davis & Galt, Phila, PA, late 19th C, water pitcher, 7¾" h, repousse, overall chased garden flower dec, 21 oz **650.00**

Dodge, Wm Waldo, Jr, Asheville, NC, early 20th C, fruit bowl and tray, 13¾" d bowl, flaring scallop edge bowl, 14¼" d deep welled round tray, hand hammered and striated textured dec,

imp logos and "Dodge/Sterling/By/
Hand," 86 oz **1,200.00**

Dominick & Haff, New York

Bowl, scrolled acanthus and floral
molded rim, claw and ball feet, retailed by J E Caldwell & Co, Phila,
PA, late 19th C, pr, 50 oz **750.00**

Compote, 7½" h, 6¾" h, circular,
spreading cylindrical foot, body and
foot repousse and chased with
flowers and leaves, matte ground,
gilt int., marked, c1880, 8 oz, 10
dwt **3,100.00**

Hot Water Kettle, 10¼" h, baluster
form teapot, sq rim, domed sq cov,
sq finial, bail handle with ivory insulating rings, partly reeded spout,
circular foot ring, fitting into two stylized foliate supports over circular
base with center burner, single wick
holder, kettle and base repousse
and chased with moths, flowers,
and leaves, flat chased ground of
maple leaves, marked, retailed by
George C Shreve, c1880, 57 oz, 10
dwt **8,800.00**

Mug, 4" h, barrel, curved handle, entire surface spot hammered, repousse cup, chased dec of pond
with waterplants and dragonfly,
Japanese taste, c1882, 9 oz **1,320.00**

Plate, 9" d, spot hammered surface,
repousse, chased dragonflies and
foliage, Japanese taste, marked,
c1881, 11 oz, 10 dwt **550.00**

Durgin Co, Wm B, Concord, NH

Coffee Set, coffeepot with ivory finial,
wood handle, open sugar and reamer, hammered pattern, band of
geometric devices, marked with
logo and "Sterling," 3 pcs, 24 oz **700.00**

Vase, 7¾" h, elongated urn shape,
pierced fret neck and two pierced
strap handles, spreading circular
foot, stylized script monogram, for
Tiffany & Co, 1910, 14 oz, pr **330.00**

Fisher, Jersey City, NJ, c1930, tray,
23¾" l, 13¾" w, round corner rect,
gadroon handles and rim, engraved
center inscription, 61½ oz **600.00**

Forbes, Wm, NY, first half 19th C, open
salt, 2½" h, Neoclassical style, openwork frame, swan's neck supports enclosing beaded ring, 9 ozs, pr **600.00**

Gale, Wm & Son, NY, 1856, waiter, 12"
l, 8⅛" w, oval, engraved bead molded
rim, crest engraved on brim, marked
on base, 17 oz **675.00**

Gale, Wood & Hughes, NY, c1836–45,
candlesticks, 11" h, shaped circular
nozzle with cast applied flowers,
scrolls, and shells, baluster shaped

standard with acanthus leaves,
scrolls, and flowers, domed shaped
hexagonal foot with flowers, scrolls,
and gadrooning, foot engraved with
family crest, marked on nozzle and
foot, 124 oz, set of 4 . . . . **30,800.00**

Gorham, Providence, RI

Bowl, 5½" h, shaped oval beaded rim,
pierced sides chased with foliate
swags, spreading base, mono-
gram, 1893, 21 oz **450.00**

Bride's Basket, 16⅞" h, pierced upright handle, flared rim, oval base,
chased and engraved foliage, floral
dec, 1917, 41 oz **1,400.00**

Cake Knife, 11⅜" l, Hizen pattern,
each side of handle cast with parcel–gilt Japanese motifs, serrated
blade, etched fish and crab,
marked, c1880, 5 oz **1,100.00**

Coffeepot, 13" h, elongated pyriform,
tall neck, domed cov, cast putti
heads on shoulders, sinous spout
and handle, ivory insulating rings,
serpentine spout, scrolled feet, repousse surface, chased scrolls and
foliage, two reserves, stylized monogram, made for L'Exposition Uni-
versalle, Paris, 1900, 38 oz **5,000.00**

Dish, 5½" d, circular, crimped edge,
repousse, chased blackberries and
leaves, gilt int., marked, c1890, 2
oz, 10 dwt **715.00**

Ice Bowl, 8¼" d, 3" h, circular, jagged
rim, sides with etched arctic
scenes, icicles etched on rim,
marked, c1885, 17 ozs, 10 dwt . . **3,300.00**

Ice Cream Spoons, 5¼" l, Florentine
pattern, gold washed bowls, mon-
ogram, 15 oz, set of 12 . . . . **325.00**

Napkin Ring, 2⅛" l, cylindrical, applied seashells, seaweed, crab,
and fish, four shell feet, center
monogrammed, gilt int., marked,
c1885, 4 oz **2,650.00**

Salt and Pepper Shakers, pr, 2⅞" h,
sq, trellis patterned sides, applied
copper peacocks, butterfly, and foliage, pierced circular cap, Japanese taste, marked, c1880, 3 oz **2,200.00**

Salt, open, 3" l, basket form, molded
socle, classical portrait medallions,
c1860, 7 ozs, pr **550.00**

Hartwell, Arthur L, for Arthur J Stone,
Gardner, MA, 1912, 9½" d, 4" h, centerpiece bowl, flaring sides, molded
rim, molded circular foot, inscription
dated 1912, marked, 27 oz **1,320.00**

Howard & Co, NY, 1899, cup, 16" h,
baluster body, domed cov, repousse,
spiral flutes and scrolling acanthus,
scrolled handles, inscription, 77 oz **1,800.00**

Jones, Ball & Poor, Boston, c1850, after dinner coffeepot, 7" h, Rococo Revival style, pyriform, repoussed acanthus leaves and flowers, mask form spout, figural finial, 12 oz **400.00**

Kidney & Johnson, NY, c1848
Ladle, 12½" l, 5 ozs **325.00**
Stuffing Spoon, 12⅜" h, Medallion pattern, Egyptian head, bright cut detail, 4 oz **500.00**

Kirk, Baltimore, MD
Sauce Boat, 8⅝ l, repousse, chased floral dec, 1903–07, 9 oz **400.00**
Water Pitcher, 9½" h, baluster, repousse, overall chased floral dec, monogram, c1925–32, 24 oz **1,200.00**

Paval, Philip Kran, dish, 6⅜" l, 3" h, rect rim on round bowl asymmetrically balanced on base, becoming large "C" curve handle attached to bowl rim, applied small strap handle, imp "Paval/Sterling", 5½ oz **400.00**

Shiebler, NY, c1880, tray, 8¾" w, shaped rect, serpentine brim, beaded edge, applied cast fish against etched seaweed, monogrammed center, marked, 9 oz, 10 dwt **1,650.00**

Shreve & Co, San Francisco
Decanter, 8½" h, hammered globular body, long neck, matching stopper, applied flowers, 11 oz **1,500.00**
Teaspoons, XIV Century pattern, twelve varying design handles, pierced monogram "D," imp logo and shopmarks, orig flannel bag, c1910, 12 oz, set of 12 .... **700.00**
Tray, 10½" d, scalloped strapwork border, round refinished oak int., imp marks **300.00**
Vase, 14¼" h, flaring cylindrical trumpet, everted undulating brim, domed circular foot with serpentine rim, applied Art Nouveau iris blossoms and stems, marked, c1905 **3,550.00**

Smith, Frederick, Denver, CO, c1889, fruit bowl, 8⅝" d, round, scalloped rim, overall chased floral pattern, 15 oz **450.00**

Stone, Arthur, Gardner, MA, early 20th C
Pen Tray, 8¼" l, 3¼" w, rect, applied rim, chased liner design, shallow well pinched at both ends, monogram, imp shopmarks, craftsman's initial "C," 6 oz **600.00**
Salad Set, 9⅜" l, fork and spoon, engraved and pierced thistle dec, imp shopmarks and craftsman's initial "B" for Charles W Brown, 7 oz .. **850.00**
Serving Fork, 8½" l, engraved and pierced thistle dec handle, imp shopmarks and craftsman's initials "B" for Charles W Brown, 3 oz .. **325.00**
Serving Spoon, 9¼" l, back tipped handle, engraved and pierced grape dec, imp shopmarks and craftsman's initials "B" for Charles W Brown, 4 oz **325.00**
Shakers, 4" h, domical cov, urn shaped body, raised foot, imp shopmarks, 8 oz, set of 4 .... **425.00**
Tray, 18" d, 20" l, shallow welled oval, two double dolphin handles, imp shopmarks and artist's initial "T" for Herbert Taylor, 125 oz **4,000.00**
Vase, 5¼" h, bud, fluted mouth tapering to foot, chased floral dec, imp shopmarks, 4 oz **350.00**

Tiffany & Co, New York, NY
Bonbonnier, 13½" l, Day and Night, heavily cast handle, with putto and rococo style cartouche, pierced foliate handle and bowl, engraved monogram, c1907, 35 oz, pr **3,850.00**
Cigar Box, 13¼" w, 6¾" d, 9" h, rect, hinged domed cov, etched cactus and palm, center cast silver finial, sides etched with palm trees, applied cast elephants on four sides, four massive cast silver cactus legs with elephant feet, gilt cov int., three part mahogany lined case, marked, attributed as presentation piece to Theodore Roosevelt .. **15,400.00**
Ice Cream Bowl, 13" d, 4½" h, circular, bowed sides repousse, chased, and engraved with stylized foliage, Indian taste, four bracket feet, surmounted by stylized peacock, marked, c1874, 55 oz, 10 dwt ... **11,000.00**
Tea Tray, 30½" l, 18½" w, oval, molded brim continues to form pierced handles, brim inlaid with gold bands, repousse well, chased laurel leaves, marked, 196 oz, 10 dwt **8,300.00**

Unger Brothers, Newark, ashtray, 6⅞" w, 4" deep, figural, Man in the Moon, smoking pipe, Art Nouveau woman's profile and curling smoke, 2 oz **800.00**

Whiting Manufacturing Co
Bowl, 9½" d, Chinese style, repousse, dragon with flaming pearl, monogram, 13 oz **1,800.00**
Dish, 5⅝" d, shaped circular, serpentine brim, repousse mask center, grape leaf wreath at brim, marked, c1900, 2 oz, 10 dwt **600.00**
Mug, 4⅛" h, cylindrical, sides deeply repousse, chased with putti and scrolling acanthus, acanthus terminals on handles, base inscribed, dated 1892, 8 oz **1,320.00**

Serving Spoon, 8½″ l, overall hammered finish, handle with applied grapevine relief in silver and patinated bronze, silver gilt bowl, retailed by Bigelow Kennard & Co, monogram, orig fitted box, c1900, 4 oz **400.00**

Wilson, Wm, Phila, PA, c1885, pitcher, 7½″ h, baluster, curved handle, narrow circular footrim, repousse body, chased underwater scenery including octopus and stingray **4,400.00**

Wood & Hughes, NY, c1885, dish, 7⅜″ l, oblong, wavy border, one end with sea form handle, etched center fish, repousse and wavy gilt int., 3 oz, 10 dwt **725.00**

Wooley, James, Boston, early 20th C, bowl, 5½″ d, 2½″ h, deep fluted, banded foot, imp co–joined "JW" and "Sterling," 6 oz **325.00**

Sheffield, silverplated, coffee urn on stand, Neoclassical style, ring handles, shaped tray with reeded edge and ball feet, 19th C, 23″ h, $5,000.00.

SILVER, CONTINENTAL

Continental silver does not have a strong following in the United States. The strong feeling of German silver cannot compete with the lightness of the English examples. In Canada, Russian silver finds a strong market.

Austrian, tray, 15½″ l, shaped rect, one corner with chased woman smoking cigarette, smoke billowing to shaped border, large chased iris on other side, stylized iris leaf handle, four double leaf and tendril feet, Art Nouveau, Vienna, c1900, maker's mark SK, 23.5 oz **2,200.00**

Danish

Cake Server, 10″ l, Rose pattern, chased handle, pierced blade, Georg Jensen, early 20th C, 5 oz **225.00**

Compote, 7½″ h, flared bowl, spiral stem, vintage detail, model 263B, Georg Jensen, 1925–32, 37 oz, pr **6,500.00**

Creamer and Sugar, flat rim handles, cone shaped bowls, Georg Jensen, mid 20th C, 11 oz **600.00**

Water Pitcher, 7″ h, flared lip, globular, fluted rosewood handle, No. 385A, Georg Jensen, c1925, 18 oz **1,600.00**

Dutch

Biscuit Box, 7″ l, rect, repousse on all sides, 18th C style genre scenes, second title, date letter "O," maker 77, 19th C, 20 oz **1,200.00**

Tobacco Box, 7″ l, oblong, rounded ends, two engraved figural reserves and inscriptions, maker's mark of a plant in shaped reserve, 7 oz **1,500.00**

French

Basket, 7″ h, cylindrical, engraved coat of arms, swing handle, 950 fine, maker's mark "SP" in lozenge, 21 oz **1,000.00**

Compote, 8½″ d, circular, chased and pierced leaf and flower dec, fluted foot, maker's mark "JG" in lozenge, 950 fine mark, 19th C, 31 oz, pr **1,000.00**

Decanter, 11″ h, fluted bottle mounted with silver neck, stopper, and foot, chased shell and scroll dec, monogram, maker mark "MJ" in diamond, dented, slight bottle chips, 19th C, pr **1,900.00**

Pot de Creme with Stand, 4″ h, fluted globular body, chased, floral strand, floral handle, matching underplate and cov, 19th C, 12 oz **600.00**

Sugar Bowl, cov, 6½″ h, Neoclassical style, pierced sides, frieze of griffins, urns, and wreaths, three splayed legs with bellflowers, hoof feet joined by swags, matching domed cov, cobalt blue liner, 18th C style hallmarks, 19th C, 13 oz **325.00**

German

Centerpiece, 15″ l, oval, shaped outline, chased scrolls, foliage, flowers, and rocaille, central circular engraved cartouche surmounted by crown enclosed by husk swags, two double scroll leaf clad handles with bifurcated joins, four matted scroll and openwork bellflower feet, Hanau, late 19th C, 45 oz **3,300.00**

Cow Creamer, 4½″ l, standing, hinged lid on back, 800 fine silver, 19th C, 3 oz **475.00**

Italian

Cruet Stand, 11½″ h, Neoclassical, central handle, gilt parrot figure, four bottle frames, caryatid supports, rect base, paw feet, pr matched cruet bottles, marked crossed keys in rect and lozenge mark, Rome, early 19th C, 44 oz **4,500.00**

Tray, 18" l, oval, pierced gallery, chased swags, shaped pierced feet, mark of head with halo above wings over NP, rim damage, foot repair, Venice, late 18th C, 38 oz **2,600.00**

Swiss, candlestick, Neoclassical style, laurel swags on nozzle, three putti seated on tripartite stem, pierced and leaf tip molded base, Bossard & Sohn, Lucerne, 935 fine mark, late 19th C, 284 oz, set of 4 . . . . **26,000.00**

SILVER, ENGLISH

From the seventeenth century to the mid-19th century, English silversmiths set the styles which American silversmiths copied. The work from the period exhibits the highest degree of craftsmanship. Active collection of English silver takes place in the American antiques marketplace.

Edward VII

Candelabra, three light, partly fluted, shaped rect stem, central baluster stem, two scrolling reeded branches rising to campana form sockets, sq wax pan and nozzle, applied gadrooned borders, raised sq base cased with flutes and shells, Woodward & Co, London, 1901, 72.5 ozs, pr **3,850.00**

Castor, 8¼" h, vase shape, pierced partly domed cov with baluster finial, rising circular base, three angular handles, two applied leaves, Boardman, Glossop & Co, Ltd., London, 1904 . . . . **350.00**

Cup, 2¾" h, tapering cylindrical with flaring rim, chased four bands of ropework, arcading, scroll handle with reeded borders, George Nathan & Ridley Hayes, 1908 . . . . . **200.00**

Pitcher, water, 9" h, urn finial over narrow waisted neck, globular body with stylized scroll and paw feet, monogram, handle dent, minor imperfections, Atkin Brothers, Sheffield, 1907–08, 23 troy oz **275.00**

Tea and Coffee Service, teapot, 9" h coffeepot, hot water jug, two handled sugar bowl, and cream jug, tapering oval shapes, chased shoulders of swirling flutes above scrolling foliage and rocaille, additional engraved scrolls, foliage,and flowers within stippled ground, central shaped oval monogrammed cartouche, leaf capped and rocaille scroll handles, oval foot with applied flowers and scrolling foliage, four scroll supports, Mappin & Webb, London, 1904, 23 oz **3,300.00**

George I Style, tea set, 6¼" h teapot, cream jug, sugar bowl, circular, molded spreading foot, wood scroll handle, paneled curved spout, wood button finial, Wakely & Wheeler, London, 1946, 41 ozs **990.00**

George II

Butter Shell, 5½" l, valve with applied reeded border, three conch feet, Robert Garrard I, London, 1817 . . **450.00**

Caster, repousse and chased designs, George Hunter, London, 1755, 6 troy oz **150.00**

Tankard, 8" h, cylindrical, applied reeded band, double scroll monogrammed handle, heart shaped terminal, domed cov with openwork thumbpiece, short spreading foot, Wm Shaw II & Wm Priest, London, 1732, 25.5 oz **3,200.00**

George III

Cann, baluster turned, scrolled handle, crown foot, inscription on base, London, 1760–61, attributed to Joseph Bell, 7 oz **550.00**

Cup, cov, 12½" h, baluster, gadrooned foot, domed cov, stylized bud finial, leafy double scroll handles, engraved coat of arms in rocaille and motto, maker "IS" with star above and cinquefoil below in circle, London, 1765–66, 48 oz . . **2,750.00**

Salt, ovoid vasiform body, bright cut dec, loop handles, spreading foot, Irish, Joseph Jackson, Dublin, one pr 1762, one pr 1770, 14½" oz, matched set of 4 . . . . **800.00**

Tankard, 8" h, domed molded cov with pierced thumb rest, baluster body, molded foot, scrolled handle, engraved "Daniel Smith/Seacaucus," maker's mark "BM," London, 1788–89, 26 oz **3,250.00**

Teapot, 11¼" l, molded oval, everted shoulder, applied tongue and dart rim, upcurved three panel spout, harp shaped handle, oblong finial, four bun feet, J McKay, Edinburgh, 1814, 21 oz **600.00**

Teapot Stand, 7" l, 5⅛" w, shaped edge rect form, engraved detail, stylized paw feet, illegible maker's mark, London, 1809–10, 4 oz . . . **375.00**

George IV

Luncheon Forks, King pattern, anthemion and reed design, monogrammed, Wm Eley & Wm Fearn, London, 1822–23, 30 oz, set of 16 .... **900.00**

Sauce Tureen, cov, 9" l, molded oval, applied rocaille and foliate scroll rim, foliate ring band, cast tied anchor finial, stylized leaf calyx and beaded border, two foliate capped upcurved loop handles, four lion's paw feet with acanthus joints, Joseph Angell, London, 1835, 35 oz **1,210.00**

George V

After Dinner Coffee Set, coffeepot, creamer, and sugar, classical form, olive branch band, hammered texture, maker's marks "A E J," Birmingham, 1929–30, 23 oz **600.00**

Bowl, 8¾" d, fluted, everted border with applied tied reeded rim, four ball and claw feet, two ring drop handles with lion's mask terminals, Reid & Sons, London, 1912, 39.5 oz **1,450.00**

Mirror, 22½" l, shaped oblong, openwork chased and engraved frame of flowers, scrolling foliage, and rocaille, worn velvet cov wood back with stand, William Comyns, London, 1910 .... **1,760.00**

Service Plate, 9¾" d, Regency style, cinquefoil serpentine gadrooned rim, monogram, Crichton Bros, London, 1930–31, 223 oz, set of 12 **4,750.00**

Regency

Candlestick, 4" h, nozzle with egg and dart, palmette moldings, gadrooned drip pan with intermittent shells, conical snuffer, engraved crest with motto, JW Story and W Elliott, London, 1812–13, 23 oz .. **1,900.00**

Salver, 21½" d, molded circular rim shaped by scrolls with shells at intervals, four scroll feet, int. later chased scrolling foliage, engraved crest, Wm Stevenson, London, 1815–16, 136 oz **5,500.00**

Victorian

Beaker, tapered cylindrical, bright cut engraving, floral festoons between stylized foliate bands, gilt liners, Daniel & Charles Houle, London, 1865, 12 oz, pr **1,320.00**

Candlestick, 12⅝" h, twisted vine stem, leaf and grape dec nozzle, spreading rococo base, E & J Barnard, London, 1853–54, 103 oz, set of 4 .... **17,000.00**

Dessert Basket, 12½" l, molded shaped oval, openwork scroll, flowerhead, and rocaille base, pierced sides at intervals below quatrefoils, chased large scrolls, tied ribbon and scrolls at each end, applied scrolls and flowersprays shaped rim, William Comyns, London, 1891, 17.5 oz **600.00**

Dresser Set, silver gilt, hammer finish, oval silver cartouche within monogram, Charles Dumenil, London, 1900, 17 pcs **900.00**

Teapot, 6" h, tapering twelve sided body, scrolled rim and handle, four trefoil feet, George Fox, London, 1894–95, 21 oz **250.00**

Vase, 12" h, flared rim, narrow tapering body repousse with floral bouquets and reeding, domed foot, weighted, Comyns & Sons, London, 1891–21, retailed by Tiffany & Co, Paris **450.00**

William III, cup, cov, 7" h, urn shape, lower body with chased swirling flutes, alternating stylized flowerheads and acorns, two scroll handles, molded domed chased cov, acorn and fluted calyx finial, short chased dentilated foot, London, 1697, 11.5 oz **2,200.00**

William IV

Mug, 4" h, broadly fluted campana form, chased stylized foliage within matting, raised circular foot with shaped border, gilt lined, foliate scroll handle, worn maker's mark, London, 1832, 5 oz **350.00**

Wine Jug, 13¾" h, compressed spherical, high relief scenes of drunken young satyrs and Bacchus, front engraved with coats of arms within foliate mantling, applied scrolling grapevine and stylized leaves, cylindrical twisted neck with applied grapevine within matting, shaped beaded rim spout, chased acanthus leaves on circular spreading foot, Robert Garrard II, London, 1836, 41.5 oz **3,200.00**

SILVER, ENGLISH, SHEFFIELD

Sheffield Silver, or Old Sheffield Plate, was made by a fusion method of silver plating used from the mid–18th century until the mid–1880s when the silver electroplating process was introduced.

Sheffield plate was discovered in 1743 when Thomas Boulsover of Sheffield, England, accidentally fused silver and copper. The process consisted of sandwiching a heavy sheet of copper between two thin sheets of silver. The result was a plated sheet of silver which could be pressed or rolled to a desired thickness. All Sheffield plate articles were worked from those plated sheets.

Most of the silver plated items found today

marked "Sheffield" are not early Sheffield plate. They are later wares made in Sheffield, England.

Bell, 4½" h, table, baluster handle, modern **200.00**

Candlestick
   Edward VII, maker Hawksworth, Eyre & Co, Ltd, 12" h, detachable bobeches, leafy composite capital, column entwined with oak leaf and acorn garland, sq shaped base with acanthus leaves and urns, gadroon rims, weighted, 1901–02, set of 4 **4,000.00**
   George V, maker Forham & Faulkner, partly fluted tapering oval, vase form socket, oval wax pan with applied husk border, molded oval base, 1913, set of 4 . . . . **2,860.00**

Tea Service, teapot, coffeepot, two handled sugar bowl, and cream jug, molded ovals, angular wooden handles, slightly raised hinged cov with wood button finial, c1963 . . . . **950.00**

Tea Tray, 29" l, Victorian, Walker & Hall, molded border, engraved broad band of flowers, foliage, scrolls, and rocaille, broad shaped rim applied with openwork matted rusticated grapevines, slightly upcurved handles, 1879, 161 oz **4,625.00**

SILVER, PLATED

Plated silver production by an electrolytic method is credited to G. R. and H. Ekington, England, in 1838.

In electroplating silver, the article is completely shaped and formed from a base metal and then coated with a thin layer of silver. In the late 19th century, the base metal was Britannia, an alloy of tin, copper, and antimony. Other bases are copper and brass. Today the base is nickel silver.

In 1847 the electroplating process was introduced in America by Rogers Bros., Hartford, Connecticut. By 1855, a number of firms were using the method to mass produce silver plated items in large quantities.

The quality of the plating is important. Extensive use or polishing can cause the base metal to show through. The prices for plated silver items are low, making it a popular item with younger collectors.

Biscuit Box, 8½" l, book form, hinged cov, engraved scrolling foliage within matting, applied tied gilt ribbon, molded spine engraved "Biscuits," engraved hinged latch, gilt pages, int. with hinged pierced gilt grille, four bun feet **600.00**

Candelabra, 23½" h, Victorian, Egyptian style, Elkington & Co, 1878, fluted campana shaped sockets with applied flowerheads and wave band, crystal pendants hung between three multi–scroll handles to vase shaped stem with Egyptian motifs, two beaded knops, three winged sphinxes, openwork palmette apron, three lion's legs with palmette foliage, stepped trefoil base with dentil band, pr **1,870.00**

Coffee and Tea Service, coffeepot, 16" h tea kettle, stand, and lamp, two handled cov sugar, cream jug, and waste bowl, partly fluted vase shape, foliate scroll supports, elaborate scroll handles, high domed fluted cov with openwork bellflower finials, shaped 30⅜" l oblong tray on four bracket feet, gadroon and rocaille rim, engraved arabesques, conforming handles **500.00**

Compote, 7" d, 5¾" h, circular, fluted brim, applied frog, stem support, circular foot, dish and base with Japanese taste relief dec, marked "Derby Silver Co, Derby, CT," late 19th C . . **200.00**

Figure, 14½" h, knight on horseback, armor suits, brandishing sword, pr . . **1,100.00**

Flatware, luncheon service, twelve knives, eleven forks, two crumbers, serving knife and fork, engraved blades, ivory handles, English **125.00**

Inkstand, 9" l, rect, two rect reeded bottle frames, cut glass bottles, cylindrical chamberstick holder, two pen trays, dentilated borders, wood stand with drawer, plated ball handle, four ball feet, c1810 . . . . **825.00**

Meat Dish Cover, 15⅛" l, partly fluted molded oval, engraved motto, crown, and monogram, foliate bifurcated reed handle **150.00**

Punch Bowl Set, 15½" d bowl with applied fruit and foliage within strapwork, twenty–four cups with flaring rims, foliage scroll handles **350.00**

Tea Service, teapot, creamer, cov sugar, flaring sq shape, bamboo form handles and spouts, cube finials, sides and cov chased and engraved with Japanese taste birds and ornaments, marked "James W Tufts, Boston," last quarter 19th C **650.00**

Tray, 30" l, shaped oval, broad border applied and engraved with scrolling foliage, flowerheads, and rocaille, two upturned handles, stamped "Mounts stamped from the Original Boulton & Watt Dies, c1774" **275.00**

Wine Coasters, 8¼" d, molded circular, wood inset, broad everted border with applied grapevine rim, pr **450.00**

SILVER DEPOSIT GLASS

History: Silver deposit glass, consisting of a thin coating of silver actually deposited on the glass by an electrical process, was popular at the turn of the century. The process was simple. The glass and a piece of silver were placed in a solution. An electric current was introduced which caused the silver to decompose, pass through the solution, and remain on those parts of the glass on which a pattern had been outlined.

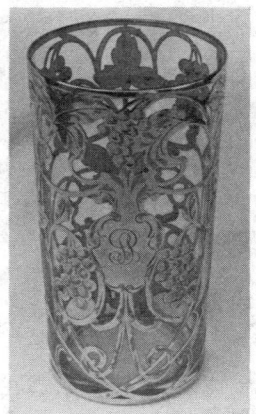

Tumbler, sterling grape, vine, and leaf motif, marked "455," 5″ h, $85.00.

Salt Shaker, partial paper label reads "Sterling Deposit," 3¼″ h, 2″ d, $15.00.

Bon Bon, 7″ d, handle, ftd	50.00
Bowl, 5½″ d, vines and leaves dec, scalloped edge	45.00
Compote, 7″ h, floral dec	75.00
Creamer and Sugar, floral dec	80.00
Decanter, 9″ h, emerald green, hollow stopper	60.00
Pitcher, 7¾″ h, green, large flowers and leaves, double horizontal ring foot ..	70.00
Serving Plate, 12½″ d, black amethyst, Art Nouveau lily dec, pierced handles	60.00
Tumbler, 4⅝″ h, flared top	24.00
Vase, 4½″ h, teardrop shape, cobalt blue glass ground, all–over silver design of leaves and vines, sgd "Boda"	100.00

SILVER OVERLAY

History: Silver overlay is silver applied directly to a finished glass or porcelain object. The overlay is cut and decorated, usually by engraving, prior to being molded around the object.

Glass usually is of high quality, either crystal or colored. Lenox used silver overlay on some porcelain pieces. The majority of design motifs are from the Art Nouveau and Art Deco periods.

Bowl	
8″ d, 2¾″ h, slightly waisted sloping sides, emerald green ground, silver overlay of scrolling stems, clematis flowers, and leaves, shaped heart form engraved medallion, Alvin Co factory marks	450.00
8¼″ d, 4″ h, waisted cylindrical sides, low circular molded foot, emerald green ground, silver overlaid stems of slender pendant leafage, scrolling tendrils, narrow borders	715.00
Goblet, 8″ h, tulip shaped bowl, hollow swollen cylindrical stem, circular foot, emerald green ground, silver overlay of entwined stems and leaves rising to three large silver tulips, silver rims, imp "Sterling"	385.00
Vase	
2¾″ h, cabinet, squatty ovoid, everted rim, irid ground, silver overlay lily pads and carnations, attributed to Loetz	825.00
3½″ h, cabinet, dimpled ovoid, everted undulating rim, gold irid, swirling leaves silver overlay, Austrian	475.00
4⅝″ h, swelled cylinder, green irid ground, silver blue spots, silver overlay of two female faces surrounded by curvilinear stems and blossoms, attributed to Loetz	675.00
6″ h, emerald green glass, SS engraved overlay	250.00
6¾″ h, ovoid, everted rim, irid yellow, blue wave and gold spotted dec, curvilinear silver overlay of stylized iris, attributed to Loetz	2,550.00

7″ h, twisted tapering triangular shake, irid gold, silvery blue waves, silver overlay lily pad descending from rim, attributed to Loetz **2,350.00**

7¼″ h, dimpled pear form, ruffled rim, green satin glass mother of pearl ground, silver rim, dogwood branches overlay, American **335.00**

SILVER RESIST

History: Silver resist ware was first produced about 1805. It is similar to silver luster in respect to the silvering process and differs in that the pattern appears on the surface.

The outline of the pattern was drawn or stenciled on the ware's body. A glue or sugar-glycerin adhesive was brushed over the part not to be lustered, causing it to "resist" the lustering solution which was applied and allowed to dry. The glue or adhesive was washed off. When fired in the kiln, the luster glaze covered the entire surface except for the pattern.

Pitcher, pine branch and pine cone dec, marked "Wedgwood & Barlaston Eturia," 5″ h, $70.00.

Bowl, 6″ d, floral border 60.00
Creamer, 3¼″ h, dark brown, flower on each side, two handles 75.00
Cup and Saucer, all–over floral dec .. 50.00
Jug, 4¼″ h, band of flowering foliage, Staffordshire, 19th C 90.00
Mug, barrel shape, jade green, all–over silver vines, buds, and flowers 50.00
Pitcher
  4⅜″ h, black transfer, enameled iron–red, blue, yellow, black, brown, and green robin on oak branch, c1815 385.00
  4½″ h, floral dec, two white reserves, Oriental scenes 150.00
  5⅜″ h, two hunters, one aiming rifle

at bird, other seated on fallen tree, Staffordshire, c1815 .... **525.00**
Wine, 4½″ h, purple–pink luster, feathering above graduated dots, cream foot and int., iron–red rim, pedestal, and foot, c1810 .... **350.00**

SMITH BROTHERS GLASS

History: After establishing a decorating department at the Mount Washington Glass Works in 1871, Alfred and Harry Smith struck out on their own in 1875. Their New Bedford, Massachusetts, firm soon became known worldwide for its fine opalescent decorated wares, similar in style to those of Mt. Washington.

Their glass often is marked on the base with a red shield enclosing a rampant lion and the word "Trademark."

Reproduction Alert: Beware of examples marked "Smith Bros."

Salt and Pepper Shakers, pr, herons, white ground, two pc pewter top, 4⅛″ h, $65.00.

Atomizer, melon shape, hp carnations outlined in gold, red rampant lion mark 595.00
Biscuit Jar
  Melon ribbed body, cream ground, large bouquets of pink spider mums, brown and gray leaves, all gold flowers and buds, SP cov and bail, sgd 825.00
  Swirled ribbed body, cream ground, crab dec, sea plants and shells, New Bedford Glass Museum accession numbers, orig fancy hardware, sgd 1,850.00
Bowl, 8¾″ d, ribbed, oak leaves and acorn dec outlined with gold, metal rim, marked 550.00
Planter, 10″ d, 4″ h, squatty, ten ribbed bulbous opal bowl, wild rose dec, gilt

outlines, raised edge, SP rim, red
rampant lion mark **600.00**
Rose Bowl, 4¼" h, pansies, cream
ground, marked **310.00**
Vase
 6½" h, swirled body, floral dec,
 beaded rim, sgd Rampant Lion
 mark on base **300.00**
 7" h, bulbous form, swirled, pink flow-
 ers and green leaves dec, raised
 gold enamel, two beaded line on
 top, sgd with Rampant Lion on
 base **225.00**
 7" h, swirl mold, delicate enameled
 daisies, marked **565.00**
 8½" h, flat sides, blue flowers and
 green leaf dec, raised gold enamel,
 short stick neck with beaded rim,
 pedestal base, sgd with Rampant
 Lion on base **400.00**
 8½" h, 6½" w, 1½" d neck, canteen
 shape, pale pink at top shading to
 cream, purple wisteria dec, raised
 heavy gold leaves and branches,
 beaded top, sgd **1,250.00**

SNOW BABIES

History: Snow babies, small bisque figurines
spattered with glitter sand, were made originally in
Germany and marketed in the early 1900s. There
are several theories about their origin. One is that
German doll makers copied the designs from the
traditional Christmas candies. Another theory, the
most widely accepted, is that they were made to
honor Admiral Peary's daughter, who was born in
Greenland in 1893 and was called the "Snow
Baby" by the Eskimos.

Reference: Ray and Eilene Early, *Snow Babies*, Collector Books, 1985.

Bear, standing on skis, 2″ h, $50.00.

Angel, sitting, outstretched arms, 1¾" **200.00**
Baby
 Holding hockey stick, 1½" **85.00**
 Kneeling on one knee, 1" **55.00**
 Laying on side, 1½" **90.00**
 Pair, one sitting on sled, other pulling,
 2½" w, 1½" h **110.00**
 Playing saxophone, marked "Ger-
 many" **75.00**
 Sitting, outstretched arms and legs,
 2¼" **135.00**
 Skating, 2" h, wearing red suit and
 hat, sgd "Germany" **30.00**
Carolers, three standing in snow, lan-
 tern, 2¼", Germany **85.00**
Figure
 Penguin, 4", Germany **70.00**
 Polar Bear, 2½D, standing **125.00**
Snow Girl, sitting upright on bisque sled,
 raised arms, 2¼" **100.00**
Snow Pup on skies, marked **110.00**

SNUFF BOTTLES

History: Tobacco usage spread from America
to Europe to China during the 17th century. Europeans and Chinese preferred to grind the dried
leaves into a powder and sniff it into their nostrils.
The elegant Europeans carried their snuff in boxes
and took a pinch with their fingertips. The Chinese
upper class, because of their lengthy fingernails,
found this inconvenient and devised a bottle with
a fitted stopper and attached spoon.

In the Chinese manner, these utilitarian objects
soon became objet d'art. Snuff bottles were fashioned from precious and semi-precious stones,
glass, porcelain and pottery, wood, metals, and
ivory. Glass and transparent stone bottles often
were enhanced further with delicate hand paintings, some done on the interior of the bottle.

Reference: Sandra Andacht, *Oriental Antiques
& Art, An Identification and Value Guide*, Wallace-
Homestead, 1987.

Collectors' Club: International Chinese Snuff
Bottle Society, 2601 North Charles Street, Baltimore, MD 21218.

Agate, carved
 Double gourd shape, c1800 . . . . . . **125.00**
 Phoenix bird, low relief floral dec on
 reverse, masks on shoulders,
 c1900 . . . . **300.00**
 Three monkeys, "hear no evil, see no
 evil, speak no evil" position, c1850 **200.00**
Amber, yellow baltic, ducks and lotus
 dec, c1890 . . . . **525.00**
Aquamarine, carved fungus trees,
 cranes, and lady in boat dec, c1860 **600.00**
Cloisonne
 Eggplant shape, flower dec, black
 ground, c1930 . . . . **60.00**

Cloisonne, floral motif on one side, forest scene with deer on other, wood base, 3⅜" h, $250.00.

Overall floral and foliate dec, blue ground, c1890	100.00
Coral, carved, high relief ducks, fish, lotus, and dragon fly dec, matching stopper with tiger eye collar, c1830	550.00
Hornbill, carved bat and dragons, red sheathing, sgd, c1850	400.00
I-Shing Pottery, rabbit in foliage dec, calligraphy, c1820	325.00
Ivory, dragon on front, clouds on corners, hornbill	500.00
Jade	
All-over low relief flowers, vines, birds, and bat, carved, c1790	475.00
Greek key dec, shou symbol center, c1760	125.00
Jadeite, double, low relief carved precious objects dec	400.00
Marbleized, purple, cut to clear, gourd shape, painted waterfall and people scene lower half, upper half with calligraphy and poem, c1910	300.00
Milk Glass	
All-over enameled floral dec, gilded sheath, ovoid, sgd, c1780	1,050.00
Royal blue overlay, carved, "The Eight Horses of Mu Wang" form, geometric leaf collar rim, Peking, c1800	400.00
Mother-of-Pearl, carved, dragon pursuing flaming pearl dec, c1890	325.00
Nephrite, double gourd shape, white, enamel and soapstone figural dec, c1880	550.00
Opal, pebble shape, carved, bread fruit, butterfly, and boy with cat dec, coral stopper with jet collar, c1930	325.00
Overlay, blue clear, carved fish dec, c1900	200.00

Porcelain	
Boy under tree, reverse with boy and sage, c1815	150.00
Enameled over-glaze vessel dec, c1825	125.00
Wine jug form, lattice cane dec, c1900	200.00
Rock Crystal, ducks in landscape dec, painted int., sgd "Wake Hsi San"	225.00
Rosewood, inlaid gold and silver floral dec, c1920	150.00
Tourmaline, relief carved bat, leaf, and floral dec, c1840	650.00

SOAPSTONE

History: The mineral steatite, known as soapstone because of its greasy feel, has been utilized for carved figural groups and other designs by the Chinese and others. Utilitarian pieces also were made. Soapstone pieces were very popular during the Victorian era.

Candlesticks, pr, red tones, flowers and vases, 5⅛" h, $85.00.

Box, 3 x 5", pearl inlay, artist sgd	40.00
Candlestick, 2½" h, trapezoidal, gray	130.00
Figure	
5" h, elderly man, standing, holding staff, fitted wood stand, artist sgd, China, late 19th C	70.00
5⅜" h, Guanyin, seated, wearing headdress, hands resting on knee, ochre, shaped teak stand, China, 19th C	500.00
6" h, Sage, carved black base, Oriental	100.00
10⅛" h, lady, tan and rust, mottled, c1900	65.00
21" h, fisherman, carved base	300.00
Inkwell, geometric carved sides	140.00
Lamp, 7½" l, spout	55.00
Paperweight, three monkeys	45.00
Toothpick Holder, figural, monkey	100.00
Urn, 7¼" d, 10¼" h, carved, figures,	

buildings, florals, and trees, elephant
head handles, wood stand **150.00**
Vase
8½″ h, highly dec and cut out chrysanthemums and birds dec, mauve
mottled ground, marked "China,"
c1900 . . . .   **200.00**
13¾″ h, carved, relief flowers and
bird, red base **60.00**

SOUVENIR AND COMMEMORATIVE CHINA AND GLASS

History: Souvenir, commemorative, and historical china and glass includes those items produced
to celebrate special events, places, and people.

Among the china plates, those by Rowland and
Marcellus and Wedgwood are most eagerly
sought. Rowland and Marcellus, Staffordshire, England, made a series of blue and white historic
plates with a wide rolled edge depicting scenes
beginning with the Philadelphia Centennial in 1876
and continuing to the 1939 New York World's Fair.
Wedgwood collaborated in 1910 with Jones,
McDuffee and Stratton to produce a series of historic dessert-sized plates depicting scenes
throughout the United States.

Many localities issued plates, mugs, glasses,
etc. for anniversary celebrations or to honor a local
historical event. These items seem to have greater
value when sold in the region from which they
originated.

Commemorative glass includes several patterns
of pressed glass which celebrate persons or
events. Historical glass includes campaign and
memorial items.

References: Bessie M. Lindsey, *American Historical Glass*, Charles E. Tuttle Company, Inc.,
1967; Frank Stefano, Jr., *Wedgwood Old Blue
Historical Plates And Other Views Of The United
States Produced For Jones, McDuffee & Stratton
Co., Boston, Importer; A Check-List with Illustrations*, published by author, 1975.

Periodical: *Travel Collector,* P.O. Box 40, Man-
awa, WI 54949.

Collectors' Club: Souvenir China Collectors
Society, Box 562, Great Barrington, MA 01230.

Additional Listings: Cup Plates, Pressed
Glass, Political Items, and Staffordshire, Historical.
Also see *Warman's Americana & Collectibles* for
more examples.

CHINA

Creamer, 6″ h, Williamsburg, VA, tankard style, blue transfer print, white
ground, marked "Made In England"   **35.00**
Cup and Saucer, Waterfront Business

Plate, Admiral Dewey, green transfer
print, marked "Semi–Vitreous/Canton
China," 8¼″ d, $7.50.

Section, Seattle, WA, Nippon, SBN
mark **40.00**
Pitcher
3½″ h, Washington Hotel, Seattle . .   **35.00**
8″ h, General Andrew Jackson, cop-
per luster, transfer print **125.00**
Plate
7″ d, Hyde Park, FDR **20.00**
7½″ d, Grant's Tomb, Riverside Drive
on the Hudson, blue transfer print,
Wedgwood **115.00**
10¼″ to 10½″ d, Wedgwood, set of
12
Columbia University **650.00**
Harvard University, red transfer
print **325.00**
New York University School of Ed-
ucation, red transfer print **200.00**
Yale University **900.00**
10½″ d, Saratoga, NY, dark blue
transfer print, rolled edges, vignette
border, Rowland and Marcellus . .   **65.00**
Tray, 11 x 7½″, sq corners, Washington's Home, Mt Vernon, VA, portraits
of George and Martha, enhanced
enameling, gold trim, marked "Ger-
many" **85.00**

GLASS

Bank, 7¼″ h, Independence Hall, clear   **75.00**
Bread Plate
Garfield Memorial, Lindsey #302 . .   **38.00**
Three Presidents, Lindsey #249 . . .   **45.00**
Bust, Admiral Dewey, emerald green,
ribbed round base **275.00**
Castor Set, Jumbo **300.00**
Compote, cov, Lutted's Cough Drops,
log cabin **275.00**
Desk Stand, 6½″ l, Memorial Hall form
inkwell, Philadelphia Exposition 1876,
clear **185.00**

Jar, 12½" h, 5" d, Statue of Liberty, clear, worn gold dec, pr	125.00
Paperweight	
Lincoln, Lindsey #275	175.00
Moses in the Bullrushes, oval	75.00
Plymouth Rock, Lindsey #18	90.00
Reclining Lion, Gillinder	225.00
Plate	
8" d, Wm H Harrison, Tippecanoe, Fort Meigs, amber	85.00
11" d, Garfield Drape, Lindsey #303	42.00
Platter	
12" l, Independence Hall, clear	65.00
13¼" l, Bunker Hill, oval, clear	50.00
Shoe, Centennial, upright holder, frosted, Gillinder	275.00
Spoon Rack, Jumbo	425.00
Toothpick, Preparedness, figural soldier and sailor standing beside toothpick holder, emb crossed flags and cannons, Spanish American War	145.00
Tray, Old State House Philadelphia, blue, Lindsey #32	110.00
Tumbler, 3⅛" h, 4" h, 4¾" h, Civil War, set of 3, Bay State Glass Co, set of 3	700.00
Vase, 6⅛" h, The Administration Building, World's Fair Chicago 1893, transfer, pale yellow satin glass, marked "Austria"	175.00
Whiskey, 3" h, Bumper to the Flag	85.00

SOUVENIR AND COMMEMORATIVE SPOONS

History: Souvenir and commemorative spoons have been issued for hundreds of years. Early American silversmiths engraved presentation spoons to honor historical personages or mark key events.

In 1881 Myron Kinsley patented a Niagara Falls spoon; in 1884 Michael Gibney patented a new flatware design. M. W. Galt, Washington, D.C., issued commemorative spoons of George and Martha Washington in 1889. From these beginnings a collecting craze for souvenir and commemorative spoons developed in the late 19th and first quarter of the 20th centuries.

References: Dorothy T. Rainwater and Donna H. Fegler, *American Spoons: Souvenir and Historical*, Schiffer Publishing Ltd., 1990; Dorothy T. Rainwater and Donna H. Fegler, *A Collector's Guide To Spoons Around The World*, Everybodys Press, Inc., 1976; *Sterling Silver, Silverplate, and Souvenir Spoons With Prices*, L-W Inc., 1988.

Collectors' Club: American Spoon Collectors, 4922 State Line, Westwood Hills, KS 66205.

Periodical: *Spoony Scoop Newsletter*, 84 Oak Avenue, Shelton, CT 06484.

Additional Listings: See *Warman's Americana & Collectibles* for more examples.

Atlantic City, NJ, skyline scene	52.00
Boston Tea Party	25.00
Carlisle, KY	25.00
Cincinnati, OH	23.00
City Hall, New York, SS, engraved New York City bowl, bridal rose figural handle	22.00
Colorado, SS, state capitol scene on bowl	18.00
Cornell University, seal on handle	30.00
Fort Ticonderoga, 1775, Ethan Allen	30.00
Illinois, SS	
Gate To Union Stockyards, Chicago on bowl	40.00
Public Library, Danville on bowl	30.00
Indianapolis 500, 1915, SS, race cars, balloons and biplane	100.00

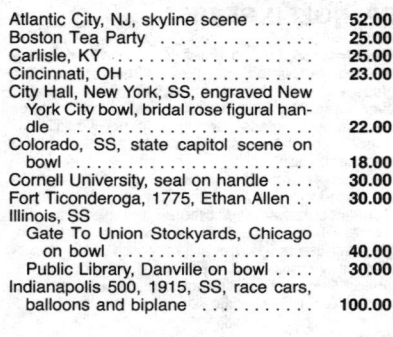

Atlantic City, skyline on handle, ocean scenes on back, boardwalk push cart in bowl, sterling silver, 6" l, $45.00.

Kaiser Wilhelm II, SP, bust handle, crest, flag, and Army and Navy figures, marked "Deutschland," plain bowl	45.00
Kansas City	35.00
Kentucky, state	28.00
Los Angeles	27.00
Mackinac Island, Mich, Indian Chief, demitasse	30.00
Minnehaha Falls, Art Nouveau handle	46.00
Montana, cowboy	40.00
Mt Tom Railway, Holyoke, MA	45.00
Niagara, Indian Head	30.00
Old City Gates	35.00
Pennsylvania, Elk's Temple, SS, Erie on bowl	15.00
St. Louis, Eads Bridge	42.00
San Francisco–Eureka, SS, Golden Gate bowl, bear figure handle	50.00
Sir Walter Rawleigh, figural	50.00
Sleepy Eye Flour Co, SP, Indian bust profile handle, plain bowl	130.00
Statue of Liberty, enamel bowl	42.00
Texas Centennial 1839–1936	60.00
Utah, SS	
Observatory Peak, Ogden in bowl	30.00
Salt Air Pavilion	18.00
Vassar College, Poughkeepsie, NY scene in bowl	35.00
Virginia, SS, engraved "Front Royal" in bowl	18.00
Wisconsin Dells, fish figural handle	25.00
Wyoming	25.00

SPANGLED GLASS

History: Spangled glass is a blown or blown molded variegated art glass, similar to spatter glass, with the addition of flakes of mica or metallic aventurine. Many pieces are cased with a white or clear layer of glass. Spangled glass was developed in the late 19th century and still is being manufactured.

Originally spangled glass was attributed only to the Vasa Murrhina Art Glass Company of Hartford, Connecticut, which distributed the glass for Dr. Flower of the Cape Cod Glassworks, Sandwich, Massachusetts. However, research has shown that many companies in Europe, England, and the United States made spangled glass, and attributing a piece to a specific source is very difficult.

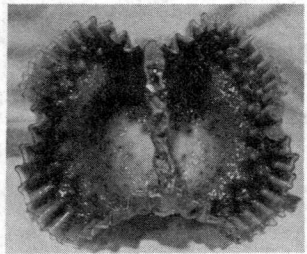

Basket, blue tones, white cased int., crimped edge, applied clear rope handle, 10 x 9", $300.00.

Basket, 8½" d, amber ground, white
casing, gold flecks, burgundy and
opal ruffled rim, applied clear looped
thorn handle 150.00
Candlesticks, pr, 8" h, green and ma-
roon, gold mica flecks, white casing 100.00
Cruet, bulbous, clear, profuse white
mottling, silver mica flecks, applied
handle, clear faceted stopper, Hobbs,
Brockunier & Company 450.00
Jack In The Pulpit Vase, 5¾" h, white
ext., pink int., clear ruffled edge, mica
flecks 125.00
Pitcher, 6¾" h, cobalt blue, gold mica
flecks, applied amber handle with
flecks 225.00
Rose Bowl, 3¾" h, 3½" d, deep pink,
mica flecks 150.00
Tumbler, red ground, silver mica flecks 90.00
Vase
8½" h, pink ground, white casing, ruffled crimped top, gold mica flecks,
applied cherries, leaf rigaree, pr . . 550.00

9¾" h, pink ground, white casing,
mica flecks, applied vaseline loop
handles, rigaree shell trim 120.00
12" h, oviform, squatty circular base,
amber, clear pinched neck 80.00

SPATTER GLASS

History: Spatter glass is a variegated blown or blown molded art glass. It originally was called "End-of-Day" glass, based on the assumption that it was made from leftover batches of glass at the end of the day. However, spatter glass was found to be a standard production item for many glass factories.

Spatter glass was developed at the end of the 19th century and still is being produced. It was made in the United States and Europe.

Reproduction Alert: Many modern examples come from Czechoslovakia.

Basket
5 x 6½", ruffled, oval top, emb swirls,
peach and white spatter, applied
clear thorn handle 160.00
6 x 7¾ x 8½", overlay, pink, blue, and
gold, white int., applied clear thorn
handle and feet 175.00
Bottle, 11" h, rubena, opal spatter . . . 115.00
Candlestick, 7½" h, yellow, red, and
white spatter, flared socket, twisted
hourglass stem, domed ribbed base 45.00
Cruet, red and white spatter, applied
clear handle, clear foot, clear ball
stopper 100.00
Darning Egg, red, yellow, and green, applied clear handle 125.00
Jar, 6½" h, cov, maroon, white, yellow,

Syrup, cranberry, clear, and white, ring neck, applied clear handle, SP top, $165.00.

and green, white cased int., applied
clear feet and finial **90.00**
Pitcher
8½" h, ribbed body, ruby and opal,
applied, clear handle **200.00**
9" h, 8" w, crimped rim, ribbed body,
white, tan, and red tortoise shell,
applied clear handle **250.00**
Rose Bowl, 3½" d, octagonal, crimped
top, rose, white cased int. **100.00**
Tumble–Up, bottle and matching tum-
bler, elongated thumbprint pattern,
green, red, yellow, and pink, white
cased int., applied clear leaf feet . . . **300.00**
Vase, 10" h, pink, yellow, and tan swirls,
white cased int., cupped goblet neck,
pr **250.00**
Water Set, Leaf Mold pattern, water
pitcher and six tumblers, vaseline
spatter **625.00**

SPATTERWARE

History: Spatterware is made of common earthenware, although occasionally creamware was
used. The earliest English examples were made
about 1780. The peak period of production was
1810–1840. Marked pieces are rare. Firms known
to have made spatterware are Adams, Barlow, and
Harvey and Cotton.

The amount of spatter decoration varies from
piece to piece. Some objects simply have decorated borders. These often are decorated with a
brush, requiring several hundred touches per
square inch to achieve the spatter effect. Other
pieces have the entire surface covered with spatter. Aesthetics of the final product is a key to value.

Collectors today focus on the patterns—Cannon, Castle, Fort, Peafowl, Rainbow, Rose, Thistle, Schoolhouse, etc. On flat ware the decoration
is in the center. On hollow pieces it occurs on both
sides.

Color of spatter is another price key. Blue and
red are most common. Green, purple, and brown
are in a middle group. Black and yellow are scarce.

Like any soft paste, spatterware was easily broken or chipped. Prices are for pieces in very good
to mint condition.

References: Susan and Al Bagdade, *Warman's
English & Continental Pottery & Porcelain, 1st Edition,* Warman Publishing Co., Inc., 1987; Kevin
McConnell, *Spongeware and Spatterware,* Schiffer Publishing Ltd., 1990; Carl and Ada Robacker,
Spatterware and Sponge, A. S. Barnes & Co.,
1978.

Reproduction Alert: "Cybris" spatter is an increasing collectible ware made by Boleslow Cybris
of Poland. The design utilizes the Adams type
peafowl and was made in the 1940s. Many contemporary craftsmen also are reproducing spatterware.

**Cup and Saucer, blue spatter, tan
ground, c1830, England, $40.00.**

Bowl, 7½" d, yellow and red spatter, pie
crust applied rim **200.00**
Creamer, 5⅜" h, octagonal paneled
form, abstract blue flower, blue, black,
red, and brown spatter **325.00**
Cup and Saucer, handleless
Acorn, two shades of green and
black, purple spatter **525.00**
Cornflowers, blue, green, and black,
red and yellow rainbow spatter bor-
der **675.00**
Plaid, blue, red, and green spatter **525.00**
Thistle, red and green flower, yellow
spatter **600.00**
Miniature, creamer, 3½" h, blue, minor
stains, small rim chip **125.00**
Pepper Pot, 4¾" h, pierced domed cov,
Peafowl, blue, ochre, rose, and black
peacock on branch, yellow spatter,
marked "Staffordshire," c1840 . . . . . **1,200.00**
Pitcher
5" h, blue, glaze edge wear, stains,
crow's foot hairline **175.00**
10" h, red transfer, cowboy scene,
blue spatter **110.00**
Plate
6" d, red stick spatter flowers and
green dotted leaves border, marked
"Staffordshire, England" **42.00**
7½" d, Schoolhouse, three color,
green spatter **625.00**
8⅛" d, Peafowl, blue, yellow, green,
and black, red spatter, wear, chips,
minor pinpoint flakes **300.00**
8⅜" d, Castle, green spatter **250.00**
9½" d, Peafowl, red, blue, yellow
ochre, and black, blue spatter,
stains and pinpoint flakes **500.00**
10" d, Peafowl, purple, green, yellow,
and black, red spatter, painted over
rim flakes **275.00**
10½" d, Peafowl in Tree, red, green,
blue, and black, blue spatter, imp
"Adams," stains, flakes on table
ring **525.00**
Soup Plate, 9½" d, Peafowl, red, blue,
green, and black peafowl, red spatter,
imp "Adams," minor stains **150.00**

Sugar, cov, Thistle, red and green
flower, yellow spatter, hairline 325.00
Teapot
  6" h, Rose, red, green, and black, red
    and purple spatter, yellowed pro-
    fessional repairs 350.00
  8½" h, paneled body, Peafowl, blue,
    green, red, and black, blue spatter,
    chips on lid and tip of spout, edge
    chips, stains, and base hairline .. 400.00
Waste Bowl, Christmas Ball, red and
  green, yellow spatter 275.00

SPONGEWARE

History: Spongeware is a specific type of decoration, not a type of pottery or glaze.

Spongeware decoration is found on many types
of pottery bodies—ironstone, redware, stoneware,
yellow ware, etc. It was made in both England and
the United States. Marked pieces indicate a start-
ing date of 1815, with manufacturing extending to
the 1880s.

Decoration is varied. In some pieces the sponging is minimal with the white underglaze dominant.
Other pieces appear to be sponged solidly on both
sides. Pieces from 1840–1860 have sponging
which appears in either a circular movement or a
streaked horizontal technique.

Examples are found in blue and white, the most
common colors. Other prevalent colors are
browns, greens, ochres, and greenish–blue. The
greenish–blue results from blue sponging which
has been overglazed in a pale yellow. A red overglaze produces a black or navy color.

Other colors are blue and red (found on English
creamware and American earthenware of the
1880s), gray, grayish–green, red, dark green on
stark white, dark green on mellow yellow, and purple.

References: Susan and Al Bagdade, *Warman's
English & Continental Pottery & Porcelain, 1st Edition,* Warman Publishing Co., Inc., 1987; Kevin
McConnell, *Spongeware and Spatterware,* Schiffer Publishing Ltd., 1990; Earl F. and Ada Robacker, *Spatterware and Sponge,* A. S. Barnes &
Co., 1978.

Bank, pig shape 65.00
Bowl
  7" d, tan and blue sponging, light gray
    ground 65.00
  12¼" d, mixing, blue sponging,
    molded design, white ground 125.00
Bread Plate, 10" l, blue sponging, double open handles 100.00
Cookie Jar, gold highlights, green,
  brown, and ochre 300.00
Cup and Saucer, earthenware, blue
  sponging, c1840 .... 130.00

Cup Plate, 3⅛" d, blue sponging, white
  ground 60.00
Cuspidor, 7½" d, blue sponge dec and
  bands, white ground 90.00
Jardiniere, 11 x 8¼", blue dec, gold
  flecked green rim, white ground ... 100.00
Mug, 4¼" h, brown sponging, yellow
  ground 70.00
Pie Plate, 9" d, brown and green
  sponge, cream ground 50.00

**Pitcher, green and brown sponging,
cream ground, 4½" h, $65.00.**

Pitcher
  4½" h, brown and green, yellow
    ground 65.00
  10" h, beige and blue sponge spatter,
    white ground, edge chips and hair-
    lines 125.00
Plate, 10¼" d, blue sponging, emb scalloped edge, white ground 175.00
Platter, 12" l, blue sponging, white
  ground, Trenton, NJ, c1865 ...... 210.00
Salt and Pepper Shakers, pr, hand
  thrown, white, green and amber
  sponge 100.00
Slop Jar, blue and white 265.00
Toddy Plate, 4¾" d, blue and white,
  marked "Burford Bros" 40.00

SPORT CARDS

History: Baseball cards date from the late 19th
century. By 1900 the most common cards, known
as "T" cards, were those produced by tobacco
companies such as American Tobacco Co., with
the majority of the tobacco-related cards being
produced between 1909 and 1915. During the
1920s American Caramel, National Caramel, and

York Caramel candy companies issued cards identified in lists as "E" cards.

From 1933 to 1941 Goudey Gum Co. of Boston, and in 1939, Gum Inc., were the big producers of baseball cards. Following World War II, Bowman Gum of Philadelphia (B.G.H.L.I.), the successor to Gum, Inc., lead the way. Topps, Inc. (T.C.G.) of Brooklyn, New York, followed. Topps bought Bowman in 1956 and enjoyed almost a monopoly in card production until 1981.

In 1941 Topps was challenged by Fleer of Philadelphia and Donruss of Memphis. All three companies annually produce sets of cards numbering 600 cards or more.

Football cards have been produced since the 1890s. However, it was not until 1933 that the first bubble gum football card appeared in the Goudey Sport Kings set. In 1935 National Chickle of Cambridge, Massachusetts, produced the first full set of gum cards devoted exclusively to football.

Both Leaf Gum of Chicago and Bowman Gum of Philadelphia produced sets of football cards in 1948. Leaf discontinued production after their 1949 issue. Bowman Gum continued until 1955.

Topps Chewing Gum entered the market in 1950 with its college stars set. Topps became a fixture in the football card market with its 1955 All-American set. From 1956 thorough 1963 Topps printed a card set of National Football League players, combining them with the American Football League players in 1961.

Topps produced sets with only American Football League players from 1964 to 1967. The Philadelphia Gum Company made National Football League card sets during this period. Beginning in 1968 and continuing to the present, Topps has produced sets of National Football League cards, the name adopted by the merger of the two leagues.

References: James Beckett, *The Official 1990 Price Guide To Baseball Cards, Ninth Edition*, House of Collectibles, 1989; James Beckett, *Sports Americana Baseball Card Price Guide, No. 10*, Edgewater Book Co., 1988; James Beckett and Denis W. Eckes, *The Sport Americana Football, Hockey, Basketball and Boxing Card Price Guide, No. 5*, Edgewater Books, 1987; Editors of Krause Publications, Sports, *Baseball Card Price Guide, Fourth Edition*, Krause Publications, 1990; Editors of Krause Publications, Sports, *Standard Catalog of Baseball Cards*, Krause Publications, 1990; Gene Florence, *The Standard Baseball Card Price Guide, Second Edition*, Collector Books, 1990; Troy Kirk, *Collector's Guide To Baseball Cards*, Wallace-Homestead Book Company, 1990.

Periodicals: *Baseball Card News, 700 East State Street, Iola, WI 54490; Beckett Baseball Monthly, 3410 Mid Court, Suite 110, Carrolto, TX 75006; Current Card Prices, P. O. Box 480, East Islip, NY 11730; Sports Collectors Digest 700 East State Street, Iola, WI 54990.*

ROCKY CASTELLANI — MIDDLEWEIGHT

Boxing, Topps, #48, Rocky Castellani, 2¹⁄₁₆ x 2¹⁵⁄₁₆", very good condition, $3.00.

BASEBALL

Bowman
  1948 Bowman (black and white)

Complete set (48)	525.00
Common player (1–36)	5.00
Common player (37–48)	7.50
5 Bob Feller	30.00
17 Enos Slaughter	18.00
32 Bill Rigney	6.00

1949 Bowman

Complete set (240)	2,975.00
Common player (1–36)	5.00
Common player (37–73)	6.00
Common player (74–144)	5.00
Common player (145–240)	20.00
19 Bobby Brown	10.00
100 Gil Hodges	30.00
214 Richie Ashburn	85.00

1951 Bowman (color)

Complete set (324)	3,850.00
Common player (1–36)	5.00
Common player (37–252)	5.00
Common player (253–324)	15.00
26 Phil Rizzuto	20.00
122 Joe Garagiola	20.00
314 Johnny Sain	18.00

1953 Bowman (black and white)

Complete set (160)	1,200.00
Common player (1–112)	10.00
Common player (113–128)	16.00
Common player (129–160)	12.00
59 Mickey Mantle	500.00
118 Billy Martin	70.00
148 Billy Goodman	15.00

1955 Bowman (color)

Complete set (320)	1,150.00

Common player (1–224)	2.50
Common player (225–320)	4.00
22 Roy Campanella	22.00
179 Hank Aaron	20.00
242 Ernie Banks	80.00

Topps Era

1951, red backs

Complete set (52)	250.00
Common player (1–52)	3.00
1 Yogi Berra	25.00
31 Gil Hodges	10.00
38 Duke Snider	20.00

1953 Topps

Complete set (280)	2,800.00
Common player (1–165)	4.50
Common player (166–220)	3.50
Common player (221–280)	16.00
27 Roy Campanella	45.00
76 Pee Wee Reese	30.00
82 Mickey Mantle	420.00
147 Warren Spahn	25.00
258 Jim Gilliam	70.00
280 Milt Bolling	25.00

1955 Topps

Complete set (210)	1,225.00
Common player (1–160)	2.50
Common player (151–160)	3.50
Common player (161–210)	4.50
28 Ernie Banks	6.00
123 Sandy Koufax	100.00
124 Harmon Killebrew	35.00
164 Roberto Clemente	130.00
194 Willie Mays	110.00

1957 Topps

Complete set (407)	1,575.00
Common player (1–264)	1.25
Common player (265–352)	5.00
Common player (353–407)	1.25
18 Don Drysdale	32.00
25 Whitey Ford	15.00
35 Frank Robinson	15.00
328 Brooks Robinson	80.00

1959 Topps

Complete set (572)	975.00
Common player (1–110)	1.00
Common player (11–506)	.70
Common player (507–572)	2.50
50 Willie Mays	27.00
150 Stan Musial	20.00
202 Roger Maris	20.00
380 Hank Aaron	25.00
514 Bob Gibson	10.00

FOOTBALL

Bowman Gum Company

1948

Common card	2.25
Sammy Baugh	20.00
Sid Luckman	18.00

1951

Common card	1.50

Norm Van Brocklin	12.00

1952

Common card, large	2.50
Tom Landry, small	30.00

1955

Common card	1.00
Doak Walker	5.00
Frank Gifford	7.50

Fleer Gum Company

1960

Common card	.35
George Blanda	3.00
Ron Mix	2.00

1961

Common card	.30
Jim Brown	12.00

Leaf Gum

1948

Common card	3.00
Bobby Layne	2.00
Jackie Jensen	18.00

1949

Common card	3.00
John Lujack	10.00

Topps Chewing Gum Inc

1950

Common card	1.25
Darryl Royal	12.00
Joe Paterno	18.00

1951

Common card	.40
Bill Wade	2.00

1955

Common card	.75
Four Horsemen	20.00
Sid Luckman	10.00
Jim Thorpe	15.00

1956

Common card	.50
Chuck Bednarik	5.00
Lenny Moore	5.00

1958

Common card	.40
John Unitas	7.50

1959

Common card	.30
Jim Brown	12.00
Ollie Spencer	5.00

SPORTS COLLECTIBLES

History: Individuals have been saving sports-related equipment since the inception of sports. Some was passed down from generation to generation for reuse. The balance occupied dark spaces in closets, attics, and basements.

In the 1980s two key trends brought collectors' attention to sports collectibles. First, decorators began using old sports items, especially in restaurant decor. Second, card collectors began to discover the thrill of owning the "real" thing.

Although the principal thrust was on baseball material, by the beginning of the 1990s all sport categories were collectible, with golf and football especially strong.

References: Mark Baker, *Sport Collectors Digest Baseball Autograph Handbook*, Krause Publications, 1990; James Beckett, *The Sports Americana Price Guide To Baseball Collectibles*, Edgewater Book Co., 1986; James Beckett and Dennis W. Eckes, *The Sports Americana Baseball Memorabilia and Autograph Price Guide*, Edgewater Book Co., 1982; Peter Capano, *Baseball Collectibles*, Schiffer Publishing Ltd., 1989; Ted Hake & Roger Steckler, *An Illustrated Price Guide To Non-Paper Sports Collectibles*, Hake's Americana & Collectibles Press, 1986; John M. and Morton W. Olman, *Encyclopedia of Golf Collectibles: A Collector's Identification and Value Guide*, Books Americana, 1985; Don Raycraft and Stew Salowitz, *Collector's Guide To Baseball Memorabilia*, Collector Books, 1987.

Periodical: *Sports Collectors Digest*, 700 East State Street, Iola, WI 54990.

Collectors' Club: Golf Collectors' Society, P. O. Box 491, Shawnee Mission, KS 66202.

Baseball, autographed photograph, Hazen "Ki Ki" Cuyler, silvered wood frame, 3½ x 5½", $25.00.

BASEBALL

Autographed Baseball
Babe Ruth, includes Lou Gehrig, Jimmie Foxx, Hank Gowdy, and Rube Walberg signatures, dated "Boston 1929" **1,430.00**
New York Giants, twenty signatures, 1957 .... **440.00**
Award, Cy Young, ebonized plaque, mounted cast metal banner with raised letters "Cy Young Awards,

baseball diamond and hand clutching baseball framed by "V" symbol, "Presented to Early Wynn Most Valuable Pitcher 1959," includes photo of Wynn receiving award **12,100.00**
Bank, baseball shape, plastic
American League All–Stars, black base, blue signatures, early 1950s **75.00**
New York Yankees, removable black base, blue signatures, incised coin slot, early 1950s **125.00**
Bat, 38" l, Ty Cobb, 125 Louisville Slugger, Hillerich and Bradsby Co, marked in pencil "Ty Cobb 6–29–25" **3,740.00**
Coaster, 4¼" d, cardboard, Ballantine Ale & Beer adv, black and white portrait illus of Bob Klinger and Virgil Davis, late 1930s **40.00**
Document, autographed, "Shoeless" Joe Jackson, 4 x 1½" cut from legal document, printed, written, and typed information on back, sgd on April 1936 .... **23,100.00**
Jacket
Boston Red Sox, Hall of Fame, wool, black, red collar, cuffs, and waist band, button front, red "B" motif, A G Spalding & Bros tag and stitched "1048" canvas tag, c1940 ...... **4,180.00**
Don Newcombe, Brooklyn Dodgers, blue faded to purple, zippered, Dodgers across front, leather sleeves with cuffs, fold felt label stitched "Newcombe 36" inside left pocket, "Butwin the Champion of Jackets" and "Dick Fisher Athletic Goods" labels **4,620.00**
Medallion, 1½" d, Babe Ruth Shrine, Ruth at bat on one side, Baltimore birthplace on other **55.00**
Money Clip, 1962 San Francisco Giants National League Champions, 14k, baseball and two bats, back engraved "Edgar Feeley 1944" **1,760.00**
Nodder
Mickey Mantle, 7½" h, composition, white and blue Yankee uniform, emb "NY" symbol on cap and chest, sq base, decal with signature, base stamped "Patent Pending, Japan," 1961–62 .... **200.00**
Willie Mays, 7" h, composition, holding baseball in one hand, decal on cap and chest, 1961–62 .... **250.00**
Painting, 18 x 12", Casey Stengel, oil on canvas, matted and framed **460.00**
Pennant, 28½" l, Yankees American League Winners 1922, fourteen bust profile line ups **1,100.00**
Photo Card, Al Bridwell, 5 x 7½", "New York National" and "Bridwell" in margin, 1911 copyright **150.00**

Photograph, 13 x 10½", Babe Ruth, black and white, inscribed black ink "To my friend Jack Lawton from Babe Ruth Dec 15th 1931" 1,870.00

Plaque, 6 x 8", Chicago Cubs, plaster, raised portraits of three players, Charley Grimm, Lon Warneke, Woody English, gold wash, dark brown shadowing, two hanging hooks, early 1930s 250.00

Press Pin
Chicago Cubs 1938 World Series, bear cub clutching enameled baseball marked "Chicago Press 1938" 825.00
New York Yankees 1938 World Series, two crossed bats, raised baseball, Press 1938, red, white and blue border marked "World Series Yankee Stadium" 825.00

Program, 11 x 9", Yankee Stadium Opening Day, April 18, 1923, portraits on cov 770.00

Ring, Jose Canseco Rookie of the Year, 10K gold, green glass set with simulated diamond, marked "American League Rookie of the Year Jose Canseco Oakland A's Athletics 33 and 1986, 117 RBI, 33 HR All Star," sgd inside band "HJ–10K" 4,400.00

Whiskey Bottle, 5" h, clear amber, center label with Pittsburgh ball player illus, late 1800s 150.00

BOXING

Autographed Photograph
Floyd Patterson, 8 x 9¾", glossy, black and white, Patterson in boxing uniform, black marker signature "To Stephen, My Sincere Best Wishes For A Healthy And Happy Life, Your Friend, Floyd Patterson" 40.00
Jack Dempsey, 13 x 11", Dempsey with bulldog and mug of Bulldog beer, inscribed "Hi Rich, Swell Job, Pal Jack Dempsey" 120.00
Jess Willard, 6½ x 8½", black and white glossy, pencil inscription on reverse "Jess Willard", early 1900s 15.00

Playing Cards, James J Jeffries Championship, 52 cards, photo boxer portrait on each card, 1909 copyright .. 100.00

FOOTBALL

Ashtray, 7½" d, Baltimore Colts Championship, china, white, blue cartoon picture, dated Dec 29, 1958, orig box 75.00
Bookends, pr, Knute Rockne, cast iron, raised portrait of Rockne, incised inscription "The Rock Of Notre Dame," early 1930s 150.00

Pennant
New York Jets, 30" l, felt, white design and inscriptions, green background, late 1960s 20.00
San Diego Chargers, 29½" l, felt, yellow–gold and white lettering and helmet design, blue background, American Football League insignia, late 1960s 15.00
New York Giants, 29" l, felt, white inscription and stadium design, dark blue background, red trim, National Football League insignia lower left, late 1960s 20.00

Program, 5½ x 8", Harvard and Yale first football match, Hamilton Park, Saturday Nov 13 1875 .... 770.00

Puzzle
Roman Gabriel, 300 pcs, full color photo action scene, 5½" h cardboard canister, American Publishing Corp, 1972 copyright 15.00
Joe Namath, 500 pcs, full color action scene, boxed, American Publishing Corp, 1971 copyright 20.00

RACING

Game, Derby Day, 72" board opened, six wood horses and hurdles, Parker Brothers, 1959 copyright 40.00
Glass, souvenir, 1964 Kentucky Derby, 5¼" h, frosted, brown horse head, gold inscription "Kentucky Derby/ Churchill Downs," reverse with white lettering listing winners from 1875 to 1963 .... 25.00
Nodder, 6½" h, Shenandoah Downs jockey, composition, gold paper sticker, 1962 copyright, Japan 50.00
Plate, Kentucky Derby Series, Nearing Finish, Reed and Barton, 1972 .... 100.00

STAFFORDSHIRE ITEMS

History: A wide variety of ornamental pottery items originated in England's Staffordshire district, beginning in the 17th century and extending to the present. The height of production was from 1820 to 1890.

These naive pieces are considered folk art by many collectors. Most items were not made carefully; some were even made and decorated by children.

The types of objects are varied, e.g., animals, cottages, and figurines (chimney ornaments). The key to price is age and condition. The older the piece, the higher the price is a general rule.

References: Susan and Al Bagdade, *Warman's English & Continental Pottery & Porcelain, 1st Edition,* Warman Publishing Co., Inc., 1987; Pat

Halfpenny, *English Earthenware Figures, 1740–1840*, Antique Collectors' Club; P. D. Gordon Pugh, *Staffordshire Portrait Figures Of The Victorian Era*, Antique Collectors' Club; Dennis G. Rice, *English Porcelain Animals Of The 19th Century*, Antique Collectors' Club.

Spill Vase, multicolored, c1860, 8½″ h, $285.00.

Animal

Bull, 6½″ w, black spotted bull being tormented by red Staffordshire bull terrier, rocky base, creamware, c1810 . . . . 990.00

Cow, 6″ h, pearlware, iron–red markings, standing before flowering tree, calf at feet, green mound base, c1820 . . . . 225.00

Dog, 12½″ h, King Charles spaniels, copper luster dec, pr 775.00

Ram, 5¼″ h, pearlware, white body, iron–red spots, standing before flowering bocage, rocky base with applied flowers, initials "ME," c1820 . . . . 450.00

Bank, 5″ h, cottage, white snow on roof, two chimneys, black outlines, c1885 200.00

Box, 3⅝″ l, rect, primrose ground, emb, painted sprays of flowers, gilt metal mounts 475.00

Figure

5¼″ h, Harlequin, pearlware, yellow hat with plumes, black mask, turquoise, yellow, iron–red, puce, and black checkered costume, standing in front of tree trunk, mound base 675.00

6½″ h, Lady with Mandolin, white dress, rose accents 245.00

6¾″ h, Prince Albert, unicorn and lion 300.00

9″ h, cloaked woman, holding child's coffin, flanking spaniel on pillow . . 725.00

9½″ h

David Garrick as Richard III, red tent, applied coleslaw dec 325.00

Two girls and dog under block . . . 340.00

10″ h

Country Couple 275.00

Man holding sheaf of wheat and woman with ewer 265.00

10¼″ h, One Legged Soldier's Dream 425.00

10½″ h, Man and Girl 300.00

11¼″ h, Dancing Couple, painted clock face 300.00

13¾″ h, Prodigal's Return 300.00

14½″ h, Robbie Burns and Highland Mary 325.00

Flask, 8″ h, man smoking pipe with cup in hand, wide leaf border, knob handles, overglazed enamel dec, early 19th C 325.00

Jug, 6½″ h, canary yellow and silver luster, commemorative, iron–red transfer print, bust length portrait of Sir Francis Burdett, inscription below, obverse with additional inscription within foliage wreath, silver luster neck, iron–red line border on rim, handle, and spout, c1810 . . . . 725.00

Mug, Dr Franklin Maxim, "Handle Your Tools Without Mittens Remember The Cat In Gloves Catches No Mice, Constant Dropping Wears Away Stones, and Little Strokes Fell Great Oaks" 165.00

Pastille Burner

5½″ h, house, white ground, leaded windows, thatched roof edged in floral encrustations, blue base with applied flowers 335.00

6½″ w, Gothic pavilion, central section with pierced cupola and tracery windows, two doors fitted with vases, outset stepped shaped rect base with applied flowers, buff ground, mid 19th C 220.00

Pipe, 8½″ l, coiled and twisted, underglaze green, blue, and raspberry enamel sponge dec, bowl molded as bust head, stem repairs, early 19th C 1,100.00

Plate, 8⅝″ d, pearlware, painted center spray of two yellow, blue, and brown pansies, blue, green, and brown leaves, scalloped rim, molded scalework and green leaves, c1860, set of 6 . . . . 1,000.00

Spill Vase

8½″ h, Tithe Pig, farmer in black hat, puce jacket, holding brown spotted piglet in right hand, staff in left, wife in black cape, holding infant, parson in black robes, basket of eggs and wheat at their feet, tree restored, pearlware, c1810 . . . . 935.00

11¼″ h, stag and hound, pr 925.00

Stirrup Cup, 5⅜″ h, ironstone, fox head, shaded iron–red and ochre mask,

gray and black muzzle and eyes,
green collar edged in back and white,
gilt center sq, c1810 . . . . **550.00**
Teapot, 4" h, saltglaze, enameled rose,
turquoise, green, iron–red, yellow,
and black bowknotted bouquet, pink,
yellow, and iron–red demi–flowerhead border within turquoise and yellow scallops, iron–red flowerhead finial, green crabstock handle, c1760 **1,870.00**
Watch Holder, 12" h, castle form **385.00**

STAFFORDSHIRE, HISTORICAL

History: The Staffordshire district of England is
the center of the English pottery industry. There
were eighty different potteries operating there in
1786, with the number increasing to 179 by 1802.
The district includes Burslem, Cobridge, Eturia,
Fenton, Foley, Hanley, Lane Delph, Lane End,
Longport, Shelton, Stoke, and Tunstall. Among the
many famous potters were Adams, Davenport,
Spode, Stevenson, Wedgwood, and Wood.

In historical Staffordshire the view is the most
critical element. American collectors pay much
less for non-American views. Dark blue pieces are
favored. Light views continue to remain underval-
ued. Among the forms, soup tureens have shown
the highest price increases.

References: David and Linda Arman, *Historical
Staffordshire: An Illustrated Check List,* published
by author, 1974, out-of-print; David and Linda Arman, *First Supplement, Historical Staffordshire:
An Illustrated Check List,* published by author,
1977, out-of-print; Susan and Al Bagdade, *Warman's English & Continental Pottery & Porcelain,
1st Edition,* Warman Publishing Co., Inc., 1987;
Ada Walker Camehl, *The Blue China Book,* Tudor
Publishing Co., 1946, (Dover reprint); A.W. Coysh
and R. K. Henrywood, *The Dictionary Of Blue And
White Printed Pottery, 1780–1880,* Antique Collectors' Club, 1982; Ellouise Larsen, *American Historical Views On Staffordshire China, 3rd Edition,*
Dover Publications, 1975.

Notes: Prices are for proof examples. Adjust
prices by 20% for an unseen chip, a faint hairline,
or an unseen professional repair; by 35% for knife
marks through the glaze and a visible professional
repair; by 50% for worn glaze and major repairs.

The numbers in parentheses refer to items in
the books by Linda and David Arman, which con-
stitute the most detailed list of American historical
views and their forms.

W.ADAMS&SONS **ADAMS**

ADAMS

The Adams family has been associated with ceramics from the mid 17th century. In 1802 William

Adams of Stoke–upon–Trent produced American
views.

In 1819 a fourth William Adams, son of William
of Stoke, became a partner with his father and
was later joined by his three brothers. The firm
became William Adams & Sons. The father died
in 1829 and William, the eldest son, became manager.

The company operated four potteries at Stoke
and one at Tunstall. American views were produced at Tunstall in black, light blue, sepia, pink,
and green in the 1830–40 period. William Adams
died in 1865. All operations were moved to Tunstall. The firm continues today under the name of
Wm. Adams & Sons, Ltd.

**Adams, plate, Headquarters of the Jun-
iata, U. S., U. S. Views Series, pink
transfer, 10½" d, $85.00.**

Hudson River Series	
Fair Mount, 4" cup plate, pink (459)	**80.00**
Fort Edwards, Hudson River, 5¼" plate, pink (460)	**60.00**
Log Cabin, medallions of Gen. Harrison on border, waste bowl, brown (458)	**250.00**
U. S. Views, Catskill Mountain House, 10¼" soup plate, light blue (445) . . .	**75.00**

CLEWS

From sketchy historical accounts that are available, James Clews took over the closed plant of
A. Stevenson in 1819. His brother Ralph entered
the business later. The firm continued until about
1836 when James Clews came to America to enter

the pottery business at Troy, Indiana. The venture was a failure because of the lack of skilled workmen and the proper type of clay. He returned to England but did not re-enter the pottery business.

Clews, plate, Christmas Eve, dark blue transfer, imp mark, 6¾″ d, $175.00.

Cities Series, dark and medium blue
Philadelphia, 5½″ plate (26)	**425.00**
Quebec, 9″ plate (28)	**225.00**
Sandusky, 17″ platter, dark blue (B-29)	**4,700.00**

Doctor Syntax, dark blue
Doctor Syntax disputing his bill with landlady, 10″ plate (38)	**225.00**
Doctor Syntax mistakes a gentleman's house for an inn, 10″ soup (42)	**150.00**
Doctor Syntax with the dairy maid, 3⅞″ cup plate (46)	**500.00**
Doctor Syntax, advertisement for a wife, 16″ platter (64)	**550.00**

Don Quixote Series, dark blue
Don Quixote, repose in woods, 6″ plate (71)	**150.00**
Mambrino's Helmet, 10″ d, plate (74) .	**150.00**
Sancho Panza and the priest and barber, 7½″ plate (75)	**150.00**

Landing of Lafayette at Castle Garden, dark blue (1)
Pitcher, 8″	**825.00**
Plate	
5½″	**250.00**
10″	**225.00**
Platter, 15″	**450.00**
Soup Plate, 9″	**275.00**
Vegetable Dish, 10″ square	**900.00**

Peace and Plenty dark blue, (A-34a)
Plate, 9″	**250.00**

Picturesque Views Series
Hudson, Hudson River
Soup Plate, 10½″ d, brown (107) . .	**60.00**
Near Hudson, Hudson River, brown, 7″ plate (113)	**60.00**

Peace and Plenty, dark blue (34)
Plate, 10″	**225.00**

Pittsfield Elm, dark blue (33)
Plate, 8″	**425.00**
Platter, 15″	**600.00**
Soup Plate, 10½″ d, Winter View of Pittsfield, MA	**325.00**

States or American and Independence Series, dark blue
Building, Deer on Lawn, 10½″ soup plate (A-2)	**500.00**
Building, Sheep on Lawn, 8⅞″ plate (5)	**225.00**
Mansion, circular drive, vegetable dish (14)	**800.00**
Mansion, winding drive, 4⅞″ h creamer, unrecorded form	**1,500.00**
Three Story Mansion, 4½″ cup plate, three small rim roughages (7) . . .	**400.00**
Two Story Building, curved drive, 8″ plate (9)	**225.00**
University Building with six chimneys, two people and eight sheep, 8¾″ d, plate	**250.00**

Wilkie, Christmas Eve, 8⅞″ d, plate, dark blue (87) . . . . | **150.00**

J.&J. JACKSON

J. & J. JACKSON

Job and John Jackson began operations at the Churchyard Works, Burslem, about 1830. The works formerly were owned by the Wedgwood family. The firm produced transfer scenes in a variety of colors, such as black, light blue, pink, sepia, green, maroon and mulberry. Over 40 different American views of Connecticut, Massachusetts, Pennsylvania, New York, and Ohio were issued. The firm is believed to have closed about 1844.

Job and John Jackson, plate, View of the Canal, Little Falls, Mohawk River, black transfer, scalloped edge, c1830, 10½″ d, $125.00.

American Scenery Series, all colors

Deaf & Dumb Asylum, Phila, 7" plate (471)	**70.00**
Fort Ticonderoga, New York, gravy tureen with cover (473)	**250.00**
State House, Boston, 10½" plate (484)	**60.00**
View of the Canal, Little Falls, Mohawk River, 10½" plate (490)	**125.00**

Miscellaneous

New York, Select Sketches series, 17" platter (496)	**400.00**
Schenectady on Mohawk River, 8" pitcher (494)	**275.00**

THOMAS MAYER

In 1829, Thomas Mayer and his brothers, John and Joshua, purchased Stubbs' Dale Hall Works of Burslem. They continued to produce a superior grade of ceramics.

Arms of the American States, dark blue

GA, 11¾" vegetable dish (500)	**3,000.00**
MA, 9½" platter (502)	**3,500.00**
MD, ftd scalloped rim punch bowl, 4⅞" h, 11½" d, unlisted form, brilliant, high glaze, soft blue, crisp transfer	**8,700.00**
NY	
9¾" plate	**650.00**
10" plate	**600.00**
Lafayette at Washington's Tomb, dark blue, sugar bowl (511)	**700.00**
Lafayette at Franklin's tomb, dark blue, waste bowl (512)	**600.00**

J.W.R.

Stone China

W. RIDGWAY

J. & W. RIDGWAY AND WILLIAM RIDGWAY & CO.

John and William Ridgway, sons of Job Ridgway and nephews of George Ridgway who owned Bell Bank Works and Couldon Place Works, produced the popular Beauties of America series at the Couldon plant. The partnership between the two brothers was dissolved in 1830. John remained at Couldon.

William managed the Bell Bank works until 1854. Two additional series were based upon the etchings of Bartlett's American Scenery. The first series had various borders including narrow lace. The second series is known as Catskill Moss.

Beauties of America is in dark blue. The other series are found in the light transfer colors of light blue, pink, brown, black, and green.

J & W Ridgway, plate, Beauties of America, City Hall of New York, blue transfer, 9½" d, $190.00.

American Scenery

Columbia Bridge on the Susquehanna Pitcher (281)	**275.00**
Peekskill Landing, Hudson River Vegetable Dish (287)	**200.00**

Beauties of America, dark blue

Almshouse, New York, 16" platter (255)	**600.00**
City Hall, New York, 10" plate, medium dark blue (A-260)	**190.00**
Court House, Boston, 10½" platter, medium dark blue	**1,100.00**
Exchange, Baltimore, cup plate (264)	**450.00**
Exchange, Charleston, 8½" gravy tureen undertray	**600.00**
Hospital, Boston, 12" platter, medium dark blue	**950.00**
Library, Phila, 8" plate (268)	**175.00**
Octagon Church, Boston, 10" soup plate, medium dark blue (A-271)	**265.00**
Pennsylvania Hospital, Philadelphia, 19" platter, medium dark blue (B-272)	**1,100.00**

Catskill Moss

Kosciusko's Tomb, 10" soup (305)	**70.00**
Meredith, 9½" plate (307)	**60.00**
President's House, tray (311)	**100.00**

Columbia Star, Harrison's Log Cabin

End View, soup (276)	**90.00**

Side View, plate, 10¼″, plowing, (277)	**90.00**
Sugar Bowl (277)	**275.00**

ROGERS

ROGERS

John Rogers and his brother George established a pottery near Longport in 1782. After George's death in 1815, John's son Spencer became a partner and the firm operated under the name of John Rogers & Sons. John died in 1816. His son continued the use of the name until he dissolved the pottery in 1842.

Boston Harbor, dark blue (441)	
Cup and Saucer	**600.00**
Sugar Bowl	**600.00**
Boston State House, dark blue (442)	
Plate, 10″	**125.00**
Platter, 14″	**475.00**
Zebra, medium dark blue	
Basket, openwork, scalloped rim, emb handles, underglaze eagle and imp marks	**575.00**
Cup and Saucer	**175.00**

R. S. W.

STEVENSON

As early as the 17th century the name Stevenson has been associated with the pottery industry. Andrew Stevenson of Cobridge introduced American scenes with the flower and scroll border. Ralph Stevenson, also of Cobridge, used a vine and leaf border on his dark blue historical views and a lace border on his series in light transfers.

The initials R. S. & W. indicate Ralph Stevenson and Williams are associated with the acorn and leaf border. It has been reported that Williams was Ralph's New York agent and the wares were produced by Ralph alone.

Acorn and Oak Leaves Border, dark blue	
Baltimore Exchange, 5½″ plate (348)	**750.00**
Harvard College, 8⅜″ d, plate, dark blue	**275.00**
Octagon Church, Boston, 4½″ cup plate (356)	**750.00**
Park Theater, New York, 10″ plate (357)	**270.00**
St Paul's Chapel, New York, 6¼″ medium blue plate (359)	**800.00**

Floral and Scroll Border, dark blue	
City Hall, New York, 7″ plate (397)	**1,100.00**
Columbia College, New York, 6½″ soup (398)	**900.00**
New York from Brooklyn Heights, 10¼″ medium blue plate	**950.00**
New York from Heights near Brooklyn, 16¼″ medium dark blue platter	**1,600.00**
Lace Border	
Erie Canal at Buffalo, 10″ soup (386)	**150.00**
Lace Border	
New Orleans	
Cup and Saucer (387)	**100.00**
Teapot (387)	**225.00**
Vine Border	
Almshouse, Boston, 14″ platter (365)	**700.00**
Capitol, Washington, 10″ soup (370)	**400.00**

STUBBS

In 1790 Stubbs established a pottery works at Burslem, England. He operated it until 1829 when he retired and sold the pottery to the Mayer brothers. He probably produced his American views about 1825. Many of his scenes were from Boston, New York, New Jersey and Philadelphia.

Rose Border, dark blue	
City Hall, NY	
Pitcher, 6″ h (335)	**375.00**
Sugar Bowl (336)	**350.00**
Teapot (336)	**500.00**
Spread Eagle Border, dark blue	
Church in the City of New York, 6⅛″ plate (322)	**750.00**
City Hall, New York, 6½″ plate, (A-323)	**200.00**
Fair Mount Near Philadelphia, 10″ plate (A-324a)	**200.00**
Upper Ferry Bridge over the River Schuykill (332)	
Plate, 8¾″	**150.00**

S. TAMS & CO.

The firm operated at Longton, England. The exact date of its beginning is not known, but believed to be about 1810–15. The company produced several dark blue American views. About 1830 the name became Tams, Anderson, and Tams.

WOOD

Enoch Wood, sometimes referred to as the Father of English Pottery, began operating a pottery at Fountain Place, Burslem, in 1783. A cousin Ralph Wood was associated with him. In 1790 James Caldwell became a partner and the firm was known as Wood and Caldwell. In 1819 Wood and his sons took full control.

Enoch died in 1840. His sons continued under the name of Enoch Wood & Sons. The American views were first made in the mid 1820s and continued through the 1840s.

It is reported that the pottery produced more signed historical views than any other Staffordshire firm. Many of the views attributed to unknown makers probably came from the Woods.

Marks vary, although always with the name Wood. The establishment was sold to Messrs. Pinder, Bourne & Hope in 1846.

Enoch Wood & Sons, plate, Erie Canal Aqueduct Bridge at Rochester, dark blue transfer, 7⅝" d, $675.00.

Celtic China, light transfer colors
Buffalo on Lake Erie, vegetable dish
(236) 275.00
Harvard College, 10" plate (240) ... 100.00
Natural Bridge, VA, 9¼" plate (244) 75.00
Pass in the Catskill Mountains, 7"
plate (247) 75.00

Trenton Falls, 8" plate (251) 60.00
Floral Border, irregular, dark blue
Commodore MacDonnough's Victory
(154)
Cream Pitcher, 3½" h, barrel
shaped 1,750.00
Plate, 6½" 350.00
Plate, 9" 250.00
Erie Canal, View of the Aqueduct
Bridge at Little Falls (158)
Pitcher, 6 1½" 1,250.00
Soup Plate, 10¼" 850.00
Sugar Bowl 750.00
Landing of the Pilgrims, Landing of the
Fathers, medium blue, 10" d, plate, pr
(218) 250.00
Shell Border, circular center, dark blue
Baltimore and Ohio Railroad, 10⅛"
soup plate (183) 700.00
Chief Justice Marshall Troy, 8⅛" plate
(127) 450.00
Chiswick on the Thames, gravy tureen, orig lid, undertray and ladle 2,000.00
City of Albany, 10¼" plate (163) ... 425.00
Highlands, Hudson River, 5¾" plate
(167)cm875.00
Mount Vernon, 7½" plate (173) 500.00
Railroad, Baltimore and Ohio, level,
10" plate (183) 600.00
Union Line, 10" plate (144) 575.00
Shell Border, irregular center, dark blue
Commodore MacDonnough's Victory
(130)
Plate, 9" 375.00
Teapot 750.00
Cowes Harbor, 6½" plate (B-132) . 215.00
Eddistone Lighthouse, 8½" open vegetable dish 700.00
Union Line, 9¼" plate (144) 375.00
Wadsworth Tower, 4½" pitcher (147) 550.00

Unknown Maker, sauce tureen, Audley End, Essex, blue transfer, 7½" l, 6½" h, $250.00.

UNKNOWN MAKERS

Anti-Slavery (608)
Cup Plate, 4″, light blue	450.00
Plate, 6″, light blue	200.00
Basket of Flowers, 4½″ cup plate, dark blue	100.00
Batahla, 11 x 8½″ oval bowl, dark blue	900.00

Erie Canal inscription
Pitcher, 5¾″, dark blue (598)	1,400.00
Plate, 10″ (597)	450.00
Maypole, 6¾″ pitcher, medium dark blue, floral border, village scene with livestock in foreground, people dancing	200.00

STAFFORDSHIRE, ROMANTIC

History: The Staffordshire district of England produced dinnerware with romantic scenes between 1830 and 1860. A large number of potters were involved and over 800 patterns have been identified.

The dinner services came in a variety of colors with light blue and pink perhaps the most popular. Usually the pattern is identified on the back of the piece. It was not uncommon for two potters to issue pieces with the same design. Therefore, check the pattern name as well as the maker's name.

It would be impossible to list all patterns. A representative selection follows. Some price ranges to keep in mind are: cups and saucers (handleless) $35–50; cup plates $40–75; plates, 9–10″, $15–50; platters $35–75.

References: Petra Williams, *Staffordshire: Romantic Transfer Patterns*, Fountain House East, 1978; Petra Williams, *Staffordshire II*, Fountain House East, 1986.

Arabesque, grayish blue, Edwards & Son
Gravy Boat	40.00
Relish, small, oblong	25.00
Vegetable Dish, open	35.00
Waste Bowl	35.00

Balantyre, J Alcock
Bowl, 8″ d	40.00
Cup Plate, twelve sided	50.00
Creamer	50.00

Plate
9½″ d, twelve sided	25.00
10½″ d, twelve sided	30.00
Relish, oblong, fluted ends	25.00

Caledonia, William Adams, c1800–1864
Creamer	50.00
Cup and Saucer	40.00

Plate
7½″ d, pink	55.00
8½″ d, dark blue	125.00
10½″ d, pink	70.00
Sugar Bowl	75.00

Cowslip, W Ridgway
Creamer	50.00
Cup and Saucer, handle	40.00
Custard Cup	25.00
Ladle, 15″ l, design on bowl and handle	100.00
Relish, shell shaped	48.00

Etruscan Vase, blue and brown, Thomas, John, Joseph Mayer, c1843–55
Bowl, 7″ d	42.00
Plate, 10½″ d	50.00
Platter, 16 x 11½″	125.00
Relish, 5″	30.00
Saucer	25.00
Soup Plate, wide flange	60.00

Plate, Corsica, brown transfer, marked "W & Co," $25.00.

Garden Scenery, pink, Mayer
Bowl, 4″ d	25.00
Cup and Saucer, handle	50.00
Cup Plate, twelve sided	30.00
Plate, twelve sided	45.00
Sauce	25.00
Soup Plate	45.00
Teapot	140.00
Vegetable, open	65.00

Ivanhoe, Podmore Walker & Co., 1834–1859
Bowl	32.50
Creamer	50.00
Plate, twelve sided	37.50
Sugar	70.00

Millenium, Ralph Stevenson & Son, 1832–1835
Bowl	30.00
Creamer	45.00
Cup and Saucer	32.50
Plate, 10½″ d, red	45.00
Vegetable Bowl, open	75.00

Oriental, Ridgway, c1830–34
Cup and Saucer, handleless	55.00
Cup Plate	50.00
Plate	48.00
Platter, 11½ x 7"	75.00
Tureen, cov, octagonal	125.00

Priory, Edward Challinor and Co., c1853–1862
Bowl	40.00
Creamer	55.00
Cup and Saucer, handleless	35.00
Plate, 9½" d, octagonal	50.00
Platter, 11½" x 17"	80.00
Sugar, cov, handles	125.00
Teapot, pagoda shape	135.00
Toddy Plate, 5" d, light blue	30.00

Undina, black and blue, J Clementson, registered Jan 7, 1852
Plate	40.00
Relish, oval, shell shape	45.00
Vista, meat tray, 19", pink, Mason's	250.00

STAINED AND/OR LEADED GLASS PANELS

History: American architects in the second half of the 19th century and the early 20th century used stained and leaded glass panels as a chief decorative element. Skilled glass craftsmen assembled the designs, the best known being Louis C. Tiffany.

The panels are held together with soft lead cames or copper wraps. When purchasing a panel, check the lead and have any necessary repairs made to protect your investment.

Collectors' Club: Stained Glass Association of America, 1125 Wilmington Avenue, St. Louis, MO 63111.

Leaded, window, semi-circular, torch center, orig frame, 22 x 42", $275.00.

LEADED

36" h, 36" w, bunch of blue grapes, green leaves, blue scroll, opal red ribbon, amber ground, self frame of blue panes, orig wood frame 575.00

43" h, 14½" w, rect, triangular flower dec, clear center panels, green, brown, and pink highlights, oak frames, Midwest, c1910, set of four ... 475.00

75" h, 7" w, asymmetrical leaded panel, clear, white, and red glass, architectural rigging motif, designed by Frank Lloyd Wright, executed by Temple Art Glass Co for Francis W Little House, Wayzata, MN, c1913 .... 6,600.00

STAINED

13¼" h, 43½" l, scenic hp outside layer of winding road with cottages, stone walls, and fences, sailboats and flamingos on river with mountain in background, deeper layer of multicolored dicroic glass, representing brilliant sky from daybreak through sunset, twenty four mottled green and red favrile glass leaded segments border, wooden window frame, attributed to Tiffany Studios Workshop 4,100.00

15¾" h, 4½" w, pair of panels, rect form, stylized rose design, red and green stained panels, early 20th C 125.00

39" h, 34" w, arched, jeweled navy border framing abstract amber and white mosaic design, faceted circles, arched wooden frame, c1900 ..... 450.00

STANGL POTTERY BIRDS

History: Stangl ceramic birds were produced from 1940 until the Stangl factory closed in 1972. The birds were produced at Stangl's Trenton plant and shipped to their Flemington, New Jersey, plant for hand painting.

During World War II the demand for these birds and Stangl pottery was so great that 40 to 60 decorators could not keep up with the demand. Orders were contracted out to private homes. These orders then were returned for firing and finishing. Colors used to decorate these birds varied according to the artist.

As many as ten different trademarks were used. Almost every bird is numbered; many are artist-signed. However, the signatures are used only for dating purposes and add very little to the value of the birds.

Several birds were reissued between 1972 and 1977. These reissues are dated on the bottom and valued at approximately one half of the older birds.

References: Harvey Duke, *The Official Identification And Price Guide To Pottery And Porcelain, Seventh Edition*, House of Collectibles, 1989; Joan Dworkin and Martha Horman, *A Guide To Stangl Pottery Birds*, Willow Pond Books, Inc., 1973; Norma Rehl, *The Collectors Handbook of Stangl Pottery*, Democrat Press, 1982.

Additional Listing: See Stangl pottery in the American Dinnerware category in *Warman's Americana & Collectibles* for more examples.

Cockatoo, #3580, 8⅞″ h, $125.00.

3250E, Drinking duck, 3¾″ h	60.00
3400, Love Bird, 4″ h	50.00
3401, Wren, 3½″ h	50.00
3401D, Wren, pr, 8″ h	90.00
3402S, Oriole, 3¼″ h, orig tag	40.00
3406S, Kingfisher, 3½″ h	50.00
3444, Cardinal, 6½″ h	55.00
3447, Yellow Warbler, 5″ h	50.00
3484, Cockatoo, 11⅜″ h	190.00
3491, Hen Pheasant, 6¼ x 11″	155.00
3492, Cock Pheasant, 6¼ x 11″	150.00
3580, Cockatoo, sgd "D C F"	125.00
3581, Mother and two babies	150.00
3582D, Parakeets, pr	145.00
3583, Parula Warbler, 4¼″ h, orig tag	50.00
3585, Rufous Hummingbird, 3″ h	50.00
3589, Indigo Bunting, 3¼″ h	35.00
3590, Chat, 4¼″ h	100.00
3594, Red–Faced Warbler, 3″ h	55.00
3595, Bobolink, 4¾″ h	125.00
3597, Wilson Warbler, 3½″ h	45.00
3598, Kentucky Warbler, 3″ h, orig tag	40.00
3599D, Hummingbird, pr, 8 x 10½″ . . .	240.00
3627, Hummingbird	40.00
3628, Rieffers Hummingbird, 4½″ h . .	125.00
3634, Allen Hummingbird, 3½″ h	40.00
3813, Bird, yellow and black, red fruit, 5¼″ h	85.00
3853, Group of Kinglets	375.00

STATUES

History: Beginning with primitive cultures, man produced statues in the shape of people and animals. During the Middle Ages most works were religious and symbolic in character and form. The Renaissance rediscovered the human and secular forms.

During the 18th and 19th centuries it was fashionable to have statues in the home. Many famous works were copied for popular consumption.

Statuette or figurine denotes smaller statues, one-fourth life size or smaller.

Reference: Anita Jacobsen (ed.), *Jacobsen's Painting and Bronze Price Guide,* published by author.

Additional Listings: Bronzes and Busts.

Bronze

8″ h, mother and child, brown patina, 19th C	200.00
9″ l, ox, detailed head turned slightly to one side, incised details, Japan, 19th C	990.00
10″ h, Pan of Rohallion, sgd and dated "F Macmonnies, 1890" . . .	1,400.00
17¼″ h, horse, standing stallion, sinister look, plaited mane and bobbed tail, brown patina, rect base sgd "Geo Malissard, 1926"	1,870.00
25″ h, peasant girl, bowed head, left hand resting on column, right hand holding sickle and wheat sheaves, golden-brown patina, inscribed "apres Math" and "n" over "Moreau," numbered "9574," late 19th C	3,000.00
Cast Iron, 33½″ eagle, American, late 19th C	1,200.00
Ivory, 23′ h, maiden, wearing ornate robe, holding flower basket in left hand, flowering branch in right, Chinese	1,650.00
Limestone, 48″ h, Guanyin, Song style, standing, wearing flowing robe, holding flower in each hand, serene features, tiara, mounted on detachable lotus petal base	6,000.00

Marble, bust, female, 13½″ h, $200.00.

Marble
    24" h, Venus at Her Bath, carrara,
        Italian, 19th C **1,100.00**
    29" h, Boy Playing Mandolin, carrara,
        white, sgd **1,600.00**
    36" h, Diana the Huntress, marble
        plinth **2,400.00**
    62" h, Draped Venus, carrara, Italian,
        1757–1822 . . . . **10,000.00**
Porcelain, 14½" h, gentleman, plumed
    hat, gilt lined cloak, molded base,
    Marseilles, late 18th C **275.00**
Wood, 42" h, Guanyin, holding lotus
    flower, dressed in multicolored robe,
    bare chest, standing on double lotus
    base, polychrome pigment highlights,
    c1900 . . . . **500.00**

STEIFF

History: Margarete Steiff, GmbH, established in
Germany in 1880, is known for very fine quality
stuffed animals and dolls as well as other beautifully made collectible toys. The company is still in
business, and its products are highly respected.

The company's first products were wool-felt elephants made by Margarete Steiff. In a few years
the elephant line was expanded to include a donkey, horse, pig, and camel.

By 1903 the company also was producing a
jointed mohair Teddy Bear, whose production dra-
matically increased to over 970,000 units in 1907.
Margarete's nephews took over the company at
this point. The bear's head became the symbol for
its label, and the famous "Button in the Ear" round,
metal trademark was added.

Newly designed animals were added: Molly and
Bully, the dogs; and Fluffy, the cat. Pull toys and
kites also were produced, as well as larger animals
on which children could ride or play.

Become familiar with genuine Steiff products before purchasing an antique stuffed animal. Plush
in old Steiff animals was mohair; trimmings usually
were felt or velvet. Unscrupulous individuals have
attached the familiar Steiff metal button to animals
that are not Steiff.

References: Peggy and Alan Bialosky, *The
Teddy Bear Catalog*, Workman Publishing, 1984,
revised edition; Shirley Conway and Jean Wilson,
Steiff Teddy Bears, Dolls, and Toys With Prices,
Wallace-Homestead, 1984; Margaret Fox Mandel,
Teddy Bears And Steiff Animals, Collector Books,
1984; Margaret Fox Mandel, *Teddy Bears, Annalee Animals & Steiff Animals, Third Series*, Collector Books, 1990; Jean Wilson, *Steiff Toys Revis-
ited*, Wallace-Homestead, 1989.

Periodical: *Steiff Collectors' Anonymous*, 1308
Park Avenue, Piqua, OH 45356.

Additional Listings: Teddy Bears. See Stuffed
Toys in *Warman's Americana & Collectibles* for
more examples.

Pull Toy, horse, 20″ h, c1900, $575.00.

Baboon, 5½" h, Coco, swivel head,
    raised script button, stock, and chest
    tag, orig collar, 1950s **135.00**
Camel, 11" h, raised script button,
    1950s **190.00**
Cat, 3" h, Tapsy, raised script button,
    orig ribbon and bell **110.00**
Dog
    Dachshund, 14" l, button and yellow
        tag in ear **55.00**
    Fox Terrier, 6½" h, mohair, white,
        standing, black and brown mark-
        ings **65.00**
Donkey, 4½" h, mohair, gray, black
    mane, red leather bridle, chest tag **135.00**
Elephant, 7" h, mohair, gray, standing,
    plastic tusks, red felt blanket and
    bells, 1950–60 . . . . **125.00**
Giraffe, 13" h, mohair, gold and brown,
    black bead eyes, incised button, stock
    tag, 1950–60 . . . . **90.00**
Goat, 6" h, mohair, frosted, brown, black
    felt horns, 1950–60 . . . . **75.00**
Koala Bear, 8" h, mohair, gray, beige,
    and cream, fully jointed, chest tag . . **500.00**
Leopard
    8½" l, baby, paper label **150.00**
    11½" l, paper label **250.00**
Lion, 11½" l, metal ear button **500.00**
Monkey, 10" h, Jocko, mohair, brown,
    fully jointed, peach felt face, incised
    button, chest tag **100.00**
Pelican, 9" h, Piccy, mohair, pink, yellow
    felt beak, white vinyl teeth, raised
    script button, chest tag **300.00**
Rabbit, 8" h, mohair, beige, tan, and
    white, jointed neck, brown glass eyes,
    pink stitched nose and mouth, blue
    ribbon around neck, chrome button **150.00**
Teddy Bear
    14" h, felt pads, black eyes, button in
        ear, voicebox **600.00**
    16" h, Limited Edition #4700, 1903
        model, orig box **425.00**

Tiger
4¼" h, baby, seated **215.00**
9" l, white **100.00**
Walrus, 4½" h, mohair, brown, black
markings, google eyes, plastic tusks,
bristly beard **100.00**

STEINS

History: A stein is a mug especially made to hold beer or ale, ranging in size from the smaller ³⁄₁₀ liters and ¼ liters to the larger 1, 1½, 2, 3, 4, and 5 liters, and in rare cases to 8 liters. (A liter is 1.05 liquid quarts.)

Master steins or pouring steins hold 3 to 5 liters and are called krugs. Most steins are fitted with a metal hinged lid with thumblift. The earthenware character-type steins usually are German in origin.

References: Susan and Al Bagdade, *Warman's English & Continental Pottery & Porcelain, 1st Edition,* Warman Publishing Co., Inc., 1987; John L. Hairell, *Regimental Steins,* published by author, 1984; Gary Kirsner and Jim Gruhl, *The Stein Book,* Glentiques, Ltd., 1984; Dr. Eugene Manusov, *Encyclopedia of Character Steins,* Wallace-Homestead, 1976; Eugene V. Manusov and Mike Wald, *Character Steins: A Collector's Guide,* Cornwall Books, 1987; Mike Wald, *HR Steins,* SCI Publications, 1980.

Collectors' Club: Stein Collectors International, P.O. Box 463, Kingston, NJ 08528.

Additional Listing: See Mettlach.

Advisor: Ron Fox.

Glass
Amber, ½ L, pewter hinged top, amber
prunts around base, colored enameled maid and cavalier scene . . . **325.00**

Mettlach #2065, 1½ L, etched, multicolored, jeweled base, sgd "Schlitt," $1,100.00.

Blown
1/2 L, ruby stained, cut **200.00**
2 L, white opaline body, blue handle **175.00**
Pressed, enamel florals, ruby prism
lid **125.00**
Faience
3/4 L, floral, pewter handle, Bayrueth
factory **130.00**
1 L, floral, South German, Mid 18th
C **300.00**
Mettlach
Etched
1/2 L, nymph drinking with large
stein, inlaid lid, sgd "Warth" . . . **410.00**
3/10 L, dwarf in nest, #2134 . . . . **520.00**
1 L, carnivalist, #2778, sgd
"Schlitt" **1,100.00**
PUG
1/4 L, polychrome enameled
gnomes drinking scene, sgd
"Schlitt" **190.00**
1/2 L, bicycle rider, train back-
ground, pewter lid **500.00**
Relief, ½ L, white musicians and dancers, blue band, inset lid **210.00**
Pewter
1/2 L, relief
Hunter and game **90.00**
Young girls **75.00**
Porcelain, ½ L
Caroline, gold beads around neck,
brown braided hair forms handle,
bonnet forms pewter lid, marked
"Musterschutz" **700.00**
Sad Radish, shaded beige ground,
pewter mountings, green radish
leaves finial, marked "Muster-
schutz" **325.00**
Pottery, ½ L
Bowling Pin, three bowling scenes **240.00**
Football, college flags with "P" **230.00**
Three Eisenbahn Regt Berlin–Hanau
1909–11, rear roster, bridge and
train scenes, locomotive finial,
thumblift with guard star **1,050.00**
Stoneware, relief
1/2 L, hunter and game animals . . . **250.00**
1 L, tavern scene **110.00**

STEUBEN GLASS

History: Frederick Carder, an Englishman, and Thomas G. Hawkes of Corning, New York, established the Steuben Glass Works in 1904. In 1918 the Corning Glass Co. purchased the Steuben Company. Carder remained with the firm and designed many of the pieces bearing the Steuben mark. Probably the most widely recognized wares are "Aurene," "Verre De Soie," and "Rosaline," but many other types were produced.

The firm continues operating, producing glass of exceptional quality.

References: Paul Gardner, *The Glass of Frederick Carder,* Crown Publishers, 1971; Paul Perrot, Paul Gardner, and James S. Plaut, *Steuben: Seventy Years Of American Glassmaking*, Praeger Publishers, 1974.

Museum: The Corning Museum of Glass, Corning, N.Y.

ACID CUT BACK

Bowl, 8" d, 1¾" h, flared, alabaster, green jade overlay, cut floral swag border, overall etched scrolling ground **300.00**
Globe, 9", schoolhouse type, Ivorene, orig air brushed brass flush mount fixture, ornate details, raised fleur–de–lis dec **345.00**
Vase
  8" h, 10" d, shouldered oval, three layers, plum jade, dark amethyst to alabaster ground, double etched, acid cut back Chinese pattern, scrolled background, fleur–de–lis mark **3,100.00**
  10¼" h, 3¾" d, heavy walled, cobalt blue Aurene ground, silver–blue irid, cut to dark cobalt, broad vintage frieze of grapes, leaves, and vines below shoulder dec of stylized leaves and berries, sgd "Steuben Aurene 2683" on base **4,000.00**

AURENE

AURENE

Basket, 14" h, gold glass basket, fancy ormolu frame and handle, sgd "Aurene, F Carder" **2,600.00**
Bowl, 7⅛" h, 6¼" d, amber, goblet shape, tapered foot, irid purple neck and fold over lip **850.00**
Candlesticks, pr, 3¾" h, everted rim tapering to stem with applied glass protrusion, circular cushioned foot, overall brilliant peacock blue irid, inscribed "Steuben Aurene L384" **800.00**
Compote, 6" d, 8¼" h, gold, quarter round bowl, elongated shaped stem, disk pedestal foot, sgd "Steuben Aurene 2642" **500.00**

Decanter, 10¼" h, gold, dimpled body, undulating rim, peaked stopper, engraved "Aurene" **660.00**
Nut Dish, gold, shaped tripartite rim, applied glass handle, inscribed "Aurene F Carder" **400.00**
Powder Box, 4", engraved copper wheel dec, orig SS enameled cov **1,250.00**
Salad Bowl, 8½" d, shallow, flared, gold, sgd "Aurene 3059," set of 4 ...... **800.00**
Vase
  6" h, 4" d, elongated cuspidor shape, gold, mirror brilliance, sgd "Steuben" **1,100.00**
  10⅜" h, baluster shape body, waisted neck, everted rim, blue **660.00**
  14¼" h, floriform, flared cylindrical body, ruffled rim, knopped stem, circular foot, blue, silver printed mark **825.00**

CALCITE

Bowl, 10" to 13¾" d, 3½" to 4¾" h, gold Aurene int., flared, small disk platform base, graduated set of four **450.00**
Compote, 9¾" d, 2¾" h, flared flattened rim, bright gold irid Aurene bowl, domed calcite pedestal foot **275.00**
Lamp Shade, green leaf and vine **250.00**
Vase, 6¼" h, 8" d, conical, blue Aurene luster on flared flattened rim, disk foot, Steuben triangular label on base **900.00**

CLUTHRA

Bowl, 15" d, 7½" h, heavy conical walls, shaded black–gray to clear and white crystal, irregular swirling bubbles throughout **800.00**
Chalice, green shaded to white, random trapped air bubbles **125.00**
Urn, 6½" h, pink, handles, sgd **650.00**

Vase, Jade, tapered cylinder, swirl, fleur-de-lis mark, 10½" h, $325.00.

JADE

Bowl, 12" d, jade bowl, alabaster base, sgd **425.00**

Compote, 6" d, 3½" h, green bowl, alabaster stem and base **115.00**

Sherbet, green jade ground, engraved flowers and festoons cut to alabaster, alabaster stem and foot, matching 7¼" underplate **450.00**

Wine, 7" h, jade bowl, alabaster stem, set of 6 .... **550.00**

MISCELLANEOUS

Candlesticks, pr, 10¼" h, swirled milky glass baluster stem, urn form nozzle, flat drip pan highlighted with purple rim, spreading deep purple circular foot **250.00**

Chandelier, 17" d, round, Ivorene, acid etched floral swag and shield dec, white painted metal ceiling mounts **475.00**

Cigarette Box, 4½", clear, Pan Am Building on cov, sgd on base **120.00**

Finger Bowl and Underplate, celeste blue, shape #1820, fleur–de–lis mark **200.00**

Lemonade Set, 5 pcs, pitcher and four glasses, amethyst, blue applied handles, ribbed design, sgd **550.00**

Pitcher, 8¾" h, clear, applied handle, sgd on base **275.00**

Salt, translucent emerald green, stenciled "Steuben" **40.00**

Vase
  10" h, green, etched tassels and flower designs, sgd on base ... **275.00**
  12¼" h, cream, eight ribs, ruffled edge **125.00**

ROSALINE

Centerpiece Set, low ftd bowl, pr 12" h candlesticks, alabaster trim **700.00**

Compote, 10" d, 4½" h, flattened pink jade bowl, applied alabaster stem and foot **325.00**

Nappy, 4½ x 5½", alabaster handle, shape #205, ground pontil **325.00**

Newel Post Ornament, 7½" h, bulbed oblique, rosaline overlay, cut back faceted roundels and star crest, applied faceted alabaster pedestal foot, gilt metal mount **500.00**

Vase, 7¼" h, flared ovoid, pink jade, domed alabaster pedestal foot, pr .. **850.00**

VERRE DE SOIE

Basket, 3½" h, 1¾" d, applied handle with prunts, ground pontil **465.00**

Champagne, 7" h, conical flute, bright

turquoise blue twisted stem and rim, set of 14 .... **1,400.00**

Jardiniere, 6 x 8", ten ribbed, swirled, quatrefoil rim **250.00**

Perfume Bottle, 5" h, melon ribbed, Rosaline Cintra dapper **525.00**

Plate, luncheon, applied opaque pink rim, set of 6 .... **450.00**

STEVENGRAPHS

History: Thomas Stevens of Coventry, England, first manufactured woven silk designs in 1854. His first bookmark was produced in 1862, followed by the first Stevengraphs, perhaps in 1874, but definitely in 1879 at the York Exhibition. The first "portrait" Stevengraphs (of Disraeli and Gladstone) were produced in 1886, and the first postcards incorporating the silk woven panels in 1903. Stevens offered many other items with silk panels, including valentines, fans, pincushions, needle cases, etc.

Stevengraphs are miniature silk pictures, matted in cardboard, and usually having a trade announcement or "label" affixed to the reverse. Thomas Stevens's name appears on the mat of the early Stevengraphs directly under the silk panel. Many of the later "portraits" and the larger silks (produced initially for calendars) have no identification on the front of the mat other than the phrase "woven in pure silk" and have no label on the back. Other companies, notably W. H. Grant of Coventry, copied this technique. Their efforts should not be confused with Stevengraphs.

American collectors favor the Stevengraphs of American interest, such as "Signing of the Declaration of Independence," "Columbus Leaving Spain," and "Landing of Columbus." Sports-related Stevengraphs such as "The First Innings" (baseball), and "The First Set" (tennis) are also popular, as well as portraits of Buffalo Bill, President and Mrs. Cleveland, George Washington, and President Harrison.

The bookmarks are longer than they are wide, have mitered corners at the bottom, and are finished with a tassel. Originally, Stevens's name was woven into the fold-over at the top of the silk, but soon the identification was woven into the fold-under mitered corners. Almost every Stevens bookmark has such identification, except the ones woven at the World's Columbian Exposition in Chicago, 1892–1893.

Postcards with very fancy embossing around the aperture in the mount almost always have Stevens's name printed on them. Embossed cards from the "Ships" and "Hands Across The Sea" series generally are not printed with Stevens's name. The most popular postcard series in the United States are "Ships" and "Hands Across the Sea," the latter incorporating two crossed flags and two hands shaking. Seventeen flag combinations have been found, but only seven are common. Stevens produced silks that were used in the "Alpha" Publishing Co. cards. Many times the silks were the top or bottom half of regular bookmarks.

References: Geoffrey A. Godden, *Stevengraphs and Other Victorian Silk Pictures,* Associated University Presses, Inc., 1971; Chris Radley, *The Woven Silk Postcard,* privately printed, 1978; Austin Sprake, *The Price Guide to Stevengraphs,* The Antique Collectors' Club, Baron Publishing, 1972.

Collectors' Club: Stevengraph Collectors' Association, 2103–2829 Arbutus Road, #2103, Victoria, British Columbia, V8N 5X5, Canada.

Museum: Coventry, England.

Note: Prices are based on pieces in mint or close to mint condition.

Advisor: John High.

The Late Frederick Archer, Prince of Wales colors, blue body, red sleeves, orig mat, $110.00.

BOOKMARK

Apostle's Creed, The	65.00
Babes in the Wood	70.00
Charles Dickens	100.00
God Speed the Plough, gilt frame	100.00
Home Sweet Home	135.00
I Love Little Pussy, 1874	75.00
Merry Christmas And A Happy New Year, pointed on both ends	100.00
Morning Hymn - Awake My Soul	75.00
New Year's Auld Lang Syne	70.00
Prince of Wales anthem, 1863	100.00
The Lady Godiva Procession, framed	225.00

STEVENGRAPH

Death of Nelson	200.00
Declaration of Independence	350.00
Finish, The	150.00
For Life or Death, fire engine rushing to burning house, orig mat and frame	325.00
Good Old Days, The	200.00

H. M. Stanley, famous explorer	300.00
Landing of Columbus, The	350.00
Last Lap, The	250.00
Park In Coventry, 7 x 13″	150.00
President Cleveland	350.00
Kaiser Wilhelm II	325.00

STEVENS AND WILLIAMS

History: In 1824 Joseph Silvers and Joseph Stevens leased the Moor Lane Glass House at "Briar Lea Hill" (Brierley Hill), England, from the Honey-borne family. In 1847 William Stevens and Samuel Cox Williams took over, giving the firm its present name. In 1870 the firm moved to its Stourbridge plant. In the 1880s the firm employed such renowned glass artisans as Frederick C. Carder, John Northwood, other Northwood family members, James Hill, and Joshua Hodgetts.

Stevens and Williams made cameo glass. Hodgetts developed a more commercial version using thinner-walled blanks, acid etching, and the engraving wheel. Hodgetts, an amateur botanist, was noted for his brilliant floral designs.

Other glass products and designs manufactured by Stevens and Williams include intaglio ware, Peach Bloom (a form of peachblow), moss agate, threaded ware, "jewell" ware, tapestry ware, and Silveria. Stevens and Williams made glass pieces covering the full range of late Victorian fashion.

After WWI the firm concentrated on refining the production of lead crystal and achieving new glass colors. In 1932 Keith Murray came to Stevens and Williams as a designer. His work stressed the pure nature of the glass form. Murray stayed with Stevens and Williams until WWII and later followed a career in architecture.

Reference: R.S. Williams-Thomas. *The Crystal Years*, Stevens and Williams Limited, England, Boerum Hill Books, 1983.

Additional Listing: Cameo Glass.

Basket, 9″ l, 6″ h, applied crimped amber glass rim, transparent blue handle, blue folded pedestal bowl, enameled florals, sgd "S & W Stourbridge"	225.00
Biscuit Jar, 8″, blue swirls, metal lid and handle	420.00
Bowl, 6¾″ d, pink, MOP satin Swirl pattern, cream lining, box pleated top	500.00
Fairy Lamp, 6″ h, 5¼″ d, blue, white, and crystal stripes, satin finish, turned	

Vase, ruffled, ruby red throat, deep gold shading to peach to buff, multicolored dec, 8″ h, $400.00.

down ruffled edge base, applied glass bottom 820.00

Pitcher, 10½″ h, cranberry overlay, blue int., applied amber feet and rim, green handle form green leaves and yellow flower 600.00

Rose Bowl, 3¾″ d, cranberry opalescent, satin finish, alternating plain panels and raised emb beaded panels, upright box pleated top 175.00

Sherbet Cup and Underplate, 4⅞″ h, 4½″ d cup, 7″ d underplate, intaglio cutting, royal blue cut to clear, cherries and pears, cut stem and base 325.00

Sweetmeat Jar, cov, 6″ h, cream, opaque, three applied amber and green leaves, pink lining, SP rim, lid,and handle 200.00

Toothpick Holder, green cut to clear, hallmarked sterling rim 350.00

Vase

5″ h, bulbous form, spiral and vertical ribbing, four lobed lip, peach, cased butterscotch 450.00

7½″ h, baluster form, white, cased cream to chocolate, spiral and vertical ribbing, four lobed neck, c1880 325.00

9¼″ h, bulbous, elongated neck, opal white body overlaid in white over amber to blue–green heat reactive layer, cameo cut and carved morning glory blossoms, leaves, and vines, circular mark "Stevens & Williams Stourbridge Art Glass" .. 3,600.00

11″ h, 4½″ d, MOP satin, Swirl pattern, orange shading to white, white lining 265.00

12″ h, conical, bright yellow cased to clear, white overlay, cameo cut foxgloves, buds, leaves, grasses, and butterfly, linear borders, marked "Stevens & Williams Stourbridge Art Glass" 2,000.00

STICKLEYS

History: There were several Stickley brothers: Albert, Gustav, Leopold, George, and John George. Gustav often is credited with creating the Mission style, a variant of the Arts and Crafts style. Gustav headed Craftsman Furniture, a New York firm, much of whose actual production took place near Syracuse. A characteristic of Gustav's furniture is exposed tenon ends. Gustav published *The Craftsman*, a magazine supporting his anti-machine points of view.

Originally Leopold and Gustav worked together. In 1902 Leopold and John George formed the L. and J. G. Stickley Furniture Company. This firm made Mission-style furniture and cherry and maple early-American-style pieces.

George and Albert organized the Stickley Brothers Company, located in Grand Rapids, Michigan.

References: David M. Cathers, *Furniture Of The American Arts and Crafts Movement*, New American Library, 1981; Bruce Johnson, *The Official Identification And Price Guide To Arts And Crafts*, House of Collectibles, 1988.

Periodical: *Arts and Crafts Quarterly*, P.O. Box 3592, Station E, Trenton, NJ 08629.

Bookrack, revolving, Model No. 90, mahogany, open handle, four wooden book compartments, pivotal base, small red Gustav Stickley decal, partial paper label, 12½″ sq, 9″ h, c1905 600.00

Candlesticks, pr, 9″ h, copper, circular removable bobeche, cylindrical column, riveted C shaped handle, bowl shaped base, orig patina, imp mark, c1913 .... 1,100.00

Catalog, The Work of L & J G Stickley Furniture Catalog, Fayetteville, NY, 1914, The Art Press, 7¼ x 9⅜″ 100.00

Clock, tall case, 70¾″ h, 12″ deep, top projecting over brass face, copper numerals, tall slightly flaring case, medium brown patina, marked "No. 3," red decal, sgd in box, c1902, pendulum, weights, and escutcheons missing 7,500.00

Desk Blotter, 25 x 15⅛″, rect, copper 335.00

Furniture

Bookcase, Model No. 645, oak, three int. shelves, glass paned doors, L & J G Stickley mark, 49″ w, 12″ d, 55″ h 3,200.00

Chair

Arm, oak, five horizontal slat back, spindled sides, Gustav Stickley decal mark, 33″ w, 37½″ d, 39½″ h 10,450.00

Morris

Model No. 332, oak, four horizontal slat back, round pivot pegs, five vertical slats beneath each arm, small red decal, 31½″ w, 38½″ d, 40″ h . . **5,500.00**

Model No. 471, oak, four horizontal slat back, six slat sides, faux leather upholstered cushions, L & J G Stickley red decal mark **1,870.00**

Side, Model No. 808, oak, five vertical slat back, leather upholstered seat, white L & J G Stickley decal mark, 38″ h **265.00**

Chest of Drawers, oak

Model No. 622, four long graduated drawers, two short drawers, panel construction sides, large red Gustav Stickley decal with "Stickley" outlined, 41″ w, 22½″ d, 50″ h, c1902 . . . . **4,500.00**

Model No. 902, arched back rail, two top drawers, four horizontal drawers, oval hammered pulls, red decal in top right drawer, 39¾″ w, 22″ d, 53½″ h **4,200.00**

Model No. 909, oak, two short drawers over three graduated drawers, panel construction sides, red Gustav Stickley decal in top right drawer, paper label, 37¼″ w, 19″ d, 42″ h **2,450.00**

Desk, lady's, writing, two drawers, shaped undertier shelf, red decal mark on back, new leather seat, 34½″ l, 20″ d, 34″ h, c1901 . . . . . **1,650.00**

Rocker, Morris, Model No. 413, oak, four horizontal slat back, orig cushions in poor condition, branded "L & J G Stickley," 29″ w, 34½″ d, 36″ h **935.00**

Settle, Model No. 265, oak, sixteen vertical slat back, slat sides, leather upholstered seat cushion, white L & J G Stickley decal mark, 75½″ l, 31″ d, 34″ h **800.00**

Server, Model No. 818, oak, rect top, horizontal back rail, row of three drawers, under shelf, red Gustav Stickley decal in top right hand drawer, 48″ l, 19½″ d, 39″ h **2,100.00**

Stool, foot, oak, rect, leather upholstered top, branded "L & J G Stickley," 16¼ x 19¾ x 13¾″ **500.00**

Table

Center, oak, round top, four sq legs joined by cross stretchers, exposed tenons, pyramidal center finial, 40″ d, 30″ h **1,550.00**

Library, Model No. 531, oak, rect, one long drawer, undertier shelf joined by through tenons to side stretchers, white "L & J G Stickley" decal in drawer, 49″ l, 30″ d, 29″ h **1,210.00**

Side, oak, octagonal, four legs joined by cross stretcher, white L & J G Stickley decal mark, 18″ d, 20″ h **1,100.00**

Tea, oak, circular top, sq section legs joined by cross stretcher, 20″ d, 26″ h **900.00**

Lamp, table, 16½″ d shade, 22½″ h, Model No. 290 hammered copper shade with cut–out panels with mica inserts, copper neck ring supporting four removable iron arms, Model No. 504 four part columnar shaft, oak flattened truncated pyramidal foot, compass mark **7,700.00**

Trophy Case, hanging, oak, slab sides, through tenons, slight curve to ends, two glazed cabinet doors, copper hinges, escutcheons, and round pulls, two adjustable int. shelves, 60½″ w, 12″ d, 48½″ h, c1904 . . . . . **8,250.00**

Umbrella Stand, 33″ h, 11½″ d, No. 54, oak, four tapering sq wooden posts joined by lower boxed shelf, copper drip pan insert, paper label, c1912 **6,100.00**

Wall Sconce, No. 400, electric, 3¾ x 5½″ bell shaped yellow opalescent glass shades, hammered copper bracket, 1906, pr **1,500.00**

STIEGEL-TYPE GLASS

History: Baron Henry Stiegel founded America's first flint glass factory at Manheim, Pennsylvania, in the 1760s. Although clear glass was the most common color made, amethyst, blue (cobalt), and fiery opalescent are found. Products included bottles, creamers, flasks, flips, perfumes, salts, tumblers, and whiskeys. Prosperity was short-lived. Stiegel's extravagant living forced the factory to close.

It is very difficult to identify a Stiegel-made item. As a result the term "Stiegel type" is used to identify glass made at that time period in the same shapes and colors.

Enamel decorated ware also is attributed to Stiegel. True Stiegel pieces are rare, an overwhelming majority is of European origin.

Reference: Frederick W. Hunter, *Stiegel Glass*, 1950, available in Dover reprint.

Reproduction Alert: Beware of modern reproductions, especially in enamel wares.

ENAMELED

Bottle, 4⅝″ h, half post, fiery opal, polychrome enameled florals **200.00**

Bride's Bottle, 7″ h, enameled flowering plants and dancing man playing French horn, orig pewter collar **185.00**

Cologne Bottle

4" h, ⅞" w, 1⅛" d, deep sapphire blue, outwardly flared tooled lip, pontiled, rect, beveled corners, multicolored floral and bird dec, c1780–1820, lip chip, mismatched collar 650.00

5" h, 2⅝" w, 2¼" d, fiery opal milk glass, tooled and expanded, pontiled, rect, beveled corners, multicolored floral and rabbit dec, c1780–1820 . . . . 675.00

Flip, 3½" h, clear, enameled flowers, berries, and running rabbit 325.00

Tumbler, 3⅛" h, clear, polychrome enameled bird and flowers 185.00

Salt, cobalt blue, twelve heavy vertical ribs, swirled to right, 2½" h, $150.00.

ENGRAVED

Cologne Bottle, 8" h, clear, pewter top, pontiled, finely engraved floral dec, c1800 . . . . 600.00

Flip, 9⅞" h, cov, clear, bird dec 225.00

Mug, 8⅞" h, cov, clear, applied ribbed handle, floral dec, flake on finial . . . 200.00

Tumbler

7" h, clear, hearts dec 400.00

7⅞" h, pale green, basket of flowers dec 175.00

OTHER

Bowl, 3" d, blown mold, Expanded DQ, deep cobalt blue, applied foot 1,200.00

Creamer, 3¾" h, Expanded DQ, deep cobalt blue, applied handle 1,200.00

Salt, 3" h, blown mold, sapphire blue, double ogee form, twelve honeycombs over diamonds, pontil scar, late 18th C 150.00

Scent Bottle, 2¾" l, swirled, deep cobalt blue 200.00

STONEWARE

History: Made from dense kaolin clay and commonly salt-glazed, stonewares were hand-thrown and high-fired to produce a simple, bold vitreous pottery. Stoneware crocks, jugs, and jars were produced for storage and utility purposes. This use dictated shape and design—solid, thick-walled forms with heavy rims, necks, and handles with little or no embellishment. When decorated, the designs were simple: brushed cobalt oxide, incised, slip trailed, stamped, or tooled.

Stoneware has been made for centuries. Early American settlers imported stoneware items at first. As English and European potteries refined their earthenware, colonists began to produce their own wares. Two major North American traditions emerged based only on the location or type of clay. North Jersey and parts of New York comprise the first area; the second was eastern Pennsylvania spreading westward and southward and into Maryland, Virginia, and West Virginia. These two distinct locations, style of decoration, and shape are discernible factors in classifying and dating early stoneware.

By the late 18th century, stoneware was manufactured in all sections of the country. During the 19th century, this vigorous industry flourished until glass "fruit jars" appeared and the widespread use of refrigeration began. By 1910, commercial production of salt-glazed stoneware came to an end.

References: Georgeanna H. Greer, *American Stoneware: The Art and Craft of Utilitarian Potters*, Schiffer Publishing, Ltd., 1981; Don and Carol Raycraft, *Country Stoneware And Pottery*, Collector Books, 1985; Don and Carol Raycraft, *Collector's Guide To Country Stoneware & Pottery*, 2nd Series, Collector Books, 1990.

Periodical: *Stoneware Collectors' Journal*, 670 Mix Avenue #5L, Hamden, CT 06514.

Apple Butter Jar, 7" h, imp "F H Cowden, Harrisburg" 85.00

Batter Jug

8" h, yellow amber salt glaze, wire handle 75.00

11" h, brown albany slip dec, wood cork 45.00

Bottle, 10" h, cobalt blue quill work inscription "J B 1870" 600.00

Bowl

4½" h, tan glaze, ribbed handle, English 25.00

10¾" d, cobalt blue stenciled design and "2" 300.00

Churn

13½" h, cobalt blue brushed floral dec, imp "1½" 125.00

15¾" h, brushed cobalt blue floral dec 175.00

26½" h, cobalt foliage and berry dec, R Woodworth, Burlington, Vermont,

3 gal, edge chip, reglued broken
out piece 100.00

Cooler

16¾″ h, emb blue and white woman
at wishing well scene 150.00

18″ h, keg shape, gray salt glaze,
greenish highlights, emb bands . . 50.00

19½″ h, brushed cobalt blue floral design, imp "3" 400.00

**Crock, two gallons, Richard C Rem-
mey, Philadelphia, cobalt blue feather
dec, $400.00.**

Crock

8″ h, cobalt blue slip dec of bird on
branch, imp label "Ottoman Bro's &
Co, Fort Edward, NY 1½," missing
one handle 90.00

10″ h, cobalt blue quill work, pecking
chicken, imp "2" 225.00

10½″ h, simple brushed cobalt blue
design and "3" 175.00

11¼″ d, cobalt dec, imp "White &
Wood Binghamton, NY," 3 gal . . . 750.00

11½″ h, cobalt dec, imp "John
Waugh, Jr, LOWELL, MASS," 2 gal 350.00

12″ h, ovoid shape, incised lines at
shoulder, imp "F Young 3" 70.00

12¾″ h, brushed cobalt blue floral design and "5" 150.00

14″ h, cobalt blue quill work dec, bouquet of flowers and "6" 225.00

17½″ h, American eagle with banner
and wreath dec, medium blue "5" 75.00

Funnel, 5″ h, brown Albany slip 155.00

Jar

6½″ h, cobalt floral dec 150.00

6⅝″ h, ovoid, four horizontal cobalt
blue stripes 150.00

9¼″ h, ovoid, applied rim handles with
daubs of cobalt blue 55.00

10½″ h, cobalt blue slip floral design,
imp "Cortland 2" 375.00

10¾″ h, ovoid, blue applied handles,
imp label "McKenzie & Jackson,
Beaver, PA" 150.00

14″ h, brown Albany slip, incised "3" 30.00

14¼″ h, cobalt blue stenciled designs,
brushed "4," applied handles 90.00

15½″ h, ovoid, grayish yellow glaze,
imp "6" 40.00

19″ h, ovoid, tooled lines at shoulder,
double ear handles, cobalt blue
quill work label "J I Ambright Newport, Ohio," reverse flourish and "6" 145.00

19¾″ h, ovoid, stenciled and freehand
cobalt blue label, eagle and "T. F.
Reppert, Greensboro, Pa. 8" 1,075.00

Jug

7¼″ h, ovoid 55.00

7¾″ h, ovoid 165.00

10½″ h, ovoid, imp "Tyler & Dillon,
Albany" highlighted in blue 200.00

10¾″ h, cobalt blue slip bird dec, imp
"J Norton & Co, Bennington, VT" 550.00

11″ h, stylized cobalt blue quill work
dec, imp "J & E Norton, Benning-
ton, VT" 550.00

11¼″ h, ovoid

Brown brushed slip stylized bird,
imp label "L. Norton & Son," mi-
nor base chips 2,700.00

Cobalt blue star shaped leaves and
"1," stenciled label "Sibb J
Beighel, Pleasant Unity, PA" . . . 275.00

13″ h, cobalt blue stenciled label,
"Jas. Benjamin Stoneware Depot,
Cincinnati, O" 65.00

13¼″ h, cobalt blue quill work, decorative "2," imp label "West Troy
Pottery 2" 325.00

13½″ h, cobalt blue simple stenciled label,
"A P Donaghho, Parkersburg, W
Va 2" 125.00

14″ h, cobalt dec, imp "J Norton & Co
Bennington, VT 2" 700.00

15¼″ h, incised and cobalt dec, imp
"Commeraws Stoneware," Thomas
Commeraws, New York, c1810 . . 1,200.00

15½″ h, cobalt blue simple floral, imp
label "Ottman Bro's & Co, Fort Edward, N. Y. 3," hairline in base of
handle 325.00

16¾″ h, ovoid, brushed cobalt blue
floral dec, imp label "Cowden &
Wilcox, Harrisburg, PA 4" 700.00

17½″ h, brown Albany slip, imp "5,"
double handle 30.00

One gallon, elaborate cobalt blue
glaze, incised dec, 19th C 225.00

Two gallon, blue and gray, handled,
bloomimg poppy leaves, sgd
"Honesdale, PA" 350.00

Three gallon, cobalt bird dec, E & L
P Norton, Bennington, VT 175.00

Milk Bowl

    11" d, brown Albany slip int., applied
handles and rim spout **100.00**

    17" d, brown glazed ext. with imp flo-
ral design, gray glazed int. with co-
balt dec, 19th C **550.00**

Milk Pitcher, green **35.00**

Mug, 4¼" l, two blue stripes **55.00**

Pitcher

    8" h, brown Albany slip **65.00**

    8½", light tan and ivory glaze, hound
handles **50.00**

    9" h, ovoid, cobalt blue brushed floral
dec **425.00**

    10¾" h, cobalt dec, imp "W K Rich-
ardson Leominster Mass" **500.00**

    11¾" h, brown Albany slip **45.00**

    13" h, stenciled and freehand cobalt
blue label, iron band around base,
"Williams and Reppert, Greens-
boro, PA 2" **1,400.00**

    13½" h, W E Howe, Worcester, MA,
2 gal, cobalt flower dec, age cracks   **100.00**

Preserving Jar

    7⅛" h, brushed cobalt blue straight
and wavy lines **155.00**

    7¼" h, brushed cobalt blue straight
and wavy lines **155.00**

    8¾" h, brushed cobalt blue foliage de-
sign **175.00**

    8⅞" h, brushed cobalt blue foliage de-
signs **245.00**

    9¾" h, cobalt blue stenciled and free-
hand label "Jas Hamilton & Co,
Greensboro" **200.00**

    10" h, stenciled and freehand cobalt
blue label "Hamilton & Jones,
Greensboro, PA" **175.00**

    11¾" h, stenciled cobalt blue label
and "2" in wreath **75.00**

Salt, 2⅝" h, cobalt blue dec, two rim
chips **500.00**

Spittoon, cobalt blue dec and "2," "M
Woodruff, Cortland" **425.00**

STONEWARE, BLUE AND WHITE

History: Blue and white stoneware refers to
molded, salt-glazed, domestic, utilitarian earthenware with a blue glaze produced in the late 19th
and early 20th centuries. Earlier stoneware was
usually handthrown and either undecorated, hand-
decorated in Spencerian script floral and other motifs, or stenciled. The stoneware of the blue and
white period is molded with a design impressed,
embossed, stenciled, or printed.

Although known as blue and white, the base
color is generally grayish in tone. The blue cobalt
glaze may coat the entire piece, appear as a series
of bands, or accent the decorative elements.

All types of household products were available

in blue and white stoneware. Bowls, crocks, jars,
pitchers, mugs, and salts are just a few examples.
The ware reached its height between 1870 and
1890. The advent of glass jars, tin containers, and
chilled transportation brought its end. The last blue
and white stoneware was manufactured in the
1920s.

References: Kathyrn McNerney, *Blue & White
Stoneware,* Collector Books, 1981; Don and Carol
Raycraft, *Collector's Guide To Country Stoneware
& Pottery,* Second Series, Collector Books, 1990.

Collectors' Club: Blue & White Pottery Club, P.
O. Box 297, Center Point, IA 52213.

Reproduction Alert: A vast majority of the blue
and white stoneware found in antiques shops and
flea markets is unmarked reproductions from
Rushville Pottery, Rushville, OH.

Pitcher, Swan, 8¼" h, $160.00.

Beater Bowl, Bassett adv **70.00**

Bowl, 10½" d, feathers, double ring . .   **100.00**

Bowl and Pitcher Set, Rose and Fish-
scales **250.00**

Butter Dish, cov

    Apple Blossom **250.00**

    Good Luck **125.00**

Cookie Jar, 9" h, Turkey Eye, diffused
bands, acorn finial **140.00**

Cooler

    11" l, barrel shape, cobalt blue dec,
three short feet **150.00**

    16¾" h, emb blue and white woman
at wishing well scene, lid **150.00**

Creamer, 4½" h, Arc and Leaf, paneled   **70.00**

Custard Cup, 4" d, 3½" h, blue and orange brush dec, wide blue band . . .   **65.00**

Match Holder, 5½" d, 5" h, Duck **65.00**

Mixing Bowl, 7½" d, Flying Bird **175.00**

Mug

    Basketweave and Flower, 5" h, bul-
bous, rolled rim, rope handle **60.00**

    Flying Bird **125.00**

Pie Plate, 10½" d, blue on blue, raised
grooved base **100.00**

Pitcher

    7" h, Good Luck **190.00**

8" h, emb tree bark with leaves, drinking scene, Gamrinus on keg 85.00
8¼" h, emb tree bark with leaves, bust of girl, and man holding beer steins 75.00
10¾" h, emb oval medallion portraits and leaves, bearded men, dog's heads, stippled ground 85.00
16" h, Fishscales and Flower 150.00

Roaster
12" d, 8½" h, Wildflower 110.00
19" l, 9" h, diffused blues, applied handles, flat finial 150.00

Rolling Pin
Swirl 475.00
Wildflower, 7" 250.00

Salt
Butterfly 65.00
Good Luck 100.00

Soap Dish, Beaded Medallion with Rose, emb lines 120.00
Soup Bowl, 6½" d, brush dec 150.00
Spittoon, basketweave 200.00
Teapot, 9" h, 6½" d, Swirl, double wire bail, wood hand grip, relief split balls, lid with finial 350.00
Toothbrush Holder, Rose and Fishscales 50.00
Umbrella Stand, 24" h, 10" d 250.00

STRETCH GLASS

History: Stretch glass was produced by many glass manufacturers in the United States between the early 1900s and the 1920s. The most prominent makers were Cambridge, Fenton (who probably manufactured more stretch glass than any of the others), Imperial, Northwood, and Steuben. Stretch glass can be identified by its iridescent, onionskin-like effect. Look for mold marks. Imported pieces are blown and show a pontil mark.

Reference: Berry Wiggins, *Stretch Glass*, Antique Publications, 1972 (1987 value update).

Collectors' Club: Stretch Glass Society, 1221 Andrews Avenue, Lakewood, OH 44107.

Compote, amber and green irid, clear stem and base, 7⅝" d, $60.00.

Bowl
7½" w, sq, orange, Imperial 50.00
9" d, 4" h, flared, orange, Imperial cross mark 50.00
9½" d, Treebark, ftd 25.00

Cake Server, center handle, green . . . 18.00

Candlesticks, pr
8½" h, vaseline 70.00
10" h, green 35.00

Candy Dish, cov
Footed, paneled, blue 30.00
Low, yellow 15.00

Compote, 9½" d, 5½" h, vaseline, treebark patterned stem, sgd "Northwood" 135.00
Lamp Shade, white 35.00

Plate
6" d, octagonal, vaseline 10.00
8" d, Laurel leaf dec, green 12.00

Ring Holder, 5" d, yellow, enamel dec 25.00
Sherbet, liner, vaseline 20.00

Vase
6" h, hp, florals and leaves, rolled rim, clear ribbed int. 35.00
6½" h, fan, green 18.00
7" h, fan, vaseline 25.00

STRING HOLDERS

History: The string holder developed as a utilitarian tool to assist the merchant or manufacturer who needed tangle-free string or twine to tie packages. The early holders were made of cast iron, some patents dating to the 1860s.

When the string holder moved to the household, lighter and more attractive forms developed, many made of chalkware. The string holder remained a key kitchen element until the early 1950s.

Man wearing top hat, plaster, 8¾" h, $8.00.

Advertising, Jaxon Soap, cast iron . . . 70.00

Apple
Chalkware, red, on branch with blackberries 15.00
Tin, 4 x 4", marked "Shenandoah Valley Apple Candy, Winchester, VA" 150.00

Beehive, 6" h, cast iron, dated "Apr 1865" 50.00
Blown Glass, clear, applied cobalt blue base and finial, 4¾" d, 4½" h, Pittsburgh 125.00
Cat, yarn holder 25.00
Chef, chalkware 30.00
Court Jester, chalkware 35.00
Dutch Girl, cast iron, hanging type ... 20.00
Girl, wearing blue bonnet, chalkware 45.00
Leaf design, emb, cast iron, 9¾" h ... 75.00
Old Lady, sitting in rocking chair, chalkware 25.00
Pear, chalkware, purple plums and leaves
  Yellow 20.00
  Red 15.00
Rooster, ceramic, Royal Bayreuth 225.00
Teapot, wood, chef decal 25.00
Victorian, oval, cast lattice pattern, recessed ball and spout, ceiling mount, 10" d 125.00

SUGAR SHAKERS

History: Sugar shakers, sugar castors, or muffineers all served the same purpose: to "sugar" muffins, scones, or toast. They are larger than salt and pepper shakers, and were produced in a variety of materials, and were in vogue in the late Victorian era.

Diamond Point and Quartered Block, Duncan and Miller #24, clear, SP metal top, pontil mark, $40.00.

CHINA

English, 5" h, cream ground, pink roses, green leaves, registry mark 50.00
Meissen, 6½" h, baluster, hp, multicolored floral spray, ozier band, pierced cov edged in puce, c1750, chip on finial 450.00
Nippon, 4¾" h, floral dec, handle, blue maple leaf mark 85.00

R S Prussia, Schlegelmilch, 4¾" h, luster finish, rose dec, scalloped base, red mark 245.00
Wedgwood, blue ground, white classical figures 55.00

GLASS

Amberina, 4" h, globular, IVT, emb floral and butterfly lid 400.00
Burmese, 4" h, globular, fall color leaves, blue enamel berries 800.00
Crown Milano, 3" h, melon ribbed, fall colored triangular leaves, enamel highlights, orange shaded to yellow satin ground, emb floral and butterfly top 525.00
Custard, 6" h, Maize, Libbey 200.00
Mt Washington, 4" h, fig, melon ribbed, textured, blue and pink asters dec, peach ground 650.00
Pattern Glass
  Banded Portland, maiden's blush, orig top 125.00
  Pineapple and Fan 35.00
  Snail, ruby stained, orig top 175.00
Peachblow
  5½" h
    New England, shiny finish 900.00
    Wheeling, shiny finish, tapered ring neck 550.00
  6" h, Mt Washington, ribbed, natural color violets and leaves, blue to white ground 500.00
Satin, 5" h, MOP, cranberry, IVT, white enamel stork and floral dec 800.00
Smith Bros, 5" h, melon ribbed, raised gold outline florals, cream ground, emb floral top 200.00

SWANSEA

History: This superb pottery and porcelain was made at Swansea (Glamorganshire, Wales) as early as the 1760s with production continuing until 1870.

Marks on Swansea vary. The earliest marks were SWANSEA impressed under glaze and DILLWAN under glaze after 1805. CAMBRIAN POTTERY was stamped in red under glaze from 1803–1805. Many fine examples, including the botanical series in pearlware, are not marked, but may have the botanical name stamped under glaze.

Fine examples of Swansea often may show imperfections, such as firing cracks. These pieces are considered mint because they left the factory in this condition.

Reference: Susan and Al Bagdade, *Warman's English & Continental Pottery & Porcelain, 1st Edition,* Warman Publishing Co., Inc., 1987.

Reproduction Alert: Swansea porcelain has

been copied for many decades in Europe and England. Marks should be studied carefully.

Dessert Tray, 9½" l, hp, creamware,
  gilding, polychrome, under glaze
  mark Swansea, c1780 . . . . **275.00**
Dish, 11 /2" d, botanical series, c1805 **325.00**

**Plate, blue and white Oriental dec, gold
rim, c1785, imp mark, 7¼" d, $125.00.**

Plate
  7¾" d, hp, creamware, flowers, reti-
    culated, marked "Dillwyn," c1805   **190.00**
  8½" d, center floral, molded foliate
    scroll rim **230.00**
Punch Bowl, earthenware, Oriental dec,
  marked "Cambrian Pottery," c1803 **1,000.00**
Serving Dish
  8" w, sq, sweetpeas, botanical, c1805 **175.00**
  11½" l, oblong, lily, pink, botanical,
    c1805 . . . . **350.00**

SWORDS

History: The first swords in America came from Europe. The chief cities for sword manufacturing were Solingen in Germany, Klingenthal in France, and Hounslow and Shotley Bridge in England. Among the American importers of these foreign blades was "Horstmann," whose mark is found on many military weapons.

New England and Philadelphia were the early centers for American sword manufacturing. By the Franco-Prussian War, the Ames Manufacturing Company of Chicopee, Massachusetts, was exporting American swords to Europe.

Sword collectors concentrate on a variety of styles: commission vs. non-commission officers' swords, presentation swords, naval weapons, and swords from a specific military branch such as cavalry or infantry. The type of sword helped identify a person's military rank and, depending on how he had it customized, his personality as well.

Following the invention of repeating firearms in the mid-19th century, the sword lost its functional importance as a combat weapon and became a military dress accessory. Condition is a key criterion determining value.

Reference: Harold L. Peterson, *The American Sword 1775–1945*, Ray Riling Arms Books Co., 1965.

Collectors' Club: Japanese Sword Society of the United States, Inc., P.O. Box 4387, Grasso Plaza Branch, St. Louis, MO 63123.

Civil War, Officer's, scalloped MOP grips, gold five pointed stars studs, feathered silver bands on grip straps, heavy gold gilt pommel and guard, Liberty bust surmounted by scrolls, wreath on head as pommel cap, floral chased knucklebow set with anthrasite stone, pierced "US," encircled by laurel spray and ornate foliage, 32" slightly curved finely etched single edge blade, reverse marked "W. Clauberg, Solingen," orig satin and blaze lined case, matching lacquered field scabbard, $14,500.00.

AMERICAN

Artillery, Model 1833,"N.P. AMES,"
  1835, brass hilt inspected "JM," "H K
  C," and "ORD," orig brass mounted
  black leather scabbard **500.00**
Cavalry, saber
  Contract of 1807, 34½" curved blade
    stamped "W Rose & Sons" **800.00**
  Model 1860, light, 30¾", brass half
    basket hilt, wood grip with leather
    and brass wire, iron scabbard . . . **200.00**
  Prahl type, 33½" curved blade, single
    fuller, brass hilt with openwork
    guard and knucklebow, faceted
    grip, c1800 . . . . **450.00**
Fraternal, Ames, regular, 29½" blade,
  19" etching, obverse with profuse fo-
  liage, "Charles S. Tanner," standing
  knight in armor, and "Ames Sword
  Co/Chicopee, Mass," gilt brass hilt
  with anchor on the langet over
  "HOPE," fitted black grip with gilt

cross, orig black leather scabbard with engraved gilt brass mounts, throat engraved with "IN HOC SIGNO/VINCES" with a snake and cross **45.00**

Musician's Sword, Model 1840, stamped at obverse ricasso "US/1863/FSS," reverse stamped "C ROBY W CHELMSFORD MS," orig issue scabbard **400.00**

Officer's, 30½" curved blade, brass hilt with five ball branch and knucklebow, pillow pommel, sq reeded ivory grip, orig black leather scabbard with brass mounts, c1815 . . . . **800.00**

Presentation, 32" blade, etched foliage, eagle, and trophy of arms and script "US signed Ames Mfg Chicopee/Mass," standard Pattern 1850 gilt brass hilt, sharkskin cov grip, twisted brass wire wrapping, elaborate brass scabbard, orig script presentation "Capt JB Parsons/Co C 10th Mass Regt/1861" **2,000.00**

EUROPEAN

English, 32½" l blade, quasi–basket hilt, fish scale cov grip, knucklebow with London hallmarks, guard with silver scrolls engraved with serpent heads, engraved counterguard with serpent design, orig leather scabbard, 1772–73 . . . . **1,100.00**

French, Officer, saber, 40½", 35¼" slightly curved blade, obverse engraved and gilt dec against blued ground and marked "Gendarmerie du Roi," reverse with military motifs and Sun King emblem, blade sgd "Coulaux Freres Klingenthal," gilted brass hilt with three branches with relief floral work, pommel emb fleur–de–lis, black leather and wire grip, steel scabbard with gilted brass carrying ring mounts **800.00**

Japanese, Wakazashi, 22¼" l, blade engraved with Japanese characters, lacquered scabbard with chiseled and inlaid mounts **750.00**

KNIVES

Bowie, 10⅛", German silver crossguard, staghorn scales, blade stamped "L F & G", 19th C **125.00**

Dirk, lady's
8", double edged blade, coin silver crossguard and ferrule, turned bone hilt, orig red morocco leather scabbard, 1825–50 . . . . **210.00**

8³⁄₁₆" l, double edged blade, coin silver crossguard and ferrule, ivory grip with silver cape, orig brown morocco leather scabbard, 1825–50 . . . . **250.00**

Japanese, Tanto, 17" blade, engraved tang with Japanese characters, one side with chiseled dragon pattern, wood carrying case, label "Tadahiro Fujiwara" **1,800.00**

Rifleman's, 11¾" blade, brass crossguard, orig black leather scabbard and frog, marked "US/WD and Ames Mfg Co/Cabotville/1849" **2,100.00**

Hunting
10⅜" l, German silver crossguard with ball finials, black horn scales, orig brown leather scabbard with German silver mounts, blade stamped "J Rodgers & Sons/No 6 Norfolk St/Sheffield" **260.00**

11³⁄₈" l, German silver crossguard with ball tips, black horn scales, leather scabbard, blade stamped "J Rodgers & Sons/No 6 Norfolk St/Sheffield" **175.00**

TEA CADDIES

History: Tea once was a precious commodity. Special boxes or caddies were used as containers to accommodate different teas, including a special cup for blending.

Around 1700, silver caddies appeared in England. Other materials, such as Sheffield plate, tin, wood, china, and pottery, also were used. Some tea caddies became very ornate.

Advertising, Lipton, brass, British Exhibition, 1924 . . . . **55.00**

Creamware, 3¾" h, cylindrical, iron–red and black dec of Samuel anointing

Rosewood, dome top, brass hinges, inlaid fruitwood on all sides, single compartment, 4⅛ x 4⅝ x 5", $500.00.

Saul, shaped cartouches, scattered foliage, Dutch dec, hairline crack in base **300.00**
Mother of Pearl, 4" h, ivory trim, Continental **600.00**
Porcelain
  4" h, polychrome dec, figures in garden scene, floral accent, Continental **125.00**
  5½" h, Chinese, blue and white, Kangxi **275.00**
  6" h, Chinese Export, Famille Rose, floral dec, monogrammed, c1785 **425.00**
Silver
  English, 5⅓" h, bombe body, chased scrolls and floral garlands, hinged lid with flame finial, marked "GN & RH," Chester, 1895 .... **325.00**
  Sterling, 4⅜" h, ginger jar shape, body and cov etched and engraved with ducks and foliage, Japanese taste, marked "J B & S M Knowles Co, Providence," c1875 .... **600.00**
Wedgwood, Jasperware, 5¾", tri-color, yellow, black, and white, classical figure **1,575.00**
Wood
  4⅛" h, 3 pcs, incised, Shinto shrine, Japanese landscape, inscription and signature **100.00**
  5½" h, pearwood, pear shape, finial and key missing, George III, late 18th C **1,500.00**
  6½" h, 8¼" w, 5½" d, mahogany, inlaid, English **275.00**
  6¾" h, fruitwood, pear shape, escutcheon and key, foil lined, early 19th C **1,400.00**

TEA LEAF IRONSTONE CHINA

History: Tea Leaf Ironstone china flowed into America from England in great quantities in the 1860-to-1910 period and graced the tables of working-class America. It traveled to California and Texas in wagons and by boat down the Mississippi River to Kentucky and Missouri. It was too plain for the rich homes; its simplicity and strength appealed to wives forced to watch pennies. Tea Leaf found its way into the kitchen of Lincoln's Springfield home; sailors ate from it aboard the *Star of India*, now moored in San Diego and still displaying Tea Leaf.

Tea Leaf was not manufactured exclusively by English potters in Staffordshire, contrary to popular opinion. Although there were more than 30 English potters producing Tea Leaf, at least 21 American potters helped satisfy the demand. However, American potters perpetuated the myth by using backstamps bearing the English coat-of-arms and

the marking "Warrented." The American housewife favored imported ware to that made by Americans.

Anthony Shaw (1850–1900) first registered the pattern in 1856 as Luster Band and Sprig. Edward Walley (1845–1856) already was decorating ironstone with luster trefoil leaf, a detached bud, and trailing green vine. Walley's products are designated Pre-Tea Leaf and are sought by eclectic collectors. Other early variants include "Morning Glory" and "Pepper" by Elsmore and Forster (Foster; 1853–1857) and "Teaberry" by Clementson Bros. (1832–1916). Clover leaf, cinquefoil, and pinwheel all may be found in a collection specializing in early ware.

The most prolific Tea Leaf makers were Anthony Shaw and Alfred Meakin (1875–). Johnson Bros. (1883–), Henry Burgess (1864–1892) and Arthur J. Wilkinson (1897–), all of whom shipped much of their ware to America and followed close behind Shaw and Meakin.

Although most of the English Tea Leaf is copper luster, Powell and Bishop (1868–1878) and their successors, Bishop and Stonier (1891–1936), worked exclusively in gold luster. Beautiful examples of gold luster by H. Burgess still are being found. Mellor, Taylor & Co. (1880–1904) used gold luster on their children's tea sets.

J. and E. Mayer, Beaver Falls, Pennsylvania, were English potters who emigrated to America and produced a large amount of copper luster Tea Leaf. The majority of the American potters decorated with gold luster, with no brown underglaze like that found under the copper luster.

East Liverpool, Ohio, potters such as Cartwright Bros. (1864–1924), East End Pottery (1894–1909), Knowles, Taylor and Knowles (1870–1934), and others decorated only in gold luster. Since no underglazing was used with the gold, much of it has been washed away.

By the 1900s Tea Leaf's popularity had waned. The sturdy ironstone did not disappear. It was stored in barns and relegated to attics and basements. Much of it was disposed in dumps, where one enterprising collector has dug up some beautiful pieces.

A frequent myth about Tea Leaf is that pieces marked "Wedgwood" are *the* Wedgwood, Josiah. This is not true! Dealers and collectors who perpetuate this myth should be confronted. Enoch Wedgwood was the only potter of that name to produce Tea Leaf. Enoch Wedgwood's product is beautiful with large showy leaves. He deserves full credit for his work.

Reference: Annise Doring Heaivilin, *Grandma's Tea Leaf Ironstone*, Wallace-Homestead, 1981.

Museums: Lincoln Home, Springfield, Ill.; Sherman Davidson House, Newark Ohio; Ox Barn Museum, Aurora, Oreg.

Reproduction Alert: There are reproductions that are collectible, and there are *reproductions*! Avoid the latter. Collectible reproductions were made by Cumbow China Decorating Co. of Abington, Virginia, from 1932 to 1980. Wm. Adams and Sons, an old English firm, made reproduction Tea Leaf from 1960 to 1972. Red Cliff, who decorated Hall China blanks with Tea Leaf and clearly marked them, worked in the late 1960s and early 1970s.

Ruth Sayer started making Tea Leaf reproductions in 1981. Although her early pieces were not marked, all of it now is marked with a leaf and the initials "RS" on the bottom. In 1968 Blakeney Pottery, a Staffordshire firm, manufactured a poor-quality reproduction of Meakin's Bamboo pattern and marked it "Victoria." It was distributed through a Pennsylvania antiques reproduction outlet.

Pitcher, marked "Mellor & Taylor," 6½" h, $135.00.

Bowl
9¼" w, sq, Meakin	50.00
9½" d, round, Meakin	70.00

Butter Dish, cov, 5⅜" w, sq, orig insert, 3 pcs Wedgwood 120.00

Butter Pat
Round, Alfred Meakin	12.00
Square, Wedgwood	12.00

Casserole, 8 x 10", cov, nut finial, marked "Rd April 7, 1856" 150.00

Child Size, Lily of the Valley blank
Creamer	200.00
Cup and Saucer, handleless	125.00
Soup Plate	45.00

Coffeepot
Elsmore & Forster variant	100.00
Meakin, 6¾" h	75.00

Compote, 9" d, rim foot, Meakin 175.00

Creamer and Sugar
Alfred Meakin	175.00
Mellor, Taylor & Co	225.00

Cup Plate, 3¼" d, unmarked 38.00

Cup and Saucer
Thomas Furnival & Sons, deep saucer	75.00
Shaw, A, handleless	110.00

Gravy Boat, 5½ x 9½" tray, Mellor, Taylor & Co 80.00

Mug, emb, Lily of the Valley, A Shaw	140.00

Nappy, 4¼" d, scalloped edge, fluted sides, Mellor, Taylor & Co 25.00

Pitcher
5¼" h, feather design on sides, bulbous top, John Edwards	130.00
6" h, cream, rooster head pattern, Thomas Furnival & Sons	115.00
7" h, milk, East End Pottery, American	100.00

Plate
8½" d, Clementson	18.00
9¾" d, Davenport	25.00
10" d, underglaze, copper luster, emb rim, Powell & Bishop	16.00

Platter
8¼" l, Meakin	50.00
9½ x 13½", molded handles, Thomas Furnival & Sons	55.00
14 x 10", Alfred Meakin	30.00

Relish
4½ x 7½", Wedgwood	30.00
8½ x 4¾", A Meakin, bamboo style	20.00

Sauce Boat, Peerless 60.00
Sauce Tureen, cov, underplate, and ladle, cable style, A Shaw 300.00
Saucer, deep, Alfred Meakin 12.00
Soap Dish, lid, drainer, Wilkinson, AJ 165.00
Soup Tureen, lid, ladle, Powell & Bishop 250.00
Spoon Rest, 5¼ x 8¾", mitten shape, cable style, Thomas Furnival & Sons 45.00
Sugar, cov, Meakin 45.00

Teapot
W Adams, Empress shape, c1960	110.00
Alfred Meakin, 7⅝" h, squatty shape, emb leafy floral design	185.00

Vegetable Dish
Covered, 9" d, rect, Meakin	50.00
Open, round, Anthony Shaw	20.00

Wash Bowl and Pitcher, 14" d, pink and copper luster, Davenport 575.00

TEDDY BEARS

History: Originally thought of as "Teddy's Bears," the name comes from President Theodore Roosevelt. These stuffed toys are believed to have originated in Germany and in the United States between 1902 and 1903.

Most of the earliest Teddy Bears had humps on their backs, elongated muzzles, and jointed limbs. The fabric used was usually mohair; the eyes were either glass with pin backs or black shoe buttons. The stuffing was generally excelsior. Kapok (for softer bears) and wood-wool (for firmer bears) also were used as stuffing materials.

Quality older bears often had elongated limbs, sometimes with curved arms, oversize feet, and felt paws. Noses and mouths were black and embroidered onto fabric.

The earliest Teddy Bears are believed to have been made by the original Ideal Toy Corporation in America and a German company, Margarete Steiff, GmbH. Bears made in the early 1900s by other companies can be difficult to identify because they had a strong similarity in appearance and because most tags or labels were lost through childhood play.

Teddy Bears are rapidly increasing as collectibles and their prices are increasing proportionately. As in other fields, desirability should depend upon appeal, quality, uniqueness, and condition. One modern bear already has been firmly accepted as a valuable collectible among its antique counterparts: the Steiff Teddy put out in 1980 for the company's 100th anniversary. This is a reproduction of that company's first Teddy and has a special box, signed certificate, and numbered ear tag; 11,000 of these were sold worldwide.

References: Peggy and Alan Bialosky, *The Teddy Bear Catalog*, Workman Publishing, 1984, revised edition; Kim Brewer and Carol-Lynn Rössel Waugh, *The Official Price Guide To Antique & Modern Teddy Bears*, House of Collectibles, 1990; Shirley Conway and Jean Wilson, *Steiff Teddy Bears, Dolls, and Toys With Prices*, Wallace–Homestead, 1984; Margaret Fox Mandel, *Teddy Bears And Steiff Animals*, Collector Books, 1984; Margaret Fox Mandel, *Teddy Bears, Annalee Animals & Steiff Animals, Third Series*, Collector Books, 1990; Helen Sieverling (comp.) and Albert C. Revi (ed.), *The Teddy Bear And Friends Price Guide*, Hobby House Press, Inc., 1983.

Periodical: *The Teddy Bear And Friends*, Hobby House Press, Inc., 900 Frederick Street, Cumberland, MD 21502.

Collectors' Club: Good Bears Of The World, P. O. Box 8236, Honolulu, HI 96815.

Additional Listing: See Steiff.

Steiff, teddy bear, light brown mohair, jointed, hump, long nose, blue and white checkered apron, 12″ h, $175.00.

BEARS

3½″ h, gold plush body, Shuco	145.00
7¼″ h, mohair, beige, full jointed, glass eyes, tag and ear button	80.00
9½″ h, wool, brown, jointed limbs, swivel head, straw stuffed, shoe button eyes, black sewn nose and mouth, felt paws, c1900	175.00
12″ h, jointed, black eyes, felt pads	450.00
13″ h, haircloth, articulated limbs, straw stuffed, button eyes, worn	110.00
14″ h, jointed, glass eyes, felt pads, musical	500.00
14½″ h	
Haircloth, gold, articulated limbs, straw stuffed, glass eyes, felt paw pads and nose, embroidered detail, voice box	300.00
Mohair, blonde, brown felt pads, marked "Merrythought, Ironbridge, Shrops, England"	125.00
15″ h, mohair, yellow, excelsior stuffed, fully jointed, shoe button eyes, long nose, felt paws, pink vest, c1918	275.00
16″ h, plush, cinnamon, black button eyes, floss nose	460.00
17″ h, mohair, blonde, black shoe button eyes, black floss nose	440.00
18½″ h, fully jointed, stuffed, black button eyes, German	175.00
19″ h	
Haircloth, gold, articulated limbs and head, glass eyes, embroidered details	165.00
Plush, pale gold, button eyes, felt paw pads, replaced ribbon, worn	40.00
23″ h, mohair, gold, jointed shoulders and hips, glass eyes, c1910	750.00
24″ h, stuffed, jointed, glass eyes, one pad replaced, worn	150.00

BEAR RELATED ITEMS

Advertising Trade Card, Roosevelt Bears scene, Cracker Jack adv, 1907	25.00
Book, *The Roosevelt Bears Abroad*, Seymour Eaton, 1908	100.00
Bottle, 4⅞″ h, figural, Teddy bear reading book	110.00
Perfume Bottle, 3¾″ h, mohair, jointed limbs, removable head, black button eyes, black sewn nose and mouth, glass bottle liner	200.00
Stickpin, tin, Roosevelt Bear litho	125.00

TELEPHONES

History: The deregulation of the nation's telephone industry and increasing interest in antique telephones has led to increasing values for old telephones and equipment.

Lovers' telegraphs and other crude sound-operated and unpatented telephones existed prior to Alexander Graham Bell's 1876 patent. However, it is generally accepted that Bell invented the telephone powered by electricity.

The most valuable antique telephones come from the pre-1895 period and must be marked, dated, or easily documented. Instruments also must be unaltered and have all major original parts. Telephones marked Charles Williams, Jr., a Boston manufacturer whose factory was the "birthplace" of the infant Bell Telephone Company, are among the most valued.

Post-1895 telephones have value if modified or converted to be compatible with today's modern phone network. Conversions should be done by an expert who will supply additional parts without removing any of the major components to accomplish conversion.

Refinishing also requires expert skills. Do not remove original circuitry. Restoring nickel and black baked enamel finishes is most desirous. Buffing original parts to expose the brass beneath will make it difficult to distinguish those parts from the many dated and old-fashioned marked, solid brass fake parts and whole telephones which have been flooding the market for a decade. No mass-produced telephone made in the United States prior to 1950 was offered with a shiny brass finish!

References: R.H. Knappen, *History And Identification Of Old Telephones*, 2 volumes, published by author, 1978; R.H. Knappen, *Old Telephones Price Guide And Picture-Index To History Of Old Telephones*, published by author, 1981.

Collectors' Clubs: Antique Telephone Collectors Association, Box 94, Abilene, KS 67410; Telephone Collectors International, P.O. Box 700165, San Antonio, TX 78270.

Advisor: Dan Golden

Automatic, Dialing Telephone
Globe Automatic, wall model	950.00
Monson Automatic, wall model	1,200.00
Ness Automatic, wall model	700.00
Select–O–Phone	200.00
Strowger Patent	
Automatic Electric, candlestick model	1,200.00
Wall Model, small	650.00
Double Box Telephone
Oak, plain, Stromberg–Carlson type, c1899	350.00
Tandem two boxes	
49 to 60" l	750.00
60 to 70" l	1,200.00
Fiddleback Telephone
Gillian, American Bell, Blake or Charles Williams transmitter	1,000.00
Vought Berger, Kellogg, Western	

Electric, Stromberg Carlson, Dean, Diamond, etc ... **275.00**

Pay Phone
Gray Pay Station
Desk Model, wood, slots for coins up to dollar, marked	3,000.00
Wall Phone, wood	2,500.00
Pay Box, cast iron, small, c1910	150.00

Single Box Wall Telephone, wood
Picture Frame Front, Cathedral Top, lightning arrestors at top	300–400.00
Plain Front, 1915–20	200.00

Stand
Gossip Bench	70.00
Ornate, carved	600.00
Plain, 1920s style	150.00

Switchboard
Hotel Annunciator	50–400.00
Mansion Annunciator, depending on size and ornateness	75–450.00
Pre–1894, wall mount, marked American Bell–Blake, Gillian, Edison, National Bell, or Charles Williams	2,000.00
Pre–1910, wall mount	500.00
Pre–1935, light bulbs	250.00
1935 to present	Surplus Value

Telephone Booth
Leaded glass, 1890s	2,000–3,500.00
1910 to 1912, single door	2,000.00
Folding Door, oak, 1914 to 1940	1,200.00

Triple Box
American Electric, Kokomo	1,200.00
Bell Telephone	1,200.00
Elliott	1,200.00
Keystone	900.00
Mianus	900.00

Note: If any of these sets are missing the 7" long exposed terminal receiver, subtract $150.00.

Upright Desk Stand (Candlestick Phones)
Oil Can shape	500.00
Potbelly shape	750.00
Straight Pipe, regular style, dial type	185.00

Notes: Extremely unusual candlestick phones made of wood or in an outrageous style may be worth in excess of $1,000.00. All phones mass produced from WWI to 1950 were made in black. The Western Electric model is now being reproduced in solid shiny brass.

TEPLITZ CHINA

History: Around 1900 twenty-six ceramic manufacturers were located in Teplitz, a town in the

Bohemian province of Czechoslovakia. Other potteries were located in the nearby town of Turn. Wares from these factories were molded, cast, and hand decorated. Most are in the Art Nouveau and Art Deco styles. Most pieces do not carry a specific manufacturer's mark. They are simply marked "Teplitz," "Turn-Teplitz," and "Turn."

Reference: Susan and Al Bagdade, *Warman's English & Continental Pottery & Porcelain, 1st Edition,* Warman Publishing Co., Inc., 1987.

Bowl, 5½" d, girl pulling rooster's tail,
  marked "Stellmacher" **65.00**
Box, cov, 5½" h, 7¾" l, figural, green
  and gray turtle, natural colored young
  boy and girl, marked "Ernst Wahliss
  Turn Teplitz Vienna," c1918 . . . . . .   **365.00**

Bust, cavalier, sepia tones, c1910, 8½" h, $175.00.

Candlestick, 5¼" h, figural, woman
  wearing flowing gown **150.00**
Dish, 7½" d, couple seated on bench,
  handles **175.00**
Ewer
  9" h, variegated purple poppies,
    bulbs, gold dec, cream ground,
    molded flowers, applied handle,
    marked "RS & K" **90.00**
  10" h, applied white florals, white narrow
    neck, cobalt blue ground, gold
    trim, ornate handle **150.00**
Loving Cup, 15" h, reticulated outer
  wall, turquoise, amber, opal, and cobalt
  blue jewels, gold scalloped rim
  and foot, twisted branch handles . . .   **325.00**
Pitcher, 4", Arab on horse, Stellmacher   **85.00**
Vase
  8¼" h, swollen cylindrical, widening
    towards base, relief band of repeating
    clover, molded vertical
    panels, mottled green and blue–
    gray glaze, sgd "Stellmacher Teplitz,"
    stamped, repaired **175.00**
  10¾" h, green, brown, white, black,
    and red modernistic motifs, marked
    "Stellmacher/Teplitz" **325.00**

12" h, bulbous upper portion with four
  pierced floriform medallions, cylindrical
  base with four handles, mottled
  brown and green glaze, blue,
  red, and gold jewels, imp mark,
  c1905–10 . . . .   **275.00**
15¾" h, trumpet form, stylized vertical
  stems, applied pendent berries
  around top, glazed, marked **650.00**
17¾" h, swollen cylindrical, molded
  free standing loop handles, stylized
  tree and flower dec, green, brown,
  pink, and gold, imp mark, c1905–
  10 . . . .   **750.00**

TERRA COTTA WARE

History: Terra cotta is ware made of a hard, semi-fired ceramic clay. The color of the pottery ranges from a light orange-brown to a deep brownish red. It is usually unglazed, but some pieces can be found partially glazed or decorated with slip designs, incised, or carved. Examples include utilitarian objects as well as statuettes and large architectural pieces. Fine early Chinese terra cotta pieces recently have brought substantial prices.

Figures, Chinese couple, 1830–40, Chinese seals, 9¼ x 9¾" h, $750.00.

Bust, 22" h, young woman, smiling, long
  hair bound at back, inscribed
  "Charles Breton, 1916," French **650.00**
Figure
  15" h, girl playing mandolin, c1870   **275.00**
  18¼" h male, 17" h female, seated
    male satyr holding tambourine
    laden with grapes, putto resting on
    right leg, facing female satyr with
    putto on left leg, another at left foot,
    each inscribed "Clodion," French,
    late 19th or early 20th C **9,900.00**
Plaque, 7½" h, 131¼" w, 3" deep beveled
  mahogany frame, rect, relief
  carved daffodils, incised sgd "S. D.

Chapman," repair and some chips,
early 20th C 300.00
Tobacco Jar, 10" h, figural, man in long
tailed coat, white vest, skull cap . . . 190.00
Urn, 27½" h, Art Nouveau nymph in
flowing gown, root form base, branching leaf handle, polychrome highlights, imp "Made in Austria Ernst
Wahliss, Wien," pr 4,400.00
Vase, 12" h, gold dragon 800.00

TEXTILES

History: Textiles are cloth or fabric items, especially anything woven or knitted. Those that survive usually represent the best since these were
the objects that were used carefully and stored by
the housewife.

Textiles are collected for many reasons—to
study fabrics, understand the elegance of a historical period, and for decorative and modern use.
The renewed interest in clothing has sparked a
revived interest in textiles of all forms.

References: William C. Ketchum, Jr., *The Knopf
Collectors' Guides to American Antiques, Quilts,*
Alfred A. Knopf, Inc., 1982; Betty Ring, *Needlework: An Historical Survey,* Main Street Press,
1984, revised edition; Helene Von Rosenstiel,
*American Rugs And Carpets: From The Seven-
teenth Century To Modern Times,* William Morrow
And Company, 1978; Carleton L. Safford and Robert Bishop, *America's Quilts And Coverlets,* Bonanza Books, 1985.

Collectors' Club: Costume Society of America,
P.O. Box 761, Elizabethtown, NJ 07726.

Additional Listings: See Clothing, Linens,
Quilts, and Samplers.

Bedspread
74 x 82", two pc, cotton, loosely
woven, pale blue and white plaid 115.00
74 x 84", two pc, cotton and wool,
woven, blue and white plaid 215.00
91 x 80", appliqued, calico, floral, and
bird printed patches, meandering
vine and flower basket motif, muslin
ground, buttonhole stitch highlights, New England, c1800 . . 2,600.00
Bolster Cover, 20 x 15", homespun, blue
and white, button closure, embroi-
dered red initials JR 300.00
Coverlet
Double Weave
70 x 80", blue and white, tulip and
snowflake, corner block reads "L
F/1855" 200.00
80 x 76", blue and white, flowers
and birds pattern, corner block
reads "Maria Sanford, Orange
1846" 700.00

**Coverlet, jacquard, blue and white,
woven by Samuel Meily, 1852, 72 x 85",
$375.00.**

81 x 96", blue and white, corners
dated "1844" 200.00
Jacquard
71 x 92", multicolored, corner
marked "J Witmer/Manor/Town-
ship for Sharlott/Sellers/1837" 700.00
76 x 84", two pc, single weave,
blue, white, natural, red, and
green floral design, corners
marked "Peter Lorenz 1846" . . 1,000.00
82 x 99", two pc, single weave, red,
blue and natural white floral design, edge labeled "E Longa-
necker 1845" 625.00
84 x 92", two pc, double weave, red
and natural floral design, corners
dated "1844" 450.00
86 x 106", one pc, single weave,
blue, red, green, and natural floral design, corners marked "Ab-
salom Klinger, Millersburg, Berks
County 1844, No 1608" 800.00
Overshot, 84 x 96", two pc, blue, red,
and white optical pattern 300.00
Single Weave, 70 x 87", two pc, floral
design, bird borders, corners
marked "John Klinhinz, Ohio 1851" 165.00
Curtains, 72" l, 62" w, linen, stenciled,
valanced borders of stylized red pomegranates and scrolls, neutral open
weave ground, c1910, pr 550.00
Picture, 12½ x 16¾", embroidered,
classical figures scene, English, 19th
C 200.00
Pillow Case, 20 x 35", homespun, white,
pieced calico star, woven and tied

fringe, embroidered name and date
"Susanna Hoch, 1884," pr **500.00**
Rug
Embroidered, 48 x 72", pastel colored
floral design, light green ground,
20th C **125.00**
Hooked
24 x 36½", yarn, folk art, "Peace-
able Kingdom," figure and wild
animals **200.00**
58" l, 50½" w, six egg shapes on
variegated colors of red, black
ground, field splint with striations
of green and brown, American,
Arts and Crafts period, early 20th
C **150.00**
80" l, 70" w, oval, wool and cotton,
multicolored, white ground, central floral bouquet, geometric
blue and white diaper design,
black border, New England, late
19th C **3,100.00**
94½ x 94½", sq, wool and cotton,
purple, green, violet, and red
paisley pattern of stylized leaves
and four peacock plumes, stylized foliate design in corners,
slate blue border, American, late
19th C **11,000.00**
Rag, hooked
26½" x 51", sheared, stagecoach
and four horses design, brown
border **125.00**
37 x 57" w, mulitcolored floral de-
sign, Centennial, dated "1776–
1876" **375.00**
Table Cover, 19½" d, yellow poppies,
green leaves, c1910 . . . . **100.00**
Table Runner
57" l, rect, cream colored, embroidered pale blue and brown stylized
flowers, crocheted ends, American,
Art Deco **100.00**
58" l, oblong, stenciled and embroi-
dered Egyptian revival motif, roses,
blues, and greens, c1910 . . . . . . **150.00**
Tapestry, 22 x 32", wool, two hills, gray,
brown, natural white, gold, and black **190.00**
Towel, 19¼ x 34½", linen, white, Washington on horseback scene, red bor-
ders marked "Washington" **55.00**
Wall Hanging, 11¾" d, stumpwork,
young couple, cottage, beehive, spinning wheel, and sailing ship, orig
frame, English, early 18th C **300.00**

THIMBLES

History: Thimbles often are thought of as common household sewing tools. Many are. However,

others are miniature works of art; souvenirs of
places, people, and events; or gadgets (thimbles
with expanded uses such as attached threaders,
cutters, or magnets).

There were many thimble manufacturers in the
United States prior to 1930. Before we became a
"throw-away" society, hand sewing was a never-
ending chore for the housewife. Garments were
mended and altered. When they were beyond repair, pieces were salvaged to make a patchwork
quilt. Thimble manufacturers tried to create a new
thimble to convince the home sewer that "one was
not enough."

By the early 1930s only one manufacturer of
gold and silver thimbles remained in business in
the United States: the Simons Brothers Company
of Philadelphia, which was founded by George
Washington Simons in 1839. Simons Brothers
thimbles from the 1904 St. Louis World's Fair and
the 1893 Columbian Exposition are prized acquisitions for any collector. The Liberty Bell thimble,
in the shape of the bell, is one of the most novel.

Today, the company is owned by Nelson Keyser
and continues to produce silver and gold thimbles.
The Simons Brothers Company designed a special
thimble for Nancy Reagan as a gift for diplomat's
wives who visit the White House. The thimble has
a picture of the White House and the initials "N.
D. R."

Thimbles have been produced in a variety of
materials: gold, silver, steel, aluminum, brass,
china, glass, vegetable ivory, ivory, bone, celluloid,
plastics, leather, hard rubber, and silk. Common
metal thimbles usually are bought by the intended
user, who makes sure the size is a comfortable fit.
Precious metal thimbles often were received as
gifts. Many of these do not show signs of wear
from constant use. This may result from ill fit of
the thimble or from it simply being too elegant for
mundane work.

During the 20th century thimbles were used as
advertising promotions. It is not unusual to find a
thimble that says "You'll Never Get Stuck Using
Our Product" or a political promotion stating "Sew
It Up—Vote for John Doe for Senator."

References: Helmut Greif, *Talks About Thimbles,* Fingerhutmuseum, Cregligen, Germany,
1983 (English edition available from Dine-Ameri-
can, Wilmington, Del.); Edwin F. Holmes, *A History
Of Thimbles,* Cornwall Books, 1985; Myrtle Lundquist, *The Book Of A Thousand Thimbles,* Wallace-Homestead, 1970; Myrtle Lundquist, *Thimble
Americana,* Wallace-Homestead, 1981; Myrtle
Lundquist, *Thimble Treasury,* Wallace-Homestead,
1975; John Heille, *Thimble Collectors Encyclopedia,* Wallace-Homestead, 1986; Gay Ann Rogers, *American Silver Thimbles,* Haggerston Press,
1989; Estelle Zalkin, *Zalkin's Handbook Of Thimbles & Sewing Implements, First Edition,* Warman
Publishing Co., 1988.

Periodical: *Thimbletter,* 93 Walnut Hill Road,
Newton Highlands, MA 02161.

Collectors' Club: Thimble Collectors International, P. O. Box 2311, Des Moines, IA 50310.

Advisor: Estelle Zalkin.

Reproduction Alert: Reproductions can be made by restrikes from an original die or cast from a mold made from an antique thimble. Many reproductions are sold as such and priced accordingly. Among the reproduced thimbles are a pre-revolution Russian enamel thimble and the Salem Witch thimble (the repro has no cap, and the seam is visible).

Sterling silver, American, 19th C, $35.00.

Advertising
Clark's O.N.T., "Our New Thread," brass	20.00
Coca Cola	2.00
Delco Light	4.00
Domestic Sewing Machine, silver	50.00
Prudential Insurance Company, brass	5.00

Bisque, American sgd "Mildred Kohls,"
modern	40.00

Brass
Be Happy message	25.00
Her Majesty's Thimble, British	25.00

Celluloid, finger shape, patent by Stella
Brophy, 1967	15.00

Dorcas
Dorcas Junior	125.00
Dreema, made by Henry Griffith	75.00
Princess May	50.00
Tailor's, open top	125.00

Enamel
Cloisonne, bird dec, Chinese	20.00
Russian, niello	250.00

Gold
Dome cap, shield cartouche, floral band, Continental, 19th C	100.00
King George and Queen Mary Commemoration	900.00
Paneled band, Continental, 19th C	75.00

Ivory, Chinese, 19th C 75.00

Porcelain
Bing and Grondahl, bird in flight dec, Denmark	35.00
Royal Worcester, fruit dec	30.00

Scrimshaw, whale bone, double heart
pierced with arrow, initials	250.00

Silver
Cupid, face and wings, French touch-mark, early 20th C	100.00
Dropped rim, holly berries and leaves cartouche, ruby set in center, Ketcham and McDougall	125.00
Louis XV pattern, Ketcham and McDougall	35.00
Scenic band, American, early 20th C	25.00
Stitch in Time Saves Nine, Simmons	200.00

Souvenir and Commemorative
Columbian Exposition, Chicago, Il, 1893, gold	550.00
Coronation of Edward and Alexandra, 1902	65.00
Exhibition of All Nations, relief Crystal Palace, London, 1851	250.00
Great Yarmouth	75.00
Lord Byron's Home	225.00
Paris Exposition, 1889	100.00
Philadelphia Sesquicentennial, 1926	75.00
Princess Anne and Mark Phillip	100.00
Queen Elizabeth's Jubilee, 1977	50.00
Rio de Janeiro, applied enamel shields, plated	20.00
St Augustine, FL, made by Ketcham and McDougall	75.00
St Peters, Rome, enamel on silver, transfer print	90.00
Washington, DC, made by Simons Brothers Company	100.00

THREADED GLASS

History: Threaded glass is glass decorated with applied threads of glass. Before the English invention of a glass threading machine in 1876, threads were applied by hand. After this invention, threaded glass was produced in quantity by practically every major glass factory.

Threaded glass was revived by the art glass manufacturers, such as Durand and Steuben, and continues to be made today.

Basket, cranberry, ruffled top, applied clear thorn handle	165.00
Bowl, white threads, clear ground, polished pontil	30.00
Cheese Dish, cov, 7½" h, light blue opal threading on upper half of bell shaped dome, faceted knop	125.00
Finger Bowl, 5" d, fluted edge, chartreuse threads	60.00
Honey Pot, cov, 5¾" h, 6½" w, pulled and twisted pattern of blue and white	

Vase, green threading, clear body, 5″ h, $60.00.

glass threads, satin finish crystal ground, twig finial on cov, twig like metal frame **450.00**

Perfume, 5½″ l, blown, machine applied threads, Lutz type **250.00**

Salt, 2¾″ d, opaque white threads, cranberry ground, applied clear petal feet **75.00**

Tumbler, 3⅛″ h, blue threads, opalescent ribbed ground, Lutz type **20.00**

Vase

  6″ h, gold threads, irid blue ground ... **300.00**

  6½″ h, cone shaped, amber, ruffled edge, three applied looped feet with strawberry pontils, English .. **50.00**

  8½″ h, pink threads, clear ground .. **125.00**

Wine, 7½″ h, green threads, random airtraps, clear stem and base, Steuben, set of 3 .... **65.00**

TIFFANY

History: Louis Comfort Tiffany (1849–1934) established a glass house in 1878 primarily to make stained glass windows. There he developed a unique type of colored iridescent glass called Favrile. His Favrile glass differed from other art glass in manufacture as it was a composition of colored glass worked together while hot. The essential characteristic is that ornamentation is found within the glass. Favrile was never further decorated. Different effects were achieved by varying the amount and position of colors which project movement in form and shape.

In 1890, in order to utilize surplus materials at the plant, Tiffany began to design and produce "small glass" such as iridescent glass lamp shades, vases, and stemware and tableware in the Art Nouveau manner.

Commercial production began in 1896. Most Tiffany wares are signed with the name L. C. Tiffany or the initials L.C.T. Some pieces also carry the word "Favrile" as well as a number. A number of other marks can be found, e.g., Tiffany Studios and Louis C. Tiffany Furnaces.

Louis Tiffany and the artists in his studio also are well known for the fine work in other areas—bronzes, pottery, jewelry, silver and enamels.

References: Victor Arwas, *Glass, Art Nouveau and Art Deco*, Rizzoli International Publications, Inc., 1977; Vivienne Couldrey, *Tiffany: The Art of Louis Comfort*, Wellfleet Press, 1989; *The Art Work of Louis C. Tiffany*, Apollo Books, 1987; Robert Koch, *Louis C. Tiffany, Rebel In Glass*, Crown Publishers, Inc., 1966; John A. Shuman III, *The Collector's Encyclopedia of American Art Glass*, Collector Books, 1988.

Note: All glass is of the Favrile type unless otherwise noted.

Lamp, bronze and Favrile glass, pink and white apple blossoms shade, green striated leaves, blue–green ground, brown–green patinated bronze urn standard, imp marks, 16″ d shade, 21½″ h, $8,000.00.

BRONZE

Ash Stand, 31½″ h, ashtray raised on ball knop, cylindrical knopped standard, bulbous ribbed base raised on ribbed spreading circular lotus base, hemispherical dish frame with radiating ribs and hinged ribbed border, brown and green patina, imp "Tiffany Studios/New York/1695," 1919–28 .. **1,980.00**

Calendar Frame, 6⅜ x 7½″, Grapevine

pattern, bronze filigree over green glass, imp "Tiffany Studios, New York" 715.00

Candelabra
9" h, gilt bronze, two arms, central stem terminating in bud, oval fluted foot, imp "Tiffany Studios, New York," bobeche inserts missing, pr 900.00
15" h, 19" l, urn shaped nozzle and bobeche, vertical stem handle, oval tripod base, six light, brown patina, impressed "Tiffany Studios/New York" and circular monogram, c1900–28 . . . . 990.00

Candlestick, 8" h, urn form nozzle, three pronged supports raised on curving branch forked with upright handle, lily pad base with etched finish, impressed "Tiffany Studios/New York/1203" and circular monogram, c1900–28 . . . . 440.00

Jardiniere, 11" d, gilt bronze, inverted rim, imp scrolling border, imp "Tiffany Studios, New York, 1702" 350.00

Lamp Base
11¾" h, harp standard, fluted cushion base, five ball feet, imp "424, Tiffany Studios, New York," depatinated 800.00
13" h, gilt bronze, harp standard, fluted circular base, imp "Tiffany Studios, 419" 700.00
17" h, three arm standard, four paw feet, circular base, imp "Tiffany Studios, New York, 427" 800.00
18½" h, gilt bronze, harp standard spreading to floriform base, eight petal form feet, imp "Tiffany Studios New York, 470" 1,100.00

Stamp Box, 5 x 3", American Indian pattern, three hinged compartments, marked "#1184" 300.00

Wall Sconce, 11" h, two scrolling arms, griffin terminals, Favrile gold quilted shades sgd "L. C. T.," pr 2,860.00

GLASS

Bowl
4½" d, circular, pinched in, scalloping rim, Favrile, gold, engraved "L. C. T." 275.00
9½" d, blue, waisted circular form and neck, ribbed sides, scalloped rim, inscribed "L C T Favrile," c1910 825.00

Compote
2¼" h, Favrile, pastel, white radiating stripes from center to mint green stretched rim, engraved "L. C. T. Favrile 1871" 385.00
3¼" h, Favrile, pastel, white feather design radiating from center to mint

green rim, engraved "L. C. T. Favrile 1700" 385.00
3½" h, Favrile, gold, engraved "L. C. T.," set of 6 . . . . 1,100.00
8¼" d, Favrile, gold, quilted pattern, knopped stem, circular foot, engraved "L. C. T. Favrile" 900.00

Cup and Saucer, irid gold, free form pulled dec, applied handle with upswept curl, sgd "L. C. Tiffany V698" 850.00

Dish
4¾" d, scalloping rim, Favrile, gold, engraved "L. C. T." 190.00
6" d, silver rim, Favrile, pastel, engraved "1898 L. C. Tiffany Favrile" 225.00

Goblet, 6½" h, Favrile, gold, intaglio carved grapes and tendrilled vines, engraved "L. C. T." 385.00

Humidor, 9½" h, cylindrical, Favrile, gold, leafy green vine descending one side, gilt bronze inner cov and monogrammed lid, imp "Tiffany Studios, New York, 22504,6" 1,450.00

Lamp Shade
4½" l, lily, Favrile, pale gold, pink and white striations, Tiffany Studios . . 275.00

Loving Cup, 7⅜" h, waisted cylindrical, Favrile, three scrolling handles, gold ground, green leaf and vine dec, engraved "471H, L. C. Tiffany–Favrile," small cracks 500.00

Salt, 2¼" d, 1⅛" h, bean pot shape, flaring rim, pulled handles, irid blue–purple gold, pr 375.00

Vase
1¾" h, cabinet, urn shape, circular foot, Favrile, engraved "L. C. T. D455" 165.00
7½" h, ovoid, sq notched rim, Favrile, green with vertical black and gold feathered stripes, intaglio rim border, engraved "L. C. T. R1605" . . 2,750.00
15" h, floriform, Favrile, white bowl, green stem, green feather pulls, gold int., domed gold foot, engraved "L. C. T. R9722" 8,250.00
11¾" h, trumpet, Favrile, cream ground, gold and green feather pull dec, engraved "LCT" on circular bronze foot, pineapple knop, imp "Tiffany Studios, New York 1043" 1,350.00
14¼" h, trumpet, Favrile, pastel, pink and white stripes, pale yellow knopped stem, circular foot, engraved "1900 L. C. Tiffany Favrile" 1,650.00
15" h, floriform, Favrile, white bowl, green stem and feather pulls, gold int., domed gold foot, engraved "L. C. T. R9722" 8,250.00
21" h, trumpet, Favrile, green and gold pulled feather, yellow throat, striped foot 9,000.00

LAMPS

Desk, 13½" h, ribbed conical gold irid shade, etched tendrils and leaves, inscribed "L. C. T. Favrile," green patinated bronze counterbalance base, adjustable curved arm, stamped "Tiffany Studios New York 416" **5,000.00**

Floor, 55½" h, conical linenfold amber Favrile glass shade, stamped "Tiffany Studios New York Pat App'd For," gilt bronze harp form base with cast petals, shaped circular foot, escalloped feet, sgd "Tiffany Studios New York 425" **4,250.00**

Piano, 9" h, three irid gold lily shades, sgd "L. C. T., Favrile," bronze base with cast petal dec, three gently curving stems, stamped "Tiffany Studios, New York 320" **3,800.00**

Table
31½" h, 20" d leaded glass shade, filigreed shade with bright red poppies, mottled blue and green panel, rim imp "Tiffany Studios, New York 1531," bronze base cast with classical maiden raising columnar standard **37,500.00**

SILVER

Centerpiece Bowl, 12¼" w, 4½" h, circular, rustic style, applied vine rim and handles, surface textured to resemble earth, applied centipede and insects, repousse twigs, spreading circular foot, marked "Tiffany & Co, New York," 1899, 51 oz, 10 dwt **3,300.00**

Child's Feeding Set, 3⅝" h mug, 5" d bowl, 7½" d plate, wide repousse border, chased farm landscape, each marked "Tiffany & Co," c1926, 22 oz, 10 dwt **2,100.00**

Cigarette Case, 3⅜" h, 2¾" w, rect, hinged cov, applied female figure standing on scrolled plinth, reaching for grapes with one hand, holding bunch in other, grapes and clasp with cabochon rubies, two pierced stays int., applied gold grapes on back, marked "Tiffany & Co," c1900, 4 oz **1,870.00**

Compote, 8⅞" d, 2⅛" h, center enameled turquoise, blue, and yellow foliage boss, enameled rim border, monogrammed, marked "Tiffany & Co," c1910, 13 oz, 10 dwt **1,210.00**

Paperweight, 10¼" l, 2⅛" w, elongated rect, pierced at one end with oval, spot hammered surface, raised stylized script monogram "LAW," marked "Tiffany & Co," c1880, 7 oz, 10 dwt **385.00**

Pitcher, 7" h, globular, curved flat chased acanthus leaf handle, circular foot, wide repousse Olympian pattern band, neck band of repousse scrolled acanthus, marked "Tiffany & Co, New York," c1880, 28 oz, 10 dwt **7,700.00**

Tea and Coffee Service, teapot, 9¼" h coffeepot, cov sugar, cream jug, waste bowl, 25" l tray with open reeded handles, globular bodies, repousse scrolls and foliage mid band, handles with ivory insulating rim, marked "Tiffany & Co," c1891, 173 oz, 10 dwt **7,700.00**

TIFFIN GLASS

History: A. J. Beatty and Sons built a glass manufacturing plant in Tiffin, Ohio, in 1888. On January 1, 1892, the firm joined the U. S. Glass Co. and was known as factory "R." Quality and production at this factory were very high and resulted in fine depression era glass.

Beginning in 1916 wares were marked with a paper label. From 1923 to 1936, Tiffin produced a line of black glassware called Black Satin. The company discontinued operation in 1980.

References: Fred Bickenheuser, *Tiffin Glassmasters, Book I*, Glassmasters Publications, 1979; Fred Bickenheuser, *Tiffin Glassmasters, Book II*, Glassmasters Publications, 1981; Fred Bickenheuser, *Tiffin Glassmasters, Book III*, Glassmasters Publications, 1985.

Collectors' Club: Tiffin Glass Collectors Club, P.O. Box 554, Tiffin, OH 44883.

Vase, bulbous, black ground, red painted poppies, green leaves, 5" h, $40.00.

Ashtray, Twilight, 6¼" d	**55.00**
Bowl, Cerise, sterling base, 9¾"	**60.00**
Candlesticks, Desert Red, pr	**195.00**
Candy Dish, cov, black satin, gold trim	**48.00**
Champagne	
Beaumont	**7.00**

Chardonnay	17.00
Nouvelle	20.00
Sylvan Pink	20.00
Cocktail	
Fuchsia, clear	20.00
June Night	18.00
Cordial, Twilight Stem	50.00
Cornucopia, Twilight	175.00
Creamer and Sugar, Cherokee Rose	30.00
Cup and Saucer, Flanders Pink	75.00
Decanter, Flanders Pink, stopper	595.00
Duck on Nest, gray slag	20.00
Flower Arranger, Empress, red and crystal, 8″	95.00
Goblet	
Camelot	10.00
Carlyle	25.00
Renaissance, gold	30.00
Willow	20.00
Iced Tea	
Cerice, ftd	20.00
Wheat	22.00
Mayonnaise Set, Fuchsia, clear, 3 pcs	42.00
Perfume, Milady, frosted	28.00
Pitcher and Lid, Flanders Pink	495.00
Plate	
Flanders Pink, 8″	20.00
Persian Pheasant, 8″	10.00
Sherbert	
Killarney Green, ftd	15.00
Montclair	10.00
Renaissance, platinum	24.00
Tiffin Rose	12.00
Tumbler	
Juice, Persian Pheasant, ftd, 5 oz	18.00
Water, Cherokee Rose, 9 oz	15.00
Vase	
Canterbury Twilite, 8½″	135.00
Floral, black satin, 10½″	95.00
Wine	
Carlyle	25.00
Montclair	17.00

TILES

History: The use of decorated tiles peaked during the latter part of the 19th century. Over one hundred companies in England alone were producing tiles by 1880. By 1890 companies had opened in Belgium, France, Australia, Germany, and the United States.

Tiles were not limited to adorning fireplaces. Many were installed into furniture, such as wash stands, hall stands, and folding screens. Since tiles were easily cleaned and, hence, hygienic, they readily were used on the floors and walls of entry halls, hospitals, butcher shops, or any place where sanitation was a concern. Many public buildings and subways also employed tiles to add interest and beauty.

Condition is an important fact in determining price. A cracked, badly scuffed and scratched, or heavily chipped tile has very little value. Slight chipping around the outer edges of a tile is, at times, considered acceptable by collectors, especially if these chips can be covered by a frame.

It is not uncommon for the highly glazed surface of some tiles to have become crazed. Crazing is not considered a deterent as long as it does not detract from the overall appearance of the tile.

References: J. & B. Austwick, *The Decorated Tile*, Pitman House Ltd., 1980; Susan and Al Bagdade, *Warman's English & Continental Pottery & Porcelain, 1st Edition*, Warman Publishing Co., Inc., 1987; Julian Barnard, *Victorian Ceramic Tiles*, N. Y. Graphic Society Ltd., 1972; Terence A. Lockett, *Collecting Victorian Tiles*, Antique Collectors Club, 1979; Hans Van Lemmen, *Tiles: A Collectors' Guide*, Seven Hills Books, 1985.

Collectors' Club: Tile & Architectural Ceramics Society, Ironbridge Gorge Museum, Ironbridge, Telford, Shropshire, England TF8 7AW.

Wedgwood, Lee Mansion, blue transfer, marked "Wedgwood, Etruria, England," 6″ sq, $150.00.

American Encaustic Tile Co, Zanesville, OH

4″ sq, Oriental junk, pagoda in background	25.00
6″ sq, The Lion In Love, transfer printed, polychrome	85.00
18 x 6″, hunting dogs, high relief, sponged pale aqua and honey brown glossy glaze	250.00
Batchelder, 4″ sq, landscape of trees, water, and bridge, deeply imp, red clay, light chalky blue brushed into recessed areas	75.00
Beaver Falls, 6″ sq, large standing squirrel, incised and outlined in black, squirrel and border in medium blue, kelly green ground, marked	60.00

California Art, 5½" sq, scenic, relief, natural colors ... 18.00

Claycraft, CA, 35 x 23½" twenty–four tile frieze, articulated scene of dirt road winding towards stone bridge, grove of fir and maple trees, Cottswald type cottage, molded wooden frame ... 2,100.00

Delft, 5" sq, purple and white, scenes, five houses, single boat, set of 6 ... 270.00

DeMorgan, William, 6" sq, hedge hog, ruby luster glaze ... 400.00

Grueby
  4½" sq, landscape, trees, stream and mountain, green, blue, yellow, and brown, orig condition, marked "Architectural" ... 600.00
  6 x 6¼", white trotting horses, green grass, light blue sky, sgd "KC" on back ... 375.00
  8" sq, mocha brown galleon, billowing white sails, choppy powder blue sea, medium blue sky, black wood frame, sgd "EH," partial black stamp ... 850.00

J. & J. G. Low, Chelsea, MA
  6" sq, boy reading book, high gloss amber glaze, back sgd, artist sgd "Arthur Osborne," on front obscured by glaze, c1881 ... 200.00
  6 x 8", President Grant, emb, amber ... 125.00
  12 x 36", frieze, six tile, rect, scene men plowing field, cream glaze, imp marks, framed ... 400.00

Minton China Works, 6" sq, transfer printed
  Alfred, black on white, from "Early English History" series by J Moyr Smith ... 50.00
  Farmyard scene, sheep, brown on white, sgd "W Wise," 1879 ... 80.00
  Hancock House, brown on white ... 30.00
  Interstate Industrial Expo, Chicago, 1880 ... 50.00
  Romeo and Juliet, sepia ... 30.00

Moravian Pottery & Tile Works, Doylestown, PA
  4" sq, Aladdin Lamp ... 40.00
  7¼ x 4", Knight in armor, on horseback, ochre and blue ... 60.00

Mosaic Tile Co., Zanesville, OH
  4" sq, German Shepherd dec, 4" sq ... 115.00
  6" sq, Little Bo Peep, blue, tan, and cream, Walter Crane ... 100.00

Pardee, 4" sq, houses and trees, matte glaze, brown and green, 1910 ... 225.00

Pewabic Pottery, Detroit, MI
  2¾" sq, bird of paradise, gray–taupe bird, cranberry red ground, high luster finish ... 60.00
  3" sq, Detroit Skyline, round, emb, brown on blue ... 70.00

Richards, H., 6" sq, Art Nouveau flower, tube lined, red and green, cream ground ... 75.00

Robertson, Los Angeles, 8" sq, scenic, cloisonne dec, winding brown road through rolling green hills, fortress ... 1,300.00

Trenton Tile Co., Trenton, NJ
  4¼" sq, portrait of woman, brown glaze ... 60.00
  6" sq, flower, tan glossy glaze ... 20.00

U. S. Encaustic Tile Works, Indianapolis, IN
  6" sq, girl with bundle of sticks, emb, amber ... 85.00
  18 x 6", Dawn, woman, emb, green glaze ... 175.00

Unmarked
  6" sq, Victorian, water lily, shaded brown painted flowers, off white ground ... 50.00
  23½ x 23¾", architectural, sailing ship in relief, round top, sq base, brown and green, suspended from brass chain ... 100.00

Wedgwood
  6" sq, Red Riding Hood and wolf, black transfer, white ground, Crane design ... 110.00
  8" sq, hunting dog and bird, brown transfer, white ground ... 100.00

TINWARE

History: Beginning in the 1700s many utilitarian household objects were made of tin. Tin is nontoxic, rust resistant, and fairly durable, so it can be used for storing food. It often was plated to iron to provide strength. Because it was cheap, tinware and tin-plated wares were in the price range of most people.

An early center of tinware manufacture in the United States was Berlin, Connecticut. Almost every small town and hamlet had its own tinsmith, tinner, or whitesmith. Tinsmiths used patterns from which to make items. They cut out the pieces, hammered and shaped them, and soldered the parts. If a piece was to be used with heat, a copper bottom was added because of the low melting point of tin. The Industrial Revolution brought about machine-made, mass-produced tinware pieces. The handmade era ended by the late 19th century.

This category is a catchall for tin objects which do not fit into other categories in our book.

Additional Listings: See Advertising, Kitchen Collectibles, Lanterns, Lamps and Lighting, and Tinware: Decorated.

Baker's Horn, 56" l, taped mouthpiece ... 35.00

Basket, 8¼ x 16¼", open lattice weave, red paint traces ... 100.00

Candle mold, eight candles, handle, $225.00.

Candle Box, 13½", cylindrical	140.00
Candle Mold	
Six tube, handle, 10¾" h	55.00
Thirty six tube, handle, 10" h	325.00
Twelve tube	
9" candles	50.00
9½" candles	50.00
15" h, round, lantern shaped finial, ring handle, soldered repair, minor battering	450.00
Twenty four tube, makes 9" candles	180.00
Chandelier, 22½" h, two tiers, "S" curved wire arms, twelve crimped sockets, 19th C	1,300.00
Chocolate Mold, 2 part, 9 x 10", eight Easter bunny cavities, clamps missing	35.00
Christmas Tree Fence, five 11" l sections, gate, green, red posts	175.00
Comb Case, 9" w, 9" h, hanging, floral emb, old worn mirror	65.00
Cookie Cutter	
3¾" h, heart, handle	60.00
5½" l, witch with broom	50.00
5¾" h, stag with antlers	175.00
Decoy, 12" h, shorebird, folding, orig polychrome paint, wood base	185.00
Lamp	
Betty, orig hangers, 19th C	125.00
Coach, 12½" h, pr, nickel plated trim, beveled glass	100.00
Miner's, 2½" h	65.00
Skater's, 6½" h, clear globe, impressed ribs	100.00
Lantern	
8" h, clear blown globe, removable base, whale oil burner, ring handle	210.00
15", circular windows, wrought iron hanger, electrified	30.00
Miniature, coffeepot, 3⅜" h	65.00
Mold, strawberries, fluted sides	10.00
Muffin Pan, 8¼ x 11½", 12 tins joined together, sunburst design on each bottom	85.00
Nutmeg Grater, 5¼" l, wood handles, patent date 1896	45.00

Pip-Squeak, 3⅜" h, wind up, bird in cage, polychrome paint, silent bellow	25.00
Sconce, pr	
11", New England, 19th C	200.00
11½" h, candle, oval mirror backs . .	190.00
12" h, mirrored, New England, 19th C	300.00

TINWARE: DECORATED

History: Decorating sheet iron, tin, and tin-coated sheet iron dates back to the mid-18th century. The Welsh called the practice pontipool, the French To'le Peinte. In America the center for tin-decorated ware in the late 1700s was Berlin, Connecticut.

Several styles of decorating techniques were used: painting, japanning, and stenciling. Designs were done by both professionals and itinerants. English and Oriental motifs strongly influenced both form and design.

A special type of decoration was the punch work on unpainted tin practiced by the Pennsylvania tinsmiths. Forms included coffeepots, spice boxes, and grease lamps.

Fruit Bowl, ftd, red, black, and gold dec, 19th C, 9½" w, 14¾" l, $125.00.

Bowl, 12", int. and ext. dec	70.00
Coal Bin, 18½" h, rect hinged top, tapering case, trifid feet, marine motifs, Victorian	1,400.00
Coffeepot, 10½" h, worn orig black paint, polychrome floral dec, resoldered spout, minor battering	425.00
Colander, 9" d, 3¾" h, punched star on bottom	35.00
Deed Box, dome top	
9" l, orig paint	
Black ground, polychrome floral dec, orig gilded brass bale handle, faded colors, minor wear . .	250.00
Red ground, yellow, green, black, white, and red floral dec, star design lid, gilded brass bale, paint flaking	500.00
9½" l, orig dark brown japanning, po-	

lychrome flowers, green, yellow, red, and white, minor wear 500.00
Document Box, white band with red berries and green leaves, asphaltum ground, early 19th C
4¾" h, 8" l, yellow swags and flourishes 300.00
6¼" h, 9½" l, yellow swags and leaf designs 500.00
Food Warmer, 8¼" h, orig brown japanning, stenciled gilded floral dec, double boiler top, font with whale oil burner 225.00
Foot Warmer
5½ x 7¾ x 9¼", punched circle and heart design, mortised wood case, turned corner posts 200.00
7¼ x 8½", 5¾" h, punched heart design with curved tail, mortised wood frame, turned corner posts, worn red repaint 225.00
Jack-O-Lantern, 6½" d, yellow and black paint 310.00
Lantern
5⅛" h, brown japanning, curved glass, folding handle 55.00
5¾" h, dark japanning, clear glass lens with cut sunburst design 55.00
13" h, Revere type, punched dec, ring handle, worn 45.00
15½" h, pierced design, gilt finish .. 75.00
16" h, pierced design, crimped wafer, bail 260.00
17" h, pierced design 75.00
21" h, pierced, double candle holders, three windows 950.00
Miniature, watering can, 4" h, green paint 85.00
Mug, blue japanning, yellow scrolls and flowers, marked "Daisy" 50.00
Sconce
9½" h, punched diamond pattern backplate, New England, 19th C 475.00
17" h, cut and stamped leaf crest, painted black, New England, 19th C 950.00
Teapot, 5½" h, orig brown japanning, red and green floral dec 105.00
Tray, 21 x 28½", polychrome stenciled and painted peacock and swan scene, gilt, orig black paint 225.00

TOBACCO CUTTERS

History: Before pre-packaging, tobacco was delivered to merchants in bulk form. Tobacco cutters were used to cut the tobacco into desired sizes.

Arrow Cupples, cast iron 65.00
Griswold, cast iron, 21" l 110.00
Keen Cutter, E C Simmons 150.00

Cast Iron, Brighton 3, $30.00.

Master Workman, orig label 100.00
Pennsylvania Hardware Co, 1900 .... 45.00
Reynolds, R J Co, orig black japanned finish 90.00
Spear Head, P J Sorg Co, cast iron, red, black lettering, 16½" l 150.00
Star Brand Tobacco, 1885 .... 50.00
Unmarked
Cast Iron, horse shape, metal wrap on handle, 7¼" l 55.00
Wood, fancy wrought iron blade and hinge, dark patina, dated 1773, 35" l, European 215.00
Wrought Iron, blade and handle mounted on oak plank, gray painted prancing horse on blade, 16½" l, 11¾" h, late 19th C 1,870.00

TOBACCO JARS

History: A tobacco jar is a container for storing tobacco. Tobacco humidors were made of various materials and in many shapes, including figurals. The earliest jars date to the early 17th century. However, most examples in today's market were made in the late 19th or early 20th centuries.

Reference: Deborah Gage and Madeleine Marsh, *Tobacco Containers & Accessories,* Gage Bluett & Company, 1988.

Bisque
Boy leaning on tree stump, marked "Austria" 175.00
Skull, wearing golf cap, sitting on book 125.00
Cut Glass
6 x 4", hobstars, large stopper with hobstars 350.00
9" h, hobstars, strawberry diamond, fan, lid, cut knob 525.00
Lead Crystal, brass lid 30.00
Porcelain, skull, ½ L 45.00
Pottery
Black Man, 5⅝" h, bust, straw hat, gold earrings 135.00
Indian, pr, seated beside cargo, smoking pipe, one labeled "St Domingo," other labeled "St Vincent," barrel of tobacco leaves and parcel monogrammed "VOC,"

Elephant, seated, gray, white tusks, pink jacket, pipe in mouth, high glaze, marked "6021" and "71," 6⅝" h, $175.00.

Dutch ship in distance, brass cov, blue "BP" marks, Dutch, mid 18th C **3,850.00**

Ovoid, 12" h, blue and white, embellished oval panel, blue foliate garlands, inscribed "N3," brass cap, Dutch, pr **1,210.00**

Skull and cigarette dec, Ed Diers, 1889 . . . . **1,650.00**

Stoneware, 6½" h, 5" d, deep blue, berry scrolls, cork lid vent, mushroom finial, ornate, marked "Duke of Monmouth" on one side, "MCC Co" on other, dated 1905 on base **200.00**

Terra Cotta, 11" h, figural, Bismark, sitting in chair **250.00**

TOBY JUGS

History: A toby jug is a drinking vessel usually depicting a full-figured, robust, genial drinking man. They originated in England in the late 18th century. The term "Toby" probably related to the character Uncle Toby from *Tristam Shandy* by Laurence Sterne.

References: Susan and Al Bagdade, *Warman's English & Continental Pottery & Porcelain, 1st Edition,* Warman Publishing Co., Inc., 1987; Vic Schuler, *British Toby Jugs,* Kevin Francis Publishing Ltd. (London), 1986.

Additional Listing: Royal Doulton.

Reproduction Alert: Within the last 100 years or more, tobies have been reproduced copiously by many potteries in the United States and England.

Bennington, 11" h, coachman, wearing tassels, Rockingham glaze, 1849 mark **425.00**

Ironstone, 10¾" h, Napoleon, multicolored enamel, marked "Napoleon Jug–patent applied for, Alfred E Evans, Philadelphia, PA" **375.00**

Leeds Type, 9¾" h, man, seated, blue and yellow mottled coat, yellow pants, brown hair, hat, and shoes, holding jug on left knee, pipe between legs, c1800 . . . . **850.00**

Pearlware, 10¾" h, green hat and jacket, brown flowered waistcoat, ochre patterned breeches, brown gloves, standing, rocky base, tree trunk forming handle, hat restored, attributed to Yorkshire, c1790 . . . . . . **550.00**

Pratt, 9½" h, man, seated, brown mottled coat, yellow vest, gray breeches, holding jug, late 18th C **600.00**

Royal Doulton, Sir Winston Churchill, marked "D 6171," 5½" h, $70.00.

Royal Doulton
  5½" h, Sir Winston Churchill **75.00**
  7¼" h, Huntsman, c1910 . . . . **350.00**
Staffordshire
  9" h, creamware, seated, holding jug of frothing ale, black hat, blue jacket, green waistcoat and breeches, black shoes, green base, c1780 . . . . **550.00**
  9¼" h, creamware, standing, smoking pipe, holding baluster jug of frothing ale, blue splashed hat, waistcoat, breeches, and shoes, brown jacket, restoration to hat and hand, c1765 . . . . **450.00**
  9¾" h, creamware, Admiral Lord Howe, holding brown jug of ale, black hat, blue jacket, cream waistcoat, yellow breeches, seated on barrel, dog under right foot, hat, hair, and belly restored, c1780 . . . **675.00**

10¾" h, brown glazed, snuff taker, standing, snuff box in left hand, taking pinch with right hand, mound base, all–over treacle glaze, hat restored, c1820 .... **600.00**

Yellow Ware, 9½" h, man, standing, glazed yellow–tan and dark brown splashes, Derbyshire, mid 19th C .. **125.00**

TOOLS

History: Before the advent of assembly line and mass production, practically everything required for living was handmade at home or by a local tradesman or craftsmen. The cooper, the blacksmith, the cabinetmaker, and the carpenter all had their special tools.

Early examples of these hand tools are collected for their workmanship, ingenuity, place of manufacture, or design. Modern-day craftsman often search out old hand tools for use to authentically recreate the manufacture of an object.

References: Ronald S. Barlow, *The Antique Tool Collector's Guide to Value*, Windmill Publishing Company, 1985, 1987 value update; Kathryn McNerney, *Antique Tools, Our American Heritage*, Collector Books, 1979; R. A. Salaman, *Dictionary of Tools*, Charles Scribner's Sons, 1974; John Walter, *Antique & Collectible Stanley Tools: A Guide To Identity and Value*, Tool Merchants, 1990.

Collectors' Club: Early American Industries Association, P. O. Box 2128, Empire State Plaza Station, Albany, NY 12220.

Museum: Shelburne Museum, Shelburne, Vt.

Plane, pine and maple, Ogontz Tool Co, 22" l, $30.00.

Axe, 7½ x 4½", Winchester **85.00**

Brace, 11" l, hand forged iron, speckled ash burl grip, "C" scroll **100.00**

Chisel, corner, two cutting edges, 18th C **75.00**

Clamp, 24" l, miter jack, bird's eye maple, metal screw shaft **140.00**

Drill, eggbeater type, brass **250.00**

Jigsaw, mounted on wood base, marked "Shipman & Binder" **100.00**

Level, 24" l, cherry, sight insight stock, sq framed round inclinometer, marked "American Combined Level and Grade Finder, Manufactured by Edward Helb, Railroad, York Co, PA, US, July 12, 1904" **225.00**

Mallet, 11¼" l, burl wood, stamped "S Coss" **50.00**

Mortise Gauge, oval head, ebony, brass face plate, solid brass rod stem ... **75.00**

Plane
Block type, Stanley No. 100½ **55.00**
Smoothing type, Sargent No. 407 .. **110.00**

Ratchet, round wood handle, Yankee No. 15 .... **10.00**

Rule, 24" l, folding type, brass edge, Stanley No. 62 .... **25.00**

Saw
Buck, 15½", mortised wood frame .. **45.00**
Hand, Winchester No. 10 .... **50.00**

Screwdriver, electrician's, insulated head, Stanley No. 45, marked "Hurwood" **8.00**

Scribe, hand forged iron, 6" carved wood handle, full bodied naked woman, hooked end **350.00**

Vise, 38" h, bench type, harness maker's, leather strap, foot treadle **175.00**

Woodgraining Set, three rollers, instruction book, Davis Co, 1904 .... **25.00**

Wrench, plier type hand lever, quick adjust crescent type, marked "Universal Wrench Co, Detroit-Windsor, patent 6-3-19" **25.00**

TOOTHPICK HOLDERS

History: Toothpick holders, indispensable table accessories of the Victorian era, are small containers used to hold toothpicks.

They were made in a wide range of materials: china (bisque and porcelain), glass (art, blown, cut, opalescent, pattern, etc.), and metals, especially silver plate. Makers include both American and European firms.

Toothpick holders were used as souvenir items by applying decals or transfers. The same blank may contain several different location labels.

References: William Heacock, *Encyclopedia Of Victorian Colored Pattern Glass, Book I, Toothpick Holders From A To Z*, Antique Publications, 1981; William Heacock, *1,000 Toothpick Holders: A Collector's Guide*, Antique Publications, 1977; William Heacock, *Rare & Unlisted Toothpick Holders*, Antique Publications, 1984.

Collectors' Club: National Toothpick Collector's Society, P. O. Box 246, Sawyer, MI 49125.

Additional Listings: See *Warman's Americana & Collectibles* for more examples.

Advisor: Judy Knauer.

ART GLASS

Alexandrite, Honeycomb pattern, shot glass shape, straight rim, 2⅛" h ... **500.00**

Amberina, Daisy and Button, intense fuchsia color **385.00**

Spearpoint Band, ruby stained top, frosted leaves, 2¼″ h, $45.00.

Burmese, florals, berries, and oak leaf dec, hexagonal rim	350.00
Mt Washington Rib, opaque, satin finish, blue flowers, white ground	145.00
Pomona, amber ruffled rim, fan shape, ftd	400.00

FIGURAL

Bird, yellow milk glass	16.00
Dutch Girl, double, bisque, Heubach	175.00
Grecian Urn, glass, clear, pedestal, applied M shape handles, 2½″ h, Steuben	125.00
Kettle, hunter on horse and dogs dec, marked "Royal Bayreuth"	110.00
Petticoat Hat, vaseline glass, gold	125.00
Roller Skate, high top, button, amber, dated 1886	20.00
Tramp Shoe, white milk glass	40.00

METAL

Bronze, emb design, Tiffany Studios	55.00
Silver Plated, figural, sailor, Victorian, Tufts	90.00
Sterling Silver	
Porcupine, Wilcox	75.00
Ruffled cone shape on base, gold washed int., 5″ h	45.00

OPALESCENT GLASS

Chrysanthemum, cranberry, white opal stripes	90.00
Ribbed Lattice, blue, Heacock #198	135.00
Wreath and Shell, blue	300.00

PATTERN GLASS

Atlas, etched	32.50
Banded Portland, gold trim	40.00
Champion	19.50
Ladders with Diamonds	30.00
Minnesota	32.00
Portland, maiden's blush	30.00
Scalloped Six Point, flared rim	30.00

Scroll with Cane Band, ruby stained	85.00
Swag with Brackets, amethyst, gold dec	65.00
Three Face	50.00
Tiny Thumbprint, custard	55.00
Vermont, green, gold dec	50.00

TORTOISESHELL ITEMS

History: For many years amber and mottled-colored tortoiseshell has been used in the manufacture of small items such as boxes, combs, dresser sets, and trinkets.

Note: Anyone dealing in the sale of tortoiseshell objects should be familiar with the Endangered Species Act and Amendment in its entirety. As of November 1978, antique tortoiseshell objects can be legally imported and sold with some restrictions.

Bracelet, bangle type, sterling silver, 3″ d, $35.00.

Bowl, 7¼″ d, ruffled rim, applied strawberry on pontil, three amber reeded feet	35.00
Box, 4 x 11″, cov, rect, fitted int.	150.00
Cigarette Case, gilded landscape and eagle dec, low relief, Oriental	150.00
Finger Bowl, 5⅝″d, ruffled rim, 6⅛″ d underplate, late 19th C	300.00
Frame, 12½ x 10½″, rect, early 20th C	500.00
Hairpin, carved, poppy blossoms	140.00
Humidor, 4½″, rect, hinged lid	150.00
Inkstand, 8 x 16″, three cut glass bottles, brass inlay, shaped handles	400.00
Jewelry Case, expandable, three compartments	340.00
Letter Opener, 17″ l, silver blade with rounded end, ribbed and fluted spiral handle, maker's mark "MH," London, 1885	325.00
Sewing Box, rect, blue silk compartment int., ivory trim, English, c1900	900.00
Shaving Brush, inlaid MOP dec handle	40.00
Snuff Box, rect, English, mid 19th C	220.00
Tea Caddy, serpentine, two int. lids, ivory trim, English, 19th C	1,200.00

TOYS

History: In America the first cast-iron toys began to appear shortly after the Civil War. Leading 19th century manufacturers include Hubley, Dent, Kenton, and Schoenhut. In the first decades of the 20th century, Arcade, Buddy L, Marx, and Tootsie Toy joined the earlier firms. Wooden toys were made by George Brown and other manufacturers who did not sign or label their work.

In Europe, Nuremberg, Germany, was the center for the toy industry from the late 18th through the mid 20th centuries. Companies such as Lehman and Marklin produced high quality toys.

Several auction houses, e.g. Lloyd Ralston Toys, have specialty auctions consisting entirely of toys.

Every toy is collectible. The key is the condition and working order if mechanical. Examples listed are considered to be in good to very good condition to mint condition unless otherwise specified.

References: Linda Baker, *Modern Toys, American Toys, 1930–1980*, Collector Books, 1985 (1988 value update); Robert Carter and Eddy Rubinstein, *Yesterday's Yesteryears: Lesney "Matchbox" Models*, Haynes Publishing Group (London), 1986; Jurgen and Marianne Cieslik, *Lehmann Toys*, New Cavendish Books, 1982; Richard Friz, *The Official Identification And Price Guide To Collectible Toys, Fifth Edition*, House of Collectibles, 1990; Gordon Gardiner and Alistair Morris, *The Illustrated Encyclopedia of Metal Toys*, Harmony Books, 1984; Lillian Gottschalk, *American Toy Cars & Trucks*, Abbeville Press, 1985; Constance King, *Metal Toys & Automata*, Chartwell Books, 1989; Ernest & Ida Long, *Dictionary of Toys Sold in America*, 2 vols, published by author; David Longest, *Character Toys and Collectibles*, Collector Books, 1984; David Longest, *Character Toys and Collectibles, Second Series*, Collector Books, 1987; David Longest, *Toys: Antique & Collectible*, Collector Books, 1990; Brian Moran, *Battery Toys*, Schiffer Publishing, 1984; Richard O'Brien, *Collecting Toys: A Collectors Identification and Value Guide, 5th Edition*, Books Americana, 1990; Richard O'Brien, *The Story of American Toys*, Abbeville Press, 1990; Maxine A. Pinsky, *Greenberg's Guide To Marx Toys, Volume I* (1988), *Volume II* (1990), Greenberg Publishing Co.; David Richter, *Collector's Guide To Tootsietoys*, Collector Books, 1990; Harry L. Rinker, *Collector's Guide To Toys, Games, And Puzzles*, Wallace–Homestead, 1991; Martyn L. Schorr, *The Guide To Mechanical Toy Collecting*, Performance Media, 1979; Peter Viemeister, *Micro Cars*, Hamilton's, 1982; Blair Whitton, *Paper Toys of The World*, Hobby House Press, Inc., 1986; Blair Whitton, *The Knopf Collector's Guide to American Toys*, Alfred A. Knopf, Inc. 1984.

Periodicals: *The Antique Toy World*, P.O. Box 34509, Chicago, IL 60634; *Toy Shop*, 700 East State Street, Iola, WI 54990; *Wheel Goods Trader*, P.O. Box 435, Fraser, MI 48026; *YesterDaze Toys*, P.O. Box 57, Otisville, MI 48463.

Collectors' Club: Antique Toy Collectors of America, Two Wall Street, New York, NY 10005.

Museums: American Museum of Automobile Miniatures, Andover, Mass.; Museum of the City of New York, New York, N.Y.; Smithsonian Institution, Washington, D.C.; Margaret Woodbury Strong Museum, Rochester, N.Y.; Toy Museum of Atlanta, Atlanta, Ga.

Additional Listings: Disneyana and Schoenhut. Also see *Warman's Americana & Collectibles* for more examples.

Arcade, Freeport, IL, 1893–1946
Dump Truck, Mack, painted red, replacement hoist mechanism, new axle, 12" l 450.00
Threshing Machine, cast iron, orig gray and white paint, red trim, orig "McCormick Deering" and "Arcade" decals, battered tin hopper, 10" l 300.00
Yellow Cab, cast iron, worn orange and black, one wheel and axle missing, 9" l 425.00
Arnold, German, 1906–Present
Airboat, litho tin, passenger ship, large rear propeller, 8½" l 715.00
Coupe, litho tin, graffiti cov 1930s style car, driver, and three passengers, c1953, 9½" l 350.00
Bergmann, Althof, American, side wheeler, painted tin, off white and dark asphaltum paint, fair paint, minor dents, c1874, 20" l 12,000.00
Bing, Gebrüder, Nürnberg, Germany
Battleship, tin windup, painted brown, dark, and light gray, three stacks, six gun emplacements, twin lifeboats, anchor, and dual masts, crow's nest, 14" l 2,860.00
Car, model T Ford sedan, lady driving four door sedan, very good finish, c1923, 6½" l 400.00
Garage, litho tin, two clockwork cars, 8" w 275.00
Ocean Liner, litho tin windup, three stacks, mast, and flag, hull professionally refinished, 8¾" l 425.00
Bliss, horse drawn trolley car, paper on wood, Jackson Park, Chicago, movable seats, open sides, dual conductors, and twin horse, some damage and repairs, 28" l 1,100.00
Bonnet, Victor, French, delivery boy, litho tin, uniformed boy pushing three wheeled cart, marked "V. B. et Cie," 7" l 880.00
Buddy L, East Moline, IL, 1921–Present
Concrete Mixer, bright green and

black accents, orig decals, paint in
very good condition 200.00
Dump Truck, metal wheels, dumping
mechanism, orig label, minor sur-
face rusting, 24½" l 400.00
Fire Truck, aerial, bell, steering
wheel, extension ladder, rotating
turret, red, 31" l 600.00
Repair It Truck, rubber tires, orig label, minor surface wear 150.00
Steam Shovel, red roof and base,
black boiler, fair paint and decal,
c1920, 20¾" l 175.00
Buffalo Toys, American
Red Streak Racer, litho tin, red, yellow wheels, spiral spring pulled at
back propels car, c1925 . . . . 245.00
Silver Dash, litho tin windup, racer,
silver body, red wheels, two yellow
figures, black hats, patent 1925,
12" l 225.00
Burnett, omnibus, litho tin windup, bat-
tery operated headlamps, litho side-
boards read "Land's End To John
O'Groats," red, black, and light green,
14½" l 1,450.00
Bush, C. G., Claremont, NH, and Prov-
idence, RI, kaleidoscope
11" h, clear and colored glass bits,
canes, and vials of colored water,
brass ships wheel turning ring, collar marked "C. G. Bush, Prov, RI,
Patent Re–Issued, Nov 11, 1873,"
turned wooden stand 475.00
13½" h, cardboard and brass cylinder,
turned walnut tripod stand, patented Nov 11, 1873 . . . . 550.00
14" h, leather bound eyepiece, brass
ship's wheel turning handle, turned
wooden base 660.00
Carette, Georges, & Cie, Nürnberg,
Germany
Ferris Wheel, painted tinplate, man-
ually operated, four seated figures,
two flags, c1900, 15" h 2,250.00
Ocean Liner, litho tin
12⅜" l, two upper decks, cream
super structure, blue, green, and
red striping, red hull two masts
with pendants, three funnels,
stern flag missing, some chip-
ping to paint, orig box, c1912 . . 1,000.00
24" l, two decks, four stacks, four
lifeboats, ramrod bow, twin
masts, open bridge, entire boat
professionally refinished 4,650.00
Champion, police motorcycle, cast iron,
7" l 170.00
Chein, A. J., Harrison, NJ, c1930
Clown, litho tin windup, doing hand-
stands, marked "Chein & Co, Made
In USA" 145.00

Disneyland Ferris Wheel 175.00
Happy Hooligan, litho tin windup,
walker, shuffles, 6" h 330.00
Ignatz Mouse, jointed wooden figure,
wire arms, leather ears, riding three
wheeled metal scooter, cord pull,
paper label marked "Ignatz Mouse,
1932 King Features Syn Inc, J
Chein & Co, 2005th Ave NY, Made
in USA," hands and one wheel
missing, 8½" h 500.00
Playland Merry–Go–Round 250.00
C. K. O.
Motorcyclist and Passenger, litho tin
windup, uniformed men, highly detailed litho motorcycle, 6" l 675.00
Passenger Liner, litho tin windup, two
single wing planes connected to
pylon on ship 425.00
Distler, Johann, Nürnberg, Germany
Autobus, litho tin windup, red, black
accents, yellow curved steps to up-
per deck, orig driver, 7" l 750.00
Packard Convertible Coupe, litho tin
windup, steering and turning front
wheels, light green, red upholstery,
10" l 200.00
Doepke, Rossmoyne, IL, aerial ladder
truck, red and aluminum ladders, rubber tires, very good decals, mid 20th
C, 34¾" l 100.00
Fallows, James & Sons, American,
painted tinplate pull toy, four jockeys
riding white horses, wheeled base,
c1885, 9" l 700.00
Fisher Price, East Aurora, NY, 1930–
Present
Jumbo Rollo, elephant, riding tricycle,
c1951 . . . . 20.00
Looky Push Car, 20" handle, plastic
steering wheel, #875 . . . . 25.00
Musical Duck, 12" l, #795 . . . . 42.00
Xylophone Pull Toy, Donald Duck,
#177, 11" h 80.00
Fleishmann, J., Nürnberg, Germany,
1887–World War II
Battleship, litho tin windup, brown and
gray, two stacks, three pivoting gun
turrets, two flags, two lifeboats, two
masts with crow's nests 850.00
Ocean Liner, tin windup, painted red,
black, and beige, twin stacks, lifeboat, decks, and masts, some re-
painting, 12½" l 425.00
Gong Bell Mfg Co, East Hampton, CT
Equestrian Bell Toy, tin, jockey on
horse, bells attached to horse, late
19th C, 9⅛" l 5,600.00
Trix Krazy Kat Race Car, black and
white wooden character, red and
black car, metal wheels containing
bells, orig label "HD Allen Trix,

Made in USA, The Gong Bell Mfg
Co, East Hampton, Conn," 10½" l   **330.00**
Gunthermann, Martin, Nürnberg, Germany, 1920–World War II
Banjo Player, painted tin, clockwork,
black figure stomps feet and strums
banjo, c1890, 7" h **550.00**
Car, litho tin windup, battery operated
headlamps, driver, royal blue,
c1935, 15" l **385.00**

**Gunthermann, painted tin, fire engine
pumper, driver and fireman, clock
mechanism drives real axle, red finish,
black trim, 8" l, $1,870.00.**

Salto, litho tin windup, black and
white bulldog, flip action **90.00**
Two Man Band, litho tin windup, two
seated black musicians, playing accordion, flute, and cymbals, keywind platform, c1895, 9" h **2,860.00**
Walking Lady, litho tin windup, hp,
black lady, full skirt, carrying umbrella and wicker basket, 6½" h . .   **990.00**
Hausser, German, litho tin, clockwork,
c1935
Army Truck, detailed camouflage
litho, nine Elastolin soldiers seated
in back, 12" l **425.00**
Army Truck with Gun on Turret, camouflage litho, reels of rope on front,
four Elastolin soldiers in back, 11"
l **600.00**
Hubley, Lancaster, PA, 1894–1965,
painted cast iron
Car Transport, red, two cars, 10" l . .   **225.00**
Plantation Wagon, repainted, 14½" l   **100.00**
Yellow Cab, nickel plated details, rubber tires **175.00**

Ives, Bridgeport, CT
General Butler, clockwork, walks, red
and blue cloth uniform, brass buttons, hp face, 10" h **2,860.00**
Preacher at the Puplit, cloth dressed
black preacher, waves hands,
thumps bible, keywind, 10" h **4,400.00**
Pull Toy, walking horse, three wheels,
orig straw tail, 6½" l **1,200.00**
Jep, French, litho tin windup
Airplane, six propeller, light blue, "Air-France-F-PA-N-AM" lithographed
on side, battery operated lights,
clockwork props, triple vertical tail
section, 21" l **575.00**
Fire Engine, red, battery operated
headlamps, driver, two fire fighters,
cloth hose, orig box and instructions in five languages, 18" l **4,400.00**
Kellermann, German, Battleship *K351*,
litho tin windup, litho detailed portholes, lifeboats, and anchors, orig
box, c1935, 14" l **350.00**
Kenton, Kenton, OH, painted cast iron
Chariot, three horses, lady driver, 10"
l **475.00**
Covered Wagon, driver, two horses,
cloth cov, unused, orig box, 15" l,
light rust **250.00**
Hansom Cab, horse, driver, lady passenger, unused, orig box, 15¾" l   **280.00**
Overland Circus, cast iron, polychrome, wagon, two horses, out riders, driver, and polar bear, unused, orig box, 14" l **450.00**
Keystone, American
Fire Truck, sheet metal, aerial ladder,
front bell, rubber tiers, red and silver, seat for child, 32" l **325.00**
Police Patrol Wagon, steering wheel,
rubber tires, black, 28" l **200.00**
Railroad Express Truck, black cab,

**Lehmann, Tut–Tut Car, painted tin,
driver blowing large horn, 7" l,
$1,000.00.**

red wheels, green body, wire sides, orig decals and paint in good condition, some rust and scratches, 1930s, 26½" h 700.00

Kosuge, Japan, racer, litho tin windup, double rear wheels, blue, American and British flags on hood and center fin, 13" l 950.00

Lehmann, Nürnberg, Germany, 1881–Present

Ajax, litho tin windup, acrobat, clubs in hands, somersaults, 9½" h 2,640.00

Autin, litho tin windup, driver at wheel of short litho wagon, 4" l 330.00

Balky Mule, litho tin windup, kicking mule rearing up against two wheel chariot, clown driver, 7" l 200.00

Bibi, litho tin, whirling top, string activated, 3" h 110.00

Climbing Monkey, litho tin windup, orig box 125.00

Dare Devil, litho tin windup, balky zebra and wagon with native driver, 7" l 275.00

Gustav Climbing Miller, string pull top, bowl on head, climbs pole to reach windmill, 18" h 220.00

Mars Sailor, litho tin windup, drunken motion, 7½" h 770.00

Na–Ob, litho tin, horsedrawn wagon, driver perched on front seat, 6" l . . 250.00

Oh My Jigger, litho tin windup, black man dancing on platform, 10" h . . 440.00

Oho, litho tin windup, automobile, two seater, green and dark blue litho, orig driver, 4" l 285.00

Paddy and the Pig, litho tin windup, 5½"

Tyras The Walking Dog, litho tin windup, detailed litho coat, 7" l . . 500.00

Uhu, litho tin windup, land and sea racer, streamlined, wheel fins, orig driver with rotating head, 9½" l . . 2,420.00

Walking Down Broadway, litho tin windup, strolling couple, rack and pinion drive, dog, walking stick, and toothed rack missing, c1890, 6⅛" h 2,000.00

Zig–Zag, litho tin windup, painted red, white, and blue 1,100.00

Linemar

Climbing Fireman, litho, battery operated, 13" h 165.00

Mickey Mouse
  Pluto Rocker, litho tin windup, Mickey rocks on Pluto's back, 6½" l 1,450.00
  Roll Over Skater, litho tin windup, skating, arms swinging, cloth pants, orig ears, 6½" h 1,775.00

Minnie Mouse, litho tin windup, knitting, rocking chair, one ear missing, 7" h 220.00

Popeye, litho tin windup, riding highwheel bicycle, cloth trousers, 6¾" h 1,550.00

Lionel, Irvington, NJ, 1906–Present

Peter Rabbit Chick Mobile, keywind hand car, painted yellow, composition glass eyed Peter Rabbit, 10½" l 330.00

Speedboat, litho tin windup, competition type, twin motors, dual drivers, cream and light green hull, 17" l 750.00

Marklin, Goppingen, Germany, 1859–Present

Army Truck, hp, three Elastolin soldiers seated in back, c1935, 8" l 450.00

Racer, tinplate, painted red, driver, four rubber tires, c1935, 11" l . . . 675.00

Martin, Ferdinand

Advocate, tin and cloth, keywind, raises and lowers hands from elevated speaker's podium, hp, 9" h 1,320.00

Chinaman Walker, tin, double independent clockwork, keywind, walks, brandishing sword in each hand, 7½" h 1,760.00

Mysterious Ball, litho tin windup, ball ascends spiral path, opens at top to reveal lady acrobat, 14" h . . 1,200.00

Marx, Louis, & Co, New York, 1921–Present

B. O. Plenty, litho tin windup, walker, holding Baby Sparkle Plenty, tilts cap, 8½" h 135.00

Benzine Buggy, litho tin windup, Charlie McCarthy, black and white litho, 8" h 825.00

Fireman, litho tin windup, climbing, two part ladder, motor not working, 1935, 21½" h 150.00

G–Man Car, litho tin windup, very good finish, 1930s, 4⅝" l 300.00

Harold Lloyd, litho tin windup, walker, cane, shuffles, 10½" h 450.00

Joe Penner and His Duck Goo–Goo, litho tin windup, walking figure, orig hat and cigar, 8" h 500.00

Mortimer Snerd Car, litho tin windup, turns head from side to side, blue and brown litho car, red and white wheels, 7½" l 300.00

Pinocchio, litho tin windup, walker, waddles forward, flicking eyes, 8½" h 135.00

Popeye and Olive Oyl, litho tin windup, Popeye dances as Olive plays the accordion, 9½" h 800.00

Ring–A–Ling Circus Roundabout, litho tin windup, center ringmaster, prods clown, elephant, monkey, and lion, 8" h 440.00

Spic and Span, litho tin windup,

seated black drummer, dancing fiddler, litho platform, orig box, 10" h **3,850.00**

Superman Rollover Tank, litho tin windup, copper colored tank, litho gun turret, hinged Superman, 4" l **285.00**

Meier, J. P. H., Nürnberg, Germany, penny toy, litho tin, baby in convertible high chair, 20th C, 3¾" h **175.00**

Nifty, German

Battling Maggie and Jiggs, litho tin, wheeled keywind base, 7" l **1,320.00**

Mickey Mouse Jazz Drummer, litho tin, plunger action causes Mickey to play drum, 6¾" h **825.00**

Powerful Katrinka, litho tin windup, Jimmy riding in wheelbarrow, 6¾" l **2,200.00**

Oro, German, litho tin windup, touring car, Packard insignia on radiator grille, driver, c1933, 9" l **11,000.00**

Performo–Toy, Middletown, PA, Ignatz, wooden, painted black and white, flexible cord limbs and tail, orig label, 5" h **90.00**

Planck, Ernest, German, coastal steamer, tinplate, steam motor, single stack, small rear cabin, painted gray and black, some hull flaking, 10½" l **700.00**

Richter & Co, blocks, boxed set, stone blocks, instructions and layouts, No. 7, early 20th C, 9⅞ x 15⅛ x 3" **75.00**

Schuco, trademark of Schreyer and Co., Germany, 1912–Present

Boy Scout, litho tin windup, playing violin **115.00**

Car, litho tin windup, coral body, striped litho tin grille with name, marked "Made in US Zone Germany," 1940s, 5½" l **115.00**

Donald Duck, litho tin windup, orig blue felt sailor shirt and hat, 6" h **400.00**

Race Car, litho tin windup, blue, steerable front wheels, orig box, 7" l . . **75.00**

Strauss, Ferdinand, Corp, New York City, 20th C, litho tin windup

Big Show Circus Wagon **450.00**

Ham and Sam **350.00**

Jazzbo Jim, 10" h **300.00**

Tip Top, black porter pushing two wheeled cart **300.00**

Tombo Dancer, tap dancing black man **330.00**

Tipp, German, litho tin windup

Cabriolet, battery operated headlamps, forward mounted doors, rear mounted spare tire, maroon, cream fenders and roof, 22" l . . . **4,125.00**

Convertible, Mercedes, hard rubber tires, opening doors and trunk, Mercedes hood ornament, orange, light green top, 9½" l **4,400.00**

Unidentified Maker

American, pedal car, pressed steel,

two passenger, twin side lights, front lamp, and horn, 80" l **3,850.00**

German

Horse, litho tin windup, Nazi soldier in full military uniform astride black and white speckled horse, 5½" h **1,000.00**

Pull Toy, Admiral Dewey, articulated, bisque head and cap, painted facial features, waving American flag, wood platform and wheels, early 1900s, 8½" l **850.00**

Racing Car, litho tin, friction drive, barrel hood, driver hunched over wheel, fully dressed, goggles, blue and cream, c1905, 6½" l **600.00**

Unique Art, Newark, NY

Dog Patch Band, litho metal, working, one arm missing, 1945, 10" l **200.00**

Hobo Train, litho boxcar, dog grabbing fleeing tramp by trousers, tinplate, keywind, 8½" l **375.00**

Jazzbo Jim, litho metal, orig box . . . **375.00**

Rap & Tap In A Friendly Scrap, litho tin windup, 4" h boxers, 5 x 4" ring, 5 x 3 x 2" base, c1825 . . . . **600.00**

Wolverine Supply & Mfg Co, 1903–Present

Crane, excellent condition **60.00**

Sunny Andy Kiddie Kampers, litho tin windup, four boy scouts, two girl scouts at campsite, 14" l **275.00**

Zilotone, litho tin windup, uniformed musician playing xylophone, four steel inserts for tune selection, 7½" w **715.00**

Wyandotte, American

Humphrey Mobile, litho tin windup, Humphrey riding tricycle and outhouse on wheels, 9" l **330.00**

Speed King Scooter, litho tin windup, boy propelling soap box three wheeled scooter, 6" l **220.00**

TRAINS, TOY

History: Railroading has always been an important part of childhood, largely because of the romance associated with the railroad and the emphasis on toy trains.

The first toy trains were cast iron and tin; windup motors added movement. The Golden Age of toy trains was 1920–1955, when electric-powered units were available and names such as Ives, American Flyer, and Lionel were household words. The construction of the rolling stock was of high quality. The advent of plastic in the late 1950s lessened this quality considerably.

Toy trains were designated by a model scale or gauge. The most popular are HO, N, O and standard. Narrow gauge was a response to the modern capacity to miniaturize. Its popularity has lessened in the last few years.

Condition of trains is critical. Items in fair condition (scratched, chipped, dented, rusted or warped) and below generally have little value to a collector. Restoration is accepted, provided it is done accurately. It may enhance the price one or two grades. Prices listed are for very good to mint condition unless noted.

References: Paul V. Ambrose, *Greenberg's Guide To Lionel Trains, 1945–1969, Volume III, sets* , Greenberg Publishing, 1990; Susan and Al Bagdade, *Collector's Guide To American Toy Trains,* Wallace–Homestead, 1990; John O. Bradshaw, *Greenberg's Guide To Kusan Trains,* Greenberg Publishing Co, 1987; Richard Friz, *The Official Identification And Price Guide To Toy Trains,* House of Collectibles, 1990; Bruce Greenberg, (edited by Christian F. Rohlfing), *Greenberg's Guide to Lionel Trains: 1901–1942, Volume 1* (1988), *Volume 2* (1988), Greenberg Publishing Co.; Bruce Greenberg (edited by Roland La Voie), *Greenberg's Guide To Lionel Trains: 1945–1969, Volume 1* (1990), *Volume 2* (1988), Greenberg Publishing Co.; John Hubbard, *The Story of Williams Electric Trains,* Greenberg Publishing Co., 1987; Steven H. Kimball, *Greenberg's Guide To American Flyer Prewar O Gauge,* Greenberg Publishing Co., 1987; Roland La Voie, *Greenberg's Guide To Lionel Trains, 1970–1988,* Greenberg Publishing Co., 1989; Lionel Book Committee, Train Collectors Association, *Lionel Trains: Standard Of The World, 1900–1943,* Train Collectors Association, 1989; Dallas J. Mallerich, III, *Greenberg's American Toy Trains: From 1900 With Current Values,* Greenberg Publishing Co., 1990; Dallas J. Mallerich, III, *Greenberg's Guide to Athearn Trains,* Greenberg Publishing Co., 1987; Eric J. Matzke, *Greenberg's Guide To Marx Trains, Volume 1,* Greenberg Publishing Co., 1989; Al McDuffie, et. al., *Greenberg Guide to Ives Trains,* 1901–1932, Greenberg Publishing Co, 1984; Robert P. Monaghan, *Greenberg's Guide to Markin OO/HO,* Greenberg Publishing Co., 1989; John R. Ottley, *Greenberg's Guide To LGB Trains,* Greenberg Publishing Co., 1989; James Patterson and Bruce C. Greenberg, *Greenberg's Guide To American Flyer S Gauge, Third Edition,* Greenberg Publishing Co., 1988; Vincent Rosa and George J. Horan, *Greenberg Guide To HO Trains,* Greenberg Publishing Co., 1986.

Note: Greenberg Publishing Company (7543 Main Street, Sykesville, MD 21784) is the leading publisher of toy train literature. Anyone interested in the subject should write for their catalog and ask to be put on their mailing list.

Collectors' Clubs: Lionel Collector's Club, P.O. Box 11851, Lexington, KY 40578; The National Model Railroad Association, P.O. Box 2186, Indianapolis, IN 46206; The Toy Train Operating Society, Inc., 25 West Walnut Street, Suite 305, Pasadena, CA 91103; The Train Collector's Association, P.O. Box 248, Strasburg, PA 17579.

Additional Listings: See *Warman's Americana & Collectibles* for more examples.

AMERICAN FLYER

Car
900, passenger car, Northern Pacific	**125.00**
979, caboose	**25.00**

Locomotive
3112, O gauge, baggage, Paul Revere on both sides, observation car with Paul Revere on one side and Lexington on other, orange with blue	**400.00**
4644, standard gauge, green and red, restored	**125.00**

Set
4637, locomotive, car 4018, 4017, 1010, 4022, and 4021, standard gauge	**650.00**
4680 locomotive, black and green, copper trim, 4693 tender, 4017 gondola, 4022 flat car, 4010 tank car, 4018 box car, 4021 caboose, standard gauge	**750.00**

IVES

Car, 64387, freight car, O gauge, Canadian Pacific RR, yellow simulated wood litho, gray enameled roof, c1913	**100.00**

Locomotive
3241, standard gauge, red brass plate, cream trim, restored	**225.00**
3255R, O gauge, rusting and surface scratches	**85.00**
Set, 3241, standard gauge, locomotive, eight cars, replaced whistle, white paint spots on locomotive	**1,000.00**

Lionel, Silver Streak Engine #616, two passenger cars #617, caboose #618, $425.00.

LIONEL

Car
213, Cattle Car, standard gauge, terra
  cotta, green floor **250.00**
900, Trailer, 2⅞ gauge, Metropolitan
  Express, maroon, black roof,
  1904–05 . . . .   **3,400.00**
Locomotive
42, standard gauge, black, NYC . . .   **250.00**
2321, O gauge, Lackawanna, AB die-
  sel **350.00**
2360, O gauge, Pennsylvania GGI   **500.00**
Set, passenger, standard gauge
408E, locomotive, green, restored . .   **1,100.00**
752E locomotive, 753 passenger, 754
  observation, Union Pacific Stream-
  line, diecast and tin, some rust . .   **650.00**

TRAMP ART

History: Tramp art was prevalent in the United
States from 1875 to the 1930s. Items were made
by itinerant artists who left no record of their identity. They used old cigar boxes and fruit and vegetable crates. The edges of items were chip-
carved and layered, creating the "Tramp Art" effect. Finished items usually were given an overall
stain. Today they are collected primarily as folk
art.

Reference: Helaine Fendelman, *Tramp Art: An
Itinerant's Folk Art Guide*, E. P. Dutton & Co.,
1975.

**Cosmetic Box, mirror inside, red lining,
10½ x 6 x 4", $85.00.**

Box
8¼" h, chip carved, one fitted drawer,
  sliding top, red velvet lined int. . . .   **600.00**
13½" l, gilded brass appliques **65.00**
Chest of drawers, miniature
6 x 12", triple arch crestrail, chip
  carved edge, rect top, three drawers, natural finish, green trimmed
  edges, ftd **160.00**
7 x 11", rect marble top, three draw-
  ers, framed oval mirror **675.00**
Frame, 17¼ x 19½", rect, chip carved,
  diamond shape projections on corners, includes German diploma,
  dated 1915 . . . .   **45.00**

Jewelry Box, 12¼" h, poplar, old dark
  finish, scrolled feet, flowers, bird finial,
  carved name "Addie," four swing out
  trays, center compartment, repair to
  lid and finial **200.00**
Mirror, 23" h, crest with confronting birds
  above horseshoe enclosing date
  "1914," center heart form frame en-
  closes mirror, applied rosettes and
  wings above two birds dec **220.00**
Sewing Box, 9½" l, pin cushion frame
  top, drawer, orig dark finish **30.00**

TRANSPORTATION MEMORABILIA

History: The first airlines in the United States
depended on subsidies form the government for
carrying mail for most of their income. The first
non-Post Office Department flight for mail carrying
was in 1926 between Detroit and Chicago. By
1930 there were 38 domestic and 5 international
airlines operating in the United States. A typical
passenger load was 10. After World War II, 4-
engine planes with a capacity of 100 or more passengers were introduced.

The jet age was launched in the 1950s. In 1955
Capitol Airlines used British-made turboprop airlin-
ers in domestic service. In 1958 National Airlines
began domestic jet passenger service. The giant
Boeing 747 went into operation in 1970 as part of
the Pan American fleet. The Civil Aeronautics
Board, which regulates the airline industry, ended
control of routes in 1982 and fares in 1983.

Transoceanic travel falls into two distinct
periods—the era of the great Clipper ships and the
era of the diesel-powered ocean liners. The later
craft reached their "Golden Age" in the period
between 1900 and 1940.

An ocean liner was a city unto itself. Many had
their own printing rooms to produce a wealth of
daily memorabilia. Companies such as Cunard,
Holland-America, and others encouraged passengers to acquire souvenirs with the company logo
and ship name.

Certain ships acquired a unique mystique. The
Queen Elizabeth, *Queen Mary*, and *United States*
became symbols of elegance and style. Today the
cruise ship has dominated the world of the ocean
liner.

References: Aeronautica & Air Label Collectors
Club of Aerophilatelic Federation of America, *Air
Transport Label Catalog*, published by club; Stan
Baumwald, *Junior Crew Member Wings*, pub-
lished by author; Trev Davis and Fred Chan, *Air-
line Playing Cards: Illustrated Reference Guide,
2nd Edition*, published by authors, 1987; Richard
R. Wallin, *Commercial Aviation Collectibles: An
Illustrated Price Guide*, Wallace-Homestead Book
Company, 1990.

The sales catalogs of Robert L. Loewenthal

(10161 Southwest 1st Court, Plantation, FL 33324) and Ken Schultz (Box M753, Hoboken, NJ 07030) are excellent substitutes for the lack of books on the subject of ocean liner collectibles.

Collectors' Clubs: Steamship Historical Society of America, Inc., 345 Blackstone Boulevard, Hall Building, Providence, RI 02906; Titanic Historical Society, P. O. Box 53, Indian Orchard, MA 01151; The World Airline Historical Society, 3381 Apple Tree Lane, Erlanger, KY 41018.

Additional Listings: See Automobilia and Railroad Items in *Warman's Antiques And Their Prices* and Aeronautica, Ocean Liner Collectibles, and Railroad Items in *Warman's Americana & Collectibles*.

Plaque, 100,000 Mile Club, United Airlines 1955, 6½ x 8½", $25.00.

AVIATION

Advertising
Calendar, Lufthansa, illustration of stewardess and child, 1956	35.00
Fan, Air India	10.00
Lighter, Air France	25.00
Pennant, Varig Airlines, silk–screen, 6 x 12"	10.00
Playing Cards, Air Florida, 1980	10.00

China
Ashtray, TWA, square, rounded corners, white, Rosenthal China	20.00
Casserole, National Airlines, brown Sun King logo, Sterling China Co	25.00
Cup and Saucer, Northwest Airlines, Regal Imperial, burgundy, tan, and gold pattern, Royal Doulton	25.00
Plate, dinner, 10½" d, Regent Air, blue and gold pattern, Spode	100.00
Sake Cup, 1½ x 1½" h, Continental, new logo, Noritake China	10.00
Salt and Pepper Shakers, pr	
Air Mauritius, Wedgwood	30.00
Air New Zealand, bullet shape, Hut-	

schenreuther and Crown Lynn China	35.00

Flatware
Fork, TWA, sp, c1930–45	35.00
Knife	
American Airlines Flagship, sp, DC3 nose stamped on solid handle, c1930	20.00
Aeroflot, stainless steel	4.00
Spoon, Chicago & Southern, sp, c1940	10.00

Glassware
Brandy, Eastern, crystal, logo on base, made by Schott Zweisel, Germany	16.00
Cocktail, Regent Air, leaded crystal, made by Atlantis, Portugal	35.00
Roly–poly, Allegheny, name and logo in red and blue	10.00
Shot, Southern Airways, 10th anniversary	35.00
Teapot, American, 3½" h, logo	50.00
Wine, United, shield logo	8.00
Wine Carafe, United Airlines, gold logo and scrollwork	15.00
Junior Wings, 1930s, "Junior Clipper Captain/Pan American World Airways"	35.00
Menu, TWA, c1960	4.00
Napkin, Delta, linen, 1958	10.00

Silver
Creamer and Sugar, United, Reed & Barton, c1960	30.00
Napkin Ring, American	25.00
Pitcher, coffee, Pan Am, International Silver Co, c1940	200.00
Serving Tray, United, International Silver Co, c1960	75.00
Timetable, American Airlines, 1951	15.00

OCEAN LINER

Ashtray, Royal Caribbean Cruise Lines, 4" octagon, 1½" h, clear glass, blue crown and anchor line logo in bowl, mottled finish	10.00
Baggage Tag, Furness Bermuda Line, *Franconia*, 3 x 6", 1931	10.00
Life Jacket, United States Lines, adult, bright orange, white belting, black stencilling, black whistle on attached cord	55.00
Matchbook, Georgian Bay Line, "Spend your 1943 'v'–cation on the Great Lakes," unused	6.00
Medallion, Panama–Pacific Line, *Virginia*, water sports, ribbon	25.00
Menu, North German Lloyd, *Bremen*, dinner, castle etching on cover, 1938	15.00
Passenger List, Anchor Line, *Transylvania II*, Jun 22, 1938	18.00

Advertising Mirror, celluloid, multicolored, American Line, Philadelphia-Liverpool-Queenstown, Whitehead & Hoag Co, Newark, NJ, 1¾″ d, $75.00.

Pinback Button
    Italia Line, *Rex,* 1⅛″ d, photo, starboard side and name 16.00
    SS Dolphin, *Zion,* 2″ d, name and logo in blue and yellow 8.00
Playing Cards, Norway, name in white, navy blue ground, unused 10.00
Postcard
    American Line, *St Paul,* color, self portrait, c1906 . . . .   14.00
    Ward Line, *Morro Castle,* photo of wreckage from beach at Asbury Park, NJ, 1934 . . . .   12.00
Poster, Holland America Line, *Rotterdam,* 37½ x 24½″, color, deck scene, line name and "Sail a Happy Ship" at top 75.00
Stationery, Norwegian–American Line, *Stavangerfjord,* buff, Hal Crest and name in blue 12.00
Stock Certificate, Cunard Line, Cunard Steam–Ship Co, Ltd, cancelled 7.00
Toothpick, United States Lines, 3″ l, line name on side, Eagle logo, set of 6   5.00
Tray, French Line, 18 x 14 x 1″, fiberglass, light green, portraits of 1960s fleet 60.00

TRUNKS

History: Trunks are portable containers that clasp shut for the storage or transportation of personal possessions. Normally "trunk" means the ribbed flat or dome-top models of the second half of the 19th century. Unrestored they sell between $50 and $150. Refinished and relined, the price rises to $200 to $400, with decorators being a principal market.

Early trunks frequently were painted, stenciled, grained, or covered with wallpaper. These are collected for their folk art qualities and as such sell for high prices.

Reference: Martin and Maryann Labuda, *Price & Identification Guide to Antique Trunks,* published by authors, 1980.

DOME TOP

Leather, 13″ l, brown, brass tack trim, iron lock and hasp, brass bale handle   **55.00**
Painted
    Norwegian, 29″ h, 46⅛″ l, yellow, green, blue, black, and white floral medallions and sprigs dec, plain int., wrought iron loop handles, inscribed **550.00**
    Sponge, 7″ h, 15″ l, black and brown, burled simulating plain int., early 19th C **145.00**

Dome top, leather covered, initialed with nail heads, iron hardware and rivets, 26½ x 15 x 12½″, $165.00.

Pine, 35″ l, fitted int. with till and four dovetailed drawers, brass bail handles **175.00**
Pine and Poplar, 35½″ l, dovetailed, orig red flame graining, black edges, imitation inlay striping, iron lock and hasp, end handles **175.00**

FLAT TOP

Chinese, 36″ l, camphor, brass bound, red pigskin facings dec, early 19th C   **1,500.00**
Grain Painted, 11¾″ h, 18½″ l, red and brown raised molded plinth base, inscribed red "1856, PWS" **170.00**
Leather
    11¼″ l, black, red trim, brass tack trim, bale and iron lock, fabric lined int., pen and ink signature **140.00**
    12¼″ l, brown and black, brass tack trim **75.00**
Pine, 27½″ l, bowed side and lid, brown graining, orig wrought iron lock and hasp, worn light blue repaint int. . . .   **175.00**

VAL SAINT-LAMBERT

History: Val Saint-Lambert, a twelfth-century Cistercian abbey, was located during different historical periods in France, the Netherlands, and Belgium (1930 to present). In 1822 Francois Kemlin and Auguste Lelievre, along with a group of financiers, bought the abbey and opened a glassworks. In 1846 Val Saint-Lambert merged with the Société Anonyme des Manufactures de Glaces, Verres à Vitre, Cristaux et Gobeletaries. The company bought many other glassworks.

Val Saint-Lambert developed a reputation for technological progress in the glass industry. In 1879 Val Saint-Lambert became an independent company employing 4,000 workers. Val Saint-Lambert concentrated on the export market, making table glass; cut, engraved, etched, and molded pieces; and chandeliers. Some pieces were finished in other countries, e.g., silver mounts added in the United States.

Val Saint-Lambert executed many special commissions for the artists of the Art Nouveau and Art Deco periods. The tradition continues. The company also made cameo-etched vases, covered boxes, and bowls. The firm celebrated its 150th anniversary in 1975.

Vase, cameo, purple overlay, tulip motif, 10″ h, $450.00.

Bottle, 6⅞″ h, green vines and flower dec, clear acid finish, green cut to clear overlay edge, sgd "Val/St Lambert"	75.00
Dresser Set, atomizer and cov powder jar, cranberry cut to clear, sgd	175.00
Goblet, 5⅜″ h, clear, blown mold, applied foot and stem	25.00

Plate, Van Dyck	65.00
Toothbrush Holder, clear, amber stain, sgd	50.00
Tumbler, 6″ h, blue cut to clear, gilt cameo classical band, set of 6	350.00
Vase	
8½″ h	
Art Deco style, gray	275.00
Cranberry to clear, sgd, orig sticker	225.00
10″ h, cameo and intaglio cut, red tulips, green frost ground	450.00

VALENTINES

History: Early cards were handmade, often containing both handwritten verses and hand-drawn pictures. Many cards also were hand-colored and contained cutwork.

Mass production of machine-made cards featuring chromolithography began after 1840. In 1847 Esther Howland of Worcester, Massachusetts, established a company to make valentines which were hand-decorated with paper lace and other materials imported from England. They had a small "H" stamped in red in the top left corner. Howland's company eventually became the New England Valentine Company (N.E.V. Co.).

George C. Whitney and his brother founded a company after the Civil War which dominated the market from the 1870s through the first decades of the twentieth century. They bought out several competitors, one of which was the New England Valentine Company.

Lace paper was invented in 1834. The 1835 to 1860 period is known as the "Golden Age" of lacy cards.

Embossed paper was used in England after 1800. Embossed lithographs and woodcuts developed between 1825–1840, with early examples being hand-colored.

References: Ruth Webb Lee, *A History of Valentines*, reprinted by National Valentine Collectors Association; Frank Staff, *The Valentine And Its Origins*, out-of-print.

Collectors' Club: National Valentine Collectors Association, Box 1404, Santa Ana, CA 92702.

Additional Listings: See *Warman's Americana & Collectibles* for more examples.

Advisor: Evalene Pulati.

Easel Back, 8½″, girl carrying red honeycomb paper parasol	50.00
Foldout	
5″, cupid, c1920	10.00
13 x 10″, diecut, lady, lacy border, c1890	25.00
Layered, 5″, hearts and flowers, c1860	15.00
Mechanical, black boy and girl, chicken and duck pop out of watermelon with cards in beaks	25.00

Sailor's, mirrored, shell encrusted, 4¾" w, 5¾" h, $95.00.

Sailor's
9" d, double, To A Lover 1,150.00
12" d, single, I'm yours/be mine . . . 600.00
Stand Up, diecut
6¾", girl holding doves, German . . . 8.00
9", Woods adv, "If You Love Your
Wife, Give Her A Woods," girl riding
in Woods car 20.00
Tuck, Raphel, 12½", Irish boy, green
jacket, top hat, string moves jointed
arms, legs 75.00

Animal Dish, cov, duck, brown top, painted green base, 4½" h, $85.00.

Butter Dish, figural, radish 75.00
Candlestick, Grecian Girl, frosted 50.00
Candy Dish, 4⅛" d, white milk glass,
basketweave, rope handles and finial 90.00
Goblet, blue, ftd 60.00
Lemon Dish, cov, figural, lemon, opaque
yellow 50.00
Plate
7½" d, floral dec, blue 35.00
8" d, Thistle pattern, green 70.00
Tumbler, 4" h, cobalt blue 45.00
Vase, 9¾" h, swelled cylinder, inverted,
scalloped rim, opalescent blue
ground, cased in burgundy, intaglio
carved crocus, engraved "Vallery-
stahl" 950.00

VALLERYSTAHL GLASS

History: Vallerystahl (Lorraine), France, has been a glass-producing center for centuries. In 1872 two major factories, Vallerystahl glassworks and Portieux glassworks, merged and produced art glass until 1898. Later, pressed glass-covered animal dishes were introduced. The factory continues operation today.

Animal Dish, cov
Fish, milk glass 85.00
Hen on nest, blue 75.00
Robin 110.00
Box
3½ x 4", cov, blue milk glass 70.00
5 x 3", cameo, dark green, applied
and cut dec, sgd 950.00

VAN BRIGGLE POTTERY

History: Artus Van Briggle, born in 1869, was a talented Ohio artist. He joined Rookwood in 1887 and studied in Paris under Rookwood's sponsorship from 1893 until 1896. In 1899 he moved to Colorado for his health and established his own pottery in Colorado Springs in 1901.

Van Briggle's work was influenced heavily by the Art Nouveau "school" he saw in France. He produced a great variety of matte glazed wares in this style. Colors varied.

The "AA" mark, a date, and "Van Briggle" were incised on all pieces prior to 1907 and sometimes into the 1910s and 1920s. After 1920, "Colorado Springs, Colorado" or an abbreviation was added. Dated pieces are the most desirable.

Artus died in 1904. Anne Van Briggle continued the pottery until 1912.

References: Barbara Arnest (ed.), *Van Briggle Pottery: The Early Years*, The Colorado Springs Fine Art Center, 1975; Scott N. Nelson, Lois Crouch, Euphemia Demmin, and Robert Newton, *Collector's Guide To Van Briggle Pottery,* Halldin Publishing, 1986.

Collectors' Club: American Art Pottery Association, 9825 Upton Circle, Bloomington, MN 55431.

Museum: Pioneer Museum, Colorado Springs, Colo.

Reproduction Alert: Van Briggle pottery still is made today. These modern pieces often are confused for older examples. Among the glazes used are Moonglo (off white), Turquoise Ming, Russet, and Midnight (black).

Vase, shades of green over tan ground, marked "86/1905/VV," $725.00.

1901–1920

Bowl
- 4¾" d, squatty, leathery purple and sky blue matte glaze, Shape #353, marked, dated 1905 . . . . 220.00
- 7¾" d, 3" h, squatty, narrow rim, stylized emb flowers, blush and light green, steel green ground, marked "III, 22," dated 1902 . . . . 990.00

Lamp, 4½" d, 6" h, ovoid, circular dished base, narrow flared neck, applied C handle, cut out oval front window, c1914 . . . . 275.00

Pot, 2 x 3", aqua, Shape #681, 1907–12 . . . . 100.00

Urn, 4 x 7", textured, rust brown, 1905   350.00

Vase
- 6¼" h, shortened baluster, all–over molding, frieze of geese heads, green–black glaze, incised mark and "Van Briggle, 1902, III" 3,300.00
- 8½" h, gourd, cylindrical collar, all–over molding, leaf and thistle dec, mauve glaze, inscribed mark and "Van Briggle, 1905, III," imp "137"   2,100.00
- 10⅛" h, conical, molded body, stylized floral panels, three open handles at neck, pinkish–red glaze, pale blue highlights, incised mark and "Van Briggle, 1904, V," imp "245" 1,650.00
- 10¾" h, baluster, small loop handles, flaring inverted rim, Shape #240, 1904 . . . . 850.00
- 13" h, relief molded abstract blossoms around rim, tall stems trailing down sides, muted gray–blue matte glaze, company cipher, c1906 . . . . 935.00
- 13⅝" h, baluster, molded body, stylized tulips, four open handles, apple–green glaze, rose highlights, incised mark and "Van Briggle, 1903, III," imp "229" 1,850.00
- 15¾" h, Shape #30, swollen cylindrical, two small angled handles, molded elongated roots, two flowers, matte green glaze, sgd 1903, marked "I," designed by Artus Van Briggle 1,400.00

1921–1968

Bookends, pr, ram's head, turquoise Ming glaze 325.00

Centerpiece Bowl, 14" l, 8¼" h, figural mermaid flower frog reclining on rim, oval shell bowl, matte blue–green, sgd "Van Briggle Colo. Sprs." 400.00

Vase
- 11½" h, Indian Chief, cylindrical, three molded Indian heads, tapering towards foot, green and brown glaze, imp logo and "Van Briggle/Colo Spgs," 1920–30 . . . . 350.00
- 14" h, ovoid, bulbous neck joined to shoulder by looping handles, molded peacock feathers, matte blue–green glaze, incised mark . . 550.00

Vasart

VASART

History: Vasart is a contemporary art glass made in Scotland by the Streathearn Glass Co. The colors are mottled, and sometimes shade from one hue to another. It is readily identified by an engraved signature on the base.

Bowl
- 5" d, light green 35.00

8" d, gray–green ground, goldstone flakes 75.00
Mug, mottled blue and white 45.00
Tray, 12" l, mottled blue shading to green 75.00
Tumbler, blue and white stripes 65.00
Vase
7½" h, swelled cylinder, internal cluthra pink and green dec, pulled and hooked swirls dec 90.00
7¾" h, waisted cylinder, internal cluthra pink and green dec, pulled and hooked swirls waist dec, sgd "Vasart" 100.00

VENETIAN GLASS

History: Venetian glass has been made on the island of Murano, near Venice, since the 13th century. Most of the wares are thin-walled. Many types of decoration have been used: embedded gold dust, lace work, and applied fruits or flowers.

Reproduction Alert: Venetian glass continues to be made today.

Paperweight, tree form, blue and goldstone, millefiori accents, crystal base, 13" h, $200.00.

Basket, 6½" d, 7½" h, flared, notched rim, purple shading to clear, controlled bubbles, gold flecked base .. 85.00
Candlesticks, pr, 10" h, figural, dragons, yellow 250.00
Chandelier, 23½" h, blown, opalescent, applied colored floral dec, eight scrolling arms 1,000.00
Cologne Bottle, light green, paperweight type stopper 65.00
Compote, 10" d, ruffled, swan handles, clear, gold aventurine flecks 85.00
Finger Bowl, amber ground, threaded, matching underplate 65.00

Goblet, frosted mauve, irid coinspots, clear amber stem, frosted base 45.00
Perfume Bottle, clear, gold spatter dec, orig stopper 375.00
Sculpture, 18" h, stylized cactus, lavender glass, etched surface, clear glass block base, engraved "Nason Aldo" 800.00
Vase, 4½" h, butterscotch ground, applied black threading and dots, applied black handles 85.00
Wine, latticino stripe, cranberry, clear, opal, and goldstone 75.00

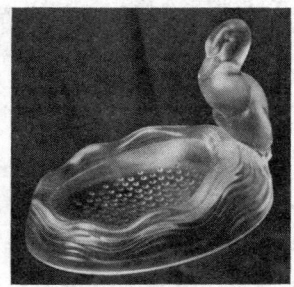

VERLYS GLASS

History: Verlys glass is an art glass originally made in France after 1930. For a period of a few months, Heisey Glass Co., Newark, Ohio, produced the identical glass, having obtained the rights and formula from the French factory.

The French-produced glass can be distinguished from the American product by the signature. The French is mold-marked; the American is etched script-signed.

Ashtray, sgd, oval, 6" l, $40.00.

Bowl
6" d, Cupids and Hearts pattern, clear 45.00
8½" d, Thistle pattern, three small feet 150.00
10" d, Chrysanthemum pattern, clear and frosted 125.00
15" d, fanning edge, carved polka dots, amber ground, molded "Verlys France" 275.00
Box, cov, 6¾" d, circular, relief molded

bouquet of coreopsis, molded "Verlys
France" on lid and base 200.00
Charger, Water Lily pattern, clear 150.00
Figure, 4¼" h, pigeon, frosted 275.00
Plate, 6¼" d, Pine Cone pattern, mold
sgd 60.00
Soap Dish, 5⅜" l, 4" h, figural, fish, clear
and frosted 75.00
Vase, 9" h, ovoid, flared flattened rim,
topaz, frosted large blossoms and
leaves, script sgd "Verlys" on base 600.00

VILLEROY AND BOCH

History: Pierre Joseph Boch established a pottery near Luxemburg, Germany, in 1767. Jean Francis, his son, introduced the first coal-fired kiln in Europe and perfected a water-power-driven potter's wheel. Pierre's grandson, Eugene Boch, managed a pottery at Mettlach; Nicholas Villeroy also had a pottery nearby.

In 1841 the three potteries were merged into the firm of Villeroy and Boch. Early production included a hard paste earthenware comparable to English ironstone. The factory continues to use this hard paste formula for its modern tablewares.

Reference: Susan and Al Bagdade, *Warman's English & Continental Pottery & Porcelain, 1st Edition,* Warman Publishing Co., Inc., 1987.

Additional Listing: Mettlach.

**Punch Bowl, etched, multicolored, 15″
h, $300.00.**

Candlestick, 8¼" h, pottery, open circular base, brick and beige geometric
dec, cream ground, imp mark 180.00
Cruet, 8½" h, blue and white 75.00
Mug, 3½" h, tan, leaf and twig dec, twig
handle 50.00

Pitcher, 10⅝" h, six sided, white int.,
dark gray raised scrolls, leaves, pods,
and birds, gray ground, beige crest
mark 250.00
Plaque
13" d, Rheinstein castle 45.00
16" d, horse race, P.U.G., Dresden 150.00
Plate, 9" h, polychrome floral dec,
gaudy stick spatter 65.00
Stein, ½ liter, five white figures, blue
ground, 6½" h, #171, Mercury mark 225.00
Teapot, 6¼" h, blue and white dec . . . 130.00
Tray
5 x 7½", Mettlach Abbey 70.00
11 x 16", cavalier, P.U.G. 155.00
Vase, 7" h, white relief floral dec, yellow
ground 100.00

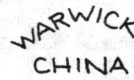

WARWICK

History: Warwick China Manufacturing Co., Wheeling, West Virginia, was incorporated in 1887 and continued until 1951. The company was one of the first manufacturers of vitreous glazed wares in the United States. Production was extensive and included tableware, garden ornaments, and decorative and utilitarian items.

Pieces were hand-painted or decorated by decals. Collectors seek portrait items and fraternal pieces for groups such as the Elks, Eagles, and Knights of Pythias.

Some experimental, eggshell-type porcelain was made before 1887. A few examples are in the market.

Bowl, 4" d, flower and stems 70.00
Chocolate Pot, 10½" h, orange thornapple branches, brown to creamy yellow
shading, ivory ground, twig handle,
marked "Warwick China" 175.00
Cream Soup, white, gold trim, underplate 10.00
Creamer, speckled blue and white,
raised leaves with gold trim on rim,
marked "Warwick China" 35.00
Humidor, cov, portrait of woman, brown
ground, marked "IOGA" 200.00
Mug
Monk drinking from mug 50.00
Monk pointing to wine glass 45.00
Pitcher
Cider, fruit dec, brown glaze 100.00
Lemonade, portrait dec, brown glaze,
marked 165.00
Portrait Plate, 10", Indian, yellow shading to brown ground 65.00

Pitcher, brown shaded ground, rose motif, marked "IOGA," 10½" h, $100.00.

Tankard, 13" h, BPOE, elk and clock, marked "IOGA"	110.00
Vase	
8" h, portrait of woman, large hat with peacock feathers, holding rose to lips, shaded brown to cream ground, ftd, marked "IOGA"	100.00
10" h, 3" w, portrait of woman, ringlet hairdo, red and brown ground, sq handles	150.00

WATCHES, POCKET

History: Pocket watches can be found from flea markets to the specialized jewelry sales at Butterfield and Butterfield, William Doyle Galleries, and Sotheby's. Condition of movement is first priority; design and detailing of case is second.

In pocket watches, listing aids are size (18/0 to 20), number of jewels in movement, open or closed (hunter) face, and whether the case is gold, gold filled, or some other metal. The movement is the critical element since cases often were switched. However, an elaborate case, especially of gold, adds significantly to value.

Pocket watches designed to railroad specifications are desirable. They are 16 to 18 in size, have a minimum of 17 jewels, adjust to at least five positions, and conform to many other specifications. All are open-faced.

Study the field thoroughly before buying. The literature is vast, including books and newsletters from clubs and collectors. Abbreviations: S = size; gf = gold filled; yg = yellow gold; j = jewels.

References: August C. Bolino, *The Watchmakers of Massachusetts,* Kensington Historical Press, 1987; Howard Brenner, *Collecting Comic Character Clocks and Watches,* Books Americana, 1987; Roy Ehrhardt & William Meggers,

American Pocket Watches Identification And Price Guide: Beginning To End . . . 1830–1980, Heart of America Press, 1987; Cedric Jagger, *The Artistry Of The English Watch,* Charles E. Tuttle Co., 1988; Reinhard Meis, *Pocket Watches: From the Pendant Watch To The Tourbillon,* Schiffer Publishing Ltd., 1987, orig published in German; Cooksey Shugart and Tom Engle, *The Official Price Guide To Watches, Tenth Edition,* House of Collectibles, 1990.

Collectors' Club: National Association of Watch & Clock Collectors, 514 Poplar Street, Box 33, Columbia, PA 17512. *Bulletin* (bi-monthly) and *Mart* (bi-monthly).

Museums: American Clock & Watch Museum, Bristol, Conn.; Hoffman Clock Museum, Newark, N.Y.; National Association of Watch and Clock Collectors Museum, Columbia, Penna.; The Time Museum, Rockford, Ill.

Open faced pocket watch, Patek Philippe, Geneve, 18 carat gold, minute repeating, split second chronograph, perpetual calendar, moon phases, register, and central alarm, c1920, $600,600.00.

Character	
Buster Brown, Buster inside circle, Ingersoll, c1928	270.00
Donald Duck, Mickey on reverse, Ingersoll, c1939	450.00
Hopalong Cassidy, rawhide strap and fob, US Time, c1950	275.00
Lone Ranger, 2" d, color portrait on reverse, New Haven Time Co, c1939	200.00
Popeye, friends on dial, New Haven Time Co, c1935	350.00
Skeezix, Ingraham, c1936	200.00
Enamelled	
56mm, transfer painted lovers, gilt case, c1761	600.00

52mm, gold enamel portrait, ¾ plate
lever movement, c1910 . . . . **1,700.00**

Railroad

Elgin, Father Time, 16 S, 21j, 12K gf
case **140.00**

Hamilton, 16 S, 23j, dial marked 23
Jewels–Railway Special, 10K ygf
case **450.00**

Illinois, 16 S, 21j, Sangamo Special,
ygf case, engraved design **250.00**

South Bend, 16 S, 21j, Studebaker,
star nickel case **185.00**

Waltham, 16 S, 23j, Vanguard, Canadian dial, Keystone base metal
case, train engraving on reverse **200.00**

Regular

Aurora, open face, 18 S, 11j, key
wind, key set, gilded, ... **165.00**

American Watch Co, hunter, 10 S,
11–15j, 14K, #1874 . . . . **325.00**

Double dial hunter, 14K yg, calendar,
engine turned cov, white enamel
dial, black Roman numerals, moon
phases, gold arrow hands, reverse
dial with chapter ring calibrated in
Russian, exposed movement,
c1900 . . . . **2200.00**

Elgin, 18 S, 11j, open face, lever set,
stem wind **70.00**

Frodsham, hunter, 18K yg, #05406,
engraved banderole and mono-
gram, gold stopwatch hand **1900.00**

Hamilton, The Banner, hunter, 18 S,
17j, #927 . . . . **150.00**

Illinois, open face, 14 S, 21j, #1–2n3,
stem wind **110.00**

Keystone Standard, hunter, 6 S, 7–
10j **125.00**

Longines, 14K yg, white matte face,
Arabic numerals, leather case . . . **200.00**

New Haven, 16 S, Angelus, two ro-
tating dials **55.00**

Rockford, 16 S, 21j, bridge plate design movement, stem wind, silver-
oid **100.00**

Seth Thomas, open face, 0 S, 15j,
gold jewel settings, No 3 . . . . **70.00**

Waltham Riverside A Model, 19j, 14K
wg, open face, engine turned bezel, silver matte dial, Arabic nu-
merals, five adjustments **175.00**

WATCHES, WRIST

History: The definition of a wristwatch is simple:
"a small watch that is attached to a bracelet or
strap and is worn around the wrist." However, a
watch on a bracelet is not necessarily a wristwatch. The key is the ability to read the time. A
true wristwatch allows you to read the time at a
glance, without making any other motions. Early
watches on a bracelet that was worn on the arm
had the axis of their dials, from 6 to 12, perpendicular to the band. Reading them required some
extensive arm movement.

The first true wristwatch appeared about 1850.
However, the key date is 1880, when the stylish
decorative wristwatch appeared and almost universal acceptance occurred. The technology to
create the wristwatch existed in the early nineteenth century with Brequet's shock-absorbing
"Parachute System" for automatic watches and
Ardien Philipe's winding stem.

The wristwatch was a response to the needs of
the entrepreneurial age with its emphasis on punc-
tuality and planned free time. By approximately
1930 the sales of wristwatches surpassed that of
pocket watches. Swiss and German manufacturers were quickly joined by American makers.

The wristwatch has undergone many technical
advances during the twentieth century, including
self-winding (automatic), shock-resistance, electric
operation, etc. It truly is the most significant and
dominant clock of the century.

References: Howard S. Brenner, *Identification
and Value Guide Collecting Comic Character
Clocks and Watches,* Books Americana, 1987;
Kahlert Mühe Brunner, *Wristwatches, History Of A
Century's Development,* Schiffer Publishing Ltd.,
1986; Sherry and Roy Ehrhardt, Joe Demesy, and
Ken Specht, *Vintage American & Europe Wrist
Watch Price Guide, Book 2,* Heart of America
Press, 1988; Sherry Ehrhardt & Peter Planes, *Vin-
tage American & European Wrist Watch Price
Guide 1987 Values,* Heart of America Press, 1987;
Cooksey Shugart & Tom Engle, *The Official Price
Guide To Watches, Tenth Edition,* House of Col-
lectibles, 1990.

Collectors' Club: National Association of
Watch & Clock Collectors, 514 Poplar Street, Box
33, Columbia, PA 17512. *Bulletin* (bi–monthly) and
Mart (bi–monthly).

Museums: American Clock & Watch Museum,
Bristol, Conn.; Hoffman Clock Museum, Newark,
N.Y.; National Association of Watch and Clock Collectors Museum, Columbia, Penna.; The Time Museum, Rockford, Ill.

Character

Captain Marvel, small size, plastic
box, New Haven, c1948 . . . . **175.00**

Dale Evans, 1 x 1¼" rect, portrait and
name on dial face, Ingraham, orig
box, c1949 . . . . **150.00**

Dick Tracy, six shooter arm action,
New Haven, c1952 . . . . **275.00**

Goofy, backward, Helbros, 1972 . . . **700.00**

Puss–N–Boots, Bradley, c1959 . . . . **250.00**

Snow White, plastic, US Time, c1962 **50.00**

Superman, 1¼" d dial, full color illus-
tration, yellow hands and border,
Dabs and Co, copyright 1977 DC
Comics **150.00**

Tom Mix, Ingersoll, c1936 . . . . 500.00
Woody Woodpecker, round dial, Ingraham, c1952 . . . . 150.00
Gentleman's
American Waltham, 21j, 14K, Albright 125.00
Baume & Mercier, 18j, stainless steel,
triple date, moon phase, ... 450.00
Bulova, 23j, 14K, waterproof 120.00
Cartier, 18j, 14K, date chapter, Le
Coultre 1,200.00
Elgin, 15j, silver, enamel dial, wire
lugs, c1915 . . . . 175.00
International Watch Co, Schaffhausen, 18K yg, circular case, molded
lugs, matte silvered dial, gold baton
numerals, hands, and sweep seconds, brown lizard band 850.00
Longines, 21j, stainless steel, Grand
Prize, c1946 . . . . 125.00
Rolex, 17j, silver, graduated bezel,
c1928 . . . . 950.00
Lady's
Cartier, 18j, 18K, European Watch Co 900.00
Hamilton, 14K yellow gold, aysmmetrical case with conforming hinged
cover set with fifty–five round diamonds and eleven baguettes, white
round face, blued hands, attached
double box link chain bracelet,
c1950 . . . . 950.00
Illinois, 15–17j, 14K 120.00
Mathey Tissot, platinum and 14K
white gold, rect case, scrolling lugs,
band of single and baguette–cut
diamonds, attached full–cut diamond line bracelet, c1930 . . . . . . 2,000.00
Movado, 18K red, white and yg,
round gold face, baton numerals
and hands, diamond set bezel, two
heart shaped lugs, flat brushed
three tone gold flexible band, 40
dwt 650.00
Patek Phillipe, 18j, 18K, c1940 . . . . 1,200.00
Universal Geneve, 14K red and yg,
sq, gold face, baton hands, flexible
two tone gold hollow link bracelet 350.00

WATERFORD

History: Waterford crystal is quality flint glass
commonly decorated with cuttings. The original
factory was established at Waterford, Ireland, in
1729. Glass made before 1830 is darker than the
brilliantly clear glass of later production. The factory closed in 1852. After 100 years it reopened
and continues in production today.

Candlestick, 7" h, pr, pear shape, hollow
center, horizontal oval cuts on wafers
between fluted top and rayed base,

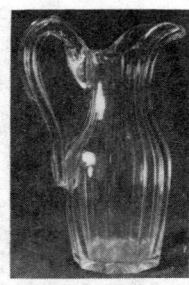

**Pitcher, ribbed, applied handle, 10½" h,
$215.00.**

looped cross cuttings in two sizes,
downward spray with star cut 150.00
Decanter
12" h, star base, paneled neck, stopper 75.00
15" h, all–over geometric cutting,
matching stopper 140.00
Goblet
Cameragh 30.00
Glengarett 35.00
Jar, 7" h, cov, fan and diamond cuts . . 125.00
Pitcher
6¾" h, shaped spout, strap handle,
Lismore 100.00
10" h, diamond cuts, applied handle 200.00
Plate, 8" d, diamond cut center 90.00
Salt, 3⅞" d, master, oval, diamond cut 65.00
Vase, 7¼" h, bulbous, top to bottom vertical cuts separated by horizontal
slash cuts, sgd 100.00

WAVE CREST
WARE

WAVE CREST

History: The C. F. Monroe Company of Meriden, Connecticut, produced the opal glassware
known as Wave Crest from 1898 until World War
I. The company bought the opaque, blown molded
glass blanks for decoration from the Pairpoint
Manufacturing Co. of New Bedford, Massachusetts, and other glassmakers, including European
factories. Florals were the most common decorative motif. Trade names used were "Wave Crest
Ware," "Kelva," and "Nakara."

References: Wilfred R. Cohen, *Wave Crest: The
Glass of C.F. Monroe*, Collector Books, 1987;
Elsa H. Grimmer, *Wave Crest Ware*, Wallace-
Homestead, 1979.

Ewer, multicolored floral dec, pink and white ground, gilt trim, metal spout and base, sgd, $500.00.

Atomizer, pink roses, white dots, new atomizer	225.00
Cigar Box, 5" sq, hinged lid, pink daisies, raised scrolled panels and lid ..	625.00
Cracker Jar, cov	
9" h, tapered, white satin ground, natural colored wild roses and leaves, metal rim, bail handle, and cov ..	175.00
9½" h, Robin Redbreast, scrolled ..	275.00
Creamer and Sugar, opal, enamel and gilt floral dec	200.00
Dresser Box, hinged lid	
3¾" d, 2½" h, blown out rose, marked "Kelva"	550.00
4" d, pink and purple emb pansy on lid, dark green base, marked "Wavecrest"	700.00
4¼" sq, 3" h, enameled pink and cream tulips, marked "Nakara, C. M. & Co"	375.00
6" d, 7" h, emb rococo mold, gold highlights, ftd	975.00
6½" d, circular, red floral clusters, enamel highlights, blue satin swirl ground	800.00
Jar, 4½" d, 2½" h, squatty, blue daisies, red–brown scrolled body, metal lid ..	155.00
Jewel Box	
3" d, round, hinged lid, pink wild roses, blue emb scrolls, marked "Wavecrest"	250.00
8" d, 3¼" h, round, satin glass, green mottled ground, large pink and white flowers, hinged, marked "Kelva"	650.00
Pin Dish	
3½" l, orig metal ormolu mounting, sgd "Wave Crest"	115.00
4", blue and white flowers, brass rim	85.00
Pin Tray, 3" d, circular, pink daisies, blue molded scrolls, double handled metal rim	115.00
Salt and Pepper Shakers, pr	
Helmschmeid swirl, floral dec	65.00
Tulip, orig lids	115.00
Sugar, cov, Helmschmeid swirl, daisy dec	145.00
Sweet Meat, cov, Helmschmeid Swirl, hp, pink and lavender pansies, twisted handle, sgd	400.00
Tray, 6½ x 4¾", ormolu feet, free form, raised scrolling, pink apple blossoms	425.00
Vase	
6⅜" h, cream ground, violets dec ..	260.00
10" h, tapered, satin ground, pale blue daisies, pale green scrolls and leaves, four gold feet	550.00
Whisk Broom Holder, 10½" l, 7¼" w, mauve holder with hp pastel flowers, bright, shiny ormolu holder, slightly frayed satin lining, red banner signature	985.00

WEATHER VANES

History: A weather vane indicates wind direction. The earliest-known examples were found on late 17th-century structures in the Boston area. The vanes were handcrafted of wood, copper, or tin. By the last half of the 19th century, weather vanes adorned farms and houses throughout the nation. Mass-produced vanes of cast iron, copper, and sheet metal were sold through mail order catalogs or at country stores.

The champion vane is the rooster. In fact, the name weathercock is synonymous with weather vane. The styles and patterns are endless. Weathering can affect the same style of vane differently. For this reason, patina is a critical element in collecting vanes.

Whirligigs are a variation of the weather vane. Constructed of wood and metal, often by unskilled craftsmen, whirligigs not only indicate the direction of the wind and its velocity, but also their unique movements served as entertainment for children, neighbors, and passersby.

Reproduction Alert: Reproduction of early models exist, and are being aged and sold as originals.

American Flag, 25½" h, 65" l, copper, gilded, painted silver, cut stars and stripes, arm holding hammer attached to flag pole, mounted on sq base, 19th C	9,350.00
Angel Gabriel, 15" h, 35½" l, sheet metal, flying position, blowing trumpet, cut and feathered wings, repousse hair and eye detail, orig gilding, 19th C	11,000.00

Eagle

11" h, 15" l, copper, molded, out-stretched wings, perched on orb with arrow directional, orig gilding, 19th C **2,090.00**

39½" w, copper, gilt finish **500.00**

Fire Chief, 52½" h, 22½" w, iron, painted, running with speaking trumpet in one hand, grappling hook in other, wrought iron reinforcing rod, c1850 ....**35,200.00**

Fish, 23¼" h, 15¼" l, pine, carved, pearl button eyes, cut sheet metal fin, harpoon projecting from mouth, orig gilding, mounted on rod on turned baluster form base, 19th C **1,100.00**

Fox, 15¾" h, 31" l, copper, running, molded and incised eye and paw, mounted on rod, weathered, 19th C **9,900.00**

Goddess of Liberty, 36" h, 28" w, copper, molded, gilded, holding American flag in one hand, pointing with other, wearing Phrygian cap, standing on octagonal shape base, mounted on two tier green painted wood base, 19th C **104,500.00**

Goose, flying, laminated body, plywood core and wings, weathered paint, 42" l **1,250.00**

Grasshopper, 16¼" h, 41½" l, copper, molded, orig gilding, 19th C **4,675.00**

Weathervane, cast iron, Black Hawk, sgd "Harris & Co.," 26" w, $1,700.00.

Horse

14" h, 27½" l, pine, carved, painted, kicking forelegs, raised rear legs with black hooves, dark brown paint, scalloped mane and tail, mounted on wrought iron rod with brass ball finial **6,050.00**

26½" h, 41" l, sheet metal, running, orig gilding, curved bar base **3,575.00**

31½" l, copper, gilded, running position, c1880 .... **1,600.00**

Horse and Sulky, copper

33" l, rod and directional 110.00

34" l, includes rider, bronze paint over orig gilt, 19th C **1,600.00**

Hunter, 29½" h, 47" l, copper, molded, holding rifle, wearing cap and jacket, standing on island shape base, 19th C **8,250.00**

Indian Chief, 49½" h, 44" l, pine and tin, painted, carved, wearing feathered headdress, kneeling position drawing bow and arrow, painted grassy base, 19th C **10,450.00**

Peacock, 26½" h, 32" l, sheet iron, standing on arrow directional, scalloped tail, one side painted yellow, other painted white, 19th C **1,430.00**

Pheasant, 9" h, 16" l, copper, molded, cut crown feathers and split tail feathers, yellow double neck ring, brown paint traces, mounted on wrought iron rod, 19th C **2,750.00**

Quill Pen, 33" l, copper, molded, yellow polychrome paint, repousse feathers, mounted on rod on black metal base, 19th C **9,900.00**

Rooster

26" h, copper, orig gilt, 19th C **900.00**

31" h, 35" l, pine, painted, incised feathers, beak, and wattle details, dark brown, red and yellow markings, wood base, 19th C **3,575.00**

Stag, 26½" h, 32" l, copper, leaping over rock work and vegetation, old yellow polychrome paint, cast zinc antlers, mounted on rod with orb, 19th C ...**18,700.00**

WEBB, THOMAS AND SONS

History: Thomas Webb and Sons was established in 1837 in Stourbridge, England. The company probably is best known for its very beautiful English cameo glass. However, many other types of colored glass were produced, including enameled glass, iridescent glass, pieces with heavy glass ornamentation, cased glass, and other art glass besides cameo.

Additional Listings: Burmese, Cameo, and Peachblow.

Bowl

3½" d, Peachblow, DQ, yellow acid finish shaded to cherry red, cased **150.00**

4½" d, 2" h, Burmese, ivy dec, eight fold–in scalloped top, imp pontil sgd "Thos Webb & Sons, Queen's Burmeseware Patented" **385.00**

5" d, 1¾" h, Alexandrite, twenty four ruffles, shaded citron yellow to rose to blue **1,100.00**

Biscuit Jar, pink satin ground, gold banding, enamel dec, Art Nouveau woman and flowers, brass cov, cone finial, block acid etched sgd, 7½″ h, 5¾″ d, $190.00.

5½″ d, 2½″ h, cameo, emerald green, white overlaid, carved apple blossoms, buds, and leafy branches, wide carved floral border, ruffled edge, mark "Thomas Webb & Sons Gem Cameo" **1,800.00**

9⅞″ d, satin, yellow, white base, frosted ruffled rim **75.00**

Cologne Bottle, 6″ h, cameo, spherical, clear frosted glass, overlaid white and red, carved blossoms, buds, leafy stems, and butterfly, linear borders, hallmarked silver cov with molded and chased blossom dec **3,200.00**

Custard Cup and Underplate, cameo, moire pattern crystal ground, delicate blue foliage and flowers with butterfly, underplate with imp Webb mark, minor rim chip on cup **600.00**

Fairy Lamp, 5¼″ h, 5⅞″ d, Burmese, acid finish, salmon pink shading to yellow dome shade, matching sq folded over base, clear marked "Clarke" cup, sgd "Thos Webb Queens Burmese" **650.00**

Finger Bowl, 5¾″ d, matching underplate, Alexandrite, ruffled and crimped edges, miniature honeycomb pattern, shaded amber, fuchsia to blue, set of 5 . . . . **3,500.00**

Perfume Bottle, 3¼″ h, cameo, pale cornflower blue ball, white overlay, carved apple blossom and leaves, circular mark "Thomas Webb & Sons Cameo," threaded rim, hallmarked silver monogrammed cap **1,000.00**

Scent Bottle, 4⅞″ l, 1¼″ w at shoulder, Queen's Burmese, delicate blush at shoulder, soft yellow base, branch of mistletoe with twelve detailed leaves, eleven white berries, sterling screw on top with hallmarks "CM," rampant lion, "N," and anchor **1,250.00**

Sweetmeat Jar, MOP, satin, Flower and Acorn pattern, deep brilliant blue ground, painted green, brown, and maroon berry, leaf, and branch design, SP top with bamboo handle . . **1,125.00**

Vase
4½″ h, ovoid, red, white lining, ornate gold and silver enameling, green and clear jewels **300.00**

7¼″ h, 4½″ d, shaded apricot satin glass, ruffled top, gold prunus dec, soft pink int., orig ormolu ftd stand **525.00**

7½″ h, ovoid, burgundy–brown ground, layered white cameo cut and hand carved ethereal portrait of dancing nude woman, gossamer drapes swirling about body, sgd "Geo Woodall" lower right, marked "Serpentina" on base rim **25,000.00**

7¾″ h, 4¾″ d, Peachblow, deep rose red to pink, rich cream lining, heavy gold prunus and bird dec **650.00**

8¼″ h
Burmese, acid finish, salmon pink shading to yellow, coral bud flowers, green leaves dec **750.00**

Simulated Ivory, flowers, vines, and six medallions of birds and butterflies, marked "Thomas Webb & Sons Ltd" **3,300.00**

9″ h, 4¼″ d, deep coral red, white lining, heavy gold branch and flowers **350.00**

9½″ h, 4½″ w top, bulbous base, deep salmon pink to pale yellow, purple cyclamen flower and green leaves and stems dec, orange enamel highlights **1,550.00**

WEDGWOOD

WEDGWOOD

History: In 1754 Josiah Wedgwood entered into a partnership with Thomas Whieldon of Fenton Vivian, Staffordshire, England. Products included marbled, agate, tortoiseshell, green glaze, and Egyptian black wares. In 1759 Wedgwood opened his own pottery at the Ivy House works, Burslem. In 1764 he moved to the Brick House (Bell Works) at Burslem. The pottery concentrated on utilitarian pieces.

Between 1766 and 1769 Wedgwood built the famous works at Etruria. Among the most renowned products of this plant were the Empress

Catherina of Russia dinner service (1774) and the Portland Vase (1790s). Product lines were cane-ware, unglazed earthenwares (drabwares), pie-crust wares, variegated and marbled wares, black basalt (developed in 1768), Queen's or cream-ware, Jasperware (perfected in 1774), and others.

Bone china was produced under the direction of Josiah Wedgwood II between 1812 and 1822 and revived in 1878. Moonlight luster was made from 1805 to 1815. Fairyland luster began in 1920. All luster production ended in 1932.

A museum was established at the Etruria pottery in 1906. When Wedgwood moved to its modern plant at Barlaston, North Staffordshire, the museum was continued and expanded.

References: Susan and Al Bagdade, *Warman's English & Continental Pottery & Porcelain, 1st Edition,* Warman Publishing Co., Inc., 1987; David Buten and Jane Clancy, *Eighteenth-Century Wedgwood: A Guide For Collectors And Connoisseurs,* Main Street Press, 1980; Robin Reilly, *The Collector's Wedgwood,* Portfolio Press/A Robert Campbell Rowe Book, 1980; Robin Reilly and George Savage, *Dictionary Of Wedgwood,* Antique Collectors Club, 1980; Geoffrey Wills, *Wedgwood,* Chartwell Books, Inc., 1989.

Periodical: American Wedgwoodian, 55 Vandam Street, New York, NY 10013.

Collectors' Clubs: The Wedgwood Society, 246 N. Bowman Avenue, Merion, PA 19066; The Wedgwood Society, The Roman Villa, Rockbourne, Fordingbridge, Hents, England, SP 6 3PG.

Basalt, figure, Cupid, imp "Cupid," and "Wedgwood," 8½" h, $600.00.

BASALT

Bust
13¾" h, Joseph Addison, modeled full head to mid chest, imp title "Addison" on back, "Wedgwood and Bentley" to both bust and raised circular base, c1775 . . . . **6,000.00**
14" h, John Bunyan, black, raised cir-

cular base, imp uppercase marks, 19th C **700.00**
17" h, 10¼" d, Mercury, black, marked "Wedgwood" **1,100.00**
18¼", Mercury, black, looking to left, winged helmet, named on reverse, socle base, imp upper case marks, mid 19th C **1,870.00**
Candlesticks, pr, 8¼" h, dolphin, upward tail, leafy molded sconces, rect base, shell border, minor repairs, imp upper case mark, late 18th C **1,300.00**
Egyptian Plaque, 8 x 8½", black, hand gilded panel scene of King Tut and Queen Ankhesenamun, titled "The Beloved of the Great Enchantress," metal fitted for hanging, limited edition of 250, numbered 195, imp and gilt marks, 1974 . . . . **450.00**
Ewer, 17¼" h
Water, entwined handle and neck molded as sea god riding dolphin's head, molded sea foliage on body, leaf tip molded base, fluted socle, imp upper case marks **2,100.00**
Wine, entwined handle and neck molded as satyr riding ram's head, molded berried vine on body, leaf tip molded base, fluted socle, imp upper case marks **2,100.00**
Inkwell
3¼" h, central urn shaped quill holder, double handles on double sided stand, circular inkwell, cov sander with shell motif, imp upper lower case mark, late 18th C **1,700.00**
3¾" h, seated model, rect base, mounted urn shaped ink pot, imp upper case mark, late 18th C . . . **1,400.00**
Lamp, oil, cov, four equally spaced shell molded wick holders, int. piping intact, sq base, minor chip repair, uppercase mark, late 18th C **900.00**
Miniature, bust, 1⅞" h, classical figure, imp mark, wooden base, 18th C . . . **400.00**
Model
Bear, 4¾" l, standing, imp upper case mark **750.00**
Elephant, 5¼" l, standing, trunk lowered, glass eyes, tusks removed, imp upper case mark **450.00**
Portrait Medallion, 4⅛ x 3⅛", King George, oval 8¼ x 6¼" mahogany frame, inlaid flame satinwood liner **225.00**
Vase
6¾" h, cov, serpent handles terminating in male masks, classical female reliefs on either side, mounted on sq base, circular stamp mark on base, handles restored, cov replacement, c1775 . . . . **2,200.00**
7" h, acanthus molded loop handles,

cherubs representing Seasons on either side, fluting to neck and socle, mounted on sq base, circular stamp mark on base, c1775 .... **1,200.00**

9¼" h, cov, loop handles, bead trim with zodiac border above scenes of children, sq base, imp "Wedgwood and Bentley" on base, c1775 .... **2,400.00**

9¾" h, cov, shoulder band of engine turned flutes, foliate scroll handles, berried laurel swags, foliate cov, ball knop, egg and dart panels on sq base, imp "Wedgwood & Bentley," c1775, minor chips **2,250.00**

10" h, 5" d, cupids on panther driven chariot, ram driven chariot on other side, grape dec handles, marked "Wedgwood" **750.00**

CANEWARE

Bulb Pot, 8½" l, D shape, engine turned basketwork, ropework borders, glazed int., cov with three bulb holders, nine small circular apertures, imp mark, c1800 .... **1,500.00**

Game Pie Dish, cov, 9¾" l, oval, glazed int., ext. with relief dec, six groups of pendant game birds, and grapevine festoons, four game groups on cov, rabbit knob, crack and int. chip **225.00**

Pastry Dish, cov, 12" l, matching undertray, piecrust rim, relief molded, lattice and acanthus leaf dec, c1800 ..... **650.00**

Solitaire Set, 5" cov teapot, cov sugar bowl, milk jug, tea cup and saucer, tray, enameled garden flowers, blue line borders, glazed int., imp mark, minor damage, c1820 .... **800.00**

Tea Caddy Spoon, 3" l, shell shaped bowl, upper lower case mark, c1790 **550.00**

Teapot, cov, pentagonal, molded cluster of bamboo stalks, inset cov, coiled bamboo sprig knob, imp "Wedgwood & Bentley," c1779 .... **3,100.00**

CREAMWARE

Argyle, 5" h, loop handle, swan neck spout, imp upper case mark, cov missing, nick on spout, late 18th C **450.00**

Basket, 10⅞" l, matching 12" l undertray, oval, green striped rims, loop handles **250.00**

Figure, 7" h, 4⅞" w, 10" l, polar bear, sgd "J Skeaping," c1927 .... **400.00**

Food Mold, jelly, 9" h, conical, painted, rose, purple, green, yellow, blue, and iron–red floral sprays and swags, bowknotted ribbons, brown line borders, four apertures on base, imp "Wedgwood" and "D," c1800, chips **2,750.00**

Montieth, 12¾" w handle to handle, heavily scalloped rim, leaf molded handles, imp upper case mark, 19th C **550.00**

Pitcher, 8¼" h, black transfer print, yellow and green enamel, hunt scene on one side inscribed "Stag Chase through the Thames," reverse with drinking scene under banner inscribed "Sportsman Festival," hunting verse below, stag and doe beneath spout and handle, imp mark with two potter's marks, late 18th C **1,600.00**

Plate, 9½" d, fable, maroon, ochre, green, and yellow, two jugs floating down stream, Spanish shaped rim, ochre and brown edges, imp mark, sgd "E Lessore," c1865 .... **500.00**

Platter, 16½" l, armorial, Duke of Clarence service, blue scallop and gilt loop border, imp upper case marks, c1816, pr **675.00**

Sock Block, 4¾" h, molded as child's foot, imp "Wedgwood," letter "J," dated cipher, c1890 .... **375.00**

Teapot, 5¼" h, globular, foliage molded spout and handle, painted loose bunches of flowers and scattered leaves, band of iron–red circlets with purple flowers, pierced ball finial, attributed to David Rhodes, c1775 ... **1,650.00**

Tureen, cov, stand, brown Water Lily pattern, floral finial, gilt handles, imp mark, c1810 .... **1,450.00**

Wine Cooler, puce scalloped rim edged with gilded darts, fluted handles, bacchic trophies, imp "Wedgwood" and "D" in gold, one handle repaired, c1790 .... **500.00**

JASPERWARE

Biscuit Jar
  5½" h, yellow and black, classical figures **725.00**
  6" h, yellow and white, acorn dec .. **575.00**
  6" h, 5¼" d, dark blue, white classical ladies dec, SP top and rim, marked "Wedgwood, England" **150.00**

Bowl, 4½" d, blue ground, white relief classical dancing figures, grape leaf swag, lion's heads border **65.00**

Brooch, 1¾ x 3¼", dark blue ground, white relief of Psyche, oval convex shape, brass frame and jeweling, polished edge, imp upper case mark .. **375.00**

Buttons, set of 5, solid blue, cut steel mounts, attributed to Matthew Boulton, late 18th C, framed **500.00**

Candlesticks, pr, 10½" h, figural, Ceres and Cybele, light green and white, each holding cornucopia, leaf molded sconce, standing on circular platforms mounted on sq bases, uppercase imp marks, c1800 .... **1,400.00**

Clock, 9¼ x 6¾", light green and white, classical figures **800.00**

Coffee Cann and Saucer, 2½" h, light blue body, applied lilac medallions and white trophies, ram's heads, and floral garlands, imp upper case marks, 19th C **800.00**

Medallion, 1½ x 1⅞", oval, portrait, solid blue, white relief bust of Frederick William II, King of Prussia, brass frame, imp Wedgwood and Bentley marks, c1780 .... **550.00**

Miniature, pitcher, 2½" h, crimson, bulbous, white relief classical figures, imp mark and "Made In England," c1920 .... **550.00**

Plaque
  6 x 12", rect, central panel of light blue with dancing hours, applied white leaf border, light green outer border, imp "Wedgwood" only, hairline crazing, c1840 .... **1,500.00**
  6 x 13½", light blue and white, Seven Graces **500.00**

Scent Bottle, dark blue and white, ⅜" classical figures on each side, 19th C **675.00**

Tea Set, 7¾" h cov teapot, creamer, cov sugar, dark blue, white classical figures, imp "England" marks **250.00**

Urn, 8¼", cov, light green and white, four medallions with garlands and ram's heads **700.00**

Vase
  3¾" h, Strapware, white body, lilac and green, base crazed, upper case mark **600.00**
  9¾" h, white body, lilac and green relief, oval medallions of classical subjects between ram's heads draped by floral garlands, imp upper case mark, early 19th C **800.00**

LUSTERS

Butterfly
  Bowl, 8" d, burgundy ext., gilt butterflies, Oriental landscape scenes, central lotus blossom, and butterflies int., gilt mark, painted number **4,400.00**
  Vase, 4⅛" d, 8⅜" h, MOP luster ext., multicolored, gold outlined butterflies, gold rim, flame luster int., Portland vase mark **400.00**

Dragon
  Bowl, 4½" h, 2½" h, mottled deep blue luster ext., gold dragons, Oriental motif, MOP luster int., Portland vase mark **200.00**

Luster, Fairyland, plate, "Imps on a Bridge and Treehouse," reverse lustered with dark blue and peacock green, 13¼" d, $4,500.00.

Box, cov, 5⅜" d, 5¼" h, mottled green luster int., gold dragons **400.00**

Vase, 3⅞" d, 8" h, mottled deep blue luster ext., gold dragons, MOP int., Portland vase mark **300.00**

Fairyland
  Bowl
    7½" d, Castle on a Road ext., Bird in a Hoop int., pattern Z5125, printed marks, c1920 .... **3,000.00**
    9½" d, Popular Trees ext., Woodland Elves III–Feather Hat int., pattern Z4968, printed marks, c1920 .... **3,000.00**
  Malfrey Pots, 7½" h, Flame Fairyland, shape #2311, Willow pattern Z5360, printed S and H within stylized flowers and Portland Vase marks, c1920, pr **2,300.00**
  Vase
    8½" h, Candlemas, shape #2034, pattern Z5157, c1920 .... **2,400.00**
    8¾" h, ftd trumpet, multicolored glazes, gilt dec of radiant maiden and mischievous fairies, stamped mark, incised "2357" **2,000.00**

Moonlight
  Compote, 10¼" l, Nautilus pattern, splashed pink luster, orange, ochre, and gray highlights, matching 11¼" l bi–valve stand, imp mark, c1810 **1,500.00**
  Pastille Burner, 4¼" h, gold luster, leafy garlands on bowl, mounted on triple dolphin supports, imp date "Feby 2 1805" and "Josiah Wedgwood" in upper case, cov missing **800.00**
  Tumbler, 2¼" h, orange and black ext., green int. with gold creatures **255.00**

MAJOLICA

Bowl, 10½" d, ftd, Cauliflower **250.00**

Match Striker, 5" h, green and brown,
sgd **200.00**
Salad Bowl, fork and spoon **550.00**
Umbrella Stand, 22" h, Aesthetic Movement, basket shape, alternating
molded rows of yellow and white
plaited raffia, green, brown, and blue
peacock feathers, pale blue ribbon,
bowknot ribbon tied at either end, int.
turquoise glaze, imp "Wedgwood,"
date cipher AJL (April 1883), May 25,
1881 registry mark, purple letters and
pattern number **2,000.00**

MISCELLANEOUS

Bust, 15" h, carrara, Sir Walter Scott,
looking to left, tartan shawl draped on
shoulders, socle base, imp "E W
Wyon F" and "Scott," c1860 ...... **675.00**
Cheese Keeper, 8 x 9", raised enamel,
Oriental style dec, bamboo blossoms
and fan shaped leaves, celadon type
pale green ground, imp "Wedgwood"
plus decorator and registry marks .. **875.00**
Plate, 8½" d, green glazed, large
molded sunflower, basketweave and
scalloped rim, c1875, imp upper case
marks, set of 6 .... **300.00**
Vase, 6" h, Moonstone, shape #4196,
printed and imp marks, designed by
Keith Murray, c1940 .... **300.00**

PEARLWARE

Bough Pot, 8½" h, urn shape, pierced
cov, mottled brown, still leaves on
pedestal base **1,000.00**
Demitasse Cup and Saucer **200.00**
Food Mold, cov, jelly, 9⅞" h, int. wedge
shape, puce, yellow, purple, iron–red,
green, and brown painted fruit clusters, bunch of grapes and strawberry
vine on end, brown line edge border,
circular base with four apertures,
plain outer cov, base imp "Wedgwood" and two J form potter's marks,
c1800, base chips **3,850.00**
Plate, 8½" d, shell shape, natural modeling, shades of pink, imp upper case
marks, set of 12 .... **660.00**
Soup Tureen, cov, matching ladle, blue
dahlias, green foliage, black rope dec **425.00**

QUEEN'S WARE

Box, cov, 4 x 5", round, light blue, relief
berries and vine, marked "Queens
Ware, Wedgwood, England" **120.00**
Chocolate Pot, 4" h, green leaf dec .. **160.00**
Platter, oval, reticulated, marked
"Wedgwood" **450.00**

TERRA COTTA WARE

Creamer, enameled flower dec **115.00**
Figure, 4¾" l, nude boy, sleeping, lying
on rect draped base, canted corners,
19th C **1,200.00**
Spillholder, 4½" h, molded bamboo
cane cluster, oval rockwork base,
c1840, pr **1,200.00**
Sugar, cov, enameled florals **150.00**
Tobacco Jar, cov, round, classical figures, marked "Wedgwood Made In
England," 20th C **200.00**
Vase, 5¼" h, Portland, flaring rim, band
of grass, angular handles, applied
masks, black relief lilies and leaves **275.00**

WELLER POTTERY

History: In 1872 Samuel A. Weller opened a
small factory in Fultonham, near Zanesville, Ohio,
to produce utilitarian stoneware, such as milk pans
and sewer tile. In 1882 he moved his facilities to
Zanesville. In 1890 Weller built a new plant in the
Putnam section of Zanesville along the tracks of
the Cincinnati and Muskingum Railway. Additions
followed in 1892 and 1894.

In 1894 Weller entered into an agreement with
William A. Long to purchase the Lonhuda Faience
Company, which had developed an art pottery line
under the guidance of Laura A. Fry, formerly of
Rookwood. Long left in 1895, but Weller continued
to produce Lonhuda under a new name, Louwelsa.
Replacing Long as art director was Charles Bab-
cock Upjohn. He, along with Jacques Sicard, Fred-
erick Hurten Rhead, and Gazo Fudji, developed
Weller's art pottery lines.

At the end of World War I, many prestige lines
were discontinued and Weller concentrated on
commercial wares. Rudolph Lorber joined the staff
and designed lines such as Roma, Forest, and
Knifewood. In 1920 Weller purchased the plant of
the Zanesville Art Pottery and claimed to be the
largest pottery in the country.

Art pottery enjoyed a revival when the Hudson
Line was introduced in the early 1920s. The 1930s
saw Coppertone and Graystone Garden ware
added. However, the depression forced the closing
of the Putnam plant and one on Marietta Street in
Zanesville. After World War II, cheap Japanese

imports took over Weller's market. In 1947 Essex Wire Company of Detroit bought the controlling stock. Early in 1948 operations ceased.

References: Sharon and Bob Huxford, *The Collectors Encyclopedia Of Weller Pottery*, Collector Books, 1979; values updated 1989; Ann Gilbert McDonald, *All About Weller: A History And Collectors Guide To Weller Pottery, Zanesville, OH,* Antique Publications, 1989.

Collectors' Club: American Art Pottery Association, P. O. 9825 Upton Circle, Bloomington, MN 55431.

Additional Listings: See *Warman's Americana & Collectibles* for more examples.

Ashtray, 4¾" h, 8" d, leaf, two stump holders, branched match box holder	**100.00**
Bowl, Kenova, 4½" d, molded lily	**125.00**
Bulb Bowl, 10¼" d, shallow round bowl, sq rose and white line dec, black ground, imp mark	**90.00**
Console Set, Silvertone, round 12" d bowl, 2¼" h pr candlesticks, 4½" d flower frog, 4 pcs	**275.00**

Creamer, brown rabbit, green branch, blue bird, cream ground, 4⅛" h, $45.00.

Ewer, Louwelsa, 7" h, brown glaze, yellow daffodil, artist sgd, half circle mark	**225.00**
Jardiniere, Hudson, 6" h, multicolored floral dec, sgd "Pillsbury"	**375.00**
Jug, Louwelsa, 6" h, corn, artist sgd "H. M.," for Hattie Mitchell	**325.00**
Mug, Dickensware, 4½" h, brown, molded white lily of the valley dec . .	**350.00**
Pitcher, Kingfisher, 7¾" h, paneled, foliage, and cattails, leaf spout, floral rim, limb handle, marked "Weller Ware"	**280.00**
Planter, Souevo, 6½" h, hanging, geometric dec, pointed base	**175.00**
Tankard, Louwelsa, 11" h, blackberries, artist sgd "HH"	**275.00**
Vase	
5" h, raised goldfish, wisteria flowers and leaves, black ground	**125.00**
5¾" h, quad shape, ftd, yellow jonquils, marked "Louwelsa Weller"	**175.00**
6½" h, bulbous, irid green, scattered oak leaves, marked "Weller Sicard"	**900.00**
7" h, cylindrical, pink apple blossoms, leafy branches, green shaded to pink ground, artist sgd "S. T." . . .	**275.00**
7⅛" h, gourd form, glazed purple, gold polka dots and blossoms, Sicard	**600.00**
7½" h, Brighton Bluebird, apple tree stump	**375.00**
9¼" h	
Eocean, high gloss, pink wild roses, long leafy stems, gray shaded to cream ground, marked "Eocean Weller"	**375.00**
Rosemont, hp, cardinals, glossy black ground	**350.00**
10" h, tapered, glossy glaze, white sea gulls over ocean, dark green to cream ground, marked "Weller Eocean"	**900.00**
11" h, cylindrical, Aurelian, glossy glaze, fall colored leaves and pods, blue and red grapes, artist sgd "E. R."	**400.00**
13½" h, shouldered ovoid, rounded everted rim, painted pale rose, lavender, and white chrysanthemum sprays, blue and green shaded leaves, pale pink ground, matte glaze, sgd "C. L. Adler," imp "Weller"	**330.00**
14⅛" h, cylindrical, gold–green lilies, purple accents, green irid lines, purple–red ground, heavy green irid drips on one side, sgd "Weller Sicard"	**1,650.00**
16" h, cylindrical, rose dec flared rim, raised blue and pink peacock, tail draped over steps, pink roses, blue matte finish, artist initials "M. T." for M. Timberlake	**1,900.00**
Wall Pocket, 10½" h, red roses, cream ground	**30.00**

WHALING

History: Whaling items are a specialized part of nautical collecting. Provenance is of prime importance since whaling collectors want assurances that their pieces are from a whaling voyage. Since ship's equipment seldom carries the ship's identification, some individuals have falsely attributed a whaling provenance to general nautical items. Know the dealer, auction house, or collector from whom you buy.

Special tools, e.g., knives, harpoons, lances, spades, etc., do not overlap the general nautical line. Makers' marks and condition determine value for these items.

Richard Bourne, Hyannis, Massachusetts, and

Chuck DeLuca, York, Maine, regularly hold auctions featuring whaling material.

Reference: Thomas G. Lytle, *Harpoons And Other Whalecraft*, Old Dartmouth Historical Society, 1984.

Periodical: *Whalebone*, P. O. Box 2834, Fairfax, VA 22031.

Museums: Cold Spring Harbor Museum, Long Island, N.Y.; Kendall Whaling Museum, Sharon, Mass.; Mystic Seaport Museum, Mystic, Conn.; National Maritime Museum, San Francisco, Calif.; Old Dartmouth Historical Society, New Bedford, Mass.; Whaling Museum, Nantucket, Mass.

Additional Listings: Nautical Items and Scrimshaw.

Stamp, whale ivory, full whale stamp, inscribed "Maria, 1837," 1¼" d, 1¾" h, $450.00.

Blubber Hook
22" l, 19th C	175.00
28" l, handwrought iron	75.00
Bottle, 3", whaling scene, marked "Pure Sperm Oil - Wm Nye"	175.00
Chest, 37¾" l, pine, dec int., dark finish, marked "Whaling Fleet Artic O" on top and bottom "Golden Gate San-Fico Cal," sgd "J N Knowles Ohio 1881," 19th C	1,000.00
Flensing Spade, 12¾" l, 18th C	30.00
Harpoon	
32¼" l, double flue	300.00
33" l, toggle, orig red paint	350.00
Killing Iron	
47¼" l, cast steel, incised letters "WB," Peters	425.00
64¼" l, sgd "J Macy & Co/Cast Steel"	325.00
Log Book	
Draco, South Atlantic Ocean voyage from July 1, 1875 to June 9, 1878, includes whale stamps, whale oil record, provisions list	1,400.00
Laetitia, voyage from 1872 to 1875,	

mate Geo Chruch, includes whale stamps	2,750.00
Lewis, Indian Ocean voyage from 1857 to 1860, Capt George F Neil	4,250.00
Richard Mitchell, departure from Edgartown, November 7, 1831 and ending November 17, 1834, includes whale stamps, burial at sea, two pen and water-color portraits, orig binding	9,500.00
Triad, voyage to South Atlantic Ocean on June 30, 1837 to April 22, 1839, contains whale stamps and drawings, cloth bound with ship portrait on front cov	5,000.00
Octant	
Ebony, ivory nameplate with the names "John Kehew" and "Capt F A Butts," oak case, 19th C	550.00
Mahogany, brass mounted claw type radial arm, boxwood scale, engraved nameplate marked "Made by In Gilbert on Tower Hill/For Capt Geo Todd Febry 24 1761"	2,700.00
Photograph	
10¼ x 13¼", titled "Last of Whalers," whaleships *Wanderer*, and *Charles W Morgan*, copyright A F Packard, dated 1902, brown toned, framed, orig matting	175.00
14 x 18", whaleship *Rousseau* and *Desdemona* tied up in New Bedford harbor, copyright J O'Neil, dated 1892, oak frame	500.00
Quadrant, ebony frame, ivory inlays, cased, includes note identifying property of Captain Goodspeed of whaling schooner *Oread* and *Idlewild*, Made by Heather of London	600.00
Telescope, single draw, ten sided tapered mahogany barrel, 62" l closed, 18th C	2,750.00
Whalebone Products	
Block, double, orig fittings, 19th C . .	650.00
Bodkin, 5⅜" l, turned, 19th C	100.00
Fid, 15" l, 19th C	200.00
Seam Rubber, 4¾" l, red wax inlay scribed lines, 19th C	450.00
Tooth, 7½" l, scrimshaw, engraved whaling scene on one side, eagle with banner reads "Tooth from a 109 bbl sperm whale, May 9th 1837" on other	600.00
Wheel, 36" d, brass mounting, 19th C	600.00

WHIELDON

WHIELDON

History: The Staffordshire potter, Thomas Whieldon, established his shop in 1740. He is best known for his mottled ware, molded in forms of vegetables, fruits, and leaves. Josiah Spode and Josiah Wedgwood, in different capacities, had connections with Whieldon.

Whieldon ware is a generic term. His wares were never marked and other potters made similar items. Whieldon ware is agate-tortoiseshell earthenware in limited shades of green, brown, blue and yellow. Most pieces are utilitarian items, e.g., dinnerware and plates, but figurines and other decorative pieces are found.

Reference: Susan and Al Bagdade, *Warman's English & Continental Pottery & Porcelain, 1st Edition,* Warman Publishing Co., Inc., 1987.

Teapot, tortoiseshell glaze, bird finial, c1760, 5¼″ h, $2,300.00.

Figure, 3¼″, pug dog, seated, ochre, brown, and gray glaze 450.00
Miniature, pitcher, scalloped rim, green, orange, ochre, brown and buff tortoiseshell glaze 150.00
Plate
  9″ d, octagonal, emb rim, brown tortoise shell glaze 450.00
  9⅛″ d, octagonal, tortoise shell glaze, black, brown, blue, and green spots 550.00
  9¼″ d, mottled gray, green, and yellow, shaped border with molded feathers and diaper pattern, c1760 325.00
  9⅜″ d, octagonal, emb rim, brown tortoiseshell glaze 400.00
  9¾″ d, octagonal, tortoise shell glaze, black, brown, blue, and green spots 475.00
  10″ d, emb scalloped rim, multicolored tortoise shell glaze 600.00
Porringer, 4¾ x 2¾″, creamware, sponged manganese, green and ochre brushed glaze, c1770 . . . . . . 600.00
Stirrup Cup, 4¹⁵⁄₁₆″ h, stag's head, creamware head, brown and green stripes, brown and ochre dots highlights, brown ears, incised eyelashes, dimpled nose, ochre whorl–molded crest, c1780, minor repairs 4,125.00

Teapot, 4½″ h, Pineapple Ware, green glazed leaves, ochre glazed lozenges, foliate spout, scaly dolphin handle, leaf cluster knob, green glaze, Wedgwood, c1760 . . . . 1,800.00

WHIMSIES, GLASS

History: Glass workers occasionally spent time during lunch or after completing their regular work schedule creating whimsies (unusual glass objects), e.g., candy striped canes, darners, hats, paperweight, pipes, witch balls, etc. Whimsies were taken home and given as gifts to family and friends.

Because of their uniqueness and infinite variety, whimsies can rarely be attributed to a specific glass house or glass worker. Whimsies occurred wherever glass was made, from New Jersey to Ohio and westward. Some have suggested that style and color can be used to pinpoint region or factory, but no one has yet developed an identification key that is adequate.

One of the most collectible types of whimsies are witch balls. They are a hollow sphere of glass, often found with a matching glass vase-type holder. Myths surround the origin and use of witch balls. Perhaps they were displayed by the fireplace to catch demon spirits as they descended the chimney, or they may have been used to store salt by the chimney to keep it dry.

Reference: Joyce E. Blake, *Glasshouse Whimsies,* published by author, 1984.

Additional Listings: See Glass, Early American and Sandwich Glass.

Witch Ball, Nailsea type, pale blue ground, white loopings, 4¼″ d, $100.00.

Bellows Bottle, 16½″ h, ftd, clear neck threading, clear quilled rigaree on each corner, cranberry body, clear applied standard and foot, pontil scar 100.00
Bird Feeder, 5¾″ h, bottle green glass, emb bird and "Don't Forget to Feed Me" 135.00
Bird Drinking Font, 4½″, blown molded, applied cobalt ball top and rim 200.00

Cane
31½" l, cased cranberry glass, swirled
ribbed ext., mid 19th C 150.00
45½ h, clear, hollow body, bulbous
end, sq shaft tapering to twisted
bottom half, mid 19th C 125.00
Fly Catcher, 7" h, removable dome cov,
clear, non–lead, 19th C 250.00
Lamp Filler, aqua glass insert, tin base,
cage, and top with handle, some orig
whale oil, mid 19th C 225.00
Milk Pail, clear, qt, base emb "Pat glass
pail, Boston, Massachusetts, June
24, 84," snap on tin cov emb "Adham
Patent Pail," ground lip 275.00
Pipe, 26½" l, Nailsea type, opaque
white, pink loopings, three separate
pcs, bowl, stem, and connector,
c1870 . . . . 145.00
Powder Horn, 14" h, cannon shaped,
twisted neck, clear non–lead glass,
blue and red loop pattern, pontil scar,
American, mid 19th C 150.00
Witch Ball
Blown, 4¾" d, aqua, white looping . . 200.00
Cranberry, 5" d, opalescent hobnails,
pr 210.00
Spatter, 8" h, tortoiseshell glass ball,
attached to amber glass stem and
foot 185.00

WHISKEY BOTTLES, EARLY

History: The earliest American whiskey bottles
were generic form bottles blown by pioneer glassmakers in the 18th century. The Biningers (1820–
1880s) were the first bottles specifically designed
for whiskey. After the 1860s distillers favored the
cylindrical "fifth" form.

The first embossed brand name bottle was the
amber E. G. Booz Old Cabin Whiskey bottle which
was issued in 1860. Many stories have been told
about this classic bottle. Unfortunately, most are
not true. Research has proved that "booze" was
a corruption of the words "bouse" and "boosy"
from the 16th and 17th centuries. It was only a
coincidence that the Philadelphia distributor also
was named Booz. This bottle has been reproduced
extensively.

Prohibition (1920–1933) brought the legal whiskey industry to a standstill. Whiskey was marked
"medicinal purposes only" and distributed by private distillers in unmarked or paper label bottles.

The size and shape of whiskey bottles are standard. Colors are limited to amber, amethyst, clear,
green, and cobalt blue (rare). Corks were the common closure in the early period, with the inside
screw top being used in the 1880–1910 period.

Bottles made prior to 1880 are the most desirable. In purchasing a bottle with a label, condition
is a critical factor. In the 1950s distillers began to
issue collectors' special edition bottles to help increase sales.

References: Ralph & Terry Kovel, *The Kovels'
Bottle Price List, 8th Edition,* Crown Publishers,
Inc., 1987; Carlo and Dorothy Sellari, *The Standard Old Bottle Price Guide,* Collector Books,
1989.

Periodical: *Antique Bottle and Glass Collector,*
P. O. Box 187, East Greenville, PA 18041.

Additional Listing: See *Warman's Americana
& Collectibles* for a listing of Collectors' Special
Editions Whiskey Bottles.

Hodico, Hollenbach, Dietrick & Co,
Reading, PA, amber, one qt, 11⅛" h,
$40.00.

A M Bininger & Co
6¾" h, bulbous, golden amber, applied tapered lip, open pontil base,
handled, emb "Bininger's Kicker-
bocker A M Biniger & Co No 19
Broad St, NY," c1850 . . . . 350.00
8⅞" h, urn shape, golden amber,
rolled lip, smooth base, handled,
emb "A M Bininger & Co/No 19
Broad St, NY," c1865 . . . . 750.00
Casper's Whiskey Made By Honest
North Carolina People, blue, round,
tooled tapered lip, 12" h, c1870–80 425.00
Diamond Club, round, medium blue–
green, applied tapered ring lip, iron
pontil, 9⁷⁄₁₆" h, 1850–60 . . . . 200.00
E G Booz's Old Cabin, Philadelphia,
amber, 1840 . . . . 60.00
Flora Temple Harness Trot, horse, to-
paz–olive, applied ring lip and handle,
smooth base, 8½" h, c1880 . . . . . . 80.00
Giffith Hyatt & Co, olive amber, label 475.00
Ginter Co, Importers, deep yellow
green, 11" h, 1860–80 . . . . 60.00
Hayner, clear, label, qt, 1916 . . . . 10.00
Hodico, Hollenbach, Dietriek & Co,
Reading, PA, amber, 11⅛" h 40.00
J A Gilka, Berlin, amber, 9½" h 25.00
Jesse Moore, dark red amber 50.00
Louis Weber Louisville, KY round, ol-

ive—green, applied tapered lip, smooth base, emb "W McCully & Co, Pittsburgh" on base, 10" h, c1870 .. **240.00**
N B Dursley, deep olive amber, qt, 1783 **525.00**
Nathans Bros 1863, Philadelphia, amber emb **125.00**
Old Joe Gideon, amber, ½ pt **10.00**
Oxford Rye Whiskey, label, 11½" h, 1880s **20.00**
Phoenix Old Bourbon, honey amber, bird and coffin, pt **115.00**
Pride of Kentucky, yellow amber **750.00**
Sour Mash 1867, amber, barrel shape, 8¼" h **20.00**
Spruance Stanley & Co, San Francisco, tooled top, 1869 .... **25.00**
Theodore Netter, barrel, clear **25.00**
Turner Brothers, sq, olive green, 9¾" h, 1860–1900 .... **65.00**

WHITE PATTERNED IRONSTONE

History: White patterned ironstone is a heavy earthenware, first patented in 1813 by Charles Mason, Staffordshire, England, using the name "Patent Ironstone China." Other English potters soon began copying this opaque, feldspathic, white china.

All white ironstone dishes first became available in the American market in the early 1840s. The first patterns had simple Gothic lines similar to the shapes used in transfer wares. Pattern shapes, such as New York, Union, and Atlantic, were designed to appeal to the American housewife. Motifs, such as wheat, corn, oats, and poppies, were embossed on the forms as the American Western prairie influenced design. Eventually over 200 shapes and patterns, with variations of finials and handles, were made.

White patterned ironstone is identified by shape names and pattern names. Many potters only named the shape in their catalogs. Pattern names usually refer to the decoration motif.

References: Jean Wetherbee, *A Look At White Ironstone,* Wallace-Homestead, 1980; Jean Wetherbee, *A Second Look At White Ironstone*, Wallace-Homestead, 1985.

Butter Pats, emb scrolled rims, set of 6 **40.00**
Cake Plate, 12" l, Cable and Ring, reticulated handles, Anthony Shaw and Son, England **10.00**
Coffeepot, Wheat and Blackberry, Clementson Bros **100.00**
Compote, Pearl Sydenham, ftd, Meakin **175.00**
Creamer
  Fuchsia, 5¼" h, unmarked **30.00**
  Wheat and Clover, Turner & Tomkinson **60.00**
Cup and Saucer
  Acorn and Tiny Oak, Pankhurst ... **25.00**

Coffeepot, Wheat and Clover pattern, melon ribbed base, ring finial, 10½" h, $125.00.

Grape and Medallion, Challinor **35.00**
Ewer, 12¾" h, Corn and Oats, Wedgwood **150.00**
Gravy Boat, Vintage **25.00**
Nappy, Prairie Flowers, Livesley Powell **15.00**
Pancake Server, octagonal, Boote, 1851 .... **40.00**
Pitcher
  8½" h, Wheat, ribbed **30.00**
  10¾" h, Ceres, Elsmore & Forster .. **130.00**
Plate
  7" d, Wheat and Clover, Turner & Tomkinson **15.00**
  8¾" d, Corn and Oats, Wedgwood, 1863 .... **20.00**
  9" d, Ceres Wheat, Elsmore & Forster **20.00**
  10½" d, Corn, Davenport **20.00**
Platter
  14½" l, Lily Of The Valley, Alfred Meakin **40.00**
  16" l, Ceres, Elsmore & Forster **55.00**
Relish Dish, parish shape, Alcock **20.00**
Sauce Tureen
  Fluted Pearl, undertray, J Wedgwood **100.00**
  Wheat and Blackberry, Clementson Bros **60.00**
Soup Plate
  8⅞" d, Paneled Grape, JF **18.00**
  9" d, Wheat and Clover, Turner & Tomkinson **25.00**
Sugar
  Fuchsia, Meakin **40.00**
  Syllabub Cup, Trumpet Vine **20.00**
Teapot, 8⅞" h, forget-me-not, Wood, Rathbone and Co, Cobridge, Staffordshire **80.00**
Toothbrush Holder
  Hyacinth, lid, Wedgwood **60.00**
  Wheat and Clover, underplate, Turner and Tomkinson **50.00**
Tureen, cov, underplate, orig ladle, Wheat pattern, marked R Froster, England, mid 19th C **325.00**

WILLOW PATTERN CHINA

History: Josiah Spode developed the first "traditional" willow pattern in 1810. The components, all motifs taken from Chinese export china, are a willow tree, "apple" tree, two pagodas, fence, two birds, and three figures crossing a bridge. The legend, in its many versions, is an English invention based on the design components.

By 1830, there were over 200-plus makers of willow pattern china in England. The pattern has remained in continuous production. Some of the English firms that still produce willow pattern china are Burleigh, Johnson Bros. (Wedgwood Group), Royal Doulton's continuation of the Booths pattern, and Wedgwood.

By the end of the 19th century, pattern production spread to France, Germany, Holland, Ireland, Sweden, and the United States. In the United States, Buffalo Pottery made the first willow pattern beginning in 1902. Many other companies followed, developing willow variants using rubber-stamp simplified patterns as well as overglaze decals. The largest American manufacturers of the traditional willow pattern were Royal China and Homer Laughlin, usually preferred because it is dated. Shenango pieces are most desired among restaurant-quality ware.

Japan began producing large quantities of willow pattern china in the early 20th century. Noritake began about 1902. Its early pieces used a Nippon "Royal Sometuke" mark. Most Japanese pieces are porous earthenware with a dark blue pattern using the tradition willow design, usually with no inner border. Noritake did put the pattern on china bodies. Unusual forms include salt and pepper shakers, one-quarter-pound butter dishes, and canisters. "Occupied Japan" may add a small percentage to the value of common table wares. Maruta and Moriyama marked pieces are especially valued. The most sought-after Japanese willow is the fine-quality NKT Co. ironstone with a copy of the old Booths pattern. Recent Japanese willow is a paler shade of blue on a porcelain body.

The most common dinnerware color is blue. However, pieces can also be found in black (with clear glaze or mustard-color glaze by Royal Doulton), brown, green, mulberry, pink (red), and polychrome. Although colors other than blue are hard to find, there is less demand; thus, prices may not necessarily be higher.

The popularity of the willow design has resulted in a large variety of willow-decorated products: candles, fabric, glass, graniteware, linens, needlepoint, plastic, tinware, stationery, watches, and wall coverings. All this material has collectible value.

References: Mary Frank Gaston, *Blue Willow: An Identification & Value Guide,* Collector Books, 1983, revised prices, 1986; Veryl Marie Worth and Louise M. Loehr, *Willow Pattern China: Collector's Guide, 3rd Edition,* H. S. Worth Co, 1986.

Periodical: *American Willow Report,* P. O. Box 900, Oakridge, OR 97463.

Reproduction Alert: The Scio Pottery, Scio, Ohio, currently manufactures a willow pattern set sold in variety stores. The pieces have no marks or back stamps, and the transfer is of poor quality. The plates are flatter in shape than those of other manufacturers.

Additional Listings: Buffalo Pottery. See *Warman's Americana & Collectibles* for more examples.

Vegetable Bowl, scalloped edge, double border, patterned center, Allerton crown mark, 8¹¹/₁₆″ d, 2⅛″ h, $30.00.

Bowl, 9″ d, marked "Royal"	5.00
Bowl and Pitcher Set, Parrot pattern	350.00
Cake Plate, flow blow pattern, pierced sides	55.00
Children's Dishes, dinner service, four plates, four cups and saucers, creamer, cov sugar, teapot, platter, cov casserole, and gravy boat, large size, marked "Japan"	225.00
Creamer, 2⅜″ h, handle, pitcher shape, marked "Shenango"	12.50
Egg Cup, 2¼″ h, border on base, marked "England"	15.00
Gravy Boat, light blue, underplate, marked "Copeland"	45.00
Plate	
8½″ d, ivory ground, scalloped edge, light brown daisy border, blue all–over willow pattern, gold bands on edge and base of border	50.00
10″ d, pink, marked "Allerton"	6.00
Platter, 8 x 11″, marked "Buffalo Pottery," c1908	46.00
Salad Bowl, 9¾″ d, fork and spoon	35.00
Salt and Pepper Shakers, pr, 4″ h, bulbous	18.00
Soup Plate, flanged, marked "Allerton"	20.00
Teapot, pink, marked "Royal"	25.00

WOODENWARE

History: Many utilitarian household objects and farm implements were made of wood. Although they were used heavily, these implements were made of the strongest woods and well taken care of by their owners.

This category serves as a catchall for wood objects which do not fit into other categories.

Additional Listings: See *Warman's Americana & Collectibles* for more examples.

Box, cov, turned urn shape, pedestal base, 6¼″ h, 2⅝″ d, $85.00.

Barrel, 19″ d, 28″ h, stave constructed, quarter sawed oak, red paint, black painted iron bands, matching lid ... **200.00**

Berry Basket, 4″ h, impressed label around side, star on bottom, varnished **95.00**

Bowl, 16 x 21″, oval, worn patina **60.00**

Box
  11½″ l, poplar, floral print wallpaper ext. **115.00**
  14″ l, pine, orig worn reddish brown flame graining, base molding, till int. **175.00**
  18½″ l, poplar, floral print wallpaper ext., int. lined with 1832 newspaper, paper label "Band Boxes Manufactured by Hannah Davis, East Jeffrey, NH" **300.00**

Bucket, 6¼″ h, stave constructed, metal bands, wire bale wood handle, orig brown graining **85.00**

Butter Paddle, 9″ l, burl, good figure, old gray scrubbed finish, traces of varnish **500.00**

Candle Box
  8 x 8 x 9½″, pine, slide cover, orig red paint, sgd and dated 1833 ...... **295.00**
  11″ l, hardwood, old blue paint, sliding lid **275.00**
  13″ l, hanging, pine, worn brown paint, peaked crest, hanging hole **125.00**

Candlestand, 21½″ h, oak, pine base,
adjustable, two candle sockets with push–up design, 19th C **1,900.00**

Candy Mold, 8½″ l, pine, fish, two parts **25.00**

Cheese Sieve, 7″ d, 3¾″ h, round, stave constructed, iron bands, four drain holes **45.00**

Chopping Bowl, 19″ l, oblong, 19th C **60.00**

Cookie Board, 4¾ x 11¾″, carved, man on one side, woman on other **255.00**

Corn Cutter, 20½″ l **55.00**

Cutting Board, 14″ d, pine, 6″ handle **35.00**

Dipper, 11¼″ l, figure and burl, scrubbed white **80.00**

Drying Rack
  26¼ x 35″, pine, shoe feet, tapered posts, three mortised bars, green paint **145.00**
  48″ w, 43″ h, poplar, three mortised and pinned bars, semicircular cut out feet, natural patina **125.00**

Foot Warmer, 8 x 8½″, 6½″ h, birch, dark patina, sliding door, drill hole date "1814" and "LF" initials, wire bale handle **105.00**

Game Board, 24½″ l, pine, scalloped edges, seven wrought iron hooks, scrubbed **100.00**

Hat Box, 17½″ l, oval, orig dec, Scandinavian, 19th C **750.00**

Hat Form, 10″ h **45.00**

Inkwell, 3½″ d, turned, glass insert, three quill holes **55.00**

Knife Tray, two sections, dovetailed, scallop arched center, open carved handle, taupe paint **250.00**

Lighting Stand, 44″ h, cross member base, peg feet, wrought iron rush holder, English **85.00**

Measure, 5¾″ d, 3½″ h, bentwood, branded label "Daniel Cragin, Manufacturer 7 Seller, Wilton, NH", refinished **60.00**

Mortar, 4″ d, 7½″ h, turned, orig dark green paint, early 1800s **150.00**

Noggin, 7″ h, repaired damage on spout **40.00**

Nut Cracker, 8½″ l, carved, gnome ... **65.00**

Piggin, 9¼″ d, 6¾″ h, stave constructed, handle, worn finish, bottom stamped "N Corthell" **160.00**

Rocking Horse, 51″ l, 34¼″ h, wood and sawdust body, horsehide cov, red and mustard dec rockers, replaced saddle, American, 19th C **500.00**

Salt Box, 10″ l, hanging, pine, old finish, European **75.00**

Sculpture, 15″ h, cherry, eagle, D James **550.00**

Shelf, hanging
  30½ x 25″, pine, orig dark finish, American, 19th C **250.00**
  32¾ x 12½ x 30″, pine, scalloped ends, handmade **175.00**

Sleigh, child's, 46″ l, orig red paint with

yellow striping, floral dec, metal tipped wood runners	450.00
Smoothing Board, 23" l, fruit wood, edge inlay, handle, dated and initialed "B St 1894"	75.00
Spoon, 7¼" l, engraved floral design handle	45.00
Sugar Bucket	
8" h, stave construction, old gray repaint, galvanized metal bottom band, wire bale, wooden handle, age crack in lid	140.00
9¾" h, stave constructed, red repaint, lid branded "C Wilder & Son"	35.00
10" h, old finish	75.00
11¾" h, stave construction, old brown finish, flat lid branded "Saratoga"	125.00
14" h, stave construction, white over gray paint	190.00
Sugar Firkin, pine, branded "William Clark," orig green paint, two minor wood losses to cov, 12" h, 12½" d	150.00
Towel Rack, 32 x 39½", pine and poplar, three mortised bars, shoe feet	100.00
Trencher, 8¾ x 9"	100.00
Writing Box, 20¼" l, mahogany, fitted int., brass bound, worn finish	125.00
Yoke, 45" l, shaped design, patina	150.00

WORLD'S FAIRS AND EXPOSITIONS

History: The Great Exhibition of 1851 in London marked the beginning of the World's Fair and Exposition movement. The fairs generally feature exhibitions from nations around the world displaying the best of their industrial and scientific achievements.

Many important technological advances have been introduced at world's fairs. Examples include the airplane, telephone, and electric lights. The ice cream cone, hot dog, and iced tea were products of vendors at fairs. Art movements often were closely connected to fairs, with the Paris Exhibition of 1900 generally considered to have assembled the best of the works of the Art Nouveau artists.

References: *American Art, New York World's Fair 1939,* Apollo Books, 1987; Carl Abbott, *The Great Extravaganza: Portland and the Lewis and Clark Exposition,* Oregon Historical Society, 1981; Stanley Appelbaum, *The New York World's Fair, 1939/1940,* Dover Publications, Inc., 1971; Patricia F. Carpenter and Paul Totah, *The San Francisco Fair, Treasure Island, 1939–1940,* Scottwall Associates, 1989; Kurt Krueger, *Meet Me In St. Louis—The Exonumia Of The 1904 World's Fair,* Krause Publications, 1979; Howard Rossen and John Kaduck, *Columbia World's Fair Collectibles,* Wallace-Homestead, 1976, revised price list 1982.

Periodical: *World's Fair,* P.O. Box 339, Corte Madera, CA 94925.

Collectors' Club: World's Fair Collectors' Society, Inc., P. O. Box 20806, Sarasota, FL 33583.

1876, Philadelphia, Centennial	
Paperweight, glass, exposition buildings	75.00
Whimsey, 3½" h, glass, boot shape, orig top	40.00
1893, Chicago, Columbian	
Admission Ticket, set of four	50.00
Advertising Trade Card, Uncle Sam and Columbus	6.00
Beer Mug, 3½" h, eight pressed panels at bottom, marked "M Gordon, World's Fair, 1893"	35.00
Fan, hand held	50.00
Jewelry Box, 3" sq, overview scene of fair	265.00
Plate, 8½" d, blue and white, Machinery Building	35.00
Rose Bowl, 3¼" h, 4" w, peach blow, wild rose pattern, eight crimp top, deep raspberry shading to white, matte acid finish, elaborate lettering and scroll dec	675.00
Spoon, SS	30.00
1901, Buffalo, Pan–American Exposition	
Hatchet, Indian head on frosted blade, berries and leaves on handle	135.00
Lamp, hurricane, green, color symbol on globe, encircled name and date	350.00
Mug, Beaded Scroll pattern, buffalo and "Pan American Exposition 1901" transfer	45.00
Plate, bread and butter, photographic scenes, pastel colored border, gold edge, Haviland	60.00
Stein, blue and gray detailing, White's Pottery, Utica, NY	385.00
1904, St Louis, Louisiana Purchase Exposition	
Bell, Liberty Bell, some gold	45.00
Cup	
Porcelain	65.00
Tin, enameled	60.00
Handkerchief, multicolored dec	20.00
Notebook, metal cov, Festival Hall Cascades on cov, suspended on chain with clip	65.00
Paperweight, hollow, shells	18.00
Plate, 7" d, metal	25.00
Reverse Painting on Glass, Varied Industrial Building, brass frame	175.00
Stein, 3" h, Manufacturing Building	275.00
Tray, 6½" l, brass	55.00
Vase, cobalt blue	30.00
1915, San Francisco, Panama–Pacific International Exposition	
Mayonnaise, china, marked "Nippon"	160.00
Napkin Ring, celluloid, pr	15.00

1933, Chicago, Century of Progress
Ashtray, brass, Chrysler Building . . .	20.00
Bottle, clear	20.00
Keychain, brass, Skyride	35.00
Paperweight	20.00
Plate, china, Science Hall scene, blue ground, Pickard	12.00
Playing Cards, one red deck, one trick deck, pr in orig box	35.00
Tapestry, silk, aerial view, Zepplin and airplanes	80.00
Thermometer, Hall of Science, framed	35.00

1939 New York Fair, souvenir spoon, SP, Oneida, 4⅜" l, $15.00.

1939, New York, New York World's Fair
Compact, enameled, Sheffield Farms giveaway to beauty contestant runner–ups	60.00
Hat, official, embroidered front, Trylon and Perisphere, women employees type	55.00
Letter Opener, logo handle, orig card	10.00
Napkin Ring, bakelite, blue, Trylon and Perisphere	40.00
Tapestry, 20 x 55½", Administration and Federal Buildings, Trylon and Perisphere	75.00

1939, San Francisco, Golden Gate International Exposition
Ashtray, metal, white	15.00
Handkerchief, embroidered	15.00
Knife, glass handle, boxed	20.00
Plate, 10", marked "Homer Laughlin"	65.00
Tablecloth, 56" sq, cotton	35.00

1964, New York, New York World's Fair
Guide Book, *Official Guide New York World's Fair*	15.00
Tray, metal, Unisphere	8.00

YELLOW WARE

History: Yellow ware is a heavy earthenware of differing weight and strength which varies in color from a rich pumpkin to lighter shades which are more tan than yellow. Although plates, nappies, and custard cups are found, kitchen bowls and other cooking utensils are most prevalent.

The first American yellow ware was produced at Bennington, Vermont. English yellow ware has additional ingredients which make its body much harder. Derbyshire and Sharp's were foremost among the English manufacturers.

References: John Gallo, *Nineteenth and Twentieth Century Yellow Ware,* Heritage Press, 1985; Joan Leibowitz, *Yellow Ware: The Transitional Ceramic,* Schiffer Publishing Ltd., 1985.

Bowl, blue band, incised dec, 10¾" d, 5¾" h, $45.00.

Bank, 3¾" h, pig, black and brown sponging, amber glaze	100.00
Bowl	
3⅞" d, blue seaweed dec on white band	500.00
7 x 8¾", oval, brown sponging	25.00
9¾" d, brown and blue sponging, marked "Red Wing Saffron Ware"	30.00
14½" d	65.00
Butter Crock, 7¼" d, dark blue stripes, ribbed bottom	100.00
Colander, round, yellow bands, white int.	175.00
Crock, 5", three brown bands	30.00
Custard Cup, brown sponging	10.00
Figure, 11⅜" h, cat, seated, oval base, brown and bluish green running glaze	2,000.00
Footwarmer, wedge shape, yellow, cork plug	100.00
Milk Pan, 11½"	60.00
Miniature, chamberpot, 2½" h, black stripes, white band with blue seaweed dec, reglued handle	90.00
Mixing Bowl, 10 to 14" d nested set of 4, white band	260.00
Mold	
Corn	90.00
Heart	85.00
Pinwheel	100.00
Mug	
2¾" h, white stripes	175.00
3¼" h, blue seaweed dec, white ground	200.00
3¾" h, white band, green seaweed dec, gray–black stripes, hairlines	150.00
Pepper Pot, 4½" h, blue and white bands	250.00
Pitcher	
9" h, green and brown seaweed mocha dec on white band	600.00
10", blue and white bands	400.00
Preserving Jar, 7¾" h	65.00

Rolling Pin, wood handles	175.00
Salt, 2⅛" h, white band with blue sea-weed dec, ftd	275.00
Wash Bowl, 12" d, plain, 1865	75.00

ZANE WARE
MADE IN U.S.A.

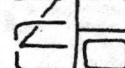

ZANE POTTERY

History: In 1921 Adam Reed and Harry Mc-Clelland bought the Peters and Reed Pottery in Zanesville, Ohio. The firm continued production of garden wares and introduced several new art lines: "Sheen," "Powder Blue," "Crystalline," and "Drip." The factory was sold in 1941 to Lawton Gonder.

Reference: Jeffery, Sherrie, and Barry Hersone, *The Peters and Reed and Zane Pottery Experience,* published by authors, 1990.

Additonal Listing: Gonder and Peters and Reed.

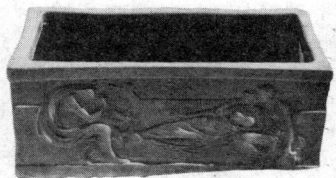

Window Box, Moss Aztec, sgd "Ferrell," 6" h, 12½" l, 5" w, $125.00.

Bowl, 5" d, blue and brown	40.00
Figure, 10⅛" h, black cat, green eyes	500.00
Jardiniere, 14½" h, variegated green semi—matte glaze, two handles, Montene	125.00
Vase	
3½" h, sq, geometric design, rich green	65.00
7" h, flowing medium green, dark forest green ground, marked	90.00
Window Box, 12½" l, 5" w, 6" h, Moss Aztec, sgd "Ferrell"	125.00

LA MORO
ZANESVILLE POTTERY

History: Zanesville Art Pottery, one of several potteries located in Zanesville, Ohio, began pro-

duction in 1900. A line of utilitarian products was first produced. Art pottery was introduced shortly thereafter. The major line was La Moro, which was hand-painted and decorated under glaze. The impressed block print mark "La Moro" appears on the high-glazed and matte-glazed decorated ware. The firm was bought by S. A. Weller in 1920 and became known as Weller Plant No. 3.

References: Louise and Evan Purviance and Norris F. Schneider, *Zanesville Art Pottery In Color,* Mid-America Book Company, 1968; Evan and Louise Purviance, *Zanesville Art Tile In Color,* Wallace-Homestead Book Co., 1972.

Teapot, souvenir type, dark green, emb "Tyces Pottery, Zanesville, Ohio," 2¾" h, $30.00.

Bowl, 6½" d, mottled blue, fluted edge	40.00
Jardiniere, 9" h, brown and gold glaze	125.00
Paperweight, A. E. Tiling Co. Ltd, 1896 calendar on back	25.00
Pitcher, tankard shape, floral dec, artist sgd	300.00
Tile, 24", sq, sixteen tiles, elk, needle-point style dec, "Mosaic" in oval and round circle mark	90.00
Vase, 8¾" h, cone shape top, bulbous base, two handles, La Moro, marked "2/802/4"	350.00

ZSOLNAY POTTERY

History: Vilmos Zsolnay (1828–1900) assumed control of his brother's factory in Pécs, Hungary, in the mid-19th century. In 1899 Miklos, Vilmos's son, became manager. The firm still produces ceramic ware.

The early wares are highly ornamental, glazed,

and have a cream color ground. "Eosin" glaze, a deep rich play of colors reminiscent of Tiffany's iridescent wares, received a gold medal at the 1900 Paris exhibition. Zsolnay Art Nouveau pieces show great creativity.

Originally no trademark was used. Beginning in 1878 a blue mark depicting the five towers of the cathedral at Pécs was used. The initials "TJM" represent the names of Miklos's three children.

Zsolnay's recent series of iridescent glazed figurines, which initially were inexpensive, now are being sought by collectors and show a steady increase in value.

Reference: Susan and Al Bagdade, *Warman's English & Continental Pottery & Porcelain, 1st Edition,* Warman Publishing Co., Inc., 1987.

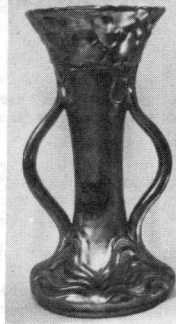

Vase, green irid glaze, marked, 8½" h, $125.00.

Bowl
  6" w, sq, reticulated, gold, burgundy,
    and blue, Persian 100.00
  7¾" d, 2¾" h, diagonally repeating irid
    blue–green lizards, gold ground,
    raised medallion mark 900.00
Dish, 8½ x 7½", fan shape, beige, gold,
  and pink dec, reticulated, fold over
  border, steeple mark 180.00
Ewer, 12" h, irid, impressed design . . . 255.00
Figure
  4½" h, sparrows, four colors, green
    stamp mark 60.00
  7" h, dog, standing, irid, bronze and
    gold 60.00
  12⅝" h, woman, standing holding
    harp, rounded triangular base, blue
    over gold iridescent glaze, "Zsol-
    nay Pecs" mark and yellow printed
    "Made in Hungary," c1950 . . . . . . 300.00
Jug, 9" h, lustered, enameled flowers,
  cream ground, handled 200.00
Plate, 12" d, pink and blue flowers in
  center, pale yellow ground, reticulated
  border, gold trim 225.00
Puzzle Jug, 6¾" h, multicolored jewel-
  ing and irid florals, reticulated roundels, three looped protrusions, pale
  beige ground, handled, blue castle
  mark 125.00
Serving Dish, 8½" d, pink and gold flow-
  ers, rolled reticulated side borders,
  beige ground 160.00
Vase
  4" h, ovoid, sq mouth, stylized land-
    scape dec, seal and imp marks . . 825.00
  9" h, 13" d, pinched bulbous, fluted
    rim, four amorphous ribbed han-
    dles, four feet, irid gold to blue
    glaze, remnants of stamp 1,300.00

PHOTO CREDITS

We wish to thank those who permitted us to photograph objects in their possession. Unfortunately, we are unable to identify the sources for all of our pictures; nevertheless, we are deeply appreciative for all who contributed to this and past editions, and to the editions of *Warman's Americana & Collectibles*.

California: Carlsbad, Dan Golden; Moor Park, Tony and Jackie Anello; Oceanside, Lois Misiewicz; San Francisco, Butterfields; Santa Ana, Evalene Pulati. **Connecticut**: New Canaan, Mildred Fishman; Sandy Hook, Bea Morgan; Stamford, Donna Schilero, West Hartford, Arnold Chase; Westport, Tom Gallagher; Woodbury, Daria of Woodbury; Woodstock, David and Linda Arman. **Delaware**: Lewes, The Price's, Sea Gert Antiques. **Florida**: Cape Coral, The Calico Cat, Elizabeth Clancey, The Collector's Den, Sandra Martz, Country Closet Antiques; Clearwater Beach, Bill Wheeler, The Oar House; Ft. Myers, Ft. Myers Antique Mall, Mina Tinsley, Things Unlimited; Hollywood, Cynthia and Joseph Klein; Miami Beach, Estelle Zalkin; Orlando, Peg Harrison, Harrison's Antiques. **Georgia**: Atlanta, Walter Glenn, Geode Ltd., Jim Marin, Art Deco Atlanta. **Illinois**: Arlington Heights, T. Johnson; Chicago, Dick and Bindy Bitterman, Eureka! Antiques and Collectibles; Lislie, Susan Nicholson; Mapleton, White's Antiques and Furniture Finishing; Monmouth, David and Betty Hallam; Northbrook, Al and Susan Bagdade, Norman Rockwell Museum; Peotone, Kathy Wojciechowski. **Iowa**: Spencer, Paul and Paula Brenner; Spirit Lake, Gaylord and Margaret Franken. **Maine**: Kennebunk, Richard W. Oliver Auction & Art Gallery; Oxford, Oxford Common; Topsham, Allan and Helen Smith, The Country House. **Maryland**: Laurel, Ken Cohen, Julie Rich; Temple Hills, John Rosenberg; **Massachusetts**: Cambridge, Stan Tillotson; Hyannis Port, Richard A. Bourne, Inc.; Winchester, Lorry and Bruce Hanes, Dad's Follies; Worcester, Ralph R. Saarinen.

Michigan: Monroe, Herb and Joyce Krueger, Mostly Majolica; Utica, Virgil Rogers and David Graves, Avant-Garde; West Bloomfield, Joan Collett Oates. **Missouri**: Sedalia, Crystal and Leyland Payton. **New Hampshire**: Peterborough, Lee and Rally Dennis; Salem, Bea and Bill Laycock, B & B Antiques & Collectibles. **New Jersey**: Bellmawr, Angie Ricciaardi Antiques; Demarest, Mimi Rudnick, The Salt Lady Antiques; Hackensack, Roz Albert; Madison, Don Fiore, The Toy Man; Magnolia, Carol Pollock, Custom Covers; Montclair, Susan Morse; Moorestown, Cindy and James Townes, Ladybug's Cupboard; Morris Plains, Elyce Litts; New Egypt, Red Barn Antiques; Old Bridge, Sue Theurich, Respectable Collectables; Paterson, Edward W. Leach; Short Hills, Cynthia Klein, Joseph Klein, C. J. K. Kollectibles; Stewartsville, Marcia and Bob Weissman, Neat Olde Things; Toms River, Shelley, Norman and Phyllis Galinkin; West Orange, Barbara and Melvin Alpern; Woodcliff Lake, Joan Raines Antiques. **New York**: Auburn, Lower Lake Collectibles; Carmel, Bob Cahn, The Primitive Man; Elmsford, Gerald and Carol Newman; Fishkill, Robert A. Doyle; Livingston, Langes Steinworld; New Platz, Charlotte and Larry Settle; New York, John High; Queens, Flamingoes; Valley Stream, Craig Dinner; Webster, Richard and Joan Randles, From The Cutter's Wheel. **North Carolina**: Chapel Hill, Alda Horner, Whitehall Shop. **Ohio**: Akron, Betty Franks; Beachwood, Rita Orons; Canton, Lewis Bettinger; Cincinnati, Connie Rogers; Newton Falls, Bob and Kathy Wujcik; Novelty, Peggy Bialosky; Urbana, Parker's Antiques. **Oklahoma**: Tulsa, Phyllis Bess.

Pennsylvania: Adamstown, Dottie Freeman and Allan Teal; Allentown, The Borgmans, Wanamaker R.R. Depot Antiques, LeFevre's Antiques, Jim Lo Antiques, Phyllis and Alvin Kahn, The Pen Man's Antiques, Arlene Rabin, Edna Stauffer, Today & Yesterday; Bath, Roy Repsher; Bethlehem, Doris M. Squyres; Cabot, Clair Bargerstock; Coatesville, Chet Ramsay Antiques; Cogan Station, Roan Bros. Auction Gallery; Coopersburg, Neil and Clodogh Wotring; Danville, Lissa L. Bryan-Smith, Dick Smith, Holiday Antiques; Doylestown, Michael Ivankovich; Eagleville, Tyler's Antiques; Easton, Harold Mellor, Coach and Four Antiques; Elkins Park, Rose Sill, The Window Sill; Emmaus, Anna M. Benner; Glen Rock, Ron Lieberman; Johnstown, Precious Metals Co; Lampeter, James S. Maxwell, Jr.; Leola, R. C. Lauchnor's Collectables; Lititz, Doug Flynn and Al Bolton, Holloway House; Montgomeryville, Clarence and Betty Maier, Burmese Cruet; Montoursville, M. Jeanne Foust, Jeanne's Glass House; New Freedom, George Theofiles, Miscellaneous Man; New Hope, Debby Bogdan, Ferry Hill, Ted and Linda Freed; Northampton, David and Sue Irons, Irons Antiques; Oley, Mrs. Lena Eyrich; Orefield, Gloria Burkos, Gloria's Collectibles; Philadelphia, Shelly Hoffman, Ed Kelberg, Marcy Kula, Ed Volkrecht, Ed's Antiques, Inc., Murray and Selma Petersons; Pittsburgh, Regis and Mary Ferson, Edward Grzybowski; Pottsville, George and Tedi Hahn, Doorway To Glass; Quakertown, Doris Castellon, Brick House Antiques, Mary Webber, Webber's Antiques; Schnecksville, David Koch; Whitehall, Herb and Nancy Hallman, The Churn Antiques; Wilkes-Barre, Al Sallitt Antiques, Golden Webb Antiques; Williamsport, Michael Rath; Yardley, Ellie Archer; York, Lookenbill's Antiques. **South Dakota**: Huron, Joan Hull. **Tennessee**: Elaine J. Luartes, Athena Antiques. **Texas**: Dallas, Ted Birbilis; Euless, The Stevensons. **Vermont**: Cavendish, Henry and Doris Sigourney, Sigourney's Antiques. **Virginia**: Arlington, Carolyn Smith; Crozet, Betty L. Loba, Rose Valley Antiques; Hopewell, Carolyn R. Morris, Yestermorrow's Collectibles and More; Portsmouth, Whitney Le Compte; Radford, Roy M. Collins. **Wisconsin**: Kaukauna, Ferill J. Rice.

INDEX

† See Warman's Americana & Collectibles, 4th Edition (1989)
for an expanded listing of these categories

Harry and the Rinkettes. Left to right: Jocelyn C. Butterer, Terese J. Oswald, Dana N. Morykan, Diane L. Sterner, Harry L. Rinker, Ellen L. Schroy, Martha S. Neff.

HARRY L. RINKER is consulting editor for Wallace-Homestead Book Company, editor of *Warman's Antiques and Their Prices* and *Warman's Americana & Collectibles;* author of *Collector's Guide to Toys, Games, and Puzzles, How to Make the Most of Your Investments in Antiques and Collectibles,* and *Rinker on Collectibles*; co-author with Frank Hill of *The Joy of Collecting with Craven Moore*; syndicated columnist of ''Rinker on Collectibles;'' and president of ''Rinker's Antiques and Collectibles Market Report.''

OTHER TOPICS COVERED BY WALLACE-HOMESTEAD

All the following books can be purchased from your local book store, antiques dealer, or can be borrowed from your public library. Books can also be purchased directly from **Chilton Book Company, Chilton Way, Radnor, PA 19089-0230.** Include code number, title, and price when ordering. Add applicable sales tax and **$2.50** postage and handling for the first book plus $ .50 for each additional book shipped to the same address. VISA/Mastercard orders call **1-800-695-1214** and ask for Customer Service Department (AK, HI, & PA residents call **215-964-4000** and ask for Customer Service Department). Prices and availability are subject to change without notice. Please call for a current Wallace-Homestead catalog.

COLLECTOR'S GUIDE SERIES

Code	Title/Author	Price
W5339	Collector's Guide to Baseball Cards, *Troy Kirk*	$12.95
W5479	Collector's Guide to Early Photographs, *O. Henry Mace*	$16.95
W5320	Collector's Guide to American Toy Trains, *Susan & Al Bagdade*	$16.95
W5568	Collector's Guide to Autographs, *George Sanders, Helen Sanders, and Ralph Roberts*	$16.95
W5487	Collector's Guide to Comic Books, *John Hegenberger*	$12.95

COLLECTIBLES

Code	Title/Author	Price
W5258	American Clocks and Clockmakers, *Robert W. & Harriett Swedberg*	$16.95
W5703	The Authorized Guide to Dick Tracy Collectibles, *William Crouch & Laurence Doucet*	$12.95
W4529	British Royal Commemoratives with Prices, *Audrey Zeder*	$24.95
W4464	Check the Oil: Gas Station Collectibles with Prices, *Scott Anderson*	$18.95
W4723	Clock Guide Identification with Prices, *Robert W. Miller*	$14.95
W569X	Collecting Antique Marbles, Second Edition, *Paul Bauman*	$17.95
W5916	Coca-Cola Collectibles, Wallace-Homestead Price Guide to, *Deborah Goldstein Hill*	$15.95
W5460	Commercial Aviation Collectibles: An Illustrated Price Guide, *Richard Wallin*	$15.95
W4731	Dolls, Wallace-Homestead Price Guide to, *Robert W. Miller*	$16.95
W4936	Dr. Records' Original 78 RPM Pocket Price Guide, *Peter A. Soderbergh Ph.D.*	$12.95
W5681	Drugstore Tins and Their Prices, *Al Bergevin*	$17.95
W5118	Food and Drink Containers and Their Prices, *Al Bergevin*	$16.95
W4901	Girl Scout Collector's Guide: 75 Years of Uniforms, Insignia, Publications & Keepsakes, *Mary Degenhardt and Judy Kirsch*	$21.95
W5797	Greenberg's American Toy Trains, From 1900 with Current Values!, *Dallas J. Mallerich III*	$17.95
W5185	Guide to Old Radios: Pointers, Pictures, and Prices, *David & Betty Johnson*	$16.95
W5711	Hake's Guide to TV Collectibles, *Ted Hake*	$14.95
W5436	Herron's Price Guide to Dolls, *R. Lane Herron*	$16.95

Code	Title/Author	Price
W0060*	Illustrated Radio Premium Catalog and Price Guide, *Tom Turnbusch*	$34.95
W5371	Jigsaw Puzzles: An Illustrated History and Price Guide, *Anne D. Williams*	$24.95
W121X*	Oil Lamps: The Kerosene Era in North America, *Catherine M. V. Thuro*	$38.95
W5312*	Petretti's Coca-Cola Collectibles Price Guide, *Allan Petretti*	$29.95
W4944	Plastic Collectibles, Wallace-Homestead Price Guide to, *Lyndi Stewart McNulty*	$17.95
W5169	Presidential and Campaign Memorabilia with Prices, Second Edition, *Stan Gores*	$18.95
W541X	Psychedelic Collectibles of the 1960s and 1970s: An Illustrated Price Guide, *Susanne White*	$21.95
W5657	Space Adventure Collectibles, *T. N. Turnbusch*	$19.95
W4154	Steiff Teddy Bears, Dolls, and Toys with Prices, *Shirley Conway & Jean Wilson*	$17.95
W538X	Steiff Toys Revisited, *Jean Wilson*	$18.95
W4847*	Thimble Collector's Encyclopedia: New International Edition, *John von Hoelle*	$35.95
W1236	Thimble Treasury, *Myrtle Lundquist*	$12.95
W3972	Tins 'N' Bins, *Robert W. & Harriett Swedberg*	$16.95
W4642	Tobacco Tins and Their Prices, *Al Bergevin*	$16.95
W5584	Tomart's Illustrated Disneyana Catalog and Price Guide, Condensed Edition, *Tom Turnbusch*	$19.95
W0140*	Zalkin's Handbook of Thimbles & Sewing Implements, *Estelle Zalkin*	$24.95
W4383	Yesterday's Toys with Today's Prices, *Fred and Marilyn Fintel*	$14.95

COUNTRY

Code	Title/Author	Price
W4499	Antiques From the Country Kitchen, *Frances Thompson*	$16.95
W5428	Baskets, Wallace-Homestead Price Guide to, Second Edition, *Frances Thompson*	$16.95
W5002	Country Sourcebook, Second Edition, *Elaine Hawley*	$19.95
W3263	Graniteware Collector's Guide with Prices, *Vernagene Vogelzang & Evelyn Welch*	$16.95
W4588	Granite Ware, Book II, *Vernagene Vogelzang & Evelyn Welch*	$18.95
W3581	Kitchens and Gadgets: 1920 to 1950, *Jane Celehar*	$16.95
W4251	Kitchens and Kitchenware: 1900 to 1950, *Jane Celehar*	$15.95
W443X	Shaker: A Collector's Source Book II, *Don & Carol Raycraft*	$15.95

FURNITURE

Code	Title/Author	Price
W4758	American Oak Furniture, Revised Edition, *Robert W. & Harriett Swedberg*	$16.95
W4243	American Oak Furniture, Volume II, *Robert W. & Harriett Swedberg*	$16.95
W4928	American Oak Furniture, Volume III, *Robert W. & Harriett Swedberg*	$16.95
W4111	Country Furniture and Accessories with Prices, *Robert W. & Harriett Swedberg*	$16.95
W376X	Country Furniture and Accessories with Prices, Book II, *Robert W. & Harriett Swedberg*	$16.95
W3883	Country Pine Furniture, Revised Edition, *Robert W. & Harriett Swedberg*	$14.95
W5401*	Macdonald Guide to Buying Antique Furniture, *Rachael Feild*	$25.00
W393X	Victorian Furniture, Book I, Revised, *Robert W. & Harriett Swedberg*	$16.95
W3875	Victorian Furniture, Book II, *Robert W. & Harriett Swedberg*	$16.95
W3964	Victorian Furniture, Book III, *Robert W. & Harriett Swedberg*	$16.95
W5207	Wicker Furniture: Styles and Prices, Revised, *Robert W. & Harriett Swedberg*	$14.95

GENERAL

Code	Title/Author	Price
W4189	Antique Radios: Restoration and Price Guide, *Betty & David Johnson*	$14.95
W5274	Antiquing in England: A Guide to Antique Centres, *Robert W. & Harriett Swedberg*	$16.95
W5614*	Bessie Pease Gutmann: Her Life and Works, *Victor J. W. Christie*	$29.95
W5304	Buy Art Smart, *Alan S. Bamberger*	$12.95
W5126	The Complete Collector's Guide to Fakes and Forgeries, *Colin Haynes*	$15.95
W5592	Flea Market Handbook: How to Make Money Selling in Flea Markets, Co-ops, and Antiques Malls, Second Edition, *Robert G. Miner*	$12.95
W3913	Flea Market Price Guide, Fifth Edition, *Robert G. Miller*	$12.95
W0121	Jewelers' Circular-Keystone Sterling Flatware Pattern Index, Second Edition, *Binder*	$69.95
W4618	Joy of Collecting, *Harry Rinker & Frank Hill*	$ 6.95
W4855	Oriental Antiques & Art: An Identification and Value Guide, *Sandra Andacht*	$17.95
W5266	Rinker on Collectibles, *Harry L. Rinker*	$14.95

GENERAL PRICE GUIDES

Code	Title/Author	Price
W5509	American Country Antiques, Wallace-Homestead Price Guide to, 10th Edition, *Don & Carol Raycraft*	$14.95
W3921	Antiques, Wallace-Homestead Price Guide to, 11th Edition, *Dan D'Imperio*	$14.95
W5576	Warman's Americana & Collectibles, 4th Edition, *Edited by Harry L. Rinker*	$14.95
W5924	Warman's Antiques and Their Prices, 25th Edition, *Edited by Harry L. Rinker*	$13.95

GLASS

Code	Title/Author	Price
W4308*	American Cut and Engraved Glass of the Brilliant Period, *Martha Louise Swan*	$35.00
W5177	Contemporary Fast-Food and Drinking Glass Collectibles, *Mark E. Chase & Michael Kelly*	$16.95
W5452*	Early American Pattern Glass — 1850 to 1910: Major Collectible Table Settings with Prices, *Bill Jenks & Jerry Luna*	$29.95
W4626	Glass Signatures, Trademarks, and Trade Names, *Anne Geffken Pullen*	$16.95
W4421	Pattern Glass, Wallace-Homestead Price Guide to, Eleventh Edition, *Robert W. Miller & Dori Miles*	$15.95
W5444*	Perfume and Scent Bottle Collecting with Prices, Second Edition, *Jean Sloan*	$35.00
W5754	Tomart's Price Guide to Character & Promotional Glasses, *Carol and Gene Markowski*	$21.95

JEWELRY

Code	Title/Author	Price
W3697	Antique Jewelry with Prices, *Doris J. Snell*	$14.95
W5746	Collectible Costume Jewelry, Revised Edition, *S. Sylvia Henzel*	$16.95
W5231*	Ladies' Compacts of The 19th and 20th Centuries, *Roselyn Gerson*	$34.95

PAPER EPHEMERA

Code	Title/Author	Price
W460X	A Collector's Guide to Autographs with Prices, *Bob Bennett*	$14.95
W4987	Currier & Ives: An Illustrated Value Guide, *Craig McClain*	$16.95
W5363	Hancer's Price Guide to Paperback Books, Third Edition, *Kevin Hancer*	$16.95
W5029	Military Postcards, 1870 to 1945, *Jack H. Smith*	$19.95
W5193*	Postcard Companion: The Collector's Reference, *Jack H. Smith*	$39.95
W5673	The Price Guide to Autographs, Second Edition, *George Sanders, Helen Sanders, & Ralph Roberts*	$21.95

POTTERY & PORCELAIN

Code	Title/Author	Price
80038*	British Studio Ceramics in the 20th Century, *Paul Rice and Christopher Gowing*	$45.00
7982X	A History of World Pottery, Revised and Updated Edition, *Emmanuel Cooper*	$24.95
W5398*	Macdonald Guide to Buying Antique Pottery & Porcelain, *Rachael Feild*	$25.00
W0116	Warman's English & Continental Pottery & Porcelain, *Susan & Al Bagdade*	$18.95

* Denotes hardcover, all others are paperback.